Company Law Handbook 2016

Company Law Handbook 2016

Saleem Sheikh
LLB (Hons), LLM (Lond), PhD (Lond)

Bloomsbury Professional

Bloomsbury Professional Ltd, Maxwelton House, 41–43 Boltro Road, Haywards Heath, West Sussex, RH16 1BJ

Bloomsbury Professional is an imprint of Bloomsbury Professional plc

A CIP Catalogue record for this book is available from the British Library.

ISBN 978 1 78043 450 6

Typeset by Phoenix Photosetting, Chatham, Kent
Printed in Great Britain by CPI Group (UK) Ltd, Croydon, CR0 4YY

Preface

Company Law Handbook 2016 aims to reflect the modernisation and future direction of UK company law by addressing updating on the increasing interrelationship between national and international laws, and the emerging significant developments. This rapid pace of change in the modernisation process renders UK company law dynamic, influential and respected internationally, owing to its ability to adapt to the constant needs of the modern society and its users. Through this approach, this *Handbook* captures the complexities, richness, variety of themes and various perspectives encountered in UK company law, thereby provoking wider discussion, debate and interpretation.

Company Law Handbook 2016 has the following objectives:

(i) to provide annual updates on key changes and developments to UK company law, including applicable European and international legislation impacting companies;

(ii) to set out the essential regulatory framework governing companies, with particular reference to the principal legislation and statutory instruments, as amended from time to time;

(iii) to highlight the significant case law that has influenced the development of UK company law including the legal and practical implications for companies;

(iv) to provide a checklist on the main areas of UK company law with a consideration of the legal and practical dimensions; and

(v) to consider the interrelationship between the various areas of law including trusts, contract, tort, agency, employment and matrimonial law and their impact on UK company law.

The *Handbook* charts the life of a company from its pre-incorporation stage through its incorporation and winding up. It addresses in detail the essential requirements for establishing a company, including the legal and practical steps, procedures and documents required during the existence and operation of the corporation. It also considers the role of the key officers in the company, their general duties within the UK corporate governance structure, and the relationship between management and shareholders in the effective governance of the corporation. Consideration is also given to the capital requirements, accounting aspects and the role of auditors and their duties. A series of checklists focus on the practical aspects of UK company law with appropriate references to the companies legislation, with the objective of assisting practitioners in navigating their way through the legislative provisions.

A significant feature of the *Handbook* is the consideration of new topics that add to the breadth, depth and variety of themes and perspectives identified in UK company law. These topics have a direct or indirect interrelationship within UK company law, with emphasis on the legal and practical implications for companies. As UK company law continues to develop, new aspects and dimensions will inevitably have a bearing on the operation and functioning of companies, with the need to ensure that proper systems, mechanisms and procedures are in place for compliance with such developments.

This *Handbook* also highlights the significant key cases that have influenced the interpretation of UK company law. The cases are addressed within the context of the Companies Act 2006 provisions, by demonstrating how some of the key provisions have been interpreted by the courts. Principal judgments are included that underpin the importance attached to the topic under consideration, with a highlighted summary of the ratio involved.

Company Law Handbook is an annual publication, serving the legal and practical needs of various users and practitioners including lawyers, accountants, directors, industrialists, entrepreneurs, company secretaries, academics and law students. It simplifies UK company law in the context of how companies operate in practice, while addressing the legal basis for the company's existence and continuing obligations during its lifetime.

UK company law, including new developments and themes at the international and European level, is constantly changing, evolving, developing and adapting through legislative reforms and landmark cases. Subsequent editions will take account of the principal changes.

In this *Company Law Handbook 2016*, consideration is given to some significant developments resulting in radical statutory reforms concerning transparency, accountability, prevention of abuse and deregulation of UK company law to further modernise company law, and to reduce administrative burdens and bureaucracy on companies. The objective of these reforms has also been to facilitate the smooth operation and functioning of companies, and to avoid unnecessary duplication of effort in the filing requirements at Companies House, and to streamline company registration.

The recent sweeping changes impact on many aspects of company law, insolvency and directors' disqualification with transitional phases for their implementation to allow companies time to adjust and comply in a timely manner.

Companies and their officers need to take on board the extent of the changes and be prepared to identify measures for their implementation. Some of the changes that are identified impose penalties on companies and their officers for non-compliance.

Company Law Handbook 2016 takes account of all the applicable recent changes to UK company law with particular reference to the following important aspects:

Deregulation Act 2015

- The main corporate features are:
- Auditors ceasing to hold office – aspects concerning their removal, resignation as auditors; notification requirements, and amendments to Part 16 of the Companies Act 2006 concerning auditors.
- Amendments to the Company Directors Disqualification Act 1986 on the application for the making of a disqualification order and new grounds for disqualification.
- Changes to the requirements of company law concerning proxies.

Small Business, Enterprise and Employment Act 2015

- The measures that affect companies aim to:
- Reduce red tape whilst increasing the quality of information on the public register.
- Enhance transparency and ensure the UK is seen as a trusted and fair place to do business.

All companies will be affected by at least some changes, as the measures will change legal requirements on companies, including what they file with Companies House - which will impact companies' systems and processes. See too: The Companies and Limited Liability Partnerships (Filing Requirements) Regulations 2015 (SI 2015/1695).

It is currently expected that changes will be implemented in three stages - those with the highest impact being delivered in the final stage. Changes to the implementation schedule may still happen during and following the passage of associated secondary legislation through Parliament.

The essential corporate aspects are:

- Streamlining company registration by making it easier to file documents at Companies House; avoiding the need to duplicate information to be provided to Companies House, Her Majesty's Revenue & Customs and other organisations.
- Definition of 'small' and 'micro' businesses in line with EU requirements and usage for the purposes of exemptions from certain requirements under the Companies Act 2006.
- Ensuring company transparency – the most significant change is the establishment of a register of people with significant control. Detailed requirements are set out on how the register will function in practice with draft regulations formulated in the form of 'Register of People with Significant Control Regulations 2015'.
- Abolition of share warrants to bearer.
- Changes in the requirement for all company directors to be natural persons (with certain exceptions for the retention of corporate directors).
- Amendments to the concept of a 'shadow director' for the purposes of the Companies Act 2006, the Insolvency Act 1986 and the Company Directors Disqualification Act 1986.
- Substantial changes to company filing requirements to take account of the following:
  - Annual return reform with a duty to deliver a confirmation statement instead of an annual return.
  - Additional information on the register – the option for companies to keep certain information on the central register rather than in the company's register.
  - Information and protection from abuse about a person's date of birth as registered at Companies House.

- Contents of statements of capital obviating the need for companies to specify the amount paid or unpaid on each shares with the only requirement to state the total amount unpaid on all shares.
- Director disputes – a requirement for filing at Companies House that the director or secretary has consented to act in the relevant capacity; and the Registrar's duty to inform new directors of their entry in the register.
- Accelerated striking off – a reduction in the notice periods for striking off companies.
- Directors disqualification – there are new grounds set out for disqualification; clearer principles for determining 'unfitness'; and compensation awards.

The Legislative Reform (Limited Partnerships) Order 2015

A draft of the Legislative Reform (Limited Partnerships) Order 2015 is currently before Parliament ('2015 Order'). The 2015 Order amends the Limited Partnerships Act 1907 ('LPA 1907') and sets out the mechanism for regulation of the private fund limited partnership ('PFLP') will operate under the regime of the LPA 1907. This Order enables a limited partnership which is a private investment fund to be designated as a PFLP on registration, and amends some of the provisions of the LPA 1907 as they apply to PFLPs and to partners in PFLPs.

Attribution of Liability

In *Jetivia SA v Bilta (UK) Ltd* [2015], the Supreme Court considered, inter alia, the doctrine of attribution and its applicability to companies and directors in identifying liability. This case is considered in detail in the *Company Law Handbook 2016.*

Proper Purpose Doctrine

In *Eclairs Group Ltd v JKX Oil & Gas plc; Glengary Overseas Ltd v JKX Oil & Gas plc* [2015] UKSC 71, the Supreme Court considered the proper purpose doctrine and its application to a company's articles of association in the context of a corporate raid. Further consideration is given to this case in the *Company Law Handbook 2016.*

The Concept of 'Establishment' under EU Regulation 1346/2000 for Winding-up Proceedings

In *Trustees of the Olympic Airlines S.A. Pension and Life Assurance Scheme v Olympic Airlines SA* [2015] UKSA 27, the Supreme Court considered the concept of 'establishment' under EU Regulations for winding up proceedings. This case is considered in detail.

De Facto Directors

The Court of Appeal's decision in *Smithton v Naggar* [2015] is an important contribution to the identification of a *de facto* director in law and practice, building upon the principles established in *Re Paycheck Services 3 Ltd; Revenue and Customs Commissioners v Holland* [2011].

The liability of the Registrar of Companies House

In *Sebry v (1) Companies House and (2) The Registrar of Companies* [2015] EWHC 115 QB, the court was required to consider whether a claim against the Registrar for negligence and breach of statutory duty could succeed, taking account of the common law principles of duty of care at common law. This case is considered in detail.

Reduction of Share Capital

There are changes to reduction of share capital provisions under the CA 2006: see The Companies Act 2006 (Amendment of Part 17) Regulations 2015 (SI 2015/472).

Financing Purchase of Own Shares

There are changes to a private company financing the purchase of its own shares: see The Companies Act 2006 (Amendment of Part 18) Regulations 2015 (SI 2015/532).

Accounts Rules

The Companies, Partnerships and Groups (Accounts and Reports) Regulations 2015 (SI 2015/980) makes important changes to the accounts rules.

The law is stated as at 31 December 2015.

Saleem Sheikh
London
1 January 2016

Acknowledgements

I owe profound gratitude and appreciation to the many people, companies, entities and organisations who encouraged me to embark on an inventive journey, which enabled me to research into areas commonly not found in company law books. I am privileged to have taken on board the invaluable comments and observations of the various people that I consulted, in ensuring that I captured their ideas and thoughts for *Company Law Handbook 2016*, which addresses some incisive legal issues balanced with practical aspects to assist practitioners in advising clients.

My family has been, and will always be, the greatest inspiration in my life. To them I owe my sincere appreciation and I thank them for their kindness, patience, understanding and immense sense of humour in giving me the time, isolation, commitment and resolute determination to write this book. I pay tribute to my wife Shabena, my daughter Iram and my two sons Kamil and Sohail, without whom the writing of this book would have been impossible; and to my son Hamza for diligently pursuing an academic course for future betterment.

I have also been blessed with my remarkable parents, Fahmida and Tahir Jamil Sheikh. I pay tribute to my late mother for her relentless efforts in encouraging me in life, for loving me, for giving me determination, hope and confidence in life and to her and my father for sharing the happiness, pain, suffering and sorrows together, for giving me the opportunity to look after them in their old age and care for their needs, and for allowing me to be with them when they needed me most. I salute them for inculcating their core values and beliefs in me which taught me to respect people of all walks of life and to give back to the community. They have made me strong, courageous and determined, and I owe my success to their laborious efforts and struggles. I only hope that I can replicate their hard work one day. I also thank my aunt, Saeeda Khan, for being there for me when I most needed her.

This edition of the *Company Law Handbook* is also dedicated to the memory of a good friend and adviser, Jolyon Frankis, who sadly passed away unexpectedly at a young age. You are deeply missed.

I am grateful to the many institutions that assisted me in my research for this book, including The Institute of Advanced Legal Studies, the London School of Economics and Political Science and the University of East London.

This book would not be complete without reference to my publishers, Bloomsbury Professional who provided me with the exciting opportunity to write this book. I owe immense gratitude and appreciation to Andy Hill, who encouraged me throughout the writing of this book and provided inspiration when I needed it most, through weekly conference calls and meetings, providing new thoughts and ideas which I incorporated in this book. Thank you also to Jane Bradford and Marianne Lee for their excellent editing in the various phases of this book and for all their assistance, patience and hard work. I also wish to acknowledge the specialist and effective marketing efforts of Jubriel Hanid and to thank Harriet Espin-Bradley, who organised the cover of this book. I am very fortunate to have worked with a team who displayed the highest professional standards in bringing their experience and skills to this book.

Writing this book and its subsequent editing has been a continuous adventure: a journey that has allowed me to introduce new subjects and topics in company law that have not been previously addressed in other UK company law books. I hope that the introduction of these new topics will give the reader a broader knowledge of the richness and depth of company law and practice, and how these topics interrelate in the dynamic shaping and development of UK company law in the wider European and international context.

Contents

Introduction

Aims and objectives

Company Law Handbook 2016 serves as a reference guide for all significant developments at a national, European and international level that impact on UK company law. It is an annual publication that takes account of the legislative and regulatory aspects including case law interpretation.

The Handbook is intended to serve as a useful guide for various groups of users ranging from the practitioner, director, secretary, industrialist, academic or student to anyone else who has an interest in company law and practice. The Handbook addresses the needs of these users in various ways. First, by analysing company law from the pre-incorporation stage to incorporation and the winding up process. Second, it provides definitions to some of the terms used in each chapter which will familiarise the reader with the terms considered in the chapter, as some of the terms are technical. Each chapter then sets out an Introduction to the topic under consideration and the key issues that will be addressed in that chapter. The paragraphs are numbered in sequential order for ease of reference. Some of the chapters comprise visual diagrams to assist with the particular topic under discussion. Other chapters also set out key cases that further explain and interpret the various legislative provisions of the Companies Act 2006. In appropriate contexts, a checklist of main aspects of the topic are provided with reference to the primary legislative provisions.

The chapters

Chapter 1 considers the regulatory framework of company law in the UK, the European and the international context. The objective of this chapter is to set out the main features of the regulatory framework, and how the legislative provisions of various Acts impact on company law, and the interrelationship between UK, European and international company law through Directives and Regulations, including the human rights of companies. This Chapter sets the key Acts of Parliament that impact on UK company law for an orderly functioning of corporations in the UK. It also sets out the other sources of UK company law including common law and principles equity. It also examines in outline the background to UK company law reform with an analysis of the key company law committees that were established to address various issues on company law. Consideration is also given to the company law reform phases that took place during the 1990s until 2005 culminating in the CA 2006. This chapter also looks at the human rights of companies.

Chapter 2 is concerned with the pre-incorporation phase before a company is established. It considers the position of founders also known as the 'promoters' who seek to establish a company for the activities contemplated and examines the concept of a 'promoter'. It also looks at the fiduciary duties of the promoters including their liability at common law with reference to case law and pre-incorporation contracts; and how the CA 2006 addresses liability in such situations including the emerging case law in this area.

The CA 2006 and the European legislation provide for various types of legal entities that may be established. *Chapter 3* sets out a classification of the companies which can be set up, and the laws and regulations governing such companies, including the steps and procedures for setting up such companies.

The company, once incorporated, is considered to be a legal entity distinct from its shareholders. The concept of corporate personality is examined in *Chapter 4*, with reference to various landmark decisions that have had an impact on the shaping of the independent personality of the corporation. The concept of 'lifting the veil' or 'piercing the veil' is considered and the circumstances in which this occurs. A particular aspect of corporate personality that may arise in matrimonial disputes is where the assets are held by the company with the effect of preventing the other party to the dispute from claiming the assets as matrimonial assets. The interrelationship between company law, employment law, matrimonial law and the law of equity is addressed in this chapter, with an analysis of the leading Supreme Court decisions.

Chapter 5 considers the legal and practical aspects of company formation, with reference to the steps and procedures involved in forming a private company limited by shares, including registration and its effect.

One of the significant constitutional documents for a company is its articles of association which regulate the effective internal governance of the company. The nature of articles of some companies that can be established under the CA 2006 is considered in *Chapter 6*, including model form articles of association and enforceability issues between the shareholders and the company. This chapter also addresses the alteration of articles and the key cases in this area.

The ability of a company to engage in activities depends upon its corporate capacity. *Chapter 7* addresses the powers of directors to bind the company and any constitutional limitations, and examines some of the aspects of the *ultra vires* doctrine in its application to corporate capacity with reference to leading case law. It also considers the execution of documents and application of the company seal.

Chapter 8 considers the use of a name for corporate, LLP and business purposes. It looks at the provisions governing prohibited and sensitive names and expressions, and those that require the consent of a third party. It discusses in detail the practical aspects of use of names and the types of organisations from whom consent is required.

Depending upon the circumstances, companies may re-register or convert into another form of corporate entity such as a private, public or an unlimited company. These aspects of re-registration are considered from a legal and practical perspective in *Chapter 9* by way of checklists, including the documentation required to be lodged at Companies House.

The company's shareholders play an important part in the corporate decision-making process. In this regard, *Chapter 10* considers the steps required to become a member of the company, with reference to the register of members and exercise of members' rights within the company.

Corporate governance has now become one of the key aspects at the heart of the operation of UK company law. The concept marks a shift away from passive shareholders and towards an active and engaging shareholders who require directors to be accountable for their actions affecting the company. Corporate governance is not limited to directors providing direction and control on the company's management and functioning – but has a broader aim of bringing together various stakeholders who have a strategic part to play in promoting the company's best interests. This necessitates close interaction and dialogue with wider stakeholders on the corporation including ensuring that objectivity and independence is prevalent within the corporation through the appointment of non-executive directors and senior independent directors who provide a balanced view of the company's position and strategic direction. *Chapter 11* addresses the topical subject of corporate governance with a consideration of the key committees that were established to look into various aspects of corporate governance in the UK that led to codes of conduct being formulated. This chapter also considers the UK Corporate Governance Code and the Stewardship Code.

Another topic closely associated with corporate governance is concerned with the legal aspects of corporate social responsibilities which some companies choose to exercise in discharging their social obligations towards society. *Chapter 12* introduces the concept of 'corporate social responsibility' and its attributes including variations of this concept with reference to the 'trusteeship' and 'philanthropic' principles that are characteristic of the concept. It examines the development of corporate social responsibilities in the United Kingdom and traces the judicial attitudes towards the concept. It also considers how the Companies Act 2006 may apply the concept to companies engaged in various social activities, including philanthropic aspects of corporate giving to regulate corporate social responsibility.

Chapter 13 looks at types of directors and their appointment and removal. The various categories of directors are considered with reference to their position within the company. Consideration is also given to significant leading cases on the directors, particularly the interrelationship between *de facto* and shadow directors.

Before 2006, the general duties of directors were fragmented and the legal position was largely governed by case law on the fiduciary and common law duties of directors which were applied in random fashion, and with some inconsistencies particularly with the low standard duty of skill and care at common law. The Companies Act 2006 has codified some of the directors' duties commonly found under the fiduciary and common law principles. *Chapter 14* examines the general statement of directors' duties as set out in the Companies Act 2006. Directors' general duties have generated emerging principal case law on the interpretation of the legislative provisions in the CA 2006 governing such duties. These aspects are examined in detail.

Chapter 15 continues the theme of directors' duties with particular reference to directors' specific statutory duties and liabilities, and situations where shareholders' consent is also required before directors can enter into a transaction. This is based on the principle of shareholder and corporate protection, and ensuring directors are transparent and accountable for their actions that impact the company and the interests of its shareholders. Shareholders have ultimate residual authority to decide whether or not to approve the transaction. It also sets out provisions concerning directors' residential addresses.

Chapter 16 addresses directors' remuneration with a consideration of the main committees that have impacted on the regulatory aspects in this area. It also considers the position under the CA 2006 and the applicable regulations governing directors' remuneration.

Chapter 17 looks at directors' disqualification and examines the grounds on which a disqualification order or undertaking may be made, including the disqualification periods under the Company Directors Disqualification Act 1986. The Act has given rise to significant case law and some of the key decisions are considered. This chapter also considers the position concerning foreign disqualification.

Within the corporate governance process, shareholders' interests need to be protected. The CA 2006 provides redress for aggrieved shareholders in certain circumstances including specific remedies available. *Chapter 18* considers the application for a derivative claim and the grounds for such application including the courts' powers to consider a derivative claim. This topic has generated some interesting case law on the interpretation of the legislative provisions, and this trend is set to continue.

Another key remedy for an aggrieved shareholder is to petition the court on the grounds of unfair prejudicial conduct and the various orders that the court may make in this regard. *Chapter 19* addresses of the judicial perspectives towards 'unfair prejudicial conduct', and the cases interpreting the legislative provisions with reference to the practical situations where unfair prejudicial conduct may arise.

For public limited companies, the role of the company secretary is significant in ensuring corporate compliance with various rules and regulations. *Chapter 20* looks at the secretary's role in this context, with a checklist of key points to consider in the appointment of the secretary.

Decisions within a company are made through resolutions and meetings, unless written resolutions apply in some circumstances. *Chapter 21* considers the different types of resolutions under the CA 2006 and the board and shareholders' meetings that may be convened. Consideration is also given to specific provisions governing public companies. The Companies Act 2006 modernises UK company law through the use of modern information technology in the form of notice and convening of meetings using modern technology. These aspects are also considered in this chapter.

Chapter 22 focuses on the control of political donations and expenditure and how the Companies Act 2006 regulates such expenditures by companies.

Chapter 23 examines the nature of a company's accounts and requirement to prepare a report including the filing of accounts and reports.

Chapter 24 sets out the requirements for a company's audit. This chapter also looks at the role and function of auditors and their liability. Some of the leading cases in this area are also considered towards their clients and third parties, including the principle of *ex turpi causa*.

The topic of shares and share capital is examined in *Chapter 25* which considers different types of shares and rights (if any) attaching to such shares. This chapter also looks at the power of directors to allot shares and pre-emption rights, including waivers and alteration of share capital as well as reduction of share capital.

Chapter 26 considers acquisition by a company of its own shares. It also addresses the redemption procedure.

The concept of a debenture is examined in *Chapter 27* and the register of debenture-holders.

Chapter 28 looks at certification and transfer of securities with reference to procedural aspects and people with significant control of a company's shares.

Chapter 29 considers information about interests in a company's shares and key cases in this area.

Chapter 30 addresses a company's distributions and circumstances where it may be permissible to declare dividends and the procedural steps required to effect distributions.

Chapter 31 looks at the position regarding a company's annual confirmation and when it is filed at Companies House.

Chapter 32 examines the nature of a charge registered by a company and the types of charges commonly found in UK company law. This aspect has been the subject of a major consultation exercise by the company law reform committee during 1999-2005, culminating in the CA 2006.

In some situations, a company may be dissolved with its removal from the register at Companies House under various grounds as set out in the CA 2006. *Chapter 33* considers the position on dissolution of a company and circumstances giving rise to its restoration at Companies House.

Companies may also be regulated through the process of company investigations leading to company inspectors being appointed with wide powers to investigate the company's affairs and its officers. The provisions under the CA 1985 (as amended by the CA 2006) establish the grounds for the investigation and the inspectors' powers. This has given rise to key case law addressing issues such as natural justice and the use of evidence obtained by the inspectors in subsequent proceedings against the company officers; and the implications under the European Convention of Human Rights, including the human rights of key corporate officers. These aspects are considered in *Chapter 34*.

Chapter 35 considers role of the Registrar of Companies in UK company law including the Registrar's powers, with reference to some key case law decisions on the Registrar's negligence.

Chapter 36 addresses the offences under the CA 2006 and the applicable penalties.

Chapter 37 considers the role, function and duties of the Statutory Auditors.

Chapter 38 addresses the role, function and duties of auditors general.

Chapter 39 considers corporate manslaughter and corporate homicide and the nature of the offence, as well as exemptions and penalties and recent cases in this area.

The subject of corporate bribery is considered in *Chapter 40* and highlights the need to ensure commercial organisations prevent bribery within their organisations. This chapter also considers the procedural aspects of corporate bribery and circumstances where the 'adequate procedures' defence may be used.

Abbreviations

AC	Appeals Cases
AGM	Annual General Meeting
AIM	Alternative Investment Market
ALL ER	All England Law Reports
APB	Auditing Practices Board
App Cas	Law Reports Appeal Cases (1875-1890)
AGM	Annual General Meeting
AIM	Alternative Investment Market
APB	Accounting Practices Board
ARD	Accounting Reference Date
ASB	Accounting Standards Board
BA 2010	Bribery Act 2010
BCC	Butterworths Company Cases
BCLC	Butterworths Company Law Cases
BERR	Department for Business, Enterprise & Regulatory Reform
BOT	Board of Trade
CA	Court of Appeal
CA 1948	Companies Act 1948
CA 1980	Companies Act 1980
CA 1981	Companies Act 1981
CA 1985	Companies Act 1985
CA 1989	Companies Act 1989
CA 2006	Companies Act 2006
C(AICE)A 2004	Companies (Audit, Investigations and Community Enterprise) Act 2004
CBI	Confederation of British Industry
CDDA 1986	Company Directors Disqualification Act 1986
CEO	Chief Executive Officer
CFO	Chief Financial officer
ChD	Law Reports Chancery Division (1876-1890)
CIB	BERR Companies Investigation Branch
CIC	Community Interest Company
CIO	Charitable Incorporated Organisation
CJA	Criminal Justice Act 1993
CLR	Commonwealth Law Reports
CPD	Common Pleas Division
CMCHA 2007	Corporate Manslaughter and Corporate Homicide Act 2007
CPD	Common Pleas Division (1875-1880)
CPS	Crown Prosecution Service
CSIH	Court of Session (Inner House)
CSR	Corporate Social Responsibilities

D&O Insurance	Directors' and Officers' Liability Insurance
DA 2015	Deregulation Act 2015
DRR	Directors' Remuneration Report
DTI	Department of Trade and Industry
DTR	Disclosure and Transparency Rule
EA	Enterprise Act 2002
E & B	Ellis and Blackburn's Queen's Bench Reports (1852-1858)
EC	European Community
ECJ	European Court of Justice
EEC	European Economic Community
ECHR	European Court of Human Rights
EEIG	European Economic Interest Grouping
EGM	Extraordinary General Meeting
ERA 1996	Employment Rights Act 1996
ERRA 2013	Enterprise and Regulatory Reform Act 2013
EU	European Union
Ex D	Exchequer Division (1875-1880)
FA	Fraud Act 2006
FCA	Financial Conduct Authority
FLR	Family Law Reports
FRC	Financial Reporting Council
FRS	Financial Reporting Standard
FSMA 2000	Financial Services and Markets Act 2000
GAAP	Generally Accepted Accounting Principles
Hare	Hare's Vice-Chancellor's Reports (1841-1853)
HL	House of Lords
HL Cas	House of Lords Cases (Clark) (1847-1866)
IA 1986	Insolvency Act 1986
IAS	International Accounting Standards
ICAEW	Institute of Chartered Accountants in England and Wales
ICSA	Institute of Chartered Secretaries and Administrators
IoD	Institute of Directors
ISC	Institutional Shareholders Committee
KB	Law Reports King's Bench
LLP	Limited Liability Partnership
LLPA 2000	Limited Liability Partnership Act 2000
LP	Limited Partnership
LR CP	Law Reports, Common Pleas (1865-1875)
LR Eq	Law Reports, Equity (1865-1875)
LR Ex	Law Reports, Exchequer (1865-1875)
LR HL	Law Reports, English and Irish Appeal Cases (1865-1875)
LR QB	Law Reports, Queen's Bench (1865-1875)
LSE	London Stock Exchange
LT	Law Times
Ltd	Limited
MCA 1973	Matrimonial Causes Act 1973
OECD	The Organisation of Economic Co-operation and Development
OFR	Operating and Financial Review
NED	Non-Executive Director
NGO	Non-Governmental Organisation

NI	Northern Ireland
PC	Privy Council
PLC	Public Limited Company
PRO NED	Promotion of Non-Executive Directors
PSC	People with Significant Control
SBEEA 2015	Small Business, Enterprise and Employment Act 2015
SE	Societas Europaea
SFO	Serious Fraud Office
S.I.	Statutory Instrument
SPE	Societas Privata Europaea
TFEU	Treaty on the Functioning of the European Union
TLR	Times Law Reports
WLR	Weekly Law Reports
UKLA	United Kingdom Listing Authority

Table of statutes

[References are to paragraph numbers.]

Company Law Handbook 2016

Saleem Sheikh
LLB (Hons), LLM (Lond), PhD (Lond)

Bloomsbury Professional

Bloomsbury Professional Ltd, Maxwelton House, 41–43 Boltro Road, Haywards Heath, West Sussex, RH16 1BJ

Bloomsbury Professional is an imprint of Bloomsbury Professional plc

A CIP Catalogue record for this book is available from the British Library.

ISBN 978 1 78043 450 6

Typeset by Phoenix Photosetting, Chatham, Kent
Printed in Great Britain by CPI Group (UK) Ltd, Croydon, CR0 4YY

Preface

Company Law Handbook 2016 aims to reflect the modernisation and future direction of UK company law by addressing updating on the increasing interrelationship between national and international laws, and the emerging significant developments. This rapid pace of change in the modernisation process renders UK company law dynamic, influential and respected internationally, owing to its ability to adapt to the constant needs of the modern society and its users. Through this approach, this *Handbook* captures the complexities, richness, variety of themes and various perspectives encountered in UK company law, thereby provoking wider discussion, debate and interpretation.

Company Law Handbook 2016 has the following objectives:

(i) to provide annual updates on key changes and developments to UK company law, including applicable European and international legislation impacting companies;

(ii) to set out the essential regulatory framework governing companies, with particular reference to the principal legislation and statutory instruments, as amended from time to time;

(iii) to highlight the significant case law that has influenced the development of UK company law including the legal and practical implications for companies;

(iv) to provide a checklist on the main areas of UK company law with a consideration of the legal and practical dimensions; and

(v) to consider the interrelationship between the various areas of law including trusts, contract, tort, agency, employment and matrimonial law and their impact on UK company law.

The *Handbook* charts the life of a company from its pre-incorporation stage through its incorporation and winding up. It addresses in detail the essential requirements for establishing a company, including the legal and practical steps, procedures and documents required during the existence and operation of the corporation. It also considers the role of the key officers in the company, their general duties within the UK corporate governance structure, and the relationship between management and shareholders in the effective governance of the corporation. Consideration is also given to the capital requirements, accounting aspects and the role of auditors and their duties. A series of checklists focus on the practical aspects of UK company law with appropriate references to the companies legislation, with the objective of assisting practitioners in navigating their way through the legislative provisions.

A significant feature of the *Handbook* is the consideration of new topics that add to the breadth, depth and variety of themes and perspectives identified in UK company law. These topics have a direct or indirect interrelationship within UK company law, with emphasis on the legal and practical implications for companies. As UK company law continues to develop, new aspects and dimensions will inevitably have a bearing on the operation and functioning of companies, with the need to ensure that proper systems, mechanisms and procedures are in place for compliance with such developments.

This *Handbook* also highlights the significant key cases that have influenced the interpretation of UK company law. The cases are addressed within the context of the Companies Act 2006 provisions, by demonstrating how some of the key provisions have been interpreted by the courts. Principal judgments are included that underpin the importance attached to the topic under consideration, with a highlighted summary of the ratio involved.

Company Law Handbook is an annual publication, serving the legal and practical needs of various users and practitioners including lawyers, accountants, directors, industrialists, entrepreneurs, company secretaries, academics and law students. It simplifies UK company law in the context of how companies operate in practice, while addressing the legal basis for the company's existence and continuing obligations during its lifetime.

UK company law, including new developments and themes at the international and European level, is constantly changing, evolving, developing and adapting through legislative reforms and landmark cases. Subsequent editions will take account of the principal changes.

In this *Company Law Handbook 2016*, consideration is given to some significant developments resulting in radical statutory reforms concerning transparency, accountability, prevention of abuse and deregulation of UK company law to further modernise company law, and to reduce administrative burdens and bureaucracy on companies. The objective of these reforms has also been to facilitate the smooth operation and functioning of companies, and to avoid unnecessary duplication of effort in the filing requirements at Companies House, and to streamline company registration.

The recent sweeping changes impact on many aspects of company law, insolvency and directors' disqualification with transitional phases for their implementation to allow companies time to adjust and comply in a timely manner.

Companies and their officers need to take on board the extent of the changes and be prepared to identify measures for their implementation. Some of the changes that are identified impose penalties on companies and their officers for non-compliance.

Company Law Handbook 2016 takes account of all the applicable recent changes to UK company law with particular reference to the following important aspects:

Deregulation Act 2015

- The main corporate features are:
- Auditors ceasing to hold office – aspects concerning their removal, resignation as auditors; notification requirements, and amendments to Part 16 of the Companies Act 2006 concerning auditors.
- Amendments to the Company Directors Disqualification Act 1986 on the application for the making of a disqualification order and new grounds for disqualification.
- Changes to the requirements of company law concerning proxies.

Small Business, Enterprise and Employment Act 2015

- The measures that affect companies aim to:
- Reduce red tape whilst increasing the quality of information on the public register.
- Enhance transparency and ensure the UK is seen as a trusted and fair place to do business.

All companies will be affected by at least some changes, as the measures will change legal requirements on companies, including what they file with Companies House - which will impact companies' systems and processes. See too: The Companies and Limited Liability Partnerships (Filing Requirements) Regulations 2015 (SI 2015/1695).

It is currently expected that changes will be implemented in three stages - those with the highest impact being delivered in the final stage. Changes to the implementation schedule may still happen during and following the passage of associated secondary legislation through Parliament.

The essential corporate aspects are:

- Streamlining company registration by making it easier to file documents at Companies House; avoiding the need to duplicate information to be provided to Companies House, Her Majesty's Revenue & Customs and other organisations.
- Definition of 'small' and 'micro' businesses in line with EU requirements and usage for the purposes of exemptions from certain requirements under the Companies Act 2006.
- Ensuring company transparency – the most significant change is the establishment of a register of people with significant control. Detailed requirements are set out on how the register will function in practice with draft regulations formulated in the form of 'Register of People with Significant Control Regulations 2015'.
- Abolition of share warrants to bearer.
- Changes in the requirement for all company directors to be natural persons (with certain exceptions for the retention of corporate directors).
- Amendments to the concept of a 'shadow director' for the purposes of the Companies Act 2006, the Insolvency Act 1986 and the Company Directors Disqualification Act 1986.
- Substantial changes to company filing requirements to take account of the following:
  - Annual return reform with a duty to deliver a confirmation statement instead of an annual return.
  - Additional information on the register – the option for companies to keep certain information on the central register rather than in the company's register.
  - Information and protection from abuse about a person's date of birth as registered at Companies House.

- Contents of statements of capital obviating the need for companies to specify the amount paid or unpaid on each shares with the only requirement to state the total amount unpaid on all shares.
- Director disputes – a requirement for filing at Companies House that the director or secretary has consented to act in the relevant capacity; and the Registrar's duty to inform new directors of their entry in the register.
- Accelerated striking off – a reduction in the notice periods for striking off companies.
- Directors disqualification – there are new grounds set out for disqualification; clearer principles for determining 'unfitness'; and compensation awards.

The Legislative Reform (Limited Partnerships) Order 2015

A draft of the Legislative Reform (Limited Partnerships) Order 2015 is currently before Parliament ('2015 Order'). The 2015 Order amends the Limited Partnerships Act 1907 ('LPA 1907') and sets out the mechanism for regulation of the private fund limited partnership ('PFLP') will operate under the regime of the LPA 1907. This Order enables a limited partnership which is a private investment fund to be designated as a PFLP on registration, and amends some of the provisions of the LPA 1907 as they apply to PFLPs and to partners in PFLPs.

Attribution of Liability

In *Jetivia SA v Bilta (UK) Ltd* [2015], the Supreme Court considered, inter alia, the doctrine of attribution and its applicability to companies and directors in identifying liability. This case is considered in detail in the *Company Law Handbook 2016.*

Proper Purpose Doctrine

In *Eclairs Group Ltd v JKX Oil & Gas plc; Glengary Overseas Ltd v JKX Oil & Gas plc* [2015] UKSC 71, the Supreme Court considered the proper purpose doctrine and its application to a company's articles of association in the context of a corporate raid. Further consideration is given to this case in the *Company Law Handbook 2016.*

The Concept of 'Establishment' under EU Regulation 1346/2000 for Winding-up Proceedings

In *Trustees of the Olympic Airlines S.A. Pension and Life Assurance Scheme v Olympic Airlines SA* [2015] UKSA 27, the Supreme Court considered the concept of 'establishment' under EU Regulations for winding up proceedings. This case is considered in detail.

De Facto Directors

The Court of Appeal's decision in *Smithton v Naggar* [2015] is an important contribution to the identification of a *de facto* director in law and practice, building upon the principles established in *Re Paycheck Services 3 Ltd; Revenue and Customs Commissioners v Holland* [2011].

The liability of the Registrar of Companies House

In *Sebry v (1) Companies House and (2) The Registrar of Companies* [2015] EWHC 115 QB, the court was required to consider whether a claim against the Registrar for negligence and breach of statutory duty could succeed, taking account of the common law principles of duty of care at common law. This case is considered in detail.

Reduction of Share Capital

There are changes to reduction of share capital provisions under the CA 2006: see The Companies Act 2006 (Amendment of Part 17) Regulations 2015 (SI 2015/472).

Financing Purchase of Own Shares

There are changes to a private company financing the purchase of its own shares: see The Companies Act 2006 (Amendment of Part 18) Regulations 2015 (SI 2015/532).

Accounts Rules

The Companies, Partnerships and Groups (Accounts and Reports) Regulations 2015 (SI 2015/980) makes important changes to the accounts rules.

The law is stated as at 31 December 2015.

Saleem Sheikh
London
1 January 2016

hard work. I also wish to acknowledge the specialist and effective marketing efforts of Jubriel Hanid and to thank Harriet Espin-Bradley, who organised the cover of this book. I am very fortunate to have worked with a team who displayed the highest professional standards in bringing their experience and skills to this book.

Writing this book and its subsequent editing has been a continuous adventure: a journey that has allowed me to introduce new subjects and topics in company law that have not been previously addressed in other UK company law books. I hope that the introduction of these new topics will give the reader a broader knowledge of the richness and depth of company law and practice, and how these topics interrelate in the dynamic shaping and development of UK company law in the wider European and international context.

Contents

Introduction

Aims and objectives

Company Law Handbook 2016 serves as a reference guide for all significant developments at a national, European and international level that impact on UK company law. It is an annual publication that takes account of the legislative and regulatory aspects including case law interpretation.

The Handbook is intended to serve as a useful guide for various groups of users ranging from the practitioner, director, secretary, industrialist, academic or student to anyone else who has an interest in company law and practice. The Handbook addresses the needs of these users in various ways. First, by analysing company law from the pre-incorporation stage to incorporation and the winding up process. Second, it provides definitions to some of the terms used in each chapter which will familiarise the reader with the terms considered in the chapter, as some of the terms are technical. Each chapter then sets out an Introduction to the topic under consideration and the key issues that will be addressed in that chapter. The paragraphs are numbered in sequential order for ease of reference. Some of the chapters comprise visual diagrams to assist with the particular topic under discussion. Other chapters also set out key cases that further explain and interpret the various legislative provisions of the Companies Act 2006. In appropriate contexts, a checklist of main aspects of the topic are provided with reference to the primary legislative provisions.

The chapters

Chapter 1 considers the regulatory framework of company law in the UK, the European and the international context. The objective of this chapter is to set out the main features of the regulatory framework, and how the legislative provisions of various Acts impact on company law, and the interrelationship between UK, European and international company law through Directives and Regulations, including the human rights of companies. This Chapter sets the key Acts of Parliament that impact on UK company law for an orderly functioning of corporations in the UK. It also sets out the other sources of UK company law including common law and principles equity. It also examines in outline the background to UK company law reform with an analysis of the key company law committees that were established to address various issues on company law. Consideration is also given to the company law reform phases that took place during the 1990s until 2005 culminating in the CA 2006. This chapter also looks at the human rights of companies.

Chapter 2 is concerned with the pre-incorporation phase before a company is established. It considers the position of founders also known as the 'promoters' who seek to establish a company for the activities contemplated and examines the concept of a 'promoter'. It also looks at the fiduciary duties of the promoters including their liability at common law with reference to case law and pre-incorporation contracts; and how the CA 2006 addresses liability in such situations including the emerging case law in this area.

The CA 2006 and the European legislation provide for various types of legal entities that may be established. *Chapter 3* sets out a classification of the companies which can be set up, and the laws and regulations governing such companies, including the steps and procedures for setting up such companies.

The company, once incorporated, is considered to be a legal entity distinct from its shareholders. The concept of corporate personality is examined in *Chapter 4*, with reference to various landmark decisions that have had an impact on the shaping of the independent personality of the corporation. The concept of 'lifting the veil' or 'piercing the veil' is considered and the circumstances in which this occurs. A particular aspect of corporate personality that may arise in matrimonial disputes is where the assets are held by the company with the effect of preventing the other party to the dispute from claiming the assets as matrimonial assets. The interrelationship between company law, employment law, matrimonial law and the law of equity is addressed in this chapter, with an analysis of the leading Supreme Court decisions.

Chapter 5 considers the legal and practical aspects of company formation, with reference to the steps and procedures involved in forming a private company limited by shares, including registration and its effect.

One of the significant constitutional documents for a company is its articles of association which regulate the effective internal governance of the company. The nature of articles of some companies that can be established under the CA 2006 is considered in *Chapter 6*, including model form articles of association and enforceability issues between the shareholders and the company. This chapter also addresses the alteration of articles and the key cases in this area.

The ability of a company to engage in activities depends upon its corporate capacity. *Chapter 7* addresses the powers of directors to bind the company and any constitutional limitations, and examines some of the aspects of the *ultra vires* doctrine in its application to corporate capacity with reference to leading case law. It also considers the execution of documents and application of the company seal.

Chapter 8 considers the use of a name for corporate, LLP and business purposes. It looks at the provisions governing prohibited and sensitive names and expressions, and those that require the consent of a third party. It discusses in detail the practical aspects of use of names and the types of organisations from whom consent is required.

Depending upon the circumstances, companies may re-register or convert into another form of corporate entity such as a private, public or an unlimited company. These aspects of re-registration are considered from a legal and practical perspective in *Chapter 9* by way of checklists, including the documentation required to be lodged at Companies House.

The company's shareholders play an important part in the corporate decision-making process. In this regard, *Chapter 10* considers the steps required to become a member of the company, with reference to the register of members and exercise of members' rights within the company.

Corporate governance has now become one of the key aspects at the heart of the operation of UK company law. The concept marks a shift away from passive shareholders and towards an active and engaging shareholders who require directors to be accountable for their actions affecting the company. Corporate governance is not limited to directors providing direction and control on the company's management and functioning – but has a broader aim of bringing together various stakeholders who have a strategic part to play in promoting the company's best interests. This necessitates close interaction and dialogue with wider stakeholders on the corporation including ensuring that objectivity and independence is prevalent within the corporation through the appointment of non-executive directors and senior independent directors who provide a balanced view of the company's position and strategic direction. *Chapter 11* addresses the topical subject of corporate governance with a consideration of the key committees that were established to look into various aspects of corporate governance in the UK that led to codes of conduct being formulated. This chapter also considers the UK Corporate Governance Code and the Stewardship Code.

Another topic closely associated with corporate governance is concerned with the legal aspects of corporate social responsibilities which some companies choose to exercise in discharging their social obligations towards society. *Chapter 12* introduces the concept of 'corporate social responsibility' and its attributes including variations of this concept with reference to the 'trusteeship' and 'philanthropic' principles that are characteristic of the concept. It examines the development of corporate social responsibilities in the United Kingdom and traces the judicial attitudes towards the concept. It also considers how the Companies Act 2006 may apply the concept to companies engaged in various social activities, including philanthropic aspects of corporate giving to regulate corporate social responsibility.

Chapter 13 looks at types of directors and their appointment and removal. The various categories of directors are considered with reference to their position within the company. Consideration is also given to significant leading cases on the directors, particularly the interrelationship between *de facto* and shadow directors.

Before 2006, the general duties of directors were fragmented and the legal position was largely governed by case law on the fiduciary and common law duties of directors which were applied in random fashion, and with some inconsistencies particularly with the low standard duty of skill and care at common law. The Companies Act 2006 has codified some of the directors' duties commonly found under the fiduciary and common law principles. *Chapter 14* examines the general statement of directors' duties as set out in the Companies Act 2006. Directors' general duties have generated emerging principal case law on the interpretation of the legislative provisions in the CA 2006 governing such duties. These aspects are examined in detail.

Chapter 15 continues the theme of directors' duties with particular reference to directors' specific statutory duties and liabilities, and situations where shareholders' consent is also required before directors can enter into a transaction. This is based on the principle of shareholder and corporate protection, and ensuring directors are transparent and accountable for their actions that impact the company and the interests of its shareholders. Shareholders have ultimate residual authority to decide whether or not to approve the transaction. It also sets out provisions concerning directors' residential addresses.

Chapter 16 addresses directors' remuneration with a consideration of the main committees that have impacted on the regulatory aspects in this area. It also considers the position under the CA 2006 and the applicable regulations governing directors' remuneration.

Chapter 17 looks at directors' disqualification and examines the grounds on which a disqualification order or undertaking may be made, including the disqualification periods under the Company Directors Disqualification Act 1986. The Act has given rise to significant case law and some of the key decisions are considered. This chapter also considers the position concerning foreign disqualification.

Within the corporate governance process, shareholders' interests need to be protected. The CA 2006 provides redress for aggrieved shareholders in certain circumstances including specific remedies available. *Chapter 18* considers the application for a derivative claim and the grounds for such application including the courts' powers to consider a derivative claim. This topic has generated some interesting case law on the interpretation of the legislative provisions, and this trend is set to continue.

Another key remedy for an aggrieved shareholder is to petition the court on the grounds of unfair prejudicial conduct and the various orders that the court may make in this regard. *Chapter 19* addresses of the judicial perspectives towards 'unfair prejudicial conduct', and the cases interpreting the legislative provisions with reference to the practical situations where unfair prejudicial conduct may arise.

For public limited companies, the role of the company secretary is significant in ensuring corporate compliance with various rules and regulations. *Chapter 20* looks at the secretary's role in this context, with a checklist of key points to consider in the appointment of the secretary.

Decisions within a company are made through resolutions and meetings, unless written resolutions apply in some circumstances. *Chapter 21* considers the different types of resolutions under the CA 2006 and the board and shareholders' meetings that may be convened. Consideration is also given to specific provisions governing public companies. The Companies Act 2006 modernises UK company law through the use of modern information technology in the form of notice and convening of meetings using modern technology. These aspects are also considered in this chapter.

Chapter 22 focuses on the control of political donations and expenditure and how the Companies Act 2006 regulates such expenditures by companies.

Chapter 23 examines the nature of a company's accounts and requirement to prepare a report including the filing of accounts and reports.

Chapter 24 sets out the requirements for a company's audit. This chapter also looks at the role and function of auditors and their liability. Some of the leading cases in this area are also considered towards their clients and third parties, including the principle of *ex turpi causa*.

The topic of shares and share capital is examined in *Chapter 25* which considers different types of shares and rights (if any) attaching to such shares. This chapter also looks at the power of directors to allot shares and pre-emption rights, including waivers and alteration of share capital as well as reduction of share capital.

Chapter 26 considers acquisition by a company of its own shares. It also addresses the redemption procedure.

The concept of a debenture is examined in *Chapter 27* and the register of debenture holders.

Chapter 28 looks at certification and transfer of securities with reference to procedural aspects and people with significant control of a company's shares.

Chapter 29 considers information about interests in a company's shares and key cases in this area.

Chapter 30 addresses a company's distributions and the circumstances in which it may be permissible to declare dividends and the procedural steps required to make distributions.

Chapter 31 looks at the position regarding a company's annual confirmation statement that is filed at Companies House.

Chapter 32 examines the nature of a charge created by a company and the types of charges commonly found in UK company law. This has also been the subject of a major reform in recent years with the reform of the charges regime during 2013 and the amendments to the CA 2006.

In some situations a company may be dissolved and/or restored to the register at Companies House under various grounds set out in the CA 2006. *Chapter 33* considers the procedure for dissolution of a company and circumstances giving rise to restoration at Companies House.

Companies may also be investigated through the Secretary of State's investigative powers, leading to a report being issued and significant penalties which may be imposed on the company, its members and its officers. The provisions under the CA 1985 (as amended by the CA 2006) establish the grounds for the investigation and the inspector's powers. This has given rise to key case law addressing issues such as natural justice and the use of evidence obtained by the inspectors in subsequent proceedings against the company's officers, and the implications under the European Convention of Human Rights, including the human rights of key company officers. These aspects are considered in *Chapter 34*.

Chapter 35 considers role of the Registrar of Companies in UK company law including the Registrar's powers, with reference to some key case law dealing with the Registrar's negligence.

Chapter 36 addresses the offences under the CA 2006 and the applicable penalties.

Chapter 37 considers the role, function and duties of the Statutory Auditors.

Chapter 38 addresses the role, function and duties of auditors general.

Chapter 39 considers corporate manslaughter and corporate homicide and the nature of the offence, as well as exemptions and penalties and recent cases in this area.

The subject of corporate bribery is considered in *Chapter 40* and highlights the need to ensure commercial organisations prevent bribery within their organisations. This chapter also considers the procedural aspects of corporate bribery and circumstances where the 'adequate procedures' defence may be used.

Abbreviations

AC	Appeals Cases
AGM	Annual General Meeting
AIM	Alternative Investment Market
ALL ER	All England Law Reports
APB	Auditing Practices Board
App Cas	Law Reports Appeal Cases (1875-1890)
AGM	Annual General Meeting
AIM	Alternative Investment Market
APB	Accounting Practices Board
ARD	Accounting Reference Date
ASB	Accounting Standards Board
BA 2010	Bribery Act 2010
BCC	Butterworths Company Cases
BCLC	Butterworths Company Law Cases
BERR	Department for Business, Enterprise & Regulatory Reform
BOT	Board of Trade
CA	Court of Appeal
CA 1948	Companies Act 1948
CA 1980	Companies Act 1980
CA 1981	Companies Act 1981
CA 1985	Companies Act 1985
CA 1989	Companies Act 1989
CA 2006	Companies Act 2006
C(AICE)A 2004	Companies (Audit, Investigations and Community Enterprise) Act 2004
CBI	Confederation of British Industry
CDDA 1986	Company Directors Disqualification Act 1986
CEO	Chief Executive Officer
CFO	Chief Financial officer
ChD	Law Reports Chancery Division (1876-1890)
CIB	BERR Companies Investigation Branch
CIC	Community Interest Company
CIO	Charitable Incorporated Organisation
CJA	Criminal Justice Act 1993
CLR	Commonwealth Law Reports
CPD	Common Pleas Division
CMCHA 2007	Corporate Manslaughter and Corporate Homicide Act 2007
CPD	Common Pleas Division (1875-1880)
CPS	Crown Prosecution Service
CSIH	Court of Session (Inner House)
CSR	Corporate Social Responsibilities

D&O Insurance	Directors' and Officers' Liability Insurance
DA 2015	Deregulation Act 2015
DRR	Directors' Remuneration Report
DTI	Department of Trade and Industry
DTR	Disclosure and Transparency Rule
EA	Enterprise Act 2002
E & B	Ellis and Blackburn's Queen's Bench Reports (1852-1858)
EC	European Community
ECJ	European Court of Justice
EEC	European Economic Community
ECHR	European Court of Human Rights
EEIG	European Economic Interest Grouping
EGM	Extraordinary General Meeting
ERA 1996	Employment Rights Act 1996
ERRA 2013	Enterprise and Regulatory Reform Act 2013
EU	European Union
Ex D	Exchequer Division (1875-1880)
FA	Fraud Act 2006
FCA	Financial Conduct Authority
FLR	Family Law Reports
FRC	Financial Reporting Council
FRS	Financial Reporting Standard
FSMA 2000	Financial Services and Markets Act 2000
GAAP	Generally Accepted Accounting Principles
Hare	Hare's Vice-Chancellor's Reports (1841-1853)
HL	House of Lords
HL Cas	House of Lords Cases (Clark) (1847-1866)
IA 1986	Insolvency Act 1986
IAS	International Accounting Standards
ICAEW	Institute of Chartered Accountants in England and Wales
ICSA	Institute of Chartered Secretaries and Administrators
IoD	Institute of Directors
ISC	Institutional Shareholders Committee
KB	Law Reports King's Bench
LLP	Limited Liability Partnership
LLPA 2000	Limited Liability Partnership Act 2000
LP	Limited Partnership
LR CP	Law Reports, Common Pleas (1865-1875)
LR Eq	Law Reports, Equity (1865-1875)
LR Ex	Law Reports, Exchequer (1865-1875)
LR HL	Law Reports, English and Irish Appeal Cases (1865-1875)
LR QB	Law Reports, Queen's Bench (1865-1875)
LSE	London Stock Exchange
LT	Law Times
Ltd	Limited
MCA 1973	Matrimonial Causes Act 1973
OECD	The Organisation of Economic Co-operation and Development
OFR	Operating and Financial Review
NED	Non-Executive Director
NGO	Non-Governmental Organisation

NI	Northern Ireland
PC	Privy Council
PLC	Public Limited Company
PRO NED	Promotion of Non-Executive Directors
PSC	People with Significant Control
SBEEA 2015	Small Business, Enterprise and Employment Act 2015
SE	Societas Europaea
SFO	Serious Fraud Office
S.I.	Statutory Instrument
SPE	Societas Privata Europaea
TFEU	Treaty on the Functioning of the European Union
TLR	Times Law Reports
WLR	Weekly Law Reports
UKLA	United Kingdom Listing Authority

Table of statutes

[References are to paragraph numbers.]

Table of statutory instruments

[*References are to paragraph numbers.*]

Table of cases

[References are to paragraph numbers.]

B

C

E

G

H

I

J

K

L

M

P

Q

R

S

T

U

V

W

Y

1 Regulatory framework of company law

Contents

Introduction

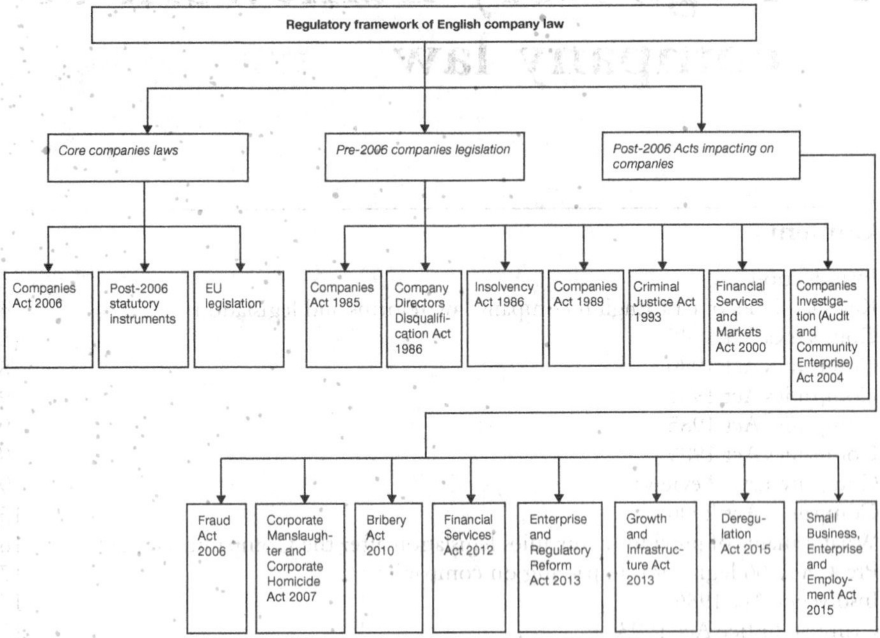

1.1 The modern corporation is a unique and remarkable institution. It is a creature of statute. It is distinguished and identified by its separate persona from the shareholders. It has particular individualistic features, attributes and characteristics that enable it to function effectively in society. The fortunes and misfortunes of the corporation are interrelated with those of its directors, shareholders and other stakeholders. At times, the corporation is helpless: it cannot act on its own and needs the support, guidance and assistance of its directors and shareholders to operate through a series of laws, rules and regulations impacting upon the daily life of the corporation.

1.2 The company's establishment and its subsequent functioning and operations owes its existence to primary companies' legislation, which regulates how the company will be set up, its composition, share ownership, capital and the effective governance between directors and shareholders. Company law legislation is at the heart of these significant issues that impact its existence: CA 2006, s 16. This aspect was aptly summarised by Lord Halsbury in *Ooregum Gold Mining Co of India Ltd v Roper* [1892] AC 125 when he stated that: '... the whole structure of a limited company owes its existence to the Act of Parliament, and it is to the Act of Parliament one must refer to see what are its powers, and within what limits it is free to act'. Similarly, in *Salomon v Salomon & Co Ltd* [1897] AC 22, when Lord Halsbury was required to consider whether a 'one-man company' could be established under the Companies Acts at the time, he stated:

> '... the important question in this case, I am not certain it is not the only question, is whether the respondent company was a company at all – whether

in truth that artificial creation of the Legislature had been validly constituted in this instance; and in order to determine that question it is necessary to look at what the statute itself has determined in that respect. I have no right to add to the requirements of the statute, nor to take from the requirements thus enacted. The sole guide must be the statute itself.'

1.3 From its inception, the company will be subject to various rules and regulations: some mandatory and others voluntary. Like a good citizen in society, the company is bound to comply with all applicable laws and procedures that affect its functioning. Internally, the corporation will be governed by a set of rules which will bind both the company and the shareholders. They reach a common consensus and understanding as to how the company will function. In this regard, the company acts in good faith. It is naive and relies on others to treat it with respect, dignity and pride and to guide it during its existence through adherence to various rules and regulations. The corporation seeks to be educated, nurtured and trained by the very people that brought it into existence, including inculcating values and ethics within the corporation. While it agrees to abide by the constitutional rules and other applicable laws, it expects its directors and shareholders to do so too. In this sense, a company has legitimate expectations that it expects its corporate officers and shareholders to honour. It expects directors to promote the long-term interests of the corporation. It expects directors to comply with their duties to the corporation. It expects directors to act as guardians and gatekeepers of the corporation by ensuring that any contracts entered into on behalf of the corporation protect the company's interests. It expects its directors not to engage in wrongful acts or misconduct in relation to the company's affairs: *Jetivia SA v Bilta (UK) Ltd* [2015] UKSA 23. In this regard, the corporation has an ego: it selfishly and jealously protects its reputation from any harm or detriment to which it might be exposed. It can also act fearlessly by initiating litigation where circumstances require, including actions against directors who falsely accuse the corporation of wrongful acts and breaches of duty, when in reality such actions may be solely conducted and orchestrated by directors for their own purpose and benefit. It also expects its shareholders to act as the ultimate residual authority, watching and towering over the directors to ensure they act primarily in the best and long-term interests of the corporation.

1.4 The regulatory aspects of English company law are governed by broad legislation that directly or indirectly impacts on companies conducting business activities. The legislation can be divided into the following primary sources:

- Acts of Parliament;
- Statutory instruments;
- EU legislation.

1.5 The principal Acts of Parliament applicable to companies can be categorised as follows:

- Core companies law:
  - Companies Act 2006;
  - Companies Act 2006 statutory instruments.

- Pre-2006 companies primary legislation:
  - Companies Act 1985;
  - Company Directors Disqualification Act 1986;
  - Insolvency Act 1986;
  - Companies Act 1989;
  - Criminal Justice Act 1993 (ss 52–64, Schs 1, 2);
  - Limited Liability Partnerships Act 2000;
  - Financial Services and Markets Act 2000;
  - Companies (Audit, Investigations and Community Enterprise) Act 2004.
- Post-2006 Acts impacting on companies:
  - Fraud Act 2006;
  - Corporate Manslaughter and Corporate Homicide Act 2007;
  - Bribery Act 2010;
  - Financial Services Act 2012;
  - Enterprise and Regulatory Reform Act 2013;
  - Growth and Infrastructure Act 2013;
  - Small Business, Enterprise and Employment Act 2015;
  - Deregulation Act 2015.

1.6 This chapter addresses the following aspects:

- an overview of the development of UK company law from a regulatory perspective which provides essential background on the development of English company law, and how the statutory framework developed to address the modern needs of company law in the UK;
- the current UK regulatory framework with a consideration of the key statutes that have an impact on UK company law including Codes and Listing Rules;
- other sources of UK company law;
- the current European regulatory framework with reference to the Directives and Regulations impacting upon UK company law;
- a checklist of the key framework statutes of English company law and company law reform reviews leading to the CA 2006; and.
- a consideration of the human rights of companies.

Key highlights of past English company law reforms and legislation

1.7 The current statutory framework of English company law can only be understood with an appreciation of past legislation and reform and how this has impacted upon and shaped the modern needs and requirements of company law in the UK. The UK companies legislation was for a long time in need of reform but the key issue centered on the nature of the reform, and whether this should be regulatory or self-regulatory, or a combination of both. At the heart of the debate was the issue of ensuring that companies were effectively regulated, whilst still allowing them some flexibility to conduct business operations without unnecessary regulatory burdens. Modern emphasis is now on deregulation and reducing unnecessary bureaucratic obstacles for companies, with measures taken to this effect under the Deregulation Act 2015 and the Small Business, Enterprise and Employment Act 2015. It was widely recognised that, before CA 2006, company law was largely fragmented and largely out of touch with modern needs and requirements of companies. This was particularly so in relation to private companies, which were also subject to some of the provisions that applied to public companies. Moreover, private companies accounted for the largest number of companies registered at Companies House, but the previous companies legislation had neglected to address how they could function more easily and effectively, without being subject to undue regulatory burdens.

1.8 Before 2006, company law in the UK proceeded on the basis of a 'think large companies first' approach, with some exceptions for private companies as an afterthought. Layers of EC provisions were also added on, addressing some of the needs of private companies in a random fashion without any clear, coherent regulatory framework.

1.9 Previously, the reform and development of company law in the UK proceeded on the basis of government committees being established to consider and recommend various amendments to the companies legislation at the time. These committees would prepare a formal report on proposed reforms to the Companies Acts at the time, to be considered and implemented by the government. The committees would usually be chaired by a senior judge with recommendations that would ultimately lead to changes in the companies legislation such as the Companies Act 1908, the Companies Act 1929 and the Companies Act 1948. Two of the earliest committees that were established to address company law reform were the Loreburn Committee reporting in 1905 and the Wrenbury Committee in 1919, but their recommendations did not have any major impact on UK company law. The next section provides a brief historical overview of the development of UK company law, with a consideration of the key committees that were established to recommend key proposed amendments to the companies' legislation.

The Greene Committee

1.10 The Greene Committee (led by Sir Wilfrid Greene) reporting in 1926 on *Company Law Amendment* (1926) Cmd 2657 proposed various amendments to companies legislation at the time. The proposed reforms included a shorter objects clause, simplifying procedures for change of company name, capital maintenance, meetings and liquidation procedures. According to the Greene Committee, the system of company law and practice in force in England and Wales had gradually evolved to meet the needs of the community at large and the commercial community in particular. It considered that in general, the companies legislation fulfilled this objective in a 'highly satisfactory manner'. It was a system well understood by those who had to deal with it; it had stood the test of time and should not be altered in any matter of principle, except where alteration was demanded. Its philosophy was to avoid radically amending the companies legislation if the provisions were working in practice, and only to make such amendments as were absolutely necessary in the circumstances.

1.11 On the issue of directors' duties, the Committee thought that 'to attempt by statute to define the duties of directors would be a hopeless task', and the proper course would be to prohibit articles and contracts directed at relieving directors and other officers of the company from liability under the general law of negligence and breach of duty or breach of trust. This type of enactment would not cause any hardship to a conscientious director or make his position more onerous, and it would not discourage otherwise desirable persons from accepting office.

1.12 It also recommended increasing disclosure to shareholders through unified accounting standards.

The recommendations were largely addressed to serve the needs of public companies with little reference to private companies. Many of the Greene Committee's recommendations were enacted in the Companies Act 1929 (19 & 20 Geo 5 c 23) which consolidated previous legislation (including the Companies Act 1928). The Companies Act 1929 was later repealed by the Companies Act 1948 (CA 1948, s 459, Sch 17).

The Cohen Committee

1.13 The Cohen Committee (chaired by Lord Cohen) with its terms of reference being 'to consider and report what major amendments are desirable in the Companies Act, 1929, and, in particular, to review the requirements prescribed in regard to the formation and affairs of companies and the safeguards afforded for investors and for the public interest', reported in 1945 in its *Report on Company Law Amendment* (1945) Cmd 6659. The areas considered for company law reform were extensive and included memoranda of association, names of companies, capital maintenance, prospectuses, private companies, charges, nominee shareholders and financial aspects. The Cohen Committee was satisfied that that the great majority of limited companies, both public and private, were honestly and conscientiously managed. It was of the view that the system of limited liability companies had been beneficial to the trade and industry of the country and essential to the prosperity of the nation as a whole. Although the Companies Acts had been amended from time to time to bring them in line with changing conditions, opportunities for abuse would inevitably exist. Accordingly the Committee considered that the fullest practicable disclosure of information concerning the activities of companies would 'lessen such opportunities and accord with a wakening social consciousness'. The Committee took account of the view that business should not be fettered unnecessarily, and that the best way to govern companies was to make available information as was reasonably required to the shareholders and creditors of the company concerned and the general public.

A large part of the Cohen Committee's recommendations were included in the Companies Act 1948 by consolidating previous companies legislation.

The Jenkins Committee

1.14 The Jenkins Committee (chaired by Lord Jenkins) with its terms of reference 'to review and report upon the provisions and workings of: the Companies Act 1948; the Prevention of Fraud (Investments) Act 1958 and Registration of Business Names Act 1916', reported in 1962 (1962 Cmd 1749). It also considered reforms to the company law system in the UK and principally to the Companies Act 1948, including a review of directors' duties and shareholders' rights.

1.15 The Committee acknowledged that since the enactment of the Companies Act 1862, later enactments had considerably increased the volume and complexity of the law relating to companies. Even the CA 1948 then comprised 462 sections with 18 schedules. The Committee recommended the need for a reduction in this 'unwieldy mass of legislation'. However, its conclusions and recommendations had the effect of increasing the level of disclosure of information by companies and added a number of provisions to the CA 1948. The Committee did not propose major reforms to company law as it believed that it would be wrong in principle to disturb in any important respect provisions designed to serve these ends, unless they had clearly outlived their usefulness or were demonstrably objectionable on other grounds. The Committee was of the view that it was necessary for the protection of shareholders, creditors and intending investors that the activities of companies and those responsible for their management should be subject to a considerable degree of statutory regulation and control. However, controls and regulations carried to excess could defeat their own object. It was therefore undesirable to impose restrictions that would seriously hamper the activities of honest business people in order to defeat an occasional wrongdoer, and it was important not to place unreasonable fetters upon business which was conducted in an efficient and honest manner.

1.16 The Committee favoured active shareholder involvement in companies and commented:

> 'But, unless the affairs of the company have gone badly wrong there is seldom any controversy. The directors of reputable companies would much prefer that meetings should be better attended and that more interest should be taken by members in the company's affairs. Members on the other hand are persistently reluctant to concern themselves with the management of their companies, and, so long as satisfactory dividends are paid, are content to leave everything to the directors. That works well in the great majority of cases but untoward events, which might have been averted by greater interest on the part of shareholders, do occur.'

There was little in terms of recommendations to ease the administrative burdens on private companies. Many of the Committee's recommendations were incorporated by way of amendments to the Companies (Amendment) Act 1967. It is interesting to note that even in 1965, the Committee suggested some regulation of directors' fiduciary duties, even as a general principle. It recommended that the Companies Act should provide that a director should observe the utmost good faith towards a company in any transaction with it or on its behalf, and should act honestly in the exercise of his powers and the discharge of the duties of his office. Further, a director should not make use of any money or other property of the company or of any information acquired by virtue of his position as a director of officer of the company, to gain directly or indirectly an improper advantage for himself at the expense of the company. A director who committed a breach of these provisions would be liable to the company for any profit made by him, and for any damage suffered by the company as a result of the breach. These aspects were not enacted in the 1967 Act.

Reform of the ultra vires rule – the Prentice Report

1.17 In 1986, the Department of Trade and Industry commissioned Dr DD Prentice to review the *ultra vires* doctrine with a view to making recommendations in this area. Dr Prentice recommended the total abolition of the *ultra vires* rule, since it no longer served any useful purpose. Some of Dr Prentice's recommendations were included in the Companies Act 1989 which amended the Companies Act 1985, but the *ultra vires* doctrine was not completely repealed at that time, with the internal effects of the *ultra vires* doctrine surviving as between the shareholders and the directors. A new CA 1985, s 3A (as amended by the CA 1989) was concerned with a statement of a company's objects by introducing a 'short form' objects clause. This provided that where a company's memorandum of association stated that the company's objects were to carry on business as a 'general commercial company', the company could carry on any trade or business whatsoever. It also had power to do all such things as were incidental or conducive to the carrying on of any trade or business by it: see now CA 2006, s 39.

Companies Act 1948

1.18 This Act received Royal Assent on 30 June 1948 and came into force on 1 July 1948. It consolidated the Companies Act 1929 and the Companies Act 1947 (other than the provisions concerning business names, bankruptcy and the prevention of fraud).

Companies Act 1980

1.19 The Companies Act 1980 came into force on 1 May 1980 and was principally enacted to harmonise UK company law with those of other Member States of the EC including the implementation of various EC Directives and Regulations impacting on company law following UK accession to the European Community in 1972. The Companies Act 1980 implemented the Second EEC Directive on Company law as regards formation of public limited companies and private companies, the maintenance of capital and protection of shareholders' interests by allowing shareholders to petition to the court on the grounds of unfair prejudicial conduct, addressing director conflicts of interest, requirement for directors generally to take employee interests into account, and rights of pre-emption for shareholders on the issue of new shares. The Act also included provisions on insider dealing which became a criminal offence and the conduct of directors in dealings with their companies. This Act was consolidated by the CA 1985.

Companies Act 1981

1.20 The Companies Act 1981 was enacted to give effect to the Fourth EEC Directive in respect of companies with limited liability. It was specifically concerned with the presentation and content of annual accounts and annual reports, the valuation methods used and their publication in respect of companies with limited liability. Companies were categorised as small, medium-sized and other companies in terms of their respective disclosure requirements. The Companies Act 1981 also introduced a mechanism to buy back and redeem shares. The use of company names was relaxed without the requirement (subject to some exceptions) to seek the consent of the Department of Trade. These provisions were subsequently consolidated under the Companies Act 1985.

Companies Act 1985

1.21 The Companies Act 1985 consolidated much of the previous companies legislation including the Companies Act 1948 and the Companies Acts 1980 and 1981. It comprised 747 sections and 25 Schedules and addressed the main company law issues including pre-incorporation, establishing a company, corporate capacity, capital maintenance, meetings, directors' statutory duties, shareholders' rights, company investigations, and financial aspects, accounts and reports. The Companies Act 1985 was largely perceived as inadequate in addressing the role of private companies with much attention paid to public companies with a 'think public companies first' approach and private companies being an after-thought through the enactment of exceptions to some of the rules applicable to public companies. Following a series of company law reviews, a large part of the Companies Act 1985 was repealed and replaced by the Companies Act 2006. Some provisions of the Companies Act 1985 still survive and these are addressed later in this chapter.

Companies Act 1989

1.22 The Companies Act 1989 was introduced to address among other matters, amendment to the law relating to company accounts; to make new provision with respect to the persons eligible for appointment as company auditors; to amend the Companies Act 1985 and certain other enactments with respect to investigations and powers to obtain information and to confer new powers exercisable to assist overseas regulatory authorities; to make new provision with respect to the registration of company charges and otherwise to amend the law relating to companies. It also addressed the issue of a company's capacity and objects clause. The CA 1989 largely amended CA 1985. Following the enactment of CA 2006, many of the provisions of CA 1989 were repealed, but some still survive and are considered at 1.48 below.

Company law reviews

1.23 English company law has undergone a period of sweeping reforms including a series of company law reviews between 1998 and 2005 on how best to ensure a deregulatory approach to company law, enabling private companies to function and operate efficiently and effectively by eradicating some of the unnecessary administrative burdens on such companies. The underlying approach was that any legislation would need to be clear, concise and intelligible to enable its users to understand and apply new provisions in a practical manner. The establishment of a company law review comprised a number of institutions, groups and people involved, including the appointment of a Project Director, a Steering Group, Working Groups and a Consultative Committee to address issues with company law at the time and to make recommendations.

1.24 From 1998 until 2000, the UK government began the process of company law reform with a series of consultation documents highlighting the need for a radical reform of company law. This process can be categorised into six phases:

1.25 *Phase 1* was the 'launch' phase for the debate on company law reform, with a consideration of the areas for reform, the rationale for change and the need for a steering committee to review the extent of reforms required and for wide consultation. This culminated in the publication of the first consultation document on company law reform: *Modern Company Law for a Competitive Economy* which highlighted the antiquated and fragmented nature of English company law legislation and the need for modernisation. This was the launch document for UK company law reform. Margaret Beckett, the President of the Board of Trade emphasised that company law lay at the heart of UK economy. Although technical, and often left to be handled by specialists, it provided the legal basis for all companies, and was fundamental to the UK's economy. The government introduced a 'fundamental review of the framework of core company law'. It contended that 40 years had passed since the last major review of company law and much of the structure of corporate law was a legacy of 19th century legislators. Although the review was under the aegis of the Board of Trade, much of the review work was undertaken by a multi-disciplinary Steering Committee, with detailed specialised company law aspects delegated to a number of working groups comprising academics, industrialists, other professionals and unions. Margaret Beckett summarised the fragmented and antiquated nature of UK companies legislation:

> 'Our current framework of company law is essentially constructed on foundations which were put in place by Victorians in the middle of the last century. There have been numerous additions, amendments and consolidations since then, but they have created a patchwork of regulation that is immensely complex and seriously out of date. The resulting costs and problems may not be obvious to all, but they are real and substantial nonetheless.'

1.26 There was a need to ensure that the UK established a framework of company law that was up to date, competitive and designed for the next century. These three concepts were categorised as the 'three key pillars' in UK's approach towards competitiveness. The consultation document set out a wide review of the companies legislation, without necessarily affecting the underlying company law principles that had stood the test of time.

1.27 The Labour Government considered that the time was right to embark on a fundamental review of the framework of core company law. Further, rapid progress in information technology had meant that in a number of areas of company law, present arrangements had held back rather than facilitated competitiveness, growth and investment.

1.28 Some of the key issues highlighted by the consultation document included the additional EU legislation that was tacked on to the companies legislation without proper consideration as to the legal and practical implications of various EU company law directives and regulations; application of large provisions of the Companies Acts to smaller companies where a deregulatory approach was required; the sheer complexity of previous companies legislation meant that directors could not clearly identify and understand their legal responsibilities – particularly directors of smaller companies; the use of over-formal language especially the Table A set of articles of association which were written in a technical and legalistic manner added to the complexities of UK companies law; in some areas, companies law over-regulated rather than offering flexibility; the previous companies law was complex in structure making it difficult to understand all the specific rules applicable to different types of companies. The previous companies legislation was, therefore, poorly laid out and complicated owing to many changes being made to meet 'short-term' needs and problems, rather than to establish solid foundations for likely future developments. Sometimes too, company law just failed to achieve its purpose; the companies legislation created obstacles to progress seeking to address problems as they arose in the past rather than to facilitate modern practices.

1.29 *Phase 2* established the strategic framework for company law reform with the publication of *Modern Company Law for a Competitive Economy – The Strategic Framework* issued in February 1999. This document laid the foundations for the work of the Steering Group and highlighted some of the substantive issues that needed to be addressed and the most appropriate mechanisms for taking company law reform forward. It considered some key areas for consideration including presumptions in favour of minimising complexity and maximising the accessibility of rules. The document highlighted that the key objective was to modernise company law, to ensure that it was well fitted to meet current and foreseeable future needs of company law users. This could involve some deregulation but the objective was to suit the law to the needs of all participants and of other relevant interests. Some Guiding Principles were developed by the review group for company law reform, namely: (i) facilitation of transactions and creating freedom for companies to make economic choices through informed decision-making processes and transparency in the decisions made – a key role for company law was to facilitate the operation of market forces through contractual and other mutual relationships; (ii) accessibility – the ease of use and identification of the law with minimum complexity and maximum accessibility; and (iii) regulatory boundaries – any overlaps, duplications and conflicts should be avoided when modernising UK companies law.

1.30 During the period of company law reform, the Law Commissions of England and Wales and Scotland published two reports which had an impact on future company legislative developments. The first report was on *Shareholder Remedies* which recommended law reform designed to make shareholder remedies more affordable and more appropriate to modern conditions. A large number of the recommendations were incorporated in the Companies Act 2006. The other report by the Law Commission of England and Wales was on *Company Directors: Regulating Conflicts* *of Interests and Formulating a Statement of Directors*. This document made the case for codifying some of the fiduciary and common law duties of directors on a statutory footing and for a revision of some of the current statutory directors' duties. Some of these recommendations were ultimately incorporated in the Companies Act 2006: see CA 2006, Part 10.

1.31 In October 1999, the steering group published *Modern Company Law for a Competitive Economy: Company General Meetings and Shareholder Communication*. This focused on the need to deregulate shareholders' meetings and for the use of effective mechanisms to ensure proper communication between the company and the shareholders, in respect of meetings including the use of company websites to announce meetings. These aspects have been included in the Companies Act 2006.

1.32 Also in October 1999, the steering group published *Modern Company Law for a Competitive Economy: Company Formation and Capital Maintenance*, with its emphasis on 'think small first' in ensuring a deregulation procedure for private companies to enable them to function effectively under modern economic and industrial conditions, including simplifying the capital maintenance rules for private companies. The Companies Act 2006 addresses these aspects with a particular emphasis on private companies.

1.33 One further consultation document was also issued by the steering group in October 1999, *Modern Company Law for a Competitive Economy: Reforming the Law Concerning Overseas Companies*. This proposed regulation of the operation of overseas branches under the English company law regime. This aspect is also addressed in the Companies Act 2006.

1.34 *Phase 3* of English company law reform was concerned with the steering group building upon the progress it had made in the series of consultation documents it had issued since 1999. In March 2000, the steering group issued *Modern Company Law for a Competitive Economy: Developing the Framework*. This document highlighted key areas of governance for companies with reference to directors' duties, and the importance of private companies in the deregulation procedure to enable them to operate effectively.

1.35 In July 2000, the steering group published *Modern Company Law for a Competitive Economy: Capital Maintenance – Other Issues*. This document addressed some residual technical issues to the main consultation document on capital maintenance.

1.36 Also in 2000, another consultation document *Modern Company Law for a Competitive Economy: Registration of Company Charges*, considered the law and practice of company charges and proposed recommendations to be considered in future companies legislation.

1.37 *Phase 4* involved completing the structure of company law reform and in November 2000, the steering group issued its consultation document *Modern Company Law for a Competitive Economy: Completing the Structure*. It specifically addressed the needs of small and private companies by simplifying and reducing unnecessary burdens on such companies.

1.38 *Phase 5* was concerned with the final report published by the steering group *Modern Company Law for a Competitive Economy: Final Report* which brought together the results of consultation and the final recommendations including draft clauses for a new Companies Bill. The Final Report highlighted the need to simplify and modernise the law for private companies; providing a legal framework reflecting the needs of the modern economy; and ensuring a flexible and responsive institutional structure.

1.39 *Phase 6* can be characterised as the government's final recommendations on company law reform by publishing two White Papers. The first, *Modernising Company Law* (July 2002), highlighted the major areas for inclusion under a future companies legislation. The second, *Company Law Reform* (March 2005), was the final document setting out the areas that would be included in a new Companies Act and summarised under the following four key objectives: (i) enhancing shareholders' engagement and a long-term investment culture; (ii) ensuring better regulation and 'think small first' approach; (iii) making it easier to set up and run a company; and (iv) providing flexibility for the future.

Companies Act 2006

1.40 Before the enactment of CA 2006, the government had introduced the Company Law Reform Bill in 2005, which was intended to amend various provisions of CA 1985, CA 1989 and related legislation, but this later changed to the Companies Bill which brought under statutory footing almost all provisions of company law from previous legislation, with some exceptions where certain provisions were retained. The Companies Bill later became CA 2006.

1.41 CA 2006 has been described as: 'an historic piece of legislation'; 'long overdue' and a 'huge piece of legislation … undertaking a root-and-branch reform of the law'; 'An archaeological approach to company law'; 'gargantuan', 'this monster'; 'incredibly long' (Lord Hodgson); 'rather like peeling back the layers of an onion' (Lord Sharman); 'lengthy and complex' (Baroness Bottomley); an Act that is 'pro-small business' (Lord Borrie); 'a model of how legislation should be introduced' (Lord Gordon).

1.42 The Companies Act 2006 is now the principal Act governing companies. It repeals many of the provisions of the Companies Act 1985 and the Companies Act 1989. The Act comprises 47 Parts with a total of 1,300 sections and 16 Schedules. Each Part of the Act sets out the main company law topic, and many of the Parts comprise a series of Chapters which further subdivide the topic. It has four main objectives: (i) enhancing shareholder engagement and a long-term investment culture; (ii) ensuring better regulation and a 'think small first' approach; (iii) making it easier to set up and operate a company; and (iv) providing flexibility for the future.

1.43 CA 2006 received Royal Assent on 8 November 2006, but was phased in over a period of time up to 1 October 2009, to allow companies time to adjust to the new regime. CA 2006 is supplemented by a number of statutory instruments elaborating on the processes and procedures of specific provisions of the Act. It was progressively brought into force by eight commencement orders made by the Secretary of State: see Companies Act 2006 (Commencement No 1, Transitional Provisions and Savings) Order 2006, SI 2006/3428; Companies Act 2006 (Commencement No 2, Consequential Amendments, Transitional Provisions and Savings) Order 2007, SI 2007/1093; Companies Act 2006 (Commencement No 3, Consequential Amendments, Transitional Provisions and Savings) Order 2007, SI 2007/2194; Companies Act 2006 (Commencement No 4 and Commencement No 3 (Amendment)) Order 2007, SI 2007/2607; Companies Act 2006 (Commencement No 5, Transitional Provisions and Savings) Order 2007, SI 2007/3495; Companies Act 2006 (Commencement No 6, Saving and Commencement Nos 3 and 5 (Amendment) Order 2008, SI 2008/674; Companies Act 2006 (Commencement No 7, Transitional Provisions and Savings) Order 2008, SI 2008/1886; Companies Act 2006 (Commencement No 8, Transitional Provisions and Savings) Order 2008, SI 2008/2860. Other key orders include: Companies Act 2006 (Consequential Amendments) (Uncertificated Securities) Order 2009, SI 2009/1889; Companies Act 2006 (Consequential Amendments, Transitional Provisions and Savings) Order 2009, SI 2009/1941; and Companies Act 2006 and Limited Liability Partnerships (Transitional Provisions and Savings) (Amendment) Regulations 2009, SI 2009/2476.

1.44 Except as otherwise provided in CA 2006 (or the context otherwise requires), the provisions of CA 2006 extend to the whole of the UK: CA 2006, s 1299. The Companies Acts as defined in CA 2006 also extend to Northern Ireland: CA 2006, s 1284. A general overview of the Parts is considered below:

Parts of CA 2006	Summary of the main areas covered
Parts 1–7	The fundamentals of what a company is, how it can be formed and what it can be called
Parts 8–12	The shareholders and officers of the company, including directors' duties and liabilities
Parts 13 and 14	How companies may take decisions (resolutions and meetings)
Parts 15 and 16	The safeguards for ensuring that the officers of a company are accountable to the shareholders (accounts and reports)
Parts 17–25	Raising share capital, capital maintenance, annual returns and company charges
Parts 26–28	Company reconstructions, mergers and takeovers
Parts 29–39	The regulatory framework, application to companies not formed under the Companies Acts, and other company law provisions
Parts 40–42	Overseas disqualification of directors, business names and statutory auditors
Part 43	Transparency obligations
Parts 44–47	Miscellaneous and general

1.45 The Companies Act 2006 also sets out the Schedules which provide further details of the main company law provisions set out in the various Parts. The main Schedules comprise the following:

Schedules to CA 2006	Summary of the main areas covered
Schedule 1	Connected persons: references to an interest in shares or debentures
Schedule 2	Specified persons, descriptions of disclosures for the purpose of CA 2006, s 948
Schedule 3	Amendments of remaining provisions of CA 1985 relating to offences
Schedule 4	Documents and information sent or supplied to a company
Schedule 5	Communications by a company
Schedule 6	Meaning of 'subsidiary' etc: supplementary provisions
Schedule 7	Parent and subsidiary undertakings: supplementary provisions
Schedule 8	Index of defined expressions
Schedule 9	Removal of special provisions about accounts and audit of charitable companies
Schedule 10	Recognised supervisory bodies
Schedule 11	Recognised professional qualifications
Schedule 12	Arrangements in which registered third-country auditors are required to participate
Schedule 13	Supplementary provisions with respect to delegation order
Schedule 14	Statutory auditors: consequential amendments
Schedule 15	Transparency obligations and related matters: minor and consequential amendments
Schedule 16	Repeals (see too CA 2006, s 1295)

1.46 The Preamble to the CA 2006 states that the objective of the Act is to reform company law and restate the greater part of the enactments relating to companies; to make other provisions relating to companies and to other forms of business organisation; to make provision about directors' disqualification, business names, auditors and actuaries and to amend Part 9 of the Enterprise Act 2002. See also the Enterprise and Regulatory Reform Act 2013 (which *inter alia*, amends the Enterprise Act 2002 and the Companies Act 2006).

1.47 All provisions of CA 2006 have been implemented except the following, which have been postponed:

- s 22(2) – limiting ability to entrench provisions of the articles of association;

- ss 327(2)(c) and 330(6)(c) – overriding articles on polls taken within 48 hours;
- s 725 – restricting the number of shares that may be held in treasury;
- s 1120 – application of criminal liability to overseas companies;
- s 1175 and Sch 9, Part 1 – application of charitable accounts rules to Northern Ireland.

Other aspects of company law are contained in separate legislation including the Insolvency Act 1986, the Company Directors Disqualification Act 1986 and the Financial Services and Markets Act 2000.

What remains of previous companies legislation after the Companies Act 2006?

1.48 The following provisions of previous companies legislation remain after CA 2006:

- Part 14 of the Companies Act 1985 on company investigations, which has a wider application and is not solely limited to companies (although this area has been amended by Part 32 of the CA 2006 and see CA 2006, ss 1035–1039);
- Part 15 of the Companies Act 1985 (orders imposing restrictions on shares (CA 1985, s 445));
- Schedule 15C to the Companies Act 1985 (specified persons) and Schedule 15D to the Companies Act 1985 (disclosures);
- Part 3 of the Companies Act 1989 (investigations and powers to obtain information);
- Part 2 of the Companies (Audit, Investigations and Community Enterprise) Act 2004 ('C(AICE) Act 2004'), dealing with the provisions on community interest companies;
- In respect of 'old public companies', the Companies Consolidation (Consequential Provisions) Act 1985 has been repealed and replaced by the Companies Act 2006 (Consequential Amendments, Transitional Provisions and Savings) Order 2009, SI 2009/1941, see art 12 and Sch 3.

1.49 The non-company law provisions that remain are:

- Part 18 of CA 1985 (floating charges and receivers (Scotland) but see now the Bankruptcy and Diligence etc (Scotland) Act 2007);
- Part 3 of the CA 1989 (powers to require information and documents to assist overseas regulatory authorities);
- Part 5 of the Companies Act 1989 (other amendments of company law), ss 112–116 of the CA 1989 (provisions on Scottish incorporated charities);
- Part 7 of the CA 1989 (provisions on financial markets and insolvency);
- Schedule 18 to the CA 1989 (amendments and savings consequential upon changes in law made by the CA 1989);

- ss 14 and 15 of the C(AICE) Act 2004 (supervision of accounts and reports);
- ss 16 and 17 of C(AICE) Act 2004 (bodies concerned with accounting standards).

1.50 In non-company law areas, CA 2006 makes amendments to other legislation. This includes the Financial Services and Markets Act 2000 and other areas of amendments including:

- overseas disqualification of company directors (Part 40 of the CA 2006 – company directors: foreign disqualification);
- business names (Part 41 of the CA 2006) – this replaces the Business Names Act 1985 but the Business Names (Chamber of Commerce etc) Act 1999 is still operative;
- statutory auditors (Part 42 of the CA 2006) – replacing Part 2 of the CA 1989; and
- transparency obligations (Part 43 of the CA 2006) – amending Part 6 of the Financial Services and Markets Act 2000.

Pre-CA 2006 legislation impacting on companies

Company Directors Disqualification Act 1986

1.51 The Company Directors Disqualification Act 1986 addresses disqualification orders and undertakings and the grounds on which disqualification orders can be made, including consequences of breach of the Act. The Act has wider significance and is not solely limited to directors. The Act is considered in detail in Chapter 17, including amendments under the Deregulation Act 2015.

Insolvency Act 1986

1.52 The Insolvency Act 1986 (as amended under the Deregulation Act 2015) addresses companies and individuals. In respect of companies, it covers corporate voluntary arrangements, receiverships, and voluntary and compulsory winding up. As regards individuals, it applies to voluntary arrangements; and bankruptcy.

Criminal Justice Act 1993

1.53 CJA 1993, ss 52–64 and Schs 1 and 2 establish the criminal offence of insider dealing. An individual who has information as an insider is guilty of insider dealing if, in the circumstances mentioned in CJA 1993, s 52(3) he deals in securities that are price-affected securities in relation to the information: CJA 1993, s 52(1).

1.54 An individual who has information as an insider is also guilty of insider dealing if:

- he encourages another person to deal in securities that are (whether or not that other knows it) price-affected securities in relation to the information, knowing or having reasonable cause to believe that the dealing would take place in the circumstances mentioned in CJA 1993, s 52(3)(a); or
- he discloses the information, otherwise than in the proper performance of the functions of his employment, office or profession, to another person: CJA 1993, s 52(3)(b).

1.55 The circumstances referred to above are that the acquisition or disposal in question occurs on a regulated market, or that the person dealing relies on a professional intermediary or is himself acting as a professional intermediary: CJA 1993, s 52(3).

There are particular defences to the insider dealing offence set out in CJA 1993, s 53.

Limited Liability Partnerships Act 2000

1.56 The Limited Liability Partnerships Act 2000 (c 12) creates an entity known as a limited liability partnership: LLP 2000, s 1. A limited liability partnership is a body corporate (with legal personality separate from that of its members) which is formed by being incorporated under the LLP 2000: LLP 2000, s 2. It has unlimited capacity: LLP 2000, s 3. The members of a limited liability partnership have such liability to contribute to its assets in the event of its being wound up as is provided for under the LLP: LLP 2000, s 4: on the application of the CA 2006 provisions to LLPs, see the Limited Liability Partnerships (Application of Companies Act 2006) Regulations 2009, SI 2009/1804.

Financial Services and Markets Act 2000

1.57 The Financial Services and Markets Act 2000 (FSMA 2000) was enacted on 14 June 2000. The Act is concerned with the regulation of financial services and markets. It provides for the transfer of certain statutory functions relating to building societies, friendly societies, industrial and provident societies and certain other mutual societies and for other connected purposes. It has been amended from time to time, including by the Financial Services Act 2012.

Companies (Audit, Investigations and Community Enterprise) Act 2004

1.58 The C(AICE) Act 2004 was introduced as part of the government's strategy to help restore investor confidence in companies and financial markets following major corporate failures. This Act amended CA 1985 and CA 1989 by strengthening the independence of the system of supervising auditors, the enforcement of accounting and reporting requirements, the rights of auditors to information and the company investigations regime and relaxing the prohibitions made by companies to indemnify directors against liability to third parties.

1.59 The Act also made provision for a new form of corporate vehicle known as the 'community interest company' ('CIC'). This type of company can be established where the CIC's profits and assets are used for the benefit of the community. Companies wishing to establish as a CIC are required to pass a community interest test and to produce an annual report showing that they have contributed to community interest aims. The Act also establishes the Regulator of Community Interest Companies who is required to maintain public confidence in the CIC model. See also the Community Interest Company Regulations 2005/1788.

The CIC is applicable to organisations in areas such as child care and social housing.

1.60 Companies formed under C(AICE) are still subject to the general framework of company law. Directors of a CIC are required to comply with their obligations under the Companies Acts, and the common law to the extent not incorporated under the CA 2006.

Fraud Act 2006

1.61 The Fraud Act 2006 creates important offences which have implications for companies and sole traders. In respect of sole traders, s 9 of the Act creates an offence for a person knowingly to be a party to the carrying on of fraudulent business. This aspect of fraudulent trading is an extension of the fraudulent trading offence under CA 2006, s 993 which is applicable to companies. Further, Fraud Act 2006, s 4 creates an offence of fraud by dishonestly abusing one's position. It applies in situations where a person has been put in a privileged position, and by virtue of his position is expected to safeguard another person's financial interests or not to act against those interests. This may apply in the context of a trustee-beneficiary relationship or a company-director situation, where in the latter case a corporate opportunity has been diverted by a director to his own business to the company's detriment. A director in this situation may be subject to a fine or imprisonment or both with a ten-year maximum prison sentence on a trial by indictment. The Fraud Act was enacted at the same time as the Companies Act 2006.

Corporate Manslaughter and Corporate Homicide Act 2007

1.62 The Corporate Manslaughter and Corporate Homicide Act 2007 applies to companies and other incorporated bodies, government departments and similar bodies, police forces and certain unincorporated associations. The organisations covered by the Act must owe a relevant duty of care to the victim. The organisation must be in breach of that duty of care as a result of the way in which the activities were managed or organised. It must also be shown that the way in which the organisation's activities were managed or organised caused the victim's death. Furthermore, the management's failure in the way the organisation's activities were managed or organised must amount to a gross breach of the duty of care. The test for 'gross' is whether the conduct constituting the breach fell far below what could reasonably have been expected. The Act also specifies the factors a jury must consider in assessing the culpability of the organisation, including the penalties and sanctions upon conviction. The Act is considered in Chapter 40.

Bribery Act 2010

1.63 The Bribery Act 2010 received Royal Assent on 8 April 2010. The principal objective of this Act has been to reform the criminal law on bribery, with a new consolidation into a single statute of the bribery offences committed in the UK and abroad. Section 7 creates a strict liability offence of failing to prevent bribery which can only be committed by a relevant commercial organisation. The main justification for the introduction of this offence is to deter commercial organisations from giving direct or indirect support to the practice or culture of bribe taking. It will be a defence for the commercial organisation to show it had adequate procedures in place to prevent persons from committing bribery offences. This is considered in Chapter 40.

Financial Services Act 2012

1.64 The Financial Services Act 2012 amends the Bank of England Act 1998, the Financial Services and Markets Act 2000 and the Banking Act 2009. It also makes other provision as to financial services and markets, including in relation to the exercise of certain statutory functions relating to building societies, friendly societies and other mutual societies. Further, it amends s 785 of the Companies Act 2006 (provision enabling procedures for evidencing and transferring title).

Enterprise and Regulatory Reform Act 2013

1.65 The Enterprise and Regulatory Reform Act 2013, *inter alia*, makes amendments to the Companies Act 2006 in respect of payments to directors of quoted companies by inserting new provisions, or amending existing provisions, notably CA 2006, ss 421(2A), 422A, 439, 439A and 226A–226F.

Growth and Infrastructure Act 2013

1.66 The Growth and Infrastructure Act 2013 Act amends the Employment Rights Act 1996 to create the employment status of employee shareholder. The employee shareholder agrees to have different employment rights to employees and receives fully paid up shares of a minimum value of £2,000 in the employing company or its parent company.

Small Business, Enterprise and Employment Act 2015

1.67 The Small Business, Enterprise and Employment Act 2015 (c 26) ('SBEEA 2015') received Royal Assent on 26 March 2015. It is concerned with improving access to finance for businesses and individuals; defines the concepts of 'small business', 'micro business' and refines the term 'shadow directors'. It also considers the status of a corporate director, and the regulation of companies including company filing requirements, and the establishment of a register of people with significant control. Part 2 of the SBEEA 2015 addresses regulatory reform and the need to streamline company registration. No later than 31 May 2017, the Secretary of State must secure a system for streamlining company registration and ensure that it is in place. A system for streamlining company legislation is a system which enables all of the registration information to be delivered by or on behalf of a person who wishes to form a company after 31 May 2017 on a single occasion to a single recipient, and by electronic means as defined under CA 2006, s 1168(4): SBEEA 2015, s 15. The objective is to provide a 'one click' registration or 'tell us once' approach in the process of company registration at Companies House, and registration for tax purposes at HMRC for VAT, corporation tax, and PAYE by means of supplying a set of data on a single occasion: SBEEA 2015, s 16. It does not require that company incorporation and tax registration is approved on the same occasion, but that the system is streamlined so as to avoid the requirement to provide the same data again. This will form a part of the on-going strategic package of better regulation by keeping unnecessary regulatory burdens on business to a minimum, and making life easier for persons setting up companies to fulfil their legal obligations by simplifying the process of incorporating and getting registered for tax by ensuring that a person can provide data once and in digital form only.

Deregulation Act 2015

1.68 The Deregulation Act 2015 (c 20) ('DA 2015') received Royal Assent on 26 March 2015. It makes provision for reducing burdens for businesses, individuals and other organisations. From a corporate perspective, it addresses the authorisation of insolvency practitioners; auditors ceasing to hold office; and various aspects of insolvency, disqualification of directors and company law issues.

City Code on Takeovers and Mergers

1.69 The City Code on Takeovers and Mergers is designed principally to ensure that shareholders in an offeree company are treated fairly and are not denied an opportunity to decide on the merits of a takeover and that shareholders in the offeree company of the same class are afforded equivalent treatment by an offeror. The Code also provides an orderly framework within which takeovers are conducted. In addition, in conjunction with other regulatory regimes, it is designed to promote the integrity of the financial markets.

1.70 The Code is not concerned with the financial or commercial advantages or disadvantages of a takeover. These are matters for the offeree company and its shareholders. In addition, it is not the purpose of the Code either to facilitate or to impede takeovers. Nor is it concerned with issues, such as competition policy, which are the responsibility of government and other bodies.

Listing Rules

1.71 Companies subscribing to the Main Market must comply with the listing and disclosure standards of the UK Listing Authority ('UKLA') and the London Stock Exchange's Admission and Disclosure Standards. For the purposes of the rules, the Financial Conduct Authority is the UKLA with a legal obligation to oversee the listing process, to assess the issuer's eligibility for the listing and to ensure that the rules are complied with. This requires the UKLA to review and approve the prospectus or the listing particulars which must satisfy the Listing Rules and the Prospectus Rules. In parallel with the UKLA application process, the issuer is also required to apply to the Exchange to have the company's securities admitted to trading on its markets and meet the requirements of the Exchange's Admission and Disclosure Standards. The Admission to list only becomes effective once all the relevant documents have been approved by UKLA, with the company becoming subject to continuing obligations once listed on the Exchange. These rules therefore serve as an essential regulatory framework and process to enable companies to operate effectively on the Main Market.

Alternative Investment Market ('AIM') Rules

1.72 AIM is the London Stock Exchange's international market for smaller growing companies. A wide range of businesses including early stage, venture capital backed as well as more established companies join AIM seeking access to growth capital. Companies seeking to join the AIM market must comply with the AIM Rules for Companies which set out the rules and responsibilities in relation to AIM companies. From time to time, the Exchange issues separate Notes on specific issues that may affect certain AIM companies and these Notes form part of the rules. The rules relating to the eligibility, responsibilities and disciplining of nominated advisers are set out in the separate rulebook, AIM Rules for Nominated Advisers. The procedures relating to disciplinary and appeals matters are set out in the Disciplinary Procedures and Appeals Handbook. The rules for trading AIM securities are set out in Rules of the London Stock Exchange.

UK Corporate Governance Code

1.73 The UK Corporate Governance Code (2014) (formerly the Combined Code) sets out standards of good practice in relation to board leadership and effectiveness, remuneration, accountability and relations with the company's shareholders.

All companies with a Premium Listing of equity shares in the UK are required under the Listing Rules to report on how they have applied the Combined Code in their annual report and accounts.

1.74 The Code contains broad principles and more specific provisions. Listed companies are required to report on how they have applied the main principles of the Code, and either to confirm that they have complied with the Code's provisions or – where they have not – to provide an explanation. A review of the Code takes every 2–3 years.

Regulations and orders

1.75 The Companies Act 2006 is the primary legislation applicable to companies established under that Act. There are, however, a number of regulations and orders that have been and continue to be enacted by way of delegated legislation that elaborate further on specific provisions of the CA 2006. The Companies Act 2006 makes references throughout the various Parts to 'regulations' and 'orders'. CA 2006, s 1288 states that unless otherwise provided, regulations and orders under the Act must be made by statutory instrument.

1.76 There are some regulations and orders that are subject to a *negative resolution procedure*. This means that the statutory instrument containing the regulation or order will be subject to annulment in pursuance of a resolution of either House of Parliament: CA 2006, s 1289.

1.77 Other regulations and orders are subject to an *affirmative resolution procedure*. This means that the regulation or order must not be made unless a draft of the statutory instrument containing them has been laid before Parliament, and approved by a resolution of each House of Parliament: CA 2006, s 1290.

1.78 Some statutory instruments are subject to *approval after being made*. This applies where the instrument is enacted and becomes operative, but it ceases to apply at the end of 28 days beginning with the day on which they were made, unless there is an affirmative resolution that is passed within this time period: CA 2006, s 1291.

1.79 The Regulations or orders under CA 2006 may:

(a) make different provision for different cases or circumstances;

(b) include supplementary, incidental and consequential provision; and

(c) make transitional provision and savings: CA 2006, s 1292(1).

1.80 Any provision that may be made by regulations under CA 2006 may be made by order; and any provision that may be made by order under CA 2006 may be made by regulations: CA 2006, s 1292(2).

Any provision that may be made by regulations or order under CA 2006 for which no Parliamentary procedure is prescribed, may be made by regulations or order subject to negative or affirmative resolution procedure: CA 2006, s 1292(3).

Any provision that may be made by regulations or order under CA 2006 subject to negative resolution procedure, may be made by regulations or order subject to affirmative resolution procedure: CA 2006, s 1292(4).

1.81 From time to time, CA 2006 makes references to 'enactment'. The term includes:

(a) an enactment contained in subordinate legislation within the meaning of the Interpretation Act 1978 (c 30);

(b) an enactment contained in, or in an instrument made under, an Act of the Scottish Parliament; and

(c) an enactment contained in, or in an instrument made under, Northern Ireland legislation within the meaning of the Interpretation Act 1978: CA 2006, s 1293.

CA 2006 also makes reference to 'prescribed' and this term means prescribed (by order or by regulations) by the Secretary of State: CA 2006, s 1167.

Other sources of UK company law

1.82 Apart from a statutory and regulatory framework, UK company law is also based on other sources such as common law and equitable principles and concepts. Company law has adapted and borrowed principles from agency, equity, partnership law, contract law and the law of trusts to apply to specific situations. For example, directors have sometimes been compared to trustees in discharging their trustee-like obligations towards the company and its stakeholders: see Sir George Jessel MR in *Re Forest of Dean Coal Mining Co* (1878) 10 Ch D 450.

1.83 Case law continues to be another main source of company law whether in terms of elaborating on the provisions of CA 2006 or developing new principles and concepts that may be applicable to company law. Indeed, common law and equitable principles under case law (including developing case law) still remain relevant for consideration under the general duties of directors. Section 170(4) states: 'The general duties shall be interpreted and applied in the same way as common law rules or equitable principles, and regard shall be had to the corresponding common law rules and equitable principles in interpreting and applying the general duties'.

1.84 In some cases, CA 2006 has codified common law principles such as the rules on capital maintenance under *Trevor v Whitworth* (1874) LR 7 HL 653; and the principle of limited liability of 'one-man' companies under *Salomon v Salomon & Co Ltd* (1897) AC.

1.85 In other cases, company law has considered international cases by way of reference and analogy to the UK position. See for example, *Coleman v Myers* (1977) 2 NZLR 225 (a New Zealand case on directors' duties).

Other sources include references to leading academics and articles which are from time to time quoted by judges: see for example Paul Finn, *Fiduciary Obligations* (1977).

1.86 UK Company law also comprises the articles of association and memorandum of association, although the articles are much more significant now than the memorandum. The articles will govern the internal relations between the shareholders and directors and set out the corporate governance structure that will be applied and implemented in the operation and functioning of the company. Companies have the flexibility and the option to prepare their own set of articles or apply the various default Model Articles of Association (depending upon the type of company that is established), or a combination of both. This represents an important source of contractual law for companies.

The European regulatory framework

1.87 The UK's membership of the EU requires compliance with various directives and regulations, particularly those applicable to the company law regulatory framework such as mergers and takeovers, market manipulation and insider trading, admission to stock exchange listing, company taxation, companies' accounts, nullity of companies, public offer of securities, capital adequacy and maintenance of capital and corporate insolvency aspects.

1.88 Under Arts 49–55 of the Treaty on the Functioning of the European Union (TFEU), companies or their branches and subsidiaries may be established in any of the Member States that are party to the TFEU based on the principle of right of establishment.

1.89 The following directives and regulations have been incorporated under the Companies Acts in the UK as part of the European regulatory framework:

- *First Council Directive 68/151/EEC of 9 March 1968* addressed the safeguards and protections for shareholders in companies through disclosure of certain corporate information including the company's constitution, appointment and termination of directors and share capital aspects. It also provided for pre-incorporation contracts and the personal liability of promoters for such contracts, including corporate capacity and *ultra vires* acts of the company and its directors and the position of third parties in respect of corporate capacity and *ultra vires* acts to protect the interests of investors and creditors. The Directive also provided for the nullity of companies on certain grounds such as illegal or unlawful objects and only for the court to declare the nullity of a company: see Case 16/89 *Marleasing SA v La Comercial International de Alimentation SA* [1990] ECR 1-4135 (a Member State cannot extend the circumstances of nullity other than those set out in the Directive); and *Ubbink Isolatie BV v Dak-en Wandtechnick BV* Case 136/87 [1988] ECR 4665 (nullity only applies where a company has legal existence). The First Directive was amended by Directive 2003/58/EC in the light of an EU Company Law Working Group Report issued in September 1999 on the simplification of the First and Second Company Law Directives which contained certain recommendations. According to Recital (3) of Directive 2003/58/EC 'The modernisation of Directive 68/151/EEC along the lines set out in those recommendations should not only help to meet the important objective of making company information more easily and rapidly accessible by interested parties, but should also simplify significantly the disclosure formalities imposed upon companies'. This Directive simplified disclosure and accessibility to company information.

- *Directive 2009/101/EC of the European Parliament and of the Council of 16 September 2009* was concerned with the co-ordination of safeguards for the protection of shareholders and third parties. The First Directive was subsequently replaced by Directive 2009/101/EC which modernised a company's disclosure obligations with reference to new technologies including electronic means. Under Art 16 of Directive 2009/101/EC, 'References to the repealed [First] Directive shall be construed as references to … Directive [2009/101/EC] and shall be read in accordance with the correlation table in Annex II'. With regard to the obligations under Directive 2009/101/EC see *Verband Deutscher-Handler eV v Daihatsu Deutschland GmbH* Case C-97/96 [1997] ECR 1-6843; and *Commission v Germany* Case C-191/95, where the European Court held that Germany had failed to provide for appropriate penalties for breaches by companies of their disclosure obligations as required under the First Directive (as subsequently amended).

  The implementation of the disclosure requirements are now set out in CA 2006, ss 9–12 which apply to both public and private companies.

- *Second Council Directive 77/91/EEC of 13 December 1976* provided for the co-ordination of safeguards for the protection of the interests of shareholders and others in respect of formation of public liability companies and the maintenance and alteration of their capital. It highlighted the need to distinguish public companies from other types of companies including the objects and minimum share capital requirements, and the need for a certificate before commencing business. It also made provision for circumstances where the number of shareholders was less than two. The Second Council Directive was amended subsequently in 2006 by *Directive 2006/68/EC* of the European Parliament and of the Council of 6 September 2006 (which took account of the Commission's Communication of 21 May 2003 to the Council and the European Parliament 'Modernising Company Law and Enhancing Corporate Governance in the European Union – A Plan to Move Forward' COM (2003) 284, which addressed, *inter alia*, easing restrictions on financial assistance and purchase of own shares including non-cash contributions. For a consideration of the Second Council Directive interpretation see: Cases C-19 and 20/90 *Karella v Minister for Industry and the Organisation for the Restructuring of Enterprises* [1991] ECR 1-2691; and Case 381/89 *Syndesmos EEC, Vasco v Greece* [1992] ECR 1-2111.

- The *Third Council Directive 78/855/EEC* was concerned with mergers of public liability companies. It set out various provisions on the regulation of mergers and the different forms of merger, including the requirements and procedures to be followed for mergers, and adequate protection for the interests of employees on a merger and the interests of creditors.
- *Directive 2011/35/EU of the European Parliament and of the Council of 5 April 2011* concerning mergers of public liability companies. This Directive superseded and consolidated many of the provisions contained in the Third Council Directive and implemented in the UK by the Companies (Reporting Requirements in Mergers and Divisions) Regulations 2011 (SI 2011 No 1606). Employees who are transferred on a merger are subject to Directive 77/187/EEC implemented in the UK by the Companies (Mergers and Divisions) Regulations 1987, SI 1987/1991, which includes the Sixth Company Law Directive concerning divisions and now forms Part 27 of CA 2006.
- *Fourth Council Directive 78/660/EEC of 25 July 1978* concerned the annual accounts of certain types of companies. It addressed the presentation and content of annual accounts with reference to the balance sheet and the profit and loss account, the valuation methods used and their publication. They are implemented in Parts 15 and 16 of CA 2006 and reduce the administrative burdens on small companies. See too the Seventh Company Law Directive.
- *Sixth Council Directive 82/891/EEC of 17 December 1982* addressed the division of public liability companies, known as a 'division by acquisition', whereby a company which is wound up but without going into liquidation transfers to more than one company all its assets and liabilities in exchange for the allocation to the shareholders of shares from the acquiring companies. The Sixth Directive was subsequently amended by Directive 2009/109 to reduce administrative burdens on companies. See too the Companies (Reporting Requirements in Mergers and Divisions) Regulations 2011 (SI 2011/1606).
- *Seventh Council Directive 83/349/EEC of 13 June 1983* concerned details for the preparation of consolidated accounts, including how and when they needed to be published. This was subsequently implemented by CA 1989. See now Part 15 of CA 2006.

- *Eighth Council Directive 84/253/EEC of 10 April 1984* (now repealed) dealt with the approval of persons responsible for carrying out the statutory audits of accounting documents. Such audits may only be undertaken by approved persons who have the requisite qualifications and fulfil the requirement to carry out statutory audits with professional integrity and independence. The Eighth Directive was subsequently replaced by the Statutory Audits Directive 2006/43/EC and is now contained in Part 16 of CA 2006
- *Tenth Council Directive 2005/56/EC of the European Parliament and of the Council of 26 October 2005* on cross-border mergers of limited liability companies provided for rules and procedures where two merging companies are based in different Member States, including the contractual terms agreed between them for the cross-border merger, the scrutiny and legality of such merger, consequences of the merger, and employee participation. It was subsequently implemented in the UK by the Companies (Cross-Border Mergers) Regulations 2007, SI 2007/2974 as amended by the Companies (Cross-Border Mergers) (Amendment) Regulations 2008, SI 2008/583.
- *Eleventh Council Directive 89/666/EEC of 21 December 1989* concerning disclosure requirements in respect of branches opened in a Member State by certain types of company governed by the law of another state. These include disclosure requirements concerning the address, activities of the branch and appointment and termination of branch members. It was subsequently implemented in the UK by the Overseas Companies and Credit and Financial Institutions (Branch Disclosure) Regulations and then by the Overseas Companies Regulations 2009, SI 2009/1801.
- *Twelfth Council Company Law Directive 89/667/EEC of 21 December 1989 on single member private limited liability companies* allowed for a private limited liability company to have a sole member to exercise the powers of the company in general meetings. It also provided for any decisions of the sole member or contracts entered into to be recorded in minutes of meetings. It was implemented in the UK by the Companies (Single Member Private Limited Companies) Regulations 1992, SI 1992/1699 and under the CA 2006 (see ss 7, 38 and 123), and see *Neptune (Vehicle Washing Equipment) Ltd v Fitzgerald* [1995] 1 BCLC 352.
- *Directive 2009/102/EC of the European Parliament and of the Council of 16 September 2009* in the area of company law on single-member private limited liability companies. This replaced and incorporated the provisions of the Twelfth Company Law Directive.
- *Council Directive 2001/86/EC of 8 October 2001* supplementing the Statute for a European company with regard to the involvement of employees. This provided for procedures for negotiation between the representatives of the company seeking to establish a European company and the employees' representatives. It also addressed specific rules for appointing the special negotiating body to represent the employees.
- *Directive 2003/58/EC of the European Parliament and of the Council of 15 July 2003 amending Council Directive 68/151/EEC* as regards disclosure requirements in respect of certain types of companies. This deals with the disclosure of certain documents at Companies House that require registration to ensure transparency,

including documents filed by electronic means, and the ability of the public to access such documents.

- *Directive 25/EC of the European Parliament and of the Council of 21 April 2004* on takeover bids established measures co-ordinating the laws, regulations, administrative provisions, codes of practice and arrangements relating to takeover bids for the securities of companies. It also considered provisions for the protection of minority shareholders and details governing the role of a supervisory authority.
- *Directive 2006/68/EC of the European Parliament and of the Council of 6 September 2006* amending Council Directive 77/91/EEC as regards the formation of public limited liability companies and the maintenance and alteration of their capital.
- Directive 2007/36/EC of the European Parliament and of the Council of 11 July 2007 on the exercise of certain rights of shareholders in listed companies.
- *Directive 2007/63/EC of the European Parliament and of the Council of 13 November 2007* amending Council Directives 78/855/EEC and 82/891/EEC as regards the requirement of an independent expert's report on the merger or division of public limited liability companies.
- *Directive 2009/109/EC of the European Parliament and of the Council of 16 September 2009* amending Council Directives 77/91/EEC, 78/855/EEC and 82/891/EEC, and Directive 2005/56/EC as regards reporting and documentation requirements for mergers and divisions.
- *Directive 2010/76/EU of the European Parliament and of the Council of 24 November 2010* amending Directives 2006/48/EC and 2006/49/EC regarding capital requirements for the trading book and for re-securitisations, and the supervisory review of remuneration policies.
- *Council Regulation (EC) No 2157/2001 of 8 October 2001 on the Statute for a European Company (SE)* provides for the rules and procedures established for the establishment of a Societas Europaea or SE including structure and provision for employee participation.
- *Council Regulation (EEC) No 2137/85 of 25 July 1985 on the European Economic Interest Grouping (EEIG)* established the basis for the structure and formation of an EEIG and the circumstances when an EEIG can be formed including its objects and activities.
- *European Private Company, COM (2008) 396*, concerns a formal proposal by the Commission on 25 June 2008 for a Regulation on a Statute for the European Private Company. It has not yet been implemented.
- *Directive 2002/14/EC*, concerns information and consulting rights of employees and applies to all firms which have over 50 employees.
- Proposal for a Directive of the European Parliament and of the Council on improving the gender balance among non-executive directors of companies listed on stock exchanges and related measures COM(2012) 614 final 14 November 2012. The proposal is founded on the principles of equality, transparency, meritocracy, justice, and common procedures and goals. The proposed Directive puts forward a temporary measure to establish a clear common strategy for all Member States in order to reach a common target: attaining the objective of

a presence of at least 40% of the under-represented sex among non-executive directors by 2020 in private listed companies and by 2018 in state-owned listed companies, and an adequate framework for Member States and companies to take efficient procedures in order to promote gender balance on boards of all listed companies. It is believed that this would improve corporate governance by offering women greater possibilities to take on a leading decisional position and enhance companies' economic performances with their skills.

Subsequently, on 25 October 2013, a draft resolution was presented to the European Parliament for consideration. It made further amendments to the text of the Directive for reconsideration by the Commission.

The human rights of companies

1.90 As companies are perceived to be legal rather than natural persons, the inference is that they do not have any human rights that require protection compared to a natural person. A company cannot be imprisoned. It cannot be tortured. Proponents of this perspective contend that a company does not possess the same characteristics, attributes, thoughts and feelings as a natural person. Further, the absence of such features renders a company devoid of any need for protection, from privacy or from any injury to its reputation or defamation, because a company does not possess the human feelings which make it vulnerable or susceptible to loss of dignity or pride, unlike an individual. The corporation is purely an abstract and metaphysical entity. There is, however, another perspective which considers that as with natural persons, companies also have human rights. It is based on the premise of 'corporate personhood' – that a company has established its reputation over a period of time for its good or services and has created an identity. Any harm to its reputation will affect its standing in the business community and with the public, and impact on the company's business trading and loss of profits, where its reputation has been damaged or injured in any way.

1.91 Various international jurisdictions offer the protection of fundamental human rights to individuals. In some of these jurisdictions, protection of human rights of individuals has also extended to afford companies basic human rights as a legal entity in its own right, which portrays the company as a 'victim' which has been the subject of a breach or violation of its human rights, or a denial of its individual freedom, liberty or free enterprise in the exercise of its legitimate and rational power or authority for a legitimate business purpose. In this regard, the company is treated as a rational person, carrying on its day to day functions like any other individual, but is subsequently denied certain rights or privileges or is affected by certain laws, rules or regulations that contravene its principal human rights.

1.92 This section addresses the relationship between fundamental human rights and its practical application to business law and business activity. It considers the circumstances that may lead to a breach of human rights of companies and protections afforded to companies similar to those given to individuals under the Convention for the Protection of Human Rights and Fundamental Freedoms (also known as the European Convention on Human Rights) ('ECHR').

1.93 The ECHR applies to individuals as well as companies and entities as stated in Art 1(1) of the Protocol to the ECHR which provides that the Convention's right to the protection of private property applies to 'every natural and legal person'. The reference to 'every' applies to business entities. Under the ECHR, companies may bring proceedings against any State that is a signatory to the Convention. The company must, however, demonstrate that it is the victim of the alleged violation. This is supported by Art 34 of the ECHR which provides that the European Court of Human Rights 'may receive applications from any persons, non-governmental organisation or group of individuals claiming to be the victim of a violation by one of the High Contracting Parties of the rights set forth in the Convention or the protocols thereto'. This would include companies, business entities, not-for-profit entities as well as NGOs: *Sunday Times v UK Series A No 30* (1980) 2 EHRR 245. Further Art 10 of the Convention ('Freedom of Expression') specifically refers to 'enterprises' and Protocol 1, Art 1, which covers the protection of property, refers to 'legal persons', which includes companies. In the UK, the Human Rights Act 1998 was enacted to give further effect to rights and freedoms guaranteed under the ECHR. The ECHR may also be used through EU law where domestic legislation contravenes any directly effective EU legislation.

1.94 The European Court of Human Rights ('ECtHR') recognises the importance and significance of companies invoking its various provisions as fundamental protections for companies. There is no definition of the term 'company' under the ECHR, but the ECtHR has never expressly rejected the premise that companies and business entities could rely upon the ECHR depending upon the specific breach or right violated. The ECtHR relies to a large extent upon each jurisdiction to define the basis for the existence of a corporation and its establishment under national laws. National laws define the essential requirement for the establishment of the corporation and the procedures required for it to come into existence. This includes the constitutional documents such as the articles of association, the memorandum of association, and the certificate of incorporation that gives the corporation a separate persona with its own unique attributes and characteristics including a purpose for its existence and functioning which is not simply limited to profit maximisation activities for the optimal benefit of the shareholders, but includes social activities for the benefit of various stakeholders in society including employees, creditors, suppliers, consumers and the wider public. The ECtHR is not, therefore, concerned about the legality of the business entity's establishment, and can assume it has been validly established for a proper purpose and objects which do not contravene public policy or are illegal or established for an unlawful activity.

Specific provisions of the European Convention of Human Rights and their applicability to companies

Article 6: Right to a fair trial and right to property

1.95 Article 6 of the ECHR is concerned with a right to a fair trial and right to property. In *Yukos v Russia* [2011], the ECtHR held that Russia violated the rights of a Russian oil company, Yukos, to property and a fair trial under Art 6. However, it dismissed charges that the acts were politically motivated by Russia. The case arose from a tax evasion investigation that made one of the country's largest companies insolvent and jailed two of its top executives.

1.96 Yukos filed a claim with the ECtHR shortly after the Russian Tax Ministry issued an initial ruling in April 2004 that because the company had used illegal tax havens, it owed more than €2.88 billion. Immediately after the ruling, the government began freezing the company's assets, and within three months, Yukos' claim in the Moscow City Commercial Court and its subsequent appeal were denied and the government sold a large part of the company. By 2007, after exhausting all domestic appeals and failing to strike an agreement with the Tax Ministry for repayment, the company dissolved. Yukos' complaint to the ECtHR alleged that the speed of the proceedings violated Russian law and prevented an adequate defence under Art 6 of the ECHR. The complaint further alleged that the tax enforcement and selling of assets were 'unlawful, arbitrary and disproportionate' under Art 1 of Protocol 1 and Arts 1, 7, 13, 14, and 18 of the ECHR.

1.97 It was decided by the ECtHR that the proceedings moved faster than the already rapid Russian legal system allowed and violated minimum protections under the ECHR, Art 6(3) by failing to provide adequate time to review all the relevant material, some of which was provided just four days before the initial trial. The ECtHR further found Russia in breach of Art 1 of Protocol 1 concerning the right to property with regard to assessing disproportionate fines and prematurely seizing company assets. The ECtHR also ruled, however, that because the tax investigation was legitimate and no evidence was provided that other companies used Yukos' methods, there were no grounds for claims of prejudicial treatment. According to the ECtHR:

> '… the Court finds that the applicant company's trial did not comply with the procedural requirements of Article 6 of the Convention for the following reasons: the applicant company did not have sufficient time to study the case file at first instance, and the early beginning of the hearings by the appeal court unjustifiably restricted the company's ability to present its case on appeal. The Court finds that the overall effect of these difficulties, taken as a whole, so restricted the rights of the defence that the principle of a fair trial, as set out in Article 6, was contravened. There has therefore been a violation of Article 6 § 1 of the Convention, taken in conjunction with Article 6 § 3 (b).'

In Comingersoll SA v Portugal [GC] Reports 2000-IV (2001) EHRR 772, the company complained to the Portuguese authorities about the inordinate delays in a civil case in which it was involved. The ECtHR was of the view that the company's right to have its case heard within a reasonable time within Art 6(1) of the ECHR had not been observed by the authorities. The company thereafter sought to claim monetary compensation for non-pecuniary loss for the delays in the national case. The ECtHR based its reasoning on a number of cases including *Immobiliare Saffi v Italy* [GC] Reports 1999-V (2000) 30 HERR 756, and *Vereinigung demokratischer Soldaten Osterreichs (VDSO) and Gubi v Austria Series* A No 302 (1995) 20 HERR 56, including the practice of the Council of Ministers and the Council of Europe that a juristic person may be awarded compensation for non-pecuniary damage. The ECtHR noted that the ECHR must be interpreted and applied in such a way as to guarantee rights that are practical and effective. In order for Art 6 of the ECHR to be effective, the ECtHR was necessarily empowered to award monetary compensation for non-pecuniary damage to commercial companies. In this regard, non-pecuniary damages suffered by such companies may include heads of claim that were to a greater or lesser extent 'objective' or 'subjective'. Accordingly, account should be taken of the company's reputation, uncertainty in decision-planning, disruption in the management of the company, and the anxiety and inconvenience caused to the members of the management team. On the facts, the proceedings in issue continued beyond a reasonable time, and this must have caused the company, its directors and shareholders considerable inconvenience and prolonged uncertainty in the conduct of the company's everyday affairs.

A corporate officer is entitled to a right to fair trial under ECHR, Art 6

Some judgments of the ECHR can impact on the functioning and operation of companies, including individuals within the companies. In *Saunders v United Kingdom* [1998] 1 BCLC 362, G plc was involved in a successful takeover bid of another company. However, G plc's share price rose dramatically during the takeover bid as a result of an unlawful share support operation. The Secretary of State for Trade and Industry appointed inspectors to investigate the matter pursuant to s 432 of the Companies Act 1985. Under ss 434 and 436 of the CA 1985, answers given by a person in the course of such inquiries could be used in evidence against him, and a refusal to co-operate with the inspectors could result in a finding of contempt of court. The inspectors found evidence that criminal offences had been committed, and it was decided that they should continue their inquiries and pass the transcripts of their interviews to the Crown Prosecution Service. The applicant was interviewed by the inspectors and was subsequently charged with offences relating to the share support operation. In the course of the applicant's trial, transcripts of those interviews were used by the prosecution to establish his involvement in the share support operation and to refute his own evidence, and he was convicted on 12 counts of conspiracy, false accounting and theft. The Court of Appeal rejected the applicant's contention that the use of those transcripts automatically rendered the proceedings unfair and denied him leave to appeal to the House of Lords. Thereafter, the applicant lodged an application with the European Commission complaining that the use at his trial of statements he had made to the inspectors under their compulsory powers had deprived him of a fair hearing in violation of Art 6(1) of the Convention for the Protection of Human Rights and Fundamental Freedoms 1950 which provides that: 'In the determination of … any criminal charge … everyone is entitled to a fair … hearing … by an independent and impartial tribunal …'.

The Commission referred the complaint to the ECtHR.

It was held by the ECtHR that the right of an individual not to incriminate himself, which was central to the notion of a fair procedure inherent in Art 6(1) of the ECHR, was primarily concerned with the right of an accused to remain silent and was not therefore confined to statements of admission of wrongdoing or to remarks which were directly incriminating. In particular, testimony obtained under compulsion which appeared to be of a non-incriminating nature, such as exculpatory remarks or mere information on questions of fact, could later be used by the prosecution in criminal proceedings to contradict or cast doubt upon other statements of the accused or otherwise to undermine his credibility. Accordingly, the question whether the applicant's right to a fair hearing had been infringed depended not on the nature of his statements but on the use made of them by the prosecution during the trial. It was clear, in the instant case, that the transcripts at issue had been used extensively by the prosecution to cast doubt upon the applicant's honesty and to establish his involvement in the share support operation. Such an infringement of the applicant's right not to incriminate himself could not be justified either by the complexity of corporate fraud or by the vital public interest in the investigation thereof, and it followed that there had been a violation of his rights under Art 6(1).

Article 8: Right to respect for private and family life, home and correspondence

1.98 Article 8 ECHR provides that everyone has the right to respect for his private and family life, his home and his correspondence: (Art 8(1)). Article 8(2) states that there shall be no interference by a public authority with the exercise of this right except such as is in accordance with the law and is necessary in a democratic society in the interests of national security, public safety or the economic well-being of the country, for the prevention of disorder or crime, for the protection of health or morals, or for the protection of the rights and freedoms of others.

In certain circumstances, ECHR, Art 8 provides protection for companies against authorities searching its corporate premises and seizure of documents

Colas Est SA and Others v France, 16 April 2002 Reports 2002-III concerned a specific provision under French Law which permitted French anti-competition authorities to search corporate premises and seize documents without a search warrant. The ECtHR held that this was in breach of Art 8 of the ECHR. The protection and 'respect for one's ... home' covered corporate premises. The ECtHR stated that the need for intervention in such situations 'must be convincingly established'. Further, Contracting States had a certain 'margin of appreciation' in determining the need for interference taking account of European rules and regulations. Moreover, relevant legislation and practice providing for a legal basis for searches and seizures should afford adequate and effective safeguards against abuse, and that operations must be regarded as strictly proportionate to the legitimate aim pursued. See too *Niemietz v Germany Series* A No 251-B, (1993) 16 EHRR 97.

Article 10: Right to freedom of expression

1.99 Article 10(1) of the ECHR states that everyone has the right to freedom of expression. This right includes freedom to hold opinions and to receive and impart information and ideas without interference by public authority and regardless of frontiers. This article does not prevent states from requiring the licensing of broadcasting, television or cinema enterprises.

1.100 Under Art 10(2), the exercise of these freedoms, since it carries with it duties and responsibilities, may be subject to such formalities, conditions, restrictions or penalties as are prescribed by law and are necessary in a democratic society, in the interests of national security, territorial integrity or public safety, for the prevention of disorder or crime, for the protection of health or morals, for the protection of the reputation or rights of others, for preventing the disclosure of information received in confidence, or for maintaining the authority and impartiality of the judiciary.

1.101 Article 10 may apply to companies in respect of their commercial expressions on various subject matters. There is, however, no definition of 'expression' under the ECHR, but it would include written or oral expressions and visual aspects communicated to the broader community. The ECtHR has on occasions considered the commercial expressions by companies.

Interference with the company's freedom of expression was not justified under Article 10(2)

In *Sunday Times v UK* (1980) 2 EHRR 153, Distillers had marketed a drug, 'thalidomide', which had been taken by a number of pregnant women who later gave birth to deformed children. Writs were issued by the parents and a lengthy period of negotiations followed without the cases proceeding to trial. The Sunday Times began a series of articles with the aim of assisting the parents in obtaining a more generous settlement of their actions. One proposed article was to deal with the history of the testing, manufacture and marketing of the drug, but the Attorney-General obtained an injunction restraining publication of the article on the ground that it would constitute a contempt of court. The injunction had been granted in the High Court, rescinded by the Court of Appeal but restored by the House of Lords. The publisher, editor and a group of journalists of The Sunday Times filed an application with the European Commission of Human Rights claiming that the injunction infringed their right to freedom of expression guaranteed by Art 10 of the ECHR. The Commission, by a majority, concluded that there had been a breach of Art 10 and referred the case to the ECtHR. The ECtHR held that the interference with the applicants' freedom of expression was not justified under Art 10(2) which permits such restrictions 'as are prescribed by law and are necessary in a democratic society … for maintaining the authority and impartiality of the judiciary'. The ECtHR deciding that, though prescribed by law and for the purpose of maintaining the authority of the judiciary, the restriction was not justified by a 'pressing social need' and could not therefore be regarded as 'necessary' within the meaning of Art 10(2). Accordingly, there had been a violation of Art 10. The ECtHR did not question the standing of the applicant as to whether a company's human rights should be protected, but simply accepted that a corporation could have human rights.

1.102 Corporate freedom of speech was also protected by the ECtHR in *Markt Intern Verlag GmbH anfd Klaus Beermann v Germany* Series A No 165, (1990) 12 HERR 161; and *Groppera Radio AG and Others v Switzerland* Series A No 173, (1990) 12 HERR 321.

There had been a breach of ECHR, Art 10 in the company's freedom of expression

In *Autronic AG v Switzerland* Series A No 178, (1990) 12 EHRR 485, the ECtHR was required to consider whether the company's transmission of satellite television signals through its aerial dish at an electronics fair fell within Art 10 of the ECHR protection. The company had applied to Swiss authorities for a licence to receive signals for its dish from a Soviet telecommunications satellite. The Swiss authorities rejected the application on the grounds that the Soviet authorities had not given their consent. The company therefore asserted that this rejection was in breach of its freedom of expression under Art 10(1) of the ECHR. The ECtHR held that the company's freedom of expression had been breached under Art 10(1). It stated that neither the company's legal status as a limited company nor the fact that its activities were commercial nor the intrinsic nature of freedom of expression could deprive the company of protection under Art 10(1). Article 10 applied to everyone – whether natural or corporate person. It applied not only to the content of information but also to the means of transmission 'since any restriction imposed on the means necessarily interferes with the right to receive and impart information …'.

1.103 The ECtHR will also have regard to the 'principle of democracy' in determining whether or not the principle of freedom of expression had been breached: *Handyside v UK* Series A No 24 (1979) 1 EHRR 737.

A refusal to broadcast a company's commercial advertisement was in breach of ECHR, Art 10

In *Verein gegen Tierfabriken Schweiz (VgT) v Switzerland (No 2)*, Case Reference Application no 32772/02, the ECtHR held that the refusal by the Swiss authorities to broadcast the company's advertisement was a breach of the company's rights under Art 10. It decided that the television commercial concerned battery pig farming and related to consumer health and animal and environmental protection, which were matters in the public interest.

Subject to certain exceptions, a company should not be denied its freedom of expression

In *Centro Europa 7 SRL and Di Stefano v Italy* Application No 38433/09, the ECtHR held that the Italian authorities should have ensured that a licensed TV company had the frequencies enabling it to broadcast. The case concerned an Italian TV company's inability to broadcast, despite having a broadcasting licence, because no television frequencies were allocated to it. There was a breach of Art 10 of the Convention but not Art 14 (Prohibition of Discrimination).

Corporate reputation and defamation

1.104 The concept of 'corporate reputation' refers to the image, goodwill, brand, logo, service or product that has been established by a company over a period of time. The general community and the public associate the company with the reputation it has built up for its products and services. Over a period of time, the company gains popularity and ingratiates with the public in the form of promotions, and loyalty programmes in order to enhance and entrench consumer loyalty. Although the process of establishing a corporate reputation takes time, it can easily be damaged by adverse comments about the company, with a detrimental effect on the company which may cause loss of business and loss of potential opportunities. The company therefore jealously guards and protects its reputation from further harm and injury just as a natural person would strive for such protection, because it believes it has not engaged in any unethical, fraudulent or criminal activities which should tarnish its reputation.

1.105 If a natural person is defamed, the tendency would be to consider an action either for slander or libel. The individual would contend that his/her reputation has been seriously affected and damaged. But what if the company has been defamed? Could the company claim that its reputation has been affected such that it seeks not only compensation, but also potential remedies to prevent future injury to its reputation? This section considers a series of significant cases impacting on corporate defamation, the position at common law and the position under the Defamation Act 2013.

The McLibel Cases

1.106 A series of libel cases were filed by McDonald's Corporation in the 1990's against two environmental activists, Morris and Steel (known as the 'McLibel Cases') concerning a pamphlet critical of McDonalds which it claimed affected its reputation.

1.107 During 1986, 'London Greenpeace', a small environmental campaign group (unrelated to Greenpeace International), distributed a leaflet 'What's wrong with McDonald's: everything they don't want you to know'. The pamphlet made various allegations against McDonald's including that: (i) it was complicit in Third World starvation; (ii) it bought from greedy rulers and elites and practised economic imperialism; (iii) it wasted huge quantities of grain and water; (iv) it destroyed rainforest with poisons and colonial invasions; (v) it sold unhealthy addictive fast food; (vi) it altered its food with artificial chemistry; (viii) it exploited children with its advertising; (ix) it exploited its workers and banned unions; and (x) it sought to hide its malfeasance.

1.108 In 1990, McDonald's brought libel proceedings against five London Greenpeace supporters of which three apologised, but Steel and Morris chose to defend the action, without legal aid and with very limited income – relying largely on pro bono lawyers to assist them in court.

In the High Court [19 June 1997, No 1990-M-No.5724], Bell J decided in favour of McDonald's for libel in some aspects of the pamphlet, but other allegations he found to be true against McDonalds, namely: (i) McDonald's endangered the health of their workers and customers by 'misleading advertising'; (ii) they 'exploit children'; (iii) they were 'culpably responsible' in the infliction of unnecessary cruelty to animals; (iv) they were 'antipathetic' to unionisation and paid their workers low wages. Bell J awarded McDonald's £60,000 damages.

1.109 The Court of Appeal [31 March 1999, QBENF 97/1281/1] held that it was a fair comment to say that McDonald's employees worldwide 'do badly in terms of pay and conditions'. It was also true to say that 'if one eats enough McDonald's food, one's diet may well become high in fat etc, with the real risk of heart disease'. The Court of Appeal stated that this latter finding 'must have a serious effect on their trading reputation since it goes to the very business in which they are engaged. In our judgment, it must have a greater impact on [McDonald's] reputation than any other charges that the trial judge had found true'. The Court of Appeal stated that it had 'considerable sympathy' with the defendants' submissions that the leaflet meant 'that there is a respectable (not cranky) body of medical opinion which links a junk food diet with a risk of cancer and heart disease', and that 'this link was accepted both in literature published by McDonald's themselves and by one or more of McDonald's own experts and in medical publications of high repute'. The Court of Appeal, however, reduced the damages award by the High Court from £60,000 to £40,000. It also rejected the 'defendants' contention that multinational corporations should no longer be able to sue for libel over public interest issues'. This was a matter for Parliament and the court was not in a position to decide which were stronger or weaker multinational corporations who could sue for libel.

1.110 Steel and Morris' appeal to the House of Lords was rejected. They subsequently filed a case before the ECtHR contesting against the UK government's policy that legal aid was not available in libel cases, and setting out the case that UK libel laws were oppressive and unfair. They further contended that lacking legal aid had breached their right to freedom of expression and a right to fair trial. The ECtHR [15 February 2005], held that the original case in the UK court had breached Art 6 (right to a fair trial) and Art 10 (right to freedom of expression) of the ECHR. The ECtHR ordered the UK government to pay Steel and Morris £57,000 compensation. The ECtHR was critical of the UK laws in failing to protect the public right to criticise corporations whose business practices affected people's lives and the environment, which was in breach of Art 10. The ECtHR also ruled that the trial was biased because of the defendants' lack of resources taking account of the complex and oppressive UK libel laws. It stated:

> 'in a democratic society even small and informal campaign groups, such as London Greenpeace, must be able to carry on their activities effectively and that there exists a strong public interest in enabling such groups and individuals outside the mainstream to contribute to the public debate by disseminating information and ideas on matters of general public interest such as health and the environment' (para 89).
>
> 'The safeguard afforded by Article 10 to journalists in relation to reporting on issues of general interest is subject to the proviso that they act in good faith in order to provide accurate and reliable information in accordance with the ethics of journalism (…), and the same principle must apply to others who engage in public debate.' (para 90).

> 'It is true that large public companies inevitably and knowingly lay themselves open to close scrutiny of their acts and, as in the case of the businessmen and women who manage them, the limits of acceptable criticism are wider in the case of such companies.' (para 94).

1.111 The ECtHR further noted in relation to multinational companies:

> 'The Court further does not consider that the fact that the plaintiff in the present case was a large multinational company should in principle deprive it of a right to defend itself against defamatory allegations or entail that the applicants should not have been required to prove the truth of the statements made. It is true that large public companies inevitably and knowingly lay themselves open to close scrutiny of their acts and, as in the case of the businessmen and women who manage them, the limits of acceptable criticism are wider in the case of such companies (see *Fayed v the United Kingdom*, judgment of 21 September 1994, Series A no 294-B, p 53, § 75). However, in addition to the public interest in open debate about business practices, there is a competing interest in protecting the commercial success and viability of companies, for the benefit of shareholders and employees, but also for the wider economic good. The State therefore enjoys a margin of appreciation as to the means it provides under domestic law to enable a company to challenge the truth, and limit the damage, of allegations which risk harming its reputation (see *Markt Intern Verlag GmbH and Klaus Beermann v Germany*, judgment of 20 November 1989, Series A no 165, pp 19–21, §§ 33–38).
>
> If, however, a State decides to provide such a remedy to a corporate body, it is essential, in order to safeguard the countervailing interests in free expression and open debate, that a measure of procedural fairness and equality of arms is provided for. The Court has already found that the lack of legal aid rendered the defamation proceedings unfair, in breach of Article 6 § 1. The inequality of arms and the difficulties under which the applicants laboured are also significant in assessing the proportionality of the interference under Article 10' (paras 94 and 95).

The position of corporate defamation at common law

1.112 At common law, corporations can sue for libel: *Metropolitan Saloon Omnibus Co Ltd v Hawkins* (1859) 4 H & N 87. The company does not have to prove actual damage.

1.113 In *South Hetton Coal Co Ltd v North-Eastern News Association Ltd* [1894] 1 QB 133, an action was brought by an incorporated colliery company against the newspaper for libel contained in the newspaper about the state of the district in which the company operated, and alleging that the company did not look after its employees, that the district was in a highly insanitary state with houses unfit for habitation, lack of water and inadequate accommodation for the occupants. Lord Esher held that an incorporated trading company could sue for libel that was calculated to injure its reputation in respect of its business, without proof of special damage. The test was whether what had been published with regard to the claimant, would tend in the minds of the people of ordinary sense to bring the claimant into contempt, hatred or ridicule, or to injure its character. See too: *Mayor Aldermen and Citizens of Manchester v Williams* [1891] 1 QB 94; and *Metropolitan Saloon Omnibus Co v Hawkins* (1899) 4 H & N 87.

1.114 In *Derbyshire County Council v Times Newspapers Ltd* [1993] AC 534, the County Council brought an action for damages for libel against the defendants where allegations were made in articles about share dealings involving the investment of monies from the local authority's superannuation fund, from a complex series of deals in companies controlled or connected by a businessman. The District County Council contended that the allegations had resulted in loss and damage by injuring its credit and reputation. The House of Lords held that it was clearly established that trading corporations were entitled to sue in respect of defamatory matters which could be seen to have damaged their business dealings. Lopes LJ stated that although a corporation could not maintain an action in libel of anything reflecting upon it personally, yet it could maintain an action for libel impacting upon their trade or business, without alleging or proving special damage. The words complained of must 'injuriously' affect the company as distinct from the individuals who compose it. The words complained of must attack the company in the method of conducting its affairs or attack its financial position. A trading company was entitled to sue in respect of defamatory matters where damage or injury occurred to the business. However, a local authority was not entitled to sue for defamation because it was a democratically elected governmental body and should be open to uninhibited public criticism.

1.115 In *Thornton v Telegraph Media Group Ltd* [2012] EWCA 383, the court stated that a defamatory meaning was one that substantially affected in an adverse manner the attitude of other people towards the claimant or had a tendency to do so.

1.116 At common law, an individual or corporation establishes a cause of action in libel by proof that the defendant published in writing or other permanent form, a statement about the claimant which bore a meaning defamatory of the claimant. The law does not require a person or company who sues for libel to surmount any preliminary hurdle by showing an established reputation: *Multigroup Bulgaria Holding AD v Oxford Analytica Ltd* [2001] EMLR 737. In *Sim v Stretch* [1936] 2 All ER 1237, Lord Atkin identified the 'threshold of seriousness' required to constitute defamation. The test of exposure of the claimant to 'hatred, ridicule or contempt' was too narrow a test and the preferred test was 'would the words tend to lower the plaintiff in the estimation of right-thinking members of society generally'?

The position of companies under the Defamation Act 2013

1.117 The Defamation Act 2013 (DA 2013) was enacted on 23 April 2013 and reforms aspects of the law of defamation. A statement will not be defamatory unless its publication has caused or is likely to cause serious harm to the reputation of the claimant: DA 2013, s 1(1). In this regard, a company may also be a claimant, and it will need to show 'serious harm' to its reputation. Harm to the reputation of a body that trades for profit is not 'serious harm', unless it has caused or is likely to cause the body 'serious financial loss': DA 2013, s 1(2).

1.118 Section 1(1) of the DA 2013 extends to situations where publication is likely to cause serious harm in order to cover situations where the harm has not yet occurred at the time the action for defamation is commenced. The section is an outcome of the judicial consideration given by the courts in a series or cases to the issue of what is sufficient to establish that a statement is defamatory.

1.119 The DA 2013 also allows for the potential for trivial cases to be struck out on the basis that they are an abuse of process and of minor importance or significance. The DA 2013 allows a potential defendant to raises defences which include truth (s 2), honest opinion (s 3) and publication on matter of public interest (s 4).

Checklist: regulatory framework of company law

1.120 *This checklist highlights some of the key aspects of the regulatory framework of UK company law including references to the CA 2006.*

No	Issue	References
1	The development of company law in the UK is the product of various reforms and recommendations by various company law committees established to review companies' legislation at the time.	Companies Acts and committees appointed by government
2	Previous approaches towards UK companies legislation were predominantly 'think large companies first' with private companies as an afterthought.	
3	EU regulations and directives were merely added on to companies legislation without proper consideration as to how these would impact on UK companies legislation.	
4	Previous companies legislation was complex and difficult to understand and did not address the needs of the users.	
5	Between 1998 and 2005, a major company law review was launched to modernise UK company law with the establishment of a Steering Group and working groups to review various aspects of UK company law.	Company law reviews
6	The product of company law review led to CA 2006 which is the primary legislation governing companies in the UK and its statutory instruments.	CA 2006 (c 46)
7	CA 2006 is based on some guiding principles including 'think small companies' first approach; modernising companies law; accessibility and flexibility of the legislation; transparency; ease of establishing legal entities; and facilitating the use of modern technology for company law.	
8	CA 2006 is one of the largest pieces of legislation in UK law, comprising 1,300 sections, 47 Parts and 16 Schedules and re-enacts many of the provisions of CA 1985.	

No	Issue	References
9	Other sources of UK company law include references to case law, principles borrowed from common law and equity adapted to the company law regime, and the company's constitution.	
10	Legislation emanating from the EU also impacts on UK company law in the form of regulations and directives. Various regulations and directives have been enacted on company law aspects which have been implemented in the companies legislation over a period of time.	
11	Companies may have certain human rights that require protection. They are subject to ensuring other people's human rights are also protected.	

Checklist: company law reform

1.121 *This checklist sets out some of the most significant UK committees involved in company law reform over the years leading to the modern Companies Acts.*

Date	Document	Coverage
1906	Loreburn Committee Report (Cmd 3052)	Examined limited aspects of company law
1918	Wrenbury Committee Report	Examined limited aspects of company law
1925–26	Greene Committee Report	Report on the whole spectrum of company law in connection with the Companies Acts 1908–17
1945	Cohen Committee Report	Consideration of various aspects of company law including objects clauses; directors' duties; accounting aspects; financial assistance; relationship between directors and shareholders
1962	Jenkins Committee Report (Cmd 1749)	Examined the CA 1948; considered whole spectrum of company law
1986	Department of Trade and Industry: The Prentice Report	Reform of the *ultra vires* rule
1997	Law Commission Report: Shareholder Remedies (No 246)	Law Commissions of England, Wales and Scotland on radical reform of shareholder remedies

Date	Document	Coverage
1997	Law Commission Report: Regulating Conflicts of Interest and Formulating a Statement of Directors' Duties (No 261)	Law Commissions of England and Wales and Scotland on radical reform of directors' duties to be placed on a statutory footing
1998	Modern Company Law for a Competitive Economy	Established the foundations for a new company law regime
1999	Company Law Steering Group – The Strategic Framework	Detailed analysis of whole spectrum of company law requiring radical change
1999	Company Law Steering Group: Modern Company Law for a Competitive Economy: Company General Meetings and Shareholder Communication	Considered proposed reforms to general meetings and effective communication between shareholders
1999	Company Law Steering Group: Modern Company Law for a Competitive Economy: Company Formation and Capital Maintenance	Detailed proposals on reform of law relating to company set-up (types of companies) and capital maintenance including financial assistance
1999	Company Law Steering Group: Modern Company Law for a Competitive Economy: Reforming the Law Concerning Overseas Companies	Proposals on reforming the laws concerning overseas companies
2000	Company Law Steering Group: Modern Company Law for a Competitive Economy: Developing the Framework (URN 00/656)	Made key proposals on governance of companies and small and private companies
2000	Company Law Steering Group: Modern Company Law for A Competitive Economy: Capital Maintenance – Other Issues	Focused on a small number of residual technical issues on capital maintenance
2000	Company Law Steering Group: Modern Company Law for a Competitive Economy: Registration of Company Charges	Reviewed previous reports on company charges and proposed options
2000	Company Law Steering Group: Modern Company Law for a Competitive Economy: Completing the Structure (URN 00/1335)	Took forward proposals of previous consultation documents towards final phase

Date	Document	Coverage
2001	Final Report presented by the Steering Group	Set out the Steering Group's final recommendations on a wide spectrum of company law reform areas addressed in previous consultation documents
2002	White Paper: Modernising Company Law (Cmd 5553-1)	Examined the Company Law Steering Group's proposals and formulation of Government policies with publication of draft Companies Bill
2005	White Paper: Company Law Reform (Cmd 6456)	Final White Paper issued with publication of draft Companies Bill.

Definitions

1.122

AIM: Alternative Investment Market.

Enactment: An enactment contained in subordinate legislation within the meaning of the Interpretation Act 1978.

LLP: Limited Liability Partnership.

Prescribed: Prescribed by order or regulations by the Secretary of State.

TFEU: Treaty on the Functioning of the European Union.

Ultra vires: An act or transaction beyond the company's capacity.

2 Pre-incorporation

Contents

Introduction

2.1 Before the life of a company begins, there is usually an initial planning process and steps to be undertaken for the establishment of a company. The process includes determining the objects of the company, its internal regulations, and identifying its potential directors, shareholders, share capital, registered office, management, governance and operational issues. The promoter has the ability and capacity to plan the setting up of the company from its incipient stages to its development – fully functional and operational with a separate legal personality of its own and which is treated in all respects as a legal person distinct from its shareholders. The company will develop its own individual personality through the directing mind and will of the promoter leading to its ultimate success or failure. The company cannot, therefore, exist in a vacuum: it requires agents for its establishment. These agents will usually be the company's promoters who may ultimately become the company's directors and shareholders, and assume all or part of the responsibility for breathing into this inanimate, lifeless creature, the soul, flesh and body of the company. The creation of the company is in the hands and mind of the promoter. The promoter decides the fate of the company even before its incorporation: whether to enter into pre-incorporation transactions in good faith with a third party, or to have such transactions tainted with illegality, fraud or deception by duping, misrepresenting and misleading others, and thereby deriving a personal benefit from such male fide activities.

2.2 This chapter considers the promoters who undertake the preliminary formalities required to establish the company. It addresses the following aspects:

- the identity of the promoters;
- the characteristics of the promoters;
- how the courts have defined promoters, and judicial attitudes towards promoters;

- the duties and obligations of promoters;
- remedies for breach of promoters' duties and obligations;
- the position on pre-incorporation contracts both at common law and under the Companies Act 2006.

Promoters

2.3 This section considers the definition of a promoter with specific reference to case law, including the characteristics and attributes of promoters. Their duties and obligations are addressed, as are judicial attitudes towards promoters.

Who is a promoter?

2.4 During the nineteenth century, the term 'promoter' was considered a pejorative expression for a person who was perceived in a bad light as a cunning, trickster, fraudster or deceiver who manipulated and misrepresented a company's status or the company's transactions with the public who believed that they were entering transactions with a *bona fide* promoter. The promoter's primary motive would typically be to make quick monetary gains and to conceal the true nature of the transaction between the promoter and the company established, including an invitation to the public by a prospectus to subscribe shares in the company set up by the promoter. The company would usually be a sham entity set up to satisfy the machinations and Machiavellian plans and motives of the promoter, including duplicity with the ulterior motive to make secret profits without any disclosure to potential shareholders. The promoter would then sell off the company to the duped shareholders and disappear from the scene causing loss to the shareholders and to the company. Lord MacNaghten recognised the nature and devious practices engaged by promoters and vehemently disapproved of such practices by a promoter in *Gluckstein v Barnes* [1900] AC 240: 'I cannot see any ingenuity or any novelty in the trick which Mr Gluckstein and his associates practised on the persons whom they invited to take shares in Olympia, Limited. It is the old story. It has been done over and over again.' He considered it timely for the law to protect potential investors and take a hard line with such promoters. Similarly in *R v Darby* [1911] 1 KB 95, Phillimore J was of the view that the promoters were 'minded to perpetrate a very great fraud'.

2.5 The term 'promoter' is not defined in the CA 2006 (nor in any previous companies legislation), and reference is often made to case law for guidance on the definition including the duties of promoters. Although there is no general consensus in English company law as to the definition of a promoter, there are some practical features and characteristics that distinguish a promoter from others:

- The term covers a broad spectrum of persons embarking on the purpose of setting up an entity for a particular project assignment. The project may be *bona fide* or a sham depending upon the promoter's intentions: *Twycross v Grant* (1877) 2 CPD 469.
- A promoter may be actively involved in the company formation, but a person who has also been passively involved in the company formation may still be a

promoter. According to Cockburn in *Twycross v Grant* (1877) 2 CPD 469, the promoters not only provisionally formed the company, but were, in fact, to the end its creators; they found the directors, and qualified them; they prepared the prospectus; they paid for printing and advertising, and the expenses incidental to the establishment of the company. So long as the work of company formation continued, those who carried on that work had retained the character of promoters.

See too: *Emma Silver Mining Co v Grant* (1879) 11 Ch D 918; *Jubilee Cotton Mills v Lewis* [1924] AC 958.

- A promoter need not necessarily be involved in the establishment of the company but will still be regarded as one if the promoter is in any way involved in the negotiation or obtaining of potential finance or negotiating agreements on behalf of the company that is to be established: *Lagunas Nitrate Co v Lagunas Syndicate* [1899] 2 Ch 392.
- A person advising promoters in a professional capacity will not be considered as a promoter: *Re Great Wheal Polgooth Co* (1883) 53 LJ Ch 42. However, if the professional goes beyond professional advice and becomes involved in becoming a director or obtaining potential investors, he may be considered as a promoter: *Lydney & Wigpool Iron Ore Co v Bird* (1886) 33 Ch D 85; *Bagnall v Carlton* (1877) 6 Ch D 371.
- One of the principal objectives of a promoter is to comply with the initial formalities required to establish a company, and to register the company at Companies House.
- The determination as to whether or not a person is a promoter is one of fact: the courts will look at all the factual circumstances in determining what role the promoter played in the establishment of the company, including any dealings with third parties before the company was established. This includes entering into pre-incorporation contracts for the company's purposes and future activities. In a public company, where securities are to be offered to the public, the promoter will usually be involved in preparing and issuing the prospectus.
- In some cases, promoters may not be involved in the initial stages of forming the company but may still be considered as promoters even if they are involved at the tail-end of company establishment: *Lagunas Nitrate Co v Lagunas Syndicate* [1899] 2 Ch 392 The promoter's role will continue until the company has been incorporated or directors have been appointed: *Twycross v Grant* (1877) 2 CPD 396.
- In some instances, promoters may seek potential funding from investors to ensure the viability and financial success of the company once it is established. Depending on the circumstances, these investors may take a passive or active part in the company's management and operations, or they may nominate their potential directors to sit on the company's board to oversee the activities of the company and guide the company in the early stages of its set up.
- Promoters may themselves become directors/shareholders in the company, but it is not a prerequisite that they do so. They may simply be arranging and co-ordinating the process of bringing together other investors into a company, without any involvement in the functional and operational aspects of the company.

- Promoters who become directors and/or shareholders in a company will be interested in ensuring the long-term success of the company, which may include profit maximisation and corporate social responsibilities towards wider stakeholders.
- Promoters usually tend to be individuals. They may also include a general partnership, a limited liability partnership, a limited partnership, an unincorporated association, or any other entity or organisation seeking to establish a company.
- Promoters may identify and purchase business assets on the company's behalf before incorporation, enter into contracts with third parties, and hire potential personnel to work for the company once it is established.
- A promoter may also a person who holds himself out or represents himself to be acting on behalf of a company that will be incorporated.

Judicial definitions of promoters

2.6 Although the term 'promoter' is referred to in the CA 2006 (see for example, the CA 2006, s 762(1)(c) on obtaining a trading certificate), there is no statutory definition of the term. Over the years, however, the English courts have developed certain features and attributes of promoters to highlight the various activities in which they are involved in the company's incorporation. Much case law in this area is old, dating back to the nineteenth century concerning rogue promoters who preyed on innocent and gullible individuals and groups. The courts during that time largely tackled and curbed attempts by promoters who conducted fraudulent and deceptive activities, by using inventive and novel devices to entrap the public into providing and securing funds ostensibly for the company's purposes, but in reality for the promoters' own unlawful motives. In this regard, the company was a sham simply to serve the whims of the fraudster. The courts established standards which a promoter should meet in dealing with third parties before incorporation. The term 'promoter' was perceived by the court as a person displaying moral probity and good standards of behaviour in the establishment of a company: anything short of this would be considered as unethical and below the standards of moral unrighteousness.

2.7 The cases on promoters are to some extent now outdated, given the strict nature of modern legislation which regulates the activities of promoters particularly in the initial public offering of securities. For example, a public company may not seek listing without first establishing a trading record, usually dating back to at least three years of trading required under the Stock Exchange listing rules, including the provisions under Part 6 of the Financial Services and Markets Act 2000 (FSMA 2000) (Official Listing), and Part 43 of the Companies Act 2006 (Transparency Obligations and Related Matters). Under FSMA 2000, s 90 for example, a promoter may be liable to pay compensation for any untrue or misleading statements contained in the listing particulars or prospectus to a person who has: (a) acquired securities to which the particulars apply; and (b) suffered loss in respect of them. However, a person will not, by reason of being a promoter of a company or otherwise, incur any liability for failing to disclose information which he would not be required to disclose in the listing particulars in respect of a company's securities if he were responsible for those particulars: FSMA 2000, s 90(8).

2.8 The courts have traditionally been reluctant to set out a detailed definition of a promoter that would capture all aspects and features of his duties and obligations. This is because the courts preferred to keep the term flexible, in order to catch as many rogues as possible who might attempt to abuse the companies legislation by using the company as a cloak for their fraudulent and deceitful activities. Usually, such fraudsters would purchase an asset well below its market price before the company was incorporated, and then sell the asset to the company at a significantly higher value in consideration for cash or shares in that company. Such transactions would also be concealed and not disclosed to the company until subsequent discovery by the company's new directors and shareholders, or by the liquidator on the company's liquidation. The cases on promoters have, therefore, concentrated largely on the standards of behaviour that promoters were required to display in their dealings with the public and third parties, including upholding standards of moral probity. The courts have applied various areas of law in imputing liability to promoters, including misrepresentation, fraud, unjust enrichment, negligence and contractual liability. This has also included applying equitable principles and imposing fiduciary duties on promoters. Although CA 2006 sets out the duties of directors, it does not provide for such duties for promoters and reliance is therefore placed on common law cases to identify such duties.

A promoter's legal existence is determined by fact not law

As long ago as 1879, in *Emma Silver Mining Co Ltd v Lewis,* 4 CPD, 36 (CP 1879), the court stated that the term 'promoter,' did not have a very definite meaning, but involved the idea of exertion for the purpose of floating a company, and also the idea of some duty towards the company, imposed by or arising from the position which the so-called promoter assumed toward it. The persons who form a company have duties towards it before it comes into existence.

One of the earliest attempts to define the term 'promoter' was set out in *Twycross v Grant* (1877) 2 CPD 469 at p 541, where Cockburn CJ stated:

> 'A promoter, I apprehend, is one who undertakes to form a company with reference to a given project and to set it going, and who takes the necessary steps to accomplish that purpose … and so long as the work of formation continues, those who carry on the work must, I think, retain the character of promoters. Of course, if a governing body, in the shape of directors, has once been formed, and they take … what remains to be done in the way of forming the company, into their own hands, the functions of a promoter are at an end.'

On occasions, the courts equated the position of a promoter to that of a person discharging trustee-like functions in the course of his duties in establishing the company.

In *Bagnall v Carlton* (1877) 6 Ch D 371, Cotton LJ described promoters as almost akin to trustees, but not identical to them: Similar to trustees, promoters had fiduciary duties to discharge and could not secretly make to themselves a profit in the transaction in which they were trustees.

In *Whaley & Bridge Calico Printing Co v Green* (1880) 5 QBD 109, Bowen J stated:

> 'The term promoter is a term not of law, but of business, usefully summing up in a single word a number of business operations familiar to the commercial world by which a company is generally brought into existence.'

It is not always the position that the promoter should personally be involved in the company formation: this aspect could be delegated to others yet the person who delegated could still be a promoter: *Lagunas Nitrate Co v Lagunas Syndicate* [1899] 2 Ch 392.

In establishing a company, the promoter may seek the assistance of a lawyer, accountant or a company formation agent. It has been held that such professionals, in undertaking their duties in that capacity, cannot be considered as the company's promoters: *Re Great Wheal Poolgooth Co Ltd* (1883) 53 LJ Ch 42.

In subsequent cases, the courts have tended to retreat from defining the term in any further detail or even using the term 'promoter', but they have instead addressed the relationship of the promoter vis-à-vis the company that is being established.

A promoter cannot be an agent of a company that does not exist

In *Lydney and Wigpool Iron Ore Co v Bird* (1886) 33 ChD 85, Lindley LJ was of the view that although a promoter could not be considered as an agent or trustee of a company that did not exist, yet the principles of agency or trustee could still apply to the promoter. He considered the term 'promoter' as ambiguous and that it was wholly inappropriate for a promoter to stand in a fiduciary relationship with an unformed company. The courts focused on the activities conducted by the promoter and dealings with third parties before incorporation. The fact that a promoter was acting as agent for the sellers in setting up a company for the purchase of their property did not exonerate him from accounting to the company, when formed, for any secret profit made by him. Lindley LJ thought that the term 'promoter' was ambiguous in the context of company law. Instead, it was necessary to ascertain in each case what the so-called promoter really did before his legal liabilities could be accurately ascertained. This would entail looking at the facts and circumstances surrounding the promoter's actions. The court would in appropriate circumstances extend the concepts of agency and trusteeship in their application to promoters for the purposes of attributing liability. Accordingly, a promoter of a company was accountable to it for all moneys secretly obtained by him from the company, similar to the relationship of principal and agent or of trustee and *cestui que trust* had really existed between them and the company when the money was so obtained.

In estimating the amount of the secret profit for which a promoter was accountable to the company he was held entitled to be allowed the legitimate expenses incurred by him in forming the company, such as the reports of surveyors, the charges of solicitors and brokers, and the cost of advertisements; but not a sum of money which he had expended in obtaining from another person a guarantee for the taking of shares. See too per Cotton LJ in *Ladywell Mining Co v Brookes* (1887) 35 ChD 400 at pp 407 and 411; and *Mann v Edinburgh Northern Tramways Co* [1893] AC 69.

Promoters' duties

2.9 Promoters' duties and liabilities are generally regulated by equity and common law. When discharging their duties and responsibilities through the process of establishing a company, promoters occupy a special relationship in their dealings with third parties and the company they are setting up. In this regard, they have not been immune from the scrutiny of the courts, for the very reason that the courts perceive promoters as individuals who have the capacity to enter into contracts and commercial dealings with third parties at a time when the company has not been formed.

2.10 Further, promoters also have full knowledge, understanding and intention as to the motives for setting up the company. Accordingly, the courts consider that some liability ought to be imposed on promoters for any of their acts or activities which are in breach of the law. The objective of the courts has also been to protect the public and third parties dealing with promoters from using any deceptive or fraudulent activities perpetrated by the promoters. Promoters cannot, therefore, shield behind the cloak of a company that is in the process of being formed, and expect to be exonerated from any liabilities that they may incur while acting in that capacity. Generally, a promoter has capacity to enter into contractual relations with third parties; to sue and be sued; as well being subject to criminal penalties and sanctions.

A promoter's duty may continue even after the company's formation

A promoter's existence does not necessarily end on the formation of the company, but any liability or accountability may still continue until all issues have been resolved between the promoter and the company: *Eden v Ridsales Rwy, Lamp & Lighting Co* (1889) 23 QBD 368.

Promoters are subject to fiduciary principles

Recognising that promoters are able to operate with unfettered powers and thereby the potential to engage in abuses of a fraudulent and deceitful nature in establishing the company, the courts have adapted the fiduciary principles applicable to trustees and directors, by applying them to promoters in order to minimise the scope of any potential abuses, and to demonstrate that promoters must be scrupulously honest and display exemplary behaviour in the conduct of their duties: *Hichens v Congreve* (1828) 4 Russ 562. Any wrongdoing conducted by the promoter in setting up the company is a wrong done to the company, and the company is the proper claimant to such action against the promoter: *Foss v Harbottle* (1843) 2 Hare 461; and see too the derivative action under the Companies Act 2006, Pt 11.

2.11 Owing to the position occupied by the promoters, the courts have developed some duties that are applicable to promoters. The next section considers some of their important duties.

Fiduciary duty

2.12 The CA 2006 does not address the duties and obligations of promoters but only considers their personal liability under a pre-incorporation context. The duties were developed by the courts largely in the nineteenth century to deal with the types of conduct and actions undertaken by promoters. The courts have traditionally applied equitable principles to promoters when addressing their duties and obligations, when determining the liability of the promoter in the steps leading to the company's establishment. As the company has no legal existence before it is established and is therefore a lifeless creature, the courts have been of the view that a promoter is not an agent of an entity which is not yet in existence, as there is no principal who can give instructions to an agent:

In some circumstances, promoters can be subject to fiduciary obligations

In *Re Leeds and Hanley Theatres of Varieties Ltd* [1902] 2 Ch 809, the promoters of a company purchased property for the purpose of selling it to the company when formed. The property was conveyed to a trustee for the promoters nominated by them, and was afterwards by the direction of the promoters conveyed by him to a trustee for the company, who was also nominated by the promoters. The promoters received from the company an increased price on the sale. They also nominated the first directors of the company. The prospectus of the company, which was issued for the purpose of inducing the public to subscribe for its shares, was prepared with the knowledge and privity of the promoters, so that, they were responsible for it. It did not disclose the fact that the promoters were the real vendors of the property to the company, but, on the contrary, represented the promoters' trustee as the vendor. The company afterwards went into liquidation. The liquidator brought an action to compel the promoters to account for the profit they had made from the resale of the property.

It was held that the promoters stood in a fiduciary position towards the persons who were invited to take shares in the company, and that it was their duty to disclose to those persons the fact that they were the real owners to the company. Further, the prospectus issued by the promoters was fraudulent, and that for their breach of duty by this non-disclosure, the promoters were liable in damages to the company. The court stated that the true measure of the damages was the profit which the promoters had obtained upon the purchase and resale of the property.

According to Vaughan Williams LJ, the fiduciary duty is owed to third parties. The promoters stood in a fiduciary relationship to the future allottees of shares – to the persons who were invited to take up the shares of the company. The promoters owed a duty to disclose the fact that they had an interest in the transaction.

A promoter must not make any secret profit from his position

In *Re British Seamless Paper Box Co* (1881) 17 Ch D 467, at 471 (2) Jessel MR said:

> 'I quite agree to this, that if promoters make an arrangement to get a profit for themselves out of what is apparently paid to the vendors, it is immaterial whether the contract with the vendors is approved of by the directors of the company, who are the promoters, just before the allotment or just after: in both cases it is intended to cheat the future shareholders; and of course it makes no difference whatever that the persons who, at the time the allotment was made, were in fact the promoters or their nominees, knew of the fraud. You can defraud future allottees as well as present allottees.'

In the same case on appeal [1902] 2 Ch 809, p 825, Brett LJ stated: 'If when parties are promoters of a company, and then become directors, and at the time when they are making a profit to themselves are intending to act not only for the then members of the company but for future members, and they keep it secret, they can be made liable to account by future shareholders ….' And Cotton LJ said that the principle 'is that the directors stand in a fiduciary relation to the whole company, that is, not only to the existing members but to all whom they intend to bring in'.

2.13 In law, the term 'fiduciary' refers to an obligation to act in a specified way towards the entity, organisation or person to whom the obligation is owed. The fiduciary is therefore placed in a special position towards the person to whom he owes duties or in his dealings with various parties. The fiduciary's intentions to act in that capacity must be *bona fide* and demonstrated by his actions towards the person he represents. Fiduciary obligations are often manifested in a duty of loyalty, honesty, good faith, the 'no profit' rule, the duty not to make secret profits, the 'no conflict' rule, or acting in any manner which may otherwise prejudicially affect the best interests of the person, entity or organisation for whom the fiduciary acts. A fiduciary is required to operate with moral probity and display exemplary standards of behaviour and professionalism in dealings with others. Fiduciaries are also required to display the utmost good faith in their dealings with third parties.

2.14 Over the years, the courts have applied these fiduciary principles borrowed from the law of trusts (based on the trustee–beneficiary relationship) towards promoters. They have considered that promoters occupy a fiduciary position: the fiduciary position is not owed so much to the directors and shareholders of the company that is ultimately formed, but towards third parties with whom promoters have dealings. This is because promoters will have knowledge as to the potential company that will be established, its objectives, activities, the amount of capital required, the identity of the potential investors that are to be targeted, any business plans that have been developed by the promoters, dealings with third parties, and in some cases, the expertise and skill that promoters may bring to the company. These aspects place the promoters in a fiduciary and advantageous position such that, should any liabilities ensue, the promoters should bear the burden of such liabilities if they are found to have breached any of the fiduciary duties that the law imposes on them.

2.15 The promoter is subject to a fiduciary duty while he is a promoter of the entity that is being formed, and therefore liable for any secret profits he has made. The psychological make-up and motive for establishing the company are important factors in the consideration of any secret profits made by the promoter. In the course of their dealings, promoters are required to make full disclosure to the company that is ultimately established of all profits made, including all material matters that affect the setting up of the company. They are also jointly and severally liable in respect of the secret profits made.

2.16 Promoters usually engage in transactions for and on behalf of a company to be formed. One of the main issues arising here is a situation where the promoter acquires an asset or property and then sells it to the company, without declaring an interest in the transaction, thereby making an undisclosed profit. This is known as a 'secret profit'. The courts have on occasions decided that a full disclosure of a secret profit made must be to an independent board of directors:

Full disclosure of a secret profit must be made to an independent board

In the House of Lords case of *Erlanger v New Sombrero Phosphate Co* [1874–1880] All ER Rep 271, a leading syndicate member, Baron Erlanger acquired a 21-year lease of a small island in the West Indies for £55,000 to work on phosphate deposits. Through Erlanger, the syndicate established New Sombrero Phosphate company, with certain prominent directors on the board, including the Lord Mayor of London who was not connected with the syndicate. Some of the other directors were abroad and others were merely acting on the instructions and directions of Erlanger. The lease was subsequently sold through another company to the New Sombrero Phosphate company for £110,000. The sale and purchase was rubber stamped without any consideration of the matter by directors at a directors' meeting once the company was established. The company offered shares to the public and many subscribed for such shares, without knowledge of the sale and purchase of the lease, until subsequent discovery when the phosphate shipments proved to be a failed transaction. The shareholders voted to remove the existing board and elected a new board of directors and to have the sale of the lease rescinded. The House of Lords held that promoters who purchase property and then create a company to purchase from them the property they possessed, stood in a fiduciary position towards that company, and they must faithfully state to the company the facts which applied to the property, and would influence the company in deciding on the reasonableness of acquiring it. According to Lord Penzance, the company never had an opportunity of exercising, through independent directors, a fair and independent judgment in respect of the transaction in question. The promoters fell below the standards of moral probity through their conduct and connivance.

Lord Cairns considered that any disclosure of a transaction by promoters should be to an independent board of directors who were the competent and partial judges as to whether or not the transaction should be entered into.

However, the *Erlanger* case imposed a strict approach towards disclosure by the promoters to an independent board including the mechanisms and composition of such a board and determining the degree of 'independency' of the board of directors. This rule was subsequently relaxed to require disclosure instead to the shareholders in a general meeting: see *Salomon v Salomon & Co Ltd* [1897] AC 22. Indeed, in *Lagunas Nitrate Co v Lagunas Syndicate* [1899] 2 CH 392, Lindley LJ stated: 'After *Salomon's* case, I think it impossible to hold that it is the duty of promoters of a company to provide it with an independent board of directors if the real truth is disclosed to those who are induced by the promoters to join the company'. Any disclosure of the actions of the promoters must be to all shareholders with a full and frank disclosure and not just to some shareholders: *Gluckstein v Barnes* [1900] AC 240.

It will not be sufficient for the disclosure of the secret profit to be made to close associates or relatives of the promoter in the company that is established, particularly where directors are charged with duties and responsibilities to act in the best interests of the company in discharging their duties.

Promoters are under a duty to disclose a secret profit

In *Gluckstein v Barnes* [1900] AC 240, a syndicate was formed by Gluckstein and others to buy the Olympia exhibition site for £140,000 in liquidation proceedings. They subsequently promoted a company which they set up called Olympia Ltd, and the Olympia site was sold to this company for £180,000. No independent directors were appointed. The syndicate then issued a prospectus inviting applications for shares and disclosing the profit made from the Olympia transaction, but they failed to disclose another profit of £20,000 which they had made from buying securities on the Olympia site. The company subsequently went into liquidation with the liquidator claiming part of the £20,000. The House of Lords held that the promoters should have disclosed to the company the profit of £20,000. The fact that the company could not now rescind the transaction was not a bar to relief, and that the promoter in question was personally liable to account to the company for the profits made.

The Earl of Halsbury LC was of the view that the company should have been informed of the transaction and consulted as to whether the company would have allowed such profit to be made. The promoters were under a duty of good faith and honesty to disclose the transaction, particularly as they had used ingenious arrangements and deception to trap investors investing in the company.

Lord MacNaghten, however, presented a more graphic view of the deceptive nature of the transaction in which promoters were involved. His Lordship stated:

> 'These gentlemen set about forming a company to pay them a handsome sum for taking off their hands a property which they had contracted to buy with that end in view. They bring the company into existence by means of the usual machinery. They appointed themselves sole guardians and protectors of this creature of theirs, half-fledged and just struggling into life, bound hand and foot while yet unborn by contracts tending to their private advantage, and so fashioned by its makers that it could only act by their hands and only see through their eyes. They issue a prospectus representing that they had agreed to purchase the property

for a sum of money largely in excess of the amount which they had, in fact, to pay. On the faith of this prospectus they collect subscriptions from a confiding and credulous public. And then comes the last act. Secretly, and therefore, dishonestly, they put into their own pockets the difference between the real and pretended price.'

A liquidator could seek to recover secret profits made by the promoter

In *Re Darby* [1911] 1 KB 95, the promoters set about establishing a company and inviting the public to subscribe for shares without disclosing the nature of secret profits that would be earned by the promoters. The company subsequently went into liquidation and the liquidator sought to recover the secret profits made by the promoters. The court held that under the circumstances the company was only an 'alias' for the promoters, and that the liquidator of the company could seek to recover the whole of the secret cash profit that the promoters had received. According to Phillimore J: '[the promoters] did not protect themselves and did not disclose the profit which they obtained. Had they called a general meeting of the shareholders and disclosed the profit and received authority from the shareholders to keep it, it might perhaps have stood. But they did not do so, and therefore they cannot keep this profit.'

A failure to disclose an interest in the transaction or contract renders the contract voidable at the company's option

In practice, the fiduciary duties of a promoter are likely to arise in his dealings with third parties and in incorporating the company. The promoter may have a dubious ulterior motive for setting up the company: typically for fraudulent and deceitful purposes and to make an undisclosed profit from various transactions with which the public is involved. One of the situations in which this fiduciary relationship arises is in respect of any profits made by the promoter which have not been disclosed to the company or its directors or shareholders upon the formation of the company. The courts have therefore imposed a fiduciary duty on promoters not to profit from their position by engaging in and making a secret profit. In *Re Lady Forrest (Murchison) Gold Mines Ltd* [1901] 1 Ch 582, Wright J considered that generally a promoter was under a fiduciary duty to disclose the profit made, albeit the profit that was made was not of a dishonest nature. On the facts, the syndicate and directors of the company were not promoters when the transaction (acquisition and resale of property to the company) was entered into. The disclosure in the prospectus of the company of the fact that the directors of the syndicate were directors of the company was a disclosure that some profit was being made. However, Simpson and the other directors were guilty of a breach of duty in not disclosing what profit had been made on the resale of the property to the company. Wright J stated: 'Although I shall have to say that Mr Simpson and the other directors, members of the syndicate, were guilty of a breach of duty in the matter, it appears to me that they were not guilty of anything which in any ordinary sense of the word can be described as fraud at all. They disclosed the fact that they were directors of the vendor syndicate, and thereby they necessarily disclosed that they were making some profit. It is quite true they did not disclose what profit they were making, and in that, as it seems to me, they were wrong and guilty of a breach of duty.' A promoter was required to bring an independent and disinterested mind when addressing the issue of whether or not to disclose the profit made.

In *Lydney and Wigpool Iron Ore Company Ltd v Bird* [1886–90] All ER Rep Ext 1686, the Court of Appeal decided that a promoter of a company was accountable for any money obtained by him from the funds of the company without the knowledge of the company, as, although before the company was formed he could not be considered as agent or trustee for it, yet the principles of the law of agency and trusteeship apply. Further, the fact that the promoter was acting for the sellers in setting up the company for the purchase of their property did not exonerate him from his liability to account to the company, when formed, for any profit secretly made by him. Lindley LJ stated that a promoter could not be characterised as an agent of a company, nor could the agent stand in such fiduciary relationship. He considered that the term 'promoter' was ambiguous, and it was necessary to ascertain in each case what the so-called 'promoter' really did before his legal liabilities could be accurately ascertained. In every case it was preferable to look at the facts, and ascertain and describe them as they are.

See too *Beck v Kantorowicz* (1857) 3 K & J 230; and *Bagnall v Carlton* (1877) 6 ChD 408.

2.17 Promoters also must not deliberately place themselves in a position where their personal interests conflict with their duty to establish the company: *Lagunas Nitrate Co v Lagunas Syndicate* [1899] 2 Ch 442. According to Lindley MR: '... in equity the promoters of a company stand in a fiduciary relation to it, and to those persons whom they induce to become shareholders in it, and cannot in equity bind the company by any contract with themselves without fully and fairly disclosing to the company all material facts which the company ought to know'.

2.18 In order to avoid liability for any potential actions, promoters would attempt to contract out of their fiduciary duties by including a 'waiver' clause in the company's articles of association. The effect of this clause was that both the company and the shareholders were denied any right of action against the promoters: *Omnium Electric Palaces v Baines* [1914] 1 Ch 332.

The need for transparency and consent

2.19 The courts have imposed a requirement that the promoter must fully, frankly and with honesty and transparency disclose all material facts to potential investors who may invest in the company. This also requires a disclosure to the company's shareholders who are members at the time of the transaction, and it is essential that the promoter makes full disclosure too in the prospectus inviting potential shareholders to subscribe so that such investors can make an informed decision as to whether or not to invest. However, where the transaction requires the public to invest in the shares of the company, the courts have required promoters fully to disclose the transaction and seek approval from an independent board of directors who are detached from the promoter in which case the promoter's liability usually ceases upon such disclosure, but with liability to potential investors who subscribed in the company based on any misrepresentation or false information provided in the prospectus. Alternatively, the disclosure should be in a prospectus offering shares to the public, so that the public are fully aware of the circumstances before purchasing shares in the company: *Lagunas Nitrate Company v Lagunas Syndicate* [1899] 2 Ch 392; *Salomon v Salomon & Co* [1897] AC 22.

Remedies

2.20 Under English law, there are various remedies available where a promoter is found to be in breach of his fiduciary obligations. The two main remedies in this area have focused on rescission of the contract entered into by the promoter; and the promoter accounting for the secret profits namely for breach of his fiduciary duties, with the remedy of tracing available.

Rescission

2.21 This may arise where there is a transfer or disposal of an asset to the company and the promoter fails to disclose the secret profit he has made from the transaction. In this situation, the company may be able to rescind the contract. In order for rescission to apply and be effective, the company must not have ratified or affirmed the contract otherwise rescission may be lost: *Erlanger v New Sombrero Phosphate Co* [1874–1880] All ER Rep 271: *Steedman v Frigidaire Corp* [1933] 1 DLR 161; *Re Leeds & Hanley Theatre of Variety* [1902] 2 Ch 809.

2.22 However, the company's right to rescind may be limited in certain circumstances. This usually arises where the company whether expressly or impliedly or by its conduct or actions, evidences an intention to affirm the contract with full knowledge of the profit made by the promoter. In such cases, the right to rescission by the company may be lost: *Re Cape Breton Co* (1885) 9 ChD 795 (affirmed sub nom *Cavendish Bentick v Fenn* (1887) 12 App Cas 652. Further, if there is a delay by the company in rescinding the contract, the company may not thereafter be able to rescind the contract: *Long v Lloyd* [1958] 1 WLR 753; and *Leaf v International Galleries* [1950] 2 KB 86. A bona fide third party without notice who obtains rights in respect of the contract will be able to enforce such rights against the company if the company has not rescinded the contract: *Re Leeds and Hanley Theatres of Varieties Ltd* [1902] 2 Ch 809. The effect of rescission is to place the parties in their original position as if the transaction had not taken place, unless this is not possible owing to the actions and conduct of the promoter: *Lagunas Nitrate Co v Lagunas Syndicate* [1899] 2 Ch 392.

2.23 Rescission will not be possible if the original asset cannot be returned back to its previous state: *Ladywell Mining Co v Brookes* (1887) 35 Ch D 400; *Smith New Court Securities v Scrimgeour Vickers (Asset Management) Limited* [1977] AC 254 per Lord Browne-Wilkinson.

Action of deceit

2.24 The parties who have been subject to fraud, may also be able to sue by an action of deceit: *Whaley Bridge Calico Printing Co v Green* (1879) 5 QBD 109.

See too *Re Olympia Limited* [1898] 1 Ch 153 under name of *Gluckstein v Barnes* [1900] AC 240.

Trusteeship

2.25 It may be possible for the company to enforce the promoter's claim on the basis of the trusteeship principle, particularly where the promoter has been promised monies, bribes or other commissions, but which have not been received by the promoter from a third party or promisor. The trusteeship principle would operate on the basis that the promoter was a trustee for the monies that he would have received from the promisor or the third party: *Whaley Bridge Calico Printing Co v Green* (1879) 5 QBD 109.

A promoter may also be liable in respect of bribes under the Bribery Act 2010.

Damages for breaches of fiduciary duties

2.26 In *Leeds and Hanley Theatres of Varieties Ltd* [1902] 2 Ch 809, the Court of Appeal stated that it may be possible for the company to claim damages against the promoter for breach of his fiduciary duties: see too *Jacobus Marler Estates Ltd v Marler* (1913) 85 LJPC 167n, PC. Damages for breaches of equitable obligations such as fiduciary duties, have also been awarded by the courts: *Target Holdings Ltd v Redferns* [1996] AC 41; *Knight v Frost* [1999] 1 BCLC 364 at p 373.

Compensation

2.27 The courts may be prepared to make an order holding the promoter liable to pay compensation to members of the public who subscribed for shares. This action is based on the information provided in the information memorandum, the prospectus or similar document, which information later proves to be false in a material particular, and where the whole objective of the scheme is to defraud the potential investors for the purposes of obtaining monies.

Account of profits

2.28 A promoter may be required by the court to account for the profits made in a transaction which has not been disclosed to the company, particularly where a secret profit has been made and rescission of the transaction is not possible to recover the secret profit: *Emma Silver Mining Co v Grant* (1879) 11 Ch D 918; and *Lydney and Wigpool Iron Ore Co v Bird* (1886) 33 ChD 85. The courts have not generally permitted account of profits where rescission has not been available: *Re Ambrose Lake Tin Co* (1880) 14 Ch D 390; *Lady Forrest (Murchison) Gold Mine* [1901] 1 Ch 582; *Jacobus*

Marler Estates v Marler (1913) 85 LJPC 167. In such cases, it will not be open to the company to require the promoter to account for the profits made from the transaction, on the basis that it would not be possible to quantify the profit or commission made by the promoter: *Re Cape Breton Co* (1885) 29 ChD 795; and *Ladywell Mining Co v Brookes* (1887) 35 ChD 400.

2.29 The courts have shown some reluctance to value the asset in question and then require the promoter to account for profits on the basis that this would be tantamount to re-writing the contract between the parties: *Re Cape Breton* (1885) 29 Ch D 795.

If it could be shown that the original purchase of the asset by the promoter was in fact for the company itself, the courts may in equity allow for account of profits, based on the initial purchase by the promoter of the asset and resale to the company: *Omnium Electric Palaces v Baines* [1914] 1 Ch 322 per Sargant J.

Action for misrepresentation

2.30 It may be possible to bring an action against the promoter for misrepresentation under the Misrepresentation Act 1967 and claim damages. It will need to be shown that the promoter made a false statement of fact which induced others to enter into the contract. There is a defence if the promoter establishes that he had reasonable grounds to believe and did believe up to the time of making the contract, that the facts that were represented were true in the circumstances. The Misrepresentation Act 1967 allows for damages instead of rescission.

2.31 Under the Misrepresentation Act 1967, s 3, any exclusion clause in connection with the misrepresentation must satisfy the requirement of reasonableness under s 11(1) of the Unfair Contract Terms Act 1977 (UCTA 1977); and it is for those claiming that the term satisfies that requirement to show that it does. UCTA 1977, s 11(1) states that 'the term shall have been a fair and reasonable one to be included having regard to the circumstances which were, or ought reasonably to have been, known to or in the contemplation of the parties when the contract was made'.

Pre-incorporation contracts

2.32 As part of their functional and operational duties in establishing the company, promoters will also be dealing with third parties by, for example, entering into contracts, before the company is established. Such contracts may be of a diverse nature, but include contracts for leasing office premises, buildings, ordering goods or equipment, or entering into contracts for the provision of services and utilities. The issue which the courts have had to address has been to identify who should be liable in the event the promoter defaults or is in breach of his obligations under the contract. The issue of liability is significant particularly where the company simply has no existence at the time the contracts are entered into by the promoter. This is because a company only acquires a separate legal personality upon incorporation – once the certificate of incorporation has been issued by the Registrar of Companies at Companies House.

In the absence of a company's legal existence, the courts have sought to impose personal liability on the promoter. This has been achieved through the application of various legal devices, including the use of contractual and agency principles.

Common law position

2.33 Under the contractual principles in English law, a contract can only be entered into with a person, entity or organisation that is in existence. A party cannot therefore contract with a non-existent being: *Rover International Ltd v Cannon Film Sales Ltd* (No 3) [1987] BCLC 540 per Harman J: 'If somebody does not exist, he cannot contract'. An argument was raised by counsel for the claimants that estoppel by convention applied based on mistake and that the contract that was entered into before the defendant company Rover was established should be enforceable on the basis of such estoppel. Harman J considered that estoppels by convention did not apply because there must be an assumption of agreed facts as the basis of a transaction into which the parties are about to enter. Therefore, the parties must make their assumption of agreed facts, on which they will not be allowed to go back, before the contract or dealing is made or conducted. However, where one party did not exist at that time it could not have made or agreed any assumption of fact, accurate or not. Estoppel by convention did not apply. Further, CA 2006, s 51 did not apply as Rover was a foreign company which was not covered by the definition of 'company' under the CA 2006 which referred to a UK company. See too: *Amalgamated Investment and Property Co Ltd (in liq) v Texas Commerce International Bank Ltd* [1981] 3 All ER 577.

2.34 Where a promoter signs a contract 'for and on behalf of a company' before the company has been established, the court is likely to impute personal liability to the promoter. However, where a promoter signs in the potential company's name with his name as a director, the courts may not impute personal liability on the basis there was no contract in existence. These contrasting principles are illustrated in *Kelner* and *Newborne* cases.

Promoters were personally liable on the contract entered into by them

In *Kelner v Baxter* (1866) LR 2 CP 174, the promoters entered into a contract for the purchase of alcohol and spirits on behalf of a hotel company which had yet to be established, but which contract was later ratified by the company upon its incorporation. All the alcohol had been consumed without any payment having been made. The company later went into liquidation. The claimants brought an action against the promoters who had contracted on behalf of the company for payment of the sums due. The defendants contended that as the company had ratified the contract, all contractual liability had been transferred to the company and the claimants must, therefore, sue the company. The court held that the promoters were personally liable on the basis that when the contract was entered into, the company had no physical existence, and that the promoters could not contract on behalf of a non-existent entity; nor could they be agents of such entity.

The contract was entered into by the company which is thereby liable

However, in *Newborne v Sensolid (GB) Ltd* [1953] 1 All ER 708, [1954] 1 QB 45, a company purported to sell goods at a time when it had not been incorporated. The company's name was attached to the contract as 'Leopold Newborne (London) Ltd' and underneath was the name of Leopold Newborne. When it was discovered that the company had not been formed, Leopold Newborne commenced proceedings for damages for breach of contract against the buyers in his own name. The Court of Appeal held that the claimant had never purported to contract to sell nor sold the goods either as principal or agent. The contract purported to be made by the company and Leopold Newborne had merely added his name to verify that the company was a party. In the circumstances, the contract was a nullity. The Court of Appeal distinguished the principle, applied in *Schmaltz v Avery* (1851) 16 QB 655, that where a person purported to contract as agent he could nevertheless disclose himself as being in truth the principal and enforce the contract. The only person who had any contract with the defendants was the company and Mr Newborne's signature merely confirmed that of the company.

2.35 Once the company is formed, it will be considered as a third party to the contract between the promoter and another person, entity or organisation, and will not be able to obtain any benefits from such contract; nor can any obligations be imposed on the company on the basis of privity of contract. Further, the Contracts (Rights of Third Parties) Act 1999 has no application to pre-incorporation contracts, and only allows enforcement by third parties where the contractual term provides some benefit being conferred to the unformed company. For some consideration, the parties could agree that once the company is formed, it will have the option of entering into a contract with the third party on terms agreed in advance. The 1999 Act only applies in respect of enforcement of rights by a third party and is not concerned with the imposition of obligations.

2.36 An agent or promoter who has not contracted personally may be liable to the other party to the contract in damages for a breach of warranty of authority: *Collen v Wright* (1857) 8 E & B 647. The personal liability arises on the basis that the promoter or agent impliedly warrants to the other party to the contract that an entity exists, when in fact it has no existence: *McRae v Commonwealth Disposals Commission* (1950) 84 CLR 377; and *Black v Smallwood* [1966] ALR 744.

The position under the Companies Act 2006

2.37 Section 51 of the CA 2006 states that a contract which purports to be made by or on behalf of a company at a time when the company has not been formed has effect, subject to any agreement to the contrary, as one made with the person purporting to act for the company or as agent for it, and he is personally liable on the contract accordingly.

2.38 This provision is the product of its predecessors CA 1985, s 36C and European Communities Act 1972, s 9(2) which implemented Art 7 of the First

Directive on Company Law (Directive 68/151/EEC). The principal objective of these sections was to remove any difficulties that were encountered by the common law cases concerning pre-incorporation contracts between promoters and third parties and to avoid any nullity of contracts including any enforceability of contractual obligations entered into between the third party and the promoter who purported to establish a company.

The promoters were personally liable on the contract entered into

The interpretation and scope of s 51 was considered by the Court of Appeal in *Phonogram Ltd v Lane* [1982] QB 938. Two pop artists decided to form a rock band under the name of 'Cheap, Mean and Nasty'. A company, 'Fragile Management Ltd', was to be formed to operate the band. Before the company was formed, the defendant entered negotiations for the financing of the group by Phonogram Ltd for £12,000, which was to be repaid in two instalments of £6,000 each. The company was never formed and never performed. The first instalment was repaid, but not the second. The issue before the Court of Appeal was who should be liable to repay the remaining £6,000 to Phonogram Ltd?

Lord Denning referred to s 9(2) of the European Communities Act 1972 (now CA 2006, s 51) and held that the defendant was personally liable for the contract with Phonogram Ltd. Secondly, in interpreting the term 'purports', Lord Denning stated that the contract can purport to be made on behalf of a company, or by a company, even though the company is known by both parties not to be formed, or that it was only about to be formed. Lord Denning also addressed the term 'subject to any agreement to the contrary' under CA 2006, s 51. It meant 'unless otherwise agreed'. If there was an express agreement that a person who was signing was not to be liable under the contract, then s 51 would not apply. But, unless there is a clear exclusion of personal liability, s 51 should be given its full effect. It means that in cases where a person purports to contract on behalf of a company not yet formed, then however he expresses his signature, he himself is personally liable on the contract.

Oliver LJ stated that the intention of parties was a relevant consideration at the time the contract was formed. He was of the view that the narrow distinguishing aspects set out in the *Kelner* and *Newborne* cases did not accurately reflect the common law position. According to Oliver LJ, although at common law the contractual liability of an agent depended on the real intent revealed by the contract, namely on whether the agent intended himself to be a party to the contract and not on the narrow distinction between a signature 'for and on behalf of' a company and a signature in the name of the company, any distinctions depending on the form of the signature which might have been raised at common law have been rendered irrelevant by s 9(2) of the 1972 Act in any case where a contract is either with a company or with the agent of a company. Instead, the position should be looked at by looking at the 'real intent' as revealed by the contract, and whether the agent intended himself to be a party to the contract.

Oliver LJ compared *Kelner v Baxter* and *Newborne v Sensolid (Great Britain) Ltd* and stated:

> 'So in *Kelner v Baxter* (1866) LR 2 CP 174, where the correspondence was directed to the agents and referred to "the proposed company" which everybody knew was not yet in existence, there really was no room for the suggestion that the purchasers were acting in any other capacity than personally. On the other hand, in *Newborne v Sensolid (Great Britain) Ltd* [1953] 1 All ER 708, [1954] 1 QB 45, where the contract was on the company's notepaper, it was clearly intended to be a company's contract (nobody realising that it had not yet been registered) and it could not be said that the individual plaintiff's signature in the company's name could possibly have been intended to make him a party to the contract. The case, in my judgment, does not rest on any narrow point as to the way in which the contract was actually signed. The result would have been exactly the same, in my judgment, if the signature there had been accompanied by some such formula as "for and on behalf of" or "per pro". The judgment of Parker J ([1954] 1 QB 45 at 47) and the judgments in the Court of Appeal of Lord Goddard CJ and Morris LJ show that the case turned on what the contract purported to do; and precisely the same applies I think in *Hollman v Pullin* (1884) Cab & El 254, where a contract, albeit signed by the plaintiff as chairman of the association, was clearly intended to be, and intended only to be, a contract directly with the association by which the defendant's services were intended to be retained.'

According to Oliver LJ, it was not sufficient simply to consider the nature of the signatures set out in the contract. If looking at the contract as a whole and the intention of the agent including his signature reveal an intention to be bound to a contract, then the agent would be personally liable at common law. It was irrelevant as to what formula was used to sign the contract.

Section 51, therefore, creates a presumption of personal liability for the promoter who enters into a contract with a third party before the company is formed. The third party, therefore, has some degree of protection. However, at common law, there is no presumption of personal liability of the promoter and consideration will be given to looking at the contract as a whole to determine the real intentions of the parties. If the real intention does not identity that the promoter should be bound, then the contract will be null and void as against the third party, unless restitution is available.

2.39 Subsequent cases have considered the scope of CA 2006, s 51.

The defendant was not liable, on the basis that the company was already registered

In *Oshkosh B'Ghosh Inc v Dan Marbel Inc* [1989] BCLC 507, the company was carrying on business under a name other than its registered name. This was because the company was purchased off-the-shelf and its change of name did not take effect until later on when the altered name was entered at Companies House. The issue was whether a director of the company was liable for the debts of the company. The Court of Appeal held that there was no basis for finding the defendant liable under CA 2006, s 51 as the company had been duly formed in 1979 before the contracts with the claimant had been entered into, and the issue of a new certificate on the alteration of the company's name could not be taken to re-form or reincorporate the company.

Section 51 did not apply to a company that has been previously struck off

The *Phonogram* principles were applied in *Cotronic (UK) Ltd v Dezonie* [1991] BCLC 721 where the Court of Appeal held that s 51 did not apply to a company which had previously been struck off the register and was no longer in existence at the time the contract was entered into by the promoter. The promoter was not therefore personally liable, as at the time he entered into the contract, he was not aware that the company had been struck off the register, and that he had meant to enter into a contract on behalf of the old company rather than the new company which had been formed to continue the old company's business. Therefore, where CA 2006, s 51 has no application, the common law cases will still be of relevance in addressing the promoter's liability. Dillon, Balcombe and Gibson LJJ were of the view that the contract was a nullity and of no effect as the company did not exist. However, it was possible for a claimant to claim by way of *quantum meruit* for work previously undertaken.

2.40 Section 51 of CA 2006 has no application where the company had already been established, but referred to by an incorrect name: *Badgerhill Properties Ltd v Cottrell* [1991] BCLC 721.

2.41 In *Hellmuth, Obata & Kassabaum Incorporated, T/a HOK Sport v King* [2000] All ER 1394, the court was required to consider the liability of a person purporting to act as agent for an unformed company by signing a letter of intent on behalf of such company. The court decided that although no contractual document had ever been signed by the parties, however, sufficient agreement had been reached between them as to the terms of the proposed contract so as to impose contractual obligations. The defendant had acted on behalf of the intended joint venture company during the negotiations. Accordingly, the defendant was personally liable under CA 2006, s 51 for sums due under the agreement to the claimant. Further, for the purposes of s 51, individuals who purported to act on behalf of an unformed company could be liable under that section for quasi-contractual obligations upon that company: *British Steel Corporation v Cleveland Bridge & Engineering Co Ltd* [1984] 1 All ER 504.

In some situations, general common law principles may apply for pre-incorporation contract formation

The issue as to whether an agent purporting to act for an unformed company can also enforce a pre-incorporation contract was considered by the Court of Appeal in *Braymist Ltd v Wise Finance Co Ltd* [2002] 1 BCLC 415. A solicitor's firm signed an agreement 'as solicitors and agents' for the sale of land on behalf of an unformed company with a purchaser, Wise Finance. The purchaser failed to complete the purchase of the property. The sellers claimed that they were entitled to enforce the contract. The Court of Appeal held that on its true construction, CA 2006, s 51 not only conferred liabilities on Wise Finance, but also rights of enforcement against Wise Finance, unless such enforcement was otherwise precluded by the ordinary common law principles governing contractual arrangements. In *Braymist*, the Court of Appeal distinguished the principle applied in *Schmaltz v Avery* (1851) 16 QB 655, that where a person who purported to contract as agent, he could nevertheless disclose himself as being in truth the principal and enforce the contract.

Arden LJ referred to the concluding words of CA 2006, s 51(1) 'and he is personally liable on the contract accordingly as 'the tailpiece'. The function of the 'tailpiece' was to establish liability only and to leave the question of whether the agent could enforce the contract to the general law. The common law therefore applied to determine whether such a person could enforce the contract.

See too: *Gibbons v Doherty* [2013] IEHC 109.

2.42 According to case law it would appear that the effect of s 51 is that the promoter is able to enforce the contract with the third party as well as obligations under the contract: *Braymist Ltd v Wise Finance Co Ltd* [2002] Ch 273; *Badgerhill Properties Ltd v Cottrell* [1991] BCLC 721. Further, s 51 does not protect third parties who contract with non-existent companies or companies that have been struck off the register. It only protects in a situation where a company has been identified as a contracting party and it has not yet been established.

Novation

2.43 Section 51 of CA 2006 holds promoters personally liable for pre-incorporation contracts before the company is formed, 'unless there is agreement to the contrary'. The Companies Act 2006 does not define this term. However, this would include situations where, in a transaction between the promoter and a third party, the third party exonerates the promoter from any personal liability in respect of the contract with the third party.

Practical points

2.44 The third party may decide to seek an indemnity from the promoter under the contract for any present or future claims arising in respect of any breach of the contractual provisions. This may also extend to the third party agreeing not to claim for any breach of warranty or representation against the promoter in order to avoid any personal liability on the promoter. These are various mechanisms to minimise personal liability for the promoter but much depends on:

- the third-party concerned;
- the type of contract that is entered into;

- the nature of protection being sought by the third party;
- whether the third party may seek further collateral from the promoter such as a personal guarantee;
- what bargaining position, if any, the promoter has to minimise or limit personal liability under the contract;
- whether a clause can be included in a contract that allows for an assignment of the contract to another party. Consent of the existing party to the contract will usually be required before the assignor can assign to an assignee. Furthermore, conditions may be set before the assignment can proceed (eg in relation to the creditworthiness of the assignee, reputation and standing and references). Consent can be withheld, based on any unfavourable or adverse position of the potential assignee.

2.45 The term 'unless there is agreement to the contrary' under CA 2006, s 51 also applies to any novation of the contract whereby the promoter, the other contracting party and the company, once it is established, agree that the company will take over all rights and obligations of the promoter under the promoter's contract with the third party. A contract cannot however be ratified by the company, simply because the company was not in existence at the time the contract was made between the promoter and the third party. It would be necessary for the company to enter into a new contract with the third party on terms similar to the old contract between the promoter and the third party: *Natal Land Co & Colonization Ltd v Pauline Colliery and Development Syndicate Ltd* [1904] AC 120 (Privy Council). The effect of a novation is that the company steps into the shoes of the promoter. Such novation contracts may also release the promoter from any liability in respect of the contractual obligations entered into, or the company agrees to indemnify the promoter against any such liability.

Checklist

2.46 *The following checklist addresses the essential issues that should be considered where promoters propose to establish a company and engage in the preliminary formalities for establishment, including contractual dealings with third parties before incorporation and liability aspects.*

No	Issue	Reference
1	Who is establishing the company?	
2	Are the promoters involved in the company formation?	
3	What are the intentions of the promoters in setting up the company?	
4	What are the objects of the company?	CA 2006, s 31
5	Will the promoters become the directors and shareholders in the company?	
6	What will be the duties and responsibilities of the promoters?	Common law

No	Issue	Reference
7	Will promoters be entering into any contracts with third parties before the company is established?	CA 2006, s 51 and the common law
8	Will promoters be contracting on behalf of an unformed company or in their own name? Consider personal liability aspects.	CA 2006, s 51 and *Kelner v Baxter* (1886) LR 2 C P 174; and *Newborne v Sensolid (Great Britain) Limited* [1954] 1 QB 45
9	Will the contract with the third parties provide for a release of liability for the promoter by the third party?	Terms of novation agreement
10	Once the company has been established, have steps been taken by the promoters:	Terms of novation agreement
	(a) To ensure that novation takes place?	
	(b) To ensure that the promoters, the existing party and the company are parties to the novation agreement?	
	(c) To ensure that the promoters are released and discharged from any past, present and future claims under the contract by the existing party to the contract?	
	(d) To declare any interests to the company's board of directors?	CA 2006, ss 177 and 182
	(e) To declare any secret profits to the company's board of directors?	CA 2006, s 176
11	Are the promoters required to account to the company for any profits made?	Terms of the non-disclosure and confidentiality agreement and the common law position
12	Have the promoters entered into any non-disclosure or confidentiality agreements? What are the terms of these agreements and the duration of the confidentiality, and in what circumstances is the confidentiality discharged or waived?	

Definitions

2.47

Account of profits: A discretionary remedy available where the promoter has made a secret profit under the cloak of company establishment, and where damages to the company will not adequately compensate the company. The promoter becomes personally liable to account to the company for any profits made from the secret profit transaction.

Promoter: A person or group of persons who embark on, or contemplate in the establishment of a company, and who partake in all or some of the formalities required to establish a company, including dealings or negotiations with third parties before the company is formed, with the exception of professionals engaged in that capacity in setting up the company.

Secret profit: A transaction or series of transactions entered into by the promoter from which profits are made, with the intention of concealing such profits from the company and/or the directors and shareholders of the company without obtaining any consent from the board of directors or all the shareholders.

3 Classification of companies

Contents

Introduction

3.1 English company law distinguishes between various types of legal entities that may be established. Depending upon the objectives of the parties, an appropriate choice of legal business vehicle may be used to enable business objectives to be achieved. The decision as to the choice of business medium will often be governed by issues such as liability, risk, tax, type of business activities, and short- and long-term objectives that are to be achieved.

3.2 This chapter addresses the following issues:

- typical unincorporated legal forms for conducting business in the UK;
- types of companies that can be established under the Companies Acts including 'small business' and 'micro business' under SBEEA 2015;
- the composition of these companies;
- the European corporate framework.

Types of business media

3.3 In English law, a distinction is often drawn between unincorporated and incorporated legal forms as vehicles for conducting business in the UK. The distinction refers to the extent of a shareholder's liability to the legal entity established rather than a liability to the creditors: *Oakes v Turquand and Harding* (1867) LR 2 HL 325. This section sets out some of the significant forms of unincorporated entities currently operating in the UK.

Unincorporated legal forms

3.4 The following are considered unincorporated legal forms as they do not have a separate legal personality, existence or independence:

Sole trader

3.5 A sole trader is a person who works in business on his/her own account and who is not in partnership with other persons. There are no formalities required to establish business as a sole trader: it is the simplest form for conducting business activities. The individual has ownership and control of the business and flexibility as to the management and operation of the business. There is no requirement to have any partners for the business. However, one disadvantage of being a sole trader is that liabilities of the business are unlimited. A creditor can pursue the sole trader personally for all or any of the sole trader's assets. A sole trader is liable for all contractual obligations entered into in respect of the business, including all debts and any tortious or other claims that may exist against the sole trader. The sole trader also runs the risk of bankruptcy and seizure of all assets by the trustee in bankruptcy, and the stigma of being classified as a bankrupt in the event the business fails, including the consequences ensuing on bankruptcy.

3.6 One of the main advantages of being a sole trader is that the sole trader owns all the assets, has freedom to appoint employees and staff for the business, and flexibility in operating the business.

Lending to sole traders can be a practical issue as lenders will usually require some security for the loan including in some cases, a personal guarantee. This limits the ability of the sole trader to raise further finance owing to restrictions in loan agreements and personal guarantees as to disposal of assets or further security on such assets.

3.7 There are not many formalities required to establish as a sole trader, unlike a company which requires a constitution and key officers in place. There are no requirements to register or file any accounts with Companies House and there is no public access to such accounts. However, a sole trader is required to make an annual tax self-assessment and account to the tax authorities for the income earned.

Unincorporated association

3.8 An unincorporated association is an association of a group of members, natural or legal, who agree to join together to pursue common specific aims or purposes of the association. The objectives of an association are usually set out in a formal constitution which establishes the rules, regulations and operation of the association. The rules set out the governance of the management committee including election of key officers for the proper functioning and operation of the association. The management committee, however, will be personally liable for any debts or liabilities of the association, unless they have an indemnity from the association. Raising finance can raise practical difficulties owing to the unlimited liability nature of the association. Examples of associations include clubs and trade unions.

3.9 Another form of unincorporated association is a friendly society which is also known as a benefit society composed of a body of people who join together for a common financial or social purpose. Before modern insurance, and the welfare state, friendly societies typically provided financial and social services to individuals, often according to their religious, political, or trade affiliations. They are governed by the Friendly Societies Act 1992, and which can be incorporated or unincorporated. Friendly societies tend to have their own set of rules governing their internal functioning and operation. One issue which arises is how the rules of a club established under the Friendly Society's Act should be construed and interpreted.

Club rules are contractual in nature and normal construction principles apply to its rules

In *Speechley v Allott* [2014] EWCA Civ 230, the Court of Appeal was required to interpret specific rules of the Blakeborough Social and Sports Club which was a working men's club registered under the Friendly Societies Act 1974. It had a set of written rules governing its internal functioning. It was a clubhouse comprising 600 members who were entitled to use the club's facilities including the bowling green and bar – known as the 'bowling members' and the 'social members'. The club had been in financial difficulties for some years and this internal dispute between the club members had led to proposals to sell the bowling green to alleviate these difficulties. The issues before the Court of Appeal were primarily related to the interpretation of special rules concerning the club including whether certain officers were validly elected, financial aspects, convening of meetings and inspection of books and records of the club; and expulsion of the club's members.

The claimant was a bowling member and at the forefront to save the bowling green and commenced proceedings with other bowling members as a representative action claiming possession of the club, and seeking declarations as to the validity of the special general meeting that was held and for the defendants to convene an AGM.

Lewison LJ held that the club's rules amounted to a contract between all the members. The club's rules must be considered and construed in the light of the various issues that arose in this case.

According to Lewison LJ the proper approach in the interpretation of rules was to consider the following questions:

- What did the rules require?
- What was the effect of non-compliance with those requirements?

The rules should be interpreted in the same way as any other contract, making due allowance for the fact that the rules were intended to be operated by non-lawyers. By interpreting the rules in this manner, the Court of Appeal held that certain committee members had not been validly elected and that the procedural irregularities were a failure not so much of form but of substance.

General partnership

3.10 General partnerships are governed by the Partnership Act 1890 and agency law including aspects of common law (PA 1890, s 5). A general partnership does not require any formal constitution for its establishment. It can be created orally or in writing and is a relation which subsists between two or more persons carrying on business in common with a view of profit: PA 1890, s 1. A partnership may still exist even where it may be trading at a loss: *Re Spanish Prospecting Company* [1911] 1 Ch 92. A partner can be a natural or legal person. In practice, however, a partnership agreement is usually entered into between the partners to create certainty and to minimise disputes between partners and this allows for flexibility to contract out of the PA 1890 adapted to the partnership's circumstances. Decisions are usually taken by the partnership management on the governance and operation of the partnership. The partnership agreement will set out details including name, type of partnership, capital contributions, sharing of profits and losses, drawings, duration of partnership, negative covenants, non-solicitation covenants and other restrictive covenants, dismissal and appointment of other partners, and termination of the partnership. The agreement will also address the issues such as the retirement of partners, how capital contributed by a partner will be returned to them, and the disposal of any partnership property.

3.11 Unlike a company, a partnership does not have separate legal personality independent of the partners. This means that the partners can be personally liable without limit for all debts and liabilities of the partnership.

Owing to the unlimited liability of the general partnership, recourse to external finance is limited, and is usually secured by personal guarantees, which can expose the partners to potential bankruptcy if they are unable to meet the partnership's debts.

The general partnership's accounts and financial information are private, and there is no requirement to disclose such details at a public registry owing to the private nature of this type of entity.

Limited partnership

3.12 The Limited Partnerships Act 1907 governs limited partnerships. A limited partnership differs from a general partnership in that there will be two types of partners in a limited partnership: a general partner whose liability is unlimited and a limited partner whose liability is limited to the contribution made by the limited partner to the partnership. A principal restriction is that the limited partner cannot participate in the management of the limited partnership, nor do they have power to bind the partnership with regard to third parties. Typically, limited partners will be passive investors who will contribute capital for investment purposes and may exit at a later date. A limited partnership must register itself at Companies House and cannot operate unless so registered. It must include the name 'LP' or 'limited partnership' in its name at Companies House: LPA 1907, ss 8A and 8B (as inserted by the Legislative Reform (Limited Partnerships) Order 2009/1940).

3.13 Limited partnerships are not required to file their financial information at any public registry and this has the advantage of a degree of privacy.

These type of partnerships are commonly used for joint venture projects and professional purposes.

3.14 The LPA 1907 will be amended to take account of private fund limited partnership ('PFLP') that is a 'collective investment scheme' (as defined in the Financial Services and Markets Act 2000, s 235) but is not a scheme authorised by the Financial Conduct Authority (FCA). A draft of the Legislative Reform (Limited Partnerships) Order 2015 (2015 Order) has been prepared setting out the mechanism for regulation of the PFLP that will operate under the regime of the LPA 1907. The 2015 Order enables a limited partnership which is a private investment fund to be designated as a PFLP on registration, and amends some of the provisions of the LPA 1907 (c 24) as they apply to PFLPs and to partners in PFLPs. A limited partnership may be designated as a PFLP only if it is constituted by an agreement in writing and is a collective investment scheme.

3.15 The following changes are proposed under the 2015 Order in respect of both limited partnerships and PFLP's:

- *Definition and constitution of limited partnership*

  Each limited partner in a limited partnership that is not a private fund limited partnership shall, at the time of entering into the partnership, contribute to the partnership a sum or sums as capital or property valued at a stated amount, and shall not be liable for the debts or obligations of the firm beyond the amount so contributed: s 4(2A).

  A limited partner in a private fund limited partnership:

  (a) is under no obligation to contribute any capital or property to the partnership unless otherwise agreed between the partners; and

  (b) is not liable for the debts or obligations of the firm beyond the amount of the partnership property which is available to the general partners to meet such debts or obligations: s 4(2B).

- *Modifications of general law in case of limited partnerships*

  If a private fund limited partnership is dissolved at a time when there is at least one general partner, the affairs of the partnership must be wound up by those who are general partners at that time, subject to any express or implied agreement between the partners as to the winding up of the affairs of the partnership by them or by a person on their behalf: s 6(3A).

  If a private fund limited partnership is dissolved at a time when there is no general partner, the affairs of the partnership must be wound up by those who are limited partners at that time, subject to any express or implied agreement between them as to the winding up of the affairs of the limited partnership by them or by a person on their behalf: s 6(3B).

  The references in sub-ss 6(3A) and (3B) to partners do not include a partner who is insolvent; and those subsections have effect subject to any order of the court as to the winding up of the affairs of the partnership: s 6(3C).

  The 2015 Order would regulate the permitted activities for limited partners in a private fund limited partnership.

For the purposes of s 6(1), a limited partner in a private fund limited partnership is not to be regarded as taking part in the management of the partnership business merely because the limited partner does anything that is under s 6A(2) a permitted activity: s 6A(1).

The permitted activities are:

(a) taking part in a decision about the variation of the partnership agreement;

(b) taking part in a decision about whether to allow:

  (i) a type of investment or a particular investment by the partnership;

  (ii) the participation by the limited partner in a particular investment by the partnership;

  (iii) the incurring, extension or discharge of debt by the partnership;

  (iv) the creation, extension or discharge of any other obligation owed by the partnership;

(c) taking part in a decision about whether the general nature of the partnership business should change;

(d) taking part in a decision about whether to dispose of the partnership business or to acquire another business;

(e) taking part in a decision about whether a person should become or cease to be a partner;

(f) taking part in a decision about whether the partnership should be dissolved;

(g) making or taking part in a decision about the winding up of the partnership;

(h) enforcing rights under the partnership agreement (unless those rights are to carry out management functions);

(i) approving the accounts of the partnership;

(j) approving the valuation of the partnership's assets;

(k) entering into a contract with the partnership or a general partner in the partnership (unless the contract requires the limited partner to take part in management functions);

(l) acting as a director, member, employee, officer or agent of, or a shareholder or partner in:

  (i) a general partner; or

  (ii) another person appointed to manage or advise the partnership in relation to the affairs of the partnership;

(m) taking part in a decision which involves an actual or potential conflict of interest that affects or relates to the partnership, its business, a partner in the partnership or a person appointed to manage or advise the partnership;

(n) discussing the prospects of the partnership business;

(o) consulting or advising a general partner, or the general partners, or any person appointed to manage the partnership, about the affairs of the partnership or about its accounts;

(p) appointing or nominating a person to represent the limited partner on a committee or revoking such an appointment or nomination;

(q) taking part in a decision regarding changes in the persons responsible for the day-to-day management of the partnership;

(r) providing surety or acting as guarantor for the partnership;

(s) taking part in a decision authorising an action that the general partner proposes to take: s 6A(2).

The Treasury or the Secretary of State may by regulations amend the list of activities in s 6A(2): s 6A(3).

Regulations under s 6A(3) are to be made by statutory instrument: s 6A(4).

- *Manner and particulars of registration*

If the application:

(a) includes a request for designation as a private fund limited partnership; and

(b) includes or is accompanied by a certificate signed by a solicitor to the effect that the limited partnership meets the private fund conditions,

the registrar must when registering the limited partnership designate it on the register as a private fund limited partnership: s 8(2).

The private fund conditions are that the partnership:

(a) is constituted by an agreement in writing; and

(b) is a collective investment scheme, or would be such a scheme but for the fact that each of the limited partners is a body corporate in the same group as the general partner: s 8(3).

The application to the registrar must state whether the application includes a request for designation as a private fund limited partnership: s 8A(1).

In the case of an application that includes a request for designation as a private fund limited partnership, the required details are:

(a) the name of each general partner;

(b) the name of each limited partner; and

(c) the address of the proposed principal place of business of the limited partnership: s 8A(3).

If the limited partnership is designated on the register as a private fund limited partnership, the certificate must also state that it is so designated: s 8C(3A).

- *Registration of changes in partnership*

If during the continuance of a limited partnership any change is made or occurs in any of the details listed in sub-s (1A), a statement, signed by the firm, specifying the nature of the change shall within seven days be sent by post or delivered to the registrar: s 9(1).

The details are:

(a) in the case of any limited partnership:

(i) the firm name;

(ii) the principal place of business;

(iii) the partners or the name of any partner;

(iv) the liability of any partner by reason of the partner becoming a limited instead of a general partner or a general instead of a limited partner;

(b) in the case of a limited partnership that is not a private fund limited partnership:

(i) the general nature of the business;

(ii) the term or character of the partnership;

(iii) the sum contributed by any limited partner: s 9(1A).

- *Striking off a private limited partnership on application*

On an application complying with s 14A(2) and (3), the registrar may strike off the register the name of a private fund limited partnership: s 14A(1).

The application must:

(a) list the relevant persons; and

(b) state that it is made with the consent of any relevant person who is not an applicant: s 14A(2).

The application must be signed or otherwise authenticated by or on behalf of:

(a) the general partner or, if there is more than one general partner, all of them;

(b) if there is no general partner, all the relevant persons; or

(c) any other person who has authority to make the application on behalf of the firm: s 14A(3).

The term 'relevant person' means:

(a) any person who is a partner at the time of the application; or

(b) if the partnership has been dissolved before the application is made, any person who was a partner immediately before that dissolution: s 14A(4).

- *Power to strike off private fund limited partnership not carrying on business or in operation*

If the registrar has reasonable cause to believe that a private fund limited partnership is not carrying on business or in operation, the registrar may send to the firm a communication inquiring whether it is carrying on business or in operation: s 14B(1).

If the registrar does not receive any answer to the communication within one month of sending it, the registrar must within 14 days after the expiration of that month send to the firm a second communication referring to the first communication and stating:

(a) that no answer to it has been received; and

(b) that if an answer is not received to the second communication within one month from its date, a notice will be published in the Gazette with a view to striking the firm's name off the register: s 14B(2).

If the registrar:

(a) receives an answer to the effect that the firm is not carrying on business or in operation; or

(b) does not within one month after sending the second communication receive any answer, the registrar may publish in the Gazette, and send to the firm, a notice that at the expiration of three months from the date of the notice the name of the firm mentioned in it will, unless cause is shown to the contrary, be struck off the register: s 14B(3).

At the expiration of the time mentioned in the notice the registrar may, unless cause to the contrary is previously shown by the firm, strike its name off the register: s 14B(4).

The registrar must publish notice in the Gazette of the firm's name having been struck off the register: s 14B(5).

The term 'Gazette' has the meaning given by s 10(2): s 14B(6).

- *Effect of striking off under section 14A or 14B*

When a firm is struck off under ss 14A or 14B, if the firm has not been dissolved:

(a) each general or limited partner in the firm remains a partner in the firm; but

(b) the firm ceases to be a limited partnership: s 14C(1).

The striking off of a firm under ss 14A or 14B does not affect the personal liability of any partner in respect of the debts or obligations of the firm incurred while the firm was registered as a limited partnership: s 14C(2).

- *Private fund limited partnerships struck off incorrectly*

A private fund limited partnership, or any partner of a private fund limited partnership, may apply for an order under this section if:

(a) the firm was struck off under s 14A or 14B;

(b) the firm continues to exist after the striking off; and

(c) the firm is subsequently registered again as a limited partnership: s 14D(1).

If such an application is made, the court may make an order under this section if it considers that:

(a) it is just and equitable to do so; and

(b) in the case of striking off under s 14A, the application for striking off was not made by, or with the consent of, all of those who were partners in the firm at the time of the application for striking off: s 14D(2).

The order may make such provision as the court thinks fit for putting the firm and any other persons:

(a) in the position they would have been in if the firm had not been struck off; or

(b) so near that position as the court considers just and equitable: s 14D(3).

The firm must deliver a copy of the order to the registrar: s 14D(4).

An application under the LPA 1907, s 14 must be made before the end of the period of three years starting with the day on which the firm was struck off: s 14D(5).

- *Designation of existing limited partnerships as private fund limited partnerships*

  Article 3 of the 2015 Order applies where a firm is registered as a limited partnership under the LPA 1907 immediately before the day on which this Order comes into force: 2015 Order, art 3(1).

  Within the 12 months beginning with the day on which this Order comes into force, the firm may apply to the registrar to be designated as a private fund limited partnership: 2015 Order, art 3(2).

  The application must:

  (a) be made in such manner and accompanied by such information as the registrar may direct; and

  (b) include or be accompanied by a certificate signed by a solicitor to the effect that the limited partnership:

    (i) meets the private fund conditions set out in s 8(3) of the Act as inserted by this Order; and

    (ii) is not an authorised contractual scheme as defined in s 237(3) of the Financial Services and Markets Act 2000(a): 2015 Order, art 3(3).

  If the application meets the requirements of para (3), the registrar must:

  (a) designate the firm on the register as a private fund limited partnership; and

  (b) issue and provide to the firm a certificate stating that the firm has been so designated.

A firm designated as a private fund limited partnership pursuant to this article is to be treated as if it had been designated as a private fund limited partnership under s 8(2) of the Act (as inserted by this Order): 2015 Order, art 3(4).

Trust

3.16 This is an unincorporated association and has no independent or separate legal existence. Most trusts are established to hold assets for an individual, company or organisation. The trust deed will set out how the assets will be employed in practice for the benefit of the trust. The trust will usually be managed by trustees who will administer the terms of the trust and account to the principal who has established the trust. The trustees remain personally liable for the debts and liabilities of the trust which are usually paid out of the trust fund. Typically, the trust will simply manage the trust assets for the specific purposes of the trust and does not usually raise finance unless specifically set out in the trust deed.

Incorporated legal forms

3.17 In English company law, there are various legal forms of business vehicles which have a separate independent legal existence from their members. They include the following:

Limited company

3.18 This is the most common form of conducting and operating a business. Once the company is established by the promoters, it acquires a separate legal existence independent of its shareholders. It therefore has a separate legal personality or corporate personality. There are, however, some formalities that are required to establish the limited company. The principal documents are the memorandum of association, where the founding shareholders agree to become members in the company; and the articles of association, which are the internal rules of the company governing the operations and functioning of the company. The articles can be amended from time to time by the company's shareholders.

3.19 The liability of the shareholders who contribute to the company's capital is usually limited to the amount they have contributed where it is a private company limited by shares. Any debts and liabilities that arise are those of the company. In general, creditors will bring proceedings against the company for any debts arising and not against the shareholders. Any enforcement will be against the company itself and not the shareholders' assets.

3.20 Section 1 of the CA 2006 sets out the definition of 'company' for the purposes of the Companies Acts. Section 1(1) defines a 'company' as one that is formed and registered under the CA 2006, that is either:

(a) a company so formed and registered after the commencement of the CA 2006, Pt 1; or

(b) a company that immediately before the commencement of the CA 2006, Pt 1:

   (i) was formed and registered under the Companies Act 1985 (c 6) or the Companies (Northern Ireland) Order 1986 (SI 1986/1032 (NI 6)); or

   (ii) was an existing company for the purposes of that Act or that Order, (which is to be treated on commencement as if formed and registered under this Act): CA 2006, s 1(1).

3.21 Certain provisions of the Companies Acts apply to:

(a) companies registered, but not formed, under this Act (see Pt 33, Ch 1), and

(b) bodies incorporated in the United Kingdom but not registered under this Act (see Ch 2 of that Part): CA 2006, s 1(2).

For provisions applying to companies incorporated outside the United Kingdom, see Part 34 (overseas companies): CA 2006, s 1(3).

3.22 Section 3 of CA 2006 states that a company is a limited company if the liability of its members is limited by its constitution. A company may be limited by shares or by guarantee.

3.23 A *company limited by shares* is a company whose shareholders have limited their liability to the amount, if any, unpaid on shares held by them: CA 2006, s 3(2). Most companies in the UK fall within this category of company. The shareholders stand only to lose the amount they have contributed in the company and no more. This form of business medium is attractive for reasons of minimising liability of the shareholders, but on occasions, the courts have pierced the corporate veil to identify those involved in the wrongdoing: see *VTB Capital plc v Nutritek International Corp* [2013] 1 BCLC 179; and *Prest v Petrodel Resources Limited* [2013] All ER 90. See also Chapter 4.

3.24 In a company limited by shares, shareholders have the ability to raise finance internally through the issue of further shares or recourse to external funding by way of a loan. Many lenders have a preference to lend to a limited liability company rather than an unincorporated association. This allows lenders to obtain a charge or security over the assets of the company. The charge is registered at Companies House as part of transparency and disclosure of the company's financial position. Profits made from the company may either be retained within the company for expansion, growth and working capital, or used and distributed by way of dividends to shareholders for their investment in the company. There is no right to a dividend, as this is at the directors' discretion and subject to shareholders' approval.

3.25 CA 2006 requires a company to have at least one shareholder. A company can also be established by a sole shareholder who may also be the company's director. A shareholder holds shares in a company. The shares usually carry voting rights, but some shares may not necessarily carry voting rights depending upon agreement between the shareholders in the company who may hold different classes of shares. The voting rights allow shareholders to vote on important decisions affecting the company.

3.26 A company's governance is based on a separation of ownership from control. The directors provide direction, strategy and execute the day-to-day operations of the company. Their objective is to act in the company's best interests for its long-term success. While shareholders have delegated some of their powers to directors, they still retain residual authority and have the ultimate authority to make any final decisions affecting the company. A private company limited by shares must have one director, whereas a public company must have at least two directors, and one of the directors must be a natural person.

3.27 Companies limited by shares may be further sub-divided into:

- *Private limited liability companies.* Section 4 of CA 2006 states that a private company is any company that is not a public company. However, a private company cannot offer shares for sale to the public: CA 2006, s 755 and FSMA 2000, s 74. If a private company offers its securities to the public, it may be subject to an order preventing such distribution or to re-register as a public company or the company may be subject to an order for compulsory winding up. Many companies begin their life as a private company and may then convert to a public company for expansion and raising further finance. CA 2006 is based on the principle of 'think small first' and allows private companies to conduct business without undue regulatory burdens.

- *Public limited liability companies.* This is a company which is able to offer its shares to the public and is subject to greater regulation and controls than a private limited liability company.' Corporate governance is an essential aspect, particularly for companies listed on the stock exchange including transparency and accountability towards shareholders. A public company must have at least two directors and a qualified company secretary. It is required to issue shares to the public up to the value of £50,000. A public company can raise additional finance by flotation on the stock exchange with stricter regulation and compliance with rules governing flotation and continuing obligations. A public company must also have a trading certificate before it can commence operations: CA 2006, s 761.
- A *company limited by guarantee* is a company whose shareholders have limited their liability to such amount as they undertake to contribute to the company's assets in the event the company is wound up: CA 2006, s 3(3). The shareholders will agree to pay a specified amount on a company's liquidation. The voting in this type of company is usually one member one vote.
- An *unlimited company* is a company which has no limit in its constitution regarding the members' liability: CA 2006, s 3(4). One advantage of a limited company is that there is no obligation to file accounts at the Companies House: CA 2006, s 448. An unlimited company may, but is not required to, have a share capital.

Unlimited companies may be established for particular purposes with certain advantages and disadvantages

Unlimited companies were the subject of consideration in *In The Matter of Lehman Brothers* [2014] EWHC 132, which concerned an application by the joint administrators of three companies in the Lehman group (Lehman Brothers International (Europe); Lehman Brothers Limited; and LB Holdings Intermediate 2 Limited). The circumstances giving rise to the application were described as both 'unexpected' and 'unusual'.

The circumstances were 'unexpected' because when the Lehman Brothers group collapsed in September 2008, it was not anticipated that there would be any surplus of assets once the general body of the unsecured creditors of any of the principal companies had been paid. The main trading company within the group in UK and Europe was Lehman Brothers International (Europe) (LBIE), and it was anticipated that LBIE was likely to have significant surplus once all unsubordinated proved debts had been paid in full.

The circumstances were 'unusual' because LBIE was an unlimited company. It had two members comprising both other companies in the group. Both had ordinary unsecured claims against LBIE and one of them had a large claim as a subordinated loan creditor. The case concerned issues as to potential liability of the members for the liabilities of LBIE, particularly its subordinated liabilities and the relationship between their liability, if any, as members and their claims as creditors.

In the course of one aspect of his judgment, Richards J considered the position of members of an unlimited company and the status of such company. He considered the position of modern company law which began with the Companies Act 1862 – a statute described by Sir Francis Palmer as the 'magna carta of co-operative enterprise'. The 1862 Act introduced a simple process of registration of companies providing for three types of companies namely, a company limited by shares, limited by guarantee and unlimited companies. These three types of companies were distinguished by the differences in the liabilities of their members.

According to Richards J, the use of unlimited companies was never great and declined during the nineteenth century. In the twentieth century, their principal advantage was an exemption from *ad valorem* stamp duty and later capital duty payable on the issue of new capital by a company. Primarily for this reason, their use for many reasons was as estate or investment companies, where estates or other properties were transferred to companies in exchange for shares issued to or owned for the benefit of the families owning them.

Companies not formed under companies legislation but authorised to register

3.28 Part 33 of the CA 2006 recognises some companies that are not formed under the companies legislation but authorised to register under the Act.

Section 1040 of the CA 2006 applies to:

(a) any company that was in existence on 2 November 1862 (including any company registered under the Joint Stock Companies Acts); and

(b) any company formed after that date (whether before or after the commencement of this Act):

  (i) in pursuance of an Act of Parliament other than this Act or any of the former Companies Acts;

  (ii) in pursuance of letters patent; or

  (iii) that is otherwise duly constituted according to law: CA 2006, s 1040(1).

Any such company may on making application register under this Act: CA 2006, s 1040(2).

3.29 Subject to the following provisions, it may register as an unlimited company, as a company limited by shares or as a company limited by guarantee: CA 2006, s 1040(3).

A company having the liability of its members limited by Act of Parliament or letters patent:

(a) may not register under this section unless it is a joint stock company; and

(b) may not register under this section as an unlimited company or a company limited by guarantee: CA 2006, s 1040(4).

3.30 A company that is not a joint stock company may not register under this section as a company limited by shares: CA 2006, s 1040(5).

The registration of a company under this section is not invalid by reason that it has taken place with a view to the company's being wound up: CA 2006, s 1040(6).

3.31 For the purposes of s 1040 (companies authorised to register under this Act) 'joint stock company' means a company:

(a) having a permanent paid-up or nominal share capital of fixed amount divided into shares, also of fixed amount, or held and transferable as stock, or divided and held partly in one way and partly in the other; and

(b) formed on the principle of having for its members the holders of those shares or that stock, and no other persons: CA 2006, s 1041(1).

Such a company when registered with limited liability under this Act is deemed a company limited by shares: CA 2006, s 1040(2).

Unregistered companies

3.32 The CA 2006, Pt 33, Ch 2 is concerned with unregistered companies.

Section 1042 of the CA 2006 applies to bodies corporate incorporated in and having a principal place of business in the United Kingdom, other than:

(a) bodies incorporated by, or registered under, a public general Act of Parliament;

(b) bodies not formed for the purpose of carrying on a business that has for its object the acquisition of gain by the body or its individual members;

(c) bodies for the time being exempted from this section by direction of the Secretary of State;

(d) open-ended investment companies: CA 2006, s 1042(1).

The Secretary of State may make provision by regulations applying specified provisions of the Companies Acts to all, or any specified description of, the bodies to which this section applies: CA 2006, s 1042(2).

The regulations may provide that the specified provisions of the Companies Acts apply subject to any specified limitations and to such adaptations and modifications (if any) as may be specified: CA 2006, s 1042(3).

3.33 Section 1042 of the CA 2006 does not:

(a) repeal or revoke in whole or in part any enactment, royal charter or other instrument constituting or regulating any body in relation to which provisions of the Companies Acts are applied by regulations under this section; or

(b) restrict the power of Her Majesty to grant a charter in lieu or supplementary to any such charter.

But in relation to any such body the operation of any such enactment, charter or instrument is suspended in so far as it is inconsistent with any of those provisions as they apply for the time being to that body: CA 2006, s 1042(4).

The term 'specified' means specified in the regulations: CA 2006, s 1042(5).

Overseas companies

3.34 Part 34 of the CA 2006 deals with overseas companies. Under the Companies Acts, an 'overseas company' means a company incorporated outside the United Kingdom: CA 2006, s 1044. The governance of overseas companies is regulated by the Overseas Companies Regulations 2009, SI 2009/1801. The Regulations impose various registration and filing requirements on overseas companies that open an establishment, whether a place of business or a branch, in the United Kingdom. The Regulations address the initial registration of particulars; usual residential addresses and; protection from disclosure; delivery of accounting documents; trading disclosures; and returns in the event of winding up.

Registration under alternative name

3.35 An overseas company that is required to register particulars under the CA 2006, s 1046 may at any time deliver to the registrar for registration a statement specifying a name, other than its corporate name, under which it proposes to carry on business in the United Kingdom: CA 2006, s 1048(1).

3.36 An overseas company that has registered an alternative name may at any time deliver to the registrar of companies for registration a statement specifying a different name under which it proposes to carry on business in the United Kingdom (which may be its corporate name or a further alternative) in substitution for the name previously registered: CA 2006, s 1048(2).

3.37 The alternative name for the time being registered under this section is treated for all purposes of the law applying in the United Kingdom as the company's corporate name: CA 2006, s 1048(3).

This does not:

(a) affect the references in this section or s 1047 to the company's corporate name;

(b) affect any rights or obligation of the company; or

(c) render defective any legal proceedings by or against the company: CA 2006, s 1048(4).

3.38 Any legal proceedings that might have been continued or commenced against the company by its corporate name, or any name previously registered under this section, may be continued or commenced against it by its name for the time being so registered: CA 2006, s 1048(5).

Small and micro business

3.39 SBEEA 2015 provides for statutory definitions of the terms 'small business' and 'micro business' with power to set out further details in regulations on the application of the concepts. The definitions are based on the approach in the widely used EU definitions of 'small enterprise' and 'microenterprise'. This is to ensure that definitions are available for use in secondary legislation made by UK Ministers where for example, the smaller businesses are exempt from new regulatory obligations.

3.40 Section 33 of the SBEEA 2015 applies where any subordinate legislation made by a Minister of the Crown (the 'underlying provision'):

(a) uses the term 'small business' or 'micro business'; and

(b) defines that term by reference to this section: SBEEA 2015, s 33(1).

3.41 In the underlying provision 'small business' means an undertaking other than a micro business (see SBEEA 2015, s 33(3)) which meets the following conditions ('the small business size conditions'):

(a) it has a headcount of staff of less than 50; and

(b) it has:

  (i) a turnover; or

  (ii) a balance sheet total,

  of an amount less than or equal to the small business threshold: SBEEA 2015, s 33(2).

3.42 In the underlying provision 'micro business' means an undertaking which meets the following conditions ('the micro business size conditions'):

(a) it has a headcount of staff of less than ten; and

(b) it has:

  (i) a turnover; or

  (ii) a balance sheet total,

  of an amount less than or equal to the micro business threshold: SBEEA 2015, s 33(3).

3.43 The Secretary of State may by regulations (referred to as 'the small and micro business regulations') make further provision about the meanings of 'small business' and 'micro business': SBEEA 2015, s 33(4).

Section 33 of the SBEEA 2015 and the small and micro business regulations are to be read subject to any modifications made by the underlying provision in any particular case: SBEEA 2015, s 33(5).

3.44 In SBEEA 2015, s 33:

- 'balance sheet total', 'headcount of staff', 'micro business threshold', 'small business threshold' and 'turnover' have such meanings as may be prescribed by the small and micro business regulations;
- 'Minister of the Crown' has the same meaning as in the Ministers of the Crown Act 1975;

- 'subordinate legislation' has the same meaning as in the Interpretation Act 1978 (see s 21 of that Act);
- 'undertaking' means:

  (a) a person carrying on one or more businesses;

  (b) a voluntary or community body within the meaning given by s 27;

  (c) a body which is formed or recognised under the law of a country or territory outside the United Kingdom and which is equivalent in nature to a body falling within the definition of voluntary or community body: SBEEA 2015, s 33(7).

3.45 Section 34 of the SBEEA 2015 sets out the permitted content of regulations under SBEEA, s 33. These regulations are known as 'the small and microbusiness regulations'. The permitted content includes provision about the following: calculation of staff headcount; turnover; and balance sheet; the extent to which connection with another business (for example, a parent-subsidiary relationship) affects the small or micro status of a particular business; the periods to be used for assessment; and how a new business will be assessed.

Community interest company

3.46 Section 6 of CA 2006 provides that in accordance with Part 2 of the Companies (Audit, Investigations and Community Enterprise) Act 2004 (c 27), the following can become a community interest company (CIC):

- companies limited by shares;
- companies limited by guarantee and not having a share capital; and
- companies limited by guarantee and having a share capital.

3.47 CICs are established for social enterprise functions and are applicable for enterprises that wish to use their profits for community and social purposes. There are relatively fewer formalities required to set up a CIC. In practice, in the event that a CIC is to be registered, it is required to lodge a community interest statement to the CIC Regulator as evidence that the CIC satisfies the legal definition of community interest, and will continue to do so for the duration of its existence and not serve an unduly restricted group of beneficiaries. The test is whether a reasonable person might consider the CIC's activities to benefit the community. CICs are required to report annually to the CIC Regulator. They must also have an 'asset lock' to prevent them from transferring any of their assets and profits, as the objective is that these be used solely for community purposes. Restrictions are also placed on dividends and interest payable, to encourage the establishment of CICs for community purposes and to ensure that their assets are used solely for community purposes.

3.48 CICs are subject to the general framework of company law. In particular, they and their directors are required to comply with their obligations under the Companies Acts and general common law.

Limited liability partnership

3.49 Limited liability partnerships (LLPs) are governed by the Limited Liability Partnership Act 2000 and regulations including the Limited Liability Partnership (Application of the Companies Act 2006) Regulations 2009, SI 2009/1804. Under the Act, a limited liability partnership will be recognised as a body corporate with a separate, independent legal personality similar to a company. Whereas a general partnership has unlimited liability, a limited liability partnership allows members to limit their liability to the amount they have contributed towards the business including any personal guarantees they have provided for raising any funds. Members take an equal share of the profits unless the partnership agreement provides otherwise.

3.50 An LLP has some characteristics of a corporate and partnership form but the provisions of CA 2006 also apply to LLPs. However, the internal governance of the LLP has partnership features rather than a board and shareholder structure.

Charitable incorporated organisation (CIO)

3.51 CIOs are relevant to charities established in England and Wales and are governed by the Charities Act 2006 which includes provisions in the Charities Act 1993 on CIOs. CIOs have the advantage of being incorporated. They also have a constitution regarding their governance, which must be in a form specified by the Charities Commission. CIOs are only required to register with the Charity Commission and will be regulated under charity law. The profits and assets of CIOs may only be used for charitable purposes.

Industrial and provident society

3.52 Industrial and provident societies are governed by the Industrial Provident Societies Acts (currently the Industrial Provident Act 2002) and can comprise the following:

- *Co-operative societies*: these are organisations operating for the mutual benefit of their members by providing them with products and services. Any surplus is put back into the organisation. Any profits made may be distributed to its members. Societies have their own rules and regulations on governance, membership and operations based on the regulations set out by the International Co-operative Alliance. They have an independent legal personality and existence from their members. The liability of members is limited to the amount unpaid on shares. Shares can be offered to the public to raise finance.
- *Community benefit societies*: this type of society engages in business for the community's benefit and not for its members. The interests of the community must be paramount. Any profits made must be returned to the community and not distributed to the members or shareholders. A community benefit society can be established as a charity if its objects are solely charitable and serve a public benefit. Finance can be raised through public grants and charitable trusts.

Employee shareholders

3.53 The Growth and Infrastructure Act 2013 addresses the issue of employee shareholders and creates a new status of 'employee shareholder'. Section 31 of that Act amends the Employment Rights Act 1996 (ERA) and inserts a new s 205 into the Employment Rights Act 1996 (ERA 1996). The effect of this provision is that the employee agrees to have different rights to other employees under the ERA 1996.

3.54 An employee who is or becomes an employee of a company is an 'employee shareholder' in the following circumstances if:

(a) the company and the individual agree that the individual is to be an employee shareholder;

(b) in consideration of that agreement, the company issues or allots to the individual fully paid up shares in the company, or procures the issue or allotment to the individual of fully paid up shares in its parent undertaking, which have a value, on the day of issue or allotment, of no less than £2,000,

(c) the company gives the individual a written statement of the particulars of the status of employee shareholder and of the rights which attach to the shares referred to in paragraph (b) ('the employee shares') (see ERA 1996, s 205A(5) and

(d) the individual gives no consideration other than by entering into the agreement and agreeing to become an employee shareholder: ERA 1996, s 205A(1).

3.55 However, there are certain restrictions and limitations on the rights of the employee shareholder under the ERA 1996. An employee who is an employee shareholder does not have:

(a) the right to make an application under ERA 1996, s 63D (request to undertake study or training),

(b) the right to make an application under ERA 1996, s 80F (request for flexible working),

(c) the right under ERA 1996, s 94 not to be unfairly dismissed (however, some unfair dismissal rights are retained – see below), or

(d) the right under s 135 to a redundancy payment: ERA 1996, s 205A(2) but there is an exception in respect of parental leave (see below).

3.56 Employee shareholders must give 16 weeks' notice before returning from maternity leave, adoption leave or additional paternity leave under the following regulations:

(a) regulation 11 of the Maternity and Parental Leave etc Regulations 1999, SI 1999/3312 (requirement for employee to notify employer of intention to return to work during maternity leave period), and

(b) regulation 25 of the Paternity and Adoption Leave Regulations 2002, SI 2002/2788 (corresponding provision for adoption leave): ERA 1996, s 205A(3).

Regulation 30 of the Additional Paternity Leave Regulations 2010, SI 2010/1055 (requirement for employee to notify employer of intention to return to work during additional paternity leave period): ERA 1996, s 205A(4).

3.57 The written statement referred to in ERA 1996, s 205A(1)(c) must:

(a) state that, as an employee shareholder, the individual would not have the rights specified in ERA 1996, s 205A(2);

(b) specify the notice periods that would apply in the individual's case as a result of ERA 1996, s 205A(3) and (4);

(c) state whether any voting rights attach to the employee shares;

(d) state whether the employee shares carry any rights to dividends;

(e) state whether the employee shares would, if the company were wound up, confer any rights to participate in the distribution of any surplus assets;

(f) if the company has more than one class of shares and any of the rights referred to in paragraphs (c) to (e) attach to the employee shares, explain how those rights differ from the equivalent rights that attach to the shares in the largest class (or next largest class if the class which includes the employee shares is the largest);

(g) state whether the employee shares are redeemable and, if they are, at whose option;

(h) state whether there are any restrictions on the transferability of the employee shares and, if there are, what those restrictions are;

(i) state whether any of the requirements of CA 2006, ss 561 and 562 are excluded in the case of the employee shares (existing shareholders' right of pre-emption), and

(j) state whether the employee shares are subject to drag-along rights or tag-along rights and, if they are, explain the effect of the shares being so subject: ERA 1996, s 205A(5).

3.58 ERA 1996, s 205A introduces the concept of a relevant independent adviser and a cooling-off period. The agreement between a company and an individual that the individual is to become an employee shareholder is of no effect unless, before the agreement is made:

(a) the individual, having been given the statement referred to in ERA 1996, s 205A(1)(c) receives advice from a relevant independent adviser as to the terms and effect of the proposed agreement, and

(b) seven days have passed since the day on which the individual receives the advice: ERA 1996, s 205A(6).

3.59 Any reasonable costs incurred by the individual in obtaining the advice (whether or not the individual becomes an employee shareholder) which would, but for this subsection, have to be met by the individual are instead to be met by the company: ERA 1996, s 205A(7). These costs are payable by the company irrespective of whether or not the individual takes up the job or not.

3.60 The reference in ERA 1996, s 205A(2)(b) to making an application under s 80F does not include a reference to making an application within the period of 14 days beginning with the day on which the employee shareholder returns to work from a period of parental leave under regulations under s 76: ERA 1996, s 205A(8).

Therefore, an employee shareholder returning from parental leave has a period of two weeks from the date of return to make a statutory request for flexible working.

3.61 The reference in ERA 1996, s 205A(2)(c) to unfair dismissal does not include a reference to a dismissal:

(a) which is required to be regarded as unfair for the purposes of Part 10 by a provision (whenever made) contained in or made under this or any other Act, or

(b) which amounts to a contravention of the Equality Act 2010: ERA 1996, s 205A(9).

The reference in ERA 1996, s 205A(2)(c) to the right not to be unfairly dismissed does not include a reference to that right in a case where ERA 1996, s 108(2) (health and safety cases) applies: ERA 1996, s 205A(10).

3.62 The effect of ERA 1996, s 205A(10) and (11) limit the exclusion of unfair dismissal rights so that an employee shareholder will still have the right not to be unfairly dismissed for automatically unfair reasons, on the grounds of discrimination, and in relation to suspension on health and safety grounds.

The Secretary of State may by order amend) ERA 1996, s 205A(1) so as to increase the minimum value of the shares to be offered as part of the employee shareholder status: ERA 1996, s 205A(11).

3.63 The Secretary of State may by regulations provide that any agreement for a company to buy back from an individual the shares referred to in ERA 1996, s 205A(1)(b) in the event that the individual ceases to be an employee shareholder or ceases to be an employee must be on terms which meet the specified requirements: ERA 1996, s 205A(12).

3.64 The term 'company' as referred in the ERA 1996 means:

(a) a company or overseas company (within the meaning, in each case, of the Companies Act 2006) which has a share capital, or

(b) a European Public Limited-Liability Company (or Societas Europaea) within the meaning of Council Regulation 2157/2001/EC of 8 October 2001 on the Statute for a European company;

'drag-along rights', in relation to shares in a company, means the right of the holders of a majority of the shares, where they are selling their shares, to require the holders of the minority to sell theirs;

'parent undertaking' has the same meaning as in the Companies Act 2006;

'relevant independent adviser' has the meaning that it has for the purposes of s 203(3)(c);

'tag-along rights', in relation to shares in a company, means the right of the holders of a minority of the shares to sell their shares, where the holders of the majority are selling theirs, on the same terms as those on which the holders of the majority are doing so: ERA 1996, s 205A(13).

3.65 The reference in this section to the value of shares in a company is a reference to their market value within the meaning of the Taxation of Chargeable Gains Act 1992 (see ss 272 and 273 of that Act): ERA 1996, s 205A(14).

3.66 A new s 47G ('Employee shareholder status') is added to the ERA 1996 to the effect that an employee has the right not to be subjected to a detriment by any act, or any deliberate failure to act, by the employee's employer done on the ground that the employee refused to accept an offer by the employer for the employee to become an employee shareholder (within the meaning of s 205A): ERA 1996, s 47G(1). There is no qualifying period for this right.

This section does not apply if the detriment in question amounts to dismissal within the meaning of Part 10: ERA 1996, s 47G(1).

3.67 A new s 104F ('employee shareholder status') is inserted in the ERA 1996 which gives the employee the right not to be unfairly dismissed as a result of refusing to accept an employee shareholder contract. There is no qualifying period for this right. It provides that an employee who is dismissed is to be regarded for the purposes of this Part as unfairly dismissed if the reason (or, if more than one, the principal reason) for the dismissal is that the employee refused to accept an offer by the employer for the employee to become an employee shareholder (within the meaning of ERA 1996, s 205A).

European Economic Interest Grouping (EEIG)

3.68 As part of the EU measures and objectives towards closer cross-border cooperation between entities formed in different Member States, the European Economic Interest Grouping (EEIG) was enacted. In the UK, the EEIG is governed by the European Economic Interest Grouping Regulations 1989 SI 1989 No 638 implementing Council Regulation 2317/85. An EEIG is established by an agreement between members from different jurisdictions for a common purpose or to provide common services incidental to the main activities of the members. Profits made by the EEIG belong to the members. Members are jointly and severally liable for the EEIG's acts. The EEIG has characteristics of both a company and a partnership. The EEIG's members may take 'any decision for the purpose of achieving the objects of the grouping'.

3.69 An EEIG is formed by a written agreement between the members. The contract for the formation of the EEIG must be lodged at Companies House, if the EEIG is to have its principal establishment in the UK. There must be at least two members and these members can be a natural or legal person. In the UK, the Regulation confers corporate personality for the EEIG where its principal establishment is in Great Britain: reg 3 as amended by the European Economic Interest Grouping Regulations 2009, SI 2009/2399.

3.70 There are, however, some restrictions with on EEIGs. These include:

- an EEIG cannot employ more than 500 employees;
- its objects must be limited to economic activities;

- it cannot exercise management over its members' activities or those of another undertaking;
- it cannot hold shares in a member company;
- it cannot be a member of another EEIG.

Many of the provisions of the Companies Act 2006, the CDDA 1986 and Insolvency Act 1986 apply to an EEIG and an EEIG is treated as a company registered under CA 2006. It can be liquidated as an unregistered company under IA 1986, Part V

European company

3.71 European companies are also known as 'Societas Europaea' or 'SE'. They are governed by Council Regulation 2157/2001 implemented by the European Public Limited-Liability Company Regulations 2004, SI 2004/2326; and Directive 2001/86 which supplements the Statute for a European Company with regard to the involvement of employees. One of the principal objectives for establishing a European company is to make it easier to establish cross-border mergers. Under UK law, the SE can only be set up by existing companies or entities. There are four methods by which an SE can be formed:

- establishing a holding SE by public or private limited companies from two different Member States;
- transformation of a public limited company which had a subsidiary in another Member State for at least two years;
- establishing a subsidiary SE;
- merging (by acquisition or formation) of two or more companies incorporated in different Member States. They must be public companies and have their registered and head office in the European Community.

The minimum capital for an SE is €120,000. The SE's registered office must be in the same Member State as its head office.

The SE's governance may be based on a unitary board structure or a supervisory and management board.

3.72 The establishment and operation of SEs is governed largely by EC law with reference, where required, to national law. National law will be applicable on issues such as liability, directors' duties, liquidation aspects, convening meetings, tax regimes, registration of documents, and preparation and filing of accounts. The Regulations set out the details of SE formation including in relation to governance, capital, rights of shareholders, convening meetings, name, liquidation, and registered and head offices. Directive 2001/86 sets out the details for the involvement of employees in the SE, their participation, role and function, issues of consultation and how employees' representatives are elected to represent them.

The impact of SEs and their ability for set up is now reduced owing to the freedom of establishment of companies and the Tenth Directive on Cross-Border Mergers which allows for transfer of companies between Member States.

European private company

3.73 The European private company ('Societas Privata Europaea' – SPE) is designed to be a European legal form intended to facilitate the establishment and operation of small and medium-sized enterprises (SMEs) in the European Single Market. At the same time, it will benefit larger groups in organising their subsidiaries abroad.

The SPE is currently at a proposal stage and yet to be implemented by the EU. Once implemented, it is expected to have the following characteristics:

Formation

3.74 The SPE can be formed *ex nihilo* by one or several natural persons and/or legal entities. It may also be formed by transforming, merging or dividing existing companies. The latter can have a statute governed by national or EU law, such as those recorded as being a European Company (Societas Europaea) or SE.

Capital and shareholders

3.75 The minimum capital of an SPE can be €1. It is divided into unquoted shares, which cannot be offered to the public or negotiated on a regulated market. Each shareholder is only liable up to the amount for which they have subscribed or agreed to subscribe.

The management body establishes a list of shareholders, which constitutes proof of ownership for the shares. All shareholdings must be notified to the management body which registers them in the list of shareholders. The procedure of excluding a shareholder is subject to a resolution of the shareholders which then leads to a request made by the SPE to the court having jurisdiction. Similarly, shareholders can withdraw from the SPE in order to protect their interests.

Registration

3.76 The registered office and the central administration or main establishment of SPEs will be established in the European Union. The company is registered in the Member State in which the statutory registered office is located. Its subsidiaries are governed by the national law where they are established. An SPE is not bound to establish its central administration or main establishment in the Member State in which the registered office is located. Administrative formalities and registration costs must be reduced as much as possible.

3.77 The registered office of an SPE may be transferred to another Member State, without having any consequences on the legal personality or on the rights and obligations created by contracts concluded previously. The transfer takes effect on the date of registration in the host Member State.

Organisation

3.78 The shareholders determine the articles of association of the SPE, as set in Annex I of the Commission Proposal (see *Proposal for a Council Regulation on the Statute* *for a European Private Company*, Com (2008), 396). Matters not covered by the articles of association are subject to the national law of the Member State in which the SPE has its registered office.

3.79 The management body is responsible for the management of the SPE and exercises all prerogatives that are not held by the shareholders.

Shareholders are responsible for the organisation of the SPE. They adopt resolutions that are binding upon shareholders, the management body and the supervisory body of the SPE and on third parties.

Accounts

3.80 Accounts management and the preparation, filing, auditing and publication of accounts are subject to national law.

Employee participation

3.81 Methods for participation are subject to the regulations of the Member State where the SPE has its registered office. Directive 2005/56/EC will apply in the case of cross-border mergers. In addition, the Proposal for the Regulation provides for a series of specific regulations on this subject if the registered office of an SPE is transferred to another Member State. This is to avoid pre-existing rights concerning employee participation being circumvented.

Small Business Act for Europe

3.82 Much emphasis has been placed on ensuring that SMEs are at the heart of conducting business activities in Europe and across borders. This concept has been transformed into a 'think small first' approach for SMEs operating in Europe.

In June 2008, the European Commission enacted the Small Business Act (SBA) for Europe reflecting the Commission's political determination to recognise the central role of SMEs in the EU economy.

The SBA applies to all independent companies which have fewer than 250 employees. One of its objectives is to reduce regulatory burdens on SMEs and for the EU to respond better to the needs of SMEs.

3.83 The SBA:

- is a set of ten principles which should guide the design and implementation of policies both at EU and national level. This is essential to create a level playing field for SMEs throughout the EU and improve the administrative and legal environment, so as to allow these enterprises to unleash their full potential to create jobs and growth;
- is an ambitious package of concrete and far-reaching new measures including four legislative proposals which translate these principles into action both at EU and Member State level; and

- was endorsed politically by the EU Council of Ministers in December 2008 to ensure the full commitment of both the Commission and the Member States together with regular monitoring of its implementation.

3.84 The EU Commission has adopted various measures to ensure an improved response to the needs of SMEs. It will engage in the following:

- Whenever possible, it will seek to exempt small businesses from EU legislation or introduce special regimes so as to minimise the regulatory burdens on them.
- It will strengthen the processes by which SMEs are consulted when reviewing existing EU legislation and preparing new EU laws.
- It will produce annual scoreboards to evaluate real benefits for businesses and to ensure a continuing focus on their needs and interests.

The SBA is currently the subject of consultation by the European Commission see: 'A Strong European Policy to Support SMEs and Entrepreneurs 2015–2020'.

Principle of freedom of establishment of companies in Member States

3.85 Article 49 (ex Art 43 TEC) of the Treaty on the Functioning of the European Union is concerned with freedom of establishment and provides:

> 'Within the framework of the provisions set out below, restrictions on the freedom of establishment of nationals of a Member State in the territory of another Member State shall be prohibited. Such prohibition shall also apply to restrictions on the setting-up of agencies, branches or subsidiaries by nationals of any Member State established in the territory of any Member State.
>
> Freedom of establishment shall include the right to take up and pursue activities as self-employed persons and to set up and manage undertakings, in particular companies or firms within the meaning of the second paragraph of Art 54, under the conditions laid down for its own nationals by the law of the country where such establishment is effected, subject to the provisions of the Chapter relating to capital.'

3.86 Article 54 (ex Art 48 TEC) of the Treaty on the Functioning of the European Union requires companies that are established in a Member State to be treated in the same way as natural persons who are nationals of Member States. It states:

> 'Companies or firms formed in accordance with the law of a Member State and having their registered office, central administration or principal place of business within the Union shall, for the purposes of this Chapter, be treated in the same way as natural persons who are nationals of Member States.
>
> "Companies or firms" means companies or firms constituted under civil or commercial law, including cooperative societies, and other legal persons governed by public or private law, save for those which are non-profit-making.'

The principle of freedom of establishment of companies has given rise to some key cases decided by the European Court of Justice.

Subject to exceptions, a Member State cannot refuse the establishment of a branch of a company from another Member State under TFEU, Arts 49 and 54

In *Centros Ltd v Erhvervs-og Selskabsstyrelsen*, Case C-212/97 [2000] 2 BCLC 68, two Danish nationals established a private limited liability company in England which had the advantage of no minimum capital requirements. The company did not engage in any activities in England. It then applied to the Danish authorities to set up a branch which would operate in Denmark. The minimum capital requirements in Denmark were of a high amount imposed on Danish nationals. The Danish authorities did not allow the branch to be established in Denmark on the basis that the two Danish nationals were carrying on their main business in Denmark which was in breach of Danish laws. The issue before the European Court was whether the refusal to register a branch in such circumstances was contrary to Arts 49 and 54 of the Treaty on the Functioning of the European Union.

According to the European Court of Justice, the Danish authorities were not entitled to refuse to register the branch as it was contrary to the principles of freedom of establishment under Arts 49 and 54. The Treaty provisions on freedom of establishment were intended specifically to enable companies formed in accordance with the law of a Member State and having their registered office, central administration or principal place of business within the European Community to pursue activities in other Member States through an agency, branch or subsidiary.

However, Member States were entitled to take measures to prevent their nationals from attempting, under cover of the Treaty rights, improperly to circumvent their national legislation or to prevent individuals from improperly or fraudulently taking advantage of Community provisions. However, the fact that a national of a Member State who wished to set up a company chose to form it in the Member State whose rules of company law seemed the least restrictive and to set up branches in other Member States did not, in itself, constitute an abuse of the right of establishment. The right to form a company in accordance with the law of a Member State and to set up branches in other Member States was inherent in the exercise, in a single market, of the freedom of establishment guaranteed by the Treaty. Furthermore, the fact that a company did not conduct any business in the Member State in which it had its registered office and pursued its activities only in the Member State in which its branch was established was not sufficient to prove the existence of abuse or fraudulent conduct which would have entitled the latter state to deny that company the benefit of the Community provisions relating to the right of establishment. It was therefore contrary to Arts 49 and 54 of the Treaty for a Member State to refuse to register a branch of a company in the circumstances of the instant case.

See too: *Segers v Bestuur van de Bedrijfsvereniging voor Bank-en Verzekeringswezen, Groothandel en Vrije Beroepen* Case 79/85 [1986] ECR 2375; and *Brennet AG v Paletta* Case C-206/94 [1996] ECR I-2357.

Subject to certain exceptions, a company incorporated in another Member State has legal capacity to bring proceedings in another Member State

In *Uberseering BV v Nordic Construction Co Baumanagement Gmbh (NCC)* [2005] 1 WLR 315, the company in question was set up in the Netherlands, but thereafter many of its business activities were undertaken in Germany. The company brought a civil action in Germany on a particular matter but was denied standing to sue by the German authorities on the ground that the company did not have any legal capacity to sue in Germany, as it was not incorporated in Germany and it did not matters that all its shareholders were German.

The European Court of Justice held that a company existed only by virtue of the national legislation which determined its incorporation and functioning. The requirement of German national law of reincorporation of the same company in Germany was therefore tantamount to outright negation of freedom of establishment. The refusal by a host Member State, B, to recognise the legal capacity of a company formed in accordance with the law of another Member State, A, in which it had its registered office on the ground that the company moved its actual centre of administration to Member State B with the result that the company could not, in Member State B, bring legal proceedings to defend rights under a contract unless it was reincorporated under the law of Member State B, constituted a restriction on freedom of establishment which was, in principle, incompatible with Arts 49 and 54 of the Treaty: see too *R v HM Treasury, ex p Daily Mail and General Trust* (Case 81/87) [1989] 1 All ER 328.

The European Court of Justice further held that it was not inconceivable that overriding requirements relating to the general interest, such as the protection of the interests of creditors, minority shareholders, employees and even taxation authorities, might, in certain circumstances and subject to certain conditions, justify restrictions on freedom of establishment. Such objectives could not, however, justify denying the legal capacity and, consequently, the capacity to be a party to legal proceedings of a company properly incorporated in another Member State in which it had its registered office. Accordingly, applying *Centros Ltd v Erhvervs-Og Selskabsstyrelsen* (Case C-212/97) [2000] All ER (EC) 481, the European Court of Justice held that the restriction on freedom of establishment that the court had found could not be justified. Therefore, Arts 49 and 54 of the Treaty required a Member State to recognise the legal capacity and, consequently, the capacity to be a party to legal proceedings which the company enjoyed under the law of its Member State of incorporation.

Subject to certain exceptions, foreign companies established in another Member State could not be subject to additional burdens and requirements that are not applied to local companies

Another issue which has arisen before the European Court of Justice on freedom of establishment is whether foreign companies that validly registered in another Member State could be subject to additional burdens and requirements owing to their 'foreign' status. This issue arose in *Kamer van Koophandel en Fabrieken voor Amsterdam v Inspire Art Ltd* [2005] 2 CLMR 34. The applicant was a company formed under the laws of England and Wales and had its registered office in England. It had a branch in Amsterdam in which it carried out all of its trade. The Dutch authorities were of the opinion that the applicant was a 'formally foreign company' within the meaning of domestic law and brought proceedings, alleging that its registration in the Netherlands had been incomplete. As a 'formally foreign company' the domestic law in question imposed obligations on the applicant, including disclosure obligations over and above those provided for by Art 2 of the Eleventh Council Directive (EEC) 89/666 concerning disclosure requirements in respect of branches opened in a Member State by certain types of company governed by the law of another state, made directors jointly and severally liable with the company and required the minimum amount of subscribed capital as prescribed for Dutch companies. The applicant disputed that its registration was incomplete and argued, *inter alia*, that the domestic law infringed the Directive and the prohibition on restrictions on freedom of establishment in Arts 49 and 54 of the Treaty.

The European Court of Justice held that it was contrary to Art 2 of the Directive to impose disclosure obligations on the branch of a company formed in accordance with the laws of another Member State that were not provided for by that Directive. On its true construction, Art 2(1) was exhaustive in formulation. Moreover, Art 2(2) contained a list of optional measures imposing disclosure requirements on branches, a measure that could have no raison d'etre unless Member States were unable to provide for disclosure measures for branches other than those laid down in the text of that Directive. Accordingly, those disclosure measures in the domestic law beyond those in Art 2 of the Directive infringed Community law.

The European Court of Justice further held that Arts 49 and 54 of the Treaty precluded national legislation that imposed on the exercise of freedom of secondary establishment in that state by a company formed in accordance with the law of another Member State certain conditions provided for in domestic law in respect of company formation relating to minimum capital and directors' liability. The reasons for which the company was formed in that other state, and the fact that it carried on its activities exclusively or almost exclusively in the Member State of establishment, did not deprive it of the right to invoke the freedom of establishment guaranteed by the Treaty, except where abuse was established on a case-by-case basis. The fact that a company was formed in a particular Member State for the sole purpose of enjoying more favourable legislation did not, applying settled principles, constitute an abuse, even if that company conducted its activities entirely or mainly in that second state. In the present case, there could be no justification of the measures in question. The justifications put forward did not fall within the scope of Art 49 and were not justified by an overriding public interest. Although a Member State was entitled to take measures designed to prevent certain of its nationals from attempting, under the cover of the rights created by the Treaty, improperly to circumvent their national legislation or to prevent individuals from improperly or fraudulently taking advantage of Community law, the provisions of the Treaty on freedom of establishment were intended specifically to enable companies formed in accordance with the law of a Member State and having their registered office within the Community, to pursue activities in other Member States through an agency, branch or subsidiary.

Subject to any exceptions, it was contrary to the principle of freedom of establishment to refuse to register a merger of legal entities from different Member States

The European Court of Justice has also considered the issue of freedom of establishment for companies in *Re Sevic Systems AG* [2006] 2 BCLC 510.

Under para 1(1)(1) of the German Law on transforming companies, it was provided that legal entities established in Germany could be transformed by merger. The Law further provided, *inter alia*, for the types of merger which would be recognised and the registration of mergers in the national commercial register. The merger contract concluded between SEVIC Systems AG (the applicant company), a company established in Germany, and Security Vision Concept SA, a company established in Luxembourg, provided for merger by way of the absorption of the Luxembourg company and its dissolution without liquidation.

SEVIC Systems AG sought registration of the merger. Its application was refused by the German authorities on the ground that para 1(1)(1) of the Law only provided for mergers between legal entities established in Germany. The applicant company brought an action against that decision. The matter was referred to the Court of Justice of the European Communities for a preliminary ruling of the question whether those provisions were to be interpreted as meaning that it was contrary to freedom of establishment for companies if a foreign European company was refused registration of its proposed merger with a German company under the Law on the ground that para 1(1)(1) of that Law only provided for the transformation of legal entities established in Germany contrary to the Treaty.

The right of establishment covered all measures which permitted or even merely facilitated access to another Member State and the pursuit of an economic activity in that state by allowing the persons concerned to participate in the economic life of the country effectively and under the same conditions as national operators. Cross-border merger operations responded to the need for co-operation and consolidation between companies established in different Member States. They constituted particular methods of exercise of the freedom of establishment, important for the proper functioning of the internal market, and were therefore amongst those economic activities in respect of which Member States were required to comply with the freedom of establishment laid down by Art 49 of the Treaty. German law established a difference in treatment between companies according to the internal or cross-border nature of a merger which was likely to deter the exercise of the freedom of establishment. Such a difference constituted a restriction within the meaning of Arts 49 and 54 of the Treaty. Whilst it was not possible to exclude the possibility that imperative reasons in the public interest could, in certain circumstances and under certain conditions, justify a measure restricting the freedom of establishment, such a measure would have to be appropriate for ensuring the attainment of the objectives pursued and not go beyond what was necessary to attain them. To refuse generally, in a Member State, to register a merger between a company established in that state and a company established in another Member State had the effect of preventing the realisation of cross-border mergers, even if imperative reasons in the public interest were not threatened. In any event, the Law went beyond what was necessary to protect those interests.

In the civil proceedings concerning *Cartesio Oktató és Szolgáltató bt* [2010] 1 BCLC 510, the applicant company, a limited partnership formed under Hungarian law, had its seat in Hungary. It filed an application with the Bács-Kiskun Megyei Bíróság (Regional Court of Bács-Kiskun), sitting as a commercial court, for registration of the transfer of its seat to Italy and, in consequence, for amendment of the entry to its company seat in the commercial register. That application was rejected on the ground that Hungarian law did not allow a company incorporated in Hungary to transfer its seat abroad while continuing to be subject to Hungarian law as its personal law. The applicant appealed against that decision with the Szegedi Ítélötábla (Court of Appeal, Szeged). The applicant claimed that Hungarian law was contrary to Arts 48 and 54 of the Treaty, because it drew a distinction between commercial companies according to the Member State in which they had their seat. The applicant also maintained that the Szegedi Ítélötábla was required to refer that question for a preliminary ruling, since it constituted a court or tribunal of a Member State against whose decisions there was no judicial remedy under national law. Taking the view that the resolution of the dispute depended on interpretation of Community law, the Szegedi Ítélötábla (the referring court) decided to stay the proceedings and referred certain questions to the Court of Justice of the European Communities for a preliminary ruling under Art 234 EC (formerly Art 177 of the EC Treaty) concerning, *inter alia*, whether Arts 48 and 54 EC Treaty precluded legislation of a Member State under which a company incorporated under that law could not transfer its seat to another Member State while retaining its status as a company governed by the law of the Member State of incorporation.

The European Court of Justice held that in respect of Arts 48 and 54 of the Treaty, these articles did not preclude the legislation of a Member State under which a company incorporated under the law of that Member State could not transfer its seat to another Member State whilst retaining its status as a company governed by the law of the Member State of incorporation.

Companies were creatures of national law and existed only by virtue of the national legislation which determined their incorporation and functioning. The legislation of the Member States varied widely in regard to both the factor providing a connection to the national territory required for the incorporation of a company and the question whether a company incorporated under the legislation of a Member State might subsequently modify that connecting factor. In defining, in Art 48, the companies which enjoyed the right of establishment, the Treaty placed on the same footing, as connecting factors, the registered office, central administration and principal place of business of a company. It could be inferred from that that the question whether a company formed in accordance with the legislation of one Member State could transfer its registered office or its actual centre of administration to another Member State without losing its legal personality under the law of the Member State of incorporation, and, in certain circumstances, the rules relating to that transfer, were determined by the national law in accordance with which the company was incorporated.

Therefore, a Member State was able, in the case of a company incorporated under its law, to make the company's right to retain its legal personality under the law of that Member State subject to restrictions on the transfer to a foreign country of the company's actual centre of administration. Consequently, in accordance with Art 48, in the absence of a uniform EU law definition of the companies which might enjoy the right of establishment on the basis of a single connecting factor determining the national law applicable to a company, the question whether Art 48 applied to a company which sought to rely on the fundamental freedom enshrined in that article was a preliminary matter which, as EU law now stood, could only be resolved by the applicable national law. Therefore, a Member State had the power to define both the connecting factor required of a company if it was to be regarded as incorporated under the law of that Member State and, as such, capable of enjoying the right of establishment, and that required if the company was to be able subsequently to maintain that status. That power included the possibility for that Member State not to permit a company governed by its law to retain that status if the company intended to reorganise itself in another Member State by moving its seat to the territory of the latter, thereby breaking the connecting factor required under the national law of the Member State of incorporation. The situation where the seat of a company incorporated under the law of one Member State was transferred to another state with no change as regards the law which governed that company fell to be distinguished from the situation where a company governed by the law of one Member State moved to another state with an attendant change as regards the national law applicable, since in the latter situation the company was converted into a form of company which was governed by the law of the Member State to which it had moved. In fact, in that latter case, the power to define the connecting factor, far from implying that national legislation on the incorporation and winding up of companies enjoyed any form of immunity from the rules of the Treaty on freedom of establishment, could not justify the Member State of incorporation, by requiring the winding up or liquidation of the company, in preventing that company from converting itself into a company governed by the law of the other Member State, to the extent that it was permitted under that law to do so. Such a barrier to the actual conversion of such a company, without prior winding up or liquidation, into a company governed by the law of the Member State to which it wished to relocate constituted a restriction on the freedom of establishment of the company concerned which, unless it served overriding requirements in the public interest, was prohibited under Art 48.

However, see now the Cross-Border Mergers Directive 2005/56/EC which specifically addresses corporate mobility for the cross-border transfer of limited companies' registered office and the Companies (Cross-Border Mergers) Regulations 2007, SI 2007/2974.

The court applies an 'open textured and purposive approach' to the interpretation of article provisions dealing with freedom of establishment

The principle of freedom of establishment was addressed in *Re Olympus UK Ltd* [2014] 2 BCLC 402.

A Japanese company resolved to transfer the operations of three of its wholly-owned English companies to Germany by two cross-border 'mergers by absorption'. By way of a first merger, an English company and its subsidiary would merge with a German company. Under a second merger another English company (an SE) would merge with an SE registered in Germany. Under both mergers, the transferor companies would be dissolved without the necessity of liquidation with their assets and liabilities transferred to the German companies (transferee companies) which would not allot shares or make any payment to the transferor companies as the shareholders had waived their right to receive payment consideration. Directive 2005/56/EC on cross-border mergers of limited liability companies ('Directive') and the Companies (Cross-Border Mergers) Regulations 2007, SI 2007/2974 established a regime to facilitate such transactions. The issue arose as to whether the 2007 Regulations contemplated that in a cross-border merger (other than a merger by absorption of a wholly-owned subsidiary), shareholders in the transferor company would actually receive, as consideration for the merger, 'shares or other securities representing the capital of the transferee company': see reg 2(2)(f) and (4)(c). In the present case, and the fact that all the companies concerned were wholly-owned by the same holding company, the draft terms of merger provided that the shareholders in the applicant transferor companies would not receive any consideration from the transferee companies. Hildyard J held that in the European context, 'cross-border merger' in Art 2(2) of the Directive was better translated as requiring members of the transferor company to be offered the 'right to receive shares in the transferee company', which right they could waive rather than requiring the actual 'issue of shares' to them. All that was required was for the shareholders to be offered the shares in the transferee company even if those shares were simultaneously declined by the transferor members. The court adopted an 'open textured and purposive approach' to the interpretation of Art 2(2).

Tax differential treatment between parent and subsidiary entities may be incompatible with TFEU, Art 49

In *Group Steria SCA v Ministere des Finances et des Comptes Publics* (Case C-386/14) (2 September 2015), concerned a certain provision of French tax law which treated dividends received by a parent company differently depending on whether the subsidiary was resident in France or another Member State. The Court of Justice held that such differential treatment was not compatible with Art 49 ('Right of establishment') of the Treaty on the Functioning of the European Union.

The concept of 'establishment' under EU Regulation 1346/2000 on insolvency proceedings referred to a fixed place of business including business activities carried on by the establishment

In *Trustees of the Olympic Airlines SA Pension and Life Assurance Scheme v Olympic Airlines SA* [2015] UKSC 27, which concerned the interpretation to be given to 'establishment' under EU Regulation 1346/2000 on insolvency proceedings, the Supreme Court decided that the term 'establishment' must be read as a whole: it referred to a fixed place of business, including business activity that was being carried on there consisting in dealings with third parties. Acts of internal administration were not in themselves sufficient.

On 2 October 2009, Olympic Airlines SA ('OA') was wound up by the Athens Court with on-going liquidation proceedings in Greece. The OA had a pension scheme but with a £16 million deficit. Under the Pensions Act 2004, s 75, it was required to make good the deficit but was unlikely to be able to do so. Under the Pensions Act 2004, members of the pension scheme were eligible for compensation from the UK's pension protection fund where there was a shortfall. The compensation fund is payable from the date when a 'qualifying insolvency event' occurred.

In this case, there were two dates for the 'qualifying insolvency event'. First, the date of 20 July 2010 when the trustees of the pension scheme presented a winding up petition in England. Under the Insolvency Act 1986 ('IA 1986'), the winding up of a company is considered as a 'qualifying insolvency event': Pensions Act 2004, s 121(3)(g). English courts therefore had jurisdiction to wind up a foreign company under the IA 1986. This is subject, however, to EU Regulation 1346/2000 on insolvency proceedings ('Regulation') which provides, inter alia, that where the company has its 'centre of main interests' in another Member State of the European Union, the English court can only wind it up if it has an 'establishment' in England namely 'any place of operations where the debtor carries out a non-transitory economic activity with human means and goods' (Art 2(h) of the Regulation).

Another possible date was 2 October 2014 which was the fifth anniversary of commencement of winding-up proceedings in Greece. This date may have been treated as the qualifying insolvency date event by the Pension Protection Fund (Entry Rules) (Amendment) Regulations 2014, SI 2014/1664.

The trustees of the pension fund preferred that compensation should be treated as payable as from 20 July 2014 rather than 2 October 2014.

The issue before the Supreme Court was whether OA had an 'establishment' in the UK on 20 July 2010 which would entitle the English court to make a winding up order under the Regulation in order to satisfy the requirement that a qualifying insolvency act occurred on 20 July 2010. However, by this date, OA had:

- closed all its offices in the UK except its head office in London;
- ceased all commercial operations;
- terminated all contracts of remaining staff except for some managers and an accounts clerk who were retained on short term contracts to coordinate with the Athens liquidator and assist in the disposal of assets.

The head office was effectively an empty shell. Its principal task was to pay any bills and undertake administrative duties at its head office in London.

At first instance, the judge decided that OA's activities were 'non-transitory economic activities' and OA therefore had an 'establishment' in the UK, so that a winding up order could be made. The Court of Appeal did not agree and held that the remaining activity consisted only in winding up the company's affairs and this was not sufficient to make a winding up order.

The Supreme Court held (Lord Sumption giving the only judgment with the other Law Lords agreeing) that the definition of 'establishment' under the Regulation must be read as a whole. It referred to a fixed place of business. Further, the business activity carried on there must consist in dealing with third parties. Merely dealing with internal administration was not sufficient. As OA was not therefore carrying on a business activity at its head office on 20 July 2010, it did not have an establishment in the UK.

The principal issue for consideration was what connection must a foreign company have with the UK to entitle the English court to wind it up where its centre of main interests ('COMI') was in another Member State of the European Union? This depended upon the interpretation to be given to the words 'economic activity' under Regulation 1346/2000 and its interrelationship with the IA 1986.

The case highlights the interconnection between European Law and English law. The IA 1986, s 221 provides that the English court has jurisdiction under domestic law to wind up a foreign company. Where, however, companies have COMI in another Member State of the EU, the English court's power is regulated by Art 3 of the Regulation concerning international jurisdiction. This provides, inter alia, that the courts of the Member States within the territory of which the centre of a debtor's main interests is situated will have jurisdiction to open insolvency proceedings. The place of the registered office will be presumed to be the centre of its main interests in the absence of proof to the contrary. Further, where the centre of a debtor's main interests is situated within the territory of a Member State, the courts of another Member State will have jurisdiction to open insolvency proceedings against the debtor only if he possesses an 'establishment' within the territory of that Member State. The effect of those proceedings will be restricted to the debtor's assets situated in the territory of the latter Member State.

The term 'centre of its main interests' ('COMI') is not defined under the Regulation. However, recital (13) of the Regulation provides that it should correspond to the place where the debtor conducts the administration of his interests on a regular basis and is therefore ascertainable by third parties.

According to the Supreme Court, the jurisdiction to bring secondary proceedings in another European jurisdiction is based on the existence of an 'establishment' within its territory. Article 2(h) of the Regulation defines an 'establishment' as 'any place of operations where the debtor carries out a non-transitory economic activity with human means and goods'. The term 'goods' effectively refers to 'assets'. The Supreme Court relied on various sources to identify the meaning of 'establishment'. First, it relied heavily on the Vigos-Schmit Report ('Report') which provided detailed commentary on the Convention on Insolvency Proceedings (which Convention was not ratified by Member States) on which the

EU Regulation is based. The Report highlighted that an 'establishment' referred to a place of operations through which the debtor carries out an economic activity on a non-transitory basis, and where he uses human resources and assets. Place of operations means a place from which economic activities are exercised on the market (externally) whether of a commercial, industrial or a professional nature. There should be a minimum level of organisation. A purely occasional place of operations cannot be an establishment. A certain degree of stability is required. The main factor is how the activity appears externally and not the intention of the debtor. See too Case C-396/09 *Interedil Srl (in liquidation) v Fallimento Interedil Srl* [2001] CCR 1-9939; and *Shierson v Vlieland-Boddy* [2005] 1 WLR 3966; and *Re Office Metro Ltd* [2012] BCC 829.

Article 2(h) definition of 'establishment' must be read as a whole and not broken down into discrete elements. The relevant activities must be:

- economic;
- non-transitory;
- carried on from a 'place of operations';
- using the debtor's assets and human agents.

There is a requirement for:

- a fixed place of business;
- business dealings with third parties;
- activities being exercised on the market;
- consideration of the character of the economic activities.

The following will not suffice:

- merely internal administration;
- where the company has no subsisting business.

OA was at the tail end of its business operations in London. It had ceased further dealings with third parties, closed its offices, and significantly reduced the number of employees to the bare minimum. OA was reduced to an empty shell. There was no further economic activity involved and it was transitory in nature. It was not a place of business operations through human resources and assets. These factors taken as a whole pointed to OA not being an 'establishment' within the meaning of the Regulation, and were not sufficient to give English courts jurisdiction to wind up OA in England. Had OA carried on some economic activity including dealings with third parties, the position may have been different.

Checklist: setting up an unlimited company

3.87 *This checklist sets out the key features governing an unlimited company which may be established under the Companies Act 2006.*

No	Issue	Reference
1	A private unlimited company's liability is unlimited. This type of legal structure is suitable for a business where the risk of insolvency is very low or non-existent, or where the owners wish to shield the financial performance and annual accounts from public view. They can be required to pay the company's debts without limit if it defaults and is wound up. It has the same features as a private company limited by shares.	CA 2006, s 3(4)
2	Consider choice of name for the unlimited company ensuring name not similar or identical to one already registered or subject to any passing off actions.	CA 2006, Part 5
3	Prepare memorandum of association and lodge at Companies House.	
4	Prepare articles of association and lodge at Companies House.	Articles of association
5	The company must have at least one shareholder – no residency requirements. A private unlimited company may or may not have share capital.	Form IN01
6	Appoint a director of the company: a sole director is sufficient – must be a natural person – no residency requirements.	Form IN01
7	The registered office must be a physical address in the UK.	Form IN01
8	There is no requirement to file accounts at Companies House	
9	Obtain certificate of incorporation from Companies House.	
10	Order company's headed paper stationery with details and address of the private unlimited company.	
11	Notify appropriate authorities of the new company's details.	

Definitions

3.88

CIC: Community Interest Company.

EEIG: European Economic Interest Grouping.

LLP: Limited Liability Partnership.

SME: Small and Medium-Size Enterprise.

4 Corporate personality

Contents

Introduction

4.1 A company acquires a separate legal personality when it is registered at Companies House, and all the formalities required for registration have been complied with: CA 2006, s 14. On the company's registration, the registrar of companies will issue a certificate of incorporation (CA 2006, s 15(1)) and a notice in the *Gazette* (CA 2006, s 1064(1)(a)) as evidence that the company has been incorporated. Prior to the date of the certificate of incorporation, a company has no legal existence: *F J Neale (Glasgow) Ltd v Vickery* 1973 SLT (Sh Ct) 88; *Mach Marketing International SA v MacColl* [1995] BCC 951. 'The company attains maturity on its birth. There is no period of minority; an interval of incapacity' (Lord Macnaghten in *Salomon v Salomon & Co Ltd* [1897] AC 22). Once the company has been registered, the subscribers to the memorandum (usually the company's promoters), together with other persons who may from time to time become members of the company, become a corporate entity by the name set out in the certificate of incorporation: CA 2006, s 16(2). From the date of registration, the company is capable of exercising all the functions of an incorporated company: CA 2006, s 16(3). The company begins a new life with a unique registration number set out in the certificate of incorporation. Under s 16(5), where the company has a share capital, the subscribers to the memorandum of association become holders of the shares from the date of the company's registration. The company's proposed officers are deemed to have been appointed as director and/or secretary as from the date of registration: CA 2006, s 16(6).

4.2 This chapter addresses the following questions:

- How does UK company law define the concept of 'corporate personality', and the circumstances in which the company is treated as a distinct legal entity from its shareholders?

- How has the landmark decision in *Salomon v A Salomon & Co Ltd* provided legitimacy to 'one-man' companies?
- What are the legal and practical implications of the *Salomon* decision?
- What is the relationship between a controlling shareholder and his employment relationship with the company?
- How has the corporate personality principle been applied to family companies and matrimonial disputes with particular reference to the Supreme Court decision in *Prest v Petrodel Resources Ltd* [2013] All ER 90?
- What are the limited circumstances in which the courts will pierce or lift the corporate veil to impose liability on the shareholders or directors with particular reference to the Supreme Court decision in *VTB Capital plc v Nutritek International* [2013] 1 BCLC 179; and *Prest v Petrodel Resources Ltd* [2013] All ER 90?

A practical checklist of issues to consider in respect of corporate personality is set out at the end of this chapter.

Setting the scene – Pre-*Salomon* Position

4.3 This section provides a brief overview of the significant developments leading to the establishment of companies with limited liability. It also provides a background to the decision in *Salomon v A Salomon & Co Ltd* [1897] AC 22.

The trading entities

4.4 At common law, the establishment of companies dates back to the fifteenth and sixteenth centuries, when common law corporations were established either by receiving charters through the exercise of the royal prerogative, or through ancient and continuous existence. Special privileges were granted to corporations which were established for specific purposes by way of royal charters. Most common law corporations were ecclesiastical including colleges of priests, convents and hospitals, deans and chapters. There were a few incorporated merchant guilds. The common law corporations had the contractual capacity of a natural person but with some differences: they could enter into contracts with third parties and could sue and be sued. They had such capacities and disposing powers that were similar to natural persons.

4.5 The other common form of business organisations were partnerships and sole traders which carried unlimited liability consequences, and in some cases, individual bankruptcies. Owing to the risks associated with unlimited liability, partnerships and sole traders were able to establish joint stock companies under the liberal provisions of the Joint Stock Companies Act 1856. Joint stock companies differed from partnerships in that partnerships were limited in their size, whereas joint stock companies comprised an unlimited number of investors with a division of capital into freely transferable shares. In joint stock companies, the members were not usually involved in the day to day management of such companies. These companies were not incorporated entities.

4.6 The growth of the popularity of joint stock companies enabled them to be fraudulently exploited and created legal issues as to whether or not they could sue and be sued. The Joint Stock Companies Act 1844 required such companies to be incorporated and to register and publicise their registration in order to combat fraud. However, this Act did not confer any limited liability for joint stock companies. Ten years later, the Limited Liability Act 1855 allowed limited liability for joint stock companies. Within a year, the joint stock company paved the way for other companies to be incorporated with limited liability under the Joint Stock Companies Act 1856. The draftsman of the 1856 Act had not however appreciated that this Act could be used by all forms of businesses from sole traders to partnerships to incorporate their business. The Act, *inter alia*, permitted the association of seven or more members to incorporate. It was thought that this Act excluded incorporation by other forms of businesses owing to the requirement for seven or more members. The path was now clear for unincorporated businesses to convert their businesses and establish a company with limited liability. The Companies Act 1862 regulated the formation and registration of companies.

The Great Depression and its impact on incorporation

4.7 Initially, the impact of the Companies Acts 1856-62 on the economic and legal forms of business was minimal. Very few businesses had registered under these Acts. However, over the next two decades, limited liability companies became an attractive form of legal vehicle for entrepreneurs to conduct business coupled with a period of the industrial revolution which significantly benefited the UK economy, trade and labour in various industrial sectors. The rise of private limited companies triumphed over joint stock companies. Entrepreneurs were largely driven by the prospect of limited liability as the main factor towards incorporation.

4.8 The 'Great Depression' from 1873 to 1896 was also an influential factor in businesses incorporating with limited liability. During this period, industrial capitalists suffered serious economic difficulties, and were exposed to the risks of personal bankruptcy and a failing business. Limited liability was perceived as a mechanism towards reducing personal risks and exposure for debts and liabilities.

Privileges of incorporation and abuse of corporate form

4.9 The concept of limited liability was also fraught with dangers particularly company fraud which involved shareholders being defrauded by the promoters through misrepresentation and concealing the nature of corporate assets and their value from potential investors. Many potential investors were duped and deceived through scams conducted by promoters at the time. Many lost their savings, with hardly any recourse in the courts against the promoters who would largely disappear from the corporate scene having defrauded the investors. As the concept of limited liability gained momentum, creditors became the subject of frauds and scams as businesses that were in financial difficulties began incorporating with limited liability status. This technique became known as 'conversion'. This involved a process whereby the owners of an unincorporated business would 'sell' their business to a limited liability company set up for that purpose which would pay them cash and/

or other types of consideration secured by a floating charge over the company's assets. In the event of a corporate failure, the owners would crystallise their charge and realise all of the company's assets as their debentures would have priority to any those of unsecured trade creditors and suppliers. This would leave outside creditors with little or nothing on the company's winding up. Many owners escaped liability by transferring their businesses to a company which was close to insolvency. At that time, there was no legislation against such activity. This meant that unsecured creditors were left with nothing after realisation of the assets of the business on the company's winding up. They were vulnerable and hardly any protection was afforded to them by the companies' legislation at the time. However, the interests of creditors were not entirely ignored. Although public companies were required to publicise their accounts, private companies were not required to do so. Vaughan-Williams (who was later to be the trial judge for the *Salomon* case), was an ardent supporter of disclosure of accounts by private companies in order to protect the interests of creditors to some extent. In an addendum to a Board of Trade report in 1895, Vaughan-Williams advocated that the publication of accounts was advisable for private companies as a guide to and for the protection of prospective creditors. He therefore championed the interests of creditors – a feature to which he returned in his first instance decision in the *Salomon* case: see P Ireland *The Triumph of the Company Legal Form 1856–1914* (1983).

Corporate personality

4.10 In company law, the concept of 'separate legal personality' or 'corporate personality' signifies that a company is distinct from its shareholders. The company has the liability and not the shareholders. The company has a legal but not a physical existence. It is neither an agent nor a trustee for its shareholders. A company acquires certain attributes upon incorporation. It is treated as a 'person' in its own right.

4.11 Upon incorporation, the company has a unique identity. It has a certificate of incorporation with its distinct registration number which distinguishes it from other corporate entities. The certificate signifies the birth of the company: a lifeless creature dependent upon the support of others for its functional and operational existence. The courts have, on occasions, resorted to anthropomorphic references to companies who are likened to a human being. It has a 'directing mind and will' – the directors and gatekeepers of the company, who guard the best interests of the company at all times. They are at the nerve centre of the company, managing the day-to-day governance, operations and functions of the company, by protecting the company's assets and striving towards profit maximisation as one of the major objectives of the company. However, the corporation also has a 'soul'. It has moral obligations in discharging its social obligations in society: it exercises a sense of social responsibility and purpose. This aspect of social responsibility awakens a sense of social consciousness within directors to address the company's role in society by enhancing the company's reputation as a good citizen in society, with a caring and a sensitive persona.

4.12 Within the corporation are the shareholders, who can be likened to the heart and soul of the corporation. They are the ultimate authority within the company. Without capital and funds from the shareholders, the company's lifeline and functional aspects, its very nerve-centre will cease to function, resulting in the death and winding up of the company through the liquidation process, when the company will cease to have any legal existence.

4.13 The corporation also needs hands that drive the company forward – these are the company's employees and officers, who participate along with the directors and shareholders, in achieving the mission and vision of the company. They are linked to the vicissitudes of the company – as the company's fortunes fluctuate – with the corporation inculcating a sense of loyalty in its employees, by offering incentives and rewards in return for corporate benefits and a long-term future, so long as the company functions profitably. The company feels a sense of pride: it has highly skilled people working for it in developing innovative products and services. The company's reputation is preserved and enhanced by investing in its employees.

A company may be compared to a natural person

In *HL Bolton (Engineering) Co Ltd v TJ Graham & Sons Ltd* [1957] 1 QB 159 at p 172, Denning LJ (as he was then) stated: 'A company may in many ways be likened to a human being. It has a brain and a nerve centre which controls what it does. It also has hands which hold the tools and act in accordance with directions from the centre.'

See however *Jetivia SA v Bilta (UK) Ltd* [2015] UKSC 23 which suggests the Supreme Court retreating from anthropomorphic references.

A company cannot act on its own and requires others for its functioning and operation

The nature of the corporation was also considered in *Lennard's Carrying Co Ltd v Asiatic Petroleum Co Ltd* [1915] AC 705, where the House of Lords decided that liability could be imposed on corporations for the directors' acts as they were the controlling minds within the corporation. The legal fiction of the corporation was set out by Viscount Haldane when he stated:

> '… a corporation is an abstraction. It has no mind of its own any more than it has a body of its own; its active and directing will must consequently be sought in the person of somebody who for some purposes may be called an agent, but who is really the directing mind and will of the corporation, the very ego and centre of the personality of the corporation. For if Mr Lennard was the directing mind of the company, then his action must, unless a corporation is not to be liable at all, have been an action which was the action of the company itself within the meaning of section 502 …'.

A company can only act through others to carry out its intentions

In *Tesco Supermarkets Ltd v Nattrass* [1972] AC 153, Lord Reid considered the nature of the personality which by a fiction the law attributed to a corporation. Lord Reid stated:

> 'A living person has a mind which can have knowledge or intention or be negligent and he has hands to carry out his intentions. A corporation has none of these: it must act through living persons, though not always one or the same person. Then the person who acts is not speaking or acting for the company. He is acting as the company and his mind which directs his acts is the mind of the company. There is no question of the company being vicariously liable. He is not acting as a servant, representative, agent or delegate. He is an embodiment of the company or, one could say, he hears and speaks through the persona of the company, within his appropriate sphere, and his mind is the mind of the company. If it is a guilt mind then that guilt is the guilt of the company.'

The corporation may have an artificial legal personality

In *Trustees of Dartmouth College v Woodward* (1819) 17 US (4 Wheat) 518 (a US case), Marshall CJ stated:

> A corporation is an artificial being, invisible, intangible, and existing only in contemplation of law. Being the mere creature of law, it possesses only those properties which the charter of its creation confers upon it, either expressly or as incidental to its very existence…Among the most important are immortality, and, if the expression be allowed, individuality, properties by which a perpetual succession of many persons are considered as the same, and may act as a single individual.'

Lord Halsbury LC in *Welton v Saffrey* [1897] AC 299, considered the corporation as an 'artificial creature' with 'an artificial creation'. A company has real legal existence distinct from its shareholders: see Lord Sumner in *Gas Lighting Improvement Co Ltd v Commissioners of Inland Revenue* [1923] AC 723.

4.14 Corporate personality is concerned with the company acquiring an existence which is independent in its own right from its shareholders. Although the shareholders give life to the company, they have delegated the day-to-day operational and governance functions to the directors by trusting the directors to manage the company in the best interests of the shareholders – both short term and long term. The shareholders may be passive or active investors. They lie waiting in the wings, guiding the company in the right direction if it sways from its primary objective; and at times acting ruthlessly where the company is in trouble. Although the shareholders may be loyal to the company they need not necessarily be so: they can sever the company's arteries and demonstrate their faithlessness by deserting and abandoning the company and selling their shares when it suits them to the company's detriment. The independent existence of a company from its shareholders means that a company can own and dispose of property. It is subject to corporation tax. It can sue and be sued. It can enter into contracts. It may also be subject to civil or criminal penalties.

The *Salomon* case

4.15 This section sets out the detailed facts and decisions in *Salomon v A Salomon & Co Ltd* – one of the major landmark cases in English company law.

The case established that a one-man company with its nominee shareholders could legally and validly establish a company in compliance with the Companies Acts.

From rags to riches

4.16 The principles legitimising one-man companies and establishing that the company was not an agent for its shareholders were established in *Salomon v Salomon & Co Ltd* [1897] AC 22. Aron Salomon's life can be categorised as one of rags to riches with his fortunes fluctuating and reaching their moral *nadir* when he was ultimately reduced to a life of abject poverty. Aron was born approximately in 1837 and came to the United Kingdom in his early twenties from Velbert in Rhenish, Prussia. He was a religious man of Jewish faith and a philanthropist at heart – giving regular donations to his local Synagogue which he frequented on a regular basis and later becoming its honorary member. He could be described as a dominant decision-maker in the family: he determined what was in the best interests of the family. He had no real need to consult his family members about the running and operation of the business: he made all the business decisions. There were no familial democratic principles applied as to how the business should operate. To some extent, Aron could be described as autocratic and authoritarian, but in other ways, he deeply cared about and was passionately committed to his family, and to ensuring that they were financially catered for in future life. He enjoyed an unblemished record for probity.

4.17 Aron set up in business on his own as a leather merchant, hide factor, wholesale and export shoe manufacturer in the East End of London, in Whitechapel High Street. With very little capital, and over a period of 30 years, he built up extensive warehouses and a large establishment. Aron had become a wealthy man and was well respected in his trade: his business received the highest award for army boots shoes and leggings at the Royal Military Exhibition in Chelsea. Aron was a proud and protective family member – perhaps too zealously over-protective, but a staunch family man with strong family values who could not accept any independence of his family from the business. His business was inextricably associated with and revolved around his family. He and his wife had a family of five sons and one daughter. Four of the sons were working with him in the business, but they were dissatisfied with their position as employees of the business. They wanted a share of the business. Apart from Aron, the only other person with some responsibility in the business was his eldest son who was practically the manager – though not formally appointed as such. The sons kept pressing their father to give them a share of the business. According to Aron, 'they troubled me, all the while'. He agreed to give his family a share of the business. In July 1892, he converted his business into a limited liability company and called it

A Salomon & Co Ltd. Although a promoter of the company, Aron still maintained control and established the terms upon which the company would be established.

4.18 All the formalities under the Companies Act 1862 for establishing Aron's limited liability company were complied with; the Act, *inter alia*, required seven members to establish a company. The company had a memorandum of association with a capital of £40,000 in 40,000 shares of £1 each. The subscribers to the memorandum were Aron, his wife and five of his children. One share each was allotted to his four sons and one each for his wife and daughter. Aron received 20,000 shares in the company. The Salomon family convened a meeting and appointed Aron and his two elder sons as the company's directors. The company also had articles of association setting out the procedure for nominating the first directors with the usual powers given to directors including a borrowing power prohibiting directors from exceeding £10,000. Aron's business was transferred to the company on 1 June 1892. The consideration paid for the transfer was £39,000 – 'a sum which represented the sanguine expectations of a fond owner rather than anything that can be called a business-like or reasonable estimate of value' per Lord Macnaghten in *Salomon v Salomon & Co Ltd* [1897] AC 22. The consideration was paid as follows: (i) £20,000 of income received from the business was paid to Aron who then returned this to the company in exchange for fully-paid shares; (ii) As part payment, Aron took up £10,000 in debentures in the company; (iii) the balance (with the exception of £1,000 which Aron seemed to have retained) went to discharge the debts and liabilities of the business at the time of the transfer. As a result, Aron received £1,000 for his business, £10,000 in debentures and half of the nominal capital of the company in fully paid shares.

Hard times

4.19 The company did not trade for long. It fell upon 'evil days'. Shortly after the company was established, there was a period of economic recession. A number of prominent shoe leather companies had collapsed. A series of general strikes took a toll on Aron's company business. Contracts with government departments which were the main source of Aron's income, were split up and divided between various other contractors. Aron's warehouses became full of unsaleable stock. He and his wife tried desperately to save the company's business from recession and collapse. They lent the company money to try and ensure its survival. During the early part of 1893, in an effort to revive the collapsing business, Aron borrowed £5,000 from a creditor, Edmund Broderip, who charged the company 10% interest. In order to obtain security for this loan to the company, the £10,000 worth of debentures (which Aron had received when the business was converted into a company) to pay off the debts were transferred to Broderip at 8% interest. This was only a temporary relief as the company was approaching insolvency. Aron's business was now ruined and his reputation was called into question. The company struggled to pay off its debts and Broderip's interest was not paid when it was due, along with other business expenses. Broderip immediately took proceedings and appointed a receiver. A meeting of creditors was called in December 1893 which was attended by the company's unsecured trade creditors: the meeting was a tense and acrimonious affair with recriminations and accusations levelled at Aron. Aron was criticised for ranking the debentures ahead of the unsecured trade creditors with whom he had dealt with over a long period of time in business and who had made his business a successful one. The unsecured trade creditors felt unhappy that they were not notified or consulted about the company's debenture to Broderip. The meeting of creditors ended on a positive note that the trade creditors would be paid in full. However, this was to no avail: the company was ultimately forced into liquidation. It was compulsorily wound up in October 1893. An order for the sale of its assets was granted in March 1894.

Aron sues as a pauper

4.20 Aron's wealth had dissipated. He now suffered the ignominy and humiliation of suing as a pauper litigant who was apparently worth nothing, in the hope of rescuing his family from abject poverty, as well as salvaging his reputation within the community and the boot trade. His name had become tarnished within the community: he was no longer perceived as a successful businessman – he had failed miserably in the business he had established. Even Aron could not escape the rigours of the Great Depression. From the sale of the company's assets, there were sufficient monies to pay Broderip but not enough to pay the debentures in full. There were no funds from the sale of the company's assets to pay any of the company's unsecured creditors. The company's liquidator counterclaimed to Broderip's claim and added Aron as a defendant to the proceedings. The liquidator also disputed the validity of the debentures issued to Broderip as a fraud on the creditors. He sought to rescind the agreement which had transferred Aron's business to the company, and claimed repayment by Aron of the balance of the purchase monies. Alternatively, the liquidator claimed payment of £20,000 on Aron's shares, alleging that nothing had been paid on them.

The decisions in Salomon

4.21 Aron's case fell within the ambit of the former Companies Act 1862. Under that Act, 'any seven or more persons associated for any lawful purpose may, by subscribing a memorandum of association and otherwise complying with the requisitions of this Act, form an incorporated company with or without limited liability'. Some of the significant issues before the court of first instance, the Court of Appeal and the House of Lords were whether this Act contemplated the establishment of 'one-man companies'; whether such companies were a mere cloak or sham established for fraudulent purposes and an abuse of the privileges granted to companies under the Companies Act; and whether creditors were at risk and exposed owing to the ease of establishing one-man companies as Aron seemed to have accomplished.

First instance – the 'agency' concept

4.22 The case of *Broderip v Salomon* was heard before Vaughan-Williams J. The liquidator's case collapsed. Vaughan-Williams J admitted Broderip's claim. He also accepted that Aron's shares were fully paid up. During the court hearing, Vaughan-Williams J provided an exit route for Aron. According to the judge, the six shareholders in the company were mere nominees or 'mere dummies'. In effect, the company was Aron, but in another form! Aron had used the company's name as an alias. The judge considered that Aron's sole intention was to take the profits from the company without accepting the risks of debts that he had contracted at his bidding and for his benefit, as well as exposing risks for unsecured creditors. Therefore, it was also necessary to consider the position of the company's unsecured trade creditors whose debts amounted to £11,000. As the company was a mere nominee or agent for Aron, Vaughan-Williams J suggested that the company had a right of indemnity against Aron as the principal for claims which the ordinary creditors advanced against the company.

4.23 The case was adjourned to allow the liquidator to amend the counterclaim to plead the agency issue and for the company to claim a right of indemnity against Aron. In February 1895, the case was again heard before Vaughan-Williams J where he made an order based on his earlier view. He pointed out that there was no allegation of fraud on Aron's part, 'but to allow a man who carries on business under another name to set up a debenture in priority to the claims of the creditors of the company would have the effect of defeating and delaying his creditors'. Vaughan- Williams J thought there was an implied agreement by Aron to indemnify the company. He was of the view that the creditors could have sued Aron directly as the company was a 'mere alias' for Aron and there was a principal–agent relationship between them.

4.24 The effect of Vaughan-Williams J's judgment signalled a major blow to individual proprietors and partnerships on the issue of establishing a limited liability company. His decision appeared to champion the rights and interests of creditors. It sent shock waves across various business sectors and cast serious doubt on the validity of establishing 'one-man companies' with mere dummies. The legal and practical implications of his decision were such that it might have prevented the success of the company as a legal entity. This decision of Vaughan-Williams J was only the start of a downward spiral and there was worse to come in the Court of Appeal judgment.

Court of Appeal – the 'trusteeship' principle

4.25 Aron appealed to the Court of Appeal in the case of *Broderip v Salomon* [1895] 2 Ch 323. In May 1895, the Court of Appeal dismissed Aron's appeal. Its decision was based not on the agency concept as was the position at first instance, but on the trusteeship principle – namely the relationship of a trustee and *cestui que trust*. It upheld Vaughan-William's decision that the company had a right to be indemnified by Aron.

4.26 According to Lindley LJ (who gave the leading judgment), the Companies Act 1862 had given rise to the establishment of 'one-man companies,' and he recognised the importance of this decision for such companies. He thought that Aron had attempted to use the Companies Act 1862 for a purpose for which it was never intended. His Lordship was of the view that the Companies Act envisaged the encouragement of trade by enabling a small number of people (no fewer than seven) to carry on business with limited liability protection. The Companies Act did not contemplate an extension of limited liability to sole traders or to fewer than seven members. Although there were seven members (as seven were required to form the company), the six members of Aron's family were subscribers simply to enable Aron to carry on the limited liability business. Lindley LJ stated that the object of the whole arrangement was to do the very thing that the Companies Act was designed to prevent. It was an 'ingenious scheme'. Lindley LJ questioned the motive behind the incorporation and thought that the company was set up for an illegitimate purpose.

4.27 Lopes LJ thought that the company had been validly incorporated. He stated that Aron had in fact fully complied with all aspects of the Companies Act, even though the business belonged solely to Aron as he had a beneficial interest in it. He was of the view that Aron had used the company as a cloak to shield against the company's debts and liabilities, and to gain priority over the unsecured creditors of the company. He considered that it would be lamentable if this scheme could not be defeated. To permit such an action as that taken by Aron would be to give vitality to that which was a myth and a fiction. The Companies Act was not intended to be used in this way. It was never intended that the company to be constituted should consist of one substantial person with a controlling interest and six 'mere dummies' who were Aron's nominees without any real interest in the company. According to Lopes LJ, the Companies Act contemplated the incorporation of six independent bona fide members, who had a mind and will of their own and were not mere puppets of Aron who carried on the same business as he did before when he was a sole trader. It would be a 'scandal' to legalise such a transaction. His Lordship stated that the liquidator should be entitled to have the sale of the business to the company set aside; to declare the company to be a trustee for Aron; and to declare that the company was a sham.

4.28 According to Kay LJ, the Companies Act was intended to allow seven or more persons bona fide associated for the purpose of the trade, to limit their liability under certain conditions and to become a company. The Act was not intended to legalise a pretended association to enable an individual to carry on his own business with limited liability. The pretended sale to the company was an 'utter fiction', because in effect the company did not pay anything to Aron for the purchase. There was no independent director to protect the company in the transaction. Kay LJ thought there was no sale at all as the business remained Aron's even after transfer of it to the company. He just carried on the business in the company's name.

4.29 The Court of Appeal's decision sent further shock waves across businesses that had intended to incorporate as one-man companies. The implications of the decision were considerable and almost signalled the end of one-man companies as well as private companies. The Court of Appeal decision did not legitimise one-man companies and cast serious doubts on the use of the corporate form for sole traders and partnerships. According to the Court of Appeal, because the Companies Act did not contemplate such companies, they could not be allowed to operate under the cloak of the Companies Act. By employing the trusteeship principle, the Court of Appeal effectively ruled out the legitimisation of one-man companies.

House of Lords: legitimisation of one-man companies

4.30 In November 1896, the six Law Lords in *Salomon v A Salomon & Co Ltd* [1897] AC 22 unanimously decided the appeal in favour of Aron, thereby reversing the earlier first instance and Court of Appeal decisions. However, each of the Law Lords gave different reasons in relation to the interpretation of the applicable sections of the Companies Act 1862 to determine what rules the Act had imposed as a condition to trading with limited liability. The House of Lords held that a one-man company was a legitimate creation under the Companies Act, provided it was validly formed and complied with all the formalities required under the Act. Further, the company was neither an agent nor a trustee for its shareholders. The House of Lords accepted that the Companies Act allowed for the establishment of a 'one-man company', even though control was practically vested in one person who was the controlling shareholder of the company.

4.31 According to Lord Halsbury, an important issue for the court to decide was whether the company, 'that artificial creation of the legislature', had been validly established under the Companies Act. The Act required, *inter alia*, seven persons as subscribers to the memorandum of association. This condition had been satisfied and as Aron's family members had been allocated a share each, they were shareholders in the company with their respective rights and liabilities. The Companies Act did not require any inquiry into the motives or intentions of persons who became shareholders in the company. Lord Halsbury stated that 'the statute enacts nothing as to the extent or degree of interest which may be held by each of the seven, or as to the proportion of interest or influence possessed by one or the majority of the shareholders over the others'. His Lordship suggested that if the requirement for seven shareholders to establish a company had not been complied with, it would have been legitimate to go behind the certificate of incorporation to show that a fraud had been committed on the officer entrusted with the duty of providing the certificate.

4.32 Lord Halsbury stated that once a company had been legally incorporated, it must be treated like any other independent person with rights and liabilities: see too *Prest v Petrodel Resources Ltd* [2013] All ER 90. The motives of those who took part in the promotion of the company were irrelevant in discussing those rights and liabilities. The establishment of the company by Aron had complied in all respects with the intention and the meaning of the Companies Act. The Act gave the company legal existence with rights and liabilities of its own. The company was a legal entity and the business belonged to the company and not Aron. The Act did not impose any prohibitions as to the independence of the shareholders and their beneficial interest: 'there was nothing in the Act requiring that the subscribers to the memorandum should be independent or unconnected, or that any of them should take a substantial interest in the undertaking'. All that was required was for a shareholder to hold one share regardless of whether he was a family member. Lord Halsbury contended that there was no fraud nor any agency aspects involved and that the establishment of the company was neither a myth nor a fiction. Lord Halsbury was critical of the Court of Appeal's decision to ignore the legal existence of the company. He contended that the Court of Appeal appeared to be struck by the inexpediency of permitting a 'one-man company', and that such a concept could not have been intended by the Companies Act. Aron had not done anything dishonest or unworthy, but he had suffered a great misfortune without any fault of his own.

4.33 According to Lord Watson, the company was legitimately and validly formed under the Companies Act. There was no requirement for the shareholders to be independent of each other. A shareholder was only required to hold one share to become a member of the company. Aron did not engage in any fraud against the company's creditors. The creditors were under a duty to make inquiries of the company before lending funds to it. His Lordship stated that whatever the moral duty of a limited company and its shareholders, when the trade of the company was not thriving, the law did not impose any obligation on them to warn those members of the public who dealt with them on credit that they ran the risk of not being paid. The apathy of a creditor could not justify an imputation of fraud against a limited company or its members. Further, a creditor who did not take adequate safeguards to protect his security, must bear the consequences of his own negligence.

4.34 Lord Herschell observed that both the first instance court and the Court of Appeal treated the company as distinct from Aron and the members who composed it, and that the company was validly constituted. He could not therefore understand why both Vaughan-Williams J and the Court of Appeal thereafter treated A Salomon & Co Ltd as an 'alias' for Aron Salomon. He stated that the company was a distinct legal person. Further, the company was not Aron's agent to carry on his business for him. Generally, a company could be established to carry on business for and on behalf of its shareholders. However, this did not give rise to a principal–agent relationship and render the shareholders liable to indemnify the company against the debts which the company incurred. As Salomon owned all the shares except six, he would be entitled to substantially the whole of the profits if the business was profitable. The Companies Act permitted the establishment of 'one-man companies'.

4.35 Lord Macnaghten thought that Aron had been dealt with harshly. The judgments at first instance and the Court of Appeal were based on the misconception that the establishment of 'one man companies' was not permissible under the Companies Act. Provided all the formalities were complied with, it did not matter whether the shareholders were strangers or were related to each other. The Companies Act did not require as a condition for establishing a company, that the shareholders should be independent or unconnected or that any one of them should take a substantial interest in the company, or that they should have a mind or will of their own, or that there should be a balance of power in the company's constitution. When all the formalities for setting up a company had been complied with, the company was thereafter capable of exercising all the functions of an incorporated company. A company attained maturity on its birth. There was no period of minority, or an interval of incapacity. The company was at law a different person from the company's shareholders, and though it may be that after incorporation the business was precisely the same as it was before, the same persons were managers and the same hands receive the profits, the company was not at law the agent of the subscribers or trustees for them. Nor were the subscribers as members liable, in any shape or form, except to the extent and manner provided by the Companies Act. His Lordship did not understand why Aron could not obtain the full advantages of the Companies Act by establishing the company as he had done. The company's creditors were not Aron's creditors. There was no evidence to suggest that Aron had acted fraudulently or dishonestly. He had demonstrated good faith by raising £5,000 for the company on debentures that belonged to him, and this also demonstrated his confidence in the company. According to Lord Macnaghten, the company's unsecured creditors may be entitled to sympathy, but they only had themselves to blame for their misfortunes. They trusted to company owing to their long-time dealings with Aron. However, they had notice that they were no longer dealing with an individual.

4.36 See too *Baglan Hall Colliery Co* (1870) LR Ch App 346; *Farrar v Farrars Ltd* (1888) 40 Ch D 395; *J H Rayner (Mincing Lane) Ltd v Department of Trade and Industry* [1990] 2 AC 418; and *North-West Transportation Co v Beatty* (1887) 12 App Cas 589.

4.37 Lord Davey thought that the company had been validly established. Upon incorporation, the company had a separate legal existence distinct from its members. The company had power to sue and be sued and to be wound up. It was not an agent or a trustee for Aron. The company was formed with corporate attributes and capable of incurring legal liabilities.

4.38 For further reference to cases illustrating the 'Salomon principle', see *Wilson v Wilson* 1999 SLT 249; *Attorney General's reference (No 2 of 1982)* [1984] QB 624; *Re Brauch (A Debtor) Ex parte Brittanic Securities & Investments* [1978] Ch 316; *Bluebell Apparel Ltd v Dickinson* 1980 SLT 157; *Barakot Ltd v Epiette Ltd* [1998] 1 BCLC 283; *National Dock Labour Board v Pinn Wheeler Ltd* [1989] BCLC 647; *EBM Co Ltd v Dominion Bank* [1937] 3 All ER 555; *Henry Browne & Son Ltd v Smith* [1964] 2 Lloyd's Rep 476; *Littlewoods Mail Order Stores v Inland Revenue Commissioners* [1969] 1 WLR 1241; *Moschi v Lep Air Services Ltd* [1971] 1 WLR 934; *Dimbleby & Sons v National Union of Journalists* [1984] 1 WLR 427; and *Multinational Gas and Petrochemical Co v Multinational Gas and Petrochemical Services Ltd* [1983] Ch 258.

Significance of *Salomon*

4.39 The decision by the House of Lords in *Salomon* led to a case note in 1895 in the Law Quarterly Review which described it as 'unfortunate' the belated discoveries that one-man companies were an abuse of the Companies Acts and that seven 'bona fide' members were required. It observed: 'Out of the thousands of private companies which have been formed in the last quarter of the century under the Companies Acts, it may be doubted if there are 10% which satisfy the new test.' The editorial note further observed that that the Court of Appeal's decision in *Broderip v Salomon* would have left these companies 'with a very questionable status' which was 'to be regretted.' The implications of the Court of Appeal decision would have led the Registrar at Companies House making an investigation as to the intentions and motives of the promoters in setting up the company – which power was not vested in the Registrar provided all the formalities of the Companies Act were complied with. With the exception of fraud, the one-man company could be legitimately established under the Companies Act.

4.40 In 1887, an article in the Law Quarterly Review raised the issue as to whether the subscribers were all required to be bona fide intending traders in partnership, or whether one trader and 'six dummies' sufficed? It observed that the House of Lords decision in *Salomon* decisively favoured the latter approach thereby, treating the statutory conditions for setting up a company under the Companies Act as mere machinery: 'You touch the requisite button and the company starts into existence, a legal entity, an independent persona.' It noted that the real significance of the *Salomon* decision was that it interpreted the policy of the Companies Act to sanction an individual trading with limited liability. However, it questioned: 'Is there anything really startling in this?' The advantages of limited liability meant that there would be no hardship to creditors: 'When once the Legislature sanctioned limited liability, it followed that the creditors must look to the capital – the limited fund – and that only. Whether there is one person behind the company or seven or 70,000 makes no difference whatever to the creditors. It is not the constituency of the company, but its capital which concerns them.'

4.41 One issue that remained even after the *Salomon* decision was whether there had been a 'real association' of seven members as required under the Companies Acts. This issue was raised only by Lord Davey in the House of Lords. Lord Davey suggested that it could be argued that because there was no 'real' association, the company could be a sham and could be disregarded. However, this aspect was not considered in subsequent cases and by that time, the *Salomon* principle was well entrenched within company law.

4.42 The *Salomon* decision paved the way for sole traders and other economic businesses to incorporate with limited liability in full compliance with the Companies Acts. This was a triumph for a one-man company with limited liability.

The *Salomon* decision legitimised the establishment of one-man companies under the Companies Act. It did not matter whether the shareholders were independent of one another, related or 'mere dummies' or nominees for the controlling shareholders. It did not matter that the shareholders were family members. It did not matter that the majority of the shareholders had only a very minority stake in the company. Providing all the formalities for establishing a company were complied with, a one-man company was a valid legal vehicle under the Companies Act. Furthermore, the company was not an agent for its shareholders. The decision did not establish that the company was a separate legal entity distinct from its shareholders. The principle was already enshrined in the Companies Act that upon incorporation the company attained an independent existence from its shareholders.

Final epilogue

4.43 As a final epilogue to the *Salomon* case, Aron's litigation experience did not end at the House of Lords. His solicitor at the time, Ralph Raphael, who had acted for Aron throughout the proceedings lodged a bills of costs which was resisted by Aron's son as administrator of his estate, and the matter proceeded to the Chancery Division before Kekewich J in *Re Raphael* [1899] 1 Ch 853. Kekewich J granted Raphael his entitlement to costs in respect of the House of Lords appeal. According to Kekewick '... though he [Aron] was not thereby made a wealthy man, he was rehabilitated and removed from the list of paupers' *ibid*, at p 856. Just six months after the House of Lords decision, Aron died of a stroke on 13 May 1897, intestate and leaving only a very modest sum as part of his estate which was probably dissipated by the legal battle with Raphael in 1899. A Salomon & Co Ltd was finally dissolved by notice in the Gazette on 27 August 1907.

One-man company contracting with its employee: the controlling shareholder concept

4.44 Following the *Salomon* decision, an issue which has arisen in the context of company and employment law has been whether a one-man company can validly enter into an employment relationship with its employee, such that the employee is able to obtain the benefits and advantages of employment protection legislation or other legislation (such as insurance). This would only be possible if the person employed by the one-man company could be treated as an 'employee' or a 'worker' within the meaning of the appropriate legislation. This section sets out the factors which have been considered by the courts and tribunals including the 'controlling shareholder' concept, in determining whether or not a person is an employee in order to obtain legislative benefits and advantages. It considers the interrelationship between company law and employment law.

A company can validly enter into a contract with its sole employee as the company and employee are distinct persons at law

In *Lee v Lee's Air Farming Ltd* [1960] 3 All ER 420, the appellant's husband, L, established a company, Lee's Air Farming specialising in aerial top-dressing for farmlands. The company's share capital was 3,000 £1 shares of which 2,999 shares were allotted to L, thereby making him a controlling shareholder in the company. He was appointed governing director of the company and was employed as its chief pilot. He received a salary for his services to the company. Article 33 of the company's articles provided that in respect of such employment, the rules of law applicable to the relationship of employer and employee should apply between the company and L. In his capacity as governing director L exercised full and unrestricted control over the company's affairs. Insurance policies were put in place by the company and its employee in the event of death, personal injury or accidents. L was killed while piloting the aircraft and L's wife claimed the benefit of an insurance policy under the New Zealand Workers' Compensation Act 1922. That Act required an employer to pay compensation on the death or injury of a worker. The term 'worker' was defined as 'any person who has entered into or worked under a contract of service ... with an employer ... whether remunerated by wages, salary or otherwise'. The Act only protected a worker who had a contract of service as opposed to a contract for services with its employer. The issue was whether L was a 'worker' within the meaning of the Act to enable his wife to claim compensation under the Act. The insurance company contended that L could not be a worker because the same person could not be both an employer and employee. The argument for the company was that L's company was not in a position to control the employment relationship. It contended that 'control' meant 'a real living person' and that 'where one gets the controller and the controlled person residing in the same person there is no control ... it is wholly illusory'. L's wife contended that it was the company and not L that was the employer. It was the company that 'was entitled under the contract to control both what L did and how he did it, and this control remained the control of the company whoever might be the agent empowered by the company to exercise it'.

Lord Morris considered the surrounding facts and circumstances in determining whether or not L was a worker employed in the one-man company. On the facts, L was paid wages for piloting the aeroplane, which belonged to the company. The company also kept a wages book in which L's wages were recorded. The work was being undertaken at the request of farmers whose contractual rights and obligations were the company's alone. In this respect, L was discharging his duties as a worker and not as a governing director. In his capacity as a worker, L had entered into a contract of employment with the company which was a separate legal entity. Both L and the company had voluntarily entered into a contract of employment relationship. According to Lord Morris, there was no suggestion that the company was a 'sham or a mere simulacrum'. Accordingly, the company's capacity to enter into a contract of employment with L could not be called into question merely because L, in his capacity as a governing director, was the company's agent in negotiating the contract. The fact that L was a controlling shareholder and that he could control the course of events, would not in itself affect the validity of his contractual relationship with the company.

The Privy Council reversed the New Zealand's Court of Appeal decision. It held that L was a worker within the meaning of the Act and his wife was entitled to compensation, since L's position as governing director and principal shareholder did not prevent him from making on the company's behalf a contract of employment with himself. It did not also prevent him from entering into or working in the capacity of an employee under a contract of service with the company. The company had validly entered into a contract of employment with L and L had acted as the company's agent in arranging the contract.

According to Lord Morris, it was a logical consequence of the decision in *Salomon*, that one person could function in dual capacities. The aspect of control would remain with the company whoever might be the agent of the company to exercise it. The existence of a right to control could not be denied once the reality of the legal existence of the company was recognised.

4.45 *Lee*'s case is, therefore, authority for two propositions. First, that an individual who owned all or almost all of the shares in the company and was its sole director with total dominion over the company, could also be employed by the company under a contract of service. Second, the issue as to whether the 'control' condition had been satisfied was irrelevant in the creation of the contract of employment. The company and the employee were not in law the same person. They were distinct in their own right. It was the company that exercised the relevant control. The control necessary for the purpose of the contract of employment was exercisable by the company, and it made no difference that in practice, so long as L remained the sole governing director, that control would be and was exercised by him as the company's agent. The close identity that in reality existed between the company and L did not prevent a contract of service being created.

Is the contract of employment with the company a sham?

4.46 Another issue that may arise not in respect of the company, but in a case where the controlling shareholder claims to have a service contract with his own company is whether the contract that has been entered into (rather than the company) is genuine or a sham. This is because the reality in such cases is that the controlling shareholder will have been the directing mind and will behind the purported creation of his own contract with the company. That factor will be likely in many cases to require careful scrutiny of the claim that a valid employment contract has been created.

Sham contracts have the appearance of creating genuine contractual obligations and rights when in reality they were not legally enforceable

In determining whether the purported *contract* might be a sham, consideration should be given to *Snook v London and West Riding Investments* [1967] 2 QB 786. In this case, Diplock LJ stated that the term 'sham' in relation to a contract meant:

> '… acts done, or documents executed by the parties to the 'sham' which are intended by them to give to third parties or the court the appearance of creating between the parties the legal rights and obligations different from the actual rights and obligations (if any) which the parties intend to create … for acts or documents to be a 'sham' with whatever legal consequences follow from this, all the parties thereto must have a common intention that the acts or documents are not to create legal rights and obligations which they give the appearance of creating. No unexpressed intentions of a 'shammer' affect the rights of a party whom he deceived.'

In *Secretary of State for Business Enterprise and Regulatory Reform v Nufeld and Howe* [2009] EWCA Civ 280, Rimer LJ stated that in most cases in which there arises a question as to whether the claimed contract is a sham, there will be what purports to be a formal written contract, or at least a board minute or memorandum purporting to evidence or record the contract: the 'shammer' is hardly likely to rest his case on the claim that his contract was an oral one. An inquiry into whether any purported contract amounted to a sham did not limit the court or tribunal considering the evidence as at the time of its making. It would also usually be highly material to see what the company on the one hand and the shareholder/director on the other have actually *done* under the purported contract which would shed light on its genuineness or otherwise.

In determining whether a document is a sham, an intention has to be established that the actual documents were not to create the legal rights and obligations which they gave the appearance of creating. The decision in *Stone v Hitch* [2001] EWCA Civ 63 emphasised the need for such a common subjective intention on the part of those concerned.

The decision of the House of Lords in *AG Securities Ltd v Vaughan* [1990] 1 AC 417 established that the term 'sham' meant an attempt to disguise the true character (of the agreement) which it was hoped would deceive the court.

According to Neuberger J (as he was then) in *National Westminster Bank plc v Jones* [2001] 1 BCLC 98, a sham agreement was one where the parties intended to give the impression that they were agreeing that which was stated in the agreement, whilst in fact they shared the common intention of not honouring their respective obligations or enjoying their respective rights under it. It was simply an agreement which the parties did not really intend to be effective, but was merely entered into for the purpose of leading a court or third party to believe that it is to be effective.

In *Protectacoat Firthglow Ltd v Miklos Szilagy* [2009] EWCA Civ 98, the Court of Appeal stated that in determining whether a written contract was a sham, the question was 'what was the true legal relationship between the parties?' If the evidence established that the true relationship was and was intended to be, different from what was described in the contractual document, then it was that relationship and not the document which defined the contract. See too *Consistent Group Ltd v Kalwak* [2008] EWCA 430; *Express & Echo Publications Ltd v Tanton* [1999] IRLR 367; *Carmicheal v National Power* [1999] ICR 1226; *Weiner v Harris* [1910] 1 KB 285; and *Street v Mountford* [1985] 1 AC 809 at p 821.

4.47 Following *Lee*'s case, the issue that has arisen before the English courts has been whether a shareholder/director or employee who works (or has worked) under a service agreement or a contract of employment, and who was the company's dominant controlling shareholder, could be prevented from obtaining protection under the employment legislation on the basis that the facts did not show that he was an employee of the company, principally because he had a controlling interest in the company. There have been a series of cases providing conflicting views as to the correct test to be applied in these circumstances, and a failure to recognise that a company is a distinct legal entity from the shareholder. Further, the significance of *Lee*'s decision as to whether a controlling shareholder could validly contract with his company was not fully appreciated in some of these cases.

4.48 In order to claim for redundancy from the state fund on an employer's insolvency, a person must show that he is (or was) an employee at the time. Section 230(1) of the Employment Rights Act 1996 ('ERA') defines an 'employee' as 'an individual who has entered into or works under (or, where the employment has ceased, worked under) a contract of employment'. A 'contract of employment' means a contract of service or apprenticeship, whether express or implied, and (if it is express) whether oral or in writing. There have been a series of cases which have considered the controlling shareholder issue, and its impact where a company enters into a contract of employment with its employee and then the employer subsequently becomes insolvent.

The controlling shareholder concept and employment legislation

4.49 The relationship between company law and employment law can be seen in the context of a controlling shareholder who has a contract of employment with the company, and the issue arises whether such a person is an employee of the company for the purposes of protections and rights under the employment legislation.

The courts must consider as a starting point the genuineness of the contract of employment between the employer and employee having regard to all facts. If no sham was involved, the next stage would be to prove that the contract was one of employment: an employee could enter into a valid contract of employment with his company

In the leading authority in this area, in *Secretary of State for Business, Enterprise and Regulatory Reform v Neufeld and Howe* [2009] EWCA Civ 280, the Court of Appeal in joint appeals, was required to consider whether the respondents were 'employees' of their respective companies which had gone into insolvency. If they were considered employees within s 182 of the Employment Rights Act 1996, then they enjoyed certain protections such as payment by the Secretary of State to the employees from the National Insurance Fund. A particular feature of each case was that the claimant was the controlling shareholder and director of the company. In effect, each operated a 'one-man' company. The Court of Appeal sought to clarify the approach that tribunals and court should take in this area. The two issues before the Court of Appeal were: (a) can a controlling shareholder and director of a company become an employee of that company under a contract of employment?; (b) if yes, are there any guidelines which may assist tribunals in deciding whether in any particular case such a shareholder/director could become an employee?

The leading judgment was given by Rimer LJ who proceeded to consider the position of a one-man company contracting with its employee with particular reference to the issue of control. It might be thought that the main conceptual barrier in the way of such a company granting a valid employment contract to its 'one man' would be that there could in practice be no relevant control of the employee so as to meet that particular condition of an employment contract. In theory, control would be exercisable by the company, a legal person separate from the individual. In practice, it would be exercisable by the employee himself since he controls the company. It is easy to conclude that that cannot be real control, with the consequence that a central condition of a contract of employment is missing. Rimer LJ stated that it was too late in the development of English law jurisprudence for the court to regard the control issue as providing a threshold obstacle to the creation of a valid contract of employment between the company and the one man who wholly controls it. The decision in *Lee's* case shows that it is not.

According to Rimer LJ, the starting point for the employment tribunal (if it arises) would be to determine whether there is a genuine contract between a company and its controlling shareholder. This would involve a consideration of all the facts relevant to such inquiry, the outcome of which will be a finding of sham or no sham. If the outcome is a finding of no sham, the next question for the tribunal will be whether the contract that has been proved amounts to one of employment. At this stage, the tribunal cannot conclude that because there was no sham the contract will automatically be regarded as a contract of employment – the tribunal will need to be satisfied as to that aspect too.

Rimer LJ decided that there was no reason in principle why someone who is a shareholder and director of a company could not also be its employee under a contract of employment. There was also no reason in principle why someone whose shareholding in the company gave him control of it – even total control (as in *Lee's* case) – could not be an employee. A person whose economic interest in a company and its business means that he is in practice properly to be regarded as its 'owner' can also be an employee of the company. It will, in particular, be no answer to his claim to be such an employee to argue that: (i) the extent of his control of the company means that the *control* condition of a contract of employment cannot be satisfied; or (ii) that the practical control that he has over his own destiny – including that he cannot be dismissed from his employment except with his consent – has the effect in law that he cannot be an employee at all. Point (i) is answered by *Lee*'s case, which decided that the relevant control is in the company; point (ii) is answered by the Court of Appeal's rejection in *Secretary of State for Trade and Industry v Bottrill* [1999] ICR 592of the reasoning in *Buchan v Secretary of State for Employment* [1997] IRLR 80.

Whether or not such a shareholder/director is an employee of the company is a question of fact for the court or tribunal before which such issue arises. In any such case there may in theory be two such issues, although in practice the evidence relevant to their resolution will be likely to overlap. The first, and logically preliminary one, will be whether the contract is a genuine contract or a sham. The second will be whether, assuming it is a genuine contract, it amounts to a contract of employment (it might, for example, instead amount to a contract for services).

In cases involving an alleged sham, there will almost invariably be what purports to be a formal written employment contract, or at least a board minute or a memorandum purporting to record or evidence the creation of such a contract. The task of the court or tribunal will be to decide whether any such document amounts to a sham in the sense of the *Snook* guidance. Any such inquiry will usually require not just an investigation into the circumstances of the creation of the document but also into the parties' purported conduct under which it will be likely to shed light into the genuineness or otherwise of the claimed contract. The fact that the employee has control over the company and the board, and so was instrumental in the creation of the very contract that he is asserting, will obviously be a relevant matter in the court's consideration of whether the contract is or is not a sham. It will usually be the feature that prompted the inquiry in the first place.

An inquiry into what the parties have done under the purported contract may show a variety of matters: (i) that they did not act in accordance with the purported contract at all, which would support the conclusion that it was a sham; or (ii) that they did act in accordance with it, which will support the opposite conclusion; or (iii) that although they acted in a way consistent with a genuine service contract arrangement, what they have done suggests a variation of the terms of the original purported contract; or (iv) that there came a point when the parties ceased to conduct themselves in a way consistent with the purported contract or any variation of it, which may invite the conclusion that, although the contract was originally a genuine one, it has been impliedly discharged. There may obviously be different outcomes of any investigation into how the parties have conducted themselves under the purported contract. It will be a question of fact as to what conclusions are to be drawn from such investigation.

In a case in which no allegation of sham is raised, or in which the claimant proves that no question of sham arises, the question for the court or tribunal will be whether the claimed contract amounts to a true contract of employment. Given the critical question as to whether the employee was in fact an employee at the time of the company's insolvency, it will or may be necessary to inquire into what has been done under the claimed contract: there will or may therefore need to be an inquiry similar to cases where there is allegation of sham. In order for the employee to make good his case, it may well be insufficient merely to place reliance on a written contract made, say, five years earlier. The tribunal will want to know that the claimed contract, perhaps as subsequently varied, was still in place at the time of the insolvency. In a case in which the alleged contract is not in writing, or is only in brief form, it is obvious that it will usually be necessary to inquire into how the parties have conducted themselves under it.

In deciding whether a valid contract of employment was in existence, consideration will have to be given to the requisite conditions for the creation of such a contract and the court or tribunal will want to be satisfied that the contract meets them. In *Lee*'s case, the position was ostensibly clear on the documents, with the only contentious issue being in relation to the control condition of a contract of employment. In some cases there will be a formal service agreement. Failing that, there may be a minute or a board meeting or a memorandum dealing with the matter. But in many cases involving small companies, with their control being in the hands of perhaps just one or two directors/shareholders, the handling of such matters may have been dealt with informally and it may be a difficult question as to whether or not the correct inference from the facts is that the employee was, as claimed, truly an employee. In particular, a director of a company is the holder of an office and will not, merely by virtue of such office, be an employee; the employee will have to prove more than his appointment as a director. It will be relevant to consider how he has been paid. Has he been paid a salary, which points towards employment? Or merely be way of director's fees, which points away from it? In considering what the employee was actually *doing*, it will also be relevant to consider whether he was acting merely in his capacity as a director of the company; or whether he was acting as an employee.

The fact of the employee's shareholding control of the company will obviously form a part of the backdrop against which the assessment will be made of what has been done under the written or oral employment contract that is being asserted. But it will not ordinarily be of any special relevance in deciding whether or not he has a valid contract. Nor will the fact that he will have a share capital invested in the company; or that he may have made loans to it; or that he has personally guaranteed its obligations; or that his personal investment in the company will stand to prosper in line with the company's prosperity; or that he has done any of the other things that the 'owner' of the business will commonly do on its behalf. These considerations are usual features of the sort of companies giving rise to the type of issue before the courts, but they will ordinarily be irrelevant to whether or not a valid contract of employment has been created so that they can and should be ignored. They show an 'owner' acting qua 'owner', which is inevitable in such a company. However, they do not show that the 'owner' cannot also be an employee.

On the facts, the Court of Appeal decided that taking away all the irrelevant considerations (such as the fact that he had given personal guarantees, lent money to the company and had a controlling interest in it), Mr Neufeld was an employee, as he had a genuine employment contract. Similarly, Mr Howe was also an employee on the facts.

See too previously *McQuisten v Secretary of State for Employment* (unreported, 11 June 1996, EAT/1298/95); *Fleming v Secretary of State for Trade and Industry*

[1997] IRLR 682; *Secretary of State for Trade and Industry v Bottrill* [1999] ICR 592; *Connolly v Letters Arenascene Ltd* [2001] ICR 760; *Hauxwell v Secretary of State for Trade and Industry* 19 June 2002, EAT 386/01; *Gladwell v Secretary of State for Trade and Industry* [2007] ICR 264; *Nesbitt v Secretary of State for Trade and Industry* [2007] IRLR 847 *Clark v Clark Construction Initiatives Ltd* [2008] IRLR 3641; *RG Bespoke Joinery Ltd v Dobson* (20 August 2009 – unreported) and *Ashby v Monterry Designs Ltd* (18 December 2009 – unreported).

Company can own property

4.50 The independent legal personality of the company means that the company can own property as a natural person. The property belongs to the company and not its shareholders. The shareholders have no interest in the company's property.

A company being a separate legal entity distinct from its shareholders can own property

In *Macaura v Northern Assurance Co Ltd* [1925] All ER Rep 51, Macaura (M) was the owner of a timber estate. He agreed to transfer his business to a company for £42,000. This amount was paid by way of an allotment to M of 42,000 fully paid shares of £1 each, which was the total amount issued by the company. As a result, M became the sole owner of shares in the company. M had also financed the company and was an unsecured creditor for £19,000. M took out insurance on the timber against fire. At a later date, a large part of the timber was destroyed by fire and M issued proceedings for recovery of monies alleged to be due under the insurance policies.

The House of Lords held that a company's shareholder did not have an interest, whether legal or beneficial, in the company's property, even though the shareholder was the sole shareholder of the company. Lord Buckmaster stated: '... no shareholder has any right to any item of property owned by the company, for he has no legal or equitable interest therein. He is entitled to a share in the profits while the company continues to carry on business and a share in the distribution of the surplus assets when the company is wound up ...' According to Lord Buckmaster it was not sufficient for a person to have a 'moral certainty' in the company's property or goods as this could not be measured in terms of the profit or loss sustained: the person needed to show he had a legal or equitable interest. This could not be shown on the facts of the case. Lord Sumner concurred stating that in his capacity as a shareholder, M could not have any interest in respect of the company's goods or property or the insurance policy: this was a matter for the company. Lord Wrenbury was of the view that the shareholder, even if he held all the shares, was not the corporation, and neither he nor any creditor had any legal or equitable interest in the company's assets.

See too *Daimler Co Ltd v Continental Tyre and Rubber Co (Great Britain) Ltd* [1916] 2 AC 307.

Company can sue and be sued

4.51 A company can sue its own directors and officers as well as third parties. This includes the company's capacity to sue for libel or slander in respect of loss of business reputation: *South Hetton Coal Co v North-Eastern News Association* [1894] 1 QB 133; and *D & L Caterers v D'Ajou* [1945] KB 364.

As the company is a separate legal entity, the legal rights belong to the company and not to its shareholders. Shareholders have separate rights of action which include an action for unfair prejudicial conduct (CA 2006, s 994) or a derivative action.

4.52 A company can also be vicariously liable for the torts committed by its agents in the course of their employment or business on the company's behalf. This includes negligence or fraudulent misrepresentation: *Citizen's Life Assurance Co Ltd v Brown* [1904] AC 423; *Lister v Hesley Hall Ltd* [2002] 1 AC 215.

In general, a company can be prosecuted for its criminal acts such as breaches of health and safety at the workplace; conspiracy to defraud (*R v ICR Haulage Ltd* [1944] KB 551) or attempted fraud (*Purcell Meats (Scotland) Ltd v McLeod* 1987 SLT 528). Although the acts are performed by the company's agents such as its directors and officers, their acts are the acts of the company. However, there are limitations on the criminal sanctions that the court may impose on the company. Although a company may be fined for its criminal acts, it cannot be imprisoned. It cannot also be prosecuted for bigamy or perjury or indecent conduct: *Dean v John Menzies (Holdings) Ltd* 1981 SLT 51; and *Chuter v Freeth & Pocock Ltd* [1991] 2 KB 832.

Perpetual succession

4.53 A company has the ability to outlive its directors and shareholders. It may be created for a fixed term or indefinitely. Unlike natural persons, a company does not suffer from any incapacitation such as mental illness or other physical defects. It is omnipresent. However, its existence may come to an end upon its dissolution on a winding up – whether on a voluntary or compulsory winding up.

The corporation has a metaphysical existence. Although invisible and not discernible to the eye, it impacts upon society and its stakeholders.

As long ago as 1937, Greer LJ in *Stepney Corporation v Osofsky* [1937] 3 All ER 289 stated that the corporation had 'no soul to be saved or body to be kicked'. Further, a corporation was considered not to be a 'person' under the Sunday Observance Act 1677 so that it was not capable of public worship.

Statutory effects of incorporation

4.54 The CA 2006, s 16 sets out the statutory effects of incorporation. On registration, the following are the effects of incorporation:

- The subscribers to the memorandum, together with such other persons as may from time to time become members of the company, are a body corporate by the name stated in the certificate of incorporation: CA 2006, s 16(2).

- That body corporate is capable of exercising all the functions of an incorporated company: CA 2006, s 16(3).
- The status and registered office of the company are as stated in, or in connection with, the application for registration: CA 2006, s 16(4).
- In the case of a company having a share capital, the subscribers to the memorandum become holders of the shares specified in the statement of capital and initial shareholdings: CA 2006, s 16(5).
- The persons named in the statement of proposed officers:

  (a) as director, or

  (b) as secretary or joint secretary of the company,

  are deemed to have been appointed to that office: CA 2006, s 16(6).

Piercing the corporate veil

4.55 It has been seen that a company has a separate legal personality distinct from its shareholders. It has rights and obligations upon incorporation. It has capacity to enter into contracts; to hold property; to sue for debts owed to it; to appoint agents and other rights and obligations conferred by law. In this respect, the corporation is treated as a natural person who has similar rights and obligations. Provided all the formalities for establishing a company have been complied with, the motives or intentions for establishing the company are irrelevant. The company must of course be set up for a lawful purpose. On incorporation, the shareholders have limited liability and are only liable up to the amount they have contributed into the company. The company, therefore, has capacity to enter into transactions as natural persons do.

4.56 However, the privileges of incorporation may sometimes lead to an abuse of corporate form. The company may not be carrying on for a lawful purpose. The motives of those setting up and controlling the company may display impropriety: the company may be used and abused to hide the real motives of the incorporators. By ignoring the separate legal personality of the company, the court can pierce or lift the veil. The separate legal personality is only ignored for certain purposes, but the corporate entity still retains its status as a corporation.

4.57 This section considers the concept of piercing the corporate veil. It then proceeds to examine the circumstances where the courts have pierced the corporate veil with particular references to *VTB Capital plc v Nutritek International Corp* [2013] 1 BCLC 179; and *Prest v Petrodel Resources Ltd* [2013] 3 WLR 1.

Defining the concept

4.58 On occasions, the courts have ignored the separate personality of the company, and they have pierced or lifted the veil to identify issues such as, for example, those who evade their legal obligations and responsibilities; or those who may conceal their personal assets from third parties because such assets are held by the company; who are the real controllers of the company; or for what purposes or motives the company was formed; or the extent of corporate abuse being perpetrated and the identity of the persons engaged in the corporate abuse or impropriety. In other situations, the courts have pierced the corporate veil to confer certain benefits and advantages to the company or group of companies. The term 'piercing the corporate veil' has traditionally been used to describe exceptions to the corporate personality concept, when the courts will look behind the company to ascertain the intention and motives of the directors or shareholders in respect of particular transactions or activities where wrongdoing or abuse is taking place.

4.59 Before the leading cases of *Prest v Petrodel Resources Ltd* [2013] All ER 90 and *VTB Capital plc v Nutritek International Corp* [2013] 1 BCLC 179, an analysis of previous cases demonstrates a remarkable degree of inconsistency in the approach by the courts in piercing or lifting the corporate veil and the circumstances in which the veil will be pierced; including some doubts raised in cases on the applicability of the principle and whether it served any useful purpose, and indeed, whether there was any real distinction between 'piercing the corporate veil' and 'lifting the corporate veil'. In *VTB Capital plc v Nutritek International Corp* [2013] 1 BCLC 179, Lord Neuberger stated that 'the terms 'piercing' and 'lifting' appeared throughout the case law authorities, sometimes interchangeably…I shall use the phrase 'piercing' in preference to 'lifting'. It is the more familiar expression and …it is unnecessary to decide whether, in truth, there is a difference in this context between 'piercing' and 'lifting' the corporate veil'. Lord Neuberger did not find any assistance to be gained in the use of pejorative expressions to describe circumstances for piercing the corporate veil echoing Justice Cardozo's reference in *Berkey v Third Ave Ry* 155 NE 58, 61 (1926), to the 'mists of metaphor' in company law, which, 'starting as devices to liberate thought,…end often by enslaving it'.

4.60 In *Tjaskemolen* [1997] 2 Lloyd's Rep 465, Clarke J was of the view that: 'The cases have not worked out what is meant by 'piercing the corporate veil'. It may not always mean the same thing'.

In *Yukong Line Ltd of Korea v Rendsbury Invest Corp of Liberia (No 2)* [1998] 2 BCLC 485, Toulson J stated that 'it may not matter what language is used [whether lifting the veil or piercing the veil] as long as the principle is clear; but there lies the rub. For the metaphor can be used to illustrate a principle, it may also be used as a substitute for analysis and may therefore obscure reasoning'.

4.61 On occasions, the courts have pierced the corporate veil by way of exceptions to the company's separate legal existence. The courts have used the terms 'piercing' or 'lifting' the corporate veil interchangeably. However, in *Atlas Marine Co SA v Avalon Maritime Ltd (No 1)* [1991] 4 All ER 769, Staughton LJ thought that there was clearly a distinction between the two concepts: 'To *pierce* the corporate veil is an expression that I would reserve for treating the rights and liabilities or activities of the company as the rights, or liabilities or activities of its shareholders.' To *lift* the corporate veil or *look behind* it, on the other hand, should mean to have regard to the shareholding in the company for some legal purpose': see too *VTB Capital plc v Nutritek International Corp* [2013] 1 BCLC 179; and Lord Neuberger in *Prest v Petrodel Resources Ltd* [2013] 3 WLR 1 with reference to the 'concealment' and 'evasion' principles (discussed below).

4.62 In the Australian case of *Pioneer Concrete Services Ltd v Yelnah Pty Ltd* (1986) 5 NSWLR 254, Young J defined 'lifting the veil' as 'whenever each individual company is formed a separate legal personality is created, the courts will on occasions, look behind the legal personality to the real controllers.' However, the effect of piercing the veil is actually to look behind the veil to determine the nature of the activities that are being carried on by the controllers. The distinction therefore does not serve any useful purpose. In *Briggs v James Hardie & Co Pty Ltd* (1989) 16 NSWLR 549, 567, Rogers AJA in the New South Wales Court of Appeal considered that 'there is no common, unifying principle, which underlies the occasional decision of courts to pierce the corporate veil', and that 'there is no principled approach to be derived from the authorities'.

4.63 In *Hashem v Shayif* [2008] EWCH 2380, Munby J expressed the view that the expressions 'piercing' and 'lifting' the corporate veil were synonymous. Munby J considered the principle of piercing the corporate veil as a remedial one.

However, Sir Andrew Morritt V-C in *Trustor AB v Smallbone* [2001] 2 BCLC 436 appears to have treated the principle of piercing the corporate veil as triggered by the finding of a 'façade'.

4.64 In *Theosophical Foundation Pty Ltd v Commissioner of Land Tax* (1966) 67 SR (NSW) 70, Herron CJ stated that the term 'lifting the corporate veil' was an 'esoteric label' and stated: 'Authorities in which the veil of incorporation has been lifted have not been of such consistency that any principle can be adduced. The cases merely provide instances in which the courts have on the facts refused to be bound by the form or fact of incorporation when justice requires the substance or reality to be investigated …'.

4.65 On the use of colourful language and of metaphors to describe the principle, Staughton LJ in *Welsh Development Agency v Export Finance Co Ltd* [1992] BCLC 148, stated that the problem was exacerbated by the use of variety of language that has been used: so words such as 'substance', 'truth', 'reality', and 'genuine' were good words. Words such as 'disguise', 'cloak', 'mask', 'colourable', 'device', 'label', 'form', 'artificial' and 'sham' were 'bad' names implying a value judgment of disapprobation. It was more important to discover the ideas which those words were intended o convey.

4.66 In *Re Polly Peck International plc (No 3)* [1996] BCLC 428, Robert Walker J referred to the concept of lifting or piercing the corporate veil as 'a vivid but imprecise metaphor which has possible application in several different contexts'. He thought that the term 'sham' was at least half-way towards becoming a term of art (requiring an intention common to all the parties). Terms such as 'cipher' and 'facade' were merely colourful language. He stated that the term 'facade' (or 'cloak' or 'mask') was most aptly used where an individual or corporation used a company either in an unconscionable attempt to evade existing obligations or to practice some other deception (a type of unilateral sham, as the corporate facade had no independent mind.

4.67 In other jurisdictions such as Canada, In *Constitution Insurance Co of Canada v Kosmopoulos* [1987] 1 SCR 2, 10, Justice Wilson in the Supreme Court of Canada stated that '[t]he law on when a court may … '[lift] the corporate veil' … follows no consistent principle'. The New Zealand Court of Appeal in *Attorney-General v Equiticorp Industries Group Ltd (In Statutory Management)* [1996] 1 NZLR 528, 541, said that "to lift the corporate veil' ... is not a principle. It describes the process, but provides no guidance as to when it can be used.' In the South African Supreme Court decision of *Cape Pacific Ltd v Lubner Controlling Investments (Pty) Ltd* 1995 (4) SA 790 (A), 802-803, Smalberger JA observed that '[t]he law is far from settled with regard to the circumstances in which it would be permissible to pierce the corporate veil'.

4.68 In the United States, some judicial attitudes have also been critical of the approach taken towards piercing the corporate veil. In *Secon Serv Sys Inc v St Joseph Bank & Trust Co* 855 F2d (7th Cir, 1988), 406, 414, Judge Easterbrook in the US Court of Appeals described the doctrine as 'quite difficult to apply, because it avoids formulating a real rule of decision. This keeps people in the dark about the legal consequences of their acts...'. In *Allied Capital Corp v GC-Sun Holdings Lp* 910 A2d (2006) 1020, 1042-1043, the Delaware Court of Chancery said that the doctrine has been 'rightfully criticized for its ambiguity and randomness', and that its application 'yield[s] few predictable results'.

4.69 Lord Neuberger in *VTB Capital plc v Nutritek International Corp* [2013] 1 BCLC 179, however, warned against the use of certain words or expressions associated with piercing the corporate veil as they served no useful purpose. He stated:

> 'Words such as "façade", and other expressions found in the cases, such as "the true facts", "sham", "mask", "cloak", "device", or "puppet" may be useful metaphors. However, such pejorative expressions are often dangerous, as they risk assisting moral indignation to triumph over legal principle, and, while they may enable the court to arrive at a result which seems fair in the case in question, they can also risk causing confusion and uncertainty in the law'.

In *Prest v Petrodel Resources Ltd* [2013] All ER 90, the Supreme Court stated that the term 'piercing the corporate veil' referred to disregarding the separate legal personality of the company. The doctrine was to be used as a last resort. There were limited circumstances for the operation of this doctrine.

4.70 This section considers the previous circumstances where the courts have considered and in some cases applied the doctrine of piercing the corporate veil, including situations where the courts have refused to pierce the veil. These cases have demonstrated that there has been no unifying definition of piercing the corporate veil that has been applicable in all the situations. Judicial attitudes have differed as to its definition and the circumstances when it may be appropriate to pierce the corporate veil. This section then considers the modern position on piercing the corporate veil with a consideration of the leading Supreme Court cases on the current approach to piercing the corporate veil.

Early attempts to pierce the corporate veil

4.71 In the landmark case of *Salomon v Salomon & Co Ltd* [1897] AC 22, judicial attempts were made to pierce the corporate veil in order to impose personal liability on Aron Salomon. At first instance, Vaughan-Williams J considered that Salomon was an agent for the company and that the company had a right of indemnity against him. The effect would have been to impose personal liability upon Aron for the company's debts. The Court of Appeal decided that Aron acted as a trustee on behalf of the company, and questioned his motive for establishing the company as being for an illegitimate purpose contrary to the spirit and intention of the Companies Acts at the time.

4.72 However, attempts to pierce the corporate veil in the *Salomon* case failed as the House of Lords rejected the position that Salomon was an agent or a trustee for the company. Lord Halsbury considered that it may be possible to go behind the veil of incorporation to show that a fraud had been committed.

Lord Halsbury was of the view that provided the company was incorporated in accordance with the Companies Acts, the motives for incorporation were irrelevant.

The House of Lords unanimously concluded that there were no grounds to pierce the corporate veil and to impose liability upon Aron.

See too *Princess of Reuss v Bos* (1871) LR 5 HL 176.

Judicial attitudes

4.73 Over the years, the courts have identified a number of exceptions to the separate legal personality concept that have resulted in piercing the corporate veil and ignoring the separate legal personality of the corporation. There has been no discernible pattern or guiding principles on the when or how exactly the doctrine of piercing the corporate veil applied – only the circumstances when the veil may be pierced, even though the doctrine had no proper basis of application to the case. This was particularly acute in cases before the Chancery Division and the inconsistent application of the doctrine in the Family Division before *Prest v Petrodel Resources Ltd* [2013] All ER 90.

4.74 In *Salomon*, Lord Halsbury had already recognised that there may be exceptions or circumstances when the court could set aside the corporate veil. He stated: 'If there was no fraud and no agency, and if the company was a real one and not a fiction or a myth, every one of the grounds upon which it is sought to support the judgment is disposed of.' Similarly, Lord Macnaghten stated that 'if, however, the declaration of the Court of Appeal means that Mr Salomon acted fraudulently or dishonestly, I must say I can find nothing in the evidence to support such an imputation'.

4.75 The idea that there is no principled basis on which it can be said that the corporate veil can be pierced has received some support from the fact that the precise nature, basis and meaning of the corporate veil principle are obscure, including the precise nature of the circumstances in which they apply: see Lord Neuberger in *VTB Capital plc v Nutritek* [2013] 1 BCLC 179.

4.76 This section sets out some of the earlier judicial attitudes towards piercing the veil. Some of the decisions in this area have confused the position by the use of metaphors and expressions that have no relevance to the modern company law position. Indeed, it is questionable whether it is really necessary to refer to 'piercing the veil' or such similar expressions when in reality, the judges should decide the matter on the factual issues before them. Perhaps a more appropriate expression should be to refer to the 'exceptions' to the *Salomon* principle rather than to 'piercing the veil'. In any event, the separate legal personality of the company has been set aside sometimes to the advantage of the shareholders, and on other occasions to their disadvantage.

Abuse of rights

4.77 Unlike English law, the position in some civil law jurisdictions is that the concept of abuse of rights is recognised in order to pierce the corporate veil. Some cases were of the view that the corporate veil could be pierced owing to abuse of rights: *Barcelona Traction Light and Power Co Ltd Case (Second Phase) (Belgium v Spain)* [1970] ICJ 3; and *La Geìneìrale des Carrières et des Mines v FG Hemisphere Associates LLC* [2013] 1 All ER 409. See too *Prest v Petrodel Resources Ltd* [2013] All ER 90.

Agency

4.78 Although the *Salomon* case established that the company is not an agent for its shareholders and is independent of them, there have been some cases which have pierced the corporate veil by establishing special circumstances giving rise to an agency situation between the company and its shareholders or individual shareholders: *Gramophone and Typewriter Ltd v Stanley* [1908] 2 KB 89; *Smith, Stone and Knight Ltd v Birmingham Corp* [1939] 4 All ER 116; *Ebbw Vale Urban District Council v South Wales Traffic Area Licensing Authority* [1951] 1 All ER 806; *Re FG (Films) Ltd* [1953] 1 All ER 615.

Certain conditions are required to be satisfied before an agency relationship could exist between a parent and a subsidiary

In one of the leading cases as to whether an agency relationship could be established, the Court of Appeal in *Adams v Cape Industries plc* [1990] BCLC 479 was required to determine whether certain US subsidiaries were agents for an English parent company. If the presence of the English parent company in America could be established, the American courts could enforce judgment against it.

In respect of the first American subsidiary, NAAC, Slade LJ found that it was not an agent for its English parent company because a substantial part of NAAC's business was its own business. Further it had no general authority contractually to bind the English parent company. NAAC had a fixed place of business in America for a substantial period of time. Slade LJ considered the factual relationship between NAAC and its English parent company. NAAC was the lessee of the premises and paid its own rent under the lease. It conducted specific activities in buying, importing, storage and marketing asbestos. NAAC also earned profits itself and paid taxes and it had creditors and debtors of its own. Slade LJ also looked at the 'functions' performed by NAAC, which included assisting in the marketing of asbestos in the USA, and generally assisting and encouraging sales in the USA of asbestos of the parent group. It also had a co-ordinating role especially of delivery of the goods. These factors and functions did not make NAAC an agent for the English parent company.

Slade LJ also considered whether another subsidiary, CPC, was an agent for the English parent company, so as to determine whether the English parent company was 'present' in America for the purposes of enforcing judgment against it. From a factual investigation, he found that the English parent company had no control over CPC. CPC was at liberty to sell materials and products other than asbestos and to engage in other commercial activities. It bought and sold manufactured textiles on its own behalf as principal. A substantial part of CPC's business was its own business. As regards the functions performed by CPC, they were very similar to those of NAAC. CPC had no authority to bind the English parent company. CPC therefore was not an agent of its English parent company.

4.79 In *Yukong Line Ltd of Korea v Rendsburg Investment Corp of Liberia (No 2)* [1998] 4 All ER 82, Toulson J thought that the starting point for considering the question of agency was to have regard to *Salomon*'s case, namely that the company was not an agent for its members. He considered that Atkinson J's six principles in *Stone* did not serve any useful purpose, in determining whether a company was carrying on the business as agent for another person. Further, he thought that it would be exceptional to find that a company was in fact an agent for its shareholders.

As a company is considered to be a separate legal entity, it is subject to corporation tax on profits made.

Interests of justice

4.80 There has been some judicial authority for the view that the courts will pierce the corporate veil where this is in the interests of justice. This principle gives the courts a wide discretion to pierce the corporate veil and has been the subject of controversy in some judicial cases as being vague with no substantive guidance on the interpretation of this concept: *Wallersteiner v Moir* [1974] 3 All ER 217; *Re A Company* [1985] BCLC 333. However, see the rejection of this principle in: *Adams v Cape Industries plc* [1990] Ch 433; *Trustor AB v Smallbone* [2001] 2 BCLC 436; *Hashem v Shayif* [2008] EWHC 2380; *Re Polly Peck International plc (No 3)* [1996] 2 All ER 433; *Ord v Belhaven Pubs Ltd* [1998] 2 BCLC 447; and *Conway v Raitu* [2005] EWCA Civ 1302; and *Kensington International Ltd v Republic of the Congo* [2006] 2 BCLC 296.

Enemy

4.81 In special circumstances, such as a state of war, or in recognition of the needs of national security, the courts have lifted the corporate veil to determine whether the company has an enemy character, by reason of the associations of those in a position to control the company: *Daimler Co Ltd v Continental Tyre & Rubber Co (Great Britain) Ltd* [1916] 2 AC 307.

Realities of the situation

4.82 On occasions, the courts have considered the realities of the situation to determine whether it would be appropriate to pierce the corporate veil: *Tunstall v Steigmann* [1962] 2 All ER 417; *Re Yenidje Tobacco Co Ltd* [1916] 2 Ch 426.

Criminal activities

4.83 The courts will pierce the corporate veil where criminal activities are being perpetrated within the company by its controllers: *Re H* [1996] 2 All ER 3.

Evading existing obligations

4.84 The courts may pierce the corporate veil where there is an attempt to avoid an existing obligation which results in a breach of that obligation.

An evasion of existing obligations may justify piercing the corporate veil

In *Gilford Motor Company Ltd v Horne* [1933] 1 Ch 935, Gilford Motor Company was in the business of purchasing various parts of motor vehicles from manufacturers. The company assembled the parts on its premises and sold the products under the name of 'Gilford Motor Vehicles'. In 1929, Horne was appointed as the company's managing director for six years and he entered into a non-solicitation clause. His employment was terminated in 1931. Shortly afterwards, he established a company whose business was concerned with the sale of spare parts of Gilford vehicles. Gilford Motors then sought to enforce the non-solicitation clause. In the Court of Appeal, Lord Hanworth MR granted an injunction prohibiting Horne 'either directly or indirectly by means of the defendant company ... to solicit his former employers' customers'. He referred to the company as having been 'formed as a device, a stratagem, in order to mask the effective carrying on of the business of Mr EB Horne'. He also described the company as a 'device, a stratagem', 'a mere cloak or a sham' and that the company was 'a mere channel' used by the defendant Horne in order to continue committing breaches of his service agreement with his previous company. Horne's objective was to carry on that business in breach of the restrictive covenant he had entered into with Gilford Motors. Horne had in fact set up his company with knowledge that he would be committing breaches of the restrictive covenant in carrying on the business, and that he might possibly avoid such liability by setting up a company. Accordingly, the corporate veil was pierced on the basis that the controllers were in control of the company and there was impropriety involved.

In *Jones v Lipman* [1962] 1 WLR 832, Lipman agreed under a contract to sell land to Mr and Mrs Jones. However, he later decided he did not want to sell the land to them. He then sold and transferred the land to a company that was wholly owned and controlled by him. His purpose was to defeat Jones' claim for specific performance. Russell J described the company as being 'under the complete control' of Lipman, and stated that the acquisition of the company and the transfer to it of the property was carried through 'solely for the purpose of defeating the plaintiff's rights to specific performance'. He further stated: 'The defendant company is the creature of the first defendant, a device and a sham, a mask which he holds before his face, in an attempt to avoid recognition in the eyes of equity.'

See application of these evasion cases in *Prest v Petrodel Resources Ltd* [2013] All ER 90.

Thwarting the rights of a minority shareholder

4.85 On occasions, the courts have been prepared to pierce the corporate veil where the company has been used as a device to thwart a minority shareholder's rights: *Re Bugle Press Ltd* [1961] Ch 270.

Determining the characteristics of the controllers and shareholders

4.86 In *The Abbey Malvern Wells Ltd v Ministry of Local Government and Planning* [1951] Ch 728, Danckwerts J thought the court was entitled to pierce the corporate veil on the basis that the company was an artificial person. Although it was a legal person, it was not a physical entity and it could only operate through human beings. It was, therefore, necessary to identify who operated the company and what was their position.

Establishing a company to divert profits and business opportunities from the existing company

4.87 In appropriate circumstances, the court may lift the corporate veil where a company is established to divert profits and business opportunities away from the existing company: *Gencor ACP Ltd v Dalby* [2000] 2 BCLC 734; *Trustor AB v Smallbone (No 2)* [2001] 3 All ER 987.

Special circumstances

4.88 In order to justify lifting the veil of incorporation, 'special circumstances' should exist indicating that the company was a mere facade concealing the true facts: *Dadourian Group International Inc v Simms* [2006] EWHC 2973, affirmed by the Court of Appeal on other grounds see [2009] EWCA Civ 169.

Corporate reorganisation

4.89 In the absence of any impropriety, sham or concealment in the restructuring of the group, the court has held that it would not be appropriate to lift the corporate veil: *Ord v Belhaven Pubs Ltd* [1998] 2 BCLC 447.

Groups and the single enterprise

4.90 In practical terms, a parent company may establish subsidiaries for various divisions of its businesses and to limit any potential liability. In *Re Southard & Co Ltd* [1979] 3 All ER 556, Templeman LJ was of the view that in the area of group companies, English company law possessed some curious features which generated some strange results. In his words:

> 'A parent company may spawn a number of subsidiary companies, all controlled directly or indirectly by the shareholders of the parent company. If one of the subsidiary companies, to change the metaphor, turns out to be the runt of the litter and declines into insolvency to the dismay of its creditors, the parent company and other subsidiary companies may prosper to the joy of the shareholders without any liability for the debts of the insolvent subsidiary.'

4.91 On occasions, the courts have been willing to pierce the corporate veil and treat a group company and subsidiary companies as one single entity for the purposes of piercing the corporate veil. In *Littlewoods Mail Order Store Ltd v IRC* [1969] 3 All ER 855, Lord Denning was willing to set aside the corporate veil by treating the group and subsidiary as one entity. He stated:

> 'I decline to treat the [subsidiary] as a separate and independent legal entity. The courts can and often do draw aside the veil. They can, and often do, pull off the mask. They look to see what really lies behind. The legislature has shown the way with group accounts and the rest. And the courts should follow suit. I think we should look at the Fork Company and see it as it really is – the wholly-owned subsidiary of the taxpayers. It is the creature, the puppet, of the taxpayer …'.

4.92 The issue as to whether a group and subsidiary should be treated as one entity was considered in *Scottish Co-operative Wholesale Society Ltd v Meyer* [1958] 3 All ER 66. This case concerned an action for oppression by a minority shareholder under the previous s 210 of the CA 1948. The Scottish Co-operative Wholesale Society had established a subsidiary, of which the respondent was a member. It was submitted on behalf of the Society that it had not conducted the company's affairs in an oppressive manner. The House of Lords did not accept this submission and held that the Society had acted in an oppressive manner. Viscount Simonds stated: 'It may be that the acts of the society of which complaint is made could not be regarded as conduct of the affairs of the company if the society and company were bodies wholly independent of each other, competitors in the rayon market, and using against each other such methods of trade warfare as custom permitted. But this is to pursue false analogy. It is not possible to separate the transactions of the society from those of the company. Each step taken by the latter was determined by the policy of the former.' In other words, the acts of the Society were the acts of its subsidiary.

In relation to a group of companies, the court was entitled to look at the realities of the situation and to pierce the corporate veil

The *Salomon* principle was disregarded in *DHN Food Distributors Ltd v London Borough of Tower Hamlets* [1976] 3 All ER 462, by piercing the corporate veil by treating a group of companies as one single enterprise. In 1965, a company DHN was established to carry on the business of importing and distributing groceries. DHN needed premises from which to trade and made certain borrowing arrangements with the bank. The agreed arrangement was that the bank would buy the property and then sell it to DHN for £120,000 with £20,000 to be paid on exchange of contracts, and the remainder within one year. The property were purchased for £115,000 and transferred to a company called Bronze, a wholly owned subsidiary of the bank. DHN then went into possession of the property and began trading. Bronze then contracted to sell the property to DHN but the contract was never completed. DHN then arranged a loan of £100,000 from a separate source and in order to save stamp duty on a conveyance by Bronze, instead agreed with the bank to purchase Bronze's share capital and repay the loan from the bank for a total sum of £120,000. This transaction was carried out and DHN and Bronze had the same directors. Bronze retained the legal title to the premises and DHN continued to use them for the purposes of the business. Later in 1969, the local authority made a compulsory purchase order and paid Bronze compensation for the value of the land. One of the main issues for consideration was whether the court should lift the corporate veil and treat DHN as owners of the property who would then become entitled to compensation for the disturbance instead of Bronze.

The Court of Appeal held that the case was one in which the court was 'entitled to look at the realities of the situation and to pierce the corporate veil'. According to Lord Denning, a group of companies could in many respects be treated together as one concern for the purpose of general accounts, balance sheet and profit and loss account. He noted that there was a general tendency to ignore the separate legal entities of various companies within a group, and to look instead at the 'economic entity' of the whole group. This was particularly the case when a parent company owned all the shares of its subsidiaries, so much that it could control every movement of the subsidiaries. The subsidiaries were 'bound hand and foqt' to the parent company and they must do what the parent company required. The group of companies on the facts was virtually the same as a partnership in which all the three companies were partners, and that they should be treated as one. Lord Denning also made reference to claims of justice in the case. He thought that the claimants should not be deprived of compensation which should justly be paid for disturbance. He decided that the three companies should be treated as one and that DHN, being the parent company, should be entitled to claim compensation not only for the value of the land, but also compensation for disturbance.

Goff LJ was of the view that the corporate veil would not be lifted in every case concerning group of companies. However, in the present case, the two subsidiaries were both wholly owned. They had no separate business operations. Further, that the owners of the business had been disturbed in their possession and enjoyment of land.

Shaw LJ referred to the 'complete identity' concept in treating the group company and subsidiaries as one single entity. The completeness of that identity manifested itself in various ways such as the directors of DHN being the same as the directors in Bronze; the shareholders of Bronze were the same as in DHN; and they had a common interest in maintaining on the property the group's business; and DHN undertook the obligation to procure its subsidiary company to make the payment which the bank required to be made. Therefore, there was complete identity and a community of interest, and so the group and subsidiaries could be treated as one entity. Shaw LJ also made reference to claims of justice: 'If each member of the group is regarded as a company in isolation, nobody at all could have claimed compensation in a case which plainly calls for it.'

The courts have not always been readily prepared to pierce the corporate veil in group enterprise situations.

The starting point for piercing the corporate veil was only where 'special circumstances' existed indicating a mere facade concealing the true facts

The case of *Woolfson v Strathclyde Regional Council* 1978 SC (HL) 90 concerned a company called Campbell Ltd ('Campbell') which carried on a retail business at a shop comprising five premises. Three of the premises were owned by Woolfson and the other two by Solfred Holdings Ltd ('Solfred'). Woolfson owned 999 shares of the 1,000 issued shares of Campbell and his wife held one share. In 1951 Woolfson became the sole director of Campbell. Woolfson also owned 20 of the issued shares in Solfred and the remaining 10 being owned by his wife. Between 1962 and 1968, Campbell paid rent to Solfred in respect of part of the premises owned by Solfred and rent for other part of the premises was credited to Woolfson in Campbell's accounts. At a later stage, all the premises were compulsorily acquired by the local authority. Woolfson and Solfred jointly sought compensation for disturbance in respect of all the premises. It was argued on behalf of Woolfson (in reliance on *DHN Food Distributors*) that the court should set aside the legalistic view that Woolfson, Campbell and Solfred were a separate legal persona and concentrate attention to the 'realities' of the situation, to the effect of finding that Woolfson was the occupier as well as the owner of the whole of the premises.

The House of Lords held that Woolfson could not be treated as beneficially entitled to the whole shareholding in Campbell as it was not found that Woolfson's wife held one share in Campbell as his nominee. Further, the court would not pierce the corporate veil by holding Woolfson to be the true owner of Campbell's business or of the assets of Solfred. According to Lord Keith, the court would not pierce the corporate veil as the facts did not reveal that the company structure was a mere facade. His Lordship stated that the starting point for piercing the corporate veil was only where 'special circumstances' existed indicating a mere facade concealing the true facts. He distinguished the *DHN Distributors* case on the basis that in that case, the company that owned the land was a wholly owned subsidiary of the company that carried on the business. The latter was in complete control of the situation as respects anything that might affect its business, and there was no one but itself having any kind of interest or right regarding the assets of the subsidiary. In the *Woolfson* case, Campbell (which carried on the business) did not have any control over the owners of the land, Solfred and Woolfson. Woolfson held two-thirds only of the shares in Solfred and Solfred held no interest in Campbell.

In relation to a group of companies, there was no general principle that all companies in a group of companies were to be regarded as one

One of the most significant cases on piercing the corporate veil in a group enterprise situation is the Court of Appeal decision in *Adams v Cape Industries plc* [1990] BCLC 479. Cape Industries plc controlled a group of companies involved in mining asbestos in South Africa and marketing in the USA. Asbestos was mined by a South African subsidiary and then sold to a factory in Owentown, South Africa. Two companies, Capacso Ltd (Capasco) which was an English company and North American Asbestos Corporation (NAAC) which was incorporated in Illinois, were marketing companies controlled by Cape. Capasco marketed worldwide, whereas NAAC marketed in the USA. NAAC was later put into liquidation. In order to carry out Cape's marketing activities in the USA, a Liechtenstein corporation, Associated Mineral Corporation (AMC) and a new Illinois corporation, Continental Productions Corporation (CPC) were formed. AMC's shares were held on behalf of a subsidiary of Cape and CPC's shares were held by the ex-President of NAAC. In 1974, employees and ex-employees of the Owentown factory brought an action (the Tyler 1 action) in the USA at Texas (the Tyler court) against Cape and Capasco claiming damages for personal injuries arising from exposure of asbestos dust. These actions were settled in 1977 and judgment entered against Cape and Capasco. A second action (the Tyler 2 action) was brought against Cape and Capasco in the same court as the Tyler 1 action, but neither Cape nor Capasco entered an appearance. A default order was made against them and the appellants sought to enforce the order in the present proceedings. At first instance, Scott J dismissed the plaintiffs' actions and they appealed to the Court of Appeal. The appellants argued that Cape, Capasco and CPC constituted a single economic unit; and that with regard to CPC, the corporate veil should be lifted so that CPC's presence in the USA should be treated as the presence of Cape/Capasco.

Slade LJ reviewed the 'single economic unit' concept. He stated that there was no general principle that all companies in a group of companies were to be regarded as one. The fundamental principle was that each company in a group of companies was a separate legal entity possessed of separate legal rights and liabilities. Therefore, Cape, Capasco, NAAC and CPC were in law separate legal entities. As to the relationship between Cape and NAAC, the very nature of a parent–subsidiary relationship was that the parent company was in a position to exercise overall control over the general policy of the subsidiary. Although this relationship was established, it was rejected based on a technical argument.

Slade LJ rejected the view that the court was entitled to pierce the corporate veil merely because it was just to do so. Further, there was no presumption at law that the business of the parent and subsidiary was being carried on by the subsidiary as agent for the parent. Also, there was no presumption that the subsidiary was the parent company's alter ego.

Slade LJ then addressed the issue of corporate veil and whether this principle applied in the *Cape* case. He approved Lord Keith's *dicta* in *Woolfson v Strathclyde Regional Council* (1978) SLT 159 that it was appropriate to pierce the corporate veil only where 'special circumstances' existed indicating that it was a 'mere facade' concealing the true facts. The appellants had alleged a mere facade by the formation and use of CPC and AMC and that the marketing arrangements were a device, sham or cloak for grave impropriety on the part of Cape or Capacso, namely ostensibly to remove their assets from the USA to avoid liability for asbestos claims whilst at the same time continuing to trade in asbestos there. Slade LJ thought that whenever a facade, device, sham or cloak is alleged, the motive of the perpetrator must be legally relevant. He did not attempt a comprehensive definition of the circumstances in which the courts would determine whether or not the arrangements of a corporate group involved a facade such that the court would lift the corporate veil. He decided that the fact that CPC was established to reduce the potential tortuous liability of Cape was a legitimate use of the corporate form. This was not a ground for piercing the corporate veil of CPC so as to treat its activities as being those of Cape.

The *Cape* case also addressed the 'agency argument', namely whether a subsidiary could be treated as an agent for the parent company. The issue was in relation to NCC and whether it was regarded as a legal entity separate from Cape/Capasco. Slade LJ decided that there was no basis for finding that NAAC was acting as an agent for Cape/Capasco because a substantial part of the business which it carried on was in every sense its own business. Further, it had no general authority to enter into contracts binding on Cape or Capasco. In determining the relationship between Cape and NAAC, the court would look into the functions performed by the subsidiary and all aspects of the relationship between it and Cape. This required a factual assessment. On the facts, an agency relationship had not been established. NAAC was carrying on business of its own and not that of Cape or Capasco. Its functions were to assist in the marketing of asbestos in the USA, and generally to assist and encourage sales in the USA of asbestos of the Cape group. It also acted as a channel of communication between Cape/Capasco and the USA customers.

4.93 Generally, the courts will not assist third parties to lift the corporate veil in a group structure. In *Multinational Gas and Petrochemical Company v Multinational Gas and Petrochemical Services Ltd* [1983] BCLC 461, the Court of Appeal refused to assist the liquidator of an insolvent subsidiary in serving a writ out of jurisdiction against three international oil companies alleging negligence. According to Lawton and Dillon LJJ, the oil companies had a good defence in law in that the misfeasance alleged by the liquidator in relation to the subsidiary company had been approved by its shareholders and directors. The Lord Justices decided that the shareholders owed no duty of care to third parties such as creditors of the company. Further, as shareholders, they owed no duties to the company.

As to the position of group companies, see CA 2006, ss 1159, 1161–1163 and Sch 7.

Proceeds of crime

4.94 In some circumstances, the courts have considered the position whether the corporate veil could be pierced in connection with criminal confiscation proceedings under the Criminal Justice Act 1988 and the Proceeds of Crime Act 2002: see *R v Seager; R v Blatch* [2009] All ER 283; *R v May* [2008] All ER 169; *Jennings v Crown Prosecution Service* [2008] All ER 126; and *R v Sale* [2013] EWCA Crim 1306.

Piercing the veil by legislation

Misfeasance

4.95 Section 212 of the Insolvency Act 1986 (IA 1986) is concerned with misfeasance and only has application in the course of a company's winding up. It has wide scope and applies to an officer of the company, liquidator, or any other person who has been concerned or has taken part in the promotion, formation or management of the company: IA 1986, s 212(1). The offences apply to misapplication or retention or becoming accountable for any money or other property of the company, any misfeasance or breach of any fiduciary or other duty in relation to the company. On the application of a liquidator or of any creditor or contributory, the court may look into the conduct of the person alleged to be involved in misfeasance and can compel him to repay, restore or account for the money or property or any part of it with interest at such rate as the court thinks just; or to contribute such sum to the company's assets by way of compensation in respect of the misfeasance or breach of the fiduciary or other duty as the court thinks just: IA 2006, s 212(3).

Fraudulent trading

4.96 Section 213 of the IA 1986 is concerned with fraudulent trading. It applies where in the course of a company's winding up, it appears that any business of the company has been carried on with intent to defraud the company's creditors or creditors of any other person, or for any other fraudulent purpose: IA 1986, s 213(1). On the application of the liquidator, the court may declare that any persons who were knowingly parties to the carrying on of the business are liable to make such contribution (if any) to the company's assets as the court thinks proper: IA 1986, s 213(2). The term 'intent' is used in the sense that a person must have been taken to intend the natural or foreseen consequences of his act: see Oliver J in *Re Murray-Watson Ltd* (unreported, 6 April 1977). Section 213 of the IA 1986 requires an intention on the part of the person to defraud creditors. In *Re Patrick Lyon Ltd* [1933] Ch 786 at 790–791, the court stated that this required actual dishonesty which involved according to current notions of fair trading among commercial men 'real moral blame'. An intention to defraud creditors may be demonstrated where the company carries on business with no prospect of paying off its debts *Re William C Leitch Bros Ltd* [1932] 2 Ch 71. It is sufficient if only one creditor is defrauded.

4.97 The Companies Act 2006 creates a criminal offence of fraudulent trading but there is no requirement of any fraudulent trading in the course of a company's winding up. Section 993 of the Companies Act 2006 states that if any business of a company is carried on with intent to defraud the company's creditors or creditors of any other persons or for any fraudulent purpose, then every person who was knowingly a party to the carrying on of the business in that manner is liable to imprisonment or a fine or both. This applies whether or not the company is in the course of being wound up. On conviction on indictment, the term of imprisonment is for a term not exceeding ten years or a fine or both: CA 2006, s 993(3)(a). In *R v Grantham* [1984] BCLC 270, the Court of Appeal stated that a person could be convicted of fraudulent trading if he took part in the management of the company's affairs and obtained credit for the company knowing that there was no reason for thinking that funds would become available to pay the debt when it became due or shortly thereafter.

Wrongful trading

4.98 Section 214 of the IA 1986 is concerned with wrongful trading. It applies where some time before commencement of the winding up, the person against whom the order is sought knew or ought to have concluded that there was no reasonable prospect that the company would avoid going into insolvent liquidation. The facts which a director of a company ought to know or ascertain, the conclusions which he ought to reach and the steps which he ought to take are those which would be known or ascertained or reached or taken by a reasonably diligent person having both: (a) the general knowledge, skill and experience that may reasonably be expected for a person carrying out the same functions as are carried out by that director in relation to the company; and (b) the general knowledge, skill and experience that the director has. The company must have gone into insolvent liquidation in that there are insufficient assets for payment of the company's debts and other liabilities and expenses of winding up. The liquidator can apply to the court for an order that the person is liable to make such contribution (if any) to the company's assets as the court thinks proper. There is a defence for the person against whom wrongful trading is alleged to show that he took every step with a view to minimising the potential loss to the company's creditors as he ought to have taken.

Matrimonial disputes: controlling shareholder and concepts of impropriety

4.99 Another strand of authority which runs parallel to the company commercial cases that has addressed the concept of piercing the corporate veil, has been in matrimonial disputes in respect of cases decided in the Family Division. In these cases, one party (usually the husband) is the controlling shareholder of a company which owns assets. The wife will be seeking ancillary financial relief and making a claim on the company's assets. The issue for the courts in the Family Division has been whether the corporate veil can be pierced to reach those assets for the benefit of the wife. Prior to *Prest*, there have been a number of inconsistent judicial decisions in the Family Division on the circumstances where it would be appropriate to pierce the corporate veil. To some extent, the cases openly revealed the division of opinion between the Family Courts and the Chancery Courts on the circumstances for piercing the corporate veil and the need for rationalisation between the two courts.

4.100 In *Green v Green* [1993] 1 FLR 326, Connell J ordered sale of land belonging to the company on the basis that it was necessary and expedient to do so.

The decision in *Green* does not appear to have applied the fundamental principles required for the courts to lift the corporate veil. The only element present here was that the husband solely controlled and owned one of the companies. There was no issue of any impropriety or culpability that would be necessary to allow the courts to lift the corporate veil, or that the company was a sham or facade to conceal the true facts, or that any special circumstances existed to pierce the corporate veil.

4.101 However, the *Green* decision did not find favour with Gibson LJ in *Wicks v Wicks* [1998] 1 FLR 465, who stated that he could not see how the application for ancillary relief could relate to land when the husband merely owned shares in two companies which owned the land. Gibson LJ thought that the court did not have the power in the *Green* case to order a sale of the land.

4.102 Connell J in *Green* had applied the sole principle of ownership and control alone as sufficient to justify piercing the corporate veil, whereas impropriety was also a required element which was not present in that case. Support for this view can be found in *Mubarak v Mubarak* [2000] 1 FLR 673. *See too Kremen v Agrest (No 2)* [2011] FLR 490.

In *Nicholas v Nicholas* [1984] FLR 285, the Court of Appeal stated that it would not pierce the corporate veil where minority interests were involved.

4.103 However, there have been cases where the courts have refused to apply the principle of piercing the corporate veil in matrimonial disputes: See *A v A* [2007] 2 FLR 467; *Ben Hashem v Al Shayif* [2009] 1 FLR 115; *Anglo German Breweries Ltd (in liquidation) v Chelsea Corp* [2012] 2 BCLC 632; *Linsen International Ltd v Humpuss Sea Transport Pte Ltd* [2012] BCLC 651.

Rationalisation of approach between the Chancery Division and Family Division on piercing the corporate veil

4.104 There had been concern that the approaches to piercing the corporate veil by the Chancery and Family Divisions were fragmented and lacked uniformity. In *Mubarak*, Bodey J thought that ideally the Family and the Chancery Divisions should have a common approach to the issue of piercing the corporate veil. He accepted however that the company law approach and the family law approach applied different considerations in determining whether the corporate veil should be lifted. The company law approach was largely concerned with parties at arm's length who were in a contractual or similar relationship or in a commercial context. The family approach was, however, concerned with the court's distributive powers as between the husband

and wife by applying discretionary considerations to what will mainly be a family-type situation.

4.105 In considering whether to lift the veil of incorporation, the Family Division appeared to be applying the concept that the courts will only pierce the corporate veil where it is just and necessary. In cases where the husband conceded that the company or trust assets could be treated as belonging to him, the case in the Family Division proceeded conveniently in allowing the courts to lift the corporate veil to allow some ancillary relief to be provided to the wife from the company's assets. This usually saved expense and was practical in the circumstances. The issue still, however, remained in defining those situations when lifting the corporate veil was appropriate by way of enforcement following a concession by the husband in ancillary relief proceedings: see *Mubarak*. The fragmented approach between the Chancery and Family Divisions on the circumstances when the corporate veil could be pierced had led to confusion in its application and it was thought to be questionable whether the doctrine had any application in such matrimonial cases.

The term 'piercing the corporate veil' refers to disregarding the company's personality. The circumstances where the corporate personality may be pierced were limited

The leading authority on whether the corporate veil can be pierced in matrimonial and other circumstances where properties are vested in companies controlled by one of the matrimonial partners was considered by the House of Lords in *Prest v Petrodel Resources Ltd* [2013] All ER 90. Although the remarks on the principle of piercing the corporate veil were *obiter*, they were intended by the Supreme Court to be of general application and not limited to matrimonial cases. The appeal arose out of proceedings following a divorce between the husband and wife. They were married in 1993, and during the marriage the matrimonial home was principally in England.

The wife petitioned for divorce in March 2008. A decree nisi was pronounced in December 2008, and a decree absolute in November 2011. The appeal concerned only the position of a number of companies belonging to the group known as the Petrodel Group which the judge found to be wholly owned and controlled (directly or through intermediate entities) by the husband.

There were originally seven companies involved, all of which were joined as additional respondents to the wife's application for ancillary relief. They were Petrodel Resources Ltd ('PRL'), Petrodel Resources (Nigeria) Ltd ('PRL Nigeria'), Petrodel Upstream Ltd ('Upstream'), Vermont Petroleum Ltd ('Vermont'), Elysium Diem Ltd, Petrodel Resources (Nevis) Ltd ('PRL Nevis') and Elysium Diem Ltd (Nevis). Three of these companies, PRL, Upstream and Vermont, all incorporated in the Isle of Man, were the respondents in this court. PRL was the legal owner of the matrimonial home, which was bought in the name of the company in 2001 but was found by the judge to be held for the husband beneficially. In addition, PRL was the legal owner of five residential properties in the United Kingdom and Vermont was the legal owner of two more. The question on the appeal was whether the court had power to order the transfer of these seven properties to the wife given that they legally belonged not to him but to his companies.

Part II of the Matrimonial Causes Act 1973 conferred wide powers on the court to order ancillary relief in matrimonial proceedings. Section 23 provided for periodical and lump sum payments to a spouse or for the benefit of children of the marriage. Under s 24(1)(a), the court may order that 'a party to the marriage shall transfer to the other party … such property as may be so specified, being property to which the first-mentioned party is entitled, either in possession reversion'. Section 25 provided for a number of matters to which the court must in particular have regard in making such orders, including, at s 25(2)(a), the 'income, earning capacity, property and other financial resources which each of the parties to the marriage has or is likely to have in the foreseeable future'.

In the High Court, Moylan J decided that there was no general principle that entitled him to reach the companies' assets by piercing the corporate veil. He nevertheless concluded that a wider jurisdiction to pierce the corporate veil was available under s 24 of the 1973 Act. In the Court of Appeal, three of the companies challenged the decision on the ground there was no jurisdiction to order their property to be conveyed to the wife. The majority of the Court of Appeal agreed and criticised the practice of the Family Division of treating assets of companies substantially owed by one party to a marriage as available for distribution under s 24 of the 1973 Act. The wife appealed to the Supreme Court.The Supreme Court, uniquely comprising seven judges (instead of five), unanimously allowed the appeal by the wife and declared that the seven disputed properties vested in the companies were held on trust for the husband on the ground that, in the particular circumstances of the case, the properties were held by the husband's companies on a resulting trust and were 'property to which the [husband] is entitled, either in possession, or reversion'. The Supreme Court addressed the concept of 'piercing the corporate veil' and the very limited circumstances in which it could apply under English law. The Court did not see the need to apply this concept in the present case, but instead applied the resulting trust concept to allow the wife's appeal. The leading judgment was given by Lord Sumption with Lord Neuberger's analysis of piercing the corporate veil.

Starting point – upholding the corporate personality principle

The starting point for analysis of piercing the veil concept was to consider the general proposition that subject to very limited circumstances (most of which were statutory), a company was a legal entity distinct from its shareholders. It had rights and liabilities of its own which were distinct from those of its shareholders. Its property was its own, and not that of its shareholders: *Salomon v A Salomon and Co Ltd* [1897] AC 22; *Macaura v Northern Assurance Co Ltd* [1925] AC 619; *Lonrho Ltd v Shell Petroleum Co Ltd* [1980] 1 WLR 627. In this regard, the Supreme Court reinforced the separate legal personality of the company which was distinct from its shareholders. The separate personality and property of a company was sometimes described as a 'fiction' but this fiction was the whole foundation of English company and insolvency law: *Bank of Tokyo Ltd v Karoon (Note)*

[1987] AC 45. Companies were both legally and economically fundamental for conducting business with third parties.

Possible legal bases for satisfying lump sum order against husband

Lord Sumption considered three possible legal bases on which the assets of the companies might be available to satisfy the lump sum order against the husband:

(1) that this is a case where, exceptionally, the court may disregard the corporate veil in order to give effective relief ('piercing the corporate veil'); or

(2) that s 24 of the 1973 Act conferred a distinct power to disregard the corporate veil in matrimonial cases ('MCA 1973, s 24'); or

(3) that the companies held the properties on trust for the husband, not by virtue of his status as sole shareholder and controller of the company, but in the particular circumstances of the case ('beneficial ownership of assets').

Piercing the corporate veil

The Supreme Court addressed the concept of piercing the corporate veil in the context of matrimonial proceedings. However, the judgments are of general application to other contexts where the term piercing the corporate veil has been used.

Defining the concept of piercing the corporate veil

Lord Sumption considered that the term 'piercing the veil' had been used indiscriminately to describe a number of different aspects. The proper use of the term referred to disregarding the separate personality of the company.

According to Lord Sumption, there were a range of situations in which the law attributed the acts or property of a company to those who controlled it, without disregarding its separate legal personality. The controller may be personally liable, generally in addition to the company, for something that he had done as its agent or as a joint actor. Property legally vested in a company may belong beneficially to the controller, if the arrangements in relation to the property were such as to make the company its controller's nominee or trustee for that purpose. For specific statutory purposes, a company's legal responsibility may be engaged by the acts or business of an associated company, for example, the provisions of the Companies Acts governing group accounts or the rules governing infringements of competition law by 'firms', which may include groups of companies conducting the relevant business as an economic unit. Equitable remedies, such as an injunction or specific performance may be available to compel the controller whose personal legal responsibility was engaged to exercise his control in a particular way. However, the term 'piercing the corporate veil' should not be applied nor attributed to such situations, but only of those cases which were true exceptions to the rule in *Salomon v A Salomon and Co Ltd* [1897] AC 22, ie where a person who owned and controlled a company was said in certain circumstances to be identified with it in law by virtue of that ownership and control.

Limited circumstances for piercing the corporate veil

The Supreme Court decided that there was a principle of English law which enabled a court in very limited circumstances to pierce the corporate veil. It applied when a person was under an existing legal obligation or liability, or subject to an existing legal restriction which he deliberately evaded or whose enforcement he deliberately frustrated by interposing a company under his control. The court may then pierce the corporate veil but only for the purpose of depriving the company or its controller of the advantage which they would otherwise have obtained by the company's separate legal personality. The principle should be used as a last resort. In most cases the facts necessary to establish this would disclose a legal relationship between the company and its controller giving rise to legal or equitable rights of the controller over the company's property, thus making it unnecessary to pierce the veil. In these cases, there was no public policy imperative justifying piercing the corporate veil. But the recognition of a small residual category of cases where the abuse of the corporate veil to evade or frustrate the law could be addressed only by disregarding the legal personality of the company was consistent with authority and long-standing principles of legal policy. The principle had no application in Prest because the husband's actions did not evade or frustrate any legal obligation to his wife, nor was he concealing or evading the law in relation to the distribution of assets of the marriage upon its dissolution.

The Supreme Court rejected the argument that a broader principle of piercing the corporate veil applied in matrimonial proceedings by virtue of s 24(1)(a) of the 1973 Act. The section invoked concepts of the law of property with an established legal meaning which could not be suspended or taken to mean something different in matrimonial proceedings. Nothing in the statutory history or wording of the 1973 Act suggested otherwise. General words in a statute were not to be read in a manner inconsistent with fundamental principles of law unless this result was required by express words or necessary implication. The trial judge's reasoning cut across the statutory scheme of company and insolvency law which were essential for protecting those dealing with companies.

It followed that the only basis on which the companies could be ordered to convey properties to the wife was that they belonged beneficially to the husband, by virtue of the particular circumstances in which the properties came to be vested in them. After examining the relevant findings about the acquisition of the seven disputed properties, the Supreme Court found that the most plausible inference from the known facts was that each of the properties was held on resulting trust by the companies for the husband. The trial judge found that the husband had deliberately sought to conceal the fact in his evidence and failed to comply with court orders with particular regard to disclosing evidence. Adverse influences could therefore be drawn against him. The Court inferred that the reason for the companies' failure to co-operate was to protect the properties, which suggested that proper disclosure would reveal them to beneficially owned by the husband. It followed that there was no reliable evidence to rebut the most plausible inference from the facts.

Having considered the various authorities, Lord Sumption stated that the considerations in the cases examined reflected the broad principle that the corporate veil may be pierced only to prevent the abuse of corporate legal personality. It may be an abuse of the separate legal personality of a company to use it to evade the law or to frustrate its enforcement. However, it was not an abuse to cause a legal liability to be incurred in the first place. It was not an abuse to rely upon the fact that a liability was not the controllers because it was the company's.

The 'concealment' and 'evasion' principles

According to Lord Sumption, the main difficulty was to identify what was the relevant wrongdoing.

It was not appropriate to make references to terms such as 'facade' or 'sham' as these terms would lead to more questions being asked than to resolve the matter. His Lordship considered that two distinct principles lay behind these 'protean terms' and that much confusion has been caused by failing to distinguish between them namely: (i) the 'concealment principle'; and (ii) the 'evasion principle'.

The 'concealment' principle was legally banal and did not involve piercing the veil. It was concerned with the interposition of a company or several companies so as to conceal the identity of the real actors, but this would not deter the courts from identifying them, assuming that their identity was legally relevant. In such cases, the court was not disregarding the 'facade', but only looking behind it to discover the facts which the corporate structure was concealing.

Under the 'evasion' principle, the court may disregard the corporate veil if there was a legal right against the person in control of it which existed independently of the person's involvement, and a company was interposed so that the separate legal personality of the company will defeat the right or frustrate its enforcement. According to Lord Sumption, some cases may fall into both the concealment and evasion principles, and in some circumstances, the difference between them may be critical. Cases such as *Guildford Motor Co Ltd v Horne* [1933] Ch 935 and *Jones v Lipman* [1962] 1 All ER 442 displayed characteristics of the evasion principle. *Gencor ACP Ltd v Dalby* [2000] 2 BCLC 734 and *Trustor AB v Smallbone (No 2)* [2001] 3 All ER 987, represented the concealment principle. These considerations reflected the broader principle that the corporate veil may be pierced only to prevent the abuse of corporate legal personality. It may be an abuse of the separate legal personality of a company to use it to evade the law or to frustrate its enforcement. It was not an abuse to cause a legal liability to be incurred by the company in the first place. It was not an abuse to rely upon the fact that a liability was not the controller's because it was the company's.

Lord Sumption concluded that there was a limited principle of English law which applied when a person was under an existing legal obligation or liability subject to an existing legal restriction, which he deliberately evaded or whose enforcement he deliberately frustrated by interposing a company under his control. The court may then pierce the corporate veil for the purpose, and only for the purpose, of depriving the company or its controller of the advantage that they would otherwise have obtained by the company's separate legal personality. The principle was properly described as a limited one, because in almost every case where the test was satisfied, the facts would in practice disclose a legal relationship between the company and its controller which would make it unnecessary to pierce the corporate veil. He further added:

'I consider that if it is not necessary to pierce the corporate veil, it is not appropriate to do so, because on that footing there is no public policy imperative which justifies that course… But the recognition of a small residual category of cases where the abuse of the corporate veil to evade or frustrate the law can be addressed only by disregarding the legal personality of the company is, I believe, consistent with authority and with long-standing principles of legal policy'.

Matrimonial Causes Act 1973, s 24(1)(a)

Lord Sumption stated that if there was no justification as a matter of general legal principle for piercing the corporate veil, it was impossible to say that a special and wider principle applied in matrimonial proceedings by virtue of s 24(1)(a) of the Matrimonial Causes Act 1973 ('MCA 1973'). The language of this provision was clear. It empowered the court to order one party to the marriage to transfer to the other 'property to which the first-mentioned party is entitled, either in possession or reversion'. An 'entitlement' was a legal right in respect of the property in question. The words 'in possession or reversion' showed that the right in question was a proprietary right, legal or equitable. This section invoked concepts with an established legal meaning and recognised legal incidents under the general law. Courts exercising family jurisdiction did not occupy a desert island in which general legal concepts were suspended or mean something different. If a right of property existed, it existed in every division of the High Court and in every jurisdiction of the county courts. If it did not exist, it did not exist anywhere. It was right to add that even where courts exercising family jurisdiction had claimed a wider jurisdiction to pierce the corporate veil than would be recognised under the general law, they had not usually suggested that this could be founded on MCA 1973, s 24. On the contrary, in *Nicholas v Nicholas [1984]* FLR 285, 288, Cumming-Bruce LJ said that it could not.

Section 24 of MCA 1973 did not allow a judge to transfer the companies' assets to the wife on the basis that the husband was the owner and controller of the company. The companies had not consented to the transfer and had opposed any such transfer to the wife. Accordingly, s 24 was not the appropriate basis in the circumstances where the properties were vested in the companies to transfer them to the wife.

Beneficial ownership of the properties

Lord Sumption decided that the only basis on which the companies could be ordered to convey the seven disputed properties to the wife was that they belonged beneficially to the husband, by virtue of the particular circumstances in which the properties came to be vested in them. Only then would they constitute property to which the husband was 'entitled, either in possession or reversion'.

The court will have regard to evidence and facts including presumptions that could be made against the party who controlled the companies which held the properties. In doing so, the court can draw inferences from the facts, take judicial notice, make inferences from the actions or inactions of a party including adverse inferences: *British Railways Board v Herrington* [1972] AC 877, per Lord Diplock; *R v Inland Revenue Commissioners, Ex P TC Coombs & Co* [1991] 2 AC 283.

Whether assets legally vested in a company were beneficially owned by its controller was a highly fact-specific issue. It was not possible to give general guidance going beyond the ordinary principles and presumptions of equity, especially those relating to gifts and resulting trusts. However, in the case of the matrimonial home, the facts were quite likely to justify the inference that the property was held on trust for a spouse who owned and controlled the company. In most cases, the occupation of the company's property as the matrimonial home of its controller would not be easily justified in the company's interest, especially if it was gratuitous. The intention would normally be that the spouse in control of the company intended to retain a degree of control over the matrimonial home which was not consistent with the company's beneficial ownership. Structures could be devised which gave a different impression, and some of them would be entirely genuine. But where the terms of acquisition and occupation of the matrimonial home were arranged between the husband in his personal capacity and the husband in his capacity as the sole effective agent of the company (or someone else acting at his direction), judges exercising family jurisdiction were entitled to be sceptical about whether the terms of occupation were really what they were said to be, or are simply a sham to conceal the reality of the husband's beneficial ownership.

Accordingly, the properties vested in the companies were held on a resulting trust for the husband.

Lord Neuberger stated that there were two types of case where judges have described their decisions as being based on piercing the veil: first, those concerned with concealment; and second, those concerned with evasion: see *Atlas Maritime Co SA v Avalon Maritime Ltd (No 1)* [1999] 4 All ER 769 where Staughton LJ sought to distinguish between 'lifting' and 'piercing' the corporate veil. The cases concerned with the concealment principle did not involve piercing the corporate veil: they simply involved the application of conventional legal principles to an arrangement which happened to include a company being interposed to disguise the true nature of that arrangement. Accordingly, if piercing the corporate veil had any role to play, it was in connection with the evasion principle.

Further, if the court had power to pierce the corporate veil, it could only do so in favour of a party when all other, more conventional, remedies had proved to be of no assistance: See *Ben Hashem v Al Shayif* [2009] 1 FLR 115 per Munby J.

According to Lord Neuberger, it was also clear from the cases that the law relating to piercing the corporate veil principle was unsatisfactory and confused. Those cases suggested that: (i) there was not a single instance in this jurisdiction where the doctrine has been invoked properly and successfully; (ii) there was doubt as to whether the doctrine should exist; and (iii) it was impossible to discern any coherent approach, applicable principles, or defined limitations to the doctrine.

His Lordship was of the view that the starting point of any discussion about the doctrine must begin with the decision in *Salomon v A Salomon and Co Ltd* [1897] AC 22, in which a unanimous House of Lords reached a clear and principled decision, which has stood unimpeached for over a century. The effect of the decision was encapsulated at pp 30–31, where Lord Halsbury LC said that a 'legally incorporated' company 'must be treated like any other independent person with its rights and liabilities appropriate to itself …, whatever may have been the ideas or schemes of those who brought it into existence'. Whether that is characterised as a common law rule or a consequence of the companies legislation (or an amalgam of both), it is a very well established principle of long standing and high authority.

Lord Neubeger stated that the decision in *Salomon* plainly represented a substantial obstacle in the way of an argument that the veil of incorporation can be pierced. Further, the importance of maintaining clarity and simplicity in this area of law meant that, if the doctrine was to exist, the circumstances in which it could apply must be limited and as clear as possible.

Since the decision in *Salomon*, there have been a number of cases where the courts have considered 'piercing' or 'lifting' the corporate veil. Lord Neuberger summarised the position as follows:

- The decision of the International Court of Justice in *In re Barcelona Traction, Light and Power Co, Ltd* [1970] ICJ 3 recognised the doctrine; however, that is in the context of a civil law system which included the principle of abuse of rights, and begs the question whether, in a common law system, the doctrine should be applicable by the courts in the absence of specific legislative sanction.

- There were judgments in family cases based on *obiter dicta* in *Nicholas v Nicholas* [1984] FLR 285 (eg the judgments of Thorpe LJ in this case and of Mostyn J in *Kremen v Agrest (No 2)* [2011] 2 FLR 490), where the doctrine had been treated as valid and applicable; but the application of the doctrine, even if it existed, in these cases was unsound, as Munby J effectively (in both senses of the word) indicated in *A v A* [2007] 2 FLR 467 and *Ben Hashem* [2009] 1 FLR 115.

- There were two cases outside the family law context which laid the ground for the establishment of the doctrine, namely the decisions of the Court of Appeal in *Gilford Motor Co Ltd v Horne* [1933] Ch 935, and of Russell J in *Jones v Lipman* [1962] 1 WLR 832. Lord Neuberger was of the view that these cases did not provide much support for the doctrine. However, the decisions could fairly be said to have rested on the doctrine if the language of the judgments were taken at face value. These cases also indicated that where a court was of the view that there was no other method of achieving justice, the doctrine provided a valuable means of doing so. Lord Neuberger thought that the courts had mistaken applied the principle of piercing the corporate veil.

- There were two subsequent decisions, one of the House of Lords, *Woolfson v Strathclyde Regional Council* 1978 SC(HL) 90, the other of the Court of Appeal, *Adams v Cape Industries plc* [1990] Ch 433, in which it was assumed or accepted that the doctrine existed, but they could not amount to more than *obiter* observations, as in neither of them did the doctrine apply.

- In subsequent cases in the Court of Appeal and High Court, it had been (unsurprisingly) assumed that the doctrine did apply, two examples being the

Court of Appeal decisions in *VTB* [2012] 2 Lloyd's Rep 313 and *Alliance Bank JSC v Aquanta Corpn* [2013] 1 Lloyd's Rep 175. However, the Supreme Court decision in *VTB Capital Plc v Nutritek International Corp* [2013] UKSC 5 rejected an extension of the principle of piercing the corporate veil to impose liability on a non-contracting party.

- However, in only two of those subsequent cases (the first instance decisions in *Gencor ACP Ltd v Dalby* [2000] 2 BCLC 734 and *Trustor AB v Smallbone (No 2)* [2001] 1 WLR 1177) had the doctrine actually been relied on, and they each could have been decided the same way without recourse to the doctrine, and therefore involved illegitimate applications of the doctrine on any view.

According to Lord Neubeger, the history of the principle of piercing the corporate veil over 80 years of its life is a result of a series of decisions, each of which could be put into one of three categories:

'i. Decisions in which it was assumed that the doctrine existed, but it was rightly concluded that it did not apply on the facts;

ii. Decisions in which it was assumed that the doctrine existed, and it was wrongly concluded that it applied on the facts;

iii. Decisions in which it was assumed that the doctrine existed and it was applied to the facts, but where the result could have been arrived at on some other, conventional, legal basis, and therefore it was wrongly concluded that it applied.'

Lord Neuberger considered that the doctrine still had a role to play in law and should not be discarded. The doctrine still represented an important legal tool that may be invoked in some wrongdoing cases or where no other principles of law were available to address the issue. He considered that the piercing the veil doctrine should only be invoked where 'a person was under an existing legal obligation or liability or subject to an existing legal restriction which he deliberately evades or whose enforcement he deliberately frustrates by interposing a company under his control'.

Lady Hale (with whom Lord Wilson agreed) agreed that the wife's appeal should succeed on the basis that the properties in question were held by the respondent companies on trust for the husband. As the husband was beneficially entitled to the properties, they fell within the court's power to make a transfer of property orders under s 24(1)(a) Matrimonial Causes Act 1973. Therefore, the court had the power to order that the companies, as bare trustees, to transfer the properties to the wife.

Lady Hale's judgment addressed specific issues arising under the Matrimonial Causes Act 1973 by emphasizing the special nature of proceedings for financial relief and property adjustment orders. There was a public interest in spouses making proper provision for one another, both during and after their marriage, especially when there were children to be cared for and educated: *Miller v Miller* [2006] 2 AC 618. The court's role was an inquisitorial one, and the parties had a duty not only to one another, but also to the court to make a full and frank disclosure of all the material facts which were relevant to the excerice of the court's powers and their resources: *Livesey (formerly Jenkins) v Jenkins* [1985] AC 424. If they did not do so, the court was entitled to draw inferences from the available material, including what has been disclosed, judicial experience of what is likely to be concealed and the inherent probabilities, in deciding what are the facts.

Section 24(1)(a) of the MCA 1973 did not suggest that it was Parliament's intention to grant to the divorce courts an express power to pierce the corporate veil in such a way as to treat property belonging to a limited company as property belonging to the spouse who owns and/or controls the company. However, in such situations, the issue was whether the courts had the power to prevent the statutes under which limited liability companies may be established as separate legal persons, being used as an engine of fraud: *R v Secretary of State for the Home Department, ex parte Puttick* [1981] QB 767. Earlier attempts at first instance and Court of Appeal to disregard the separate personality of the company failed in the House of Lords decision *Salomon v A Salomon and Co Ltd*; and that no fraud was involved in using a limited liability company as a vehicle for conducting a legitimate business.

However, Lady Hale was not convinced whether it was possible to classify previous cases addressing piercing the corporate veil neatly into cases of either concealment or evasion:

> 'They may simply be examples of the principle that the individuals who operate limited companies should not be allowed to take unconscionable advantage of the people with whom they do business. But what the cases do have in common is that the separate legal personality is being disregarded in order to obtain a remedy against someone other than the company in respect of a liability which would otherwise be that of the company alone (if it existed at all). In the converse case, where it is sought to convert the personal liability of the owner or controller into a liability of the company, it is usually more appropriate to rely on the concepts of agency and of the 'directing mind'.

Lord Mance agreed with the decisions of Lords Sumption and Neubeger. Although Lord Mance considered the rationalisation made by Lord Sumption of previous cases falling either within the evasion or concealment principles, he cautioned against compartmentalising future cases under these principles without reference to further developments in the law.

> 'It is however often dangerous to seek to foreclose all possible future situations which may arise and I would not wish to do so. What can be said with confidence is that the strength of the principle in Salomon's case and the number of other tools which the law has available mean that, if there are other situations in which piercing the veil may be relevant as a final fall-back, they are likely to be novel and very rare'.

However, according to Lord Mance it may not be easy in the future to develop any further exceptions to the evasion principle set out by Lord Sumption as exceptions to piercing the corporate veil.

Lord Clarke agreed with Lord Sumption. He was of the view that the principle of piercing the corporate veil existed in English company law but its limits had not been clear. He agreed with Munby J's reasoning in *Ben Hashem v Al Shayif* [2009] to the effect that the court only had power to pierce the corporate veil when all the other more conventional remedies had proved to be of no assistance. Lord Clarke thought that the principle would most likely be deployed in a very rare case – perhaps in evasion type situations and not concealment. However, Lord Clarke cautioned that this distinction between the evasion and concealment principles should not be definitively adopted unless and until the court has heard detailed submissions upon it. It would be dangerous to foreclose all possible future situations which may arise and any possible exceptions in the future should be left open for the court to decide. He agreed also with Lord Walker that the situations in which piercing the corporate veil may be available as a fall-back were likely to be very rare and no one should be encouraged to think that any further exception in addition to the evasion principle will be easy to establish.

Lord Walker agreed with Lord Sumption relating to the beneficial ownership of the London properties held by Mr Prest based on the positive evidence of the sources from which the properties were funded. Lord Walker did not add further to the debate on the 'vexed question' of piercing the corporate veil. He thought that the concept of 'piercing the corporate veil' was not a doctrine at all in the sense of a coherent principle or rule of law: 'it is simply a label – often …used indiscriminately – to describe the disparate occasions on which some rule of law produces apparent exceptions to the principle of the separate juristic personality of a body corporate reaffirmed by the House of Lords in *Salomon v A Salomon and Co Ltd* [1897] AC 22'.

The court could order assets in the name of the company to be transferred to the other spouse on the basis that the assets were held by the husband by way of a resulting trust

Following the *Prest* decision, in *M v M* [2013] All ER 133, King J held that whether assets legally vested in a company were beneficially owned by its controller was a highly fact-specific issue. The court had to search for evidence of the subjective intention of the transferor or evidence of actual intention. In determining the intention of the parties, the court might, where appropriate, draw adverse inferences against the parties, either in respect of their failure to give or call evidence to rebut the presumption, or by their failure to make proper disclosure within the proceedings. Only in the absence of evidence of intention would the law of presumption apply, which presumption would be easily rebutted by evidence of the transferor's intention to make an outright transfer.

Where the company in whose name the property in question was held was owned by the same individual who asserted he had retained the beneficial interest by virtue of a resulting trust, there was less room for such a resulting trust to be established by a presumption in the absence of evidence of intention. However, the burden remained on the transferee to rebut the presumption, and positive evidence of the source from which the purchases were funded established the ordinary inference that the provider of the funds was the beneficial owner of the property absent any evidence to rebut that ordinary presumption of equity. In the case of the matrimonial home, the facts were likely to justify the inference that the property was held on trust for a spouse who owned and controlled the company (see [210] of the judgment).

In the present case, the husband was a shadow director and at all times the directing mind of each of the companies. He and he alone had made each and every decision in relation to the purchase and operation of the companies, and the directors whom from time to time had been put in place were acquiescent employees or family members who would have had neither the skill nor the knowledge to carry out any of the duties of a company director. Adverse findings could be drawn against the husband by virtue of his failure to comply with orders to provide disclosure, his failure to attend court to give evidence, and his silence in the face of the case against him. Adverse findings could also be drawn against the companies. Having drawn such adverse inferences as were appropriate against the backdrop of the wilful lack of disclosure and engagement by the husband and the companies, there was no difficulty in concluding that the inherent probabilities were that the husband, and the companies that he controlled, had throughout been endeavouring to defeat the claims of the wife. In particular, they had sought to disguise the fact that the husband had retained the beneficial interest in the UK properties. It was no coincidence that those were the only assets in respect of which the wife would have had little difficulty in enforcing any order of the court. The husband's actions in relation to the properties was at all times that of a beneficial owner. At all times he had intended to retain the beneficial interest in the UK properties and the only reason the companies had, on the husband's direction, failed to co-operate in the instant proceedings was because proper disclosure of documents or exposure of the directors to cross-examination would very quickly have revealed that the properties concerned had at all times been held beneficially by the husband. The court therefore ordered, *inter alia*, that the UK properties be transferred to the wife, the release to the wife of the husband's share of the balance of the proceeds of the family matrimonial home, and the payment by the husband to the wife of a lump sum.

However, see *Smith v Bottomley* [2013] EWCA Civ 953.

Based on the concealment principle established in Prest, directors were liable for breaches of their fiduciary duties towards the company and it was not appropriate to apply the evasion principle

In *Pennyfeathers Ltd v Pennyfeathers Property Co Ltd* [2013] EWHC 3530, a claim arose out of a large plot of land being a farm ('Farm'). Pennyfeathers UK was established by the second and third claimants Mr Steer and Mr Taylor to exploit the opportunity to develop the Farm. The claimants allege that the second and third defendants (Mr Bowdery and Mr Attwell) who were then directors of Pennyfeathers UK breached their fiduciary duties towards Pennyfeathers UK by causing Pennyfeathers Jersey (first defendant) to contract with the Farm's owners on terms which were in their own interests and not the interests of Pennyfeathers UK, and entering into options over land surrounding the Farm when those options should have been acquired by Pennyfeathers UK.

Rose J held that the company directors were liable for breach of their fiduciary duty on the basis that they diverted a corporate opportunity to themselves in circumstances where it could not be said that there was any informed consent by the shareholders. The directors had also acted in bad faith towards the shareholders. This was not a case concerning the evasion principle, only the concealment principle applied and therefore it was not necessary to pierce the corporate veil.

Attribution of liability to a non-contracting party

4.106 The Supreme Court has considered the position of whether the doctrine of lifting the corporate veil could be extended to attribute liability to a non-contracting party.

The principle of piercing the corporate veil cannot be extended to attribute liability to a non-contracting party

In one of the leading cases on piercing the corporate veil, *VTB Capital plc v Nutritek International Corp* [2013] 1 BCLC 179, VTB was a bank established in England and was a subsidiary of a Russian bank. It lent about $225 million to a Russian company, RAP to finance the purchase of some dairy companies and associated companies in Russia from Nutritek which was a British Virgin Islands company owned by two Russian companies. The loan was set out in a facility agreement and governed by English law. Although RAP made some payments on the loan, it defaulted subsequently leaving VTB with a security of no more than $40 million.

Proceedings were issued by VTB in England for damages for deceit and/or conspiracy against Nutritek. VTB's contention was that the dairy companies were significantly overvalued based on information provided by Nutritek's management, and that VTB was induced to enter into the loan by fraudulent misrepresentations made by Nutritek as to the value of the dairy companies. VTB sought to amend the claim to add a claim in contract against a controlling shareholder of RAP for breach of the facility, even though he was not a party to the agreement and that the court should 'pierce the corporate veil of RAP' to impose liability on him under two contracts together with RAP. One of the principal issues in this case was whether the principle of piercing the corporate veil could be extended to impose liability on a person who controlled the company, as if he had been a co-contracting party with the company concerned, but where the company was in actual reality the party to the contract, and not the person controlling the company? In this case, VTB sought to pierce RAP's corporate veil to impose personal liability on RAP's controlling shareholder.

The trial judge refused to allow VTB to amend its claim to plead the contract claim on the grounds that the corporate veil of the company could not be pierced to support a claim for damages for breach of contract. The Court of Appeal upheld the trial judge's decision not to pierce the corporate veil in order to permit a claim in contract to proceed. The Supreme Court held that the principle of piercing the veil of incorporation could not be extended to hold that a person controlling the company was liable as if he had been a co-contracting party with the company concerned, to a contract to which the company was a party but he was not. To do so would be contrary to a fundamental principle on which the contractual liabilities and rights were based, namely what would an objective reasonable observer believe was the effect of what the parties to the contract, or alleged contract, communicated to each other by words and actions, as assessed in their context: see *Smith v Hughes* (1871) LR 6 QB 597.

Further, even where a person could be identified as controlling the respondent companies, he could not be held liable as if he was a co-contracting party to the facility or other agreements, since: (i) at the time the agreements were entered into, none of the actual parties to the agreements had intended to contract with the controlling shareholder and he did not intend to contract with them; and (ii) thereafter, he never conducted himself as if, or led any other party to believe, he was liable under the agreements.

The leading judgment on piercing the corporate veil was given by Lord Neuberger (whose opinion was shared by Lords Mance, Reed, Clarke and Wilson). He observed that early attempts to pierce the corporate veil were unanimously rejected by the Supreme Court in *Salomon v Salomon & Co Ltd* [1897] AC 22. Further, the decision of the Supreme Court in *Woolfson v Strathclyde Regional Council* 1978 SC (HL) 90, to refuse to pierce the corporate veil on the facts unless 'special circumstances' existed had made further judicial inroads in limiting the circumstances when the corporate veil could be pierced. Lord Neuberger further stated:

> 'There is obvious attraction in the proposition that the court can pierce the veil of incorporation on appropriate facts, in order to achieve a just result … The brief discussion of the principle in *Woolfson* does not justify the contention that it was somehow affirmed or approved by the House: Lord Keith's remarks were *obiter*, and the power of the court to pierce the corporate veil does not appear to have been in issue in that case. The most that can be said about *Woolfson* from the perspective of VTB is that the House was prepared to assume that the power existed.
>
> The notion that there is no principled basis upon which it can be said that one can pierce the veil of incorporation receives some support from the fact that the precise nature, basis and meaning of the principle are all somewhat obscure, as are the precise nature of circumstances in which

the principle can apply. Clarke J in *The Tjaskemolen* [1997] 2 Lloyd's Rep 465 at 471 rightly said that "[t]he cases have not worked out what is meant by 'piercing the corporate veil'. It may not always mean the same thing" (and to the same effect, see *Palmer's Company Law* para 2.1533). Munby J in *Ben Hashem v Ali Shayif* seems to have seen the principle as a remedial one, whereas Sir Andrew Morritt V-C in *Trustor AB v Smallbone* [2001] 2 BCLC 436, [2001] 3 All ER 987, [2001] 1 WLR 1177 appears to have treated the principle as triggered by the finding of a "façade".

The "façade" mentioned by Lord Keith is often regarded as something of a touchstone in the cases – eg per Munby J in *Ben Hashem* [2009] 1 FLR 115 at [164], and per Sir Andrew Morritt V-C in *Trustor* [2001] 2 BCLC 436 at [23]. Words such as "façade", and other expressions found in the cases, such as "the true facts", "sham", "mask", "cloak", "device", or "puppet" may be useful metaphors. However, such pejorative expressions are often dangerous, as they risk assisting moral indignation to triumph over legal principle, and, while they may enable the court to arrive at a result which seems fair in the case in question, they can also risk causing confusion and uncertainty in the law. The difficulty which Diplock LJ expressed in *Snook v London and West Riding Investments Ltd* [1967] 1 All ER 518 at 528, [1967] 2 QB 786 at 802, as to the precise meaning of "sham" in connection with contracts, may be equally applicable to an expression such as "façade".'

According to Lord Neuberger, there was a case for retaining the principle of piercing the corporate veil in certain circumstances 'in order to defeat injustice', though it is not clear what aspects of 'injustice' are being referred to that would allow for such piercing. It resonates to some extent with cases that have considered piercing the corporate veil in the interests of justice. This suggests a broader category of situations where the court may pierce the corporate veil.

Lord Neuberger considered that it was not appropriate to decide that the court could not pierce the corporate veil because the matter before the court was on an interlocutory appeal, and this issue of major importance could not be decided in this manner. Instead, his Lordship proceeded on the assumption that the court could pierce the corporate veil based on the English law jurisdiction, and proceeded to consider the circumstances whether such a piercing could be justified in VTB's favour. However, Lord Neuberger did not accept VTB's contention that the corporate personality could be pierced, as this would involve an extension to the circumstances where it has traditionally been held that the corporate veil could be pierced, namely to impose liability on a non-contracting party: 'It is an extension because it would lead to the person controlling the company being held liable as if he had been a co-contracting party with the company concerned to a contract where the company was a party and he was not.' The effect would have been to treat a non-contracting party as if he has been a co-contracting party with other companies.

There was no justification for extending the principle of piercing the corporate veil to impose liability on a non-contracting party. Lord Neuberger reasoned as follows: VTB had amended their claim to hold the controlling shareholder 'jointly and severally liable with RAP'. Even accepting that the court could pierce the corporate veil in some circumstances, 'the notion of such joint and several liability was inconsistent with the reasoning and decision in *Salomon v Salomon*: 'A company should be treated as being a person by the law in the same way as a human being. The fact that a company can only act or think through humans does not call that point into question: it just means that the law of agency will always potentially be in play, but, it will, at least normally, be the company which is the principal, not an agent. On VTB's case, if the agency analogy is relevant, the company, as the contracting party, is the quasi-agent, not the quasi-principal'.

Lord Neuberger stated that the facts relied upon by VTB to justify piercing of the corporate veil did not involve RAP being used as 'a facade concealing the true facts.' His Lordship considered that if the corporate veil was to be pierced, 'the true facts' must mean that, in reality, it was the person behind the company, rather than the company, which was the relevant actor or recipient (as the case may be). On the facts, VTB's case as to 'the true facts' related to the control, trading performance, the value of the Dairy companies, and the genuineness of the underlying arrangement involving transfer of assets between companies in common ownership. However, none of these features could be said to involve RAP being used as a facade to conceal the true facts; and added nothing to Lord Keith's characterisation in *Woolfson v Strathclyde*, or it may be an additional requirement before the corporate veil could be pierced.

Checklist

4.107 *This checklist sets out the current law on piercing the corporate veil and practical implications based on the decisions in VTB Capital plc v Nutritek International Corp [2013] 1 BCLC 179 and Prest v Petrodel Resources Ltd [2013] All ER 90 particularly in identifying circumstances when the courts will lift the corporate veil to impose liability, including the consequences of a company's separate legal personality.*

No	Issue	Reference
1	The starting position for the separate legal personality of a company is the Companies Act 2006. A company is a legal entity distinct from its shareholders.	CA 2006, ss 1–5 and 16
2	*Salomon v A Salomon and Co Ltd* legitimised the establishment of 'one-man' companies provided there is compliance with the Companies Acts on registration formalities; and that a company was not an agent for its shareholders.	[1897] AC 22
3	The effect of a separate legal personality is that a company has rights and liabilities of its own; it can sue and be sued; it can enter into contracts	CA 2006, s 16

No	Issue	Reference
4	The separate legal personality also applies to a sole owner and controller of a company, who can contract with his company as an employee	*Macaura v Northern Assurance Co Ltd* [1925] AC 619; *Lee v Lee's Air Farming Limited* [1960] 3 All ER 420
5	Previously, the courts set aside the separate legal personality of a company on the basis of exceptions to the corporate personality principle. This was usually through 'piercing the veil' or lifting the veil of incorporation and has been used in circumstances such as interests of justice; enemy situation; group enterprise; corporate abuse; agency; proceeds of crime; where the company was a sham or facade	
6	However, the term 'piercing the corporate veil' has been used indiscriminately. It means disregarding the separate personality of the company. The circumstances for piercing the corporate veil must be true exceptions to the principle established in *Salomon* namely, where a person owns and controls a company and is identified with it in law by virtue of that ownership and control	*Petrodel Resources Ltd v Prest* [2013] 1 BCLC 30
7	In other jurisdictions, the term 'piercing the corporate veil' has been associated with abuse of rights, misuse, fraud, malfeasance or evasion of legal obligations	*In re Barcelona Traction, Light and Power Co Ltd* [1970] ICJ 3
8	English law has a different approach to piercing the corporate veil. Legal relationships are based on honesty and good faith which can be vitiated where fraud is present. Fraud unravels everything. This principle has been traditionally used in the context of contracts or other consensual arrangements. It has also been applied on grounds of public policy to set aside a public act such as a judgment or the evasion of law was dishonest	*Lazarus Estates Ltd v Beasley* [1956] 1 QB 702 *Duchess of Kingston's Case* (1776) 2 Smith's LC, 13th ed 644; *R v Secretary of State for the Home Department, Ex p Puttick* [1981] QB 767; *Welwyn Hatfield Borough Council v Secretary of State for Communities and Local Government* [2011] 2 AC 304
9	It is appropriate to pierce the corporate veil where special circumstances exist indicating it is a mere facade concealing the true facts	*Woolfson v Strathclyde Regional Council* 1978 SC (HL) 90

No	Issue	Reference
10	The corporate veil could be disregarded only in cases where it was being used for a deliberately dishonest purpose; or the company was a 'facade' or 'sham' or where the company was involved in some impropriety. It did not apply where 'interests of justice' so required	*Adams v Cape Industries plc* [1990] Ch 433 *Trustor AB v Smallbone (No 2)* [2001] 1 WLR 1177
11	Previously in matrimonial cases, the Family Division has on occasions pierced the corporate veil where the company was a one-man company and alter ego of husband; where it was 'just and necessary' to do so; where there was a strong practical reason why the cloak should be penetrable even absent a finding of wrongdoing	*Nicholas v Nicholas* [1984] FLR 285; *Green v Green* [1993] 1 FLR 326; *Mubarak v Mubarak* [2001] 1 FLR 673; *Kremen v Agrest (No 2)* [2001] 2 FLR 490
12	However, other judges in the Family Division had reservations about the application of the doctrine in ancillary relief proceedings and that it only applied where there was a relevant impropriety and control aspects	*A v A* [2007] 2 FLR 467; *Ben Hashem v Al Shayif* [2009] 1 FLR 115; *VTB Capital plc v Nutritek International Corp* [2013] UKSC 5
13	The court may be justified in piercing the corporate veil if the company's separate legal personality is being abused for the purpose of some relevant wrongdoing	*VTB Capital plc v Nutritek International Corp* [2013] 1 BCLC 179
14	The corporate veil may not be pierced to impose liability on a non-contracting party	*Petrodel Resources Ltd v Prest* [2013] 1 BCLC 30
15	A distinction can be made between two principles in determining when the concept of piercing the corporate veil applies: the 'concealment principle' and the 'evasion principle'. The concealment principle does not involve the application of piercing the corporate veil. Under this principle, the company is used to conceal the real actors in the company and the courts can look to see who are these persons to discover the facts which the corporate structure is concealing. The evasion principle allows the court to disregard the corporate veil if there is a legal right against the person in control of it which exists independently of the company's involvement, and a company is interposed so that the separate legal personality of the company will defeat the right or frustrate its enforcement	See *Jones v Lipman* [1962] 1 WLR 832; *Gencor ACP Ltd v Dalby* [2000] 2 BCLC 734; and *Trustor AB v Smallbone (No 2)* [2001] 1 WLR 1177 on the concealment principle See *Gilford Motor Co Ltd v Horne* [1933] Ch 935 on application of the evasion principle

No	Issue	Reference
16	The corporate veil may be pierced only to prevent an abuse of corporate legal personality such as to evade the law or to frustrate its enforcement. It is not an abuse of the law to cause a legal liability to be incurred by the company.	*Nokes v Doncaster Amalgamated Collieries Ltd* [1940] AC 1014 per Lord Atkin; *Multinational Gas & Petrochemical Co v Multinational Gas & Petrochemical Services Ltd* [1983] Ch 258; *Belmont Finance Corp Ltd v Williams Furniture Ltd* [1979] Ch 250; *Attorney-General's Reference (No 2 of 1982)* [1984] QB 624; *Director of Public Prosecutions v Gomez* [1993] AC 422
17	There is a limited principle of English law which applies when a person is under an existing legal obligation or liability or subject to an existing legal restriction which he deliberately evades or whose enforcement he deliberately frustrates by interposing a company under his control. The court may then pierce the corporate veil only for the purpose of depriving the company or its controller of the advantage that they would otherwise have obtained by the company's separate legal personality. It is a limited principle because in almost every case where the test is satisfied, the facts will in practice disclose a legal relationship between the company and its controller which will make it unnecessary to pierce the corporate veil	*Prest v Petrodel Resources Limited* [2013] 1 BCLC 30; *M v M* [2013] All ER 133
18	The doctrine of piercing the corporate veil did not have any special or wider significance in relation to Matrimonial Causes Act 1973, s 24(1)(a). There was nothing in the MCA 1973 and nothing in its purpose or broader social context to indicate that the legislature intended to authorise the transfer by one party to the marriage to the other of property which was not his to transfer. The company must usually consent to any transfer of property. The general statutory words must not be read in a way which 'would overthrow fundamental principles, infringe rights, or depart from the general system of law, without expressing its intention with irresistible clearness'.	

No	Issue	Reference
19	One of the basis on which companies could be ordered to convey properties to the wife is that they belonged beneficially to the husband based on the concept of a resulting trust	

Definitions

4.108

Corporate Personality:	signifies that a company is distinct from its shareholders.
Piercing the corporate veil:	disregarding the separate personality of the company.

5 Formation and registration of a company

Contents

Introduction

5.1 This chapter addresses the formation and registration of both a private and public company under the Companies Act 2006 (as amended by the Small Business, Enterprise and Employment Act 2015 ('SBEEA 2015'). It considers the legal and procedural aspects of establishing these entities. The Companies Act 2006 is fundamentally based on 'think small first approach' with emphasis on deregulation and facilitating the establishment of private limited companies. This aspect is reflected in the incorporation process of private companies and post-incorporation.

5.2 The aim of this chapter is to consider the following:

- the differences between 'off-the-shelf' companies and 'tailor-made' companies;
- how to establish a private company limited by shares or a public limited company;
- how a company can change its registered address;

- the forms and documents required to register a company; and
- checklists on incorporation steps and procedures.

Off-the-shelf companies

5.3 Off-the-shelf companies are companies that have already been established, but typically remain dormant until purchased.

Some of the issues to consider are:

Costs

5.4 It is often cheaper to purchase an off-the-shelf company than one which is specifically formed for the purpose. Costs differ depending upon the incorporation history of the company, including suitability of the name as this type of company will already have a name as evidenced by the certificate of incorporation. However, this should be balanced against the cost and procedures involved in the event that, for example, the name needs to be changed, capital needs to be increased or the articles of association require amendment.

Name

5.5 The company has already been established with a name and is able to function with immediate effect upon purchase. The purchasers of the company may need to change the company name to one suited for their purposes, provided the name is not similar or identical to one already registered at Companies House: see Chapter 8. Also, consideration should be given to any common law actions for passing off in the use of the name.

Articles

5.6 The articles of an off-the-shelf company may not be suitable for the company's internal management and administration. Once purchased, the company's articles of association may require changes with the adoption of model articles or amendment to these articles or the company may wish to draft a new set of articles specifically suited for its purposes: see Chapter 6.

Capital

5.7 The capital clause may need to be amended as the share capital may not be adequate for the company. It may need to be increased.

Registered office

5.8 The company's registered office will need to change as the current registered office of the founding shareholders will not suffice. Accordingly, Companies House will need to be notified: see section 5.14 below.

Director's residential addresses

5.9 The directors' residential addresses will need to be changed, and if required, for such residential addresses not to be disclosed by the registrar to Companies House: see Chapter 13.

Tailor-made company

5.10 A tailor-made company is one which is formed in the very initial stages of setting up a new company. Some of the essential features to consider are:

Name

5.11 The name will be selected by promoters provided it is not similar to or identical to one already registered at Companies House. The selected name may be suited to the company's activities. Consideration should also be given to any common law actions for passing off.

Articles

5.12 These can be specifically tailored to the needs and requirements of the promoters, or it may adopt the Model Articles or a combination of such articles and specific articles suited for the company's particular purposes.

Cost

5.13 It will cost more to form a tailor-made company than an off-the-shelf company because of the specific requirements of the company's promoters which require adaptation.

Registered office

5.14 The promoters will select their own registered office for receipt of correspondence and notices.

Capital

5.15 The promoters will determine the amount of capital best suited to the company's operations.

Time

5.16 It will take longer to form a tailor-made company depending upon complexities involved in the articles of association and any other factors that may delay the company formation.

Purposes of the company

5.17 A company cannot be formed for an 'unlawful purpose': CA 2006, s 7(2). The term 'unlawful purpose' is not defined. However, case law provides some guidance.

An 'unlawful purpose' is one which is contrary to the general law or illegal

In *R v Registrar of Joint Stock Companies, ex parte More* [1931] 2 KB 197, an Irish group of people sought to incorporate a company whose objects would be to market Irish Sweepstakes Tickets. This activity was lawful in Ireland but not in the UK. The registrar refused to register this company on the grounds that the objects of the company were unlawful or illegal, and the applicants sought judicial review of the registrar's decision.

The Court of Appeal upheld the registrar's decision to refuse to register the company on the basis that the proposed company's activities were not lawful, and that the company was carrying on activities which involved 'an offence against the general law'.

The court will have regard to the purpose and activity carried on by the company under its name

In *R v Registrar of Companies ex parte Bowen* [1914] 2 KB 1611, an order was made against the registrar on the basis that the activity was lawful, and that all the statutory conditions had been complied with by the proposed company and its founders. The registrar was therefore bound to register the company.

In this case, an application was made for the registration, under the Companies Act of a company with the name of 'The United Dental Service, Limited'. One of the objects of the company was 'to carry on the practice, profession, or business of practitioners in dentistry in all its branches', which it was intended to carry on by practitioners not registered under the Dentists Act 1878.

It was held by the court that that the use of the proposed name by the company when carrying on business by unregistered practitioners would not constitute an offence under s 3 of the Dentists Act 1878, and that therefore the object of the company was not unlawful. Therefore, the Registrar of Companies had no power to refuse registration upon the ground that the name of the company would be calculated to deceive people into the belief that the business was carried on by registered practitioners. According to Lord Reading CJ, the Registrar has discretion to refuse to register a company which is not formed for a lawful purpose, which would include names that contained 'scandalous' or 'obscene' words.

A company cannot be established if it offends the general law

In *R v Registrar of Joint Stock Companies, ex parte More* [1931] 2KB 197, a group of Irish people sought to incorporate a company whose objects would be to market Irish Sweepstake tickets. This activity was lawful in Ireland but not in the UK. The registrar refused to register this company, and a mandamus was sought by the applicants to overturn the registrar's decision. The Court of Appeal upheld the registrar's decision to refuse to register the company, on the basis that the proposed company's activities were not lawful. According to Greer LJ: 'The question is whether the persons proposing to register the company are persons associated for a lawful purpose.' Slesser LJ stated: 'It is clear that a company cannot be formed whose proposed constitution necessarily involves an offence against the general law.'

The court will have regard to the specific objects of the company to determine whether or not they are lawful

In *Bowman v Secular Society* [1917] AC 406, the Secular Society Ltd, was registered as a company limited by guarantee under the Companies Acts. The main object of the company, as stated in its memorandum of association, was 'to promote … the principle that human conduct should be based upon natural knowledge, and not upon super-natural belief, and that human welfare in this world is the proper end of all thought and action'.

The issue was whether these objects were lawful.

The House of Lords held that assuming that this object involved a denial of Christianity, that it was not criminal, inasmuch as the propagation of anti-Christian doctrines, apart from scurrility or profanity, did not constitute the offence of blasphemy. Further (by Lord Dunedin, Lord Parker of Waddington, Lord Sumner, and Lord Buckmaster; Lord Finlay LC dissenting), that it was not illegal in the sense of rendering the company incapable in law of acquiring property by gift, and that a bequest 'upon trust for the Secular Society Limited' was valid.

The term 'unlawful purpose' would therefore apply to the object, or activities in which the company is engaged. The activities may be considered illegal or contrary to public interest or law or public morals, either upon incorporation or after the company has been established.

The registrar's discretion is, therefore, subject to judicial review. This is the case even where the company has already been registered at Companies House.

A company's objects which are considered sexually immoral by the courts may be illegal and for an unlawful purpose

In *R v Registrar of Companies, ex parte Attorney General* [1991] BCLC 476, the court applied *Bowman v Secular Society* and held that where a company was registered with objects which involved it entering into contracts which were sexually immoral and hence illegal, the court would grant judicial review of the registrar's decision to register the company and would strike it off the register.

In this case, the Attorney General applied to quash the incorporation and registration by the Registrar of Companies in 1979 of Lindi St Claire (Personal Services) Ltd as a limited company under the provisions of the Companies Acts.

The grounds of the application were that in certifying the incorporation of a company and in registering the same, the Registrar of Companies acted *ultra vires* or misdirected himself or otherwise erred in law, in particular as to the proper construction and application of the Companies Act in that the company was not formed for any lawful purpose but, on the contrary, was formed expressly with the primary object of carrying on the business of prostitution (this being an unlawful purpose involving the commission of acts which are immoral and contrary to public policy).

The founders of the company had previously asked the registrar whether the name 'Prostitute Ltd' was available for registration as a limited company, pointing out the main object of the company would be that of organising the services of a prostitute. The registrar did not like that name and did not accept it, nor did he accept another name 'Hookers Ltd' which was offered. But subsequently two further names were offered, 'Lindi St Claire (Personal Services) Ltd' and 'Lindi St Claire (French Lessons) Ltd', and it was the former which the registrar registered. The memorandum of association stated that the objects of the company was 'To carry on the business of prostitution'. The Court of Appeal held that the association was for the purpose of carrying on a trade which involved illegal contracts because the purpose was a sexually immoral purpose and as such against public policy.

According to Ackner LJ, a contract which was made upon a sexually immoral consideration or for a sexually immoral purpose was against public policy and was illegal and unenforceable. The fact that it did not involve or may not involve the commission of a criminal offence in did not prevent the contract being illegal, being against public policy and therefore being unenforceable.

Registration documents

5.18 The memorandum of association must be delivered to the Registrar together with an application for registration of the company, the documents required by this section and a statement of compliance: CA 2006, s 9(1).

The application for registration must state:

(a) the company's proposed name;

(b) whether the company's registered office is to be situated in England and Wales (or in Wales), in Scotland or in Northern Ireland;

(c) whether the liability of the members of the company is to be limited, and if so whether it is to be limited by shares or by guarantee; and

(d) whether the company is to be a private or a public company: CA 2006, s 9(2).

If the application is delivered by a person as agent for the subscribers to the memorandum of association, it must state his name and address: CA 2006, s 9(3).

5.19 The application must contain:

(a) in the case of a company that is to have a share capital, a statement of capital and initial shareholdings (see s 10): CA 2006, s 9(4);

(b) in the case of a company that is to be limited by guarantee, a statement of guarantee (see s 11);

(c) a statement of the company's proposed officers (see s 12): CA 2006, s 9(5);

(d) a statement of initial significant control: CA 2006, s 9(4)(d) (as inserted by SBEEA 2015, Sch 3, Pt 2).

5.20 The application must also contain:

(a) a statement of the intended address of the company's registered office;

(b) a copy of any proposed articles of association (to the extent that these are not supplied by the default application of model articles: see s 20); and

(c) a statement of the type of company it is to be and its intended principal business activities: CA 2006, s 9(5) (as inserted by the SBEEA 2015, s 93).

5.21 The information as to the company's type must be given by reference to the classification scheme prescribed for the purposes of CA 2006, s 5: CA 2006, s 9(5A) (as inserted by SBEEA 2015, s 93).

The information as to the company's intended principal business activities may be given by reference to one or more categories of any prescribed system of classifying business activities: CA 2006, s 9(5B) (as inserted by the SBEEA 2015, s 93).

5.22 The application must be delivered:

(a) to the Registrar of Companies for England and Wales, if the registered office of the company is to be situated in England and Wales (or in Wales);

(b) to the Registrar of Companies for Scotland, if the registered office of the company is to be situated in Scotland;

(c) to the Registrar of Companies for Northern Ireland, if the registered office of the company is to be situated in Northern Ireland: s.9(6) CA 2006.

Statement of capital and initial shareholdings

5.23 SBEEA 2015, Sch 6 amends the CA 2006 to alter the content of statements of capital required under various provisions of that Act: SBEEA 2015, s 97.

Where a company is to have a share capital, a statement of capital and initial shareholdings is required to be delivered to the registrar. The statement must set one of the following details: CA 2006, s 10(1):

- the total number of shares of the company to be taken on formation by the subscribers to the memorandum of association;
- the aggregate nominal value of those shares;
- the aggregate amount (if any) to be unpaid on those shares (whether on account of their nominal value or by way of premium); and
- for each class of shares:

  (i) the prescribed particulars of the rights attached to the shares;

  (ii) the total number of shares that class;

  (iii) the aggregate nominal value of the shares that class: CA 2006, s 10(2) (as inserted by SBEEA 2015, Sch 6);
- such information as may be prescribed for the purpose of identifying the subscribers to the memorandum of association: CA 2006, s 10(3).

5.24 With respect to each subscriber to the memorandum of association, the statement must also contain the following details:

- The number, nominal value (of each share) and class of shares to be taken by him on formation. Further, where the subscriber to the memorandum of association is to take shares of more than one class, the information that is required (as to the number, nominal value and class of shares), for each class of shares, CA 2006, s 10(4).
- The amount to be paid up and the amount of (if any) to be unpaid on each share (whether on account of the nominal value of the share or by way of premium): CA 2006, s 10(3).

Statement of guarantee

5.25 A statement of guarantee is required to be delivered to the registrar for a company limited by guarantee: CA 2006, s 11(1).

The statement must provide such information as may be prescribed for the purposes of identifying the subscribers to the memorandum of association – this includes: the names and addresses of the subscribers to the memorandum of association.

It must also state that each member undertakes that, if the company is wound up while he is a member, or within one year after he ceases to be a member, he will contribute to the assets of the company such amounts as may be required for the following:

(i) payment of the debts and liabilities of the company contracted before he ceases to be a member:

(ii) payment of the costs, charges and expenses of winding up; and

(iii) adjustment of the rights of the contributories among themselves,

not exceeding a specified amount: CA 2006, s.11(3).

Statement of proposed officers

5.26 The statement of proposed officers of the company which is required to be delivered to the registrar must contain the required particulars of the following: CA 2006, s 12(1):

- the person who is, or persons who are, to be the first director or directors of the company;
- where a company is to be a private company, any person who is (or the persons who are) to be the first secretary (or joint secretary) of the company;
- where the company is to be a public company, the person who is (or the persons who are) to be the first secretary (or joint secretaries) of the company).

5.27 References to 'required particulars' are to the required particulars that will be required (or in the absence of an election under ss167A or 279A, would be required) in the company's register of directors and register of directors' residential addresses (see CA 2006, ss 162–166) or, as the case may be for a secretary, its register of secretaries (see CA 2006, ss 277–279): CA 2006, s12(2) (as inserted by the SBEEA 2015, Sch 5, Pt 1).

5.28 The statement must also include a statement by the subscribers to the memorandum of association that each of the persons named as a director, as secretary or as one of the joint secretaries has consented to act in the relevant capacity. If all the partners in a firm are to be joint secretaries, consent may be given by one partner on behalf of all of them: CA 2006, s 12(3) (as inserted by the SBEEA 2015, s 100(2)).

Statement of initial significant control

5.29 The statement of initial significant control required to be delivered to the registrar must:

(a) state whether, on incorporation, there will be anyone who will count for the purposes of s 790M (register of people with significant control over a company) as either a registrable person or a registrable relevant legal entity in relation to the company;

(b) include the required particulars of anyone who will count as such; and

(c) include any other matters that on incorporation will be required (or, in the absence of an election under s 790X, would be required) to be entered in the company's PSC register by virtue of s 790M: CA 2006, s 12A(1) (as inserted by the SBEEA 2015, Sch 3, Pt 2).

5.30 It is not necessary to include under sub-s (1)(b) the date on which someone becomes a registrable person or a registrable relevant legal entity in relation to the company: CA 2006, s 12A(2) (as inserted by the SBEEA 2015, Sch 3, Pt 2).

If the statement includes required particulars of an individual, it must also contain a statement that those particulars are included with the knowledge of that individual: CA 2006, s 12A(3) (as inserted by SBEEA 2015, Sch 3, Pt 2).

'Registrable person', 'registrable relevant legal entity' and 'required particulars' have the meanings given in Pt 21A (see ss 790C and 790K): CA 2006, s 12A(4) (as inserted by the SBEEA 2015, Sch 3, Pt 2).

Statement of compliance

5.31 The statement of compliance required to be delivered to the registrar of companies is a statement that the requirements of CA 2006 as to registration have been complied with: CA 2006, s 13(1).

The registrar may accept the statement of compliance as sufficient evidence of compliance: CA 2006, s 13(2).

Memorandum of Association

5.32 The memorandum of association is not part of the company's constitution. Its function will be simply to provide details of the company's subscribers at the date of the company's formation. It cannot be amended or updated. The memorandum of association must be authenticated by each subscriber which will provide validity by adding their signatures next to their names: CA 2006, s 8(2). It is therefore a much shorter document. It is a registerable document. The memorandum of association must be delivered to the registrar at Companies House for formal registration of a company.

5.33 For companies formed under CA 2006, the memorandum of association will contain limited information evidencing the intention to form the company. For companies formed before CA 2006, the memorandum will contain key constitutional information of a type which will in future be set out in the articles of association or provided to the registrar in another format. Such material is treated for the future as part of the company's articles of association: CA 2006, s 28.

A company's memorandum must be in a prescribed form as set out under SI 2008/3014.

Articles of Association

5.34 The articles of association are the internal regulations of the company setting out the governance aspects and regulating the relationship between directors and shareholders. Every company must have articles of association. See Chapter 6 on the Company's Constitution.

Registration

5.35 If he is satisfied that the requirements of CA 2006 are complied with, the registrar must register the documents delivered to him: CA 2006, s 14.

Issue of certificate of incorporation

5.36 On the registration of a company, the registrar of companies must provide a certificate that the company is incorporated: CA 2006, s 15(1).

The certificate must state:

(i) the name and registered number of the company;

(ii) the date of its incorporation;

(iii) whether it is a limited or unlimited company, and if it is limited, whether it is limited by guarantee;

(iv) whether it is a private or a public company;

(v) whether the company's registered office is situated in England and Wales (or in Wales), in Scotland or in Northern Ireland: CA 2006, s 15(2).

The certificate must be signed by the registrar or authenticated by the registrar's official seal: CA 2006, s 15(3). Under s 15(4), it is conclusive evidence that requirements of the Act as to registration have been complied with and that the company is duly registered.

5.37 The word 'conclusive' means what it says – the registrar's certificate is conclusive and unassailable and it is not possible to go behind the certificate: *Re CL Nye Ltd* [1971] Ch 442; *Bank of Beirut SAL v HRH Prince Adel El-Hashemite* [2015] EWHC 1451. The issue of 'conclusive evidence' of the certificate of incorporation has the effect that all registration formalities for establishing a company have been complied with notwithstanding any issues discovered subsequently, unless exceptions can be found to declare the company a nullity. This could apply where, for example, the company was set up for an unlawful purpose: *Bowman v Secular Society* [1971] AC 406; and *R v Registrar of Companies, ex p Attorney General* [1991] BCLC 476. However, in *Exeter Trust v Screenways Ltd* [1991] BCC 477, the Court of Appeal refused to order rectification of the register of charges at Companies House on the basis that the registrar's certificate was conclusive evidence that the requirements as to registration had been satisfied. One issue in this regard has been whether an exception to the conclusivity of the certificate can apply where there is fraud on the basis of the principle that 'fraud unravels all'? See *HIH Casualty & General Insurance v Chase Manhattan Bank* [2003] UKHL 6. The effect of fraud is to vitiate 'judgments, contracts and all transactions whatsoever': *Lazarus Estates Ltd v Beasley* [1956] 1 QB 702; and *Arab National Bank v The Registrar of Companies* [2005] EWHC 3047. The issue is whether the fraud principle could be an exception and therefore vitiate or set aside the conclusive evidence of the certificate of incorporation? In *Bank of Beirut SAL v HRH Prince Adel El-Hashemite* [2015] EWHC 1451, Nugee J was of the view that the principle that fraud unravels all was not a sufficient basis to go behind the conclusivity of a certificate of incorporation as this would be adding provisos to the provisions on conclusivity which were not intended by applicable legislation, particularly as the registrar at Companies House would have acted in good faith in registering a legal entity even though any mistake by the registrar in registering the entity's documents were procured by fraud by an applicant. The position is less clear where, for example, the registration of documents is effected by the registrar in a fraudulent manner and not a mistake.

Effect of registration

5.38 The registration of a company has the following effects as from the date of incorporation: CA 2006, s 16(1) (see too *Jubilee Cotton Mills Ltd v Lewis* [1924] AC 958):

- The subscribers to the memorandum, together with such other persons as may from time to time become members of the company, are a body corporate by the name stated in the certificate of incorporation: CA 2006, s 16(2).
- That body corporate is capable of exercising all the functions of an incorporated company: CA 2006, s 16(3).
- The status and registered office of the company are as stated in the application for registration: CA 2006, s 16(4).
- In the case of a company having a share capital, the subscribers to the memorandum become holders of the shares specified in the statement of capital and initial shareholdings: CA 2006, s 16(5).
- The persons named in the statement of proposed officers as directors or as secretary, or joint secretary of the company are deemed to have been appointed to that office: CA 2006, s 16(6).

Company: registered office and change of address

5.39 Associated with the establishment of a company, is the company's registered office.

A company must at all times have a registered office to which all communications and notices may be addressed: CA 2006, s 86. This is particularly important for service of documents. Under s 1139(1), a document may be served on a company registered under CA 2006 by leaving it at, or sending it by post to, the company's registered office. The term 'registered address' is defined as any address for the time being shown as a current address in relation to that person in the part of the register available for public inspection: CA 2006, s 1139(3).

5.40 A company may change the address of its registered office by giving notice to the registrar: CA 2006, s 87. The change takes effect upon the notice being registered by the registrar, but until the end of the period of 14 days, beginning with the date on which it is registered, a person may validly serve any document on the company at the address properly registered.

5.41 For the purpose of any duty of a company:

- to keep available for inspection at its registered office any register, index, or other documents; or
- to mention the address of its registered office in any document: CA 2006, s 87(3)

a company that has given notice to the registrar of a change in the address of its registered office, may act on the change as from such date, not more than 14 days after the notice is given, as it may determine: CA 2006, s 87(4).

5.42 There is a defence for the company if it cannot perform its duties within the time period to change its registered office address. Where a company unavoidably ceases to perform at its registered office any such duty as is mentioned in s 87(3)(a) in circumstances in which it was not practicable to give prior notice to the registrar of a change in the address of its registered office, but:

(a) resumes performance of that duty at other premises as soon as practicable, and

(b) gives notice accordingly to the registrar of a change in the situation of its registered office within 14 days of doing so,

it is not to be treated as having failed to comply with that duty: CA 2006, s 87(4).

Checklist: incorporation of a private company limited by shares

5.43 *The following checklist sets out the steps and procedures required to establish a private company limited by shares, including the documentation involved both during incorporation and post-incorporation.*

No	Issue	Reference
1	Who will form the private limited company? It may be formed by a sole subscriber and be a single member company. Any enactment or rule of law applicable to companies formed by two or more persons or having two or more members applies with any necessary modification in relation to a company formed by one person or having only one person as a member.	CA 2006, s 7 CA 2006, s 38
2	The company must not be formed for an unlawful purpose.	CA 2006, s 7(2)
3	Search in index of names for existing company names and choice of name. Ensure that name proposed to be registered is not the same as or identical to one already registered at Companies House. Consider any sensitive names and whether any consent is required from a government/regulatory body or organisation. Take account of any potential passing-off issues. Consider any exemption for company to use 'limited' (Ltd) as part of its name.	CA 2006, Pt 5 and Pt 41
4	Prepare a memorandum of association for subscribers to the company. Ensure signature by subscriber(s) and witnessed by at least one witness.	CA 2006, s 8
5	There must be at least one director.	CA 2006, s 154
6	A company secretary may be appointed but this is not a requirement.	CA 2006, s 270

No	Issue	Reference
7	Prepare articles of association. Either specifically tailored or model articles for a company limited by shares or a combination. Ensure articles are signed by subscriber(s) and witnesses.	CA 2006, s 18
8	Prepare statement of capital and initial shareholdings.	CA 2006, s 10
9	Prepare statement of proposed officers.	CA 2006, s 12
10	Prepare statement of compliance (either by proposed officer or secretary or solicitor) that the requirements of CA 2006 as to registration have been complied with.	CA 2006, s 13
11	Prepare Form IN01 setting out the following details: • company name; • any restrictions on company name; • company type; • registered office address; • articles of association; • proposed officers; • secretary (if required); • statement of capital; • statement of initial shareholdings; • statement of compliance.	Form IN01
12	Lodge at Companies House: • Form IN01; • fee for filing (either £100 for same day incorporation or £40 for hard copy filing), or £14 if using appropriate software package or £18 if using WebFiling service; • memorandum of association; • articles of association (unless model articles adopted then no need to lodge as accepted by Companies House by default); • If required Form NE01 (exemption from requirement to use 'Limited'); • Consent of government authority/regulatory body or organisation on name use.	

No	Issue	Reference
13	Obtain certificate of incorporation from the registrar which will set out: • registered number; • name of company; • private company limited by shares; • date of incorporation.	CA 2006, s 15
14	Call a board meeting. Prepare letterhead including invoices with company's name, registered address and company registration number.	
15	Notify tax authorities of incorporation for tax purposes.	
16	Appoint company chairman.	
17	Appoint company bankers. Ensure bank mandate prepared with appropriate signatories.	
18	Appoint auditors and accountants.	CA 2006, s 485
19	Fix the company's accounting reference date.	Form AA01
20	Allot shares to the shareholders and issue share certificates.	CA 2006, s 188
21	If required, prepare service contracts for directors and seek approval if required under CA 2006.	
22	Obtain directors' indemnity insurance and employers' liability insurance.	
23	Do directors need to declare any interests in contracts or any other proposed interests?	CA 2006, ss 177, 182
24	Update: • register of directors; • register of directors' interests; • register of secretary (if appropriate); • register of charges (if appropriate); • register of members.	
25	Notify registrar if service contract or statutory books will be kept at a location other than at the company's registered office.	

Checklist: incorporation of a public company limited by shares

5.44 *The following checklist sets out the steps and procedures required to establish a public limited company, including the documentation involved both during incorporation and post-incorporation.*

No	Issue	Reference
1	Who will form the public limited company (plc)? It may be formed by a sole subscriber and be a single member company. Any enactment or rule of law applicable to companies formed by two or more persons or having two or more members applies with any necessary modification in relation to a company formed by one person or having only one person as a member.	CA 2006, s 7 CA 2006, s 38
2	The company must not be formed for an unlawful purpose.	CA 2006, s 7(2)
3	Search in index of names for existing company names and choice of name. Ensure that name proposed to be registered is not the same as or identical to one already registered at Companies House. Consider any sensitive names and whether any consent is required from a government/regulatory body or organisation. Take account of any potential passing-off issues.	CA 2006, Pt 5 and Pt 41
4	Prepare a memorandum of association for subscribers to the company. Ensure signature by subscriber(s) and witnessed by at least one witness.	CA 2006, s 8
5	There must be at least two directors. The company must have at least one director who is an individual. All individual directors must be aged 16 or over.	CA 2006, s 154
6	A company secretary must be appointed and ensure secretary is appropriately qualified.	CA 2006, ss 271 and 273
7	Prepare articles of association. Either specifically tailored or model articles for public limited companies or a combination. Ensure articles are signed by subscriber(s) and witnesses.	CA 2006, s 8
8	Prepare statement of capital and initial shareholdings.	CA 2006, s 10
9	Prepare statement of proposed officers.	CA 2006, s 12
10	Prepare statement of compliance (either by proposed officer or secretary or solicitor) that the requirements of CA 2006 as to registration have been complied with.	CA 2006, s 13
11	Prepare Form IN01 setting out the following details: • company name; • any restrictions on company name; • company type; • registered office address; • articles of association; • proposed officers; • secretary (if required);	Form IN01

No	Issue	Reference
	• statement of capital; • statement of initial shareholdings; • statement of compliance.	
12	Lodge at Companies House: • Form IN01; • fee for filing (either £100 for same-day incorporation or £40 for hard copy filing), or £14 if using appropriate software package, or £18 if using WebFiling service; • memorandum of association; • articles of association (unless model articles for a plc adopted then no need to lodge as accepted by Companies House by default); • consent of government authority/regulatory body or organisation on name use.	
13	Obtain certificate of incorporation from the registrar which will set out: • registered number; • name of company; • public limited company; • date of incorporation.	CA 2006, s 15
14	Call a board meeting. Prepare letterhead including invoices with company's name, registered address and company registration number.	
15	Notify tax authorities of incorporation for tax purposes.	
16	Appoint company chairman.	
17	Appoint company bankers. Ensure bank mandate prepared with appropriate signatories.	
18	Appoint auditors and accountants.	
19	Fix the company's accounting reference date.	
20	Allot shares to the shareholders and issue share certificates.	CA 2006, s 489
21	If required, prepare service contracts for directors and seek approval if required under CA 2006.	Form AA01 CA 2006, s 188
22	Obtain directors' indemnity insurance and employers' liability insurance.	
23	Do directors need to declare any interests in contracts or any other proposed interests?	CA 2006, ss 177, 182

No	Issue	Reference
24	Update: ● register of directors; ● register of directors' interests; ● register of secretary (if appropriate); ● register of charges (if appropriate); ● register of members.	
25	Notify registrar if service contract or statutory books will be kept at a location other than at the company's registered office.	CA 2006, s 228(4)
26	Consider if any appropriate governance structures need to be in place such as: ● non-executive directors; ● audit committee; ● nomination committee; ● remuneration committee.	
27	Ensure company has nominal issued capital of at least £50,000. A public company must not allot shares except as paid up at least as to one-quarter of its nominal value and the whole of any premium on it.	CA 2006, s 761 CA 2006, s 586
28	Apply for a trading certificate. A company that is a public company (otherwise than by virtue of re-registration as a public company) must not do business or exercise any borrowing powers unless the registrar has issued it with a certificate under this section (a 'trading certificate').	CA 2006, s 761
	An application for a certificate under the CA 2006, s 761 must: (a) state that the nominal value of the company's allotted share capital is not less than the authorised minimum; (b) specify the amount, or estimated amount, of the company's preliminary expenses; (c) specify any amount or benefit paid or given, or intended to be paid or given, to any promoter of the company, and the consideration for the payment or benefit; (d) be accompanied by a statement of compliance; and (e) be accompanied by a statement of the aggregate amount paid up on the shares of the company on account of their nominal value.	CA 2006, s 762 (as inserted by SBEEA 2015, s 98(3))

No	Issue	Reference
	The statement of compliance is a statement that the company meets the requirements for the issue of a certificate under s 761. The registrar may accept the statement of compliance as sufficient evidence of the matters stated in it.	
29	The registrar must issue a trading certificate if, on an application made in accordance with CA 2006, s 762 he is satisfied that the nominal value of the company's allotted share capital is not less than the authorised minimum. A trading certificate has effect from the date on which it is issued and is conclusive evidence that the company is entitled to do business and exercise any borrowing powers.	Form SH50

Checklist: differences between a private and a public company

5.45 *The following checklist sets out some of the key differences between a private and a public company under CA 2006.*

Issue	Private	Public
Name	Must end with Ltd or Limited (or Welsh equivalent) unless exempt	Must end with plc or public limited company (or Welsh equivalent) unless exempt
Securities	Cannot offer securities to the public	Can offer securities to the public
Trading certificate	No need for a trading certificate. The company can start business immediately upon obtaining the certificate of incorporation	Trading certificate required
Share capital	No minimum share capital	The nominal value of the company's share capital must not be less than the authorised minimum £50,000
Secretary	No requirement	Required and with appropriate qualifications
Directors	One director required	Two directors required of whom one must be a natural person
Accounting/ audit requirement	Exemptions apply for small or medium-sized companies	No exemptions

Issue	Private	Public
Annual general meetings	No requirement for AGMs	Must hold AGMs
Written resolutions	May be used	Cannot be used
Allotment of shares	May allot shares in accordance with its capital requirements	A public company may not allot shares unless at least one-quarter of their nominal value and the whole of any premium has been paid up
Non-cash consideration for shares		A public company may not allot shares as fully or partly paid up (as to their nominal value or any premium on them), otherwise than in cash if the consideration for the allotment is or includes an undertaking which is to be, or may be, performed more than five years after the date of the allotment. If the allotment for non-cash consideration is permissible, then an expert's prior valuation and report on the consideration given is usually required. Further, a public company may not allot shares in consideration of an undertaking to do work or perform services
Pre-emption rights	May disapply	Limited period for disapplication of pre-emptive rights
Dividends distribution	No restrictions apply	Prohibition from making a distribution if its net assets are less than the aggregate in value of its called-up share capital and its undistributable reserves
Loss of capital	No particular restrictions where losses suffered	Where the company's net assets are reduced to half or less of its called-up share capital, directors are obliged to convene an extraordinary general meeting, for shareholders to determine what steps should be taken to address the losses
Dormant company	Where a private company is classified as a 'small' company, it need not appoint auditors but must file an abbreviated balance sheet	No such requirement

Issue	**Private**	**Public**
Financial assistance	Exemption for private companies (subject to certain conditions) to give financial assistance for the acquisition of its shares	Cannot give financial assistance for acquisition of its shares
Purchase or redemption of shares	Exemption for private companies (subject to certain conditions) for a private company to redeem or purchase its shares	No such exemption
Interest in shares	No requirement of disclosure of interest in shares	Disclosure required including keeping a register of interest in shares
Proxy	A proxy who attends a general or class meeting of shareholders in a private company has the same right as the shareholder appointing him to speak at such meeting	No such requirement

Definitions

5.46

Director's Service Contract: a director's 'service contract', in relation to a company, means a contract under which:

(a) a director of the company undertakes personally to perform services (as director or otherwise) for the company, or for a subsidiary of the company, or

(b) services (as director or otherwise) that a director of the company undertakes personally to perform are made. available by a third party to the company, or to a subsidiary of the company.

Required Particulars: the required particulars that must be stated in the company's register of directors and register of directors' residential addresses (see CA 2006, ss 162–166) or, as the case may be for a secretary, its register of secretaries (see CA 2006, ss 277–279).

6 The company's constitution

Contents

Introduction

6.1 The company's constitution will set out the essential internal functioning and operation of the company, including the powers and authorities vested in the directors and shareholders. It provides an insight into the company's main activities, its share capital, increase or reduction of capital, the company's name, transfer or transmission of shares, procedural rules such as convening meetings at the board and shareholder levels, the company's financial year, and other issues concerning the company's operations including appointment of key company officers. It also regulates the relationship between the shareholders and the company and the shareholders *inter se*. As the articles of association are a public document, they must be registered at Companies House. Subject to any other provision in the CA 2006, a company has the flexibility in the articles it chooses to govern its internal relations and governance structure. This chapter addresses the following issues:

- the statutory definition of the term 'constitution' and the context in which the term is used;
- the company's articles of association;
- an overview of the standard company's model articles of association;

- the procedure for amending the company's articles of association and the test applied on alteration;
- the contractual status of the articles of association;
- the status of the memorandum of association; and
- construction of the articles of association.

The company's constitution

6.2 Chapter 1 of Part 3 to CA 2006 sets out the definition and scope of a 'company's constitution'. Section 17 of CA 2006 provides that unless the context otherwise requires, references in the Companies Acts to a 'company's constitution' include:

- the company's articles of association; and
- any resolutions and agreements to which Chapter 3 of Part 3 of CA 2006 applies. Section 29 of CA 2006 refers to resolutions and agreements affecting a company's constitution. The resolutions include:
  - any special resolution;
  - any resolution or agreement agreed to by all the members of a company that, if not so agreed to, would not have been effective for its purpose unless passed by a special resolution;
  - any resolution or agreement agreed to by all the members of a class of shareholders that, if not agreed to, would not have been effective for its purpose unless passed by some particular majority or otherwise in some particular manner;
  - any resolution or agreement that effectively binds all members of a class of shareholders though not agreed to by all those members; any other resolution or agreement to which Chapter 3 of Part 3 applies.

6.3 The term 'company's constitution' as used in CA 2006, s 17 is non-exhaustive and will apply throughout the Companies Acts 'unless the context requires otherwise'. Therefore, a wider or restricted meaning could be attributed to the term under specific provisions of the Companies Acts.

Under s 257, however, the definition of a 'company's constitution' takes on a wider significance for the purpose of Part 10 of the Act in respect of company directors, to include resolutions and decisions made by members of the company.

In addition to the provisions of a company's articles of association, and the resolutions and agreements to which Chapter 3 of Part 3 of CA 2006 applies, the contents of certain other documents will be of constitutional relevance for certain purposes. For example, a company's certificate of incorporation summarises key information applicable to the company by setting out whether it is a public or a private company.

Articles of association

6.4 Under CA 2006, the company's constitution includes its articles of association. The company's articles are internal rules governing the internal function and operation of the company. They form a statutory contract between the company and its shareholders, and between each of the shareholders, and are an integral part of the company's constitution, and are legally binding on the company and its shareholders. Articles of association establish the division of power and responsibility between the directors and the shareholders, which creates a separation of management and ownership between the two groups. Companies formed under the Companies Act 2006 or the Companies Acts are required to have their articles of association for the internal functioning of the company.

6.5 As the company's memorandum of association is no longer part of a company's constitution, the articles of association will contain all the essential powers, objects and activities of the company. The articles are intended to provide flexibility for both directors and shareholders to facilitate effective governance of the company, and to provide some degree of transparency in the relationship between directors and shareholders for the proper functioning of the company.

The articles of association are decided by the shareholders and they are intended to ensure the smooth functioning of the company's internal governance system, and how matters should proceed in the event that decisions are required to be made or actions are required to be undertaken. Articles of association cannot address every issue, but they usually emphasise the important aspects that typically arise within the corporate establishment.

6.6 Before the Companies Act 2006, companies limited by shares typically adopted Table A 1985 or Table A 1948 articles of association to govern their internal functioning. Table A was adopted either in full, or subject to certain amendments tailored to the company's requirements.

As from 1 October 2009, companies may adopt model articles for a private or public company under the Companies (Model Articles) Regulations 2008, SI 2008/3229. The model articles do not set out the provisions of the Companies Act 2006 and consideration should be given to any amendments that a company may need to make to ensure that the provisions are suitably adapted for the proper functioning of the company.

The nature of the company's articles of association

6.7 A company must have articles of association setting out relevant regulations: CA 2006, s 18(1). Unless it is a company to which model articles apply by virtue of s 20 (default application of model articles in case of limited company), it must register the articles of association with the Registrar of Companies at Companies House.

Under s 18(3), the articles of association registered by a company must be contained in a single document and be divided into paragraphs numbered consecutively.

6.8 The Secretary of State may by regulations prescribe model articles of association for various types of companies: CA 2006, s 19(1); and a company may adopt all or any of the provisions of the model articles. The Secretary of State has already enacted model articles for a private company limited by shares under the Companies (Model Articles) Regulations 2008, SI 2008/3229 as set out in Schedule 1. Schedule 2 to these Regulations sets out the model articles for a company limited by guarantee.

The articles of association are therefore the main form of constitution under CA 2006.

6.9 In some cases, a default application of the model articles can apply. On the formation of a limited company, if the company's articles of association are not registered, or if the articles are registered, but they do not exclude or modify the relevant model articles, then the relevant model articles (so far as practicable) will form part of the company's articles of association, in the same manner and to the extent as if articles in the form of those articles had been duly registered: CA 2006, s 20. Under s 20(1)(a), the term 'relevant model articles' means the model articles prescribed for a company of that description as in force at the date on which the company is registered.

6.10 The adoption of the model articles by companies formed under CA 2006 will be entirely a matter for individual companies. They are able to incorporate provisions from the model articles (with or without amendment); and/or add to those provisions; and/or exclude such provisions as they think fit.

Companies can also adopt the provisions of model articles by reference. This is a common practice, which enables a company that wishes to incorporate specific provisions to do so, without the necessity of having to copy out the provisions in question.

6.11

Example:

A company's registered articles may have the following variations in its articles of association:

- 'The Model Articles apply except for articles x, y and z'; or
- 'The company's articles are a, b and c, plus model articles 'g, p and q''; or
- 'Model article 'n' applies but it is amended as follows …'

Alteration of articles of association

6.12 The company may amend its articles of association by special resolution: CA 2006, s 21(1). This is subject to the rules on entrenchment as set out in s 22. Private companies can, however, amend their articles by a written resolution procedure.

Where a company is a charity, this is subject to:

(a) in England and Wales, ss 197 and 198 of the Charities Act 2011;

(b) in Northern Ireland, art 9 of the Charities (Northern Ireland) Order 1987,SI 1987/2048 (NI 19): CA 2006, s 21(2).

6.13 In the case of a company that is registered in the Scottish Charity Register, this is subject to:

(a) s 112 of the Companies Act 1989 (c 40); and

(b) s 16 of the Charities and Trustee Investment (Scotland) Act 2005 (asp 10).

See too the Companies Act 2006 (Commencement No 8, Transitional Provisions and Savings) Order 2008, SI 2008/2860, Sch 2, para 4.

Judicial attitudes towards alteration of articles of association

6.14 Over the years, there has developed a principle in English company law, that subject to any restrictions under statute or any entrenchment provision and where appropriate, the interests of minority shareholders, a company is generally free to amend its articles of association. The principle has also been based on majority rule – if the majority of the shareholders have decided on a particular transaction, the minority must accept majority decisions based on the rule in *Foss v Harbottle* (1843) 2 Hare 46, subject to certain exceptions (such as fraud or illegality).

6.15 Traditionally, English courts have stated the power to alter the articles of association under the CA 2006 must be exercised 'bona fide for the benefit of the company as a whole', and this expression appears to have been inextricably linked to CA 2006, s 21 and its predecessors. This concept derives from partnership law, and was enshrined in English company law to ensure that the majority did not abuse its powers of expulsion to the detriment of the minority. In some cases, this has been based on the ability of the majority shareholders to bind the minority. There has been no clear explanation in case law as to the meaning of the term 'bona fide'. Subsequent cases have, therefore, developed other tests applicable to alteration of articles while still retaining aspects of the bona fide test. The cases also demonstrate judicial reluctance by the courts to intervene in commercial business decisions of companies in determining the bona fides of their decisions, based on principles established in *Foss v Harbottle* (1843) 2 Hare 461, that where wrongs are done to the company then only the company is the proper claimant, and the majority control over corporate decisions: see too *Burland v Earle* [1902] AC 83; and *MacDougall v Gardiner* (1875) 1 Ch D 13; and *Edwards v Halliwell* [1950] 2 All ER 1064. Articles of association can be the subject of challenge even if passed by the requisite majority of shareholders as being invalid in certain circumstances.

Test of bona fide for the benefit of the company

One of the earliest cases to set out the 'bona fide' test was *Allen v Gold Reefs of West Africa Ltd* [1900] 1 Ch 656, the articles of a limited company provided that it should have a lien for all debts and liabilities of any member to the company 'upon all shares (not being fully paid) held by such member'. The company had a lien on partly paid shares of one shareholder. On the shareholder's death, he owed arrears on his partly paid shares to the company. The company therefore sought to extend the lien to all fully paid shares which were part of the deceased shareholder's estate. The Court of Appeal was required to consider whether such alteration could be effected by the company. The Court of Appeal held (Lindley MR, Vaughan Williams and Romer LJJ), that the company had power to alter its articles by extending its lien to fully paid shares. It decided that as the power to alter articles enabled the majority shareholders to bind the minority, it must be exercised 'bona fide for the benefit of the company'. According to Lindley LJ:

> 'The power thus conferred on companies to alter the regulations contained in their articles is limited only by the provisions contained in the statute and the conditions contained in the company's memorandum of association. Wide, however, as the language of s 50 [now s.21 CA 2006] is, the power conferred by it must, like all other powers, be exercised subject to those general principles of law and equity which are applicable to all powers conferred on majorities and enabling them to bind minorities. It must be exercised, not only in the manner required by law, but also bona fide for the benefit of the company as a whole, and it must not be exceeded. These conditions are always implied, and are seldom, if ever, expressed. But if they are complied with I can discover no ground for judicially putting any other restrictions on the power conferred by the section than those contained in it.'

6.16 *Allen's* case was not concerned with compulsory transfer provisions (or 'expropriation clauses' or 'exclusion' clauses) which compels a majority shareholder to purchase some or all shares of the minority shareholder with a view to excluding any further participation by the minority shareholder. However, some subsequent cases have involved compulsory transfer provisions which have applied the *Allen* test, namely that any alteration must be exercised 'bona fide for the benefit of the company' and the courts will take account of minority shareholders' interests in this regard. However, the courts have never clearly articulated the concept of 'bona fide for the benefit of the company' in respect of amendments to articles of association.

Notions of conscience, oppression and natural justice

There have been some cases that have associated alteration of articles with aspects of conscience, equity, natural justice and fair play. The courts would consider it unconscionable for majority shareholders to alter articles of association where minority shareholders would be subjected to a detriment or oppression. In this regard, the courts addressed the subjective intentions of the shareholders as decision makers, and whether such intentions were tainted with any bad faith or mala fides on their part in effecting the alteration, including purely selfish motives, desires or intentions on the part of the majority shareholders.

In *Brown v British Abrasive Wheel Co* [1919] 1 Ch 290, there were two groups of shareholders in the company with the majority shareholders wishing to put more capital into the company with a view to ousting the minority shareholders. The majority shareholders held 98% of the company capital and they wanted to alter the company's articles of association to acquire the remaining 2% from the minority shareholders in anticipation that further capital would be required to expand the company's operations. The minority shareholders challenged the alteration and sought an injunction preventing the alteration from going ahead. It should be noted that the claimant did not challenge the bona fides of the majority and the judge accepted that the majority shareholders were frank and transparent in their actions.

The court was of the opinion that the alteration was not bona fide for the company's benefit. The resolution was therefore invalid. According to Astbury J, the issue involved a consideration of whether the majority should be allowed to continue with alteration to the articles on an unwilling minority. It was contended by the minority shareholder that this was an oppressive attempt to buy out the minority forcibly for the benefit of the majority shareholders. The issue was whether this proposition was contrary to natural justice. If the proposition was fair and just, in the interests of the company and the shareholders generally, the court could not interfere, but if, on the other hand, it was oppressive and unfair, the court could prevent it being carried out. In effect the issue was whether the alteration of the articles was one where the majority was entitled to enforce on the minority?

Astbury J was of the view that it was not just and equitable to compulsorily purchase the minority shareholding, and that the proposed alteration was not for the company's benefit. The majority shareholders had acted for their own benefit in effecting the alteration rather than for the company as a whole. Astbury J granted the injunction to prevent the company from effecting alterations to the articles.

Astbury J also addressed notions of 'conscience' and natural justice including fair play in the company effecting alteration to the articles of association. This included incidences of oppressiveness on minority shareholders that results or may result from the alteration. These aspects would enable the court to interfere and provide justice to minority shareholders who may be expropriated.

Astbury J decided that the introduction of a compulsory transfer provision (which is dependant solely on the will of the majority to acquire minority interest) was contrary to ordinary principles of justice, and not for the benefit of the company. Further, he also decided that a provision in the articles which was in actual reality for the mere benefit of the majority could not be regarded as for the company's benefit even where the compulsory transfer could lead to future advantages for the company.

6.17 Subsequent cases have been critical of and distinguished *Brown v British Abrasive Wheel Co*.

Retreat from natural justice and oppressiveness and restating the bona fide test

In *Sidebottom v Kershaw, Leese & Co Ltd* [1920] 1 Ch 154, a company in which the majority of the shares were held by the directors, passed a special resolution to alter its articles by introducing a power for the directors to require any shareholder who competed with the company's business to transfer his shares, at their full value, to nominees of the directors. The claimants, who carried on a competing business, held the minority of the shares, and had voted against the resolution. They brought an action for a declaration that it was invalid as against them. The Court of Appeal upheld an alteration to the articles as it was for the company's benefit. The company had power to introduce into its altered articles anything that might have been included in its original articles, provided that the alteration was made bona fide for the benefit of the company as a whole. A power to expel a shareholder by buying him out was valid in the case of original articles, and could therefore be included in altered articles, subject to the same limitation. Further, the resolution was passed bona fide for the benefit of the company as a whole, and was therefore valid, and enforceable by the majority against the minority.

According to Lord Sterndale, the issue concerned the validity or invalidity of an alteration in the articles of association of the company. He stated that Astbury J was incorrect to treat the question of ordinary principles of justice and the question of the benefit of the company as two separate matters: 'if they are bona fide for the benefit of the company they are consonant with the ordinary principles of justice'.

The alteration was not directed at the minority shareholder director. Thus, one aspect of considering bona fides according to the *Sidebottom* case is to consider whether the proposed alteration was calculated to directly harm the shareholder? Were the motives malicious or in bad faith? What would be the detriment to the company if the alteration was not effected? According to Lord Sterndale, the resolution in *Sidebottom* was passed for the company's benefit owing to the competing nature of the minority shareholders and not directed at a particular shareholder.

Warrington LJ expressed the position that when a person became a shareholder in a company, it was based on a 'bargain' he had entered into which included an alteration in the future to the company's articles of association, and if the power was not exercised bona fide for the company's benefit, it could be challenged.

Warrington LJ considered that the objective behind the alteration was to protect the company's interest even though there was no dishonest or mala fide motive involved. The *Brown* case was distinguished on the facts and that Astbury J may have wrongly applied the test to include two aspects, namely bona fide and for the benefit of the company, whereas there was only one test involved.

Eve J thought that expressions such as 'the ordinary principles of justice', 'just and equitable' or 'oppressive' in the context of alteration of articles confused rather than resolved issues. The proper test was whether the resolution that was adopted or the alteration was made for the benefit of the company or for the benefit of some section of the company, without reference to the benefit of the company as a whole. Where the circumstances established that the purpose of an alteration was to get rid of an individual shareholder, that circumstance may furnish evidence of male fides.

All three members of the Court of Appeal agreed that it could be for the company's benefit to exclude its direct competitors, and that this aspect was for commercial businessmen to decide rather than for the courts. The only aspect for consideration thereafter would be whether the decision was taken in a bona fide manner. They thought that where the resolution was passed with the intention of getting rid of an individual shareholder, this may be evidence but not conclusive evidence of bad faith on the part of the shareholders.

The court considers honesty and real intention behind the proposed alteration

However, in *Dafen Tinplate Co Ltd v Llanelly Steel Co (1907) Ltd* [1920] 2 Ch 124, the defendant company, not having power under its original articles of association compulsorily to acquire the shares of members, passed special resolutions altering its articles and introducing a power enabling the majority of the shareholders to determine that the shares of any member (other than a certain named company) should be offered for sale by the directors to such person or persons (whether a member or members or not) as they should think fit at the fair value to be fixed from time to time at stated intervals by the directors. The company made steel bars which were used in the manufacture of tinplate. There was an expectation that the members, who were tinplate manufacturers, would take the steel they required from the company. However, the claimant, who was a shareholder in the company, formed a rival steel company and stopped taken any steel from the defendants.

Peterson J decided that the directors who had proposed the alteration to the company's articles were honestly convinced that it was not in the company's interests that the claimant should remain as a shareholder: the real objective of the alteration was to protect the company against the conduct of any shareholder whose actions would be detrimental to the company's interests. However, Peterson J held that resolutions in conferring an unrestricted and unlimited power on the majority of the shareholders to expropriate any shareholder they might think proper at their will and pleasure, went much further than was necessary for the protection of the company from the conduct of shareholders detrimental to the company's interests. The power thereby conferred could not be bona fide or genuinely for the benefit of the company as a whole and was not such a power as could be assumed by the majority.

6.18 The decision in this case was criticised in subsequent cases.

It was for the company to decide what was in its best interests and not the court

Shuttleworth v Cox Bros & Co (Maidenhead) Ltd [1927] 2 KB 9 was not concerned with a compulsory transfer provision unlike previous cases. In this case, the company's articles of association provided that the claimant and four others should be the first directors of the company, and that they should be permanent directors; and further that each of them should be entitled to hold office so long as he should live unless he should become disqualified from any one of six specified events. Owing to irregularities in the accounts furnished by the claimant of sums received by him on the company's account, an extraordinary general meeting of the company was held and a special resolution was passed that the articles should be altered by adding a seventh event disqualifying a director – namely, a request in writing by all his co-directors that he should resign his office. Such a request was subsequently made to the claimant. There was no evidence of bad faith on the part of the shareholders.

The director challenged the validity of the alteration to the articles.

The Court of Appeal disapproved of the case of *Dafen Tinplate Co Ltd v Llanelly Steel Co Ltd* [1920] 2 Ch 124. It decided that the contract, if any, between the claimant and the company contained in the articles in their original form was subject to the statutory power of alteration; and that if the alteration was bona fide for the benefit of the company, it was valid and there was no breach of that contract. There was no ground for saying that the alteration could not reasonably be considered for the benefit of the company, and in the absence of bad faith, there was no ground for questioning the decision of the shareholders that the alteration was for the benefit of the company; and, consequently, that the claimant was not entitled to the relief claimed.

In effect, the Court of Appeal decided that it was not for the court to determine what was in the company's interests: this was a matter for the company to decide.

The Court of Appeal held that there was only one test for determining alteration of the articles – namely that the alteration must be bona fide for the benefit of the company.

Further, that it was for the shareholders, and not for the court to say whether an alteration of the articles is for the benefit of the company, provided that it is not of such a character that no reasonable men could so regard it.

Bankes LJ stated that the courts will interfere with the alteration of articles if the alteration is 'so oppressive as to cast suspicion on the honesty of the persons responsible for it, or so extravagant that no reasonable men could really consider it for the benefit of the company'. On the facts, there was no vindictiveness or bad motive on the company's part. He further stated that the alteration of articles would be invalid 'if it is such that no reasonable men could consider it for the benefit of the company'.

According to Scrutton LJ, the words 'exercised bona fide for the benefit of the company' meant that the shareholders must act honestly having regard to and endeavouring to act for the benefit of the company:

> '... Now when persons, honestly endeavouring to decide what will be for the benefit of the company and to act accordingly, decide upon a particular course, then, provided there are grounds on which reasonable men could come to the same decision, it does not matter whether the Court would or would not come to the same decision or a different decision. It is not the business of the Court to manage the affairs of the company. That is for the shareholders and directors. The absence of any reasonable ground for deciding that a certain course of action is conducive to the benefit of the company may be a ground for finding lack of good faith or for finding that the shareholders, with the best motives, have not considered the matters which they ought to have considered. On either of these findings their decision might be set aside.'

The Court of Appeal criticised the decision of Peterson J in *Dafen Tinplate* case. There was only one test and not two tests to determine whether the alteration was valid: namely that the alteration must be bona fide for the benefit of the company. This required the shareholders to determine the issue honestly. However, the bona fides of shareholders may not be enough. The Court will however go further in determining that the alteration may not be valid if no reasonable person could consider it as for the benefit of the company. However, none of the members of the Court of Appeal considered that the *Dafen* case was wrongly decided on its facts. They did however express the view that a resolution to alter the articles of association might be bad even if the majority shareholders had honestly convinced themselves that it was in the best interests of the company. Each of the judges appears to have reasoned differently in putting forward the appropriate test, but nevertheless arriving at the same conclusion in connection with the alteration.

The test to be applied in expropriation cases was whether the alteration was bona fide for the company's benefit

In *Constable v Executive Connections Ltd* [2005] 2 BCLC 638, the claimant was a minority shareholder in the company and had no right to vote at general meetings. A special resolution was passed introducing an article enabling a member's shares to be compulsorily transferred on failure to accept an offer approved by 75% of shareholders and to sell his shares. The minority shareholder was being offered more than a fair value for his shares. The minority shareholder sought to prevent implementation of the expropriation article. The issue before the court was whether the introduction of the expropriation article was an abuse by the majority shareholders of their powers.

Christopher Nugee QC (sitting as a Deputy Judge of the High Court) held that the test to be applied when determining the validity of a resolution introducing a compulsory transfer provision, was whether it was bona fide for the benefit of the company as a whole. In the present case it was impossible to conclude that there was no serious issue to be tried. First, the claimant was entitled to test in cross-examination the assertion of the defendants as to the reasons for introducing the new article. If the substantive motive for doing so was to acquire his shareholding so that the offer or any similar offer could be accepted, or so that the company could achieve a better price for its own shares in the company, it was arguable that the decision was not really taken in the interests of the company but in the interests of the company's shareholders or the company itself. Secondly, the law in this area was not clear or easy to apply and the present case raised the issue in a particularly stark form. The article was virtually a naked compulsory transfer provision, namely one in which no reason had to be ascribed for it being invoked. The court recognised that in some cases, the alterations 'cannot be regarded as being for the benefit of the company, no matter how honestly the majority believe them to be'.

6.19 The principle of 'bona fide for the benefit of the company' was further elucidated in subsequent cases.

Shareholders must collectively decide what in their honest opinion is for the company's benefit

In *Greenhalgh v Arderne Cinemas Ltd* [1950] 2 All ER 1120, Evershed MR stated:

> 'In the first place, it is now plain that "bona fide for the benefit of the company as a whole" means not two things but one thing. It means that the shareholder must proceed on what, in his honest opinion, is for the benefit of the company as a whole. Secondly, the phrase, "the company as a whole", does not (at any rate in such a case as the present) mean the company as a commercial entity as distinct from the corporators. It means the corporators as a general body. That is to say, you may take the case of an individual hypothetical member and ask whether what is proposed is, in the honest opinion of those who voted in its favour, for that person's benefit.'

The cases have also shown that provided the alteration is bona fide and within the powers, it will be upheld by the courts.

However, shareholders do not need to take the company's interests into account. They are not obliged to act in the best interests of the company; they do not owe duties to the company or the directors; they are not partners with the company; they are not trustees for the company; and they are not the company's keepers or keepers of the company's conscience. They can vote against the interests of the company. Their intentions may be male fide, but they owe no duties to the directors or the company.

Provided the power to alter the articles of association is exercised bona fide by the shareholders, the courts will be reluctant to interfere in such decisions

In *Rights & Issues Investment Trust Ltd v Stylo Shoes Ltd* [1965] Ch 250, in which, together with a substantial increase in the issued ordinary share capital, the articles were amended to double the number of votes attached to special management shares in order to maintain the control of the existing management. Some 92% of the ordinary shareholders voted in favour.

The court held that the members of a company acting in accordance with the Companies Act and the constitution of the company, and subject to any necessary consent on the part of the class affected, could alter the relative voting powers attached to various classes of shares. Further, since the resolution for the alteration of voting rights was passed in good faith for the benefit of the company as a whole, it could not be said to be oppressive, and that, accordingly, the court would not interfere by interlocutory injunction to restrain the company from acting on the resolution.

6.20 However, the test for alterations to articles of association cannot solely be based on bona fide for the company's benefit. In *Hutton v West Cork Rly Co* (1893) 23 Ch D 654, Bowen LJ stated: 'Bona fides cannot be the sole test, otherwise you might have a lunatic conducting the affairs of the company, and paying away its money with both hands in a manner perfectly bona fide yet perfectly irrational'.

The 'bona fide' test has been the subject of some criticism in other jurisdictions.

The power to alter the articles must be exercised for a proper purpose and not oppressively towards the minority

The bona fide for the benefit of the company test was rejected by the Australian court in *Gambotto v WCP Ltd* (1995) 182 CLR 432. In this case, an alteration to the company's articles of association was being effected to allow a 90% shareholder to buy out minority shareholders at a fixed price which would lead to certain tax and commercial advantages for the company. The court favoured a more objective approach towards alteration of articles having regard to the proper purpose for the exercise of the power.

The High Court of Australia decided that where the purpose of altering a company's articles of association by resolution was to confer on the majority power to expropriate the shares of the minority, such a power would only be valid to the extent it was exercisable for a proper purpose and would not operate oppressively in relation to minority shareholders. Whether the alteration was bona fide for the benefit of the company as a whole was not a relevant consideration in such determination. Exceptional circumstances would be required to justify an amendment to a company's articles authorising the compulsory expropriation by the majority of the minority's interests. An alteration might be justified where the purpose of such was to secure the company from significant detriment and the alteration was not oppressive to the minority, provided that the process used to expropriate was fair, which required the majority shareholders to disclose all relevant information leading up to the alteration, and that the terms of the expropriation itself were fair. However, to allow expropriation where it would advance the interests of a company as a legal and commercial entity or those of the general body of corporators would be to fail to attach sufficient weight to the proprietary nature of a share and tantamount to expropriation by the majority for personal gain and thus improper. The nature of proprietary rights attaching to ownership of shares required that the onus of proving whether or not the power to expropriate was validly exercised lay on those supporting an expropriation. On the facts, there was no suggestion that the appellants' continued presence as members put the company's business activities at risk or that the appellants acted in some way to its detriment. The fact that taxation advantages and administrative benefits would flow to the company if minority shareholdings were expropriated did not therefore constitute a proper purpose for the resolution altering the articles.

Gambotto v WCP Ltd, however, is not binding in English law and does not support the English authorities in the area of compulsory transfer of shares by majority shareholders from the minority shareholders.

The shareholders' opinion should be considered as to whether the alteration of the articles was for the company's benefit

In *Citco Banking Corp NV v Pusser's Ltd* [2007] 2 BCLC 483, a Privy Council decision, the amendment (by way of resolutions) to the company's articles of association gave voting control to the chairman and unqualified control of the company. The appellant brought proceedings in the British Virgin Islands High Court to have the resolutions declared invalid because they were passed in the interests of the chairman to give him indisputable control, and were not bona fide in the interests of the company. The appellant contended that the chairman was disqualified from voting, because he was a shareholder who particularly stood to gain a personal advantage from the amendment. The trial judge applied the objective test of whether the amendment to the articles was for the benefit of the company, in holding that it was not in the company's interests for a single shareholder to have permanent control of the company for the duration of his life, without being removable if the other shareholders lost confidence in his management.

On appeal, the British Virgin Islands, Court of Appeal reversed the judge on the grounds that it was reasonable for the other shareholders to accept in good faith the reasons put forward by the chairman as to why the amendment would be in the interests of the company. The appellant appealed to the Privy Council.

The Privy Council held that the proper test was whether, in the opinion of the shareholders, the alteration of the articles was for the benefit of the company and whether there were grounds on which reasonable men could come to the same decision. Since reasonable shareholders could have accepted in good faith the reasons put forward by the chairman as to why the amendment of the articles was in the interests of the company even though the amendment had the effect of vesting of voting control in him, and since there was no dispute as to whether the chairman had acted bona fide the appellant's challenge to the special resolutions failed. Nor was the chairman barred from voting simply because the special resolutions were advantageous to him. Accordingly, the appellant's appeal was unsuccessful.

According to Lord Hoffmann:

> 'It must however be acknowledged that the test of "bona fide for the benefit of the company as a whole" will not enable one to decide all cases in which amendments of the articles operate to the disadvantage of some shareholder or group of shareholders. Such amendments are sometimes only for the purpose of regulating the rights of shareholders in matters in which the company as a corporate entity has no interest, such as the distribution of dividends or capital or the power to dispose of shares'.

The Privy Council applied the *Shuttleworth* case principles, including whether reasonable shareholders could have considered that the amendment was for the benefit of the company. To this extent, the position on alteration of articles is that the courts are likely to apply both a subjective and objective test in determining the validity and effectiveness of the alteration.

In considering the power to exercise alteration of articles, the court would consider the competing interests of the shareholders

The Australian case of Peters' American Delicacy Co Ltd v Heath (1939) 61 CLR 457 did not apply the bona fides test, and considered the position in terms of the competing interests of shareholders. The High Court of Australia held that an alteration of the articles which discriminated against holders of partly paid shares in favour of the majority shareholders did not constitute a fraud on the minority. In the course of his judgment, Latham CJ (with whom McTiernan J agreed) expressed the view that, although the power to alter articles must be exercised bona fide, the fact that an alteration prejudiced or diminished some (or all) of the rights of the shareholders was not in itself a ground for attacking the validity of an alteration. On the contrary, his Honour considered that such an alteration must be valid unless the party complaining could establish that the resolution was passed fraudulently or oppressively or was 'so extravagant that no reasonable person could believe that it was for the benefit of the company'. His Honour noted that the criterion of the 'benefit of the company as a corporation' could not be invoked as the sole solution to the problem where the amendment in question affected the relative rights of different classes of shareholders.

Dixon J also considered that the amendment was valid, although his Honour arrived at that conclusion by a different route. Dixon J declined to leave any analysis of this question to general notions of fairness and propriety, preferring instead to focus on the purpose of the proposed amendment. According to Dixon J a share in a company was property consisting of proprietary rights as defined by the articles of association. The power of alteration of the articles might be used by the majority shareholders for their own aggrandizement at the expense of the minority shareholders. It has seemed incredible that this could be so. But reliance on the doctrine that powers shall be exercised bona fide and for no extraneous purpose presented difficulties. The power of alteration was not a fiduciary power and the right to vote was an incident of property which may be exercised for the shareholder's personal advantage. Prima facie, rights dependent upon the articles were not enduring and indefeasible but were liable to modification or destruction by special resolution. So, 'if a resolution is regularly passed with the single aim of advancing the interests of a company considered as a corporate whole, it must fall within the scope of the statutory power to alter the articles and could never be condemned as mala fides'.

According to Dixon J:

> 'The chief reason for denying an unlimited effect to widely expressed powers such as that of altering a company's articles is the fear or knowledge that an apparently regular exercise of the power may in truth be but a means of securing some personal or particular gain, whether pecuniary or otherwise, which does not fairly arise out of the subjects dealt with by the power and is outside and even inconsistent with the contemplated objects of the power. It is to exclude the purpose of securing such ulterior special and particular advantages that Lord Lindley used the phrase "bonâ fide for the benefit of the company as a whole".'

His Honour considered that 'benefit as a whole' was a very general expression negativing purposes foreign to the company's affairs and that the 'bonâ fide for the benefit of the company as a whole' test was 'inappropriate, if not meaningless' where the amendment proposed to adjust the rights of conflicting interests. Although his Honour did not expressly state which test or tests might be applied in such circumstances, he upheld the resolution in question on the basis that it 'involved no oppression, no appropriation of an unjust or reprehensible nature and did not imply any purpose outside the scope of the power'.

See too the application of the bona fide test in directors' powers to allot shares: *Richard Brady Franks Ltd v Price* (1937) 58 CLR 112 at 135, *Mills v Mills* (1938) 60 CLR 150 at 187–188, *Ngurli Ltd v McCann* (1953) 90 CLR 425 at 440, *Harlowe's Nominees Pty Ltd v Woodside (Lakes Entrance) Oil Co NL* (1968) 121 CLR 483 at 493 and *Whitehouse v Carlton Hotel Pty Ltd* [1988] LRC (Comm) 725, (1987) 162 CLR 285).

Therefore, the use of the expression 'for the benefit of the company as a whole' is no longer influential in the context of an alteration of the articles designed to effect or authorise the expropriation of a minority's shares. The courts will look to the reasonableness in the decisions arrived at by the shareholders.

Key principles derived from cases on alteration of the company's articles of association and 'drag' rights

In the leading case of *Arbuthnott v Bonnyman* [2015] All ER 218, the issues concerned transfer of shares and the validity of the transfer. The claimant owned shares in the company. Other shareholders formed a new corporate vehicle to acquire the company and sold their shares to the new corporate vehicle. The claimant refused to sell his shares claiming: (a) unfair prejudicial conduct; and (b) that the company had sought to expropriate his shares at a gross undervalue. The Court of Appeal considered the construction of the 'drag' rights (compulsory sale of shares of minority shareholder if majority sell their shares) and of the amendment to the company's articles of association. It dismissed the claimant's claim. It set out the following principles from some of the key cases on the conditions for effecting a challenge to an alteration to the articles of association.

(1) The limitations on the exercise of the power to amend a company's articles arise because, as in the case of all powers, the manner of their exercise is constrained by the purpose of the power and because the framers of the power of a majority to bind a minority will not, in the absence of clear words, have intended the power to be completely without limitation. These principles may be characterised as principles of law and equity or as implied terms: *Allen v Gold Reefs of West Africa Ltd* [1900] Ch 656 at 671; *Assenagon Asset Management SA v Irish Bank Resolution Corpn Ltd* [2013] Bus LR 2660 at 278–280.

(2) A power to amend will be validly exercised if it is exercised in good faith in the interests of the company: *Sidebottom v Kershaw Leese and Co Ltd* [1920] 1 Ch 154 at 163.

(3) It is for the shareholders, and not the court, to say whether an alteration of the articles is for the benefit of the company but it will not be for the benefit of the company if no reasonable person would consider it to be such: Shuttleworth at 18–19, 23–24, 26–27; *Peters' American Delicacy Co v Heath* (1939) 61 CLR 457 at 488.

(4) The view of shareholders acting in good faith that a proposed alteration of the articles is for the benefit of the company, and which cannot be said to be a view which no reasonable person could hold, is not impugned by the fact that one or more of the shareholders was actually acting under some mistake of fact or lack of knowledge or understanding: *Peters' American Delicacy Co* at 491. In other words, the court will not investigate the quality of the subjective views of such shareholders.

(5) The mere fact that the amendment adversely affects, and even if it is intended adversely to affect, one or more minority shareholders and benefit others does not, of itself, invalidate the amendment if the amendment is made in good faith in the interests of the company: *Sidebottom* at 161, 163–167, 170–173; *Shuttleworth*; *Citco* at 490, 493; *Peters' American Delicacy Co* at 480, 486.

(6) A power to amend will also be validly exercised, even though the amendment is not for the benefit of the company because it relates to a matter in which the company as an entity has no interest but rather is only for the benefit of shareholders as such or some of them, provided that the amendment does not amount to oppression of the minority or is otherwise unjust or is outside the scope of the power: *Peters' American Delicacy Co* at 481, 504, 513, 515; *Assenagon*.

(7) The burden is on the person impugning the validity of the amendment of the articles to satisfy the court that there are grounds for doing so: *Citco* at 491; *Peters' American Delicacy Co* at 482.

It is clear from Arbuthnott that the courts will not generally interfere in shareholders' decisions when effecting an alteration to the company's articles of association provided the alteration is exercised in good faith. The term 'good faith' signifies that the alteration must be for the company's benefit or some group of shareholders in respect of a matter in which the company has no interest. The circumstances in which a minority shareholder may successfully mount a challenge to the articles of association are limited to demonstrating: (a) lack of good faith; (b) unfair prejudicial conduct; (c) the amendment was outside the scope of power or beyond the company's capacity. The minority shareholder also has the heavy burden of showing that the alteration was not in good faith when requesting the court to set aside the alteration. The Arbuthnott case demonstrates the court's unwillingness to intrude in corporate affairs where shareholders make a decision in the company's best interests unless circumstances arise which require intervention by the court. The Court of Appeal was persuaded by the following factors in upholding the drag rights by way of amendment into the articles of association:(a) there would be a better alignment of ownership as part of the management buyout and achieving such alignment was in the company's best interests; (b) the drag rights were not specifically targeted at the claimant nor was he singled out, but applied to all shareholders: the claimant was entitled to be bought out on the same terms as the exiting majority shareholders; (c) the company's shareholder's agreement and its articles of association when read together already contained drag rights which formed one of the bases of the original commercial bargain between the shareholders.

Further effects of alteration of articles of association on company members

6.21 The further effects of an alteration of the articles on the company's shareholders is governed by CA 2006, s 25. This states that a company's shareholder is not bound by an alteration to its articles after the date on which he became a shareholder in the following circumstances:

- if and so far as the alteration requires him to take or subscribe for more shares in the company than the number held by him at the date on which the alteration was made; or
- the alteration has the effect in any way of increasing his liability to the company as at that date, to contribute to the company's share capital or otherwise to pay money to the company: CA 2006, s 25(1).

Under CA 2006, s 25(2), a shareholder may, however, give his written consent to such an alteration and, where he does so, he will be bound by the alteration.

Registrar to be sent a copy of amended articles

6.22 Where a company amends its articles, it must send a copy of the amended articles to the registrar not later than 15 days after the amendment takes effect: CA 2006, s 26(1).

Section 26 does not require a company to set out in its articles any provisions of model articles that:

(a) are applied by the articles; or

(b) apply by virtue of s 20 (default application of model articles): CA 2006, s 26(2).

6.23 If a company fails to comply with this section, an offence is committed by:

(a) the company; and

(b) every officer of the company who is in default: CA 2006, s 26(3).

Under s 26(4), a person guilty of an offence under this section will be liable on summary conviction to a fine not exceeding level 3 on the standard scale and, for continued contravention, a daily default fine not exceeding one-tenth of level 3 on the standard scale.

Registrar's notice to comply in case of failure with respect to amended articles

6.24 If it appears to the registrar that a company has failed to comply with any enactment requiring it to send to the registrar a document making or evidencing an alteration in the company's articles; or to send to the registrar a copy of the company's articles as amended, the registrar may give notice to the company requiring it to comply: CA 2006, s 27(1). The notice must state the date on which it was issued; and require the company to comply within 28 days of the date of the notice: CA 2006, s 27(2). If the company complies with the notice within the specified time, it will not be subject to legal proceedings. However, if it does not so comply, it will be liable to a civil penalty of £200 and any criminal proceedings: CA 2006, s 27(3). The fine may be recovered by the registrar, and is then paid into the Consolidated Fund: CA 2006, s 27(4).

Other aspects in connection with the company's constitution

6.25 The Companies Act 2006 sets out other areas that have an impact on the company's constitution. These include constitutional documents to be provided to the shareholders; and notification to the registrar where amendments to the articles of association are effected.

Constitutional documents to be provided to members

6.26 A company must, on request by any member, send to him the following documents:

(a) an up-to-date copy of the company's articles;

(b) a copy of any resolution or agreement relating to the company to which Chapter 3 applies (resolutions and agreements affecting a company's constitution) and that is for the time being in force;

(c) a copy of any document required to be sent to the registrar under:

  (i) s 34(2) (notice where company's constitution altered by enactment); or

  (ii) s 35(2)(a) (notice where order of court or other authority alters company's constitution);

(d) a copy of any court order under s 899 (order sanctioning compromise or arrangement) or s 900 (order facilitating reconstruction or amalgamation);

(e) a copy of any court order under s 996 (protection of members against unfair prejudice: powers of the court) that alters the company's constitution;

(f) a copy of the company's current certificate of incorporation, and of any past certificates of incorporation;

(g) in the case of a company with a share capital, a current statement of capital;

(h) in the case of a company limited by guarantee, a copy of the statement of guarantee: CA 2006, s 32(1).

6.27 The statement of capital required by CA 2006, s 34(1)(g) is a statement of:

(a) the total number of shares of the company;

(b) the aggregate nominal value of those shares;

(ba) the aggregate amount (if any) unpaid on those shares (whether on account of their nominal value or by way of premium); and

(c) for each class of shares:

  (i) prescribed particulars of the rights attached to the shares;

  (ii) the total number of shares of that class; and

  (iii) the aggregate nominal value of shares of that class: CA 2006, s 32(2) (as inserted by SBEEA 2015, Sch 6).

If a company fails to comply with this section, an offence is committed by every officer of the company who is in default: CA 2006, s 32(3).

Under s 32(4), any person guilty of an offence under this section will be liable on summary conviction to a fine not exceeding level 3 on the standard scale.

Notice to registrar where company's constitution altered by enactment

6.28 Section 34 of CA 2006 applies where a company's constitution is altered by an enactment, other than an enactment amending the general law: CA 2006, s 34(1). The company must give notice of the alteration to the registrar, specifying the enactment, not later than 15 days after the enactment comes into force.

Under s 34(2), in the event of a special enactment, the notice must be accompanied by a copy of the enactment.

If the enactment amends:

(a) the company's articles; or

(b) a resolution or agreement to which Chapter 3 applies (resolutions and agreements affecting a company's constitution),

the notice must be accompanied by a copy of the company's articles, or the resolution or agreement in question, as amended: CA 2006, s 34(3).

6.29 A 'special enactment' means an enactment that is not a public general enactment, and includes:

(a) an Act for confirming a provisional order;

(b) any provision of a public general Act in relation to the passing of which any of the standing orders of the House of Lords or the House of Commons relating to private business applied; or

(c) any enactment to the extent that it is incorporated in or applied for the purposes of a special enactment: CA 2006, s 34(4).

6.30 If a company fails to comply with this section, an offence is committed by:

(a) the company; and

(b) every officer of the company who is in default: CA 2006, s 34(5).

A person guilty of an offence under this section will be liable on summary conviction to a fine not exceeding level 3 on the standard scale and, for continued contravention, a daily default fine not exceeding one-tenth of level 3 on the standard scale: CA 2006, s 34(6).

Notice to registrar where company's constitution altered by order

6.31 Where a company's constitution is altered by an order of a court or other authority, the company must give notice to the registrar of the alteration not later than 15 days after the alteration takes effect: CA 2006, s 35(1).

The notice must be accompanied by:

(a) a copy of the order; and

(b) if the order amends:

  (i) the company's articles; or

  (ii) a resolution or agreement to which Chapter 3 applies (resolutions and agreements affecting the company's constitution),

  a copy of the company's articles, or the resolution or agreement in question, as amended: CA 2006, s 35(2).

6.32 If a company fails to comply with this section, an offence is committed by:

(a) the company; and

(b) every officer of the company who is in default: CA 2006, s 35(3).

A person guilty of an offence under this section will be liable on summary conviction to a fine not exceeding level 3 on the standard scale and, for continued contravention, a daily default fine not exceeding one-tenth of level 3 on the standard scale: CA 2006, s 35(4).

This section does not apply where provision is made by another enactment for the delivery to the registrar of a copy of the order in question: CA 2006, s 35(5).

Entrenched provision of the articles of association

6.33 A company's articles of association may provide that specified provisions of the articles may not be altered or repealed, or may be altered or repealed only if certain conditions are met, or procedures are complied with, that are more restrictive than those applicable in the case of a special resolution: CA 2006, s 22(1). This is known as 'provision for entrenchment'.

Any provision for entrenchment may only be made in the company's articles, either on the company's formation, or by an amendment of its articles of association agreed to by all the company's shareholders: CA 2006, s 22(2). All provisions of the articles of association cannot be entrenched as this would prevent the company from the power contained under the CA 2006 to amend the articles.

The provision for entrenchment does not prevent amendment of the company's articles of association by agreement of all the company's shareholders, or by a court order or other authority having power to alter the company's articles: CA 2006, s 22(3).

Companies formed under CA 2006 cannot provide in their articles of association that an entrenchment provision can never be repealed or amended.

Notwithstanding the provision for entrenchment, the court or any other authority still has power to alter a company's articles of association: CA 2006, s 22(4).

Notice to registrar of existence of restriction on amendment of articles

6.34 The company must provide notice to the registrar on the provision for entrenchment in the following situations: CA 2006, s 23:

- if the company's articles of association contain provision for entrenchment on formation; or
- where a company's articles are amended so as to include such provision; or
- where a company's articles are altered by a court or other authority so as to restrict or exclude the power of the company to amend its articles: CA 2006, s 23(1);
- where a company's articles are amended so as to remove provision for entrenchment; or
- where a company's articles are altered by order of the court or other authority so as to remove such provision; or
- the removal of any other restriction on, or any exclusion of, the power of the company to amend its articles: CA 2006, s 23(2).

Statement of compliance where amendment of articles restricted

6.35 Section 24 of CA 2006 applies where a company's articles are subject to provision for entrenchment, or to an order of a court or other authority restricting or excluding the company's power to amend the articles: CA 2006, s 24(1). Under s 24(2), if a company amends its articles and is required to send to the registrar a document making or evidencing the amendment, the company must deliver a statement of compliance to accompany that document.

This statement of compliance will be a statement certifying that the amendment has been made in accordance with the company's articles and, where relevant, any applicable order of the court or other authority: CA 2006, s 24(3). Under s 24(4), the registrar may rely on the statement of compliance as sufficient evidence of the matters stated in it. The objective is to ensure that the registrar, and any person searching the public register, is put on notice that the articles contain entrenching provisions and that special rules therefore apply to the company's articles.

Shareholders' agreement

6.36 Although the articles of association are the principal internal rules governing the company, they may from time to time be supplemented by other rules and regulations which may elaborate further on the articles of association. A shareholders' agreement may be supplemental to a company's articles of association and will set out further provisions governing relations between the shareholders on issues such as voting, capital, transfer of shares, possible 'lock in' periods for shareholders, detailed governance aspects and exit provisions. Shareholders' agreements are usually drafted to ensure consistency with the articles. The shareholders' agreement may prevail over the company's articles of association provided it is not inconsistent with the Companies Act 2006.

As the shareholders' agreement is a private document, it does not require registration at Companies House.

Typically, new shareholders joining the shareholders' agreement will do so by a deed of adherence where they agree to comply with all aspects of the shareholders' agreement.

Model articles of association

6.37 Companies have the freedom to draft and set their internal rules, but in some cases they can rely on a standard prescribed set of articles to govern their relationships, with adaptations to such articles specifically applicable to their particular situation. Under CA 2006, companies have the option to adopt model articles of association, which are set out in standard form. These model articles may be adopted either in their entirety, or in part depending upon the company's requirements.

6.38 Under CA 2006, s 19(1) the Secretary of State has power by regulations, to prescribe model articles of association for companies. Different model articles may be prescribed for different types of company: CA 2006, s 19(2).

A company may adopt all or any of the provisions of the model articles: CA 2006, s 19(3). Under s 19, any amendment of model articles by regulations will not affect a company registered before the amendment takes effect.

Under s 19(4), 'amendment' here includes addition, alteration or repeal.

6.39 On 16 December 2008, the Secretary of State enacted the Companies (Model Articles) Regulations 2008, SI 2008/3229 and these came into force on 1 October 2009. The model articles apply to private and public companies incorporated on or after 1 October 2009, where companies decide to adopt them in their entirety or with amendments. They also apply by default to companies formed under CA 2006, unless they register their own articles. Where the proposed company decides to adopt model articles without any amendments, it does not need to send a copy of the articles to Companies House.

6.40 The three model articles enacted are:

- Model Articles for Private Companies Limited by Shares: reg 2, Sch 1 to the Companies (Model Articles) Regulations 2008;
- Model Articles for Private Companies Limited by Guarantee: reg 3 of the Companies (Model Articles) Regulations 2008;
- Model Articles for Public Companies: reg 4 of the Companies (Model Articles) Regulations 2008.

Contractual status of the articles of association: 'insider' and 'outsider' rights – a statutory contract

6.41 The provisions of the company's constitution bind the company and its members, to the same extent as if there were covenants on the part of the company and of each member to observe those provisions: CA 2006, s 33(1). The effect of s 33(1) is that the articles of association are a statutory contract created by the Companies Act 2006 (and its predecessors): *Bratton Seymour Services Co Ltd v Oxborough* [1992] BCLC 693. This contract is also enforceable between the shareholders. However, under this statutory contract, certain provisions under the articles of association may not be enforceable, unlike a typical contractual document, as enforceability depends upon the capacity in which a person brings an action, as considered below. The contractual status of the articles is likely to arise on a transfer of shares, on a right of pre-emption, or where an obligation is placed on the directors to purchase the shares of a shareholder who is leaving the company: *Borland's Trustees v Steel* [1901] 1 Ch 279.

However, s 33 does not clearly define the relationship between the members, or the relationship between the company and its members.

6.42 Over the years, there have been a number of cases that have considered the effect of s 33(1) (previously CA 1985, s 14) as to the enforcement rights between the different parties depending on whether a person is an 'insider' and able to enforce the provisions of the articles of association, or an 'outsider' who is excluded from enforceability. At common law, only those who are parties to a contract can enforce it having regard to the doctrine of privity of contract. In the context of company law, a shareholder may enforce terms in the articles of association as an 'insider', but a director may be excluded from enforcing the articles of association even where he is closely involved with the company because the law treats him/her as outsider owing to the capacity in which the person brings an action.

It should be noted that the Contracts (Rights of Third Parties) Act 1999 does not apply to the company's constitution: s 6(2).

This section considers four different situations where enforceability has been considered by the courts.

(i) A company's enforcement of the articles of association against a shareholder

6.43 Section 33(1) of CA 2006 allows a company to enforce the articles against a shareholder, as both are parties to such contract as set out in the articles. The articles bind the members in their capacity as members of the company.

A company can enforce provisions of the articles against shareholders

Hickman v Kent or Romney Marsh Sheepbreeders' Association **[1915] 1 Ch 851**

According to the company's articles of association, any disputes between the shareholders were to be referred to arbitration. One of the company's shareholders was in a dispute with the company and issued legal proceedings. The company applied to prevent such legal proceedings from going ahead and to refer the dispute to arbitration in accordance with the company's articles of association. The court decided that the shareholder was bound by the provisions of the articles of association and that the dispute be referred to arbitration.

According to Astbury J:

> '… first, no article can constitute a contract between the company and a third person; secondly, that no right merely purporting to be given by an article to a person, whether a member or not, in a capacity other than that of a member, as for instance, as solicitor, promoter, director, can be enforced against the company; and, thirdly, that articles regulating the rights and obligations of the members generally as such do create rights and obligations between them and the company respectively.'

Further he stated:

> 'An outsider to whom rights purport to be given by the articles in his capacity as such outsider, whether he is or subsequently becomes a member, cannot sue on those articles treating them as contracts between himself and the company to enforce those rights.'

Articles are enforceable against shareholders and they cannot enforce in any other capacity

However, *in Beattie v Beattie* [1938] Ch 708, the articles provided that any dispute between a company and a shareholder should be referred to arbitration. The Court of Appeal applied *Hickman's* case and held that a dispute between the company and a director who was also a member, was not subject to the articles, as the dispute was simply concerned with the company and its director, and not the company with its shareholder.

According to Sir Wilfrid Greene MR: 'The question as to the precise effect of [CA 2006, s 33(1)] has been the subject of considerable controversy in the past, and it may very well be that there will be considerable controversy about it in the future. But it appears to me that this much, at any rate, is good law: that the contractual force given to the articles of association by the section is limited to such provisions of the articles as apply to the relationship of the members in their capacity as members.'

Proceedings can only be brought in the capacity of a shareholder

In *Quinn & Axtens Ltd v Salmon* [1909] 1 Ch 311, the articles of association of a company stipulated that the general management of the business of the company was vested in the directors subject to such regulations – not being inconsistent with the provisions of the articles – as might be prescribed by the company in general meeting. Further, it was provided that no resolution of a meeting of the directors having as its object (among other things) the acquisition or letting of any premises should be valid unless 24 hours' notice of the meeting should have been given to each of the managing directors A and B and that neither of them should have dissented therefrom in writing before or at the meeting. A and B held the bulk of the ordinary shares in the company. Resolutions were passed by the directors for the acquisition of certain premises and for the letting of certain other premises, but B dissented from each of these resolutions in accordance with the articles. At an extraordinary general meeting of the company resolutions to the same effect were passed by a simple majority of the shareholders. B sought an injunction to restrain the company from such transactions.

The Court of Appeal held that an injunction should be granted to prevent such transactions from proceeding. The effect of this decision was that although the dispute affected the directors in question, it was possible to sidestep the *Hickman* case and for the managing director in his capacity as a shareholder to bring such proceedings.

A substantive procedural irregularity may entitle a shareholder to bring an action against the company

A member may also bring proceedings where the articles require a special voting procedure to be followed but this is not so implemented in practice. In *Edwards v Halliwell* [1950] 2 All ER 1064, two trade union members brought an action against the trade union on grounds that a motion to increase members' contributions which required a two-thirds majority was not obtained. It was held by the Court of Appeal that as the matter in question was not a mere irregularity in the internal management of the union, but was a matter of substance and tinctured with oppression, the court would grant the claimants relief if it was proper to do so.

The Court of Appeal further stated that it was implicit in the rule in *Foss v Harbottle* (1843) 2 Hare 461 that the matter relied on as constituting the cause of action should be a cause of action properly belonging to the general body of members of the association in question, as opposed to a cause of action which some individual member could assert in his own right. In the present case, the personal and individual rights of membership of the claimants had been invaded and particular damage inflicted by the invalid alteration of the members' contributions. In such circumstances the rule in *Foss v Harbottle* had no application to individual members who were suing, not in the right of the union, but in their own right to protect from invasion their individual rights as members, and, therefore, the claimants were entitled to their declaration.

According to Jenkins LJ, the rule in *Foss v Harbottle* does not prevent an individual member suing if the matter in respect of which he was suing could validly be done, not by a simple majority of the members of the association, but only by some special majority. See too *Cotter v National Union of Seamen* [1929] 2 Ch 58.

A mere internal irregularity may not entitle a shareholder to bring proceedings if the majority can cure the irregularity

In *MacDougall v Gardiner* (1875) 1 Ch D 13, in breach of the company's articles, the chairman of the meeting refused to request a poll by the shareholders. It was held this was an internal irregularity and the shareholders had no right of action. The decision was based on the majority rule principle. However, see now, CA 2006, Pt 11 derivative actions.

A shareholder may bring proceedings where personal rights are infringed

The *MacDougall* case can be compared with *Pender v Lushington* (1877) 6 ChD 70, a case in which the chairman had refused to recognise the votes of a nominee shareholder. The court held that the personal rights of the shareholder had been infringed. Jessel MR stated that according to the articles, a member of the company was a person whose name was on the register of shareholders. Furthermore, the register was the only evidence by which the rights of members to vote at a general meeting could be ascertained; and that at a general meeting no votes of shareholders properly qualified and whose names had been three months on the register should be rejected on the ground that their shares had been transferred to them by other shareholders for the purpose of increasing their own voting power, or with an object alleged to be adverse to the interests of the company, or on the ground that the holders were not beneficial owners of the shares.

(ii) A shareholder may enforce provisions of the articles of association against another shareholder

6.44

> ***A shareholder may be able to enforce articles against another shareholder***
>
> In *Rayfield v Hands* [1960] Ch 1, the claimant was a shareholder in a company. Article 11 of the articles of association required him to inform the directors of his intention to transfer shares in the company, and provided that the directors 'will take the said shares equally between them at a fair value'. In accordance with article 11, the claimant notified the directors of his intention to transfer the shares. However, the directors contended that they need not take and pay for the claimant's shares on the ground that the articles imposed no such liability upon them. The claimant applied to the court for a determination of the fair value of his shares, and for an order that the directors should purchase such shares at a fair value.
>
> It was held that the shareholder could enforce article 11 against the other shareholders and that they were required to purchase his shares at a fair value. According to Vaisey J, the article was concerned with the relationship between a shareholder and other shareholders, even though it provided for the directors to purchase the shares of the outgoing shareholder. See too *Re Leicester Club and County Racecourse Co* (1885) 30 Ch D 629; *Dean v Prince* [1954] Ch 409.

(iii) Can a shareholder enforce the articles of association against the company?

6.45 Some of the cases in this area provide conflicting positions as to whether a shareholder can enforce the articles against the company. It may not always be possible for a shareholder to enforce articles of association against the company.

> ***A shareholder may be able to enforce some provisions of the articles against the company***
>
> In *Hickman v Kent or Romney Marsh Sheepbreeders' Association* [1915] Ch 851, Astbury J stated that it may be possible for a shareholder to enforce provisions of the articles of association in his capacity only as a shareholder in the company and not in any other capacity. See also *Re Severn and Wye and Severn Bridge Railway Co* (1896) 1 Ch 559 (a shareholder's right to have his vote recorded by the company).

> ***Members of the company may enforce certain provisions of the articles against the company***
>
> In *Pender v Lushington* (1877) 6 Ch D 70, the company's chairman failed to follow proper procedure in recording the votes of the shareholders. This affected the rights of shareholders. The shareholders in their capacity as such succeeded in obtaining an injunction to prevent the passing of any resolution.

> ***A shareholder may bring proceedings against a company for declaration of dividends***
>
> In *Wood v Odessa Waterworks Co* (1889) 42 Ch D 636, a shareholder in his capacity as such was able to bring proceedings against the company to compel declaration of a dividend as provided by the articles: see too *Kaye v Croydon Tramways* [1898] 1 Ch 358; *Baillie v Oriental Telephone and Electric Co Ltd* [1915] 1 Ch 503.

6.46 Section 33(1) of CA 2006 creates a contract which is enforceable by a shareholder against the company. A shareholder may bring proceedings against the company where directors propose to take certain action that could threaten or jeopardise the interests of the company by a potential breach of the articles of association: *Irvine v Union Bank of Australia* (1877) 2 App Cas 366.

(iv) Outsiders cannot enforce the articles of association

6.47 A person who is not suing in his capacity as a member is considered as an 'outsider'. Some cases have not allowed a shareholder to sue in any capacity other than as a member of the company. Such cases have prevented 'outsider rights' from being enforced on the basis that the statutory contract is between the company and its shareholders who are entitled to enforce against each other. Any rights of the outsider are likely to be governed by another contractual arrangement and not the articles of association:

> ***A professional adviser is considered as an 'outsider'***
>
> In *Eley v Positive Life Association* (1876) 1 Ex D 88, the articles of association contained a clause in which it was stated that the claimant, a solicitor, should be the solicitor to the company and transact its legal business. The articles were registered and the company incorporated, and 11 months later the claimant became a member. The claimant was not appointed solicitor by any resolution of the directors, nor by any instrument bearing the seal of the company, but he acted as such for a time. Subsequently, the company ceased to employ him and he brought an action for breach of contract against the company. Amphlett B stated: 'The articles, taken by themselves, are simply a contract between the shareholders *inter se*, and cannot, in my opinion, give a right of action to a person like the plaintiff, not a party to the articles, although named therein'.

> ***A seller of a mine was considered as an 'outsider'***
>
> In *Pritchard's Case* L R 8 Ch 956, the articles of association of a mining company provided that the company should immediately after incorporation enter into an agreement with De Thierry, the vendor, for the purchase of a mine for £2,000 and 3,200 fully paid shares. The articles were signed by the vendor and six other persons, and the directors allotted the 3,200 shares to the vendor or his nominees, but no further agreement was made with him. It was held, affirming the decision

of Wickens V-C, that the articles of association did not constitute a contract in writing between the vendor and the company within CA 2006, s 33, and that the shares could not therefore be considered as fully paid. Mellish LJ stated that the articles of association were simply a contract as between the shareholders *inter se* in respect of their rights as shareholders.

Articles could not be enforced where directors had a discretion vested in them

In *Melhado v Porto Alegre Ry Co* L R 9 C P 503, the articles of association of a joint stock company provided that the company should defray such expenses incurred in its establishment as the directors should consider might be deemed and treated as preliminary expenses to an amount not exceeding £2,000. The claimants, who were promoters of the company, had incurred preliminary expenses in its establishment, but it was held that no action for these expenses would lie in an action brought by the claimants against the company under the articles as the claimants were not parties to the articles of association and the directors had a discretion as to payment of corporate expenses.

In some situations, outsiders' rights may be enforceable under another agreement and not the articles

In *Re New British Iron Co, ex p Beckwith* [1898] 1 Ch 324, the articles of association of a company required its directors to possess a share qualification; and provided that the remuneration of the board 'shall be an annual sum of £1000 to be paid out of the funds of the company'. It was held by Wright J that that although these provisions in the articles were only part of the contract between the shareholders *inter se*, the provisions were, on the directors being employed and accepting office on the footing of them, embodied in the contract between the company and the directors; that the remuneration was not due to the directors in their character of members, but under the contract so embodying the provisions. Further, that, in the winding-up of the company, the directors were entitled to rank as ordinary creditors in respect of the remuneration due to them at the commencement of the winding-up. He stated that the remuneration 'is not due to the directors in their character as members. It is not due to them by their being members of the company, but under a distinct contract with the company.'

Companies (Tables A to F) Regulations 1985

6.48 Before CA 2006, companies established under the Companies Act 1985 had the option to adopt Tables A to F of the Companies (Tables A to F Regulations) 1985, SI 1985/805 and SI 2000/3373 depending upon the type of company established. This was commonly known as Table A. Tables A to F are standardised model articles which companies can use or adopt as their own articles of association. In the absence of a company's own articles of association, Tables A to F apply by default. Table A is most commonly used, as it is a prescribed format of articles of association of a company limited by shares under the previous Companies Act 1985 and earlier legislation.

The Companies Tables A to F Regulations have been amended to ensure the articles are in line with changes in company law and the Companies Act 2006.

6.49 Accordingly, *the Companies (Tables A to F) (Amendment) Regulations 2007 (2007/2541)* and the *Companies (Tables A to F) (Amendment) (No 2) Regulations 2007 (2007/2826)* which came into force on 1 October 2007, have been enacted as part of the modernisation process. These new regulations apply to companies incorporated on or after 1 October 2007 which do not register articles of their own when they apply to be incorporated. Companies are not required to use any of the Tables A to F and can prepare their own articles of association based on the Tables A to F model articles. If companies do not register their own articles of association, then Tables A to F apply by default.

6.50 Whereas Tables A to F apply to companies incorporated after 1 October 2007, the model articles were prepared in December 2008 and commenced on 1 October 2009. The changes to Tables A to F have no impact on the model articles or the timing of the introduction. When the model articles came into force in 2009, they replaced Tables A to F as default articles. However, a company which already has the revised Tables A to F and its articles will not be affected by the model articles, unless it decides to adopt them.

The new Tables A to F do not affect existing companies, unless these companies decide to adopt the Table. Existing companies can decide to amend their current articles of association by special resolution to bring them in line with the changes in the law, as expressed in the revised Tables A to F and CA 2006.

6.51 With regard to changes to Tables C and E, in April 2005, cl 54 of Table C and cl 2 of Table E were amended to bring them in line with CA 2006. Clause 54 of Table C (vote of members) was ambiguous in terms of whether it allowed proxies acting on behalf of the members of a company limited by guarantee to vote on a show of hands prescribed by CA 2006, s 324. With the revision, proxies are now specifically mentioned in the regulation.

Regulation 38 of Table E sets a notice period of seven days for general meetings of unlimited companies. This was in conflict with CA 2006, s 307 which requires at least 14 days' notice. Regulation 38 has, therefore, been deleted from Table E.

6.52 The Table A which applies to a company, is the Table A in force at the date of the company's incorporation. If Table A is subsequently altered, the changes do not affect a company registered before the alteration took effect. In order to ensure that the correct Table A is being used, the starting point is to establish the date of the company's incorporation, and which version of Table A was in force on that date. The table below sets out the various Acts/Regulations in force at the time in respect of Table A and the dates when Table A was effective.

Status of the memorandum of association

6.53 Companies that are established under the Companies Act 2006, on or after 1 October 2009, will adopt a new format for the memorandum of association. However, the memorandum of association does not fall within the definition of a company's constitution. It simply represents a 'snapshot' of the company at the time of incorporation compared to the wider format of the memorandum of association under the Companies Act 1985. Its function is only to set out the agreement of the shareholders to establish the company.

6.54 Section 81(1) of CA 2006 provides that a memorandum of association is a memorandum stating that the subscribers (the founding shareholders) wish to engage in two respects:

- They agree to form a company under CA 2006. This evidences their intention to form a company in compliance with the formalities under the Act.
- The subscribers also agree to become members of the company and, in the case of a company that is to have a share capital, to take at least one share each. By taking their respective allocation of shares, the subscribers will be shareholders in the company.

6.55 The memorandum of association must, however, be in a prescribed form and must be authenticated by each member. The prescribed format for the memorandum of association is set out in the Companies (Registration) Regulations 2008 (2008/3014). Companies are not required to set out any objects clauses in the memorandum of association, as the objects clause is unrestricted, unless the company specifically restricts the objects clause in its articles of association: CA 2006, s 31(1). The objects clause, including any restrictions in the objects, will now be contained in the articles of association. For any company incorporated before 1 October 2009, its objects are deemed to be contained in the articles of association, and if they previously contained restrictions then such restrictions can be removed by special resolution to make the objects unrestricted. This also includes any entrenching provisions that were set out in the memorandum of association. These are now deemed to be contained in the articles of association: CA 2006, s 28.

6.56 As from 1 October 2009, the memorandum of association will not be required to set out the company's authorised share capital. Where a company's memorandum of association referred to its authorised share capital clause before 1 October 2009, this is now deemed to be contained in the articles of association. This clause may be removed by the company's shareholders by an ordinary resolution.

As from 1 October 2009, it is no longer a requirement to include a statement in the memorandum of association that the liability of the shareholders is limited, whether by shares or guarantee. These provisions are now deemed to be contained in the company's articles of association and these provisions are also included in the model articles for both a private and a public company. If a company chooses not to adopt the model articles, it must include a limited liability statement in its articles of association.

Construction of the articles of association

6.57 A company's articles of association constitute a contract, which is in the nature of a statutory contract between the company and the shareholders as well as between the shareholders: CA 2006, s 31. It is considered as a commercial or business document. According to Jenkins LJ in *Holmes v Keyes* [1958] 2 All ER 129:

'... the articles of association of the company should be regarded as a business document and should be construed so as to give them reasonable business efficacy, where a construction tending to that result is admissible on the language of the articles, in preference to a result which would or might prove unworkable.'

In *Re Hartley Baird Ltd* [1955] Ch 143, Wynn-Parry J, where he stated: 'In the interpretation of such a commercial document as articles of association, the maxim *ut res magis valeat quam pereat* should be applied, namely "It is better for a thing to have effect than to be made void".'

6.58 This approach was considered in *BWE International Limited v Jones* [2004] 1 BCLC 406, where the Court of Appeal held that the interpretation of articles of association was very much the same approach as was to be applied to other commercial documents, and accordingly they should be construed so as to give them reasonable business efficacy where that was admissible on the language. However, they should not be construed so as to cut down the shareholder's rights to his property unless that was a fair interpretation of the articles. Further, it was not in general possible to have regard in the interpretation of articles of association to extrinsic evidence. Additionally, the articles of association could not be rectified. The articles could only be construed so as to give it reasonable business efficacy where that was admissible on the language; and there must be close attention to the particular words of the article's provision (see Arden LJ).

6.59 The courts will not rectify a mistake in the articles of association or add provisions to articles which should have been included by the parties: *Scott v Frank F Scott* [1940] 1 Ch 794; and *Evans v Chapman* (1902) 86 LT 381. In some situations, the court may add words to articles of association to avoid any absurdities: *Folkes Group plc v Alexander* [2002] 2 BCLC 254.

Provisions of articles cannot be rewritten by the court nor the implication of terms

In *Bratton Seymour Service Co Ltd v Oxborough* [1992] BCLC 693, the issue before the Court of Appeal was whether it was possible to imply into the articles of association of a company set up to manage a development of flats a term that the shareholders, who were the owners of the flats, should make contributions for the upkeep of the amenity areas of the development. The Court of Appeal held that the articles of association constituted a statutory contract with its own distinctive features. For example, unlike an ordinary contract, it was not defensible on the grounds of misrepresentation and it could not be rectified on the grounds of mistake. Whereas the court might be able to infer a term purely by way of constructional implication, it was not possible to go further and to imply a term from extrinsic circumstances. Dillon LJ was of the view that the articles of association differed from a normal contract because they had statutory force and were subject to a statutory regime in the alteration process.

Steyn LJ thought that the articles of association were a statutory contract of a special nature with its own distinctive features. The articles derived their binding force not from a bargain struck between parties but from the terms of the statute.

It was binding only insofar as it affected the rights and obligations between the company and the members acting in their capacity as members. If it contained provisions conferring rights and obligations on outsiders, then those provisions do not bite as part of the contract between the company and the members, even if the outsider was coincidentally a member. Similarly, if the provisions were not truly referable to the rights and obligations of members as such they did not operate as a contract. Moreover the contract could be altered by a special resolution without the consent of all the contracting parties. Unlike an ordinary contract, the articles were not defensible on the grounds of misrepresentation, common law mistake, mistake in equity, undue influence or duress.

Sir Christopher Slade LJ also considered the articles of association as constituting a form of contract between a shareholder and the company of a special nature having statutory operation. However, he accepted that in construing the articles of association of a company, evidence of surrounding circumstances may be admissible for the limited purpose of identifying persons, places or other subject matter referred to. It was not possible to use extrinsic evidence for the purposes of adding obligations on shareholders as this would place shareholders in an intolerable position. The admission of additional extrinsic evidence that has the effect of increasing obligations would be contrary to the principles governing this type of statutory contract. The shareholders were entitled to rely on the meaning of the language of the memorandum and articles of association, as such meaning appeared from the language used.

See also: *Wambo Coal Pty Ltd v Sumiseki Materials Co Ltd* [2014] NSWCA 326.

Certain principles of construction and interpretation on implying terms may apply to articles of association

One of the leading cases on implication of terms in articles of association is *AG of Belize v Belize Telecom* [2009] 2 BCLC 148, which is a Privy Council decision. This concerned construction of the articles of association. There were various classes of shareholders who had the ability to appoint and remove directors. However, the articles made no express provision as to what would be the position for appointment of directors where a shareholder's shareholding fell below a certain threshold.

Lord Hoffmann set out some basic principles of implication of terms:

- The court had no power to improve upon an instrument which it was called upon to construe, whether it was a contract, a statute or articles of association.
- It was concerned only to discover what the instrument meant.
- When an instrument did not provide expressly for what was to happen when some event occurred, the most usual inference was that nothing was to happen.

- Although in certain cases the court would imply a term, the purpose of such an implication was to spell out the meaning of the instrument, not to make an addition to the instrument.
- In every case in which it was said that some provision ought to be implied in an instrument, the question for the court was whether such a provision would spell out in express words what the instrument, read against the relevant background, would reasonably be understood to mean. That question could be reformulated in various ways which a court might find helpful in providing an answer – the implied term had to 'go without saying', it had to be 'necessary to give business efficacy to the contract' and so on – but those were not to be treated as different or additional tests. There was only one question: was that what the instrument, read as a whole against the relevant background, would reasonably be understood to have meant.

Lord Hoffmann decided that the implication was also required in such a case to avoid defeating what appeared to be the overriding purpose of the machinery of appointment and removal of directors, namely to ensure that the board reflected the appropriate shareholder interests in accordance with the scheme laid out in the articles. The implication as to the composition of the board was based not on extrinsic evidence known to a limited number of persons but upon the scheme of the articles themselves and, to a limited extent, such background as was apparent from the memorandum and the fact that all in Belize knew that telecommunications was a state monopoly. See too *Stena Line Ltd v Merchant Navy Ratings Pension Fund Trustees Ltd* [2011] EWCA Civ 543.

A plain and ordinary interpretation and construction should be given to the articles unless this produced a commercial absurdity

In *Thompson v Goblin Hill Hotels Ltd* [2011] 1 BCLC 587, the company's articles of association stated that the maintenance charges for the villas were to be borne by 'each member' of the company. The company levied maintenance charges on the leaseholder shareholders and not investor shareholders too. The case turned on the construction of the words in the articles of association. The Privy Council held that applying the principle that the plain and ordinary meaning of the words used in a commercial contract could only be displaced if it produced a commercial absurdity, the provision under the company's articles was to be given its plain and ordinary meaning that the amount assessed for maintenance was to be borne by each member of the company, including the investor shareholders, in the proportion that his shareholding bore to the entire issued share capital of the company, since the respondents, on whom the onus lay, had not shown that such an interpretation resulted in a commercial absurdity. As a matter of ordinary language the particular provision in the articles of association could only reasonably be understood to bear their literal meaning so that 'each member' meant exactly that, namely each shareholder and not just leaseholder shareholders. Furthermore, in the face of the plain and ordinary meaning it was impossible to imply a term that the assessments should be borne only by leaseholder shareholders.

The Privy Council considered that the plain and ordinary meaning of the words used in the company's articles could only be displaced if it produced a commercial absurdity. It preferred the approach taken by Lord Diplock in *Antaios Cia Naviera SA v Salen Rederierna AB, The Antaios* [1985] AC 191:

> 'If a detailed semantic and syntactical analysis of words in a commercial contract is going to lead to a conclusion that flouts business common sense, it must be made to yield to business common sense'.

If there is no express provision in a contract, a term cannot be implied

In *Marks and Spencer plc v BNP Paribas Securities Services Trust Company (Jersey) Limited* [2014] ECWA Civ 603, the Court of Appeal was required to consider a 'break clause' in a lease which allowed the tenant to terminate the lease earlier than the last date of the lease term upon payment of a 'break premium'. Although the parties had negotiated the break premium, the lease did not mention anything on the apportionment of rent which the lease required the tenant to pay in advance. The issue was whether the court could imply a term which enabled the tenant to get back that part of the advance payment of rent which related to a broken period after the break date? Arden LJ considered that the principles of interpretation enabled the court to take account of the parties' common aim in entering into a transaction or any provision in it (see *Investors Compensation v West Bromwich Building Society* [1998] 1 WLR 896). It was a different exercise from implying a term using the conventional pre-Belize test which involved asking whether the term implied was necessary in order to give effect to the agreement. The *Belize* test required the court to ask whether the agreement has the meaning that such a term would achieve, because even though the parties did not expressly include that term in their agreement, that is what their agreement meant. This required the court to pay close regard to the contractual terms and a high level of loyalty to the parties' agreement read against the admissible background. The party seeking to establish an implied term must therefore show not simply that the term *could* be part of the agreement, but that a term *would* be part of the agreement. The starting point in implying terms was that if there was no express term none could be implied because if the parties intended that a particular term should apply to their relationship, they would have indicated a term to that effect rather than leave it to implication. On the facts, the Court of Appeal held that there was no implied term for repayment of the break premium. The Supreme Court dismissed the tenant's appeal.

Implied duty of good faith and fair dealing in shareholders' agreements

Haughton J in the Irish High Court case of *Flynn v Breccia* [2015] IEHC 547 decided that in the context of a commercial relationship, there was an implied duty for the parties to act in good faith and fair dealing. Haughton J referred to the approach adopted by Leggatt J in *Yam Seng PTE Ltd v International Trade Corporation Ltd* [2013] EWHC 111:

'The case for a wider implication of a term of good faith and fair dealing in ordinary commercial contracts based on the presumed intentions of the parties put forward by Leggatt J in Yam Seng is persuasive, and on the level of principle there is much to recommend his approach. While it has certainly not received universal acceptance in the UK High Court, it has not been rejected by any clear cut authoritative decision of a higher court, and it appears to have some support from the Court of Appeal.

In principle, but with certain caveats that Leggatt J enunciates, I see no reason why this Court should not follow his lead in an appropriate case. Implying such a term is heavily dependent on context, and may only be appropriate in a "relational" type contract where there is a long term commitment. I also agree with Andrews J in Greenclose where she said that such a term will be more readily implied in a situation where a contracting party is given a discretion such that "the discretion should not be exercised in bad faith or in an arbitrary or capricious manner."'

The court will have regard to the duty to act honestly in the performance of contractual obligations

In the Canadian case of *Bhasin v Hrynew* (2014) SCC 71, Cromwell J considered that there was a general organising principle of good faith underlying various aspects of contract law. Further, there was a new common law duty which applied to all contracts, namely, to act honestly in the performance of contractual obligations and not capriciously or arbitrarily. Under this duty of honesty, the parties must not lie or otherwise knowingly mislead each other about matters directly linked to the performance of the contract.

The principle of duty of honesty could be applied to interpreting articles of association to ensure that one part to the statutory contract does not mislead the other in the functional and operational performance of the articles. The test is similar to the duty to act bona fide when effecting alteration of the articles but is more concerned with the performance of obligations under the contract.

The court will have regard to the express terms in the articles of association as representing the true bargain entered into between the parties

In *Jackson v Dear* [2014] 1 BCLC 186, the Court of Appeal stated that the starting point was to consider the nature of the express terms in the articles of association. In some circumstances, the articles may be silent on a particular point. The test was to identify whether the consequences would contradict what a reasonable person would understand the contract to mean taking account of the fact that the opinions of reasonable people may differ in any given set of circumstances. The Court of Appeal also stated that the express terms agreed between the parties represented the true bargain between them, and it was not necessary for the commercial workability of a contract to imply terms in it. Further, it was not obvious that the parties would have agreed to terms being implied into the contract.

> ***In interpreting provisions of articles of association, the court looks to see whether the provisions are clear and unambigious***
>
> In *Sugarman v CJ Investments LLP* [2015] 1 BCLC 1, the Court of Appeal was required to consider a provision in the company's articles of association concerning voting for the appointment of directors. Article 13 provided that every member of the company present in person or by proxy should have one vote. The defendants argued that Article 13 should be read as restricted to a show of hands only and that the issue of voting on a poll was regulated by the CA 2006. The Court of Appeal held that the language of Article 13 was 'clear and ambiguous', and that the words 'present in person or by proxy' did not indicate that the draughtsman was only considering a show of hands. A reasonable person seeking to understand these words would not react by saying 'it cannot mean what it says'. It was clear that Article 13 meant what it said.

Checklist: alteration of articles of association

6.60 *This checklist sets out the law, practice and procedure for amending articles of association.*

No	Issue	Reference
1	Prepare an agenda for the board meeting	Articles and Agenda
2	Draft appropriate amendments to the company's articles of association – check also whether any specific requirements may be set out in any shareholders' agreement	Articles and Shareholders' Agreement
3	Send notice of the board meeting to the company's directors giving date, time and place of the meeting	Articles
4	Can directors dispense with a board meeting by a written resolution procedure?	Articles
5	Is a quorum present?	Articles
6	Has a chairman been appointed for the board meeting?	Articles
7	Directors to vote on the resolution to amend the company's articles of association on a show of hands	
8	Prepare minutes of the board meeting	Minutes
9	Company or secretary to send notice of extraordinary general meeting to the shareholders. Meeting to state date, time, place and proxy	Notice
10	Can the EGM be dispensed with?	Articles
11	Is a quorum present at the EGM?	
12	Appoint chairman for the EGM	CA 2006, s 21(1)
13	Shareholders to vote on the special resolution on a show of hands or on a poll	CA 2006, s 26(1)

No	Issue	Reference
14	Prepare minutes of the EGM	CA 2006, s 355
15	Lodge the special resolution at Companies House	CA 2006, s 26(1)
16	Lodge the amended articles of association at Companies House within 15 days after the amendments have been made	CA 2006, s 26(1)

Checklist: model articles for private company limited by shares

6.61 *This checklist sets out in summary form the Model Articles of Association for a company limited by shares.*

No	Issue	Articles
1	*Defined Terms* – sets out the main interpretation terms used in these Model Articles	Part 1, article 1
2	*Liability of Members* – the liability of members is limited to the amount, if any, unpaid on the shares held by them	Part 1, article 2
3	*Directors' General Authority* – directors are responsible for management of the company's business for which purpose they may exercise all powers of the company, subject to the articles	Part 2, article 3
4	*Shareholders' Reserve Power* – shareholders have residual authority by special resolution which can direct the directors to take or refrain from taking specified action	Part 2, article 4
5	*Directors May Delegate* – directors may delegate their powers to certain persons on such terms as thought fit, subject to the articles	Part 2, article 5
6	*Committees* – where directors delegate any of their powers to committees, such committees must follow procedures within the articles governing the taking of decisions by directors. Directors can also make procedural rules for committees	Part 2, article 6
7	*Directors to take decisions collectively* – any decision of directors should be by majority decision or under article 8. If only one director, he may take decisions without regard to any of the provisions in the articles on directors' decision making	Part 2, article 7
8	*Unanimous Decisions* – directors may take unanimous decisions where they share a common view on a matter and in this case, a written resolution procedure may be used	Part 2, article 8

No	Issue	Articles
9	*Calling a Directors' Meeting* – any director can call a board meeting or by authorising the company secretary (if any) to give notice of the meeting with specific contents of the notice	Part 2, article 9
10	*Participation in Directors' Meetings* – subject to the articles, directors may participate in Board meetings or in part	Part 2, article 10
11	*Quorum for Directors' Meetings* – two directors unless otherwise determined by directors	Part 2, article 11
12	*Chairing of Directors' Meetings* – directors may appoint a director to chair meetings of the board which appointment can be terminated any time	Part 2, article 12
13	*Casting Vote* – chairman has casting vote in the event of a deadlock	Part 2, article 13
14	*Conflicts of Interest* – in the event that a director is involved in a proposed or actual conflict of interest that director cannot vote or count in a quorum subject to exceptions	Part 2, article 14
15	*Record of Decisions to be Kept* – all unanimous or majority decisions of directors to be kept for ten years by directors	Part 2, article 15
16	*Directors' discretion to make further rules* – directors can make further rules as thought fit as to how they take decisions and how rules are recorded or communicated to directors	Part 2, article 16
17	*Method of Appointing Directors* – a director can be appointed by ordinary resolution or by a decision of the directors	Part 2, article 17
18	*Termination of directors' appointment* – sets out the circumstances when a person ceases to be a director	Part 2, article 18
19	*Directors' remuneration* – directors are entitled to remuneration as they determine	Part 2, article 19
20	*Directors' expenses* – the company may pay any reasonable expenses which the directors properly incur in respect of their meetings	Part 2, article 20
21	*All shares to be fully paid up* – a share cannot be issued for less than the aggregate of its nominal value	Part 3, article 21
22	*Powers to issue different classes of share* – a company may issue shares with such rights or restrictions as determined by ordinary resolution, subject to the articles and rights attached to any existing share	Part 3, article 22

No	Issue	Articles
23	*Company not bound by less than absolute interests* – company is not bound by and need not recognise any interest in a share other than the holder's absolute ownership	Part 3, article 23
24	*Share certificates* – the company must issue share certificates to each shareholder free of charge with specific details set out in the share certificate	Part 3, article 24
25	*Replacement of share certificates* – in certain circumstances a shareholder can obtain a replacement share certificate upon indemnity and payment of a reasonable fee to the directors	Part 3, article 25
26	*Share transfers* – shares may be transferred by instrument of transfer or as determined by directors	Part 3, article 26
27	*Transmission of shares* – sets out the procedure where shares are transmitted on death of a shareholder or on bankruptcy	Part 3, article 27
28	*Exercise of transmittees' rights* – sets out the procedure for transmittees to hold shares in the company	Part 3, article 28
29	*Transmittees bound by prior notices* – where notice is given to a shareholder in respect of shares and transmittee is entitled to those shares, transmittee bound by the notice if given to the shareholder before transmittee 's name entered in register of members	Part 3, article 29
30	*Procedure for declaring dividends* – by ordinary resolution and the directors may decide to pay interim dividends	Part 3, article 30
31	*Payment of dividends and other distributions* – addresses how a dividend will be paid once declared	Part 3, article 31
32	*No interest on distributions* – general rule that a company will not pay interest on dividends subject to exceptions	Part 3, article 32
33	*Unclaimed distributions* – deals with procedure where dividends unclaimed by shareholders	Part 3, article 33
34	*Non-cash distributions* – subject to ordinary resolution, company may decide to pay all or part of dividends by non-cash assets	Part 3, article 34
35	*Waiver of distributions* – deals with circumstances when dividends may be waived	Part 3, article 35
36	*Authority to capitalise and appropriation of capitalised sums* – directors may decide to capitalise the company's profits subject to ordinary resolution	Part 3, article 36
37	*Attendance and speaking at general meetings* – the right of a person to attend and speak, communicate any information or opinions concerning that meeting	Part 4, article 37

No	Issue	Articles
38	*Quorum for general meetings* – no business can be conducted at a general meeting unless quorum is present except appointment of chairman	Part 4, article 38
39	*Chairing general meetings* – the chairman will chair general meetings if appointed and the procedure where a chairman has not been appointed and who can chair	Part 4, article 39
40	*Attendance and speaking by directors and non-shareholders* – directors may attend and speak at general meetings whether or not they are shareholders. At chairman's discretion, others may be entitled to attend and speak	Part 4, article 40
41	*Adjournment* – where a meeting is not quorate within half an hour of the meeting time, it may be adjourned in circumstances set out	Part 4, article 41
42	*Voting: general* – on a show of hands unless poll demanded	Part 4, article 42
43	*Errors and disputes* – An objection as to the qualification of the person voting at a general meeting can only be raised at the general meeting or adjourned meeting	Part 4, article 43
44	*Poll votes* – deals with circumstances when a poll vote is taken	Part 4, article 44
45	*Content of proxy notices* – sets out what is required in a proxy notice	Part 4, article 45
46	*Delivery of proxy notices* – deals with appointment and revocation of proxy notices	Part 4, article 46
47	*Amendments to resolutions* – deals with procedure for amendments to ordinary and special resolutions	Part 4, article 47
48	*Means of communication to be used* – this is subject to the articles and means of communication prescribed under CA 2006 in respect of notices or documents	Part 4, article 48
49	*Company seals* – any common seal may only be used by authority of the directors	Part 4, article 49
50	*No right to inspect accounts and other records* – accounting or other records cannot be inspected by a shareholder unless authorised by directors or by ordinary resolution	Part 4, article 50
51	*Provision for employees on cessation of business* – directors may make provision for the benefit of employees or former employees of the company on a cessation or transfer of business	Part 4, article 51
52	*Indemnity* – deals with indemnifying a director in certain circumstances and form of indemnity	Part 4, article 52
53	*Insurance* – directors may decide to take out insurance in respect of any loss or liability incurred by the director	Part 4, article 53

Checklist: effective date of Table A

6.62 *This checklist sets out the further changes to Table A since its enactment.*

The effective date of each Table A	
Table A prescribed by:	*Effective from:*
Joint Stock Companies Act 1856	14 July 1856
The Companies Act 1862	7 August 1862
Board of Trade Order 1906	1 October 1906
Companies Consolidation Act 1908	1 April 1909
Companies Act 1929	1 November 1929
Companies Act 1948	1 July 1948
– as amended by Companies Act 1967	27 January 1968
– as amended by Companies Act 1976 (3 commencement dates)	18 April 1977, 1 June 1977, and 1 October 1977
– as amended by the Stock Exchange (Completion of Bargains) Act 1976, Part 1 – as amended by the Stock Exchange (Completion of Bargains) Act 1976, Part 2 – as amended by the Stock Exchange (Completion of Bargains) Act 1976, Part 3	2 February 1979
– as amended by Companies Act 1980	22 December 1980
– as amended by Companies Act 1981	3 December 1981
Companies (Tables A to F) Regulations 1985	1 July 1985
– as amended by Companies (Tables A to F) (Amendment) Regulations 1985	1 August 1985
– as amended by Companies Act 1985 (Electronic Communications) Order 2000	22 December 2000
– as amended by Companies (Tables A to F) (Amendment) Regulations 2007 and The Companies (Tables A to F) (Amendment) (No 2) Regulations 2007 for private companies limited by shares	
– as amended by Companies (Tables A to F) (Amendment) Regulations 2007 and The Companies (Tables A to F) (Amendment) (No 2) Regulations 2007 for public companies limited by shares	1 October 2007

Checklist: articles of association

6.63

No	Issue	Reference
1	Articles are defined as part of the company's 'constitution' and are registered at Companies House	CA 2006, s 17
2	The company's 'constitution' also includes resolutions of directors and shareholders	CA 2006, s 29
3	The memorandum of association is not part of the company's constitution	CA 2006, s 8
4	Articles regulate the internal relations between the company, directors and the shareholders and every company must have articles	CA 2006, s 18
5	A company may either have tailor-made articles, or adopt the default Model Articles or combine both the Model Articles and its own articles	
6	Articles may be supplemented by a shareholders' agreement setting out in more detail the governance between shareholders and directors including exit mechanisms and restrictive covenants	
7	Certain provisions of the articles may be entrenched for the protection of certain shareholders	CA 2006, s 22(1)
8	A company may alter its articles of association	CA 2006, s 21(1)
9	Judicial attitudes towards articles of association range from various tests employed for the alteration including: (i) bona fide for the benefit of the company; (ii) notions of conscience, oppression and (iii) shareholders to consider the alteration honestly as to whether for the company's benefit.	*Allen v Gold Reefs of West Africa Ltd* [1900] 1 Ch 656; *Brown v British Abrasive Wheel* [1919] 1 Ch 290; *Sidebottom v Kershaw, Leese & Co Ltd* [1920] 1 Ch 154.
10	Provisions of the company's constitution bind the company and its members to the same extent as if there were covenants on the part of the company and of each member to observe those provisions	CA 2006, s 33(1)
11	A company may enforce articles against a shareholder	*Hickman v Kent or Romney Marsh Sheepbreeders' Association* [1915] Ch 851
12	A shareholder may enforce provisions of the articles of association against another shareholder	Ch 851; *Rayfield v Hands* [1960] Ch 1

No	Issue	Reference
13	A shareholder may be able to enforce some of the provisions of the articles against the company	*Pender v Lushington* (1877) 6 Ch D 70
14	Outsiders cannot enforce the articles of association	*Eley v Positive Life Association* (1876) 1 Ex D 88

Definitions

6.64

Bona fide: good faith intention.

Constitution: includes articles of association and resolutions and agreements to which Ch 3 of Pt 3 to CA 2006 applies: CA 2006, s 17.

Special enactment: an enactment that is not a public general enactment, and includes:

(a) an Act for confirming a provisional order;

(b) any provision of a public general Act in relation to the passing of which any of the standing orders of the House of Lords or the House of Commons relating to private business applied; or

(c) any enactment to the extent that it is incorporated in or applied for the purposes of a special enactment: CA 2006, s 34(4).

7 Corporate capacity and related matters

Contents

Introduction

7.1 As the company is considered a separate legal entity distinct from its shareholders, it has legal capacity to enter into contracts with third parties, and internally with shareholders and directors: CA 2006, s 16; *Salomon v Salomon & Co Ltd* [1897] AC 22.

Previously, a company's capacity to enter into transactions was strictly regulated and controlled by various mechanisms, including restricting or expanding its ability to enter into certain transactions through provisions contained in the objects clause in the memorandum of association. Corporate capacity could also be restricted through judicial intervention by the use of the doctrine of *ultra vires*. The aim of the *ultra vires* doctrine, as it applied to companies, was to protect investors and creditors against unauthorised corporate activities and depletion of their funds. In the strict sense of the term, any transaction which was beyond the company's capacity as defined in its objects clause in the memorandum of association would be void and could not be ratified by the members: *Ashbury Railway Carriage and Iron Company v Riche* (1875) LR HL 653.

7.2 At times, the *ultra vires* doctrine created obstacles for companies and third parties by restricting their commercial freedom to enter into transactions, and progressively the practice grew of expanding a companies' objects clauses to allow them to undertake a wide range of business activities without invoking the *ultra vires* doctrine: *Bell Houses Ltd v City Wall Properties Ltd* [1966] 1 QB 207. This technique of expanding the objects clauses as widely as possible to allow for any activity by a company was at times met with judicial disapproved. Although the House of Lords in *Cotman v Brougham* [1918] AC 514 viewed this activity as 'pernicious practice: confusing power with purpose', Lord Wrenbury felt he had to 'yield to it'.

However, the application of the ultra vires doctrine created judicial uncertainty owing to the confusion between corporate capacity and a company's powers. In *Rolled Steel*

Products v British Steel Corporation [1985] 3 All ER 52, the Court of Appeal decided that the term *ultra vires* was only applicable to acts beyond the company's capacity as opposed to powers.

7.3 Corporate capacity is now regulated by the CA 2006 and the company's articles of association. This section addresses the following issues:

- consideration of the concept of corporate capacity;
- how corporate capacity may be restricted;
- the effect of corporate capacity;
- the powers of directors to bind the company;
- related matters including execution of documents by companies.

Corporate capacity

Nature of corporate capacity

7.4 A company's capacity refers to its ability to carry out specific activities or enter into transactions, through the board of directors, the shareholders or third parties for the purposes of the company's business. Historically, the activities were governed by the company's objects clause and powers that were supplementary to the company's objects as set out in the company's memorandum of association. However, there is no longer a requirement for a company to provide an objects clause in its constitution. Section 31 of CA 2006 states that a company will have unlimited objects, unless the objects are specifically restricted by the articles. In practice, this means that unless a company makes a deliberate choice to restrict its objects or activities, the objects will have no bearing on what a company can do. This allows freedom for companies to engage in commercial dealings without any impediment or restrictions in the objects clause. Any restrictions or limitations in the company's articles of association will not affect the company's capacity to engage in transactions, but it may impact on the powers and duties of directors who had entered into the prohibited transaction or activity.

7.5

Example:

Company A decides to restrict its objects clause in its articles of association with the following provision:

> 'Notwithstanding any other provision in the Company's Articles of Association, the Company shall not at any time engage in any philanthropic activities or provide any donations to any organisations, persons, charities or entities without the unanimous resolution of the shareholders.'

In breach of the restrictions in its articles, Company A provides financial donations to charities and seconds some of its employees to local organisations to discharge its corporate social responsibilities, and to demonstrate that it is a good, responsible and caring corporate citizen.

The effects of CA 2006, ss 31 and 39 are that Company A's capacity to enter into the transaction cannot be challenged. The external effects of the *ultra vires* doctrine, therefore, have no application. The directors may also be in breach of their general duties set out in CA 2006, Pt 10 unless they can demonstrate that they acted in good faith to promote the success of the company. They may consider CA 2006, s 1157 (relief from liability) as exoneration from liability for breach of duty. Shareholders may have an action against the directors for exceeding their powers, or acting in breach of their general duties or in breach of the contractual provisions of the articles of association. The internal effects of the *ultra vires* doctrine may still apply.

7.6 Under CA 2006, s 31(2) where a company changes its articles to add, remove or alter a statement of the company's objects, it must give notice to the registrar at Companies House. The registrar must register the notice, and the alteration will not take effect until the notice has been registered.

Section 31(3) of CA 2006 ensures that any such amendment to the company's articles of association will not affect any rights or obligations of the company, or render defective any legal proceedings by or against it.

Companies that are charities will still apply CA 2006, s 31 in respect of their objects. However, the charities are subject to the charities legislation, depending upon the jurisdiction where they were established: see s 64 of the Charities Act 1993 in England and Wales; in Northern Ireland: Charities (Northern Ireland) Order 1987 (SI 1987/2048) (NI); and in Scotland where a company is entered the Scottish Charity Register, the Charities and Trustee Investment (Scotland) Act 2005 applies: CA 2006, s 31(4).

Under CA 2006, directors still have a duty to observe the company's constitution. Section 171 of the Act requires directors to act within their powers. However, restrictions in a company's objects will have little effect outside of the internal operations of the company because of the effect of s 39 (company's capacity) and s 40 (power of directors to bind the company).

Effect of corporate capacity

7.7 Part 4 of CA 2006 is concerned with the company's capacity and related matters. Section 39(1) of CA 2006 applies to a company's capacity to enter into obligations or to carry out a transaction with third parties. It states that the validity of a company's acts will not be called into question on the ground of lack of capacity by reason of anything in a company's constitution.

The effect of s 39 is that there are no limits to a company's capacity to enter into transactions or undertake various acts, and the company has full contractual and commercial freedom in its dealings with third parties. Therefore, whatever the 'act' in which the company engages, it cannot be called into question. However, the company cannot engage in illegal activities or activities that are contrary to public policy or morals. Also, the courts can and will question a company's capacity to enter into transactions or undertake acts by lifting the corporate veil to identify any evasive wrongdoing: *Prest v Petrodel Ltd* [2013] All ER 90.

Section 7(2) of CA 2006 states that a company cannot be established for an unlawful purpose.

Powers of directors to bind the company

7.8 Section 40(1) of CA 2006 provides that in favour of a person dealing with the company in good faith, the power of the directors to bind the company, or authorise others to do so, is deemed not to be constrained by the company's constitution. The internal aspects of the *ultra vires* doctrine still survive as between the shareholders and directors, which means that directors' powers may be open to challenge by the shareholders.

The concept of 'good faith'

7.9 The effect of CA 2006, s 40(1) is that a third party dealing with a company in good faith need not be concerned about whether a company is acting within its constitution. The term 'good faith' is not defined by CA 2006. Instead, there is a presumption of good faith in favour of the third party. Therefore, only some third parties will benefit from CA 2006, s 40. The third party is presumed to have acted in good faith unless the contrary is proved. He is not to be regarded as acting in bad faith by reason only of his knowing that an act is beyond the powers of the directors under the company's constitution.

7.10 In practice, it may be difficult to demonstrate bad faith owing to the protections given to the third party in the following circumstances:

- There is no obligation on the third party to enquire into the limitations on the powers of directors to bind the company. Therefore, the doctrine of constructive notice does not apply: *Royal British Bank v Turquand* (1856) 6 E & B 327.
- The onus is on the company to show that the third party was not acting in good faith unless the contrary is proved.
- A third party who knows that the act in question is beyond the powers of directors under the company's constitution, will not be considered to have acted in bad faith.

Aspects of 'good faith'

The concept of 'good faith' was considered in *Barclays Bank v TOSG Trust Fund Ltd* [1984] BCLC 1, where Nourse J stated that a person had to act 'genuinely and honestly in the circumstances of the case'.

This case went on appeal to the Court of Appeal on other grounds.

A third party put on notice could not benefit from CA 2006, s 40

In *Wrexham Associated Football Club Ltd v Crucialmove* [2007] BCC 139, the third party in question was put on notice that the director entering into a transaction was involved in a conflict of interest. The Court of Appeal did not allow the third party to take the benefit of CA 2006, s 40 even though he was aware that the directors had exceeded their powers in respect of the transaction in question. As he was put on notice, he was bound to make further enquiries which he failed to do, and could not also rely on the ostensible authority of the officers concerned. Sir Peter Gibson LJ was of the view that the CA 2006, s 40(1) could not absolve a person dealing with the company from any duty to inquire whether the persons acting for the company have been authorised by the board to enter into the transaction when the circumstances were such as to put that person on inquiry. As the third party was put on inquiry, he could not satisfy the requirement of good faith.

A third party did not act in bad faith by knowing of the limitations on directors' powers

Ford v Polymer Vision Ltd [2009] 2 BCLC 160, concerned a company which was in financial difficulties. To address this aspect, a debenture and option agreement was executed in favour of an investor and signed by the chief executive officer. The company's articles authorised transactions by meetings of directors. The issue was whether the meetings were properly convened in accordance with requirements of the company's articles and the shareholders' agreement and whether the third party could rely upon CA 2006, s 40. Blackburne J held that the grant of the debenture to a third party and, later, the option agreement were acts or transactions within the scope of the Companies Act 2006, s 40. The defects in the two meetings, namely the failure to give notice to all of the special directors and the fact that, given the identity of the two directors who did attend and the manner of their attendance, the meetings were deemed to have taken place in the UK, were within the scope of the expression 'limitation under the company's constitution' appearing in s 40(1) and 'beyond the powers of the directors under the company's constitution' appearing in s 40(2)(b)(iii). He decided that the third party had not acted in bad faith simply by knowing about the limitations on directors' powers in the company's articles of association.

'Person dealing with the company'

7.11 CA 2006, s 40(2) states that a person 'deals with' a company if he is a party to any transaction or other act to which the company is a party. The 'transaction' referred to may be a contract or an obligation that is entered into. The term 'act' may refer to consideration paid for the transaction or services performed. This section has given rise to some case law as to what meaning is to be given to 'person' and 'dealing with the company'.

A third party could rely upon CA 2006, s 40 in respect of the bonus shares allocated

In *EIC Services Ltd v Phipps* [2004] 2 BCLC 589, the central issue for the Court of Appeal was whether a shareholder was entitled to rely on s 40 in respect of the bonus shares that were allotted to them. The Court of Appeal held that shareholders could not rely on the section. According to Peter Gibson LJ, the bonus issue could not be validated by the application of s 40 because shareholders receiving bonus shares were not persons 'dealing with the company'. Section 40 contemplated a bilateral transaction between the company and the person dealing with the company, and as a matter of ordinary language, and having regard to the nature of a bonus issue and the fact that it was an internal arrangement in which there was no diminution or increase in the assets or liabilities of the company, no change in the proportionate shareholdings and no action was required from any shareholders, a shareholder receiving bonus shares could not be regarded as a person dealing with the company.

A third party is a constructive trustee for monies knowingly improperly received

In *International Sales and Agencies Ltd v Marcus* [1982] 3 All ER 551, a cheque was drawn by a director on the company's account. The director appropriated the company's funds to settle a personal debt incurred by a deceased director. The creditor knew that the payment was made in breach of trust. The issue was whether the creditor was a constructive trustee for the company of the money received and whether he was a person dealing with the company in good faith. Lawson J considered s 9(1) of the European Communities Act 1972, which later led to s 40 CA 2006. He held that applying the principles of constructive trust, monies received by a third party knowing that it came improperly from the company's funds was a breach of trust: the defendants became constructive trustees of the money received by them, since they had actual notice that the money received belonged to the company: see too Ungoed-Thomas J in *Selangor United Rubber Estates Ltd v Cradock (a bankrupt) (No 3)* [1968] 2 All ER at 1093, and Lord Dunpark in *Thompson v J Barke & Co (Caterers) Ltd* 1975 SLT at 75; and *Belmont Finance Corp v Williams Furniture Ltd (No 2)* [1980] 1 All ER 393. Further, in applying CA 2006, s 40 Lawson J stated that with regard to the concept of 'good faith, a third party who had actual knowledge that the payments to them were in breach of duty and trust and were *ultra vires* the company could not be said to be acting in good faith under s 40.

The position of directors under CA 2006, s 40

7.12 CA 2006, s 40 concerns directors and allows any limitations on their powers to bind the company or authorise others to do so to be removed. One issue that arises is where there is a properly convened board of directors' meeting (ie proper notice served), but the requisite quorum is not present, and the transaction is entered into by the directors who bind the company with the third party. The issue is whether the third party can benefit from CA 2006, s 40 in these circumstances.

A person must be a director to fall within CA 2006, s 40

In *Smith v Henniker-Major & Co (a firm)* [2002] 2 BCLC 655, a director convened a meeting of the company at which he alone attended without the requisite quorum (which was two). He approved and executed an assignment as director and chairman of certain of the company's claims to himself in the mistaken belief that he had power to act alone under the articles. The principal issue was whether the director was entitled to rely on his own mistake to invoke CA 2006, s 40 concerning powers of the board of directors to bind the company to validate his act.

The Court of Appeal was divided on the issue. It held that the requirement for a quorum was a limitation on the power of the board of directors to bind the company within the meaning of s 40. The irreducible minimum if s 40 was to apply was a genuine decision taken by a person or persons who could on substantial grounds claim to be the board of directors acting as such, even though the proceedings of the board were marred by procedural irregularities.

The majority in the Court of Appeal thought that although the expression 'person dealing with the company' in s 40 was wide enough to include a director of the company, it did not apply to a person such as the claimant, who was not simply a director dealing with the company and having some incidental involvement in the decision, but the chairman of the company, whose duty it was to ensure that the constitution was properly applied. Accordingly the claimant could not rely on his own mistake in order to give validity to something which had no validity of any kind under the company's constitution. The requirement for a quorum was a limitation on the power of the board of directors to bind the company within the meaning of s 40.

Robert Walker LJ, however, dissented and thought that the chairman could rely on s 40 to validate what had happened, whereas Schiemann and Carnwath L JJ thought that he could not.

According to Carnwath LJ, the issue was to identify the 'irreducible minimum' needed to bring s 40 into play. Literal interpretation would not be of assistance. Section 40 concerned the 'power of the board of directors' to bind the company, in favour of a person who is party to 'any transaction … to which the company is a party'. There were two questions to which s 40 provided no direct answer: first, how did the 'board of directors' exercise its power; and second, in what circumstances was a transaction to be treated as one to which the company was a 'party'? He thought that both questions could only be answered, under the ordinary law, by looking at the company's constitution. Yet that is the very inquiry which s 40 sought to avoid.

Carnwath LJ was also of the view that the matter under s 40 could not be decided by distinguishing between 'procedural irregularity' and 'nullity' as set out by Robert Walker LJ who thought that the absence of a quorum was a mere procedural irregularity and would still allow a person to have protection under s 40.

Schiemann LJ explained the policy behind CA 2006, s 40:

> 'This provision was clearly intended to prevent the company from relying as against a third party on limits on the powers of the organs of the company. I do not consider that it was intended to prevent the company from relying on those limits as against the very director ("the delinquent director") who breached those limits. The fact that the directive makes no mention of good faith seems to lend support to this view. It is to me inconceivable that it was intended that a company should not be able to sue a director who knowingly acted beyond his powers so as to dispose of the company's assets. This leads me to the conclusion that such a director falls out with the concept of a third party as used in the directive.'

He thought that the heart of the issue was:

> 'Does … [section 40] enable a director, who has made an honest mistake as to the meaning of a provision in the articles of the company of which he is a director, himself to rely on his own mistake in order to give validity to something which would lack validity were it not for that mistake? In the phraseology of judges who lived in a different sartorial era, to pull himself up by his own bootstraps.'

He was of the view that s 40 did not apply in this situation.

Application of 'good faith' under CA 2006, s 40

The concept of 'good faith' was considered in *Sargespace Ltd v Natasha Anastasia Eustace* [2013] EWHC 2944, which concerned Mr Baxendale-Walker ('BW') who acquired and operated a company making pornographic films in which he starred, and whose lifestyle was described by the judge as essentially involving casual relationships with multiple sex partners – a group or club of women known as his 'hunny bunnies' or the 'hunny bunnies club' to whom, in return for their sexual favours, he made lavish gifts, including money, clothes and holidays, as well as providing flats and cars for their use.

The defendant, Natasha Eustace, was one of the members of the club. According to BW, they had what was no more than a casual and (on both sides) non-exclusive sexual relationship beginning in the summer of 2010 and lasting until December 2011, at which time their sexual relationship ended – although they remained friends. BW claimed that she was a TV stripper and glamour model who provided sex and occasional companionship in exchange for a comfortable and conditional standard of living. Eustace's account was however different. She claimed that they had a loving and close relationship and although there were arguments over BW's sexual activities with other women, it was intended to be a long term and faithful relationship which would eventually lead to marriage. Various emails from BW to Eustace described his love for Eustace and described the emptiness in BW's playboy life and describing his other girlfriends as 'the shit girls'. According to the judge, while BW's emails would not win any literary prize, BW appeared to have genuinely described his ardent love for Eustace.

The action concerned a flat in the UK of which Eustace was the registered legal owner and a Range Rover vehicle, also in her name. The claimant, Sargescape Ltd, a company of which BW is a director and shareholder, maintained that it provided the funds for the purchase of the flat on terms that the legal title would be held by Eustace as a bare trustee, and that it was beneficially entitled to the flat and a right to possession. Further, it claimed that the Range Rover was lent to Eustace who had no legal or beneficial ownership. The application was by the company for summary judgment on its claims for both the flat and the vehicle.

It was contended on behalf of BW that the flat did not belong to BW but to the company and that BW was unable to effect such a gift, because to do so would be either *ultra vires* or would entail a major breach of his fiduciary and common law duties as a director, which would be unthinkable when the company was in independent ownership.

Justice Males considered CA 2006, s 40 and stated that Eustace was clearly a person 'dealing with the company'. So that if there were any limitation on the powers of the directors to bind the company, that limitation would not affect her, unless it could be proved, the burden being on the company, that she was not acting in good faith. He stated that it seemed unlikely that this was a burden which would be able to discharge. He made no further decision on this point.

Justice Males also considered the applicability of CA 2006, s 41 which concerned transactions whose validity depended upon s 40 to be voidable if the parties to the transaction included 'a person connected with' a director of the company. He decided that the definition of connected persons included spouses, civil partners and those with whom the director was living as a partner. However, it did not include Eustace as she did not live together with BW but was considered as his mistress and s 41 could not assist her.

Justice Males was of the opinion that the proper analysis was likely to be concerned with breach of the directors' duties rather than powers of the company. Accordingly, if BW and his fellow director were acting in breach of their duties to the company in transferring title to Eustace, that would leave the company with a remedy against BW and his fellow director, but would not affect Eustace's position, unless she was complicit in the wrongdoing – but this was not a matter for summary determination. He did not, however, accept that there was any breach of duty. This would depend upon such matters as the identity of the beneficial owners of the company and what they knew about the transaction or the way BW used the company as a vehicle for providing benefits to the members of his bunnies club.

The judge dismissed the company's claim for summary judgment in respect of the flat and vehicle, as Eustace had a real prospect of defending the claims against her by the company on the ownership of the assets.

The references to limitations on the directors' powers under the company's constitution include limitations deriving from a resolution of the company or of any class of shareholders; or from any agreement between the members of the company or any class of shareholders: CA 2006, s 40(3).

The internal effects of the *ultra vires* doctrine still survive. Despite directors exceeding the limitations on their powers, shareholders can still take action. CA 2006, s 40(4) provides that it does not affect any right of a member of a company to bring proceedings to restrain the doing of an action that is beyond the powers of the directors. This procedure allows shareholders to bring an action (usually seeking an injunction) to prevent directors from entering into future obligations that are beyond their powers. However, no such proceedings lie in respect of an act to be done in fulfilment of a legal obligation arising from a previous act of the company.

7.13

Example:

The chairman of the board of directors of Company Z has circulated an agenda to all directors, which contains an item for the proposed sale of one of the company's property at what is considered to be at a substantial undervalue and which is not permitted under its articles of association. A minority shareholder of Company Z receives a copy of the agenda in error. The shareholder proposes to prevent Company Z from voting on this item at the board meeting.

Section 40(4) of CA 2006 allows the shareholder to petition to the court by applying, for example, for an injunction preventing Company Z's board of directors voting on the item and passing the resolution.

Now suppose that for this particular property, Company Z had previously entered into a lease, but failed to send notice to the landlord for non-renewal of the lease in a timely manner to the landlord or its agents. The lease provides that in such event, the lease is deemed renewed for a further year. In this situation, Company Z will be bound by the terms of the lease and it will be difficult for the shareholders to bring proceedings as the renewal of the lease will be considered as an act to be done in fulfilment of an obligation arising from a previous act of Company Z.

7.14 Further, s 40 does not affect any liability incurred by the directors, or any other person, by reason of the directors exceeding their powers: CA 2006, s 40(5). Section 40 is also subject to s 41 (transactions with directors or their associates), and s 42 (companies that are charities).

Constitutional limitations: transactions involving directors or their associates

7.15 Section 41 of CA 2006 applies to a transaction if, or to the extent that, its validity depends on s 40. It provides that nothing in s 41 is to be read as excluding the operation of any other enactment or rule of law by virtue of which the transaction may be called into question or any liability to the company may arise: s 41(1). The term 'transaction' includes any act: CA 2006, s 41(7).

This section also addresses the position of the nature of the transaction between the company and its director or connected persons. Where a company enters into a transaction of the type contemplated under s 41(1), and the parties to the transaction include a director of the company or of its holding company, or a person connected with any such director, the transaction is voidable at the instance of the company. The reference to a person connected with a director has the same meaning as in Part 10 (company directors): CA 2006, s 41(7).

Section 41 of CA 2006 refers to a transaction with an 'insider' such as a director or person connected with a director. Irrespective of whether the transaction is voided, the 'insider' and any director of the company who authorised the transaction is liable to account to the company for any gain he has made directly or indirectly as a result of the transaction, and to indemnify the company for any loss or damage that the company has incurred resulting from the transaction.

7.16 Under s 41(4) a transaction will cease to be voidable in certain circumstances:

- if restitution of any money or assets that have been lost as a result of the transaction is no longer possible; or
- the company is indemnified for any loss or damage resulting from the transaction; or
- rights acquired bona fide for value without actual notice of the directors exceeding their powers by a person who is not a party to the transaction would be affected by voiding the transaction; or
- the transaction is affirmed by the company.

However, where the 'insider' is not a director of the company, it may be possible for him to avoid liability under s 41(3) if he can show that at the time he entered into the transaction with the company, he did not know that the directors were exceeding their authority: CA 2006, s 41(5).

However, nothing in the preceding provisions of s 41 affects the rights of any party to the transaction not within s 41(2)(b)(i) or (ii). But the court may, on the application of the company or any such party, make an order affirming, severing or setting aside the transaction on such terms as appear to the court to be just: CA 2006, s 41(6). See too *Re Torvale Group Ltd* [1999] 2 BCLC 605.

Constitutional limitations: companies that are charities

7.17 Sections 39 and 40 (company's capacity and power of directors to bind company) do not apply to the acts of a company that is a charity, except in favour of a person who:

(a) does not know at the time the act is done that the company is a charity; or

(b) gives full consideration in money or money's worth in relation to the act in question and does not know (as the case may be):

  (i) that the act is not permitted by the company's constitution; or

  (ii) that the act is beyond the powers of the directors: CA 2006, s 42(1).

7.18 Where a company that is a charity purports to transfer or grant an interest in property, the fact that (as the case may be):

(a) the act was not permitted by the company's constitution; or

(b) the directors in connection with the act exceeded any limitation on their powers under the company's constitution,

does not affect the title of a person who subsequently acquires the property or any interest in it for full consideration without actual notice of any such circumstances affecting the validity of the company's act: CA 2006, s 42(2).

7.19 In any proceedings arising out of sub-ss (1) or (2) the burden of proving:

(a) that a person knew that the company was a charity; or

(b) that a person knew that an act was not permitted by the company's constitution or was beyond the powers of the directors,

lies on the person asserting that fact: CA 2006, s 42(3).

7.20 In the case of a company that is a charity, the affirmation of a transaction to which s 41 applies (transactions with directors or their associates) is ineffective without the prior written consent of:

(a) in England and Wales, the Charity Commission;

(b) in Northern Ireland, the Department for Social Development: CA 2006, s 41(4).

This section does not extend to Scotland (but see s 112 of CA 1989 (c 40)): CA 2006, s 42(5).

Formalities of doing business under the law of England and Wales and Northern Ireland

7.21 This section considers related matters concerning corporate capacity where a company undertakes business activities.

Company contracts

7.22 Under the law of England and Wales or Northern Ireland a contract may be made:

(a) by a company, by writing under its common seal; or

(b) on behalf of a company, by a person acting under its authority, express or implied: CA 2006, s 43(1).

Any formalities required by law in the case of a contract made by an individual also apply, unless a contrary intention appears, to a contract made by or on behalf of a company: CA 2006, s 43(2).

Execution of documents

7.23 Under the law of England and Wales or Northern Ireland, a document is executed by a company:

(a) by the affixing of its common seal; or

(b) by signature in accordance with the following provisions: CA 2006, s 44(1).

7.24 A document is validly executed by a company if it is signed on behalf of the company:

(a) by two authorised signatories; or

(b) by a director of the company in the presence of a witness who attests the signature: CA 2006, s 44(2).

7.25 The following are 'authorised signatories' for the purposes of CA 2006, s 44(2):

(a) every director of the company; and

(b) in the case of a private company with a secretary or a public company, the secretary (or any joint secretary) of the company: CA 2006, s 44(3).

7.26 A document signed in accordance with s 44(2) and expressed, in whatever words, to be executed by the company has the same effect as if executed under the common seal of the company: CA 2006, s 44(4).

In favour of a purchaser a document is deemed to have been duly executed by a company if it purports to be signed in accordance with s 44(2). A 'purchaser' means a purchaser in good faith for valuable consideration and includes a lessee, mortgagee or other person who for valuable consideration acquires an interest in property: CA 2006, s 44(5).

Where a document is to be signed by a person on behalf of more than one company, it is not duly signed by that person for the purposes of this section unless he signs it separately in each capacity: CA 2006, s 44(6).

7.27 References in this section to a document being (or purporting to be) signed by a director or secretary are to be read, in a case where that office is held by a firm, as references to its being (or purporting to be) signed by an individual authorised by the firm to sign on its behalf: CA 2006, s 44(7).

This section applies to a document that is (or purports to be) executed by a company in the name of or on behalf of another person whether or not that person is also a company: CA 2006, s 44(8).

Application of CA 2006, s 44

Section 44 was the subject of interpretation in *Williams v Redcard Ltd* [2011] 2 BCLC 350. The appellants were purchasers of some flats in a building including freehold interest in the building belonging to Redcard Ltd ('Redcard'). The sale and purchase agreement had various signatures under the words 'signed … seller', as well as two individuals who were authorised signatories of Redcard. The names of these two individuals were included in the agreement as 'Seller' and they agreed to sell their leasehold interests in the flats. Redcard was also defined as 'Seller' in the same agreement. The agreement did not have Redcard's common seal or separate signatures stated to be 'for and on behalf of Redcard'.

The purchasers contended that there was no contract which they could be compelled to complete as the sellers' part of the contract was not properly executed by Redcard. They submitted that the valid execution of the documents by Redcard required that, in the absence of a common seal, the documents should contain the words expressly stating that the signatures of the authorised signatories were 'by or on behalf of' Redcard.

Under English law, for the sale of land, the contract has to be signed 'by or on behalf of' each party to the contract under s 2 of the Law of Property (Miscellaneous Provisions) Act 1989. The 1989 Act applies to a contract made by or on behalf of a company or a contract entered into by an individual, under CA 2006, s 43(2).

The Court of Appeal held that the words 'expressed in whatever words to be executed by the company' in s 44(4) had to add something to the provision in subs (2) that a document was validly executed by a company if it was signed on behalf of the company by two authorised signatures. In the circumstances there was no need for the use of words spelling out that those signatures were 'by or on behalf of' the company. The signatures to the agreement were under the words 'signed … seller' and 'seller' was defined in the agreement as including both Redcard selling its freehold and the individuals selling their leaseholds; the signatures included the signatures of two authorised signatories; and the use of the defined term 'seller' above those signatures meant that the document was expressed to be simultaneously executed both by Redcard and by the individuals, all being included in the term 'seller'. Thus, the agreement was properly executed by Redcard.

According to Mummery LJ, CA 2006, s 44 expressly stated that a company neither required a common seal, nor was it required to execute a document under its common seal: CA 2006, s 45. He set out the following aspects in connection with s 44:

- Section 44, like its neighbouring sections, ss 43 and 45, relates to the formalities of doing business, in particular the formalities for the making of contracts and the execution of documents by companies.
- The purpose of s 44 was to facilitate the formalities of the execution of documents by companies by allowing signatures either of two authorised signatories or of one director, if attested, to count as execution by a company under its the common seal.
- In order to achieve that result s 44 uses the familiar legislative technique of 'deeming'. Thus, in the case of a document signed in accordance with s 44, the document has the same effect 'as if' executed under the common seal.

- The legal effect of words in subs (4) 'and expressed in whatever words to be executed by the company' are central to the appellants' contention that, in order to give rise to a deemed execution of a document by a company, the signatures relied on must be expressed in words conveying that they are by or on behalf of the company.
- As for subsequent purchasers for value in good faith, subs (5) deems, in their favour, that a document was duly executed by a company, if it purports to be signed in accordance with subs (2).
- Similarly, subs (6) did not apply here, because only one company was involved. It provides that, where a document is to be signed by a person on behalf of more than one company, it must, for the purposes of due execution, be signed separately in each capacity. See the recommendations of the Law Commission No 253, 1998, *The Execution of Deeds and Documents by or on behalf of Bodies Corporate* paras 3.30–3.33, which preceded the enactment of s 44(6).

According to Mummery LJ, in order for a document to be executed by a company, it must either bear the company's seal, or it must comply with s 44(4) in order to take effect as if it had been executed under seal. Section 44(4) required that the document must not only be made on behalf of the company by complying with one of the two alternative requirements for signature in s 44(2): it must also be 'expressed, in whatever words, to be executed by the company'. This meant that the document must purport to have been signed by persons held out as authorised signatories and held out to be signing on the company's behalf. It must be apparent from the face of the document that the people signing it were doing something more than signing it on the company's behalf. It must be apparent that they were signing it on the company's behalf in such a way that the document is to be treated as having been executed 'by' the company for the purposes of s 44(4), and not merely by an agent 'for' the company.

The supplementary agreement did not state on whose behalf each signatory was signing it, or identify the relationship between the signatories and Redcard. The appellants submitted that it could not be said that the supplementary agreement was executed 'by' Redcard within s 44, as there was no expression in words in the supplementary agreement that Redcard itself was executing it, rather than by an agent. There was nothing in it to indicate who was executing it on behalf of Redcard, or whether Redcard was executing it by any one of the signatures.

The appeal turned on what the words 'expressed in whatever words to be executed by the company' in subs (4) added to the presence of signatures by two authorised signatories in accordance with subs (2) and whether that added requirement was satisfied in this case. Mummery LJ was of the view that those words must add something to the provision in subs (2), that a document was validly executed by a company if it was signed on behalf of the company by two authorised signatories. Subsection (4) did not simply provide that a document signed in accordance with subs (2) had the same effect as if executed under the common seal of the company.

The words did not require that, in addition to the signatures of the individuals who were the authorised signatories, there must be words spelling out that those signatures were 'by or on behalf of' the company.

Common seal

7.28 A company may have a common seal, but need not have one: CA 2006, s 45(1). If a company has a common seal, it must have its name engraved in legible characters on the seal: CA 2006, s 45(2). If a company fails to comply with s 45(2), an offence is committed by:

(a) the company; and

(b) every officer of the company who is in default: CA 2006, s 45(3).

An officer of a company, or a person acting on behalf of a company, commits an offence if he uses, or authorises the use of, a seal purporting to be a seal of the company on which its name is not engraved as required by s 45(2): CA 2006, s 45(4).

A person guilty of an offence under this section is liable on summary conviction to a fine not exceeding level 3 on the standard scale: CA 2006, s 45(5).

This section does not form part of the law of Scotland: CA 2006, s 45(6).

Execution of deeds

7.29 A document is validly executed by a company as a deed for the purposes of s 1(2)(b) of the Law of Property (Miscellaneous Provisions) Act 1989 (c 34) and for the purposes of the law of Northern Ireland if, and only if:

(a) it is duly executed by the company; and

(b) it is delivered as a deed: CA 2006, s 46(1).

For the purposes of s 46(1)(b) a document is presumed to be delivered upon its being executed, unless a contrary intention is proved: CA 2006, s 46(2).

Execution of deeds or other documents by attorney

7.30 Under the law of England and Wales or Northern Ireland a company may, by instrument executed as a deed, empower a person, either generally or in respect of specified matters, as its attorney to execute deeds or other documents on its behalf: CA 2006, s 47(1).

A deed or other document so executed, whether in the UK or elsewhere, has effect as if executed by the company: CA 2006, s 47(2).

Scotland – execution of documents by companies

7.31 The following provisions form part of the law of Scotland only: s 48(1).

Notwithstanding the provisions of any enactment, a company need not have a company seal: CA 2006, s 48(2).

For the purposes of any enactment:

(a) providing for a document to be executed by a company by affixing its common seal; or

(b) referring (in whatever terms) to a document so executed,

a document signed or subscribed by or on behalf of the company in accordance with the provisions of the Requirements of Writing (Scotland) Act 1995 (c 7) has effect as if so executed: CA 2006, s 48(3).

Official seal for use abroad

7.32 A company that has a common seal may have an official seal for use outside the UK: CA 2006, s 49(1). The official seal must be a facsimile of the company's common seal, with the addition on its face of the place or places where it is to be used: CA 2006, s 49(2). The official seal when duly affixed to a document has the same effect as the company's common seal.

This subsection does not extend to Scotland: CA 2006, s 49(3).

A company having an official seal for use outside the UK may:

(a) by writing under its common seal; or

(b) as respects Scotland, by writing subscribed in accordance with the Requirements of Writing (Scotland) Act 1995,

authorise any person appointed for the purpose to affix the official seal to any deed or other document to which the company is party: CA 2006, s 49(4).

7.33 As between the company and a person dealing with such an agent, the agent's authority continues:

(a) during the period mentioned in the instrument conferring the authority; or

(b) if no period is mentioned, until notice of the revocation or termination of the agent's authority has been given to the person dealing with him: CA 2006, s 49(5).

The person affixing the official seal must certify in writing on the deed or other document to which the seal is affixed the date on which, and place at which, it is affixed: CA 2006, s 49(6).

Official seal for share certificates etc

7.34 A company that has a common seal may have an official seal for use:

(a) for sealing securities issued by the company; or

(b) for sealing documents creating or evidencing securities so issued: CA 2006, s 50(1).

7.35 The official seal:

(a) must be a facsimile of the company's common seal, with the addition on its face of the word 'Securities'; and

(b) when duly affixed to the document has the same effect as the company's common seal: CA 2006, s 50(2).

Bills of exchange and promissory notes

7.36 A bill of exchange or promissory note is deemed to have been made, accepted or endorsed on behalf of a company if made, accepted or endorsed in the name of, or by or on behalf or on account of, the company by a person acting under its authority: CA 2006, s 52.

Checklist

7.37 *This checklist sets out the key issues governing corporate capacity and matters that need to be considered where corporate capacity is challenged. It also addresses the main provisions and case law impacting on corporate capacity*

No	Issue	Reference
1	Previously, a company's objects clause was set out in its memorandum of association.	Memorandum of association
2	Acts outside the company's objects were considered *ultra vires* the company.	*Ashbury Railway Carriage and Iron Company v Riche* (1875) LR HL 653
3	A practice grew of mitigating the effects of the *ultra vires* doctrine by expanding the objects clause to enable the widest interpretation to be given to each activity of the objects clause, including those incidental or conducive to the company's objects.	*Bell Houses Ltd v City Wall Properties Ltd* [1966] 1 QB 207
4	The combined effects of the reforms in 1972 and 1989 led to a short-form objects clause in the memorandum of association.	European Communities Act 1972 Companies Act 1989, s 3A
5	Under CA 2006, companies no longer need an objects clause.	CA 2006, s 31
6	If a company chooses to have an objects clause, it will appear in the articles of association.	Articles of association
7	A company is deemed to have unrestricted objects unless it chooses to place limitations or restrictions on its activities.	CA 2006, s 31

No	Issue	Reference
8	A company cannot be established for an unlawful purpose.	CA 2006, s 7(2)
9	A company's capacity refers to its ability to carry out acts or transactions whether through its board, directors, shareholders or third parties.	CA 2006, s 39
10	The validity of an act done by a company cannot be called into question on the ground of lack of capacity by reason of anything in the company's constitution.	CA 2006, s 39
11	Where a person deals with the company in good faith, the powers of the directors to bind the company or authorise others to do so, is deemed not to be constrained by the company's constitution.	CA 2006, s 40
12	Transactions between the company and its directors or their associates are voidable at the instance of the company but there are exceptions where the transaction ceases to be voidable.	CA 2006, s 41
13	There are formalities to be observed for company contracts.	CA 2006, s 43
14	There are formalities to be observed for the execution of documents by a company.	CA 2006, s 44
15	A company need not have a common seal.	CA 2006, s 45
16	There are formalities to be observed for the execution of deeds by a company.	CA 2006, s 46

Definitions

7.38

Deals with: a person 'deals with' a company if he is a party to any transaction or other act to which the company is a party: CA 2006, s 40(2)(a).

Purchaser: a purchaser in good faith for valuable consideration and includes a lessee, mortgagee or other person who for valuable consideration acquires an interest in property: CA 2006, s 44(5).

Transaction: includes any act: CA 2006, s 41(7).

Ultra vires: any act or transaction beyond the company's capacity: *Rolled Steel Products v British Steel Corporation* [1985] 3 All ER 52.

8 Company and business names

Contents

Introduction

8.1 In order to establish a company, a name must be selected which must not be similar or identical to one which has already been registered at Companies House, or which could give rise to any issues of 'passing off' at common law, or any trade mark infringements.

The choice of name is, therefore, a significant issue in setting up the company to minimise or avoid the threat or any litigation in the future.

8.2 This chapter addresses the following issues:

(a) the requirements on the choice of a company name under CA 2006;

(b) the circumstances in which prohibited, sensitive words or expressions or use of inappropriate words cannot be used;

(c) the situation, in which objections can be raised to company names;

(d) the regulator of names; and

(e) trading disclosures.

This chapter takes into account the Company, Limited Liability Partnership and Business (Names and Trading Disclosures) Regulations 2015, SI 2015/17, and the Company, Limited Liability Partnership and Business Names (Sensitive Words and Expressions) Regulations 2014, SI 2014/3140.

Searches

8.3 Before any final selection of name can be made, a search should be undertaken using the Companies House 'WebCHeck' service to ensure that the selected name is not the same as an existing name on the index of company names. The WebCHeck service provides access to company information for no more than £1 per document, with some information free of charge. While there is a minimal fee of £1 for documents, basic company details are free, including:

- the registered office address;
- date of incorporation;
- the nature of the business and details of previous names;
- company type;
- company status (eg live, dissolved, etc);
- insolvency details or actions registered against the company;
- key filing dates.

A company name search should also be undertaken at the Trade Marks Register of the UK Intellectual Property Office, to avoid any infringement of an existing trademark.

Company name

8.4 Parts 6 and 41 of CA 2006 and companies regulations set out the details on the choice of company name and the restrictions that apply. The rules on the change of name are governed by Pt 5 of CA 2006.

Indications of company type in name

8.5 This section sets out the required indications in a name for limited companies under CA 2006.

Public limited companies

8.6 Under CA 2006, s 58(1) if the company is a public company, its name must end with 'public limited company' or 'plc'.

If the company's registered office is stated as being situated in Wales (ie a 'Welsh' company), its name may instead end with 'cwmni cyfyngedig cyhoeddus' or 'ccc': CA 2006, s 58(2).

This does not apply to community interest companies: CA 2006, s 58(3) (but see ss 33(3) and (4) of the Companies (Audit, Investigations and Community Enterprise) Act 2004.

Private limited companies

8.7 Under CA 2006, s 59(1), where a company is a private company, its name must end with 'limited' or 'ltd'.

If the company's registered office is stated as being situated in Wales (ie a 'Welsh' Company), its name may instead end with 'cyfyngedig' or 'cyf': CA 2006, s 59(2).

This does not however, apply to community interest companies: CA 2006, s 59(4) (but see ss 33(1) and (2) of the Companies (Audit, Investigations and Community Enterprise) Act 2004.

Exemptions

8.8 A private company is exempt from the requirement to have 'limited' or 'ltd' at the end of its name in the following circumstances:

- It is a charity: CA 2006, s 60(1)(a).
- It is exempted from the requirements by regulations made by the Secretary of State: CA 2006, s 60(1)(b). The relevant regulations are the Company, Limited Liability Partnership and Business (Names and Trading Disclosures) Regulations 2015, SI 2015/17.
- The Registrar of Companies may refuse to register a private limited company with a name that does not include the word 'limited' (or a permitted alternative), unless a statement has been delivered to him that the company meets the conditions for exemption: CA 2006, s 60(2). Further, the registrar may accept the statement as sufficient evidence of the matters stated in it: CA 2006, s 60(3).
- Where the private company is a company limited by shares, which has an existing exemption and it can continue with that exemption in accordance with the conditions set out in s 61: CA 2006, s 60(1)(c). Section 61 applies to a private company limited by shares:
  - (a) that on 25 February 1982:
    - (i) was registered in Great Britain; and
    - (ii) had a name that, by virtue of a licence under s 19 of the Companies Act 1948 (c 38) (or corresponding earlier legislation), did not include the word 'limited' or any of the permitted alternatives; or

(b) that on 30 June 1983:

   (i) was registered in Northern Ireland; and

   (ii) had a name that, by virtue of a licence under s 19 of the Companies Act (Northern Ireland) 1960 (c 22 (NI)) (or corresponding earlier legislation), did not include the word 'limited' or any of the permitted alternatives: CA 2006, s 61(1).

A company to which s 61 applies is exempt from s 59 (the requirement to have a name ending with 'limited' or permitted alternative), as long as:

(a) it continues to meet the following two conditions; and

(b) it does not change its name: CA 2006, s 61(2).

The first condition is that the objects of the company are the promotion of commerce, art, science, education, religion, charity or any profession, and anything incidental or conducive to any of those objects: CA 2006, s 61(3).

The second is that the company's articles:

(a) require its income to be applied in promoting its objects;

(b) prohibit the payment of dividends, or any return of capital, to its members; and

(c) require all the assets that would otherwise be available to its members generally to be transferred on its winding up either:

   (i) to another body with objects similar to its own; or

   (ii) to another body the objects of which are the promotion of charity and anything incidental or conducive thereto,

(whether or not the body is a member of the company): CA 2006, s 61(4).

- Where the company is a company limited by guarantee, which has an existing exemption and it can continue with that exemption in accordance with the conditions set out in s 62: CA 2006, s 60(1)(d). Under s 62, a private company limited by guarantee that immediately before the commencement of Part 5 of CA 2006:

(a) was exempt by virtue of s 30 of the Companies Act 1985 (c 6) or art 40 of the Companies (Northern Ireland) Order 1986 (SI 1986 No 1032 (NI 6)) from the requirement to have a name including the word 'limited' or a permitted alternative; and

(b) had a name that did not include the word 'limited' or any of the permitted alternatives,

is exempt from s 59 (requirement to have name ending with 'limited' or permitted alternative) so long as it continues to meet the following two conditions and does not change its name: CA 2006, s 62(1).

The first condition is that the objects of the company are the promotion of commerce, art, science, education, religion, charity or any profession, and anything incidental or conducive to any of those objects: CA 2006, s 62(2).

The second is that the company's articles:

(a) require its income to be applied in promoting its objects;

(b) prohibit the payment of dividends to its members; and

(c) require all the assets that would otherwise be available to its members generally to be transferred on its winding up either:

  (i) to another body with objects similar to its own; or

  (ii) to another body the objects of which are the promotion of charity and anything incidental or conducive thereto,

(whether or not the body is a member of the company): CA 2006, s 61(3).

Restriction on amendment of articles

8.9 A private company that is exempt under ss 61 or 62 from the requirement to use 'limited' (or a permitted alternative) as part of its name, and whose name does not include 'limited' or any of the permitted alternatives, must not amend its articles so that it ceases to comply with the conditions for exemption under the section: CA 2006, s 63(1).

8.10 In the event that s 63 is contravened, an offence is committed by the company and by every company officer who is in default. Under s 63(2), a shadow director is treated as an officer of the company. A person guilty of an offence under s 63 is liable on summary conviction to a fine not exceeding level 5 on the standard scale, and for continued contravention, a daily default fine not exceeding one-tenth of level 5 on the standard scale: CA 2006, s 63(3).

8.11 Where immediately before 1 October 2009, a company was exempt by virtue of s 30 of the Companies Act 1985 (c 6) or art 40 of the Companies (Northern Ireland Order 1986 (SI 1986 No 1032 (NI 6)) from the requirement to have a name including the word 'limited' (or a permitted alternative), and the company's memorandum or articles contained a provision preventing their alteration without the approval of the Board of Trade or a Northern Ireland Department (or any other department or Minister), or the Charity Commission, that provision and any condition of such licence, as stated in s 61(1)(a)(ii) or (b)(ii) requiring such provision, shall cease to have effect. This does not apply, if the provision is required by or under any other enactment: CA 2006, s 63(4).

Power to direct change of name where company ceases to be entitled to exemption

8.12 If it appears to the Secretary of State that a company whose name does not include 'limited' or any of the permitted alternatives has ceased to be entitled to exemption under CA 2006, s 60(1)(a) or (b) or in the case of a company within s 61 or s 62 (which impose conditions as to the objects and articles of the company):

(i) has carried on any business other than the promotion of any of the objects set out in s 61(3) or s 62(2); or

(ii) has acted inconsistently with the provisions required by s 61(4)(a) or (b) or s 62(3) (a) or (b),

the Secretary of State may direct the company to change its name so that it ends with 'limited' or one of the permitted alternatives: CA 2006, s 64(1).

8.13 The direction must be in writing and must specify the period within which the company is to change its name: CA 2006, s 64(2). A change of name in order to comply with a direction under s 64 may be made by a resolution of the directors. This is without prejudice to any other method of changing the company's name: CA 2006, s 64(3).

Where a resolution of the directors is passed in accordance with s 64(3), the company must give notice to the registrar of the change. Sections 80 and 81 of CA 2006 apply as regards the registration and effect of the change: CA 2006, s 64(4).

8.14 If the company fails to comply with a direction under s 64, an offence is committed by the company, and every officer of the company who is in default: CA 2006, s 64(5).

A person guilty of an offence under s 64 is liable on summary conviction to a fine not exceeding level 5 on the standard scale and for continued contravention, a daily default fine not exceeding one-tenth of level 5 on the standard scale: CA 2006, s 64(6).

Inappropriate use of indications of common type or legal form

8.15 The Secretary of State may make provision by regulations prohibiting the use in a company name of specified words, expressions or other indications:

(a) that are associated with a particular type of company or form of organisation; or

(b) that are similar to words, expressions or other indications associated with a particular type of company or form of organisation: CA 2006, s 65(1).

8.16 The regulations may prohibit the use of words, expressions or other indications:

(a) in a specified part, or otherwise than in a specified part, of a company's name;

(b) in conjunction with, or otherwise than in conjunction with, such other words, expressions or indications as may be specified: CA 2006, s 65(2). The term 'specified' means specified in the regulations: CA 2006, s 65(4).

Under s 65(3), a company must not be registered under the Act by a name that consists of or includes anything prohibited by regulations under the section.

8.17 The following restrictions are applicable under the Company, Limited Liability Partnership and Business (Names and Trading Disclosures) Regulations 2015, SI 2015/17:

- A company must not be registered under CA 2006 by a name that includes, otherwise than at the end of the name, an expression or abbreviation specified in inverted commas in paragraphs 3(a)–(f) of Schedule 2 (or any expression or abbreviation specified as similar): paragraph 4(1) of the Regulations. The expressions and abbreviations specified are that the following should appear at the end of the company's name:

  (a) 'PUBLIC LIMITED COMPANY' or (with or without full stops) the abbreviation 'PLC';

  (b) 'CWMNI CYFYNGEDIG CYHOEDDUS' or (with or without full stops) the abbreviation 'CCC';

  (c) 'COMMUNITY INTEREST COMPANY' or (with or without full stops) the abbreviation 'CIC';

  (d) 'CWMNI BUDDIANT CYMUNEDOL' or (with or without full stops) the abbreviation 'CBC';

  (e) 'COMMUNITY INTEREST PUBLIC LIMITED COMPANY' or (with or without full stops) the abbreviation 'COMMUNITY INTEREST PLC';

  (f) 'CWMNI BUDDIANT CYMUNEDOL CYHOEDDUS CYFYNGEDIG' or (with or without full stops) the abbreviation 'CWMNI BUDDIANT CCC'.

  Further, a company cannot be registered under CA 2006 by a name that includes any 'expression or abbreviation specified as similar'.

- A company must not be registered under CA 2006 by a name that includes in any part of the name an expression or abbreviation specified in inverted commas in paragraph 3(g) or (h) of Schedule 2 (or any expression or abbreviation specified as similar) unless that company is an RTE company within the meaning of s 4A of the Leasehold Reform, Housing and Urban Development Act 1993(1): paragraph 4(2) of the Regulations. These are:

  (g) 'RIGHT TO ENFRANCHISEMENT' or (with or without full stops) the abbreviation 'RTE';

  (h) 'HAWL I RYDDFREINIAD'.

  Further, a company cannot be registered under CA 2006 by a name that includes any 'expression or abbreviation specified as similar' unless that company is an RTE company within the meaning of s 4A of the Leasehold Reform, Housing and Urban Development Act 1993(1): para 4(2) of the Regulations.

- A company must not be registered under CA 2006 by a name that includes in any part of the name an expression or abbreviation specified in inverted commas in paragraph 3(i) or (j) of Schedule 2 (or any expression or abbreviation specified as similar), unless that company is an RTM company within the meaning of s 73 of the Commonhold and Leasehold Reform Act 2002(2): paragraph 4(3) of the Regulations. These are:

(i) 'RIGHT TO MANAGE' or (with or without full stops) the abbreviation 'RTM';

(j) 'CWMNI RTM CYFYNGEDIG'.

- Further, a company cannot be registered under CA 2006 by a name that includes in any part of the name an expression or abbreviation specified in inverted commas in para 3(k) to (x) to Sch 2 (or any expression or abbreviation specified as similar): para 4(4) of the Regulations. These are:

  (k) 'EUROPEAN ECONOMIC INTEREST GROUPING' or (with or without full stops) the abbreviation 'EEIG';

  (l) 'INVESTMENT COMPANY WITH VARIABLE CAPITAL';

  (m) 'CWMNI BUDDSODDI A CHYFALAF NEWIDIOL';

  (n) 'LIMITED PARTNERSHIP';

  (o) 'PARTNERIAETH CYFYNGEDIG';

  (p) 'LIMITED LIABILITY PARTNERSHIP';

  (q) 'PARTNERIAETH ATEBOLRWYDD CYFYNGEDIG';

  (r) 'OPEN-ENDED INVESTMENT COMPANY';

  (s) 'CWMNI BUDDSODDIANT PENAGORED';

  (t) CHARITABLE INCORPORATED ORGANISATION';

  (u) 'SEFDYDLIAD ELUSENNOL CORFFOREDIG';

  (v) 'INDUSTRIAL AND PROVIDENT SOCIETY';

  (w) 'CO-OPERATIVE SOCIETY';

  (x) 'COMMUNITY BENEFIT SOCIETY'.

  Further, a company cannot be registered under CA 2006 by a name that includes immediately before an expression or abbreviation specified in inverted commas in para 3(a) to (j) to Sch 2 an abbreviation specified in inverted commas in para 3(y) of that Schedule (or any abbreviation specified as similar): paragraph 4(5) of the Regulations.

- The following abbreviations (with or without full stops) of the expressions specified in sub-paragraphs (n), (o), (p), (q), (t) and (u) respectively, namely 'LP', 'PC', 'LLP', 'PAC', 'CIO' and 'SEC': paragraph 3(y) of Schedule 2 to the Regulations.

- The reference to the term 'expressions or abbreviations specified as similar' applies where:

  (a) one or more permitted characters has been omitted;

  (b) one or more permitted characters has been added; or

  (c) each of one or more permitted characters has been substituted by one or more other permitted characters, in such a way as to be likely to mislead the public as to the legal form of a company or business if included in the registered name of the company or in a business name: paragraph 2 to Schedule 2 of the Regulations.

- A company which is exempt from the requirement of CA 2006, s 59 (requirement to have name ending with 'limited' or permitted alternative) under s 60 must not be registered under the Companies Act 2006 by a name that concludes with:

  (a) a word specified in inverted commas in paragraph 1(c) or (d) of Schedule 2 (or any word specified as similar): paragraph 5 of the Regulations.

  These are:

  (c) 'UNLIMITED'; and

  (d) 'ANGHYFYNGEDIG' (including any 'word specified as similar');

  or

  (b) an expression or abbreviation specified in inverted commas in paragraph 3(a)–(f) or (y) of Schedule 2 (or any expression or abbreviation specified as similar): paragraph 5 of the Regulations.

  These are:

  (a) 'PUBLIC LIMITED COMPANY' or (with or without full stops) the abbreviation 'PLC';

  (b) 'CWMNI CYFYNGEDIG CYHOEDDUS' or (with or without full stops) the abbreviation 'CCC';

  (c) 'COMMUNITY INTEREST COMPANY' or (with or without full stops) the abbreviation 'CIC';

  (d) 'CWMNI BUDDIANT CYMUNEDOL' or (with or without full stops) the abbreviation 'CBC';

  (e) 'COMMUNITY INTEREST PUBLIC LIMITED COMPANY' or (with or without full stops) the abbreviation 'COMMUNITY INTEREST PLC';

  (f) 'CWMNI BUDDIANT CYMUNEDOL CYHOEDDUS CYFYNGEDIG' or (with or without full stops) the abbreviation 'CWMNI BUDDIANT CCC';

  (g) 'COMMUNITY BENEFIT SOCIETY'; and

  (h) 'LP', 'PC', 'LLP', 'PAC', 'CIO' and 'SEC'.

- An unlimited company must not be registered under the Act by a name that concludes with:

  (a) a word or abbreviation specified in inverted commas in paragraph 1(a) or (b) of Schedule 2 (or any word or abbreviation specified as similar): paragraph 6 of the Regulations.

These are:

(a) 'LIMITED' or (with or without full stops) the abbreviation 'LTD';

(b) 'CYFYNGEDIG' or (with or without full stops) the abbreviation 'CYF';

or

(b) an expression or abbreviation specified in inverted commas in paragraph 3(a)–(f) or (y) of Schedule 2 (or any expression or abbreviation specified as similar). These are:

(a) 'PUBLIC LIMITED COMPANY' or (with or without full stops) the abbreviation 'PLC';

(b) 'CWMNI CYFYNGEDIG CYHOEDDUS' or (with or without full stops) the abbreviation 'CCC';

(c) 'COMMUNITY INTEREST COMPANY' or (with or without full stops) the abbreviation 'CIC';

(d) 'CWMNI BUDDIANT CYMUNEDOL' or (with or without full stops) the abbreviation 'CBC';

(e) 'COMMUNITY INTEREST PUBLIC LIMITED COMPANY' or (with or without full stops) the abbreviation 'COMMUNITY INTEREST PLC';

(f) 'CWMNI BUDDIANT CYMUNEDOL CYHOEDDUS CYFYNGEDIG' or (with or without full stops) the abbreviation 'CWMNI BUDDIANT CCC';

(g) 'COMMUNITY BENEFIT SOCIETY'; and

(h) 'LP', 'PC', 'LLP', 'PAC', 'CIO' and 'SEC'.

- An overseas company must not be registered under the Act by a name that concludes with a word or abbreviation specified in inverted commas in paragraph 1(a) or (b) of Schedule 2 (or any word or abbreviation specified as similar), unless the liability of the members of the company is limited by its constitution: Part 4, paragraph 13(1) of the Regulations. These are:

(a) 'LIMITED' or (with or without full stops) the abbreviation 'LTD';

(b) 'CYFYNGEDIG' or (with or without full stops) the abbreviation 'CYF'.

- An overseas company must not be registered under the Act by a name that concludes with a word specified in inverted commas in paragraph 1(a) or (b) of Schedule 2 (or any word specified as similar) unless the liability of the members of the company is not limited by its constitution: Part 4, paragraph 13(2) of the Regulations. These are:

(c) 'UNLIMITED'; and

(d) 'ANGHYFYNGEDIG' (including any 'word specified as similar').

- An overseas company must not be registered under the Act by a name that includes in any part of the name an expression or abbreviation specified in inverted commas in paragraph 3 of Schedule 2 (or any expression or abbreviation specified as similar): Part 4, paragraph 13(3) of the Regulations. These are:

  (a) 'PUBLIC LIMITED COMPANY' or (with or without full stops) the abbreviation 'PLC';

  (b) 'CWMNI CYFYNGEDIG CYHOEDDUS' or (with or without full stops) the abbreviation 'CCC';

  (c) 'COMMUNITY INTEREST COMPANY' or (with or without full stops) the abbreviation 'CIC';

  (d) 'CWMNI BUDDIANT CYMUNEDOL' or (with or without full stops) the abbreviation 'CBC';

  (e) 'COMMUNITY INTEREST PUBLIC LIMITED COMPANY' or (with or without full stops) the abbreviation 'COMMUNITY INTEREST PLC';

  (f) 'CWMNI BUDDIANT CYMUNEDOL CYHOEDDUS CYFYNGEDIG' or (with or without full stops) the abbreviation 'CWMNI BUDDIANT CCC';

  (g) 'RIGHT TO ENFRANCHISEMENT' or (with or without full stops) the abbreviation 'RTE';

  (h) 'HAWL I RYDDFREINIAD';

  (i) 'RIGHT TO MANAGE' or (with or without full stops) the abbreviation 'RTM';

  (j) 'CWMNI RTM CYFYNGEDIG';

  (k) 'EUROPEAN ECONOMIC INTEREST GROUPING' or (with or without full stops) the abbreviation 'EEIG';

  (l) 'INVESTMENT COMPANY WITH VARIABLE CAPITAL';

  (m) 'CWMNI BUDDSODDI A CHYFALAF NEWIDIOL';

  (n) 'LIMITED PARTNERSHIP';

  (o) 'PARTNERIAETH CYFYNGEDIG';

  (p) 'LIMITED LIABILITY PARTNERSHIP';

  (q) 'PARTNERIAETH ATEBOLRWYDD CYFYNGEDIG';

  (r) 'OPEN-ENDED INVESTMENT COMPANY';

  (s) 'CWMNI BUDDSODDIANT PENAGORED';

  (t) 'CHARITABLE INCORPORATED ORGANISATION';

  (u) 'SEFDYDLIAD ELUSENNOL CORFFOREDIG';

> (v) 'INDUSTRIAL AND PROVIDENT SOCIETY';
>
> (w) 'CO-OPERATIVE SOCIETY';
>
> (x) 'COMMUNITY BENEFIT SOCIETY'; and
>
> (y) 'LP', 'PC', 'LLP', 'PAC', 'CIO' and 'SEC'.

Prohibited names

8.18 Part 5 of CA 2006 sets out the general requirements on prohibited names.

A company must not be registered under CA 2006 by a name if, in the opinion of the Secretary of State:

(a) its use by the company would constitute an offence; or

(b) it is offensive: CA 2006, s 53.

Sensitive words and expressions

8.19 Some words and expressions are sensitive and therefore require consent. The following aspects should be considered when addressing choice of name:

Names suggesting a connection with government and public authority

8.20 The approval of the Secretary of State is required for a company to be registered under CA 2006 by a name that would be likely to give the impression that the company is connected with:

(a) Her Majesty's Government, any part of the Scottish administration, the Welsh Assembly Government or Her Majesty's Government in Northern Ireland;

(b) a local authority; or

(c) any public authority specified for the purposes of s 54 by regulations made by the Secretary of State: CA 2006, s 54(1).

8.21 For the purposes of CA 2006, s 54 the term 'local authority' means:

(a) a local authority within the meaning of the Local Government Act 1972 (c 70), the Common Council of the City of London or the Council of the Isles of Scilly;

(b) a council constituted under s 2 of the Local Government etc (Scotland) Act 1994 (c 39); or

(c) a district council in Northern Ireland.

The term 'public authority' includes any person or body having functions of a public nature: CA 2006, s 54(2).

8.22 The regulations referred to are the Company, Limited Liability Partnership and Business (Names and Trading Disclosures) Regulations 2015, SI 2015/17. Under reg 9, the persons and bodies set out in col (1) of Sch 4 is specified for the purposes of CA 2006, s 54. An applicant must seek the view of the government department or other body set out opposite that public authority in col (2) of Sch 4: paras 9(1) and (2).

Limited Liability Partnership names

8.23 Under reg 9 of the Company, Limited Liability Partnership and Business (Names and Trading Disclosures) Regulations 2015, SI 2015/17, any reference to CA 2006, s 54 includes a reference to that section as applied by reg 8 of the Limited Liability Partnerships (Application of Companies Act 2006) Regulations 2009: SI 2015/17, reg 11(1). Further SI 2015/17, Sch 5 amends the Limited Liability Partnerships (Application of Companies Act 2006) Regulations 2009 for applicability to LLPs: SI 2015/17, reg 11(2).

Other sensitive words or expressions

8.24 The approval of the Secretary of State is required for a company to be registered under CA 2006 with a name that includes a word or expression for the time being specified in regulations made by the Secretary of State under CA 2006, s 55(1).

Part 1 of Sch 1 of the Company, Limited Liability Partnership and Business Names (Sensitive Words and Expressions) Regulations 2014, SI 2014/3140 sets out the words and expressions for the purposes of CA 2006, ss 55(1) and 1194(1) which are specified by the Secretary of State as requiring prior approval for use in the names of companies, LLPs and businesses. Part 2 of Sch 1 sets out words and expressions that the Secretary of State is specifying as requiring prior approval when used in the names of companies or LLPs only. Regulations 3(1)(b) and (c), and 4(b) and (c) provide that the specified words and expressions are specified in all their plural, possessive and (where relevant) feminine forms and, in the case of Gaelic and Welsh words, in their grammatically mutated forms.

8.25 The following are the words and expressions specified for the purposes of CA 2006, ss 55(1) and 1194(1):

Accredit
Accreditation
Accredited
Accrediting
Adjudicator
Association
Assurance
Assurer
Audit office
Auditor General
*Banc
Bank
Banking
Benevolent
*Breatannach
*Breatainn
*Brenhinol
*Brenin
*Brenhiniaeth
Britain
British
Chamber of commerce
Charitable
Charity
Charter
Chartered
Child maintenance
Child support
*Coimisean
*Comhairle
*Comisiwn
Commission
Co-operative
Council
*Cyngor
Dental

Dentistry
*Diùc
*Dug
Duke
Ei Fawrhydi
England
English
Federation
Friendly Society
Foundation
Fund
Government
*Gwasanaeth iechyd
Health centre
Health service
Health visitor
His Majesty
HPSS
HSC
Inspectorate
Institute
Institution
Insurance
Insurer
Judicial appointment
King
Licensing
*Llywodraeth
Medical centre
Midwife
Midwifery
*Mòrachd
Mutual
NHS
Northern Ireland
Northern Irish
Nurse
Nursing
Oifis sgrùdaidh
*Oilthigh
Ombudsman
*Ombwdsmon
*Parlamaid
Parliament
Parliamentarian
Parliamentary
Patent
Patentee
Police
Polytechnic
Post office
*Prifysgol
Prince
*Prionnsa
*Prydain
*Prydeinig
Queen
Reassurance
Reassurer
Registrar
Regulator
Reinsurance
Reinsurer
*Riaghaltas
*Rìgh
Rìoghachd Aonaichte
Rìoghail
Rìoghalachd
Royal
Royalty
Scotland
Scottish
Senedd
Sheffield
Siambr fasnach
Social service
Society
Special school
Standards
Stock exchange
Swyddfa archwilio
*Teyrnas Gyfunol
*Teyrnas Unedig
Trade union
Tribunal
Trust
*Tywysog
Underwrite
Underwriting
University
Wales
Welsh
Windsor

8.26 The following are the words and expressions specified for the purposes of CA 2006, s 55(1):

Alba
Albannach
Na h-Alba
*Cymru
*Cymraeg
*Cymreig

Duty to seek comments of government department or other specified body

8.27 The Secretary of State may by regulations under:

(a) CA 2006, s 54 (name suggesting connection with government or public authority); or

(b) CA 2006, s 55 (other sensitive words or expressions),

require that, in connection with an application for the approval of the Secretary of State under that section, the applicant must seek the view of a specified government department or other body: CA 2006, s 56(1).

Where such a requirement applies, the applicant must request the specified department or other body (in writing) to indicate whether (and if so why) it has any objections to the proposed name: CA 2006, s 56(2). Under s 56(5) the term 'specified' means specified in the regulations.

8.28 Where a request under s 56 is made in connection with an application for the registration of a company under CA 2006, the application must:

(a) include a statement that a request under the section has been made; and

(b) be accompanied by a copy of any response received: CA 2006, s 56(3).

8.29 Where a request under the section is made in connection with a change in a company's name, the notice of the change sent to the registrar must be accompanied by:

(a) a statement by a director or secretary of the company that a request under the section has been made; and

(b) a copy of any response received: CA 2006, s 56(4).

8.30 Sections 56(1) and 1195(1) of the Act, including s 56(1) as applied to LLPs, give the Secretary of State the power to require that, in connection with an application for use of a sensitive word or expression, the applicant must seek the view of a specified government department or other body. Schedule 2 lists the government departments and other bodies whose views must be sought. Part 2 of Sch 2 identifies the relevant government department or public authority whose view must be sought where the situation of the company's or LLP's registered office is relevant.

8.31 The reference in reg 6(a)(i) of the Company, Limited Liability Partnership and Business Names (Sensitive Words and Expressions) Regulations 2014, SI 2014/3140 (applications where situation of registered office or principal place of business is relevant) to a registered office which is situated in England and Wales arises because England and Wales are usually treated in the CA 2006 as a single jurisdiction for the purposes of the situation of the registered office. However, a company whose registered office is situated in Wales can require the Register of Companies to state that its registered office is situated in Wales. In this case, the company will be governed by reg 6(b)(i) rather than reg 6(a)(i). The position is similar for an LLP whose registered office is situated in Wales.

Since overseas companies are not required by the Overseas Companies Regulations 2009, SI 2009/1801 to register in a specified part of the United Kingdom, they are treated for the purposes of reg 6 in the same way as companies registered in England and Wales.

Permitted characters

8.32 The Secretary of State may make provision by regulations:

(a) as to the letters or other characters, signs or symbols (including accents and other diacritical marks) and punctuation that may be used in the name of a company registered under this Act; and

(b) specifying a standard style or format for the name of a company for the purposes of registration: CA 2006, s 57(1).

The regulations may prohibit the use of specified characters, signs or symbols when appearing in a specified position (in particular, at the beginning of a name): CA 2006, s 57(2). Under s 57(5), the term 'specified' means specified in the regulations.

A company may not be registered under CA 2006 by a name that consists of or includes anything that is not permitted in accordance with regulations under the section: CA 2006, s 57(3).

8.33 The regulations referred to are the Companies, Limited Liability Partnership and Business (Names and Trading Disclosures) Regulations 2015, SI 2015/17. Under reg 2(1) of the regulations, the following are the permitted characters:

(a) any character, character with an accent or other diacritical mark, sign or symbol set out in table 1 in Sch 1;

(b) 0, 1, 2, 3, 4, 5, 6, 7, 8 or 9;

(c) full stop, comma, colon, semi-colon or hyphen; and

(d) any other punctuation referred to in column 1 of table 2 in Sch 1 but only in one of the forms set out opposite that punctuation in column 2 of that table.

8.34 The signs and symbols set out in table 3 in Sch 1 are permitted characters that may be used but not as one of the first three permitted characters of the name.

The name must not consist of more than 160 permitted characters. For the purposes of computing the number of permitted characters, any blank space between one permitted character and another in the name shall be counted as though it was a permitted character: SI 2015/17, para 2(4).

Schedule 1 to SI 2015/17, sets out the following permitted characters, which extends the list of characters that may be used in a company name which allows for the use of accents, diacritical marks and ligatures:

Table 1: Characters, Signs, Symbols (including Accents and other Diacritical Marks) and Punctuation

8.35

Characters, signs and symbols				
A	À	Á	Â	Ã
Ä	Å	Ā	Ă	Ą
Ǻ	Æ	Ǽ	B	C
Ç	Ć	Ĉ	Ċ	Č
D	Þ	Ď	Đ	E
È	É	Ê	Ë	Ē
Ĕ	Ė	Ę	Ě	F
G	Ĝ	Ğ	Ġ	Ģ
H	Ĥ	Ħ	I	Ì
Í	Î	Ï	Ĩ	Ī
Ĭ	Į	İ	J	Ĵ
K	Ķ	L	Ĺ	Ļ
Ľ	Ŀ	Ł	M	N
Ñ	Ń	Ņ	Ň	Ŋ
O	Ò	Ó	Ô	Õ
Ö	Ø	Ō	Ŏ	Ő
Ǿ	Œ	P	Q	R
Ŕ	Ŗ	Ř	S	Ś
Ŝ	Ş	Š	T	Ţ
Ť	Ŧ	U	Ù	Ú
Û	Ü	Ũ	Ū	Ŭ
Ů	Ű	Ų	V	W
Ŵ	Ẁ	Ẃ	Ẅ	X
Y	Ỳ	Ý	Ŷ	Ÿ
Z	Ź	Ż	Ž	&
@	£	$	€	¥

Table 2

8.36

Column 1 (type of punctuation)	*Column 2 (punctuation mark)*
Apostrophe	‘
	’
	‘
Bracket	(
	)
	[
	]
	{
	}
	<
	>
Exclamation mark	!
Guillemet	«
	»
Inverted comma	“
	”
	“
Question mark	?
Solidus	\
	/

Table 3

8.37

Signs and symbols
*
=
#
%
+

Similarity to other names on registrar's index

8.38 Specific rules apply in connection with registration of a name that already exists at the registrar's index of names. A company must not be registered under the Act by a name that is the same as another name appearing in the index of company names: CA 2006, s 66(1).

The Secretary of State may make provision by regulations supplementing s 66: CA 2006, s 66(2).

The regulations may make provision:

(a) as to matters that are to be disregarded; and

(b) as to words, expressions, signs or symbols that are, or are not, to be regarded as the same, for the purposes of the section: CA 2006, s 66(3).

8.39 The regulations may provide:

(a) that registration by a name that would otherwise be prohibited under s 66 is permitted:

  (i) in specified circumstances; or

  (ii) with specified consent; and

(b) that if those circumstances obtain or that consent is given at the time a company is registered by a name, a subsequent change of circumstances or withdrawal of consent does not affect the registration: CA 2006, s 66(4).

8.40 With reference to the changes in the permitted characters under the Company, Limited Liability Partnership and Business (Names and Trading Disclosures) Regulations 2015, SI 2015/17, a proposed company name cannot be registered if it is considered the 'same as' another name already registered. For example:

The character 'Ř' will be considered the same as 'R' and 'É' the same as 'E'.

So: 'ŘEAL COFFEE CAFÉ' will be considered the same name as 'REAL COFFEE CAFÉ LTD'.

'PLUM TECHNOLOGY LTD' will be considered the same name as 'PLUM TECHNOLOGY COMPANY LTD'.

'STONE COMPANY LTD' is treated the same as 'STONE AND COMPANY LIMITED'.

8.41 However, the Company, Limited Liability Partnership and Business (Names and Trading Disclosures) Regulations 2015, SI 2015/17 has removed a list of words or expressions (previously under the 2009 Regulations) which are to be ignored when considering whether a name is the 'same as' another. For example:

'CATERING EXPORTS LTD' under SI 2015/17 will be considered different from 'CATERING IMPORTS LTD'.

- In determining whether a name is the same as another name appearing in the Registrar's index of company names, SI 2015/17, Sch 3, paras 1 and 2 are applied. The permitted character set out in column 1 below will be treated the same as a corresponding permitted character or combination of permitted characters in column 2:

Column 1 (permitted characters)	*Column 2 (to be treated the same as)*	
À Á Â Ã Ä Å Ā Ă Ą Ǻ	A	
Æ Ǽ	AE	
Ç Ć Ĉ Ċ Č	C	
Þ Ď Đ	D	
È É Ê Ë Ē Ĕ Ė Ę Ě	E	
Ĝ Ğ Ġ Ģ	G	
Ĥ Ħ	H	
Ì Í Î Ï Ĩ Ī Ĭ Į İ	I	
Ĵ	J	
Ķ	K	
Ĺ Ļ Ľ Ŀ Ł	L	
Ñ Ń Ņ Ň Ŋ	N	
Ò Ó Ô Õ Ö Ø Ō Ŏ Ő Ǿ	O	
Œ	OE	CE
Ŕ Ŗ Ř	R	
Ś Ŝ Ş Š	S	
Ţ Ť Ŧ	T	
Ù Ú Û Ü Ũ Ū Ŭ Ů Ű Ų	U	
Ŵ Ẁ Ẃ Ẅ	W	
Ỳ Ý Ŷ Ÿ	Y	
Ź Ż Ž	Z	

Under s 66(6), the term 'specified' means specified as set out in the Company, Limited Liability Partnership and Business (Names and Trading Disclosures) Regulations 2015, SI 2015/17. Under the Regulations, para 7, for the purposes of CA 2006, s 66 (determining whether a name to be registered under the Act is the same as another name appearing in the registrar's index of company names), Sch 3 will apply for setting out:

(a) the matters that are to be disregarded; and

(b) the words, expressions, signs and symbols that are to be regarded as the same.

Under Sch 3, para 3 taking the name remaining after application of para 2, there shall be disregarded any word, expression or abbreviation set out in inverted commas in Sch 2 where it appears at the end of the name:

- 'LIMITED' or (with or without full stops) the abbreviation 'LTD';
- 'CYFYNGEDIG' or (with or without full stops) the abbreviation 'CYF';

- 'UNLIMITED';
- 'ANGHYFYNGEDIG' (including any 'word specified as similar');
- 'PUBLIC LIMITED COMPANY' or (with or without full stops) the abbreviation 'PLC';
- 'CWMNI CYFYNGEDIG CYHOEDDUS' or (with or without full stops) the abbreviation 'CCC';
- 'COMMUNITY INTEREST COMPANY' or (with or without full stops) the abbreviation 'CIC';
- 'CWMNI BUDDIANT CYMUNEDOL' or (with or without full stops) the abbreviation 'CBC';
- 'COMMUNITY INTEREST PUBLIC LIMITED COMPANY' or (with or without full stops) the abbreviation 'COMMUNITY INTEREST PLC';
- 'CWMNI BUDDIANT CYMUNEDOL CYHOEDDUS CYFYNGEDIG' or (with or without full stops) the abbreviation 'CWMNI BUDDIANT CCC';
- 'RIGHT TO ENFRANCHISEMENT' or (with or without full stops) the abbreviation 'RTE';
- 'HAWL I RYDDFREINIAD';
- 'RIGHT TO MANAGE' or (with or without full stops) the abbreviation 'RTM';
- 'CWMNI RTM CYFYNGEDIG';
- 'EUROPEAN ECONOMIC INTEREST GROUPING' or (with or without full stops) the abbreviation 'EEIG';
- 'INVESTMENT COMPANY WITH VARIABLE CAPITAL';
- 'CWMNI BUDDSODDI A CHYFALAF NEWIDIOL';
- 'LIMITED PARTNERSHIP';
- 'PARTNERIAETH CYFYNGEDIG';
- 'LIMITED LIABILITY PARTNERSHIP';
- 'PARTNERIAETH ATEBOLRWYDD CYFYNGEDIG';
- 'OPEN-ENDED INVESTMENT COMPANY';
- 'CWMNI BUDDSODDIANT PENAGORED';
- 'CHARITABLE INCORPORATED ORGANISATION';
- 'SEFDYDLIAD ELUSENNOL CORFFOREDIG';
- 'INDUSTRIAL AND PROVIDENT SOCIETY';
- 'CO-OPERATIVE SOCIETY';
- 'COMMUNITY BENEFIT SOCIETY'; and
- the following abbreviations (with or without full stops) 'LP', 'PC', 'LLP', 'PAC', 'CIO', and 'SEC'.

- Under paragraph 4 of Schedule 3, taking the name after application of paragraph 2 above, the following words, expressions, signs and symbols are to be regarded as the same where they are each followed by:

  (a) a blank space; or

  (b) if at the beginning of the name, followed by a blank space.

  The words, expressions, signs and symbols are:

  - 'AND' and '&';
  - 'PLUS' and '+';
  - '0', 'ZERO' and 'O';
  - '1' and 'ONE';
  - '2', 'TWO', 'TO' and 'TOO';
  - '3' and 'THREE';
  - '4', 'FOUR' and 'FOR';
  - '5' and 'FIVE';
  - '6' and 'SIX';
  - '7' and 'SEVEN';
  - '8' and 'EIGHT';
  - '9' and 'NINE';
  - '£' and 'POUND';
  - '€'and 'EURO';
  - '$' and 'DOLLAR';
  - ¥ and 'YEN'.
  - '%', 'PER CENT', 'PERCENT', 'PER CENTUM' and 'PERCENTUM'; and
  - '@' and 'AT'.

- Taking the name remaining after the application of paragraphs 2 and 4 of Schedule 3, disregard at the end of the name the matters set out below (or any combination of such matters), where the matter (or combination) is preceded by:

  (a) a blank space;

  (b) a full stop; or

  (c) '@'.

  The matters are:

  - '& CO';
  - '& COMPANY';
  - 'AND CO';

- 'BIZ';
- 'CO';
- 'CO UK';
- 'CO.UK';
- 'COM';
- 'COMPANY';
- 'EU';
- 'GB';
- 'GREAT BRITAIN';
- 'NET';
- 'NI';
- 'NORTHERN IRELAND';
- 'ORG';
- 'ORG UK';
- 'ORG.UK';
- 'UK';
- 'UNITED KINGDOM';
- 'WALES';
- '& CWMNI';
- 'A 'R CWMNI';
- 'CWMNI';
- 'CYM';
- 'CYMRU';
- 'DU';
- 'PF';
- 'PRYDAIN FAWR'; and
- 'Y DEYRNAS UNEDIG'.

The matters in Sch 3, para 2 include any matter in inverted commas that is preceded by and followed by brackets set out in column 2 of table 2 in Sch 1: Sch 3, para 5(3).

- Taking the name remaining after the application of paras 2 to 5 to Sch 3, disregard the following matters in any part of the name:

  (a) any full stop, comma, colon, semi-colon or hyphen;

  (b) any of the following types of punctuation as stated below:

(i) '*';

(ii) '=';

(iii) '#'

(iv) apostrophe;

(v) bracket;

(vi) exclamation mark;

(vii) guillemet;

(viii) inverted comma;

(ix) question mark; and

(x) solidus.

(Schedule 3, para 6.)

- Taking the name remaining after the application of paragraphs 2 to 6 of Schedule 3 of CA 2006, disregard the letter 'S' at the end of the name: Sch 3, para 7.
- Taking the name remaining after the application of paragraphs 2 to 7 of Schedule 3 of CA 2006, disregard any permitted character after the first 60 permitted characters of the name: paragraph 8(1) to Schedule 3. For the purpose of computing the number of permitted characters in this paragraph, any blank space between one permitted character and another in the name shall be counted as though it was a permitted character: paragraph 8(2) to Schedule 3.
- Taking the name remaining after the application of paragraphs 2 to 8 of Schedule 3 of CA 2006, disregard the following matters or any combination of the following matters set out in inverted commas where they appear at the beginning of the name:

  (a) '@';

  (b) 'THE' (but only where followed by a blank space); and

  (c) 'WWW: Sch 3, para 9.
- Taking the name remaining after the application of paragraphs 2 to 9 of Schedule 3 of CA 2006, disregard blank spaces between permitted characters: Sch 3, para 10.

Exception

Paragraph 8 of the Regulations sets out exceptions to the rule that a company cannot be registered with the same name. It applies in the context of a group of companies. This provides that a company may be registered under CA 2006 by a proposed same name if the conditions below are met: reg 8(1):

The conditions are:

(a) the company or other body whose name already appears in the registrar's index of company names ('Body X') consents to the proposed same name being the name of a company ('Company Y');

(b) Company Y forms, or is to form, part of the same group as Body X; and

(c) Company Y provides to the registrar a copy of a statement made by Body X indicating:

  (i) the consent of Body X as referred to in sub-paragraph (a); and

  (ii) that Company Y forms, or is to form, part of the same group as Body X: reg 8(2).

If the proposed same name is to be taken by a company which has not yet been incorporated, the copy of such statement must be provided to the registrar instead by the person who delivers to the registrar the application for registration of the company: reg 8(3).

The registrar may accept the statement referred to in paragraph (2)(c) as sufficient evidence that the conditions referred to in paragraph (2)(a) and (b) have been met: reg 8(4).

If the consent referred to in paragraph (2)(a) is given by Body X, a subsequent withdrawal of that consent does not affect the registration of Company Y by that proposed same name: reg 8(5).

The term:

(a) 'group' has the meaning given in CA 2006, s 474(1); and

(b) 'proposed same name' means a name which is, due to the application of reg 7 and Schedule 3, considered the same as a name appearing in the registrar's index of company names and differs from that name appearing in the index only by one of the matters set out in inverted commas in paragraph 5 of Schedule 3: reg 8(6).

Power to direct a change of name in case of similarity to existing name

8.42 The Secretary of State may direct a company to change its name if it has been registered in a name that is the same as or, in the opinion of the Secretary of State, too like:

(a) a name appearing at the time of the registration in the registrar's index of company names; or

(b) a name that should have appeared in that index at that time: CA 2006, s 67(1).

The Secretary of State may make provision by regulations supplementing this provision: CA 2006, s 67(2).

8.43 The regulations may make provision:

(a) as to matters that are to be disregarded; and

(b) as to words, expressions, signs or symbols that are, or are not, to be regarded as the same,

for the purposes of s 67: CA 2006, s 67(3).

8.44 The regulations may provide:

(a) that no direction is to be given under s 67 in respect of a name:

(i) in specified circumstances; or

(ii) if specified consent is given, and

(b) that a subsequent change of circumstances or withdrawal of consent does not give rise to grounds for a direction under the section: CA 2006, s 67(4).

The term 'specified' means specified in the regulations: CA 2006, s 67(6).

Direction to change name: supplementary provisions

8.45 The following provisions have effect in relation to a direction under CA 2006, s 67 (power to direct change of name in case of similarity to existing name): CA 2006, s 68(1).

Any such direction:

(a) must be given within 12 months of the company's registration by the name in question; and

(b) must specify the period within which the company is to change its name: CA 2006, s 68(2).

The Secretary of State may by a further direction extend this period. Any such direction must be given before the end of the period for the time being specified: CA 2006, s 68(3).

A direction under s 67 or s 68 must be in writing.

8.46 If a company fails to comply with the direction, an offence is committed by:

(a) the company; and

(b) every officer of the company who is in default.

For this purpose a shadow director is treated as an officer of the company: CA 2006, s 68(4).

A person guilty of an offence under s 68 is liable on summary conviction to a fine not exceeding level 3 on the standard scale and, for continued contravention, a daily default fine not exceeding one-tenth of level 3 on the standard scale: CA 2006, s 68(5).

8.47 According to the Companies House Guidance Booklet GP1 *Incorporation of Names*, in general a name is 'too like' an existing name if:

- the differences are so trivial that the public are likely to be confused by the simultaneous appearance of both names on the index;
- the names look and sound the same.

In practice this means that a name will be regarded as being 'too like' an existing name if they:

- differ by one or two letters or characters, although the length of the names involved will be taken into account;

- differ because of punctuation or spacing of letters or words or the order of words;
- look and sound the same.

8.48 Names that differ by the inclusion of additional words (as opposed to a few characters) will not be treated as 'too like', regardless of whether the additional word does or does not describe an activity in detail. For example, there is no difference in the treatment of 'trading' or 'plastics' in terms of additional words. However, names that differ only by the inclusion of words that are normally associated with a name ending such as 'company' or 'partnership' will be regarded as 'too like' one another.

When deciding whether a name is 'too like' another no consideration will be given to other factors, such as:

- trademarks/patents infringement;
- disputes between directors;
- trading/business names;
- nature and location of the companies' activities;
- arguments over proprietary rights in the name;
- suggestions of passing off;
- suggestions of implied association; and
- dormancy or non-trading status.

(See Chapter 8 of the GPI Guidance Booklet issued by Companies House.)

Similarity to another name in which a person has goodwill

8.49 There are specific rules and procedures that apply under CA 2006 where a name has a similarity to another name in which a person has goodwill. This includes 'opportunistic registration'. According to Companies House Guidance Booklet GP1 *Incorporation of Names*, opportunistic registration is the term applied to a company or LLP which registers a similar name to one in which another person has goodwill. There is no restriction on who can complain. Complaints about opportunistic registration are handled by the Company Names Tribunal (not Companies House) which provides a remedy for parties who are damaged by the registration of a company or LLP name in which they have a goodwill/reputation. Objections are also based on the suspicion that the name has been registered in order to extract money or to prevent the aggrieved party from registering the name.

Objection to company's registered name

8.50 A person ('the applicant') may object to a company's registered name on the ground:

(a) that it is the same as a name associated with the applicant in which he has goodwill; or

(b) that it is sufficiently similar to such a name that its use in the UK would be likely to mislead by suggesting a connection between the company and the applicant: CA 2006, s 69(1).

The objection must be made by application to a company names adjudicator (see s 70): CA 2006, s 69(2). The company concerned will be the primary respondent to the application and any of its members or directors may be joined as respondents: CA 2006, s 69(3).

8.51 If the ground specified in s 69(1)(a) or (b) is established, it is for the respondents to show:

(a) that the name was registered before the commencement of the activities on which the applicant relies to show goodwill; or

(b) that the company:

  (i) is operating under the name; or

  (ii) is proposing to do so and has incurred substantial start-up costs in preparation; or

  (iii) was formerly operating under the name and is now dormant; or

(c) that the name was registered in the ordinary course of a company formation business and the company is available for sale to the applicant on the standard terms of that business; or

(d) that the name was adopted in good faith; or

(e) that the interests of the applicant are not adversely affected to any significant extent.

If none of the above is shown, the objection will be upheld: CA 2006, s 69(4).

If the facts mentioned in subs (4)(a), (b) or (c) are established, the objection shall nevertheless be upheld if the applicant shows that the main purpose of the respondents (or any of them) in registering the name was to obtain money (or other consideration) from the applicant or prevent him from registering the name: CA 2006, s 69(5).

If the objection is not upheld under subs (4) or (5), it shall be dismissed: CA 2006, s 69(6).

Under s 69(7), the term 'goodwill' includes reputation of any description.

Company names adjudicators

8.52 The Secretary of State may appoint company names adjudicators under CA 2006, s 70(1). The persons appointed must have such legal or other experience as, in the Secretary of State's opinion, makes them suitable for appointment: CA 2006, s 70(2).

An adjudicator:

(a) holds office in accordance with the terms of his appointment;

(b) is eligible for re-appointment when his term of office ends;

(c) may resign at any time by notice in writing given to the Secretary of State; and

(d) may be dismissed by the Secretary of State on grounds of incapacity or misconduct: CA 2006, s 70(3).

One of the adjudicators will be appointed Chief Adjudicator and will perform such functions as the Secretary of State may assign to him: CA 2006, s 70(4). The other adjudicators will undertake such duties as the Chief Adjudicator may determine: CA 2006, s 70(5).

8.53 The Secretary of State may:

(a) appoint staff for the adjudicators;

(b) pay remuneration and expenses to the adjudicators and their staff;

(c) defray other costs arising in relation to the performance by the adjudicators of their functions;

(d) compensate persons for ceasing to be adjudicators: CA 2006, s 70(6).

Procedural rules

8.54 Under s 71(1), the Secretary of State may make rules regarding proceedings before a company names adjudicator. The rules are set out in the Company Names Adjudicator Rules 2008, SI 2008/1738, which came into force on 1 October 2008 ('rules'). See too the Practice Direction issued by the Company Names Tribunal.

In particular, the rules may make provision:

(a) as to how an application is to be made and the form and content of an application or other documents;

(b) for fees to be charged;

(c) about the service of documents and the consequences of failure to serve them;

(d) as to the form and manner in which evidence is to be given;

(e) for circumstances in which hearings are required and those in which they are not;

(f) for cases to be heard by more than one adjudicator;

(g) setting time limits for anything required to be done in connection with the proceedings (and allowing for such limits to be extended, even if they have expired);

(h) enabling the adjudicator to strike out an application, or any defence, in whole or in part:

    (i) on the ground that it is vexatious, has no reasonable prospect of success or is otherwise misconceived; or

    (ii) for failure to comply with the requirements of the rules;

(i) conferring power to order security for costs (in Scotland, caution for expenses);

(j) as to how far proceedings are to be held in public;

(k) requiring one party to bear the costs (in Scotland, expenses) of another and as to the taxing (or settling) the amount of such costs (or expenses): CA 2006, s 71(2).

The rules may confer on the Chief Adjudicator power to determine any matter that could be the subject of provision in the rules: CA 2006, s 71(3). Rules under this provision will be made by statutory instrument and will be subject to annulment in pursuance of a resolution of either House of Parliament: CA 2006, s 71(4).

Decision of adjudicator to be made available to public

8.55 Within 90 days of determining an application under s 69, a company names adjudicator must make his decision and the reasons for making such decision available to the public: CA 2006, s 72(1). He may do this by means of a website, or by such other means as appear to him to be appropriate: CA 2006, s 72(2).

Order requiring name to be changed

8.56 If an application under s 69 is upheld, the adjudicator must make an order:

(a) requiring the respondent company to change its name to one that is not an offending name; and

(b) requiring all the respondents:

  (i) to take all such steps as are within their power to make, or facilitate the making, of that change; and

  (ii) not to cause or permit any steps to be taken calculated to result in another company being registered with a name that is an offending name: CA 2006, s 73(1).

8.57 An 'offending name' means a name that, by reason of its similarity to the name associated with the applicant in which he claims goodwill, would be likely:

(a) to be the subject of a direction under s 67 (power of Secretary of State to direct change of name); or

(b) to give rise to a further application under s 69: CA 2006, s 73(2).

8.58 The order must specify a date by which the respondent company's name is to be changed, and may be enforced:

(a) in England and Wales or Northern Ireland, in the same way as an order of the High Court;

(b) in Scotland, in the same way as a decree of the Court of Session: CA 2006, s 73(3).

If the respondent company's name is not changed in accordance with the order by the specified date, the adjudicator may determine a new name for the company: CA 2006, s 73(4).

8.59 If the adjudicator determines a new name for the respondent company he must give notice of his determination:

(a) to the applicant;

(b) to the respondents; and

(c) to the registrar: CA 2006, s 73(5).

For the purposes of s 73 a company's name is changed when the change takes effect in accordance with s 81(1) (on the issue of the new certification of incorporation): CA 2006, s 73(6).

Appeal from adjudicator's decision

8.60 Under s 74(1), an appeal lies to the court from any decision of a company names adjudicator to uphold or dismiss an application under s 69. Notice of appeal against a decision upholding an application must be given before the date specified in the adjudicator's order by which the respondent company's name is to be changed: CA 2006, s 74(2).

If notice of appeal is given against a decision upholding an application, the effect of the adjudicator's order is suspended: CA 2006, s 74(3).

If on appeal the court:

(a) affirms the decision of the adjudicator to uphold the application; or

(b) reverses the decision of the adjudicator to dismiss the application,

the court may specify the date by which the adjudicator's order is to be complied with, remit the matter to the adjudicator, or make any order or determination that the adjudicator might have made: CA 2006, s 74(4).

8.61 If the court determines a new name for the company, it must give notice of the determination:

(a) to the parties to the appeal; and

(b) to the registrar: CA 2006, s 74(5).

Other powers of the Secretary of State

8.62 CA 2006 sets out further powers of the Secretary of State in connection with the use of a name.

Provision of misleading information

8.63 If it appears to the Secretary of State:

(a) that misleading information has been given for the purposes of a company's registration by a particular name; or

(b) that an undertaking or assurance has been given for that purpose and has not been fulfilled,

the Secretary of State may direct the company to change its name: CA 2006, s 75(1).

8.64 Any such direction:

(a) must be given within five years of the company's registration by that name; and

(b) must specify the period within which the company is to change its name: CA 2006, s 75(3).

The Secretary of State may by a further direction extend the period within which the company is to change its name. Any such direction must be given before the end of the period for the time being specified: CA 2006, s 75(3).

Any direction under s 75 must be in writing: CA 2006, s 75(4).

8.65 If a company fails to comply with a direction under s 75, an offence is committed by:

(a) the company; and

(b) every officer of the company who is in default.

For this purpose a shadow director is treated as an officer of the company: CA 2006, s 75(5).

A person guilty of an offence under this provision is liable on summary conviction to a fine not exceeding level 3 on the standard scale and, for continued contravention, a daily default fine not exceeding one-tenth of level 3 on the standard scale: CA 2006, s 75(6).

Misleading indication of activities

8.66 If in the opinion of the Secretary of State the name by which a company is registered gives so misleading an indication of the nature of its activities as to be likely to cause harm to the public, the Secretary of State may direct the company to change its name: CA 2006, s 76(1). This direction must be in writing: s 76(2) CA 2006 and must be complied with within a period of six weeks from the date of the direction or such longer period as the Secretary of State may think fit to allow.

8.67 This does not apply if an application is duly made to the court under the following provisions: CA 2006, s 76(3):

- the company may apply to the court to set the direction aside;
- the application must be made within the period of three weeks from the date of the direction: CA 2006, s 76(4).

The court may set the direction aside or confirm it.

If the direction is confirmed, the court shall specify the period within which the direction is to be complied with: CA 2006, s 76(5).

8.68 If a company fails to comply with a direction under s 76, an offence is committed by:

(a) the company; and

(b) every officer of the company who is in default.

For this purpose a shadow director will be treated as an officer of the company: CA 2006, s 76(6).

A person guilty of an offence under s 76 will be liable on summary conviction to a fine not exceeding level 3 on the standard scale and, for continued contravention, a daily default fine not exceeding one-tenth of level 3 on the standard scale: CA 2006, s 76(7).

Change of name

8.69 A company may change its name under CA 2006, Pt 5, Ch 5. This sets out the various ways in which the change of name may be effected.

A company may change its name:

(a) by special resolution (see CA 2006, s 78); or

(b) by other means provided for by the company's articles (see CA 2006, s 79): CA 2006, s 77(1).

8.70 A company may also change its name:

(a) by resolution of the directors acting under s 64 (change of name to comply with direction of Secretary of State under that section);

(b) on the determination of a new name by a company names adjudicator under s 73 (powers of adjudicator on upholding objection to company name);

(c) on the determination of a new name by the court under s 74 (appeal against decision of company names adjudicator);

(d) under s 1033 (company's name on restoration to the register): CA 2006, s 77(2).

Change of name by special resolution

8.71 Where a change of name has been agreed to by a company by special resolution, the company must give notice to the registrar. It must also forward a copy of the resolution to the registrar: CA 2006, s 78(1).

Where such a change of name is conditional on the occurrence of an event, the notice given to the registrar of the change must:

(a) specify that the change is conditional; and

(b) state whether the event has occurred: CA 2006, s 78(2).

8.72 If the notice states that the event has not occurred:

(a) the registrar is not required to act under s 80 (registration and issue of new certificate of incorporation) until further notice;

(b) when the event occurs, the company must give notice to the registrar stating that it has occurred; and

(c) the registrar may rely on the statement as sufficient evidence of the matters stated in it: CA 2006, s 78(3).

Change of name by means provided for in company's articles

8.73 Where a change of a company's name has been made by other means provided for by its articles:

(a) the company must give notice to the registrar; and

(b) the notice must be accompanied by a statement that the change of name has been made by means provided for by the company's articles: CA 2006, s 79(1).

The registrar may rely on the statement as sufficient evidence of the matters stated in it: CA 2006, s 79(2).

Change of name: registration and issue of new certificate of incorporation

8.74 Section 80 applies where the registrar receives notice of a change of a company's name: CA 2006, s 80(1).

If the registrar is satisfied:

(a) that the new name complies with the requirements of CA 2006; and

(b) that the requirements of the Companies Acts, and any relevant requirements of the company's articles, with respect to a change of name are complied with,

the registrar must enter the new name on the register in place of the former name: CA 2006, s 80(2).

On the registration of the new name, the registrar must issue a certificate of incorporation which has been altered to meet the circumstances of the case: CA 2006, s 80(3).

Change of name: effect

8.75 A change of a company's name will have effect from the date on which the new certificate of incorporation is issued: CA 2006, s 81(1). The change will not affect any rights or obligations of the company, or render defective any legal proceedings by or against it: CA 2006, s 81(2). Any legal proceedings that might have been continued or commenced against it by its former name may be continued or commenced against it under its new name: CA 2006, s 81(3).

Trading disclosures

8.76 There are specific rules that apply in respect of a name once a company begins to trade under that name. CA 2006, Pt 5, Ch 6 also sets out the civil and criminal consequences.

Requirement to disclose company name

8.77 The Secretary of State may by regulations make provision requiring companies:

(a) to display specified information in specified locations;

(b) to state specified information in specified descriptions of document or communication; and

(c) to provide specified information on request to those they deal with in the course of their business: CA 2006, s 82(1).

The regulations must in every case require disclosure of the name of the company and may make provision as to the manner in which any specified information is to be displayed, stated or provided: CA 2006, s 82(2).

Under s 82(3), the regulations may provide that, for the purposes of any requirement to disclose a company's name, any variation between a word or words required to be part of the name and a permitted abbreviation of that word or those words (or vice versa) shall be disregarded.

The term 'specified' means specified in the regulations: CA 2006, s 82(4).

The regulations are the Company, Limited Liability Partnership and Business (Names and Trading Disclosures) Regulations 2015, SI 2015/17. Part 6 of the regulations applies to trading disclosures as follows.

Legibility of displays and disclosures

8.78 Any display or disclosure of information required by SI 2015/17, Pt 6 must be in characters that can be read with the naked eye: Pt 6, reg 20.

Requirement to display registered name at registered office and inspection place

8.79 A company shall display its registered name at:

(a) its registered office; and

(b) any inspection place: SI 2015/17, Pt 6, reg 21(1).

But reg 21(1) does not apply to any company which has at all times since its incorporation been dormant: SI 2015/17, Pt 6, reg 21(2).

8.80 Regulation 21(1) shall also not apply to the registered office or an inspection place of a company where:

(a) in respect of that company, a liquidator, administrator or administrative receiver has been appointed; and

(b) the registered office or inspection place is also a place of business of that liquidator, administrator or administrative receiver: SI 2015/17, Pt 6, reg 21(3).

Requirement to display registered name at other business locations

8.81 SI 2015/17, Pt 6, reg 22 applies to a location other than a company's registered office or any inspection place: Pt 6, reg 22(1).

A company shall display its registered name at any such location at which it carries on business: Pt 6, reg 22(2).

But reg 22(2) shall not apply to a location which is primarily used for living accommodation: Pt 6, reg 22(3).

Regulation 22(2) shall also not apply to any location at which business is carried on by a company where:

(a) in respect of that company, a liquidator, administrator or administrative receiver has been appointed; and

(b) the location is also a place of business of that liquidator, administrator or administrative receiver: Pt 6, reg 22(4).

Regulation 22(2) shall also not apply to any location at which business is carried on by a company of which every director who is an individual is a relevant director: Pt 6, reg 22(5).

The following terms apply for the purposes of Pt 6, reg 21:

(a) 'administrative receiver' has the meaning given—

  (i) in England and Wales or Scotland, by section 251 of the Insolvency Act 1986, and

  (ii) in Northern Ireland, by Article 5 of the Insolvency (Northern Ireland) Order 1989;

(b) 'credit reference agency' has the meaning given in section 243(7) of the Act;

(c) 'protected information' has the meaning given in section 240 of the Act; and

(d) 'relevant director' means an individual in respect of whom the registrar is required by regulations made pursuant to section 243(4) of the Act to refrain from disclosing protected information to a credit reference agency: Pt 6, reg 22(6).

Manner of display of registered name

8.82 SI 2015/17, Pt 6, reg 23 applies where a company is required to display its registered name at any office, place or location: Pt 6, reg 23(1).

Where that office, place or location is shared by no more than five companies, the registered name:

(a) shall be so positioned that it may be easily seen by any visitor to that office, place or location; and

(b) shall be displayed continuously: Pt 6, reg 23(2).

Where any such office, place or location is shared by six or more companies, each such company must ensure that either:

(a) its registered name is displayed for at least fifteen continuous seconds at least once every three minutes; or

(b) its registered name is available for inspection on a register by any visitor to that office, place or location: Pt 6, reg 23(3).

Registered name to appear in communications

8.83 Every company shall disclose its registered name on:

(a) its business letters, notices and other official publications;

(b) its bills of exchange, promissory notes, endorsements and order forms;

(c) cheques purporting to be signed by or on behalf of the company;

(d) orders for money, goods or services purporting to be signed by or on behalf of the company;

(e) its bills of parcels, invoices and other demands for payment, receipts and letters of credit;

(f) its applications for licences to carry on a trade or activity; and

(g) all other forms of its business correspondence and documentation: SI 2015/17, Pt 6, reg 24(1).

Every company shall disclose its registered name on its websites: Pt 6, reg 24(2).

Further particulars to appear in business letters, order forms and websites

8.84 Every company shall disclose the particulars set out in SI 2015/17, Pt 6, reg 25(2) on:

(a) its business letters;

(b) its order forms; and

(c) its websites: Pt 6, reg 25(1).

8.85 The particulars are:

(a) the part of the United Kingdom in which the company is registered;

(b) the company's registered number;

(c) the address of the company's registered office;

(d) in the case of a limited company exempt from the obligation to use the word 'limited' as part of its registered name under section 60 of the Act, the fact that it is a limited company;

(e) in the case of a community interest company which is not a public company, the fact that it is a limited company; and

(f) in the case of an investment company within the meaning of section 833 of the Act, the fact that it is such a company: SI 2015/17, Pt 6, reg 25(2).

8.86 If, in the case of a company having a share capital, there is a disclosure as to the amount of share capital on:

(a) its business letters;

(b) its order forms; or

(c) its websites,

that disclosure must be as to paid up share capital: SI 2015/17, Pt 6, reg 25(3).

Disclosure of names of directors

8.87 Where a company's business letter includes the name of any director of that company, other than in the text or as a signatory, the letter must disclose the name of every director of that company: SI 2015/17, Pt 6, reg 26(1).

In paragraph (1), 'name' has the following meanings:

(a) in the case of a director who is an individual, 'name' has the meaning given in section 163(2) of the Act; and

(b) in the case of a director who is a body corporate or a firm that is a legal person under the law by which it is governed, 'name' means corporate name or firm name: Pt 6, reg 26(2).

Disclosures relating to registered office and inspection place

8.88 A company shall disclose:

(a) the address of its registered office;

(b) any inspection place; and

(c) the type of company records which are kept at that office or place,

to any person it deals with in the course of business who makes a written request to the company for that information: SI 2015/17, Pt 6, reg 27(1).

The company shall send a written response to that person within five working days of the receipt of that request: Pt 6, reg 27(2).

Offence

8.89 Where a company fails, without reasonable excuse, to comply with any requirement in regs 20 to 27, an offence is committed by:

(a) the company; and

(b) every officer of the company who is in default: SI 2015/17, Pt 6, reg 28(1).

8.90 A person guilty of an offence under paragraph (1) is liable on summary conviction to:

(a) a fine not exceeding level 3 on the standard scale; and

(b) for continued contravention, a daily default fine not exceeding one-tenth of level 3 on the standard scale: SI 2015/17, Pt 6, reg 28(2).

For the purposes of this regulation a shadow director is to be treated as an officer of the company: Pt 6, reg 28(3).

Interpretation

8.91 The following definitions apply in SI 2015/17, Pt 6:

(a) 'company record' means:

  (i) any register, index, accounting records, agreement, memorandum, minutes or other document required by the Companies Acts to be kept by a company; and

  (ii) any register kept by a company of its debenture holders;

(b) 'inspection place' means any location, other than a company's registered office, at which a company keeps available for inspection any company record which it is required under the Companies Acts to keep available for inspection;

(c) a reference to any type of document is a reference to a document of that type in hard copy, electronic or any other form; and

(d) in relation to a company, a reference to 'its websites' includes a reference to any part of a website relating to that company which that company has caused or authorised to appear: Pt 6, reg 29.

Civil consequences of failure to make required disclosure

8.92 Section 83 applies to any legal proceedings brought by a company to which s 82 applies (requirement to disclose company name etc) to enforce a right arising out of a contract made in the course of a business in respect of which the company was, at the time the contract was made, in breach of regulations under that section.

The proceedings will be dismissed if the defendant (in Scotland, the defender) to the proceedings shows:

(a) that he has a claim against the claimant (pursuer) arising out of the contract that he has been unable to pursue by reason of the latter's breach of the regulations, or

(b) that he has suffered some financial loss in connection with the contract by reason of the claimant's (pursuer's) breach of the regulations,

unless the court before which the proceedings are brought is satisfied that it is just and equitable to permit the proceedings to continue: CA 2006, s 83(2).

The section does not affect the right of any person to enforce such rights as he may have against another person in any proceedings brought by that person: CA 2006, s 83(3).

Criminal consequences of failure to make required disclosures

8.93 Regulations under s 82 may provide:

(a) that where a company fails, without reasonable excuse, to comply with any specified requirement of regulations under that section an offence is committed by:

  (i) the company; and

  (ii) every officer of the company who is in default;

(b) that a person guilty of such an offence is liable on summary conviction to a fine not exceeding level 3 on the standard scale and, for continued contravention, a daily default fine not exceeding one-tenth of level 3 on the standard scale: CA 2006, s 84(1). In subs (1)(a), the term 'specified' means specified in the regulations: CA 2006, s 84(3).

The regulations may provide that, for the purposes of any provision made under subs (1), a shadow director of the company is to be treated as an officer of the company: CA 2006, s 84(2).

Minor variations in form of name

8.94 For the purposes of Chapter 6 of CA 2006, in considering a company's name no account is to be taken of:

(a) whether upper or lower case characters (or a combination of the two) are used;

(b) whether diacritical marks or punctuation are present or absent;

(c) whether the name is in the same format or style as is specified under s 57(1)(b) for the purposes of registration;

provided there is no real likelihood of names differing only in those respects being taken to be different names: CA 2006, s 85(1).

This does not affect the operation of regulations under s 57(1)(a) permitting only specified characters, diacritical marks or punctuation: CA 2006, s 85(2).

Business names

8.95 The CA 2006, Pt 41 is concerned with the regulation of business names. It is supplemented by Pt 5 to the Company, Limited Liability Partnership and Business (Names and Trading Disclosures) Regulations 2015, SI 2015/17, which specifically addresses business names.

Restricted or prohibited names

8.96 Chapter 1 of Pt 41 applies to a person carrying on business in the UK: CA 2006, s 1192(1). The provisions under Pt 41 do not prevent:

(a) an individual carrying on business under a name consisting of his surname without any addition other than a permitted addition; or

(b) individuals carrying on business in partnership under a name consisting of the surnames of all the partners without any addition other than a permitted addition: CA 2006, s 1192(2).

8.97 The permitted additions are as follows:

(a) in the case of an individual his forename as initial;

(b) in the case of a partnership:

  (i) the forenames of individual partners as the initials of those forenames; or

  (ii) where two or more individual partners have the same surname, the addition of 's' as the end of that surname.

(c) in either case, an addition merely indicating that the business is carried on in succession to a former owner of the business: CA 2006, s 1192(3).

Name suggesting connection with government or public authority

8.98 A person must not, without the approval of the Secretary of State, carry on business in the UK under a name that would be likely to give the impression that the business is connected with:

(a) Her Majesty's Government. Any part of the Scottish administration, the Welsh Assembly Government or Her Majesty's Government in Northern Ireland;

(b) any local authority; or

(c) any public authority specified for the purposes of CA 2006, s 1193 by regulations made by the Secretary of State: CA 2006, s 1193(1).

8.99 The term 'local authority' means:

(a) a local authority within the meaning of the Local Government Act 1972 (c 70), the Common Council of the City of London or the Council of the Isles of Scilly;

(b) a Council constituted under s 2 of the Local Government, etc (Scotland) Act 1994 (c 39); or

(c) a District Council in Northern Ireland.

The term 'public authority' includes any person or body having functions of a public nature: CA 2006, s 1193(2).

Any person who contravenes s 1193 commits an offence.

Where an offence under CA 2006, s 1193 is committed by a body corporate, an offence will also be committed by every officer of that body who is in default: CA 2006, s 1193(5).

A person found guilty of an offence under s 1193 will be liable on summary conviction to a fine not exceeding level 3 on the standard scale and, for continued contravention, a daily default fine not exceeding one-tenth of level 3 on the standard scale: CA 2006, s 1193(6).

Other sensitive words or expressions

8.100 Under s 1194 a person must not, without the approval of the Secretary of State, carry on business in the UK under a name that includes a word or expression for the time being specified in the regulations made by the Secretary of State.

A person who contravenes s 1194 commits an offence, and where an offence under the section is committed by a body corporate, an offence is also committed by every officer of the body who is in default: CA 2006, s 1194(4). A person who is guilty of an offence under this provision is liable on summary conviction to a fine not exceeding level 3 on the standard scale and, for continued contravention, a daily default fine not exceeding one-tenth of level 3 on the standard scale: CA 2006, s 1194(5).

The regulations in respect of sensitive words or expressions are set out in the Company, Limited Liability Partnership and Business Names (Sensitive Words and Expressions) Regulations 2014, SI 2014/3140.

Requirement to seek comments of government department or other relevant body

8.101 The Secretary of State may by regulations under CA 2006, s 1193 or s 1194 require that in connection with an application for the approval of the Secretary of State under either of those sections, the applicant must seek the view of a specified government department or other body: CA 2006, s 1195(1).

Where such a requirement applies, the applicant must request the specified department or other body (in writing) to indicate whether (and if so why) it has any objections to the proposed name: CA 2006, s 1195(2). He must submit to the Secretary of State a statement that such a request has been made and a copy of any response received from the specified body: CA 2006, s 1195(3).

If these requirements are not complied with, the Secretary of State may refuse to consider the application for approval: CA 2006, s 1195(5).

The applicable regulations are the Company, Limited Liability Partnership and Business Names (Sensitive Words and Expressions) Regulations 2014, SI 2014/3140.

Withdrawal of Secretary of State's approval

8.102 In respect of any of applications under CA 2006, s 1193 or s 1194, if it appears to the Secretary of State that there are overriding considerations of public policy that require such approval to be withdrawn, the approval may be withdrawn by notice in writing given to the person concerned: CA 2006, s 1196(2).

The notice must create the date as from which the approval is withdrawn: CA 2006, s 1196(3).

Misleading names

8.103 Part 41 of CA 2006 also sets out provisions concerning misleading business names.

Name containing inappropriate indication of company type or legal form

8.104 The Secretary of State may make provision by regulations prohibiting a person from carrying on business in the UK under a name consisting of or containing specified words, expressions or other indications:

(a) that are associated with a particular type of company or form of organisation; or

(b) that are similar to words, expressions or other indications associated with a particular type of company or form of organisation: CA 2006, s 1197(1).

8.105 The regulations may prohibit the use of words, expressions or other indications:

(a) in a specified part, or otherwise than in a specified part, of a name;

(b) in conjunction with, or otherwise than in conjunction with, such other words, expressions or indications as may be specified: CA 2006, s 1197(2).

The term 'specified' means specified in the regulations: CA 2006, s 1197(3).

Under s 1197(5), a person who uses a name in contravention of regulations under the section will be guilty of an offence. Where an offence under this section is committed by a body corporate, the offence is also committed by every officer of the body who is in default: CA 2006, s 1197(6). A person guilty of an offence under the section will be liable on summary conviction to a fine not exceeding level 3 on the standard scale and, for continued contravention, a daily default fine not exceeding one-tenth of level 3 on the standard scale: CA 2006, s 1197(7).

8.106 The CA 2006 includes provisions with respect to the use of names by companies (in Pt 5 of CA 2006, LLPs in CA 2006, Pt 5 as applied by Pt 3 of the Limited Liability Partnerships (Application of Companies Act 2006) Regulations 2009, SI 2009/1804, and business names in CA 2006, Pt 41. These set out the characters and words that may or must be used in the name of companies, LLPs or businesses, or powers for the Secretary of State to make additional or supplementary provisions relating to the use of names. Under the Company, Limited Liability Partnership and Business (Names and Trading Disclosures) Regulations 2015, SI 2015/17, the following rules apply in respect of business names:

- A person must not carry on business in the UK under a name that:
  - ends with 'LIMITED' or (with or without full stops) the abbreviation 'LTD';
  - 'CYFYNGEDIG' or (with or without full stops) the abbreviation 'CYF' (or any word or abbreviation specified as similar),

  unless that person is:
  - a company or an overseas company registered in the UK by that name;

- an overseas company incorporated with that name;
- a society registered under the Industrial and Provident Societies Act 1965(1) or the Industrial and Provident Societies Act (Northern Ireland) 1969(2) by that name;
- an incorporated friendly society (as defined in section 116 of the Friendly Societies Act 1992(c)) which has that name; or
- a company to which section 1040 of the Act (companies authorised to register under the Companies Act 2006) applies which has that name: Pt 5, reg 16(1).

- A person must not carry on business in the UK under a name that concludes with any word or abbreviation specified as similar to any word or abbreviation set out below:
  - 'LIMITED' or (with or without full stops) the abbreviation 'LTD';
  - 'CYFYNGEDIG' or (with or without full stops) the abbreviation 'CYF'.

  (Pt 5, reg 16(2)).
- A person must not carry on business in the UK under a name that includes any expression or abbreviation specified as similar to any expression or abbreviation set out below, unless that person is such a company, partnership, grouping or organisation as is indicated in that expression or abbreviation: Pt 5, reg 17(1):
  - 'PUBLIC LIMITED COMPANY' or (with or without full stops) the abbreviation 'PLC';
  - 'CWMNI CYFYNGEDIG CYHOEDDUS' or (with or without full stops) the abbreviation 'CCC';
  - 'COMMUNITY INTEREST COMPANY' or (with or without full stops) the abbreviation 'CIC';
  - 'CWMNI BUDDIANT CYMUNEDOL' or (with or without full stops) the abbreviation 'CBC';
  - 'COMMUNITY INTEREST PUBLIC LIMITED COMPANY' or (with or without full stops) the abbreviation 'COMMUNITY INTEREST PLC';
  - 'CWMNI BUDDIANT CYMUNEDOL CYHOEDDUS CYFYNGEDIG' or (with or without full stops) the abbreviation 'CWMNI BUDDIANT CCC';
  - 'RIGHT TO ENFRANCHISEMENT' or (with or without full stops) the abbreviation 'RTE';
  - 'HAWL I RYDDFREINIAD';
  - 'RIGHT TO MANAGE' or (with or without full stops) the abbreviation 'RTM';
  - 'CWMNI RTM CYFYNGEDIG';
  - 'EUROPEAN ECONOMIC INTEREST GROUPING' or (with or without full stops) the abbreviation 'EEIG';

- 'INVESTMENT COMPANY WITH VARIABLE CAPITAL';
- 'CWMNI BUDDSODDI A CHYFALAF NEWIDIOL';
- 'LIMITED PARTNERSHIP';
- 'PARTNERIAETH CYFYNGEDIG';
- 'LIMITED LIABILITY PARTNERSHIP';
- 'PARTNERIAETH ATEBOLRWYDD CYFYNGEDIG';
- 'OPEN-ENDED INVESTMENT COMPANY';
- 'CWMNI BUDDSODDIANT PENAGORED';
- 'CHARITABLE INCORPORATED ORGANISATION';
- 'SEFDYDLIAD ELUSENNOL CORFFOREDIG'.
- 'INDUSTRIAL AND PROVIDENT'
- 'LP', 'PC', 'LLP', 'PAC', 'CIO' and 'SEC'.

The words and abbreviations specified as similar or an expression or abbreviation specified as similar is any in which:

(a) one or more characters has been omitted;

(b) one or more characters, signs, symbols or punctuation has been added; or

(c) each of one or more characters has been substituted by one or more other characters, signs, symbols or punctuation,

in such a way as to be likely to mislead the public as to the legal form of a company or business if included in the registered name of the company or in a business name: see paragraph 2 of Schedule 2 to the Regulations.

- A person must not carry on business in the UK under a name that includes any expression or abbreviation specified as similar to any expression or abbreviation set out in inverted commas in paragraph 3 of Schedule 2: Pt 5, reg 17(2).

Certain exceptions, however, apply to existing lawful business names under reg 19. In the following situations, the provisions for approval of sensitive words and expressions and for prohibition on inappropriate indications of company type do not apply. They are:

- The carrying on of a business under a name by a person who:

  (a) carried on that business under that name immediately before the 2015 Regulations came into force; and

  (b) continues to carry it on under that name,

  if it was lawful for the business to be carried on under that name immediately before these Regulations came into force: reg 19(1).

Regulation 17 does not apply to the carrying on of a business under a name by a person to whom the business is transferred on or after the date on which the 2015 Regulations came into force in the following circumstances:

(a) where that person continues to carry on the business under that name; and

(b) where it was lawful for the business to be carried on under that name immediately before the transfer,

during the period of 12 months beginning with the date of the transfer: reg 19(2).

The term 'lawful business name', in relation to a business, means a name under which the business was carried on without contravening the provisions of Chapter 1 of Part 41 of the CA 2006: reg 19(5).

Name giving misleading indication of activities

8.107 A person must not carry on business in the UK under a name that gives so misleading an indication of the nature of the activities of the business as to be likely to cause harm to the public: CA 2006, s 1198(1).

Under s 1198(2), a person who uses a name in contravention of this section commits an offence, and where such an offence is committed by a body corporate, it is also committed by every officer of the body who is in default: CA 2006, s 1198(3).

A person guilty of an offence under this provision is liable on summary conviction to a fine not exceeding level 3 on the standard scale and, for continued contravention, a daily default fine not exceeding one-tenth of level 3 on the standard scale: CA 2006, s 1198(4).

Savings for existing lawful business names

8.108 Section 1199 of CA 2006 has effect in relation to:

- ss 1192–1196 (sensitive words or expressions); and
- s 1197 (inappropriate indication of company type or legal form): CA 2006, s 1199(1).

Those sections do not apply to the carrying on of a business by a person who:

(a) carried on the business immediately before the date on which this chapter of CA 2006 came into force; and

(b) continues to carry it on under the name that immediately before that date was its lawful business name: CA 2006, s 1199(2).

Where:

(a) a business is transferred to a person on or after the date on which the chapter came into force; and

(b) that person carries on the business under the name that was its lawful business name immediately before the transfer,

those sections do not apply in relation to the carrying on of the business under that name during the period of 12 months beginning with the date of the transfer: CA 2006, s 1199(3).

The term 'lawful business name', in relation to a business, means a name under which the business was carried on without contravening:

(a) s 2(1) of the Business Names Act 1985 (c 7) or article 4(1) of the Business Names (Northern Ireland) Order 1986, SI 1986/1033 NI 7; or

(b) after this chapter of CA 2006 has come into force, the provisions of this chapter: CA 2006, s 1199(4).

Disclosure required in case of individual or partnership

8.109 CA 2006, Pt 41, Ch 2 sets out the provisions governing disclosure of business names where an individual or partnership is concerned. The chapter applies to an individual or partnership carrying on business in the UK under a business name. The references in Chapter 2 to 'a person to whom this chapter applies' are to such an individual or partnership: CA 2006, s 1200.

For the purposes of Chapter 2, a 'business name' means a name other than:

(a) in the case of an individual, his surname without any addition other than a permitted addition;

(b) in the case of a partnership:

  (i) the surnames of all partners who are individuals; and

  (ii) the corporate names of all partners who are bodies corporate,

  without any addition other than a permitted addition: CA 2006, s 1200(2).

8.110 The following are the permitted additions:

(a) in the case of an individual, his forename or initial;

(b) in the case of a partnership:

  (i) the forenames of individual partners or the initials of those forenames; or

  (ii) where two or more individual partners have the same surname, the addition of 's' at the end of that surname;

(c) in either case, an addition merely indicating that the business is carried on in succession to a former owner of the business: CA 2006, s 1200(3).

Information required to be disclosed

8.111 The 'information required by Chapter 2 is:

(a) in the case of an individual, the individual's name;

(b) in the case of a partnership, the name of each member of the partnership;

and, in relation to each person so named, an address at which service of any document relating in any way to the business will be effective: CA 2006, s 1201(1).

If the individual or partnership has a place of business in the UK, the address must be in the UK: CA 2006, s 1201(2).

If the individual or partnership does not have a place of business in the UK, the address must be an address at which service of documents can be effected by physical delivery and the delivery of documents is capable of being recorded by the obtaining of an acknowledgement of delivery: CA 2006, s 1201(3).

Disclosure required: business documents

8.112 A person to whom Chapter 2 applies must state the information required by the chapter, in legible characters, on all:

(a) business letters;

(b) written orders for goods or services to be supplied to the business;

(c) invoices and receipts issued in the course of the business; and

(d) written demands for payment of debts arising in the course of the business.

This subsection has effect subject to s 1203 (exemption for large partnerships if certain conditions met): CA 2006, s 1202(1).

A person to whom Chapter 2 applies must secure that the information required by that chapter is immediately given, by written notice, to any person with whom anything is done or discussed in the course of the business and who asks for that information: CA 2006, s 1202(2).

Under s 1202(3), the Secretary of State may by regulations require that such notices be given in a specified form.

Exemption for large partnerships if certain conditions met

8.113 Section 1202(1) of CA 2006 (disclosure required in business documents) does not apply in relation to a document issued by a partnership of more than 20 persons if the following conditions are met: CA 2006, s 1203(1):

(a) the partnership maintains at its principal place of business a list of the names of all the partners;

(b) no partner's name appears in the document, except in the text or as a signatory; and

(c) the document states in legible characters the address of the partnership's principal place of business and that the list of the partners' names is open to inspection there: CA 2006, s 1203(2).

Where a partnership maintains a list of the partners' names for the purposes of this provision, any person may inspect the list during office hours: CA 2006, s 1203(3).

Where an inspection required by a person in accordance with s 1203 is refused, an offence is committed by any member of the partnership concerned who without reasonable excuse refused the inspection or permitted it to be refused: CA 2006, s 1203(4).

A person guilty of an offence under subs (4) is liable on summary conviction to a fine not exceeding level 3 on the standard scale and, for continued contravention, a daily default fine not exceeding one-tenth of level 3 on the standard scale: CA 2006, s 1203(5).

Disclosure required: business premises

8.114 A person to whom Chapter 2 of CA 2006 applies must, in any premises:

(a) where the business is carried on; and

(b) to which customers of the business or suppliers of goods or services to the business have access,

display in a prominent position, so that it may easily be read by such customers or suppliers, a notice containing the information required by the chapter: CA 2006, s 1204(1).

The Secretary of State may by regulations require that such notices be displayed in a specified form: CA 2006, s 1204(2).

Criminal consequences of failure to make required disclosure

8.115 A person who without reasonable excuse fails to comply with the requirements of:

- s 1202 (disclosure required: business documents etc); or
- s 1204 (disclosure required: business premises),

commits an offence: CA 2006, s 1205(1).

Where an offence under s 1205 is committed by a body corporate, an offence is also committed by every officer of the body who is in default: CA 2006, s 1205(2). A person guilty of an offence under this provision is liable on summary conviction to a fine not exceeding level 3 on the standard scale and, for continued contravention, a daily default fine not exceeding one-tenth of level 3 on the standard scale: CA 2006, s 1205(3).

The references in s 1205 to the requirements of ss 1202 or 1204 include the requirements of regulations under that section: CA 2006, s 1205(4).

Civil consequences of failure to make required disclosure

8.116 Section 1206 of CA 2006 applies to any legal proceedings brought by a person to whom this chapter applies to enforce a right arising out of a contract made in the course of a business in respect of which he was, at the time the contract was made, in breach of s 1202(1) or (2) (disclosure in business documents etc) or s 1204(1) (disclosure at business premises): CA 2006, s 1206(1).

The proceedings will be dismissed if the defendant (in Scotland, the defender) to the proceedings shows:

(a) that he has a claim against the claimant (pursuer) arising out of the contract that he has been unable to pursue by reason of the latter's breach of the requirements of this chapter of CA 2006; or

(b) that he has suffered some financial loss in connection with the contract by reason of the claimant's (pursuer's) breach of those requirements, unless the court before which the proceedings are brought is satisfied that it is just and equitable to permit the proceedings to continue: CA 2006, s 1206(2).

The references in s 1206 to the requirements of this chapter of CA 2006 include the requirements of regulations under the Chapter: CA 2006, s 1206(3). This section does not affect the right of any person to enforce such rights as he may have against another person in any proceedings brought by that person: CA 2006, s 1206(4).

Application of general provisions about offences

8.117 The provisions of ss 1121–1123 (liability of officer in default) and 1125–1131 (general provisions about offences) apply in relation to offences under this part of the Act as in relation to offences under the Companies Acts: CA 2006, s 1027.

Checklist: procedural rules before the company names adjudicator

8.118 *This checklist sets out the rules of procedure before the Company Names Adjudicator under the Company Names Adjudicator Rules 2008 SI 2008 No 1738 which came into force on 1 October 2008.*

Under the rules, the following definitions apply:

- 'the Act' means the Companies Act 2006 and references to a 'section' are to a section of CA 2006;
- 'the appropriate form' means the form determined by the Chief Adjudicator in relation to a particular matter; and
- 'the Office' means the office of the company names adjudicator at the Intellectual Property Office, Concept House, Cardiff Road, Newport, South Wales, NP10 8QQ.

No	Issue	Reference
1	**Procedure for objecting to a company's registered name** • An application under s 69(2) shall: (a) be made on the appropriate form (Form CNA 1); (b) include a concise statement of the grounds on which the application is made; (c) include an address for service in the UK; and (d) be filed at the Office. • The adjudicator shall send a copy of the appropriate form to the primary respondent. • The adjudicator shall specify a period within which the primary respondent must file its defence.	Company Names Adjudicator Rules 2008, r 3

No	Issue	Reference
	• The primary respondent, before the end of that period, shall file a counter-statement on the appropriate form, otherwise the adjudicator may treat it as not opposing the application and may make an order under CA 2006, s 73(1). • In its counter-statement the primary respondent shall: (a) include an address for service in the UK; (b) include a concise statement of the grounds on which it relies; (c) state which of the allegations in the statement of grounds of the applicant it admits and which it denies; and (d) state which of the allegations it is unable to admit or deny, but which it requires the applicant to prove. • Any member or director of the primary respondent who is joined as a respondent to the application must be joined before the end of a period specified by the adjudicator. • The adjudicator shall send a copy of the appropriate form referred to in paragraph (4) to the applicant.	
2	**Evidence rounds** • When the period specified under r 3(3) has expired, the adjudicator shall specify the periods within which evidence may be filed by the parties. • All evidence must be: (a) accompanied by the appropriate form; and (b) copied to all other parties in the proceedings.	Company Names Adjudicator Rules 2008, r 4
3	**Decision of adjudicator and hearings** • Where the applicant files no evidence in support of its application the adjudicator may treat it as having withdrawn its application. • Any party may, by filing the appropriate form, request to be heard in person before a decision is made by the adjudicator under the Act or these Rules. • Any party may, by filing the appropriate form, request to be heard in person before a decision is made by the adjudicator under the Act or these Rules.	Company Names Adjudicator Rules 2008, r 5

No	Issue	Reference
	• Following a request under r 5(3) the adjudicator shall decide whether a decision can be made without an oral hearing in circumstances where: (a) the primary respondent files no evidence; or (b) the applicant files no evidence in reply to the respondent's evidence; or (c) the decision will not terminate the proceedings. • Where the adjudicator decides that a decision can be made without an oral hearing the adjudicator will specify a period for the parties to submit written submissions before making a decision. • Where the adjudicator decides that a hearing is necessary he shall require the parties or their legal representatives to attend a hearing and shall give the parties at least 14 days' notice of the hearing. • When the adjudicator has made a decision on the application under s 69(2) he shall send to the parties written notice of it, stating the reasons for his decision. • The date on which the decision was sent to the parties shall be taken to be the date of the decision for the purposes of any appeal.	
4	**General powers of adjudicator in relation to proceedings before him** • At any stage of proceedings before him, the adjudicator may direct that the parties to the proceedings attend a case management conference or pre-hearing review. • The adjudicator may give such directions as to the management of the proceedings as he thinks fit, and in particular he may: (a) direct a document to be filed or to be copied to a party to proceedings within a specified period; (b) allow for the electronic filing and sending of documents; (c) direct how documents filed or sent electronically are to be authenticated; (d) direct that a document shall not be available for public inspection; (e) require a translation of any document;	Company Names Adjudicator Rules 2008, r 6

No	Issue	Reference
	(f) direct that a witness be cross-examined; (g) consolidate proceedings; (h) direct that proceedings are to be heard by more than one adjudicator; (i) direct that part of any proceedings be dealt with as separate proceedings; or (j) suspend or stay proceedings. • The adjudicator may control the evidence by giving directions as to: (a) the issues on which he requires evidence; (b) the nature of the evidence which he requires to decide those issues; and (c) the way in which the evidence is to be placed before him, and the adjudicator may use his power under this paragraph to exclude evidence which would otherwise be admissible.	
5	**Requests for extension of time** • Any party to the proceedings may apply to the adjudicator for the hearing to be held in private. • The adjudicator may extend (or further extend) any period which has been specified under any provision of these Rules even if the period has expired. • Any party can request an extension of any time period specified under any provision of these Rules. • Any request for a retrospective extension must be filed before the end of the period of two months beginning with the date the time period in question expired. • Any request made under paragraph (2) shall be made on the appropriate form and shall include reasons why the extra time is required. A request for a retrospective extension shall also include reasons why the request is being made out of time. Para 7, Company Names Adjudicator Rules 2008	Company Names Adjudicator Rules 2008, r 7
6	**Public proceedings** • Subject to paragraphs (3) and (4), any hearing before the adjudicator of proceedings relating to an application under s 69(2) shall be held in public.	Company Names Adjudicator Rules 2008, r 8

No	Issue	Reference
	● The adjudicator shall only grant an application under paragraph (2) where: (a) it is in the interests of justice for the hearing to be in held in private; and (b) all the parties to the proceedings have had an opportunity to be heard on the matter, and where the application is granted the hearing shall be held in private. ● Any hearing of an application under paragraph (2) shall be held in private. ● In this rule a reference to a hearing includes any part of a hearing. ● Nothing in this rule shall prevent a member of the Administrative Justice and Tribunals Council or of its Scottish Committee from attending a hearing. ● All documents connected to proceedings shall be available for public inspection unless the adjudicator directs otherwise.	
7	**Evidence in proceedings before the adjudicator** ● Subject to r 6(3), evidence filed under these Rules may be given: (a) by witness statement, affidavit or statutory declaration; or (b) in any other form which would be admissible as evidence in proceedings before the court, and a witness statement may only be given in evidence if it includes a statement of truth. ● For the purposes of these Rules, a statement of truth: (a) means a statement that the person making the statement believes that the facts stated in a particular document are true; and (b) shall be dated and signed by the maker of the statement. ● In these Rules, a witness statement is a written statement signed by a person that contains the evidence which that person would be allowed to give orally.	Company Names Adjudicator Rules 2008, r 9

No	Issue	Reference
8	**Correction of irregularities of procedure** • Any irregularity in procedure may be rectified on such terms as the adjudicator may direct. • Where rectification includes the amendment of a document by the adjudicator the parties will be given notice of this amendment.	Company Names Adjudicator Rules 2008, r 10
	Costs or expenses of proceedings The adjudicator may, at any stage in any proceedings before him under the Act, award to any party by order such costs (in Scotland, expenses) as he considers reasonable, and direct how and by what parties they are to be paid.	Company Names Adjudicator Rules 2008, r 11
	Security for costs or expenses An application for security for costs (in Scotland, caution for expenses) shall be made on the appropriate form. The adjudicator may require a person to give security for costs (in Scotland, caution for expenses) if he is satisfied, having regard to all the circumstances of the case, that it is just to require such security or caution.	Company Names Adjudicator Rules 2008, r 12
	Address for service • Where a person has provided an address for service in the UK under r 3 he may substitute a new address for service in the UK by notifying the adjudicator on the appropriate form. • Where the primary respondent has a registered office in the UK the adjudicator may treat this as the address for service in the UK unless and until an alternative address is provided.	Company Names Adjudicator Rules 2008, r 12
	Hours of business • For the transaction of relevant business by the public under the Act the Office shall be open: (a) on Monday to Friday between 9.00 am and midnight; and (b) on Saturday between 9.00 am and 1.00 pm, unless the day is an excluded day (see r 15). • For the transaction of all other business by the public under the Act the Office shall be open on Monday to Friday between 9.00 am and 5.00 pm unless the day is an excluded day (see r 15). • In this rule and in r 15 'relevant business' means the filing of any application or other document.	Company Names Adjudicator Rules 2008, r 14

No	Issue	Reference
	Excluded days • The following shall be excluded days for the transaction of any business by the public under the Act: (a) a Sunday; (b) Good Friday; (c) Christmas Day; (d) a day which is specified or proclaimed to be a bank holiday by or under s 1 of the Banking and Financial Dealings Act 1971(1); or (e) a Saturday where the previous Friday and the following Monday are both excluded days. • Any application or document received on an excluded day shall be treated as having been filed on the next day on which the Office is open for relevant business. • Where any period for filing any document ends on an excluded day that period shall be extended to the next day on which the Office is open for relevant business.	Company Names Adjudicator Rules 2008, r 15

Checklist: prescribed forms for applications before the Company Names Tribunal

8.119 *The following are the prescribed forms required for proceedings and hearing before the Company Names Tribunal:*

Form	Description	Fee
CNA 1	Application form	£400
CNA 2	Notice of defence	£150
CNA 3	Notice of giving evidence	£150
CNA 4	Request for a hearing to be appointed	£100
CNA 5	Request for an extension of time	£100
CNA 6	Request for security for costs	£150
CNA 7	Appointment or change of agent or contact address	Nil

Checklist: change of company name

8.120 *This Checklist sets out the steps and procedures required to change a company's name from one that is already registered at Companies House. The company should refer to its articles of association for the practice of calling meetings.*

Issue		**Reference**
1	Consider proposed name that is to be selected and is not already registered at Companies House	CA 2006, ss 66, 1080, 1085
2	Search at Trade Marks Registry	CA 2006, ss 55–57, 58, 1193–1198
3	Ensure no potential infringements of use of name and name not sensitive or requiring prior consent or misleading and ensure name ends with 'limited' or 'Ltd' or 'public limited company' or 'plc' or Welsh equivalents	
4	Prepare Agenda and call a Board meeting – date, time and place of the meeting	
5	Ensure quorum present	
6	Directors vote by simple majority to put a special resolution on change of name to the shareholders at EGM	
7	Consider whether a Board meeting can be dispensed with and a written resolution is used	
8	After the Board meeting, prepare minutes of the meeting	
9	Convene an EGM	
10	Notice of the EGM to state date, time, place of meeting and a note on proxy – at least 14 days before the EGM unless consent to short notice applies	
11	Ensure quorum present	
12	Voting on the special resolution by a show of hands	
13	Consider whether the EGM can be dispensed with by use of written resolution procedure	
14	After the EGM:	
	Prepare minutes of EGM	
	• Lodge special resolution at Companies House within 15 days	CA 2006, ss 78–79
	• Notice of change of name	Form RES15
	• Pay fee: £15	Form NM01, NM02, NM04 or NM05
	• Amend Memorandum of Association with change of name	

Issue		Reference
	• Amend Articles of Association with new name • Change company headed paper • Inform bank and other authorities	CA 2006, s 26
	• Obtain an amended certificate of incorporation • Change email/website details	CA 2006, ss 80–82

List of Government Departments and other bodies whose views must be sought

8.121 *The Company, Limited Liability Partnership and Business Names (Sensitive Words and Expressions) Regulations 2014, SI 2014/3140, Sch 2 sets out a list of Government Departments and other Bodies whose views must be sought.*

Part 1 of Schedule 2 to the 2014 Regulations sets out the applications where the situation of the registered office or principal place of business is irrelevant:

8.122

Column (1) *Word or expression specified under regulation 3*	*Column (2)* *Specified Government department or other body whose view must be sought*
Accredit	Department for Business, Innovation & Skills
Accreditation	Department for Business, Innovation & Skills
Accredited	Department for Business, Innovation & Skills
Accrediting	Department for Business, Innovation & Skills
Assurance	Financial Conduct Authority
Assurer	Financial Conduct Authority
Banc	Financial Conduct Authority
Bank	Financial Conduct Authority
Banking	Financial Conduct Authority
Brenhinol	The Welsh Assembly Government
Brenin	The Welsh Assembly Government
Brenhiniaeth	The Welsh Assembly Government
Child maintenance	Department for Work and Pensions
Child support	Department for Work and Pensions
Dental	General Dental Council
Dentistry	General Dental Council

Column (1) *Word or expression specified under regulation 3*	*Column (2)* *Specified Government department or other body whose view must be sought*
Diùc	The Scottish Government
Dug	The Welsh Assembly Government
Ei Fawrhydi	The Welsh Assembly Government
Friendly Society	Financial Conduct Authority
Fund	Financial Conduct Authority
Gwasanaeth iechyd	The Welsh Assembly Government
Health visitor	Nursing & Midwifery Council
HPSS	Department of Health, Social Services and Public Safety
HSC	Department of Health, Social Services and Public Safety
Insurance	Financial Conduct Authority
Insurer	Financial Conduct Authority
Judicial appointment	Ministry of Justice
Llywodraeth	The Welsh Assembly Government
Medical centre	Department of Health, Social Services and Public Safety
Midwife	Nursing & Midwifery Council
Midwifery	Nursing & Midwifery Council
Mòrachd	The Scottish Government
Mutual	Financial Conduct Authority
NHS	Department of Health
Nurse	Nursing & Midwifery Council
Nursing	Nursing & Midwifery Council
Oifis sgrùdaidh	Audit Scotland
Oilthigh	The Scottish Government
Parlamaid	The Scottish Parliamentary Corporate Body
Parliament	The Corporate Officer of the House of Lords and The Corporate Officer of the House of Commons
Parliamentarian	The Corporate Officer of the House of Lords and The Corporate Officer of the House of Commons
Parliamentary	The Corporate Officer of the House of Lords and The Corporate Officer of the House of Commons
Patent	The Patent Office
Patentee	The Patent Office
Polytechnic	Department for Business, Innovation & Skills

Column (1) *Word or expression specified under regulation 3*	*Column (2)* *Specified Government department or other body whose view must be sought*
Prifysgol	The Welsh Assembly Government
Prionnsa	The Scottish Government
Reassurance	Financial Conduct Authority
Reassurer	Financial Conduct Authority
Reinsurance	Financial Conduct Authority
Reinsurer	Financial Conduct Authority
Riaghaltas	The Scottish Government
Rìgh	The Scottish Government
Rìoghail	The Scottish Government
Rìoghalachd	The Scottish Government
Senedd	The National Assembly for Wales
Sheffield	The Company of Cutlers in Hallamshire
Swyddfa archwilio	Auditor General for Wales
Tywysog	The Welsh Assembly Government
Underwrite	Financial Conduct Authority
Underwriting	Financial Conduct Authority

Part 2 of Schedule 2 to the 2014 Regulations sets out applications where situation of registered office or principal place of business is relevant:

8.123

Column (1)	*Column (2)*	*Column (3)*	*Column (4)*	*Column (5)*
Word or expression specified under regulation 3	*Specified Government department or other body whose view must be sought*			
	under regulation 6(a)	*under regulation 6(b)*	*under regulation 6(c)*	*under regulation 6(d)*
Audit office	Comptroller & Auditor General	Auditor General for Wales	Audit Scotland	Northern Ireland Audit Office
Charitable Charity	The Charity Commission	The Charity Commission	Office of the Scottish Charity Regulator	The Charity Commission

Column (1)	*Column (2)*	*Column (3)*	*Column (4)*	*Column (5)*
Word or expression specified under regulation 3	*Specified Government department or other body whose view must be sought*			
	under regulation 6(a)	*under regulation 6(b)*	*under regulation 6(c)*	*under regulation 6(d)*
Duke His Majesty King Prince Queen Royal Royalty Windsor	Ministry of Justice	The Welsh Assembly Government	The Scottish Government	Ministry of Justice
Health centre Health service	Department of Health	The Welsh Assembly Government	The Scottish Government	Department of Health, Social Services and Public Safety
Police	The Home Office	The Home Office	The Scottish Government	Department of Justice in Northern Ireland
Special school	Department for Education	The Welsh Assembly Government	The Scottish Government	Department of Education
University	Department for Business, Innovation & Skills	The Welsh Assembly Government	The Scottish Government	Department for Employment and Learning

Definitions

8.124

Business: includes a profession

Initial: includes a recognised abbreviation of a name

Partnership: means:

(a) a partnership within the Partnership Act 1890 (c 39); or

(b) a limited partnership registered under the Limited Partnerships Act 1907 (c 24), or a firm or entity of a similar character formed under the law of a country or territory outside the UK.

Surname: in relation to a peer or person usually known by a British title different from his surname means the title by which he is known.

9 Company re-registration

Contents

Introduction

9.1 Once a company is established it retains its legal identity and status as evidenced by the certificate of incorporation, which sets out the nature and type of entity concerned. This status is maintained until an event or circumstance arises which necessitates the company re-registering its status (eg where the company proposes to effect a flotation on the stock exchange, or a reduction in the share capital of the company for the purposes of downsizing).

The Companies Act 2006 provides a procedure and mechanism that allows companies to alter their legal status by converting into another corporate legal form. This allows for flexibility and convenience and avoids the process of having to dissolve one company and to establish the desired company.

This chapter addresses the following issues:

- the companies that may be allowed to re-register to enable them to alter their status;
- the steps and procedures that are required to alter their status; and
- a checklist of legal and practical issues in connection with the re-registration process.

Part 7 of CA 2006, ss 89–111 (as amended by the Small Business, Enterprise and Employment Act 2015 (SBEEA 2015)) sets out the requirements for re-registration as a means of altering a company's legal status. It also sets out the procedures required for the re-registration process. As the process is essentially procedural, the method of conversion or re-registration is provided by way of checklists.

Companies that may alter their status

9.2 The following companies may re-register to alter their status: CA 2006, s 89:

- from a private company to a public company: CA 2006, ss 90–96;
- from a public company to a private company: CA 2006, ss 97–101;
- from a private limited company to an unlimited company: CA 2006, ss 102–104;
- from an unlimited private company to a limited company: CA 2006, ss 105–108;
- from a public company to an unlimited private company: CA 2006, ss 109–111.

Checklist: Private company becoming public

9.3 A private company (whether limited or unlimited) may be re-registered as a public company limited by shares if the following are satisfied (CA 2006, s 90(1)).

This checklist sets out the procedures required to effect a change of status where a private company wishes to convert its status to a public company.

No	Issue	Reference
1	Ensure the company has a minimum of at least two directors and at least one director must be a natural person	CA 2006, ss 154 and 155
2	Ensure that the company meets the authorised minimum share capital requirements (see below)	CA 2006, s 90
3	Ensure that a suitably qualified company secretary is appointed (see below)	CA 2006, s 271
4	The private company must pass a special resolution that it should be re-registered as a public company. The procedure will be:	CA 2006, s 90(1)(a)
	• call a board meeting upon reasonable notice;	Articles of association/ Notice to board members
	• prepare an agenda for the meeting including any background papers and briefs particularly on responsibilities and obligations of a public company including directors;	Agenda
	• board meeting may be dispensed with if written resolution used;	Written resolution
	• ensure quorum present;	
	• ensure all five conditions present for alteration of status (see below);	CA 2006, s 90

No	Issue	Reference
	• board meeting votes on altering the status of the private company to a public company;	
	• prepare minutes of the board meeting;	
	• call an EGM by notice to the shareholders setting out date, time and place of the meeting including nature of special resolution and reference to appointment of a proxy, or consent to short notice;	CA 2006, s 307(1) Notice to shareholders
	• consider if written resolution may be used;	
	• ensure quorum present;	
	• voting on a show of hands (unless poll demanded) – 75% required for approval by majority;	
	• prepare minutes of the EGM for circulation;	Minutes
	• lodge the special resolution/written resolution at Companies House;	CA 2006, s 307(5) Written resolution
	• lodge statement of compliance;	Compliance statement
	• lodge form at Companies House;	Form R01 (Application by a private company for re-registration as a public company)
	• printed copy of the articles of association;	
	• copy of balance sheet dated no more than seven months before receipt of Form RR01;	
	• auditor's statement;	
	• auditor's report;	
	• fee for re-registration;	
	• change company headed notepaper/business cards;	
	• change company signage at Head Office;	
	• notify suppliers/third parties/banks/HMRC/VAT/PAYE.	
	• revise, draft and lodge a memorandum of association for a public company limited by shares (see below)	
	• obtain a certificate of re-registration from the Registrar of Companies	
	• if required, obtain a new company seal	
	• change company's bank account details	

No	Issue	Reference
5	The following five conditions for altering the status from private company to public company must be satisfied: • the company must have a share capital; • the requirements of CA 2006, s 91 are met as regards share capital (see below); • the requirements of CA 2006, s 92 are met as regards its net assets; • compliance with CA 2006, s 93 (recent allotment of shares for non-cash consideration if this section applies); and • the company has not previously re-registered as unlimited.	CA 2006, s 90(1)(b) and (2)
6	The company must make such changes in its name and in its articles as are necessary in connection with it becoming a public company (articles of association for plc to be prepared and reference to 'plc' or 'public liability company' or Welsh equivalent).	CA 2006, s 90(3)
7	If the company is unlimited it must also make such changes in its articles of association as are necessary in connection with it becoming a company limited by shares.	CA 2006, s 90(4)
8	The following requirements as to share capital must be met at the time the special resolution is passed that the company should be re-registered as a public company: (a) the nominal value of the company's allotted share capital must not be less than the authorised minimum; (b) each of the company's allotted shares must be paid up at least as to one-quarter of the nominal value of that share and the whole of any premium on it; (c) if any shares in the company or any premium on them have been fully or partly paid up by an undertaking given by any person that he or another should do work or perform services (whether for the company or any other person), the undertaking must have been performed or otherwise discharged; and (d) if the shares have been allotted as fully or partly paid up as to their nominal value or any premium on them otherwise than in cash, and the consideration for the allotment consists of or includes an undertaking to the company, then either: (i) the undertaking must have been performed or otherwise discharged; or	CA 2006, s 91(1)

No	Issue	Reference
	(ii) there must be a contract between the company and some person pursuant to which the undertaking is to be performed within five years from the time the special resolution is passed. For the purpose of determining whether the above requirements under (b), (c) and (d) are met, the following may be disregarded: (i) shares allotted before 22 June 1982 in the case of a company then registered in Great Britain; or (ii) shares allotted before 31 December 1984 in the case of a company then registered in Northern Ireland; (iii) shares allotted in pursuance of an employee's share scheme by reason of which the company, but for CA 2006, s 91(2)(b), be precluded under CA 2006, s 91(1)(b) (but not otherwise) from being re-registered as a private company.	
	• No more than one-tenth of the nominal value of the company's allotted share capital is to be disregarded under CA 2006, s 91(2)(b). The allotted share capital is treated as not including shares disregarded under CA 2006, s 91(2)(b).	CA 2006, s 91(3)
	• Shares disregarded under CA 2006, s 91(2) are treated as not forming part of the allotted share capital for the purposes of CA 2006, s 91(1)(a).	CA 2006, s 91(4)
	• A company must not be re-registered as a public company if it appears to the registrar that: (a) the company has resolved to reduce its share capital; (b) the reduction is made under CA 2006, s 626 (reduction in connection with the redenomination of share capital). It is supported by a solvency statement in accordance with CA 2006, s 643; or it has been confirmed by an order of the court under CA 2006, s 648; and the effect of the reduction is, or will be, that the nominal value of the company's allotted share capital is below the authorised minimum.	CA 2006, s 91(5)
9	With regard to the requirement as to net assets, a company applying to re-register as a public company must obtain:	CA 2006, s 92(1)

No	Issue	Reference
	(a) a balance sheet prepared as at a date not more than seven days before the date on which the application is delivered to the registrar; (b) an unqualified report by the company's auditor on that balance sheet; and (c) a written statement by the company's auditor that it is his opinion at the balance sheet date that the amount of the company's net assets was not less than aggregate of its called up share capital and undistributable reserves.	
	• Between the balance sheet date and the date on which the application for re-registration is delivered to the registrar, there must be no change in the company's financial position that results in the amount of its net assets becoming less than the aggregate of its called up share capital and distributable reserves.	
	• The term 'unqualified report' means: (a) if the balance sheet was prepared for a financial year of the company, a report stating without material qualification the auditor's opinion that the balance sheet has been properly prepared in accordance with the requirements of CA 2006; or (b) if the balance sheet was not prepared for a financial year of the company, a report stating without material qualification the auditor's opinion that the balance sheet has been properly prepared in accordance with the provisions of CA 2006 which would have applied if it had been prepared for a financial year of the company.	CA 2006, s 92(3)
	• For the purpose of an auditor's report on the balance sheet that was not prepared for a financial year of the company, the provisions of CA 2006 apply with such modifications as are necessary by reason of the fact.	CA 2006, s 92(4)
	• For the purposes of CA 2006, s 92(3), a qualification is material unless the auditor states in his report that the matter giving rise to the qualification is not material for the purpose of determining (by reference to the company's balance sheet) whether, at the balance sheet date, the amount of the company's net assets were less than the aggregate of its called-up share capital and 'undistributable reserves'.	

No	Issue	Reference
10	With regard to recent allotment shares for non-cash consideration, this is governed by CA 2006, s 93 which applies where: (a) shares are allotted by the company in the period between the date as to which the balance sheet required by CA 2006, s 92 is prepared and the passing of the resolution that the company should re-register as a public company; and (b) the shares are allotted as fully or partly paid up as to their nominal value or any premium on them otherwise than in cash.	CA 2006, s 93(1)
	• The registrar must not entertain an application by the company for re-registration as a public company unless: (a) the requirements of s 593(1)(a) and (b) have been complied with (independent valuation of non-cash consideration: valuer's report to company not more than six months before allotment); or (b) the allotment is in connection with: (i) a share exchange (see sub-ss (3)–(5) below); or (ii) a proposed merger with another company (see sub-s (6) below).	CA 2006, s 93(2)
	• An allotment is in connection with a share exchange if: (a) the shares are allotted in connection with an arrangement under which the whole or part of the consideration for the shares allotted is provided by: (i) the transfer to the company allotting the shares of shares (or shares of a particular class) in another company; or (ii) the cancellation of shares (or shares of a particular class) in another company; and (b) the allotment is open to all the holders of the shares of the other company in question (or, where the arrangement applies only to shares of a particular class, to all the holders of the company's shares of that class) to take part in the arrangement in connection with which the shares are allotted.	CA 2006, s 93(3)

No	Issue	Reference
	• In determining whether a person is a holder of shares for the purposes of sub-s (3), there shall be disregarded: (a) shares held by, or by a nominee of, the company allotting the shares; (b) shares held by, or by a nominee of: (i) the holding company of the company allotting the shares; (ii) a subsidiary of the company allotting the shares; or (iii) a subsidiary of the holding company of the company allotting the shares.	CA 2006, s 93(4)
	• It is immaterial, for the purposes of deciding whether an allotment is in connection with share exchange, whether or not the arrangement in connection with which the shares are allotted involves the issue to the company allotting the shares of shares (or shares of a particular class) in the other company.	CA 2006, s 93(5)
	• There is a proposed merger with another company if one of the companies concerned proposed to acquire all the assets and liabilities of the other in exchange for the issue of its shares or other securities to shareholders of the other (whether or not accompanied by a cash payment). 'Another company' includes anybody corporate.	CA 2006, s 93(6)
	• For the purposes of CA 2006, s 93: (a) the consideration for an allotment does not include any amount standing to the credit of any of the company's reserve accounts, or of its profit and loss account, that has been applied in paying up (to any extent) any of the shares allotted or any premium on those shares; and (b) 'arrangement' means any agreement, scheme or arrangement, including an arrangement sanctioned in accordance with: (i) Part 26 CA 2006 (arrangement and reconstruction); or	CA 2006, s 93(7)

No	Issue	Reference
	(ii) s 110 of the Insolvency Act 1986 (c 45) or art 96 of the Insolvency (Northern Ireland) Order 1989 (SI 1989/2405 (NI 19)) (liquidator in winding up accepting shares as consideration for sale of company's property)).	
11	An application for re-registration as a public company must contain: (a) a statement of the company's proposed name on re-registration; and (b) in the case of a company without a secretary, a statement of the company's proposed secretary under CA 2006, s 95.	CA 2006, s 94(1)
	• The application must be accompanied by: (a) a copy of the special resolution that the company should re-register as a public company unless a copy has already been forwarded to the registrar under CA 2006, Pt 3, Ch 3; (b) a copy of the company's articles as proposed to be amended; (c) a copy of the balance sheet and other documents referred to in CA 2006, s 92(1); (d) if CA 2006, s 93 applies (recent allotment of shares for non-cash consideration), a copy of the valuation report (if any) under CA 2006, s 93(2)(a); and (e) a statement of the aggregate amount paid up on the shares of the company on account of their nominal value.	CA 2006, s 94(2) CA 2006 (as inserted by SBEEA 2015, s 98(2))
	• The statement of compliance required to be delivered together with the application is a statement that the requirements so as to re-registration as a public company have been complied with.	CA 2006, s 94(3)
	• The registrar may accept the statement of compliance as sufficient evidence that the company is entitled to be re-registered as a public company.	CA 2006, s 94(4)

No	Issue	Reference
	• The statement of compliance is conclusive evidence that requirements of CA 2006 as to re-registration have been complied with.	
12	The statement of the company's proposed secretary must contain the required particulars of the person who is or the persons who are to be the secretary or joint secretaries of the company.	CA 2006, s 95(1)
	• The required particulars are the particulars that will be required to be stated in the company's register of secretaries (CA 2006, ss 277–279).	CA 2006, s 95(2)
	• The statement must also include a statement by the company that the person named as secretary, or each of the persons named as joint secretaries, has consented to act in the relevant capacity. If all the partners in the firm are to be joint secretaries, consent may be given by one partner on behalf of all of them.	CA 2006, s 95(3) (as inserted by SBEEA 2015, s 100(3))
13	With regard to the issue of a certificate of incorporation on re-registration, if on the application for re-registration as a public company, the registrar is satisfied that the company is entitled to be so re-registered the company shall be re-registered accordingly.	CA 2006, s 96(1)
	• The registrar must issue a certificate of incorporation altered to meet the circumstances of the case.	CA 2006, s 96(2)
	• The certificate must state that it is issued on re-registration and the date on which it is issued.	CA 2006, s 96(3)
	• On the issue of the certificate the following take effect: (a) the company becomes a public company; (b) the changes in the company's name and articles take effect; and (c) where the application contained a statement under CA 2006, s 95 (Statement of proposed secretary), the person or persons named in the statement as secretary or joint secretary of the company are deemed to have been appointed to that office.	CA 2006, s 96(4)

Checklist: Public company becoming private

9.4 *A public company may re-register as a private company under CA 2006. This checklist sets out the conditions, steps and procedures required to effect such re-registration.*

No	Issue	Reference
1	A public company may be re-registered as a private company limited by shares or by guarantee if the following are satisfied:	CA 2006, s 97(1)
	(a) A special resolution that the public company should be re-registered as a private company is passed.	
	(b) An application for re-registration is delivered to the registrar in accordance with CA 2006, s 100 together with other documents required by that section and a statement of compliance.	
	• Call a board meeting upon reasonable notice.	Notice
	• Prepare an agenda for the meeting including any background papers and briefs.	Agenda
	• Board meeting may be dispensed with if written resolution used.	Special/written resolution
	• Ensure quorum present.	
	• Ensure all conditions present for alteration of status (see below).	
	• Board meeting votes on altering the status of the public company to a private company.	
	• Prepare minutes of the board meeting.	Minutes
	• Call an EGM by notice to the shareholders setting out date, time and place of the meeting including nature of special resolution and reference to appointment of a proxy.	Notice
	• Ensure quorum present.	
	• Voting on a show of hands (unless poll demanded).	
	• Prepare minutes of the EGM for circulation.	Minutes
	• Lodge the special resolution/written resolution at Companies House and copy court order (if appropriate).	CA 2006, s 30
	• Lodge statement of compliance.	Statement of compliance
	• Lodge Form RR02 or RR05 at Companies House with fee.	Form RRO2 (Application by a public company for registration as a private limited company)
	• Lodge printed copy of articles of association and memorandum of association	

No	Issue	Reference
	• Obtain certificate of re-registration from the Registrar of Companies • If required, obtain a new company seal • Notify suppliers/third parties/banks/HMRC/ VAT/PAYE. • Printed copy of the amended articles of association.	Articles of association
	• Fee for re-registration. • Change company headed notepaper/business cards. • Change company signage at Head Office. • Notify suppliers/third parties/banks/HMRC/ VAT/PAYE.	
	• The following conditions must be complied with: (a) where no application under CA 2006, s 98 for cancellation of the resolution has been made: (i) having regard to the number of members who consented to or voted in favour of the resolution, no such application may be made; or (ii) the period within which such an application could be made has expired; (a) where such an application has been made – (i) the application has been withdrawn; or (ii) an order has been made confirming the resolution and a copy of that order has been delivered to the registrar.	CA 2006, s 97(2)
	• The company must make such changes in its name and in its articles as are necessary in connection with its becoming a private company limited by shares, or as the case may be, by guarantee.	CA 2006, s 97(3)
2	Where a special resolution by a public company to be re-registered as a private limited company has been passed, and application to the court for the cancellation of the resolution may be made: (a) by the holders of not less in the aggregate than 5% in nominal value of the company's issued share capital on any class of the company's issued share capital (disregarding any shares held by the company at treasury shares);	CA 2006, s 98(1)

No	Issue	Reference
	(b) if the company is not limited by shares, by not less than 5% of its members; or (c) by not less than 50 of the company's members. However, the above do not apply to a person who has consented to or voted in favour of the resolution.	
	• The application must be made within 28 days after the passing of the resolution and may be made on behalf of the persons entitled to make it by such one or more of their number as they may appoint for the purpose.	CA 2006, s 98(2)
	• On the hearing of the application, the court must make an application either cancelling or confirming the resolution.	CA 2006, s 98(3)
	• The court may: (a) make an order on such terms and conditions as it thinks fit; (b) if it thinks fit, adjourn the proceedings in order that an arrangement may be made to the satisfaction of the court for the purchase of the interests of dissentient members; and (c) give such directions and make such orders, as it thinks expedient for facilitating or carrying into effect any such arrangement.	CA 2006, s 98(4)
	• The court's order may if the court thinks fit: (a) provide for the purchase by the company of the shares of any of its members and for the reduction accordingly of the company's capital; and (b) make such other alteration in the company's articles as may be required in consequence of that provision.	CA 2006, s 98(5)
	• The court's order may, if the court thinks fit, require the company not to make any, or any specified, amendments to its articles without the leave of the court.	CA 2006, s 98(6)
3	• On making an application under CA 2006, s 98 (application to court to cancel resolution) the applicants or the person making the application on their behalf, must immediately give notice to the registrar. This is without prejudice to any provisions of rules of court as to service of notice of the application.	CA 2006, s 99(1)

No	Issue	Reference
	• On being served with notice of any such application, the company must immediately give notice to the registrar.	Form RR05 (Notice by the applicants of application to the court for cancellation of resolution for re-registration) CA 2006, s 99(2)
	• Within 15 days of making of the court's order on the application, or such other longer period as the court may at any time direct, the company must deliver to the registrar a copy of the order.	CA 2006, s 99(3)
	• If a company fails to comply with CA 2006, s 99(2) or (3), the offence is committed by the company and every officer of the company who is in default.	CA 2006, s 99(4)
	• A person guilty of an offence under CA 2006, s 99 is liable on summary conviction to a fine not exceeding level 3 on the standard scale and, for continued contravention, a daily default fine not exceeding one-tenth of level 3 on the standard scale.	CA 2006, s 99(5)
4	• An application for re-registration as a private limited company must contain a statement of the company's proposed name on re-registration.	CA 2006, s 100(1)
	• The application must be accompanied by: (a) a copy of the resolution that the company should re-register as a private limited company (unless a copy has already been forwarded to the registrar under Chapter 3 of Part 3); and (b) a copy of the company's articles as proposed to be amended.	CA 2006, s 100(2)
	• The statement of compliance required to be delivered together with the application is a statement that the requirements as to re-registration as a private limited company have been complied with.	CA 2006, s 100(3)
	• The registrar may accept the statement of compliance as sufficient evidence that the company is entitled to be re-registered as a private limited company.	CA 2006, s 100(4)

No	Issue	Reference
	• If, on an application for re-registration as a private limited company, the registrar is satisfied that the company is entitled to be so re-registered, the company shall be re-registered accordingly.	CA 2006, s 101(1)
	• The registrar must issue a certificate of incorporation altered to meet the circumstances of the case.	CA 2006, s 101(2)
	• The certificate must state that it is issued on re-registration and the date on which it is issued.	CA 2006, s 101(3)
	• On the issue of the certificate: (a) the company becomes a private limited company and; (b) the changes in the company's name and articles take effect.	CA 2006, s 101(4)
	• The certificate is conclusive evidence that the requirements of CA 2006, as to re-registration have been complied with.	CA 2006, s 101(5)

Checklist: Private limited company becoming unlimited

9.5 *This checklist sets out the legal and practical steps and procedures for altering the status of a private limited company to become unlimited. This process of re-registration is not common in practice but some companies may become unlimited to keep their accounts private without the need to file them at Companies House. Advantage of this re-registration may also include ease of distribution of funds to the shareholders under an unlimited company than a private limited liability company.*

No	Issue	Reference
1	A private limited company may be re-registered as an unlimited company if: (a) all the members of the company have assented to its being so re-registered; (b) an application for re-registration is delivered to the registrar in accordance with CA 2006, s 103, together with the other documents required by that section and a statement of compliance; and	CA 2006, s 102(1)
	(c) there is compliance with the condition that the company has not been previously re-registered as limited.	CA 2006, s 102(2)

No	Issue	Reference
2	• The company must make such changes in its name and its articles as are necessary in connection with its becoming an unlimited company; and if it is to have a share capital, as are necessary, in connection with its becoming an unlimited company having a share capital.	CA 2006, s 102(3)
3	• Call a board meeting upon reasonable notice.	Notice
4	• Prepare agenda for the meeting including any background papers and briefs.	Agenda
5	• Board meeting may be dispensed with if written resolution used.	Written resolution
6	• Ensure quorum present for the board meeting.	
7	• Board meeting votes on altering the status of the limited liability company to an unlimited company.	
8	• Prepare minutes of the board meeting.	Minutes
9	• Call an EGM by notice to the shareholders setting out date, time and place of the meeting including nature of special resolution and reference to appointment of a proxy.	Notice
10	• Consider if written resolution may be used.	
11	• Make appropriate changes to the articles of association and memorandum of association.	
12	• Ensure quorum present for the EGM.	
13	• Voting on a show of hands (unless poll demanded). Unanimous consent required.	
14	• Prepare minutes of the EGM for circulation.	Minutes
15	• Lodge the written resolution at Companies House.	CA 2006, s 30
16	• Lodge Form RR05 at Companies House.	Form RR05 (Application by a private limited company for re-registration as an unlimited company)
17	• Printed copy of the amended articles of association for an unlimited company and memorandum of association.	Articles and memorandum
18	• Fee for re-registration.	Fee
19	• Change company headed notepaper/business cards.	
20	• Change company signage at Head Office.	

No	Issue	Reference
21	• Notify suppliers/third parties/banks/HMRC/ VAT/PAYE.	
22	• Obtain certificate of re-registration from the Registrar of Companies	
23	• If required, obtain a new company seal	
24	• Change company's bank account details	
25	• A trustee in bankruptcy of a member of the company is entitled, to the exclusion of the member, to assent to the company's becoming an unlimited company. The personal representative of a deceased member of the company may assert on behalf of the deceased.	CA 2006, s 102(4)
26	• The reference to a 'trustee in bankruptcy of a member of the company' includes: (a) a permanent trustee or an interim trustee (within the meaning of the Bankruptcy (Scotland) Act 1985 (c 66)) on the sequestrated estate of a member of the company; and (b) a trustee under a protected trustee deed (within the meaning of the Bankruptcy (Scotland) Act 1985) granted by a member of the company.	CA 2006, s 102(5)
27	• An application for re-registration as an unlimited company must contain a statement of the company's proposed name on re-registration.	CA 2006, s 103(1)
28	• The application must be accompanied by the following: (a) the prescribed form of assent to the company being registered as an unlimited company authenticated by or on behalf of all the members of the company; (b) a copy of the company's articles as proposed to be amended.	CA 2006, s 103(2)
29	• The statement of compliance delivered together with the application is a statement that the requirements as to re-registration as an unlimited company have been complied with.	CA 2006, s 103(3)
30	• The statement must contain a statement on the directors of the company:	CA 2006, s 103(4)

No	Issue	Reference
	(a) that the persons by whom or on whose behalf the form of assent is authenticated constitute the whole membership of the company; and (b) if any of the members have not authenticated that form themselves, that the directors have taken all reasonable steps to satisfy themselves that each person who authenticated it on behalf of a member was lawfully empowered to do so.	
31	• The registrar may accept the statement of compliance as sufficient evidence that the company is entitled to be re-registered as an unlimited company.	CA 2006, s 103(5)
32	• If, on an application for re-registration of a private limited company as an unlimited company, the registrar is satisfied that the company is entitled to be so re-registered, the company shall be registered accordingly.	CA 2006, s 104(1)
33	• The registrar must issue a certificate of incorporation altered to meet the circumstances of the case.	CA 2006, s 104(2)
34	• The certificate must state that it is issued on re-registration and the date on which it is issued.	CA 2006, s 104(3)
35	• On the issue of the certificate: (a) the company becomes an unlimited company; and (b) the changes in the company's name and articles take effect.	CA 2006, s 104(4)
36	• The certificate is conclusive evidence that the requirements of CA 2006, as to re-registration, have been complied with.	CA 2006, s 104(5)

Checklist: Unlimited private company becoming limited

9.6 *This checklist sets out how an unlimited private company may alter its status to become a limited company – whether limited by shares or guarantee. It considers the steps and procedures required to effect the change.*

No	Issue	Reference
1	An unlimited company may be re-registered as a private limited company if: (a) a special resolution that it should be so re-registered is passed; (b) the application for re-registration is delivered to the registrar in accordance with CA 2006, s 106 together with the other documents required by that section; and a statement of compliance; and (c) there is compliance with the condition that the company has not previously re-registered as an unlimited company.	CA 2006, s 105(1); CA 2006, s 105(2)
2	• Call a board meeting upon reasonable notice.	Notice
3	• Prepare agenda for the meeting including any background papers and briefs.	Agenda
4	• A board meeting may be dispensed with if written resolution used.	
5	• Ensure quorum present at the Board Meeting.	
6	• Board meeting votes on altering the status of the unlimited company to a limited liability company (whether limited by shares or guarantee).	
7	• Prepare minutes of the board meeting.	Minutes
8	• Call an EGM by notice to the shareholders setting out date, time and place of the meeting including nature of special resolution and reference to appointment of a proxy. The special resolution must state whether the company is to be limited by shares or guarantee.	Notice, CA 2006, s 105(3)
9	• Consider if written resolution may be used.	Written resolution
10	• Make appropriate changes to the articles of association and memorandum of association.	
11	• Ensure quorum present at the EGM	
12	• Voting on a show of hands (unless poll demanded).	
13	• Prepare minutes of the EGM for circulation.	Minutes
14	• Lodge the special resolution at Companies House.	CA 2006, s 30
15	• Lodge Form RR06 at Companies House.	Form RR06
16	• Printed copy of the amended articles of association for a limited company and memorandum of association.	Articles and memorandum
17	• Fee for re-registration.	
18	• Statement of compliance.	

No	Issue	Reference
19	• Change company headed notepaper/business cards.	
20	• Change company signage at head office.	
21	• Notify suppliers/third parties/banks/HMRC/ VAT/PAYE.	
22	• The company must make such changes in its name and in its articles, as are necessary in connection with its becoming a company limited by shares, or as the case may be, by guarantee.	CA 2006, s 105(4)
23	• An application for re-registration as a limited company must contain a statement of the company's proposed name on re-registration.	CA 2006, s 106(1)
24	• The application must be accompanied by: (a) a copy of the resolution that the company should re-register as a private limited company (unless a copy has already been forwarded to the registrar under CA 2006, Pt3, Ch 3); (b) if the company is to be limited by guarantee, a statement of guarantee; and (c) a copy of the company articles as proposed to be amended.	CA 2006, s 106(2)
25	• The statement of guarantee required to be delivered in the case of a company that is to be limited by guarantee must state that each member undertakes that, if the company is wound up while he is a member, or within one year after he ceases to be a member, he will contribute to the assets of the company such amount as may be required for: (a) payment of the debts and liabilities of the company contracted before he ceases to be a member; (b) payment of the costs, charges and expenses of winding-up; and (c) adjustment of the rights of the contributories among themselves; not exceeding a specified amount.	CA 2006, s 106(3)
26	• The statement of compliance required to be delivered together with the application is a statement that the requirements as to re-registration as a limited company have been complied with.	CA 2006, s 106(4)

No	Issue	Reference
27	• The registrar may accept the statement of compliance as sufficient evidence that the company is entitled to be re-registered as a limited company.	CA 2006, s 106(5)
28	• If, on an application for registration of an unlimited company as a limited company, the registrar is satisfied that the company is entitled to be re-registered, the company shall be re-registered accordingly.	CA 2006, s 107(1)
29	• The registrar must issue a certificate of incorporation altered to meet the circumstances of the case.	CA 2006, s 107(2)
30	• The certificate must state that it is issued on re-registration and the date on which it is issued.	CA 2006, s 107(3)
31	• On the issue of the certificate, the company becomes an unlimited company; the changes in the company's name and articles take effect.	CA 2006, s 107(4)
32	• The certificate is conclusive evidence that the requirements for re-registration have been complied with.	CA 2006, s 107(5)
33	• A company, which on re-registration under CA 2006, s 107 already has allotted share capital, must deliver a statement of capital to the registrar within 15 days after the re-registration.	CA 2006, s 108(1)
34	• The requirement under CA 2006, s 108(1) does not apply if the information which would be included in the statement has already been sent to the registrar in: (a) payment of the debts and liabilities of the company contracted before he ceases to be a member; (b) payment of the costs, charges end expenses of winding up; and (c) a statement of capital and initial shareholdings: CA 2006, s 10; or (d) (if different) the last statement of capital sent by the company.	CA 2006, s 108(2) (as inserted by SBEEA 2015, s 93(4))
35	• The statement of capital must state with respect to the company's share capital on re-registration: (a) the total number of shares of the company; (b) the aggregate nominal value of those shares; (c) for each class of shares:	CA 2006, s 108(3)

No	Issue	Reference
	(i) prescribed particulars of the rights attached to the shares; (ii) the total number of shares of that class; and (iii) the aggregate nominal value of shares of that class, and (d) the amount paid up and the amount (if any) unpaid on each share (whether on account of the nominal value of the share or by way of premium).	
36	• If default is made in complying with CA 2006, s 108, an offence is committed by the company and every officer of the company who is in default.	CA 2006, s 108(4)
37	• A person guilty of an offence under CA 2006, s 108 is liable, on summary conviction, to a fine not exceeding level 3 on the standard scale and for continued contravention, a daily default fine not exceeding one-tenth of level 3 on the standard scale	CA 2006, s 108(5)

Checklist: Public company becoming private and unlimited

9.7 *This checklist sets out the legal steps and procedures required to effect an alteration in the status from a public company becoming private and unlimited.*

No	Issue	Reference
1	• A public company limited by shares may be re-registered as an unlimited private company with a share capital if: (a) all the members of the company have assented to its being so re-registered; (b) the application for re-registration is delivered to the registrar in accordance with CA 2006, s 110 together with the other documents required by that section; and a statement of compliance; and (c) the satisfaction of the condition that the company has not previously been registered as limited or unlimited.	CA 2006, s 109(1)
2	• The company must make such changes in its name and in its articles as are necessary in connection with its becoming an unlimited private company.	CA 2006, s 109(2)
3	• Call a board meeting upon reasonable notice.	Notice

No	Issue	Reference
4	• Prepare an agenda for the meeting including any background papers and briefs.	Agenda
5	• Board meeting may be dispensed with if a written resolution used.	Written resolution
6	• Ensure quorum present.	
7	• The board meeting votes on altering the status of the public company to an unlimited private company.	
8	• Prepare minutes of the board meeting.	Minutes
9	• Call an EGM by notice to the shareholders setting out the date, time and place of the meeting including the appointment of a proxy.	
10	• Consider if written resolution may be used.	Written resolution
11	• Make appropriate changes to the articles of association and memorandum of association for the private unlimited company.	
12	• Voting by a show of hands (unless poll demanded).	CA 2006, s 109(3)
13	• Prepare minutes of the EGM for circulation.	Minutes
14	• Lodge the written resolution at Companies House.	CA 2006, s 30
15	• Lodge Form RR07 at Companies House.	Form RR07 (Application by a public company for re-registration as a private unlimited company)
16	• Printed copy of the amended articles of association for the private unlimited company and memorandum of association	
17	• Fee for re-registration	
18	• Statement of compliance.	
19	• Change company headed notepaper/business cards.	
20	• Change company signage at head office.	
21	• Notify suppliers/third parties/banks/HMRC/ VAT/PAYE.	
22	• For the purpose of CA 2006, s 109:	CA 2006, s 109(4)

No	Issue	Reference
	(a) a trustee in bankruptcy of a member of the company is entitled to the exclusion of the member to assent the company's re-registration; and (b) the personal representative of a deceased member of the company may assent on behalf of the deceased.	
23	• The reference to 'a trustee in bankruptcy of a member of a company' includes: (a) a permanent trustee or an interim trustee (within the meaning of the Bankruptcy (Scotland) Act 1985 (c 66) on the sequestered estate of a member of the company; and (b) a trustee under a protected trustee deed (within the meaning of the Bankruptcy (Scotland) Act 1985) granted by a member of the company.	CA 2006, s 109(5)
24	• An application for re-registration of a public company as an unlimited private company must contain a statement of the company's proposed name on re-registration.	CA 2006, s 110(1)
25	• The application must be accompanied by: (a) the prescribed form of assent to the company's being registered as an unlimited company authenticated by or on behalf of all the members of the company; and (b) a copy of the company's articles as proposed to be amended.	CA 2006, s 110(2)
26	• The statement of compliance required to be delivered together with the application is a statement to re-registration as an unlimited private company have been complied with.	CA 2006, s 110(3)
27	• The statement must contain a statement by the directors of the company: (a) that the persons by whom or on whose behalf the form of assent is authenticated constitute the whole membership of the company; and	CA 2006, s 110(4)

No	Issue	Reference
	(b) if any of the members have not authenticated that form themselves, that the directors have taken all reasonable steps to satisfy themselves that each person who authenticated it on behalf of a member was lawfully empowered to do so.	
28	• The registrar may accept the statement of compliance as sufficient evidence that the company is entitled to be re-registered as an unlimited private company.	CA 2006, s 110(5)
29	• If, on an application for re-registration of a public company as an unlimited private company, the registrar is satisfied that the company is entitled to be so re-registered, the company shall be re-registered accordingly.	CA 2006, s 111(1)
30	• The registrar must issue a certificate of incorporation altered to meet the circumstances of the case.	CA 2006, s 111(2)
31	• The certificate must state that it is issued on a re-registration and the date on which it is so issued.	CA 2006, s 111(3)
32	• On issue of the certificate, the company becomes an unlimited private company, and the changes in the company's name and articles take effect.	CA 2006, s 111(4)
33	• The certificate is conclusive evidence that the requirements under the CA 2006, as to re-registration have been complied with.	CA 2006, s 111(5)

Definitions

9.8

Another company: includes any body corporate.

Arrangement: means any agreement, scheme or arrangement, (including an arrangement sanctioned in accordance with:

(i) Part 26 of CA 2006 (arrangements and reconstructions), or

(ii) s 110 of the Insolvency Act 1986 (c 45) or Art 96 of the Insolvency (Northern Ireland) Order 1989 (SI 1989/2405 (NI 19)) (liquidator in winding up accepting shares as consideration for sale of company's property).

Trustee in bankruptcy of a member of the company:	(a)	a permanent trustee or an interim trustee (within the meaning of the Bankruptcy (Scotland) Act 1985 (c 66)) on the sequestrated estate of a member of the company; and
	(b)	a trustee under a protected trustee deed (within the meaning of the Bankruptcy (Scotland) Act 1985) granted by a member of the company.

10 Shareholders and exercise of rights

Contents

Introduction

10.1 Shareholders occupy an important position and function in the company's corporate governance system. They have the ultimate residual authority over corporate matters. Traditionally, shareholders were perceived as passive or 'absentee' owners, delegating the most part of their authority to the company's directors to determine their fortunes without guarding their interests and the long-term success of the company. Shareholders merely accepted the consequences of their investments and were content to receive dividends. Following the collapse of several large companies (eg Polly Peck and BCCI in the UK and Enron in the US), the need to strengthen the corporate governance system of companies became apparent, with various UK committees (eg Cadbury and Hampel) publishing reports requiring companies to ensure the quality of their financial reporting, transparency and accountability. These reforms have resulted in shareholders becoming more active within their companies; they are prepared to ask questions at meetings, including the annual general meeting, and are prepared to make their voices heard.

The Companies Act (CA) 2006 sets out the position of shareholders within the company including exercise of their rights. It recognises and reinforces the significant position occupied by shareholders within the corporate governance system, and the need to ensure that directors perform their duties effectively in the company's management.

10.2 This chapter address the following issues:

- who constitute the members of the company;
- the steps required to register a person as a company member;
- the register of members and the option for a private company to register information in the central registry at Companies House as an alternative method of record keeping;
- the position regarding overseas branch registers;
- the exercise of members' rights.

Part 8 of CA 2006 (as amended by the Small Business, Enterprise and Employment Act 2015 (SBEEA 2015)) is concerned with company members. It comprises four chapters. It defines the members of a company as part of the corporate governance process. It also deals with the register of members, overseas branch registers and prohibition on a subsidiary being a member of its holding company.

This chapter also addresses the provisions dealing with the exercise of members' rights in the corporate governance process. This is governed by CA 2006, Pt 9.

Company's members

10.3 The Companies Act 2006 does not use the term 'shareholder' under any of its provisions. Instead, the term 'member' is used to describe a shareholder who holds shares in the company. CA 2006, Pt 8, Ch 1 deals with members of a company. The subscribers of a company's memorandum are deemed to have agreed to become members of the company, and on its registration become members and must be entered as such in its register of members (CA 2006, s 112(1)). The definition applies to all bodies corporate which are formed and registered under the legislation: *Enviroco Ltd v Farstad Supply A/S* [2011] 2 BCLC 165.

10.4 There are two aspects to the recognition of membership under this provision:

- The subscribers (namely the founding shareholders) must subscribe to the company's memorandum of association by setting out their names and stating their desire to become members of the company. This statement must be witnessed. At this stage, they cannot be treated as members. However, they must agree to become members of the company. Consent of a member is, therefore, required.
- The subscribers' names must then be registered in the company's register of members.

A person must 'agree' to become a member of the company. There is no requirement for a bilateral agreement between the company and the prospective member: only the member needs to consent to becoming a member of the company

The issue of agreeing to become a member was addressed in *Re Nuneaton Borough Association Football Club Limited (No 1)* [1989] BCLC 454. The case concerned an appeal to the Court of Appeal by Mr Shooter from a first instance decision where his claim for unfair prejudicial conduct was struck out in relation to the affairs of Nuneaton Borough Association Football Club Limited, on the ground that Mr Shooter has no locus standi to present the petition because on the evidence, he was not a member of the company.

At a board meeting in 1986, the directors resolved to issue 10,000 ordinary shares of £1 each in the company to Mr Shooter, who paid the company for the shares and he was registered in the register of members in respect of these shares. Subsequently, he agreed to purchase an additional 10,000 shares but these additional shares were never registered in the register of members.

The issue before the Court of Appeal was did Mr Shooter 'agree' to become a member of the company?

It was held by the Court of Appeal that the phrase 'agrees to become a member' in s 112 of CA 2006 was satisfied where a person assented to become a member: it did not require that there be a binding contract between the person and the company. Accordingly, where the name of a person was entered in the register of members with his consent he was a member of the company. According to Fox LJ, CA 2006, s 112 made no reference to a bilateral agreement but merely required the agreement of the person to become a member.

Nicholls LJ was of the view that the expression 'agrees to become a member' referred to 'consents to become a member'. It envisaged entry on the register with the consent and authority of the person in question.

See too: *Re Railway Time Tables Publishing Co, ex p Sandys* (1889) 42 Ch D 98; *Re Disderi & Co* (1870–71) LR 11 Eq 242; *Re James Pilkin & Co Ltd* (1916) 85 L J Ch 318.

10.5 Entry in the register of members, usually by the company secretary or directors, is essential for the recognition of membership.

It was a fundamental principle of UK company law – reflected in the definition of 'member' in s 112 – that a member of a company was the person entered on the register as a member, to the exclusion of any other person

Enviroco Ltd v Farstad Supply A/S [2011] 2 BCLC 165, concerned issues regarding a charterparty. In this case, the court was required to determine whether a parent company was a 'member' of the subsidiary and had control of its subsidiary under CA 2006, s 1159(1)(c).

The parent company owned shares in its subsidiary but had given security of the shares to a bank. The shares were registered in the name of the bank's nominee. Accordingly, the register of members had identified the bank's nominee as the member, not the parent company. The issue was whether the parent company was a 'member' of its subsidiary even though the bank's nominee was registered in the register of members.

The Supreme Court, having considered the historical background to CA 2006, s 1159 held (per Lord Collins) that it was a fundamental principle of UK company law – reflected in the definition of 'member' in s 112 – that a member of a company was the person entered on the register as a member, to the exclusion of any other person, unless special provision was made for another person to be deemed to be a member on the register, and that the person so entered on the register had all the relevant rights and liabilities of a member: *Re Sussex Brick Co* [1904] 1 Ch 598 (retrospective rectification of register did not invalidate notices).

Accordingly, the parent company was not a member of the subsidiary.

A registration of a member under a false or fictitious name renders that person liable to contribution up to the amount subscribed

An application by a person in a false or fictitious name to become a member and shares are allotted to him under such name renders that person as a member of the company and liable for contribution up to the amount subscribed: *Re Hercules Insurance Co, Pugh and Sharman's Case* (1872) LR 13 Eq 566.

An entry of a member in the register of members may not by itself be sufficient and may require other actions to become registered as a member

In some situations, entry of a member in the register of members may not be sufficient by itself as other requirements may still have to be met. In *POW Services Ltd v Clare* [1995] 2 BCLC 435, admission to membership required the consent of the Council (an administrative body) under the articles of association. The issue was whether an EGM was validly constituted by its members, particularly where one member's membership to the company had not been approved by the Council. The court held that the EGM had not been validly constituted.

According to Jacobs J, admission to membership of the company required a decision of the company's Council as to whether a person should be admitted as a member. The procedure adopted by the company was a virtual automatic admission on an administrative basis of any person who applied for membership, and this was not sufficient to comply with the company's articles of association.

10.6 Section 112(2) of CA 2006 states that 'every other person who agrees to become a member of a company, and whose name is entered in its register of members, is a member of the company'. This addresses other situations once incorporation has been effected, for a person to become a member of the company. It may be through the following types of situations:

- on a sale of shares;
- on a transfer of shares;
- an allotment of shares; or
- on a transmission of shares (death or bankruptcy).

10.7 Where an election under CA 2006, s 128B is in force in respect of a company:

(a) the requirement in CA 2006, s 112(1) to enter particulars of members in the company's register of members does not apply; and

(b) CA 2006, s 112(2) has effect as if the reference to a person whose name is entered in the company's register of members were a reference to a person with respect to whom the following steps have been taken:

    (i) the person's name has been delivered to the registrar under CA 2006, s 128E; and

    (ii) the document containing that information has been registered by the registrar: CA 2006, s 112(3) (as inserted by SBEEA 2015, Sch 5, Pt 2).

Alternative method of record-keeping

10.8 The CA 2006, Pt 8, Ch 2 must be read with Ch 2A (which allows for an alternative method of record-keeping in the case of private companies). The CA 2006, Pt 8, Ch 2A is concerned with an option for private companies to keep information on a central register. It sets out rules allowing private companies to keep information on the register kept by the registrar instead of entering it in their register of members: CA 2006, s 128A(1).

The register kept by the registrar (see s 1080) is referred to in Ch 2A as 'the central register': CA 2006, s 128A(2).

Right to make an election

10.9 An election may be made under CA 2006, s 128B:

(a) by the subscribers wishing to form a private company under the CA 2006; or

(b) by the private company itself once it is formed and registered: CA 2006, s 128B(1).

10.10 In the latter case, the election is of no effect unless, before it is made:

(a) all the members of the company have assented to the making of the election; and

(b) any overseas branch registers that the company was keeping under Ch 3 have been discontinued and all the entries in those registers transferred to the company's register of members in accordance with s 135: CA 2006, s 128B(2).

10.11 An election under s 128B is made by giving notice of election to the registrar: CA 2006, s 128B(3).

If the notice is given by subscribers wishing to form a private company:

(a) it must be given when the documents required to be delivered under s 9 are delivered to the registrar; and

(b) it must be accompanied by a statement containing all the information that:

 (i) would be required (in the absence of the notice) to be entered in the company's register of members on incorporation of the company; and

 (ii) is not otherwise included in the documents delivered under s 9: CA 2006, s 128B(4).

10.12 If the notice is given by the company, it must be accompanied by:

(a) a statement by the company:

 (i) that all the members of the company have assented to the making of the election; and

 (ii) if the company was keeping any overseas branch registers, that all such registers have been discontinued and all the entries in them transferred to the company's register of members in accordance with s 135, and

(b) a statement containing all the information that is required to be contained in the company's register of members as at the date of the notice in respect of matters that are current as at that date: CA 2006, s 128B(5).

The company must where necessary update the statement sent under s 128B(5)(b) to ensure that the final version delivered to the registrar contains all the information that is required to be contained in the company's register of members as at the time immediately before the election takes effect (see s 128C) in respect of matters that are current as at that time: CA 2006, s 128B(6).

10.13 The obligation in s 128B(6) to update the statement includes an obligation to rectify it (where necessary) in consequence of the company's register of members being rectified (whether before or after the election takes effect): CA 2006, s 128B(7).

If default is made in complying with s 128B(6), an offence is committed by:

(a) the company; and

(b) every officer of the company who is in default.

For this purpose a shadow director is treated as an officer of the company: CA 2006, s 128B(8).

A person guilty of an offence under s 128B is liable on summary conviction to a fine not exceeding level 3 on the standard scale and, for continued contravention, a daily default fine not exceeding one-tenth of level 3 on the standard scale: CA 2006, s 128B(9).

10.14 A reference in Ch 2A to matters that are current as at a given date or time is a reference to:

(a) persons who are members of the company as at that date or time; and

(b) any other matters that are current as at that date or time: CA 2006, s 128B(10).

Effective date of election

10.15 An election made under se 128B takes effect when the notice of election is registered by the registrar: CA 2006, s 128C(1).

The election remains in force until either:

(a) the company ceases to be a private company; or

(b) a notice of withdrawal sent by the company under s 128J is registered by the registrar,

whichever occurs first: CA 2006, s 128C(2).

Effect of election on obligations under Chapter 2

10.16 The effect of an election under s 128B on a company's obligations under Ch 2 is as follows: CA 2006, s 128D(1).

The company's obligation to maintain a register of members does not apply with respect to the period when the election is in force: CA 2006, s 128D(2).

This means that, during that period:

(a) the company must continue to keep a register of members in accordance with Ch 2 (a 'historic' register) containing all the information that was required to be stated in that register as at the time immediately before the election took effect; but

(b) the company does not have to update that register to reflect any changes that occur after that time: CA 2006, s 128D(3).

Sections 128D(2) and (3) apply to the index of members (if the company is obliged to keep an index of members) as they apply to the register of members: CA 2006, s 128D(4).

10.17 The provisions of Ch 2 (including the rights to inspect or require copies of the register and to inspect the index) continue to apply to the historic register and, if applicable, the historic index during the period when the election is in force: CA 2006, s 128D(5).

The company must place a note in its historic register:

(a) stating that an election under s 128B is in force;

(b) recording when that election took effect; and

(c) indicating that up-to-date information about its members is available for public inspection on the central register: CA 2006, s 128D(6).

Section 113(7) and (8) apply if a company makes default in complying with s 128D(6) as they apply if a company makes default in complying with that section: CA 2006, s 128D(7).

The obligations under s 128D with respect to a historic register and historic index do not apply in a case where the election was made by subscribers wishing to form a private company: CA 2006, s 128D(8).

Duty to notify registrar of changes

10.18 The duty under s 128E(2) applies during the period when an election under s 128B is in force: CA 2006, s 128E(1).

The company must deliver to the registrar any relevant information that the company would during that period have been obliged under this Act to enter in its register of members, had the election not been in force: CA 2006, s 128E(2).

10.19 'Relevant information' means information other than:

(a) the date mentioned in s 113(2)(b) (date when person registered as member);

(b) the date mentioned in s 123(3)(b) (date when membership of limited company increases from one to two or more members); and

(c) the dates mentioned in the following provisions, but only in cases where the date to be recorded in the central register is to be the date on which the document containing information of the relevant change is registered by the registrar:

   (i) s 113(2)(c) (date when person ceases to be member);

   (ii) s 123(2)(b) (date when company becomes single member company) CA 2006, s 128E(3).

The relevant information must be delivered as soon as reasonably practicable after the company becomes aware of it and, in any event, no later than the time by which the company would have been required to enter the information in its register of members: CA 2006, s 128E(4).

In a case of the kind described in s 128E(3)(c), the company must, when it delivers information under s 128E(2) of the relevant change, indicate to the registrar that, in accordance with s 1081(1A), the date to be recorded in the central register is to be the date on which the document containing that information is registered by the registrar: CA 2006, s 128E(5).

10.20 If default is made in complying with this section, an offence is committed by:

(a) the company; and

(b) every officer of the company who is in default: CA 2006, s 128E(6).

For this purpose a shadow director is treated as an officer of the company.

A person guilty of an offence under this section is liable on summary conviction to a fine not exceeding level 3 on the standard scale and, for continued contravention, a daily default fine not exceeding one-tenth of level 3 on the standard scale: CA 2006, s 128E(7).

Information as to state of central register

10.21 When a person inspects or requests a copy of material on the central register relating to a company in respect of which an election under s 128B is in force, the person may ask the company to confirm that all information that the company is required to deliver to the registrar under this Chapter has been delivered: CA 2006, s 128F(1).

If a company fails to respond to a request under s 128F(1), an offence is committed by:

(a) the company; and

(b) every officer of the company who is in default: CA 2006, s 128F(2).

A person guilty of an offence under s128F is liable on summary conviction to a fine not exceeding level 3 on the standard scale: CA 2006, s 128F(3).

Power of court to order company to remedy default or delay

10.22 Section 128G applies if:

(a) the name of a person is without sufficient cause included in, or omitted from, information that a company delivers to the registrar under this Chapter concerning its members, or

(b) default is made or unnecessary delay takes place in informing the registrar under this Chapter of:

  (i) the name of a person who is to be a member of the company; or

  (ii) the fact that a person has ceased or is to cease to be a member of the company: CA 2006, s 128G(1).

10.23 The person aggrieved, or any member of the company, or the company, may apply to the court for an order:

(a) requiring the company to deliver to the registrar the information (or statements) necessary to rectify the position; and

(b) where applicable, requiring the registrar to record under s 1081(1A) the date determined by the court: CA 2006, s 128G(1) .

The court may either refuse the application or may make the order and order the company to pay any damages sustained by any party aggrieved: CA 2006, s 128G(3).

10.24 On such an application the court may decide:

(a) any question relating to the title of a person who is a party to the application to have the person's name included in or omitted from information delivered to the registrar under this Chapter about the company's members, whether the question arises between members or alleged members, or between members or alleged members on the one hand and the company on the other hand; and

(b) any question necessary or expedient to be decided for rectifying the position: CA 2006, s 128G(4).

Nothing in this section affects a person's rights under ss 1095 or 1096 (rectification of register on application to registrar or under court order): CA 2006, s 128G(5).

Central register to be evidence

10.25 The central register is prima facie evidence of any matters about which a company is required to deliver information to the registrar under this Chapter: CA 2006, s 128H(1).

Section 128H(1) does not apply to information to be included in a statement under s 128B(5)(b) or in any updated statement under s 128B(6): CA 2006, s 128H(1).

Time limits for claims arising from delivery to registrar

10.26 Liability incurred by a company:

(a) from the delivery to the registrar of information under this Chapter; or

(b) from a failure to deliver any such information,

is not enforceable more than ten years after the date on which the information was delivered or, as the case may be, the failure first occurred: CA 2006, s.128I(1).

This is without prejudice to any lesser period of limitation (and, in Scotland, to any rule that the obligation giving rise to the liability prescribes before the expiry of that period): CA 2006, s 128I(2).

Withdrawing the election

10.27 A company may withdraw an election made by or in respect of it under s 128B: CA 2006, s 128J(1).

Withdrawal is achieved by giving notice of withdrawal to the registrar: CA 2006, s 128J(2).

The withdrawal takes effect when the notice is registered by the registrar: CA 2006, s 128J(3).

The effect of withdrawal is that the company's obligation under Ch 2 to maintain a register of members applies from then on with respect to the period going forward: CA 2006, s 128J(4).

This means that, when the withdrawal takes effect:

(a) the company must enter in its register of members all the information that is required to be contained in that register in respect of matters that are current as at that time;

(b) the company must also retain in its register all the information that it was required under s 128D(3)(a) to keep in a historic register while the election was in force; but

(c) the company is not required to enter in its register information relating to the period when the election was in force that is no longer current: CA 2006, s 128J(5).

10.28 The company must place a note in its register of members:

(a) stating that the election under s 128B has been withdrawn;

(b) recording when that withdrawal took effect; and

(c) indicating that information about its members relating to the period when the election was in force that is no longer current is available for public inspection on the central register: CA 2006, s 128J(6).

Sections 113(7) and (8) apply if a company makes default in complying with sub-s (6) as they apply if a company makes default in complying with that section: CA 2006, s 128J(7).

Power to extend option to public companies

10.29 The Secretary of State may by regulations amend this Act:

(a) to extend ss 128A to 128J (with or without modification) to public companies or public companies of a class specified in the regulations; and

(b) to make such other amendments as the Secretary of State thinks fit in consequence of that extension: CA 2006, s 128K(1).

Register of members

10.30 Every company must keep a register of its members: CA 2006, s 113(1). The following details must be entered in the register:

(a) the names and addresses of the members;

> ***The term 'address' refers to an address provided by the member***
>
> In respect of the 'addresses of members' there is no requirement for the members to give their residential address. A member may provide any other address. In *POW Services Ltd v Clare* [1995] 2 BCLC 435, Jacob J was of the view that 'address' must mean the address the member himself gives, not some other address provided by someone else.

(b) the date on which each person was registered as a member; and

(c) the date at which any person ceased to be a member: CA 2006, s 113(2).

10.31 For companies having a share capital, there must be entered in the register, with the names and addresses of the members, a statement of:

(a) the shares held by each member, distinguishing each share:

  (i) by its number (as long as the share has a number); and

  (ii) where the company has more than one class of issued shares, by its class; and

(b) the amount paid or agreed to be considered as paid on the shares of each member: CA 2006, s 113(3).

If the company has converted any of its shares into stock, and given notice of the conversion to the registrar, the register of members must show the amount and class of stock held by each member instead of the amount of shares and the particulars relating to shares specified above: CA 2006, s 113(4).

In the case of joint holders of shares or stock in a company, the company's register of members must state the names of each joint holder.

In other respects, joint holders are regarded for the purposes of this chapter of CA 2006 as a single member (so that the register must show a single address): CA 2006, s 113(5).

In the case of a company that does not have a share capital but has more than one class of members, there must be entered in the register, with the names and addresses of the members, a statement of the class to which each member belongs: CA 2006, s 113(6).

10.32 If a company defaults in complying with s 113 an offence is committed by:

(a) the company; and

(b) every officer of the company who is in default: CA 2006, s 113(7).

A person guilty of an offence under s 113 is liable on summary conviction to a fine not exceeding level 3 on the standard scale and, for continued contravention, a daily default fine not exceeding one-tenth of level 3 on the standard scale: CA 2006, s 113(3).

Register to be kept available for inspection

10.33 A company's register of members must be kept available for inspection:

(a) at its registered office; or

(b) at a place specified in regulations under s 1136: CA 2006, s 114(1).

A company must give notice to the registrar of the place where its register of members is kept available for inspection and of any change in that place: CA 2006, s 114(2).

No such notice is required if the register has, at all times since it came into existence (or, in the case of a register in existence on the relevant date, at all times since then) been kept available for inspection at the company's registered office: CA 2006, s 114(3).

10.34 The relevant date is:

(a) 1 July 1948 in the case of a company registered in Great Britain; and

(b) 1 April 1961 in the case of a company registered in Northern Ireland: CA 2006, s 114(4).

10.35 If a company defaults for 14 days before complying with s 114(2), an offence is committed by:

(a) the company; and

(b) every officer of the company who is in default: CA 2006, s 114(5).

A person guilty of an offence under s 114 is liable, on summary conviction, to a fine not exceeding level 3 on the standard scale and, for continued contravention, a daily default fine not exceeding one-tenth of level 3 on the standard scale: CA 2006, s 114(6).

Index of members

10.36 Every company having more than 50 members must keep an index of the names of the members of the company, unless the register of members is in such a form as to constitute in itself an index: CA 2006, s 115(1).

The company must make any necessary alteration in the index within 14 days after the date on which any alteration is made in the register of members: CA 2006, s 115(2).

The index must contain, in respect of each member, a sufficient indication to enable the account of that member in the register to be readily found: CA 2006, s 115(3).

The index must be at all times kept available for inspection at the same place as the register of members: CA 2006, s 115(4).

If default is made in complying with s 115, an offence is committed by:

(a) the company; and

(b) every officer of the company who is in default: CA 2006, s 115(5).

A person guilty of an offence under s 115 is liable, on summary conviction, to a fine not exceeding level 3 on the standard scale and, for continued contravention, a daily default fine not exceeding one-tenth of level 3 on the standard scale: CA 2006, s 115(6).

Right to inspect and require copies

10.37 The register and the index of members' names must be open to the inspection:

(a) of any member of the company without charge; and

(b) of any other person on payment of such fee as may be prescribed: CA 2006, s 116(1).

10.38 Any person may require a copy of a company's register of members, or of any part of it, on payment of such fee as may be prescribed: CA 2006, s 116(2). A person seeking to exercise either of the rights conferred by s 116 must make a request to the company to that effect: CA 2006, s 116(3). This request must contain the following information:

(a) in the case of an individual, his name and address;

(b) in the case of an organisation, the name and address of an individual responsible for making the request on behalf of the organisation;

(c) the purpose for which the information is to be used; and

(d) whether the information will be disclosed to any other person, and if so:

   (i) where that person is an individual, his name and address;

   (ii) where that person is an organisation, the name and address of an individual responsible for receiving the information on its behalf; and

   (iii) the purpose for which the information is to be used by that person: CA 2006, s 116(4).

Register of members: response to request for inspection or copy

10.39 Where a company receives a request under CA 2006, s 116 (register of members: right to inspect and require copy), it must within five working days either:

(a) comply with the request; or

(b) apply to the court: CA 2006, s 117(1).

If it applies to the court it must notify the person making the request: CA 2006, s 117(2).

10.40 If on an application under s 117, the court is satisfied that the inspection or copy is not sought for a proper purpose:

(a) it shall direct the company not to comply with the request; and

(b) it may further order that the company's costs (in Scotland, expenses) on the application be paid in whole or in part by the person who made the request, even if he is not a party to the application: CA 2006, s 117(3).

If the court makes such a direction and it appears to the court that the company is or may be subject to other requests made for a similar purpose (whether made by the same person or different persons), it may direct that the company is not to comply with any such request.

The order must contain such provision as appears to the court appropriate to identify the requests to which it applies: CA 2006, s 117(4).

If on an application under s 117, the court does not direct the company not to comply with the request, the company must comply with the request immediately upon the court giving its decision or, as the case may be, the proceedings being discontinued: CA 2006, s 117(5).

The words 'proper purposes' under CA 2006, s 117(3) must be given their ordinary, natural meaning

The issue as to what is considered a 'proper purpose' under CA 2006, s 117(3) was considered in *Burry & Knight Ltd v Knight* [2015] 1 BCLC 61. K was a shareholder in two family companies and for a period of time complained about improprieties within these companies. Subsequently he sought to obtain a copy of the share register from the companies. K's purpose of obtaining a copy was to inform other shareholders of the improprieties and past conduct of directors. The companies applied to the court for an order not to comply with the request. The issue before the Court of Appeal was the meaning to be applied to 'proper purposes'. It held that the words 'proper purposes' were to be given their ordinary, natural meaning. A proper purpose ought generally, in the case of a member of the company, relate to the interest of the member in that capacity, and/or to the exercise of shareholder rights. Where there were multiple purposes of which some were proper and some were not, a proper purpose was not necessarily tainted by being coupled to an improper purpose. The reference to 'proper purposes' involved the court first finding what the purpose of the request was which would be found in the request itself, but Parliament had not stated that the court was restricted to the purpose as stated in that document. The onus in a s 117(3) application was on the company to demonstrate to the court that it should be satisfied that the request was for an improper purpose, and 'satisfied' meant satisfied on the balance of probabilities. Therefore, it was not enough that the purpose was capable of being or could possibly be an improper one if the court was not satisfied that it was in fact proper.

According to Arden LJ, the requirement that, unless a company obtained an order under s 117(3), it must comply with a request for access and the imposition of a criminal penalty for non-compliance signalled the importance that Parliament had attached to the exercise of the right of access to the share register; the way the statutory provisions were framed reflected a strong presumption in favour of shareholder democracy and a policy of upholding principles of corporate transparency and good corporate governance. Those factors pointed in favour of the court exercising its discretion sparingly and with circumspection where requests were made by shareholders to communicate with fellow shareholders. A strong case would be required to prevent access, because if a shareholder could not communicate with fellow shareholders the corporate governance of the company would be weakened. Moreover, it was in principle for shareholders to assess whether a communication was of value to them and what action they should take. Parliament could not be taken to have intended the court to take a view about how far the information which the member requesting access wished to give was information of value; that would involve the court making a commercial judgment as to the merits of the view of the member requesting access and would lead to satellite litigation which would delay a decision on access. Although in some cases it would be obvious that the information was of no value, as where it was already known to members, if the court was in any doubt, it should not make a no-access order.

Further, Arden LJ stated that the structure of s 117(3) also showed that it was not for the court to rule out access on discretionary grounds; if the court could not conclude that it was satisfied that access was not sought for an improper purpose, the member had a right to access under s 117(5). The policy behind s 117(3) was that access was to be refused where a person was disqualified by his purpose; thus the court was not necessarily required to be satisfied that there was no substance in, for example, allegations of misconduct which an applicant made against a company, if his purpose in pursuing those allegations was not a 'proper purpose'. Where a member sought access to the share register so that he could communicate with other members, the proposed communication, if it was to be for a proper purpose, had to be relevant in some way to the members' interests as members of the company. In the instant case, the inference of improper purpose which the registrar had drawn from K's failure to bring forward more evidence and to provide some explanation for the delay had been on so strong a basis that he had been entitled to draw it despite the witness statement containing a statement of truth. The information which K had sought to convey to fellow company members was not now apt to confer any benefit on the members and K had asserted no corporate purpose in pursuing the matters. Accordingly, K's purpose was not a proper one in so far as he sought access to the share registers in order to pursue with other shareholders his long-standing allegations. The words 'a proper purpose' in s 117(3) were to be read as including 'proper purposes' where there was more than one purpose, so that the court would have to make a no-access order if any of the purposes were improper; for the court to be satisfied that the purpose of a request was a proper purpose simply because it was satisfied that one of several purposes was a proper purpose would undermine the protection which the no-access provision was intended to give. Moreover, a purpose could be improper not only because of the end it sought to achieve, but also because of the way in which it sought a proper purpose. An order enabling a party to communicate with shareholders but which at the same time permitted the company to keep the details of the shareholders on the register private, such as had been made in the instant case, could still be made under s 117(3) as under the earlier legislation; such an order enabled access for a proper purpose to take place because if such an order could not be made, the court would be bound to conclude that it was satisfied that the access would not be for a proper purpose.

In *Burberry Group PLC v Fox-Davies* [2015] All ER (D) 185 (Feb), the defendant, who ran a tracing agency, requested a copy of the register of members of the claimant company (Burberry), for the purpose of assisting shareholders who might be unaware of their entitlements to reassert ownership or recover the benefit of their property. The defendant was not a member of Burberry. Burberry refused the request and applied for relief, under CA 2006, s 117(3). The Companies Court allowed Burberry's application, held, among other things, that the request was for an improper purpose. Accordingly, it directed Burberry not to comply with the request. Registrar Briggs reasoned that the right to inspect and to make copies of a company's register of members were subject to restrictions, which were set out in ss 116 and 117 of the Act. Section 117 of the Act informed a company receiving such a request that it had two options: (i) to comply with the request within five working days; and (ii) to apply to the court. Where a member sought access, the court would consider the real purpose behind the request and determine, as a matter of fact, if the information was to be used for improper purposes, such as to harangue shareholders. As a result of a strong presumption in favour of shareholder democracy, a policy of corporate transparency and the promotion of good corporate governance, the approach of the courts to a request by a member would be that he should be granted access where the purpose related to his or her rights. However, where access was refused by the board and an application was made to the court, the company might satisfy the court on the balance of probabilities that the request was not for a proper purpose. A person other than a member might have a legitimate interest in accessing the information on the register. The decision to disallow inspection and apply to the court was that of a company, which might be a subjective decision, but the test applied by the court was objective, namely, whether the purpose was proper in the context of the company, its relationship with its shareholders, its trading and the request made. Generally, the issue required a fact sensitive inquiry. Another relevant factor when undertaking the inquiry was the public policy need for strong corporate governance: the relationship between the board and the shareholders was relevant. If an application was made to the court, it was legitimate for the court to consider, not only the stated purpose for the request, but also how the purpose was carried out.

Another issue in *Burberry Group PLC*, concerned the fact that Burberry was out of time to make the application to court pursuant to CA 2006, s 117. The issue for consideration was whether the letter of request by the defendant constituted a valid request within the meaning of CA 2006, s 116. Registrar Briggs held that the CA 2006 was worded in mandatory terms. A company had to make an application within five days and the person seeking the information had to set out the names and addresses of any individual with whom he was going to share the information. If that information was not provided, the company receiving the request would not know whether to oppose the request or not. The legislation had a provision that dealt with failure to comply with the requirements. However, the mandatory language required compliance and a failure to comply with the requirements would invalidate the request. On the facts, the defendant's letter of request failed as it had not accurately set out the purpose of the request.

Register of members: refusal of inspection or default in providing copy

10.41 If an inspection required under CA 2006, s 116 (register of members: right to inspect and require copy) is refused or default is made in providing a copy required under that section, otherwise than in accordance with an order of the court, an offence is committed by:

(a) the company; and

(b) every officer of the company who is in default: CA 2006, s 118(1).

A person guilty of an offence under s 118 is liable on summary conviction to a fine not exceeding level 3 on the standard scale and, for continued contravention, a daily default fine not exceeding one-tenth of level 3 on the standard scale: CA 2006, s 118(2).

In the case of any such refusal or default the court may by order compel an immediate inspection or, as the case may be, direct that the copy required be sent to the person requesting it: CA 2006, s 118(3).

Register of members: offences in connection with request for or disclosure of information

10.42 It is an offence for a person knowingly or recklessly to make in a request under s 116 (register of members: right to inspect or require copy) a statement that is misleading, false or deceptive in a material particular: CA 2006, s 119.

It is an offence for a person in possession of information obtained by exercise of either of the rights conferred by that section:

(a) to do anything that results in the information being disclosed to another person; or

(b) to fail to do anything with the result that the information is disclosed to another person,

knowing, or having reason to suspect, that person may use the information for a purpose that is not a proper purpose: CA 2006, s 119(2).

10.43 A person guilty of an offence under s 119 is liable:

(a) on conviction on indictment, to imprisonment for a term not exceeding two years or a fine (or both);

(b) on summary conviction:

  (i) in England and Wales, to imprisonment for a term not exceeding 12 months or to a fine not exceeding the statutory maximum (or both);

  (ii) in Scotland or Northern Ireland, to imprisonment for a term not exceeding six months, or to a fine not exceeding the statutory maximum (or both): CA 2006, s 119(3).

Information as to state of register and index

10.44 When a person inspects the register, or the company provides him with a copy of the register or any part of it, the company must inform him of the most recent date (if any) on which alterations were made to the register and whether there are further alterations to be made: CA 2006, s 120(1). When a person inspects the index of members' names, the company must inform him whether there is any alteration to the register that is not reflected in the index: CA 2006, s 120(2).

If a company fails to provide the information required under subs (1) or (2), an offence will be committed by:

(a) the company; and

(b) every officer of the company who is in default: CA 2006, s 120(3).

A person guilty of an offence under s 120 is liable on summary conviction to a fine not exceeding level 3 on the standard scale: CA 2006, s 120(4).

Removal of entries relating to former members

10.45 An entry relating to a former member of the company may be removed from the register following the expiration of ten years from the date on which he ceased to be a member: CA 2006, s 121.

Special cases

10.46 The Companies Act 2006 sets out some special cases in connection with members that require particular consideration.

Share warrants

10.47 Until a share warrant issued by a company is surrendered the following are deemed to be the particulars required to be entered in the register of members in respect of the warrant:

(a) the fact of the issue of the warrant;

(b) a statement of the shares included in the warrant, distinguishing each share by its number so long as the share has a number; and

(c) the date of the issue of the warrant: CA 2006, s 122(1) (as amended by SBEEA 2015, Sch 4).

The bearer of a share warrant may, if the articles of the company so provide, be deemed a member of the company within the meaning of CA 2006, either to the full extent or for any purposes defined in the articles: CA 2006, s 122(3).

The company is responsible for any loss incurred by any person by reason of the company entering in the register the name of a bearer of a share warrant in respect of the shares specified in it without the warrant being surrendered and cancelled: CA 2006, s 122(5).

On the surrender of a share warrant, the date of the surrender must be entered in the register: CA 2006, s 122(6).

Single member companies

10.48 The Companies Act 2006 allows for the establishment of single member companies. Section 123 addresses the position of register of members for such a company.

If a limited company is formed under the Act with only one member there must be entered in the company's register of members, with the name and address of the sole member, a statement that the company has only one member: CA 2006, s 123(1).

If the number of members of a limited company falls to one, or if an unlimited company with only one member becomes a limited company on re-registration, there must, upon the occurrence of that event, be entered in the company's register of members, with the name and address of the sole member:

(a) a statement that the company has only one member; and

(b) the date on which the company became a company having only one member: CA 2006, s 123(2).

10.49 If the membership of a limited company increases from one to two or more members, there must upon the occurrence of that event be entered in the company's register of members, with the name and address of the person who was formerly the sole member:

(a) a statement that the company has ceased to have only one member; and

(b) the date on which that event occurred: CA 2006, s 123(3).

10.50 If a company makes default in complying with s 123, an offence is committed by:

(a) the company; and

(b) every officer of the company who is in default: CA 2006, s 123(4).

A person guilty of an offence under s 123 is liable on summary conviction to a fine not exceeding level 3 on the standard scale and, for continued contravention, a daily default fine not exceeding one-tenth of level 3 on the standard scale: CA 2006, s 123(5).

Company holding its own shares as treasury

10.51 Where a company purchases its own shares in circumstances in which CA 2006, s 724 (treasury shares) applies:

(a) the requirements of s 113 (register of members) need not be complied with if the company cancels all of the shares forthwith after the purchase; and

(b) if the company does not cancel all of the shares forthwith after the purchase, any share that is so cancelled shall be disregarded for the purposes of that section: CA 2006, s 124(1).

Subject to s 124(1) where a company holds shares as treasury shares the company must be entered in the register as the member holding those shares: CA 2006, s 124(2).

Power of court to rectify register

10.52 In certain circumstances, the company may refuse to register a member or prospective member's shares. CA 2006, s 125 allows an aggrieved person to seek the remedy of rectification. Thus, if:

(a) the name of any person is, without sufficient cause, entered in or omitted from a company's register of members; or

(b) default is made or unnecessary delay takes place in entering on the register the fact of any person having ceased to be a member,

the person aggrieved, or any member of the company, or the company, may apply to the court for rectification of the register: CA 2006, s 125(1).

The court may refuse the application, or may order rectification of the register and payment by the company of any damages sustained by any party aggrieved: CA 2006, s 125(2).

10.53 On such an application the court may decide any question relating to the title of a person who is a party to the application to have his name entered in or omitted from the register, whether the question arises between members or alleged members, or between members or alleged members on the one hand and the company on the other hand, and generally may decide any question necessary or expedient to be decided for rectification of the register: CA 2006, s 125(3).

In the case of a company required by CA 2006 to send a list of its members to the registrar of companies, the court, when making an order for rectification of the register, shall by its order direct notice of the rectification to be given to the registrar: CA 2006, s 125(4).

Section 125 appears to be restricted to rectification of a name or that a person has ceased to become a member. It does not, however, address errors concerning a person's shareholding or share interest in the company.

Rectification by court may allow correction of errors concerning a person's shareholding

This issue came before the court in *Re Transatlantic Life Assurance Co* [1980] 1 WLR 79, where there was an error in the member's shareholding. The issue was whether such error could be rectified under CA 2006, s 125. Slade J decided that rectification was possible because the wording of CA 2006, s 125 was wide enough in its terms to empower the court to order the rectification of a company's register by deleting a reference to some only of a registered shareholder's shares. The section could still operate even though the proposed rectification did not involve the entire deletion of the name of the registered holder as a member of the company concerned.

10.54 On occasions the court has ordered rectification in the following circumstances:

- where there had been no allotment of shares: *Re Homer District Consolidated Gold Mines ex parte Smith* (1888) 39 ChD 546 (per North J); and *Re Portuguese Consolidated Copper Mines Ltd* (1889) 42 ChD 160; or
- on an irregular allotment of shares.

It may be possible to apply the common law concept of mistake in order to allow rectification of the register of members

In *Re Cleveland Trust plc* [1991] BCLC 424, bonus shares had mistakenly been allotted by the company. The court applied the common law concept of mistake as a justification for rectification of the register applying the principles set out by Lord Atkin in *Bell v Lever Bros* [1932] AC 161 where he stated:

> '… the rules of law dealing with the effect of mistake on contract appear to be established with reasonable clearness. If mistake operates at all it operates so as to negative or in some cases to nullify consent. The parties may be mistaken in the identity of the contracting parties, or in the existence of the subject-matter of the contract at the date of the contract, or in the quality of the subject-matter of the contract. These mistakes may be by one party, or by both, and the legal effect may depend upon the class of mistake above mentioned.'

On a further elaboration of the principle of mistake, Steyn J in *Associated Japanese Bank (International) Ltd v Credit du Nord SA* [1988] 3 All ER 902 at 912–913, [1989] 1 WLR 255 at 268 stated:

> 'The first imperative must be that the law ought to uphold rather than destroy apparent contracts. Second, the common law rules as to a mistake regarding the quality of the subject matter, like the common law rules regarding commercial frustration, are designed to cope with the impact of unexpected and wholly exceptional circumstances on apparent contracts. Third, such a mistake in order to attract legal consequences must substantially be shared by both parties, and must relate to facts as they existed at the time the contract was made. Fourth, and this is the point established by *Bell v Lever Bros Ltd* [1932] AC 161, [1931] All ER Rep 1, the mistake must render the subject matter of the contract essentially and radically different from the subject matter which the parties believed to exist.'

It would therefore appear that on occasions, the court may use the principle of mistake to justify rectification under CA 2006, s 125.

See also: *Welch v Bank of England* [1955] 1 All ER 811; *Re New Cedos Engineering Co Ltd* [1994] 1 BCLC 797; *International Credit and Investment Co (Overseas) Ltd v Adham* [1994] 1 BCLC 66.

The power given to the court to order rectification of the register of members may apply retrospectively

In *Re Sussex Brick Co* [1904] 1 Ch 598, the Court of Appeal stated that the power given to the court by s 125 of CA 2006 of rectifying the register of members of a limited company was exercisable in any of the cases mentioned namely under s 125(1)(a) and (b) and, whether a company was in liquidation or not.

In ordering rectification of the register under s 125 of CA 2006, whether the company is in liquidation or not, the court had power, in a proper case, to fix a particular date at which the registration would become operative, even to the extent of making it retrospective; but subject, if necessary, to conditions protecting the rights of third persons.

See too *Barbor v Middleton* 1988 SLT 288.

10.55 In some cases, the court has refused rectification of the register where a mistake is involved.

Where a large group of shareholders is involved, the concept of mistake may not be sufficient to order rectification of the register of members

In *Re Thundercrest Ltd* [1995] 1 BCLC 117, the court ordered a rectification of the register by cancellation of the allotment to two of the shareholders. In his judgment, Baker J referred to the concept of mistake particularly where large groups of shareholders were involved, which may make rectification of the register difficult:

> 'One can see in the case of a large allotment the grave difficulties of undoing an allotment of shares where third party rights have become involved. If some mistake has occurred in allotting the shares among a group of shareholders when some have paid their money, it may well be that the allotment cannot be undone and the register cannot be rectified where those rights have accrued. Hence the person who has suffered an injury or wrong because of the mishandling of the allotment is left with a remedy of compensation or damages. One can see the sense of all that. But, in my judgment, there is nothing to prevent the setting aside of allotments to directors in their own favour, the directors themselves being responsible for managing the allotments. In appropriate circumstances it would be possible to rectify by removing a name from

the register. Otherwise directors might be taking advantage of their own wrong. Therefore, I reject the submission that the proceedings are misconceived, having been brought by way of originating motion but that does not mean to say that they are bound to succeed. We have to see whether there should be some degree of rectification of the register in the particular circumstances of this case, and that in turn depends on whether the supplementary allotment was valid.'

The order for rectification is a discretionary one and the court will consider all appropriate circumstances

In *Re Piccadilly Radio plc* [1989] BCLC 683, the Independent Broadcasting Authority's consent was required to transfer shares, but consent was not obtained by a radio company and shares were transferred in breach of the company's articles of association. Some of the company's shareholders sought to prevent certain proposals being agreed at an EGM and brought an action for rectification of the register by deleting the transferees' names and substituting the existing transferor. According to Millett J, although there had been a breach of the articles of association, there would not be an order for rectification for the following reasons:

- the order for rectification was discretionary – it was not automatic;
- the court must consider the circumstances in which and the purpose for which the relief is sought;
- the applicants had no interest in the shares;
- the applicants were not requiring their own names to be restored on the register;
- the transferor had not sought rectification; and
- they were searching for a means to disenfranchise the expected opposition to their offer, and they seized on a breach of the articles which did not endanger the licence because of a failure to obtain the IBA's consent of which the IBA itself had not complained.

Trusts not to be entered on register

10.56 No notice of any trust, expressed, implied or constructive, shall be entered on the register of members of a company registered in England and Wales or Northern Ireland, or be receivable by the registrar: CA 2006, s 126.

Register to be evidence

10.57 The register of members is *prima facie* evidence of any matters which are by CA 2006 directed or authorised to be inserted in it, except for any matters of which the central register is prima facie evidence by virtue of s 128H: CA 2006, s 127 (as inserted by SBEEA 2015, Sch 5, Pt 2). See *Reese River Silver Mining Co v Smith* (1869) LR 4 HL 64; *Re Baku Consolidated Oilfields Ltd* (1993) *The Times*, 7 July; and *Re Briton Medical and General Life Association* (1888) 39 Ch D 61.

Time limit for claims arising from entry in register

10.58 Any liability incurred by a company:

(a) from the making or deletion of an entry in the register of members; or

(b) from a failure to make or delete any such entry,

is not enforceable more than ten years after the date on which the entry was made or deleted or, as the case may be, the failure first occurred: CA 2006, s 128(1).

This is without prejudice to any lesser period of limitation (and, in Scotland, to any rule that the obligation giving rise to the liability prescribes before the expiry of that period): CA 2006, s 128(2).

Overseas branch registers

10.59 A company having a share capital may, if it transacts business in a country or territory to which Chapter 3 of Part 8 of CA 2006 applies, cause to be kept there a branch register of members resident there (an 'overseas branch register'): CA 2006, s 129(1).

Chapter 3 applies to:

(a) any part of Her Majesty's dominions outside the UK, the Channel Islands and the Isle of Man; and

(b) the countries or territories listed below: CA 2006, s 129(2):

Bangladesh	Malaysia
Cyprus	Malta
Dominica	Nigeria
The Gambia	Pakistan
Ghana	Seychelles
Guyana	Sierra Leone
The Hong Kong Special Administrative Region of the People's Republic of China	Singapore
India	South Africa
Ireland	Sri Lanka
Kenya	Swaziland
Kiribati	Trinidad and Tobago
Lesotho	Uganda
Malawi	Zimbabwe

10.60 The Secretary of State may make provision by regulations as to the circumstances in which a company is to be regarded as keeping a register in a particular country or territory: CA 2006, s 129(3).

Any references:

(a) in any Act or instrument (including, in particular, a company's articles) to a dominion register; or

(b) in articles registered before 1 November 1929 to a colonial register,

are to be read (unless the context otherwise requires) as a reference to an overseas branch register kept under this section: CA 2006, s 129(5).

Notice of opening of overseas branch register

10.61 A company that begins to keep an overseas branch register must give notice to the registrar within 14 days of doing so, stating the country or territory in which the register is kept: CA 2006, s 130(1).

If default is made in complying with s 130(1), an offence is committed by:

(a) the company; and

(b) every officer of the company who is in default: CA 2006, s 130(2).

A person guilty of an offence under s 130(2) is liable, on summary conviction, to a fine not exceeding level 3 on the standard scale and, for continued contravention, a daily default fine not exceeding one-tenth of level 3 on the standard scale: CA 2006, s 130(3).

Keeping of overseas branch register

10.62 An overseas branch register is regarded as part of the company's register of members ('the main register'): CA 2006, s 131(1).

The Secretary of State may make provision by regulations modifying any provision of Chapter 2 (register of members), as it applies in relation to an overseas branch register: CA 2006, s 131(2).

Subject to the provisions of the Companies Act 2006, a company may by its articles make such provision as it thinks fit as to the keeping of overseas branch registers: CA 2006, s 131(4).

Register or duplicate to be kept available for inspection in the UK

10.63 A company that keeps an overseas branch register must keep available for inspection:

(a) the register; or

(b) a duplicate of the register duly entered up from time to time,

at the place in the UK where the company's main register is kept available for inspection: CA 2006, s 132(1).

10.64 Any such duplicate is treated for all purposes of the Act as part of the main register: CA 2006, s 132(2).

If default is made in complying with s 132(1), an offence is committed by:

(a) the company; and

(b) every officer of the company who is in default: CA 2006, s 132(3).

A person guilty of an offence under s 132(3) is liable, on summary conviction, to a fine not exceeding level 3 on the standard scale and, for continued contravention, a daily default fine not exceeding one-tenth of level 3 on the standard scale: CA 2006, s 132(4).

Transactions in shares registered in overseas branch register

10.65 Shares registered in an overseas branch register must be distinguished from those registered in the main register: CA 2006, s 133(1). No transaction with respect to shares registered in an overseas branch register may be registered in any other register: CA 2006, s 133(2).

An instrument of transfer of a share registered in an overseas branch register:

(a) is regarded as a transfer of property situated outside the UK; and

(b) unless executed in a part of the UK, is exempt from stamp duty: CA 2006, s 133(3).

Jurisdiction of local courts

10.66 A competent court in a country or territory where an overseas branch register is kept may exercise the same jurisdiction as is exercisable by a court in the UK:

(a) to rectify the register (see s 125); or

(b) in relation to a request for inspection or a copy of the register (see CA 2006, s 117): CA 2006, s 134(1).

10.67 The offences:

(a) of refusing inspection or failing to provide a copy of the register (see CA 2006, s 118); and

(b) of making a false, misleading or deceptive statement in a request for inspection or a copy (see CA 2006, s 119),

may be prosecuted summarily before any tribunal having summary criminal jurisdiction in the country or territory where the register is kept: CA 2006, s 134(2).

Section 134 extends only to those countries and territories to which paragraph 3 of Schedule 14 to the Companies Act 1985 (c 6) (which made similar provision) extended immediately before the coming into force of Chapter 3: CA 2006, s 134(3).

Discontinuance of overseas branch register

10.68 A company may discontinue an overseas branch register: CA 2006, s 135(1). If it does so, all the entries in that register must be transferred:

(a) to some other overseas branch register kept in the same country or territory; or

(b) to the main register: CA 2006, s 135(2).

The company must give notice to the registrar within 14 days of the discontinuance: CA 2006, s 135(3).

10.69 If default is made in complying with CA 2006, s 135(3), an offence will be committed by:

(a) the company; and

(b) every officer of the company who is in default: CA 2006, s 135(4).

A person guilty of an offence under this provision will be liable on summary conviction to a fine not exceeding level 3 on the standard scale and, for continued contravention, a daily default fine not exceeding one-tenth of level 3 on the standard scale: CA 2006, s 135(5).

Prohibition on subsidiary being a member of its holding company

10.70 Except as provided by Chapter 3 of Part 8 of CA 2006:

(a) a body corporate cannot be a member of a company that is its holding company; and

(b) any allotment or transfer of shares in a company to its subsidiary is void: CA 2006, s 136(1).

The exceptions are provided for in:

- CA 2006, s 138 (subsidiary acting as personal representative or trustee); and
- CA 2006, s 141 (subsidiary acting as authorised dealer in securities): CA 2006, s 136(2).

Shares acquired before prohibition became applicable

10.71 Where a body corporate became a holder of shares in a company:

(a) before the relevant date; or

(b) on or after that date and before the commencement of this chapter of CA 2006 in circumstances in which the prohibition in s 23(1) of the Companies Act 1985 or art 33(1) of the Companies (Northern Ireland) Order 1986 (SI 1986 No 1032 (NI 6)) (or any corresponding earlier enactment), as it then had effect, did not apply; or

(c) on or after the commencement of this chapter of the Act in circumstances in which the prohibition in s 136 did not apply, it may continue to be a member of the company: CA 2006, s 137(1).

10.72 The relevant date for the purposes of subs (1)(a) is:

(a) 1 July 1948 in the case of a company registered in Great Britain; and

(b) 1 April 1961 in the case of a company registered in Northern Ireland: CA 2006, s 137(2).

As long as it is permitted to continue as a member of a company by virtue of s 137, an allotment to it of fully paid shares may be validly made by way of capitalisation of reserves of the company: CA 2006, s 137(3).

But, as long as the prohibition in CA 2006, s 136 would (apart from this section) apply, it has no right to vote in respect of the shares mentioned in CA 2006, s 137(1), or any shares allotted as mentioned in CA 2006, s 137(3) on a written resolution or at meetings of the company or of any class of its members: CA 2006, s 137(4).

Subsidiary acting as personal representative or trustee

10.73 The prohibition in CA 2006, s 136 (prohibition on subsidiary being a member of its holding company) does not apply where the subsidiary is concerned only:

(a) as personal representative; or

(b) as trustee,

unless, in the latter case, the holding company or a subsidiary of it is beneficially interested under the trust: CA 2006, s 138(1).

10.74 For the purpose of ascertaining whether the holding company or a subsidiary is so interested, there shall be disregarded:

(a) any interest held only by way of security for the purposes of a transaction entered into by the holding company or subsidiary in the ordinary course of a business that includes the lending of money;

(b) any interest within:

  (i) CA 2006, s 139 (interests to be disregarded: residual interest under pension scheme or employees' share scheme); or

  (ii) CA 2006, s 140 (interests to be disregarded: employer's rights of recovery under pension scheme or employees' share scheme);

(c) any rights that the company or subsidiary has in its capacity as trustee, including in particular:

  (i) any right to recover its expenses or be remunerated out of the trust property; and

  (ii) any right to be indemnified out of the trust property for any liability incurred by reason of any act or omission in the performance of its duties as trustee: CA 2006, s 138(2).

Interests to be disregarded: residual interest under pension scheme or employees' share scheme

10.75 Where shares in a company are held on trust for the purposes of a pension scheme or employees' share scheme, there shall be disregarded for the purposes of s 138 any residual interest that has not vested in possession: CA 2006, s 139(1).

A 'residual interest' means a right of the company or subsidiary ('the residual beneficiary') to receive any of the trust property in the event of:

(a) all the liabilities arising under the scheme having been satisfied or provided for; or

(b) the residual beneficiary ceasing to participate in the scheme; or

(c) the trust property at any time exceeding what is necessary for satisfying the liabilities arising or expected to arise under the scheme: CA 2006, s 139(2).

10.76 In s 139(2):

(a) the reference to a right includes a right dependent on the exercise of a discretion vested by the scheme in the trustee or another person; and

(b) the reference to liabilities arising under a scheme includes liabilities that have resulted, or may result, from the exercise of any such discretion: CA 2006, s 139(3).

10.77 For the purposes of s 139, a residual interest vests in possession:

(a) in a case within s 139(2)(a), on the occurrence of the event mentioned there (whether or not the amount of the property receivable pursuant to the right is ascertained);

(b) in a case within s 139(2)(b) or (c), when the residual beneficiary becomes entitled to require the trustee to transfer to him any of the property receivable pursuant to the right: CA 2006, s 139(4).

The term 'pension scheme' means a scheme for the provision of benefits consisting of or including relevant benefits for or in respect of employees or former employees: CA 2006, s 139(5).

10.78 In s 139(5):

(a) 'relevant benefits' means any pension, lump sum, gratuity or other like benefit given or to be given on retirement or on death or in anticipation of retirement or, in connection with past service, after retirement or death; and

(b) 'employee' shall be read as if a director of a company were employed by it: CA 2006, s 139(6).

Interests to be disregarded: employer's rights of recovery under pension scheme or employees' share scheme

10.79 Where shares in a company are held on trust for the purposes of a pension scheme or employees' share scheme, there shall be disregarded for the purposes of s 138, any charge or lien on, or set-off against, any benefit or other right or interest under the scheme for the purpose of enabling the employer or former employer of a member of the scheme to obtain the discharge of a monetary obligation due to him from the member: CA 2006, s 140(1).

10.80 In the case of a trust for the purposes of a pension scheme there shall also be disregarded any right to receive from the trustee of the scheme, or as trustee of the scheme to retain, an amount that can be recovered or retained, under s 61 of the Pension Schemes Act 1993 (c 48) or s 57 of the Pension Schemes (Northern Ireland) Act 1993 (c 49) (deduction of contributions equivalent premium from refund of scheme contributions) or otherwise, as reimbursement or partial reimbursement for any contributions equivalent premium paid in connection with the scheme under Part 3 of that Act: CA 2006, s 140(2).

10.81 The term 'pension scheme' means a scheme for the provision of benefits consisting of or including relevant benefits for or in respect of employees or former employees. 'Relevant benefits' here means any pension, lump sum, gratuity or other like benefit given or to be given on retirement or on death or in anticipation of retirement or, in connection with past service, after retirement or death: CA 2006, s 140(3).

The terms 'employer' and 'employee' should be read as if a director of a company were employed by it: CA 2006, s 140(4).

Subsidiary acting as authorised dealer in securities

10.82 The prohibition in s 136 (prohibition on subsidiary being a member of its holding company) does not apply where the shares are held by the subsidiary in the ordinary course of its business as an intermediary: CA 2006, s 141(1).

For this purpose a person is an intermediary if he:

(a) carries on a bona fide business of dealing in securities;

(b) is a member of, or has access to, a regulated market; and

(c) does not carry on an excluded business: CA 2006, s 141(2).

10.83 The following are excluded businesses:

(a) a business that consists wholly or mainly in the making or managing of investments;

(b) a business that consists wholly or mainly in, or is carried on wholly or mainly for the purposes of, providing services to persons who are connected with the person carrying on the business;

(c) a business that consists in insurance business;

(d) a business that consists in managing or acting as trustee in relation to a pension scheme, or that is carried on by the manager or trustee of such a scheme in connection with or for the purposes of the scheme; and

(e) a business that consists in operating or acting as trustee in relation to a collective investment scheme, or that is carried on by the operator or trustee of such a scheme in connection with and for the purposes of the scheme: CA 2006, s 141(3).

10.84 For the purposes of s 141:

(a) the question whether a person is connected with another must be determined in accordance with s 1122 of the Corporation Tax Act 2010;

(b) 'collective investment scheme' has the meaning given in s 235 of the Financial Services and Markets Act 2000 (c 8);

(c) 'insurance business' means business that consists in the effecting or carrying out of contracts of insurance;

(d) 'securities' includes:

  (i) options;

  (ii) futures; and

  (iii) contracts for differences,

  and rights or interests in those investments;

(e) 'trustee' and 'the operator' in relation to a collective investment scheme shall be construed in accordance with s 237(2) of the Financial Services and Markets Act 2000 (c 8): CA 2006, s 141(4).

Expressions used in s 141 that are also used in the provisions regulating activities under the Financial Services and Markets Act 2000 have the same meaning here as they do in those provisions: CA 2006, s 141(5).

See s 22 of that Act, orders made under that section and Schedule 2 to that Act.

Protection of third parties in other cases where subsidiary acting as dealer in securities

10.85 Section 142 of CA 2006 applies where:

(a) a subsidiary that is a dealer in securities has purportedly acquired shares in its holding company in contravention of the prohibition in s 136, and

(b) a person acting in good faith has agreed, for value and without notice of the contravention, to acquire shares in the holding company:

  (i) from the subsidiary; or

  (ii) from someone who has purportedly acquired the shares after their disposal by the subsidiary: CA 2006, s 142(1).

A transfer to that person of the shares mentioned in subs (1)(a) has the same effect as it would have had if their original acquisition by the subsidiary had not been in contravention of the prohibition: CA 2006, s 142(2).

Application of provisions to companies not limited by shares

10.86 In relation to a company other than a company limited by shares, the references in Chapter 3 of Part 8 of CA 2006 to shares should be read as references to the interest of its members as such, whatever the form of that interest: CA 2006, s 143.

Application of provisions to nominees

10.87 The provisions of Chapter 3, Part 8 of CA 2006 apply to a nominee acting on behalf of a subsidiary as to the subsidiary itself: CA 2006, s 144.

Exercise of members' rights

10.88 Part 9 of CA 2006 is concerned with the exercise of members' rights. The provisions in this part of the Act are designed to make it easier for investors to exercise their governance rights fully and responsibly and allow indirect investors to exercise their governance rights such as information rights through the registered member.

Effect of provisions of articles as to enjoyment or exercise of members' rights

10.89 Section 145 applies where provision is made by a company's articles enabling a member to nominate another person or persons as entitled to enjoy or exercise all or any specified rights of the member in relation to the company: CA 2006, s 145(1).

So far as is necessary to give effect to that provision, anything required or authorised by any provision of the Companies Acts to be done by or in relation to the member shall instead be done, or (as the case may be) may instead be done, by or in relation to the nominated person (or each of them) as if he were a member of the company: CA 2006, s 145(2). This applies, in particular, to the rights conferred by:

(a) ss 291 and 293 (right to be sent proposed written resolution);

(b) s 292 (right to require circulation of written resolution);

(c) s 303 (right to require directors to call general meeting);

(d) s 310 (right to notice of general meetings);

(e) s 314 (right to require circulation of a statement);

(ea) s 319A (right to ask question at meeting of traded company) (as inserted by the Companies (Shareholders' Rights) Regulations 2009, SI 2009/1632, reg 12(2));

(f) s 324 (right to appoint proxy to act at meeting);

(g) s 338 (right to require circulation of resolution for AGM of public company); and

(ga) s 338A (traded companies: members' power to include matters in business dealt with at AGM) (as inserted by the Companies (Shareholders' Rights) Regulations 2009, SI 2009/1632, reg 17(2) (with application as stated in reg 1(2)).

(h) s 423 (right to be sent a copy of annual accounts and reports): CA 2006, s 145(3).

10.90 This section and any such provision as are mentioned in s 145(1):

(a) do not confer rights enforceable against the company by anyone other than the member, and

(b) do not affect the requirements for an effective transfer or other disposition of the whole or part of a member's interest in the company: CA 2006, s 145(4).

Traded companies: nomination of persons to enjoy information rights

10.91 Section 146 of CA 2006 applies to a company whose shares are admitted to trading on a regulated market: CA 2006, s 146(1).

A member of such a company who holds shares on behalf of another person may nominate that person to enjoy information rights: CA 2006, s 146(2).

The term 'information rights' means:

(a) the right to receive a copy of all communications that the company sends to its members generally or to any class of its members that includes the person making the nomination; and

(b) the rights conferred by:

  (i) ss 431 or 432 (right to require copies of accounts and reports); and

  (ii) s 1145 (right to require hard copy version of document or information provided in another form): CA 2006, s 146(3).

10.92 The reference in s 146(3)(a) to communications that a company sends to its members generally includes the company's annual accounts and reports.

For the application of s 426 (option to provide summary financial statement) in relation to a person nominated to enjoy information rights, see subs (5) of that section: CA 2006, s 146(4).

A company need not act on a nomination purporting to relate to certain information rights only: CA 2006, s 146(5).

Information rights: form in which copies to be provided

10.93 Section 147 of CA 2006 applies as regards the form in which copies are to be provided to a person nominated under s 146 (nomination of person to enjoy information rights): CA 2006, s 147(1).

If the person to be nominated wishes to receive hard copy communications, he must:

(a) request the person making the nomination to notify the company of that fact; and

(b) provide an address to which such copies may be sent.

This must be done before the nomination is made: CA 2006, s 147(2).

10.94 If, having received such a request, the person making the nomination:

(a) notifies the company that the nominated person wishes to receive hard copy communications; and

(b) provides the company with that address,

the right of the nominated person is to receive hard copy communications accordingly: CA 2006, s 147(3).

This is subject to the provisions of Parts 3 and 4 of Schedule 5 of CA 2006 (communications by company) under which the company may take steps to enable it to communicate in electronic form or by means of a website: CA 2006, s 147(4).

10.95 If no such notification is given (or no address is provided), the nominated person is taken to have agreed that documents or information may be sent or supplied to him by the company by means of a website: CA 2006, s 147(5).

That agreement:

(a) may be revoked by the nominated person; and

(b) does not affect his right under s 1145 to require a hard copy version of a document or information provided in any other form: CA 2006, s 147(6).

Termination or suspension of nomination

10.96 The following provisions have effect in relation to a nomination under s 146 (nomination of person to enjoy information rights): CA 2006, s 148(1).

The nomination may be terminated at the request of the member or of the nominated person: CA 2006, s 148(2).

The nomination ceases to have effect on the occurrence in relation to the member or the nominated person of any of the following:

(a) in the case of an individual, death or bankruptcy;

(b) in the case of a body corporate, dissolution or the making of an order for the winding up of the body otherwise than for the purposes of reconstruction: CA 2006, s 148(3).

10.97 In s 148(3):

(a) the reference to bankruptcy includes:

  (i) the sequestration of a person's estate; and

  (ii) a person's estate being the subject of a protected trust deed (within the meaning of the Bankruptcy (Scotland) Act 1985 (c 66)); and

(b) the reference to the making of an order for winding up is to:

  (i) the making of such an order under the Insolvency Act 1986 (c 45) or the Insolvency (Northern Ireland) Order 1989, SI 1989/2405 (NI 19); or

  (ii) any corresponding proceeding under the law of a country or territory outside the UK: CA 2006, s 148(4).

The effect of any nominations made by a member is suspended at any time when there are more nominated persons than the member has shares in the company: CA 2006, s 148(5).

10.98 Where:

(a) the member holds different classes of shares with different information rights; and

(b) there are more nominated persons than he has shares conferring a particular right,

the effect of any nominations made by him is suspended to the extent that they confer that right: CA 2006, s 148(6).

10.99 Where the company:

(a) enquires of a nominated person whether he wishes to retain information rights, and

(b) does not receive a response within the period of 28 days beginning with the date on which the company's enquiry was sent,

the nomination ceases to have effect at the end of that period.

Such an enquiry is not to be made of a person more than once in any 12-month period: CA 2006, s 148(7).

The termination or suspension of a nomination means that the company is not required to act on it.

It does not prevent the company from continuing to do so, to such extent or for such period as it thinks fit: CA 2006, s 148(8).

Information as to possible rights in relation to voting

10.100 Section 149 applies where a company sends a copy of a notice of a meeting to a person nominated under s 146 of CA 2006 (nomination of person to enjoy information rights): CA 2006, s 149(1).

The copy of the notice must be accompanied by a statement that:

(a) he may have a right under an agreement between him and the member by whom he was nominated to be appointed, or to have someone else appointed, as a proxy for the meeting; and

(b) if he has no such right or does not wish to exercise it, he may have a right under such an agreement to give instructions to the member as to the exercise of voting rights: CA 2006, s 149(2).

10.101 Section 325 of CA 2006 (notice of meeting to contain statement of member's rights in relation to appointment of proxy) does not apply to the copy, and the company must either:

(a) omit the notice required by that section; or

(b) include it, but state that it does not apply to the nominated person: CA 2006, s 149(3).

Information rights: status of rights

10.102 Section 150 has effect as regards the rights conferred by a nomination under s 146 (nomination of person to enjoy information rights): CA 2006, s 150(1).

Enjoyment by the nominated person of the rights conferred by the nomination is enforceable against the company by the member as if they were rights conferred by the company's articles: CA 2006, s 150(2).

Any enactment and any provision of the company's articles having effect in relation to communications with members has a corresponding effect (subject to any necessary adaptations) in relation to communications with the nominated person: CA 2006, s 150(3).

In particular:

(a) where under any enactment, or any provision of the company's articles, the members of a company entitled to receive a document or information are determined as at a date or time before it is sent or supplied, the company need not send or supply it to a nominated person:

 (i) whose nomination was received by the company after that date or time; or

 (ii) if that date or time falls in a period of suspension of his nomination; and

(b) where under any enactment, or any provision of the company's articles, the right of a member to receive a document or information depends on the company having a current address for him, the same applies to any person nominated by him: CA 2006, s 150(4).

10.103 The rights conferred by the nomination:

(a) are in addition to the rights of the member himself; and

(b) do not affect any rights exercisable by virtue of any such provision as is mentioned in s 145 (provisions of company's articles as to enjoyment or exercise of members' rights): CA 2006, s 150(5).

A failure to give effect to the rights conferred by the nomination does not affect the validity of anything done by or on behalf of the company: CA 2006, s 150(6).

10.104 References in s 150 to the rights conferred by the nomination are to:

(a) the rights referred to in s 146(3) (information rights); and

(b) where applicable, the rights conferred by ss 147(3) (right to hard copy communications) and 149 (information as to possible voting rights): CA 2006, s 150(7).

Information rights: power to amend

10.105 The Secretary of State may by regulations amend the provisions of ss 146–150 (information rights) so as to:

(a) extend or restrict the classes of companies to which s 146 applies;

(b) make other provision as to the circumstances in which a nomination may be made under that section; or

(c) extend or restrict the rights conferred by such a nomination: CA 2006, s 151(1).

The regulations may make such consequential modifications of any other provisions of this part of the Act, or of any other enactment, as appear to the Secretary of State to be necessary: CA 2006, s 151(2).

Exercise of rights where shares held on behalf of others: exercise in different ways

10.106 Where a member holds shares in a company on behalf of more than one person:

(a) rights attached to the shares; and

(b) rights under any enactment exercisable by virtue of holding the shares,

need not all be exercised, and if exercised, need not all be exercised in the same way: CA 2006, s 152(1).

A member who exercises such rights but does not exercise all his rights, must inform the company as to the extent to which he is exercising the rights: CA 2006, s 152(2).

A member who exercises such rights in different ways must inform the company of the ways in which he is exercising them and the extent to which they are exercised in each way: CA 2006, s 152(3).

10.107 If a member exercises such rights without informing the company:

(a) that he is not exercising all his rights; or

(b) that he is exercising his rights in different ways,

the company is entitled to assume that he is exercising all his rights and is exercising them in the same way: CA 2006, s 152(4).

Exercise of rights where shares held on behalf of others: members' requests

10.108 Section 153 applies for the purposes of:

(a) s 314 (power to require circulation of statement);

(b) s 338 (public companies: power to require circulation of resolution for AGM);

(ba) s 338A (traded companies: members' power to include matters in business dealt with at AGM);

(c) s 342 (power to require independent report on poll); and

(d) s 527 (power to require website publication of audit concerns): CA 2006, s 153(1).

10.109 A company is required to act under any of those sections if it receives a request in relation to which the following conditions are met:

(a) it is made by at least 100 persons;

(b) it is authenticated by all the persons making it;

(c) in the case of any of those persons who is not a member of the company, it is accompanied by a statement:

  (i) of the full name and address of a person ('the member') who is a member of the company and holds shares on behalf of that person;

  (ii) that the member is holding those shares on behalf of that person in the course of a business;

  (iii) of the number of shares in the company that the member holds on behalf of that person;

  (iv) of the total amount paid up on those shares;

  (v) that those shares are not held on behalf of anyone else or, if they are, that the other person or persons are not among the other persons making the request;

  (vi) that some or all of those shares confer voting rights that are relevant for the purposes of making a request under the section in question; and

  (vii) that the person has the right to instruct the member how to exercise those rights;

(d) in the case of any of those persons who is a member of the company, it is accompanied by a statement:

  (i) that he holds shares otherwise than on behalf of another person; or

  (ii) that he holds shares on behalf of one or more other persons but those persons are not among the other persons making the request;

(e) it is accompanied by such evidence as the company may reasonably require of the matters mentioned in paragraph (c) and (d);

(f) the total amount of the sums paid up on:

  (i) shares held as mentioned in paragraph (c); and

  (ii) shares held as mentioned in paragraph (d);

  divided by the number of persons making the request, is not less than £100;

(g) the request complies with any other requirements of the section in question as to contents, timing and otherwise: CA 2006, s 153(2).

Checklist:

10.110 *This checklist sets out some of the key issues concerning a member of a company and exercise of some of the rights in the capacity of a member.*

No	Issue	Reference
1	A 'member' refers to a person (whether natural or legal) who holds shares in a company	CA 2006, Pt 8, Ch 1

No	Issue	Reference
2	The subscribers of a company's memorandum are deemed to have agreed to become members of the company, and on its registration become members and must be entered as such in its register of members	CA 2006, s 273
3	The agreement to become a member requires assent and does not require a bilateral agreement between the company and the prospective member	*Re Nuneaton Borough Association Football Club Limited* [1989] BCLC 454
4	It was a fundamental principle of UK company law – reflected in the definition of 'member' in s 112 – that a member of a company was the person entered on the register as a member, to the exclusion of any other person	*Enviroco Ltd v Farstad Supply A/S* [2011] 2 BCLC 165
5	A registration of a member under a false or fictitious name renders that person liable to contribution up to the amount subscribed	*Re Hercules Insurance Co, Pugh and Sharman's Case* (1872) LR 13 Eq 566
6	An entry of a member in the register of members may by itself not be sufficient and may require other actions to become registered as a member	*POW Services Ltd v Clare* [1995] 2 BCLC 435
7	Every company must keep a register of its members	CA 2006, s 113
8	A company's register of members must be kept available for inspection	CA 2006, s 114
9	Every company having more than 50 members must keep an index of the names of the members of the company, unless the register of members is in such a form as to constitute in itself an index	CA 2006, s 115
10	The register and the index of members' names must be open to the inspection: (a) of any member of the company without charge; and (b) of any other person on payment of such fee as may be prescribed:	CA 2006, s 116 CA 2006, s 125
11	The court has power to rectify the register of members	*Re Transatlantic Life Assurance Co* [1980] 1 WLR 79
12	Rectification by court may allow correction of errors concerning a person's shareholding	*Re Cleveland Trust plc* [1991] BCLC
13	The power given to the court to order rectification of the register of members may apply retrospectively	*Re Sussex Brick Co* [1904] 1 Ch 598

No	Issue	Reference
14	The order for rectification is a discretionary one and the court will consider all appropriate circumstances	*Re Piccadilly Radio plc* [1989] BCLC 683
15	Consider option for private companies to keep information on central register instead of in the register of members	Chapter 2A of Part 8 CA 2006

Definitions

10.111

Insurance business: A business that consists in the effecting or carrying out of contracts of insurance: CA 2006, s 141(4).

Member: A person who has agreed to become a member of the company and is entered in the register of members.

Pension scheme: A scheme for the provision of benefits consisting of or including relevant benefits for or in respect of employees or former employees: CA 2006, s 139(5).

Relevant benefits: Any pension, lump sum, gratuity or other like benefit given or to be given on retirement or on death or in anticipation of retirement or, in connection with past service, after retirement or death: CA 2006, s 139(6).

Securities: Includes options, futures, and contracts for differences, and rights or interests in those investments: CA 2006, s 141(4).

11 Corporate governance and the Code

Contents

Introduction

Definition of corporate governance

11.1 The term 'corporate governance' can be described as the system by which companies are directed and controlled. Within the corporate governance system, the board of directors are responsible for the governance of their companies. The shareholders' role in the governance is to appoint the directors and the auditors and to satisfy themselves that an appropriate governance structure is in place. The responsibilities of the board include setting the company's strategic aims, providing the leadership to put them into effect, supervising the management of the business and reporting to shareholders on their stewardship. The board's actions are subject to laws, regulations and the shareholders in a general meeting.

As a system, corporate governance is concerned with the boards and key executives who control, manage and operate the company. These executives are driven by corporate values, corporate ethics, norms and beliefs, and manage the operational aspects of the company's daily interaction with its internal and external stakeholders. The corporate governance system also addresses how a board can add value to a company, ensuring that its long-term strategy is not only profit maximisation and long-term success, but also discharging its corporate social responsibilities towards wider stakeholders in society.

11.2 Corporate governance is also interrelated to corporate social responsibilities. Previously, in English company law, corporate bodies were usually perceived as inanimate objects, whose primary function was to earn profits in an impersonal way by providing services of a material nature to the community. Subsequently, however, the modern corporation began to be perceived as a private institution with public obligations. The traditional belief that corporations were solely profit maximisers was no longer sustainable. Corporations had 'souls'. The modern corporation was perceived as a 'caring corporation' discharging social as well as economic obligations in society. The rise of professional managers and directors within the corporation had symbolised a new 'managerial revolution' within the corporate governance system. Industrial leaders had often urged more participation by the business community to resolve some of the community's social problems. They believed that a company should be a good citizen and neighbour in society.

The debate on corporate governance is essentially concerned with the accountability, responsibilities and duties of directors within the corporation. It is also concerned with the role of shareholders in the system. The issues that need to be addressed in this regard are: Why have shareholders delegated their powers of management to directors? What role should shareholders play within the system? What are the duties and responsibilities of shareholders towards other potential claimants on the corporation? Is 'shareholder democracy' an effective mechanism to monitor the powers and duties of directors? These issues also have an impact on the wider community. Pressures from the community are now powerful forces which can require directors and shareholders to reflect on their policies before they are implemented. To this extent, the debate on corporate governance should be widened in scope. Corporate governance should also be perceived as a 'social contract' between the company and its wider constituencies which imposes on it a moral obligation to take account of the interests of its other 'stakeholders'.

Corporate governance is also concerned with the ethics, values and morals of a corporation and its directors. Do corporations care about their environment? Do corporations care about the atmosphere they pollute? Do corporations care about the adverse publicity they attract from various constituencies? Do corporations take account of the demands of consumer lobbyists? These are all issues of ethics and morals which must form part of corporate culture and corporate decision making.

11.3 An effective corporate governance system should provide mechanisms for regulating directors' duties to stop them from abusing their powers and to ensure that they act in the best interests of the company in its broad sense. There are various methods of regulating directors' duties. In English company law, this is achieved in a somewhat random fashion by employing the following control mechanisms:

(1) By legislation: under CA 2006, certain safeguards (eg unfair prejudicial conduct and the derivative action) exist for the protection of shareholders and creditors. The Insolvency Act 1986 provides further protection and safeguards for the company's creditors who invest in the company. Directors bear a high level of responsibility to the company's creditors to ensure that a company is not involved in fraudulent or wrongful trading.

(2) The application of other common law and fiduciary duties to directors that have not been codified under CA 2006 on the general duties of directors.

(3) Directors may also be subject to civil liability for breach of their fiduciary duties.

(4) Compliance with the UK Code of Corporate Governance. Companies are subject to the City Code on Takeovers and Mergers and SARs and the Listing Rules.

(5) Shareholders are given some rights to monitor directors' actions under the articles of association as well as some statutory rights under the Companies Act 2006.

(6) Auditors ensure that the risk of financial irregularities is minimised by auditing the company's accounts and ensuring that a company's accounts provide a 'true and fair view' of its financial position.

11.4 This chapter examines the corporate governance debate, particularly the concept of 'corporate governance' and its essential features. This is followed by an analysis of the growth and development of the concept in England. The legal aspects of the corporate governance debate are examined with particular reference to directors' duties and shareholders' rights to control the abuse of power by directors.

This chapter addresses the following:

- defining the concept of 'corporate governance';
- the development of corporate governance in England;
- the separation of ownership from control;
- the establishment of various committees on corporate governance;
- consideration of the UK Corporate Governance Code; and
- the Stewardship Code.

A brief overview of the development of corporate governance in the UK

11.5 The development of corporate governance in the UK owes its historical origins to a number of company law committees that were established to examine the efficiency, effectiveness, operational and functional aspects of corporate governance and how the system could be better improved to ensure more accountability and transparency by directors in managing the corporation as well as their dealings with shareholders.

This section briefly considers the key origins of corporate governance dating back to the 1990s and traces the developments over the years culminating in the publication of the Code on Corporate Governance in the United Kingdom.

The principle of profit maximisation

11.6 In England, the concept of corporate governance was largely entrenched in the traditional theory of the firm which advocated that the only objective of companies was to maximise profits with shareholders' welfare as its paramount consideration. This structure of corporate governance mandated directors to carry out the shareholders' directions. Directors were, therefore, perceived as agents for their shareholders.

Adam Smith, in *An Inquiry into the Causes of the Wealth of Nations* (first published 1776, published by The Modern Library in 1937), believed that individual entrepreneurs, who relied on their own efforts and market forces, would be led by an 'invisible hand' to achieve the rewards which the markets were prepared to offer. The success of the entrepreneur was conditional on risk taking. He was not complimentary to directors when he wrote:

> 'The directors of such companies, however, being the managers of other people's money than of their own, it cannot well be expected, that they should watch over it with the same anxious vigilance with which the partners in a private co-partnery frequently watch over their own ... Negligence and

> profusion, therefore, must always prevail more or less, in the management of the affairs of such a company.'

Smith also observed that directors:

> 'seldom pretend to understand anything of the business of the company; and when the spirit of faction happens not to avail among them, give themselves no trouble about it, but receive contentedly such half yearly or yearly dividend, as the directors think proper to make to them'.

English company law has clearly reinforced the profit maximisation principle within the corporate governance system:

Previous case law established the principle of profit maximisation by companies

In *North-West Transportation v Beatty* (1887) 12 App Cas 589, the claimant, Henry Beatty, sued the directors of the company and claimed an order to set aside a sale made to the company of his steamer *The United Empire*, which he had owned before she was sold. Sir Richard Baggallay stated that the resolution of a majority of the shareholders, duly adopted, upon any question coming under the pinnacle of a company's mandate, was binding upon the majority and consequently upon the company. Further, every shareholder had a right to vote on any such question, although he might have a personal interest in the subject matter opposed to, or different from, the general or particular interests of the company.

The rule in *North-West Transportation* seems to have gained solid ground in England as it is in conformity with the traditional notion on which English company law is based. It is not, therefore, surprising that initiatives for amending companies' legislation in England prior to 1980 were sporadic, unconstructed and akin to the traditional notion that social responsibilities must not enter the realm of the company's activities.

The separation of ownership from control

11.7 In the 1930s in the United States, Berle and Means, in *The Modern Corporation and Private Property,* highlighted the separation of ownership from control in large US companies. English company law similarly functions on the basis of a separation of ownership from control. The directors control the company and have been delegated the day-to-day functions and operation by the shareholders. The shareholders are the owners of the company and provide the financial capital to ensure the sustainability and survival of the company.

In 1945, the Cohen Committee was set up to consider whether company legislation needed to be amended to address corporate governance aspects, particularly with concern over lack of shareholder participation. It was satisfied that a large majority of limited companies, both public and private, were honestly and conscientiously managed and that the system of limited liability companies was beneficial to trade and industry. The Cohen Committee recommended disclosure of a company's activity. It emphasised the need for 'a wakening social consciousness'. The lack of active participation of shareholders within their corporations was highlighted by the Cohen Committee when it stated that:

> 'The illusory nature of the control theoretically exercised by shareholders over directors has been accentuated by the dispersion of capital among an increasing number of small shareholders who pay little attention to their investments, so long as satisfactory dividends are forthcoming, who lack sufficient time, money and experience to make full use of their rights as occasions arise and who are, in many cases, too numerous and too widely dispersed to be able to organise themselves.'

The Cohen Committee believed that the separation of ownership from control was largely responsible for the lack of shareholder participation in corporate affairs:

> 'The growth of investment trust companies and of unit trusts in recent years has tended to divorce the investor still further from the management of his investments. Executive power must inevitably be vested in the directors and is generally used to the advantage of the shareholders. There are, however, exceptional cases in which directors of companies abuse their power and it is, therefore, desirable to devise provisions which will make it difficult for directors to secure the hurried passage of controversial measures, and as far as possible, to encourage shareholders carefully to consider any proposals required by law to be put before them by the directors.'

The Cohen Committee that drew the attention of the business community in England to the need for a separation of ownership from control of a company. The directors were to be treated as mere managers of a company and they should manage in accordance with the policies adopted by the company's shareholders, although directors, as managers, should be required to advise their shareholders as to whether a particular investment or venture would be profitable and beneficial to their interests.

11.8 Reporting in 1962, the Jenkins Committee set out to consider, *inter alia*, '... in the light of modern conditions ... what should be the duties of directors and the rights of shareholders; and generally to recommend what changes in the law are desirable'. It recommended wider disclosure of information as a means of remedying abuse within a corporation. On the issue of corporate governance, the Jenkins Committee thought that the protection of shareholders, creditors, intending investors and those responsible for their management, should be subject to a considerable degree of statutory regulation and control. However, the Committee warned that:

> 'controls and regulations carried to excess may defeat their own object; and we share the views of the Greene and Cohen Committees as to the undesirability of imposing restrictions which would seriously hamper the activities of honest men in order to defeat an occasional wrongdoer, and the importance of not placing unreasonable fetters upon business which is conducted in an efficient and honest manner.'

The Committee considered proposals for giving shareholders closer control over their directors, to allow them a more 'effective voice' in the management of their company's business. In other words, according to the Committee, a separation of control from ownership would be essential for the general good of the company. The Jenkins Committee also addressed such issues as directors' duties and shareholder control within a corporation. It recognised that, although the Companies Act established certain duties for directors, a large part of them were still determined by case law. A number of proposals made by witnesses suggested that the directors' duties ought to be codified in a new Act. Some witnesses suggested that the law on directors' duties should be set out as simply as possible. The Committee felt that it would be impossible exhaustively to define the duties of directors.With specific reference to directors' powers and shareholders' control, the Jenkins Committee was of the view that, although the articles of association gave directors a wide degree of powers to manage a company's affairs, shareholders still had a reasonable degree of control. It stated that, unless the affairs of the company had gone badly wrong, there would seldom be any controversy from the shareholders. It may be deduced, therefore, that corporate governance is primarily concerned with keeping the shareholders content in terms of monetary returns – which, according to the Committee, is precisely what should be avoided.

The fact remains that it is the shareholders who may need directions from directors as to how the company's image and future profitability might be secured by being conscious of corporate social responsibilities. In other words, the Jenkins Committee was concerned with another issue, that is, whether shareholders who contribute to the equity of a company should really be involved in the management of a company; they can simply guide the managers where necessary, but the directors should perform their duties without being involved in the ownership of a company, as this would give rise to a conflict of interest. The Committee argued that if directors were to manage their company efficiently, they must, within broad limits, have a free hand to do what they may think best in the interests of the company.

The separation of ownership from control in some cases, has given rise to issues of the degree of control vested in directors and the powers of shareholders to restrain or control the exercise of directors' powers.

11.9 During the 19th century, the English courts considered directors as agents of the shareholders: the shareholders could give directions by an ordinary resolution which would be binding on the directors. This had the effect that directors' powers could be controlled and regulated from time to time as dictated by the shareholders. The shareholders reigned supreme. Two lines of authorities governed the principle that the courts would not interfere in the decisions of the shareholders. First, the courts could declare that that any breach of articles was a mere irregularity that could be cured by the shareholders: *MacDougall v Gardiner* (1875) 1 Ch D 13. Secondly, the courts considered that a breach of articles infringed the personal rights of shareholders: *Pender v Lushington* (1877) 6 Ch D 70.

Shareholders could mandate directors to act in a certain manner

In *Isle of Wight Railway v Tahourdin* (1883) 25 Ch D 320, a number of shareholders required the directors of a railway company to call a meeting of the company to appoint a committee to inquire into the working and general management of the company, and the means of reducing the working expenses, to empower such committee to consolidate offices, to remove any of the officers and appoint others, and to authorise and require the directors to carry out the recommendations of the committee. The requisitionists gave notice that they would not attend the meeting, as the notice did not provide for all their objects. Ultimately they did not attend, and they subsequently issued a notice calling a meeting for the purposes mentioned in their requisition. The directors brought an action in the name of the company to restrain the requisitionists from holding the meeting.

The Court of Appeal held that the requisitionists were entitled to hold a meeting under the terms of the requisition. The shareholders were entitled to intervene and interfere in the company's management if they believed that the course of action taken by directors was not for the company's benefit. According to Cotton LJ, although directors had wide powers of management, the powers could be constrained by the shareholders' residual authority at general meetings.

11.10 The decision of the Court of Appeal in the *Tahourdin* case demonstrated that shareholder power reigned supreme within the corporate decision making functions. The shareholders were considered as active participants within the company with powers to mandate directors to function in a particular manner. It also signalled the court's desire not to interfere in the internal management of the company's affairs unless required to do so in the company's interests. The court accepted that the shareholders' authority was final, ultimate and binding on the directors.

Subsequently, some judicial attitudes considered that the articles of association governed the powers vested in directors and the shareholders. Where the articles provided for directors to manage the company's affairs, the shareholders could not interfere with such powers.

As shareholders had delegated certain powers to the directors, they could not interfere in directors' decisions

In *Automatic Self-Cleansing Filter Syndicate Co v Cunninghame* [1906] 2 Ch 34, a company had power under its memorandum of association to sell its undertaking to another company having similar objects. Under its articles of association, the general management and control of the company were vested in the directors, subject to such regulations as might from time to time be made by extraordinary resolution. In particular, the directors were empowered to sell or otherwise deal with any property of the company on such terms as they might think fit.

At a general meeting of the company, a resolution was passed by a simple majority of the shareholders for the sale of the company's assets on certain terms to a new company formed for the purpose of acquiring them, and directing the directors to carry the sale into effect. The directors were of opinion that a sale on those terms was not for the benefit of the company and declined to implement the sale.

The Court of Appeal held that, under the construction of the articles, the directors could not be compelled to comply with the resolution on the basis that the shareholders had delegated wide powers to the directors. According to Collins MR, the directors were not agents for the shareholders but they acted as agents for the company as principal.

Cozens Hardy LJ considered that under the articles of association which constituted a contract between the shareholders and the company, the shareholders had delegated day-to-day powers to the directors and the shareholders could not interfere unless the constitution was amended by shareholders in general meeting. The Court of Appeal distinguished the *Tahourdin* case on the grounds that the wording in that company's articles of association was different from the present case.

Directors were not agents for the shareholders and had powers to conduct the day-to-day operations of the company

The principles established in *Automatic Self-Cleansing Filter Syndicate Co* were subsequently considered by the Court of Appeal in *Gramaphone & Typewriter Ltd v Stanley* [1908] 2 KB 89.

Fletcher Moulton LJ cited with approval the *Automatic* case and the fact that directors were not agents of their shareholders and were not required to comply with shareholder directions unless required by the company's constitution and resolutions passed at general meetings.According to Buckley LJ, as the shareholders had delegated a significant degree of control to the directors, they could not interfere with the powers delegated to them.

11.11 The *Automatic* case, however, did not gain support from some subsequent cases as the effect of the case would be that directors may act on their own volition with their powers becoming uncontrollable. In this situation, shareholders would simply be perceived as passive with no voice and accepting all decisions made by directors, whether or not in the company's best interests.

A retreat from Automatic – shareholders had the right to control directors' actions

Marshalls Valve Gear Co v Manning Wardle & Co [1909] 1 Ch 267 distinguished the *Automatic* case. In the *Marshalls* case, M Company was incorporated under the Companies Acts and acquired and worked a patent. The powers of its directors were governed by art 55 in Sch 1 to the Companies Act 1862, which provides:

> 'the business of the company shall be managed by the directors, who may …. exercise all such powers of the company as are not by the foregoing Act, or by these articles, required to be exercised by the company in general meeting, subject nevertheless to any regulations of these articles, to the provisions of the foregoing Act, and to such regulations, being not inconsistent with the aforesaid regulations or provisions, as may be prescribed by the company in general meeting.'

A and three other persons were the four directors of the company and between them held substantially the whole of the subscribed share capital of the company. A held a majority, but not a three-fourths majority, of the shares and votes. Disputes arose at the board between A and the other three directors, who were interested in a patent vested in the N Company, which, so A was advised, infringed the M Company's patent and was admittedly a competing patent. The three directors bona fide declining to sanction any proceedings against the N Company, A commenced an action against the N Company in the name of the M Company to restrain the alleged infringement. Subsequently, the three acting on behalf of the M Company proceeded to strike out the name of that company as claimant and to dismiss the action on the ground that the name of the M Company had been used without authority.

Neville J held that on the construction of art 55, the majority of the shareholders had the right to control the action of the directors in the matter, and that the motion must be dismissed.

Applying Automatic – directors has powers vested in them to conduct daily corporate matters with which shareholders could not interfere

However, in *Quin & Axtens Ltd v Salmon* [1909] 1 Ch 311, the Court of Appeal reverted to the position established in the *Automatic* case thereby maintaining a complete separation of ownership from control, the effect of which was to prevent shareholders from generally interfering in the day-to-day management of the company.

Under the articles of association of a company, the general management of the business of the company was vested in the directors subject to such regulations (being not inconsistent with the provisions of the articles) as might be prescribed by the company in general meeting, and it was provided that no resolution of a meeting of the directors having for its object (among other things) the acquisition or letting of any premises should be valid unless 24 hours' notice of the meeting should have been given to each of the managing directors A and B and neither of them should have dissented therefrom in writing before or at the meeting. A and B held the bulk of the ordinary shares in the company. Resolutions were passed by the directors for the acquisition of certain premises and for the letting of certain other premises, but B dissented from each of these resolutions in accordance with the articles. At an extraordinary general meeting of the company, resolutions to the same effect were passed by a simple majority of the shareholders.

The Court of Appeal held, applying the principle of *Automatic Self-Cleansing Filter Syndicate Co v Cuninghame* [1906] 2 Ch 34, that the resolutions of the company were inconsistent with the provisions of the articles, and that the company ought to be restrained from acting upon them.

Where powers were vested in directors, they alone could make corporate decisions without interference from shareholders – there was a clear demarcation between the role of directors and shareholders

The modern view expressing the separation of ownership from control was established in *Shaw & Sons (Salford) Ltd v Shaw* [1935] 2 KB 113. The Court of Appeal decided that if powers of management were vested in the directors of a company, they and they alone could exercise those powers. The only way in which the general body of the shareholders could control the exercise of powers vested by the articles in the directors was by altering the articles of the company or refusing to re-elect the directors of whose actions they disapproved. They could not usurp the powers which, by the articles, were vested in the directors.

According to Greer LJ , a company was a distinct entity from its shareholders and directors. Some of the company's powers may, according to its articles, be exercised by directors; certain other powers may be reserved for the shareholders in general meeting. If the powers of management were vested in the directors they alone could exercise these powers. The only way in which the general body of the shareholders could control the exercise of the powers vested by the articles in the directors was by altering their articles, or, if opportunity arose under the articles, by refusing to reelect the directors of whose actions they disapproved. The shareholders could not themselves usurp the powers which by the articles were vested in the directors any more than the directors could usurp the powers vested by the articles in the general body of shareholders.

See too *Rose v McGivern* [1998] 2 BCLC 593 per Neuberger J; and *Scott v Scott* [1943] 1 All ER 582.

11.12 The Model Articles for a private company limited by shares vests authority in directors to manage the day-to-day affairs of the company, but this is 'subject to the articles'. The Model Articles also provide for ultimate residual power ('members reserve') vested in the shareholders to mandate directors to act in a particular manner by way of a special resolution.

(Model Articles of Association of a Private Company Limited by Shares)

PART 2
DIRECTORS

DIRECTORS' POWERS AND RESPONSIBILITIES

Directors' general authority

3. Subject to the articles, the directors are responsible for the management of the company's business, for which purpose they may exercise all the powers of the company.

Shareholders' reserve power

4.—(1) The shareholders may, by special resolution, direct the directors to take, or refrain from taking, specified action.

(2) No such special resolution invalidates anything which the directors have done before the passing of the resolution.

The establishment of corporate governance committees

Cadbury Committee

11.13 The Cadbury Committee was established in May 1991 under the chairmanship of Sir Adrian Cadbury by the Financial Reporting Council (FRC), the London Stock Exchange and the accountancy profession to address the financial aspects of corporate governance, and produced a report on 1 December 1992 on *The Financial Aspects of Corporate Governance*. The Report was published against the background of collapse and failure of major corporations such as BCCI and the Maxwell Group, including concerns about directors' remuneration and the low level of confidence in financial reporting and the ability of auditors to provide the safeguards which users of company reports sought and expected. The Committee's recommendations focused on the control and reporting functions of boards and on the role of directors, with the objective of strengthening the unitary board system and increasing its effectiveness and strengthening trust in the corporate governance system.

11.14 It defined 'corporate governance' as 'the system by which companies were directed and controlled'. The board of directors were responsible for the governance of their companies. The shareholders' role in governance was to appoint the directors and the auditors to satisfy themselves that an appropriate governance structure was in place. Within the corporate governance system, the responsibilities of the board included setting the company's strategic aims, providing the leadership to put them into effect, supervising the management of the business and reporting to the shareholders on their stewardship. The board's actions were subject to laws, regulations and the shareholders in general meeting.

The principal recommendations of the Cadbury Committee included that all boards of listed companies registered in the UK should comply with a Code of Best Practice which the Committee had developed. The Code was designed to achieve high standards of corporate behaviour expected of such companies. Its principles were based on openness, integrity and accountability. The Code addressed various aspects such as the role of auditors, the board of directors, shareholders and non-executive directors (NEDs) including reporting and controls.

Greenbury Committee

11.15 In January 1995, a Study Group on Directors' Remuneration was established on the initiative of the CBI in response to public and shareholder concerns about the pay and other remuneration of company directors in the UK. This group became known as the 'Greenbury Committee' as it was headed by Sir Richard Greenbury whose terms of reference were 'to identify good practice in determining directors' remuneration and prepare a Code of such practice for use by UK plcs'.

On 17 July 1995, the Greenbury Committee published a report on 'Directors' Remuneration' which focused exclusively on plc directors' remuneration in listed companies. The report was published against a background of concerns about executive remuneration with large pay increases and large gains from share options in privatised utility industries, including the amounts of compensation paid to some departing directors. The Committee did not recommend statutory controls, but action to strengthen accountability and encourage enhanced performance coupled with proper reporting to shareholders and transparency about directors' remuneration.

11.16 The Committee emphasised the need for directors to delegate responsibility for determining directors' remuneration to independent non-executive directors (NEDs) and to ensure that any directors' remuneration packages linked rewards to performance by both the company and the director and aligned the interests of directors and shareholders in promoting the company's progress.

The Committee published a new Code of Best Practice on Directors' Remuneration which recommended that all listed companies in the UK should comply with the Code, and report annually to the shareholders about their compliance. The Code required boards to establish a remuneration committee to address the executive compensation of directors independently monitored by NEDs.

Hampel Committee

11.17 The Hampel Committee on Corporate Governance was established in November 1995 by the Financial Reporting Council (FRC). This followed the recommendations by both the Cadbury and Greenbury Committees that a new committee should review the implementation of their findings.

The Committee published its Final Report in January 1998. It emphasised the need for listed plcs to apply principles of corporate governance in practice and for companies to be ready to explain their governance policies including any circumstances justifying departing from best practice. Boards had a duty to consider the best interests of the company and the need to appoint independent non-executive directors on plc boards to consider various aspects of the company's business including appointment to remuneration, audit and nomination committees. It published a Combined Code on Corporate Governance which applied to listed plcs.

Turnbull – Internal Control: Guidance for Directors on the Combined Code

11.18 In September 1999, Nigel Turnbull, as Chairman of the Internal Control Working Party of the Institute of Chartered Accountants in England and Wales, published a report entitled *Internal Control: Guidance for Directors on the Combined Code*.

The work involved preparing guidance for directors of UK incorporated listed companies in respect of Principle D.2 of the Combined Code and its associated Provisions D.2.1 and D.2.2 in assessing how the company had applied Code Principle D.2; implementing the requirements of Code Provisions D.2.1 and D.2.2; and reporting on these matters to shareholders in the annual report and accounts.

11.19 The Turnbull guidance emphasised the following aspects:

- *The need to maintain a sound system of internal control*

  This included a consideration by the board of the following:

  - the nature and extent of the risks facing the company;
  - the extent and categories of risk which it regards as acceptable for the company to bear;
  - the likelihood of the risks concerned materialising;
  - the company's ability to reduce the incidence and impact on the business of risks that do materialise; and
  - the costs of operating particular controls relative to the benefit thereby obtained in managing the related risks.

  Further, a sound system of internal control encompassed the policies, processes, tasks and behaviours to facilitate its effective and efficient operation, and to help ensure the quality of internal and external reporting, including compliance with applicable laws and regulations.

- *Reviewing the effectiveness of internal control*

  This included the board forming its own view on effectiveness after due and careful enquiry based on the information and assurances provided to it by management. Board committees also have an essential role in the review process.

  The process of reviewing effectiveness required continuous monitoring of the internal control system including those of an operational and compliance nature through receipts of reports by management and reviews undertaken by the board.

  When reviewing reports during the year, the board should:

  - consider the significant risks and assess how they have been identified, evaluated and managed;
  - assess the effectiveness of the related system of internal control in managing
  - the significant risks, having regard, in particular, to any significant failings or weaknesses in internal control that have been reported;

- consider whether necessary actions are being taken promptly to remedy any significant failings or weaknesses; and
- consider whether the findings indicate a need for more extensive monitoring of the system of internal control.

The board's annual assessment should consider:

- the changes since the last annual assessment in the nature and extent of significant risks and the company's ability to respond to changes in its business and the external environment;
- the scope and quality of management's ongoing risk monitoring and internal control systems and, where applicable, the work of its internal audit function and other providers of assurance;
- the extent and frequency of the communication of the results of the monitoring to the board (or board committee(s)) which enables it to build up a cumulative assessment of the levels of control in the company and the effectiveness with which risk is being managed;
- the incidence of significant control failings or weaknesses that have been identified at any time during the period and the extent to which they have resulted in unforeseen outcomes or contingencies that have had, could have had, or may in the future have, a material impact on the company's financial performance or condition; and
- the effectiveness of the company's public reporting processes.

- *The board's statement on internal control*

  The Guidance provides that the board should, in its narrative statement of how the company applied Code principle D.2, disclose that there is an ongoing process for identifying, evaluating and managing the significant risks faced by the company, that this process has been in place for the year under review and, up to the date of approval of the annual report and accounts, it is regularly reviewed by the board and is in accordance with the guidance in this document.

  The board may wish to provide additional information in the annual report and accounts to assist understanding of the company's risk management processes and systems of internal control.

  The disclosures relating to the application of principle D.2 should include an acknowledgement by the board that it is responsible for the company's system of internal control and for reviewing its effectiveness. It should also explain that such a system is designed to manage rather than eliminate the risk of failure to achieve business objectives and can only provide reasonable and not absolute assurance against material misstatement or loss.

Higgs – Review of the Role and Effectiveness of Non-executive Directors

11.20 In January 2003, Derek Higgs published a report entitled *Review of the Role and Effectiveness of Non-executive Directors*. It addressed the role of the board and the participation of non-executive directors (NEDs) within it. Higgs emphasised the need for board collectivity in promoting the company's success by directing and supervising its affairs. The board's role is to provide entrepreneurial leadership of the company within a framework of prudent and effective controls which enables risk to be assessed and managed.

The board should set the company's strategic aims, ensure that the necessary financial and human resources are in place so that it can meet its objectives and review management performance.

The board should also set the company's values and standards and ensure that its obligations to its shareholders and others were both understood and met.

Within the board, the chairman is responsible for effective leadership and coordination with shareholders.

Higgs also recommended that the role of independent NEDs should include strategy, performance, risk, and people management when determining directors' remuneration. He also made suggestions for a revision of the Code to take account of his recommendations.

Smith – Report on Audit Committees – Combined Code Guidance

11.21 In January 2003, Sir Robert Smith published a report entitled *Report on Audit Committees – Combined Code Guidance* which set out guidance designed to assist company boards in making suitable arrangements for their audit committees and to assist directors serving on audit committees in carrying out their role. The report highlighted the fact that the audit committee had a particular role, acting independently from the executive, to ensure that the interests of shareholders were properly protected in relation to financial reporting and internal control.

11.22 Some of the key recommendations included the following:

- The board should establish an audit committee, the main role and responsibilities of which should be:
  - to monitor the integrity of the financial statements of the company;
  - to review both the company's internal financial control system and risk management systems (unless these are addressed by a separate risk committee or by the board itself);
  - to monitor and review the effectiveness of the company's internal audit function;
  - to make recommendations to the board in relation to the appointment of the external auditor and to approve the remuneration and terms of engagement of the external auditor following appointment by the shareholders in a general meeting;
  - to monitor and review the external auditor's independence, objectivity and effectiveness; and
  - to develop and implement policy on the engagement of the external auditor to supply non-audit services.

- Audit committees should include at least three members, who should all be independent non-executive directors; and the chairman of the company should not be an audit committee member.
- The audit committee should be provided with sufficient resources to undertake its duties.
- The board should provide written terms of reference for the audit committee.
- The audit committee should review the significant financial reporting issues and judgements made in connection with the preparation of the company's financial statements, interim reports, preliminary announcements and related formal statements. The audit committee should also review the clarity and completeness of disclosures in the financial statements.
- The audit committee should monitor the integrity of the company's internal financial controls. Further, the audit committee, in the absence of other arrangements (eg a risk committee), should assess the scope and effectiveness of the systems established by management to identify, assess, manage and monitor financial and non-financial risks.
- The directors' report should contain a separate section that describes the role and responsibilities of the audit committee and the actions taken by the audit committee to discharge those responsibilities.

Walker – a Review of Corporate Governance in UK Banks and other Financial Industry Entities

11.23 On 26 November 2009, David Walker published a report entitled *A Review of Corporate Governance in UK Banks and other Financial Industry Entities* in the light of the experience of critical loss and failure of the banking system during the period of economic recession.

It made a number of recommendations, some of which included:

- an effective role for non-executive directors to enable them to contribute towards a better understanding of the business including induction, training and development;
- dedicated support for NEDs;
- overall time commitment of NEDs to their tasks should be up to 30–36 days in a major bank;
- NEDs should test the effectiveness of board strategy and challenge it where necessary;
- the chairman should commit a substantial amount of his time to the business of the entity;
- the chairman has the responsibility for leadership of the board and ensuring its effectiveness;
- there should be a senior independent director to assist the chairman and coordinate with the NEDs;

- the board should undertake a formal and vigorous evaluation of its performance;
- institutional shareholders should play an effective role in communication and engagement with the board; and
- the Stewardship Code should be ratified by the FRC.

Regulatory framework of corporate governance in the UK

11.24 In the UK, corporate governance is subject to the following principal regulations:

- the Companies Act 2006 and its regulations;
- the Listing Rules of the London Stock Exchange under the aegis of the Financial Conduct Authority;
- the Disclosure and Transparency Rules;
- the UK Corporate Governance Code; and
- the Stewardship Code.

These aspects are considered in relation to the UK Corporate Governance Code. The Stewardship Code is considered separately.

For small and medium-sized enterprises, the Quoted Companies Alliance has published the *Corporate Governance Code for Small and Mid-Size Quoted Companies* (QCA Code) which helps quoted companies put into practice appropriate corporate governance arrangements and encourage positive engagement between companies and shareholders.

The QCA Code is widely recognised as an industry standard for those growing companies for which the UK Corporate Governance Code is not applicable. This includes standard listed companies, those on the AIM and the ICAP Securities and Derivatives Exchange.

The QCA Code adopts key elements of the UK Corporate Governance Code, current policy initiatives and other relevant guidance and then applies these to the needs and particular circumstances of small and medium-sized quoted companies on a public market. It focuses on 12 principles and a set of minimum disclosures. The QCA Code encourages companies to consider how – or indeed whether – they should apply each principle to achieve good governance and provide quality explanations to their shareholders about what they have done.

11.25 In addition, there has been much guidance by key regulatory authorities on corporate governance in the UK. The FRC, in its publication *The UK Approach to Corporate Governance* (2010), set out the following keys aspects to corporate governance in the UK:

- a single board collectively responsible for the sustainable success of the company;
- checks and balances including:
  - a separate chairman and chief executive;
  - a balance of executive and independent NEDs;

- strong, independent audit and remuneration committees; and
- annual evaluation by the board of its performance.

- transparency on appointments and remuneration;
- effective rights for shareholders, who are encouraged to engage with the companies in which they invest; and
- the fact that the UK Corporate Governance Code operates on the basis of the 'comply or explain' principle and is regularly reviewed in consultation with both companies and investors.

The UK Corporate Governance Code

Introduction

11.26 A revised UK Corporate Governance Code (the Code) was published by the FRC in September 2014 (replacing the previous Code in June 2012) and applies to reporting periods beginning on or after 1 October 2014. The FRC has the responsibility for revisions to the Code. Previous reviews of the Code were in 2005, 2007, 2008, 2010 and 2012. Another revision is expected in 2016.

The Code applies to all companies with a Premium Listing of equity shares regardless of whether they are incorporated in the UK or elsewhere.

The Code is based on the 'comply or explain' principle for good corporate governance in the UK. Since its inception, it has never been a rigid set of rules, but comprises a set of principles on effective governance with main principles and supporting provisions. The Code effectively represents a guide to a number of aspects for effective board practice. Owing to its flexibility, it is also recognised by the Code that there may be reasons justifying departure from the principles of the Code in particular circumstances if good governance can be achieved by other effective means.

Objectives of the Code

11.27 The objective of the Code is to facilitate effective, entrepreneurial and prudent management that can deliver the long-term success of the company. It is a guide to key components of effective board practice. It is based on the underlying principles of all good governance: accountability, transparency, probity and focus on the sustainable success of an entity over the longer term.

The comply or explain approach

11.28 At the heart of the Code is the 'comply or explain' approach which is required to be undertaken by all companies with a premium listing. The Code consists of principles (main and supporting) and provisions.

The Listing Rules require companies to apply the main principles and report to shareholders about how they have done so. The principles are the core of the Code and the way in which they are applied should be the central question for a board as it determines how it is to operate.

It is recognised that an alternative to following a provision may be justified in particular circumstances if good governance can be achieved by other means. A condition of so doing is that the reasons for it should be explained clearly and carefully to shareholders, who may wish to discuss the position with the company and whose voting intentions may be influenced as a result.

In providing an explanation, the company should aim to illustrate how its actual practices are consistent with the principle to which the particular provision relates, contribute to good governance and promote the delivery of business objectives. It should set out the background, provide a clear rationale for the action it is taking and describe any mitigating actions being taken to address any additional risk and maintain conformity with the relevant principle. Where deviation from a particular provision is intended to be limited in time, the explanation should indicate when the company expects to comply with the provision.

11.29 In their response to explanations, shareholders should pay due regard to companies' individual circumstances and should bear in mind the size and complexity of the company and the nature of the risks and challenges it faces. Whilst shareholders have every right to challenge companies' explanations if they are unconvincing, they should not be evaluated in a mechanistic way; departures from the Code should not be automatically treated as breaches. Shareholders should be careful to respond to the statements from companies in a manner that supports the 'comply or explain' process bearing in mind the purpose of good corporate governance. They should put their views to the company and both parties should be prepared to discuss the position.

Smaller listed companies, in particular those new to listing, may judge that some of the provisions are disproportionate or less relevant in their case. Some of the provisions do not apply to companies below the FTSE 350. Such companies may nonetheless consider that it would be appropriate to adopt the approach in the Code and they are encouraged to do so. Externally managed investment companies typically have a different board structure which may affect the relevance of particular provisions; the Association of Investment Companies' *Corporate Governance Code and Guide* can assist them in meeting their obligations under the Code.

11.30 Under the Listing Rules, there is a requirement to include in their annual report and accounts:

> '(5) a statement of how the listed company has applied the Main Principles set out in the UK Corporate Governance Code, in a manner that would enable shareholders to evaluate how the principles have been applied;
>
> (6) a statement as to whether the listed company has:
>
> (a) complied throughout the accounting period with all relevant provisions set out in the UK Corporate Governance Code; or
>
> (b) not complied throughout the accounting period with all relevant provisions set out in the UK Corporate Governance Code and if so, setting out:

(i) those provisions, if any it has not complied with;

(ii) in the case of provisions whose requirements are of a continuing nature, the period within which, if any, it did not comply with some or all of those provisions; and

(iii) the company's reasons for non-compliance; and

(7) a report to the shareholders by the board which contains all the matters set out in LR 9.8.8 R.' (This latter aspect is in connection with directors' remuneration.)

Under the Disclosure and Transparency Rules (DTR 7.2), the following aspects apply in respect of corporate governance statements:

'DTR 7.2.1: An issuer to which this section applies must include a corporate governance statement in its directors' report. That statement must be included as a specific section of the directors' report and must contain at least the information set out in DTR 7.2.2R to DTR 7.2.7R and, where applicable, DTR 7.2.10R.

DTR 7.2.2: The corporate governance statement must contain a reference to:

(1) the corporate governance code to which the issuer is subject; and/or

(2) the corporate governance code which the issuer may have voluntarily decided to apply; and/or

(3) all relevant information about the corporate governance practices applied beyond the requirements under national law.

DTR 7.3.3:

(1) An issuer which is complying with DTR 7.2.2R(1) or DTR 7.2.2R(2) must:

(a) state in its directors' report where the relevant corporate governance code is publicly available; and

(b) to the extent that it departs from that corporate governance code, explain which parts of the corporate governance code it departs from and the reasons for doing so.

(2) Where DTR 7.2.2R(3) applies, the issuer must make its corporate governance practices publicly available and state in its directors' report where they can be found.

(4) If an issuer has decided not to apply any provisions of a corporate governance code referred to under DTR 7.2.2R(1) and DTR 7.2.2R(2), it must explain its reasons for that decision.

DTR 7.2.4: A listed company which complies with LR 9.8.6R(6) (the 'comply or explain' rule in relation to the UK Corporate Governance Code) will satisfy the requirements of DTR 7.2.2R and DTR 7.2.3R.

DTR 7.2.5: The corporate governance statement must contain a description of the main features of the issuer's internal control and risk management systems in relation to the financial reporting process.

DTR 7.2.6: The corporate governance statement must contain the information required by paragraph 13(2)(c), (d), (f), (h) and (i) of Schedule 7 to the Large and Medium-sized Companies and Groups (Accounts and Reports) Regulations 2008 (SI 2008 No 410) (information about share capital required under Directive 2004/25/EC (the Takeover Directive)) where the issuer is subject to the requirements of that paragraph.

DTR 7.2.7: The corporate governance statement must contain a description of the composition and operation of the issuer's administrative, management and supervisory bodies and their committees.

DTR 7.2.8: In the FCA's view, the information specified in provisions A.1.1, A.1.2, B.2.4, D.2.11 and C.3.3 of the UK Corporate Governance Code will satisfy the requirements of DTR 7.2.7R.

DTR: 7.2.9: An issuer may elect that, instead of including its corporate governance statement in its directors' report, the information required by DTR 7.2.1R to DTR 7.2.7R may be set out:

(1) in a separate report published together with and in the same manner as its annual report. In the event of a separate report, the corporate governance statement must contain either the information required by DTR 7.2.6 R or a reference to the directors' report where that information is made available; or

(2) by means of a reference in its directors' report to where such document is publicly available on the issuer's website.

DTR: 7.2.10: Subject to DTR 7.2.11R, an issuer which is required to prepare a group directors' report within the meaning of s 415(2) of CA 2006 must include in that report a description of the main features of the group's internal control and risk management systems in relation to the process for preparing consolidated accounts. In the event that the issuer presents its own annual report and its consolidated annual report as a single report, this information must be included in the corporate governance statement required by DTR 7.2.1R.

DTR 7.2.11: An issuer that elects to include its corporate governance statement in a separate report as permitted by DTR 7.2.9R(1) must provide the information required by DTR 7.2.10R in that report.'

Approval and signing of separate corporate governance statement

11.31 Under s 419A of CA 2006, any separate corporate governance statement must be approved by the board of directors and signed on behalf of the board by a director or the secretary of the company: see *The Companies Act 2006 (Accounts, Reports and Audit) Regulations 2009*, SI 2009/1581, reg 2 (with application as stated in reg 1(3)).

The main principles of the UK Code on Corporate Governance

11.32 The Code is based on five sections that set out the main principles. Each main principle is followed by supporting principles and Code provisions.

Main principles

Section A: Leadership

Every company should be headed by an effective board which is collectively responsible for the long-term success of the company.

There should be a clear division of responsibilities at the head of the company between the running of the board and the executive responsibility for the running of the company's business. No one individual should have unfettered powers of decision.

The chairman is responsible for leadership of the board and ensuring its effectiveness on all aspects of its role.

As part of their role as members of a unitary board, non-executive directors should constructively challenge and help develop proposals on strategy.

Section B: Effectiveness

The board and its committees should have the appropriate balance of skills, experience, independence and knowledge of the company to enable them to discharge their respective duties and responsibilities effectively.

There should be a formal, rigorous and transparent procedure for the appointment of new directors to the board.

All directors should be able to allocate sufficient time to the company to discharge their responsibilities effectively.

All directors should receive an induction on joining the board and should regularly update and refresh their skills and knowledge.

The board should be supplied in a timely manner with information in a form and of a quality appropriate to enable it to discharge its duties.

The board should undertake a formal and rigorous annual evaluation of its own performance and that of its committees and individual directors.

All directors should be submitted for re-election at regular intervals, subject to continued satisfactory performance.

In respect of Sections A and B, the FRC has published the *Guidance on Board Effectiveness* (the Guidance) in March 2011. This is not prescriptive but is intended to stimulate boards' thinking on how they can carry out their role most effectively. Ultimately, it is for each individual board to decide on the governance arrangements most appropriate to their circumstances. According to the Guidance:

The role of an effective board is to provide entrepreneurial leadership of the company within a framework of prudent and effective controls, which enables risk to be assessed and managed.

An effective board develops and promotes its collective vision of the company's purpose, its culture, its values and the behaviours it wishes to promote in conducting its business. In particular it:

- provides direction for management;
- demonstrates ethical leadership, displaying – and promoting throughout the company – behaviours consistent with the culture and values it has defined for the organisation;
- creates a performance culture that drives value creation without exposing the company to excessive risk of value destruction;
- makes well-informed and high-quality decisions based on a clear line of sight into the business;
- creates the right framework for helping directors to meet their statutory duties under the Companies Act 2006 and/or other relevant statutory and regulatory regimes;
- is accountable, particularly to those that provide the company's capital; and
- thinks carefully about its governance arrangements and embraces evaluation of their effectiveness.

The *Guidance* provides that the chairman's role should include:

- demonstrating ethical leadership;
- setting a board agenda which is primarily focused on strategy, performance, value creation and accountability, and ensuring that issues relevant to these areas are reserved for board decision;
- ensuring a timely flow of high-quality supporting information;
- making certain that the board determines the nature, and extent, of the significant risks the company is willing to embrace in the implementation of its strategy, and that there are no 'no go' areas which prevent directors from operating effective oversight in this area;
- regularly considering succession planning and the composition of the board;
- making certain that the board has effective decision-making processes and applies sufficient challenge to major proposals;
- ensuring the board's committees are properly structured with appropriate terms of reference;
- encouraging all board members to engage in board and committee meetings by drawing on their skills, experience, knowledge and – where appropriate – independence;

- fostering relationships founded on mutual respect and open communication – both in and outside the boardroom – between the NEDs and the executive team;
- developing productive working relationships with all executive directors, particularly the CEO, providing support and advice while respecting executive responsibility;
- consulting the senior independent director on board matters in accordance with the Code;
- taking the lead on issues of director development, including induction programmes for new directors and regular reviews with all directors;
- acting on the results of board evaluation;
- being aware of, and responding to, his or her own development needs, including people and other skills, especially when taking on the role for the first time; and
- ensuring effective communication with shareholders and other stakeholders and, in particular, that all directors are made aware of the views of those who provide the company's capital.

The *Guidance* also recommends the appointment of a senior independent director who should act as a sounding board for the chairman, provide support in the delivery of his or her objectives and lead the evaluation of the chairman on behalf of the directors. The senior independent director may intervene in some of the following circumstances in order to maintain board and company stability:

- if there is a dispute between the chairman and CEO;
- where shareholders or NEDs have expressed concerns that are not being addressed by the chairman or CEO;
- if the strategy being followed by the chairman and CEO is not supported by the entire board;
- where the relationship between the chairman and CEO is particularly close and decisions are being made without the approval of the full board; or
- if succession planning is being ignored.

Section C: Accountability

The board should present a fair, balanced and understandable assessment of the company's position and prospects.

The board is responsible for determining the nature and extent of the significant risks it is willing to take in achieving its strategic objectives. The board should maintain sound risk management and internal control systems.

The board should establish formal and transparent arrangements for considering how they should apply the corporate reporting, risk management and internal control principles and for maintaining an appropriate relationship with the company's auditors.

Section D: Remuneration

Levels of remuneration should be sufficient to attract, retain and motivate directors of the quality required to run the company successfully, but a company should avoid paying more than is necessary for this purpose.

A significant proportion of executive directors' remuneration should be structured so as to link rewards to corporate and individual performance.

There should be a formal and transparent procedure for developing policy on executive remuneration and for fixing the remuneration packages of individual directors. No director should be involved in deciding his or her own remuneration.

Section E: Relations with shareholders

There should be a dialogue with shareholders based on the mutual understanding of objectives. The board as a whole has responsibility for ensuring that a satisfactory dialogue with shareholders takes place.

The board should use the AGM to communicate with investors and to encourage their participation.

The Stewardship Code

11.33 The FRC published *The Stewardship Code* which was revised in September 2012 and implemented 1 October 2012. The origins of the Code date back to a publication by the Institutional Shareholders Committee (ISC) of *The Responsibilities of Institutional Shareholders and Agents: Statements of Principles* which was first published in 2002 and subsequently converted into a code in 2009. Following the Walker Review, the FRC was invited to take responsibility for the Code. In 2010, the FRC published the first version of the *UK Stewardship Code*, which closely mirrored that of the ISC. This edition of the Code does not change the spirit of the original Code.

The Code is aimed at institutional investors who are typically asset owners and asset managers with equity holdings in UK listed companies. It allows institutional shareholders to outsource to external service providers some of the activities associated with stewardship but they cannot delegate their responsibility.

According to the FRC, stewardship aims to promote the long-term success of companies in such a way that the ultimate providers of capital also prosper. Effective stewardship benefits companies, investors and the economy as a whole.

In publicly listed companies, responsibility for stewardship is shared. The primary responsibility rests with the board, which oversees the actions of its management. Investors in the company also play an important role in holding the board to account for the fulfilment of its responsibilities.

11.34 The UK Corporate Governance Code identifies the principles that underlie an effective board. The UK Stewardship Code sets out the principles of effective stewardship by investors. In so doing, the Code helps institutional investors better to exercise their stewardship responsibilities, which in turn gives force to the 'comply or explain' system.

For investors, stewardship is more than just voting. Activities may include monitoring and engaging with companies on matters such as strategy, performance, risk, capital structure, and corporate governance, including culture and remuneration. Engagement is purposeful dialogue with companies on these matters as well as on issues that are the immediate subject of votes at general meetings.

Institutional investors' activities include decision-making on matters such as allocating assets, awarding investment mandates, designing investment strategies, and buying or selling specific securities. The division of duties within and between institutions may span a spectrum, such that some may be considered asset owners and others asset managers.

Broadly speaking, asset owners include pension funds, insurance companies, investment trusts and other collective investment vehicles. As the providers of capital, they set the tone for stewardship and may influence behavioural changes that lead to better stewardship by asset managers and companies. Asset managers, with day-to-day responsibility for managing investments, are well positioned to influence companies' long-term performance through stewardship.

11.35 Compliance with the Code does not constitute an invitation to manage the affairs of a company or preclude a decision to sell a holding where this is considered in the best interests of clients or beneficiaries.

As with the UK Corporate Governance Code, the Stewardship Code is based on a 'comply or explain' basis. The Code is not a rigid set of rules. It consists of principles and guidance. The principles are the core of the Code and it should be the way in which these are applied that should be the central question for the institutional investor. The guidance recommends how the principle might be applied.

Those signatories who neither choose to comply with one of the principles nor follow the guidance, should deliver meaningful explanations that enable the reader to understand their approach to stewardship. In providing an explanation, the signatory should aim to illustrate how its actual practices contribute to good stewardship and promote the delivery of the investment objectives of either the institution or its clients. They should provide a clear rationale for their approach.

11.36 The Financial Services Authority (FSA) requires any firm authorised to manage funds, which is not a venture capital firm and which manages investments for professional clients that are not natural persons, to disclose 'the nature of its commitment' to the Code or 'where it does not commit to the Code, its alternative investment strategy' (under Conduct of Business Rule 2.2.31).

The FRC recognises that not all parts of the Code are relevant to all signatories. For example, smaller institutions may judge that some of its principles and guidance are disproportionate in their case. In these circumstances, they should take advantage of the 'comply or explain' approach and set out why this is the case.

In their responses to explanations, clients and beneficiaries should pay due regard to the signatory's individual circumstances and bear in mind the size and complexity of the signatory, the nature of the risks and challenges it faces and the investment objectives of the signatory or its clients.

Whilst clients and beneficiaries have every right to challenge a signatory's explanations if they are unconvincing, they should not evaluate explanations in a mechanistic way. Departures from the Code should not automatically be treated as breaches. A signatory's clients and beneficiaries should be careful to respond to the statements from the signatory in a manner that supports the 'comply or explain' process and bears in mind the purpose of good stewardship. They should put their views to the signatory and both parties should be prepared to discuss the position.

The seven stewardship principles

11.37 The Stewardship Code is based on seven principles.

> *The principles of the Code*
>
> So as to protect and enhance the value that accrues to the ultimate beneficiary, institutional investors should:
>
> (1) publicly disclose their policy on how they will discharge their stewardship responsibilities;
>
> (2) have a robust policy on managing conflicts of interest in relation to stewardship which should be publicly disclosed;
>
> (3) monitor their investee companies;
>
> (4) establish clear guidelines on when and how they will escalate their stewardship activities;
>
> (5) be willing to act collectively with other investors where appropriate;
>
> (6) have a clear policy on voting and disclosure of voting activity;
>
> (7) report periodically on their stewardship and voting activities.
>
> Each principle sets out detailed Guidance on how it operates.

11.38 With regard to the application of the Stewardship Code, the FRC expects signatories of the Code to publish on their website, or if they do not have a website in another accessible form, a statement that:

- describes how the signatory has applied each of the seven principles of the Code and discloses the specific information requested in the guidance to the principles; or
- if one or more of the principles have not been applied or the specific information requested in the guidance has not been disclosed, explains why the signatory has not complied with those elements of the Code.

Disclosures under the Code should improve the functioning of the market for investment mandates. Asset owners should be better equipped to evaluate asset managers, and asset managers should be better informed, enabling them to tailor their services to meet asset owners' requirements.

In particular the disclosures should, with respect to conflicts of interest, address the priority given to client interests in decision making; with respect to collective engagement, describe the circumstances under which the signatory would join forces with other institutional investors to ensure that boards acknowledge and respond to their concerns on critical issues and at critical times; and with respect to proxy voting agencies, how the signatory uses their advice.

The statement of how the Code has been applied should be aligned with the signatory's role in the investment chain.

11.39 Asset owners' commitment to the Code may include engaging directly with companies or indirectly through the mandates given to asset managers. They should clearly communicate their policies on stewardship to their managers. Since asset owners are the primary audience of asset managers' public statements as well as client reports on stewardship, asset owners should seek to hold their managers to account for their stewardship activities. In so doing, they better fulfil their duty to their beneficiaries to exercise stewardship over their assets.

An asset manager should disclose how it delivers stewardship responsibilities on behalf of its clients. Following the publication in 2011 of the Stewardship Supplement to Technical Release AAF 01/06, asset managers are encouraged to have the policies described in their stewardship statements independently verified. Where appropriate, asset owners should also consider having their policy statements independently verified.

11.40 Overseas investors who follow other national or international codes that have similar objectives should not feel the application of the Code duplicates or confuses their responsibilities. Disclosures made in respect of those standards can also be used to demonstrate the extent to which they have complied with the Code. In a similar spirit, UK institutions that apply the Code should use their best efforts to apply its principles to overseas equity holdings.

Institutional investors with several types of funds or products need to make only one statement, but are encouraged to explain which of their funds or products are covered by the approach described in their statements. Where institutions apply a stewardship approach to other asset classes, they are encouraged to disclose this.

11.41 The FRC encourages service providers to disclose how they carry out the wishes of their clients with respect to each principle of the Code that is relevant to their activities.

Signatories are encouraged to review their policy statements annually and to update them where necessary to reflect changes in actual practice.

This statement should be easy to find on the signatory's website, or if they do not have a website in another accessible form, and should indicate when the statement was last reviewed. It should include contact details of an individual who can be contacted for further information and by those interested in collective engagement. The FRC hosts on its website the statements of signatories who do not have their own website.

The FRC also retains on its website a list of asset owners, asset managers and service providers who have published a statement on their compliance or otherwise with the Code. It requests that signatories notify the FRC when both they have done so, and if the statement is updated.

The FRC regularly monitors the take-up and application of the Code. It expects the content of the Code to evolve over time to reflect developments in good stewardship practice, the structure and operation of the market and the broader regulatory framework. Unless circumstances change, the FRC does not envisage proposing further changes to the Code until 2014 at the earliest.

Checklist: corporate governance framework

11.42 *This checklist sets out an overview of the regulatory framework governing corporate governance in the United Kingdom*

No	Issue	Reference
1	There is no universally accepted definition of 'corporate governance'. It may be described as the system by which companies are directed and controlled.	See Cadbury Committee on the Financial Aspects of Corporate Governance (1992)
2	Traditionally in the UK, corporate governance had been concerned with the drive by companies towards profit maximisation	*North-West Transportation v Beatty* (1887) 12 App Cas 589
3	The UK corporate governance system is based on the separation of ownership from control: directors control the management of the company and shareholders are the owners	
4	The traditional view was that shareholders could mandate directors to act in a certain manner	*Isle of Wight v Tahourdin* (1883) 25 Ch D 320
5	However, the traditional view gave way to a modern view that since shareholders had delegated some of their powers to the directors under the company's constitution, they could not interfere with such powers	*Automatic Self-Cleansing Filter Syndicate Co v Cunninghame* [1906] 2 Ch 34; *Shaw & Sons (Salford) Ltd v Shaw* [1935] 2 KB 113
6	Since the 1990s, various committees were established to address issues concerning corporate governance – the key ones being: • Cadbury Committee • Greenbury Comittee • Hampel Committee • Turnbul • Higgs • Smith • Walker	

No	Issue	Reference
7	In the UK, the UK Corporate Governance Code applies to all companies with a Premium Listing of equity shares	2014 edition published by the FRC
8	The Stewardship Code applies to institutional investors	2012 edition published by the FRC

Definitions

11.43

Corporate governance:	the system by which companies are directed and controlled.
Separation of ownership from control:	the division of responsibilities between directors who control the company and the shareholders as the company's owners.

12 Legal aspects of corporate social responsibility

Contents

Introduction

12.1 One of the primary difficulties in dealing with the legal aspects of corporate social responsibility is that no identifiable and acceptable definition of the concept can be found. Consequently, both the dimensions and the nature of the concept remain unclear, although its role in the corporate world and the business world at large cannot be denied. In this section, an attempt is made to examine various definitions of corporate social responsibility.

There seems to be a broad consensus among many commentators that a definition of 'corporate social responsibility' contains two main principles: the philanthropic and the trusteeship principles. When a company discharges a social service role it is then concerned with corporate philanthropy. In such circumstances, companies participate in society by engaging in social activities themselves and by encouraging philanthropic activities in the form of the resolution of chosen social problems of the community without any direct monetary benefits.

12.2 The trusteeship principle, perceives directors as trustees for shareholders, creditors, employees, consumers and the wider community. However, there seems to exist an apparent hierarchy between these groups. For example, directors' responsibilities towards shareholders and creditors of the company primarily relate to the protection of their monetary interests. The nature of the interests to be protected in respect of employees, consumers and the wider community seems to be of a much broader nature and may be impossible to quantify in monetary terms.

Corporate philanthropy is, therefore, concerned with the company's role in society. The trusteeship principle is, however, more concerned with the awareness of a sense of responsibility on the part of directors towards the various groups with whom they are directly concerned.

The concept of corporate social responsibilities may not, therefore, be accurately defined; it may only be described.

Features of corporate social responsibility

12.3 One of the features of corporate social responsibility is to provide a 'good service' to the community and to the various 'stakeholders' in a company. This idea was advanced by Berle and Means in the 1930s in *The Modern Corporation and Private Property*, although they never expressly refer to the concept in their work. They thought the modern corporation should be a 'social institution' involving the interrelation of a wide diversity of economic interests. These 'interests' included the owners who supply capital, the workers who 'create' and the consumers who give credence to the company's products. Social pressure requires companies to exercise their power equally for the benefit of all these groups. Berle and Means claimed that directors, therefore, held their power in trust for these groups. This was:

> 'a wholly new concept of corporate activity. The various affected groups had placed the company in a position to demand that the modern corporation serve not only the shareholders but also society. The interests of the community were paramount'.

In his later writing, Berle believed that corporate social responsibility had 'revolutionalised' the modern company. Management provided a social service and a 'good life' for the community. Corporate social responsibility required the management of a company to have an orientation which contributed to a corporation's philanthropic activities and those based on the trusteeship principle. There is also a voluntary commitment by corporations to pursuing social objectives. The spill-over effect of such a commitment should automatically improve the quality of management and thereby contribute to the welfare of society. This 'voluntary assumption' of responsibilities includes corporate involvement in charitable contributions, community service, employee welfare, charging reasonable prices, improving existing products and introducing new ones, locating plants according to community needs, providing for the conservation of natural resources and promoting fundamental scientific research for the benefit of the community.

Corporate social responsiveness

12.4 The concept of corporate social responsiveness developed in the 1970s in response to the vagueness of the concept of social responsibility. Some critics argued that the emphasis on motivation alone was not sufficient. Instead, corporate social responsiveness should be identified with the managerial task of implementing social policies within the financial framework of the company's activities. Managers should be required to restructure their companies and to adapt corporate behaviour, to ensure that it is socially responsive to the community and other groups in society.

12.5 This perspective emerged as a result of increasing demands from various consumer pressure groups, employees, trade unions and other interest groups. It involves three basic phases. The first is the 'identification phase' which reflects the process of companies identifying current social issues and formulating future developments. The second phase is the 'commitment stage', when companies select specific social issues requiring responsive action and they specify their level of commitment to them. The final phase is 'implementation', which focuses on the initiation and execution of the agreed social policies.

Without awareness amongst the general public as to corporate social responsibility, corporate social responsiveness may not be effectively achieved. In this sense, there is a correlation between corporate social responsiveness and an awareness of corporate social responsibility in the general public.

Corporate social rectitude

12.6 Corporate social rectitude is concerned with the ethical aspects of corporate social behaviour. Although the concept is close to the general features of corporate social responsibility, nevertheless it is possible to identify the meaning of corporate social rectitude and its role in developing and activating general corporate social responsibility.

As the expression suggests, it is concerned with the ethical dimensions of corporate activities. In other words, corporate social rectitude provides the foundation of corporate social responsibility. Corporate social rectitude apparently conflicts with the attitudes maintained by profit maximisers, but a standard of responsible behaviour for corporate bodies requires that the concept of corporate social rectitude is maintained.

12.7 Corporate social rectitude is based on the developments that took place in the business community in the US under the pioneering movement launched by the pressure groups, including the US Chamber of Commerce, initially in the field of consumer protection, but which gradually extended to the protection of the environment and other related areas. The ethical aspects of corporate social rectitude are linked to the value element. This emphasises the need for directors to adopt ethical values towards shareholders, creditors, employees and other persons having a legal interest in the company which may be enshrined in corporate codes of conduct and mission statements formulated by some companies.

Corporate social performance

12.8 This concept refers to a system of assessing a company's performance in achieving its social objectives, based on social policies of a participatory nature. One method of assessing the social performance of companies is to measure the social objectives they are implementing. This requires a system to measure and report on social issues and ultimately assessing the performance of directors in achieving the company's social objectives.

Corporate social performance may be assessed either by financial accounting procedures or by social audit systems. A social audit system could measure social issues such as equal employment opportunity programmes, conditions of work in the workplace, pollution control, job satisfaction and the quality of working life, the ethical performance of corporate executives, as well as community and urban redevelopment programmes by companies. The data extrapolated from social auditing could be useful for companies in assessing their social performance over the years.

The term corporate social performance is a relative term in that, in a dynamic society, its dimensions will change alongside society's perceptions, attitudes and understandings of the concept. Effective social audit may suffer unless a socially responsible society has articulated what is expected of a corporation in terms of its corporate social responsibilities. Government initiatives in this regard are essential for developing corporate social responsibility to assess corporate social performance.

The legal regulation of corporate social responsibility

12.9 One aspect of corporate social responsibility involves corporate philanthropy – the use of corporate funds for social or charitable purposes. It is not concerned with political donations as these are separately regulated by UK legislation: see Chapter 22 on the control of political donations by companies.

In most companies, directors control corporate funds. They are vested with powers delegated to them by shareholders to use corporate funds in the best interests of their company. In this respect, directors must exercise their powers and discretion bona fide for the company's best interests, not for improper purposes. However, directors cannot embark on philanthropic activities by depleting corporate funds at their discretion. They must comply with the legal framework which is intended to safeguard the interests of both creditors and investors from the unauthorised use of corporate funds, including observing their duties under the Companies Act 2006, in both equity and at common law.

12.10 This section considers the legal regulation of corporate philanthropy and gratuitous distributions. The starting point is a consideration of the *ultra vires* doctrine. Although the doctrine is now largely of historical interest, the purpose of considering it here is to demonstrate its influence on the development of corporate social responsibility in UK law and practice. The impact of the doctrine on corporate philanthropy is also considered. The existence of various judicial approaches reveals the inconsistency with which the courts have applied the doctrine in this area. The statutory regime under the Companies Act 2006 for regulating corporate philanthropy is considered.

Although companies are regulated to some extent as to how they may pursue social obligations, there has been no attempt to date to consolidate this very fragmented and piecemeal legal framework under a unifying regulatory system. There is a need for a coherent legal framework on corporate philanthropy and gratuitous distributions.

Ultra vires doctrine

12.11 The legal implications of and judicial approaches to corporate philanthropy can only be explained and understood by reference to the *ultra vires* doctrine. This section outlines the historical development of the doctrine and the sequence of reforms culminating in the enactment of the Companies Act 2006. Particular consideration will be given to the developments since 1985, notably the Prentice Report in 1986 and its partial implementation in the Companies Act 1989. It also looks at the courts' application of the doctrine and suggests that in some cases it has been misunderstood and incorrectly applied. This has resulted in a series of inconsistent judicial approaches in some of the cases on corporate philanthropy.

History and nature of the ultra vires doctrine – the position before 2006

12.12 The aim of the *ultra vires* doctrine as it applied to companies was to protect investors and creditors against unauthorised corporate activities and depletion of their funds. In the strict sense of the term, any transaction which was beyond the company's capacity as defined in its objects clause in the memorandum of association would be void and could not be ratified by the members. The common form of business organisations before the establishment of joint stock companies in 1844 was a partnership, but the *ultra vires* doctrine had no application to partnerships. Their liability was based on the concept of agency under actual or apparent authority and any change in the nature of partnership business required unanimous consent.

12.13 The incorporation of joint stock companies under the Companies Act 1844 required them to register their constitution in the form of a deed of settlement at Companies House. The deed of settlement was an extended form of partnership deed and the 1844 Act required such companies to provide a statement of the nature and purpose of their business. These companies had no corporate personality and, therefore, the *ultra vires* doctrine did not apply to them. Section 25 of that Act stated that the main powers and privileges of a deed of settlement company included a power to 'perform all other Acts necessary for carrying into effect the Purposes of such Company, and in all respects as other Partnerships are entitled to do'. Although the 1844 Act referred to the word 'company', the deed-of-settlement company was still just an extended form of partnership which had been granted certain corporate attributes. The doctrine also did not apply to chartered corporations even though they had a legal personality distinct from their members. Subsequent legislation particularly the Joint Stock Companies Act 1856, defined the limits and boundaries of corporate capacity when entering into transactions. This was achieved by compelling registered incorporated companies to state their object(s) or purpose(s) which could not be altered later by the members in a general meeting.

12.14 The *ultra vires* doctrine was first applied in its strict sense to registered and statutory companies in the mid-nineteenth century, with particular application to the railway and public utility companies. In the landmark decision of *Ashbury Railway Carriage and Iron Company v Riche* (1875) LR HL 653, the House of Lords was concerned with the effect of the railway company entering into a transaction which was not permitted by its objects clause. It held that a company incorporated under the Companies Acts had capacity to do only those acts which were expressly or impliedly authorised by its memorandum of association. The House of Lords clearly distinguished acts which were *ultra vires* the directors because they were beyond the powers delegated to them under their company's articles and, therefore, capable of ratification by the members, from those acts which were *ultra vires* the company because they were beyond the objects as expressed in the memorandum. These latter acts were correctly termed *ultra vires* and not ratifiable by the members in general meeting.

12.15 The strict rule in the *Ashbury* case was relaxed in subsequent cases which had gradually diminished the scope of the doctrine. Various devices were used to mitigate the extreme effects of the doctrine. In *A-G v Great Eastern Railway Company* (1880) 5 App Cas 473, the House of Lords concluded that, in addition to the express powers given to the company under its memorandum, a company had implied powers to do whatever was reasonably incidental to the carrying out of the express objects. Lord Selborne LC stated that 'the doctrine ought reasonably, and not unreasonably to be understood and applied …'. The doctrine could also be circumvented by the corporate practice of providing an extensive list of objects and powers in the memorandum and allowing companies the freedom to engage in a wide range of activities without being restricted by the doctrine. Although the House of Lords in *Cotman v Brougham* [1918] AC 514 viewed this activity as 'pernicious practice: confusing power with purpose', Lord Wrenbury felt he had to 'yield to it' but nevertheless expressed his dissatisfaction: 'It has arrived now at a point at which the fact is that the function of the memorandum is taken to be not to specify, not to disclose, but to bury beneath a mass of words the real object or objects of the company, with the intent that every conceivable form of activity shall be found included somewhere within its terms.'

12.16 This issue was resolved by the judicial practice of analysing and construing various objects and powers in the memorandum and defining the main as opposed to the ancillary objects of the company's activities. The courts applied the '*ejusdem generis*' rule of construction by deciding that the powers could only be used in relation to the company's objects. This became known as the 'main objects rule of construction'. In *Re Haven Gold Mining Company* (1882) 20 ChD 151, the court held that where the company's objects were expressed in a series of paragraphs, the court would look for those paragraphs which contained the company's main objects. All other sub-paragraphs would be considered ancillary to its main objects.

12.17 Some companies, nevertheless, evaded the distinction between powers and objects and thereby avoided the application of the *ultra vires* rule. This was achieved by the practice of including a provision at the end of the objects clause which stated that the objects should not be construed restrictively and that both paragraphs should be interpreted as a separate and an independent object. This was known as the *Cotman v Brougham* clause [1918] AC 514. The courts subsequently took a restrictive view of this form of clause. In *Re Introductions Limited v National Provincial Bank Limited* [1970] Ch 199, Harman J considered that not all powers could be objects: 'You cannot have an object to do every mortal thing you want, because that is to have no object at all.'

12.18 The legal rationale of allowing the main objects rule of construction to defeat the *ultra vires* doctrine was extended to subjective objects clauses. These were drafted to empower a company 'to carry on any other trade or business whatever, which can in the opinion of the board of directors, be advantageously carried on by, in connection with, or ancillary to, any of the above businesses or general business of the company'. The validity of this clause was upheld by the Court of Appeal in *Bell Houses Ltd v City Wall Properties Ltd* [1966] 1 QB 207, where the court applied a 'natural and ordinary meaning' to the clause and concluded that as long as the directors honestly and genuinely formed the view that a particular business could be carried on advantageously, any activity undertaken in reliance of such a clause would be within the company's capacity.

The doctrine sometimes impacted unfairly on innocent third parties to the transaction because of the doctrine of constructive notice which deems a party to have notice of the company's objects and capacity.

Reform of the law

12.19 Upon joining the European Community in 1972, the UK was required to implement the First Directive of the European Community on Company Law. Article 9 of the Directive required all Member States to provide protection for third parties dealing with companies. It stated that 'acts done by the organs of the company shall be binding upon it even if those acts are not within the objects of the company, unless such acts exceed the powers that the law confers, or allows to be conferred, on those organs.'

Article 9 also provided that if Member States could not comply with this provision, they could implement an alternative provision which stated that: '... the company shall not be bound where such acts are outside the objects of the company, if it proves that the third party knew that the act was outside those objects or could not in view of the circumstances have been unaware of it; disclosure of the statutes shall not of itself be sufficient proof thereof'.

12.20 The UK implemented the latter alternative in the form of s 9 of the European Communities Act 1972 which was later consolidated and became s 35 of the Companies Act 1985 which was concerned with the company's capacity.

The effect of s 35 was that a company would be bound by the decision of its directors regardless of whether the transaction with the third party was outside the company's objects clause, unless it could be shown that the third party was not acting in good faith. It was presumed that the third party was acting in good faith unless the contrary could be proved. The third party was not, however, required to examine the company's articles or memorandum to enquire into any limitations imposed on directors or the company's capacity to act by virtue of the contents of the constitution.

12.21 Section 35 did not completely abolish the *ultra vires* rule. It could not be relied upon by the company and only protected the third party dealing with the company in good faith. The section did not provide any definition of the words 'good faith'. It was also unclear whether 'directors' could also include a sole director. In construing s 35, some courts considered the First Directive as an aid to its interpretation.

The requirement of 'good faith' was considered in *International Sales and Agencies v Marcus* [1982] 3 All ER 551, where Lawson J decided that: '... the test of good faith in someone entering into obligations with a company will be found either in proof of his actual knowledge that the transaction was *ultra vires* the company or where it can be shown that such a person could not in view of all the circumstances have been unaware that he was a party to a transaction *ultra vires*.'

12.22 In *Barclays Bank Ltd v TOSG Trust Fund Ltd* [1984] BCLC 1, Nourse J was emphatic that the test of good faith was not objective but subjective requiring a person to act 'genuinely and honestly in the circumstances of the case'. See further Chapter 7 on corporate capacity.

In 1985, the Court of Appeal reconsidered the *ultra vires* rule in *Rolled Steel Products v British Steel Corporation* [1985] 3 All ER 52. Browne-Wilkinson LJ clarified the confusion which had existed in previous cases:

> 'The critical distinction is, therefore, between acts done in excess of the capacity of the company on the one hand and acts done in excess or abuse of the powers of the company on the other. If the transaction is beyond the capacity of the company it is in any event a nullity and wholly void: whether or not the third party had notice of the invalidity, property transferred or money paid under such a transaction will be recoverable from a third party. If, on the other hand, the transaction (although in excess or abuse of powers) is within the capacity of the company, the position of the third party depends upon whether or not he had notice that the transaction is beyond the capacity of the company or merely in excess or abuse of its power: in either event the shareholders will be able to restrain the carrying out of the transaction or hold liable those who have carried it out. Only if the question of ratification by all the shareholders arises will it be material to consider whether the transaction is beyond the capacity of the company since it is established that, although all the shareholders can ratify a transaction within the company's capacity, they cannot ratify a transaction falling outside its objects.'

However, this statement by Browne-Wilkinson LJ identified the proper definition to be attributed to the *ultra vires* doctrine. There clearly exists a distinction between 'acts done in excess of the capacity of the company' and 'acts done in excess or abuse of the powers of the company'. Unfortunately, this distinction was not maintained by the courts in some cases decided before *Rolled Steel Products*. Where a company acts in excess of its capacity, then its acts are *ultra vires*, but where it abuses its powers, it is liable to legal sanctions; the question of its acts being *ultra vires* does not arise. An abuse of power by the company can be disregarded if it is ratified by the company's shareholders. It is in light of this distinction that one should consider whether acts of corporate philanthropy in the form of donations or other forms of monetary or non-monetary consideration should be regarded as *ultra vires* or an abuse of power of the company. It is, however, to be emphasised that corporate philanthropy may be justified provided it is not regarded as an act in abuse of the power of the company.

12.23 In 1986 the Department of Trade and Industry commissioned Dr DD Prentice to review the *ultra vires* doctrine with a view to making recommendations in this area. A Consultative Document was produced to seek comments from various interested parties. According to the Department of Trade and Industry, 'in practice, it (ie the *ultra vires* doctrine) represents an obstacle to enterprise and works so capriciously that it is doubtful whether it offers any real protection to anyone'.

The Prentice Report recommended the complete abolition of the *ultra vires* doctrine since it no longer served any useful purpose. His recommendations, *inter alia*, were that a company should have the capacity to do any act whatsoever; a third party dealing with a company should not be affected by the contents of any document merely because it was registered with the registrar of companies or with the company (this could be made the subject of appropriate exceptions); a company should be bound by the acts of its board or an individual director; a third party should be under no obligation to determine the scope of the authority of a company's board or an individual director, or the contents of a company's articles or memorandum (this should extend to documents which have to be registered under s 380 of the Companies Act 1985); a third party who has actual knowledge that a board or an individual director does not possess authority to enter into a transaction on behalf of the company should not be allowed to enforce it against the company but the company should be free to ratify it. The same result should obtain where a third party has actual knowledge that the transaction falls outside the company's objects but in this case ratification should be by special resolution; knowledge in this context will require understanding and it will only be the knowledge of the individual entering into the particular transaction which will be relevant. As regards actual knowledge, Prentice recommended that the rules should be modified where a third party is an officer or director of the company and in this situation, constructive knowledge should be sufficient to render the transaction unenforceable and, for this purpose, constructive knowledge which may reasonably be expected of a person carrying out the functions of that director or officer of that company.

12.24 Although the Companies Act 1989 had virtually repealed the *ultra vires* doctrine, the Act has not adopted the recommendations proposed by Prentice. It instead inserted a new s 3A into the Companies Act 1985 ('Statement of Company's Objects'). This provided that where the memorandum states that the company's object is to carry on business as a 'general commercial company', the company can carry on any trade or business whatsoever. It also had the power to do all such things as are incidental or conducive to the carrying on of any trade or business by it, including philanthropic acts. Section 3A was intended to encourage companies to use the 'short form' objects clause rather than the 'long form' objects clause which was widely drafted to avoid the *ultra vires* doctrine.

Further steps towards the virtual abolition of the *ultra vires* doctrine were achieved by substituting the original s 35 above (CA 2006, ss 35, 35A and 35B as amended), which sections have now been transposed under the Companies Act 2006.

Judicial approaches to corporate philanthropy and gratuitous distributions

12.25 Some complex legal issues can arise where a company engages in corporate philanthropy or gratuitous distributions in the form of gifts to institutions and political parties or by way of remuneration and pensions to directors, which are of an altruistic nature. The cases show that the courts have, over the years, viewed such payments with no great enthusiasm, and sometimes with outright hostility.

In some cases, the courts have misapplied the doctrine by referring to the term *ultra vires* as an abuse or misuse of power by directors rather than to the company's capacity. This section considers the various judicial approaches that the courts have taken in addressing corporate philanthropy and gratuitous distributions, including the circumstances when they are permissible or declared as *ultra vires*.

Business judgment approach

12.26 This approach was one of the first to be applied by the English courts to some cases on corporate philanthropy. It allows corporate gifts to be made where decisions are taken by directors bona fide as to what they consider (not what the court considers) is in the best interests of their company. It appears that the courts are reluctant to interfere with directors' business decisions, as they are best placed to manage their company's business. This approach is also concerned with the extent to which the wishes of the majority can be questioned by minority shareholders. The courts will not generally entertain any shareholders' proceedings against a company under the rule in *Foss v Harbottle* (1843) 2 Hare 461.

In what has come to be regarded as a seminal exposition of the rule, Jenkins LJ in *Edwards v Halliwell* [1950] 2 All ER 1064, stated that it was based upon two propositions: first, the proper plaintiff in an action in respect of a wrong alleged to be done to a company is *prima facie* the company; and second, only the majority of the shareholders can decide to bring proceedings where a wrong has been done to the company.

Directors should not be prevented from carrying on business in a manner most conducive to the company's welfare

One of the earliest English applications of the business judgment approach to corporate philanthropy is *Taunton v Royal Insurance Company* (1864) 2 H & M 135. A minority shareholder in the insurance company attempted to restrain the company and its directors from offering to pay compensation to 80 householders in Liverpool whose houses were damaged by a gunpowder explosion on board a vessel. He also sought a declaration that the directors were personally liable to account for any payments already made to those affected by the explosion. The company's articles of association gave directors the power to settle and adjust claims and also general powers to conduct the company's business – including insurance – against any form of casualty according to their discretion as might be for the company's welfare. Counsel for the plaintiff argued that the payments by the insurance company to the owners of the houses were not covered by such risks under the terms of the insurance policy. Relying on *Foss v Harbottle*, the defendants, however, contended that the payment of compensation to those affected by the explosion was an internal business arrangement with which the court should not interfere. Counsel for the defendants argued: 'Could not the directors give a Christmas Box? If either the directors or the company in general meeting can do this, the Plaintiff is out of court on the principle of *Foss v Harbottle*.'

Further, it was also 'customary' for officers to pay compensation even where such explosions were excluded by the company's insurance policy. The company benefited in dealing 'liberally with customers, even to the extent of paying losses not strictly within the terms of their policies'.

Vice-Chancellor, Sir Page Wood, stated that it was not in the interests of companies that the conduct of their business should be 'needlessly hampered'. Directors should not be prevented from carrying on business in a manner most conducive to the company's welfare. The expenditure of corporate funds was 'designed to secure to the company the largest possible amount of profit in its own proper business'. The Vice Chancellor stated that the payment was made not on the ground of legal liability but because the directors thought it 'judicious' to do so. The action therefore failed. There was also concern for the company's welfare and reputation in the community if these payments were not made.

The company wished to avoid any questions which its customers could raise at law as to its strict obligations or any imputation on its liberality when paying compensation for the losses which were incurred: 'It is said that the payment is a mere gratuity. Let it be so called, it does not follow that it is beyond the power of the company if to give such gratuities be the generally received method of conducting such a business.'

Directors had acted bona fide in approving payments to their employees for their hard work and effort

This business judgment approach was followed in *Hampson v Price's Patent Candle Company* (1876) 45 LJ Ch 437, where as a matter of factory management policy, the directors had proposed to make one week's *ex-gratia* payment (in addition to the usual wages) to their employees 'in recognition of the fact that their exertions have helped to make the company's profits larger than they have been for the last sixteen years'. These payments were for employees who had 'worked there with good character throughout the year'. There was no express power in the memorandum to pay these gratuities. A majority of the shareholders had approved the payments, but the plaintiff, who was one of the dissenting shareholders, brought an action against the company. Hampson alleged that the company could not, under its constitution, authorise voluntary expenditure from the corporate funds. He contended that the resolution approving the payment was void and illegal and that the company should be restrained from making these payments. He also argued that the distribution of funds to the employees was beyond the scope of the directors' authority.

Jessel MR decided that the company's articles gave wide powers of management to its directors. They could, therefore, lawfully exercise all the powers of the company. In approving the payments he reasoned: 'Can anything be more reasonable than that, when the employer has had a very good year through the exertions of the workmen employed by him, he should give them something more than their ordinary wages by encouraging them to exert themselves for the future?'

The directors had clearly acted *bona fide* by seeking approval for the payment from their shareholders. The court would not interfere where directors had decided that the proposed payment to their employees would encourage them to work for the company's benefit. This was the 'best mode' of conducting the company's affairs as determined by the directors and 'no judge ought to give an opinion on matters of this kind, which he does not understand'. Jessel MR concluded that: '… the managers and directors of the company whose business it is, and who ought to know how to conduct the business to the most advantage, ought to be allowed to judge whether what is about to be done is advantageous and reasonable or not'.

Liberal approach

12.27 A liberal approach has, on occasions, been applied by the English courts in allowing companies to engage in corporate philanthropy. In the absence of an express power in the company's constitution to make gratuitous payments, the courts have, in some cases, implied a power to make these donations provided they are reasonably incidental or conducive to the company's business. In 1962, the Jenkins Committee on Company Law Reform reasserted this liberal approach and went so far as to say that: 'The practice, which has developed, of companies (without express powers) making donations to general charities of no direct interest to the companies' business has never been challenged in the courts in this country and we venture to think that this practice, which is regarded by businessmen as necessary to create or preserve goodwill for their companies, would on that ground, be acceptable to the court today.'

A corporate donation may be made provided it is reasonably incidental to the company's objects

The case of *Evans v Brunner Mond* [1921] 1 Ch 359 is one of the first applications of this liberal approach. One of the company's objects, in clause 3 of its memorandum, stated that it could do 'all such business and things as may be incidental or conducive to the attainment of the above objects, or any of them'. The shareholders had passed a resolution authorising their directors to distribute £100,000 to various universities and scientific institutions in furtherance of scientific education and research. A dissenting shareholder sought an injunction to restrain the company from making this payment claiming a declaration that the resolution was *ultra vires* the objects and powers of the company. The plaintiff's counsel argued that the donation was not within the company's objects and there was no direct benefit to the company. Counsel for the company argued, however, that the donation was reasonably incidental and conducive to the company's main objects because the company required persons equipped to undertake research work and the donation to the universities would assist the company in this respect. According to the evidence presented by the directors by way of affidavits, the company, by its contribution, wished to encourage a class of persons who would cultivate scientific study and research generally. According to the plaintiff's counsel, therefore, in the event of a donation being conducive to the company, it may be regarded as lawful.

Eve J construed the company's objects as permitting donations for the furtherance of scientific education and research. He appreciated the past practice by the courts of distinguishing between objects and powers, but thought that it was not now necessary to distinguish between the two. It was merely sufficient to interpret the extent and scope of the company's objects. His Lordship concluded: 'The wide and general objects are to be construed as ancillary to the company's main purpose, and I apprehend that the act to be intra vires must be one which can fairly be regarded as incidental or conducive to the main or paramount purpose for which the company was formed.'

12.28 In *Tomkinson v South-Eastern Railway Company* (1887) 35 ChD 675, at a meeting of the shareholders of a railway company (which was established by statute), a resolution was passed authorising the directors to subscribe a sum of £1,000 out of the company's funds by way of a donation towards the Imperial Institute for the purposes of exhibitions and sporting events. Kay J held that the proposed donation to the Imperial Institute was not within the objects of the railway company, nor was it reasonably incidental to the company's main purpose. Kay J stated: 'To say…that any expenditure which may indirectly conduce to the benefit of the company, is *intra vires*, seems to me to be extravagant'. Accordingly an injunction was granted to prevent such donation.

A corporate donation must be reasonably incidental to the company's objects

The liberal approach has also been applied in some US cases on corporate philanthropy. In *A P Smith Mfg v Barlow* (1953) 13 NJ 145, the directors proposed to donate '$1,500 to Princeton University and a further contribution towards its maintenance'. Some of the minority shareholders brought an action to prevent this distribution of corporate funds on the ground that the company's objects did not expressly permit such donations. Further, there was no implied power to make them.

The company's president testified that he considered the payment was a good investment and that the public expected companies to aid philanthropic and benevolent institutions. He expressed the view that, in contributing to the liberal arts institutions, companies 'were furthering self-interest' in ensuring the free flow of properly trained personnel for administrative and corporate employment. Jacobs J reviewed the historical literature on corporate social responsibility and observed that the early corporate charters referred to services to the public in their recitals: 'The corporate object was the public one of managing and ordering the trade as well as the private one of profit for the members.' He upheld the validity of the donation because it was reasonably incidental to the company's objectives and benefited the company's reputation by establishing a closer relationship with local educational institutions. The court also upheld the donation on the general grounds of a company's wider obligations to the community. Jacobs J stated:

> 'Modern conditions require that corporations acknowledge and discharge social as well as private responsibilities as members of the communities within which they operate.'

The liberal approach, therefore, justifies corporate philanthropy by referring to its role in contributing to the socio-economic health of the community.

The restrictive approach

12.29 Where the company is no longer a 'going concern' because of its insolvency or near insolvency, and is not in a position to exercise corporate philanthropy nor is capable of discharging any social obligations, the courts have applied a restrictive approach. The expenditure of corporate funds in these circumstances would, therefore, be *ultra vires*. The rationale for this approach is protection of the interests of creditors and shareholders investing in the company against the unlawful depletion of corporate funds by directors. A further justification for this restrictive approach is that a company which is in the process of winding up cannot be in a position to maximise profits for the shareholders. This approach reflects the traditional economic perspective that the only social responsibilities of companies are to maximise profits for the benefit of their shareholders. According to Sealy, 'the 'shareholders' money' approach rests on the basic assumption that companies *are* formed with the paramount aim of earning profits, and the investors contribute their capital on that understanding'.

Corporate funds could not be used where the company was no longer a going concern

This restrictive approach was applied in the English case of *Hutton v West Cork Railway Company* (1883) 23 ChD 654. An action was brought by the holder of a debenture stock who did not approve of a resolution by the company to make certain payments to the company's officers. The court was required to decide whether the sum of £1,050 could lawfully be paid by the company as compensation to its managing director and other officers for loss of their employment. It was also required to determine whether another sum of £1,500 could be paid to directors as remuneration for their past services in circumstances where the company was no longer a going concern. The railway company had sought to sell its undertaking to another company but it had no express provisions in its articles for the payment of remuneration to its directors and had never previously made such payments. The Act authorised the transfer of business provided that, on completion of the transfer, the company would be dissolved except for the purposes of regulating its internal affairs and using the proceeds of the sale in the manner resolved by the company. The Court of Appeal held that a power to make these payments could not be implied after the company had ceased to be a going concern. The powers could be implied only as incidental to the company's business but not where the company was moribund.

Cotton LJ distinguished this case from the *Taunton* and *Hampson* cases where payments were made by companies which were going concerns. In the present case, the company was no longer a going concern. The proposed payment of £1,050 to the company's directors was a gratuity but without any prospect of it being in any way reasonably conducive to the company's benefit. His lordship considered that payment as *ultra vires*. The other proposed payment of £1,500 to the directors was not a reasonable sum as remuneration for their past services. It was instead 'a sum which might with reasonable generosity be paid to them taking into consideration the fact that they never received anything during the years when they carried on the railway'. This payment was also held to be beyond the company's powers and *ultra vires*.

Bowen LJ sympathised with the directors' dilemma, but felt that their interests must be balanced against the interests of the dissenting shareholders:

> 'They can only spend money which is not theirs but the company's, if they are spending it for purposes which are reasonably incidental to the carrying on of the business of the company.'

Bowen LJ reasoned that *bona fides* could not be the sole test 'otherwise you might have a lunatic conducting the affairs of the company, and paying away its money with both hands in a matter perfectly *bona fide* yet perfectly irrational'. The test was whether the payment was reasonably incidental to and within the reasonable scope of carrying on the company's business. In the absence of any express provisions in the company's articles, the payments to the directors would amount to a gratuity. Thus:

> 'A railway company, or the directors of the company, might send down all the porters at a railway station to have tea in the country at the expense of the company. Why should they not? It is for the directors to judge, provided it is a matter which is reasonably incidental to the carrying on of the business of the company; and a company which always treated its employees with Draconian severity, and never allowed them a single inch more than the strict letter of the bond, would soon find itself deserted – at all events, unless labour was very much more easy to obtain in the market than it often is …
>
> It is no charity sitting at the board of directors because … charity has no business to sit at the board of directors qua charity. The law does not say that there are to be no cakes and ale, but there are to be no cakes and ale except such as are required for the benefit of the company.'

12.30 This statement by Bowen LJ clearly suggests that a company has the sole authority to determine what would be regarded as being for the benefit of the company. However, where the company had ceased to be a going concern it could not derive any benefit from the gratuitous distribution. The company had a special and limited business 'and that business was to preside at its own funeral, to wind itself up and to carry on its own internal affairs'.

Redundancy payments from corporate funds could not be made where the company was no longer a going concern

The restrictive policy was applied in *Parke v Daily News Limited* [1962] Ch 927. The defendant company was in the process of selling its two main associated newspapers which had incurred losses, to Associated Newspapers. The directors of the *Daily News* had intended to distribute the proceeds of the sale to the company's employees who were to be made redundant. Before a meeting of *Daily News* shareholders could be convened to approve the proposed payment to the employees, the plaintiff brought an action against the company claiming that the proposed payment was *ultra vires* the company.

Plowman J decided that the directors were not acting in the best interests of their shareholders. The directors' decision was actuated by other motives, predominant among which was 'a desire to treat the employees generously beyond all legal entitlement'.

In considering the directors' affidavits which provided substantive evidence that 'the employees had claims to consideration' which it was proper for the company to consider, Plowman J accepted:

> 'The view that directors, in having regard to the question "what is in the best interests of their company" are entitled to take into account the interests of the employees, irrespective of any consequential benefit to the company, is one which may be widely held.'

However, in answer to the affidavit of the *Daily News* accountant that companies had an obligation to their employees, Plowman J replied 'but no authority to support that proposition as a proposition of law was cited to me. I know of none, and in my judgment, such is not the law'. The directors were prompted by motives which, however laudable and however enlightened from the point of view of industrial relations, were such that the law would not recognise as sufficient the justification for making the proposed payments to the employees. This was based on the reasoning that the *Daily News* would cease to be a going concern after the business was sold to Associated Newspapers.

The 'three pertinent questions' approach

12.31 When considering the nature of corporate transactions (including corporate philanthropic and gratuitous distributions), the court should consider three questions in determining the validity of such transactions.

The court will have regard to three pertinent 'questions' in determining whether corporate payments could be made

This approach derives from *Re Lee Behrens & Company Limited* [1932] 2 Ch 46, in which the company's directors had resolved to provide an annuity for a period of five years to the widow of the company's former managing director on his death. The company's constitution contained an express power to that effect. At a later date, a resolution was passed for a voluntary winding up of the company. The widow lodged a proof in winding up for the capitalised value of the annuity. Counsel for the widow argued that the pension payment was not *ultra vires* since there was power under the company's articles to provide for the welfare of persons employed or formerly employed by the company, including the employees' widows and children. But the company's liquidator argued that the annuity payment granted to the widow was a gratuitous payment.

Eve J held that the transaction was not 'for the benefit of the company or reasonably incidental to the company's business'. The power to provide for the annuity was not within the terms of the company's articles. The company had failed to seek the approval of the shareholders in a general meeting and it was, consequently, *ultra vires*. According to Eve J, whether or not payments could be made under an express or implied power depended upon the answers to 'three pertinent questions', namely:

(1) Is the transaction reasonably incidental to the carrying on of the company's business?

(2) Is it a *bona fide* transaction?

(3) Is it done for the benefit, and to promote the prosperity, of the company?

He decided that the predominant and only consideration in the minds of the directors was a desire to provide for the widow without considering whether any benefit could be derived by the company as a result. Another ground for rejecting the pension payment was that it was a gift from the company's assets by the directors. They could not use corporate assets unless authorised to do so by the company's constitution. However, it is submitted that if Eve J's decision related to the company's capacity, then it is erroneous since there was an express power to provide the pension in this case. This case misapplied the *ultra vires* rule. The decision can only be defended on the grounds that there was of a breach of duty by the directors.

The application of the 'three pertinent questions' meant that corporate funds could not be used to benefit a director's widow

In *Re W & M Roith Limited* [1967] 1 All ER 427, the company's articles were altered to enable the directors to award pensions and annuities to certain persons including widows of directors. There was a service agreement between Roith in his capacity as a director and the company, whereby Roith was appointed as a general manager for the remainder of his life and devoted the whole of his time and abilities to the company's business. One of the provisions of his service agreement provided for payments to his wife in the event of his death. A few months after his death, the company went into a creditors' voluntary liquidation. However, Plowman J held that the true inference from the circumstances was that the service agreement was not reasonably incidental to the carrying on of the company's business nor was it entered into *bona fide* for the benefit, and to promote the prosperity, of the company. He applied the three tests enumerated by Eve J in *Re Lee Behrens*. He decided that the whole object of these payments was to benefit the widow, not the company. The payments were, therefore, *ultra vires* the company. In light of subsequent cases, *Re Roith* must now be regarded as dubious authority.

12.32 The decision in *Re Lee Behrens* (and the cases which have applied this test) is now largely of historical interest as it was criticised and distinguished by Pennycuick J in *Charterbridge Corporation Limited v Lloyds Bank Limited* [1970] Ch 62, as inappropriate to the scope of express powers. This case concerned a group guarantee. Lloyds Bank had advanced money to the property development subsidiary in a group, provided that each other company in the group gave a guarantee of the indebtedness secured by a debenture on its assets. The issue in this case was whether the guarantees and debentures given by the other companies were *ultra vires*. The objects clause contained an express power providing for the giving of guarantees and debentures by the companies. In commenting on the three tests in the *Behrens* case, Pennycuick J stated that the first of the three pertinent questions posed by Eve J was only appropriate to the scope of the implied powers of a company which did not have an express power. The second test was appropriate in part to the duties of directors and not corporate capacity. The third test was wholly inappropriate to the scope of express powers and notwithstanding the words 'whether they may be made under an express or implied power' at the beginning of the power. He doubted whether Eve J really intended the last test to apply to express powers. Pennycuick J stated:

> 'Apart from authority, I should feel little doubt that where a company is carrying out the purposes expressed in its memorandum, and does an act within the scope of a power expressed in its memorandum, that act is an act within the powers of the company. The memorandum of a company sets out its objects and proclaims them to persons dealing with the company and it would be contrary to the whole function of a memorandum that objects unequivocally set out in it should be subject to some implied limitation by reference to the state of mind of the parties concerned. Where directors misapply the assets of their company, that may give rise to a claim based on breach of duty. Again, a claim may arise against the other party to the transaction, if he has notice that the transaction was effected in breach of duty. Further, in a proper case, the company concerned may be entitled to have the transaction set aside. But all that results from the ordinary law of agency and has not of itself anything to do with the corporate powers of the company.'

The *Re Lee Behrens* three questions approach has now been finally laid to rest in *Rolled Steel Products (Holdings) Limited v British Steel Corporation* [1986] Ch 246. The Court of Appeal stated that the *Behrens* case was of no assistance and 'positively misleading when the relevant question is whether a particular gratuitous transaction was within a company's corporate capacity'. The Court of Appeal stated that the confusion had arisen from the misuse of the term *ultra vires*. In the correct usage of the term, it referred to acts in excess of the company's capacity in which case the transaction would be void and not capable of ratification. Those acts which were in excess or an abuse of the power of directors were not *ultra vires* and could be ratified by the members in general meeting. Both the *Behrens* and the *Roith* decisions were concerned with the latter aspect.

Modern approaches

12.33 There have been a series of decisions in the 1980s on gratuitous distributions in which the propriety of the application of the *ultra vires* doctrine have been considered. These cases have concerned express provisions in the company's constitution enabling such payments to be made.

Payments from corporate fund may be genuine and not a disguised gift out of capital

In *Re Halt Garage (1964) Limited* [1982] 3 All ER 1016, the company's general meeting resolved to award remuneration to both the husband and wife who were its only directors. Its articles provided an express power, *inter alia*, to award remuneration to directors. Oliver J held that the competence of the company to award the remuneration pursuant to the company's express power depended upon whether the payments were 'genuine directors' remuneration' as opposed to a 'disguised gift out of capital'. Therefore, if a transaction was *intra vires*, the test was to consider the genuineness and honesty of the transaction including the exercise of that power. He rejected the test that payments were required to be for the 'benefit of the company' and considered the previous cases on the application of the *ultra vires* principle to gratuitous distributions to be incorrect. The test of '*bona fide*' or 'benefit to the company' was only appropriate to the question of propriety of the exercise of a power rather than the capacity to exercise it.

Oliver J stated:

> 'In the absence of fraud on the creditors or on minority shareholders, the quantum of such remuneration is a matter for the company. There is no implication or requirement that it must come out of profits only and, indeed, any requirement that it must be so restricted would, in many cases, bring businesses to a halt and prevent a business which had fallen on hard times from being brought round … I cannot help thinking, if I may respectfully say so, that there has been a certain confusion between the requirements for a valid exercise of the fiduciary powers of directors (which have nothing to do with the capacity of the company but everything to do with the propriety of acts done within that capacity), the extent to which powers can be implied or limits be placed, as a matter of construction, on express powers, and the matters which the court will take into consideration at the suit of a minority shareholder in determining the extent to which his interests can be overridden by a majority vote. These three matters, as it seems to me, raise questions which are logically quite distinct but which have sometimes been treated as if they demanded a single, universal answer leading to the conclusion that, because a power must not be abused, therefore, beyond the limit of propriety it does not exist …
>
> The real test must, I think, be whether the transaction in question was a genuine exercise of the power. The motive is more important than the label. Those who deal with a limited company do so on the basis that its affairs will be conducted in accordance with its constitution, one of the express incidents of which is that the directors may be paid remuneration. Subject to that, they are entitled to have the capital kept intact. They have to accept the shareholders' assessment of the scale of that remuneration, but they are entitled to assume that, whether liberal or illiberal, what is paid is genuinely remuneration and that the power is not used as a cloak for making payments out of capital to the shareholders as such.'

Corporate philanthropy may be exercised by a company provided the objects expressly allow for such activities

In *Re Horsley and Weight Limited* [1982] Ch 442, the Court of Appeal was also required to consider the applicability of the *ultra vires* rule to gratuitous distributions. It held that if an act which was expressed in the company's memorandum was capable of being an 'independent substantive object', it could not be *ultra vires* because it was by definition something which the company was established to do. Buckley LJ appeared to sanction gratuitous distributions for philanthropic purposes provided they were expressly stated in the objects clause:

> 'The objects of a company do not need to be commercial; they can be charitable or philanthropic; indeed they can be whatever the original incorporators wish, provided that they are legal. Nor is there any reason why a company should not part with its funds gratuitously or for non-commercial reasons if to do so is within its objects.'

12.34 In *Aveling Barford Ltd v Perion Ltd* [1989] BCLC 626, the company's balance sheet (which was now in liquidation) showed that, on a going concern basis, its assets exceeded its liabilities but that it had an accumulated deficit on its profit and loss account and therefore was not in a position to make any distribution to its shareholders. The company sold property, valued by an independent valuer at £650,000, to the first defendant company, a company which was controlled by L who also controlled the plaintiff company. The purchase price of the property was £350,000. The purchase was to be financed in part by a mortgage and the mortgagee company valued the property at £1,150,000. It also appeared that the company and the defendant had agreed that should the defendant sell the property within a year of the transaction then the defendant would pay the company £400,000 if the sale price exceeded £800,000. Within a year of the transaction the defendant sold the property for £1,526,000. The company obtained judgment in default on the ground that the first defendant was a constructive trustee of the proceeds of the sale of the property. The first defendant sought to have the judgment set aside. It was held by the court that as L knew that the property was worth £650,000, it was a breach of L's fiduciary duty to arrange to sell the property for £350,000 and, since the first defendant was aware of the facts constituting the breach, it was accountable as a constructive trustee. The sale to the defendant was not a genuine exercise of the power of the plaintiff to sell its property. It was a sale at an undervalue for the purpose of enabling L, the sole beneficial owner of the plaintiff, to obtain an unauthorised return of capital and hence was *ultra vires* and unratifiable.

12.35 Hoffmann J stated:

> 'So it seems to me in this case that looking at the matter objectively, the sale to Perion was not a genuine exercise of the company's power under its memorandum to sell its assets. It was a sale at a gross undervalue for the purpose of enabling a profit to be realised by an entity controlled and put forward by its sole beneficial shareholder. This was as much a dressed-up distribution as the payment of excessive interest in *Ridge Securities* or excessive

remuneration in *Halt Garage*. The company had at the time no distributable reserves and the sale was therefore *ultra vires* and incapable of validation by the approval or ratification of the shareholder.'

12.35 In *Commissioners of Inland Revenue v. Richmond and Jones*, [2003] EWCA 999 (Ch), the court decided that directors who caused their company to make *ultra vires* payments were in the same position as trustees who make payments in breach of trust, and are liable to make good the money so applied: see too *Re Lands Allotment Company* [1894] 1 Ch 616.

The courts will also have regard to the genuineness of the transaction

In *Progress Property Co Ltd v Moorgarth Group Ltd* [2010] 1 BCLC 1, the issue concerned the sale of shares where the sale was negotiated by a director in the genuine belief that the transaction was a commercial sale at market value. The court was required to decide whether the sale of the shares was an unlawful distribution of assets and *ultra vires*.

The Court of Appeal decided that the well-settled common law rule devised for the protection of the creditors of a company was that a distribution of a company's assets to a shareholder, except in accordance with specific statutory procedures such as the winding up of a company, was an unlawful return of capital which was *ultra vires* the company. However, what made the sale of a company's asset to a shareholder an unlawful distribution and *ultra vires* was the fact that it was known and intended to be a sale at an undervalue and was not a genuine sale. The correct test to be applied by the court on the issue of *ultra vires* was to look to the true nature and substance of the payment and assess whether it was genuine by determining the facts as they were genuinely perceived to be and, having regard to the nature and character of the payment, it could properly be characterised as something other than a gratuitous distribution to one or more shareholders.

In this case, there was no *mala fides* intended: the transaction was genuine and not a disguised distribution of assets.

For a wider interpretation as to 'capacity' in an international conflict of laws perspective to enter into transactions, see *Haugesund Kommune and another v Depfa ACS Bank (Wikborg Rein & Co, Part 20 defendant)* [2011] 1 All ER (Comm) 985.

12.36 Historically, the business judgment approach facilitated corporate philanthropy by allowing corporate gifts to be made where decisions were taken *bona fide* by the directors in the company's best interests or by a majority of the shareholders in a general meeting. This was a nineteenth-century approach before the strict *ultra vires* doctrine was devised by the courts. The liberal approach, which survived for a longer period, was compatible with the *ultra vires* doctrine by allowing companies to engage in corporate philanthropy provided the donation was reasonably incidental or conducive to the company's business. The restrictive approach, on the other hand, was not inconsistent with the liberal approach but it applied in limited circumstances, especially where a company was either insolvent or near insolvency. In the *Hutton* and *Parke* cases, the companies were no longer 'going concerns' so that the interests of shareholders and creditors were considered paramount in the circumstances. The

Re Lee Behrens 'three questions' approach was inconsistent and inappropriate to the doctrine of corporate philanthropy. The 'three questions' approach survived for at least 50 years but it misapplied the *ultra vires* doctrine confusing corporate capacity with directors' powers. *Re Lee Behrens* must now be regarded as dubious authority in the light of criticisms of the *Behrens'* case in *Charterbridge* and *Rolled Steel Products*. The modern judicial approaches, however, accord a proper interpretation of the *ultra vires* doctrine and its application to corporate philanthropy by clearly distinguishing between acts beyond the corporate capacity and, therefore, *ultra vires*, from acts in excess of directors' powers which are not *ultra vires* and are capable of ratification by shareholders in a general meeting.

These various judicial approaches, therefore, demonstrate the inconsistent manner in which the courts have applied the *ultra vires* doctrine to corporate philanthropy. Although the recent judicial approaches have clarified the confusion which had previously existed on the *ultra vires* doctrine, the position has now changed since the external effect of the doctrine has been repealed by the Companies Act 2006.

Statutory regime for corporate social responsibility

12.37 The starting point for a consideration of legal aspects of companies exercising corporate social responsibility is the Companies Act 2006. The following form the statutory basis for regulation of corporate social responsibilities:

Objects clause

12.38 Under s 31(1) of CA 2006, 'unless a company's articles specifically restrict the objects of the company, its objects are unrestricted'. The effect of this section is that a company's objects are unlimited: it can carry on any trade or business or service. The objects must, however, be legal and the company must be established for a legal purpose. A company may not be so formed for an unlawful purpose: CA 2006, s 7(2). The effect of having an unrestricted objects clause is that it allows contractual freedom for the company to enter into transactions internally and externally with third parties. It obviates any barriers or obstacles that may previously have existed. Companies do not need to amend their articles of association to add other business activities: the very nature of the unrestricted objects means that, practically, the company is able to engage in transactions and conclude agreements in a timely manner.

12.39 Although a company may have unrestricted objects, s 31(1) still allows it specifically to restrict the company's objects if it so requires. So, although certain objects may be permitted to be conducted by the company, other activities or acts may be expressly prohibited. For example, the company's objects may provide the following:

> 'The company's objects shall be unrestricted except that it shall not be engaged in any charitable or philanthropic donations.'

Here, the company specifically restricts its capacity to provide these activities. It would be open to interpretation as to what exactly constituted 'charitable' or 'philanthropic' donations as the objects here do not define these terms. Would, for example, the provision of corporate facilities (such as the use of a hall for events/workshop training) to a voluntary organisation constitute a charitable donation? Is the term 'donation' strictly limited to financial contributions? Or does it include other forms of charitable services including voluntary work within the community? The terms may need to be further defined or refined to ensure, with absolute clarity, the nature of the activities or services that were to be restricted (eg financial donations may be expressly prohibited, but not other forms of voluntary services).

12.40 The revised objects clause may then appear as follows:

> 'The company's objects shall be unrestricted except that it shall not be engaged in any charitable or philanthropic donations. The term "donations" in this context shall mean any financial contributions by the Company, but shall exclude any voluntary services or assumption of voluntary responsibilities by the Company in relation to charitable or philanthropic activities.'

The extent of the restriction can therefore be set out and defined as required by the company depending upon the circumstances and such restrictions, if any, will be set out in the company's articles of association, and not the memorandum of association.

Company's capacity

12.41 Assuming that there is a restriction in the company's objects clause as set out in the articles of association on the corporate or philanthropic donations and the company, in breach of this restriction, engages in providing donations to a charity or for a charitable cause. Is the provision of the financial donation beyond the company's capacity?

Section 39(1) of CA 2006 provides that the validity of an act done by a company shall not be called into question on the ground of lack of capacity by reason of anything in the company's constitution. This means that the 'act' (ie the financial contribution to a charity or for a philanthropic cause) will not be beyond the company's capacity. The company still has the capacity to undertake this prohibited or restricted act. It will not be *ultra vires*. It cannot be challenged as exceeding the company's capacity. As between the third party and the company, the financial contribution is valid and cannot be questioned even where the company lacked the capacity to do so in its articles of association.

The effect is that there is no longer any *ultra vires* (external effects) to be invoked to prevent the financial contribution being made. Companies have the flexibility and freedom to engage in such prohibited transactions with third parties. For further analysis, see Chapter 7 on corporate capacity and related matters.

Power of directors to bind the company

12.42 However, as between the company and the directors, the internal effects of the *ultra vires* doctrine still survive and apply to directors.

Section 40(1) of CA 2006 begins with a presumption of 'good faith' in favour of a person dealing with the company. The power of the directors to bind the company, or authorise others to do so, is deemed to be free of any limitation under the company's constitution. The term 'constitution' includes the company's articles of association. For this purpose:

(a) a person 'deals with' a company if he is a party to any transaction or other act to which the company is a party;

(b) a person dealing with a company:

(i) is not bound to enquire as to any limitation on the powers of the directors to bind the company or authorise others to do so;

(ii) is presumed to have acted in good faith unless the contrary is proved; and

(iii) is not to be regarded as acting in bad faith by reason only of his knowing that an act is beyond the powers of the directors under the company's constitution.

12.43 The third party is not bound to enquire into the company's constitution as to any limitations or restrictions or powers of authority. The third party can assume that the directors have the powers to act on the company's behalf.

The references above to limitations on the directors' powers under the company's constitution include limitations deriving:

(a) from a resolution of the company or of any class of shareholders; or

(b) from any agreement between the members of the company or of any class of shareholders.

However, as between the directors and the shareholders, s 40 does not affect any right of a member of the company to bring proceedings to restrain the doing of an action that is beyond the powers of the directors. But no such proceedings lie in respect of an act to be done in fulfilment of a legal obligation arising from a previous act of the company. The right of a member to bring proceedings applies to any present or future actions in which the directors have engaged and which was beyond their powers. A member will not be able to bring an action where the company was already bound to fulfil a legal obligation which also includes any contractual obligation which the company was bound to fulfil.

12.44 In practice, it may be very difficult for shareholders to ascertain the future intentions of directors on donations or directors' policy on corporate philanthropy. Directors still have obligations to the company under s 40, which states, *inter alia*, that 'it remains the duty of the directors to observe any limitations on their powers flowing from the company's memorandum'. If any loss to the company is caused by their entering into a legal obligation (eg a cash donation) they may be liable to their company for a breach of their fiduciary duties. Therefore, irrespective of shareholders' application for an injunction, the requirement for directors to perform their fiduciary duties properly operates as a blocking mechanism in this regard.

In the context of corporate philanthropy, the 'transaction' could be a contract entered into with, for example, a charitable institution and the 'act' could include directors making gratuitous distributions or *ex-gratia* payments. The act or transaction which is entered into must be approved by the board of directors acting collectively or by any person authorised by them. Section 40 also provides that a third party will not be acting in bad faith by reason of his knowing that the act is beyond the powers of directors under the company's constitution. A third party will be presumed to have acted in good faith unless the contrary is proved: *Barclays Bank Limited v TOSG Trust Fund* [1984] BCLC 1.

12.45 Any 'limitations' imposed upon the powers of directors will be ineffective as against the third party. These are limitations in the company's memorandum or articles of association including those imposed by the resolutions of the general meeting. If an act or transaction is beyond the powers of directors or any other person, it could be ratified by an ordinary resolution: *Grant v UK Switchback Rys* (1880) 40 ChD 135. The third party is further protected by the abolition of the doctrine of constructive notice and will not be required to inquire whether the act or transaction with the company is valid under the company's constitution.

Section 40 does not affect any liability incurred by the directors, or any other person, by reason of the directors' exceeding their powers. For further analysis, see Chapter 7 on corporate capacity and related matters.

General duties of directors

12.46 Directors must still, nevertheless, observe any restrictions placed on their powers when engaging in, for example, corporate social responsibility. Section 171 of CA 2006 requires a director to act in accordance with the company's constitution. Further, the director must only exercise powers for the purposes for which they were conferred.

When considering whether to engage in corporate philanthropy, there will be a duty on a director to ensure that, in any given case, he acts in a way he decides in good faith would be most likely to promote the company's success for the benefit of the members as a whole: CA 2006, s 172. The courts will apply a subjective test in deciding whether the director in question exercised good faith in promoting corporate success by engaging in corporate philanthropic activities. They are likely to question the motive of a director in the transaction and how the company has benefited by the transaction including shareholder welfare.

12.47 In the context of corporate philanthropy, in deciding whether this would promote the company's success, the director is required to take account, in good faith, all the 'material factors' that it is practicable in the circumstances for him to identify. A consideration of the 'material factors' means: (i) the likely consequences (short and long term) of the actions open to a director, so far as a person of care and skill would consider them relevant; and (ii) all such factors as a person of care and skill would consider relevant. It is generally accepted within some companies that corporate philanthropy, in whatever form, may be beneficial to the corporation in the long term as it may enhance the company's reputation in the local community and may also benefit the community in some way. Again, motives of a director will be considered by the courts who will in particular have regard to the following matters that a director would have considered (among others) before engaging in corporate philanthropy:

- The company's need to foster its business relationships, including those with its employees and suppliers and the customers for its products and services. A director may be justified in making a gratuitous payment to its employees because the company has performed well over the years as this would foster its business relations with its employees. A company may second some of its employees to a supplier or a particular customer which could be justified as fostering business relationships as part of the social responsibilities of companies.
- The company's need to have regard to the impact of its operations on the communities affected and on the environment. Although this may suggest any adverse effects of the corporation's activities on communities and the environment, it also includes the beneficial effects of, for example, a donation made by the company towards the establishment of a school or hospital for the community. It is unlikely to be disputed that this was for the company's as well as the local community's benefit. This should be compared to a situation where a company proposes to build a chemical plant where the chemicals and facilities used at the plant are considered hazardous and dangerous to both the local community and environment. The exercise of corporate philanthropy requires a consideration by the directors as to how the local community and the environment would benefit from the company's operations.
- The company's need to maintain a reputation for high standards of business conduct. Directors must not deplete corporate assets to either the company's detriment, or its shareholders or creditors. From the viewpoint of corporate philanthropy, a company must engage in such activities with the highest standards of ethics and conduct that can be expected and not for any wrongful or fraudulent motives that could affect the company's future. So, for example, a company that engages in money laundering activities and uses some of the proceeds for philanthropic purposes would have violated the high standard of conduct and ethics by engaging in such criminal activities. It is not denied that a company must engage in profit maximisation but not at any cost and only ethically in the best interests of the corporation.
- The company's need to achieve outcomes that are fair as between its members. Although directors have the discretion to decide whether or not to engage in philanthropic activities, they should ensure that such activities are transparent to shareholders and appropriate disclosure is made to demonstrate that these activities are *bona fide* in the best interests of the company.

12.48 A director must also exercise independent judgment: CA 2006, s 173.

The courts are also likely to have regard to other aspects of the directors' general duties under the CA 2006 in considering the validity of corporate philanthropy. They include exercising care, skill and diligence when engaging in philanthropic transactions by a consideration of the knowledge, skill and experience which may reasonably be expected of a director in his position and any additional knowledge, skill and experience that the director has: CA 2006, s 174.

Further, the director must not be involved in any philanthropic transactions that would involve a conflict of interest: CA 2006, s 175.

12.49 Corporate philanthropy may involve use of corporate funds or services to third parties. The courts may have regard to any personal use by the director of the company's property, information or opportunity whereby the director benefits from such use in the performance of his functions. Any benefits or rewards received by a director or former director from third parties in respect of the philanthropic activities may be challenged as contrary to directors' duties: CA 2006, s.176.

It is, however, possible for more than one of the general duties to apply in any given case: CA 2006, s 179.

The consequences of breach (or threatened breach) of ss 171–177 are the same as would apply if the corresponding common law rule or equitable principle applied. The duties in those sections (with the exception of s 174 (duty to exercise reasonable care, skill and diligence)) are, accordingly, enforceable in the same way as any other fiduciary duty owed to a company by its directors: CA 2006, s 178.

Other legal mechanisms to regulate corporate social responsibility

12.50 At times, the courts have resorted to other legal mechanisms to regulate corporate social responsibility, particularly when faced with a depletion or misapplication of corporate funds (especially in light of the virtual abolition of the *ultra vires* doctrine).

Breach of directors' fiduciary duties

12.51 The courts could declare that directors have acted unconstitutionally by exceeding their authority, or by abusing their powers, they may have acted in breach of their fiduciary duties: *ANZ Executors and Trustees Co Ltd v Quintex Ltd* (1990) 8 ACLC 980. The transaction may then be set aside. The third party in receipt of corporate funds and with knowledge of the misapplication of funds by directors, may be treated as a constructive trustee and therefore liable to reimburse the company for any sums received: *Selangor United Rubber Estates Ltd v Craddock (No 3)* [1968] 1 WLR 1555; *Belmont Finance Corp Ltd v Williams Furniture Ltd (No 2)* [1980] 1 All ER 393. Some breaches of directors' duties, however, will not be capable of ratification: *Kinsela v Russell Kinsela Pty Ltd* (1986) 10 ACLR 395; *Polly Peck International plc v Nadir (No 2)* [1993] BCLC 187.

Disguised gifts out of capital

12.52 The courts may resort to the capital maintenance doctrine by holding that the company's capital cannot be reduced without complying with the procedures under the Companies Act 2006, otherwise the payments by the company will be 'dressed-up gifts of capital'. The courts may, therefore, declare the payments *ultra vires*. In *Ridge Securities Ltd v IRC* [1964] 1 All ER 275, Pennycuick J stated:

> 'A company can only lawfully deal with its assets in furtherance of its objects. The corporators may take assets out of the company by way of a dividend or, with leave of the court, by way of a reduction of capital, or in a winding up. They may of course acquire them for full consideration. They cannot take assets out of the company by way of a voluntary disposition, however described, and if they attempt to do so, the disposition is *ultra vires* the company.'

Insolvency aspects

12.53 Where the company is insolvent, the courts may set aside certain transactions under s 212 of the Insolvency Act 1986 which states, *inter alia*, that if in the course of a company's winding up, it appears that a director has 'misapplied or retained or become accountable for, any money or other property of the company, or been guilty of any misfeasance or breach of any fiduciary or other duty in relation to the company', the court can compel the director to repay the money or property or to personally contribute to the company's assets as the court thinks just. Donations by directors for philanthropic purposes would be caught by this provision.

12.54 Corporate donations could also be set aside where directors have been involved in fraudulent trading under s 213 of the Insolvency Act 1986. This applies where, in the course of a company's winding up, it appears that any business of the company has been carried on with intent to defraud the company's creditors or any other person, or for any fraudulent purpose. The company's liquidator can apply to the court for a declaration that any persons who were 'knowingly parties' to fraudulent trading, should make such contributions (if any) to the company's assets as the court thinks proper: *Re Augustus Barnett & Sons Ltd* [1986] BCLC 170; *Re Gerald Cooper Chemicals Ltd* [1978] Ch 262; *Re Patrick & Lyon Ltd* [1933] Ch 786.

12.55 The courts could also apply s 214 of the Insolvency Act 1986 to set aside corporate donations on grounds of wrongful trading. This applies where an insolvent company has gone into liquidation, and at some time before the commencement of the company's winding up, the director knew or ought to have concluded that there was no reasonable prospect that the company would avoid going into insolvent liquidation. The company's liquidator can apply to the court for a declaration that the director should make such contribution (if any) to the company's assets as the court thinks proper: *Re Produce Marketing Consortium Ltd (No 2)* [1989] BCLC 520; *Re DKG Contractors Ltd* (1990) BCC 903.

12.56 It is submitted that corporate donations may also be set aside as transactions at an undervalue under s 238 of the 1986 Act. A company enters into a transaction at an undervalue if:

> '(a) the company makes a gift to that person or otherwise enters into a transaction with that person on terms that provide for the company to receive no consideration, or
>
> (b) the company enters into a transaction with that person for a consideration the value of which, in money or money's worth, is significantly less than the value, in money or money's worth, of the consideration provided by the company.'

However, the court will not declare a transaction to be at an undervalue if it is satisfied that the company entered into the transaction in good faith and for the purpose of carrying on its business and that at the time it did so, there were reasonable grounds for believing that the transaction would benefit the company. Another alternative which the judiciary might resort to would be to declare the philanthropic donations as a transaction defrauding creditors under ss 423–425 of the Insolvency Act 1986. This applies where a company enters into a transaction at an undervalue with the intention of putting the company's assets beyond the reach of creditors. This transaction can be set aside whenever it was made by the company. It is to be emphasised that the above procedures are available only in respect of insolvent companies.

Unfair prejudicial conduct

12.57 Where, however, shareholders have not been granted an injunction under CA 2006, s 40(4) by virtue of the company already entering into a contractual obligation with a third party, it is arguable that shareholders could petition the court under CA 2006, s 994 on grounds that 'the company's affairs are being or have been conducted in a manner which is unfairly prejudicial to the interests of its members generally or some part of its members …' Shareholders may argue that the unlawful depletion or misapplication of corporate funds by directors for philanthropic activities constitutes unfair prejudicial conduct.

12.58 If a shareholder succeeds in demonstrating unfair prejudicial conduct under s 994, the court could make one or more orders under s 996, which may take the form of:

(a) regulating the future conduct of the company's affairs by, for example, imposing a limit on the amount companies could donate for philanthropic purposes; or

(b) by requiring the company to refrain from doing or continuing an act complained of by the petitioner by, for example, preventing the company from engaging in specific philanthropic activities; or by requiring the company to do an act which the petitioner has complained the company has omitted to do; or

(c) by authorising civil proceedings to be brought in the name and on behalf of the company by such person or persons and on such terms as the courts may decide; or

(d) require the company not to make any or any specified alterations in its articles without the leave of the court; or

(e) provide for the purchase of shares of any members of the company by other members, or by the company itself and, in the case of a purchase by the company itself, the reduction of the company's capital accordingly.

In the case of (a), the company may only be ordered to reduce its donation but not refrain from making it altogether or order the company not to make the donation, whereas under the second alternative, it is possible for the court to order the company to change the beneficiary of the corporate social responsibilities. Under (c), however, the petitioner could bring civil proceedings on the company's behalf where, for example, the company has engaged in corporate social responsibilities and this has unfairly prejudiced the shareholder.

Derivative action

12.59 There may be a challenge to corporate philanthropy or corporate social responsibility by a shareholder bringing a statutory derivative claim under CA 2006,

Pt 11, Ch 1 where: (a) a cause of action is vested in the company; and (b) the shareholder is seeking relief on the company's behalf: CA 2006, s 260.

The shareholder is required to apply to the court for permission to continue the derivative action. At the first stage, if it appears to the court that the application and evidence filed by the applicant in support of it does not disclose a *prima facie* case for giving permission, the court must dismiss the application; and may make any consequential order it considers appropriate: CA 2006, s 261(2).

12.60 At the second stage, if the application is not dismissed under s 262(2), the court may give directions as to the evidence to be provided by the company; and it may adjourn proceedings to enable the evidence to be obtained: CA 2006, s 261(3).

Upon hearing the application, the court may give permission to continue the claim on such terms as it thinks fit; or refuse permission and dismiss the claim; or adjourn the proceedings on the application and give such directions as it thinks fit: CA 2006, s 261(4).

The application by the shareholder for permission to continue the claim as a derivative claim, will apply where a company has brought a claim; and the cause of action on which the claim is based could be pursued as a derivative claim: CA 2006, s 262. The shareholder must satisfy one of the grounds for application under s 262(2) with the court's powers set out under s 262(3). See further Chapter 18 on derivative claims.

Legal aspects of corporate social responsibility

Checklist

12.61 *This checklist sets out the key issues likely to be encountered in respect of the legal aspects of corporate social responsibility. It also addresses possible challenges to the validity or legality of companies engaging in this area.*

No	Issue
1	Develop a policy and strategy towards corporate social responsibility.
2	What are the social issues affecting the company that require immediate attention?
3	Consider the interests of shareholders and shareholder maximisation with long-term interests of other potential claimants on the corporation.
4	What are the concerns of shareholders that require immediate action (eg directors' remuneration, corporate leadership and direction)?
5	Nominate senior independent director for accountability to shareholders on specific issues.
6	Ensure transparency and openness towards shareholders by channels including IT and use of website and links for shareholder communication.
7	Consider interests of employees and appropriate corporate disclosure to employees.

No	Issue
8	Consider whether employees may be involved in indirect participation in corporate decision-making.
9	Identify interests of creditors and for corporations to avoid any transactions that impact adversely on the interests of creditors.
10	Identify the interests of the consumers and the wider public in the high quality and services provided to these groups and how the company can be ethically responsible towards them.
11	What is the company's environmental policy? Consider steps to minimise any harm to the environment.
12	How does the company integrate within the community? Consider ways in which the company can benefit the community such as sponsorship programmes.
13	Does the company have a policy on political or charitable donations? Identify criteria for the donations.
14	Has the company produced a code of ethics? Identify the key issues with which the company will comply and to which it will adhere.
15	Company to review its policy on transparency, openness and disclosure of information towards the potential claimants on the corporation.
16	Consider other philanthropic activities of the corporation, such as helping the disadvantaged, secondments of employees to worthy organisations, free advice and assistance to beneficial organisations.
17	Consider whether nominee directors may be suitable for appointment to the board.
18	Identify induction courses for directors with emphasis on corporate social policy issues.
19	Identify tax advantages in corporate philanthropic activities.
20	Consider corporate social policy at a European level particularly where company is multinational – ensure uniformity and consistency in application of social policies at a European level.
21	Consider possible challenges to corporate social responsibility: • Is it a disguised gift out of capital? • Is it a breach of directors' general duties (including any fiduciary and common law)? • Will the act of CSR have any implications upon the company's insolvency? • Could the transaction be considered as unfair prejudicial conduct? • Could the shareholder bring a derivative claim?

Definitions

12.62

CSR:	Corporate Social Responsibility
ESF:	European Social Fund
IIRC:	International Integrated Reporting Council
ILO:	International Labour Organisation
OECD:	Organisation for Economic Cooperation and Development
SEE:	Social, environmental and Ethical
SME:	Small and Medium-sized Enterprises
SRI:	Socially Responsible Investment
Ultra vires:	An act beyond the company's capacity
UN:	United Nations

13 Directors: types, appointment and removal

Contents

Introduction

13.1 Although a company is a separate legal entity independent from its shareholders and recognised as a legal person, it cannot act nor function on its own. It is a passive and voiceless creature, which requires agents to operate on its behalf: *Jetivia SA v Bilta (UK) Ltd* [2015] UKSC 23. It requires the custodians, gatekeepers, trustees and guardians to guide the company throughout its existence. In *Ferguson v Wilson* (1866) LR 2 Ch App 77, Cairns LJ stated that 'the company itself cannot act in its own person … it can only act through directors'. See too *Ernest v Nicholls* (1857) 6 HL Cas 401 per Lord Wensleydale.

13.2 The company relies on the directors to manage its day-to-day activities – to provide a strategy and direction for the company. The company, therefore, has legitimate demands. It demands that its directors do not deceive or enter into illegal or fraudulent activities. It demands that its directors promote the long-term interests of the company. It demands loyalty. It requires directors to act in the company's best interests at all times free from any conflicts of interest. It requires its directors to ensure that they are not involved in making secret profits. It demands directors to be accountable to the company for their actions and responsibilities, through proper disclosure of interests and transparency towards the company's shareholders and other stakeholders.

13.3 Throughout its existence, the company wishes to ensure that it appoints quality directors who will promote the company and ensure its success. It recognises the need to validly appoint directors with proper authorisation and powers to conduct the company's operations. However, from time to time, perhaps owing to the exigencies of business, the company accepts that some of its directors may not have been validly appointed and who act in a *de facto* capacity – but this gives rise to issues as to the capacity of *de facto* directors and their powers and authority to bind the company.

13.4 The company also accepts that from time to time, its directors may accept instructions and directions from others who act as a shadow director – previously portrayed as that dark, mysterious, distant figure who lurks in the background hovering over the directors as it were, whispering instructions and directions to the directors who are accustomed to act upon such instructions or directions. In some situations, the silhouette of the shadow director exercises real influence over the company's affairs, such that the directors become mere puppets of the person who pulls the strings. In modern times, the shadow director is no longer perceived as such a dark, dingy, dishevelled character, but one who may be smart, sophisticated, and shrewd, actively involved in the corporate governance of the company, while the directors either actively, passively or subserviently continue to accept instructions and directions from a calculating, and domineering shadow director, who may hide his true motive and intentions, while ostensibly pretending to act in the company's best interests. The company has no knowledge of the shadow director. Why does he give instructions and directions to the directors? Why are the directors accepting such instructions or directions and for how long? What is the persona and psychological motive of the shadow director? Does he have an evil intent towards the company or is he of good character? Will he trouble the company while the company conducts its daily activities? Will the shadow director affect the company's fate? Will the directors disclose the true motives of the shadow director to the company? Are the directors also implicated along with the shadow director in any wrongful actions? Will they implicate, use or abuse the company for their own purposes?

13.5 In troubled times, the company, therefore, hopes that it can rely upon its ardent supporters to dismiss directors who have abused the company's trust or engaged in wrongful actions, breaches of duty or negligence. Though the company may choose to condone such actions and ratify a director's conduct, it can also act ruthlessly and unforgiving by removing its directors from office in an unceremonious manner only to be replaced by new ones. In this regard, the company becomes wiser through experience, knowledge and more cautious – but also optimistic that the new replacements will safeguard the company's interests.

13.6 This chapter addresses the following issues:

- identifying who is a 'director' of the company;
- distinguishing between different types of directors;
- the requirement to have a director(s);

- the appointment process, including the minimum requirements to be satisfied before a person can become a director;
- the need for a register of directors and the particulars of directors to be registered;
- appointing a director; and
- the process for removing a director from office.

Definition of director

13.7 Under the Companies Act 2006, the term 'director' includes any person occupying the position of director, by whatever name called: CA 2006, s 250. The term is similarly used in the Insolvency Act 1986 (IA 1986), s 251 and the Company Directors Disqualification Act 1986 (CDDA 1986), s 22(4). However, this definition is not exhaustive and does not identify who is a director of the company. The title occupied by a person is not the determining factor in identifying whether that person is a director of a company. A person need not be called a 'director' in order to act in that capacity. In some cases, a person may occupy the position of a 'manager' or a 'governor', but could still exercise the functions of a director under CA 2006. The term 'director' is sometimes used in a misleading way in employment law where some personnel are described as 'marketing director' or 'operations director' but do not perform the essential management functions of a director as contemplated under CA 2006.

A director is a person who has ultimate control of management or any part of the company's business

In *Smithton Ltd v Naggar* [2015] 2 BCLC 22, Arden LJ was of the view that 'the question who is a director of a company is important because of the substantial duties which a director has. It is usually easy to tell if a person is a director if he has been duly appointed as such by the company (and is then a de jure director or 'director in law'), but much less easy if he has not been even purportedly appointed as a director but has simply acted as a director on occasions (when he might be a de facto director or director 'in fact') or if he has persuaded the directors to act in a particular way (when he might be a shadow director).' Further, having regard to the usual split of powers between directors and shareholders and shareholders' delegation of day to day management powers to directors (which can be intervened by the exercise of a special resolution), a director was a person 'who either alone or with others has ultimate control of the management or any part of the company's business …it does not include a purely negative role of giving or receiving permission for some business activity'.

In *Re Eurostem Maritime Ltd* [1987] PCC 190, Mervyn Davies J considered that the words in s 250(1) 'occupying the position of director' covered any *de facto* director. However, *Re Lo-Line Electric Motor Ltd* took a different approach.

The definition of 'director' is inclusive and not exhaustive and may include a de facto director

In *Re Lo-Line Electric Motor Ltd* [1988] BCLC 698, Sir Nicolas Browne-Wilkinson VC noted that the definition of 'director' was inclusive not exhaustive and stated that its meaning had to be derived from the words of the Companies Act as a whole. The meaning of 'director' varied according to the context in which it is to be found. It was not possible to treat a *de facto* director as a 'director' for all the purposes of the 2006 Act. The definition extended to persons who were validly appointed as directors. He stated that s 250(1) of CA 2006 did not purport to define the meaning of 'director' but merely provided that certain persons were to be included in the definition. The reference to 'by whatever name called' showed that the subsection is dealing with nomenclature; for example where the company's articles provided that the conduct of the company was committed to 'governors' or 'managers'.

Distinguishing between various types of directors

13.8 In company law and practice, a distinction is often made between the following types of directors:

- *de jure* director;
- *de facto* director;
- shadow director; and
- directors of corporate directors.

De jure director

13.9 A *de jure* director ('director in law') is a person who has been validly and formally appointed to the company's board following the proper procedures for appointment under the company's constitution and CA 2006. He agrees to become a director of the company and has not been disqualified as a director under the CDDA 1986.

The *de jure* director will also be registered at Companies House and his name entered in the register of directors.

De facto director

13.10 A distinction has often been made between *de jure* and *de facto* directors and their responsibilities and duties on the board of directors. Although the term *de jure* director has a generally accepted meaning, the concept of a *de facto* director has been problematic and has given rise to a number of cases, particularly in relation to director's disqualification proceedings. A *de facto* director (director 'in fact') is a term applied to a person who assumes the position of a *de jure* director within the corporate governance structure without having been validly appointed as a *de jure* director. He then treated or assumes some or all of the functions of a *de jure* director, including any liabilities that may ensue.

13.11 The essential nature of the distinction often arises where a *de facto* director has become liable to a claim, penalty or fine and attempts to evade such liability by claiming that he was not properly appointed. The cases have shown that this distinction usually arises in cases of disqualification, misfeasance, wrongful trading and fraudulent trading, or when things go wrong within the company and liability is imputed to the *de facto* director. Judicial cases have not often been consistent in their approach towards determining whether a person was, in reality, a *de facto* or a *de jure* director or indeed a shadow director, and what tests or factors should be taken into account in distinguishing between a *de facto* director and a shadow director, and whether in practice there was any real distinction between the two. Until *Re Paycheck Services 3 Ltd; Revenue and Customs Commissioners v Holland* [2011] 1 BCLC 141, there were differing and conflicting judicial interpretations as to who was a *de facto* director, the tests used to identify such director in law and practice, and how a *de facto* director differed from a shadow director. As Lord Collins remarked in the leading case of *Re Paycheck*, for over 150 years *de facto* directors in English law were persons who assumed their position, role and functions as directors, but whose appointment was defective, or had come to an end, but nevertheless acted or continued to act as directors. Many of the cases on *de facto* directors were concerned with the validity of their acts.

Earlier cases on de facto directors

13.12 Some of the earlier cases on *de facto* directors concerned persons who purported to be directors, but whose appointment was defective: they had not been validly appointed, but assumed the role of a director through carrying out the functions that would normally be attributed to a *de jure* director. The earlier cases were also concerned with whether the acts of such persons were legally valid or effective. Other cases involved applications of the principle under the Companies Acts and articles of association that, notwithstanding that it might afterwards be discovered that there was some defect or error in the appointment of directors, any acts of those directors were to be valid (see for example CA 2006 s 161 (validity of acts of directors), and reg 92 of the Table A Companies (Tables A to F) Regulations 1985, SI 1985/805.

13.13 Some of the earlier cases have addressed such similar provisions to reg 92 contained in the company's articles of association. The effect of such provisions was to cure any defect that might have occurred in the director not having been validly appointed. See for example: *Charles Edward Mangles v Grand Collier Dock Co* (1840) 10 Sim 519; *Foss v Harbottle* (1843) 2 Hare 4; *Re County Life Assurance Co* (1870) 5 Ch App 288; *Murray v Bush* (1873) LR 6 HL 37; *Mahony v East Holyford Mining Co* (1875) LR 7 HL 869; *Rama Corp Ltd v Proved Tin and General Investments Ltd* [1952] 1 All ER 554; *Royal British Bank v Turquand* (1856) 6 El & Bl 327; 119 ER 886; *Freeman and Lockyer (a firm) v Buckhurst Park Properties (Mangal) Ltd* [1964] 1 All ER 630; *John Morley Building Co v Barras* [1891] 2 Ch 386 and *Channel Collieries Trust Ltd v Dover St Margaret's and Martin Mill Light Rly Co* [1914] 2 Ch 506; *Morris v Kanssen* [1946] 1 All ER 586.

The modern approach to de facto directors

13.14 Although previous cases on *de facto* directors were principally concerned with the defective appointment of a director or who had ceased to be a director and their liability, the modern concept of *de facto* directors has extended to disqualification proceedings, insolvency including wrongful trading by directors: see *Re Eurostem Maritime Ltd* (1987) PCC 190.

The acts of de facto directors extended to liability in disqualification proceedings

In *Re Lo-Line Electric Motors Ltd* [1988] BCLC 698, the issue concerned s 300 of the CA 1985 (disqualification order) (now CDDA 1986). The respondent had been a director of company A; he resigned as a director but continued as production manager. After the sole remaining director had absconded to the United States, the respondent took over the running of the company, but was not appointed as a director. The respondent also acted as a director of company B, although he was never appointed as such. Sir Nicolas Browne-Wilkinson V-C held that for the purposes of a disqualification order under the 1985 Act, in considering whether a person was unfit to be a director, only his conduct 'as director' was relevant, and that, as a matter of construction, 'director' in s 300 included a person *de facto* acting as a director, though not appointed as such.

A de facto director is one who assumes to act as a director though not validly appointed

Re Hydrodam (Corby) Ltd [1994] 2 BCLC 180 was concerned with Hydrodam, which had two corporate directors, which were companies incorporated in the Channel Islands. It was a subsidiary of Eagle Trust plc. The liquidator commenced proceedings against Eagle Trust plc (the ultimate parent company of Hydrodam through two other subsidiaries) and all of Eagle Trust's directors, alleging that they were liable as *de facto* or shadow directors of Hydrodam under s 214 of the Insolvency Act 1986, for wrongful trading. The decision concerned an application by two of the directors to strike out the proceedings. It was alleged that as directors of Eagle Trust they were, with the other directors, collectively responsible for the conduct of Eagle Trust in relation to Hydrodam. The proceedings were struck out because the liquidator had neither pleaded nor adduced evidence to support any allegation that either of the respondents was a director of Hydrodam.

Millett J stated that a *de jure* director is one who has been validly appointed by the board of directors with proper authority and powers to manage the company's business.

Millett J considered that a *de facto* director was a person who assumed to act as a director. He was held out as a director of the company and claimed and purported to be a director, although he was never actually or validly appointed as such. To establish that a person was a *de facto* director, it was necessary to show that he undertook functions in relation to the company which could properly be discharged only by a director. It was not sufficient to show that he was concerned in the management of the company's affairs, or undertook tasks in relation to its business which could properly be performed by a manager below board level:

> 'Those who assume to act as directors and who thereby exercise the powers and discharge the functions of a director, whether validly appointed or not, must accept the responsibilities which are attached to the office.'

Accordingly, Millett J held that the liquidator had neither pleaded nor adduced evidence that either of the directors was a director of Hydrodam. As regards one of them, Dr Hardwick, he had never acted as a director, and as regards the other, Mr Thomas, it was not alleged that he acted in any way in relation to the company's affairs. Although Millett J had used terms such as 'held out as a director' and 'claims and purports to be a director' as elements for identifying a *de facto* director, subsequent cases have considered these as only factors and not determinative.

This case raised questions as to whether it was a necessary ingredient of *de facto* directorship that the person in question should have been held out by the company). Authorities subsequent to *Re Hydrodam* have tended to downplay this aspect to being a useful indicator, but not an essential requirement.

Since *Hydrodam*, there have been a number of cases that have considered the position of a *de facto* director. A large number of these cases have been concerned with directors' disqualification proceedings. These cases have treated *Hydrodam* as the starting position before applying the principles to the facts in question. However, some of the previous judicial decisions (mainly first instance decisions) applied different tests in determining whether a person was a *de facto* director.

Holding out and the label of 'director' were not a necessary precondition in identifying a de facto director but assumption of role as director was an important factor

In Re Moorgate Metals [1995] BCLC 143, Warner J decided that it was not a necessary condition of a *de facto* directorship that the person concerned was held out as a director, by having the label of 'director' expressly attached to that person. This principle was supported by Etherton J in *Secretary of State for Trade and Industry v Hollier* [2007] BCC 11 where he stated that it was not a necessary characteristic for a de facto director to be 'held out' as a company director. Such 'holding out' may be important evidence in support of the conclusion that a person had in fact acted a director, but this was a far too narrow a test to embrace all those who had discharged functions normally and most appropriately carried out by a director: see Jacob J in *SSTI v Tjolle* [1998] BCC 282, 291 to the same effect.

In *Re H Laing Demolition Building Contractors Ltd, Secretary of State for Trade and Industry v Laing* [1996] 2 BCLC 324, the court stated that a person had to assume the role of a director to constitute being a *de facto* director. The period of assuming such directorship would be relevant in determining the existence of a *de facto* director.

It was necessary to show that the de facto director was the sole person directing the affairs of the company or, if there were others who were true directors, that he acted on an equal footing with such persons in directing the affairs of the company

In *Re Richborough Furniture Limited* [1996] 1 BCLC 507, Timothy Lloyd QC stated that the term '*de facto* director' referred to a situation where a person has acted as a director even though he has not been validly appointed or even if there has been no appointment at all. For a person to be treated as a *de facto* director there would have to be clear evidence that he had been the sole person directing the affairs of the company or, if there were others who were true directors, that he acted on an equal footing with such persons in directing the affairs of the company. Where it is unclear that what the person did was referable to an assumed directorship or to some other capacity such as shareholder or consultant, the person in question is to be given the benefit of the doubt (see also *Morris v Kanssen* [1946] AC 459).

In *Secretary of State for Trade and Industry v Ashby (No 1915 of 1992)* (unreported), Anthony Mann QC considered that it was not a requirement in all respects for a de facto director to be on an exactly equal footing to all the other directors. For example, a de facto director would be expected to defer to the properly appointed marketing director in matters of marketing in the same way as a de jure appointed finance director would. In investigating the qualities of the acts performed by the person whose status is in question, it was necessary to look for someone who is essentially operating at the same level as the properly appointed directors, that is to say they are not in reality subordinate to them at all times.

The 'equal footing' test was also applied by His Honour Judge Cooke in *Secretary of State for Trade and Industry v Elms* (16 January 1997, unreported) who considered that the test was not so much about equality of power, but 'equality of ability' to participate in the notional board room. In this regard, It is necessary to ask:

> 'Is he somebody who is simply advising and, as it were, withdrawing having advised, or somebody who joins the other directors, de facto or de jure, in decisions which affect the future of the company?'

He stated that in determining whether a person was a shadow director, consideration should be given to the following:

- Was he directing others?
- Was he committing the company to major obligations?
- Was he taking part in an equally based collective decision-making process at board level (ie at the level of a director with a foot in the board room)?

There was no one test in identifying a de facto director and regard must be had to various factors

In *Secretary of State for Trade and Industry v Tjolle* [1998] 1 BCLC 333, Jacob J stated that it was difficult to postulate one decisive test of whether a person was a *de facto* director. The court had to take account of all the relevant factors, including whether or not there was a holding out by the company of the individual as a director, whether the individual used the title, whether the individual had proper information (eg management accounts) on which to base decisions, and whether the individual had to make major decisions and so on. The question was whether the individual was part of the corporate governing structure. There would be no justification for the law making a person liable to misfeasance or disqualification proceedings unless they were truly in a position to exercise the powers and discharge the functions of a director. An alleged *de facto* director was in a different position to a *de jure* director in that he might not have had certain knowledge and no right or means to have that knowledge, which was important when the Secretary of State's case in part relied on what K ought to have known. It followed that someone who had no, or only peripheral, knowledge of matters of vital company concern (eg financial state) and had no right, legal or *de facto*, to access to such matters was not to be regarded by the law as in substance a director. Jacob J stated that on the facts, the use of the title 'director' with added words did not make K a *de facto* director, because she was not in fact directing the company. There was clear evidence of K's lack of involvement in anything financial. Her attendance at a meeting did not make her a *de facto* director. K was a manager, but she did not form part of the real corporate governance of the company. There was no function she performed that could only properly be discharged by a director. Nor did she accept the responsibilities of office; no one could properly do so who did not have access to the company's financial position in reasonable detail.

13.15 In *Re Sykes (Butchers) Ltd, Secretary of State of Trade and Industry v Stokes* [1996] BCC 155, the court was of the view that a strong evidence of holding out could strengthen the inference of equality between a *de facto* director and the appointed board.

A de facto director's actions may be directorial and either acting in an individual capacity or as a director of the company

In *Secretary of State for Trade and Industry v Jones* [1999] BCC 336, Jonathan Parker QC held that a management consultant was a de facto director of his client company. He had signed a letter to the client's auditors confirming their appointment on headed notepaper and described himself as the company's managing director. He was also signatory on the company's bank account, dealt directly with the company's creditors and negotiated with the company's suppliers. His actions were principally directorial in nature, acting alone.

Assumption of the status and functions of a company director were important elements in identifying whether or not a person was a de facto director

In *Re Kaytech International plc, Secretary of State for Trade and Industry v Kaczer* [1999] 2 BCLC 351, a public limited company went into voluntary liquidation after 12 months trading with an estimated deficiency as regards creditors of about £1.6m. The Secretary of State for Trade and Industry issued an originating summons under s 6 of the Company Directors Disqualification Act 1986 seeking disqualification orders against the three respondents, said to have been directors of the company, alleging that they had been parties to a false declaration and return to the companies registry and to those dealing with the company that it had a paid up share capital of £2.5m whereas in fact its paid up capital was only £2, that they had continued its business beyond the time when it had no reasonable prospect of paying its creditors, had failed to keep proper accounting records and had failed to co-operate with the liquidator. The first respondent admitted that he was a director of the company but disputed that anything he did justified a finding that he was unfit to be concerned in the management of a company. The main defence of the second and third respondents was that they were never directors of the company at all, whether *de jure*, *de facto* or shadow, so that the claim against them must fail.

The Court of Appeal held that in ascertaining whether an individual was a *de facto* director of a company, the crucial question was whether he had assumed the status and functions of a company director so as to make himself responsible under the 1986 Act as if he were a *de jure* director. On the facts, the second respondent had been deeply and openly involved in the company's affairs from the outset, and although he had done his best to avoid being seen to act as a director, using his office as *de jure* secretary and his professional status as camouflage, on some very important occasions he openly acted as a director. Accordingly he was a *de facto* director of the company and therefore a director for the purposes of s 6 of the CDDA 1986. A de facto director was a person who exercised 'real influence' in the company's corporate governance system: on occasions, that influence may be concealed or it may be open or a mixture of both.

Similarly, in *IRC v McEntaggart* [2006] 1 BCLC 476, the person in question acted in the company's affairs while an undischarged bankrupt and was involved in the negotiation and signing of contracts with third parties as well as 'moving spirits' within the company. It was held that the person was a *de facto* director.

Various factors should be taken into account in identifying whether or not a person was a de facto director

In *Gemma Ltd v Davies* [2008] 2 BCLC 281, the wife of the sole director of a building company was appointed as company secretary and performed clerical tasks for the company. The issue was whether she had real influence on the corporate decision-making process such that she would be liable as a *de facto* director for the company's debts.

Jonathan Gaunt QC was of the view that the tests to be applied were: whether she undertook functions in relation to the company which could properly be discharged only by a director, whether she participated in directing the affairs of the company on an equal footing with her husband and not in a subordinate role, and whether she was shown to have assumed the status and functions of a company director and to have exercised real influence in the corporate governance of the company. Although she was held out as a director on the company notepaper that was by her husband, not her and although she signed some letters on company notepaper she never signed or described herself as a director. Moreover, her functions for the company were purely clerical and involved no decision making; she played no role in the major decisions affecting the company. Accordingly, it had not been shown that she had real influence on the corporate decision-making process, and it could not be inferred from the fact that she did not vociferously object to her husband's actions that she had an influential role in the corporate decision-making of the company. It followed that she did not act as a *de facto* director, was not a person concerned in the promotion, formation or management of the company and was not guilty of any misfeasance or breach of any fiduciary or other duty in relation to the company.

13.16 A person may still be a *de facto* director even if he does not have day-to-day control over the company's affairs, and even though he acts as a director only in relation to part of the company's activities: *Secretary of State for Trade and Industry v Deverell* [2001] Ch 340.

Actions of the de facto director in practice were indicative in determining the capacity in which he acted and that he was part of a corporate governance structure

In *Secretary of State for Trade and Industry v Hollier* [2007] BCC 618, Etherton J stated that in considering whether a person 'assumes to act as a director', the important aspect was not what he called himself but what he did. A *de facto* director was one who claimed and purported to act as a director, although not validly appointed as such. The touchstone was whether the defendant had been part of the corporate governing structure. Inherent in that touchstone was the distinction between someone who participated, or had the right to participate, in collective decision making on corporate policy and strategy and its implementation, and others who might advise or act on behalf of, or otherwise for the benefit of, the company, but did not participate in decision making as part of the corporate governance of the company. The issue whether a person had acted so as to become a *de facto* director was to be judged objectively in the light of all relevant facts.

Assumption of status and functions of a person were determinative as to whether he was a de facto director

In *Secretary of State for Trade and Industry v Hall* [2009] BCC 190, the question which the court had to consider was whether the second respondent was a *de facto* director of the company by reason of the fact that he owned, controlled and was the sole director of its corporate director. The case against the second respondent failed because he had not, either individually or through his control of the corporate director, taken any steps which indicated that either he or his company had assumed the status and functions of a director of the subject company. He did not fit the description of a *de facto* director, because the description required positive action by an individual which showed that he was acting as if he was a director. Evans-Lombe J stated that the crucial issue was whether the individual in question had assumed the status and function of a company director so as to make himself responsible under the CDDA as if he were a *de jure* director. It seemed that, to be constituted a *de facto* director of a subject company, a director of a corporate *de jure* director had to cause the corporate director to take action with relation to the subject company as would have constituted it a *de facto* director of that company. The degree of control which the director of the corporate director exercised over that company would be of relevance. Equally, the shareholder control of the corporate director might be relevant.

Assumption of responsibility and involvement in the corporate governance structure were significant indications of participation by a de facto director in corporate matters

In the leading Supreme Court case of *Re Paycheck Services 3 Ltd, Revenue and Customs Commissioners v Holland* [2011] 1 BCLC 141, the court stated that there was no one test for determining and identifying whether a person was a *de facto* director. It was clear from established authority that the circumstances in which a person could be held to be a *de facto* director for the purposes of the remedy provided for by s 212 of the 1986 Act varied widely from case to case, and was very much a question of fact and degree. All the relevant factors had to be taken into account. The purpose of the section was to impose liability on those who had been in a position to prevent damage to creditors by taking proper steps to protect their interests. Those who assumed to act as directors and who thereby exercised the powers and discharged the functions of a director, whether validly appointed or not, had to accept the responsibilities of the office. Accordingly, one had to look at what the person had actually done to see whether he had assumed those responsibilities in relation to the subject company. The question was one of law and it was a question of principle. The guiding principle could be expressed in that way, unless and until Parliament provided otherwise. So long as the relevant acts had been done by the individual entirely within the ambit of the discharge of his duties and responsibilities as a director of the corporate director, it was to that capacity that his acts had to be attributed.

The term could not be universally applied to all situations and statutory provisions which imposed liability on a director. The court would look at the purpose for the rule being applied, whether the director was acting alone and directing the company's affairs or on an equal footing with other directors in directing the company's affairs, whether there was any holding out by that person, and whether, having regard to all the facts and circumstances, the person was part of the company's governance structure.

According to Lord Collins, the original basis of liability as a de facto director was that a person had been appointed a director by an invalid process and acted as such. Accordingly, the original basis of liability was the assumption of responsibility as a director. Where a person had never been even invalidly appointed a director, it was necessary to examine the governance system of the company in order to assess whether he acted as a director. Lord Collins further stated:

> 'It does not follow that "de facto director" must be given the same meaning in all of the different contexts in which a "director" may be liable. It seems to me that in the present context of the fiduciary duty of a director not to dispose wrongfully of the company"s assets, the crucial question is whether the person assumed the duties of a director. Both Sir Nicolas Browne-Wilkinson V-C in *Re Lo-Line Electric Motors Ltd* [1988] BCLC 698 at 707, [1988] Ch 477 at 490) and Millett J in *Re Hydrodam (Corby) Ltd* [1994] 2 BCLC 180 at 183 referred to the assumption of office as a mark of a de facto director. In *Fayers Legal Services Ltd v Day* (11 April 2001, unreported), a case relating to breach of fiduciary duty, Patten J, rejecting a claim that the defendant was a de facto director of the company and had been in breach of fiduciary duty, said that in order to make him liable for misfeasance as a de facto director the person must be part of the corporate governing structure, and the claimants had to prove that he assumed a role in the company sufficient to impose on him a fiduciary duty to the company and to make him responsible for the misuse of its assets. It seems to me that that is the correct formulation in a case of the present kind. See also *Primlake Ltd (in liq) v Matthews Associates* [2006] EWHC 1227 (Ch) at [284], [2007] 1 BCLC 666 at [284]'.

Having considered the cases on *de facto* directors, Lord Hope stated that the circumstances for determining whether or not a person was a *de facto* director, varied from case to case. There was no single decisive test for identifying a *de facto* director. All the relevant factors must be taken into account. Assumption of responsibility and discharging the functions as a director was important. Also, regard must be had to what the person actually did to see whether he assumed those responsibilities in relation to the subject company. Lord Hope considered the separate legal personality of the corporate director as the key consideration. He held that the question whether the director was a de facto director of the other company had to be approached on the basis that the companies were separate legal persons: 'So long as the relevant acts are done by the individual entirely within the ambit of the discharge of his duties and responsibilities as a director of the corporate director, it is to that capacity that his acts must be attributed.'

The director in question had done no more than simply discharge his duties as a director of the corporate director. As his acts had been done 'within the ambit' of the discharge of those duties, his acts were required to be attributed to that capacity without any further inquiry as to whether they also fell 'within the ambit' of what a director of the composite companies would have done.

See now s 156A(1) of the CA 2006 (as inserted by SBEEA 2015, s 87(4)) which prevents the appointment of corporate directors).

Post-Re Paycheck Services Ltd

Since *Re Paycheck Services Ltd* was decided, there has been a uniform and consistent approach towards determining the test to be used to for identifying a *de facto* director.

Assumption of responsibility was a significant factor in determining whether or not a person was a de facto director

In *Re Idessa (UK) Ltd (in liquidation); Burke and another v Morrison* [2012] 1 BCLC 80, the first respondent was held out as director in business plan and paid same salary as director. He was appointed a director of affiliated companies, having equal authority in financial matters. The issue was whether he exercised real influence over company's affairs, whether the respondent was fairly to be regarded as part of the company's corporate governance, and whether the respondent assumed the duties of a director.

Lesley Anderson QC held that in deciding whether a person was a *de facto director* in the context of a director's fiduciary duty not to dispose wrongfully of the company's assets, the crucial question was whether that person had assumed the duties of a director. On the facts, the first respondent was to be treated as having acted as a *de facto* director from the time of the incorporation of the company until its liquidation, because it was clear from a draft shareholders' agreement and the evidence that it was always intended that he would be a director and shareholder, he was held out as a promoter and director of the company in a business plan, he was a *de jure* director of the English and American affiliated companies, he was paid the same salary as a director, ie the second respondent, he had equal access with the second respondent to the company's bank accounts, the company's accountant or accounts clerk dealt with them both equally in regard to financial matters, a business card was printed stating that he was a director, he operated a loan account with the company, and both respondents were listed as debtors on liquidation, all of which showed that he exercised real influence over the company's affairs and acted on an equal footing with the second respondent, so that he was fairly to be regarded as part of the company's corporate governance.

Directing the company's affairs and involvement were indicative that a person was a de facto director

In *Re Snelling House Ltd* [2012] EWHC 440 (Ch), the court was required to determine whether one of the respondents in question was a *de facto* director and therefore liable on the company's liquidation along with the other directors. On the facts, the respondent was involved in the day-to-day running of the company; he was a signatory on the company account and had full power to withdraw monies under a bank mandate; he gave all instructions to the company's accountants as well as dealing with VAT. Moss QC, therefore, decided that, given the evidence of the respondent's activities and the absence of any evidence to explain away his actions as being those of a consultant, the only reasonable inference was that the respondent was acting as a *de facto* director throughout. He was, in reality, the person directing the affairs of the company. In terms of the policy of and principle underlying the *de facto* director concept, he was the person at the company in a position to prevent damage to creditors by taking proper steps to protect their interests.

13.17 See too: *Re UKLI Ltd Secretary of State for Business, Innovation and Skills v Chohan* [2013] EWHC 680.

In order to determine whether a person was a de facto director, it was necessary to consider that person's role within the corporate governance process

In *Smithton Ltd v Naggar* [2015] 2 BCLC 22, the Court of Appeal was required to consider the test that should be applied in identifying whether a person was a shadow director. It held that having regard to the usual split of powers between shareholders and directors under Table A of the Companies (Tables A to F) Regulations 1985 on the basis that the powers of management of the company's business were delegated to the directors and the shareholders could not intervene except by special resolution, a director was a person who either alone or with others had ultimate control of the management of any part of the company's business. In the usual case a purely negative rôle of giving or receiving permission for some business activity or being consulted about directorial decisions or for approval did not make a person a director.

Further, whether a person was a de facto or shadow director depended on whether he was part of the system of corporate governance of the company, and if so, in what capacity he acted in relation to the corporate governance structure and whether, objectively, he had assumed the status and function of a director so as to assume responsibility to act as a director. The assessment of the capacity in which a person acted was one of fact and degree and all the circumstances had to be taken into account but relevant factors included whether the company considered him to be a director, whether it held him out as such, and whether third parties considered him to be a director.

Arden LJ set out the following factors in identifying whether or not a person could be a de facto director:

- The concepts of shadow director and de facto are different but there is some overlap.
- A person may be de facto director even if there was no invalid appointment. The question is whether he has assumed responsibility to act as a director.
- To answer that question, the court may have to determine in what capacity the director was acting (as in *Holland*).
- The court will in general also have to determine the corporate governance structure of the company so as to decide in relation to the company's business whether the defendant's acts were directorial in nature.
- The court is required to look at what the director actually did and not any job title actually given to him.
- A defendant does not avoid liability if he shows that he in good faith thought he was not acting as a director. The question whether or not he acted as a director is to be determined objectively and irrespective of the defendant's motivation or belief.
- The court must look at the cumulative effect of the activities relied on. The court should look at all the circumstances 'in the round' (per Jonathan Parker J in *Secretary of State for Trade and Industry v Jones* [1999] BCC 336).
- It is also important to look at the acts in their context. A single act might lead to liability in an exceptional case.
- Relevant factors include:

  (i) whether the company considered him to be a director and held him out as such;

  (ii) whether third parties considered that he was a director.
- The fact that a person is consulted about directorial decisions or his approval is sought for such decisions does not in general make him a director because he is not making the decision.
- Acts outside the period when he is said to have been a de facto director may throw light on whether he was a de facto director in the relevant period.
- The question whether a director is a de facto or shadow director is a question of fact and degree.

Shadow director

13.18 Under the Companies Act 2006, a 'shadow director' means a person in accordance with whose directions or instructions the directors of the company are accustomed to act: CA 2006, s 251(1).

The following rules apply in respect of those who are not regarded as shadow directors:

- A person is not a shadow director by reason only of the fact that the directors act:

  (a) on advice given by that person in a professional capacity;

  (b) in accordance with instructions, a direction, guidance or advice given by that person in the exercise of a function conferred by or under an enactment;

  (c) in accordance with guidance or advice given by that person in that person's capacity as a Minister of the Crown (within the meaning of the Ministers of the Crown Act 1975): CA 2006, s 251(2) (as inserted by s 90(3) SBEEA 2015).

The term 'enactment' under s 1293 of CA 2006 also refers to legislation made in Wales: see s 1293(aa) of CA 2006 (as inserted by SBEEA 2015, s 90(4)).

For the position of shadow directors in Northern Ireland see s 91 of SBEEA 2015.

- A body corporate is not to be regarded as a shadow director of any of its subsidiary companies for the purposes of:

  – Chapter 2 (general duties of directors);

  – Chapter 4 (transactions requiring members' approval); or

  – Chapter 6 (contract with sole member who is also a director),

  by reason only that the directors of the subsidiary are accustomed to act in accordance with its directions or instructions: CA 2006, s 251(3).

Various provisions of CA 2006 and the Insolvency Act 1986 (s 251 as amended by SBEEA 2015, s 90(1)) make references to a shadow director in the regulation and disclosure of transactions. These Acts impute liability to a person if he is influential in running the company's affairs through other directors, while not himself on the company board; and if the directors are accustomed to acting in accordance with that person's directions and instructions. The issue concerning shadow directors also arises in the context of CDDA 1986 proceedings including the insolvency proceedings dealing with wrongful trading. Section 22(5) of the CDDA 1986 (as inserted by SBEEA 2015, s 90(2)) provides an identical definition of a 'shadow director' as s 251 of the CA 2006.

13.19 The words of the definition 'shadow director', as opposed to the term defined, are not new: see Morritt LJ in *Secretary of State for Trade and Industry v Deverell* [2000] 2 BCLC 133. With the omission of the exception, it was previously added by s 3 of the Companies (Particulars as to Directors) Act 1917 to the definition of the word 'director' in ss 26, 75 and 274 of the Companies (Consolidation) Act 1908, it was included in the definition of 'officer' in s 73(3) and 'director' in s 75(5) of the Companies Act 1928. What is now the exception was added by s 380(2) of the Companies Act 1929. Since then it has been carried forward through the various consolidations effected in 1948 and 1985. The words 'shadow director' first appeared as the defined term in s 63 of the Companies Act 1980. Currently the defined term also appears in s 417(1) of the Financial Services and Markets Act 2000.

Various cases have considered the statutory definition of 'shadow director' and the test to be applied in determining whether a person was a shadow director.

A shadow director is the éminence grise controlling the directors

In *Re Lo-Line Electric Motors Ltd* [1988] BCLC 698, Browne-Wilkinson V-C was concerned with an allegation that the person in question was a *de facto* director, not a shadow director. He said of the latter that the definition presupposes that there is a board of directors 'who act in accordance with instructions from someone else, the éminence grise or shadow director'.

A shadow director is a puppet master controlling the Board actions

In *Re Unisoft Group Ltd (No 3)* [1994] 1 BCLC 609 Harman J was concerned with an application to strike out a minority shareholder's petition. One of the relevant allegations was that a particular individual was a shadow director within the meaning of the definition contained in s 251 of the CA 2006. In respect of that definition, Harman J stated:

> '... those words can only mean ... that the shadow director must be, in effect, the puppet master controlling the actions of the board. The directors must be (to use a different phrase) the 'cat's paw' of the shadow director. They must be people who act on the directions or instructions of the shadow director as a matter of regular practice. That last requirement follows from the reference in the subsection to the directors being 'accustomed to act'. That must refer to acts not on one individual occasion but over a period of time and as a regular course of conduct.'

A shadow director lurks in the shadows sheltering behind others and is not held out as a director

In *Re Hydrodam (Corby) Limited* [1994] 2 BCLC 180, Millett J contrasted a *de facto* director with a shadow director. He considered that the terms did not overlap: 'They are alternatives, and in most and perhaps all cases are mutually exclusive.' He suggested that it would be embarrassing to allege, without distinguishing between them, that the respondent acted as a *de facto* or alternatively a shadow director. He further stated:

> 'A shadow director ... does not claim or purport to act as a director. On the contrary, he claims not to be a director. He lurks in the shadows, sheltering behind others who, he claims, are the only directors of the company to the exclusion of himself. He is not held out as a director by the company. To establish that a defendant is a shadow director of a company it is necessary to allege and prove: (1) who are the directors of the company, whether de facto or de jure; (2), that the defendant directed those directors how to act in relation to the company or that he was one of the persons who did so; (3) that those directors acted in accordance with such directions; and (4) that they were accustomed

> so to act. What is needed is first, a board of directors claiming and purporting to act as such; and secondly, a pattern of behaviour in which the board did not exercise any discretion or judgment of its own, but acted in accordance with the directions of others.'

13.20 However, this graphic view of a passive shadow director may not necessarily accord with the position in practice. A shadow director is likely to be proactive, planning, scheming his instructions or directions to the directors. He may also be impulsive – acting on the spur of the moment, catching directors off-guard and requiring them to act immediately in respect of a particular matter or transaction.

In determining the position of the shadow director, the court will enquire as to the locus for effective decision making

In *Australian Securities Commission v AS Nominees Ltd* (1995) 133 ALR 1, Finn J, sitting in the Federal Court of Australia, was concerned with petitions to wind up various trust companies of which Windsor was a manager. Section 60 of the Corporations Law (Australia) is in the same terms as s 22(5) save that the proviso is not confined to advice given in a professional capacity, but extends to advice given in the proper performance of the functions attaching to a business relationship with the directors. Finn J stated that the reference in the section to a person in accordance with whose directions or instructions the directors are 'accustomed to act' did not require that there be directions or instructions embracing all matters involving the board. Rather it only required that, as and when the directors were directed or instructed, they were accustomed to act as the section required.

Various factors may be identified in determining whether or not a person was a shadow director

In the leading case on shadow directors of *Secretary of State for Trade and Industry v Deverell* [2000] 2 BCLC 133, E Ltd went into creditors voluntary liquidation with an estimated deficiency with regard to creditors of £4.6m. The Secretary of State subsequently sought disqualification orders against D and H under the Company Directors Disqualification Act 1986, contending that they had been shadow directors of E Ltd.

Section 22(5) of the 1986 Act (as amended by s 90(2) SBEEA 2015) defines 'shadow director' as a person in accordance with whose directions or instructions the directors of the company were accustomed to act. It further provides that a person was not deemed to be a shadow director merely because the directors acted on advice given by him in a professional capacity; or in accordance with instructions, a direction, guidance or advice given by that person in the exercise of a function conferred by or under an enactment; or in accordance with guidance or advice given by that person in that person's capacity as a Minister of the Crown (within the meaning of the Ministers of the Crown Act 1975).

The Court of Appeal held that for the purposes of s 22(5) of the 1986 Act, the question whether a particular communication constituted a direction or instruction had to be answered in the light of all the evidence, and it was not necessary to prove the understanding or expectation of either giver or receiver. Evidence of such an understanding or expectation might be relevant, but it could not be conclusive.

Furthermore, non-professional advice could fall within s 22(5). Such a conclusion appeared to be assumed by the proviso excepting advice given in a professional capacity, and in any event the concepts of 'direction' and 'instruction' did not exclude the concept of 'advice' since all three shared the common feature of 'guidance'.

Moreover, although it would be sufficient to show that properly appointed directors had cast themselves in a subservient role or surrendered their discretions in the face of 'directions or instructions' from the alleged shadow director, it would not always be necessary to do so. Such instructions or directions did not have to extend over all or most of the corporate activities of the company. Also, it was not necessary to demonstrate a degree of compulsion in excess of that implicit in the fact that the board was accustomed to act in accordance with them. Moreover, it was not necessary for the shadow director to lurk in the shadows, although he might frequently do so. The judge had therefore applied too strict a test, and he had been wrong to conclude that D and H had not been shadow directors of E Ltd.

In the course of his judgment, Morritt LJ stated the following propositions that would be applicable to a shadow director:

'(1) The definition of a shadow director is to be construed in the normal way to give effect to the parliamentary intention ascertainable from the mischief to be dealt with and the words used.

(2) The purpose of the legislation is to identify those, other than professional advisers, with real influence in the corporate affairs of the company. But it is not necessary that such influence should be exercised over the whole field of its corporate activities …

(3) Whether any particular communication from the alleged shadow director, whether by words or conduct, is to be classified as a direction or instruction must be objectively ascertained by the court in the light of all the evidence. In that connection I do not accept that it is necessary to prove the understanding or expectation of either giver or receiver. In many, if not most, cases it will suffice to prove the communication and its consequence … Certainly the label attached by either or both parties then or thereafter cannot be more than a factor in considering whether the communication came within the statutory description of direction or instruction.

(4) Non-professional advice may come within that statutory description. The proviso excepting advice given in a professional capacity appears to assume that advice generally is or may be included. Moreover the concepts of "direction" and "instruction" do not exclude the concept of "advice" for all three share the common feature of "guidance".

(5) It will, no doubt, be sufficient to show that in the face of "directions or instructions" from the alleged shadow director the properly appointed directors or some of them cast themselves in a subservient role or surrendered their respective discretions. But I do not consider that it is necessary to do so in all cases … Such a requirement would be to put a gloss on the statutory requirement that the board are "accustomed to act in accordance with" such directions or instructions … .'

On the facts, the Court of Appeal held that the two individuals concerned, who claimed that they were the company's consultants, were, in fact, shadow directors who were involved at a senior level in the governance of the company's affairs.

A pattern of conduct of accepting instructions was an important factor in identifying a shadow director – one single event will not suffice

In *Secretary of State for Trade and Industry v Becker* [2003] 1 BCLC 555, the case against the two individuals concerned disqualification proceedings under CDDA 1986. The conduct relied on by the Secretary of State in regard to both the individuals included causing and/or allowing the transfer of the company's assets to a new company without valuable consideration and to the detriment of creditors, failing to recover or assist in the recovery of monies properly due to the company, causing it to make preferential payments to the respondent and his son, and failing to pay PAYE and National Insurance contributions to the Inland Revenue.

The issue was whether both shadow directorships had been established.

Sir Donald Rattee decided that in order to establish that a person was a 'shadow director', there had to be proof of a pattern of conduct in which a *de jure* director of a company was accustomed to act on the instructions or directions of the alleged shadow director. In order to establish that a person was a de facto director it was necessary to show that he undertook functions in relation to the company which could properly be discharged only by a director. The test for a shadow director was not satisfied if all that could be shown was that a *de jure* director acted on the instructions or directions of the alleged shadow director in relation to one event at the end of the company's life. Accordingly, the fact that the respondent's son, as the director of the old company, caused it to cease trading and took no steps to stop the new company taking the benefit of its contracts, as the result of the respondent's influence, as the sole shareholder of both companies, did not establish either that the son, as the *de jure* director, was accustomed to act as a director of the company on the instructions or directions of his father, the respondent, or that the respondent undertook functions in relation to the company which could properly be discharged only by a director.

Accordingly, the Secretary of State had not established the existence of a shadow directorship.

The level of influence exerted over directors was significant in identifying a shadow director

In *Re Mea Corporation, Secretary of State for Trade and Industry v Aviss* [2007] 1 BCLC 618, the allegation against the individuals concerned was that they were involved in dictating the policy of three companies as to application of trade income and payment of trade creditors. Certain creditors were preferred to others in payment priority. Money received by companies in the group was paid into a central fund and this was used to support companies outside the group. The issue was whether the individuals were directors or shadow directors of the group companies.

The court decided that the individuals' level of influence over the company's affairs were sufficient for them to be identified as shadow directors.

According to Lewison J, persons who undertook the functions of directors, even though not formally appointed as such, were called *de facto* directors or directors 'in fact'. A person was not deemed a shadow director by reason only that the directors acted on advice given by him in a professional capacity. Moreover, the role of a shadow director did not necessarily extend over the whole range of the company's activities, and there was no conceptual difficulty in concluding that a person could be both a shadow director and a *de facto* director In each case, it was necessary to examine the facts, bearing in mind that the purpose of the legislation was to identify those, other than professional advisers, with real influence in the corporate affairs of the company.

In the critical areas of the application of trading income and the payment of trade creditors, the policy of all three companies had been dictated by the respondents. The respondents had been responsible for the failure of the companies to satisfy its creditors caused by the application of the companies' funds to assist outside companies in which the first respondent had an interest. In doing so they had failed to respect the fundamental principle that the director of a company owed a duty to exercise his powers in the best interests of the company.

A shadow director must exercise real influence in the corporate affairs of the company

In the *matter of Coroin Ltd (sub nom Mckillen v Misland (Cyprus) Investments Ltd)* [2012] EWHC 1158, the judge confirmed the position on the definitions of *de facto* and shadow directors and stated that shareholders may be found to be acting as directors and, therefore, to owe duties to companies.

This case concerns control of an English company, 'C Ltd', which owned some of the most exclusive hotels in London. The claimant, 'M', owned 36 per cent of C Ltd's shares. Unable to reach agreement for the purchase of C Ltd, two other shareholders 'B1' and 'B2' executed a plan aimed at the acquisition of full control and ownership of C Ltd. M commenced proceedings under s 994 of CA 2006 and then sought permission to introduce significant amendments to the petition and the particulars of claim which were opposed by the defendants. M claimed that B1 and B2 were *de facto* or shadow directors, owed fiduciary and/or statutory duties to C Ltd, and breached those duties by causing the directors appointed by the companies associated with, or controlled by, them to take steps to pursue the plan. As regards shadow directors, the judge stated that 'the purpose of the legislation is to identify those, other than professional advisers, with real influence in the corporate affairs of the company. But it is not necessary that such influence should be exercised over the whole field of its corporate activities' (*Secretary of State for Trade and Industry v Deverell* [2000] 2 All ER 365 followed). It is enough that a majority of directors act in accordance with the directions of the shadow director. It is not necessary that the shadow director should exercise control through the instructions which he gives over all the matters which are decided by the board. All relevant circumstance have to be taken into account as there is no single decisive test (*HMRC v Holland* [2010] All ER (D) 255 (Nov).

Do shadow directors owe fiduciary duties?

13.21 There appears to be a position, now taken by the courts that shadow directors owe a duty, like directors, to act in the best interests of the company. The position is supported by CA 2006, s 170(5) (as amended by SBEEA 2015, s 89).

A shadow director does not generally owe fiduciary duties to the company

In *Ultraframe (UK) Limited v Fielding* [2005] EWHC 1638, Lewison J was of the view that the fact that a person was determined to be a shadow director did not imply that he owed fiduciary duties to the company similarly to those imposed on directors. He stated:

> 'The indirect influence exerted by a paradigm shadow director who does not directly deal with or claim the right to deal directly with the company's assets will not usually, in my judgment, be enough to impose fiduciary duties upon him; although he will, of course, be subject to those statutory duties and disabilities that the Companies Act creates. The case is the stronger where the shadow director has been acting throughout in furtherance of his own, rather than the company's, interests. However, on the facts of a particular case, the activities of a shadow director may go beyond the mere exertion of indirect influence.'

Lewison J went on to stress that the real question was as to the nature of the activities undertaken, and not a label attached to their perpetrator.

However, in *Re Mea Corporation, Secretary of State for Trade and Industry v Aviss* [2007] 1 BCLC 618, Lewison J appeared to have assumed that a shadow director owed duties to the company to act in the best interests of the company.

Significance of the distinction between a de facto director and a shadow director

13.22 In *Re Hydrodam (Corby) Ltd* [1994] 2 BCLC 180, Millett J was of the view that that the *de facto* and shadow directorships did not overlap and that there were clear distinctions between the two. They were alternatives and in most and perhaps all cases, are mutually exclusive.

However, according to Lord Collins in *Re Paycheck Services 3 Ltd; Revenue and Customs Commissioners v Holland* [2011] 1 BCLC 141, over the years the distinction between de facto directors and shadow directors has become blurred and eroded and impossible to maintain owing to the extension of the *de facto* directorship concept and the consideration of such matters as the taking of major decisions by the individual, which might be through instructions to the de jure directors, and the evaluation of his real influence in the company's affairs: see *Re Kaytech International plc, Secretary of State for Trade and Industry v Kaczer* [1999] 2 BCLC 351.

13.23 Another consequence has been that the courts were confronted with the very difficult problem of identifying what functions were in essence the sole responsibility of a director or board of directors. In this regard, a number of tests have been suggested of which the following are the most relevant:

- First, whether the person was the sole person directing the affairs of the company (or acting with others equally lacking in a valid appointment), or if there were others who were true directors, whether he was acting on an equal footing with the others in directing its affairs: *Re Richborough Furniture Ltd*.
- Secondly, whether there was a holding out by the company of the individual as a director, and whether the individual used the title: *Secretary of State for Trade and Industry v Tjolle.*
- Thirdly, taking all the circumstances into account, whether the individual was part of 'the corporate governing structure': *Secretary of State for Trade and Industry v Tjolle*, approved in *Re Kaytech International plc, Secretary of State for Trade and Industry v Kaczer,* where Robert Walker LJ also approved the way in which Jacob J in *Secretary of State for Trade and Industry v Tjolle* had declined to formulate a single test. He also said that the concepts of shadow director and *de facto* director had in common 'that an individual who was not a *de jure* director is alleged to have exercised real influence (otherwise than as a professional adviser) in the corporate governance of a company' (at 424). See also especially *Re Mea Corp Ltd, Secretary of State for Trade and Industry v Aviss* [2006] EWHC 1846 (Ch), [2007] 1 BCLC 618 (Lewison J); *Ultraframe (UK) Ltd v Fielding, Northstar Systems Ltd v Fielding* [2005] EWHC 1638 (Ch), [2005] All ER (D) 397 (Jul) (Lewison J); *Secretary of State for Trade and Industry v Hollier* [2006] EWHC 1804 (Ch), [2007] BCC 11 (Etherton J). In fact it is just as difficult to define 'corporate governance' as it is to identify those activities which are essentially the sole responsibility of a director

or board of directors, although perhaps the most quoted definition is that of the Cadbury Report: 'Corporate governance is the system by which companies are directed and controlled' (Report of the Committee on the Financial Aspects of Corporate Governance, 1992, para 2.5).

In modern times, the courts look more towards various factors in determining the degree of control exercised over the company's affairs by either the de facto director or the shadow director. Indeed, it may be possible for a person to be both a shadow director and a *de facto* director in certain circumstances. The distinction may matter in respect of a shadow director who will be liable only under the statutory provisions that impose obligations on a shadow director. It would seem that the *de facto* director will be liable to a larger extent than a shadow director and that more cases are likely to be brought against a *de facto* director than a shadow director based on the extent of control exercised over the company's governing structure.

Directors of corporate directors

13.24 Can a *de jure* director of one company, while acting in that role, become a *de facto* director of another company? Does the *de jure* role in one company protect against liability to the other?

All relevant factors must be taken into account to determine whether a person was a de facto director of another company

These issues were raised in the leading case of *Re Paycheck Services 3 Ltd; Revenue and Customs Commissioners v Holland* [2011] 1 BCLC 141, the husband and wife established an intricate structure of companies (composite companies) whose activities included the administration of the business and tax affairs of contracting workers in different sectors. Each of the contractors became an employee of one of the composite companies and was given a share which carried no voting rights. This meant that the employees received both a salary and a dividend. The structure of the composite companies was such that each company was only liable to pay corporation tax at the small companies' rate. However, under UK legislation, these composite companies were in reality associated companies, which meant that each company was liable to pay corporation tax at the main rate. Provision had not been made for the payment of tax at the main rate. Further, each company had, throughout its life, declared and paid dividends that should not have been paid because there were insufficient distributable reserves to permit them. All the composite companies stopped trading and went into liquidation and thereafter into a creditors' voluntary liquidation. The Revenue was the only creditor.

HMRC applied to the court in respect of each composite company alleging that, as *de facto* directors of the composite companies, it had been guilty of misfeasance and breaches of duty in causing the payments of unlawful dividends.

At first instance, the judge dismissed the applications against the wife, but allowed, in part, those against the husband, and ordered him to make a contribution to the assets of the insolvency companies under s 212 of the Insolvency Act 1986 as a result of misfeasance, where a person had been an officer of the company, which included a *de facto* director.

At the Court of Appeal, its appeal was allowed taking the view that there was no reason why a director of a corporate director who was doing no more than discharging his duties should thereby become a *de facto* director of the subject company. HMRC appealed to the Supreme Court.

Supreme Court

A majority of the House of Lords decided 3:2 (Lord Walker and Lord Clarke dissenting) that it was clear from established authority that the circumstances in which a person could be held to be a *de facto* director for the purposes of s 212 of the Insolvency Act 1986 varied widely from case to case, and was very much a question of fact and degree. All the relevant factors had to be taken into account.

The objective of s 212 of the Insolvency Act 1986 was to impose liability on those who had been in a position to prevent damage to creditors by taking proper steps to protect their interests. Those who assumed to act as directors and who thereby exercised the powers and discharged the functions of a director, whether validly appointed or not, had to accept the responsibilities of the office.

Accordingly, one had to look at what the person had actually done to see whether he had actually assumed those responsibilities in relation to the subject company. The question was one of law and it was a question of principle. The guiding principle could be expressed in that way unless and until Parliament provided otherwise.

As long as the relevant acts had been done by the individual entirely within the discharge of his duties as the director of the corporate director, it was to that capacity that his acts had to be attributed.

In the present case, he had been doing no more than discharging his duties as a director of the composite companies. Everything that he had done had been done under that umbrella.

Further, the Revenue had been unable to point to anything that he had done which could not be said to have been done by him in his capacity as a director of the corporate director. It had not been shown that he had been acting as *de facto* director of the composite companies so as to make him responsible for the misuse of the assets.

Lord Hope considered whether Mr Holland was, in fact, a *de facto* director of the composite companies. He stated that all the relevant factors must be taken into account. The liability is imposed on those who were in a position to prevent damage to creditors by taking proper steps to protect their interests. Those who assume to act as directors and who exercise the powers and discharge the functions of a director, whether validly appointed or not, must accept the responsibilities of the office. It is essential to look at what the person actually did, to see whether he assumed those responsibilities in relation to the subject company. The problem that was presented by this case, however, is that Mr Holland was doing no more than discharging his duties as the director of the corporate director of the composite companies.

Lord Hope considered that the question of whether Mr Holland was acting as a *de facto* director of the composite companies must be approached on the basis that Paycheck Directors (the sole corporate director of each of the composite companies) and Mr Holland were, in law, separate persons, each with their own separate legal personality (see *Salomon v Salomon & Co Ltd*). The mere fact of acting as a director of a corporate director would not be enough for an individual to become a *de facto* director of the subject company. It was necessary to consider what a person actually did to see whether he assumed the responsibilities of the office of director. Everything Mr Holland did was under the umbrella of being the director of a sole corporate director. Until Parliament provided otherwise, if acts were entirely within the ambit of the duties and responsibilities of a director of the corporate director, it is to that capacity that acts were attributed.

Lord Collins provided a different reasoning but agreed with Lord Hope and held that whether a person is a *de facto* director was not simply a question of fact: the question was whether all of his acts could be attributed in law solely to the activities of the corporate director. It did not follow from the fact that Mr Holland took all the relevant decisions that he was a *de facto* director of the composite companies; if that were so, the guiding mind of every sole corporate director would find themselves the *de facto* director of another company. The basis of liability for a *de facto* director was an assumption of responsibility and being part of the governing structure. Parliament had already intervened in the Companies Act 2006 to ensure that there is a natural person to whom responsibility is attributed. The further extension of the concept of *de facto* director contended for by HMRC was a matter for the legislature, not for the Supreme Court.

Lord Saville agreed with Lord Hope and Lord Collins.

Lord Walker considered that if a person took all the important decisions affecting a company and saw that they were carried out, then he was acting as a director of that company. Lord Walker considered that to attribute acts on the basis of capacity in a corporate structure was the most arid formalism.

Lord Clarke agreed with Lord Walker and held that capacity should be irrelevant to the question of whether an individual was a *de facto* director. Lord Clarke thought it artificial and wrong to hold that Mr. Holland was doing no more than merely discharging his duties as a *de jure* director of Paycheck Directors.

13.25 The statutory position on corporate directors is governed by s 156A(1) of CA 2006 (as inserted by SBEEA 2015, s 87(4)). This provides that a person may not be appointed a director of a company unless the person is a natural person. However, this does not prohibit the holding of the office of director by a natural person as a corporation sole or otherwise by virtue of an office: s 156A(2). An appointment made in contravention of s 156A of CA 2006 is void. Nothing in s 156A affects any liability of a person under any provision of the Companies Acts or any other enactment if the person:

(a) purports to act as a director; or

(b) acts as a shadow director,

although the person could not, by virtue of s 156A, be validly appointed as a director: s 156A(4) CA 2006.

Section 156A is subject to s 156B (power to provide for exceptions from requirement that each director be a natural person): CA 2006, s 154(5).

13.26 If a purported appointment is made in contravention of s 156A, an offence is committed by:

(a) the company purporting to make the appointment;

(b) where the purported appointment is of a body corporate or a firm that is a legal person under the law by which it is governed, that body corporate or firm; and

(c) every officer of a person falling within paragraph (a) or (b) who is in default.

13.27 For this purpose, a shadow director is treated as an officer of a company: s 156A(6) CA 2006.

A person guilty of an offence under s 156A CA 2006 is liable on summary conviction in England and Wales to a fine; in Scotland or Northern Ireland, to a fine not exceeding level 5 on the standard scale: s 156A(7) CA 2006.

13.28 The Secretary of State may make provision by regulations for cases in which a person who is not a natural person may be appointed a director of a company: s 156B(1) of CA 2006. The regulations must specify the circumstances in which, and any conditions subject to which, the appointment may be made: s 156B(2) of CA 2006. This may include a provision that an appointment may be made only with the approval of a regulatory body specified in the circumstances: s 156B(3) of CA 2006. The regulations must include provision that a company must have at least one director who is a natural person. This requirement is met if the office of director is held by a natural person as a corporation sole or otherwise by virtue of an office: s 156B(4) of CA 2006. The regulations may amend s 164 of CA 2006 so as to require particulars relating to exceptions to be contained in a company's register of directors: s 156B(5) of CA 2006. The regulations may make different provisions for different parts of the United Kingdom. This is without prejudice to the general power to make different provision for different cases: s 156B(6) of CA 2006.

13.29 Section 156C of CA 2006 deals with an existing director who is not a natural person. It sets out the transition period for companies with corporate directors. After one year of coming into force of s 156A, a corporate director not within the scope of exceptions defined in the regulations under s 156B will cease to be a director. The company will need to make the necessary register alterations and notifications to the registrar.

The Government is required to review the provisions of s 87 of SBEEA 2015 every five years with the first review taking place no later than five years after these provisions come into force: s 88 of SBEEA 2015.

Director's appointment

13.30 The CA 2006 does not address in any detail how directors may be appointed and the procedure for such appointment. Much is therefore left to the company's articles of association to set out the mechanism for such appointment. Under Model Article 17 for private companies limited by shares, a person may be appointed as a director provided he is 'willing to act as a director' and is permitted by law to do so. The appointment may be by ordinary resolution or a decision of the directors. The person must agree to the appointment: *Re British Empire Match Co Ltd* (1888) 59 LT 291. In *Re CEM Connections Limited* [2000] BCC 917, Registrar Rawson stated that for the appointment of a director of a company to be valid it was necessary that the person appointed should give informed consent of that appointment. The fact that a person signed a form of consent was strong prima facie evidence that consent was given, but it was not conclusive, and may be rebutted by evidence which indicates that the signature was obtained without the person signing the document appreciating what he or she was doing.

The power to appoint a director for public companies is contained in Model Articles for public companies Article 20, with the director holding office only until the next annual general meeting: Article 21(2).

Others who may appoint the directors

13.31 Under CA 2006, s 154(1), every private company must have at least one director; and a public company must have at least two directors: CA 2006, s 154(2). Where a public company's directors is reduced to one, that sole director cannot act on own, and he must then appoint another director if such power exists under the articles: *Channel Collieries Trust Ltd v Dover St Margaret's and Martin Hill Light Railway Co* [1914] 2 Ch 506. Such power is provided for under Article 11(3)(a) of the Model Articles for a private company, and Article 17(1)(b) Model Articles for a public company. In relation to a private company, Model Article 17(2) provides that in any case where, as a result of death, the company has no shareholders and no directors, the personal representatives of the last shareholder to have died have the right, by notice in writing, to appoint a person to be a director.

13.32 It is also possible for the Secretary of State under CA 2006, s 156 to require the company to appoint a director within a period of one to three months where the company has less than the statutory minimum number of directors or there is no natural director appointed. Failure to comply with s 156 will be an offence. A person guilty of an offence under s 156 is liable on summary conviction to a fine not exceeding level 5 on the standard scale and, for continued contravention, a daily default fine not exceeding one-tenth of level 5 on the standard scale: CA 2006, s 156(7).

Minimum age

13.33 A person may not be appointed a director of a company unless he has attained the age of 16: CA 2006, s 157(1).

However, this does not affect the validity of an appointment that is not to take effect until the person attained that age: CA 2006, s 157(2).

Where the office of a company is held by a corporation sole, or otherwise by virtue of another office, the appointment to that other office of a person who has not attained the age of 16 is not effective also to make him a director of the company until he attains the age of 16 years: CA 2006, s 157(3).

Any appointment made in contravention of s 157 is void: CA 2006, s 157(4).

13.34 Nothing in s 157 affects any liability of a person under any provision of the Companies Acts if he purports to act as director, or acts as a shadow director, although he could not, by virtue of s 157, be validly appointed as a director: CA 2006, s 157(5).

Section 157 is subject to exception from minimum age requirements under s 158 (power to provide for exceptions from minimum age requirement): CA 2006, s 157(6).

Power to provide for exceptions from minimum age requirement

13.35 As an exception to CA 2006, s 157 the Secretary of State may make provision by regulation for cases in which a person who has not attained the age of 16 may be appointed a director of a company: CA 2006, s 158(1). Further, the regulations must specify the circumstances in which, and any conditions subject to which, the appointment may be made: CA 2006, s 158(2).

If the specified circumstances cease to obtain, or any specified conditions cease to be met, a person who was appointed by virtue of the regulations and who has not since attained the age of 16 ceases to hold office: CA 2006, s 158(3).

The regulations may make different provisions for different parts of the UK. This is without prejudice to the general power to make a different provision for different cases: CA 2006, s 158(4).

Existing under age directors

13.36 Section 159 of CA 2006 applies where:

(a) a person was appointed a director before 1 October 2008 and has not attained the age of 16 as at that date; or

(b) the office of director of a company is held by a corporation sole, or otherwise by virtue of another office, and the person appointed to that other office has not attained the age of 16 years when that section comes into force,

and the case is not one excepted from that section by regulations under s 158(2): CA 2006, s 159(1).

13.37 That person ceases to be a director upon s 157 coming into force: CA 2006, s 158(2).

The company must make the necessary consequential alteration in its register of directors but need not give notice to the registrar of the change: CA 2006, s 159(3).

If it appears to the registrar (from other information) that a person has ceased, by virtue of s 159, to be a director of a company, the registrar shall note the fact on the register: CA 2006, s 159(4).

Appointment of directors of public company to be voted individually

13.38 At a general meeting of a public company a motion for the appointment of two or more persons as directors of the company by a single resolution must not be made unless a resolution that it should be so made has first been agreed by the meeting without any vote being given against it: CA 2006, s 160(1).

A resolution moved in contravention of s 160 is void, whether or not so moved was objected to at the time. But where a resolution so moved is passed, no provision for the automatic reappointment of retiring directors in default of another appointment applies: CA 2006, s 160(2).

A motion for approving a person's appointment or for nominating a person for appointment is treated as a motion for his appointment: CA 2006, s 160(3). This does not affect a resolution amending the company's articles of association: CA 2006, s 160(4).

Validity of acts of directors

13.39 The acts of a person acting as a director are valid notwithstanding that it is afterwards discovered that:

- there was a defect in his appointment;
- he was disqualified from holding office;
- he had ceased to hold office;
- he was not entitled to vote on the matter in question: CA 2006, s 160(1).

This applies even if the resolution for his appointment is void under s 160: CA 2006, s 161(2).

13.40 This section address defective appointments of directors that may have arisen during the company's existence which are then validated: see *Morris v Kanssen* [1946] AC 459. A person seeking to rely on the validation provisions must ensure he has acted in good faith to invoke such provisions: *Channel Collieries Trust Ltd v Dover, St Margaret's and Martin Hill Light Railway Co* [1914] 2 Ch 506.

In *British Asbestos Co Ltd v Boyd* [1903] 2 Ch 439, Farwell stated that the aim of the validation provision was 'to make the honest acts of *de facto* directors as good as the honest acts of *de jure* directors … although there may be some slip which has been overlooked, if it has been bona fide overlooked, then the acts of the *de facto* directors are as good as the acts of the *de jure* directors.'

Register of directors

13.41 Every company must keep a register of its directors: CA 2006, s 162(1).

The register must contain the required particulars (see ss 163–165) of each person who is a director of the company: CA 2006, s 162(2).

The register must be kept available for inspection:

- at the company's registered office; or
- at a place specified in regulations under s 1136: CA 2006, s 162(3).

The company must give notice to the registrar:

- of the place at which the register is kept available for inspection; and
- of any change of that place: CA 2006, s 162(4),

unless it has, at all times, been kept at the company's registered office: CA 2006, s 162(4).

The register must be open to the inspection:

- of any member of the company without charge; and
- of any other person on payment on such fee as may be prescribed: CA 2006, s 162(5).

13.42 If default is made in complying with s 162(1), (2), or (3) or if default is made in complying with s 162(4), or if an inspection required under s 162(5) is refused, an offence is committed by:

- the company; and
- every officer of the company who is in default: CA 2006, s 162(6).

A person guilty of an offence under s 162 is liable on summary conviction to a fine not exceeding level 5 on the standard scale and for continued contravention, a daily default fine not exceeding one-tenth of level 5 on the standard scale: CA 2006, s 162(7).

In case of refusal of inspection of the register, the court may, by order, compel an immediate inspection of it: CA 2006, s 162(8).

Particulars of directors to be registered – individuals

13.43 A company's register of directors must contain the following particulars in the case of an individual:

- name and any former name;
- service address;
- country and state (or part of the UK) in which he usually resides;
- nationality;
- business occupation (if any); and
- date of birth: CA 2006, s 163(1).

13.44 The term 'name' means a person's Christian name (or any forename) and surname, except in the case of:

- a peer; or
- an individual usually known by a title.

In these situations, the title may be stated instead of his Christian name (or other forename) and surname or in addition to either or both of them: CA 2006, s 163(2).

13.45 The term 'former name' means a name by which the individual was formerly known for business purposes: CA 2006, s 163(3). Where a person is, or was, formerly known by more than one such name, each of them must be stated.

It is not necessary for the register to contain particulars of a former name in the following cases:

- In the case of a peer or an individual normally known by a British title, where the name is one by which the person was known previous to the adoption of or succession to the title.
- In the case of any person, where the former name:
  - was changed or disused before the person attained the age of 16; or
  - has been changed or disused for 20 years or more: CA 2006, s 163(4)(b).

A person's service address may be stated to be 'The company's registered office': CA 2006, s 163(5).

Particulars of directors to be registered: corporate directors and firms

13.46 Under s 164 of CA 2006, a company's register of directors must contain the following particulars in the case of a body corporate, or a firm that is a legal person under the law by which it is governed:

(a) corporate or firm name;

(b) registered or principal office;

(c) in the case of an EEA company to which the First Company Law Directive (68/151/EEC) applies, particulars of:

- the register in which the company file mentioned in Article 3 of that Directive is kept (including details of the relevant state); and
- the registration number of the register.

(d) in any other case, particulars of:

- the legal form of the company or firm and the law by which it is governed; and
- if applicable, the register in which it is entered (including details of the state) and its registration number in that register.

Register of directors' residential addresses

13.47 Every company must keep a register of directors' residential addresses: CA 2006, s 165(1). This must state the usual residential address of each of the company's directors: CA 2006, s 165(2).

If a director's usual residential address is the same as his service address (as stated in the company's register of directors), the register of directors' residential addresses need only contain an entry to that effect: CA 2006, s 165(2). This does not apply if his service address is stated to be 'The company's registered office'.

If default is made in complying with s 165, an offence is committed by the company, and every officer of the company who is in default. For this purpose a shadow director is treated as an officer of the company: CA 2006, s 165(4).

13.48 A person guilty of an offence under s 165 is liable, on summary conviction, to a fine not exceeding level 5 on the standard scale and, for continued contravention, a daily default fine not exceeding one-tenth of level 5 on the standard scale: CA 2006, s 165(5).

Section 165 applies only to directors who are individuals, not where the director is a body corporate or a firm that is a legal person under the law by which it is governed: CA 2006, s 165(6).

Under s 166, the Secretary of State has the power to make regulations in respect of the particulars of directors to be registered including amendments, adding and removing items from the particulars required to be contained in the company's register of directors' residential addresses. This has been enacted under the *Companies (Disclosure of Address) Regulations 2009, SI 2009/214 and the Companies (Disclosure of Address) (Amendment) Regulations 2015, SI 2015/842.*

Protected information

13.49 Chapter 8 of Part 10 to the CA 2006 makes provision for protecting an individual company director regarding information as to his usual residential address; and the information that his service address is his usual residential address.

This type of information is categorised as 'protected information': CA 2006, s 240(2). The information does not cease to be protected information on the individual ceasing to be a director of the company: CA 2006, s 240(3).

Chapter 8 applies to both the current director of a company and, where appropriate, to a former director: CA 2006, s 240(3).

Protected information: restriction on use or disclosure by company

13.50 A company must not use or disclose protected information about any of its directors except for the following situations:

- for communicating with the director concerned;

- in order to comply with any requirement of the Companies Acts as to the particulars to be sent to the registrar; and
- in accordance with CA 2006, s 244 (disclosure under court order): CA 2006, s 241(1).

Section 241(1), however, does not prohibit any use or disclosure of protected information with the consent of the director concerned: CA 2006, s 241(2). The reference to a director includes, to that extent, a former director.

Protected information: restriction on use or disclosure by registrar

13.51 The registrar must omit protected information from the material on the register that is available for inspection where:

- it is contained in a document delivered to him in which such information is required to be stated; and
- in the case of a document having more than one part, it is contained in a part of the document in which such information is required to be stated: CA 2006, s 242.

The registrar is not required to check other documents or (as the case may be) other parts of the document to ensure the absence of protected information; or to omit from the material that is available for public inspection anything registered before 1 October 2008: CA 2006, s 242(2).

The registrar must not use or disclose protected information except as permitted by s 243 (permitted use or disclosure by registrar); or in accordance with s 244 (disclosure under court order): CA 2006, s 242(3).

Permitted use or disclosure by the registrar

13.52 Section 243 of CA 2006 sets out the circumstances where the registrar may use the protected information.

The protected information may be used and disclosed by the registrar for communicating with the director in question: CA 2006, s 243(1).

The registrar may disclose protected information to a public authority under regulations made by the Secretary of State, or to a credit reference agency: CA 2006, s 243(2).

13.53 The term 'credit reference agency' means a person carrying on a business comprising the furnishing of information relevant to the financial standing of individuals, being information collected by the agency for that purpose: CA 2006, s 243(7).

The Secretary of State may make provision by regulations:

(a) specifying conditions for the disclosure of protected information in accordance with s 243, and

(b) providing for the charging of fees: CA 2006, s 243(3).

The Secretary of State may make provision by regulations requiring the registrar, on application, to refrain from disclosing protected information relating to a director to a credit reference agency: CA 2006, s 243(4).

13.54 The Regulations under s 243(4) may make provision as to:

(a) who may make an application;

(b) the grounds on which an application may be made;

(c) the information to be included in and documents to accompany an application; and

(d) how an application is to be determined: CA 2006, s 243(5).

The provision under s 243(5)(d) may, in particular:

(a) confer a discretion on the registrar; or

(b) provide for a question to be referred to a person other than the registrar for the purposes of determining the application: CA 2006, s 243(6).

The Secretary of State has enacted the Companies (Disclosure of Address) Regulations 2009 (SI 2009/214) which came into force on 1 October 2009; and the Companies (Disclosure of Address) (Amendment) Regulations 2015, SI 2015/ 842.

Disclosure under court order

13.55 The court may make an order for the disclosure of protected information by the company or by the registrar if:

(a) there is evidence that service of documents at a service address other than the director's usual residential address is not effective to bring them to the notice of the director, or

(b) it is necessary or expedient for the information to be provided in connection with the enforcement of an order or decree of the court,

and the court is otherwise satisfied that it is appropriate to make the order: CA 2006, s 244(1).

13.56 An order for disclosure by the registrar is to be made only if the company:

(a) does not have the director's usual residential address, or

(b) has been dissolved: CA 2006, s 244(2).

The order may be made on the application of a liquidator, creditor or member of the company, or any other person appearing to the court to have a sufficient interest: CA 2006, s 244(3).

The order must specify the persons to whom, and purposes for which, disclosure is authorised: CA 2006, s 244(4).

Circumstances in which registrar may put address on the public record

13.57 The registrar may put a director's usual residential address on the public record if:

(a) communications sent by the registrar to the director and requiring a response within a specified period remain unanswered, or

(b) there is evidence that service of documents at a service address provided in place of the director's usual residential address is not effective to bring them to the notice of the director: CA 2006, s 245(1).

13.58 The registrar must give notice of the proposal:

(a) to the director, and

(b) to every company of which the registrar has been notified that the individual is a director: CA 2006, s 245(2).

13.59 The notice must:

(a) state the grounds on which it is proposed to put the director's usual residential address on the public record, and

(b) specify a period within which representations may be made before that is done: CA 2006, s 245(3).

It must be sent to the director at his usual residential address, unless it appears to the registrar that service at that address may be ineffective to bring it to the individual's notice, in which case it may be sent to any service address provided in place of that address: CA 2006, s 245(4).

The registrar must take account of any representations received within the specified period: CA 2006, s 245(5).

What is meant by putting the address on the public record is explained in section 246: CA 2006, s 245(6).

Putting the address on the public record

13.60 The registrar, on deciding in accordance with section 245 that a director's usual residential address is to be put on the public record, shall proceed as if notice of a change of registered particulars had been given:

(a) stating that address as the director's service address, and

(b) stating that the director's usual residential address is the same as his service address: CA 2006, s 246(1).

The registrar must give notice of having done so:

(a) to the director, and

(b) to the company: CA 2006, s 246(2).

13.61 On receipt of the notice the company must:

(a) enter the director's usual residential address in its register of directors as his service address, and

(b) state in its register of directors' residential addresses that his usual residential address is the same as his service address: CA 2006, s 246(3).

But:

(a) s 246(3)(a) does not apply if an election under s 167A is in force in respect of the company's register of directors, and

(b) s 246(3)(b) does not apply if an election under s 167A is in force in respect of the company's register of directors' residential addresses: CA 2006, s 246(3A) (as inserted by SBEEA 2015, Sch 5, Pt 2).

If the company has been notified by the director in question of a more recent address as his usual residential address, it must:

(a) enter that address in its register of directors as the director's service address, and

(b) give notice to the registrar as on a change of registered particulars: CA 2006, s 246(4).

If an election under s 167A is in force in respect of the company's register of directors, the company must, in place of doing the things mentioned in sub-s (4)(a) and (b), deliver the particulars to the registrar in accordance with s 167D: CA 2006, s 246(4A) (as inserted by SBEEA 2015, Sch 5, Pt 2).

If a company fails to comply with s 246(3), (4) or (4A), an offence is committed by:

(a) the company, and

(b) every officer of the company who is in default: CA 2006, s 246(5) (as inserted by SBEEA 2015, Sch 5, Pt 2).

A person guilty of an offence under s 246(5) is liable on summary conviction to a fine not exceeding level 5 on the standard scale and, for continued contravention, a daily default fine not exceeding one-tenth of level 5 on the standard scale: CA 2006, s 246(6).

A director whose usual residential address has been put on the public record by the registrar under this section may not register a service address other than his usual residential address for a period of five years from the date of the registrar's decision: CA 2006, s 246(7).

Duty to notify registrar of change

13.62 A company must within the period of 14 days from:

- a person becoming or ceasing to be a director; or
- the occurrence of any change in the particulars contained in its register of directors or its register of directors' residential addresses;

give notice to the registrar of the change and of the date on which it occurred: CA 2006, s 167(1).

Notice of a person having become a director of the company must contain a statement of the particulars of the new director that are required to be included in the company's register of directors and its register of directors' residential addresses, and be accompanied by a statement by the company that the person has consented to act in that capacity CA 2006, s 167(2) (as inserted by SBEEA 2015, s 100(4)). For newly appointed directors and secretaries, a statement will be added by Companies House to the relevant appointment and incorporation forms (paper and electronic) that the person has consented to act in their relevant capacity. Companies will be required to agree to this statement. As part of this, Companies House will write to all newly appointed directors to make them aware that their appointment has been filed on the public register and explain their statutory general duties.

13.63 Where a company gives notice of a change of a director's service address as stated in the company's register of directors, and the notice is not accompanied by notice of any resulting change in the particulars contained in the company's register of directors' residential addresses, the notice must be accompanied by a statement that no such change is required: CA 2006, s 167(3).

If default is made in complying with this section, an offence will be committed by the company, and every officer of the company who is in default: CA 2006, s 167(4). For this purpose a shadow director is treated as an officer of the company.

A person guilty of an offence under s 167 will be liable, on summary conviction, to a fine not exceeding level 5 on the standard scale and, for continued contravention, a daily default fine not exceeding one-tenth of level 5 on the standard scale: CA 2006, s 167(5).

Removing a director

13.64 A company may, by ordinary resolution, at a meeting remove a director before the expiration of his period of office, notwithstanding anything in any agreement between it and him: CA 2006, s 168.

Special notice is required of a resolution to remove a director under s 168 or to appoint somebody instead of a director so removed at the meeting at which he is removed: CA 2006, s 168(2).

A vacancy created by the removal of a director, if not filled at the meeting at which he is removed, may be filled as a casual vacancy: CA 2006, s 168(3).

13.65 A person appointed director in place of a person removed under s 168 is treated, for the purpose of determining the time at which he or any other director is to retire, as if he had become director on the day on which the person in whose place he is appointed was last appointed a director: CA 2006, s 168(4).

Section 168 is not to be taken:

(a) as depriving a person removed under it of compensation or damages payable to him in respect of the termination of his appointment as director or of any appointment terminating with that as director; or

(b) as derogating from any power to remove a director that may exist apart from s 168.

The Model Articles of Association for a private company limited by shares only sets out the grounds for termination of a director's appointment: Article 18. However, some articles of association may require a director to resign following a request from the other directors of the company.

A power contained in the articles of association for two life directors, was exercisable by the survivor on the death of the other

In *Bersel Manufacturing Co v Berry* [1968] 2 All ER 552, the appellant B and his wife were the first directors of a private company and were appointed permanent life directors by the articles of association. Article 16 (H)a of the articles provided that the permanent life directors 'shall have power to terminate forthwith the directorship of any of the ordinary directors by notice in writing'. B's wife died and the question arose whether this power was exercisable by B, who survived her.

The House of Lords held that the power which was conferred on the two life directors was exercisable by the survivor, on whose death the office would cease.

The expulsion provisions in the articles of association were valid and effective in removing a director

In *Lee v Chou Wen Hsien* [1984] 1 WLR 1201, the articles of association of Ocean-Land Development Ltd (the company), the eighth defendant, of which the claimant and the other seven defendants had become directors on its incorporation, provided that the office of a director 'shall be vacated' if a director was 'requested in writing by all his co-directors to resign'. Such a notice was served on the claimant just two days before the holding of a board meeting, which the claimant had requested the secretary of the company to convene to discuss the sale of some of the company's holdings in subsidiary and associated companies about which he had become concerned, and he suspected that at least one of the sales had been made to a company which was owned by two of his co-directors.

The claimant in his personal capacity commenced proceedings for a declaration that the notice of removal was ineffective and void and that he remained a director of the company. The defendants sought to have the claimant's action dismissed and the writ struck out on the grounds, *inter alia*, that the claimant's action was irregularly constituted and that the writ showed no reasonable cause of action. At first instance, Fuad J dismissed the action and the plaintiff's appeal was dismissed by the Court of Appeal of Hong Kong.

It was held by the Privy Council that the appeal would be dismissed. Although the power of expulsion vested in the directors was a fiduciary power and accordingly, in exercising it, they had to act in what they believed to be the best interests of the company and not for ulterior purposes, the expulsion provision in the company's articles of association was so drafted as to require a director to vacate immediately his office once he had been requested to do so by all the other directors. Even if one or more of the requesting directors acted from ulterior motives the expulsion would be effective provided the stated events for a valid expulsion had been satisfied. Accordingly, as the claimant had been requested in writing to vacate his office by all the other directors, he had been validly removed from his directorship.

Lord Brightman was of the view that the courts could not interfere in the management of the company's affairs: where bad faith was pleaded by the aggrieved director against other directors.

13.66 In some cases, it is possible for the removal of a director to be blocked where a director who is also a shareholder can exercise his weighted voting rights to prevent his removal from office.

Weighted voting rights may validly and effectively prevent the removal of a director

This aspect was reinforced by the House of Lords in *Bushell v Faith* [1970] AC 1099. Article 9 of the articles of association of a private company provided that, in the event of a resolution being proposed at a general meeting of the company for the removal of a director, any shares held by that director should carry three votes per share. The company had an issued capital of £300 in £1 shares, which were distributed equally between the claimant, the defendant (her brother) and B, their sister. The claimant and defendant were the only directors of the company. The two sisters, being dissatisfied with their brother's conduct as a director, requisitioned a general meeting of the company for the purpose of passing a resolution removing him from office as a director. On a poll at the meeting they both voted for the resolution, and he voted against it. A dispute having arisen as to whether the resolution had been passed or defeated, the claimant contended that it had been passed by 200 votes, being those of herself and her sister, to 100, those of the defendant. The defendant contended that in accordance with article 9, his 100 shares carried 300 votes, and that, therefore, the resolution had been defeated by 300 votes to 200. The claimant claimed a declaration that the resolution had been validly passed and an injunction restraining the defendant from acting as a director of the company.

It was held by the House of Lords (Lord Morris dissenting) that Article 9 was valid and applicable, despite the provisions of CA 2006, s 168, since Parliament was only seeking to make an ordinary resolution sufficient to remove a director, and had not sought to fetter a company's right to issue a share with such rights or restrictions as it thought fit and these need not be of general application, but could be attached to special circumstances and particular types of resolution. Accordingly the resolution had been defeated.

13.67 It may also be possible to use the entrenchment provisions under CA 2006, s 22 which provides that a company's articles may contain provision ('provision for entrenchment') to the effect that specified provisions of the articles may be amended or repealed only if conditions are met, or procedures are complied with, that are more restrictive than those applicable in the case of a special resolution. This may be a basis for circumventing the removal provisions under CA 2006, s168.

Another basis on which CA 2006, s 168 may be circumvented is that an agreement may be made between the directors and the shareholders which has the effect of preventing the removal of a director. This is because s 168 deals with an agreement between the company and its director so that s 168 overrides such agreement: *Walker v Standard Chartered Bank plc* [1992] BCLC 535.

13.68 It may be possible for the director who may also be the shareholder to petition on grounds of unfair prejudicial conduct under CA 2006, s 994 based on the view that the director had a legitimate expectation of participating in the company's management: see *Re Westbourne Galleries Limited* [1973] AC 360.

Assuming there is a service contract in place, a director may be entitled to compensation where there is a breach of the service contract by the company. Companies Act 2006, s 168(5)(a) removal of a director does not deprive him of compensation or damages payable to him. The company would therefore be advised to check the provisions of the service contract (if any) with the director to identify the extent of any compensation payable to the director. It applies to termination of his appointment as director or of any appointment terminating with that as director. The director may be entitled to damages for breach of contract where the service contract was for a fixed term which has not expired, or that compensation is payable to the director as part of his terms under the service contract on termination of office.

A director's appointment and termination provisions may be set out in the company's articles of association. In this case, the ordinary contractual principles would apply and provided proper procedures were followed under the articles, it would appear that the director may not have entitlement to claim for damages.

There was no service agreement entitling the director to notice of termination

In *Read v Astoria Garage (Streatham) Ltd* [1952] Ch 637, the company's articles of association consisted of the old Table A of the First Schedule to the Companies Act 1929, with certain modifications and included art 68 of Table A which empowered the directors to appoint one of their body as managing director for such term and at such remuneration as they think fit. It also provided that 'his appointment shall be subject to determination ipso facto … if the company in general meeting resolve that his tenure of the office of managing director … be determined.'

At the first meeting of the company in January, 1932, the claimant was appointed managing director at a salary of £7 a week. In 1948 he became a sick man and the company was doing badly, and on 15 March 1949, the directors decided to remove the plaintiff from being managing director; this was afterwards confirmed at an Extraordinary General Meeting of the company on 28 September 1949.

Early in 1950 the claimant brought proceedings claiming damages for wrongful dismissal on the ground that he was removed from being managing director without notice.

It was held by the Court of Appeal, (affirming Harman J), that as there was no service agreement entitling the claimant to notice, his tenure of the office of managing director could under art 68 be determined ipso facto by resolution of the company in general meeting without notice.

See too: *Swabey v Port Darwin Gold Mining Co* (1889) 1 Meg 385.

13.69 In other cases, a director may have a service contract with the company which has been breached because, for example, termination occurred within the fixed term period of the contract. In such cases, the director may be entitled to damages.

In some circumstances, the courts may imply terms between the parties

In *Southern Foundries (1926) Ltd v Shirlaw* [1940] AC 701, Southern Foundries ('Southern'), by an agreement dated 21 December 1933, appointed the respondent, who was then a director, to be managing director for a term of ten years. Article 91 of the company's articles of association provided that a managing director should 'subject to the provisions of any contract between him and the company be subject to the same provisions as to .... removal as the other directors of the company and if he cease to hold the office of director he shall ipso facto and immediately cease to be a managing director.' Article 105 gave the company power to remove a director before the expiration of his period of office.

In 1935 Federated Foundries Ltd. ('Federated'), which was a company formed to take over the shares of a number of companies, including Southern, acquired all the shares of that company. By a special resolution passed on 17 April 1936, the existing articles of association of Southern were abrogated and new articles adopted. Article 8 empowered Federated by an instrument subscribed by two directors and the secretary to remove any director of the company. Article 9 provided that a director need not hold a share qualification. The new articles incorporated a large part of Table A, including art. 68, which made a managing director's appointment subject to determination ipso facto if he ceased to be a director. On 27 March 1937, an instrument subscribed as above was delivered to Southern removing the respondent from the office of director, and the company thereupon treated him as ceasing to be managing director. The respondent commenced proceedings claiming damages as against Southern for wrongful repudiation of the agreement and as against the Federated for wrongly procuring, causing or inducing the company's breach of the agreement.

It was held by the House of Lords, (Viscount Maugham and Lord Romer dissenting), that it was an implied term of the agreement of 21 December 1933, that Southern should not remove the respondent from his position as director during the term of years for which he was appointed managing director. Further, that in respect of the breach of the agreement, the respondent was entitled to the damages awarded by the trial judge.

Resignation

13.70 A director may leave office by an act of resignation. This may be effected by a notice served on the company setting out the date of resignation. Such notice when once given cannot be withdrawn without the consent of the company: *Glossop v Glossop* [1907] 2 Ch 370. Typically, the service contract between a director and the company will set out the notice period required to be given and much will depend upon the executive position occupied by the director in the company: the more senior the executive, the longer the notice period required: *CMS Dolphin Ltd v Simonet* [2001] 2 BCLC 704.

Director's right to protest against removal

13.71 On receipt of notice of an intended resolution to remove a director under s 168, the company must send a copy of the notice to the director concerned: CA 2006, s 169(1). The director (whether or not a member of the company) is entitled to be heard on the resolution at the meeting: CA 2006, s 169(2).

- Where notice is given of an intended resolution to remove a director under s 169, and the director concerned makes with respect to it representations in writing to the company (not exceeding a reasonable length) and requests their notification to members of the company, the company shall, unless the representations are received by it too late for it to do so:
- in any notice of the resolution given to members of the company state the fact of the representations having been made; and
- send a copy of the representations to every member of the company to whom notice of the meeting is sent (whether before or after receipt of the representations by the company): CA 2006, s 169(3).

If a copy of the representations is not sent as required by s 169(3) because it was received too late or because of the company's default, the director may (without prejudice to his right to be heard orally) require that the representations shall be read out at the meeting: CA 2006, s 169(4).

Copies of the representations need not be sent out and the representations need not be read out at the meeting if, on the application either of the company or of any other person who claims to be aggrieved, the court is satisfied that the rights conferred by s 169 are being abused: CA 2006, s 169(5).

The court may order the company's costs (in Scotland, expenses) on an application under s 165(5) to be paid in whole or in part by the director, notwithstanding that he is not a party to the application: CA 2006, s 169(6).

Checklist: Appointment of a director

13.72 *This checklist sets out the steps and procedures for appointing a director. Notwithstanding the CA 2006 provisions which partially address the appointment of a director, check the company's articles of association on procedure and practice.*

No	Issue	Reference
1	Prepare an agenda for the board meeting	Agenda
2	Check articles of association on procedure for appointing a director – whether by directors or shareholders. Ensure proposed director not disqualified and check Companies House on register of directors' disqualifications; undertake World Check if necessary. See articles on number of directors (minimum/ maximum that may be appointed). Check also any provisions of a shareholders' agreement/joint venture agreement on procedure for nomination and appointment of directors.	Articles of association or Model Articles/ Shareholders' Agreement
3	Ensure director is at least 16 years of age.	CA 2006, s 157(1)
4	Send notice of the board meeting to the company's directors of date, time and place of the meeting.	Notice
5	Can directors dispense with a board meeting by a written resolution procedure? Is a quorum present?	Articles of association
6	Has a chairman been appointed for the board meeting?	Articles of Association
7	Directors to vote on the resolution to appoint the director. Voting will be on a show of hands by simple majority.	Articles of Association
8	Prepare minutes of the board meeting.	
9	Is shareholders' approval required to appoint a director? Company or company secretary to send notice of extraordinary general meeting to the shareholders. Meeting to state date, time, place and proxy.	Articles of Association
10	Can the EGM be dispensed with?	Articles of Association
11	Is a quorum present at the EGM?	
12	Appoint chairman for the EGM.	Articles of Association
13	Shareholders to vote on the appointment of the director on a show of hands or on a poll.	
14	Prepare minutes of the EGM.	
15	File Form AP01 (Appointment of Director) or AP02 (Appointment of Corporate Director) at Companies House.	
16	Inform bank, insurers, HMRC, company personnel, change letterhead/invoices to include director's name. Consider whether obligation to notify if listed company	

No	Issue	Reference
17	Will director be entering into service contract? Consider terms. Does service contract require approval of shareholders?	CA 2006, s 188
18	Update register of directors and register of directors' residential addresses.	
19	Lodge the amended articles of association at Companies House within 15 days after the amendments have been made.	
20	Consider whether director has any interest in contracts or dealings that require disclosure?	CA 2006, ss 177, 182
21	Consider providing director with induction on company and duties in law	

Checklist: Removal of a director

13.73 *This checklist sets out the steps and procedures required to remove a director from office under the CA 2006. References are also made to the model articles of association though companies should consider their own articles of association governing the procedures for convening the meetings.*

No	Issue	Reference
	Steps and procedures	
1	Consider any service contract entered into between company and director and consequences of termination including compensation payable.	Model Articles 9(1) and 18
2	Convene a board meeting on reasonable notice (or such notice as required by the articles of association).	Model Article 9(2)
3	Notice to set out the date, time and place of the board meeting.	Agenda
4	Prepare an agenda for the board meeting setting out the proposed removal of the director.	Model Article 9(4)
5	A written resolution cannot be used at the board meeting.	Model Article 10
6	Ensure quorum is present. Consider the voting at the board meeting – usually by simple majority on a show of hands unless the articles of association provide otherwise.	Model Article 11
7	Directors to put the ordinary resolution to remove the director to the shareholders. Is Chairman appointed? Does Chairman have a casting vote? Are there any conflicts of interest?	Model Articles 12, 13 and 14

No	Issue	Reference
8	After the board meeting, prepare minutes of the board meeting.	Model Article 15
9	Prepare ordinary resolution to remove a director and notice to shareholders.	CA 2006, s 168
10	Notice to set out the date, time, place of meeting and resolution proposed including a note on proxy.	CA 2006, s 169
11	Consider providing the director to be removed from office on opportunity to make some representations. Representation must be of reasonable length.	Model Articles 37, 38, 39, 40, 42, 44, 45
12	Ensure quorum present. Has Chairman been appointed? Shareholders to vote on the resolution. Voting is on a show of hands unless a poll is demanded.	
13	After the EGM, prepare minutes of the meeting.	Minutes
14	Update Register of Directors and Register of Directors' residential addresses.	
15	Ensure any authorities given to directors (bank mandate etc) are revoked immediately and check any personal guarantees given to bank.	
16	Remove name of director from all letterheads, invoices.	
17	Inform insurance company where director's name is on the directors' indemnity policy.	
18	File Form TM01 (Termination of appointment of director) to Companies House within 14 days.	Form TM01
19	Inform the company's auditors.	
20	Inform HMRC.	
21	Check director's service contract/contract of employment on obligations – reminding director (if applicable) of post-termination covenants; duty of confidentiality; non-solicitation clause; non-dealing; intellectual property aspects; use of company name and logo; prohibition on making disparaging remarks. Consider whether any compensation payable to director arising from the service contract?	
22	Consider whether director entering into a settlement agreement? Was independent advice taken?	
23	Consider whether any Stock Exchange obligations to be satisfied for notification on director's removal.	

Definitions

13.74

De facto director:	a person who has not been validly appointed but assumes the role and function of a de jure director
De jure director:	a person who has been validly appointed to undertake the functions of an executive director
Director:	includes any person occupying the position of director, by whatever name called: CA 2006, s 250
Executor de son tort:	a person who has not been lawfully appointed as executor or administrator, who by reason of his intrusion upon the affairs of the deceased is treated for some purposes a having assumed the executorship
Shadow director:	a person in accordance with whose directions or instructions the directors of the company are accustomed to act: CA 2006, s 251(1)

14 Directors' duties

Contents

Introduction

14.1 Traditionally in the UK, before the Companies Act 2006, directors' duties had been fragmented partly comprising case law, common law principles and fiduciary duties that impacted upon directors' duties, including legislation such as the Company Directors Disqualification Act 1986, the Insolvency Act 1986 and the Financial Services and Markets Act 2000. Case law and legislation were combined with voluntary self-reform by directors towards corporate governance, transparency and accountability. Corporate governance becomes more effective with the impact of legal obligations that are placed on directors to ensure corporate control and power is exercised responsibly in the interests of the main stakeholders.

14.2 At the heart of the issue has been the effect and consequences of the separation of ownership from control. Although shareholders in most companies have delegated many of managerial powers to directors through the articles of association, there is a real risk that directors may abuse the powers vested in them: the powers may be used for purposes unconnected with the company's activities, and these powers may become uncontrollable without any effective mechanisms to monitor directors' powers, which could affect the shareholders' investment in the company. Although shareholders risk their capital investment in the company, they also have a vested interest in ensuring that their investment is maximised for their benefit. The debate on directors' duties is, therefore, concerned with the legal regulation and control of their powers within the corporate governance system. Although company law permits directors to have some flexibility in the management of the company's affairs, it also compels directors to have regard to the use of their powers, duties and functions in the performance of their managerial duties within the corporation.

14.3 The regulation and statutory codification of some directors' duties owes much of its origin to the Law Commission and the various government initiatives leading up to the Companies Act 2006. Following a series of company law reviews initiated by the government in the 1990s which spanned over a decade, there was a perceived need for a clear statement of directors' general duties and to regulate such duties in a codified form, and for directors to be aware of where such general duties could be found. A combination of the Company Law Review and the Law Commission Report on *Directors' Duties* recommended that directors' general duties should be set out in a new Companies Act to enable directors to adhere to their duties in the course of the company's operations. The CA 2006 codifies some of the directors' fiduciary and common law duties as part of the general duties of directors.

This chapter considers addresses the following aspects:

- a consideration of the trusteeship of directors based on the application of and interrelationship with the law of trusts;
- the concept of a 'fiduciary' and its application to directors' duties taking account of the 2014 Law Commission Report *Fiduciary Duties of Investment Intermediaries*;
- the general duties of directors and attribution of liability with a consideration of the Supreme Court case of *Jetivia SA v Bilta (UK) Ltd* [2015] UKSA 23;
- a consideration of the proper purpose rule and the Supreme Court decision in *Eclairs Group Ltd v JKX Oil & Gas plc; Glengary Overseas Ltd v JKX Oil & Gas plc* [2015] UKSC 71;
- the remedies available under the CA 2006, the common law and equity including the proprietary nature of claims, having regard to the Supreme Court's decision in *FHR European Ventures LLP and others v Cedar Capital Partners LLC* [2014] EWSC 45; and
- an examination of relief from liability available for directors and officers.

Are corporate managers trustees?

14.4 In English company law, the courts have sometimes referred to directors as 'trustees' or 'fiduciaries' of the company in performing their duties under the corporate governance system. On occasions, the courts have borrowed from the law of trusts to impose trusteeship principles on directors. This section considers the 'trusteeship' of directors and their 'fiduciary' duties as these concept has been used by the courts for example, to impose an obligation on a director to hold property, assets or profits as a constructive trustee for the company.

The concept of 'fiduciary'

14.5 The concept of 'fiduciary', 'fiduciary duties' and 'fiduciary undertaking' are familiar to the law of trusts: they are equitable principles developed over a period of time by the Chancery Courts in their application to trustees who administered assets on behalf of the beneficiaries of a trust. The concept involved notions of conscience: acting in good faith; a sense of loyalty; acting selflessly; and ensuring the best interests of the beneficiaries at all times. The trustees acted with a moral conscience to ensure that trust assets were not misapplied, nor trust funds depleted unnecessarily without cause or reason. Trustees were required to undertake their fiduciary obligations with a sense of purpose and objective which was fundamental to the status of a trustee. They generally acted voluntarily in the performance of their duties without any expectation of any remuneration or reimbursement: *Robinson v Pett* (1734) 3 P Wms 249; *Re Barber* (1886) 34 Ch D 77. Such remuneration or reimbursement was only claimable if trustees could demonstrate a specific entitlement,

Further, trustees were required to ensure that they did not place themselves in a position where their duties and interests might conflict.

A fiduciary is liable to account for breach of his fiduciary duty

In *Boardman v Phipps* [1967] 2 AC 46, Viscount Dilhorne advocated that equity, may, where there has been some impropriety of conduct on the part of a person in a fiduciary relationship (eg a trustee purchasing trust property), require that person to account. Further, where trustees have entered into engagements in which they had or could have had a personal interest conflicting with the interests of those they were bound to protect, clearly they would be liable for doing so.

See too *Aas v Benham* [1891] 2 Ch 244.

A person in a fiduciary position must not make any secret profit or put himself in a conflict of interest situation

In *Bray v Ford* [1896] AC 44, Lord Herschell stated: 'It is an inflexible rule of a court of equity that a person in a fiduciary position ... is not, unless otherwise expressly provided, entitled to make a profit; he is not allowed to put himself in a position where his interest and duty conflict.'

Any benefit gained from renewal of a lease was held on trust for the beneficiary

The concept of "fiduciary" signifies that the person occupying a fiduciary position must not personally profit from that position to the detriment of the beneficiary. In *Keech v Sandford* (1726) Sel Cas T King 61, the court held that a trustee could not personally benefit from a renewal of a lease and that the benefit must be held on trust for the beneficiary.

See too *Chan v Zacharia* (1984) 154 CLR 178; *Don King Productions Inc v Warren* [2000] Ch 291; and *Thompson's Trustee in Bankruptcy v Heaton* [1974] WLR 605.

There are various types of fiduciary relationships existing in law and practice

However, in *Coomber v Coomber* [1911] 1 Ch 723, Fletcher Moulton LJ warned against resorting to verbal formulae in connection with the concept of 'fiduciary duty' on the basis that there were different types of fiduciary relationships that existed between various parties which extended 'to the most intimate and confidential relations which can possibly exist between one party and another where the one is wholly in the hands of the other because of his infinite trust in him'.

However, not every fiduciary situation may give rise to a claim for a breach of such duty.

The term 'fiduciary' has different meanings in various circumstances

In *Girardet v Crease & Co* (1987) 11 BCLR (2d) 361, 362, Southin J stated:

> 'The word "fiduciary" is flung around now as if it applied to all breaches of duty by solicitors, directors of companies and so forth .... That a lawyer can commit a breach of the special duty [of a fiduciary] ... by entering into a contract with the client without full disclosure ... and so forth is clear. But to say that simple carelessness in giving advice is such a breach is a perversion of words.'

These remarks were approved by La Forest J in *LAC Minerals Ltd v International Corona Resources Ltd* (1989) 61 DLR (4th) 14, 28 where he said: 'not every legal claim arising out of a relationship with fiduciary incidents will give rise to a claim for breach of fiduciary duty'.

Not every breach of duty by a fiduciary is a breach of fiduciary duty

In *Bristol & West Building Society v Mothew* [1998] Ch 1, the Court of Appeal addressed in detail the concept of 'fiduciary duty'. According to Millett LJ, the term 'fiduciary duty' was confined to those duties which were peculiar to fiduciaries and the breach of which attracted legal consequences differing from those consequent upon the breach of other duties. Unless the expression was so limited it was lacking in practical utility. In this sense, not every breach of duty by a fiduciary was a breach of fiduciary duty.' The expression may not be appropriate to apply to a trustee or other fiduciary to use proper skill and care in the discharge of his duties, particularly where the standard of care in equity and at common law had different meaning and significance.

See too: *Henderson v Merrett Syndicates Ltd* [1995] 2 AC 145.

In *Permanent Building Society v Wheeler* (1994) 14 ACSR 109, 157, Ipp J elucidated further on the concept of a 'fiduciary':

> 'A fiduciary is someone who has undertaken to act for or on behalf of another in a particular matter in circumstances which give rise to a relationship of trust and confidence. The distinguishing obligation of a fiduciary is the obligation of loyalty. The principal is entitled to the single-minded loyalty of his fiduciary. This core liability has several facets. A fiduciary must act in good faith; he must not make a profit out of his trust; he must not place himself in a position where his duty and his interest may conflict; he may not act for his own benefit or the benefit of a third person without the informed consent of his principal. This is not intended to be an exhaustive list, but it is sufficient to indicate the nature of fiduciary obligations. They are the defining characteristics of the fiduciary. As Dr Finn pointed out in his classic work *Fiduciary Obligations* (1977), p 2, he is not subject to fiduciary obligations because he is a fiduciary; it is because he is subject to them that he is a fiduciary.
>
> The nature of the obligation determines the nature of the breach. The various obligations of a fiduciary merely reflect different aspects of his core duties of loyalty and fidelity. Breach of fiduciary obligation, therefore, connotes disloyalty or infidelity. Mere incompetence is not enough. A servant who loyally does his incompetent best for his master is not unfaithful and is not guilty of a breach of fiduciary duty.
>
> Even if a fiduciary is properly acting for two principals with potentially conflicting interests he must act in good faith in the interests of each and must not act with the intention of furthering the interests of one principal to the prejudice of those of the other: see Finn, p 48. I shall call this "the duty of good faith". But it goes further than this. He must not allow the performance of his obligations to one principal to be influenced by his relationship with the other. He must serve each as faithfully and loyally as if he were his only principal.'

The extension of trusteeship to directors as fiduciaries

14.6 In his book *Fiduciary Obligations* (1977), Paul Finn sets out various situations in which the 'fiduciary' obligations can arise. These include trustee–beneficiary, solicitor–client and director–shareholder relationships: see *Imperial Mercantile Credit Association v Coleman* (1873) LR 6 HL 189, where it was held that a director of a joint-stock company was in a fiduciary position towards the company. Finn has highlighted the importance of an undertaking to act for or on behalf of another person, as one of the key aspects of a fiduciary relationship in some particular matter or matters. According to Finn:

> 'For a person to be a fiduciary he must first and foremost have bound himself in some way to protect and/or to advance the interests of another. This is perhaps the most obvious of the characteristics of the fiduciary office for Equity will only oblige a person to act in what he believes to be another's interests if he himself has assumed a position which requires him to act for or on behalf of that other in some particular matter' (para 15).

See too Millett LJ in *Bristol and West Building Society v Mothew* [1998] Ch 1.

14.7 Another aspect of the fiduciary relationship is the concept of 'legitimate expectations', in that one party is entitled to expect that the other will act in his interests in and for the purposes of the relationship. Aspects such as ascendancy, influence, vulnerability, trust confidence or dependency are only evidence of a relationship suggesting that entitlement. This view has received judicial support by the Privy Council in *Arklow Investments Ltd v Maclean* [2000] 1 WLR 594, where the Council stated that:

> 'The [fiduciary] concept encaptures a situation where one person is in a relationship with another which gives rise to a legitimate expectation, which equity will recognise, that the fiduciary will not utilise his or her position in such a way which is adverse to the interests of the principal'.

Fiduciary relationships may also have the characteristics of 'vulnerability and discretion'. In the Canadian case of *Frame v Smith* [1987] 2 SCR 99, Bertha Wilson J stated:

> 'Relationships in which a fiduciary obligation have been imposed seem to possess three general characteristics: (1) The fiduciary has scope for the exercise of some discretion or power. (2) The fiduciary can unilaterally exercise that power or discretion so as to affect the beneficiary's legal or practical interests. (3) The beneficiary is peculiarly vulnerable to or at the mercy of the fiduciary holding the discretion or power'.

14.8 The concept of vulnerability is now considered by the courts as only an indicator of fiduciary status rather than its defining feature. In *Hodgkinson v Simms* [1994] 3 SCR 377, the Supreme Court of Canada was of the view that 'the concept of vulnerability is not the hallmark of fiduciary relationship'. Also, in *Hospital Products Limited v United States Surgical Corp* (1984) 156 CLR 41, Mason J stated that although the primary test is whether there is an undertaking or agreement by the fiduciary to act for or on behalf of or in the interests of another person, it is:

> 'partly because the fiduciary's exercise of the power or discretion can adversely affect the interests of the person to whom the duty is owed and because the latter is at the mercy of the former that the fiduciary comes under a duty to exercise his power or discretion in the interests of the person to whom it is owed'.

There has also been much uncertainty as to when fiduciary duties arise as well as what the fiduciary duties require as not all fiduciaries owe the same fiduciary duties: *Henderson v Merrett Syndicates Ltd (No 1)* [1995] 2 AC 145. It is clear, however, that the most fundamental aspect of the content of the fiduciary duty is the duty of loyalty, which may be sub-divided into the 'no-conflict rule' and the 'no-profit rule'. These aspects are considered in later sections with particular reference to directors' duties.

14.9 In its report in 2014 entitled *Fiduciary Duties of Investment Intermediaries* (No 350), the Law Commission considered the concept of a 'fiduciary', including fiduciary duties within the legal framework. The Law Commission considered how the law of fiduciary duties applied to investment intermediaries and to evaluate whether the law worked in the interests of the ultimate beneficiaries following the Kay review – *UK Equity Markets and Long-Term Decision Making: Final Report* (July 2012).

The Law Commission acknowledged that the term, 'fiduciary duty' has been used in different contexts. In some cases, the term has been used by pension trustees to emphasise their ethos, which is to act in the interests of the beneficiaries. To others, the term denotes judge-made law often associated with trusts and equities, and the term has also been used in a broad sense to encompass all the various duties owed by fiduciaries to their principles, including duties of care and duties arising from the exercise of a power. At times, the courts have emphasised that the core of fiduciary duty is 'the obligation of loyalty' so that breach 'connotes disloyalty or infidelity': *Bristol & West Building Society v Mothew* [1998] Ch 1, per Millett LJ. Mere incompetence is not enough.

14.10 According to the Law Commission, 'fiduciary duties cannot be understood in isolation. Instead they are better viewed as 'legal polyfilla', moulding themselves flexibly around other legal structures, and sometimes plugging the gaps'. The term 'fiduciary duty' means different things to lawyers and non-lawyers, and has been used in a broad sense to cover all the various duties a fiduciary owes, which also reflects much of judicial thinking in this area: *Aequitas v AEFC* [2001] NSWSC 14. However, the courts have issued stern warnings against using the term in this way. Although it has been recognised that fiduciaries will owe both fiduciary duties and non-fiduciary duties, however, only those duties that are peculiar to fiduciaries are properly termed fiduciary duties: *Breen v Williams* (1996) 186 CLR 74. Therefore, not every breach of duty by a fiduciary is a breach of fiduciary duty: *AG v Blake* [1998] Ch 439; *John Youngs Insurance Services Ltd v Aviva Insurance Service UK Ltd* [2011] EWHC 1515; *Ocular Sciences Ltd v Aspect Vision Care Ltd* [1997] RPC 289; *Base Metal Trading Ltd v Shamurin* [2004] EWCA Civ 1316; *Hilton v Barker Booth & Eastwood* [2005] UKHL 8.

14.11 The Law Commission was of the view that the distinguishing duty of a fiduciary was 'the duty of loyalty'. However, this duty was combined with other statutory, equitable and common law duties which a fiduciary might owe. An example is the duty to exercise reasonable care and skill which is not a fiduciary duty recognised in law: see *Permanent Building Society v Wheeler* (1994) 14 ACSR 109. In *Hilton v Barker Booth & Eastwood* [2005] UKHL 8, the House of Lords stated: 'If a solicitor is careless in investigating a title or drafting a lease, he may be liable to pay damages for breach of his professional duty, but that that is not a breach of a fiduciary duty of loyalty; it is simply the breach of duty of a duty of care'.

14.12 In practice, fiduciary relationships may arise in two circumstances: first in relation to 'status-based fiduciaries' such as a solicitor-client relationship and such fiduciary relationships represent a settled basis of relationship and include trustee and beneficiary (*Keech v Sandford* (1726) Sel Cas Ch 61)); principal and agent (*De Busshe v Alt* (1878) 8 Ch D 286)); company directors and the company (*Sinclair v Brougham* [1914] AC 398)); (*Regal (Hastings) v Gulliver* [1967] 2 AC 134); and secondly, 'fact-based fiduciaries', where the particular facts and circumstances of a relationship justify the imposition of fiduciary duties: *Chimside v Fay* [2006] NZSC 68.

However, the categories of fiduciary relationships are not closed: *Tate v Williamson* (1866) LR 2 Ch App 55; *English v Dedham Vale Properties Ltd* [1978] 1 WLR 93. The courts have traditionally declined to provide a clear definition of the fiduciary duty concept, but have instead preferred preserving flexibility as to its meaning and adapted to different circumstances: *Lloyds Bank Ltd v Bundy* [1975] QB 326; *Hospital Products Ltd v United States Surgical Corp* (1984) 156 CLR 41.

Directors are accountable to the company for unlawful dividends paid and were in a fiduciary relationship with their company

In *Bairstow v Queens Moat Houses plc* [2001] 2 BCLC 531, which concerned dividends which had been unlawfully paid. There was a requirement under the CA 2006 that distributions may be made only in accordance with company's financial statements strict and mandatory in character. The issue was whether the directors were accountable to the company for unlawfully paid dividends. The Court of Appeal held that the principle that directors were accountable to the company for unlawful dividends paid in contravention of the provisions of the CA 2006, whether or not the dividends were demonstrably paid out of capital, applied regardless of whether the company was solvent or insolvent. On the principle that a corporation was a legal person separate from the persons who were from time to time its members or shareholders, the right to reclaim dividends unlawfully paid belonged to the company for the protection of both creditors and shareholders and if directors caused a company to pay a dividend which was *ultra vires* and unlawful, the fact that the company was still solvent was not a defence to a claim against the directors to make good the unlawful distribution. Furthermore, any unfair windfall for the shareholders arose because they were not required to account for the original unlawful dividend, rather than because the repayment might again be distributed by way of dividend: *Re Exchange Banking Co, Flitcroft's Case* (1882) 21 Ch D 519.

In the course of their judgment, the Court of Appeal considered the trusteeship nature of directors' duties.

Robert Walker LJ stated that the fiduciary obligations undertaken in this case by the former directors involved heavy and continuing responsibilities for the stewardship of the company's assets. They were not strictly speaking trustees, as title to the assets was not vested in them; but they had trustee-like responsibilities, because they had the power and the duty to manage the company's business in the interests of all its members. He stated:

> 'It may be that a more satisfactory dividing line is not that between the traditional trust and the commercial trust, but between a breach of fiduciary duty in the wrongful disbursement of funds of which the fiduciary has this sort of trustee-like stewardship and a breach of fiduciary duty of a different character (for instance a solicitor's failure to disclose a conflict of interest.'

Directors owe continuing fiduciary duties to their company

In *Gwembe Valley Development Co Ltd v Koshy* [1998] 2 BCLC 613, Harman J emphasised the continuing nature of the fiduciary duties of directors while a director of a company on the basis that a director was an officer of the company and his duties are continuous while he holds such office.

However, in some cases a director may not owe fiduciary duties to the company. In *Plus Group Ltd v Pyke* [2002] 2 BCLC 201, the Court of Appeal held that although the fiduciary duty of a director to his company was uniform and universal, there was no completely rigid rule that a director could not be involved in the business of another company which was in competition with a company of which he was a director. Every decision whether a fiduciary relationship existed in relation to the matter complained of was fact-specific, and in exceptional circumstances, where a director had been effectively excluded from the company it was not a breach of fiduciary duty for him to work for a competing company.

Not all duties of a director are in the nature of fiduciary duties

In *Extrasure Travel Insurances Ltd v Scattergood* [2003] 1 BCLC 598, Jonathan Crow (sitting as a Deputy Judge of the High Court) stated that:

> 'Fiduciary duties are not less onerous than the common law duty of care: they are of a different quality. Fiduciary duties are concerned with concepts of honesty and loyalty, not with competence. In my view, the law draws a clear distinction between fiduciary duties and other duties that may be owed by a person in a fiduciary position. A fiduciary may also owe tortious and contractual duties to the *cestui que trust*: but that does not mean that those duties are fiduciary duties. Bearing all that in mind, I find nothing surprising in the proposition that crass incompetence might give rise to a claim for breach of a duty of care, or for breach of contract, but not for a breach of fiduciary duty.'

A person who assumes a senior position in a company which is akin to a director may owe fiduciary duties to the company.

A person in a senior position may owe fiduciary duties towards the company

In *ODL Securities Ltd v McGrath* [2013] EWHC 1865, a person was appointed as head of risk which involved the management and reduction of risk to the company, and authorised the transfer of funds including granting loans and advances to non-trading clients, when he had no such authority to do so. The company's junior staff regarded him as having a position akin to a director. The company contended that he owed fiduciary duties: (a) to act in good faith in the best interests of the company; (b) not to act so as to place himself in a position where his personal interests did or might conflict with the interests of the company; and (c) to inform the company of all matters which he considered in good faith to be matters of which the company would wish to be informed.

Flaux J held that as head of risk, McGrath was clearly in a senior position within the company and was trusted by management. He was in effect treated as a director. The other employees were accustomed to following his instructions specifically in relation to payments or transfers from client accounts. He was essentially running the business. That situation of vulnerability for the company was precisely the situation in which such fiduciary duties would be imposed. Although not a director of the company. McGrath was in a closely analogous position and owed the same fiduciary duties as he would if he had been a director. These duties encompassed a duty to disclose matters which were in the interests of the company to know, including where appropriate, his own misconduct.

In *Helmet Integrated Systems Ltd v Tunnard* [2007] IRLR 126, the Court of Appeal held that an employee's duty of fidelity imposed no inhibition on his competing against his former employer once he had left. This freedom to compete, once an employee had left, carried with it a freedom to prepare for future activities, which the employee planned to undertake once he had left. The mere fact that activities during the course of employment were 'preparatory', however, would not necessarily be dispositive of whether the employee acted in breach of his obligations to his employer. Many activities might be described as reasonable and necessary for the purposes of future competition, but that did not assist in deciding whether they were in breach of the employee's obligations.

The employee's activities would have amounted to 'competitor activity' if undertaken by a competitor, and he owed an obligation as a fiduciary not to misuse information about such activity for his own benefit or for the benefit of someone other than his employers. This was because the employers would have no control over how the employee deployed what he had learned as a salesman, and would be dependent upon him to pass on the information. Were it not so, the employee could pick or choose what he did or did not pass on and the employers would be vulnerable to any misuse of such information, the dissemination of which was outside the employers' control.

It did not follow, however, that the employee was under any obligation, fiduciary or otherwise, to inform his employers of his own activities or such activities undertaken on his behalf. The words of the job specification did not restrict his freedom to prepare for competition on leaving. Clear words are needed to restrict the ordinary freedom of an employee who is considering setting up in competition to his former employer. Nor could any relevant fiduciary obligation be identified. The employee owed no fiduciary duties in relation to the development of a preliminary concept. His own preparatory activity could not legitimately be described as 'competitor activity' in the context of his employment as a salesman and his right to prepare for competition once he had left employment as a salesman.

In *Item Software v Fassihi* [2005] ICR 450 where Arden LJ compared the duties of an employee with those of a director and concluded that the duties of a director were in general higher than those imposed by law on an employee because a director was not simply a senior manager of the company, he was a fiduciary and with his fellow directors he had responsibility for the success of the company's business. The fundamental duty to which a director was subject was the duty to act in what he, in good faith, considered to be the best interests of his company. There was no authority for the proposition that a director, as opposed to an employee, owed no duty to disclose his own misconduct. Moreover, there were policy reasons for imposing such a duty of disclosure, in making the remedy for an existing liability of a director to account for secret profits and for the diversion of corporate opportunities more effective.

See too: *Ranson v Customer Systems plc* [2012] IRLR 769.

14.13 In the context of company law and practice, the courts have applied the trusteeship principle to directors based on the view that directors' duties were similar to those of a trustee. It was sufficient for the courts to reason that, since directors had accepted an appointment with obligations towards stakeholders, they were considered as trustees and therefore accountable to the company for breaches of trust: *York and North-Midland Rly v Hudson* (1853) 16 Beav 485; *Charitable Coro v Sutton* (1742) 2 Atk 400.

Another reason for treating directors as trustees was that historically the deeds of settlement of the earliest form of companies usually constituted directors as trustees of their funds and properties. In these situations, directors would be held accountable to their companies and shareholders for mismanagement of the trust fund.

14.14 Although company directors are not strictly speaking trustees, they are in a closely analogous position because of the fiduciary duties which they owe to the company. Lord Selborne in *Great Eastern Rly Co v Turner* (1872) 8 Ch App 149 was of the view that the directors were the mere trustees or agents of the company – trustees of the company's money and property and agents in the transactions which they enter into on behalf of the company.

There has been a growing development of case law addressing the issue as to whether directors are trustees for the company and other stakeholders of the corporation.

The cases have drawn analogous references to the duties of trustees with those of directors in determining the extent and scope of trusteeship of directors.

Directors' duties are sometimes analogous to those of trustees

In comparing a trustee with a director of a company Sir George Jessel MR, in *Re Forest of Dean Coal Mining Co* (1878) 10 Ch D 450, stated that:

> 'Directors have sometimes been called trustees, or commercial trustees, and sometimes they have been called managing partners, it does not much matter what you call them so long as you understand what their true position is, which is that they are really commercial men managing a trading concern for the benefit of themselves and of all the other

> shareholders in it. They are bound, no doubt, to use reasonable diligence having regard to their position, though probably an ordinary director, who only attends at the board occasionally, cannot be expected to devote as much time and attention to the business as the sole managing partner of an ordinary partnership, but they are bound to use fair and reasonable diligence in the management of their company's affairs, and to act honestly.'

Some judicial attitudes have considered the concepts of trustees and the trust as useful mechanisms for addressing the duties of directors.

An analogy of directors' duties with trustees may serve useful purposes in imposing obligations on directors

Bowen LJ in *Imperial Hydropathic Hotel Co v Hampson* (1882) 23 Ch D 1, was of the view that when persons who are directors of a company are from time to time spoken of by judges as agents, trustees, or managing partners of the company, it was essential to recollect that such expressions were used not as exhaustive of the powers or responsibilities of those persons, but only as indicating useful points of view from which they may for the moment and for the particular purpose be considered.

See too: *Flitcroft's Case* (1882) 21 Ch D 519.

The concept of trusteeship and trust was developed further in subsequent cases.

Directors may in some situations be likened to trustees

In re Lands Allotment Co. [1894] 1 Ch 616 Lindley LJ stated that although directors were not properly speaking trustees, yet they have always been considered and treated as trustees of money which comes to their hands or which is actually under their control.

From time to time, there has been some criticism by some courts as to the view that directors were in reality trustees for their company.

Directors stand in a fiduciary relationship to their company

In *Re City Equitable Fire Insurance Co Ltd* [1924] All ER Rep 485, Romer J was of the view that the view that directors were trustees meant no more than that directors in the performance of their duties stood in a fiduciary relationship to the company. However, directors' duties and responsibilities could not be compared to those of trustees.

The decision at first instance was approved by the Court of Appeal [1925] Ch 407.

Directors are not identical to the position of trustees of a will or settlement but there are similarities in their duties

In *Selangor United Rubber Estates Ltd v Cradock (No 3)* [1968] 1 WLR 1555, Ungoed Thomas J was of the opinion that directors were clearly not trustees identically with trustees of a will or marriage settlement. In particular, they have business to conduct and business functions to perform in a business manner, which are not normally rate associated with trustees of a will or marriage settlement. All their duties, powers and functions qua directors are fiduciary for and on behalf of the company.

See too: *Regal (Hastings) Ltd v Gulliver* [1967] 2 AC 134, per Lord Porter; *Belmont Finance Corporation v Williams Furniture Limited (No 2)* [1980] 1 All ER 393; and *Target Holdings v Redferns* [1996] AC 421.

The statutory regime: scope and nature of general duties under the CA 2006

14.15 The statutory regime on the general duties of directors owes much of its origins to the Law Commission Report *Company Directors: Regulating Conflicts of Interest and Formulating a Statement of Duties* Law Com No 261 (1999) and the Company Law Review's consideration of this issue. The Law Commission recommended a statutory codification of only the principal duties of directors enshrined in case law while leaving the common law to develop some of the other rules on directors' duties. There is no comprehensive statutory codification of directors' interests towards creditors and this aspect may be developed further by case law. However, the Company Law Review preferred a codification of all the duties of the directors. Both favoured a high level statement of directors' duties. In the end, Pt 10 of the CA 2006 came closer to the Law Commission's view of partial codification of the key directors' duties found in case law.

14.16 Section 170 of CA 2006 addresses the question to whom directors owe the general duties. It follows the well-established principle under case law and states that the general duties specified in ss 171–177 are owed by a director of the company to a company (as defined by s 250). The duties are also owed by a *de facto* director in the same way and to the same extent they are owed by a properly appointed (*de jure*) director: CA 2006, s 170(1). The duties will apply to a *de facto* director where it can be shown that the person was part of the corporate governing structure, and had assumed a role in the company sufficient to impose a duty on him: *Re Paycheck Services 3 Ltd, Revenue and Customs Commissioners v Holland* [2011] 1 BCLC 141.

Duty to the company

14.17 Section 170(1) of CA 2006 establishes that directors owe their duties to the company and not to its individual shareholders, nor to its employees or any other person or third party. These duties can only be enforced by those who act for or on behalf of the company, including bringing a derivative action under Pt 11 of the CA 2006.

This duty is owed collectively to the shareholders as a group and not to individual shareholders generally. This follows the fiduciary principle that directors must act bona fide in the best interest of the company. In *Re Smith & Fawcett* [1942] Ch 304, the court stated that directors must act at all times bona fide in which they consider (not what the court may consider) to be in the best interest of the company. This principle reflects the court of equity and reluctance to interfere with or second-guess the commercial judgement of directors. The requirement that directors owe a duty to the company means that when taking any decision concerning the management of a company, they must positively apply their minds to the question of what are the best interests of the company. If they fail to carry out the task, the court may intervene and imposed the decision: *Inland Revenue Commissioners v Richmond* [2003] EWHC 99 (Ch).

Directors owe primary duty to their company

The application of this duty can be found in *Percival v Wright* [1902] 2 Ch 421. The shareholders offered to sell their shares to the company's directors and chairman at a price of £12.50 per share. The directors and chairman, however, negotiated a higher price for the shares with a third party. The headnote to the decision stated: 'The directors of a company are not trustees for individual shareholders, and may purchase their shares without disclosing pending negotiations for the sale of the company's undertaking.'

Swinfen Eady J decided that directors of a company did not normally stand in a fiduciary position with their shareholders individually. He stated:

> 'The true rule is that a shareholder is fixed with knowledge of all the directors' powers, and has no more reason to assume that they are not negotiating a sale of the undertaking than to assume that they are not exercising any other power.'

In this case, the directors were under no obligation to disclose the negotiations which had taken place between themselves and the third party. There was no question of unfair dealing. Further, the directors did not approach the shareholders with a view to purchasing their shares. The shareholders approached the directors and named the price at which they would be prepared to sell their shares. The directors did not take any initiative to buy the shares.

Directors do not generally owe duties towards their shareholders

However, in *Re Chez Nico (Restaurants) Ltd* [1992] BCLC 192, Nicolas Browne-Wilkinson V-C (as he was then) doubted the breadth of the proposition said to be contained in *Percival v Wright. He was of the view that* in general directors did not owe fiduciary duties to shareholders, but owed them to the company: however, in certain special circumstances fiduciary duties, carrying with them a duty of disclosure, could arise which placed directors in a fiduciary capacity vis-à-vis the shareholders.

14.18 Although the duty is owed to the company rather than the shareholders, the interests of the company are synonymous with the interests of the shareholders as a general body, both present and future: *Greehalgh v Arderne Cinemas Limited* [1951] Ch 286.

Directors are also required to balance a long-term view against short-term interests of present members: *Gaiman v National Association for Mental Health* [1971] Ch 317.

Directors stand in a fiduciary relationship to their company

In *Multinational Gas and Petrochemical Company v Multinational Gas and Petrochemical Services Limited* [1983] Ch 258, Dillon LJ stated: 'The directors indeed stand in a fiduciary relationship to the company, as they are appointed to manage the affairs of the company and they owe fiduciary duties to the company though not to the creditors, present or future, or to individual shareholders.'

See too *Brant Investments Ltd v Keeprite Inc* (1991) 80 DLR (4th) 161.

14.19 The company is, therefore, the proper claimant in any proceedings against directors and can enforce compliance with such duties (subject to certain exceptions in the form of a derivative action or unfair prejudicial conduct proceedings which may be brought by shareholders).

However, the company may not in some circumstances sue for a breach of a director's duty particularly where a company had acquired improper intentions from its corporate officers and thereby sought an indemnity from these officers:

The Competition Act did not impose personal liability on the directors but on undertakings for breach of its provisions

In *Safeway Stores Ltd v Twigger* [2011] 2 All ER 841, the issue before the Court of Appeal was whether an undertaking, such as Safeway, which had infringed provisions of the Competition Act 1998 relating to anti-competitive activity and was duly penalised by the Office of Fair Trading (OFT), could recover the amount of such penalties from its directors or employees who were themselves responsible for the infringement.

The Court of Appeal held that an undertaking which infringed provisions of the 1998 Act relating to anti-competitive activity and was penalised by the OFT was precluded by the application of the maxim *ex turpi causa non oritur* action from recovering the amount of such penalty from its directors or employees who were themselves responsible for the infringement. The liability of the claimants under the 1998 Act was not a vicarious one.

Duty towards individual shareholders?

14.20 The CA 2006 does not address the issue as to whether directors may owe duties towards individual shareholders. At common law, there was reluctance by the courts to recognise that directors owed duties towards individual shareholders owing to the cohesion of shareholders who are treated as a collective group within the company, and to the fact that the enforcement of directors' duties should only be vested in the company and not through individual shareholders engaging in litigation, who may be protecting their own interests in the company by bringing such action.

> ***In some situations, directors may owe duties towards shareholders***
>
> In *Towcester Racecourse Co Ltd v The Racecourse Association* [2003] 1 BCLC 260, Patten J rejected the view that apart from owing duties to the company, directors also owed duties to individual shareholders through the implied terms under the company's articles of association. According to Patten J, having regard to the well-established principle that in the absence of special provisions in the articles or some collateral agreement between the company and its members, neither the company nor its directors owed any direct legal duties to the members as such. It would be inconsistent for the company to owe its members direct contractual duties under the articles.

However, on occasions, the courts have recognised that in some situations, directors may owe duties towards individual shareholders, such as in the course of dealings with the individual shareholder concerned.

> ***Directors may in some situations owe duties towards individual shareholders***
>
> In *Allen v Hyatt* (1914) 30 TLR 444, the directors undertook to act as agents of their shareholders in the sale of their shares. According to Viscount Haldane LC, the directors presented themselves to individual shareholders as acting for them on the same footing as they were acting for the company itself, that is, as agents for the shareholders.
>
> See too: *Platt v Platt* [1999] 2 BCLC 745 (the matter went on appeal to the Court of Appeal, but it did not address the fiduciary duty issue).

> ***Directors may in some situations owe duties towards individual shareholders***
>
> *Coleman v Myers* (1977) 2 NZLR 225 extended the agency approach established in *Allen v Hyatt.* It concerned a takeover bid whereby minority shareholders were compelled to sell their shares to the company's ultimate controller. The Court of Appeal decided that a fiduciary duty was established between directors and shareholders in view of the 'special circumstances' that existed between them, namely: the company was a private company with shares held largely by members of one family; the other members of the family had habitually looked to the defendants for business advice; the information affecting the true value of

the shares had been withheld from shareholders by the defendants. Woodhouse J stated that the standard of conduct required from a director in relation to dealings with a shareholder will differ depending upon all the surrounding circumstances and the nature of the responsibility which in a real and practical sense the director has assumed towards the shareholder. Although it would be difficult to establish a general test as to when this fiduciary duty would arise, the court would have regard to various "factors" such as: dependence upon information and advice; the existence of a relationship of confidence; the significance of some particular transaction for the parties; and the extent of any positive action taken by or on behalf of the director or directors to promote it.

The *Coleman v Myers* case was followed by the English courts in *Re Chez Nico (Restaurants) Limited* [1992] BCLC 192, where Browne-Wilkinson V-C stated that in general directors did not owe fiduciary duties to shareholders but owed them to the company: however, in certain special circumstances fiduciary duties, carried with them a duty of disclosure, could arise which placed directors in a fiduciary capacity vis-à-vis the shareholders.

14.21 In some situations there may be dual fiduciary duties in operation.

There may be 'special circumstances' where directors may owe duties to shareholders

In *Stein v Blake and Others (No 2)* [1998] 1 BCLC 573, Millett LJ recognised that there may be special circumstances in which a fiduciary duty is owed by a director to a shareholder personally and in which breach of such a duty has caused loss to him directly (eg by being induced by a director to part with his shares in the company at an undervalue), as distinct from loss sustained by him by a diminution in the value of his shares (eg by reason of the misappropriation by a director of the company's assets), for which he (as distinct from the company) would not have a cause of action against the director personally.

Directors may also be personally liable to the shareholders where they misrepresent or provide misleading advice or abuse their position:

Directors have a duty to be honest and not misrepresent facts to shareholders

In *Gething v Kilner* [1972] 1 All ER 1166, Brightman J held that the directors of an offeree company owed a duty to their shareholders which included the duty to be honest and not to mislead in connection with a takeover offer. See too: *Briess v Woolley* [1954] AC 333.

Directors must not mislead shareholders in the course of their duties

In *Dawson International plc v Coats Paton plc* [1989] BCLC 233, Lord Cullen decided that in a takeover position, a company could have an interest in the identity of its shareholders on a takeover and therefore it was not beyond the capacity of a company to enter into a contract not to co-operate with a rival bidder. The directors of a company did not owe a fiduciary duty to current shareholders as sellers of shares but only had a duty to consider the interests of such shareholders in the discharge of their duty to the company. However, if directors took it upon themselves to advise shareholders they had to do so in good faith and not mislead the shareholders, whether deliberately or carelessly.

Similarly, in the context of a takeover, directors owe duties to the shareholders not to mislead them in respect of advice given to the shareholders.

Directors owe a duty not to mislead shareholders

In *Re A Company* [1986] BCLC 382, Hoffmann J stated that where rival bids were made for a private company and its directors proposed to exercise their rights as shareholders to accept the lower bid, they were not under a duty to advise shareholders to accept the higher offer. However, where directors decide to advise the shareholders on the merits of the competing bids, they must provide sufficient information and advice to enable shareholders to reach an informed decision and must refrain from giving misleading advice or exercising their fiduciary powers in ways that would prevent shareholders from being able to make an uninhibited choice. Normally, the giving of such advice would be within the authority of the board and would constitute an aspect of the conduct of a company's affairs.

According to Hoffmann J, directors were not under an obligation to advise shareholders on a bid, but if they did advise, it must be 'with a view to enabling the shareholders … to sell, if they so wish, at the best price'.

On occasions, the courts have also decided that where there are competing bids concerning a takeover, the shareholders must have complete freedom to decide on the best price for the sale shares: see *Heron International Ltd v Lord Grade* [1983] BCLC 244.

Directors may in some situations owe duties to the shareholders

The duty of directors to the company and in some cases to individual shareholders was upheld by the Court of Appeal in *Peskin v Anderson* [2001] 1 BCLC 372. The Court of Appeal highlighted the principal duty owed by directors to the company, and the particular circumstances where a director(s) may owe duties towards individual shareholders.

The Court of Appeal held that fiduciary duties owed by directors to shareholders only arose if there was a special factual relationship between the directors and the shareholders in the particular case, capable of generating fiduciary obligations, such as a duty of disclosure of material facts, or an obligation to use confidential information and valuable commercial opportunities for the benefit of shareholders and not to prefer and promote the directors' own interests at the expense of shareholders. On the facts, the directors did not owe any fiduciary duty to the shareholders.

See too *Sharp v Blank* [2015] EWMC 3220.

Duties towards other groups?

14.22 English company law has not generally recognised the duties of directors towards employees or creditors, nor a wider group of potential stakeholders or claimants on the corporation. According to Toulson J in *Yukong Line Ltd of Korea v Rendsberg Investments Corp of Liberia (The Rialto)* [1998] 1 WLR 294, stated that a director did not owe a direct fiduciary duty towards an individual creditor, nor was an individual creditor entitled to sue for breach of the fiduciary duty owed by the director to the company. See too *Parke v Daily News (No 2)* [1962] Ch 927.

Applicability of certain general duties to former directors

14.23 Some of the directors' general duties continue to apply even where a person is no longer a director of the company. The objective is to ensure that former directors do not easily avoid their fiduciary duties after having left the company, and that such specific duties continue to apply to them. This is particularly the case in respect of the following two of the seven general directors' duties:

- The duty to avoid conflicts of interest under CA 2006, s 175 with particular regard to exploitation of any property, information or opportunity of which he became aware at a time when he was director: CA 2006, s 170(2)(a).
- The duty not to accept benefits from third parties under s 176 with particular regard to things done or omitted by him before he ceased to be a director: CA 2006, s 170(2)(b).

The term 'exploitation' is not defined, but suggests use of the property, information or opportunity for personal benefit or for another person's benefit. It is immaterial whether the company could take advantage of the property, information, or opportunity.

14.24 There is no definition of 'benefits' and a wide interpretation will be given to the term, including gratuitous benefits, pecuniary advantages, services performed, secret profits, or any gains received whether directly or indirectly in his capacity as a director of the company.

The 'benefits' must be received from 'third parties'. The term 'third party' means a person other than the company, an associate body, corporate, or a person or an associate body corporate: CA 2006, s 176(2).

The duty not to accept benefits from third parties applies to 'things done or omitted by him' before a person ceased to be a director of the company. This refers to positive action undertaken by the director or any lack of action on the director's part. It may also include any preparatory work undertaken by the former director. The word 'omissions' would refer to inaction, lack of action, inactivity, failure to act, or silence, where the matter required some effort on the part of the director to avoid receipt of the benefit.

14.25 The specific statement of general duties that are applicable to a former director are subject to any 'necessary adaptations'. This recognises the fact that any such duties on a former director must not be too onerous, as they would apply to an existing director of the company. For example, where the former director may not have up-to-date knowledge concerning the company or its detailed functioning since he left. Depending on the circumstances, a lower or higher standard may be expected of a former director depending on the degree of his involvement in respect of the above specific duties before he left the company.

In *Allfiled UK Ltd v Eltis* [2015] EWHC 1300 (Ch), Hildyard J accepted that the rigour of fiduciary accountability may occasionally be abated where resignation has been forced upon the director and he or she has not actively sought to seduce the company's customers or to exploit any opportunity belonging to it: see too *Hunter Kane Ltd v Watkins* [2003] EWHC 186 (Ch), approved by the Court of Appeal in *Foster Bryant Surveying Ltd v Bryant* [2007] EWCA Civ 200.

Application of common law rules and equitable principles

14.26 The general duties of directors are based on certain common law rules and equitable principles as they apply in relation to directors. The general duties have effect in place of those rules and principles: CA 2006, s 170(3).

The general duties must be interpreted and applied in the same way as common law rules or equitable principles. Regard will also be taken of the corresponding common law rules and equitable principles in interpreting and applying the general duties: CA 2006, s 170(4). The courts will therefore still have regard to existing case law on directors' duties in the common law and the fiduciary duties in equity in the interpretation of the statement of the general duties of directors. Further, where future developments in common law or equity take place, the courts will have regard to such new developments as they occur. This will be the case in particular regarding developments in equity, trusts and fiduciaries, and other areas of law that may impact upon directors' duties, particularly, for example, in the analogy that the courts have used at common law between the law of trusts and its application to directors as trustees for the company, which area may be developed further by the courts. The effect of s 170(3) and (4) is that the court will have regard to developments in the common law and equity rules as well as previous case law in the application to directors' general duties.

14.27 The general duties are based on some of the common law rules and equitable principles, as they apply to directors, and have effect in place of these rules and principles as regards the duties owed to a company by a director. The general duties in effect replace the common law rules and equitable principles, but preserve other rules and principles at common law and equity that have not been codified. The objective of s 170(3) is to make clear that the general duties partially codify only some of the common law rules and equitable principles as they apply to directors based on established principles, established over the years under case law. In future, any action for breach of directors' duties should be in respect of the seven general duties set out in Pt 10 of the CA 2006. However, although the CA 2006 has partially codified directors' duties and attained clarity in respect of such duties, it has also introduced new concepts and principles that were not inherent at common law, and in such situations, the courts will have no corresponding common law or equitable principles to consider. Where however the general duties correspond to common law and equity principles, the courts will continue to have regard to case law in these areas. The key to understanding the interrelationship between s 170(3) and (4) and the common law and equity principles is identifying those general duties that correspond directly or indirectly with common law and equity principles and their interpretation through case law.

14.28 What other duties remain uncodified, and will be subject to case law interpretation? For example, the duty to consider the interests of creditors where an insolvency is threatened will still continue to be governed by common law principles.

The court will still have regard to previous applicable case law on common law rules and equitable principles concerning directors to assist in the statutory interpretation of directors' duties. However, there are some differences in approach by way of departures from the common law position towards the codified general duties of directors and the position that operated at common law, such as for example, the need for authorisation from independent directors where there are conflicts of duty. Where there are such differences, previous case law may not always assist and the courts will need to consider the statutory wording of the provision in clarifying the position. This also requires an understanding of the differences that exist under the general directors' duties from those at common law and equity. In *Madoff Securities International Ltd v Raven* [2013] EWHC 3147, the directors' conduct occurred largely before 2007 and therefore fell to be considered under the common law principles, but Popplewell J thought that such conduct could equally be considered under the statutory statement of directors' general duties, to the extent that there was not any distinction between the duty at common law and the statutory principle.

14.29 However, s 170(4) allows for future flexibility, as company law borrows from various equitable principles and common law rules in its application to directors. The process of developing and expanding on directors' duties will still continue. This provision, therefore, takes account of new developments that may occur in law on the interpretation and applicability to the general duty and directions.

The scope and nature of general duties of directors as set out in ss 171–177 of CA 2006 apply to a shadow director of a company where and to the extent that they are capable of so applying: CA 2006, s 170(5) (as amended by SBEEA 2015, s 89). The Secretary of State is empowered to make regulations about the application of the general duties of directors to shadow directors. The regulations may make provision for prescribed general duties of directors to apply to shadow directors with such adaptations as may be prescribed; and for prescribed general duties of directors not to apply to shadow directors. This provision inserted by SBEEA 2015, s 89 recognises that the starting point with shadow directors is that all the general duties as set out in ss 171–177 of

CA 2006 will apply to them, and no general distinction is maintained. However, the words "where and to the extent that they are capable of so applying" has several effects: first, not all the general duties are suited to applying to shadow directors. Second, the Secretary of State may by regulations directly apply or disapply one or more of the general duties to shadow directors with or without modifications, to facilitate their applying to shadow directors. The rationale of this provision is to ensure that the shadow directors are made accountable for their actions and activities on the same level as directors (unless some of the provisions do not apply or are excluded). Once the shadow director is identified, he must comply with the general duties.

> ***Directors' duties are not considered as public duties***
>
> In *Ailakis v Olivero (No 2)* [2014] WASCA 127, Martin CJ of the Court of Appeal of Western Australia was of the view that although the scope of a director's duties, and the standards which must be met in the discharge of those duties, are embodied in a statute and can be enforced by the exercise of the remedies conferred by a statute does not of itself mean that the duties have a public character, analogous, for example, to the duty to attend court in answer to a subpoena, or the duty to care for a dependent child. The duties of a director are owed to the company and are enforceable by the company.

Duty to act within powers

14.30 There are two aspects in this duty that must be observed by a director of a company:

A director must:

(a) act in accordance with the company's constitution; and

(b) only exercise powers for the purposes for which they conferred: CA 2006, s 171.

14.31 The term 'constitution' is defined for the purposes of directors' general duties under CA 2006, s 257 to include the following:

(a) any resolution or other decision come to in accordance with the constitution: CA 2006, s 257(1); and

(b) any decision by the members of the company, or class of members, that is treated by virtue of any enactment or rule of law as equivalent to a decision by the company. This is in addition to the matters set out in CA 2006, s 17 (general provision as to matter contained in the company's constitution): CA 2006, s 257(2).

14.32 Prior to s 171, the position at common law was that directors were required to ensure that they exercised their powers for a proper and not any collateral purpose. This latter duty was known as the 'proper purpose' doctrine. Under this doctrine at common law, where directors acted beyond their powers, this was considered ultra vires the company: *Re Lands Allotment Company* [1894] 1 Ch 616; *Re Oxford Benefit Building and Investment Society* (1886) 35 Ch D 502; and *Leeds Estate Building and Investment Company v Shepherd* (1887) 36 Ch D 787. This rule has now been codified under the CA 2006 and amplified further in *Eclairs Group Ltd v JKX Oil & Gas plc; Glengary Overseas Ltd v JKX Oil & Gas plc* [2015] UKSC 71.

Acting in accordance with the company's constitution

14.33 Under CA 2006, s 171(a), the duty to act in accordance with the company's constitution means that the directors must observe any limitations or restrictions on their powers. They cannot usurp the powers of the shareholders. The objective of s 171(a) is to ensure that the demarcation of responsibilities between directors and shareholders is maintained under the corporate governance system as set out in the company's constitution. While directors will manage the day-to-day operations of the company, they are ultimately responsible to their shareholders who have residual authority on major matters affecting the company.

14.34 Section 171 should also be considered with s 40, which provides that the directors must take account of limitations on their powers as set out in the company's constitution, as well as any resolutions of the company or of any class of shareholders; or from any agreement between the members of the company or any class of shareholders. While s 40 may not be an issue for a third-party dealing with the company, it will be an internal matter between shareholders and directors, where directors are held accountable for their actions. A breach of s 40 may also be a breach of s 171. Directors must observe any limitations or restrictions in the articles of association as part of their obligations to the company. The definition of 'constitution' is broader to include resolutions of the general meeting or agreements notified to the Registrar, which may limit the powers or authority of directors to act in a certain manner.

Exercising powers for the purposes conferred

14.35 Section 171(b) of CA 2006 also imposes a duty on directors only to exercise powers for the purposes for which they were conferred. Some of the leading cases decided before CA 2006 considered the proper purposes doctrine and its application to directors' powers. In such cases, the improper purposes typically involved directors maintaining control of the company for personal advantage to the detriment of the shareholders: *Fraser v Whalley* (1864) 2 Hem & M 10. The nature of improper purposes arises because directors exercise powers outside their limits for which they were conferred: in effect, it is an abuse of authority by the director who misuses his power to usurp power and position within the company. The court will not consider the subjective intentions of the director concerned who has exercised the powers for improper purposes – the test is objective: *Howard Smith Ltd v Ampol Petroleum Ltd* [1974] AC 821. Where directors have exercised their powers for a proper purposes, the courts are unlikely to second-guess such decisions based on the reasonabless or unreasonableness of directors' decisions: *Edge v Pensions Ombudsman* [2000] Ch 602.

The issuing of new shares was an abuse of power by directors

In *Punt v Symons Co Ltd* [1903] 2 Ch 506, in order to secure the passing of a special resolution, the directors had issued new shares to five additional shareholders. Byrne J held that this was an abuse of the directors' powers. The shares were not issued bona fide for the general benefit of the company; but were issued with the immediate object of controlling the shareholding in the company and of obtaining the necessary majority for passing the special resolution, while at the same time, not conferring upon the minority the power to demand a poll.

In *Piercy v S Mills & Co Ltd* [1920] 1 Ch 77, the directors decided to allot shares with the intention of preventing the majority shareholders from exercising control of the company. This was held to be an improper exercise of directors' powers.

In *Re Smith & Fawcett Ltd* [1942] Ch 304, the court stated that directors must act for a proper purpose. Where directors act for an improper or 'collateral' purpose, the court will intervene and set aside the act in question.

In *Hogg v Cramphorn* [1967] Ch 254, the company directors issued shares that carried special voting rights for the trustees of a scheme established for the benefit of the company's employees. The directors' objective was to prevent a takeover bid. They had acted in good faith throughout the transaction. Buckley J held that this was an improper purpose, but that it could be ratified by shareholders at a general meeting. He further stated that unless a majority in a company was acting oppressively towards the minority, the court should not and will not itself interfere with the exercise by the majority of its constitutional rights or embark upon any inquiry into the respective merits of the views held or policies followed by the majority and the minority.

However, judicial authorities in Australia and Canada rejected the decision in *Hogg v Cramphorn* and decided that directors' decisions to use their powers to thwart a threatened takeover could be upheld by the courts.

In *Harlowe's Nominees Ptd Ltd v Woodside Oil Co* [1968] 121 Ch 483 and *Teck Corp Ltd v Miller* [1972] 33 ALR 3 at 288, the High Court of Australia and the Canadian Court respectively upheld directors' decisions to prevent a takeover.

Bamford v Bamford [1970] Ch 212, also illustrates an improper exercise of power by directors in the context of a takeover of the company.

The raising of capital and issuing shares was an abuse of power by directors where the predominant purpose was to thwart a takeover attempt

In the Privy Council case concerning improper purposes of *Howard Smith Ltd v Ampol Petroleum* [1974] AC 821, the issue of directors acting for the improper purposes was considered by the Privy Council. The case also concerned attempts by directors to prevent a takeover. The directors contended that the only proper purpose for which the power was being exercised was to raise new capital and issue new shares. This argument was rejected by the House of Lords, which held that the power to raise new capital and issue shares was used for the predominant purposes of defeating a takeover by the directors. The decision concerning a takeover should have been a matter for the shareholders to decide. According to Lord Wilberforce, when considering the powers to directors, it was:

> '... necessary to start with consideration of the power whose exercise is in question; in this case, a power to issue shares. Having ascertained, on a fair view, the nature of this power and having defined as can best be done in the light of the modern conditions the, or some, limits within which it may he exercised, it is then necessary for the court, if a particular exercise of it is challenged, to examine the substantial purpose for which it was to be exercised, and to reach a conclusion whether that purpose was proper or not. In doing so, it will necessarily give credit to the bona fide opinion of the directors, if such is found to exist, and will respect their judgment as to the matter of the management having done this, the ultimate conclusion has to be as to the side of a fairly broad time on which the case falls.'

In determining whether directors have acted for improper purposes, the court will consider the powers conferred for directors and the limitations placed upon them in the exercise of that power. The court will then consider the actual purpose for which the power was exercised. In this regard, the court is entitled to '... look at the situation objectively, in order to estimate how critical or pressing a substantial, as per contra insubstantial an alleged requirement may have been.'

14.36 In some cases, the courts have considered that it may be a legitimate use of power by directors to forestall a takeover bid: *Criterion Properties plc v Stratford UK Properties LLC* [2002] 2 BCLC 151 and [2003] 2 BCLC 129.

Once a breach of CA 2006, s 171(a) is found, directors cannot establish a defence that they were unaware of the limitations under the company's constitution: they are required to have read and fully understood the provisions of the articles of association and any restrictions on their powers. The common law position where directors acted for improper purposes was that any such exercise of their powers was void; and where misuse of the company's capital was concerned or unlawful distribution of dividends, directors are treated as constructive trustees owing to a breach of trust and liable to account to the company.

Where directors act in breach of CA 2006, s 171(b), the position at common law is that their actions are voidable and liable to set aside by the company, unless third party rights apply: *Hunter v Senate Support Services Ltd* [2004] EWHC 1085 (Ch). The company may also consider ratification of directors' actions in such situations: *Bamford v Bamford* [1970] Ch 212; *Criterion Properties plc v Stratford UK Properties LLC* [2004] 1 WLR 1846.

14.37–14.41 Section 40 of CA 2006 also has application and assists a third party dealing with the company with a statutory presumption of good faith in favour of a third party. CA 2006, s 40(5) states that s 40 does not affect any liability incurred by the directors, or any other person, by reason of the directors exceeding their powers. Directors therefore must take account of and have full knowledge of any restrictions or limitations on their powers. Section 41 of CA 2006 also has application in respect of constitutional limitations on the powers of directors, particularly where a director is the contracting party with the company or a person connected with the director. Under s 41 the liability falls on both the directors authorising the transaction and the actual director or connected person entering into a contract with the company. The remedy is liability to account for any gain made and to indemnify the company for any loss as a consequence of entering into the transaction: s 41(3) and (4).

In the application of CA 2006, s 793 (restriction notice), the issue of the board acting for improper motives did not arise, as the failure by the shareholder to respond fully to the questions posed by the board demonstrated that the shareholder was a victim of his own disenfranchisement.

Although the Supreme Court decided that the proper purpose rule applied to an article provision which imposed restrictions, there was no unanimity on the appropriate test that should be applied in identifying whether or not directors acted for a proper purpose within the powers conferred on them, particularly where multiple purposes were involved

Facts

Part 22 of the CA 2006 is concerned with information about interests in a company's shares. The purpose of Part 22 of CA 2006 is to seek information about a person's 'interest' in the company's shares, whether past or present: *Re TR Technology Investment Trust plc* [1988] BCLC 256. Sections 793–797 of CA 2006 allow a company to issue a statutory disclosure notice requiring information about persons interested in a company's shares. Part 22 of CA 2006 also empower the court to restrict the exercise of rights in shares where there is non-compliance in providing the requisite information. JKX Oil & Gas plc had a provision under its articles of association in the form of Article 42 ('Article 42'), which empowered the board of directors (instead of the court under Part 22 of CA 2006) to impose such restrictions where a statutory disclosure notice had not been complied with. Article 42 provided that the board was entitled to treat a response to a disclosure notice as non-compliant where it knew or had reasonable cause to believe that the information provided was false or materially incorrect.

JKX's directors believed that the company had become the target of a corporate raid (an attempt to exploit a minority shareholding in a company to obtain effective management or voting control without paying what other shareholders would regard as a proper price) by two minority shareholders, Eclairs and Glengary. JKX issued disclosure notices requesting information from Eclairs and Glengary about the number of shares held, their beneficial ownership, and any agreements or arrangements between the persons interested in them. Subsequently at a board meeting, JKX's directors considered that there were agreements or arrangements between the addressees of the disclosure notices which had not been disclosed in the responses. The board resolved to exercise powers under Article 42 by issuing restriction notices in relation to the shares held by Eclairs and Glengary. This had the effect of suspending their right to vote at general meetings and restricting the right of transfer of shares.

The restriction notices were challenged by Eclairs and Glengary who relied on the proper purpose rule under s 171(b) of CA 2006, which provides that a director must only exercise powers for the purposes for which they were conferred. At first instance, Mann J held that the board's decision was invalid. The power conferred by Article 42 could be exercised only to provide an incentive to remedy the default or a sanction for failing to do so. Although the board had reasonable cause to believe that there was an arrangement or agreement between Eclairs and Glengary, the board's purpose was to influence the fate of the resolutions at the AGM. The Court of Appeal, however, allowed the appeal by a majority. It held that the proper purpose rule did not apply to Article 42, because the shareholders only had to answer the questions more fully in order to avoid the imposition of restrictions on the exercise of their rights, and because the application of the rule was inappropriate in the course of a battle for control. Eclairs and Glengary appealed to the Supreme Court.

Decision

The Supreme Court allowed the appeal. It held that the proper purposes rule applied to the exercise of power by directors under Article 42, and that the directors of JKX had acted for improper purposes. Although the main judgment was given by Lord Sumption (with whom Lord Hodge agreed), the other Law Lords had some reservations on some aspects of the proper purpose rule identified by Lord Sumption, and preferred to defer their views and opinions for another subsequent case on this issue.

Origins of the Proper Purposes Rule

The early origins of the proper purposes rule had its roots in equity and its application to trustees with discretionary powers given under a trust. A trustee was not permitted to use the powers which the trust conferred upon him at law except for the legitimate purposes of the trust. The trustee was required to act bona fide and in the best interests of the trust: *Balls v Strutt* (1841) 1 Hare 146. In equity, the doctrine was known as 'fraud on the power', and the Chancery Courts attached consequences of fraud to acts which were honest and unexceptional at common law, but unconscionable under equitable principles. Equity would intervene and set aside dispositions under powers conferred by trust deeds if, although within the language conferring the power, they were outside the purpose for which they were conferred: *Lane v Page* (1754) Amb 233; *Aleyn v Belchier* (1758) 1 Eden 132. Equity did not require the proof of any fraud to intervene in cases dealing with proper purposes: *Vatcher v Paull* [1915] AC 372.

Modern View of the Proper Purpose Rule

The fiduciary duty of directors to ensure that they exercise their powers for proper purposes has been codified under s 171(b) of CA 2006, which requires that a company director must 'only exercise powers for the purposes for which they were conferred'. This section is based on certain common law rules and equitable principles as they apply to directors and have effect in place of those rules and principles as regards duties owed to a company by a director: s 170(3) of CA 2006. Further, this duty is to be interpreted and applied in the same way as the common law rules or equitable principles, and regard shall be had to the corresponding rules and equitable principles in interpreting and applying the general duties: s 170(4) of CA 2006.

The proper purpose rule is not concerned with excess of power by doing an act which is beyond the scope of the instrument creating it as a matter of construction or implication. It is concerned with an abuse of power by directors – by doing acts which are within the scope of authority but carried out for an improper reason. The exercise of directors' powers are limited to the purpose for which they were conferred. For example, an abuse of directors' powers would apply where the directors attempted to influence the outcome of a general meeting. This would be an abuse of power for a collateral purpose. It would also offend the constitutional distribution of powers between the different organs of the company, because it involves the use of the board's powers to control or influence a decision, which the company's constitution assigns to the general body of shareholders: *Fraser v Whalley* (1864) 2 H & M 10; *Anglo-Universal Bank v Baragnon* (1881) 45 LJ 362; *Hogg v Cramphorn Ltd* [1967] 1 Ch 254.

According to Lord Sumption, although a company's articles of association are part of the contract of association, to which successive shareholders accede on becoming members of the company, a term limiting the exercise of powers conferred on directors to their proper purpose may sometimes be implied on the ordinary principles of law governing the implication of terms. However, this was not the basis of the proper purpose rule. The rule was not a term of the contract and did not necessarily depend on any limitation on the scope of the power as a matter of construction. The proper purpose rule was a principle by which equity controlled the exercise of the fiduciary powers in respects which were not or not necessarily determined by the instrument. Ascertaining the purpose of a power where the instrument was silent depended upon an inference from the mischief of the provision conferring it, which was itself deducted from its express terms, from an analysis of their effect and from the court's understanding of the business context.

The purpose of a power conferred by a company's articles was rarely expressed in the instrument itself – but it was obvious from its context and effect why a power had been conferred.

On the facts, Lord Sumption was of the view that the purpose of Article 42 was threefold:

- To induce the shareholder to comply with a disclosure notice.
- To protect the company and its shareholders against having to make decisions about their respective interests in ignorance of relevant information.
- The restrictions had a punitive effect – they were imposed as sanctions on account of the failure or refusal of the addressee of a disclosure notice to provide the information for as long as it persisted, on the footing that a person interested in shares who had not complied with obligations attaching to that status should not be entitled to the benefits attaching to the shares.

These three purposes were all directly related to the non-provision of information requisitioned by the disclosure notice. The imposition of the restrictions under

Article 42 was a serious interference with the financial and constitutional rights which existed for the benefit of the shareholder and the company.

According to Lord Sumption, the rule that the fiduciary powers of directors may be exercised only for the purposes for which they were conferred was one of the main means by which equity enforced the proper conduct of directors. It was also fundamental to the constitutional distinction between the respective domains of the board and the shareholders. These considerations were particularly important when the company was in play between the competing groups seeking to control or influence its affairs.

Lords Neuberger, Mance and Clarke agreed that the appeals should be allowed, but declined to express a concluded view on some of the issues raised by Lord Sumption. Lord Mance believed that the restriction notices were issued for the principal purpose of improving the prospects of passing at the forthcoming AGM two special resolutions to authorise market purchases and to disapply the pre-emption rights.

On the interpretation of s 171(b) of CA 2006, Lord Mance was of the view that the purpose had to be a legitimate one for it to be a proper purpose. However, further clarity was required as to the scope of the duty under s 171(b) of CA 2006.

Tests for Determining 'Proper Purpose'

Although their Lordships were in agreement on the nature and context of the proper purpose rule and its application to Article 42, there was neither consensus nor agreement on the test that should be applied in identifying whether or not the powers exercised by the directors were for proper purposes. A majority of their Lordships preferred to defer a decision as to the test to be applied until a subsequent case in this area.

The issue is further compounded by the fact that there may be multiple purposes which directors have in mind in exercising their powers under s 171(b) of CA 2006 – some may be for proper purposes while others may be improper. The issues for consideration have been: which purpose should prevail; and what should be the test?

Set out below are various tests that may be associated with the proper purpose rule and its application to directors in company law.

Subjective Test

According to the Supreme Court, the test to be applied for determining whether the directors acted for proper purposes was subjective: the state of mind of those who acted, and the motive on which they acted were all important aspects for consideration: *Hindle v John Cotton Ltd* (1919) 56 ScLR 625.

The 'Trusteeship' Test

A test which has previously been applied by the Chancery Courts has been to consider directors' duties as similar or analogous to those of a trustee. The courts have adapted this trusteeship principle to apply to directors in the company law sphere, particularly in respect of the exercise of discretionary powers by trustees under the trust instrument and its analogy with directors' powers under the proper purpose rule. This would have some support particularly when considered against the background and origins of the proper purpose rule. However, in *Mills v Mills* (above), Dixon J stated that the application of trusteeship principles to directors was not the same or analogous to those that applied to a trustee of a trust instrument.

Bona Fide Test

Under this test, the courts are reluctant to be involved in management issues as directors are best placed to decide what is in the best interests of the company as a whole. The courts prefer not to 'second-guess' directors' decisions. However, where powers are usurped for improper purposes the courts have intervened to prevent power manipulation by the board. A test that has previously applied in identifying what are the proper purposes for which the directors' powers are exercised has been to consider whether the directors acted honestly and bona fide when exercising the power. In *Harlowe's Nominees Pty Ltd v Woodside (Lakes Entrance) Oil Co NL* (1968) 121 CLR 483, an issue of shares was made to a large oil company in order to secure the financial stability of the company. This was upheld as being within the power conferred on directors, although it had the effect of defeating the attempt of the claimant to secure control by buying up the company's shares. The Australian High Court stated that the ultimate question must always be whether in truth the power which was exercised by the directors was made honestly in the interests of the company: 'Directors in whom are vested the right and the duty of deciding where the company's interests lie and how they are to be served may be concerned with a wide range of practical considerations, and their judgment, if exercised in good faith and not for irrelevant purposes, is not open to review in the courts'.

However, subsequent cases have shown that honesty and bona fide aspects in the decision making process are not sufficient to demonstrate that directors exercised their powers for proper purposes. In *Hutton v West Cork Railway Company* (1883) 23 Ch D 654, Bowen LJ stated that bona fides could not be the sole test 'otherwise you might have a lunatic conducting the affairs of a company, and paying away its money with both hands in a matter perfectly bona fide yet perfectly irrational'. See too *Howard Smith Ltd v Ampol Petroleum Ltd* [1974] AC 821.

Public Law Test

One test that could be used to identify proper purposes is to adapt the public law principles for company law. Accordingly, a decision which has been materially influenced by a legally irrelevant consideration should generally be set aside, even if legally relevant considerations were more significant: *R (FDA) v Secretary of State for Work and Pensions* [2013] 1 WLR 444; and Smith v North East Derbyshire Primary Care Trust [2006] 1 WLR 3315. Although such public law test has not been applied in the context of directors' duties, there was a suggestion by Dixon J in *Mills v Mills* (1938) 60 CLR 150 that the public law test may be applied in the context of company law.

Primary/Dominant Purpose

Directors' decisions may generally be set aside only if the primary or dominant purpose for which it was made was improper. This is because the courts of equity are concerned to uphold the integrity of the decision making process, but also to limit its intervention in the conduct of the company's affairs to cases in which an injustice has resulted from the directors having taken irrelevant considerations into account.

The court will compare the relative significance of different considerations which influenced the directors in arriving at their decision. However, in determining what is the 'primary' or 'dominant' purpose and how this is identified, the court may consider what was the 'weightiest' purpose – one about which the directors felt most strongly. According to Lord Sumption, this test would be difficult to justify because it would involve a forensic inquiry into the relative intensity of the directors' feelings about the various considerations that influenced them.

Further, the test is also met with a fundamental point of principle. Under s 171(b) of CA 2006, the directors must exercise their powers 'only' for the purposes for which they were conferred. The duty is broken if they allow themselves to be influenced by any improper purpose.

'Moving Cause' Test

The issue for determination here is which considerations led the directors to act as they did (ie the 'moving cause')? In this regard, the court may have regard to the 'moving cause' of the decision: *Hindle v John Cotton*; *Mills v Mills*, above. However, this test may not assist where the board was concurrently moved by multiple causes – some proper and others improper.

Causation/But-For Test

According to Lord Sumption, the focus should be on identifying the improper purpose and ask whether the board decision would have been made if the directors had not been moved by it. If the answer is that without the improper purpose(s), the decision impugned would never have been made, then it would be irrational to allow it to stand simply because the directors had other, proper considerations in mind, to which they attached greater importance: *Mills v Mills, supra.* However, if there were proper reasons for exercising the power, and it would still have been exercised for those reasons even if the absence of improper ones, the decision may be a valid one and not one that would be set aside.

In formulating the 'but-for' test, Lord Sumption gave weight to the High Court of Australia decision in *Whitehouse v Carlton House Pty* (1987) 162 CLR, namely, that regardless of whether the impermissible purpose was the dominant one or but one of a number of significantly contributing causes, the allotment will be invalidated if the impermissible purpose was causative in the sense that, but for its presence, the power would not have been exercised. Lord Sumption thought that this was consistent with the rationale of the proper purpose rule, and which corresponded with the view of the court of equity about the exercise of powers of appointment by trustees.

Lord Mance thought that further consideration needed to be given on the test for determining the proper purpose. The test may involve a director exercising his powers primarily or substantially only for the purpose for which they were conferred. Alternatively, further consideration would need to be given to Lord Sumption's proposed test which was to treat s 171(b) of CA 2006 as requiring a director's power to be used 'with an entire and single view to the real purpose and object of the power', by assimilating a director's power in this respect with the exercise of discretionary powers by trustees. Although Lord Sumption relied on the dictum of Dixon J in *Mills v Mills* to some extent, but Dixon J did not necessarily consider the powers of directors and directors to be analogous. Dixon J thought that consideration should be given to the substantial object the accomplishment of which formed the real ground of the board's action. If this was within the scope of the power, then the power had been validly exercised.

Although Lord Mance had sympathy with Lord Sumption's view that the 'but for' causation offered a single test which it might be possible or preferable to substitute for references to the principal or primary purposes, he was not persuaded that it should be undertaken as this would be a new development of company law.

On Lord Sumption's view in the difficulties of identifying the primary or substantial purpose, Lord Mance considered that the difficulties would also be prevalent in the 'but for' test. It was just as likely to give rise to artificial and defensive attempts to justify what was done. The principal or primary purpose in mind would be likely to be easier to identify, since it was likely to be reflected in directors' exchanges before and at the time of the decisions under examination, than the answer to a question whether they would have acted as they did taking into account their main expressed purpose. They will have been less likely to have directed express attention to this.

Lord Mance also stated that if the 'but for' test were to be adopted, attention should be given to the standard to which the directors (on whom the onus would lie) would have to show that they would have reached the same decision even if they had not had the illegitimate purpose in mind. It was unclear whether probability would be enough to satisfy this test or whether the test should be that the decision would inevitably have been the same.

Practical Implications

- If a power has been validly exercised for the purpose(s) for which it was conferred, this is a proper exercise of power by the directors and in compliance with the statutory duty under s 171(b) of CA 2006.
- If a power has been exercised for an improper purpose, contrary to the purpose for which it has been conferred, the court will intervene and may declare this to be an abuse of power or authority.

- JKX's case failed on the basis that Article 42 was exercised for improper purposes and an abuse of the directors' powers. But would the board have reached the same decisions even if they had not taken account of the impact of the restriction notices on the resolutions at the AGM? At first instance, Mann J thought that the board would inevitably have reached the same conclusions even if they had confined themselves to the proper purposes of inducing the addressees of the disclosure notices to comply with them, and imposing sanctions on their failure to do so. Lord Sumption thought that on that hypothesis, it would have been difficult to regard the impact on the resolutions as a primary consideration. The lack of information would have been a sufficient justification of the restrictions and the resolutions would have been irrelevant as no more than a welcome incidental consequence. JKX however did not contest its case on the basis of the hypothesis set out by Mann J. JKX's case was that once the corporate raiders had failed to provide the information, the power to make a restriction order could properly be exercised for the purpose of defeatin their attempt to influence or control the company's affairs, provided that this was conceived in good faith to be in the company's interests. JKX's case should not have addressed the desire to defeat the raiders but one of imposing restrictions for want of information.
- Although we now have clarification as to what is meant by proper purposes and its relationship to the scope of authority and powers, the Supreme Court was unable to agree in identifying the test to be applied in determining whether or not directors exercised their powers for proper purposes. The law is still not clear on the actual test that should be applied in these circumstances. This aspect has been left for further debate and discussion for a subsequent case addressing this point in the future.
- Consideration should be given to s 170(3) and (4) of CA 2006. Section 170(3) provides that the general duties of directors (including the proper purpose rule under s 171(b) of CA 2006 is based on certain common law rules and equitable principles as they apply to directors and have effect in place of those rules and principles as regards duties owed to a company by a director: s 170(3) of CA 2006. Further, this duty is to be interpreted and applied in the same way as the common law rules or equitable principles, and regard shall be had to the corresponding rules and equitable principles in interpreting and applying the general duties: s 170(4) of CA 2006. The courts can therefore have regard to previous cases and developments at common law and equity in interpreting the proper purpose rule and its particular application to company law. For example, the courts may adapt and develop principles relating to trustees exercising discretionary powers under the trust instrument, as such principles may apply to directors exercising their powers for proper purposes. Previous cases have demonstrated that directors may be considered as trustees for the company and its shareholders collectively: *Re Forest of Dean Coal Mining Co* (1878) 10 Ch D 450. This 'trusteeship' principle may be appropriately applied to directors' general duties because s 170(3) and (4) permit such applications and developments to apply in these circumstances.

- Proper consideration was not given to the leading Privy Council decision in *Howard Smith Ltd v Ampol Petroleum Ltd* [1974] AC 821. This case was concerned with attempts by directors to prevent a takeover. The directors contended that the only proper purpose for which the power was being exercised was to raise new capital and to issue new shares. The Privy Council held that the power to raise capital and to issue shares was used for the predominant purposes of defeating a takeover by the directors. The decision concerning the takeover was a matter for the shareholders to decide. Lord Wilberforce applied the 'primary purpose' test. The starting point was to look at the power whose exercise was in question. A wider investigation as to the facts would need to be made to determine the purposes for which the powers were conferred. This is evident from Viscount Finlay's dictum in *Hindle v John Cotton Ltd* (1919) 56 ScLR 625, 630-631:

  > 'Where the question is one of abuse of powers, the state of mind of those who acted, and the motive on which they acted, are all important, and you may go into the question of what their intention was, collecting from the surrounding circumstances all the materials which genuinely throw light upon that question of the state of mind of the directors so as to show whether they were honestly acting in discharge of their powers in the interests of the company or were acting from some bye-motive, possibly of personal advantage, or for any other reason.'

- Next, according to Lord Wilberforce, having ascertained on a fair view the nature of this power and having defined in the light of modern conditions any limits within which the power may be exercised, it was then necessary for the court to examine the 'substantial purpose' for which the power was exercised and to reach a conclusion as to whether or not that power was exercised for a proper purpose. In this regard the court would give credit to any bona fide opinion of directors and will also respect their judgment. The court is entitled to look at the situation objectively in order to estimate how critical or pressing a substantial or insubstantial requirement may have been. If it finds that a particular requirement though real, was not urgent or critical at the relevant time, it may have reason to doubt or discount the assertions of individuals that they acted solely for proper purposes. According to Lord Sumption, the terms 'substantial or primary purpose' as used by Lord Wilberforce meant the purpose which accounted for the board's decision. Lord Sumption was of the view that Lord Wilberforce had adopted Dixon J's test in *Mills v Mills* and concluded that although the directors in *Howard Smith* case were influenced by the company's need for capital, the decisive factor was that but for their desire to convert the majority shareholders into a minority, the directors would not have sought to raise capital by means of a share issue, nor at that point in time. It is respectfully submitted that Lord Wilberforce was not advocating a 'but for' test but simply to address the substantial or primary purpose after examining the power that was in question. The predominant test remains the 'substantial or primary purpose' in the exercise of the power(s) conferred on directors. This test would still require an examination into the minds of directors, background of facts, surrounding circumstances, exchanges between directors to ascertain the

> substantial or primary purpose. It would also require the court to undertake a balancing exercise in weighing up the proper against improper purposes (assuming there are multiple purposes involved), and then consider overall whether the directors were motivated by proper or improper purposes.

Duty to promote the success of the company

14.42 This modern formulation of duty arises from the common law duty of loyalty by the directors towards the company.

Under CA 2006, a director of a company must act in the way he considers, in good faith, would be the most likely, to promote the success of the company for the benefit of its members as a whole, and in doing so, have regard (amongst other matters) to:

(a) the likely consequence of any decision in the long term;

(b) the interests of the company's employees;

(c) the need to foster the company's business relationships with suppliers, customers and others;

(d) the impact on the company's operations on the community and the environment;

(e) the desirability of the company maintaining a reputation for high standards of business conduct; and

(f) the need to act fairly as between members of the company: CA 2006, s 172(1).

At common law directors were required to act in good faith in the interests of the company. This was a fundamental duty of loyalty that a director owed to his company. This aspect of duty towards the company has now been reformulated under s 171 of the CA 2006. However, the common law requirement that directors act in the interests of the company did not address clearly in whose interests, owing to the inanimate legal entity nature of the corporation – whether of shareholders individually or collectively or other broader stakeholders? In *Gaiman v National Association for Mental Health* [1971] Ch 317, Sir Robert Megarry VC was of the view that the interests of the association could not be considered in isolation: they referred to the interests of members both present and future. Similarly, in *Brady v Brady* [1988] BCLC 20, Nourse LJ was of the view that 'the interests of a company, as an artificial person, cannot be distinguished from the interests of the persons who are interested in it'. The common law position also at times recognised the interests of other stakeholders such as employees: *Parke v Daily News (No 2)* [1962] Ch 927; *Hutton v West Cork Railway Co* (1883) 23 Ch D 654.

> ***Directors must act bona fide in the company's interests***
>
> In *Smith & Fawcett Ltd* [1942] Ch 304, the court stated that the interests of the company signified the interests of the shareholders collectively as a whole which has as its objective the need to balance the interests of the present shareholders against the long-term interests of future shareholders. According to Lord Greene the directors 'must exercise their discretion bona fide in what they consider– not what a court may consider – to be in the interests of the company, and not for any collateral purpose'.

> ***Mere incompetence is not sufficient for breach of fiduciary duty***
>
> According Millett LJ in *Bristol and West Building Society v Mothew (t/a Stapley & Co)* [1998] Ch 1 at 18, the various obligations of a fiduciary merely reflect different aspects of his core duties of loyalty and fidelity. Breach of fiduciary obligation, therefore, connotes disloyalty or infidelity. Mere incompetence is not enough. A servant who loyally does his incompetent best for his master is not unfaithful and is not guilty of a breach of fiduciary duty.

> ***The term 'bona fide in the interests of the company' is reflected in CA 2006, s 172***
>
> In *Re Southern Counties Fresh Foods Limited* [2008] All ER 195, Warren J stated that 'the perhaps old-fashioned phrase acting "bona fide in the interests of the company" is reflected in the statutory words acting "in good faith in a way most likely to promote the success of the company for the benefit of its members as a whole". They come to the same thing with the modern formulation giving a more readily understood definition of the scope of the duty'.

14.43 Section 172 of CA 2006 upholds the primacy of shareholder consideration in promoting the company's success. The Company Law Review addressed the issue of profit maximisation for the benefit of shareholders and the pluralist approach, which focuses on company's interests towards other stakeholders including employees, creditors, consumers, suppliers, and the wider public. Section 172 is based on the premise of profit maximisation in the shareholders' interests as the primary objective of the company. However, in undertaking this objective, directors must have regard to consideration of other stakeholders though not on equal par to the shareholders as only shareholders may enforce directors' duties and not other stakeholders. There is no requirement for the directors to balance the interests of the stakeholder groups under s 172 in determining the success of the company, particularly as these stakeholders do not have enforceable rights under the section which they can bring against the company or the directors. In practice, it may be difficult to demonstrate that the directors did not act in good faith when taking account of the interests of various stakeholders under s 172.

The duty to promote the success of the company codifies the fiduciary principle imposed on a director having regard to 'enlightened shareholder value'. This has two elements:

(1) the director must act in a way he considers in good faith, would be most likely to promote the success of the company for the benefit of the members as a whole; and

(2) in doing so, the director must have regard, *inter alia*, to the factors listed in CA 2006, s 172(1).

A duty to act in good faith

14.44 The first aspect of CA 2006, s 172(1) is the requirement for directors to act in good faith. It is addressed to each director who 'must act in the way he considers' in good faith to promote the company's success. The duty is subjective. The promotion of the success of the company is based on the business judgment decision of directors: they are best-placed to decide what will constitute the company's success having regard to the various factors. The duty must be considered as a whole, together with the factors set out. This is one of the core duties that will apply in any aspect of directors' day-to-day management of the company; in their decision-making functions; in the closure of a branch of a business; in their conduct of all company affairs. There is no objectivity test involved in what a reasonable director would have done in the circumstances.

The test of 'bona fide in the interests of the company' was a subjective one

In *Regentcrest plc v Cohen* [2001] 2 BCLC 80, the company had operated a successful property development business since 1990. Subsequently, the company waived a clawback claim of £1.5 million under a share sale agreement with the sellers. The directors voted in favour of a resolution to waive a claim by the company against the sellers of the shares. Subsequently, the company went into liquidation. The liquidator brought a claim against the directors for breach of fiduciary duty in voting in favour of the resolution. The issue before the court was whether the directors had acted in the best interests of the company.

According to Jonathan Parker J, the duty imposed on directors to act bona fide in the interests of the company was a subjective one, the question being whether the director honestly believed that his act or omission was in the interests of the company. Although where it was clear that the act or omission under challenge resulted in substantial detriment to the company a director would have a harder task persuading the court that he honestly believed it to be in the company's interest, this did not detract from the subjective nature of the test.

In this case, there were good commercial reasons why the directors voted in favour of the resolution and they honestly believed they were acting in the company's best interests.

Jonathan Parker J stated:

> 'The question is not whether, viewed objectively by the court, the particular act or omission which is challenged was in fact in the interests of the company; still less is the question whether the court, had it been in the position of the director at the relevant time, might have acted differently. Rather, the question is whether the director honestly believed that his act or omission was in the interests of the company. The issue is as to the director's state of mind.'

14.45 Directors must also have a 'good faith' belief that they acted to promote the company's success. They are required to address their minds to the issue in question and demonstrate some supporting reasoning how they had acted in good faith.

A director would not be in breach of his duties if he acted honestly in the circumstances

In *Extrasure Travel Insurances Limited v Scattergood* [2003] 1 BCLC 598, Jonathan Crow (sitting as a Deputy Judge) decided that breach of the fiduciary duty owed by a director to his company could be demonstrated by showing either that he did not exercise his powers in what he honestly believed to be the company's best interests, or that he did not exercise those powers for the proper purposes for which they were conferred on him. Accordingly, although crass incompetence on the part of a director might give rise to a claim for breach of a duty of care or breach of contract, it would not give rise to a claim for a breach of fiduciary duty. It followed that a company director, in carrying out his duty to do what he honestly believed to be in the company's best interests, was not in breach of his fiduciary duty if he acted on an honest, but unreasonable and mistaken, view.

On the facts, the directors had acted in the company's best interests.

Usually the courts will not second-guess the decisions of directors

14.46 Although the courts will not second-guess directors' business decisions (see *Burland v Earle* [1902] AC 83; *Carlen v Drury* (1812) 1 Ves & B 154), they are still required to determine whether directors have satisfied the aspect of good faith under s 172. This would require the courts to determine not only directors' acting bona fide, but a demonstration (whether active or otherwise) that they addressed their minds honestly to the issue in question.

In addressing the issue of good faith, the court will also consider whether any bad faith was exercised by the directors in considering the promotion of the company's interests. In *Primlake v Matthews Associates* [2007] 1 BCLC 666, Lawrence Collins J, was of the view that on the facts the directors acted in bad faith in making excessive payments by way of directors' remuneration to another director: the directors had not held an honest belief that such excessive payments should be made.

14.47 In *Simtel Communications Ltd v Rebak* [2006] 2 BCLC 571, one of the allegations against the directors was releasing stock held on the claimant's behalf in Nigeria, notwithstanding that no payment had been received by the claimant for those goods. Forbes J held that in relation to the release of stock, the first defendant had also acted in breach of his duty to act bona fide in the interests of the company, and in breach of his contractual duty to carry out his services with reasonable skill and care. Furthermore, all the defendants had been acting pursuant to a common design or agreement to set up a competing business. In the furtherance of that common design, they had acted in breach of fiduciary duty and contract, diverting the company's business, destroying and transferring data, with the intention to injure the company by unlawful means.

> ***Directors must have regard to the purposes for which the company was formed under CA 2006, s 172 in considering its long term success***
>
> In *Southern Private Landlords Association* [2010] BCC 387, Pelling J considered CA 2006, s 171 and stated that s 171(1) was to be read as providing that a director must act in a way that he considered in good faith would be most likely to achieve those purposes. Section 171(1) was to be construed as meaning that a director of a company with mixed objects must act in a way that he considered in good faith would most likely promote the success of the company for the benefit of its members as a whole whilst at the same time achieving its other purposes. Where there was a conflict between promoting the success of the company for the benefit of its members and the achievement of the other objectives, a balancing exercise will be required.

The term 'good faith' is not defined but the directors' intentions and motive will be taken into account as well as whether they acted bona fide in arriving at their decision. Bad faith may apply where directors acted illegally, fraudulently, or where an improper motive or intent is enacted and embraces high expectation of such type of behaviour. Aspects of good faith also include integrity, ethical behaviour, professionalism, honour, respect, adherence to the company's values. Good faith is a wide term and should be interpreted broadly, to embrace such well-intentioned types of behaviour.

The concept of 'success'

14.48 Section 172(1) of the CA 2006 requires a director to act in good faith in a way he considers '... would be most likely to promote the success of the company for the benefit of its members as a whole ...'. There is no definition of 'success'. It is, however, considered as the pivotal factor in directors exercising their discretion under s 172. The test is subjective and almost on par with Lord Greene MR's statement in *Re Smith & Fawcett* [1942] Ch 304 where he stated that the directors were to act 'bona fide in what they consider – not what a court may consider – is in the interests of the company'. For some companies, the term success would be measured in terms of profit maximisation for the benefit of shareholders. Indeed, some shareholders would view this as the primary objective of commercially driven companies. However, not all companies that are established have as their objective profit maximisation: for some companies, the distribution of dividends is not the main motive – they may be charitable companies or shareholders forming a management company for the operation of a block of flats. Their motives are not profit maximisation and success would be measured in terms of the objectives they have established at the outset in operating such companies. This aspect is addressed in s 172(2) of the CA 2006 which states that:

> 'where or to the extent that the purposes of the company consist of or include purposes other than the benefit of its members, [s 172(1) CA 2006] has effect as if the reference to promoting the success of the company for the benefit of its members were to achieving those purposes'.

14.49 The effect is that it will be the shareholders who will define the company's success whether measured in terms of profitability or value, and for directors to implement the concept of success in practice. The purpose of objectives of the company may be either established in the company's constitutional documents or communicated to the directors through, for example, a shareholders' agreement. Although directors are given a degree of flexibility in promoting the company's success, they are still ultimately responsible and accountable to the company's shareholders for the decisions that they reach.

It requires the director(s) in question (and not a reasonable or a prudent director since the concept is applied to the particular company under consideration) to determine how to promote the long-term success of the company. The words 'most likely' suggest that the director his mind by projecting forward in determining whether the decisions that he makes will be for the long-term success of the company. The term 'promote' would suggest an enhancement or furtherance of the company's interest. Therefore, promoting the success of the company signifies profit maximisation and enlightened shareholder value. The primary objective is to ensure optimal shareholder maximisation of wealth as a result of the capital contribution made by its shareholders collectively.

14.50 According to the ministerial statements of the government on the concept 'success', Lord Goldsmith stated that the starting point was that it was essentially for the members of the company is define the objectives they wanted to achieve. Success meant what the members collectively wanted the company to achieve. For a commercial company, success now normally means 'long-term' increase in value. For certain companies such as charities and community interim companies, it will mean the attainment of the objective for which the company has been established.

Although, for a commercial company, 'success' will normally mean long-term increase of its value, the company, constitution and the decisions made under it will also lay down the appropriate success model for the company. Shareholders should, therefore, define the success that they wish to achieve.

14.51 Although the primary duty to promote the long-term success of the company is rational and essential for the company's survival and well-being, the directors must also exercise a sense of corporate social responsibility towards other shareholders of the company. Any decision made by the directors will have an impact on the shareholders and others in society. CA 2006, s 176 therefore, compels the director to address his mind towards other shareholders affected by the decisions which the director will make.

It may be that afterwards it transpires that the director was mistaken in his judgment – his decision does not promote the long-term success of the company. It proves a failure and a loss to the company. Provided the director has exercised his decision in good faith. The court will not second-guess the director's business judgment.

14.52 The decision to promote the success of the company must be for the benefit of the members as a whole. This clearly prohibits directors from favouring one class of shareholders over another, or starting one class inequitably or unfairly, in arriving at a decision or treating minority shareholders with prejudice or oppression as compared to majority shareholders. The term applies to shareholders as a group.

Although for a commercial company, 'success' would normally mean long-term increase in value, the company's constitution and decisions made under it may also lay down the appropriate success model for the company. For most companies, success would be measured in terms of profit maximisation. However, success may be measured in terms of the company's wider social responsibilities as part of the wider objectives of companies and not just profit maximisation. This is envisaged by CA 2006, s 172(2) which states that where or to the extent that the purposes of the company consist of or include purposes other than the benefit of its members, s 172(1) has effect as if the reference to promoting the success of the company for the benefit of its members were to achieving those purposes.

The six factors

14.53 In determining whether a director's actions would promote the interests of the company, the director must 'have regard to' the six factors identified in s 172(1) of CA 2006. The list is not exhaustive as other factors may also be applicable depending upon the circumstances when the director makes his decision. The reference to 'amongst other matters' is significant because it requires the director to address his mind to other aspects, situations or circumstances that may impact on the decision to promote the interest of the company.

Not all factors will be appropriate or relevant for a director at a particular board meeting to consider. In that case, the director only needs to consider the most appropriate factors set out in s 172(1).

14.54 The six factors are subservient to the main principle that the director must consider in good faith what would be most likely, to promote the success of the company for the benefit of the members as a whole. The primacy is shareholder value or maximisation: all other aspects are subservient to this primary objective.

Further, the six factors are not in any order of priority, a hierarchical level, or order of precedence. All six factors are given equal weight but it may not be unreasonable to suppose that some of the factors may require the particular attention of directors, depending upon the facts, circumstances, events or situations that they encounter.

In having regard to the six factors (and other matters), there is no distinction as to the emphasis placed on the factors for public and private companies. The factors to be considered by a large public company may not be the same as those for a sole director/shareholder company. Much will depend upon the background, circumstances, events, and situations that would invoke a consideration of all or some of the six factors for public and private companies.

14.55 Further, a failure by directors to direct their minds to the six factors may constitute a breach of duty on their part, but such breach may only be enforceable by the company or the shareholders: *Re W & M Roith* [1967] 1 WLR 432. Even where directors have addressed their minds to the six factors and concluded as to what would promote the company's success, the courts are unlikely to second-guess directors' decisions by substituting their own views as to what would promote the company's success: *Edge v Pensions Ombudsman* [2000] Ch 602, where Chadwick LJ stated that the duty to act impartially was no more than the ordinary duty which the law imposed on a person entrusted with the exercise of a discretionary power to exercise such power for a proper purpose, giving proper consideration to relevant matters and excluding from consideration irrelevant matters. Provided they acted in this matter, those exercising such power could not be criticised if they reached a decision which appeared to prefer the claims of one interest over another: such a preference would be the result of a proper exercise of the discretionary power.

The duty to promote the success of the company also includes a duty on a director to disclose his own wrongdoing including disclosing breaches of his fiduciary duty to the company: *Item Software (UK) Limited v Fassihi* [2005] 2 BCLC 91.

Factor (a) – 'the likely consequences of any decision in the long term'

14.56 This factor requires a director to address his mind by acting positively or proactively, in determining the likely consequence of any decision in the long term. The decision must not be reached on a short-term basis or for short-term gains or benefits. This principle is also set out in the UK Corporate Governance Code A.1 – Main Principle.

Directors will apply their mind to the likely future consequences of any decision they reach. They are not required to be certain about the consequences, as this would be onerous. They will ask themselves: 'What is likely to result from the decisions we make today in the long term?'

Factor (b) – 'the interests of the company's employees'

14.57 Previously CA 1985, s 309 addressed the requirement for directors to have regard to the interests of the company's employees. In some cases, where directors were challenged on certain decisions by the shareholders, they would invoke s 309 as a defensive measure against an attack by the shareholders: *Re Saul D Harrison & Sons plc* [1995] 1 BCLC 14.

Judicial attitudes towards directors considering the interests of employees have varied and the law has not been applied consistently by the courts. Legal issues have arisen where a company has engaged in corporate philanthropy or gratuitous distributions of an altruistic nature towards, for example, its employees. Some cases have shown that the courts have viewed gratuitous payments by companies to employees with no great enthusiasm; and in other cases, the courts have permitted gratuitous payments to employees as a recognition of directors taking account of employees' interests within the corporation.

14.58 In *Hampson v Price's Patent Candle Co* (1876) 45 LJ Ch 437 where, as a matter of factory management policy, the directors had proposed to make one week's ex gratia payment (in addition to the usual wages) to their employees 'in recognition of the fact that their exertions have helped to make the company's profits larger than they have been for the last 16 years'. These payments were for employees who had 'worked there with good character throughout the year'. There was no express power in the memorandum to pay these gratuities.

A majority of the shareholders had approved the payments, but the applicant, who was one of the dissentient shareholders, brought an action against the company. Hampson alleged that the company could not, under its constitution, authorise voluntary expenditure from the corporate funds. He contended that the resolution approving the payment was void and illegal and that the company should be restrained from making these payments. He also contended that the distribution of funds to the employees was beyond the scope of the directors' authority.

Jessel MR decided that the company's articles gave wide powers of management to its directors. They could lawfully exercise all the powers of the company. In approving the payments he stated:

> 'Can anything be more reasonable than that, when the employer has had a very good year through the exertions of the workmen employed by him, he should give them something more than their ordinary wages by encouraging them to exert themselves in the future?'

The directors had acted bona fide by seeking approval for the payment from the shareholders. The courts would not interfere where directors had decided that the proposed payment to their employees would encourage them to work for the company's benefit. This was the 'best mode' of conducting the company's affairs as determined by the directors and 'no judge ought to give an opinion on matters of this kind, which he does not understand'.

Payments to directors may only be made if within the objects and the company was a going concern

In *Hutton v West Cork Railway Co* (1883) 23 Ch D 654, an action was brought by the holder of debenture stock who did not approve of a resolution by the company to make certain payments to the company's officers. The court was required to decide whether the sum of £1,050 could lawfully be paid by the company as compensation to its managing director and other officers for loss of their employment. It was also required to determine whether another sum of £1,500 could be paid to directors as remuneration for their past services in circumstances where the company was no longer a going concern.

The railway company had sought to sell its undertaking to another company, but it had no express provisions in its articles for the payment of remuneration to its directors and had never previously made such payments. The Act authorising the transfer of business provided that, on completion of the transfer, the company would be dissolved except for the purposes of regulating its internal affairs and using the proceeds of the sale in the manner resolved by the company.

The Court of Appeal held that the power to make these payments could not be implied after the company had ceased to be a going concern.

Cotton LJ distinguished this case from the *Hampson* case where payments were made by companies that were going concerns. In the present case, the company was no longer a going concern. The proposed payment of £1,050 to the company's directors was a gratuity, but without any prospect of it being in any way reasonably conducive to the company's benefit. The other proposed payment of £1,500 to the directors was not a reasonable sum as remuneration for their past services. It was instead 'a sum which might with reasonable generosity be paid to them taking into consideration the fact that they never received anything during the years when they carried on the railway'. This payment was also held to be beyond the company's powers and *ultra vires*.

Bowen LJ reasoned that bona fide could not be the sole test 'otherwise you might have a lunatic conducting the affairs of the company and paying away its money with both hands in a manner perfectly bona fide yet perfectly irrational'. The test was whether the payment was reasonably incidental to, and within the reasonable scope of, carrying on the company's business. In the absence of any express provisions in the company's articles, the payments to the directors would amount to a gratuity. Thus:

> 'A railway company, or the directors of the company, might send down all the porters at a railway station to have tea in the country at the expense of the company. Why should they not? It is for the directors to judge, provided it is a matter which is reasonably incidental to the carrying on of the business of the company, and a company which always treated its employees with Draconian severity, and never allowed them a single inch more than the strict letter of the bond, would soon find itself deserted – at all events, unless labour was very much more easy to obtain in the market than it often is. The law does not say that there are to be no cakes and ale, but there are to be no cakes and ale except such as are required for the benefit of the company.'

This statement by Bowen LJ clearly suggests that a company has the sole authority to determine what would be regarded as being for the benefit of the company in consideration of the 'interests of the employees'. However, where the company had ceased to be a going concern, it could not derive any benefit from the gratuitous distribution. The company had a special and limited business, and that business was to preside at its own funeral, to wind itself up and to carry on its own internal affairs.

Directors could not make payments to employees as this was not in the best interests of the company

In *Parke v Daily News Limited* [1962] Ch 927, the defendant company was in the process of selling its two main associated newspapers, which had incurred losses, to Associated Newspapers. The directors of *Daily News* had intended to distribute the proceeds of the sale to the company's employees who were to be made redundant. Before a meeting of *Daily News* shareholders could be convened to approve the proposed payment to the employees, the claimant brought an action against the company claiming that the proposed payment was *ultra vires* the company.

Plowman J decided that the directors were not acting in the best interests of their shareholders. The directors' decision was actuated by other motives, predominant among which was 'a desire to treat the employees generously beyond all legal entitlement'. Plowman J accepted 'the view that directors, in having regard to the question "what is in the best interests of their company?" are entitled to take account the interests of the employees, irrespective of any consequential benefit to the company, is one which may be widely held'.

However, in response to an affidavit of the *Daily News* accountant, that companies had an obligation to their employees, Plowman J stated: '... but no authority to support that proposition was a proposition of law was cited to me. I know of none, and in my judgment such is not the law'. The directors were prompted by motives which, however laudable, and however enlightened from the point of view of industrial relations, were such that the law would not recognise them as sufficient justification for making the proposed payments to the employees.

14.59 With regard to employees, CA 2006, s 247 deals with the power for directors to make gratuitous provision for employees on cessation or transfer of business. The powers of the directors of a company include (if they would not otherwise do so) power to make provision for the benefit of persons employed or formerly employed by the company, or any of its subsidiaries, in connection with the cessation or the transfer to any person of the whole or part of the undertaking of the company or that subsidiary: CA 2006, s 247(1).

This power is exercisable notwithstanding the general duty imposed by s 172 (duty to promote the success of the company): CA 2006, s 247(2).

In the case of a company that is a charity it is exercisable notwithstanding any restrictions on the directors' powers (or the company's capacity) flowing from the objects of the company: CA 2006, s 247(3).

14.60 The power may only be exercised if sanctioned:

(a) by a resolution of the company; or

(b) by a resolution of the directors,

in accordance with the following provisions: CA 2006, s . 247(4). A resolution of the directors:

(a) must be authorised by the company's articles; and

(b) is not sufficient sanction for payments to or for the benefit of directors, former directors or shadow directors: CA 2006, s 247(5).

Any other requirements of the company's articles as to the exercise of the power conferred by s 247 must be complied with: CA 2006, s 247(6).

Any payment under s 247 must be made:

(a) before the commencement of any winding up of the company; and

(b) out of profits of the company that are available for dividend: CA 2006, s 247(7).

Factor (c) – 'the need to foster the company's business relationship with suppliers, customers and others'

14.61 A company will have business dealings with various third parties. This factor provides for directors to address the requirement to foster the company's business relationships with suppliers, customers and others. The word 'foster' would suggest the need to promote growth or develop business relationships with such third parties. Developing such business relationships is vital for the company's sustainability and viability to ensure growth and success. It signifies the need to have a business understanding with the company's suppliers, customers and others: how the parties can work together for mutual benefit and gain. A company cannot operate or function in a vacuum: it has dealings with other businesses and in some cases, relies on suppliers and customers for its very existence. It signifies the need for a regular dialogue with such third parties on how the company can conduct better business in society. For example, the dialogue with customers will be how the company can provide a better service or a better product. What will it take to extract a sense of loyalty from customers towards the company? How does the company better promote its services or products? How does the company effectively address customer complaints or grievances? Is the after-sales service provided effectively to customers? The list set out in factor (c) is not exhaustive and the category is not closed, as it includes, 'others'. This may include lenders, creditors, professional advisers and other third parties with whom the company has dealings.

This factor does not permit suppliers, consumers and others to bring proceedings where directors have failed to have regard to this factor.

Factor (d) – 'the impact of the company's operations on the community and the environment'

14.62 This requires directors to have regard, *inter alia*, to the environment and to avoid any pollution or harm to the local community through the company's activities or operations; to for example, prevent any leakage of hazardous substances into the community that could cause harm or damage or reasonable foreseeability of such harm or damage occurring. In this regard, the company would need to assess the magnitude of risk involved and have in place effective measures to address the level of risk.

Another situation may involve the proposed closure of the company's operations in a particular district location, where the local community is heavily dependent upon local businesses for employment. The closure of the company's branch could lead to redundancies and reflect poorly on the company's image. In such circumstances, the directors must have regard to the impact the closure would have on the local community.

The term 'operations' is not defined but would signify its activities, functions and procedures. Although under separate legislation, the Corporate Manslaughter and Corporate Homicide Act 2007 has significant implications for a company conducting or organising its operations and activities in the wider community.

Factor (e) – 'the desirability of the company maintaining a reputation for high standards of business conduct'

14.63 This factor is concerned with business ethics and conduct – the manner, behaviour and values of a company. The ethics may be enshrined in various forms ranging from mission statements, vision statements or codes of conduct. In some cases, companies may also be affiliated to trade organisations to demonstrate high standards of business conduct.

The wording under factor (e) only requires 'desirability' – this is voluntary and not an obligation for companies. The term 'maintain' suggests regularising a specific standard and keeping up with such standard by, for example, frequent reviews or updates. Some companies have international standards in place that regularise their systems and procedures, as well as compliance standards. The standard is not an ordinary or reasonable one – but it is a high standard. Factor (e) also displays characteristics of corporate social rectitude, which is concerned with the ethical aspects of corporate social behaviour – the need to adopt ethical values towards shareholders, creditors, employees and other wider potential claimants and stakeholders of the company.

Factor (f) – 'the need to act fairly as between members of the company'

14.64 Directors must not take advantage of one group of shareholders to the detriment of the others. They must be transparent with all members concerned and not engage in partial disclosure of information to one group to the exclusion of the other.

The key term is 'fairly': directors must exercise impartial judgment and decisions affecting various groups of members. For example, in the context of takeovers and mergers, the City Code on Takeovers and Mergers provides, *inter alia*, that the Code is designed principally to ensure that shareholders are treated 'fairly' and not denied the opportunity to debate the merits of a takeover and that shareholders of the same class are afforded equivalent treatment by the offeror. General Principle 1 states that all holders of securities of an offeree company of the same class must be afforded equivalent treatment.

14.65 This factor may give rise to litigation because of the potential for enforcement by the members concerned, and may give rise to a judicial review on the rights and interests of the shareholders within the company. In *Equitable Life Assurance Society v Hyman* [2000] 2 All ER 331, Lord Woolf stated that there were similarities between the role of the courts on judicial review and in relation to a fiduciary duty based on similar principles as those established by Lord Greene MR in *Associated Provincial Picture Houses Ltd v Wednesbury Corp* [1947] 2 All ER 680. With regard to public authorities, they are very much in the same position as if fiduciary powers were conferred on them: the powers are entrusted to them so that they can exercise them for the benefit of the public or a section of the public. The public places its trust in the public bodies to exercise their powers for the purposes for which they were conferred. Similarly, with respect to public or private companies, the powers are entrusted to the board to be used equitable for the benefit of members both present and future having regard to the interests of the company as a whole.

The directors in making the allotment of shares had exercised their power bona fide in the interests of the company

Mutual Life Insurance Co of New York v Rank Organisation Limited [1985] BCLC 11, concerned discrimination against a group of shareholders on the allotment of shares. In 1975 The Rank Organisation Ltd (Rank), the first defendant, offered for sale to the public 20 million A ordinary shares, half of which were made available on a preferential basis to existing Rank A ordinary shareholders except those resident in the US or Canada, or their agents, who were excluded from the offer because of the securities legislation in those countries. The articles of association of Rank vested in the directors of the company a power to allot, deal with or dispose of the company's shares 'on such terms as they think proper'. The issue was whether the principle of equal treatment had been breached by the directors.

Goulding J held that the power to allot shares had been conferred in the widest terms on the board of directors of Rank and it was subject to only two implied terms: that the power would be exercised by the directors in good faith and in the interests of the company and that it would be exercised fairly as between different shareholders (which did not require that they be treated identically). On the facts, the directors in making the allotment had exercised their power bona fide in the interests of the company. The US and Canadian shareholders had not been treated unfairly, in that their exclusion from participation in the offer did not affect the existence of their shares or the rights attached to them; there was no suggestion that the terms of the offer were improvident; no shareholder in Rank had any right to expect his interest to remain constant forever; and the reason for the exclusion of the North American shareholders was because of a difficulty resulting only from their own personal situation. In addition, there was no justification for implying a term that the directors of Rank should only proceed with the discriminatory allotment if, after having considered the inherent unfairness of such a distribution, they concluded that no alternative method of allotment not involving discrimination was practicable and that it was essential for the prosperity of Rank that the shares be allotted.

Directors must exercise their powers fairly as between different classes of shareholders

In *Re BSB Holdings Ltd (No 2)* [1996] 1 BCLC 155, Arden J stated that where a proposal affected the rights of different groups of shareholders as against each other, then the directors were required not only to exercise their powers in good faith in the interests of the company, but also to exercise them fairly as between the different classes or groups of shareholders. The law did not require the interests of the company to be sacrificed in the particular interests of a group of shareholders.

On the facts there was no breach by the directors of unfair treatment of the shareholders nor any unfair prejudicial conduct.

See too: *Re Sunrise Radio Ltd, Kohli v Lit* [2010] 1 BCLC 367; and *Re McCarthy Surfacing Ltd Hequet v McCarthy* [2009] 1 BCLC 622.

Combination of the factors

14.66 In some cases, the courts will have regard to a combination of factors, as set out in CA 2006, s 172(2).

> ***Directors must have regard to the factors in CA 2006, s 172 when considering the long term success of the company***
>
> In *Shepherd v Williamson* [2010] All ER 142, the company operated as a quasi-partnership. The petitioner was prevented from participating in the company's management and from contributing to the prosperity of business. The issue was whether the petitioner's interests as a member were unfairly prejudiced.
>
> Proudman J held that a balancing exercise was required by the director in question (Mr Shepherd) when considering the factors under CA 2006, s 172(2) namely whether anti-competitive practices should be disclosed to a major customer as well as the Office of Fair Trading. The decision as to what promotes the success of the company within s 172(1) was one for a director's subjective judgment exercised in good faith.

Interests of creditors?

14.67 Section 172 of the CA 2006 does not address the interests of creditors. This aspect will continue to be governed by the common law position and the Insolvency Act 1986. Of particular importance is IA 1986, s 214 which is concerned with wrongful trading. It imposes upon directors a duty of care to take account of the interests of creditors to take all reasonable steps to minimise further loss to the company's creditors where there is no reasonable prospect of the company avoiding insolvent liquidation. Section 214 is enforceable by the company's liquidator. Under CA 2006, s 172(3), the duty imposed by IA 1986, s 214 'has effect subject to any enactment...requiring directors, in certain circumstances, to consider or act in the interests of creditors of the company'. Therefore, in exercising their duties under s 172 of the CA 2006, directors must also have regard to the provision on wrongful trading under IA 1986, s 214.

At common law, directors have a duty to consider the interests of creditors where the company is insolvent or near insolvency: *Walker v Wimborne* (1976) 137 CLR 1. This approach was followed in *West Mercia Safetywear Ltd v Dodd* [1988] BCLC 250; *Re Welfab Engineers Limited* [1990] BCLC 833; *Lonrho Ltd v Shell Petroleum Co* [1980] 1 WLR 627.

14.68 In some situations, the interests of creditors may need to be taken into account well before the company's suspected insolvency: *Brady v Brady* [1988] BCLC 20. In *Nicholson v Permakraft (NZ) Ltd* [1985] 1 NZLR 242, the court was of the view that the duty of care by directors towards creditors would apply by 'a course of action which would jeopardise solvency'. The courts have also stated at common law that the duty by the directors is not owed to creditors individually, but is rather a duty owed to the company: *Winkworth v Edward Baron Development Co Ltd* [1986] 1 WLR 1512; and *Yukong Line Ltd of Korea v Rendsburg Investment Corp of Liberia* [1998] 1 WLR 294. Further, directors may still continue to trade even though the company may be in financial problems provided they continue to take account of creditors' interests in these circumstances: *Facia Footwear Ltd v Hinchcliffe* [1998] 1 BCLC 218.

Duty to exercise independent judgment

14.69 A director of a company must exercise independent judgment: CA 2006, s 173(1).

Section 173 of CA 2006 has codified the common law position that directors must not fetter their future position or discretion.

Section 173 does not prevent directors from seeking advice from other advisers or professional advisers in arriving at an informed decision. For example, the UK Corporate Governance Code requires directors to seek independent advice as and when required for the proper discharge of their duties. However, the board must thereafter take its own decision upon the advice received. It may also be possible for directors to delegate some of their authority to others. At common law, directors were prohibited from entering into agreements which fettered their future discretion as to how they would vote or exercise their powers despite any advantage or personal gain involved.

However, directors may still act in good faith in respect of the contract they have entered into to vote at board meetings in order to carry out the provisions of the contract into effect

In *Thorby v Goldberg* (1964) 112 CLR 597, the directors undertook to allot shares at a specific time and date but failed to honour the undertaking. They contended that the undertaking unlawfully fettered their discretion. The High Court of Australia held that if, at the time when a contract was negotiated on behalf of a company, the directors bona fide thought it in the interests of the company as a whole that the transaction should be entered into and carried into effect, they could bind themselves by the contract to do whatever was necessary to effectuate it. The directors had bound themselves at the time of entering into the undertaking.

In some situations, directors could bind themselves to fetter their future discretion

Thorby v Goldberg was followed by the Court of Appeal in *Fulham Football Club Ltd v Cabra Estates plc* [1994] 1 BCLC 363. Undertakings were given by the directors of the company to support planning applications for redevelopment by the other party and not to object in any way to such applications. In return, the directors would receive substantial compensation. The issue was whether the undertakings were enforceable, or whether the undertakings were illegal or contrary to public policy and an improper fetter on future exercise of directors' fiduciary powers. The Court of Appeal held that directors could bind themselves to fetter their future discretion.

14.70 The duty to exercise independent judgment under CA 2006, s 173 is not infringed by a director acting:

(a) in accordance with an agreement duly entered into by the company that restricts the future exercise of discretion by its directors; or

(b) in a way authorised by the company's constitution: CA 2006, s 173(2). The definition of 'constitution' is set out in s 257.

Section 173(a) captures the principle in *Cabra Estates*, and reference to 'duly entered into' suggest that directors must act bona fide and in good faith in the best interests of the company in the future exercise of their discretion. Further, s 173(b) requires directors to also have regard to the company's constitution to identify any restrictions or limitations on their powers. They will not be in breach of s 173 if they act in a manner authorised by the company's articles of association.

Duty to exercise reasonable care, skill and diligence

14.71 A director of a company must exercise reasonable care, skill and diligence: CA 2006, s 174(1). This means the care, skill and diligence that would be exercised by a reasonably diligent person with:

(a) the general knowledge, skill and experience that may reasonably be expected of a person carrying out the functions carried out by the director in relation to the company; and

(b) the general knowledge, skill and experience that the director has: CA 2006, s 174(2).

Section 174 of CA 2006 codifies the common law position for directors to exercise reasonable skill and care in the exercise of their functions. This is a common law duty, as opposed to a fiduciary one: CA 2006, s 178(2). The position at common law was to ascertain the standard of skill and care required of a director in discharging his duty. At common law, a lower standard of duty was required of a director, which explains why many directors were not held liable for decisions that they made. The courts applied a subjective test in the application of this duty, namely what the director did in the circumstances and not what a reasonable director would have done.

At common law, a lower standard of skill and care is expected of a director

In *Re City Equitable Fire Fire Insurance Co* [1924] All ER Rep 485 and [1925] Ch 407, Romer J (with whom the Court of Appeal agreed on this issue stated the following principles governing the standard of skill and care at common law:

In ascertaining the duties of a director of a company, it is necessary to consider the nature of the company's business and the manner in which the work of the company is, reasonably in the circumstances and consistently with the articles of association, distributed between the directors and the other officials of the company.

In discharging those duties, a director:

(a) must act honestly, and

(b) must exercise such degree of skill and diligence as would amount to the reasonable care which an ordinary man might be expected to take, in the circumstances, on his own behalf. However:

(c) he need not exhibit in the performance of his duties a greater degree of skill than may reasonably be expected from a person of his knowledge and experience; in other words, he is not liable for mere errors of judgment;

(d) he is not bound to give continuous attention to the affairs of his company; his duties are of an intermittent nature to be performed at periodical board meetings, and at meetings of any committee to which he is appointed, and though not bound to attend all such meetings he ought to attend them when reasonably able to do so; and

(e) in respect of all duties which, having regard to the exigencies of business and the articles of association, may properly be left to some other official, he is, in the absence of grounds for suspicion, justified in trusting that official to perform such duties honestly.

Directors engaging in business ventures which proved disastrous were not in breach of their duty of skill and care

In *Re Brazilian Rubber Plantations and Estates Ld* [1911] 1 Ch 425, the court held that that the conduct of the directors did not amount to gross negligence. Even if it had been gross negligence, the directors were protected by the provision in the articles.

Directors were not negligent in engaging in ruinous business ventures

In *Overend & Gurney Co v Gibb* (1871–72) LR 5 HL 480, the House of Lords held that in a company formed for the purchase of a business where the power to make the purchase was distinctly conferred on the directors, though the character of the business turned out to be ruinous, unless that character was obviously apparent when the purchase was made, the directors will not be personally responsible for making it. The directors in this case were not held negligent for their actions in the circumstances.

The attendance at only one board meeting was not in breach of a director's duty of skill and care

In *Re Cardiff Savings Bank* [1892] 2 Ch 100 (also known as the Marquis of Bute's case), where the Marquis had been elected as 'President' of bank at the age of six months and then subsequently after attaining adulthood, attended only one meeting of the board of directors, was held not liable nor had he fallen below the standard of skill and care. Stirling J decided that that omission to attend the meetings of the bank was not the same as neglect or omission of the duties which ought to have been performed at those meetings; and that under the circumstances the Marquis was not liable.

14.72 The common law position changed subsequently when the courts began to address the test for determining the standard of skill and care that should be exercised by a director in the performance of his duties. In *Dorchester Finance Co v Stebbing* [1989 [BCLC 498, where Foster J held that a director in carrying out his duties (i) was required to exhibit in the performance of his duties such a degree of skill as may reasonably be expected from a person with his knowledge and experience, (ii) had, in the performance of his duties, to take such care as an ordinary man might be expected to take on his own behalf, and (iii) must exercise any power vested in him in good faith and in the interests of the company. In applying these standards no distinction was to be drawn between executive and non-executive directors. On the facts, the non-executive director had fallen below the duty of skill and care expected of him.

Similarly, in *Norman v Theodore Goddard* [1991] BCLC 1027, Hoffmann J equated the standard of skill and care to that of IA 1986, s 214(4) as an objective test and not a subjective one. As to the distinction between the duties at common law and equity, see: *Bristol & West Building Society v Mothew* [1996] 4 All ER 698.

14.73 Section 174 of CA 2006 closely reflects s 214 of IA 1986 in connection with wrongful trading. Under IA 1986, s 214(4) the director's conduct is judged against the facts which a director of a company ought to know or ascertain, the conclusions which he ought to reach and the steps which he ought to take are those which would be known or ascertained, or reached or taken, by a reasonably diligent person having both:

(a) the general knowledge, skill and experience that may reasonably be expected of a person carrying out the same functions as are carried out by that director in relation to the company; and

(b) the general knowledge, skill and experience that that director has: see *Norman v Theodore Goddard* ['1991] BCLC 1028; *Re D'Jan of London Limited, sub nom Copp v D'Jan* [1994] 1 BCLC 561.

Under CA 2006, s 174 there is a collective as well as individual responsibility on the part of directors to exercise reasonable care, skill and diligence. However, in practice there will be a difference in the functions carried on by an executive and non-executive director including the types of companies in which they operate so that liability under s 174 may not be imputed to all types of directors: much will depend upon the functions that were discharged by different types of directors and the nature of their duties for s 174 to apply. For example, in the Australian case of *Daniels v Anderson* (1995) 16 ACSR 607, the non-executive directors were held not liable for their failure to discover fraud committed by an employee. The Court of Appeal also stated however that an objective approach required non-executive directors to 'take reasonable steps to place themselves in a position to guide and monitor the management of a company'.

14.74 Further, any delegation by the director to another person, for example, an employee, does not absolve that director from the application of s 174 to supervise and monitor the activities of the person to whom the delegation has been made: *Equitable Life Assurance Society v Bowley* [2004] 1 BCLC 180, where Langley J decided that the extent to which a non-executive director could reasonably rely on the executive directors and other professionals to perform their duties was an area in which the law was developing and was plainly 'fact sensitive'. It was arguable that a company could reasonably at least look to non-executive directors for independence of judgment and supervision of the executive management; and *Re Barings plc (No 5)* [1999] 1 BCLC 433.

14.75 However, on occasions the court have stated that directors 'have a continuing duty to acquire and maintain a sufficient knowledge and understanding of the company's business to enable them properly to discharge their duties as directors': *Lexi Holdings plc v Luqman* [2009] 2 BCLC 1.

In *Re Denham & Co* (1883) 25 Ch D 752, Chitty J held that an innocent director of a company was not liable for the fraud of his co-directors in issuing to the shareholders false and fraudulent reports and balance sheets, if the books and accounts of the company had been kept and audited by duly appointed and responsible officers, and he had no ground for suspecting fraud. The director was therefore entitled to rely upon others to discharge their duties.

See too: *Re Westmid Packing Services Ltd, Secretary of State for Trade and Industry v Griffiths* [1998] 2 BCLC 646.

14.76 The test and the standard under CA 2006, s 174 is an objective one which must be discharged. In *Re Brian D Pierson (Contractors) Ltd* [2001] 1 BCLC 275, the court stated that the standard was an objective minimum, although it may be raised by the particular attributes of the director in question. See too *Re Continental Assurance Co of London plc* [2007] 2 BCLC 287 where Park J stated that even where the directors were accountants by profession who were expected to understand ordinary accounting principles, they could not be expected to have the level of accounting knowledge required for the insurance industry as this would raise the standard of duty of skill and care required of a director.

The court will have regard to the nature of duties and functions carried on by the director:

In *Re Barings plc (No 5), Secretary of State for Trade and Industry v Baker (No 5)* [1999] 1 BCLC 433 (subsequently affirmed by the Court of Appeal [2000] 1 BCLC 523), Park J stated that the existence and extent of any particular duty would depend upon how the particular business was organised and upon what part in the management of that business the respondent could reasonably be expected to play: see *Bishopsgate Investment Management Limited (in liquidation) v Maxwell (No 2)* [1993] BCLC 1285.

A director was to be judged by the standards of what can reasonably be expected of a person fulfilling his functions

In *Re Produce Marketing Consortium Ltd (No 2)* [1989] BCLC 520, Knox J stated that the director in question was to be judged by the standards of what can reasonably be expected of a person fulfilling his functions, and showing reasonable diligence in doing so. In this connection, the requirement to have regard to the functions to be carried out by the director in question, in relation to the company in question, involved having regard to the particular company and its business. Further, the general knowledge, skill and experience postulated would be much less extensive in a small company in a modest way of business, with simple accounting procedures and equipment, than it would be in a large company with sophisticated procedures. However, certain minimum standards were to be assumed to be attained such as a duty to keep accounting records.

A director must properly discharge his functions within the corporate governance system

In *Re AG (Manchester) Ltd, Official Receiver v Watson* [2008] 1 BCLC 321, the finance director in question was at fault in not discharging his functions, but instead leaving it to the inner group which continued to make all the key financial decisions including those relating to dividends and effectively reduced the role of the other directors to departmental managers with no serious input at board meetings on issues affecting the running of the company. It was the finance director's duty to ensure that the company was operated in accordance with its articles of association and under CA 2006.

Non-executive directors must also discharge their duties effectively within the corporate governance system

With regard to a non-executive director (NED), in *Secretary of State for Trade and Industry v Swan* [2005] BCC 596, Etherton J stated that the NED was required to discharge his duties effectively, and if a serious matter arose to discuss it with senior management of the company as well as auditors or fellow NEDs.

Certain propositions apply in respect of directors' duties

The nature of the duties exercised by a director under CA 2006, s 174 was considered by Jonathan Parker in *Re Barings plc (No 5) Secretary of State for Trade and Industry v Baker (No 5)* [1999] 1 BCLC 433 stated the following propositions:

(a) Each individual director owed duties to the company to inform himself about its affairs and to join with his co-directors in supervising and controlling them.

(b) Subject to the articles of association of the company, a board of directors might delegate specific tasks and functions. Some degree of delegation was almost always essential if the company's business was to be carried on efficiently: to that extent, there was a clear public interest in delegation by those charged with the responsibility for the management of a business.

(c) The duty of an individual director, however, did not mean that he might not delegate. Having delegated a particular function it did not mean he was no longer under any duty in relation to the discharge of that function, notwithstanding that the person to whom the function had been delegated appeared both trustworthy and capable of discharging the function.

(d) Where delegation had taken place the board (and the individual directors) remained responsible for the delegated function or functions and retained a residual duty of supervision and control. The precise extent of that residual duty will depend on the facts of each particular case, as will the question of whether it had been breached.

(e) A person who accepted the office of director of a particular company undertook the responsibility of ensuring that he understood the nature of the duty a director was called upon to perform. That duty would vary according to the size and business of that particular company and the experience or skills that the director held himself out to have in support of appointment to the office. The duty included that of acting collectively to manage the company.

(f) Where there was an issue as to the extent of a director's duties and responsibilities in any particular case, the level of reward which he was entitled to receive or which he might reasonably have expected to receive from the company might be a relevant fact in resolving that issue. It was not that the unfitness depended on how much he was paid. The point was that the higher the level of reward, the greater the responsibilities which might reasonably be expected (prima facie, at least) to go with it.

(g) The following general propositions could be stated with respect to the director's duties:

(i) Directors had, both collectively and individually, a continuing duty to acquire and maintain a sufficient knowledge and understanding of the company's business to enable them properly to discharge their duties as directors.

Directors must therefore understand the business in which they are involved to discharge their duties effectively: see *Re Queen's Moat Houses plc, Secretary of State for Trade and Industry v Bairstow (No 2)* [2005] 1 BCLC 136; *Re Westmid Packing Services Ltd, Secretary of State for Trade and Industry v Griffiths* [1998] 2 BCLC 646; and *Re Kaytech International plc, Secretary of State for Trade and Industry v Kaczer* [1999] 2 BCLC 351.

(ii) Whilst directors were entitled (subject to the articles of association of the company) to delegate particular functions to those below them in the management chain, and to trust their competence and integrity to a reasonable extent, the exercise of the power of delegation did not absolve a director from the duty to supervise the discharge of the delegated functions.

In *Re Landhurst Leasing plc, Secretary of State for Trade and Industry v Ball* [1999] 1 BCLC 286, Hart J stated that a director might rely on his co-directors to the extent that: the matter in question lay within their sphere of responsibility given the way in which the particular business was organised; and that there existed no grounds for suspicion that that reliance might be misplaced. However, even where there were no reasons to think the reliance was misplaced, a director might still be in breach of duty if he left to others matters for which the board as a whole had to take responsibility. A proper degree of delegation and division of responsibility by the board was permissible, but not a total abrogation of responsibility since this would undermine the collegiate or collective responsibility of the board of directors which was of fundamental importance to corporate governance.

See too *A G (Manchester) Ltd, Official Receiver v Watson* [2008] 1 BCLC 321; *Re Westminster Property Management Limited, Official Receiver v Stern (No 2)* [2001] BCC 305; and *Lexi Holdings plc v Luqman* [2009] 2 BCLC 1.

(iii) No rule of universal application can be formulated as to the duty referred to in (ii) above. The extent of the duty, and the question whether it had been discharged, depended on the facts of each particular case, including the director's role in the management of the company.

See too the Court of Appeal decision in [2000] 1 BCLC 523.

14.77 In assessing the standard of care expected of a director, the court will apply the test under s 174, which has both subjective and objective aspects. This test is similar to s 214 of IA 2006 and in line with the developing standards of negligence at common law. In determining the objective standards, the courts are likely to adopt a robust approach in defining the functions of directors at board level and whether the director discharged his functions. Consideration is likely to be given to the director's role within the corporate governance system and how that role was implemented in practice.

In the event there is a breach of s 174, the appropriate remedy will be compensation for loss caused by the director's negligence towards the company. Under CA 2006, s 178(2), the duties under ss 171–177 of CA 2006 (with the exception of s 174 (duty to exercise reasonable care, skill and diligence)) are, accordingly, enforceable in the same way as any other fiduciary duty owed to a company by its directors. The distinction as to whether compensation is payable under common law and equitable principles has been blurred: *Bristol and West Building Society v Mothew* [1998] Ch 1.

Duty to avoid conflicts of interest

14.78 A director of a company must avoid a situation in which he has, or can have, a direct or indirect interest that conflicts, or possibly may conflict, with the interests of the company: CA 2006, s 175(1).

The term 'possibly may conflict' refers to a real sensible possibility of conflict

The words 'possibly may conflict' were considered by Lord Upjohn in *Boardman v Phipps* [1966] 3 All ER 721 where he stated:

> 'The phrase "possibly may conflict" requires consideration. In my view it means that the reasonable man looking at the relevant facts and circumstances of the particular case would think that there was a real sensible possibility of conflict; not that you could imagine some situation arising which might, in some conceivable possibility in events not contemplated as real sensible possibilities by any reasonable person, result in a conflict.'

This applies in particular to the exploitation of any property, information or opportunity (and it is immaterial whether the company could take advantage of the property, information or opportunity): CA 2006, s 175(2).

14.79 Under s 175(3), the duty does not apply to a conflict of interest arising in relation to a transaction or arrangement with the company. This excludes self-dealing transactions with the company which are subject not to the board scrutiny but approval by the shareholders usually by an ordinary resolution: *Bell v Lever Bros Ltd* [1932] AC 161 and *Sinclair Investments (UK) Ltd v Versailles Trade Finance Ltd* [2011] EWCA Civ 347.

This duty is not infringed:

(a) if the situation cannot reasonably be regarded as likely to give rise to a conflict of interest – In *Eastford Ltd v Gillespie* [2010] CSIH 12, the court interpreted the word 'likely' as referring to 'a real sensible possibility'; or

(b) if the matter has been authorised by the directors: CA 2006, s 175(4).

14.80 Authorisation may be given by the directors:

(a) where the company is a private company and nothing in the company's constitution invalidates such authorisation, by the matter being proposed to and authorised by the directors; or

(b) where the company is a public company and its constitution includes provision enabling the directors to authorise the matter, by the matter being proposed to and authorised by them in accordance with the constitution: CA 2006, s 175(5).

14.81 The authorisation is effective only if:

(a) any requirement as to the quorum at the meeting at which the matter is considered is met without counting the director in question or any other interested director; and

(b) the matter was agreed to without their voting or would have been agreed to if their votes had not been counted: CA 2006, s 175(6).

Any reference in s 175 to a conflict of interest includes a conflict of interest and duty and a conflict of duties: CA 2006, s 175(7).

14.82 Section 175 derives from the fiduciary duty to avoid conflicts of interest. At common law, directors as fiduciaries were required to ensure that they did not put themselves in a conflict of interest position between their duties to the company and their personal interests.

As Lord Herschell in *Bray v Ford* [1896] AC 44 stated that there was an inflexible rule of the court of equity that a person in a fiduciary position was not, unless otherwise expressly provided, entitled to make a profit; he was not allowed to put himself in a position where his interest and duty conflict.

The 'no-conflict' rule applies to various transactions in which a director may be involved including: his dealings with the company; a duty not to receive a benefit from a third party; and a duty for a director not to make personal use of the company's property, information or opportunities (also known as 'corporate opportunities').

A director must not put himself in a position where his interests to the company conflict with his personal interests

In *Aberdeen Rly Co v Blaikie Bros* (1854) 1 Macq 461, a contract between the company and a partnership of which one of the directors was a partner was set aside by the court on the basis of a conflict of interest arising, and owing to the fiduciary and trusteeship nature of a director's duties.

In the course of his judgment, Lord Carnworth stated that it was the duty of a director of a company to act so as best to promote the interests of the company. That duty was of a fiduciary character, and no one who had such duties to discharge could be allowed to enter into engagements in which he had, or could have, a personal interest which would conflict, or possibly conflict, with the interests of the company. A director, therefore, was precluded from entering on behalf of the company into a contract with himself or with a firm or company of which he was a member, and so strictly is this principle adhered to that no question can be raised as to the fairness or unfairness of a contract so entered into.

The 'no-conflict' rule is designed to prevent any self-interest from arising and is associated in some cases with the 'no-profit' rule: *CMS Dolphin Ltd v Simonet* [2001] 2 BCLC 704; and *Quarter Master UK v Pyke* [2005] 1 BCLC 245.

The no-conflict duty continues until resignation of a director. However, under CA 2006, s 170(2)(a) a former director will be subject to the no-conflict rule regarding exploitation of property, information or opportunity of which he became aware when he was a director.

Section 175 of CA 2006 and the common law has given rise to a number of cases on corporate opportunities arising where a director diverts an opportunity which properly belonged to the company for his own personal advantage or gain, and where the director property, information or opportunity.

Directors may in in breach of the 'no-conflict' duty where this conflicted between his interests towards the company and his personal interests

In *Bhullar v Bhullar* [2003] 2 BCLC 241, a diversion of business opportunity was available to the company. However, directors purchased investment property adjacent to the company's property without informing the company of the existence of an opportunity to acquire the property, which would have significantly increased the value of the company's property. The issue was whether the no-conflict rule applied.

Jonathan Parker LJ held that the directors were in breach of the no-conflict rule. The rule that a fiduciary was not allowed to enter into engagements in which he had, or could have, a personal interest conflicting, or which might possibly conflict, with the interests of those whom he is bound to protect was universal and inflexible. The test was whether 'reasonable men looking at the facts would think there was a real sensible possibility of conflict' and where a fiduciary, such as the director of a company, exploited a commercial opportunity for his own benefit, the relevant question was not whether the party to whom the duty was owed (ie the company) had some kind of beneficial interest in the opportunity but whether the fiduciary's exploitation of the opportunity was such as to attract the application of the rule. Since the only capacity in which the appellants carried on business was as directors of the company, in which capacity they were in a fiduciary relationship with the company, and since at the material time the company was still trading and acquisition of the property would have been commercially attractive to the company, the appellants were under a duty to communicate the existence of opportunity to acquire the property to the company. Applying the test that 'reasonable men looking at the facts would think there was a real sensible possibility of conflict', the appellants had acted in breach of their fiduciary duty to the company.

14.83 The principle behind the no-conflict rule is that the company is entitled to expect the exclusive loyalty of its directors in the pursuit of business opportunities.

See too: *Quarter Master (UK) Ltd v Pyke* [2005] 1 BCLC 245.

Earlier cases on conflict of interest have highlighted the conflict between personal interests and the company's interests.

A director is under a duty to disclose all information which he received in the course of his dealings with another company

In *Industrial Development Consultants Limited v Cooley* [1972] 2 All ER 162 a managing director diverted a business opportunity from the gas board to himself, instead of to his company. Roskill J stated that while the defendant was managing director of the company, a fiduciary relationship existed between him and the company. Accordingly, information which came to him while he was managing director and was of concern to the company, was information which it was his duty to disclose to the company. He was under a duty therefore to disclose all information which he received in the course of his dealings with the gas board. Instead, he had embarked on a deliberate course of conduct which had put his personal interests as a potential contracting party with the gas board in direct conflict with his pre-existing and continuing duty as managing director to the company. He was therefore in breach of his fiduciary duty to the company in failing to pass on to it all the relevant information received in the course of his dealings with the gas board and in guarding it for his own personal purposes and profit.

Directors will be in breach of their fiduciary duty in diverting contract opportunities away from the company

In *Cook v Deeks* [1916] 1 AC 554, the directors of a construction company negotiated with a railway company a contract on their own behalf, but in exactly the same manner as that in which they had previously acted when negotiating contracts for the construction company, and with the advantage of the successful completion by the construction company of contracts for the railway company in the past. When all the necessary preliminaries of the contract had been concluded, the directors formed a new company to carry it out, and at a meeting of the construction company, owing to their voting power, they secured the passing of a resolution declaring that the construction company had no interest in the contract and authorising them as directors to defend an action brought by the claimant, a minority shareholder, against them and the new company for a declaration that they and the new company were trustees of the benefit of the contract for the construction company.

The House of Lords held that the directors were guilty of a breach of duty in the course they took to secure the contract; they could not retain the benefit of that contract for themselves, but must be regarded as holding it on behalf of the construction company; the resolution the passing of which they had secured was ineffective to regularise the position.

A director may not divert a maturing opportunity away from his company

In *Canadian Aero Service v O'Malley* [1973] 40 DLR (3d) 371, Laskin J in the Supreme Court of Canada considered the misuse of the corporate opportunity giving rise to a conflict of interest and stated:

> 'An examination of the case law … shows the pervasiveness of a strict ethic in this area of law. In my opinion this ethic disqualifies a director or senior director from usurping for himself or diverting to another person or company with whom or with which he is associated a maturing business opportunity which his company is actively pursuing; he is only precluded from so acting even after his resignation where the resignation may fairly be said to be prompted or influenced by a wish to acquire for himself the opportunity sought by the company, or where it was his position with the company rather than a fresh initiative which led him to the opportunity which he later acquired'.

14.84 In considering the no-conflict view, the courts will have regard to the nature of the company's business and wide-ranging scope.

The rationale of the 'no conflict' and 'no profit' rules was to underpin the fiduciary's duty of undivided loyalty to his beneficiary

In *O'Donnell v Shanahan* [2009] 2 BCLC 666, there was a diversion by directors of a business opportunity belonging to the company. The issue was whether the directors were in breach of fiduciary duty; and whether the relevant opportunity was within the scope of the company's business in determining whether the directors were entitled to decide that the company would not be interested in taking up opportunity.

The Court of Appeal held that the rationale of the 'no conflict' and 'no profit' rules was to underpin the fiduciary's duty of undivided loyalty to his beneficiary. The principle of accountability by directors who breached the rules derived from the strict rule affecting trustees that if an opportunity came to a person in his capacity as a fiduciary, his principal was entitled to know about it. Because the rule was applied strictly, it was irrelevant whether an opportunity which presented itself to a director was within the scope of the company's business and, moreover, he could not without the authority of the company appropriate an opportunity to himself simply on the basis of his own decision that the company would not be interested. Unlike the duties owed by a partner, which were circumscribed by the contract of partnership, a director owed an unlimited duty of undivided loyalty to his company akin to a general trusteeship, which put him under a duty to inform his company of the existence of any opportunity which it was relevant for the company to know.

Further, the company had operated on the basis of a relationship of trust and confidence between the shareholders which meant that when the opportunity to invest in a property arose the respondents could not properly decide to take up the opportunity for their own benefit, because that opportunity came to them in the course of acting as directors of the company. Since they had in fact, without the company's informed consent (which in practice was that of the petitioner), adopted the business opportunity for their own private benefit, using information obtained in the course of acting as directors, they were in principle accountable to the company under the 'no profit' and 'no conflict' rules for any profit derived from the investment.

The company had a wide range of activities that prohibited the directors from engaging in any conflicts of interest. See too: *Commonwealth Oil & Gas Co Ltd v Baxter* [2009] CSIH 75.

14.85 The no-conflict duty can arise in the context of the exploitation of any property, information or opportunity. Section 175(2) of CA 2006 does not allow for such exploitation by a director.

Directors were liable to account to the company profit made from a transaction unless ratified by the shareholders

In *Regal (Hastings) Ltd v Gulliver* [1942] 1 All ER 378, the directors of the company were interested in acquiring further cinemas from a subsidiary and as the company did not have additional capital to pay for the acquisition, they paid personally by acquiring shares in the subsidiary and sold at a profit.

The House of Lords held applying the trusteeship principles of equity, that the directors, other than the chairman, were in a fiduciary relationship to the appellant company and liable, therefore, to repay to it the profit they had made on the sale of the shares.

Although the directors may have acted in good faith, they were still accountable to the company for the profits made based on the personal gain they made from exploitation of the corporate opportunity where it was identified that '(i) what the directors did was so related to the affairs of the company that it can properly be said to have been done in the course of their management and in utilisation of their opportunities and special knowledge as directors; and (ii) that what they did resulted in a profit to themselves'.

It was irrelevant that the company could not have taken up a business opportunity that came to the company's director

Gencor ACP Ltd v Dalby [2000] 2 BCLC 734 concerned a dishonest diversion of assets and business opportunities belonging to or available to the company by the director. The director of an asphalt equipment manufacturer arranged sales of second-hand and refurbished equipment through his own private company. The issue was whether this was within the no-conflict rule.

Rimer J held that there was such a breach and that it was irrelevant that the company could not have taken up the business opportunity.

14.86 Similarly, a director is obliged to disclose corporate opportunities to which he comes across: *Crown Dilmun v Sutton* [2004] 1 BCLC 468.

Directors are obliged to disclose full facts of a transaction to the company

In *Sharma v Sharma* [2013] All ER 291, various family members were involved in establishing a company which operated as a dental practice. Subsequently, the wife established another company for the purposes of acquisition of other dental practices. Matrimonial difficulties arose between the husband and wife. During the course of financial relief proceedings, an issue arose as to the legal and beneficial interests in dental practices which had been acquired by the wife in her own name and by a company owned and controlled by her. She was also the sole director and a shareholder of a company owned by her husband's family which also acquired and operated dental practices. The wife maintained that the family had consented to her acting on her own behalf as well as on behalf of the family company. The High Court judge found that the wife had not been in breach of either her fiduciary duty or her statutory duty under CA 2006, s 175 (Duty to avoid conflicts of interest) in that (accepting the wife's witness statement), at a family meeting, the family had consented to the wife's acquisition of other dental practices. The husband and his family members appealed against this decision and contended that the wife had exploited the acquisition of dental practice opportunities for her own benefit and breached her duty under s 175. The central issue in the appeal was whether the shareholders with knowledge of the material facts, had acquiesced in the wife's proposed course of conduct to acquire further dental practices in her own name.

Jackson LJ summarised the position on CA 2006, s 175 by application of the facts as follows:

(a) A company director is in breach of his fiduciary or statutory duty if he exploits for his personal gain:

  (i) opportunities which come to his attention through his role as director; or

  (ii) any other opportunities which he could and should exploit for the benefit of the company.

(b) If the shareholders with full knowledge of the relevant facts consent to the director exploiting those opportunities for his own personal gain, then that conduct is not a breach of the fiduciary or statutory duty.

(c) If the shareholders with full knowledge of the relevant facts acquiesce in the director's proposed conduct, then that may constitute consent. However, consent cannot be inferred from silence unless:

  (i) the shareholders know that their consent is required; or

  (ii) the circumstances are such that it would be unconscionable for the shareholders to remain silent at the time and object after the event.

(d) For the purposes of propositions (b) and (c) full knowledge of the relevant facts does not entail an understanding of their legal incidents. In other words the shareholders need not appreciate that the proposed action would be characterised as a breach of fiduciary or statutory duty.

It was held that the wife was not in breach of her duty under CA 2006, s 175 on the basis that silence by the other family members constituted consent to the wife acquiring further dental practices in her own name.

See too: *Pennyfeathers Ltd v Pennyfeathers Property Company Ltd* [2013] EWHC 3530.

A director was precluded from diverting to himself a maturing business opportunity which his company was actively pursuing

In *Island Export Finance Ltd v Umunna* [1986] BCLC 460, a director resigned from his company and at a later date pursued a business opportunity in which the company had not then been interested. Hutchison J set out the position that a director was precluded from diverting to himself a maturing business opportunity which his company was actively pursuing even after his resignation where the resignation was prompted or influenced by a desire to acquire that opportunity for himself. However, the no-conflict duty did not apply here. Although a director's fiduciary duty did not necessarily come to an end when he ceased to be a director, on the facts, the company was not actively pursuing the business opportunity.

However, the intention to resign may in certain situations trigger the no-conflict rule.

See too: *Colman Taymar Ltd v Oakes* [2001] 2 BCLC 749; and *Shepherds Investments Limited v Walters* [2007] 2 BCLC 202.

14.87 The exploitation of property, information or opportunity is illustrated in *CMS Dolphin Ltd v Simonet* [2001] 2 BCLC 704. The director of an advertising agency resigned without giving notice and set up a new business, first in partnership and later through a company controlled by him. He recruited all the staff of the agency, and the principal clients switched their business to him. Further, he diverted the business and the benefit of existing contracts to his partnership/company. He had not personally made profits, as the profits were made by his company. Lawrence Collins J held that the underlying basis of the liability of a director of a company who, following his resignation, exploited a maturing business opportunity of the company of which he had knowledge as a result of his being a director, was that the opportunity was to be treated as if it were property of the company in relation to which the director had fiduciary duties. By seeking to exploit the opportunity after his resignation, he was appropriating that property for himself and became a constructive trustee of the fruits of his abuse of the company's property, which he had acquired in circumstances where he knowingly had a conflict of interest, and exploited it by resigning from the company. He was liable to account for the profits made. He compared this to a position of a trustee who has obligations leaving matters unattended without properly accounting for trust property.

A resigning director who had acted honestly and in good faith and whose resignation was forced on him, was not in breach of the no-conflict rule

However, in *Foster Bryant Surveying Ltd v Bryant* [2007] 2 BCLC 239, the director resigned and established a competing business during his notice period and took major customers from his previous company. The Court of Appeal held that there had not been any breach of the no-conflict rule.

On the facts, the director was not disloyal nor did he act in bad faith. His resignation was forced on him. He did not resign to exploit company property or information. Therefore, there was no breach of the no-conflict rule.

14.88 In respect of remedies available under s 175 of CA 2006, where the corporate opportunity has not yet matured, the company may seek an injunction to prevent the director taking up the corporate opportunity. Where the corporate opportunity has been taken by the director, a breach of duty will have been committed with the company claiming compensation for loss occasioned as a result of the exploitation of the corporate property, information or opportunity.

In conflict of interest cases where expoitation of corporate information, property or information is concerned, the courts have tended to disgorge the director of the profits made and to account to the company for such profits. Where no profit has been made then there is no liability to account to the company. The court has also considered whether the disgorging of profits is a proprietary remedy or a personal remedy: *FHR European Ventures LLP v Cedar Capital Partners LLC* [2014] EWSC 45. Under the no-conflict cases, however, the company is not entitled generally to recover losses sustained.

Duty not to accept benefits from third parties

14.89 A director of a company must not accept a benefit from a third party conferred by reason of:

(a) his being a director; or

(b) his doing (or not doing) anything as director: CA 2006, s 176(1).

A 'third party' means a person other than the company, an associated body corporate or a person acting on behalf of the company or an associated body corporate: CA 2006, s 176(2). This is an exception to the prohibition set out in s 176(1) which allows the director to perform services for such corporate body.

14.90 Benefits received by a director from a person by whom his services (as a director or otherwise) are provided to the company are not regarded as conferred by a third party: CA 2006, s 176(3). This is an exception to the prohibition set out in s 176(1) in respect of directors' remuneration and service contracts entered into by the director.

This duty is not infringed if the acceptance of the benefit cannot reasonably be regarded as likely to give rise to a conflict of interest: CA 2006, s 176(4). This is also an exception to the prohibition set out in s 176(1). There is no guidance on the level or type of benefit that is subject to the exception, but it is unlikely to catch aspects such as entertainment tickets, small gifts or travel vouchers. The test would appear to be objective having regard to the reasonableness of the situation.

Any reference in s 176 to a conflict of interest includes a conflict of interest and duty and a conflict of duties: CA 2006, s 176(5).

14.91 Section 176 of CA 2006 does not define the term 'benefits' and it could include gifts as well as bribes, with bribery being a criminal offence under the Bribery Act 2010 (see **Chapter 40**). English law takes a broad view as to what constitutes a bribe for the purposes of a civil claim: *Fiona Trust & Holding Corp v Privalov* [2010] EWHC 3199; *Daraydan Holdings Limited v Solland International Limited* [2005] Ch 119. The rationale for CA 2006, s 176 is that the taking of benefits by a director would conflict with his duty to the company and the benefit received from the third party. Section 176 is not limited to bribes but has wider significance to include payment of monies or other benefit received by the person concerned which has not been disclosed to the company: *Industries and General Mortgage Co Ltd v Lewis* [1949] 2 All ER 573. The common law does not require any motive or intention to be shown on the part of the person receiving the payment or the bribe.

14.92 It is possible for the shareholders to ratify the acceptance of benefits from third parties under CA 2006, s 180(4)(a) which provides that 'the general duties have effect subject to any rule of law enabling the company to give authority, specifically or generally, for anything to be done (or omitted) by the directors, or any of them, that would otherwise be a breach of duty', or as set out in the company's articles of association: see also CA 2006, s 239. However, under the Bribery Act 2010, it is not possible to ratify any giving or receiving of bribes.

> ***CA 2006, s 176 did not apply where a person received the benefits as a trustee***
>
> In *Pullan v Wilson* [2014] EWHC 126 (Ch), the court was required to consider the application of CA 2006, s 176 prohibiting directors from accepting benefits from third parties. A trustee had been appointed as a non-executive director of various companies in which the trusts had invested, and issues arose as to the reasonableness of the remuneration charged to a number of family trusts by the trustee.
>
> Hodge J held that s 176 did not apply because the benefits in question were received by the person in his capacity as a trustee. He did not obtain the benefits because he was a director or undertaking any role as a director for the various trusts.

14.93 The remedies for breach of s 176 of CA 2006 are set out in s 178 of CA 2006 and the effect is that the common law remedies will be applicable in the circumstances with remedies against the director including the third party. Common law provides a wide range of remedies in these situations which include recission of the contract between the company and the third party where the director has received a third party benefit and the third party had knowledge of the position of the director: *Taylor v Walker* [1958] 1 Lloyd's Rep 490.

At common law, the director and the third party may also be liable to pay damages where bribery or fraud is involved subject to the company demonstrating proof of loss: *Mahesan v Malaysia Government Officers' Co-Operative Housing Society Limited* [1979] AC 374.

In other situations, the court may impose a constructive trust on the person concerned who has received the benefit of an asset or interest: *Attorney-General of Hong Kong v Reid* [1994] 1 AC 324. However, the Court of Appeal in *Sinclair Investments (UK) Ltd v Versailles Trade Finance Ltd* [2011] 4 All ER 335 rejected the Privy Council view, but subsequently, *FHR European Ventures LLP v Cedar Capital Partners LLC* [2014] UKSC 45, has overruled *Sinclair.*

Duty to declare interest in proposed transaction or arrangement

14.94 If a director of a company is in any way, directly or indirectly, interested in a proposed transaction or arrangement with the company, he must declare the nature and extent of that interest to the other directors: CA 2006, s 177(1). The disclosure must, therefore, be to the board of directors and not to a committee of directors: *Guinness plc v Saunders* 1990] 2 AC 663. Whereas s 177 addresses disclosure of interest in proposed transactions and therefore a general duty imposed on directors under Pt 10, Ch 2, CA 2006, s 182 is concerned with disclosure of interest in existing transactions and is governed by CA 2006, Pt 10, Ch 3.

The effect of s 177 is to put the company's directors on notice of a proposed interest in a transaction or arrangement. This in turn will enable the directors to put themselves into a position to protect the company's position for the future. Although section 177 does not set out what steps such directors who are put on notice should take, in practice they will owe a duty of care to the company to act on the notice and take appropriate action.

14.95 The duty to declare only arises in respect of a proposed arrangement with the company and not otherwise. It could be in respect of a transaction with the company such as purchase of an asset or disposal between the two parties; or in respect of a service contract to be entered into between the director and the company. The duty to declare an interest only arises in respect of a proposed transaction or arrangement with the company – transactions or arrangements yet to be entered into or contemplated being entered into in the future. The effect is to alert the board of such arrangement or transaction or such possibility and to provide consent so as to avoid any conflict of interest in due course: the company still has the ability to decide whether or not to proceed with the transaction because the arrangement or transaction will take place in the future. Section 177 of CA 2006 is not concerned with transactions or arrangements with the holding company or subsidiary – but only the direct company of which the person is a director. It may relate to a contractual arrangement or a non-contractual one whether by the board of directors or by the director: *Re Duckwari (No 2)* [1998] 2 BCLC 315; *Neptune (Vehicle Washing Equipment) Ltd v Fitzgerald* [1996] Ch 274.

14.96 Section 177 also catches 'indirect' transactions which may not necessarily involved the director in his capacity as such but possibly as a shareholder or a person connected with the director (as an interest 'in any way'): *Transvaal Lands Co v New Belgian (Transvaal) Land & Development Co* [1914] 2 Ch 488. In *Newgate Stud Co v Penfold* [2008] 1 BCLC 46, the court stated that indirect transactions are caught such that there is a 'real risk of conflict between duty and personal loyalties'.

Section 177 makes it clear that not only is disclosure required by the director but also the 'extent' of such disclosure. This refers to providing some detailed content of the information to be disclosed as part of the disclosure requirements.

The duty to declare under s 177 may also apply to a shadow director 'where and to the extent that the corresponding common law rules or equitable principles so apply': CA 2006, s 170(5).

The situation arises where the director may be involved in a dual relationship in respect of the transaction contemplated.

A director's personal interest must not conflict with the interests of the company

The position was highlighted in *Aberdeen Rly Co v Blaikie Bros* (1854) 1 Macq 461, where a director of a railway company, also a member of a mercantile firm, entered into a contract in his capacity as a company director with the firm for the supply of certain iron chairs at a fixed price.

The House of Lords held that it was the duty of a director of a company to act so as best to promote the interests of the company. That duty was of a fiduciary character, and no one who had such duties to discharge could be allowed to enter into engagements in which he had, or could have, a personal interest which conflicted, or possibly may conflict, with the interests of the company. A director, therefore, was precluded from entering on behalf of the company into a contract with himself or with a firm or company of which he was a member. This was a strict principle that should be adhered to so that no question could be raised as to the fairness or unfairness of a contract so entered into.

Directors must declare the nature of their personal interest to the company

Movitext Ltd v Bulfield [1988] BCLC 104 concerned a potential conflict of interest in the purchase of a freehold property by the company's directors through another company which they had set up. There was no breach by directors of their duties as they had properly declared their interests and sought approval from the board. The directors had not preferred their own interests to those of the company.

A director must disclose his interest in a transaction in which he has a personal interest

In *Gwembe Valley Development Co Ltd v Koshy* [2004] 1 BCLC 131, a director procured the company to enter into loan transactions with a company controlled by him without making proper disclosure to other directors or its shareholders of his personal interest. He concealed a secret profit made from currency transactions when investing in the company. The Court of Appeal held that the director had failed to disclose his interest in the transaction as required under the CA 2006.

14.97 The director need only declare the nature and extent of the interest to the board of directors: there is no requirement for board nor shareholder approval: see *Neptune (Vehicle Washing Equipment) Ltd v Fitzgerald* [1995] 1 BCLC 352. Disclosure of interest to a committee of directors will not be sufficient to comply with CA 2006, s 177: *Guinness plc v Saunders* [1990] BCLC 402. A sole director is not required to make a disclosure to himself but the declaration should be minuted in the company's minutes and to show appropriate compliance of the directors' general duties under the CA 2006.

If the declaration is not made, any contract that is entered into is voidable at the company's option and may be set aside: *Hely-Hutchinson v Brayhead Ltd* [1967] 3 All ER 98. The company may elect to affirm or rescind the contract.

One of the civil consequences where declaration was not timely made and the contract is avoided is that the company may seek an order requiring the director to account to the company for any profits made. In *Gwembe Valley Development Co Ltd v Koshy* [2004] 1 BCLC 131, the director was liable to account to the company for the loss suffered owing to his non-disclosure of his interest in the transaction. This was on the basis that the contract in question could not be set aside.

A director who failed to disclose his interest to the company may be liable for damages to the company for any personal benefit obtained

In *Re MDA Investment Management Limited, Whalley v Doney* [2004] 1 BCLC 217, there was a diversion of consideration received from the sale of a business by the director concerned. The contract in the nature of the sale transaction had already been performed. Park J held that breach by directors of duties owed to their company was customarily expressed as common law misfeasance or breach of fiduciary duty in equity. The latter duty extended to transactions where the director acted improperly in his own interest rather than in the interests of the company. Neither duty was limited to circumstances in which the company was insolvent but when the company, whether technically insolvent or not, was in financial difficulties to the extent that its creditors were at risk, the duties owed by directors to the company were extended to encompass the interests of the company's creditors as a whole, as well as those of the shareholders.

The director had failed to disclose his interest in the transaction as required under CA 2006. He was therefore liable in damages to, or alternatively accountable to, the liquidator for the personal benefit which he obtained.

See too, Bowen LJ in *Re Cape Breton Co* (1885) 29 Ch D 795.

14.98 There is nevertheless a duty on the company to mitigate any losses that it may have suffered regardless of the lack of disclosure by the director: see *Bishopsgate Investment Management Limited v Maxwell (No 2)* [1993] BCLC 1282.

Section 177 sets out three situations as to how the declaration may be made by the director: the methods of disclosure are not exhaustive and may include other forms of disclosure. The declaration may (but need not) be made:

(a) at a meeting of the directors; or

(b) by notice to the directors in accordance with:

  (i) CA 2006, s 184 (notice in writing); or

  (ii) s 185 (general notice): CA 2006, s 177(2). Although not expressly stated under CA 2006, this may include situations where even though the director is not interested, but the interest arises between the company and a connected person. The general notice is likely to apply where a specific transaction or arrangement has not yet been identified but serves as an advance notice but with further details still to be provided by the director to the company. A General notice is notice given to the directors of a company to the effect that the director:

  - has an interest (as member, officer, employee or otherwise) in a specified body corporate or firm and is to be regarded as interested in any transaction or arrangement that may, after the date of the notice, be made with that body corporate or firm, or
  - is connected with a specified person (other than a body corporate or firm) and is to be regarded as interested in any transaction or arrangement that may, after the date of the notice, be made with that person. .

  The notice must state the nature and extent of the director's interest in the body corporate or firm or, as the case may be, the nature of his connection with the person. Further the general notice is not effective unless: (a) it is given at a meeting of the directors; or (b) the director takes reasonable steps to secure that it is brought up and read at the next meeting of the directors after it is given: CA 2006, s 185.

If a declaration of interest under s 177 proves to be, or becomes, inaccurate or incomplete, a further declaration must be made: CA 2006, s 177(3).

Any declaration required by s 177 must be made before the company enters into the transaction or arrangement: CA 2006, s 177(4).

14.99 There is a requirement to make a full and frank disclosure of the interest so that the board can make an informed decision.

Section 177 provides certain gateways to the duty of disclosure in existing transactions by the director to the company. It does not require a declaration of an interest of which the director is not aware or where the director is not aware of the transaction or arrangement in question: CA 2006, s 177(5).

For this purpose a director is treated as being aware of matters of which he ought reasonably to be aware.

14.100 A director need not declare an interest:

(a) if it cannot reasonably be regarded as likely to give rise to a conflict of interest: *Boardman v Phipps* [1967] 2 AC 46;

(b) if, or to the extent that, the other directors are already aware of it (and for this purpose the other directors are treated as aware of anything of which they ought reasonably to be aware): see *Re Marini Ltd* [2004] BCC 172; and *Lee Panavision Ltd v Lee Lighting Ltd* [1992] BCLC 22; *Runciman v Walter Runciman plc* [1992] BCLC 1084; and *MacPherson v European Strategic Bureau Ltd* [1999] 2 BCLC 203; or

(c) if, or to the extent that, it concerns terms of his service contract that have been or are to be considered:

   (i) by a meeting of the directors; or

   (ii) by a committee of the directors appointed for the purpose under the company's constitution: see *Runciman v Walter Runciman plc* [1992] BCLC 22: CA 2006, s 177(6).

It should also be noted that s 177 will not apply to a single member company: CA 2006, s 231.

14.101 A breach of s 177 is subject to civil consequences as set out in CA 2006, s 178 because it is a breach of a general duty as compared to existing transactions under CA 2006, s 182 which impose criminal sanctions.

The civil consequences that apply are that the proposed transaction or arrangement entered into is voidable at the company's option subject to any third party rights. The remedy of recission may be available as in the position at common law: *Breton v Fenn* (1887) 12 App Cas 652.

14.102 Another consequence is that provided the director declares his interest under CA 2006, s 177, s 180(1)(b) states that the 'the transaction or arrangement is not liable to be set aside by virtue of any common law rule or equitable principle requiring the consent or approval of the members of the company'. This has the effect that the company will not be able to set aside the transaction or arrangement. It may, however, be possible to establish further restrictions in the company's articles of association on the nature and extent of the disclosure and to which other body it should be made as additional protections for the company, subject to third party rights under CA 2006, s 40.

Attribution of liability

14.103 The scope of the doctrine of attribution of liability has been considered in the leading Supreme Court case of *Jetivia SA v Bilta (UK) Ltd* [2015] UKSC 23. In November 2009, Bilta was wound up compulsorily based on a winding up petition presented by HMRC, as a creditor. Subsequently, Bilta's liquidators issued proceedings against its two former directors ('directors'), and against Jetivia SA (a Swiss company) and Jetivia's chief executive ('appellants'). The allegations were that the directors and appellants were parties to an 'unlawful means conspiracy' to injure Bilta by a fraudulent scheme by the directors breaching their fiduciary duties in their capacity as Bilta's directors, and Jetivia and its chief executive in dishonestly assisting them in this process.

The nature of the conspiracy was that Bilta's directors caused Bilta to enter into transactions relating to the European Emissions Trading Scheme Allowances with various parties including Jetivia, and that these transactions amounted to a 'carousel fraud' (VAT fraud).

14.104 Bilta's liquidators claimed: (i) damages in tort from Bilta's directors, Jetivia and its chief executive; (ii) compensation based on constructive trust from Jetivia and its chief executive; and (iii) a contribution from each of the four defendants under s 213 of IA 1986 (fraudulent trading).

The appellants applied to strike out Bilta's claim on the basis of the defence of illegality and that s 213 of IA 1986 did not have extra territorial effect. The appellants claimed that Bilta's claim against its directors could not be upheld because of the criminal nature of Bilta's conduct while under the directors' control. They contended that, in effect, Bilta served as a vehicle for defrauding HMRC and the illegality defence prevented Bilta from suing the directors to recover the company's loss for the benefit of Bilta's creditors.

The case before the Supreme Court addressed three principal issues on appeal:

(1) The circumstances in which the knowledge of directors and other persons is attributed to a legal person such as a company ('Attribution').

(2) The purpose of the illegality defence and its application to Bilta's claims ('illegality defence'); and

(3) The extra territorial effect of s 213 of IA 1986 ('Extra Territorial Effect').

The Supreme Court held that the illegality defence could not bar Bilta's claims against the appellants. This was because the conduct of the directors could not be attributed to Bilta in respect of a claim against directors for breach of their duties. Further, s 213 of IA 1986 had extra territorial effect and could be invoked against the appellants.

Attribution

14.105 The Supreme Court's starting point on attribution was that that a company had a separate legal personality distinct from its shareholders: *Salomon v Salomon & Co Ltd* [1897] AC 22 and *Prest v Petrodel Resources Limited* [2013] 2 AC 415. A company has a real legal existence regardless of whether it was controlled by one or more persons.

However, as a company was not a natural person, it could not operate in vacuum: it must act through its directors and agents who control how the company will function in its day to day existence: *Aberdeen Railway Co v Blaikie Brothers* (1854) 1 Macq 461. They are also accountable to their company and owe fiduciary duties to the company through common law, equity and their general duties under the Companies Act 2006. The independent existence of the company signifies that the company can incur liabilities; it can enter into contracts; it can sue and be sued, whether in contract, tort or otherwise. Generally, directors can be described as the 'directing mind and will' of the company, in that their acts and state of mind may be attributed to the company through application of the agency principles at common law. However, this attribution rule was not of general application but was subject to limitations, and consideration must be given to the very specific and particular context or situation in which the acts and state of mind of the directors could be attributed to the company. In this regard, the court will consider the nature of the agency relationship between the company and its directors, and the nature of the principal's or the other party's claim.

14.106 In this case, Bilta was being used by its directors as a vehicle to commit a fraud on a third party causing losses to the company in breach of the directors' fiduciary duties to the company. Under these particular circumstances, it was not appropriate to attribute to the company the fraud to which the alleged breach of duty related, even if this was being practiced by a person whose acts and state of mind would be attributed to the company in other contexts. The Supreme Court identified three situations in a civil law context concerning attribution of knowledge to a company:

- In relation to a claim by a defrauded third party against the company. Here under the agency rules, the company should be treated as a perpetrator of the fraud. The acts and state of mind of the director are attributed to the company. The company is treated as an absent human owner of a business who leaves it to his managers to operate the business.
- In respect of a claim between the company against its directors for breach of a duty (whether fiduciary or otherwise), the delinquent directors should not be able to rely on their own breach of duty nor should their actions or state of mind be attributed to the company. It would also defeat the policy of the Companies Act provisions, which provisions were intended to protect the company including the interests of the company's creditors on where the company is insolvent or near insolvency – the 'statutory policy' argument put forward by Lords Toulson and Hodge.

  Where a company claims against a third party, whether or not there is attribution of the director's act or state of mind will depend upon the nature of the claim that is in issue.
- The application of the Attribution principles in the context of a company/director relationship makes it clear that there is no place to hide for a director who breaches his duties. The director cannot attribute his acts and state of mind as those of the company.

Illegality defence

14.107 The Supreme Court did not consider the *Jetivia* case as an appropriate forum to address fully the illegality defence and stated the urgency in reviewing this defence in any forthcoming case on this issue. Many of their Lordships comments were therefore obiter with differing perspectives of their Lordships as to the proper application of this defence. According to Lords Toulson and Hodge, the defence of illegality was a rule of public policy dependent upon the nature of the particular claim brought by the claimant and the relationship between the parties. Owing to the fiduciary duties of directors towards an insolvent company, directors must have proper regard to creditors' interests: a position addressed under s 172 of CA 2006 and at common law and equity: *Kinsella v Russell Kinsela Pty Ltd (*in liquidation) (1986) 4 NSWR 722; and *West Mercia Safetywear v Dodd* [1988] BCLC 250. The significant feature of the illegality defence was based on public policy grounds, and directors could not escape liability for breach of their fiduciary duty on the ground that they were in control of the company. A different perspective put forward by Lord Sumption was that the defence of illegality was a rule of law independent of any judicial value judgment about the balance of equities in each case. However, Lord Sumption did not agree with Lords Toulson and Hodge on the 'statutory policy' argument defeating the claim of illegality defence.

Section 213 of IA 1986 and its extra territorial effect

14.108 The Supreme Court unanimously held that that s 213 of IA 1986 (fraudulent trading) had extra territorial effect. Section 213 applies where any person who has knowingly become a party to the carrying of that company's business for a fraudulent purpose. The section applied to companies registered in Great Britain; however the effect of a winding up order was worldwide. It would seriously affect the efficient winding up of a British company if the jurisdiction of the court responsible for the winding up of an insolvent company did not extent to people and corporate bodies resident overseas who had been involved in the carrying on of the company's business.

- The doctrine of attribution is applied generally in a variety of situations and contexts under general agency principles. However, when attributing liability, consideration should be given to the particular factual context and circumstances in which the doctrine is being used. In the company context, a company has independent legal existence separate from its shareholders. However, the company cannot act or function alone: it acts through the directors and agents who control the company's operations. The issue is: where directors are in breach of their duties, can they attribute that breach and state of mind (if appropriate) to the company? In this regard, the attribution doctrine becomes more significant in the particular context of the company/director relationship. Where the company has been the victim of wrong-doing by its directors or of which directors had notice, the wrong-doing or knowledge of the directors cannot be attributed to the company as a defence to a claim brought against the directors by the company's liquidator, in the name of the company and/or on the company's behalf. This principle will apply even where the directors were the only directors and shareholders of the company, and even though the wrong-doing or knowledge of the directors may be attributed to the company in many other ways.

- The Supreme Court could not reach any unanimous opinion as to the proper approach which should be adopted to the illegality defence. Their Lordships held differing views and approaches to the defence, but agreed to defer further discussion when the appropriate case arises in the future. Lord Sumption was of the view that the law on the defence of illegality was established in Tinsley v Milligan [1994] 1 AC 340 and developed in *Les Laboratoires Servier v Apotex Inc* [2014] UKSC 55 and their consistency with the decision in *Hounga v Allen* [2014] UKSC 47. Lords Toulson and Hodge adopted the Court of Appeal's approach in *Tinsley* with *Hounga* as supporting the Court of Appeal's approach to the defence of illegality.

- Their Lordships also addressed the role of statutory policy with reference to the illegality defence, with Lords Toulson and Hodge dismissing the appellants' appeal based on statutory policy in that it would be contrary to statutory policy and duties contained under s 172(3) of CA 2006 if directors against whom a claim was brought under that provision, could rely on the illegality defence. The codification of general duties of directors derived from common law and equity and the statutory general duties of directors merely restated these rules. It would, therefore, be contrary to statutory policy to apply the illegality defence in this context.

  The Supreme Court was also divided in the proper analysis to be attributed to *Stone & Rolls Limited v Moore Stephens* [2009] 1 AC 1391. In *Stone & Rolls*, the majority of the Lords reached different conclusions as to how the illegality defence should be applied, including the difficulty of identifying the ratio of the case. However, there was agreement that *Stone & Rolls* was particular to its facts and should be confined to such particular facts and not looked at again. See too and *Safeway Stores Ltd v Twigger* [2010] EWCA Civ 1472.

- While the Supreme Court has to some extent clarified some of the law relating to the doctrine of Attribution and the contexts of its application where a company is involved, it has not clarified the scope and application of the illegality defence and its application in *Stone & Rolls*. The diverse views of their Lordships as to the proper approach will need much further analysis in a future case addressing this issue. *Stone & Rolls* will most probably be left to gather dust as confined to its particular facts with no pertinent ratio that serves any useful purpose. The attribution rules in the context of a company will bite most in the company/director relationship, where directors are in breach of their fiduciary duties, and they cannot exonerate themselves by attributing liability to the company, because the acts and state of mind are clearly not those of the company. Directors' duties should not, therefore, be taken lightly and a heavy burden is imposed on directors to act in the best interests of the company and its various stakeholders. Directors can no longer shield behind the company for their wrongful acts.

Civil consequences of breach of general duties

Application of CA 2006, s 178

14.109 The consequences of breach (or threatened breach) of CA 2006, ss 171–177 are the same as would apply if the corresponding common law rule or equitable principle applied: CA 2006, s 178(1).

The duties in those sections (with the exception of s 174 (duty to exercise reasonable care, skill and diligence)) are, accordingly, enforceable in the same way as any other fiduciary duty owed to a company by its directors: CA 2006, s 178(2). The exception in respect of the duty to exercise reasonable care, skill and diligence is that this is a common law duty and not a fiduciary one.

The application of s 178 is only to the general duties of directors under Ch 2 of Pt 10 to CA 2006 and not to Chs 3 or 4 of Pt 10 of CA 2006.

Damages

14.110 Most typically the remedy that will be sought by the company will be damages or compensation for the loss sustained. Often, precise measurement of damages or quantification of loss may be problematic for the courts. The damages sought may be in respect of breach of articles of association or failure by the director to comply with his service contract.

Injunction

14.111 The company may also seek an injunction for any threatened or continuing actions by the director concerned. This is often assessed on the balance of probabilities and may be effective to prevent the director from further damaging the company.

Setting aside the contract

14.112 A contract or arrangement entered into between the company and the director may be set aside where it breaches the no-conflict rule, provided it has not been ratified by the company.

Application of the constructive trust principle

14.113 In some cases the courts have treated directors as trustees of the company's property or asset particularly where the asset which belonged to the company becomes vested or in the possession of the director. In such situations, the court may treat the director as a constructive trustee so that the asset or property is restored back to the company; and the remedy of tracing may apply to bring the asset back to the company: *JJ Harrison (Properties) Ltd v Harrison* [2002] 1 BCLC 162. Where the asset is with a third party, the court may order the director to restore the asset to the company concerned: *Bairstow v Queen Moat Houses plc* [2001] 2 BCLC 531.

The nature of proprietary versus personal interests

14.114 In other situations, the courts may consider the remedy of accounting for profits (as recission will not be available) made by the director from a transaction with a third party, which profit may have been made by the company had it entered into the transaction. This may arise from a breach of fiduciary duty in receiving benefits from third parties or breach of the no-conflict duty. In these cases, the company will not need to demonstrate proof of loss or damage but to require to account for the profits made from the transaction: *Murad v Al-Saraj* [2005] EWCA Civ 959; *Regal (Hastings) Ltd v Gulliver* [1967] 2 AC 134. In respect of accounting for profits, the courts have considered whether the duty to account is proprietary or a personal duty.

14.115 This section examines the leading Supreme Court decision of *FHR European Ventures LLP and others v Cedar Capital Partners LLC* [2014] UKSC 45, and the position after this case.

Over the years, the courts have considered the issue whether a bribe or secret commission received by an agent could be held on trust for his principal, or whether the principal merely had a claim for equitable compensation in a sum equal to the value of the bribe or commission? Judicial attitudes had revealed a number of inconsistent decisions over 200 years. There are significant legal and practical effects flowing from this question. If the bribe or commission is held on trust, then the principal has a proprietary claim to it. However, if the principal merely has a claim for equitable compensation, then the principal has no proprietary claim. The effect is twofold: first, if the agent becomes insolvent, a proprietary claim would give the principal priority over the agent's unsecured creditors; and if the principal only had a claim for compensation, he would rank equally with other unsecured creditors. Secondly, where the principal has a proprietary claim to the bribe or commission, he may trace and follow it in equity; and if the claim is for equitable compensation, the principal has no right to trace in equity.

14.116 A number of 19th century cases considered the position of an agent or fiduciary who made an unauthorised profit by taking advantage of an opportunity which came to his attention as a result of his agency, and some judicial decisions ruled that the equitable rule applied so that the profit was held on trust for the principal: see for example, *Carter v Palmer* (1842) 8 Cl & F 657; *Bowes v City of Toronto* (1858) 11 Moo PC 463; and *Bagnall v Carlton* (1877) 6 Ch D 371.

Where an agent acquires a benefit which came to his notice as a result of his fiduciary position, or pursuant to an opportunity which results from his fiduciary position, the general equitable rule ('the Rule') is that he is to be treated as having acquired the benefit on behalf of his principal by way of constructive trust, so it is beneficially owned by the principal. The Rule applies to both bribes and secret commissions received by the agent. The principal, therefore, has a proprietary claim against the agent

In the leading case of *FHR European Ventures LLP and others v Cedar Capital Partners LLC* [2014] UKSC 45, the issue before the Supreme Court was whether an agent who received a secret commission held the sum paid on constructive trust for his principal(s), giving rise to proprietary rights, or whether the principal merely had a claim for equitable compensation in a sum equal to the value of the bribe or commission?

On 22 December 2004, FHR European Ventures LLP purchased the issued share capital of Monte Carlo Grand Hotel SAM from Monte Carlo Grand Hotel Ltd ('the Seller') for €211.5m. The purchase was a joint venture between the claimants in these proceedings, for whom FHR was the vehicle. Cedar Capital Partners LLC provided consultancy services to the hotel industry, and it had acted as the claimants' agent in negotiating the purchase. Cedar accordingly owed fiduciary duties to the claimants. Cedar had also entered into an 'Exclusive Brokerage Agreement' with the Seller, which provided for the payment to Cedar of a €10m fee following a successful conclusion of the sale and purchase of the issued shared capital of Monte Carlo Grand Hotel SAM. The Seller paid Cedar €10m on or about 7 January 2005.

On 23 November 2009 the claimants began these proceedings for recovery of the sum of €10m from Cedar. The main issue at trial was whether Cedar had made proper disclosure to the claimants of the Exclusive Brokerage Agreement. Simon J found against Cedar on that issue, and made a declaration of liability for breach of fiduciary duty on the part of Cedar for having failed to obtain the claimants' fully informed consent in respect of the €10m, and ordered Cedar to pay that sum to the claimants. However, he refused to grant the claimants a proprietary remedy in respect of the monies. However, Simon J held that there was no constructive trust giving rise to a proprietary right; the claim gave rise only to a personal remedy.

The claimants successfully appealed to the Court of Appeal, who made a declaration that Cedar received the €10m fee on constructive trust for the claimants absolutely. The CA overruled Simon J and held that in receiving the secret commission, Cedar had exploited an opportunity properly belonging to the consortium. Accordingly the sum was held on constructive trust for the consortium, giving rise to the consortium's consequential proprietary rights in respect of the €10m secret commission. Cedar appealed to the Supreme Court on this issue.

The Supreme Court unanimously dismissed the appeal. Lord Neuberger gave the judgment of the court. Where an agent acquired a benefit which came to his notice as a result of his fiduciary position, or pursuant to an opportunity which resulted from his fiduciary position, the general equitable rule ('the Rule') was that he was to be treated as having acquired the benefit on behalf of his principal, so it was beneficially owned by the principal. The dispute in this case was the extent to which the Rule applied where the benefit was a bribe or secret commission obtained by an agent in breach of his fiduciary duty to his principal. While it was not possible, as a matter of pure legal authority, to identify any plainly right or plainly wrong answer to the issue of the extent of the Rule, considerations of practicality and principle supported the case that a bribe or secret commission accepted by an agent was held on trust for his principal.

The only point on this appeal was whether the claimants were entitled to the proprietary remedy in respect of the €10m received by Cedar from the Seller. According to the Supreme Court, the following principles were not in doubt:

(1) An agent owed a fiduciary duty to his principal because he was someone who had undertaken to act for or on behalf of his principal in a particular matter in circumstances which gave rise to a relationship of trust and confidence.

(2) As a result, an agent must not make a profit out of his trust, and must not place himself in a position in which his duty and his interest may conflict (see *Boardman v Phipps* [1967] 2 AC 46).

(3) A fiduciary who acted for two principals with potentially conflicting interests without the informed consent of both was in breach of the obligation of undivided loyalty, by putting himself in a position where his duty to one principal may conflict with his duty to the other (see Millett LJ in *Bristol and West Building Society v Mothew* [1998] Ch 1.

Another well-established principle, which applied where an agent received a benefit in breach of his fiduciary duty, was that the agent was obliged to account to the principal for such a benefit, and to pay, in effect, a sum equal to profit by way of equitable compensation: see *Regal (Hastings) Ltd v Gulliver* [1967] 2 AC 134. The principal's right to seek an account undoubtedly gave him a right in equitable compensation in respect of the bribe or secret commission, which equalled the quantum of that bribe or commission. In cases to which the Rule applied, the principal had a proprietary remedy in addition to his personal remedy against the agent, and the principal could elect between the two remedies.

What was in dispute was the extent to which the Rule applied where the benefit was a bribe or secret commission obtained by an agent in breach of his fiduciary duty to his principal. The appellant contended that the Rule should not apply to a bribe or secret commission paid to an agent, because it was not a benefit which can properly be said to be the property of the principal. The respondents argued that the Rule did apply to bribes or secret commissions received by an agent, because, in any case where an agent received a benefit, which was, or resulted from, a breach the fiduciary duty owed to his principal, the agent held the benefit on trust for the principal.

According to the Supreme Court, it was not possible to identify any plainly right or plainly wrong answer to the issue of the extent of the Rule, as a matter of pure legal authority. The respondents' formulation of the Rule had the merit of simplicity: any benefit acquired by an agent as a result of his agency and in breach of his fiduciary duty was held on trust for the principal. In contrast, the appellant's position was more likely to result in uncertainty. Wider policy considerations also supported the respondents' case that bribes and secret commissions received by an agent should be treated as the property of his principal, rather than merely giving rise to a claim for equitable compensation. Bribes and secret commissions undermined trust in the commercial world, and one would expect the law to be particularly stringent in relation to a claim against an agent who has received a bribe or secret commission.

The argument that the respondents' version of the Rule would tend to prejudice the agent's unsecured creditors had limited force in the context of a bribe or secret commission. In the first place, the proceeds of a bribe or secret commission consisted of property which should not be in the agent's estate at all. Secondly, the bribe or commission would very often have reduced the benefit from the relevant transaction which the principal would have obtained, and therefore could fairly be said to be his property. Finally, it was just that a principal whose agent had obtained a bribe or secret commission should be able to trace the proceeds of the bribe or commission into other assets and to follow them into the hands of knowing recipients.

Considerations of practicality and principle supported the case that a bribe or secret commission accepted by an agent was held on trust for his principal. While the position was less clear when one examined the decided cases, taken as a whole the authorities supported the respondents' case. The cases, with the exception of *Tyrrell v Bank of London* (1862) 10 HL Cas 26, were consistently in favour of bribes or secret commissions being held on trust for the principal or other beneficiary until the decision in *Metropolitan Bank v Heiron* (1880) 5 Ex D 319, which was then followed in *Lister & Co v Stubbs* (1890) 45 Ch D 1. The domestic cases subsequent to *Lister* were explicable on the basis that the issue was either conceded, or decided on the basis that *Lister* was binding. The decision in *Tyrrell* should not stand in the way of the conclusion that the law took a wrong turn in *Heiron* and *Lister*, and that those decisions, and any subsequent decisions in so far as they relied on or followed *Heiron* and *Lister*, should be treated as overruled including *Powell & Thomas v Evan Jones & Co* [1905] 1 KB 11. The Supreme Court also overruled the Court of Appeal decision in *Sinclair Investments (UK) Ltd v Versailles Trade Finance Ltd* [2012] Ch 453.

The decision in *FHR* effectively allows the principal's claim to rank ahead of ordinary unsecured creditors based on the proprietary claim. The principal can also trace the proceeds of the bribe or secret commission into the hands of a third party, namely those who are not bona fide purchasers for value without notice. The Supreme Court reached the result of prevent the agent from benefiting from the bribe or secret commission which he had obtained in breach of his fiduciary duty and obligation towards the principal, and instead determined that the principal should obtain this benefit rather than set out the circumstances in which the principal should benefit.

Cases within more than one of the general duties

14.117 Except as otherwise provided, more than one of the general duties may apply in any given case: CA 2006, s 179.

More than one of the general duties under Pt 10 of CA 2006 may apply in a case

There have been several cases where breaches of more than one of the general duties of directors has been alleged. This arose in *Madoff Securities International Ltd (in liquidation) v Raven* [2013] EWHC 3147 where various breaches of general duties were alleged against the directors. Popplewell J held that it was settled law that a director owed a fiduciary duty to a company to act in what he considered to be the interests of the company. The test was a subjective one. The directors of a company were in a similar position in respect of the company's property as trustees. The predominant interests to which the directors of a solvent company had to have regard were the interests of the shareholders as a whole, present and future. A trustee who knowingly permitted a co-trustee to commit a breach of trust was also in breach of trust.

On the issue of the exercise of skill, care and diligence, where a director failed to address his mind to the question of whether a transaction was in the interests of a company, he was not thereby, and without more, liable for the consequences of the transaction. The court would ask whether an honest and intelligent man in the position of a director of the company concerned could, in the whole of the existing circumstances, have reasonably believed that the transaction was for the benefit of the company. The standard of care required of a director was to be determined, not only subjectively, by reference to his particular knowledge, skill and experience, but on general objective criteria.

> On the issue of exercise of powers for proper purposes, a director owed a fiduciary duty to exercise the powers conferred on him by the constitution for the purposes for which they were conferred. The court would apply a four-stage test, which involved identifying:
>
> (i) the power whose exercise was in question;
>
> (ii) the proper purpose for which such power was conferred;
>
> (iii) the substantial purpose for which the power had been exercised; and
>
> (iv) whether that purpose had been proper.
>
> A power might be exercised for an improper purpose notwithstanding that the directors bona fide believed it was being exercised in the company's best interest.
>
> Popplewell J also held that liability was fault based: a director's liability in relation to misapplication of a company's property by exercising a power otherwise than that for which it was conferred could not arise unless he knew that it was an improper purpose or of the facts which made the purpose improper. A director had a duty to exercise reasonable care, skill and diligence. A limited company, not in liquidation, might not return assets to its shareholders except by way of a reduction of capital approved by the court. A company should not make a distribution except out of the profits available for that purpose. A transaction which offended that principle was to be treated as ultra vires.

Consent, approval or authorisation by members

14.118 In a case where:

(a) s 175 of CA 2006 (duty to avoid conflicts of interest) is complied with by authorisation by the directors; or

(b) s 177 (duty to declare interest in proposed transaction or arrangement) is complied with,

the transaction or arrangement is not liable to be set aside by virtue of any common law rule or equitable principle requiring the consent or approval of the members of the company.

This is without prejudice to any enactment, or provision of the company's constitution, requiring such consent or approval: CA 2006, s 180(1).

14.119 The application of the general duties is not affected by the fact that the case also falls within Chapter 4 (transactions requiring approval of members), except that where that chapter applies and:

(a) approval is given under that chapter; or

(b) the matter is one as to which it is provided that approval is not needed,

it is not necessary also to comply with s 175 (duty to avoid conflicts of interest) or s 176 (duty not to accept benefits from third parties): CA 2006, s 180(2).

14.120 Compliance with the general duties does not remove the need for approval under any applicable provision of Chapter 4 (transactions requiring approval of members): CA 2006, s 180(3).

The general duties:

(a) have effect subject to any rule of law enabling the company to give authority, specifically or generally, for anything to be done (or omitted) by the directors, or any of them, that would otherwise be a breach of duty; and

(b) where the company's articles contain provisions for dealing with conflicts of interest, are not infringed by anything done (or omitted) by the directors, or any of them, in accordance with those provisions: CA 2006, s 180(4).

Otherwise, the general duties have effect (except as otherwise provided or the context otherwise requires) notwithstanding any enactment or rule of law: CA 2006, s 180(5).

Declaration of interest in existing transaction or arrangement

14.121 Where a director of a company is in any way, directly or indirectly, interested in a transaction or arrangement that has been entered into by the company, he must declare the nature and extent of the interest to the other directors in accordance with s 182: CA 2006, s 182(1). This duty applies to existing transactions or arrangements which a director has recently concluded or acquired. It applies to concluded arrangements or transactions unlike s 177 of CA 2006, which refers to proposed arrangements or transactions.

Section 182 does not apply if or to the extent that the interest has been declared under s 177 (duty to declare interest in proposed transaction or arrangement).

14.122 Section 182 sets out three methods for declaration of existing transactions. The declaration must be made:

(a) at a meeting of the directors; or

(b) by notice in writing (see s 184); or

(c) by general notice (see s 185): s 182(2) CA 2006.

If a declaration of interest under this section proves to be, or becomes, inaccurate or incomplete, a further declaration must be made: s 182(3) CA 2006.

14.123 Any declaration required by this section must be made as soon as is reasonably practicable.

Failure to comply with this requirement does not affect the underlying duty to make the declaration: CA 2006, s 182(4).

This obligation applies also to shadow directors: CA 2006, s 187(1) but with adaptations. The method of giving notice for declaration at a meeting of directors does not apply. Further, the notice to be given at or brought up and read at meeting of directors does not apply to a shadow director. The general notice by a shadow director is not effective unless given by notice in writing in accordance with s 184: CA 2006, s 187(2)–(4).

A failure by a director to disclose an interest in a transaction, renders the transaction voidable at the option of the company: *Hely-Hutchinson v Brayhead Ltd* [1967] 3 All ER 98; and *Guinness plc v Saunders* [1990] 1 All ER 652 per Lord Goff.

> ***A director owed a duty to declare his interest in a transaction to the company***
>
> In *Coleman Taymar Ltd v Oakes* [2001] 2 BCLC 749, Judge Robert Reid QC stated that CA 2006, s 182, which imposed a statutory duty on a director of a company who was directly or indirectly interested in a contract or a proposed contract with the company to disclose his interest at a meeting of the directors of the company and rendered him liable to a fine for failure to do so, did not give the company a separate right of action for damages against the director. Any right of action arose from the breach of fiduciary duty and not from the section. Further, a company was entitled to elect whether to claim damages or an account of profits against a director for breach of his fiduciary duty.

14.124 Section 182 of CA 2006 does not require a declaration of an interest of which the director is not aware, or where the director is not aware of the transaction or arrangement in question.

For this purpose a director is treated as being aware of matters of which he ought reasonably to be aware: CA 2006, s 182(5).

A director need not declare an interest under s 182:

(a) if it cannot reasonably be regarded as likely to give rise to a conflict of interest;

(b) if, or to the extent that, the other directors are already aware of it (and for this purpose the other directors are treated as aware of anything of which they ought reasonably to be aware); or

(c) if, or to the extent that, it concerns terms of his service contract that have been or are to be considered:

  (i) by a meeting of the directors; or

  (ii) by a committee of the directors appointed for the purpose under the company's constitution: CA 2006, s 182(6).

Offence of failure to declare interest

14.125 A director who fails to comply with the requirements of CA 2006, s 182 (declaration of interest in existing transaction or arrangement) commits an offence: CA 2006, s 183(1).

A person guilty of an offence under s 183 is liable:

(a) on conviction on indictment, to a fine;

(b) on summary conviction, to a fine not exceeding the statutory maximum: CA 2006, s 183(2).

Declaration made by notice in writing

14.126 Section 184 of CA 2006 applies to a declaration of interest made by notice in writing: CA 2006, s 184(1).

The director must send the notice to the other directors: CA 2006, s 184(2).

The notice may be sent in hard copy form or, if the recipient has agreed to receive it in electronic form, in an agreed electronic form: CA 2006, s 184(3).

The notice may be sent:

(a) by hand or by post; or

(b) if the recipient has agreed to receive it by electronic means, by agreed electronic means: CA 2006, s 184(4).

Where a director declares an interest by notice in writing in accordance with this section:

(a) the making of the declaration is deemed to form part of the proceedings at the next meeting of the directors after the notice is given; and

(b) the provisions of CA 2006, s 248 (minutes of meetings of directors) apply as if the declaration had been made at that meeting: CA 2006, s 184(5).

General notice treated as sufficient declaration

14.127 General notice in accordance with CA 2006, s 185 is a sufficient declaration of interest in relation to the matters to which it relates: CA 2006, s 185(1).

General notice is notice given to the directors of a company to the effect that the director:

(a) has an interest (as member, officer, employee or otherwise) in a specified body corporate or firm and is to be regarded as interested in any transaction or arrangement that may, after the date of the notice, be made with that body corporate or firm; or

(b) is connected with a specified person (other than a body corporate or firm) and is to be regarded as interested in any transaction or arrangement that may, after the date of the notice, be made with that person: CA 2006, s 185(2).

The notice must state the nature and extent of the director's interest in the body corporate or firm or, as the case may be, the nature of his connection with the person: CA 2006, s 185(3).

General notice is not effective unless:

(a) it is given at a meeting of the directors; or

(b) the director takes reasonable steps to secure that it is brought up and read at the next meeting of the directors after it is given: CA 2006, s 185(4).

Declaration of interest in case of company with sole director

14.128 Where a declaration of interest under CA 2006, s 182 (duty to declare interest in existing transaction or arrangement) is required of a sole director of a company that is required to have more than one director:

(a) the declaration must be recorded in writing;

(b) the making of the declaration is deemed to form part of the proceedings at the next meeting of the directors after the notice is given; and

(c) the provisions of CA 2006, s 248 (minutes of meetings of directors) apply as if the declaration had been made at that meeting: CA 2006, s 186(1).

Nothing in s 186 affects the operation of s 231 (contract with sole member who is also a director: terms to be set out in writing or recorded in minutes): CA 2006, s 186(2).

Declaration of interest in existing transaction by shadow director

14.129 The provisions of CA 2006, Pt 10, Ch 3 relating to the duty under s 182 (duty to declare interest in existing transaction or arrangement) apply to a shadow director as to a director, but with the following adaptations (CA 2006, s 187(1)):

- Section 182(2)(a) (declaration at meeting of directors) does not apply: CA 2006, s 187(2).
- In s 185 (general notice treated as sufficient declaration), CA 2006, s 185(4) (notice to be given at or brought up and read at meeting of directors) does not apply: CA 2006, s 187(3).
- General notice by a shadow director is not effective unless given by notice in writing in accordance with s 184: CA 2006, s 187(4).

Ratification of acts giving rise to liability

Ratification of acts of directors

14.130 Section 239 of CA 2006 applies to the ratification by a company of conduct by a director amounting to negligence, default, breach of duty or breach of trust in relation to the company: CA 2006, s 239(1). The decision of the company to ratify such conduct must be made by resolution of the members of the company: CA 2006, s 239(2).

Where the resolution is proposed as a written resolution, neither the director (if a member of the company) nor any member connected with him is an eligible member: CA 2006, s 239(3).

14.131 Where the resolution is proposed at a meeting, it is passed only if the necessary majority is obtained disregarding votes in favour of the resolution by the director (if a member of the company) and any member connected with him. This does not prevent the director or any such member from attending, being counted towards the quorum and taking part in the proceedings at any meeting at which the decision is considered: CA 2006, s 239(4).

For the purposes of CA 2006, s 239:

(a) 'conduct' includes acts and omissions;

(b) 'director' includes a former director;

(c) a shadow director is treated as a director; and

(d) in CA 2006, s 252 (meaning of 'connected person'), s 239(3) (exclusion of person who is himself a director) does not apply: CA 2006, s 239(5).

14.132 Nothing in s 239 affects:

(a) the validity of a decision taken by unanimous consent of the members of the company; or

(b) any power of the directors to agree not to sue, or to settle or release a claim made by them on behalf of the company: CA 2006, s 239(6).

Section 239 of CA 2006 does not affect any other enactment or rule of law imposing additional requirements for valid ratification or any rule of law as to acts that are incapable of being ratified by the company: CA 2006, s 239(7).

Where the interests of creditors intrude on insolvency or doubtful solvency, a sole shareholder owes a duty to the shareholder and cannot use CA 2006, s 239 to ratify his own breach

In *Goldtrail Travel Ltd v Aydin* [2014] EWHC 1587, a holiday tour operator which had been established for 15 years went into liquidation by its sole director and shareholder, Aydin. The liquidator brought an action against Aydin for misapplication of corporate funds and breaches of his fiduciary duties to the company. Rose J held that a company's sole shareholder could not ratify his own misconduct as the company's sole director in respect of misapplication of corporate funds and breaches of his fiduciary duties. Aydin should have considered the interests of creditors particularly where the company was near insolvency or of doubtful solvency: *Vivendi SA v Richards* [2013] EWHC 3006. Further, Aydin could not use CA 2006, s 239 to ratify his conduct. Aydin could not also rely on the *Duomatic* principle to ratify his own breaches: see *Ultraframe (UK) Ltd v Fielding* [2004] RPC 24.

Rose J also held that the sole director could not take advantage of CA 2006, s 175 ('Duty to avoid conflicts of interest'), which provides that the duty to avoid a conflict of interest is not infringed if the director is authorised by the directors to put himself into the situation where the conflict arises. However, s 175(6) provides that authorisation for that purpose is effective only if the matter was agreed to by the directors without counting the director in question or would have been agreed to if his vote was not counted. As Mr Aydin was the only director, it was not possible for him to take advantage of the authorisation provision.

See too: *Bilta (UK) Ltd (in liquidation) v Nazir (No 2)* [2013] EWCA Civ 968, where the Court of Appeal stated that a sole director/shareholder owed to the company the fiduciary duties set out in s 172 of CA 2006 and could not use his control of the company to ratify his fraudulent acts against the company, particularly where the interests of creditors would be prejudiced: see Companies Act s 239(3) and (7).

Relief from liability

14.133 Where directors or other officers are found to be in breach of their duties, apart from seeking relief from liability from the shareholders, they may be able to apply to the court to seek relief from the impact of Pt 10 of CA 2006.

Section 1157 of CA 2006 is concerned with the power of the courts to grant relief in certain circumstances. It states that if in proceedings for negligence, default, breach of duty or breach of trust against:

(a) an officer of a company, or

(b) a person employed by a company as auditor (whether he is or is not an officer of the company),

it appears to the court hearing the case, that the officer or person is or may be liable but that he acted honestly and reasonably, and that having regard to all the circumstances of the case (including those connected with his appointment) he ought fairly to be excused, the court may relieve him, either wholly or in part, from his liability on such terms as it thinks fit: CA 2006, s 1157(1).

14.134 Further, If any such officer or person has reason to apprehend that a claim will or might be made against him in respect of negligence, default, breach of duty or breach of trust:

(a) he may apply to the court for relief, and

(b) the court has the same power to relieve him as it would have had if it had been a court before which proceedings against him for negligence, default, breach of duty or breach of trust had been brought: CA 2006, s 1157(2).

Where a case to which s 1157(1) applies is being tried by a judge with a jury, the judge, after hearing the evidence, may, if he is satisfied that the defendant (in Scotland, the defender) ought in pursuance of s 1157(1) to be relieved either in whole or in part from the liability sought to be enforced against him, withdraw the case from the jury and forthwith direct judgment to be entered for the defendant (in Scotland, grant decree of absolvitor) on such terms as to costs (in Scotland, expenses) or otherwise as the judge may think proper: CA 2006, s 1157(3).

14.135 The effect of s 1157 is to provide relief to a director or officer from past acts or future acts. It provides a wide discretion to the court to provide partial, full or such relief as the court thinks fit. The starting point is that there has been negligence, default, breach of duty or breach of trust on the part of the director or officer in connection with the company's affairs. The director must show as an absolute precondition that he acted honestly and reasonably: *Bairstow v Queens Moat Houses plc* [2001] 2 BCLC 531, where on the facts the directors had acted dishonestly in falsifying the company's accounts, it was not open to the court to find aspects of honesty. Further, as Lord Nicholls stated in *Royal Brunei Airlines Sdn Bhd v Tan* [1995] 3 All ER 97 at 106:

> 'The standard of what constitutes honest conduct is not subjective. Honesty is not an optional scale, with higher or lower values according to the moral standards of each individual. If a person knowingly appropriates another's property, he will not escape a finding of dishonesty simply because he sees nothing wrong in such behaviour.'

Although the question as to whether a director has acted honestly is tested subjectively, the question whether he has acted reasonably is an objective one: *Coleman Taymar Ltd v Oakes* [2001] 2 BCLC 749.

14.136 See too *Inland Revenue Commissioners v Richmond; Re Loquitur Ltd* [2003] 2 BCLC 442.

The court will have regard to all the circumstances of the case in assessing whether the director 'ought fairly to be excused' from liability. In *Ultraframe (UK) Ltd v Fielding* [2005] EWHC 1638, Lewison J stated that 'the expression "the case" does not mean "the litigation"; but primarily means the circumstances in which the breach took place ... [and] include a review of the director's stewardship of the company; but they do not involve a more wide-ranging inquiry into the director's character and behaviour'.

Section 1157 of CA 2006 applies to a breach of director's duty of skill and care.

In respect of the concept of reasonableness, *Equitable Life Assurance Society v Bowley* [2004] 1 BCLC 180, the case concerned the liability of a non-executive director in an interlocutory application found to have been in breach of the common law duty of skill and care, and whether s 1157 applied to such duty. Langley J held that s 1157 applied to a breach of director's duty of skill and care. The court would as a minimum have to be satisfied that the officer had acted 'reasonably' and that it was aware of 'all the circumstances' which enabled a determination to be made.

The duty of care that a director owed to a company at common law of exercising reasonable skill and care was equivalent to that in s 214(4) of the Insolvency Act 1986: *Re D'Jan of London Limited* [1994] 1 BCLC 561.

Section 1157 of CA 2006 will have no application where there are third party claims against the director. In *Customs and Excise Commissioners v Hedon Alpha Limited* [1981] 2 All ER 697, Stephenson LJ stated that although s 1157 of CA 2006 was expressed in wide language, in its context of company law and on its true construction the only proceedings for which relief under s 1157 could be claimed were proceedings against a director by, on behalf of or for the benefit of his company for breach of his duty to the company as a director, or penal proceedings against a director for a breach of the CA 2006. Section 1157(1) accordingly did not apply to claims by a third party to the company against a director to enforce a civil liability, for example, a debt.

Section 1157 CA 2006 will not be able to relieve a director who is involved in proceedings such as wrongful trading. In *Re Produce Marketing Consortium Ltd* [1989] 1 WLR 745, Knox J decided that s 1157 of CA 2006 did not apply to relieve a director for proceedings under s 214 of IA 1986.

Section 1157 of CA 2006 will not be able to relieve a director from liability in respect of ss 216 and 217 of IA 1986 in using a phoenix name: *First Independent Factors & Finance Ltd v Mountford* [2008] 2 BCLC 297. The relief is also not available in respect of disqualification proceedings under s 15 of IA 1986 (liability of disqualified person for debts incurred while disqualified): *IRC v McEntaggart* [2006] 1 BCLC 476.

The court may be unwilling to relieve a director from liability under s 1157 where he has obtained a personal gain or benefit from his actions. In *a Flap Envelope Co Ltd* [2004] 1 BCLC 64, Jonathan Crow J was of the view that even if a director showed that he acted honestly and reasonably, it would require an extremely powerful case to persuade the court to exercise its discretion under s 1157 to relieve him from liability if he obtained a material personal benefit through the breach of duty. See too *Re Marini Ltd* [2004] BCC 172.

The court also may not provide relief to a director under s 1157 at the expense of the company's creditors. In *Inn Spirit Ltd v Burns* [2002] 2 BCLC 780, where Rimer J stated that the court should not excuse directors from liability at the creditors' expense. Similarly, in *First Global Media Group Ltd v Larkin* [2003] EWCA Civ 1765, the Court of Appeal stated it was out of the question to fairly excuse the director from repaying a loan to a creditor. Further, in *Queensway Systems Ltd v Walker* [2007] 2 BCLC 577, Paul Girolami J stated that the defendants who had misapplied company funds were not entitled to be relieved of liability under s 1157 of CA 2006, because although they had not acted dishonestly, they had not acted reasonably and the circumstances were not such that they ought fairly to be excused liability. In particular, ignorance of a person's duties as a director and/or that the payments could involve a contravention of the CA 2006, or a misapplication of company funds was not a reason for excusing a person from liability, and to do so would prejudice the company's creditors.

Certain factors may apply in considering relief from liability under s 1157

The Northampton Regional Livestock Centre Co Ltd v Cowling [2014] EWHC 30 (QB), involved a director of the company who had placed himself in a position of conflict by acting for both the vendor and purchaser in a commercial property transaction.

Green J considered the application of CA 2006, s 1157 to grant a director relief from liability in respect of negligence, default, breach of duty or breach of trust. He considered the following factors to be appropriate in granting relief:

- good faith and honesty;
- claimant's allegations against the director;
- whether the director sought board approval;
- the severity of the breach involved;
- economic reality of the transaction concerned; and
- the probability of material loss being caused to the company.

Complete inactivity by a director will be a bar to relief under CA 2006, s 1157

In *Finch v Finch* [2015] (13 August 2015), Judge Hodge QC refused to grant relief to the director under s.1157 CA 2006 owing to inactivity on the part of the director, and his failure to seek any legal advice on his duties as director. The judge found that Mr Finch has not acted honestly or reasonably, nor ought he fairly to be excused. Nor should such relief be granted to Mrs Finch, who completely abrogated the discharge of her duties as director, leaving everything to her husband. As Briggs J observed in *Lexi Holdings Plc v Luqman* [2007] EWHC 2652 (Ch) at [224]: 'Complete inactivity as a director is by definition unreasonable'. This case serves as a warning to directors that they cannot completely abrogate or delegate their duties to others and escape liability. Directors need to demonstrate a certain degree of proactivity and understanding of their duties and responsibilities and to discharge their duties effectively. They must demonstrate that they acted honestly and in good faith and did all that could reasonably be expected of them in the circumstances in order to be considered for relief under s.1157.

Dishonesty will be a bar to any relief under CA 2006, s 1157

In the Scottish case of *McGivney Construction Ltd v Kaminski* [2015] CSOH 107, Lord Woolman refused to grant relief to a director on the basis that the director did not act honestly in connection with misappropriation of a Council contract. The test of honesty was to be judged objectively: *Royal Brunei Airlines* v *Tan Sdn. Bhd.* [1995] 2 AC 378, 389B per Lord Nichols. In McGivney, Lord Woolman stated that: 'no honest man could think that it was appropriate for a director and foreman to poach a sizeable contract'. Further, there must be a strong case to allow relief if the director has obtained personal benefit, even if it is relatively trivial: *Towers* v *Premier Waste Management Ltd* CA [2012] BCC 72.

Checklist: directors' general duties

14.137 *The checklist considers the general duties of directors under Pt 10 of CA 2006 based on some of the fiduciary and common law duties of directors which have been codified. Those duties which have not been codified remain to be assessed through developments in common law and equity.*

No	Issue	Reference
1	Directors have sometimes been likened to trustees fulfilling trusteeship and fiduciary duties in the performance of their duties	*Re Forest of Dean Coal Mining Co* (1878) 10 Ch D 450
2	Directors primary duty is to the company and not to individual shareholders generally	CA 2006, s 170
3	In some situations directors may owe duties towards individual shareholders particularly where 'special circumstances' may exist to demonstrate such relationship	*Peskin v Anderson* [2001] 1 BCLC 372

No	Issue	Reference
4	Some of the general duties of directors apply to former directors particularly the duty to avoid conflicts of interest; and the duty not to accept benefits from third parties	CA 2006, ss 175, 176
5	The general duties are based on certain common law rules and equitable principles as they apply in relation to directors	CA 2006, s 170(3)
6	Directors must act within their powers by: (a) Acting in accordance with the company's constitution; and (b) Exercising powers for the purposes conferred	CA 2006, s 171 *Eclairs Group Ltd v JKX Oil & Gas plc; Glengary Overseas Ltd v JKX Oil & Gas plc* [2015] UKSC 71
7	Directors have a duty to promote the company's success – to act in good faith in considering in good faith what would most likely promote the long term success of the company for the members having regard to the six factors	CA 2006, s 172
8	Directors must exercise independent judgment in the performance of their functions	CA 2006, s 173
9	Directors must exercise reasonable care, skill and diligence – the test is both subjective and objective (based on IA 1986, s 214)	CA 2006, s 174
10	A director must avoid conflicts of interest situation	CA 2006, s 175
11	A director must not accept benefits from third parties	CA 2006, s 176
12	A director must declare interest in a proposed transaction or arrangement	CA 2006, s 177
13	Certain civil consequences flow from breach of the general duties with the application of the common law and equitable principles	CA 2006, s 178
14	Where an agent acquires a benefit which came to his notice as a result of his fiduciary position, or pursuant to an opportunity which results from his fiduciary position, the general equitable rule ('the Rule') is that he is to be treated as having acquired the benefit on behalf of his principal, so it is beneficially owned by the principal. The Rule applies to both bribes or secret commissions received by the agent	*FHR European Ventures LLP v Cedar Capital Partners LLC* [2014] UKSC 45
15	A director has a duty to declare his interest in an existing transaction or arrangement	CA 2006, s 182
16	In some situations, it may be possible to ratify act of directors amounting to negligence, default, breach of duty or breach of trust in relation to the company	CA 2006, s 239

No	Issue	Reference
17	Where directors or other officers are found to be in breach of their duties, apart from seeking relief from liability from the shareholders, they may be able to apply to the court to seek relief from the impact of Pt 10 of CA 2006 in respect of negligence, default, breach of duty or breach of trust provided they acted honestly and reasonably	CA 2006, s 1157

15 Directors: specific duties

Contents

Introduction

15.1 This chapter addresses the specific duties of directors and their liabilities under the CA 2006. It is concerned with specific transactions between directors and the company that require approval from the shareholders, rather than mere disclosure by directors at the board meeting. The requirement for shareholder approval strengthens the system of corporate governance. It enables legal controls and mechanisms to be in place to regulate the conduct and actions of directors; and ensure that they do not misuse the trust that shareholders have placed on them.

15.2 Under the UK corporate governance system, shareholders have delegated the day-to-day management, operation and functions to directors. Although directors owe duties to the company primarily and not the shareholders, the system of corporate governance is able to vest residual authority and ultimate control in the shareholders. This is achieved by the CA 2006 setting out particular transactions that are considered so significant in the company's operations. Chapter 4 of Pt 10 deals with a company's transactions with directors requiring approval of members.

15.3 This chapter addresses the following aspects:

- It considers the provisions of Chapter 3 of Part 10 of CA 2006 on declaration by directors of interest in existing transactions or arrangements.
- Directors' long-term service contracts.
- Substantial property transactions.
- Loans to directors.

- Credit transactions and related arrangements; and
- Payment for loss of office.

Declaration of interest

15.4 Chapter 3 of Part 10 of CA 2006 addresses the issue of declaration of interest by a director in an existing transaction or arrangement. It comprises six sections. The pattern that is followed in these provisions is first to set out the nature of the specific duty and then the offence.

Declaration of interest in existing transaction of arrangement

15.5 There is a specific obligation on a director to declare an interest which he has in an existing transaction or arrangement. Section 182 of the CA 2006 provides that where a director of a company is in any way, directly or indirectly, interested in a transaction or arrangement that has been entered into by the company, he must declare the nature and extent of the interest to the other directors: CA 2006, s 182(1). This also applies to a shadow director: CA 2006, s 187. This would apply where, for example, a director has just been appointed to the company's board and he has an interest in the company's contracts or arrangements.

15.6 Section 182 does not apply if or to the extent that the interest has been declared under CA 2006, s 177 (duty to declare interest in proposed transaction or arrangement).

The declaration must be made by any of the following methods:

(a) at a meeting of the directors; or

(b) by notice in writing (see CA 2006, s 184); or

(c) by general notice (see CA 2006, s 185): CA 2006, s 182(2).

If a declaration of interest under s 182 proves to be, or becomes, inaccurate or incomplete, a further declaration must be made: CA 2006, s 182(3).

Any declaration required by s 182 must be made as soon as is reasonably practicable. Failure to comply with this requirement does not affect the underlying duty to make the declaration: CA 2006, s 182(4).

15.7 Section 182 does not require a declaration of an interest of which the director is not aware, or where the director is not aware of the transaction or arrangement in question. For this purpose, a director is treated as being aware of matters of which he ought reasonably to be aware: CA 2006, s 182(5).

However, a director need not declare an interest under s 182 under the following circumstances:

(a) if it cannot reasonably be regarded as likely to give rise to a conflict of interest;

(b) if, or to the extent that, the other directors are already aware of it (and for this purpose the other directors are treated as aware of anything of which they ought reasonably to be aware); or

(c) if, or to the extent that, it concerns terms of his service contract that have been or are to be considered by a meeting of the directors; or by a committee of the directors appointed for the purpose under the company's constitution: CA 2006, s 182(6).

Offence of failure to declare interest

15.8 A director who fails to comply with the requirements of CA 2006, s 182 (declaration of interest in existing transaction or arrangement) will be guilty of an offence: CA 2006, s 183(1).

On conviction on indictment, the maximum liability is an unlimited fine; on summary conviction the fine must not exceed the statutory maximum (currently £5,000): CA 2006, s 183(2). This provision does not affect the validity of the transaction or impose any other civil consequences for a failure to make the declarations of interest required by s 182.

In *Hely-Hutchinson v Brayhead Ltd* [1967] 3 All ER 98, Lord Pearson stated that s 182 only created a statutory duty of disclosure. However, s 182 goes further and imposes a fine for non-compliance, but it does not affect the validity of transaction entered into by the company. Therefore, it will be necessary to look to any other breaches of director's fiduciary or other general duties that may be applicable to the circumstances in question.

A director has a duty to disclose to the board any existing transaction or arrangement with the company

In *Coleman Taymar Ltd v Oakes* [2001] 2 BCLC 749, Judge Robert Reid (sitting as a High Court Judge) held that CA 2006, s 182 imposed a statutory duty on a director of a company who was directly or indirectly interested in a contract or a proposed contract with the company, to disclose his interest at a meeting of the directors of the company, and rendered him liable to a fine for failure to do so. The section did not give the company a separate right of action for damages against the director. Any right of action arose from the breach of fiduciary duty and not from the section. Therefore, a company was entitled to elect whether to claim damages or an account of profits against a director for breach of his fiduciary duty.

Declaration made by notice in writing

15.9 Section 184 of CA 2006 applies to a declaration of interest made by notice in writing: CA 2006, s 184(1). Under s 184(2), the director must send the notice to the other directors. The notice must be sent in hard copy form or, if the recipient has agreed to receive it in electronic form, in an agreed electronic form: CA 2006, s 184(3).

The notice may be sent by hand or by post; or if the recipient has agreed to receive it by electronic means, by agreed electronic means: CA 2006, s 182(4).

Where a director declares an interest by notice in writing in accordance with s 184, the making of the declaration is deemed to form part of the proceedings at the next meeting of directors after the notice is given; and the provisions of CA 2006, s 248 (minutes of meetings of directors) apply as if the declaration had been made at the meeting: CA 2006, s 184(5).

General notice treated as sufficient declaration

15.10 A general notice in accordance with CA 2006, s 184 is a sufficient declaration of interest in relation to the matters to which it relates: CA 2006, s 185(1). A general notice is notice given to the directors of the company to the effect that the director:

(a) has an interest (as member, officer, employee or otherwise) in a specified body corporate or firm, and is to be regarded as interested in any transaction or arrangement that may, after the date of the notice, be made with that body corporate or firm; or

(b) is connected with a specified person (other than a body corporate or firm), and is to be regarded as interested in any transaction or arrangement that may, after the date of the notice, be made with that person: CA 2006, s 184(2).

The notice must state the nature and extent of the director's interest in the body corporate or firm or, as the case may be, the nature of his connection with the person: CA 2006, s 184(3).

15.11 However, a general notice is not effective unless it is given at a meeting of directors, or the director takes reasonable steps to secure that it is brought up and read at the next meeting of the directors after it is given: CA 2006, s 184(4).

Declaration of interest in case of company with sole director

15.12 Section 186(1) of CA 2006 provides that where a declaration of interest under s 182 is required of a sole director of a company that is required to have more than one director, the following apply:

(a) the declaration must be recorded in writing;

(b) the making of the declaration is deemed to form part of the proceedings at the next meeting of the directors after the notice is given; and

(c) the provisions of CA 2006, s 248 (minutes of meetings of directors) apply as if the declaration had been made at that meeting: CA 2006, s 186(1).

However, nothing in s 186 affects the operation of CA 2006, s 231 (contract with sole member who is also a director: terms to be set out in writing or recorded in minutes): CA 2006, s 186(2).

Declaration of interest in existing transaction by shadow director

15.13 Section 187 of CA 2006 applies in respect of a declaration of interest in an existing transaction by a shadow director. The provisions of Chapter 3 of Part 10 of CA 2006 relating to the duty under s 182 (duty to declare interest in an existing transaction or arrangement) apply to a shadow director as to a director but with adaptations: CA 2006, s 187(1).

However, s 182(2)(a) (declaration at meeting of directors) does not apply: CA 2006, s 187(2).

In s 185 (general notice treated as sufficient declaration), subs (4) (notice to be given at or brought up and read at meeting of directors) does not apply: CA 2006, s 187(3).

A general notice by a shadow director is not effective, unless given by notice in writing in accordance with s 184: CA 2006, s 187(4).

Transactions with directors requiring approval of members

15.14 Chapters 4 and 5 of Part 10 contain several provisions designed to deal with particular situations in which a director has a conflict of interest. There is a requirement for member approval in relation to four different types of transaction by a company:

- long-term service contracts;
- substantial property transactions;
- loans, quasi-loans and credit transactions;
- payments for loss of office.

The rules relating to each type of transaction tend to adopt a common structure: they begin with the rule requiring approval from the shareholders; then follow the exceptions to that rule; and then the consequences of breaching that rule.

Service contracts

Directors' long-term service contracts: requirement of members' approval

15.15 Sections 188–189 of CA 2006 are concerned with directors' service contracts. Section 188 deals with directors' long-term service contracts that require members' approval. It applies to a provision under which the 'guaranteed term' of a director's employment:

(a) with the company of which he is a director; or

(b) where he is a director of a holding company, within the group consisting of that company and its subsidiaries,

is or may be longer than two years: CA 2006, s 188(1).

15.16 A company may not agree to such provision unless it has been approved by a resolution of the members of the company; and, in the case of a director of a holding company, by resolution of the members of that company: CA 2006, s 188(2).

The 'guaranteed term' of a director's employment is:

(a) the period (if any) during which the director's employment:

   (i) is to continue, or may be continued otherwise that at the instance of the company (whether under the original agreement or under a new agreement entered into in pursuance of it); and

   (ii) it cannot be terminated by the company by notice, or can be so terminated only in specified circumstances; or

(b) in the case of employment terminable by the company by notice, the period of notice required to be given;

or in the case of employment having a period within paragraph (a) and a period within paragraph (b), the aggregate of those periods: CA 2006, s 188(3).

15.17 If more than six months before the end of the guaranteed term of a director's employment, the company enters into a further service contract (otherwise than in pursuance of a right conferred by or under the original contract on the other party to it), s 188 applies if there were added to the guaranteed term of the new contract the unexpired period of the guaranteed term of the original contract: CA 2006, s 188(4).

A resolution approving provision to which CA 2006, s 188 applies must not be passed unless a memorandum setting out the proposed contract incorporating the provision is made available to the members in the following circumstances:

(a) in the case of a written resolution, by being sent or submitted to every eligible member at or before the time at which the proposed resolution is sent or submitted to him;

(b) in the case of a resolution at a meeting, by being made available for inspection by members of the company both at the company's registered office for not less than 15 days ending with the date of the meeting; and at the meeting itself: CA 2006, s 188(5).

15.18 No approval is required under s 188 on the part of the members of a body corporate that is not a UK-registered company, or is a wholly-owned subsidiary of another body corporate: CA 2006, s 188(6).

The term 'employment' means any employment under a director's service contract: CA 2006, s 188(7).

Under s 227, a 'service contract' in relation to a company means a contract under which:

(a) a director of the company undertakes personally to perform services (as director or otherwise) for the company, or for a subsidiary of the company; or

(b) services (as director or otherwise) that a director of the company undertakes personally to perform are made available by a third party to the company, or to a subsidiary of the company: CA 2006, s 227(1).

15.19 The provisions of CA 2006, Pt 10 relating to directors' service contracts apply to the terms of a person's appointment as a director of a company. They are not restricted to contracts for the performance of services outside the scope of the ordinary duties of a director: CA 2006, s 227(2).

A company must keep available for inspection:

(a) a copy of every director's service contract with the company or with a subsidiary of the company; or

(b) if the contract is not in writing, a written memorandum setting out the terms of the contract: CA 2006, s 228(1).

All the copies and memoranda must be kept available for inspection at the company's registered office, or a place specified in regulations under CA 2006, s 1136: CA 2006, s 228(2). The copies and memoranda must be retained by the company for at least one year from the date of termination or expiry of the contract and must be kept available for inspection during that time: CA 2006, s 228(3).

15.20 The company must give notice to the registrar:

(a) of the place at which the copies and memoranda are kept available for inspection; and

(b) of any change in that place,

unless they have at all times been kept at the company's registered office: CA 2006, s 228(4).

If default is made in complying with s 228(1), (2) or (3), or default is made for 14 days in complying with s 228(4), an offence will be committed by every officer of the company who is in default: CA 2006, s 228(5). A person guilty of an offence under s 228 will be liable on summary conviction to a fine not exceeding level 3 on the standard scale and, for continued contravention, a daily default fine not exceeding one-tenth of level 3 on the standard scale: CA 2006, s 228(6).

The provisions of s 228 apply to a variation of a director's service contract in the same way as to the original contract: CA 2006, s 228(7).

15.21 Every copy or memorandum required to be kept under s 228 must be open to inspection by any member of the company without charge: CA 2006, s 229(1).

Any member of the company is entitled, on request and on payment of such fee as may be prescribed, to be provided with a copy of any such copy or memorandum. The copy must be provided within seven days after the request is received by the company: CA 2006, s 229(2).

If an inspection required under s 229(1) is refused, or default is made in complying with that provision, an offence will be committed by every officer of the company who is in default: CA 2006, s 229(3).

15.22 A person guilty of an offence under s 299 will be liable on summary conviction to a fine not exceeding level 3 on the standard scale and, for continued contravention, a daily default fine not exceeding one-tenth of level 3 on the standard scale: CA 2006, s 229(4).

In the case of any such refusal or default the court may by order compel an immediate inspection or, as the case may be, direct that the copy required be sent to the person requiring it: CA 2006, s 229(5).

A shadow director will be treated as a director for the purposes of CA 2006, Pt 10, Ch 5: CA 2006, s 230.

Directors' long-term service contracts: civil consequences for contravention

15.23 Section 189 of CA 2006 deals with the civil consequences of contravention of s 188. If a company agrees to a provision in contravention of s 188 (directors' long-term service contracts: requirement of members' approval), the provision will be void, to the extent of the contravention. Further, the contract is deemed to contain a term entitling the company to terminate at any time by giving reasonable notice.

Substantial property transactions

Requirement of members' approval

15.24 Sections 190–196 of CA 2006 deal with substantial property transactions. Section 190 states that a company may not enter into an arrangement under which:

(a) a director of the company or of its holding company, or a person connected with such a director, acquires or is to acquire from the company (directly or indirectly) a substantial non-cash asset;

(b) or where the company acquires or is to acquire a substantial non-cash asset (directly or indirectly) from a director or a person so connected).

Such non-cash asset may only be acquired if the arrangement has been approved by a resolution of the members of the company, or is conditional on such approval being obtained: CA 2006, s 190(1).

15.25 The term 'substantial non-cash asset' is defined in s 191. It is also defined in CA 2006, s 1163 as 'any property or interest in property other than cash'. The meaning is wide-ranging and may include intellectual property, lease, s tock, license or assets: *Ultraframe (UK) Ltd v Fielding* [2005] UKHC 1638 (Ch); and *Re Duckwari plc (No 1)* [1997] 2 BCLC 713. The asset may be described as the benefit of the purchase contract or the beneficial interest in the asset itself.

If the director or connected person is a director of the company's holding company or a person connected with such a director, the arrangement must also have been approved by a resolution of the members of the holding company, or be conditional upon such approval being obtained: CA 2006, s 190(2).

The objective of s 190 of CA 2006 is to safeguard a company from any losses resulting from transactions between a company and a director

In *British Racing Drivers' Club Ltd v Hextell Erskine & Co* [1997] 1 BCLC 182, the solicitors had failed to advise on the need for a resolution for shareholders' approval where a holding company was involved. Carnwath J held that the purpose of s 190 was to safeguard a company from losses resulting from transactions between the company and its directors; if the decision to enter into a transaction was left to the directors there was a risk that their judgment might be distorted by conflicts of interest and loyalties, even in cases where there was no actual dishonesty. On the facts, the solicitors had been negligent in failing to advise on members' approval.

The *Duomatic* principle of informal unanimous shareholders' assent may be used for the purposes of s 190: *NBH Ltd v Hoare* [2006] 2 BCLC 649.

A company will not be subject to any liability by reason of a failure to obtain the approval required: CA 2006, s 190(3).

However, approval will not be required from shareholders of a body corporate that is not a UK-registered company, or is a wholly owned subsidiary of another body corporate: CA 2006, s 190(4).

An arrangement involving more than one non-cash asset, or an arrangement that is one of a series involving non-cash assets, will be treated as if they involved a non-cash asset of a value equal to the aggregate value of all the non-cash assets involved in the arrangement or, as the case may be, the series: CA 2006, s 190(5).

Section 190(6) does not apply to a transaction so far as it relates to anything to which a director of a company is entitled under his service contract. It does not apply to payment for loss of office as defined in CA 2006, s 215 (payments requiring member's approval): CA 2006, s 190(6).

In *Granada Group Ltd v The Law Debenture Pension Trust Corporation plc* [2015] EWHC 1499, the claimant challenged the legality of, and sought to set aside, arrangements granting the defendant trustee a first fixed equitable charge over gilts on the basis that the arrangements had been entered into in contravention of s.190 CA 2006. The Chancery Division, in dismissing the application, held that the scheme was not voidable under s.190, as the directors were contingent beneficiaries, and the trustee had been acting in its capacity as trustee of a pension scheme and had not been a 'connected person'. Further, the trustee was entitled to indemnification and interest concerning the costs of the proceedings.

Shareholder approval under CA 2006, s 190 was not required where there was only a possibility of acquiring a non-cash asset

Section 190 of CA 2006 was considered by the Court of Appeal in *Smithton Ltd v Naggar* [2015] 2 BCLC 22. The case concerned an acquisition of a non-cash asset by a director from the company or by the company from the director. The company bought shares at defendant's request to hedge contracts for difference. The company was not informed of the identity of the counterparty at the time of purchase. The issue for consideration was whether the defendant director acted in breach of restriction of non-cash asset without shareholders' approval. The Court of Appeal held that the defendant's instructions to the claimant to purchase shares to hedge contract for difference without the purchaser being identified did not contravene s 190 of CA 2006, because although the claimant was not aware of the name of the purchaser at the time of purchase, the nomination of the ultimate purchaser by the end of the day of purchase had the effect that the purchase was ratified in that purchaser's name from the earliest moment in that day, with the result that for the purposes of s 190 the defendant did not acquire an asset from the claimant or the claimant from him in the course of the trading day. Moreover, shareholder approval under s 190 was only required for arrangements under which a director or a person connected to him definitely acquired 'or is to acquire' an interest in shares, and was not required for arrangements under which his or their acquisition of an interest in shares was only a possibility. Since at the time the defendant made an arrangement for the claimant to write contracts for difference, the arrangement only provided a means whereby the contracts for difference holders might ultimately acquire non-cash assets and there was no certainty that when the contracts for difference was closed out the contracts for difference holder would opt to acquire the referenced shares, s 190 did not apply to those arrangements.

Meaning of 'substantial'

15.26 The definition of 'substantial' non-cash asset is set-out in s 191: CA 2006, s 191(1). An asset is a substantial asset in relation to the company if its value exceeds 10% of the company's assets value and is more than £5,000; or exceeds £100,000: CA 2006, s 191(2). The 'value' represents the capital value of the asset: *Ultraframe (UK) Limited v Fielding* [2005] EWCH 1638. The onus is on the applicant to show that the transaction in question exceeded the financial limits of s 191: *Joint Receivers and Managers of Niltan Carson Ltd v Hawthorne* [1988] BCLC 298 at 321.

Under CA 2006, s 190 the onus is on the person alleging the contravention to prove that the value of the non-cash asset exceeded the requisite value

In *Niltan Carson Limited v Hawthorne* [1998] BCLC 298, Hodgson J stated that where it was alleged that CA 2006, s 190 had been contravened because a director had entered into an arrangement to acquire a non-cash asset from the company in excess of the 'requisite value', the onus would be on the person alleging the contravention to prove that the value of the non-cash asset exceeded the requisite value.

Under CA 2006, s 190, the relevant value of the asset is the value to the director, or person connected with him, who acquired the asset and not the objective market value of the asset

In *Micro Leisure Ltd v County Properties and Developments Limited* [2000] BCC 872, Lord Hamilton considered that where a director of a company, or a person connected with that director, acquired a non-cash asset from the company, the relevant value of the asset in terms of s 190, was held to be the value to the director, or person connected with him, who acquired the asset and not the objective market value of the asset. He stated that the purpose of s 190 was to increase the control of members of the company over specific transactions between the company and its directors. In this regard, the use of an objective concept of value was consistent with that purpose. It would be inappropriate to construe s 190 simply to meet unusual circumstances. The members of a company had other remedies, including remedies based on the fiduciary obligations of directors.

15.27 A company's 'asset value' at any time is the value of the company's net assets determined by reference to its most recent statutory accounts or if no statutory accounts have been prepared, the amount of the company's called-up share capital: CA 2006, s 191(3).

A company's 'statutory accounts' means its annual accounts prepared in accordance with CA 2006, Pt 15 and its 'most recent' statutory accounts means those in relation to which the time for sending them out to members (see CA 2006, s 424) is most recent: CA 2006, s 191(4).

Whether an asset is a substantial asset must be determined as at the time the arrangement is entered into: CA 2006, s 191(5). A 'non-cash asset' means any property or interest in property, other than cash: CA 2006, s 1163.

A lease may be a non-cash asset if at a premium

In *Ultraframe (UK) Limited v Fielding* [2005] EWCH 1638, Lewison J decided that the grant of a lease at a premium constituted a non-cash asset: 'If, s ay, a director grants a long lease to a company at a substantial premium, I can see no policy reason for holding that the literal words of section [190 CA 2006] do not apply to such a transaction'.

A bilateral agreement between the director and the company gave rise to seeking an approval from the shareholders

In *Re Duckwari plc (No 1)* [1997] 2 BCLC 713, Millett LJ determined that on the facts there was a bilateral agreement between the parties for one party to acquire property from the other. This agreement gave rise to approval under CA 2006, s 190 which had not been obtained. Accordingly, there was a breach of this provision.

Exception for transactions with members or other group companies

15.28 Approval will not be required under CA 2006, s 190 (requirement of members' approval for substantial property transactions):

(a) for a transaction between a company and a person in his character as a member of that company; or

(b) for a transaction between a holding company and its wholly owned subsidiary; or

(c) two wholly-owned subsidiaries of the same holding company: CA 2006, s 192.

Exception in the case of company in winding up or administration

15.29 Section 193 of CA 2006 applies to a company:

(a) that is being wound up (unless the winding up is a member's voluntary winding up); or

(b) that is in administration within the meaning of Schedule B1 to the Insolvency Act 1986 or the Insolvency (Northern Ireland) Order 1989, SI 1989 No /2405 (NI 19): CA 2006, s 193(1).

In such circumstances, approval is not required under s 190 (requirement of member's approval for substantial property transactions) on the part of the members of a company; or for an arrangement entered into by a company: CA 2006, s 193(2).

Exceptions for transactions on recognised investment exchange

15.30 Approval is not required under CA 2006, s 190 (requirement of members' approval for substantial property transactions) for a transaction on a recognised investment exchange effected by a director, or a person connected with him, through the agency of a person who in relation to the transaction acts as an independent broker: CA 2006, s 194(1).

An 'independent broker' means a person who, independently of the director or any person connected with him, s elects the person with whom the transaction is to be effected. A 'recognised investment exchange' has the same meaning as in Part 18 of the Financial Services and Markets Act 2000: CA 2006, s 194(2).

Property transactions: civil consequences of transaction

15.31 There are a number of civil remedies available where a breach of s 190 is found to exist.

Section 195 of CA 2006 applies where a company enters into an arrangement in contravention of s 190: CA 2006, s 195(1).

The arrangement and any transaction entered into in pursuance of the arrangement (whether by the company or any other person) is voidable at the insurance of the company, unless:

(a) restitution of any money or other asset that was the subject matter of the arrangement or transaction is no longer possible;

(b) the company has been indemnified by any other persons for the loss or damage suffered by it;

(c) rights acquired in good faith, for value and without actual notice of the contravention by a person who is not a party to the arrangement or transaction would be affected by the avoidance: CA 2006, s 195(2).

15.32 Whether or not the arrangement or any such transaction has been avoided, each of the persons specified in s 195(4) is liable:

(a) to account to the company for any gain that has been made directly or indirectly by the arrangement or transaction; and

(b) (jointly and severally with any other person so liable under s 195) to indemnify the company for any loss or damage resulting from the arrangement or transaction: CA 2006, s 195(3).

Where a company did not make a loss on the asset, any extra profit may be retained by the director

NBH Ltd v Hoare [2006] 2 BCLC 649, concerned an asset which was sold to the company at an over value. The company did not make any loss on the resale of the asset. The issue was whether the director was liable for extra profit company might have made on the sale and whether he could retain the profit he had made?

Park J held that as the company had not made any loss, the director was able to retain the extra profit made.

The main objective of CA 2006, s 190 was to give shareholders specific protection against transactions that may be beneficial to the directors

In *Re Duckwari (No 2)* [1998] 2 BCLC 315, the transaction involved was the sale of land and a substantial property transaction within s 190 of CA 2006. Although board approval was obtained, s hareholder approval was not sought.

The Court of Appeal allowed the company to recover by way of indemnity. It stated that the principal purpose of s 190 of CA 2006 was to give shareholders specific protection in respect of arrangements and transactions which would or might benefit directors to the detriment of the company. Section 195(3) of CA 2006 provided an indemnity for loss incurred on the realisation of a property for less than the cost of its acquisition. The loss suffered by the company was the difference between the value of the property at acquisition and realisation. However, see *Smithton Ltd v Naggar* [2015] 2 BCLC 22.

In *Re Duckwari (No 3)* [1999] 1 BCLC 168, the Court of Appeal held that the loss or damage recoverable under s 195(3)(b) of CA 2006 was limited to that resulting from the acquisition of the property. The transaction was entered into in pursuance of the arrangement which breached s 190 of CA 2006. Accordingly Duckwari was entitled to the difference between the cost of acquiring the property and the proceeds of sale, plus interest. Duckwari was not entitled to recover actual interest paid or owing on its bank borrowing or to notional interest on its own money used to fund the purchase, since the borrowing and the application of its own money did not contravene s 190 of CA 2006.

15.33 The persons who will be liable are:

(a) any director of the company or of its holding company with whom the company entered into the arrangement in contravention of CA 2006, s 190;

(b) any person with whom the company entered into the arrangement in contravention of that section who is connected with a director of the company or of its holding company;

(c) the director of the company or of its holding company with whom any such person is connected; and

(d) any other director of the company who authorised the arrangement or any transaction entered into in pursuance of such an arrangement: CA 2006, s 195(4).

However, s 195(3), (4) is subject to s 195(6), (7): CA 2006, s 195(5).

15.34 In the case of an arrangement entered into by a company in contravention of s 190 with a person connected with a director of the company or of its holding company, that director is not liable by virtue of s 195(4)(c) if he shows he took all reasonable steps to secure the company's compliance with that section: CA 2006, s 195(6).

In any case:

(a) a person so connected is not liable by virtue of s 195(4)(b); and

(b) a director is not liable under s 195(4)(d),

if he shows that, at the time the arrangement was entered into, he did not know the relevant circumstances constituting the contravention: CA 2006, s 195(7).

Nothing in s 195 will be read as excluding the operation of any other enactment or rule of law by virtue of which the arrangement or transaction may be called in question or any liability to the company may arise: CA 2006, s 195(8).

Property transactions: effect of subsequent affirmation

15.35 Where a transaction or arrangement is entered into by a company in contravention of CA 2006, s 190 (requirement of member's approval) but, within reasonable period, it is affirmed:

(a) in the case of a contravention of s 190(1) by resolution of the members of the company; and

(b) in the case of a contravention of s 190(2) by resolution of the members of the holding company,

the transaction or arrangement may no longer be avoided by s 195: CA 2006, s 196.

Loans, quasi-loans and credit transactions

15.36 Sections 197–214 of CA 2006 address loans, quasi-loans and credit transactions.

Loans to directors: requirement of members' approval

15.37 Section 197 of CA 2006 is concerned with loans to directors with reference to the requirement of members' approval. Under this section, a company may not:

(a) make a loan to a director of the company or its holding company; or

(b) give a guarantee or provide security in connection with a loan or quasi-loan made by any person to such a director,

unless the transaction has been approved by a resolution of the members: CA 2006, s 197(1).

15.38 If the director is a director of the company's holding company, the transaction must also have been approved by a resolution of the members of the holding company: CA 2006, s 197(2).

A resolution approving a transaction under s 197 must not be passed unless a memorandum setting out the matters in s 197(4) is made available to the members, in the following two circumstances:

(a) in the case of a written resolution, by being sent or submitted to every eligible member at or before the time at which the proposed resolution is sent or submitted to him; and

(b) in the case of a resolution at a meeting, by being made available for inspection by members of the company both at the company's registered office for not less than 15 days ending with the date of the meeting; and at the meeting itself: CA 2006, s 197(3).

15.39 The matters that must be disclosed are:

(a) the nature of the transaction;

(b) the amount of the loan and the purpose for which it is required; and

(c) the extent of the company's liability under any transaction connected with the loan: CA 2006, s 197(4).

However, no approval is required from the members of a body corporate that is not a UK-registered company, or a company associated with a public company: CA 2006, s 197(5).

No definition of a 'loan' is set out in this and the preceding sections. In *Champagne Perrier-Jouet SA v HH Finch Limited* [1982] 3 All ER 717, Walton J was content to use the Oxford Dictionary meaning as 'A sum of money lent for a time to be returned in money or money's worth': see too *Potts's Exors v IRC* [1951] 1 All ER 76. In *First Global Media Group Ltd v Larkin* [2003] EVCA Civ 1765, the Court of Appeal stated: 'A loan ordinarily involves an advance of money pursuant to an agreement providing for its repayment.' In *Currencies Direct Ltd v Ellis* [2002] 2 BCLC 482, the Court of Appeal was required to consider whether a sum of money payable to a director constituted a loan or remuneration for services performed. It held that on the facts, the services performed by the director and payment made was remuneration and not advances made to a director that were payable.

The consequences of a contravention of CA 2006, s 197 is that it is a breach of the CA and might constitute a misapplication of the company's funds including a breach of director's duty: *Queensway Systems Ltd v Walker* [2007] 2 BCLC 577.

Quasi-loans to directors: requirement of members' approval

15.40 Section 198 of CA 2006 applies to a company if it is a public company, or a company associated with a public company: CA 2006, s 198(1). Under this provision, a company may not:

(a) make a quasi-loan to a director of the company or of its holding company; or

(b) give a guarantee or provide security in connection with a quasi-loan made by any person to such a director,

unless the transaction has been approved by a resolution of the members of the company: CA 2006, s 198(2).

If the director is a director of the company's holding company, the transaction must also have been approved by a resolution of the members of the holding company: CA 2006, s 198(3).

15.41 A resolution approving a transaction must not be passed unless a memorandum setting out the matters mentioned in s 198(5) is made available to the members, in the following two circumstances:

(a) in the case of a written resolution, by being sent or submitted to every eligible member at or before the time at which the proposed resolution is sent or submitted to him;

(b) in the case of a resolution at a meeting, by being made available for inspection by members of the company both at the company's registered office for not less than 15 days ending with the date of the meeting; and at the meeting itself: CA 2006, s 198(4).

15.42 In respect of s 198(4), the matters to be disclosed are:

(a) the nature of the transaction;

(b) the amount of the quasi-loan and the purpose for which it is required; and

(c) the extent of the company's liability under any transaction connected with the quasi-loan: CA 2006, s 198(5).

However, no approval is required under s 198 on the part of the members of a body corporate that is not a UK-registered company; or is a wholly-owned subsidiary of another body corporate: CA 2006, s 198(6).

Meaning of 'quasi-loan' and related expressions

15.43 A 'quasi-loan' is defined as a transaction under which one party known as the creditor 'agrees to pay', or pays otherwise than in pursuance of an agreement; a sum for another person, known as 'the borrower', or agrees to reimburse, or reimburses otherwise than in pursuance of an agreement, expenditure incurred by another party for another ('the borrower'):

(a) on terms that the borrower (or a person on his behalf) will reimburse the creditor; or

(b) in circumstances giving rise to a liability on the borrower to reimburse the creditor: CA 2006, s 199(1).

Any reference to the person to whom a quasi-loan is made is a reference to the borrower: CA 2006, s 199(2).

The liabilities of the borrower under a quasi-loan include the liabilities of any person who has agreed to reimburse the creditor on behalf of the borrower: CA 2006, s 199(3).

Loans or quasi-loans to persons connected with directors: requirement of members' approval

15.44 Section 200 of CA 2006 applies to a company if it is a public company; or a company associated with a public company: CA 2006, s 200(1).

A company may not:

(a) make a loan or quasi-loan to a person connected with a director of the company or of its holding company; or

(b) give a guarantee or provide security in connection with a loan or quasi-loan made by any person to a person connected with such a director,

unless the transaction has been approved by a resolution of the members of the company: CA 2006, s 200(2).

15.45 If the connected person is a person connected with a director of the company's holding company, the transaction must also have been approved by a resolution of the members of the holding company: CA 2006, s 200(3).

A resolution approving a transaction must not be passed unless a memorandum setting out the matters mentioned in CA 2006, s 198(5) is made available to the members, in the following two circumstances:

(a) in the case of a written resolution, by being sent or submitted to every eligible member at or before the time at which the proposed resolution is sent or submitted to him;

(b) in the case of a resolution at a meeting, by being made available for inspection by members of the company both at the company's registered office for not less than 15 days ending with the date of the meeting; and at the meeting itself: CA 2006, s 200(4).

15.46 In respect of s 198(4), the matters to be disclosed are:

(a) the nature of the transaction;

(b) the amount of the quasi-loan and the purpose for which it is required; and

(c) the extent of the company's liability under any transaction connected with the quasi-loan: CA 2006, s 200(5).

However, no approval is required under s 198 on the part of the members of a body corporate that is not a UK-registered company; or is a wholly-owned subsidiary of another body corporate: CA 2006, s 200(6).

15.47 Sections 197–214 of CA 2006 require member approval for loans, quasi-loans, credit transactions and related guarantees or security made by a company for:

- a director of the company; or
- a director of its holding company.

In the case of a public company, or a private company associated with a public company, CA 2006, ss 197, 198, 200 and 201 require member approval for loans, quasi-loans (as defined in s 199), credit transactions (as defined in s 202) and related guarantees or security made by the company for:

- a director of the company;
- a director of its holding company;
- a person connected with a director of the company; or
- a person connected with a director of its holding company.

15.48 Section 256 of CA 2006 sets out what is meant by references to associated companies. A holding company is associated with all its subsidiaries, and a subsidiary is associated with its holding company and all the other subsidiaries of its holding company.

Member approval is not required by these sections for:

- loans, quasi-loans and credit transaction to meet expenditure on company business. The total value of transaction under this exception made in respect of a director and any person connected to him must not exceed £50,000 (CA 2006, s 204);
- money lent to fund a director's defence costs for legal proceedings in connection with any alleged negligence, default, breach of duty or breach of trust by him in relation to the company or an associated company (CA 2006, s 205) or in connection with regulatory action or investigation under the same circumstances (CA 2006, s 206);
- small loans and quasi-loans, as long as the total value of such loans and quasi-loans made in respect of a director and any person connected to him does not exceed £10,000 (CA 2006, s 207(1));
- small credit transactions, as long as the total value of such credit transaction made in respect of a director and any person connected to him does not exceed £15,000 (CA 2006, s 207(2));
- credit transactions made in the ordinary course of the company's business (CA 2006, s 207(3));
- intra-group transactions (CA 2006, s 208); and

- loans and quasi-loans made by a money-lending company in the ordinary course of the company's business (as long as the requirements of CA 2006, s 209 are met).

Credit transactions

15.49 Sections 201–214 of CA 2006 are concerned with credit transactions and related arrangements.

Credit transactions: requirement of members' approval

15.50 Section 201 of CA 2006 applies to a company if it is a public company; or a company associated with a public company: CA 2006, s 201(1).

A company may not:

(a) enter into a credit transaction as creditor for the benefit of a director of the company or of its holding company, or a person connected with such a director; or

(b) give a guarantee or provide security in connection with a credit-transaction entered into by any person for the benefit of such a director, or a person connected with such a director,

unless the credit transaction, the giving of the guarantee or the provision of security (as the case may be) has been approved by a resolution of the members of the holding company: CA 2006, s 201(2).

15.51 If the director or connected person is a director of its holding company or a person connected with such a director, the transaction must also have been approved by a resolution of the members of the holding company: CA 2006, s 201(3).

A resolution approving a transaction under CA 2006, s 201 cannot be passed unless a memorandum setting out the matters in s 201(4) is made available to the members in the following two circumstances:

(a) in the case of a written resolution, by being sent or submitted to every eligible member at or before the time at which the proposed resolution is sent or submitted to him;

(b) in the case of a resolution at a meeting, by being made available for inspection by members of the company both at the company's registered office for not less than 15 days ending with the date of the meeting, and at the meeting itself: CA 2006, s 201(4).

15.52 The matters that must be disclosed are:

(a) the nature of the transaction;

(b) the value of the transaction and the purpose for which the land, goods and services sold or otherwise disposed of, leased, hired or supplied under the credit transaction are supplied; and

(c) the extent of the company's liability under any transaction connected with the credit transaction: CA 2006, s 201(5).

However, no approval is required from the members of a body corporate that is not a UK-registered company; or is a wholly owned subsidiary of another body corporate: CA 2006, s 201(6).

Meaning of credit transaction

15.53 A 'credit transaction' is defined as a transaction under which one party known as 'the creditor' does any of the following:

(a) supplies any goods or sells any land under a hire-purchase agreement or a conditional sale agreement; or

(b) leases or hires any land or goods in return for periodical payments; or

(c) otherwise disposes of land or supplies goods or services on the undertaking that payment (whether in lump sum or instalments or by way of periodical payments or otherwise) is to be deferred: CA 2006, s 202(1).

Any reference to the person for whose benefit a credit transaction is entered into is to the person to whom goods, land or services are supplied, s old, leased, hired, or otherwise disposed of under the transaction: CA 2006, s 202(2).

A reference to a 'conditional sale agreement' has the same meaning as in the Consumer Credit Act 1974. The term 'services' means anything other than goods or land: CA 2006, s 202(3).

Related arrangements: requirement of members' approval

15.54 A company may not:

(a) take part in an arrangement under which:

  (i) another person enters into a transaction that, if it had been entered into by the company, would have required approval under CA 2006, ss 197, 198, 200 or 201; and

  (ii) that person, in pursuance of the arrangement, obtains a benefit from the company or a body corporate associated with it; or

(b) arrange for the assignment to it, or assumption by it, of any rights, obligations or liabilities under a transaction that, if it had been entered into by the company, would have required such approval,

unless the arrangement in question has been approved by a resolution of the members of the company: CA 2006, s 203(1).

15.55 If a director or connected person for whom the transaction is entered into is a director of its holding company or a person connected with such a director, the arrangement must also have been approved by a resolution of the members of the holding company: CA 2006, s 203(2).

A resolution approving an arrangement to which s 203 applies must not be passed unless a memorandum setting out the matters mentioned in s 203(4) is made available to members:

(a) in the case of a written resolution, by being sent or submitted to every eligible member at or before the time at which the proposed resolution is sent or submitted to him: CA 2006, s 203(3).

(b) in the case of a resolution at a meeting, by being made available for inspection by members of the company both at the company's registered office for not less than 15 days ending with the date of the meeting, and at the meeting itself: CA 2006, s 203(3).

15.56 The matters to be disclosed are:

(a) the matters that would have to be disclosed if the company were seeking approval of the transaction to which the arrangement relates;

(b) the nature of the arrangement; and

(c) the extent of the company's liability under the arrangement or any transaction connected with it: CA 2006, s 203(4).

No approval is required on the part of the members of a body corporate that is not a UK-registered company, or is a wholly-owned subsidiary of another body corporate: CA 2006, s 203(5).

In determining whether a transaction is one that would have required approval under CA 2006, ss 197, 198, 200 or 201, if it had been entered into by the company, the transaction must be treated as having been entered into on the date of the arrangement: CA 2006, s 203(6).

Exception for expenditure on company business

15.57 Approval is not required under CA 2006, s 197, 198, 200 or 201 (requirement of members' approval for loans etc) for anything done by a company:

(a) to provide a director of the company or of its holding company, or a person connected with any such director, with funds to meet expenditure incurred or to be incurred by him:

 (i) for the purposes of the company; or

 (ii) for the purpose of enabling him properly to perform his duties as an officer of the company; or

(b) to enable any such person to avoid incurring such expenditure: CA 2006, s 204(1).

Section 204 does not authorise a company to enter into a transaction if the aggregate of the value of the transaction in question; and the value of any other relevant transactions or arrangements, exceeds £50,000: CA 2006, s 204(2).

Exception for expenditure on defending proceedings etc

15.58 Approval is not required under CA 2006, ss 197, 198, 200 or 201 (requirement of members' approval for loans etc) for anything done by a company:

(a) to provide a director of the company or of its holding company with funds to meet expenditure incurred or to be incurred by him:

  (i) in defending any criminal or civil proceedings in connection with any alleged negligence, default, breach of duty or breach of trust by him in relation to the company or an associated company; or

  (ii) in connection with an application for relief (see CA 2006, s 205(5)); or

(b) to enable any such director to avoid incurring such expenditure, if it is done on the following terms: CA 2006, s 205(1).

15.59 The terms are:

(a) that the loan is to be repaid, or (as the case may be) any liability of the company incurred under any transaction connected with the thing done is to be discharged, in the event of:

  (i) the director being convicted in the proceedings;

  (ii) judgment being given against him in the proceedings; or

  (iii) the court refusing to grant him relief on the application; and

(b) that it is to be so repaid or discharged not later than:

  (i) the date when the conviction becomes final;

  (ii) the date when the judgment becomes final; or

  (iii) the date when the refusal of relief becomes final: CA 2006, s 205(2).

15.60 For this purpose a conviction, judgment or refusal of relief becomes final:

(a) if not appealed against, at the end of the period for bringing an appeal;

(b) if appealed against, when the appeal (or any further appeal) is disposed of: CA 2006, s 205(3).

An appeal is disposed of if it is determined and the period for bringing any further appeal has ended; or if it is abandoned or otherwise ceases to have effect: CA 2006, s 205(4).

The reference in s 205(1)(a)(ii) to an application for relief is to an application for relief under s 661(3) or (4) (power of court to grant relief in case of acquisition of shares by innocent nominee), or s 1157 (general power of court to grant relief in case of honest and reasonable conduct): CA 2006, s 205(5).

Exception for expenditure in connection with regulatory action or investigation

15.61 Approval is not required under CA 2006, s 197, 198, 200 or 201 (requirement of members' approval for loans etc) for anything done by a company:

(a) to provide a director of the company or of its holding company with funds to meet expenditure incurred or to be incurred by him in defending himself:

  (i) in an investigation by a regulatory authority; or

  (ii) against action proposed to be taken by a regulatory authority, in connection with any alleged negligence, default, breach of duty or breach of trust by him in relation to the company or an associated company; or

(b) to enable any such director to avoid incurring such expenditure: CA 2006, s 206.

Exceptions for minor and business transactions

15.62 Approval is not required under CA 2006, s 197, 198 or 200 for a company to make a loan or quasi-loan, or to give a guarantee or provide security in connection with a loan or quasi-loan, if the aggregate of:

(a) the value of the transaction; and

(b) the value of any other relevant transactions or arrangements,

does not exceed £10,000: CA 2006, s 207(1).

15.63 Approval is not required under CA 2006, s 201 for a company to enter into a credit transaction, or to give a guarantee or provide security in connection with a credit transaction, if the aggregate of:

(a) the value of the transaction (ie, of the credit transaction, guarantee or security), and

(b) the value of any other relevant transactions or arrangements,

does not exceed £15,000: CA 2006, s 207(2).

15.64 Approval is not required under CA 2006, s 201 for a company to enter into a credit transaction, or to give a guarantee or provide security in connection with a credit transaction, if:

(a) the transaction is entered into by the company in the ordinary course of the company's business; and

(b) the value of the transaction is not greater, and the terms on which it is entered into are not more favourable, than it is reasonable to expect the company would have offered to, or in respect of, a person of the same financial standing but unconnected with the company: CA 2006, s 207(3).

Exceptions for intra-group transactions

15.65 Approval is not required under CA 2006, ss 197, 198 or 200 for:

(a) the making of a loan or quasi-loan to an associated body corporate; or

(b) the giving of a guarantee or provision of security in connection with a loan or quasi-loan made to an associated body corporate: CA 2006, s 208(1).

Approval is not required under CA 2006, s 201:

(a) to enter into a credit transaction as creditor for the benefit of an associated body corporate; or

(b) to give a guarantee or provide security in connection with a credit transaction entered into by any person for the benefit of an associated body corporate: CA 2006, s 208(2).

Exceptions for money-lending companies

15.66 Approval is not required under CA 2006, s 197, 198 or 200 for the making of a loan or quasi-loan, or the giving of a guarantee or provision of security in connection with a loan or quasi-loan, by a money-lending company if:

(a) the transaction (ie the loan, quasi-loan, guarantee or security) is entered into by the company in the ordinary course of the company's business; and

(b) the value of the transaction is not greater, and its terms are not more favourable, than it is reasonable to expect the company would have offered to a person of the same financial standing but unconnected with the company: CA 2006, s 209(1).

A 'money-lending company' means a company whose ordinary business includes the making of loans or quasi-loans, or the giving of guarantees or provision of security in connection with loans or quasi-loans: CA 2006, s 209(2).

The condition specified in s 209(1)(b) does not of itself prevent a company from making a home loan:

(a) to a director of the company or of its holding company; or

(b) to an employee of the company,

if loans of that description are ordinarily made by the company to its employees and the terms of the loan in question are no more favourable than those on which such loans are ordinarily made: CA 2006, s 209(3).

15.67 For the purposes of s 209(3) a 'home loan' means a loan:

(a) for the purpose of facilitating the purchase, for use as the only or main residence of the person to whom the loan is made, of the whole or part of any dwelling-house together with any land to be occupied and enjoyed with it;

(b) for the purpose of improving a dwelling-house or part of a dwelling-house so used or any land occupied and enjoyed with it; or

(c) in substitution for any loan made by any person and falling within paragraph (a) or (b): CA 2006, s 209(4).

Other relevant transactions or arrangements

15.68 Section 210 of CA 2006 applies for determining what are 'other relevant transactions or arrangements' for the purposes of any exception to ss 197, 198, 200 or

201. In the following provisions 'the relevant exception' means the exception for the purposes of which that falls to be determined: CA 2006, s 210(1).

Other relevant transactions or arrangements are those previously entered into, or entered into at the same time as the transaction or arrangement in question in relation to which the following conditions are met: CA 2006, s 210(2).

15.69 Where the transaction or arrangement in question is entered into:

(a) for a director of the company entering into it; or

(b) for a person connected with such a director,

the conditions are that the transaction or arrangement was (or is) entered into for that director, or a person connected with him, by virtue of the relevant exception by that company or by any of its subsidiaries: CA 2006, s 210(3).

15.70 Where the transaction or arrangement in question is entered into:

(a) for a director of the holding company of the company entering into it; or

(b) for a person connected with such a director,

the conditions are that the transaction or arrangement was (or is) entered into for that director, or a person connected with him, by virtue of the relevant exception by the holding company or by any of its subsidiaries: CA 2006, s 210(4).

15.71 A transaction or arrangement entered into by a company that at the time it:

(a) was entered into was a subsidiary of the company entering into the transaction or arrangement in question; or

(b) was a subsidiary of that company's holding company,

is not a relevant transaction or arrangement if, at the time the question arises whether the transaction or arrangement in question falls within a relevant exception, it is no longer such a subsidiary: CA 2006, s 210(5).

The value of transactions and arrangements

15.72 For the purposes of CA 2006, ss 197–214 (loans etc):

(a) the value of a transaction or arrangement is determined as follows; and

(b) the value of any other relevant transaction or arrangement is taken to be the value so determined reduced by any amount by which the liabilities of the person for whom the transaction or arrangement was made have been reduced: CA 2006, s 211(1).

The value of a loan is the amount of its principal: CA 2006, s 211(2).

The value of a quasi-loan is the amount, or maximum amount, that the person to whom the quasi-loan is made is liable to reimburse the creditor: CA 2006, s 211(3).

15.73 The value of a credit transaction is the price that it is reasonable to expect could be obtained for the goods, services or land to which the transaction relates if they had been supplied (at the time the transaction is entered into) in the ordinary course of business and on the same terms (apart from price) as they have been supplied, or are to be supplied, under the transaction in question: CA 2006, s 211(4).

The value of a guarantee or security is the amount guaranteed or secured: CA 2006, s 211(5).

The value of an arrangement to which CA 2006, s 203 (related arrangements) applies is the value of the transaction to which the arrangement relates: CA 2006, s 211(6).

If the value of a transaction or arrangement is not capable of being expressed as a specific sum of money:

(a) whether because the amount of any liability arising under the transaction or arrangement is unascertainable, or for any other reason; and

(b) whether or not any liability under the transaction or arrangement has been reduced,

its value is deemed to exceed £50,000: CA 2006, s 211(7).

The person for whom a transaction or arrangement is entered into

15.74 Section 212 of CA 2006 elaborates on the concept of 'the person for whom a transaction or arrangement is entered into'. For the purposes of ss 197–214 (loans etc), the person for whom a transaction or arrangement is entered into is:

(a) in the case of a loan or quasi-loan, the person to whom it is made;

(b) in the case of a credit transaction, the person to whom goods, land or services are supplied, s old, hired, leased or otherwise disposed of under the transaction;

(c) in the case of a guarantee or security, the person for whom the transaction is made in connection with which the guarantee or security is entered into;

(d) in the case of an arrangement within s 203 (related arrangements), the person for whom the transaction is made to which the arrangement relates: CA 2006, s 212.

Loans etc: civil consequences of contravention

15.75 Section 213 of CA 2006 applies where a company enters into a transaction or arrangement in contravention of ss 197, 198, 200, 201 or 203 (requirement of members' approval for loans etc): CA 2006, s 213(1).

The transaction or arrangement is voidable at the instance of the company, unless:

(a) restitution of any money or other asset that was the subject matter of the transaction or arrangement is no longer possible;

(b) the company has been indemnified for any loss or damage resulting from the transaction or arrangement; or

(c) rights acquired in good faith, for value and without actual notice of the contravention by a person who is not a party to the transaction or arrangement would be affected by the avoidance: CA 2006, s 213(2).

15.76 Whether or not the transaction or arrangement has been avoided, each of the persons specified in CA 2006, s 213(4) is liable:

(a) to account to the company for any gain that he has made directly or indirectly by the transaction or arrangement; and

(b) (jointly and severally with any other person so liable under this section) to indemnify the company for any loss or damage resulting from the transaction or arrangement: CA 2006, s 213(3).

In some circumstances, salary paid to a director may in reality be a loan

In *Broadside Colours and Chemicals Ltd, Brown v Button* [2011] 2 BCLC 597, the company went into voluntary liquidation and the liquidator sought to recover loans made to directors under CA 2006, s 197, which loans were repaid by substantial dividends. It was contended that all three directors were jointly liable in respect of all sums due and to indemnify the company for the unlawful loans. As the application was not issued until more than six years after the allegedly unlawful loans an issue also arose as to whether the claims were statute-barred.

Judge Behrens held that on the facts the salaries paid to the directors were in reality loans. Further, the limitation defence in respect of loans they had individually received could not be relied upon, s ince the usual six-year limitation period did not apply where the claim was to recover trust property such as a case where a director had obtained property from the company in breach of trust. Therefore the claims against them succeeded in respect of the monies actually received by them. However, the claim against another director failed, because the joint liability of the directors to indemnify the company in respect of the amount of the unlawful loans arose when the loans were made and was not a continuing obligation.

15.77 The persons who are liable are:

(a) any director of the company or of its holding company with whom the company entered into the transaction or arrangement in contravention of CA 2006, ss 197, 198, 201 or 203;

(b) any person with whom the company entered into the transaction or arrangement in contravention of any of those sections who is connected with a director of the company or of its holding company;

(c) the director of the company or of its holding company with whom any such person is connected; and

(d) any other director of the company who authorised the transaction or arrangement: CA 2006, s 213(4).

Section 213(3) and (4) are subject to 213(6) and (7): CA 2006, s 213(5).

15.78 In the case of a transaction or arrangement entered into by a company in contravention of s 200, 201 or 203 of CA 2006 with a person connected with a director of the company or of its holding company, that director is not liable by virtue of s 213(4)(c) if he shows that he took all reasonable steps to secure the company's compliance with the section concerned: CA 2006, s 213(6).

15.79 In any case:

(a) a person so connected is not liable by virtue of s 213(4)(b), and

(b) a director is not liable by virtue of s 213(4)(d),

if he shows that, at the time the transaction or arrangement was entered into, he did not know the relevant circumstances constituting the contravention: CA 2006, s 213(7): see *Lexi Holdings plc v Luqman* [2008] 2 BCLC 725 appeal to [2009] 2 BCLC 1.

Nothing in CA 2006, s 213 should be read as excluding the operation of any other enactment or rule of law by virtue of which the transaction or arrangement may be called in question or any liability to the company may arise: CA 2006, s 213(8).

An issue that arises is whether a director can be liable for improper loans to other directors without knowledge of such transactions.

A director may be held accountable for making unauthorised loans contrary to CA 2006

In *Neville v Krikorian* [2007] 1 BCLC 1, improper loans were made to directors of the company. The issue was whether a director could be jointly and severally liable for such unauthorised loans to other directors.

The Court of Appeal held that a director who knowingly allowed a practice of lending by his company to a co-director to be treated as acceptable and to continue, could properly be said to have authorised individual payments made in accordance with that practice, notwithstanding that he did not have actual knowledge of each individual payment at the time that it was made. A director could be jointly and severally liable if he took no steps to bring such practice of unauthorised loans to an end. See too: *Re Carriage Co-operative Supply Association* (1884) 27 Ch D 322.

A director is obliged to ascertain and identify the nature of payments made by the company

In *Queensway Systems Ltd v Walker* [2007] 2 BCLC 577, Paul Girolami QC (sitting as a Deputy High Court Judge) held that although the director in question was not aware of each individual payment, s he was aware of the general practice throughout the company's trading history of monies being paid out to or for the benefit of both defendants to fund their joint lifestyle. By allowing that practice to continue without applying her mind to the questions what payments were being made and whether they were justified, which it was her obligation to do, or preventing what was occurring, which she was in a position to do, she was to be taken to have authorised the practice as an arrangement or transaction for the purposes of the CA 2006, and also to have sufficiently participated in, or given her sanction to, both the practice and the payments or alternatively sufficiently failed in her duty of care, that she was liable for breach of her duty as a director. Both the director defendants were therefore jointly and severally liable to the claimants for the sum claimed.

Loans etc: effect of subsequent affirmation

15.80 Where a transaction or arrangement is entered into by a company in contravention of CA 2006, s 197, 198, 200, 201 or 203 (requirement of members' approval for loans etc) but, within a reasonable period, it is affirmed:

(a) in the case of a contravention of the requirement for a resolution of the members of the company, by a resolution of the members of the company; and

(b) in the case of a contravention of the requirement for a resolution of the members of the company's holding company, by a resolution of the members of the holding company,

that the transaction or arrangement may no longer be avoided under s 213: CA 2006, s 214.

Payments for loss of office

The nature of payments

15.81 Section 215 of CA 2006 sets out provisions dealing with payments for loss of office. The term 'payment for loss of office' means a payment made to a director or past director of a company:

(a) by way of compensation for loss of office as director of the company;

(b) by way of compensation for loss, while director of the company or in connection with his ceasing to be a director of it, of:

  (i) any other office or employment in connection with the management of the affairs of the company; or

  (ii) any office (as director or otherwise) or employment in connection with the management of the affairs of any subsidiary undertaking of the company;

(c) as consideration for or in connection with his retirement from his office as director of the company; or

(d) as consideration for or in connection with his retirement, while director of the company or in connection with his ceasing to be a director of it, from:

  (i) any other office or employment in connection with the management of the affairs of the company; or

(ii) any office (as director or otherwise) or employment in connection with the management of the affairs of any subsidiary undertaking of the company: CA 2006, s 215(1). See *Taupo Totara Timber Co Ltd v Rowe* [1978] AC 537.

The references to 'compensation' and 'consideration' include benefits otherwise than in cash, and references in CA 2006 Pt 10, Ch 4 to payment have a corresponding meaning: Chapter 4 s 215(2).

15.82 For the purposes of CA 2006, ss 217–221 (payments requiring members' approval):

(a) payment to a person connected with a director; or

(b) payment to any person at the direction of, or for the benefit of, a director or a person connected with him,

is treated as payment to the director: CA 2006, s 215(3).

References in those sections to payment by a person include payment by another person at the direction of, or on behalf of, the person referred to: CA 2006, s 215(4).

Amounts taken to be payments for loss of office

15.83 Section 216 of CA 2006 applies where in connection with any such transfer as is mentioned in ss 218 or 219 (payment in connection with transfer of undertaking, property or shares) a director of the company:

(a) is to cease to hold office; or

(b) is to cease to be the holder of:

   (i) any other office or employment in connection with the management of the affairs of the company; or

   (ii) any office (as director or otherwise) or employment in connection with the management of the affairs of any subsidiary undertaking of the company: s 216(1) CA 2006.

15.84 If in connection with any such transfer:

(a) the price to be paid to the director for any shares in the company held by him is in excess of the price which could at the time have been obtained by other holders of like shares; or

(b) any valuable consideration is given to the director by a person other than the company,

the excess or, as the case may be, the money value of the consideration is taken for the purposes of those sections to have been a payment for loss of office: CA 2006, s 216(2).

Payment by company: requirement of members' approval

15.85 A company may not make a payment for loss of office to a director of the company unless the payment has been approved by a resolution of the members of the company: CA 2006, s 217(1).

A company may not make a payment for loss of office to a director of its holding company unless the payment has been approved by a resolution of the members of each of those companies: CA 2006, s 217(2).

15.86 A resolution approving a payment to which s 217 applies must not be passed unless a memorandum setting out particulars of the proposed payment (including its amount) is made available to the members of the company whose approval is sought:

(a) in the case of a written resolution, by being sent or submitted to every eligible member at or before the time at which the proposed resolution is sent or submitted to him;

(b) in the case of a resolution at a meeting, by being made available for inspection by the members both:

 (i) at the company's registered office for not less than 15 days ending with the date of the meeting, and

 (ii) at the meeting itself: CA 2006, s 217(3).

No approval is required under s 217 on the part of the members of a body corporate that is not a UK-registered company, or is a wholly-owned subsidiary of another body corporate: CA 2006, s 217(4).

Payment in connection with transfer of undertaking etc: requirement of members' approval

15.87 No payment for loss of office may be made by any person to a director of a company in connection with the transfer of the whole or any part of the undertaking or property of the company unless the payment has been approved by a resolution of the members of the company: CA 2006, s 218(1).

No payment for loss of office may be made by any person to a director of a company in connection with the transfer of the whole or any part of the undertaking or property of a subsidiary of the company unless the payment has been approved by a resolution of the members of each of the companies: CA 2006, s 218(2).

15.88 A resolution approving a payment to which s 218 applies must not be passed unless a memorandum setting out particulars of the proposed payment (including its amount) is made available to the members of the company whose approval is sought:

(a) in the case of a written resolution, by being sent or submitted to every eligible member at or before the time at which the proposed resolution is sent or submitted to him;

(b) in the case of a resolution at a meeting, by being made available for inspection by the members both:

 (i) at the company's registered office for not less than 15 days ending with the date of the meeting; and

 (ii) at the meeting itself: CA 2006, s 218(3).

No approval is required under s 218 on the part of the members of a body corporate that is not a UK-registered company; or is a wholly-owned subsidiary of another body corporate: CA 2006, s 218(4).

15.89 A payment made in pursuance of an arrangement:

(a) entered into as part of the agreement for the transfer in question, or within one year before or two years after that agreement; and

(b) to which the company whose undertaking or property is transferred, or any person to whom the transfer is made, is privy, is presumed, except in so far as the contrary is shown, to be a payment to which s 218 applies: CA 2006, s 218(5).

Payment in connection with share transfer: requirement of members' approval

15.90 No payment for loss of office may be made by any person to a director of a company in connection with a transfer of shares in the company, or in a subsidiary of the company, resulting from a takeover bid unless the payment has been approved by a resolution of the relevant shareholders: CA 2006, s 219(1). The relevant shareholders are the holders of the shares to which the bid relates and any holders of shares of the same class as any of those shares: CA 2006, s 219(2).

15.91 A resolution approving a payment to which s 219 applies must not be passed unless a memorandum setting out particulars of the proposed payment (including its amount) is made available to the members of the company whose approval is sought:

(a) in the case of a written resolution, by being sent or submitted to every eligible member at or before the time at which the proposed resolution is sent or submitted to him;

(b) in the case of a resolution at a meeting, by being made available for inspection by the members both:

  (i) at the company's registered office for not less than 15 days ending with the date of the meeting, and

  (ii) at the meeting itself: CA 2006, s 219(3).

15.92 Neither the person making the offer, nor any associate of his (as defined in CA 2006, s 988), is entitled to vote on the resolution, but:

(a) where the resolution is proposed as a written resolution, they are entitled (if they would otherwise be so entitled) to be sent a copy of it; and

(b) at any meeting to consider the resolution they are entitled (if they would otherwise be so entitled) to be given notice of the meeting, to attend and speak and if present (in person or by proxy) to count towards the quorum: CA 2006, s 219(4).

If at a meeting to consider the resolution a quorum is not present, and after the meeting has been adjourned to a later date a quorum is again not present, the payment is (for the purposes of s 219) deemed to have been approved: CA 2006, s 219(5).

15.93 No approval is required under s 219 on the part of shareholders in a body corporate that is not a UK-registered company, or is a wholly-owned subsidiary of another body corporate: CA 2006, s 219(6).

A payment made in pursuance of an arrangement entered into as part of the agreement for the transfer in question, or within one year before or two years after that agreement; and to which the company whose shares are the subject of the bid, or any person to whom the transfer is made, is privy, is presumed, except in so far as the contrary is shown, to be a payment to which s 219 applies: CA 2006, s 219(7).

Exception for payments in discharge of legal obligations etc

15.94 Section 220 of CA 2006 deals with the exceptions for payments in discharge of legal obligations. Approval is not required under ss 217, 218 or 219 (payments requiring members' approval) for a payment made in good faith in the following circumstances:

(a) in discharge of an existing legal obligation (as defined below);

(b) by way of damages for breach of such an obligation;

(c) by way of settlement or compromise of any claim arising in connection with the termination of a person's office or employment; or

(d) by way of pension in respect of past services: CA 2006, s 220(1).

In relation to a payment within s 217 (payment by company) an existing legal obligation means an obligation of the company, or any body corporate associated with it, that was not entered into in connection with, or in consequence of, the event giving rise to the payment for loss of office: CA 2006, s 220(2).

15.95 In relation to a payment within s 218 or 219 (payment in connection with transfer of undertaking, property or shares), an existing legal obligation means an obligation of the person making the payment that was not entered into for the purposes of, in connection with or in consequence of, the transfer in question: CA 2006, s 220(3).

In the case of a payment within both s 217 and s 218, or within both s 217 and s 219, s 220(2) above applies and not s 220(3): CA 2006, s 220(4).

A payment part of which falls within s 220(1) above and part of which does not is treated as if the parts were separate payments: CA 2006, s 220(5).

Exception for small payments

15.96 Approval is not required under CA 2006, ss 217, 218 or 219 (payments requiring members' approval) if the payment in question is made by the company or any of its subsidiaries; and the amount or value of the payment, together with the amount or value of any other relevant payments, does not exceed £200: CA 2006, s 221(1).

For this purpose 'other relevant payments' are payments for loss of office in relation to which the following conditions are met: CA 2006, s 221(2).

15.97 Where the payment in question is one to which CA 2006, s 217 (payment by company) applies, the conditions are that the other payment was or is paid:

(a) by the company making the payment in question or any of its subsidiaries;

(b) to the director to whom that payment is made; and

(c) in connection with the same event: CA 2006, s 221(3).

Where the payment in question is one to which CA 2006, ss 218 or 219 applies (payment in connection with transfer of undertaking, property or shares), the conditions are that the other payment was (or is) paid in connection with the same transfer to the director to whom the payment in question was made; and by the company making the payment or any of its subsidiaries: CA 2006, s 221(4).

Payments made without approval: civil consequences

15.98 If a payment is made in contravention of CA 2006, s 217 (payment by company) it is held by the recipient on trust for the company making the payment; and any director who authorised the payment is jointly and severally liable to indemnify the company that made the payment for any loss resulting from it: CA 2006, s 222(1).

If a payment is made in contravention of s 218 (payment in connection with transfer of undertaking etc), it is held by the recipient on trust for the company whose undertaking or property is or is proposed to be transferred: CA 2006, s 222(2).

15.99 If a payment is made in contravention of s 219 (payment in connection with share transfer) it is held by the recipient on trust for persons who have sold their shares as a result of the offer made; and the expenses incurred by the recipient in distributing that sum amongst those persons shall be borne by him and not retained out of that sum: CA 2006, s 222(3).

If a payment is in contravention of s 217 and s 218, s 222(2) applies rather than s 222(1): CA 2006, s 222(4).

If a payment is in contravention of s 217 and s 219, s 222(3) applies rather than s 222(1), unless the court directs otherwise: CA 2006, s 222(5).

Transactions requiring members' approval: application of provisions to shadow directors

15.100 Section 223 of CA 2006 applies to shadow directors. For the purposes of:

(a) ss 188 and 189 (directors' service contracts);

(b) ss 190–196 (property transactions);

(c) ss 197–214 (loans etc); and

(d) ss 215–222 (payments for loss of office),

a shadow director is treated as a director: CA 2006, s 223(1).

Any reference in those provisions to loss of office as a director does not apply in relation to loss of a person's status as a shadow director: CA 2006, s 223(2).

Approval by written resolution: accidental failure to send memorandum

15.101 Where approval under Chapter 4 of Part 1 of CA 2006 is sought by written resolution, and a memorandum is required under that chapter to be sent or submitted to every eligible member before the resolution is passed, any accidental failure to send or submit the memorandum to one or more members will be disregarded for the purpose of determining whether the requirement has been met: CA 2006, s 224(1).

Section 224(1) applies subject to any provision of the company's articles: CA 2006, s 224(2).

Cases where approval is required under more than one provision

15.102 Section 225 of CA 2006 recognises that there may be circumstances where approval is required under more than one provision. Approval may be required under more than one provision of CA 2006, Pt 1, Ch 4: CA 2006, s 225. If so, the requirements of each applicable provision must be met: CA 2006, s 225(2).

This does not require a separate resolution for the purposes of each provision: CA 2006, s 225(3).

Contracts with sole members who are directors

Contract with sole member who is also a director

15.103 Section 231 of CA 2006 applies where:

(a) a limited company having only one member enters into a contract with the sole member;

(b) the sole member is also a director of the company; and

(c) the contract is not entered into in the ordinary course of the company's business: CA 2006, s 231(1).

The company must, unless the contract is in writing, ensure that the terms of the contract are either set out in a written memorandum; or recorded in the minutes of the first meeting of the directors of the company following the making of the contract: CA 2006, s 231(2).

15.104 If a company fails to comply with s 231, an offence will be committed by every officer of the company who is in default: CA 2006, s 231(3). A person who is guilty of an offence under the section is liable on summary conviction to a fine not exceeding level 5 on the standard scale: CA 2006, s 231(4).

For the purposes of CA 2006, s 231 a shadow director is treated as a director: CA 2006, s 231(5).

Failure to comply with s 231 in relation to a contract does not affect the validity of the contract: CA 2006, s 231(6). Nothing in the section excludes the operation of any other enactment or rule of law applying to contracts between a company and a director of the company: CA 2006, s 231(7).

Directors' liabilities

Provision protecting directors from liability

15.105 Any provision that purports to exempt a director of a company (to any extent) from any liability that would otherwise attach to him in connection with any negligence, default, breach of duty or breach of trust in relation to the company is void: CA 2006, s 232(1).

Any provision by which a company directly or indirectly provides an indemnity (to any extent) for a director of the company, or of an associated company, against any liability attaching to him in connection with any negligence, default, breach of duty or breach of trust in relation to the company of which he is a director is void, except as permitted by:

(a) s 233 (provision of insurance),

(b) s 234 (qualifying third party indemnity provision), or

(c) s 235 (qualifying pension scheme indemnity provision): CA 2006, s 232(2).

Section 232 of CA 2006 applies to any provision, whether contained in a company's articles or in any contract with the company or otherwise: CA 2006, s 232(3).

Nothing in s 232 prevents a company's articles from making such provision as has previously been lawful for dealing with conflicts of interest: CA 2006, s 232(4).

See in particular the position of non-executive directors in respect of liability in *Equitable Life Assurance Society v Bowley* [2004] 1 BCLC 180.

Provision of insurance

15.106 Section 232(2) (voidness of provisions for indemnifying directors) does not prevent a company from purchasing and maintaining for a director of the company, or of an associated company, insurance against any such liability as is mentioned in that subsection: CA 2006, s 232(2).

Qualifying third party indemnity provision

15.107 Section 232(2) of CA 2006 (voidness of provisions for indemnifying directors) does not apply to qualifying third party indemnity provision: CA 2006, s 234(1). Third party indemnity provision means provision for indemnity against liability incurred by the director to a person other than the company or an associated company: CA 2006, s 234(2). Such provision is a qualifying third party indemnity provision if certain requirements are met.

The provision must not provide any indemnity against:

(a) any liability of the director to pay:

 (i) a fine imposed in criminal proceedings; or

 (ii) a sum payable to a regulatory authority by way of a penalty in respect of non-compliance with any requirement of a regulatory nature (however arising); or

(b) any liability incurred by the director:

 (i) in defending criminal proceedings in which he is convicted; or

 (ii) in defending civil proceedings brought by the company, or an associated company, in which judgment is given against him; or

 (iii) in connection with an application for relief (see CA 2006, s 234(6)) in which the court refuses to grant him relief: CA 2006, s 234(3).

15.108 The references in CA 2006, s 234(3)(b) to a conviction, judgment or refusal of relief are to the final decision in the proceedings: CA 2006, s 234(4).

For this purpose:

(a) a conviction, judgment or refusal of relief becomes final:

 (i) if not appealed against, at the end of the period for bringing an appeal; or

 (ii) if appealed against, at the time when the appeal (or any further appeal) is disposed of; and

(b) an appeal is disposed of:

 (i) if it is determined and the period for bringing any further appeal has ended; or

 (ii) if it is abandoned or otherwise ceases to have effect: CA 2006, s 234(5).

15.109 The reference in CA 2006, s 234(3)(b)(iii) to an application for relief is to an application for relief under:

(a) CA 2006, s 661(3) or (4) (power of court to grant relief in case of acquisition of shares by innocent nominee); or

(b) CA 2006, s 1157 (general power of court to grant relief in case of honest and reasonable conduct): CA 2006, s 234(6).

Qualifying pension scheme indemnity provision

15.110 Section 232(2) of CA 2006 (voidness of provisions for indemnifying directors) does not apply to qualifying pension scheme indemnity provision: CA 2006, 235(1).

Pension scheme indemnity provision means provision indemnifying a director of a company that is a trustee of an occupational pension scheme against liability incurred in connection with the company's activities as trustee of the scheme.

15.111 Such provision is qualifying pension scheme indemnity provision if certain requirements are met: CA 2006, s 235(2). The provision must not provide any indemnity against:

(a) any liability of the director to pay:

  (i) a fine imposed in criminal proceedings; or

  (ii) a sum payable to a regulatory authority by way of a penalty in respect of non-compliance with any requirement of a regulatory nature (however arising); or

(b) any liability incurred by the director in defending criminal proceedings in which he is convicted: CA 2006, s 235(3).

15.112 The reference in s 235(3)(b) to a conviction is to the final decision in the proceedings: CA 2006, s 235(4). For this purpose:

(a) a conviction becomes final:

  (i) if not appealed against, at the end of the period for bringing an appeal; or

  (ii) if appealed against, at the time when the appeal (or any further appeal) is disposed of; and

(b) an appeal is disposed of:

  (i) if it is determined and the period for bringing any further appeal has ended; or

  (ii) if it is abandoned or otherwise ceases to have effect: CA 2006, s 235(5).

The term 'occupational pension scheme' means an occupational pension scheme as defined in s 150(5) of the Finance Act 2004 that is established under a trust: CA 2006, s 235(6).

Qualifying indemnity provision to be disclosed in directors' report

15.113 Section 236 of CA 2006 requires disclosure in the directors' report of:

(a) qualifying third party indemnity provision; and

(b) qualifying pension scheme indemnity provision.

Such provision is referred to in s 236 as 'qualifying indemnity provision': CA 2006, s 236(1).

15.114 If when a directors' report is approved any qualifying indemnity provision (whether made by the company or otherwise) is in force for the benefit of one or more directors of the company, the report must state that such provision is in force: CA 2006, s 236(2).

If at any time during the financial year to which a directors' report relates any such provision was in force for the benefit of one or more persons who were then directors of the company, the report must state that such provision was in force: CA 2006, s 236(3).

15.115 If when a directors' report is approved qualifying indemnity provision made by the company is in force for the benefit of one or more directors of an associated company, the report must state that such provision is in force: CA 2006, s 236(4).

If at any time during the financial year to which a directors' report relates any such provision was in force for the benefit of one or more persons who were then directors of an associated company, the report must state that such provision was in force: CA 2006, s 236(5).

Copy of qualifying indemnity provision to be available for inspection

15.116 Section 237 of CA 2006 applies where qualifying indemnity provision is made for a director of a company, and applies:

(a) to the company of which he is a director (whether the provision is made by that company or an associated company); and

(b) where the provision is made by an associated company, to that company: CA 2006, s 237(1).

15.117 That company or, as the case may be, each of them must keep available for inspection:

(a) a copy of the qualifying indemnity provision; or

(b) if the provision is not in writing, a written memorandum setting out its terms: CA 2006, s 237(2).

15.118 The copy or memorandum must be kept available for inspection at:

(a) the company's registered office; or

(b) a place specified in regulations under CA 2006, s 1136: CA 2006, s 237(3).

The copy or memorandum must be retained by the company for at least one year from the date of termination or expiry of the provision and must be kept available for inspection during that time: CA 2006, s 237(4).

15.119 The company must give notice to the registrar:

(a) of the place at which the copy or memorandum is kept available for inspection; and

(b) of any change in that place,

unless it has at all times been kept at the company's registered office: CA 2006, s 237(5).

If default is made in complying with CA 2006, s 237(2), (3) or (4), or default is made for 14 days in complying with s 237(5), an offence is committed by every officer of the company who is in default: CA 2006, s 237(6).

15.120 A person guilty of an offence under s 237 is liable on summary conviction to a fine not exceeding level 3 on the standard scale and, for continued contravention, a daily default fine not exceeding one-tenth of level 3 on the standard scale: CA 2006, s 237(7).

The provisions of s 237 apply to a variation of a qualifying indemnity provision as they apply to the original provision: CA 2006, s 237(8).

Under s 237, the term 'qualifying indemnity provision' means:

(a) qualifying third party indemnity provision; and

(b) qualifying pension scheme indemnity provision: CA 2006, s 237(9).

Right of member to inspect and request copy

15.121 Every copy or memorandum required to be kept by a company under CA 2006, s 237 must be open to inspection by any member of the company without charge: CA 2006, s 238(1).

Any member of the company is entitled, on request and on payment of such fee as may be prescribed, to be provided with a copy of any such copy or memorandum: CA 2006, s 238(2).

The copy must be provided within seven days after the request is received by the company.

15.122 If an inspection required under CA 2006, s 238(1) is refused, or default is made in complying with s 238(2), an offence is committed by every officer of the company who is in default: CA 2006, s 238(3).

A person guilty of an offence under s 238 is liable on summary conviction to a fine not exceeding level 3 on the standard scale and, for continued contravention, a daily default fine not exceeding one-tenth of level 3 on the standard scale: CA 2006, s 238(4).

In the case of any such refusal or default the court may by order compel an immediate inspection or, as the case may be, direct that the copy required be sent to the person requiring it: CA 2006, s 238(5).

Checklist: Approving directors' long-term service contracts

15.123 *This checklist sets out the steps and procedures involved in approving directors' long-term service contracts under CA 2006, s 188. The practice and procedure will depend upon the Articles of Association adopted by the company and appropriate adaptations should be made depending upon the circumstances.*

No	Issue	Reference
1	Consider whether the service contract is short term or long term?	CA 2006, ss 188–189 and s 227

No	Issue	Reference
2	Approval of shareholders is required where the service contract has a "guaranteed term" and that the period of employment is or may be longer than two years. The guaranteed term' of a director's employment is: (a) the period (if any) during which the director's employment: (i) is to continue, or may be continued otherwise that at the instance of the company (whether under the original agreement or under a new agreement entered into in pursuance of it); and (ii) it cannot be terminated by the company by notice, or can be so terminated only in specified circumstances; or (b) in the case of employment terminable by the company by notice, the period of notice required to be given; or where the employment is within the periods (a) and (b) above, the aggregate of those periods.	CA 2006, s 188(3)
3	The long term service contract may be with the company itself or where he is a director of the holding company, within the group consisting of that holding company and its subsidiaries	CA 2006, s 188(1)
4	Prepare a draft of the service contract or memoranda and ensure all appropriate terms are included (including duties, rights, obligations, restrictions during employment, post-termination covenants, confidentiality, protection of intellectual property, remuneration, pension, expenses, holidays, illness, disciplinary aspects, termination)	
5	Call a Board meeting upon reasonable notice: either a director or secretary (if there is one) may call a board meeting. Set out: • Date • Time • Place • Attach a memorandum of key terms of the service contract	Notice
6	Prepare Agenda for the Board meeting	Agenda

No	Issue	Reference
7	At the Board meeting: ● Ensure quorum present ● Any director to declare interest in the contract ● Chairman presides at the Board meeting. Whether Chairman has a casting vote? ● Voting on a show of hands to convene an EGM for shareholders' approval to the service contract ● Alternatively consider dispensing with a Board meeting and use the written resolution procedure attaching the memorandum to the resolution	CA 2006, ss 177, 182
8	Prepare minutes of the Board meeting	Minutes
9	Call an EGM for every eligible member and set out: ● Date ● Time ● Place ● Ordinary resolution ● Note on proxy ● Attach memorandum of key provisions of the service contract ● Ensure memorandum available for inspection by members at least 15 days before the EGM unless consent to short notice applies	Notice
10	At the EGM: ● Ensure quorum present ● Chairman presides at the EGM. Whether Chairman has a casting vote? ● Voting on a show of hands unless a poll is demanded ● Shareholders' approval to the service contract ● Alternatively consider dispensing with the EGM and use the written resolution procedure attaching the memorandum to the resolution ● Where a company agrees to a provision in contravention of CA 2006, s .188, the provision is void to the extent of the contravention. The service contract is deemed to contain a term entitling the company to terminate at any time by giving reasonable notice	CA 2006, ss 228, 229 CA 2006, s 188(2) CA 2006, s 189

No	Issue	Reference
11	After the EGM:	Minutes
	• Prepare minutes of the EGM	
	• Ensure a copy of the director's service contract is kept available for inspection by the company or subsidiary of the company, or a written memorandum setting out terms of the contract	CA 2006, s 228(1)
	• Ensure the copy or memorandum of the service contract is kept available for inspection at the company's registered office or a place specified in the regulations	CA 2006, s 228(2)
	• The copy of the service contract or memoranda must be retained by the company for at least one year from the date of termination or expiry and available for inspection during that time	
	• Company must give notice to the registrar of the place at which copies and memoranda are kept available for inspection; and a change in that place unless at all times kept at the company's registered office	CA 2006, s 228(3)
	• The above aspects apply also to any variation in the director's service contract or memoranda	CA 2006, s 228(7)
	• Ensure that a copy of the service contract or memoranda is available for inspection by a member of the company without charge. If inspection is refused or default is made, the court may compel an immediate inspection or direct that the copy required be sent to the person requiring it.	CA 2006, s 229(1), 229(5)
	• If a member of the company requests a copy of the service contract or memoranda, the company must send such copy upon payment of such fee as may be prescribed. Ensure a copy is provided within 7 days of request	CA 2006, s 229(2)
	There are criminal penalties where inspection of the service contract or memoranda is refused.	CA 2006, ss 228(6), 229(2)

Definitions

15.124

Compensation and consideration: Includes benefits otherwise than in cash

Employment:	Employment under a director's service contract
Independent broker:	A person who, independently of the director or any person connected with him, s elects the person with whom the transaction is to be effected
Services:	Anything other than goods or land
Value:	Capital value of the asset

16 Directors' remuneration

Contents

Introduction

16.1 Directors' remuneration has long provoked controversy in the UK owing to substantial financial compensation packages being awarded to chairmen or chief executives on their resignation or departure from the company, particularly where the company has performed badly during their tenure of office. The problem usually arises where ailing companies are seeking a potential chairman or chief executive to revive the company's fortunes. The company will seek to recruit a person of high repute with a proven history of success. Recruiting such key officers is likely to be an expensive exercise for the company owing to the expectations that key officers may have regarding the financial packages to be provided to them. The company will try and maintain a balance between the best interests of the company in terms of payments it can afford to make, and the potential candidate's financial requirements. In some cases, the company may be faced with no other option but to accede to the financial package that a chairman or chief executive may request. There has also been public concern over increases in the size of financial packages given to key officers on the board upon their departure from office. This has heightened awareness amongst shareholders and the need to question the financial packages awarded, and to act as an effective control mechanism for preventing directors from awarding excessive remuneration packages.

16.2 This chapter addresses in outline the work of various UK committees that have considered, *inter alia*, directors' remuneration, some of the recommendations of which have been incorporated in a revised UK Code on Corporate Governance. It analyses the information required to be included in the Directors' Remuneration Report, and consideration is given to the consequences for listed companies. The legal position at common law on directors' remuneration is addressed, with particular reference to judicial attitudes towards excessive remuneration when faced with an action by minority shareholders. It also considers actions by minority shareholders under CA 2006, s 994 based on unfair prejudicial conduct based on excessive remuneration to directors are also considered. This chapter also addresses the statutory position concerning directors' remuneration under the CA 2006.

UK committees on directors' remuneration issues

16.3 In the UK, various committees were established to consider corporate governance issues. Some of these committees have specifically addressed directors' remuneration and some of their recommendations now form part of the UK Code on Corporate Governance.

Cadbury Committee

16.4 In 1992, the Cadbury Committee, *inter alia,* considered the issue of directors' remuneration. It stated that the overriding principle in respect of board remuneration was that of openness and transparency. Shareholders were entitled to a full and clear statement of directors' present and future benefits, and how they had been determined. Cadbury recommended that in disclosing directors' total emoluments and those of the chairman and highest paid UK director, separate figures should be given for their salary and performance – related elements and that the criteria on which performance was measured should be explained. Relevant details of stock options, stock appreciation rights, and pension contributions should also be provided. It also recommended that future service contracts should not exceed three years without shareholders' approval, and that this would strengthen shareholder control over levels of compensation for loss of office.

16.5 Cadbury further recommended that boards should appoint remuneration committees, which have now become a conspicuous feature of modern boardroom practice. Cadbury perceived these remuneration committees as comprised wholly or mainly of non-executive directors and chaired by a non-executive director, recommending to the board the remuneration of the executive directors and taking account of outside advice as necessary. Executive directors would not be permitted to participate in decisions on their own remuneration. The composition of members of the remuneration committee should be disclosed in the Director's Report.

Greenbury Committee

16.6 The Greenbury Committee reporting, on 17 July 1995, specifically considered directors' remuneration, owing to public and shareholder concerns about significantly high levels of pay and other remuneration packages of company directors in the UK. Its terms of reference were to identify good practice in determining directors' remuneration and to prepare a specific code of practice for use by UK plcs. Concerns about executive remuneration had largely centred on some large pay increases and large gains from share options in privatised utility industries. Greenbury also acknowledged that there were public and shareholder concerns on the amounts of compensation paid to some departing directors. This adverse publicity had sparked some wider concerns about accountability for directors' remuneration, especially in industries that operated in a less competitive environment.

16.7 Greenbury was of the view that UK companies mostly dealt with directors' remuneration in a sensible and responsible way, and that much had been done in recent years to raise standards and improve procedures for this and other aspects of corporate governance. There was also a key issue about performance which had received too little attention in public discussion. Although the UK's industrial performance had greatly improved in recent years, the performance of companies depended, to an important extent, on the directors and senior executives who led them. In this respect, the remuneration packages that UK companies offered had to be sufficient to attract, retain and motivate directors and managers of the highest quality.

16.8 Greenbury did not advocate statutory controls over directors' remuneration as these would be unnecessary and harmful, preferring voluntary self-reform as the best way forward. The Greenbury Committee considered that it was necessary to strengthen accountability and encourage as well as enhance performance, and to build on progress already made. Greenbury believed that the key to strengthening accountability lay in proper allocation of responsibility for determining directors' remuneration, proper reporting to shareholders and transparency.

Many of Greenbury's recommendations were incorporated in a separate Code of Best Practice alongside the Cadbury Code. The Listing Rules also implemented some of Greenbury's recommendations as part of the listing's procedure and continuing responsibilities of company directors.

Hampel Committee

16.9 The Hampel Committee reporting in 1998, revisited the issue of directors' remuneration, taking into account Cadbury and Greenbury recommendations and best practice procedures.

Hampel emphasised that directors' remuneration was of legitimate concern to shareholders. They were entitled to expect that remuneration would be 'sufficient to attract and retain the directors needed to run the company successfully; and that the remuneration of executive directors should link rewards to corporate and individual performance.' Hampel acknowledged that more generally, now that details of individual directors' remuneration were disclosed, they were liable to have an impact both on the company's reputation and on morale within the company.

16.10 Hampel believed that the remuneration needed to attract and retain executive directors of the required calibre would be largely determined by the market. For directors of international companies, the market was increasingly global. The board, through its remuneration committee, was best qualified to judge the appropriate level; the shareholders were entitled to information which enabled them to judge whether remuneration was appropriate, and whether the structure of remuneration packages would align the directors' interests with their own.

Hampel's recommendations led to a Combined Code, merging together both the Cadbury and Greenbury Codes of Best Practice.

Turnbull Report

16.11 The Turnbull Report published in 2003 was largely concerned with going concern, risk and internal control. However, it established some issues for the Board to address including:

> 'Do the company's culture, code of conduct, human resources policies, and performance reward systems support the business objectives and risk management and internal control systems?'

Boards should take account of directors' remuneration policy and the risk factors associated with such policy.

Higgs' Review

16.12 Although Higgs' Review in 2003 was generally concerned with the role and effectiveness of non-executive directors, the Review also addressed the issue of remuneration paid to non-executive directors.

Higgs was of the view that remuneration for directors needed to be sufficient to attract and retain high calibre candidates but no more than was necessary for this purpose. The level of remuneration appropriate for any particular non-executive director role should reflect the likely workload, the scale and complexity of the business and the responsibility involved. Higgs suggested that, in practice, it may be helpful in assessing remuneration for non-executive directors to use as a benchmark the daily remuneration of a senior representative of the company's professional advisers. The risk of high levels of remuneration (or a large shareholding) prejudicing independence of thought was real and should be avoided. Where a non-executive director had extra responsibilities (such as membership or chairmanship of board committees), the total remuneration should reflect these. Higgs accordingly recommended that non-executive directors' fees should be more clearly built up from an annual fee, meeting attendance fees (to include board committee meetings) and an additional fee for the chairmanship of committees or role as senior independent director. The level of remuneration for non-executive directors should be a matter for the chairman and the executive directors of the board.

Walker Review

16.13 The Walker Review in 2009 addressed corporate governance aspects in UK banks owing to the failures of the banking system during that period. The review also included a consideration of the following aspects concerning remuneration:

- The effectiveness of risk management at board level, including the incentives in remuneration policy to manage risk effectively;
- The balance of skills, experience and independence required on the boards of UK banking institutions;
- The effectiveness of board practices and the performance of audit, risk, remuneration and nomination committees;
- The role of institutional shareholders in engaging effectively with companies and monitoring of boards;

- Whether the UK approach is consistent with international practice and how national and international best practice can be promulgated; and
- The applicability of the recommendations to other financial institutions.

Some of the key aspects of Walker's recommendations included giving more power to remuneration committees to determine directors' remuneration, and to have oversight of highly-paid executives who were not on the company Boards. It also highlighted the need for more disclosure of pay for highly-paid executives.

Kay Review

16.14 In July 2012, the Kay Review published its report entitled 'UK Equity Markets and Long-Term Decision Making'. One of the key recommendations was to link incentives to long-term business performance rather than a short-termism approach, which would not be conducive to a company's financial position.

Other stakeholders

16.15 Institutional shareholders also have an effective voice in respect of directors' remunerations. The Association of British Insurers (ABI) and the National Association of Pension Funds (NAPF) have produced guidelines on directors' remuneration and severance payments.

Other interested potential stakeholders include the Trades Union Congress (TUC), Institute of Directors, Confederation of British Industry (CBI) and Pensions and Investment Research Consultants (PIRC), who have, from time to time, addressed issues concerning directors' remuneration.

Impact of the UK Corporate Governance Code on directors' remuneration

16.16 The UK Corporate Governance Code makes particular references to directors' remuneration that should be addressed by listed companies. This section sets out references to the remuneration regime under the Code with specific reference to the main provisions and supporting principles. This section will shortly be amended following the Financial Reporting Council's consultation on revisions to the Code.

Section D: Remuneration

D.1: The Level and Components of Remuneration

MAIN PRINCIPLE

Levels of remuneration should be sufficient to attract, retain and motivate directors of the quality required to run the company successfully, but a company should avoid paying more than is necessary for this purpose. A significant proportion of executive directors' remuneration should be structured so as to link rewards to corporate and individual performance.

Supporting Principle

The performance-related elements of executive directors' remuneration should be stretching and designed to promote the long-term success of the company.

The remuneration committee should judge where to position their company relative to other companies. But they should use such comparisons with caution, in view of the risk of an upward ratchet of remuneration levels with no corresponding improvement in performance.

They should also be sensitive to pay and employment conditions elsewhere in the group, especially when determining annual salary increases.

Code Provisions

D.1.1. In designing schemes of performance-related remuneration for executive directors, the remuneration committee should follow the provisions in Schedule A to this Code.

D.1.2. Where a company releases an executive director to serve as a non-executive director elsewhere, the remuneration report[21] should include a statement as to whether or not the director will retain such earnings and, if so, what the remuneration is.

D.1.3. Levels of remuneration for non-executive directors should reflect the time commitment and responsibilities of the role. Remuneration for non-executive directors should not include share options or other performance-related elements. If, exceptionally, options are granted, shareholder approval should be sought in advance and any shares acquired by exercise of the options should be held until at least one year after the non-executive director leaves the board. Holding of share options could be relevant to the determination of a non-executive director's independence (as set out in provision B.1.1).

D.1.4. The remuneration committee should carefully consider what compensation commitments (including pension contributions and all other elements) their directors' terms of appointment would entail in the event of early termination. The aim should be to avoid rewarding poor performance. They should take a robust line on reducing compensation to reflect departing directors' obligations to mitigate loss.

D.1.5. Notice or contract periods should be set at one year or less. If it is necessary to offer longer notice or contract periods to new directors recruited from outside, such periods should reduce to one year or less after the initial period.

D.2: Procedure

Main Principle

There should be a formal and transparent procedure for developing policy on executive remuneration and for fixing the remuneration packages of individual directors. No director should be involved in deciding his or her own remuneration.

Supporting Principles

The remuneration committee should consult the chairman and/or chief executive about their proposals relating to the remuneration of other executive directors. The remuneration committee should also be responsible for appointing any consultants in respect of executive director remuneration. Where executive directors or senior management are involved in advising or supporting the remuneration committee, care should be taken to recognise and avoid conflicts of interest.

The chairman of the board should ensure that the company maintains contact as required with its principal shareholders about remuneration.

Code Provisions

D.2.1. The board should establish a remuneration committee of at least three, or in the case of smaller companies[22] two, independent non-executive directors. In addition the company chairman may also be a member of, but not chair, the committee if he or she was considered independent on appointment as chairman. The remuneration committee should make available its terms of reference, explaining its role and the authority delegated to it by the board[23]. Where remuneration consultants are appointed, they should be identified in the annual report and a statement made as to whether they have any other connection with the company.

D.2.2. The remuneration committee should have delegated responsibility for setting remuneration for all executive directors and the chairman, including pension rights and any compensation payments. The committee should also recommend and monitor the level and structure of remuneration for senior management. The definition of 'senior management' for this purpose should be determined by the board but should normally include the first layer of management below board level.

D.2.3. The board itself or, where required by the Articles of Association, the shareholders should determine the remuneration of the non-executive directors within the limits set in the Articles of Association. Where permitted by the Articles, the board may however delegate this responsibility to a committee, which might include the chief executive.

D.2.4. Shareholders should be invited specifically to approve all new long-term incentive schemes (as defined in the Listing Rules[24]) and significant changes to existing schemes, save in the circumstances permitted by the Listing Rules.

Schedule A: The design of performance-related remuneration for executive directors

The remuneration committee should consider whether the directors should be eligible for annual bonuses. If so, performance conditions should be relevant, stretching and designed to promote the long-term success of the company. Upper limits should be set and disclosed. There may be a case for part payment in shares to be held for a significant period.

The remuneration committee should consider whether the directors should be eligible for benefits under long-term incentive schemes. Traditional share option schemes should be weighed against other kinds of long-term incentive scheme. Executive share options should not be offered at a discount save as permitted by the relevant provisions of the Listing Rules.

In normal circumstances, shares granted or other forms of deferred remuneration should not vest, and options should not be exercisable, in less than three years. Directors should be encouraged to hold their shares for a further period after vesting or exercise, subject to the need to finance any costs of acquisition and associated tax liabilities.

Any new long-term incentive schemes which are proposed should be approved by shareholders and should preferably replace any existing schemes or, at least, form part of a well-considered overall plan incorporating existing schemes. The total rewards potentially available should not be excessive.

Payouts or grants under all incentive schemes, including new grants under existing share option schemes, should be subject to challenging performance criteria reflecting the company's objectives, including nonfinancial performance metrics where appropriate.

Remuneration incentives should be compatible with risk policies and systems.

Grants under executive share option and other long-term incentive schemes should normally be phased rather than awarded in one large block.

Consideration should be given to the use of provisions that permit the company to reclaim variable components in exceptional circumstances of misstatement or misconduct.

In general, only basic salary should be pensionable. The remuneration committee should consider the pension consequences and associated costs to the company of basic salary increases and any other changes in pensionable remuneration, especially for directors close to retirement.

21 As required for UK incorporated companies under the Large and Medium-Sized Companies and Groups (Accounts and Reports) Regulations 2008.
22 See footnote 6.
23 This provision overlaps with FSA Rule DTR 7.2.7 R (see Schedule B).
24 Listing Rules LR 9.4. Copies are available from the FSA website.

The Directors' Remuneration Report

Preparation of report and disclosure

16.17 The CA 2006 sets out the basic requirements for directors to prepare the directors' remuneration report and disclosure of the report. Various changes have been introduced by the Enterprise and Regulatory Reform Act 2013 and the Large and Medium-sized Companies and Groups (Accounts and Reports) (Amendment)

Regulations 2013, SI 2013/1981. The effect of these legislative provisions is to give shareholders more power to prevent rewards for failure and to ensure that pay is linked to performance. They also make it easier for shareholders to understand what directors are paid and will be paid; and encourage better relationships between companies and shareholders.

16.18 The directors of a quoted company must prepare a directors' remuneration report for each financial year of the company: CA 2006, s 420(1).

In the case of failure to comply with the requirement to prepare a directors' remuneration report, every person who:

(a) was a director of the company immediately before the end of the period for filing accounts and reports for the financial year in question, and

(b) failed to take all reasonable steps for securing compliance with that requirement,

commits an offence: CA 2006, s 420(2).

16.19 A person guilty of an offence under CA 2006, s 420 is liable:

(a) on conviction or indictment, to a fine;

(b) on summary conviction, to a fine not exceeding the statutory maximum: CA 2006, s 420(3).

With regard to the disclosure of the directors' remuneration report, it is the duty of:

(a) any director of a company, and

(b) any person who is or has at any time in the preceding five years been a director of the company,

to give notice to the company of such matters relating to himself as may be necessary for the purposes of the directors' remuneration report: CA 2006, s 421(1).

A person who makes default in complying with s 421(3) commits an offence and is liable on summary conviction to a fine not exceeding level 3 on the standard scale: CA 2006, s 421(4).

Content of Directors' Remuneration Report

16.20 The Secretary of State may make provision by regulations as to:

(a) the information that must be contained in a directors' remuneration report,

(b) how information is to be set out in the report, and

(c) what is to be the auditable part of the report: CA 2006, s 421(1).

The regulations must provide that any information required to be included in the report as to the policy of the company with respect to the making of remuneration payments and payments for loss of office (within the meaning of Ch 4A of Pt 10) is to be set out in a separate part of the report: CA 2006, s 421(2A).

16.21 Under the *Large and Medium-sized Companies and Groups (Accounts and Reports) (Amendment) Regulations 2008, SI 2008/410,* as amended by the *Large and Medium-sized Companies and Groups (Accounts and Reports) (Amendment) Regulations 2013 SI 2013 No 1981* (the latter came into force on 1 October 2013) ('Regulations'), the remuneration report which the directors of a quoted company are required to prepare under CA 2006 s 420 (duty to prepare directors' remuneration report) must contain the information specified in Schedule 8 to these Regulations, and must comply with any requirement of that Schedule as to how information is to be set out in the report: regulation 11(1). Further, the document setting out a revised directors' remuneration policy in accordance with CA 2006 s 422A must contain the information specified in Schedule 8 to these Regulations, and must comply with any requirements in that Schedule as to how that information is to be set out: regulation 11(1A). Section 422A provides for revisions to directors' remuneration policy and states that the directors' remuneration policy contained in a company's directors' remuneration report may be revised. Any such revision must be approved by the board of directors. The policy as so revised must be set out in a document signed on behalf of the board by a director or the secretary of the company. Any regulations under s 421(1) may make provision as to:

(a) the information that must be contained in a document setting out a revised directors' remuneration policy; and

(b) how information is to be set out in the document.

Sections 422(2) and (3), 454, 456 and 463 of CA 2006 will apply in relation to such a document as they apply in relation to a directors' remuneration report.

Under s 422A, the term 'directors' remuneration policy' means the policy of a company with respect to the matters mentioned in s 421(2A).

16.22 The information to be provided relates to remuneration committees, performance related remuneration, consideration of conditions elsewhere in company and group and liabilities in respect of directors' contracts: regulation 11(1). It also relates to detailed information about directors' remuneration (information included under Part 3 of Schedule 8 to the Regulations) is required to be reported on by the auditor. For the purposes of s 497 in Part 16 of CA 2006 (auditor's report on auditable part of directors' remuneration report), 'the auditable part' of a directors' remuneration report is the part containing the information required by Part 3 of Schedule 8 to these Regulations.

Schedule 8 to the Regulations requires information to be given only so far as it is contained in the company's books and papers, available to members of the public or the company has the right to obtain it: Schedule 8, para 49 of the Regulations.

16.23 However, the directors' remuneration policy as specified in Part 4 of Schedule 8 to the Regulations may, subject to Schedule 8 para 1(3), be omitted from the directors' remuneration report for a financial year, if the company does not intend, at the accounts meeting at which the report is to be laid, to move a resolution to approve the directors' remuneration policy in accordance with s 439A of CA 2006: Schedule 8 para 1(2).

Where the directors' remuneration policy is omitted from the report in accordance with Schedule 8 para 1(2), there must be set out in the report the following information:

(a) the date of the last general meeting of the company at which a resolution was moved by the company in respect of that directors' remuneration policy and at which that policy was approved; and

(b) where, on the company's website or at some other place, a copy of that directors' remuneration policy may be inspected by the members of the company: Schedule 8, para 1(3).

The information required to be shown in the report for or in respect of a particular person must be shown in the report in a manner that links the information to that person identified by name: Schedule 8, para 2(1).

16.24 Nothing in Schedule 8 to the Regulations prevents the directors setting out in the report any such additional information as they think fit, and any item required to be shown in the report may be shown in greater detail than required by the provisions of the Schedule: Schedule 8, para 2(2).

Where the requirements of Schedule 8 to the Regulations make reference to a 'director', those requirements may be complied with in such manner as to distinguish between directors who perform executive functions and those who do not: Schedule 8, para 2(3).

Any requirement of Schedule 8 to the Regulations to provide information in respect of a director may, in respect of those directors who do not perform executive functions, be omitted or otherwise modified where that requirement is not applicable to such a director. In such a case, particulars of, and the reasons for, the omission or modification must be given in the report: Schedule 8, para 2(4).

16.25 Any requirement of Schedule 8 to the Regulations to provide information in respect of performance measures or targets does not require the disclosure of information which, in the opinion of the directors, is commercially sensitive in respect of the company: Schedule 8, para 2(5).

Where information that would otherwise be required to be in the report is not included in reliance on Schedule 8 para 2(5), particulars of, and the reasons for, the omission must be given in the report and an indication given of when (if at all) the information is to be reported to the members of the company: Schedule 8, para 2(6).

Where any provision of Schedule 8 to the Regulations requires a sum or figure to be given in respect of any financial year preceding the relevant financial year, in the first directors' remuneration report prepared in accordance with this Schedule, that sum or figure may, where the sum or figure is not readily available from the reports and accounts of the company prepared for those years, be given as an estimate and a note of explanation provided in the report: Schedule 8, para 2(7).

Definitions applicable under Schedule 8

16.26 Part 7 of Schedule 8 to the Regulations sets out particular definitions that are used in the various paragraphs.

'Amounts to be shown'

16.27 Under Schedule 8, Part 7 to the Regulations, the amount in each case includes all relevant sums paid by or receivable from:

(a) the company; and

(b) the company's subsidiary undertakings; and

(c) any other person,

except sums to be accounted for to the company or any of its subsidiary undertakings or any other undertaking of which any person has been a director while director of the company, by virtue of s 219 of CA 2006 (payment in connection with share transfer: requirement of members' approval), to past or present members of the company or any of its subsidiaries or any class of those members: para 46(2).

The reference to amounts paid to or receivable by a person include amounts paid to or receivable by a person connected with him or a body corporate controlled by him (but not so as to require an amount to be counted twice): para 46(3).

16.28 The amounts to be shown for any financial year under Part 3 Schedule 8 to the Regulations are the sums receivable in respect of that year (whenever paid) or, in the case of sums not receivable in respect of a period, the sums paid during that year: para 47(1). But where:

(a) any sums are not shown in the directors' remuneration report for the relevant financial year on the ground that the person receiving them is liable to account for them as mentioned in para 46(2), but the liability is thereafter wholly or partly released or is not enforced within a period of two years; or

(b) any sums paid by way of expenses allowance are charged to United Kingdom income tax after the end of the relevant financial year or, in the case of any such sums paid otherwise than to an individual, it does not become clear until the end of the relevant financial year that those sums would be charged to such tax were the person an individual,

those sums must, to the extent to which the liability is released or not enforced or they are charged as mentioned above (as the case may be), be shown in the first directors' remuneration report in which it is practicable to show them and must be distinguished from the amounts to be shown apart from this provision: para 47(2).

'Compensation'

16.29 The term includes benefits otherwise than in cash; and in relation to such compensation references in this Schedule to its amounts are to the estimated money value of the benefit: para 44(3).

Compensation in respect of loss of office

16.30 The term includes compensation received or receivable by a person for:

(a) loss of office as director of the company, or

(b) loss, while director of the company or on or in connection with his ceasing to be a director of it, of:

  (i) any other office in connection with the management of the company's affairs, or

(ii) any office as director or otherwise in connection with the management of the affairs of any undertaking that, immediately before the loss, is a subsidiary undertaking of the company or an undertaking of which he is a director by virtue of the company's nomination (direct or indirect);

(c) compensation in consideration for, or in connection with, a person's retirement from office; and

(d) where such a retirement is occasioned by a breach of the person's contract with the company or with an undertaking that, immediately before the breach, is a subsidiary undertaking of the company or an undertaking of which he is a director by virtue of the company's nomination (direct or indirect):

(i) payments made by way of damages for the breach; or

(ii) payments made by way of settlement or compromise of any claim in respect of the breach: para 44(2).

Emoluments of a person

16.31 The term 'emoluments of a person':

(a) includes salary, fees and bonuses, sums paid by way of expenses allowance (so far as they are chargeable to United Kingdom income tax or would be if the person were an individual), but

(b) does not include any of the following, namely:

(i) the value of any share options granted to him or the amount of any gains made on the exercise of any such options;

(ii) any company contributions paid, or treated as paid, in respect of him under any pension scheme or any benefits to which he is entitled under any such scheme; or

(iii) any money or other assets paid to or received or receivable by him under any long term incentive scheme: para 44(1).

Qualifying services

16.32 The term 'qualifying services', in relation to any person, means his services as a director of the company, and his services at any time while he is a director of the company:

(a) as a director of an undertaking that is a subsidiary undertaking of the company at that time;

(b) as a director of any other undertaking of which he is a director by virtue of the company's nomination (direct or indirect); or

(c) otherwise in connection with the management of the affairs of the company or any such subsidiary undertaking or any such other undertaking: para 44(1).

Shares

16.33 The term 'shares' means shares (whether allotted or not) in the company, or any undertaking which is a group undertaking in relation to the company, and includes a share warrant as defined by CA 2006, s 779(1): para 44(1).

Share option

16.34 The term 'share option' means a right to acquire shares: para 44(1).

Value

16.35 The term 'value', in relation to shares received or receivable on any day by a person who is or has been a director of the company, means the market price of the shares on that day: para 44(1).

Schedule 8, Part 2

16.36 Part 2 of Schedule 8 to the Regulations deals with information that is not the subject of audit.

Annual Statement

16.37 Under Part 2 of Schedule 8 to the Regulations, the directors' remuneration report must contain a statement by the director who fulfils the role of chair of the remuneration committee (or, where there is no such person, by a director nominated by the directors to make the statement) summarising for the relevant financial year:

(a) the major decisions on directors' remuneration;

(b) any substantial changes relating to directors' remuneration made during the year; and

(c) the context in which those changes occurred and decisions have been taken: Schedule 8, para 3.

Annual Report on Remuneration

16.38 Part 3 sets out details to be included in the annual report on remuneration.

Single total figure of remuneration for each director

16.39 The directors' remuneration report must, for the relevant financial year, for each person who has served as a director of the company at any time during that year, set out in a table in the form set out in para 5 ('the single total figure table') the information prescribed by paras 6 and 7 below: Schedule 8, para 4(1).

The report may set out in separate tables the information to be supplied in respect of directors who perform executive functions and those who do not: Schedule 8, para 4(2).

Unless otherwise indicated the sums set out in the table are those in respect of the relevant financial year and relate to the director's performance of, or agreement to perform, qualifying services: Schedule 8, para 4(3).

The form of the table required by para 4 is set out below: Schedule 8, para 5(1):

Single Total Figure Table						
	a	b	c	d	e	Total
Director 1	xxx	xxx	xxx	xxx	xxx	xxx
Director 2	xxx	xxx	xxx	xxx	xxx	xxx

The directors may choose to display the table using an alternative orientation, in which case references in Schedule 8 to columns are to be read as references to rows: Schedule 8, para 5(2).

In addition to the columns described in para 7, columns:

(a) must be included to set out any other items in the nature of remuneration (other than items required to be disclosed under para 15) which are not set out in the columns headed '(a)' to '(e)'; and

(b) may be included if there are any sub-totals or other items which the directors consider necessary in order to assist the understanding of the table: Schedule 8, para 6(1).

16.40 Any additional columns must be inserted before the column marked 'Total': Schedule 8, para 6(2).

Subject to para 9, in the single total figure table, the sums that are required to be set out in the columns are:

(a) in the column headed 'a', the total amount of salary and fees;

(b) in the column headed 'b', all taxable benefits;

(c) in the column headed 'c', money or other assets received or receivable for the relevant financial year as a result of the achievement of performance measures and targets relating to a period ending in that financial year other than:

   (i) those which result from awards made in a previous financial year and where final vesting is determined as a result of the achievement of performance measures or targets relating to a period ending in the relevant financial year; or

   (ii) those receivable subject to the achievement of performance measures or targets in a future financial year;

(d) in the column headed 'd', money or other assets received or receivable for periods of more than one financial year where final vesting:

   (i) is determined as a result of the achievement of performance measures or targets relating to a period ending in the relevant financial year; and

   (ii) is not subject to the achievement of performance measures or targets in a future financial year;

(e) in the column headed 'e', all pension related benefits including:

   (i) payments (whether in cash or otherwise) in lieu of retirement benefits;

   (ii) all benefits in year from participating in pension schemes;

(f) in the column headed 'Total', the total amount of the sums set out in the previous columns: Schedule 8, para 7(1).

Where it is necessary to assist the understanding of the table by the creation of sub-totals the columns headed 'a' to 'e' may be set out in an order other than the one set out in para 5: Schedule 8 para 7(2).

16.41 In respect of any items in para 7(1)(c) or (d) where the performance measures or targets are substantially (but not fully) completed by the end of the relevant financial year:

(a) the sum given in the table may include sums which relate to the following financial year; but

(b) where such sums are included, those sums must not be included in the corresponding column of the single total figure table prepared for that following financial year; and

(c) a note to the table must explain the basis of the calculation: Schedule 8, para 8(1).

16.42 Where any money or other assets reported in the single total figure table in the directors' remuneration report prepared in respect of any previous financial year are the subject of a recovery of sums paid or the withholding of any sum for any reason in the relevant financial year:

(a) the recovery or withholding so attributable must be shown in a separate column in the table as a negative value and deducted from the column headed 'Total'; and

(b) an explanation for the recovery or withholding and the basis of the calculation must be given in a note to the table: Schedule 8, para 8(2).

Where the calculations in accordance with para 10 (other than in respect of a recovery or withholding) result in a negative value, the result must be expressed as zero in the relevant column in the table: Schedule 8, para 8(3).

16.43 Each column in the single total figure table must contain, in such manner as to permit comparison, two sums as follows:

(a) the sum set out in the corresponding column in the report prepared in respect of the financial year preceding the relevant financial year; and

(b) the sum for the relevant financial year: Schedule 8, para 9(1).

16.44 When, in the single total figure table, a sum is given in the column which relates to the preceding financial year and that sum, when set out in the report for that preceding year was given as an estimated sum, then in the relevant financial year:

(a) it must be given as an actual sum;

(b) the amount representing the difference between the estimate and the actual must not be included in the column relating to the relevant financial year; and

(c) details of the calculation of the revised sum must be given in a note to the table Schedule 8, para 9(2).

16.45 The methods to be used to calculate the sums required to be set out in the single total figure table are:

(a) for the column headed 'a', cash paid to or receivable by the person in respect of the relevant financial year;

(b) for the column headed 'b', the gross value before payment of tax;

(c) for column 'c', the total cash equivalent including any amount deferred, other than where the deferral is subject to the achievement of further performance measures or targets in a future financial year;

(d) for column 'd':

   (i) the cash value of any monetary award;

   (ii) the value of any shares or share options awarded, calculated by:

      (aa) multiplying the original number of shares granted by the proportion that vest (or an estimate);

      (bb) multiplying the total arrived at in (aa) by the market price of shares at the date on which the shares vest; and

   (iii) the value of any additional cash or shares receivable in respect of dividends accrued (actually or notionally);

(e) for the column headed 'e':

   (i) for the item in para 7(1)(e)(i), the cash value;

   (ii) for the item in para 7(1)(e)(ii), what the aggregate pension input amount would be across all the pension schemes of the company or group in which the director accrues benefits, calculated using the method set out in s 229 of the Finance Act 2004 where:

      (aa) references to 'pension input period' are to be read as references to the company's financial year, or where a person becomes a director during the financial year, the period starting on the date the person became a director and ending at the end of the financial year;

      (bb) all pension schemes of the company or group which provide relevant benefits to the director are deemed to be registered schemes;

      (cc) all pension contributions paid by the director during the pension input period are deducted from the pension input amount;

      (dd) in the application of s 234 of that Act, the figure 20 is substituted for the figure 16 each time it appears;

      (ee) ss 229(3) and (4) do not apply; and

      (ff) s 277 of that Act is read as follows:

      '277 Valuation assumptions

      For the purposes of this Part the valuation assumptions in relation to a person, benefits and a date are:

      (a) if the person has not left the employment to which the arrangement relates on or before the date, that the person left that employment on the date with a prospective right to benefits under the arrangement,

(b) if the person has not reached such age (if any) as must have been reached to avoid any reduction in the benefits on account of age, that on the date the person is entitled to receive the benefits without any reduction on account of age, and

(c) that the person's right to receive the benefits had not been occasioned by physical or mental impairment.' Schedule 8, para 10(1).

16.46 For the item in para 7(1)(e)(ii) where there has not been a company contribution to the pension scheme in respect of the director, but if such a contribution had been made it would have been measured for pension input purposes under s 233(1)(b) of the Finance Act 2004, when calculating the pension input amount for the purposes of sub-paragraph (1)(e)(ii) it should be calculated as if the cash value of any contribution notionally allocated to the scheme in respect of the person by or on behalf of the company including any adjustment made for any notional investment return achieved during the relevant financial year were a contribution paid by the employer in respect of the individual for the purposes of s 233(1)(b) of the Finance Act 2004: Schedule 8, para 10(2).

For the purposes of the calculation in sub-paragraph (1)(d)(ii):

(a) where the market price of shares at the date on which the shares vest is not ascertainable by the date on which the remuneration report is approved by the directors, an estimate of the market price of the shares shall be calculated on the basis of an average market value over the last quarter of the relevant financial year; and

(b) where the award was an award of shares or share options, the cash amount the individual was or will be required to pay to acquire the share must be deducted from the total: Schedule 8, para 10(3).

Definitions applicable to the single total figure table

16.47 In para 7(1)(b) 'taxable benefits' includes:

(a) sums paid by way of expenses allowance that are:

  (i) chargeable to United Kingdom income tax (or would be if the person were an individual, or would be if the person were resident in the United Kingdom for tax purposes), and

  (ii) paid to or receivable by the person in respect of qualifying services; and

(b) any benefits received by the person, other than salary, (whether or not in cash) that:

  (i) are emoluments of the person, and

  (ii) are received by the person in respect of qualifying services: Schedule 8, para 11(1).

A payment or other benefit received in advance of a director commencing qualifying services, but in anticipation of performing qualifying services, is to be treated as if received on the first day of performance of the qualifying services: Schedule 8, para 11(2).

ADDITIONAL REQUIREMENTS IN RESPECT OF THE SINGLE TOTAL FIGURE TABLE

16.48 In respect of the sum required to be set out by para 7(1)(b), there must be set out after the table a summary identifying:

(a) the types of benefits the value of which is included in the sum set out in the column headed 'b'; and

(b) the value (where significant): Schedule 8, para 12(1).

For every component the value of which is included in the sums required to be set out in the columns headed 'c' and 'd' of the table by paras 7(1)(c) and (d), there must be set out after the table the relevant details: Schedule 8, para 12(2).

16.49 In sub-paragraph (2) 'the relevant details' means:

(a) details of any performance measures and the relative weighting of each;

(b) within each performance measure, the performance targets set at the beginning of the performance period and corresponding value of the award achievable;

(c) for each performance measure, details of actual performance relative to the targets set and measured over the relevant reporting period, and the resulting level of award; and

(d) where any discretion has been exercised in respect of the award, particulars must be given of how the discretion was exercised and how the resulting level of award was determined: Schedule 8, para 12(3).

For each component the value of which is included in the sum set out in the column headed 'c' of the table, the report must state if any amount was deferred, the percentage deferred, whether it was deferred in cash or shares, if relevant, and whether the deferral was subject to any conditions other than performance measures: Schedule 8, para 12(4).

16.50 Where additional columns are included in accordance with para 6(1)(a), there must be set out in a note to the table the basis on which the sums in the column were calculated, and other such details as are necessary for an understanding of the sums set out in the column, including any performance measures relating to that component of remuneration or if there are none, an explanation of why not): Schedule 8, para 12(5).

Total pension entitlements

16.51 The directors' remuneration report must, for each person who has served as a director of the company at any time during the relevant financial year, and who has a prospective entitlement to defined benefits or cash balance benefits (or to benefits under a hybrid arrangement which includes such benefits) in respect of qualifying services, contain the following information in respect of pensions:

(a) details of those rights as at the end of that year, including the person's normal retirement date;

(b) a description of any additional benefit that will become receivable by a director in the event that that director retires early; and

(c) where a person has rights under more than one type of pension benefit identified in column headed 'e' of the single total figure table, separate details relating to each type of pension benefit: Schedule 8, para 13(1).

For the purposes of this paragraph, 'defined benefits', 'cash balance benefits' and 'hybrid arrangement' have the same meaning as in s 152 of the Finance Act 2004: Schedule 8, para 13(2).

16.52 'Normal retirement date' means an age specified in the pension scheme rules (or otherwise determined) as the earliest age at which, while the individual continues to accrue benefits under the pension scheme, entitlement to a benefit arises:

(a) without consent (whether of an employer, the trustees or managers of the scheme or otherwise), and

(b) without an actuarial reduction,

but disregarding any special provision as to early repayment on grounds of ill health, redundancy or dismissal: Schedule 8, para 13(3).

Scheme interests awarded during the financial year

16.53 The directors' remuneration report must for each person who has served as a director of the company at any time during the relevant financial year contain a table setting out:

(a) details of the scheme interests awarded to the person during the relevant financial year; and

(b) for each scheme interest:

  (i) a description of the type of interest awarded;

  (ii) a description of the basis on which the award is made;

  (ii) the face value of the award;

  (iv) the percentage of scheme interests that would be receivable if the minimum performance was achieved;

  (iii) for a scheme interest that is a share option, an explanation of any difference between the exercise price per share and the price specified under para 14(3);

  (iv) the end of the period over which the performance measures and targets for that interest have to be achieved (or if there are different periods for different measures and targets, the end of whichever of those periods ends last); and

  (vii) a summary of the performance measures and targets if not set out elsewhere in the report: Schedule 8, para 14(1).

16.54 In respect of a scheme interest relating to shares or share options, 'face value' means the maximum number of shares that would vest if all performance measures and targets are met multiplied by either:

(a) the share price at date of grant or

(b) the average share price used to determine the number of shares awarded: Schedule 8, para 14(2).

16.55 Where the report sets out the face value of an award in respect of a scheme interest relating to shares or share options, the report must specify:

(a) whether the face value has been calculated using the share price at date of grant or the average share price;

(b) where the share price at date of grant is used, the amount of that share price and the date of grant;

(c) where the average share price is used, what that price was and the period used for calculating the average: Schedule 8, para 14(3).

Payments to past directors

16.56 The directors' remuneration report must, for the relevant financial year, contain details of any payments of money or other assets to any person who was not a director of the company at the time the payment was made, but who had been a director of the company before that time, excluding:

(a) any payments falling within para 16;

(b) any payments which are shown in the single total figure table;

(c) any payments which have been disclosed in a previous directors' remuneration report of the company;

(d) any payments which are below a de minimis threshold set by the company and stated in the report;

(e) payments by way of regular pension benefits commenced in a previous year or dividend payments in respect of scheme interests retained after leaving office; and

(f) payments in respect of employment with or any other contractual service performed for the company other than as a director: Schedule 8, para 15.

Payments for loss of office

16.57 The directors' remuneration report must for the relevant financial year set out, for each person who has served as a director of the company at any time during that year, or any previous year, excluding payments which are below a de minimis threshold set by the company and stated in the report:

(a) the total amount of any payment for loss of office paid to or receivable by the person in respect of that financial year, broken down into each component comprised in that payment and the value of each component;

(b) an explanation of how each component was calculated;

(c) any other payments paid to or receivable by the person in connection with the termination of qualifying services, whether by way of compensation for loss of office or otherwise, including the treatment of outstanding incentive awards that vest on or following termination; and

(d) where any discretion was exercised in respect of the payment, an explanation of how it was exercised: Schedule 8, para 16.

Statement of directors' shareholding and share interests

16.58 The directors' remuneration report for the relevant financial year must contain, for each person who has served as a director of the company at any time during that year:

(a) a statement of any requirements or guidelines for the director to own shares in the company and state whether or not those requirements or guidelines have been met;

(b) in tabular form or forms:

 (i) the total number of interests in shares in the company of the director including interests of connected persons (as defined for the purposes of s 96B(2) of the Financial Services and Markets Act 2000(4));

 (ii) total number of scheme interests differentiating between:

  (aa) shares and share options; and

  (bb) those with or without performance measures;

 (iii) details of those scheme interests (which may exclude any details included elsewhere in the report); and

 (iv) details of share options which are:

  (aa) vested but unexercised; and

  (bb) exercised in the relevant financial year: Schedule 8, para 17.

Performance graph and table

16.59 The directors' remuneration report must:

(a) contain a line graph that shows for each of:

 (i) a holding of shares of that class of the company's equity share capital whose listing, or admission to dealing, has resulted in the company falling within the definition of 'quoted company', and

 (ii) a hypothetical holding of shares made up of shares of the same kinds and number as those by reference to which a broad equity market index is calculated, a line drawn by joining up points plotted to represent, for each of the financial years in the relevant period, the total shareholder return on that holding; and

(b) state the name of the index selected for the purposes of the graph and set out the reasons for selecting that index: Schedule 8, para 18(1).

16.60 The report must also set out in tabular form the following information for each of the financial years in the relevant period in respect of the director undertaking the role of chief executive officer:

(a) total remuneration as set out in the single total figure table;

(b) the sum set out in the table in column headed 'c' in the single total figure table expressed as a percentage of the maximum that could have been paid in respect of that component in the financial year; and

(c) the sum set out in column headed 'd' in the single total figure table restated as a percentage of the number of shares vesting against the maximum number of shares that could have been received, or, where paid in money and other assets, as a percentage of the maximum that could have been paid in respect of that component in the financial year: Schedule 8, para 18(2).

For the purposes of sub-paragraphs (1), (2) and (6), 'relevant period' means the specified period of financial years of which the last is the relevant financial year: Schedule 8, para 18(3).

16.61 Where the relevant financial year:

(a) is the company's first financial year for which the performance graph is prepared in accordance with this paragraph, 'specified' in sub-paragraph (3) means 'five';

(b) is the company's 'second', 'third', 'fourth', 'fifth' financial year in which the report is prepared in accordance with this Schedule, 'specified' in sub-paragraph (3) means 'six', 'seven', 'eight', 'nine' as the case may be; and

(c) is any financial year after the fifth financial year in which the report is prepared in accordance with Schedule 8, 'specified' means 'ten': Schedule 8, para 18(4).

16.62 Sub-paragraph (2) may be complied with by use of either:

(a) a sum based on the information supplied in the directors' remuneration reports for those previous years, or,

(b) where no such report has been compiled, a suitable corresponding sum: Schedule 8, para 18(5).

16.63 For the purposes of sub-paragraph (1), the 'total shareholder return' for a relevant period on a holding of shares must be calculated using a fair method that:

(a) takes as its starting point the percentage change over the period in the market price of the holding;

(b) involves making:

    (i) the assumptions specified in sub-paragraph (7) as to reinvestment of income, and

    (ii) the assumption specified in sub-paragraph (9) as to the funding of liabilities; and

(c) makes provision for any replacement of shares in the holding by shares of a different description;

and the same method must be used for each of the holdings mentioned in sub-paragraph (1): Schedule 8, para 18(6).

16.64 The assumptions as to reinvestment of income are:

(a) that any benefit in the form of shares of the same kind as those in the holding is added to the holding at the time the benefit becomes receivable; and

(b) that any benefit in cash, and an amount equal to the value of any benefit not in cash and not falling within paragraph (a), is applied at the time the benefit becomes receivable in the purchase at their market price of shares of the same kind as those in the holding and that the shares purchased are added to the holding at that time: Schedule 8, para 18(7).

In sub-paragraph (7) 'benefit' means any benefit (including, in particular, any dividend) receivable in respect of any shares in the holding by the holder from the company of whose share capital the shares form part: Schedule 8, para 18(8).

16.65 The assumption as to the funding of liabilities is that, where the holder has a liability to the company of whose capital the shares in the holding form part, shares are sold from the holding:

(a) immediately before the time by which the liability is due to be satisfied, and

(b) in such numbers that, at the time of the sale, the market price of the shares sold equals the amount of the liability in respect of the shares in the holding that are not being sold: Schedule 8, para 18(9).

In sub-paragraph (9) 'liability' means a liability arising in respect of any shares in the holding or from the exercise of a right attached to any of those shares: Schedule 8, para 18(10).

Percentage change in remuneration of director undertaking the role of chief executive officer

16.66 The directors' remuneration report must set out (in a manner which permits comparison) in relation to each of the kinds of remuneration required to be set out in each of the columns headed 'a', 'b' and 'c' of the single total figure table the following information:

(a) the percentage change from the financial year preceding the relevant financial year in respect of the director undertaking the role of the chief executive officer; and

(b) the average percentage change from the financial year preceding the relevant financial year in respect of the employees of the company taken as a whole: Schedule 8, para 19(1).

Where for the purposes of sub-paragraph (1)(b), a comparator group comprising the employees taken as a whole is considered by the company as an inappropriate comparator group of employees, the company may use such other comparator group of employees as the company identifies, provided the report contains a statement setting out why that group was chosen: Schedule 8, para 19(2).

Where the company is a parent company, the statement must relate to the group and not the company, and the director reported on is the director undertaking the role of chief executive officer of the parent company, and the employees are the employees of the group: Schedule 8, para 19(3).

Relative importance of spend on pay

16.67 The directors' remuneration report must set out in a graphical or tabular form that shows in respect of the relevant financial year and the immediately preceding financial year the actual expenditure of the company, and the difference in spend between those years, on:

(a) remuneration paid to or receivable by all employees of the group;

(b) distributions to shareholders by way of dividend and share buyback; and

(c) any other significant distributions and payments or other uses of profit or cash-flow deemed by the directors to assist in understanding the relative importance of spend on pay: Schedule 8, para 20(1).

There must be set out in a note to the report an explanation in respect of sub-paragraph (1)(c) why the particular matters were chosen by the directors and how the amounts were calculated: Schedule 8, para 20(2).

Where the matters chosen for the report in respect of sub-paragraph (1)(c) in the relevant financial year are not the same as the other items set out in the report for previous years, an explanation for that change must be given: Schedule 8, para 20(3).

Statement of implementation of remuneration policy in the following financial year

16.68 The directors' remuneration report must contain a statement describing how the company intends to implement the approved directors' remuneration policy in the financial year following the relevant financial year: Schedule 8, para 21(1).

The statement must include, where applicable, the:

(a) performance measures and relative weightings for each; and

(b) performance targets determined for the performance measures and how awards will be calculated: Schedule 8, para 21(2).

Where this is not the first year of the approved remuneration policy, the statement should detail any significant changes in the way that the remuneration policy will be implemented in the next financial year compared to how it was implemented in the relevant financial year: Schedule 8, para 21(3).

This statement need not include information that is elsewhere in the report, including any disclosed in the directors' remuneration policy: Schedule 8, para 21(4).

Consideration by the directors of matters relating to directors' remuneration

16.69 If a committee of the company's directors has considered matters relating to the directors' remuneration for the relevant financial year, the directors' remuneration report must:

(a) name each director who was a member of the committee at any time when the committee was considering any such matter;

(b) state whether any person provided to the committee advice, or services, that materially assisted the committee in their consideration of any such matter and name any person that has done so;

(c) in the case of any person named under para (b), who is not a director of the company (other than a person who provided legal advice on compliance with any relevant legislation), state:

   (i) the nature of any other services that that person has provided to the company during the relevant financial year;

   (ii) by whom that person was appointed, whether or not by the committee and how they were selected;

   (iii) whether and how the remuneration committee has satisfied itself that the advice received was objective and independent; and

   (iv) the amount of fee or other charge paid by the company to that person for the provision of the advice or services referred to in para (b) and the basis on which it was charged: Schedule 8, para 22(1).

In sub-paragraph (1)(b) 'person' includes (in particular) any director of the company who does not fall within sub-paragraph (1)(a): Schedule 8, para 22(2).

Sub-paragraph (1)(c) does not apply where the person was, at the time of the provision of the advice or service, an employee of the company: Schedule 8, para 22(3).

This paragraph also applies to a committee which considers remuneration issues during the consideration of an individual's nomination as a director: Schedule 8, para 22(4).

Statement of voting at general meeting

16.70 The directors' remuneration report must contain a statement setting out in respect of the last general meeting at which a resolution of the following kind was moved by the company:

(a) in respect of a resolution to approve the directors' remuneration report, the percentage of votes cast for and against and the number of votes withheld;

(b) in respect of a resolution to approve the directors' remuneration policy, the percentage of votes cast for and against and the number of votes withheld; and,

(c) where there was a significant percentage of votes against either such resolution, a summary of the reasons for those votes, as far as known to the directors, and any actions taken by the directors in response to those concerns: Schedule 8, para 23.

Directors' Remuneration Policy

16.71 Part 4 of Schedule 8 to the Regulations sets out the directors' remuneration policy.

Introductory

16.72 The information required to be included in the directors' remuneration report by the provisions of this Part must be set out in a separate part of the report and constitutes the directors' remuneration policy of the company: Schedule 8, para 24(1).

Where a company intends to move a resolution at a meeting of the company to approve a directors' remuneration policy and it is intended that some or all of the provisions of the last approved directors' remuneration policy are to continue to apply after the resolution is approved, this fact must be stated in the policy which is the subject of the resolution and it must be made clear which provisions of the last approved policy are to continue to apply and for what period of time it is intended that they shall apply: Schedule 8, para 24(2).

16.73 Notwithstanding the requirements of this Part, the directors' remuneration policy part of the report must set out all those matters for which the company requires approval for the purposes of Chapter 4A of Part 10 of CA 2006: Schedule 8, para 24(3).

Where any provision of the directors' remuneration policy provides for the exercise by the directors of a discretion on any aspect of the policy, the policy must clearly set out the extent of that discretion in respect of any such variation, change or amendment: Schedule 8, para 24(4).

The directors' remuneration policy (or revised directors' remuneration policy) of a company in respect of which a company moves a resolution for approval in accordance with s 439A of CA 2006 must, on the first occasion that such a resolution is moved after 1 October 2013 set out the date from which it is intended by the company that that policy is to take effect: Schedule 8, para 24(5).

Future policy table

16.74 The directors' remuneration report must contain in tabular form a description of each of the components of the remuneration package for the directors of the company which are comprised in the directors' remuneration policy of the company: Schedule 8, para 25(1).

Where the report complies with sub-paragraph (1) by reference to provisions which apply generally to all directors, the table must also include any particular arrangements which are specific to any director individually: Schedule 8, para 25(2).

References in Part 4 of Schedule 8 to 'component parts of the remuneration package' include, but are not limited to, all those items which are relevant for the purposes of the single total figure table: Schedule 8, para 25(3).

16.75 In respect of each of the components described in the table there must be set out the following information:

(a) how that component supports the short and long-term strategic objectives of the company (or, where the company is a parent company, the group);

(b) an explanation of how that component of the remuneration package operates; .

(c) the maximum that may be paid in respect of that component (which may be expressed in monetary terms, or otherwise);

(d) where applicable, a description of the framework used to assess performance including:

(i) a description of any performance measures which apply and, where more than one performance measure applies, an indication of the weighting of the performance measure or group of performance measures;

(ii) details of any performance period; and

(iii) the amount (which may be expressed in monetary terms or otherwise) that may be paid in respect of:

(aa) the minimum level of performance that results in any payment under the policy, and

(bb) any further levels of performance set in accordance with the policy;

(e) an explanation as to whether there are any provisions for the recovery of sums paid or the withholding of the payment of any sum: Schedule 8, para 26.

16.76 There must accompany the table notes which set out:

(a) in respect of any component falling within para 26(d)(i)–(iii), an explanation of why any performance measures were chosen and how any performance targets are set;

(b) in respect of any component (other than salary, fees, benefits or pension) which is not subject to performance measures, an explanation of why there are no such measures;

(c) if any component did not form part of the remuneration package in the last approved directors' remuneration policy, why that component is now contained in the remuneration package;

(d) in respect of any component which did form a part of such a package, what changes have been made to it and why; and

(e) an explanation of the differences (if any) in the company's policy on the remuneration of directors from the policy on the remuneration of employees generally (within the company, or where the company is a parent company, the group): Schedule 8, para 27.

16.77 The information required by para 25 may, in respect of directors not performing an executive function, be set out in a separate table and there must be set out in that table the approach of the company to the determination of:

(a) the fee payable to such directors;

(b) any additional fees payable for any other duties to the company;

(c) such other items as are to be considered in the nature of remuneration: Schedule 8, para 28.

Approach to recruitment remuneration

16.78 The directors' remuneration policy must contain a statement of the principles which would be applied by the company when agreeing the components of a remuneration package for the appointment of directors: Schedule 8, para 29(1).

The statement must set out the various components which would be considered for inclusion in that package and the approach to be adopted by the company in respect of each component: Schedule 8, para 29(2).

The statement must, subject to sub-paragraph (4), set out the maximum level of variable remuneration which may be granted (which can be expressed in monetary terms or otherwise): Schedule 8, para 29(3).

Remuneration which constitutes compensation for the forfeit of any award under variable remuneration arrangements entered into with a previous employer is not included within sub-paragraph 29(3), but is subject to the requirements of sub-paragraphs 29(1) and (2): Schedule 8, para 29(4).

Service contracts

16.79 The directors' remuneration policy must contain a description of any obligation on the company which:

(a) is contained in all directors' service contracts;

(b) is contained in the service contracts of any one or more existing directors (not being covered by paragraph (a)); or

(c) it is proposed would be contained in directors' service contracts to be entered into by the company

and which could give rise to, or impact on, remuneration payments or payments for loss of office but which is not disclosed elsewhere in this report: Schedule 8, para 30.

Where the directors' service contracts are not kept available for inspection at the company's registered office, the report must give details of where the contracts are kept, and if the contracts are available on a website, a link to that website: Schedule 8, para 31.

The provisions of paras 30 and 31 relating to directors' service contracts apply in like manner to the terms of letters of appointment of directors: Schedule 8, para 32.

Illustrations of application of remuneration policy

16.80 The directors' remuneration report must, in respect of each person who is a director (other than a director who is not performing an executive function), set out in the form of a bar chart an indication of the level of remuneration that would be received by the director in accordance with the directors' remuneration policy in the first year to which the policy applies: Schedule 8, para 33.

The bar chart must contain separate bars representing:

(a) minimum remuneration receivable, that is to say, including, but not limited to, salary, fees, benefits and pension;

(b) the remuneration receivable if the director was, in respect of any performance measures or targets, performing in line with the company's expectation;

(c) maximum remuneration receivable (not allowing for any share price appreciation): Schedule 8, para 34(1).

16.81 Each bar of the chart must contain separate parts which represent:

(a) salary, fees, benefits, pension and any other item falling within sub-paragraph 34(1)(a);

(b) remuneration where performance measures or targets relate to one financial year;

(c) remuneration where performance measures or targets relate to more than one financial year: Schedule 8, para 34(2).

Each bar must show:

(a) percentage of the total comprised by each of the parts; and

(b) total value of remuneration expected for each bar: Schedule 8, para 34(3).

A narrative description of the basis of calculation and assumptions used to compile the bar chart must be set out to enable an understanding of the charts presented: Schedule 8, para 35(1).

In complying with sub-paragraph 35(1) it is not necessary for any matter to be included in the narrative description which has been set out in the future policy table required by para 25: Schedule 8, para 35(2).

Policy on payment for loss of office

16.82 The directors' remuneration policy must set out the company's policy on the setting of notice periods under directors' service contracts: Schedule 8, para 36.

The directors' remuneration policy must also set out the principles on which the determination of payments for loss of office will be approached including:

(a) an indication of how each component of the payment will be calculated;

(b) whether, and if so how, the circumstances of the director's loss of office and performance during the period of qualifying service are relevant to any exercise of discretion; and

(c) any contractual provision agreed prior to 27 June 2012 that could impact on the quantum of the payment: Schedule 8, para 37.

Statement of consideration of employment conditions elsewhere in company

16.83 The directors' remuneration policy must contain a statement of how pay and employment conditions of employees (other than directors) of the company and, where the company is a parent company, of the group of other undertakings within the same group as the company, were taken into account when setting the policy for directors' remuneration: Schedule 8, para 38.

The statement must also set out:

(a) whether, and if so, how, the company consulted with employees when drawing up the directors' remuneration policy set out in this part of the report;

(b) whether any remuneration comparison measurements were used and if so, what they were, and how that information was taken into account: Schedule 8, para 39.

Statement of consideration of shareholder views

16.84 The directors' remuneration policy must contain a statement of whether, and if so how, any views in respect of directors' remuneration expressed to the company by shareholders (whether at a general meeting or otherwise) have been taken into account in the formulation of the directors' remuneration policy: Schedule 8, para 40.

Approval and signing of the Directors' Remuneration Report

16.85 The directors' remuneration report must be approved by the board of directors and signed on behalf of the board by a director or the secretary of the company: CA 2006, s 422(1).

If a directors' remuneration report is approved that does not comply with the requirements of this Act, every director of the company who:

(a) knew that it did not comply, or was reckless as to whether it complied, and

(b) failed to take reasonable steps to secure compliance with those requirements or, as the case may be, to prevent the report from being approved,

commits an offence: CA 2006 s 422(2).

A person guilty of an offence under CA 2006, s 422 is liable:

(a) on conviction on indictment, to a fine;

(b) on summary conviction, to a fine not exceeding the statutory maximum: CA 2006, s 422(3).

16.5.5.10 Quoted companies: members' approval of directors' remuneration report

16.86 A quoted company must, prior to the accounts meeting, give to the members of the company entitled to be sent notice of the meeting notice of the intention to move at the meeting, as an ordinary resolution, a resolution approving the directors' remuneration report for the financial year other than the part containing the directors' remuneration policy (as to which see section 439A): CA 2006, s 439(1).

The notice may be given in any manner permitted for the service on the member of notice of the meeting: CA 2006, s 439(2).

The business that may be dealt with at the accounts meeting includes the resolution: CA 2006, s 439(3).

This is so notwithstanding any default in complying with s 439(1) or (2) of CA 2006.

16.87 The existing directors must ensure that the resolution is put to the vote of the meeting: CA 2006, s 439(4).

No entitlement of a person to remuneration is made conditional on the resolution being passed by reason only of the provision made by s 439 of CA 2006: CA 2006, s 439(5).

Under s 439 of CA 2006:

- 'the accounts meeting' means the general meeting of the company before which the company's annual accounts for the financial year are to be laid; and
- 'existing director' means a person who is a director of the company immediately before that meeting: CA 2006, s 439(6).

Quoted companies: members' approval of directors' remuneration policy

16.88 A quoted company must give notice of the intention to move, as an ordinary resolution, a resolution approving the relevant directors' remuneration policy:

(a) at the accounts meeting held in the first financial year which begins on or after the day on which the company becomes a quoted company; and

(b) at an accounts or other general meeting held no later than the end of the period of three financial years beginning with the first financial year after the last accounts or other general meeting in relation to which notice is given under this subsection: CA 2006, s 439A(1).

16.89 A quoted company must give notice of the intention to move at an accounts meeting, as an ordinary resolution, a resolution approving the relevant directors' remuneration policy if:

(a) a resolution required to be put to the vote under s 439 was not passed at the last accounts meeting of the company; and

(b) no notice under this section was given in relation to that meeting or any other general meeting held before the next accounts meeting: CA 2006, s 439A(2).

Section 439A(2) does not apply in relation to a quoted company before the first meeting in relation to which it gives notice under s 439A(1): CA 2006, s 439A(3).

A notice given under s 439A(2) is to be treated as given under s 439A(1) for the purpose of determining the period within which the next notice under s 439A(1) must be given: CA 2006, s 439A(4).

16.90 Notice of the intention to move a resolution to which this section applies must be given, prior to the meeting in question, to the members of the company entitled to be sent notice of the meeting: CA 2006, s 439A(5).

Section 439(2) to (4) applies for the purposes of a resolution to which this section applies as it applies for the purposes of a resolution to which s 439 applies, with the modification that, for the purposes of a resolution relating to a general meeting other than an accounts meeting, subsection (3) applies as if for 'accounts meeting' there were substituted 'general meeting': CA 2006, s 439A(6).

16.91 For the purposes of s 439A, the relevant directors' remuneration policy is:

(a) in a case where notice is given in relation to an accounts meeting, the remuneration policy contained in the directors' remuneration report in respect of which a resolution under s 439 is required to be put to the vote at that accounts meeting;

(b) in a case where notice is given in relation to a general meeting other than an accounts meeting:

  (i) the remuneration policy contained in the directors' remuneration report in respect of which such a resolution was required to be put to the vote at the last accounts meeting to be held before that other general meeting; or

  (ii) where that policy has been revised in accordance with s 422A, the policy as so revised: CA 2006, s 439A(7).

16.92 The following terms apply under s 439A:

(a) 'accounts meeting' means a general meeting of the company before which the company's annual accounts for a financial year are to be laid;

(b) 'directors' remuneration policy' means the policy of the company with respect to the matters mentioned in s 421(2A): CA 2006, s 439A(8).

Quoted companies: offences in connection with procedure for approval

16.93 In the event of default in complying with CA 2006, s 439(1) (notice to be given of resolution for approval of directors' remuneration report), an offence is committed by every officer of the company who is in default: CA 2006, s 440(1).

If the resolution is not put to the vote of the accounts meeting, an offence is committed by each existing director: CA 2006, s 440(2).

It is a defence for a person charged with an offence under CA 2006, s 440(2) to prove that he took all reasonable steps for securing that the resolution was put to the vote of the meeting: CA 2006, s 440(3).

A person guilty of an offence under CA 2006, s 440 is liable on summary conviction to a fine not exceeding level 3 on the standard scale: CA 2006, s 440(4).

Under CA 2006, s 440:

- 'the accounts meeting' means the general meeting of the company before which the company's annual accounts for the financial year are to be laid; and
- 'existing director' means a person who is a director of the company immediately before that meeting: CA 2006, s 440(5).

Legal regulation of directors' remuneration

16.94 This section considers the common law position and the challenge that can be made by shareholders to directors' excessive remuneration. It then considers the options available to shareholders under the CA 2006 to enable them to bring proceedings where the remuneration may not in the best interests of the company.

It also addresses the provisions of Chapter 4A of Part 10 of the CA 2006 in respect of special provisions concerning remuneration for directors of quoted companies (as amended by the Enterprise and Regulatory Reform Act 2013).

The common law position

Presumption

16.95 There is a presumption at common law that directors are expected to work for nothing unless there is express provision in the company's articles of association or a service contract provides for a director's remuneration.

There is no implied term at common law that directors should be paid for their services to the company

In *Hutton v West Cork Railway Company Co* [1883] 23 Ch D 654, a railway company which had no provision in its articles for paying remuneration to directors, and had never paid any, sold its undertaking to another company at a price to be determined by an arbitrator. By an Act authorising the transfer it was provided that on completion of the transfer the company should be dissolved except for the purpose of regulating their internal affairs and of winding up the same, and of dividing up the purchase money. The purchase money was to be applied in paying the costs of the arbitration and in paying off any revenue debts or charges of the company, with the residue being divided among the debenture holders and shareholders. After completion of the transfer, a general meeting of the company was held, at which a resolution was passed to apply a certain amount of the purchase money in compensating the paid officials of the company for their loss of employment, although it was accepted that they had no legal claim for any compensation including any remuneration to them for their past services.

The directors proposed to apply £1,050 in compensating the managing director of the company as well as other paid officers for loss of their employment. The remainder after payment of expenses, which the directors estimated at about £1,050, would be paid by way of remuneration for directors' past services, as they had never received any remuneration. The action was in fact brought by one of the holders of the debenture stock of West Cork Company who was seeking an injunction restraining the company from making the proposed payments to the detriment of the creditors.

According to Bowen LJ, the directors had not done anything wrong in proposing to make these payments. The company had done what nine out of ten companies would do without the least objection being made. They were directors who for many years had served the company for nothing and it was always intended that they would always serve the company for nothing. The payments by way of remuneration were not in respect of the measure of service rendered by the directors but a general view that the company entertained of the directors' past merits. According to Bowen LJ, the money that was to be paid to the directors and officers did not belong to the majority. It was the company's money, which the majority shareholders wanted to spend. However, they could only spend money which was not theirs but the company's if they were spending it for purposes which were reasonably incidental to the carrying on of the business of the company. Further, bona fides could not be the sole test, otherwise:

'you might have a lunatic conducting the affairs of the company, and paying away its money with both hands in a manner perfectly bona fide yet perfectly irrational. The test must be what is reasonably incidental to, and within the reasonable scope of carrying on, the business of the company.'

According to Bowen LJ, the remuneration payable to directors was in the form of a gratuity analogous to a compensation for loss of the services of a managing director. A director was not a servant. He was a person who was doing business for the company, but not upon ordinary terms. It was not implied from the mere fact that he was a director that he was to have a right to be paid for it. In some companies, there is a special provision for the way in which directors are to be paid and regards must be had to that provision to see how the remuneration is to be paid. Where there is no special provision the payment would be in the form of a gratuity.

There must be a genuine exercise of the power of directors to award remuneration otherwise such payments will be considered ultra vires

The courts will not permit payment of director's remuneration that is in reality a disguised gift out of capital

In *Re Halt Garage (1964) Ltd* [1982] 3 All ER 1016, the husband acquired a ready-made company and carried on a garage business through the company. He and his wife were the only shareholders in the company and its directors. The company's articles under its Regulation 76 gave the company the following powers: 'The remuneration of the directors shall from time to time be determined by the company in general meeting. Such remuneration shall be deemed to accrue from day to day.' The company's article also included an express power for the company to determine and pay directors' remuneration for the mere assumption of the post of director. The husband and wife built up the company together and drew weekly sums from the business as their director's remuneration. When the wife became ill, the husband continued to work full time, but gradually the company's profits began to decline and the company went into voluntary liquidation and subsequently compulsory winding up. During a certain period of time, the husband and wife's remuneration was largely out of capital because the company was suffering a trading loss.

The liquidator brought proceedings against the directors on the basis that the remuneration exceeded the market value of his services to the company and that the directors were guilty of misfeasance and breach of trust in making the drawings. The liquidator submitted that although the amounts drawn by the husband and wife were either formally determined by the company in general meeting as directors' remuneration or were otherwise sanctioned as such by the company, and although they were made in good faith, they were still ultra vires the company as being gratuitous payments made out of capital, otherwise than for consideration, unless it could be shown that they were made for the benefit of the company and to promote its prosperity.

> Oliver J decided that where payments of remuneration to a director were made under the authority of the company in general meeting under an express power in its articles to award director's remuneration and there was no question of fraud on the company's creditors or on minority shareholders, the competence of the company to award the remuneration depended on whether the payments were genuinely director's remuneration (as opposed to a disguised gift out of capital) and not an abstract test of benefit to the company. The amount of remuneration awarded in such circumstances was a matter of company management. Provided there had been a genuine exercise of the company's power to award remuneration, it was not for the court to determine. There was, however, evidence that having regard to the company's turnover, the husband's drawings were excessive or they were disguised gifts of capital rather than genuine awards of remuneration. But the court would not inquire into whether it would have been more beneficial to the company to have made lesser awards of remuneration to him, since this was a matter for the company.
>
> With regards to the wife's drawings, although the company's articles included power to award remuneration for the mere assumption of directorship, the power under the company's articles assumed that a director would receive remuneration for services rendered or to be rendered. Having regard to the wife's inactivity during the period in question, the whole of the amounts drawn by the wife during her period of illness were not genuine awards of remuneration to her for holding the directorship office and would be considered disguised gifts out of capital. They were ultra vires the company and repayable.

Lack of corporate capacity

16.96 A challenge could also be made by shareholders on the ground that the payment of excessive remuneration was ultra vires and beyond the company's objects. However, under CA 2006, s 39, the validity of an act undertaken by a company cannot be called into question on grounds of lack of capacity by reason of anything in the company's memorandum. This effectively abolishes the external ultra vires rule. However, the internal aspects of the doctrine still survive as between the company and the shareholders. Directors must still observe any limitations under the company's constitution: CA 2006, ss 40 and 41.

Unfair prejudicial conduct

16.97 Under the CA 2006, minority shareholders could bring proceedings under s 994 by way of a challenge to the excessive remuneration.

Section 994 allows a shareholder to petition to the court on grounds that the company's affairs have been or are being conducted in a manner unfairly prejudicial to the interests of the company. Under CA 1985, s 996, the court can make such order as it thinks fit. This includes an order regulating the future affairs of the company. This could mean that the court could be involved in deciding whether or not the remuneration was excessive, although traditionally the courts have been reluctant to get involved in second-guessing directors' management decisions. However, a shareholder could invite the court to decide on the nature of the remuneration. It may be possible for the court to set aside the remuneration or reduce the remuneration awarded to directors.

Another order under s 996 is for the court to order the company from doing an act or to refrain from acting. This could mean that the court could prevent any future payment being made to a director or chairman or the court could order only a certain amount to be paid to such officers.

> ***Directors had not abused their fiduciary position in awarding excessive directors' remuneration***
>
> In *Re Saul D Harrison & Sons plc* [1995] 1 BCLC 14, the petitioner who held 8 per cent of shares in the company sought an order under CA 2006, s 994 on the grounds that the directors had kept the company in business in order to earn remuneration in circumstances in which it was operating at a loss, and that they had paid themselves excessive remuneration and had failed to keep proper and complete accounting records. Hoffmann LJ (as he was then) stated that in order to determine what was unfair for the purposes of s 994, the test of unfairness should be judged in a commercial context. The Articles of Association determined the powers of the board of directors; the starting point under s 994 was to determine whether the allegedly unfair prejudicial conduct was in accordance with the articles of association. They may be situations where the articles of association did not reflect the understandings upon which the shareholders were associated, and this may entail that an exercise of powers in compliance with the articles was unfair. Hoffmann LJ decided that there were no grounds for finding that the relationship between the company members was other than that set out in the articles. There was no basis for finding that the directors had abused their fiduciary positioning awarding excessive remuneration, nor had they conducted the company's affairs in breach of the company's articles of association.

Directors of quoted companies: special provision

16.98 Section 226A of CA 2006 (as inserted by the Enterprise and Regulatory Reform Act 2013) introduces Ch 4A of Pt 10 of CA 2006 concerning special provisions on remuneration for directors of quoted companies.

Key definition

16.99 Under Chapter 4A, the following terms apply:

- 'directors' remuneration policy' means the policy of a quoted company with respect to the making of remuneration payments and payments for loss of office;
- 'quoted company' has the same meaning as in Part 15 of the CA 2006;
- 'remuneration payment' means any form of payment or other benefit made to or otherwise conferred on a person as consideration for the person:

(a) holding, agreeing to hold or having held office as director of a company, or

(b) holding, agreeing to hold or having held, during a period when the person is or was such a director:

(i) any other office or employment in connection with the management of the affairs of the company, or

(ii) any office (as director or otherwise) or employment in connection with the management of the affairs of any subsidiary undertaking of the company,

other than a payment for loss of office;

- 'payment for loss of office' has the same meaning as in Chapter 4 of Part 10 CA 2006: CA 2006, s 226A(1).

16.100 Section 226A(3) applies where, in connection with a relevant transfer, a director of a quoted company is:

(a) to cease to hold office as director, or

(b) to cease to be the holder of:

(i) any other office or employment in connection with the management of the affairs of the company, or

(ii) any office (as director or otherwise) or employment in connection with the management of the affairs of any subsidiary undertaking of the company: CA 2006, s 226A(2).

16.101 If in connection with the transfer:

(a) the price to be paid to the director for any shares in the company held by the director is in excess of the price which could at the time have been obtained by other holders of like shares, or

(b) any valuable consideration is given to the director by a person other than the company,

the excess or, as the case may be, the money value of the consideration is taken for the purposes of section 226C to have been a payment for loss of office: CA 2006, s 226A(3).

16.102 Under s 226A(2), 'relevant transfer' means:

(a) a transfer of the whole or any part of the undertaking or property of the company or a subsidiary of the company;

(b) a transfer of shares in the company, or in a subsidiary of the company, resulting from a takeover bid: CA 2006, s 226A(4).

The references in Chapter 4A of Part 10 CA 2006 to the making of a remuneration payment or to the making of a payment for loss of office are to be read in accordance with this section: CA 2006, s 226A(5).

16.103 The references in Chapter 4A of Part 10 CA 2006 to a payment by a company include a payment by another person at the direction of, or on behalf of, the company: CA 2006, s 226A(6).

The references in Chapter 4A of Part 10 CA 2006 to a payment to a person ('B') who is, has been or is to be a director of a company include:

(a) a payment to a person connected with B, or

(b) a payment to a person at the direction of, or for the benefit of, B or a person connected with B: CA 2006, s 226A(7).

Section 252 CA 2006 applies for the purposes of determining whether a person is connected with a person who has been, or is to be, a director of a company as it applies for the purposes of determining whether a person is connected with a director: CA 2006, s 226A(8).

The references in Chapter 4A of Part 10 CA 2006 to a director include a shadow director but references to loss of office as a director do not include loss of a person's status as a shadow director: CA 2006, s 226A(9).

Restrictions relating to remuneration or loss of office payments

16.104 In connection with remuneration payments:

A quoted company may not make a remuneration payment to a person who is, or is to be or has been, a director of the company unless:

(a) the payment is consistent with the approved directors' remuneration policy, or

(b) the payment is approved by resolution of the members of the company: CA 2006, s 226B(1).

The approved directors' remuneration policy is the most recent remuneration policy to have been approved by a resolution passed by the members of the company in general meeting: CA 2006, s 226B(2).

16.105 In respect of loss of office payments:

No payment for loss of office may be made by any person to a person who is, or has been, a director of a quoted company unless:

(a) the payment is consistent with the approved directors' remuneration policy, or

(b) the payment is approved by resolution of the members of the company: CA 2006, s 226C(1).

The approved directors' remuneration policy is the most recent remuneration policy to have been approved by a resolution passed by the members of the company in general meeting: CA 2006, s 226C(2).

Chapter 4A also sets out supplementary provisions in respect of ss 226B and 226C:

16.106 A resolution approving a payment for the purposes of s 226B(1)(b) or 226C(1)(b) must not be passed unless a memorandum setting out particulars of the proposed payment (including its amount) is made available for inspection by the members of the company:

(a) at the company's registered office for not less than 15 days ending with the date of the meeting at which the resolution is to be considered, and

(b) at that meeting itself: CA 2006, s 226D(1).

The memorandum must explain the ways in which the payment is inconsistent with the approved directors' remuneration policy (within the meaning of the section in question): CA 2006, s 226D(2).

The company must ensure that the memorandum is made available on the company's website from the first day on which the memorandum is made available for inspection under s 226D(1) until its next accounts meeting: CA 2006, s 226D(3).

16.107 Failure to comply with s 226D(3) does not affect the validity of the meeting at which a resolution is passed approving a payment to which the memorandum relates or the validity of anything done at the meeting: CA 2006, s 226D(4).

Nothing in section 226B or 226C authorises the making of a remuneration payment or (as the case may be) a payment for loss of office in contravention of the articles of the company concerned: CA 2006, s 226D(5).

Nothing in ss 226B or 226C applies in relation to a remuneration payment or (as the case may be) a payment for loss of office made to a person who is, or is to be or has been, a director of a quoted company before the earlier of:

(a) the end of the first financial year of the company to begin on or after the day on which it becomes a quoted company, and .

(b) the date from which the company's first directors' remuneration policy to be approved under s 439A takes effect: CA 2006, s 226D(6).

Under s 226D, the 'company's website' is the website on which the company makes material available under s 430: CA 2006, s 226D(7).

16.108 In respect of payments made without approval: civil consequences, the following apply:

An obligation (however arising) to make a payment which would be in contravention of ss 226B or 226C has no effect: CA 2006, s 226E(1).

If a payment is made in contravention of ss 226B or 226C:

(a) it is held by the recipient on trust for the company or other person making the payment, and

(b) in the case of a payment by a company, any director who authorised the payment is jointly and severally liable to indemnify the company that made the payment for any loss resulting from it: CA 2006, s 226E(2).

16.109 If a payment for loss of office is made in contravention of s 226C to a director of a quoted company in connection with the transfer of the whole or any part of the undertaking or property of the company or a subsidiary of the company:

(a) s 226E(2) does not apply, and

(b) the payment is held by the recipient on trust for the company whose undertaking or property is or is proposed to be transferred: CA 2006, s 226E(3).

16.110 If a payment for loss of office is made in contravention of s 226C to a director of a quoted company in connection with a transfer of shares in the company, or in a subsidiary of the company, resulting from a takeover bid:

(a) s 226E(2) does not apply,

(b) the payment is held by the recipient on trust for persons who have sold their shares as a result of the offer made, and

(c) the expenses incurred by the recipient in distributing that sum amongst those persons shall be borne by the recipient and not retained out of that sum: CA 2006, s 226E(4).

16.111 If in proceedings against a director for the enforcement of a liability under s 226E(2)(b):

(a) the director shows that he or she has acted honestly and reasonably, and

(b) the court considers that, having regard to all the circumstances of the case, the director ought to be relieved of liability,

the court may relieve the director, either wholly or in part, from liability on such terms as the court thinks fit: CA 2006, s 226E(5).

Section 226F(1) of CA 2006 ('relationship with requirements under Chapter 4') provides that Ch 4A does not affect any requirement for approval by a resolution of the members of a company which applies in relation to the company under Ch 4 of Pt 10 to the CA 2006.

Where the making of a payment to which ss 226B or 226C applies requires approval by a resolution of the members of the company concerned under Ch 4, approval obtained for the purposes of that Chapter is to be treated as satisfying the requirements of s 226B(1)(b) or (as the case may be) s 226C(1)(b): CA 2006, s 226F(2).

Directors' remuneration under the Listing Rules

16.112 Companies listed on the London Stock Exchange are required to comply with the Listing Rules as part of the directors' remuneration disclosure. Details of the requirements for disclosure are set out primarily in *LR 9.4: Documents requiring prior approval*. Changes to the remuneration disclosure requirements were set out in the Financial Conduct Authority's policy statement (PS13/11) and consultation (CP13/7: 'Consequential Changes to the Listing Rules resulting from BIS Directors' Remuneration Reporting Regulations and Narrative Reporting Regulations in August 2013.

Definitions

16.113

Accounts meeting:	a general meeting of the company before which the company's annual accounts for a financial year are to be laid.
Directors' remuneration policy:	the policy of the company with respect to the matters set out in CA 2006, s 421(2A).

17 Directors' disqualification

Contents

Introduction

17.1 A typical situation leading to the disqualification of directors is where the company has misused by some or all of the directors: they have engaged in wrongful conduct subsequent to the establishment of the company by, for example, engaging in transactions defrauding or misleading the public or the creditors, or failure to keep proper accounting records, or using phoenix companies. The directors may have used the company as a cloak for their delinquent acts. They hide behind the veil of incorporation by, for example, misapplying and siphoning off corporate funds for their own personal gain and use and incurring significant losses for the company.

Although the wrongful actions of directors may to some extent fall within the breach of their general duties under the CA 2006 (such as duty to the company), the CA 2006 falls short of imposing disqualification sanctions against directors or other persons. In the circumstances, therefore, the Company Directors Disqualification Act 1986 (CDDA 1986) was enacted to address disqualification sanctions various persons. This Chapter incorporates amendments made to the CDDA 1986 by SBEEA 2015 and under the DA 2015.

Objectives of the Company Directors Disqualification Act 1986

17.2 In the Preamble to the Company Directors Disqualification Act 1986 (CDDA 1986), it states that the objective of the Act is to consolidate certain enactments relating to the disqualification of persons from being directors of companies, and from being otherwise concerned with a company's affairs.

The CDDA 1986 applies not only to directors but is wider in scope, and certain provisions apply to a wide range of potential defendants, including company secretaries, liquidators, and other officers within the company.

17.3 The objective of the CDDA was set out in *Re Blackspur Group plc, Secretary of State for Trade and Industry v Davies* [1998] 1 BCLC 676, where Lord Woolf MR stated:

> 'The purpose of the 1986 Act is the protection of the public, by means of prohibitory remedial action, by anticipated deterrent effect on further misconduct and by encouragement of higher standards of honesty and diligence in corporate management, from those who are unfit to be concerned in the management of a company.
>
> Parliament has designated the Secretary of State as the proper public officer to discharge the function of making applications to the court for disqualification orders. There is a wide discretion to do so in cases where it appears, in the prescribed circumstances, that "it is expedient in the public interest that a disqualification order should be made". In any particular case it may be decided that the public interest is best served by making and continuing an application to trial; or by not making an application at all; or by not continuing a pending application to trial; or by not contesting at trial points raised by way of defence or mitigation. All these litigation decisions are made by the Secretary of State according to what is considered by her to be "expedient in the public interest". They are not made by the court or by other parties to the proceedings'.

The principal objective is to ensure public protection as well as protection of the creditors. The effect of the CDDA 1986 is that directors who are disqualified for a certain period of time lose the privilege of limited liability company, owing to their wrongful action or misconduct in acting as a director of the company. In effect, directors who subsequent upon disqualification, conduct business activities on their own account become personally liable with the threat of bankruptcy if they cannot pay their debts: this is the consequence of abuse of the privilege of incorporation. In 1982, the Cork Committee highlighted the need for 'proper safeguards for the public'.

17.4 In *Re Tech Textiles Ltd, Secretary of State for Trade and Industry v Vane* [1998] 1 BCLC 259, Arden J stated that 'the public' for this purpose includes all relevant interest groups, such as shareholders, employees, lenders, customers and other creditors – the stakeholders of the company. Further, in *Hill v Secretary of State for the Environment, Food and Rural Affairs* [2006] 1 BCLC 601, Hart J was of the view that the public policy underlying the CDDA 1986 was the protection of the public from those individuals who are not regarded as trustworthy persons to be involved in the management of a limited liability company. The relevant section of the public also consisted of, as a primary class, those who might extend credit to a company.

The CDDA 1986 concerns civil proceedings against directors and the sanction is not penal, though the effect is to restrict individual freedom. Judicial attitudes have varied as to the nature of the conduct required to disqualify a director. It may include unethical behaviour towards third parties – a disregard to the interests of creditors or suppliers demonstrates values and conduct unbefitting a director. It may also include recklessness, incompetence, or breach of commercial morality towards wider stakeholders on the company.

17.5 According to Browne-Wilkinson VC in *Re Lo-Line Electric Motors Limited* [1988] 2 All ER 692:

> 'The primary purpose of the section is not to punish the individual but to protect the public against the future conduct of companies by persons whose past records as directors of insolvent companies have shown them to be a danger to creditors and others. Therefore, the power is not fundamentally penal. But, if the power to disqualify is exercised, disqualification does involve a substantial interference with the freedom of the individual. It follows that the rights of the individual must be fully protected. Ordinary commercial misjudgment is in itself not sufficient to justify disqualification. In the normal case, the conduct complained of must display a lack of commercial probity, although I have no doubt that in an extreme case of gross negligence or total incompetence disqualification could be appropriate'.

Under the CDDA 1986, depending upon the grounds for disqualification, the court will either make a disqualification order or a disqualification undertaking.

17.6 The CDDA is also supplemented by:

- Practice Direction: Directors Disqualification Proceedings;
- the Insolvent Companies (Reports on Conduct of Directors) (Amendment) Rules 1996 as amended by The Insolvent Companies (Reports on Conduct of Directors) (Amendment) Rules 2001, SI 2001/764;
- the Insolvent Companies (Disqualification of Unfit Directors) Proceedings Rules 1987 (as amended by The Insolvent Companies (Disqualification of Unfit Directors) Proceedings (Amendment) Rules 2007; and
- the Companies (Disqualification Orders) Regulations 2009, SI 2009/2471.

17.7 This chapter addresses the following:

- the role of the Insolvency Service;
- the circumstances when disqualification orders may be applied;
- the use of disqualification undertakings;
- grounds on which the directors' disqualification operates;
- the period of disqualification; and
- foreign directors' disqualification.

The role of the Insolvency Service

17.8 One of the roles of the Insolvency Service is to investigate a director and/or his company where it has been involved in insolvency proceedings, or where there has been a complaint lodged with the Insolvency Service by a third party.

Where the Insolvency Service believe that the director who is the subject of an investigation, has not complied with his legal responsibilities as a company director, it will contact him in writing informing him:

- what the director has done that makes him unfit to be a director;
- the intention of the Insolvency Service to start the disqualification process; and
- how the director may respond.

17.9 The director can either:

- wait for the Insolvency Service to take him to court to disqualify him and defend the case against him; or
- give the Insolvency Service a 'disqualification undertaking' by voluntarily disqualifying himself with the cessation of further court action against him.

On receiving a report from a practitioner on the company's insolvency, the Insolvency Service will consider it carefully. It has to decide whether there appears to be sufficient unfit conduct for seeking disqualification to be in the public interest, and if so, from reading the report and any other information, whether adequate evidence appears to be available. From the information available, if public and evidential tests are met, it will target the case for investigation, grading it according to the level of public interest in taking enforcement action. Then, in consultation with the practitioner and his staff, the following steps are taken:

- The Insolvency Service's Investigation Team conducts an investigation into the facts of the case, prioritising matters on the basis of the public interest grading. This will usually involve an inspection of the company records held by the practitioner's office, as well as the practitioner's own files relating to the conduct of the insolvency, and extensive enquiries of third parties and the directors themselves. Alternatively, the Insolvency Service may allocate the investigation to a solicitor, or the local official receiver, who carries out the same duties.
- Every report is considered on its own merits. The evidence must be sound and of substance. The courts regard disqualification as a severe restriction on the individual's rights, so the Insolvency Service must be satisfied there is a reasonable prospect of success. It cannot seek disqualification based on unsubstantiated assertions, presumptions or assumptions, or a general feeling of 'unhappiness' about the director's conduct, or the circumstances around the company's failure.
- Following investigation, the Insolvency Service may conclude the case on the basis that the allegations of unfitness cannot be proved, are insufficiently serious or there are other reasons why proceedings should not be brought in the public interest. Alternatively, the Insolvency Service will prepare a draft affidavit/ affirmation (or draft report for Scottish companies) which is considered by the Secretary of State and who will, if appropriate, issue an authority for proceedings to be issued.
- Notify the defendant(s) of the intention to issue proceedings and, through the defendant liaison team, consider and administer voluntary disqualification undertakings (CDDA 1986, s 1A).
- If the undertakings are not initially obtained from the defendants, the defendant liaison team will instruct solicitor agents to issue proceedings in court. Undertakings

may still be accepted after the issue of proceedings, or alternatively the matter will progress to disposal at court either on an uncontested basis, or through full trial. Legal input is obtained from solicitors or counsel as and when required.

17.10 The Insolvency Service has a time period of two years within which to bring disqualification proceedings against a director under CDDA 1986, s 7(2). The CDDA 1986 allows the Secretary of State to make an application out of time but he must show a good reason for an extension. The matter was considered by Scott LJ in *Re Probe Data Systems Ltd (No 3), Secretary of State for Trade and Industry v Desai* [1992] BCLC 405 at 416 where he said:

> 'In considering an application under s 7(2) for leave to commence disqualification proceedings out of time the court should, in my opinion, take into account the following matters: (1) the length of the delay, (2) the reasons for the delay, (3) the strength of the case against the director and (4) the degree of prejudice caused to the director by the delay.'

17.11 In *Re Copecrest Limited* [1994] 2 BCLC 284, the Secretary of State sought to apply for disqualification proceedings out of time. The Court of Appeal held that owing to the delays on the part of the director, this was a good reason to apply out of time.

Issues may, therefore, arise as to the human rights of directors who may not receive a fair trial based on the fact that they cannot afford the cost of legal proceedings in contrast to the State-funded Insolvency Service, particularly where the company operated by the director has become insolvent.

The court may not grant an extension of time to bring proceedings where there was an inordinate delay by the Secretary of State

In *Re Manlon Trading Limited* [1996] Ch 136, the official receiver sought an order under CDDA 1986, s 6 that the applicant should not, without leave of the court, be a director of or in any way concerned in the promotion, formation or management of a company for such period as the court thought fit.

The proceedings were issued on the day before the expiry of the two-year limitation period for the bringing of such proceedings and thereafter were not advanced during a period of 17 months. The official receiver accepted that that delay was inordinate and inexcusable and due to him. Thereafter the official receiver did not serve his evidence in support of the proceedings for another 15 months.

The applicant applied to have the proceedings dismissed for want of prosecution. The judge concluded that the applicant had not suffered specific prejudice as a result of the delay and it was still possible to have a fair trial but he granted the application and dismissed the proceedings on the ground that the public interest in obtaining the protection of a disqualification order diminished as time passed and that such an obvious public interest no longer existed. The judge held, in the alternative, that the serious prejudice to the applicant inherent in having disqualification proceedings pending for such a period warranted the dismissal of the proceedings.

The official receiver appealed. The Court of Appeal held that disqualification proceedings under the Company Directors Disqualification Act 1986 were brought in the public interest, which did not diminish with the passage of time, but that, even where a fair trial was still possible, serious collateral prejudice arising from inordinate and inexcusable delay in prosecuting such proceedings might be sufficient to justify granting an application to dismiss them for want of prosecution if, in the circumstances of the case, it outweighed the public interest in obtaining the disqualification order; that where disqualification proceedings were issued towards the end of the two-year limitation period provided by the Act, greater diligence was required in their prosecution, and that, in all the circumstances, the delay in prosecuting the proceedings was inordinate and inexcusable and, the prejudice inherent in having disqualification proceedings pending over such a period coupled with the effect of delay on the memories of witnesses, outweighed the public interest in obtaining the order and justified the dismissal of the proceedings.

The reasonableness of the length of proceedings under the CDDA 1986 was to be assessed in the light of the circumstances of the case, having regard in particular to its complexity, the conduct of the parties to the dispute and the relevant authorities

In *Davies v United Kingdom (42007/98)* [2006] 2 BCLC 351, a disqualification order had been made against a director of a large company. There had been inordinate delay in disposing of the proceedings. It was contended that the disqualification proceedings were not pursued with required diligence by the State whereby the proceedings took five and a half years. The applicant filed for compensation for distress, anxiety and frustration and for costs and expenses and applied to the European Court of Human Rights contending the delay prejudiced him.

The European Court of Human Rights held that the reasonableness of the length of proceedings was to be assessed in the light of the circumstances of the case, having regard in particular to its complexity, the conduct of the parties to the dispute and the relevant authorities.

Furthermore, the applicant's position as a company director and the considerable impact which disqualification proceedings would have on his reputation and ability to practise his profession meant that special diligence was called for in bringing those proceedings to an end expeditiously.

Although the case against the applicant was based on complex evidence and some of the delay in disposing of the proceedings was attributable to his conduct of the proceedings, the State was responsible for the greater part of the five and a half years it took to dispose of the proceedings.

In all the circumstances the proceedings had not been pursued with the diligence required by Art 6 and the failure to determine the applicant's 'civil rights and obligations' within 'a reasonable time' amounted to a violation of Art 6.

The applicant was therefore awarded €4,500 for non-pecuniary damage to compensate him for the distress, anxiety and frustration resulting from the unreasonable length of the proceedings and £10,000 in respect of costs and expenses, but no award would be made in respect of his costs before the domestic courts because he had voluntarily agreed to pay such costs as part of the *Carecraft* settlement and such pecuniary loss was not attributable to the unreasonable length of the proceedings.

There was no infringement of the European Convention of Human Rights where the applicant was given an opportunity to voluntarily enter into a disqualification undertaking

In *Eastaway v Secretary of State for Trade and Industry* [2007] BCC 550, the Court of Appeal did not set aside a disqualification undertaking entered into by a director despite the fact that the European Court of Human Rights had held that the proceedings had taken too long.

The Court of Appeal held that the Secretary of State did not violate the applicant's Art 6 rights by accepting the disqualification undertaking. The applicant had not been obliged to give the 1999 undertaking or the disqualification undertaking. He had not been faced with a choice between a fair trial and none at all or an unfair trial but was given the option of disposing of the proceedings on mutually agreed terms. It had benefited him in that it avoided the cost and publicity of a full trial, at which some serious allegations were to be raised. The interests of the public were protected by the provisions of s 7 of the 1986 Act which enabled the Secretary of State to accept a disqualification undertaking only if 'it appears to him that it is expedient in the public interest that he should do so (instead of applying, or proceeding with an application, for a disqualification)'. The public interest was also protected by the requirement in s 18 of the 1986 Act for a register of disqualification orders and undertakings. In those circumstances, there was no important public interest preventing the waiver of the right to a fair trial by the giving of either undertaking.

Although s 7 of the Human Rights Act 1998 created a mechanism whereby a person could bring proceedings against a public authority for violation of a Convention right if he had no other means of doing so, that mechanism was limited to a person who was a 'victim'. The definition of 'victim' in s 7(7) of the Act turned on whether proceedings could be brought in the European Court of Human Rights in respect of the act complained of. In the present case the act complained of would be the continuance of the disqualification proceedings when no fair trial was possible. Thus the statutory hypothesis in s 7(7) must be applied not to the proceedings, which had already been brought in European Court of Human Rights, but to some new proceedings brought on the same basis as his new complaint and at the same time. The applicant would thus be a victim for the purpose of s 7 if he had been entitled to assert a seriously arguable claim. However, he was not able to do so.

> There was no sufficiently arguable claim that the disqualification proceedings should have been dismissed on the grounds that the applicant had suffered prejudice as a result of the delay because of his professional position. Disqualification proceedings inevitably involved prejudice to a professional person and the evidence of prejudice in the present case was a quite inadequate basis for a conclusion that the prolongation of the proceedings resulted in sufficient substantial prejudice to justify the dismissal of those proceedings.

These cases would demonstrate that where proceedings are inordinate or delay on the part of the Secretary of State to bring proceedings, the director may be able to petition to the European Court of Human Rights for compensation in respect of distress and suffering including costs incurred in the proceedings.

Disqualification orders

17.12 A disqualification order is made by the court. In the circumstances specified in 37.3 below a court may, and under CDDA 1986, ss 6 and 9A shall, make against a person a disqualification order, that is to say an order that for a period specified in the order:

(a) he shall not be a director of a company, act as receiver of a company's property or in any way, whether directly or indirectly, be concerned or take part in the promotion, formation or management of a company unless (in each case) he has the leave of the court, and

(b) he shall not act as an insolvency practitioner: CDDA 1986, s 1(1).

The scope of the order is, therefore, broad and wide-ranging and not just limited to a person being simply disqualified as a director. In *Re Gower Enterprises (No 2)* [1995] 2 BCLC 201, Robert Reid J was of the view that the the 'or' under CDDA 1986, s 1(1) (a) was intended to be conjunctive and that the meaning of s 1(1) of the Act was that a disqualification order was an order that a person without the leave of the court shall not be a director of a company, and shall not be a liquidator or an administrator of a company, and shall not be a receiver or manager of a company's property, and shall not be in any way, whether directly or indirectly concerned and shall not take part in the promotion, formation or management of a company. Further, an order which did not prevent a person from doing all of those things was not a disqualification order within the terms of s 1(1) of the Act. See too: *Re Seagull Manufacturing Co Ltd* [1996] 1 BCLC 51; and *Re Polly Peck International plc* [1994] 1 BCLC 574.

17.13 In each section of the CDDA 1986 which gives a court power to or, as the case may be, imposes on it the duty to make a disqualification order there is specified the maximum (and, in CDDA 1986, ss 6 and 8ZA, the minimum) period of disqualification which may or (as the case may be) must be imposed by means of the order. Unless the court otherwise orders, the period of disqualification so imposed shall begin at the end of the period of 21 days beginning with the date of the order: CDDA 1986, s 1(2) (as inserted by SBEEA 2015, Sch 7 Part 1).

Where a disqualification order is made against a person who is already subject to such an order or to a disqualification undertaking, the periods specified in those orders or, as the case may be, in the order and the undertaking shall run concurrently: CDDA 1986, s 1(3).

17.14 A disqualification order may be made on grounds which are or include matters other than criminal convictions, notwithstanding that the person in respect of whom it is to be made may be criminally liable in respect of those matters: CDDA 1986, s 1(4).

In making the disqualification order, the objective is to ensure that the director is prevented for a specified period of time from engaging in management decisions or in any way connected with management matters within a company.

The term 'management' is broadly interpreted and includes not just taking part in the company's affairs but also holding a managerial post

In *R v Campbell* [1984] BCLC 83, the Court of Appeal stated that the widest interpretation will be given to the words in CDDA 1986, s 1. According to Bedlam J, a person subject to a disqualification order made under s 1 would contravene that order if, as a management consultant, he advised on the financial management and restructuring of a company. This was because s 1 was very widely cast and was designed to make it impossible for a person disqualified under s 1 to be part of the management and central direction of a company's affairs. In particular, the words in s 1 'be concerned in' should not be narrowly construed to mean 'take part in'.

See too: *Re Market Wizard Systems (UK) Ltd* [1998] 2 BCLC 282; *Drew v HM Advocate* [1996] SLT 1062.

Entering into contracts on the company's behalf is taking part in the company's management

In *Hill v Secretary of State for the Environment, Food and Rural Affairs* [2006] 1 BCLC 601, an undischarged bankrupt entered into two contracts on behalf of the company. Hart J held that the undischarged bankrupt was effectively concerned with managing the company. The objective was the protection of the public from those individuals who were not regarded as trustworthy persons to be involved in the management of a limited liability company.

17.15 Where an order is made under CDDA 1986, s 1, the courts are not required to select which aspect of the order to make: the order is made as a whole for all aspects of CDDA 1986, s 1(1)(a).

When making a disqualification order, all activities under s 1(1) must be included in the order

In *R v Cole* [1998] 2 BCLC 234, the Court of Appeal stated that CDDA 1986, s 1(1) envisaged only one disqualification with a number of different consequences and not five different categories of disqualification. A pick and choose approach could not be adopted by the courts.

Disqualification undertakings

17.16 Whereas the disqualification order is made by the court, a disqualification undertaking may be agreed between the director and the Disqualification Unit of the Insolvency Service. There is no requirement for judicial proceedings. The disqualification undertaking has a similar effect to a disqualification order.

In the circumstances specified in CDDA 1986, ss 5A, 7, 8, 8ZC and 8ZE, the Secretary of State may accept a disqualification undertaking, that is to say an undertaking by any person that, for a period specified in the undertaking, the person:

(a) will not be a director of a company, act as receiver of a company's property or in any way, whether directly or indirectly, be concerned or take part in the promotion, formation or management of a company unless (in each case) he has the leave of a court, and

(b) will not act as an insolvency practitioner: CDDA 1986, s 1A(1) (as inserted by SBEEA 2015, Sch 7, Part 1).

The maximum period which may be specified in a disqualification undertaking is 15 years; and the minimum period which may be specified in a disqualification undertaking under s 7 or 8ZC is two years: CDDA 1986, s 1A(2) (as inserted by SBEEA 2015, Schedule 7, Part 1).

17.17 Where a disqualification undertaking by a person who is already subject to such an undertaking or to a disqualification order is accepted, the periods specified in those undertakings or (as the case may be) the undertaking and the order shall run concurrently: CDDA 1986, s 1A(3).

In determining whether to accept a disqualification undertaking by any person, the Secretary of State may take account of matters other than criminal convictions, notwithstanding that the person may be criminally liable in respect of those matters: CDDA 1986, s 1A(4).

The Secretary of State has discretion to decide whether or not to accept a disqualification undertaking

In *Re Blackspur Group plc (No 3), Secretary of State for Trade and Industry v Davies (No 2)* [2002] 2 BCLC 263, the Court of Appeal held that the CDDA 1986 legislation reflected Parliament's view that the Secretary of State was in a much better position than the court to gauge what the public interest required in relation to the regulation of directors' conduct. Accordingly, it was for the Secretary of State, and not for the court, to determine whether it was expedient in the public interest that a disqualification order under CDDA 1986, s 6 should be made, and if the Secretary of State decided to accept an undertaking instead of seeking an order, he had to be satisfied not only that the conduct of the director offering the undertaking made him unfit to be concerned in the management of a company, but also that it was expedient in the public interest to accept the undertaking in lieu of a disqualification order.

The court may on occasions decide to order a stay of a disqualification order pending an appeal

In *Cathie v Secretary of State for Business, Innovation & Skills* [2011] EWHC 2234, two directors were subject to a disqualification order. One of the directors applied for a stay of that order on the grounds that he had established a significant reputation in his expertise service and would not be conducting business through a company but individually. Judge Purle granted a stay order pending an appeal against the disqualification order. During the stay period, the disqualification order is not registered with the Registrar at Companies House.

17.18 In some situations, it may arise that the court makes a disqualification order against a company director and then subsequently, the court grants permission for a disqualified director to act as a company director on terms set out in the court order. The director may have contributed to the drafting of the court order. The issue arises as to whether the court is entitled to have regard to the intentions of the person drafting the order for the purposes of its construction?

The principles of contractual interpretation could be considered in the interpretation of a court order

In *Feld v Secretary of State for Business, Innovation & Skills* [2014] EWHC 1383, the court stated that the principles of contractual interpretation were appropriate to be considered in the interpretation of a court order. It would give the court insight into the person's intention in drafting the order. Judge Edward Murray relied on the Court of Appeal decision in Court of Appeal decision in *R* v *Evans* [2004] EWCA Crim 3102 as providing support for the proposition that the proper approach to interpretation of a court order was, broadly, to apply the principles of statutory interpretation.

In some circumstances, there have been successful appeals by directors in respect of the length of their disqualification undertakings.

In some circumstances, it may be possible for directors to have the length of their disqualification period reduced

In *R v Randhawa* [2008] EWCA Crim 2599, two directors were successful in having the length of their disqualification periods reduced.

In this case, the directors gave undertakings under CDDA 1986, s 1A that that for a period of ten years from 2003 they would not take part in any company's management. Subsequently, they were disqualified for 12 years from 2007. Taking together the undertakings and disqualification orders, this meant that they would be disqualified from acting as directors for 16 years. They contended that 12 years was too long a period of disqualification. The Court of Appeal accordingly reduced the period of disqualification taking account of the directors' undertakings and their acceptance of the gravity of the criminal offences they had committed.

Grounds for disqualification – disqualification for general misconduct in connection with companies

17.19 The CDDA 1986 sets out various grounds for disqualification in connection with companies.

Disqualification on conviction of indictable offence

17.20 The court may make a disqualification order against a person where he is convicted of an indictable offence (whether on indictment or summarily) in connection with the promotion, formation, management, liquidation or striking off of a company with the receivership of a company's property or with his being an administrative receiver of a company: CDDA 1986, s 2(1).

In subsection (1), 'company' includes overseas company: CDDA 1986, s.2(1A) (as inserted by SBEEA 2015, Sch 7, Part 1).

17.21 The term 'the court' is defined as:

(a) any court having jurisdiction to wind up the company in relation to which the offence was committed, or

(aa) in relation to an overseas company not falling within paragraph (a), the High Court or, in Scotland, the Court of Session, or

(b) the court by or before which the person is convicted of the offence, or

(c) in the case of a summary conviction in England and Wales, any other magistrates' court acting in the same local justice area;

and for the purposes of CDDA 1986, s 2, the definition of 'indictable offence' in Schedule 1 to the Interpretation Act 1978 applies for Scotland as well as for England and Wales: CA 2006, s 2(2) (as inserted by SBEEA 2015, Sch 7, Part 1).

17.22 The maximum period of disqualification under CDDA 1986, s 2 is:

(a) where the disqualification order is made by a court of summary jurisdiction, five years, and

(b) in any other case, 15 years: CDDA 1986, s 2(3).

Disqualification for persistent breaches of companies legislation

17.23 The court may made a disqualification order against a person where it appears to it that he has been persistently in default in relation to provisions of the companies legislation requiring any return, account or other document to be filed with, delivered to or sent to, or notice of any matter to be given to, the registrar of companies: CDDA 1986, s 3(1).

On an application to the court for an order to be made under CDDA 1986, s 3, the fact that a person has been persistently in default in relation to such provisions as are mentioned above may (without prejudice to its proof in any other manner) be conclusively proved by showing that in the five years ending with the date of the application he has been adjudged guilty (whether or not on the same occasion) of three or more defaults in relation to those provisions: CDDA 1986, s 3(2).

17.24 A person is to be treated under s 3(2) as being adjudged guilty of a default in relation to any provision of that legislation if:

(a) he is convicted (whether on indictment or summarily) of an offence consisting in a contravention of or failure to comply with that provision (whether on his own part or on the part of any company), or

(b) a default order is made against him, that is to say an order under any of the following provisions:

   (i) CA 2006, s 452 (order requiring delivery of company accounts),

   (ia) CA 2006, s 456 (order requiring preparation of revised accounts),

   (ii) CA 2006, s 1113 (enforcement of company's filing obligations),

   (iii) the Insolvency Act 1986, s 41 (enforcement of receiver's or manager's duty to make returns), or

   (iv) the Insolvency Act 1986, s 170 (corresponding provision for liquidator in winding up),

   in respect of any such contravention of or failure to comply with that provision (whether on his own part or on the part of any company): CDDA 1986, s 3(3).

In this section, 'company' includes overseas company: CDDA 1986, s 3A (as inserted by SBEEA 2015, Sch 7, Part 1).

17.25 The term 'the court' means:

(a) any court having jurisdiction to wind up any of the companies in relation to which the offence or other default has been or is alleged to have been committed; or

(b) in relation to an overseas company not falling within paragraph (a), the High Court or, in Scotland, the Court of Session: CDDA 1986, s 3(4) (as inserted by SBEEA 2015, Sch 7, Part 1).

The term 'companies legislation' means the Companies Acts and Parts 1 to 7 of the Insolvency Act 1986 (company insolvency and winding up): CDDA 1986, s 3(4A).

The maximum period of disqualification under this section is five years: CDDA 1986, s 3(5).

Disqualification for fraud, etc, in winding up

17.26 The court may make a disqualification order against a person if, in the course of the winding up of a company, it appears that he:

(a) has been guilty of an offence for which he is liable (whether he has been convicted or not) under CA 2006, s 993 (fraudulent trading), or

(b) has otherwise been guilty, while an officer or liquidator of the company receiver of the company's property or administrative receiver of the company, of any fraud in relation to the company or of any breach of his duty as such officer, liquidator, receiver or administrative receiver: CDDA 1986, s 4(1).

A liquidator had standing to bring disqualification proceedings against a former liquidator of a company

In *Wood v Mistry* [2012] EWHC 1899 (Ch), applications under the CDDA 1986 are normally made by the Secretary of State for Business, Innovation and Skills or the Official Receiver against individuals who are or have been company directors. In this case however, the application concerned Mr Mistry's conduct in relation to companies of which he was a liquidator. The application was not brought by the Secretary of State or Official Receiver but by liquidators by reason of CDDA 1986, s 4(1)(b). The issue was whether the claimant liquidators had locus standi to bring proceedings to disqualify the previous company liquidator?

Section 16(2) of CDDA 1986 states :

> An application to a court with jurisdiction to wind up companies for the making against any person of a disqualification order under any of sections 2 to 4 may be made by the Secretary of State or the official receiver, or by the liquidator or any past or present member or creditor of any company in relation to which that person has committed or is alleged to have committed an offence or other default.'

Therefore, the potential applicants included liquidators. Newey J disqualified the liquidator for 12 years. The period of disqualification reflected the serious breaches of misconduct by the liquidator.

17.27 The term 'the court' means any court having jurisdiction to wind up any of the companies in relation to which the offence or other default has been or is alleged to have been committed, and 'officer' includes a shadow director: CDDA 1986, s 4(2).

The term 'shadow director' is set out in CDDA 1986, s 22(5) (as amended by SBEEA 2015, s 90(2), which provides that the term 'shadow director', in relation to a company, means a person in accordance with whose directions or instructions the directors of the company are accustomed to act, but so that a person is not deemed a shadow director by reason only that the directors act:

(a) on advice given by that person in a professional capacity;

(b) in accordance with instructions, a direction, guidance or advice given by that person in the exercise of a function conferred by or under an enactment;

(c) in accordance with guidance or advice given by that person in that person's capacity as a Minister of the Crown (within the meaning of the Ministers of the Crown Act 1975).

The maximum period of disqualification under CDDA 1986, s 4 is 15 years: CDDA 1986, s 4(3).

Disqualification on summary conviction

17.28 An offence counting for the purposes of CDDA 1986, s 5 is one of which a person is convicted (either on indictment or summarily) in consequence of a contravention of, or failure to comply with, any provision of the companies legislation requiring a return, account or other document to be filed with, delivered or sent, or notice of any matter to be given, to the registrar of companies (whether the contravention or failure is on the person's own part or on the part of any company): CDDA 1986, s 5(1).

Where a person is convicted of a summary offence counting for those purposes, the court by which he is convicted (or, in England and Wales, any other magistrates' court acting for the same petty sessions area) may make a disqualification order against him if the circumstances specified in the next subsection are present: CDDA 1986, s 5(2).

17.29 Those circumstances are that, during the five years ending with the date of the conviction, the person has had made against him, or has been convicted of, in total not less than three default orders and offences counting for the purposes of this section; and those offences may include that of which he is convicted as mentioned in CDDA 1986, s 5(2) and any other offence of which he is convicted on the same occasion: CDDA 1986, s 5(3).

Under CDDA 1986, s 5, the following definitions apply:

(a) the definition of 'summary offence' in Schedule 1 to the Interpretation Act 1978 applies for Scotland as for England and Wales, and

(b) 'default order' means the same as in s 3(3)(b) of CDDA 1986: CDDA 1986, s 5(4).

In this section, 'the companies legislation' means the Companies Acts and Parts 1 to 7 of the Insolvency Act 1986 (company insolvency and winding up): CDDA 1986, s 5(4A).

In this section, 'company' includes overseas company: CDDA 1986, s 5(4B) (as inserted by SBEEA 2015, Sch 7, Part 1.

The maximum period of disqualification under s 5 is five years: CDDA 1986, s 5(5).

New grounds for disqualification

Convictions abroad

Disqualification for certain convictions abroad

17.30 If it appears to the Secretary of State that it is expedient in the public interest that a disqualification order under s 5A of CDDA 1986 should be made against a person, the Secretary of State may apply to the court for such an order: CDDA 1986, s 5A(1).

The court may, on an application under s 5A(1) of CDDA 1986, make a disqualification order against a person who has been convicted of a relevant foreign offence: CDDA 1986, s 5A(2).

A 'relevant foreign offence' is an offence committed outside Great Britain:

(a) in connection with:

  (i) the promotion, formation, management, liquidation or striking off of a company (or any similar procedure),

  (ii) the receivership of a company's property (or any similar procedure), or

  (iii) a person being an administrative receiver of a company (or holding a similar position), and

(b) which corresponds to an indictable offence under the law of England and Wales or (as the case may be) an indictable offence under the law of Scotland: CDDA 1986, s 5A(3).

17.31 Where it appears to the Secretary of State that, in the case of a person who has offered to give a disqualification undertaking:

(a) the person has been convicted of a relevant foreign offence, and

(b) it is expedient in the public interest that the Secretary of State should accept the undertaking (instead of applying, or proceeding with an application, for a disqualification order),

the Secretary of State may accept the undertaking: CDDA 1986, s 5A(4).

In s 5A CDDA 1986, the terms 'company' includes an overseas company; and 'the court' means the High Court or, in Scotland, the Court of Session.

17.32 The maximum period of disqualification under an order under this section is 15 years: CDDA 1986, s 5A(5).

Section 5A(2) and (4) of the Company Directors Disqualification Act 1986, as inserted by s 104 of SBEEA 2015, applies in relation to a conviction of a relevant foreign offence which occurs on or after the day on which this section comes into force regardless of whether the act or omission which constituted the offence occurred before that day: SBEEA 2015, s 104(2).

See The Small Business, Enterprise and Employment Act 2015 (Commencement No 2 and Transitional Provisions) Regulations 2015, SI 2015/1689.

Disqualifications relating to unfit directors

Duty of court to disqualify unfit directors of insolvent companies

17.33 The court must make a disqualification order against a person in any case where, on an application under CDDA 1986, s 6, it is satisfied:

(a) that he is or has been a director of a company which has at any time become insolvent (whether while he was a director or subsequently), and

(b) that his conduct as a director of that company (either taken alone or taken together with his conduct as a director of one or more other companies or overseas companies) makes him unfit to be concerned in the management of a company: CDDA 1986, s 6(1) (as inserted by SBEEA 2015, s 106(2)(a).

In this section, references to a person's conduct as a director of any company or overseas company include, where that company or overseas company has become insolvent, references to that person's conduct in relation to any matter connected with or arising out of the insolvency: CDDA 1986, s 6(1A) (as inserted by SBEEA 2015, s 106(2)(b).

17.34 For the purposes of CDDA 1986, ss 6 and 7, a company becomes insolvent if:

(a) the company goes into liquidation at a time when its assets are insufficient for the payment of its debts and other liabilities and the expenses of the winding up,

(b) an administration order is made in relation to the company, or

(c) an administrative receiver of the company is appointed: CDDA 1986, s 6(2) (as amended by SBEEA 2015, s 106(2)(c).

For the purposes of this section, an overseas company becomes insolvent if the company enters into insolvency proceedings of any description (including interim proceedings) in any jurisdiction: CDDA 1986, s 6(2A) (as inserted by SBEEA 2015, s 106(2)(d).

The term 'liquidation' is defined as the time when a company passes a resolution for the voluntary winding up of the company or the time of the court order where there is a compulsory winding up of the company: Insolvency Act 1986, s 247 (as incorporated under CDDA 1986, s 22(3)).

17.35 Under CDDA 1986, ss 6 and 7(2), 'the court' means:

(a) where the company in question is being or has been wound up by the court, that court,

(b) where the company in question is being or has been wound up voluntarily, any court which has or (as the case may be) had jurisdiction to wind it up,

(d) where neither of the preceding paragraphs applies but an administration order has at any time been made, or an administrative receiver has at any time been appointed, in relation to the company in question, any court which has jurisdiction to wind it up: CDDA 1986, s 6(3).

17.36 Sections 117 and 120 of the Insolvency Act 1986 (jurisdiction) will apply for the purposes of CDDA 1986, s 6(3) as if the references in the definitions of 'registered office' to the presentation of the petition for winding up were references:

(a) in a case within paragraph (b) of that subsection, to the passing of the resolution for voluntary winding up,

(b) in a case within paragraph (c) of that subsection, to the making of the administration order or (as the case may be) the appointment of the administrative receiver: CDDA 1986, s 6(3A).

Nothing in s 6(3) invalidates any proceedings by reason of their being taken in the wrong court; and proceedings:

(a) for or in connection with a disqualification order under s 6, or

(b) in connection with a disqualification undertaking accepted under s 7, may be retained in the court in which the proceedings were commenced, although it may not be the court in which they ought to have been commenced: CDDA 1986, s 6(3B).

17.37 Under CDDA 1986, ss 6 and 7, 'director' includes a shadow director: CDDA 1986, s 6(3B).

Under s 6 the minimum period of disqualification is two years, and the maximum period is 15 years: CDDA 1986, s 6(4).

CDDA 1986, s 6 has given rise to much case law in the interpretation and legal and practical implications involved in the term "unfit", and this is the section under which a large number of legal proceedings ensue, including disqualification orders and undertakings.

Section 6 applies to a *de jure* director, shadow director or a *de facto* director. The aim of this section is to protect the public from unfit directors including protection of the creditors and other stakeholders of the company.

The court will have regard to the conduct of the director when deciding to make a disqualification order

In *Re Lo-Line Electric Motors Ltd* [1988] 2 All ER 692, Sir Nicolas Browne-Wilkinson (as he was then) held that when deciding whether a director should be disqualified under CDDA 1986, s 6, the court was required to have regard to his conduct as a director regardless of whether he had been validly appointed or was merely assuming to act as a director without any appointment at all, since the conduct relevant to his future suitability to act as a director depended on his past record as a director irrespective of the circumstances in which he came to act as such. On the facts, the respondent had behaved in a commercially culpable manner in trading through limited companies when he knew them to be insolvent, and in using unpaid Crown debts to finance such trading, and he would be disqualified generally from being a director for three years. However, he would in the circumstances be permitted to be a director of two particular companies subject to certain conditions.

The provisions of CDDA 1986, s 6 also apply to a shadow director

Similarly, in *Re Kaytech International plc, Secretary of State for Trade and Industry v Kaczer* [1999] 2 BCLC 351, Rimer J decided that, in ascertaining whether an individual was a de facto director of a company, the crucial question was whether he had assumed the status and functions of a company director so as to make himself responsible under the CDDA 1986 as if he were a de jure director. In the present case, the second respondent had been deeply and openly involved in the company's affairs from the outset, and although he had done his best to avoid being seen to act as a director, using his office as de jure secretary and his professional status as camouflage, on some very important occasions he openly acted as a director. Accordingly he was a de facto director of the company and therefore a director for the purposes of CDDA 1986, s 6.

In connection with the third respondent who was a non-executive director, although he honestly believed that he was not a director of the company, that belief was thoroughly unreasonable since he was a professional man who made his living by holding nominee directorships. Accordingly, he was not released from his duty to inform himself about the affairs of the company. Since he had been totally inactive in the performance of any of his duties as a non-executive director of the company, he was liable not only for failure to ensure the keeping of proper accounting records but also for the false representations to the companies registry and its creditors and for continuing its business for as long as it did. He was therefore unfit to be concerned in the management of a company and was therefore disqualified.

The CDDA also applies to a corporate director: *Official Receiver v Brady* [1999] BCC 847. It also applies to a shadow director: CDDA 1986, s 6(3C).

Abdication of responsibility may lead to a director being disqualified

In the Scottish case of *Secretary of State for Business Innovation and Skills v Reza* [2013] CSOH 86, the Secretary of State applied under CDDA 1986, s 6 for a disqualification order against the respondent for failure to discharge her obligations as a director in the company particularly in relation to non-payment of tax. Over the whole of her 18 years in office as a director, the respondent failed to carry out even the most basic of her duties. This neglect continued when the company was in difficulties and defaults occurred in respect of tax liabilities. Throughout she abdicated all interest in and responsibility for the company's affairs, leaving them to her husband. Mr Reza was the driving force, and she was only made a director because of perceived tax advantages, and in case it might be helpful to have a director in the care home and available to sign documents.

Lord Malcolm stated:

> 'If someone accepts a directorship and then abdicates all responsibility for the affairs of the company, on any common sense view they have demonstrated unfitness for the office to a high degree … The public interest demands that directors of companies take an active interest in the affairs of the company, and are mindful of their personal responsibilities for the proper running of the business'.

See too: *Re Grayan Ltd* [1995] Ch 241, where Hoffmann LJ stated that the court should not shrink from its duty to disqualify a director who has fallen below the required standard.

Determining 'unfitness'

17.38 The Secretary of State must demonstrate not only that the company is insolvent but that, at the time, the person was unfit. Typically, the director has been trading through the company and entered into transactions causing losses to the company and mounting debts including tax debts and liabilities, and continues to trade while the company is insolvent. During this period, the directors may have paid themselves excessive remuneration or diverted corporate funds for other purposes, which may have the effect of placing corporate assets beyond the reach of creditors, including preferences.

Some examples of 'unfitness'

17.39

The court will have regard to the evidence in the application to disqualify to determine whether the 'unfitness' test has been met

In *Amaron Ltd, Secretary of State for Trade and Industry v Lubrani* [2001] 1 BCLC 562, the directors (husband and wife) carried on business of the company sustaining losses and mounting Crown debts while the company was insolvent. Neuberger J held that the circumstances merited a disqualification order being made.

In *Secretary of State for Trade and Industry v Gray* [1995] 1 BCLC 276, the allegations against the directors were that they had: (1) caused the company to trade while insolvent; (2) failed to keep proper accounting records; (3) failed to file the appropriate year audited accounts on time; and (4) made preferential payments contrary to s 239 of the Insolvency Act 1986.

The Court of Appeal held that the question of whether a director's conduct made him unfit to be concerned in the management of a company within the meaning of CDDA 1986, s 6(1) was to be determined by reference to the matters and evidence relied on in the application for the disqualification order, and not by reference to whether, at the date of the hearing, the future protection of the public might or might not require a period of disqualification. CDDA 1986, s 6 imposed a duty on the court to disqualify a person whose conduct had shown him to be unfit. The purpose of making disqualification mandatory was to ensure that everyone whose conduct had fallen below the appropriate standard was disqualified for at least two years (s 6(4)), whether in the individual case the court thought this was necessary in the public interest or not.

In *The Official Receiver v Watson* [2008] EWHC 64 (Ch), the director was disqualified on the basis of his acquiescence and participation in the corporate governance system involving breaches of company law.

The court is required to have regard to addressing the concept of 'unfitness' and not a breach of duty by a director, though a breach of duty could ultimately result in unfitness being demonstrated, but may not necessarily do so. The court will also consider whether any creditors were affected, particularly where phoenix companies are established and the previous companies still have unpaid creditors: *Re Travel Mondial (UK) Ltd* [1991] BCLC 120.

Unfitness may be demonstrated by mere incompetence or dishonesty

In *Re Barings plc (No 5), Secretary of State for Trade and Industry v Baker (No 5)* [1999] 1 BCLC 433, the issue arose whether mere incompetence was sufficient by itself to render the three directors unfit under CDDA 1986, s 6.

Jonathan Parker J held that s 6 imposed a duty on the court to make a disqualification order where the respondent was or had been a director of a company which had become insolvent, and his conduct as a director of that company (whether taken alone or taken together with his conduct as a director of any other company or companies) made him 'unfit to be concerned in the management of a company'.

The expression 'unfit to be concerned in the management of a company' would appear to mean 'unfit to be concerned in the management of any company', without qualification. However, in the light of s 17 of the CDDA 1986 whereby the court can grant a disqualified director leave to act as a director, it would appear that the expression 'unfit to be concerned in the management of a company' in s 6 could not have the wholly unqualified meaning which, on face value, it appeared to have.

The primary purpose of the jurisdiction under s 6 was to protect the public against the future conduct in the management of companies by persons whose past records as directors of insolvent companies had shown them to be a danger to others.

Unfitness might be shown by conduct which was dishonest (including conduct showing a want of probity or integrity) or by conduct which was merely incompetent. In every case the function of the court in addressing the question of unfitness was to decide whether the conduct of which complaint was made by the Secretary of State, viewed cumulatively and taking into account any extenuating circumstances, had fallen below the standards of probity and competence appropriate for persons fit to be directors of companies.

In addressing that question in the context of an application under s 6 of the CDDA 1986, ie where the company has become insolvent, the court was required by s 9 of the Act to have regard to the various matters listed in Sch 1 to the Act. But the list in Sch 1 was not exhaustive: the matters to which the court might have regard were not limited to the matters listed in the Schedule.

In considering the question of unfitness, the respondent's conduct had to be evaluated in context. Thus the only extenuating circumstances which might be taken into account in addressing the question of unfitness were those which accompanied the conduct in question. For example, the fact that a respondent might have shown himself unlikely to offend again was irrelevant to the question of unfitness – although it might be relevant to the question of the length of the disqualification order.

See also [2000] 1 BCLC 523.

In *Secretary of State for Business, Enterprise and Regulatory Reform v Sullman* [2009] 1 BCLC 397, the directors had misled customers over insurance policies coverage. Norris J held that the ascertainment of unfit conduct was essentially the application to the found facts of the ordinary words 'unfit to be concerned in the management of a company'. Being a jury question, and one to be considered in a broad way, it was not appropriate to put a judicial gloss on the words of s 8 of the 1986 Act. However, 'conduct in relation to [a] company' encompassed conduct as a director which bore upon the company's business or its affairs, whether that conduct occasioned prejudice to the company itself or its shareholders, or to its customers or funders or anyone else with whom it had commercial relationships. The phrase referred to the way the business was run.

On the facts, the misrepresentation rendered directors unfit under CDDA 1986, s 6.

In considering whether a person is fit to be a director, the court should apply the facts of the case to the standard of conduct established by the courts

In *Secretary of State for Trade and Industry v Goldberg* [2004] 1 BCLC 597, there was an allegation of breach of fiduciary duty. The director in question was aware that the chairman was bypassing the board and misusing company funds. The director caused or permitted board minute to be produced when he knew no resolution had been passed.

Lewinson J was of the view that a director could not escape disqualification under CDDA 1986, s 6 simply by showing that he had not been incompetent, had complied with the company's statutory obligations to keep proper records and file accounts and returns, and was not dishonest. The court was required to take a broad brush approach in making its value judgment about a director's fitness or otherwise to be a director and although the criteria of competence, discipline in complying with the duties regarding records, accounts and returns, and honesty were highly relevant in assessing fitness or unfitness, the question for the court was the much broader issue of applying to the facts of the case the standard of conduct laid down by the courts appropriate to a person fit to be a director, that being a question of mixed law and fact.

In particular, unfitness by reason of incompetence could be established without proof of a breach of duty. On the other hand, although dishonesty was not the acid test, the court had to be very careful before holding that a director was unfit because of conduct that did not amount to a breach of any duty (whether contractual, tortious, statutory or equitable) to anyone, and was not dishonest.

The court will focus on the conduct of the director when making the appropriate disqualification order

In *Re Bunting Electric Manufacturing Co Ltd, Secretary of State for Trade and Industry v Golby* [2006] 1 BCLC 550, Judge McCahill stated that although the focus of the CDDA 1986 was on the conduct of the director, not its consequences, the consequences were not irrelevant or immaterial since they were relevant to the court's assessment of the seriousness or relative seriousness of the conduct complained of, and were important not only in considering whether an order for disqualification should be made but also in determining any appropriate period of any disqualification. There was no unfairness in this approach to the defendant. Further, the standard of proof was on the balance of probabilities. However, because of the defendant's good character and the seriousness of the allegations against him, the court would require much more cogent evidence to establish the relevant wrongdoing. His good character was relevant both to his credibility and to his propensity, or lack of it, to engage in dishonest behaviour. Dishonesty required both an objective and subjective element and the conduct must be viewed cumulatively taking into account any extenuating circumstances. Furthermore, the court was required to take a broadbrush approach.

The disqualification procedure under CDDA 1986, s 6 is a two-stage procedure

In *Secretary of State for Trade and Industry v Swan* [2005] BCC 597, Etherton J stated that the determination of unfitness under CDDA 1986, s 6 was a two-stage process. First, the Secretary of State had to establish as facts, to the requisite standard of proof, namely on a balance of probabilities, the matters on which the allegation of unfitness was based. Second, the court had to be satisfied that the conduct alleged was sufficiently serious to warrant disqualification.

Other courts have decided that there is a three-stage process under CDDA 1986, s 6 in disqualifying a director

In *Official Receiver v Key* [2009] 1 BCLC 22, Mithani J held that in determining whether a defendant was unfit to be a director the decision whether the requirements of CDDA 1986, s 6(1)(b) were met involved a three stage process: first, did the matters relied on amount to misconduct; second, if so, did they justify a finding of unfitness; and, third, if so, what period of disqualification ought to be imposed. The court was required to take a broad brush approach in making a value judgment about the defendant's fitness or otherwise to be a director, and that required little more than a common sense decision about whether the facts of the case, when applied to the standard of conduct laid down by the court, ought to result in a finding of unfitness being made against the defendant.

17.40 The court will have regard to CDDA 1986, Sch 1 in connection with determining the director's conduct. In all cases, the following is taken into account:

1. Any misfeasance or breach of any fiduciary or other duty by the director in relation to the company.
2. Any misapplication or retention by the director of, or any conduct by the director giving rise to an obligation to account for, any money or other property of the company.

3. The extent of the director's responsibility for the company entering into any transaction liable to be set aside under Part XVI of the Insolvency Act 1986 (provisions against debt avoidance).
4. The extent of the director's responsibility for any failure by the company to comply with any of the following aspects of the CA 2006, namely:
   (a) s 113 (register of members);
   (b) s 114 (register to be kept available for inspection);
   (c) s 162 (register of directors);
   (d) s 165 (register of directors' residential addresses);
   (e) s 167 (duty to notify registrar of changes: directors);
   (f) s 275 (register of secretaries);
   (g) s 276 (duty to notify registrar of changes: secretaries);
   (h) s 386 (duty to keep accounting records);
   (i) s 388 (where and for how long accounting records to be kept);
   (j) s 854 (duty to make annual returns);
   (k) s 860 (duty to register charges); and
   (l) s 878 (duty to register charges: companies registered in Scotland).

The extent of the director's responsibility for any failure by the directors of the company to comply with the following provisions of the CA 2006:

(a) ss 394 or 399 (duty to prepare annual accounts);

(b) ss 414 or 450 (approval and signature of abbreviated accounts); and

(c) s 433 (name of signatory to be stated in published copy of accounts)

17.41 The court will take the following into account in determining unfitness where the company is insolvent:

- The extent of the director's responsibility for the causes of the company becoming insolvent.
- The extent of the director's responsibility for any failure by the company to supply any goods or services which have been paid for (in whole or in part).
- The extent of the director's responsibility for the company entering into any transaction or giving any preference, being a transaction or preference:

  (a) liable to be set aside under s 127 or ss 238 to 240 of the Insolvency Act 1986, or.

  (b) challengeable under s 242 or 243 of that Act or under any rule of law in Scotland.
- The extent of the director's responsibility for any failure by the directors of the company to comply with s 98 of the Insolvency Act 1986 (duty to call creditors' meeting in creditors' voluntary winding up).

- Any failure by the director to comply with any obligation imposed on him by or under any of the following provisions of the Insolvency Act 1986.
  (a) s 22 (company's statement of affairs in administration);
  (b) s 47 (statement of affairs to administrative receiver);
  (c) s 66 (statement of affairs in Scottish receivership);
  (d) s 99 (directors' duty to attend meeting; statement of affairs in creditors' voluntary winding up);
  (e) s 131 (statement of affairs in winding up by the court);
  (f) s 234 (duty of any one with company property to deliver it up);
  (g) s 235 (duty to co-operate with liquidator, etc).

Other aspects of a director's conduct may be relevant in disqualification proceedings

In *Re Migration Services Services International Limited, Official Receiver v Webster* [2000] 1 BCLC 666, Neuberger J held that other aspects of a director's conduct could still be taken into account even though not mentioned specifically under CDDA 1986, Sch 1.

Under CA 2006, s 172(3), directors are required to take account of creditors' interests in promoting the company's success. The interests of creditors or failure to take account of their interests is one of the significant aspects for application under CDDA 1986, s 6 by the Secretary of State against a director. Typically, the allegation will be that the carried on business while the company was insolvent without regard to creditors' interests.

Unfitness may be demonstrated by the company's insolvency and that the director knew that the company had no reasonable prospect of meeting creditors' claims

In *Secretary of State v Creggan* [2002] 1 BCLC 99, the Court of Appeal held that it was well established that the test of whether a director should be disqualified pursuant to CDDA 1986, s 6 for acting incompetently, was whether he caused the company to trade while it was insolvent and had no reasonable prospect of meeting creditors' claims. In applying that test both elements had to be satisfied, and it was not enough for the company to have been insolvent and for the director to have known that it was. Insolvency, especially when it was only apparent on the face of the balance sheet and not in an inability to pay debts as they fell due, was not to be equated with there being no reasonable prospect of meeting creditors' claims, and it had to be shown that he knew or ought to have known that there was no reasonable prospect of meeting creditors' claims.

Significant company debts and engaging in preferring a creditor could demonstrate unfitness

In *Secretary of State for Trade and Industry v Collins* [2000] 2 BCLC 223, the allegations were that the directors' conduct involved causing the company to trade for a significant period of time when it was recognised to be heavily insolvent; and entering into transactions concerning contingency insurance policies when the company's position was precarious and causing the company to give a preference to another company.

The Court of Appeal disqualified the directors for up to seven to nine years.

Where the facts demonstrate competence and no dishonesty nor improper purpose, unfitness may not have been satisfied

However, in *Secretary of State for Trade and Industry v Gill* [2004] All ER 345, Blackburne J did not find that 'unfitness' had been established. There was no suggestion that the directors had not viewed seriously the professional advice they had received in connection with the company's business. There was also no suggestion that any part of the directors' motivation was to line their own pockets or that they had some other dishonest or consciously improper purpose in mind in continuing to trade. Further, they had not acted incompetently. The court did not make a disqualification order.

The importance of creditors' interests is recognised by the courts in deciding whether or not to disqualify a director under CDDA 1986, s 6.

Creditors' interests are of major significance in considering whether unfitness has been demonstrated

In *Mea Corporation Ltd, Secretary of State for Trade and Industry v Aviss* [2007] 1 BCLC 618, the directors concerned established a policy for three companies that they had established, as to the application of trade income and payment of trade creditors. Monies received by companies in the group were paid into a central fund. The monies in the central fund were used to support companies outside the group.

Lewinson J held that in respect of the application of trading income and the payment of trade creditors, the policy of all three companies had been dictated by the directors. They had been responsible for the failure of the companies to satisfy its creditors caused by the application of the companies' funds to assist outside companies in which the first respondent had an interest. In doing so they had failed to respect the fundamental principle that the director of a company owed a duty to exercise his powers in the best interests of the company. Accordingly, the directors were unfit to be concerned in the management of a company. The disqualification orders were for seven and eleven years for each director respectively.

The Secretary of State is required to set out the factual basis of allegations of unfitness with supporting evidence

In *Secretary of State for Business, Innovation and Skills v Doffman* [2011] 2 BCLC 541, Newey J held that in deciding whether the Secretary of State had made out the allegations of unfitness, the court was required to have regard to, but was not restricted to, the statutory matters in paras 1, 2 and 6 of Sch 1 to the CDDA 1986 on which the Secretary of State relied, namely misfeasance or breach of fiduciary or other duty, misapplication or retention of, or failure to account for, money, and responsibility for the company's insolvency.

The Secretary of State was required to establish the allegations of unfitness on the balance of probabilities, but in so far as serious impropriety, in particular fraudulent conduct, was alleged against the defendants, who were both solicitors and against whom there was no other evidence of dishonesty, the court would regard the allegations as inherently improbable and would require cogent evidence before accepting them.

If dishonesty was to be alleged against a defendant, the allegation had to be fairly and squarely made in the case against him and had to be fairly and squarely put in cross-examination.

However, the Secretary of State was not precluded from alleging fraud at trial if it was evident in the context that a 'matter determining unfitness' which was expressed in terms that the defendant 'knew or ought to have known' of the wrongdoing was intended to encompass an alternative allegation of dishonesty. What was crucial was that the defendant had fair notice of an allegation and a fair opportunity to respond to it.

In some cases, directors may prefer one creditor over others in the payment of debts. In such cases, the courts may find unfitness being established.

Disqualification orders fell into three main brackets depending upon the seriousness of the offence

This aspect was considered in *Re Sevenoaks Stationers (Retail) Limited* [1991] BCLC 325. The director in question had been a director of five companies which had gone into insolvent liquidation. The accounts of the companies had not been properly audited and with respect to one of the companies the accounting records of the company were inadequate. There were other allegations of impropriety in the management of the company's affairs and substantial Crown debts were owing. The director was disqualified for seven years and he appealed against his sentence.

The Court of Appeal held that in determining the length of a disqualification order under CDDA 1986, s 6, the top bracket of disqualification should be reserved for serious cases. The minimum bracket of two to five years should be reserved for cases which were relatively not serious and the middle bracket of six to ten years should apply to serious cases that did not deserve the maximum sentence. However, non-payment of Crown debts could not be treated as automatic grounds for disqualification.

Furthermore, it was of paramount importance that a director facing a disqualification order should know the charges that he had to meet. This may have implications for a director to plead the Human Rights Act 1998 and the European Convention on Human Rights including the right to a fair trial and natural justice concepts.

A lower standard of fairness is required in civil proceedings than criminal actions as disqualification proceedings are civil in nature

In *R v Secretary of State for Trade and Industry ex p McCormick* [1998] BCC 379, the applicant contended that the Secretary of State should not to be allowed to use the evidence obtained against him from company investigations in subsequent disqualification proceedings.

It was agreed that if disqualification proceedings involved a criminal charge, the Secretary of State's power to use compelled evidence ought to be exercised so as to give effect to the obligations of the United Kingdom under the Convention. That question had to be determined in accordance with national law. Although the consequences of a disqualification order were severe and had been described as penal, they did not involve a deprivation of liberty, livelihood or property. The disqualification order did not prevent the person subject to its terms carrying on a commercial activity in his own name. Instead, its effect was to remove the privilege of doing so through the vehicle of a limited liability company.

The court also rejected the applicant's submission that, as art 6.1 applied to civil rights and obligations, the Secretary of State was obliged to follow the same procedure as applied in criminal proceedings. As was established by the jurisprudence of the European Court of Human Rights, the requirement of fairness did not demand the same treatment in civil proceedings as in criminal. In the former, compelled evidence in the form of discovery and interrogatories was allowed by the rules of court, but those rules were designed to produce a fair trial. The Secretary of State was not bound to treat these proceedings as if they involved a criminal charge, and her decision to use compelled evidence did not make the proceedings unfair.

See too *DC v United Kingdom (39031/97)* [2000] BCC 710.

The use in disqualification proceedings of statements obtained under s 235 of the Insolvency Act 1986 did not necessarily involve a breach of art 6(1) of the Convention

In *Official Receiver v Stern* [2000] 1 WLR 2230, the Official Receiver sought disqualification orders against two directors under the Company Directors Disqualification Act 1986. In those proceedings, he wanted to rely on interviews given by the directors to the insolvency service under s 235 of the Insolvency Act 1986, a provision which required them to attend and answer questions.

The directors contended that the use of these statements in disqualification proceedings breached the right to a fair hearing under art 6(1) of the European Convention for the Protection of Human Rights and Fundamental Freedoms 1950. That contention was rejected by Sir Richard Scott, the Vice-Chancellor, and the directors applied to the Court of Appeal for permission to appeal.

The Court of Appeal held that the use in disqualification proceedings of statements obtained under s 235 of the Insolvency Act 1986 did not necessarily involve a breach of art 6(1) of the convention. The issue of fair trial was one which had to be considered in the round, having regard to all relevant factors. Those factors included, but were not limited to, the fact that disqualification proceedings, though they were not criminal proceedings and were primarily for the protection of the public, often involved serious allegations and almost always carried a degree of stigma for anyone who was disqualified.

It also stated that there were degrees of coercion involved in different investigative procedures available in corporate insolvency, and those differences might be reflected in different degrees of prejudice involved in the admission in disqualification proceedings of statements obtained by such procedures; and that, in directors' disqualification proceedings, as in most other fields, it was generally best for issues of fairness or unfairness to be decided by the trial judge, either at a pre-trial review or in the course of the trial.

The court could not make an order under IA 1986, s 236 for production of documents by third parties for subsequent use in disqualification proceedings – this would be an abuse of power by the Official Receiver

In *Re Pantmaenog Timber Co Ltd* [2001] 4 All ER 588, the issue arose whether, under IA 1986, ss 235 and 236, evidence obtained by the liquidator or the official receiver could be used by the Secretary in subsequent disqualification proceedings under the CDDA 1986.

The Court of Appeal held that the court had no power to make an order, on an application by the Official Receiver under s 236 of the Insolvency Act 1986, for the production of documents by third parties in circumstances where the sole purpose of the application was to obtain documents for use as evidence in pending proceedings under the Disqualification Act. Such an application fell outside the scope of s 236 and would therefore be an application for an improper purpose.

The Court of Appeal set out two reasons for its decision: first, in a case where the company was not being wound up by the court, the applicant in any disqualification proceedings had to be the Secretary of State, and he was not a person who could invoke directly the powers conferred by ss 235 and 236 of the Insolvency Act. Those powers were conferred on the liquidator for the better discharge of his functions in the winding up, not to enable the Secretary of State to obtain, indirectly, information and documents which Parliament had not thought it necessary or appropriate to enable him to obtain directly. There was no reason to think that Parliament intended that the powers to obtain information and documents for use in disqualification proceedings should be any greater in a case where the company was being wound up by the court than in a case where the company was in a voluntary winding up.

Secondly, in a case where the company was being wound up by the court, the function of the Official Receiver under the Insolvency Act was to investigate the causes of failure and to report to the court. Although it was plainly intended that the Official Receiver should be able to invoke the powers under ss 235 and 236 for the purpose of discharging that function, it could not have been intended that he should invoke those powers either for the purpose of carrying out his role under s 7(3) of the Disqualification Act or for the purpose of obtaining evidence for use in disqualification proceedings of which he had conduct under s 7(1)(b) of that Act, save in so far as either purpose was incidental to the discharge of his function under s 132 of the Insolvency Act.

Disqualification orders under s 6: applications and acceptance of undertakings

17.42 If it appears to the Secretary of State that it is expedient in the public interest that a disqualification order under CDDA 1986, s 6 should be made against any person, an application for the making of such an order against that person may be made:

(a) by the Secretary of State, or

(b) if the Secretary of State so directs in the case of a person who is or has been a director of a company which is being or has been wound up by the court in England and Wales, by the official receiver: CDDA 1986, s 7(1).

Except with the leave of the court, an application for the making under that section of a disqualification order against any person shall not be made after the end of the period of three years beginning with the day on which the company of which that person is or has been a director became insolvent: CDDA 1986, s 7(2) (as inserted by SBEEA 2015, s 108(1)). Section 108(1) of SBEEA 2015 applies only to an application relating to a company which has become insolvent after the commencement of that subsection: SBEEA 2015, s 108(2). Section 6(2) of the CDDA 1986 (meaning of 'becoming insolvent') applies for the purposes of s 108(2) of SBEEA 2015 as it applies for the purposes of s 6 of that Act: SBEEA 2015, s 108(3).

17.43 If it appears to the Secretary of State that the conditions mentioned in CDDA 1986, s 6(1) are satisfied as regards any person who has offered to give him a disqualification undertaking, he may accept the undertaking if it appears to him that it is expedient in the public interest that he should do so (instead of applying, or proceeding with an application, for a disqualification order): CDDA 1986, s 7(2A).

17.44 The Secretary of State or the official receiver may require the liquidator, administrator or administrative receiver of a company, or any person:

(a) to furnish him with such information with respect to that person's or another person's conduct as a director of a company which has at any time become insolvent (whether while the person was a director or subsequently), , and

(b) to produce and permit inspection of such books, papers and other records as are considered by the Secretary of State or (as the case may be) the official receiver to be relevant to that person's or another person's conduct as such a director,

as the Secretary of State or the official receiver may reasonably require for the purpose of determining whether to exercise, or of exercising, any function of his under CDDA 1986, s 7: CDDA 1986, s 7(4) (as inserted by DA 2015, Sch 6, Part 4).

Subsections (1A) and (2) of s 6 apply for the purposes of this section as they apply for the purposes of that section: CDDA 1986, s 7(5) (as inserted by SBEEA 2015, Sch 7, Part 1).

The issue of whether or not it is 'expedient' in the public interest for a disqualification order to be made is a matter for determination by the Secretary of State and not by the court

In *Re Blackspur Group plc, Secretary of State for Trade and Industry v Davies* [1998] 1 BCLC 676, Lord Woolf MR set out the following points:

(1) The purpose of the CDDA 1986 is the protection of the public, by means of prohibitory remedial action, by anticipated deterrent effect on further misconduct and by encouragement of higher standards of honesty and diligence in corporate management, from those who are unfit to be concerned in the management of a company.

(2) Parliament has designated the Secretary of State as the proper public officer to discharge the function of making applications to the court for disqualification orders. There is a wide discretion to do so in cases where it appears, in the prescribed circumstances, that 'it is expedient in the public interest that a disqualification order should be made'. In any particular case it may be decided that the public interest is best served by making and continuing an application to trial; or by not making an application at all; or by not continuing a pending application to trial; or by not contesting at trial points raised by way of defence or mitigation. All these litigation decisions are made by the Secretary of State according to what is considered by her to be 'expedient in the public interest'. They are not made by the court or by other parties to the proceedings.

(3) Once proceedings have been brought to trial, it is for the court, not for the Secretary of State or for any other party, to decide whether a disqualification order should or should not be made. A court can only make a disqualification order if it is 'satisfied' on the prescribed statutory matters. As the court must be 'satisfied' of those matters, it is not appropriate for the court to act, or even for the court to be asked to act, as a rubber stamp on a proposed consent order, without regard to its factual basis.

    However, this does not prevent the court from taking into account the agreement of the parties in concluding that it is satisfied that the case warrants disqualification and in determining the period of disqualification which is appropriate, thus allowing the issues to be determined by the court to be disposed of summarily.

(4) Applications under the CDDA 1986 are not ordinary private law proceedings, even when heard and determined by a civil court. They are made, and can only be properly made, in cases where it is considered 'expedient in the public interest' to seek a disqualification order in the specified statutory form which, when made, has serious penal consequences. The unique form of the order and the special procedure for obtaining it are prescribed by the CDDA 1986. Significantly, the CDDA 1986 does not expressly equip the court with a discretion to deploy the armoury of common law and equitable remedies to restrain future misconduct (injunction or undertaking in lieu of injunction), to punish for disregard of restraints imposed by court order (contempt powers of imprisonment or fine), to compensate for past loss unlawfully inflicted (damages) or to restore benefits unjustly acquired (restitution).

The Secretary of State and not the court is required to decide whether or not to bring disqualification proceedings before the court

In *Re Barings plc (No 3), Secretary of State for Trade and Industry v Baker* [1999] 1 BCLC 226, Chadwick LJ stated that the decisions whether or not to commence, and thereafter to pursue, applications to the court for disqualification orders have been entrusted by Parliament to the Secretary of State. It is for her, and not for the court, to make those decisions.

Further, a court was not entitled to intervene and stay proceedings because it may take the view that the Secretary of State is acting in a manner that it may regard as over-zealous. That would be to substitute the court's view of what is expedient in the public interest for her view. That is no part of the court's role. The basis upon which the court can interfere, by granting a stay of proceedings, is to protect its own process from abuse.

An abnegation of responsibility by a director in the company's affairs was a significant failure rendering him unfit and subject to disqualification proceedings

In *Secretary of State for Business, Innovation and Skills v Aaron & Ors* [2009] EWHC 3263 (Ch) the Secretary of State successfully brought proceedings for the disqualification of two directors under CDDA 1986, s 7 for breaches of the Financial Services rules.

The directors contended that their disqualification would be unfair because their breaches of FSA rules were not connected with the general management of the company. Proudman J stated:

> 'The fact that he [the director] has not shown himself unfit to manage any business, or to undertake a different management role, is, like the likelihood or otherwise of offending again … a matter which goes to leave to be concerned in the management of a company under s 17 CDDA and to length of disqualification. It is not a matter which goes

> to disqualification itself. Secondly, there is the simple fact that the abnegation of responsibility by a director is a matter affecting the ability to conduct ordinary corporate governance. A director's failure to ensure that he was sufficiently concerned with relevant responsibilities is a grass roots failure'.

Office-holder's report on conduct of directors

17.45 The office-holder in respect of a company which is insolvent must prepare a report (a 'conduct report') about the conduct of each person who was a director of the company:

(a) on the insolvency date, or

(b) at any time during the period of three years ending with that date: CDDA 1986, s 7A(1) (as inserted by SBEEA 2015, s 107(2)).

For the purposes of this section a company is insolvent if:

(a) the company is in liquidation and at the time it went into liquidation its assets were insufficient for the payment of its debts and other liabilities and the expenses of the winding up,

(b) the company has entered administration, or

(c) an administrative receiver of the company has been appointed;

and s 6(1A) applies for the purposes of this section as it applies for the purpose of that section: CDDA 1986, s 7A(2) (as inserted by SBEEA 2015, s 107(2)).

A conduct report must, in relation to each person, describe any conduct of the person which may assist the Secretary of State in deciding whether to exercise the power under section 7(1) or (2A) in relation to the person: CDDA 1986, s 7A(3) (as inserted by SBEEA 2015, s 107(2)).

The office-holder must send the conduct report to the Secretary of State before the end of:

(a) the period of three months beginning with the insolvency date, or

(b) such other longer period as the Secretary of State considers appropriate in the particular circumstances: CDDA 1986, s 7A(4) (as inserted by SBEEA 2015, s 107(2)).

If new information comes to the attention of an office-holder, the office-holder must send that information to the Secretary of State as soon as reasonably practicable: CDDA 1986, s 7A(5) (as inserted by SBEEA 2015, s 107(2)).

17.46 The term 'New information' is information which an office-holder considers should have been included in a conduct report prepared in relation to the company, or would have been so included had it been available before the report was sent: CDDA 1986, s 7A(6) (as inserted by SBEEA 2015, s 107(2)).

If there is more than one office-holder in respect of a company at any particular time (because the company is insolvent by virtue of falling within more than one paragraph of subsection (2) at that time), subsection (1) applies only to the first of the office-holders to be appointed: CDDA 1986, s 7A(7) (as inserted by SBEEA 2015, s 107(2)).

In the case of a company which is at different times insolvent by virtue of falling within one or more different paragraphs of subsection (2):

(a) the references in subsection (1) to the insolvency date are to be read as references to the first such date during the period in which the company is insolvent, and

(b) subsection (1) does not apply to an office-holder if at any time during the period in which the company is insolvent a conduct report has already been prepared and sent to the Secretary of State: CDDA 1986, s 7A(8) (as inserted by SBEEA 2015, s 107(2)).

The 'office-holder' in respect of a company which is insolvent is:

(a) in the case of a company being wound up by the court in England and Wales, the official receiver;

(b) in the case of a company being wound up otherwise, the liquidator;

(c) in the case of a company in administration, the administrator;

(d) in the case of a company of which there is an administrative receiver, the receiver: CDDA 1986, s 7A(9) (as inserted by SBEEA 2015, s 107(2)).

17.47 The 'insolvency date':

(a) in the case of a company being wound up by the court, means the date on which the court makes the winding-up order (see s 125 of IA 1986);

(b) in the case of a company being wound up by way of a members' voluntary winding up, means the date on which the liquidator forms the opinion that the company will be unable to pay its debts in full (together with interest at the official rate) within the period stated in the directors' declaration of solvency under s 89 of IA 1986;

(c) in the case of a company being wound up by way of a creditors' voluntary winding up where no such declaration under section 89 of that Act has been made, means the date of the passing of the resolution for voluntary winding up;

(d) in the case of a company which has entered administration, means the date the company did so;

(e) in the case of a company in respect of which an administrative receiver has been appointed, means the date of that appointment: CDDA 1986, s 7A(10) (as inserted by SBEEA 2015, s 107(2)).

For the purposes of subsection (10)(e), any appointment of an administrative receiver to replace an administrative receiver who has died or vacated office pursuant to section 45 of the Insolvency Act 1986 is to be ignored: CDDA 1986, s 7A(11) (as inserted by SBEEA 2015, s 107(2)).

In this section, the terms 'court' has the same meaning as in s 6 of CDDA 1986; and 'director' includes a shadow director: CDDA 1986, s 7A(12) (as inserted by SBEEA 2015, s 107(2)).

Disqualification of director on finding of unfitness

17.48 If it appears to the Secretary of State that it is expedient in the public interest that a disqualification order should be made against a person who is, or has been, a director or shadow director of a company, he may apply to the court for such an order: CDDA 1986, s 8(1).

The court may make a disqualification order against a person where, on an application under CDDA 1986, s 8, it is satisfied that his conduct in relation to the company (either taken alone or taken together with his conduct as a director or shadow director of one or more other companies or overseas companies), makes him unfit to be concerned in the management of a company: CDDA 1986, s 8(2) (as inserted by SBEEA 2015 s 106(3)(a)).

17.49 Where it appears to the Secretary of State that, in the case of a person who has offered to give him a disqualification undertaking:

(a) the conduct of the person in relation to a company of which the person is or has been a director or shadow director (either taken alone or taken together with his conduct as a director or shadow director of one or more other companies or overseas companies), makes him unfit to be concerned in the management of a company, and

(b) it is expedient in the public interest that he should accept the undertaking (instead of applying, or proceeding with an application, for a disqualification order) he may accept the undertaking: CDDA 1986, s 8(2A) (as inserted by SBEEA 2015, s 106(3)(b)) and s 109(1)).

Subsection (1A) of section 6 applies for the purposes of this section as it applies for the purposes of that section: CDDA 1986, s 8(2B) (as inserted by SBEEA 2015, s 106(3)(c)).

The term 'the court' means the High Court or, in Scotland, the Court of Session: CDDA 1986, s 8(3).

The maximum period of disqualification under this section is 15 years: CDDA 1986, s 8(4).

Persons instructing unfit directors

Order disqualifying person instructing unfit director of insolvent company

17.50 The court may make a disqualification order against a person ('P') if, on an application under section 8ZB, it is satisfied:

(a) either:

  (i) that a disqualification order under s 6 has been made against a person who is or has been a director (but not a shadow director) of a company, or

  (ii) that the Secretary of State has accepted a disqualification undertaking from such a person under s 7(2A), and

(b) that P exercised the requisite amount of influence over the person.

That person is referred to in this section as 'the main transgressor': CDDA 1986, s 8ZA(1).

17.51 For the purposes of s 8ZA, P exercised the requisite amount of influence over the main transgressor if any of the conduct:

(a) for which the main transgressor is subject to the order made under section 6, or

(b) in relation to which the undertaking was accepted from the main transgressor under section 7(2A),

was the result of the main transgressor acting in accordance with P's directions or instructions: CDDA 1986, s 8ZA(2).

But P does not exercise the requisite amount of influence over the main transgressor by reason only that the main transgressor acts on advice given by P in a professional capacity: CDDA 1986, s 8ZA(3).

Under s 8ZA, the minimum period of disqualification is two years and the maximum period is 15 years: CDDA 1986, s 8ZA(4).

17.52 In this s 8ZA and s 8ZB 'the court' has the same meaning as in s 6 CDDA 1986; and subsection (3B) of s 6 applies in relation to proceedings mentioned in subsection (6) below as it applies in relation to proceedings mentioned in s 6(3B)(a) and (b):CDDA 1986, s 8ZA(5).

The proceedings are proceedings:

(a) for or in connection with a disqualification order under this section, or

(b) in connection with a disqualification undertaking accepted under section 8ZC:CDDA 1986, s 8ZA(6).

Application for order under s 8ZA

17.53 If it appears to the Secretary of State that it is expedient in the public interest that a disqualification order should be made against a person under s 8ZA, the Secretary of State may:

(a) make an application to the court for such an order, or

(b) in a case where an application for an order under section 6 against the main transgressor has been made by the official receiver, direct the official receiver to make such an application: CDDA 1986, s 8ZB(1).

Except with the leave of the court, an application for a disqualification order under s 8ZA must not be made after the end of the period of three years beginning with the day on which the company in question became insolvent (within the meaning given by s 6(2)): CDDA 1986, s 8ZB(2).

Section 8ZB(4) of CDDA 1986 applies for the purposes of this section as it applies for the purposes of that section: CDDA 1986, s 8ZB(3).

Disqualification undertaking instead of an order under s 8ZA

17.54 If it appears to the Secretary of State that it is expedient in the public interest to do so, the Secretary of State may accept a disqualification undertaking from a person ("P") if:

(a) any of the following is the case:

(i) a disqualification order under s 6 has been made against a person who is or has been a director (but not a shadow director) of a company,

(ii) the Secretary of State has accepted a disqualification undertaking from such a person under s 7(2A), or

(iii) it appears to the Secretary of State that such an undertaking could be accepted from such a person (if one were offered), and

(b) it appears to the Secretary of State that P exercised the requisite amount of influence over the person.

That person is referred to in this section as 'the main transgressor': CDDA 1986, s 8ZC(1).

17.55 For the purposes of this section, P exercised the requisite amount of influence over the main transgressor if any of the conduct:

(a) for which the main transgressor is subject to the disqualification order made under s 6,

(b) in relation to which the disqualification undertaking was accepted from the main transgressor under s 7(2A), or

(c) which led the Secretary of State to the conclusion set out in sub-s (1)(a)(iii),

was the result of the main transgressor acting in accordance with P's directions or instructions: CDDA 1986, s 8ZC(2).

But P does not exercise the requisite amount of influence over the main transgressor by reason only that the main transgressor acts on advice given by P in a professional capacity: CDDA 1986, s 8ZC(3).

Sections (4) of s 7 applies for the purposes of this section as it applies for the purposes of that section: CDDA 1986, s 8ZC(4).

Order disqualifying person instructing unfit director: other cases

17.56 The court may make a disqualification order against a person ('P') if, on an application under this section, it is satisfied:

(a) either:

(i) that a disqualification order under section 8 has been made against a person who is or has been a director (but not a shadow director) of a company, or

(ii) that the Secretary of State has accepted a disqualification undertaking from such a person under section 8(2A), and

(b) that P exercised the requisite amount of influence over the person.

That person is referred to in this section as 'the main transgressor': CDDA 1986, s 8ZD(1).

17.57 The Secretary of State may make an application to the court for a disqualification order against P under this section if it appears to the Secretary of State that it is expedient in the public interest for such an order to be made: CDDA 1986, s 8ZD(2).

For the purposes of s 8ZD, P exercised the requisite amount of influence over the main transgressor if any of the conduct:

(a) for which the main transgressor is subject to the order made under section 8, or

(b) in relation to which the undertaking was accepted from the main transgressor under section 8(2A),

was the result of the main transgressor acting in accordance with P's directions or instructions: CDDA 1986, s 8ZD(3).

But P does not exercise the requisite amount of influence over the main transgressor by reason only that the main transgressor acts on advice given by P in a professional capacity: CDDA 1986, s 8ZD(4).

Under s 8ZD the maximum period of disqualification is 15 years: CDDA 1986, s 8ZD(5).

In s 8ZD CDDA 1986, 'the court' means the High Court or, in Scotland, the Court of Session: CDDA 1986, s 8ZD(6).

Disqualification undertaking instead of an order under s 8ZD

17.58 If it appears to the Secretary of State that it is expedient in the public interest to do so, the Secretary of State may accept a disqualification undertaking from a person ('P') if:

(a) any of the following is the case:

  (i) a disqualification order under s 8 has been made against a person who is or has been a director (but not a shadow director) of a company,

  (ii) the Secretary of State has accepted a disqualification undertaking from such a person under s 8(2A), or

  (iii) it appears to the Secretary of State that such an undertaking could be accepted from such a person (if one were offered), and

(b) it appears to the Secretary of State that P exercised the requisite amount of influence over the person.

That person is referred to in this section as 'the main transgressor': CDDA 1986, s 8ZE(1).

17.59 For the purposes of s 8ZE of CDDA 1986, P exercised the requisite amount of influence over the main transgressor if any of the conduct:

(a) for which the main transgressor is subject to the disqualification order made under s 8,

(b) in relation to which the disqualification undertaking was accepted from the main transgressor under s 8(2A), or

(c) which led the Secretary of State to the conclusion set out in subsection (1)(a)(iii),

was the result of the main transgressor acting in accordance with P's directions or instructions: CDDA 1986, s 8ZE(2).

But P does not exercise the requisite amount of influence over the main transgressor by reason only that the main transgressor acts on advice given by P in a professional capacity: CDDA 1986, s 8ZE(3).

Further provision about disqualification undertakings

Variation etc of disqualification undertaking

17.60 The court may, on the application of a person who is subject to a disqualification undertaking:

(a) reduce the period for which the undertaking is to be in force, or

(b) provide for it to cease to be in force: CDDA 1986, s 8A(1).

On the hearing of an application under s 8A(1), the Secretary of State shall appear and call the attention of the court to any matters which seem to him to be relevant, and may himself give evidence or call witnesses: CDDA 1986, s 8A(2).

17.61 Subsection (2) does not apply to an application in the case of an undertaking given under s 9B, and in such a case on the hearing of the application whichever of the OFT or a specified regulator (within the meaning of s 9E) accepted the undertaking:

(a) must appear and call the attention of the court to any matters which appear to it or him (as the case may be) to be relevant;

(b) may give evidence or call witnesses: CDDA 1986, s 8A(2A).

The term 'the court':

- in the case of an undertaking given under s 8ZC has the same meaning as in s 8ZA;
- in the case of an undertaking given under s 8ZE means the High Court or, in Scotland, the Court of Session:
- in the case of an undertaking given under 9B means the High Court or (in Scotland) the Court of Session;
- in any other case has the same meaning as in s 5A(5), 7(2) or 8 (as the case may be): CDDA 1986, s 8A(3) (as inserted by SBEEA 2015, Sch 7, Pt 1).

Disqualification for competition infringements

Competition disqualification order

17.62 The court must make a disqualification order against a person if the following two conditions are satisfied in relation to him: CDDA 1986, s 9A(1).

The first condition is that an undertaking which is a company of which he is a director commits a breach of competition law: CDDA 1986, s 9A(2).

The second condition is that the court considers that his conduct as a director makes him unfit to be concerned in the management of a company: CDDA 1986, s 9A(3).

An undertaking commits a breach of competition law if it engages in conduct which infringes any of the following:

(a) the Chapter 1 prohibition (within the meaning of the Competition Act 1998) (prohibition on agreements etc preventing, restricting or distorting competition);

(b) the Chapter 2 prohibition (within the meaning of that Act) (prohibition on abuse of a dominant position);

(c) Article 81 of the Treaty establishing the European Community (prohibition on agreements etc preventing, restricting or distorting competition);

(d) Article 82 of that Treaty (prohibition on abuse of a dominant position): CDDA 1986, s 9A(4).

17.63 For the purpose of deciding under s 9A(3) whether a person is unfit to be concerned in the management of a company the court:

(a) must have regard to whether s 9A(6) applies to him;

(b) may have regard to his conduct as a director of a company in connection with any other breach of competition law;

(c) must not have regard to the matters mentioned in Schedule 1: CDDA 1986, s 9A(5).

CDDA 1986, s 9A(6) applies to a person if as a director of the company:

(a) his conduct contributed to the breach of competition law mentioned in s 9A(2);

(b) his conduct did not contribute to the breach but he had reasonable grounds to suspect that the conduct of the undertaking constituted the breach and he took no steps to prevent it;

(c) he did not know but ought to have known that the conduct of the undertaking constituted the breach: CDDA 1986, s 9A(7).

17.64 For the purposes of s 9A(6)(a), it is immaterial whether the person knew that the conduct of the undertaking constituted the breach.

For the purposes of s 9A(4)(a) or (c), references to the conduct of an undertaking are references to its conduct taken with the conduct of one or more other undertakings: CDDA 1986, s 9A(8).

The maximum period of disqualification under this section is 15 years: CDDA 1986, s 9A(9).

An application under s 9A for a disqualification order may be made by the OFT or by a specified regulator: CDDA 1986, s 9A(1).

Competition undertakings

17.65 CDDA 1986, s 9B applies if:

(a) the OFT or a specified regulator thinks that in relation to any person an undertaking which is a company of which he is a director has committed or is committing a breach of competition law,

(b) the OFT or the specified regulator thinks that the conduct of the person as a director makes him unfit to be concerned in the management of a company, and

(c) the person offers to give the OFT or the specified regulator (as the case may be) a disqualification undertaking: CDDA 1986, s 9B(1).

The OFT or the specified regulator (as the case may be) may accept a disqualification undertaking from the person instead of applying for or proceeding with an application for a disqualification order: CDDA 1986, s 9B(2).

17.66 A disqualification undertaking is an undertaking by a person that for the period specified in the undertaking he will not:

(a) be a director of a company;

(b) act as receiver of a company's property;

(c) in any way, whether directly or indirectly, be concerned or take part in the promotion, formation or management of a company;

(d) act as an insolvency practitioner: CDDA 1986, s 9B(3).

But a disqualification undertaking may provide that a prohibition falling within s 9B(3)(a) to (c) does not apply if the person obtains the leave of the court: CDDA 1986, s 9B(4).

The maximum period which may be specified in a disqualification undertaking is 15 years.

If a disqualification undertaking is accepted from a person who is already subject to a disqualification undertaking under this Act or to a disqualification order the periods specified in those undertakings or the undertaking and the order (as the case may be) run concurrently: CDDA 1986, s 9B(6).

Competition investigations

17.67 If the OFT or a specified regulator has reasonable grounds for suspecting that a breach of competition law has occurred it or he (as the case may be) may carry out an investigation for the purpose of deciding whether to make an application under CDDA 1986, s 9 for a disqualification order: CDDA 1986, s 9C(1).

For the purposes of such an investigation ss 26 to 30 of the Competition Act 1998 apply to the OFT and the specified regulators as they apply to the OFT for the purposes of an investigation under s 25 of that Act: CDDA 1986, s 9C(2).

17.68 CDDA 1986, s 9C(4) applies if as a result of an investigation under this section the OFT or a specified regulator proposes to apply under s 9A for a disqualification order: CDDA 1986, s 9C(3).

Before making the application the OFT or regulator (as the case may be) must:

(a) give notice to the person likely to be affected by the application, and

(b) give that person an opportunity to make representations: CDDA 1986, s 9C(4).

Co-ordination

17.69 The Secretary of State may make regulations for the purpose of co-ordinating the performance of functions under ss 9A–9C (relevant functions) which are exercisable concurrently by two or more persons: CDDA 1986, s 9D(1).

Section 54(5) to (7) of the Competition Act 1998 applies to regulations made under this section as it applies to regulations made under that section and for that purpose in that section:

(a) references to Part 1 functions must be read as references to relevant functions;

(b) references to a regulator must be read as references to a specified regulator;

(c) a competent person also includes any of the specified regulators: CDDA 1986, s 9D(2).

17.70 The power to make regulations under s 54 of the Competition Act 1998 must be exercised by statutory instrument subject to annulment in pursuance of a resolution of either House of Parliament: CDDA 1986, s 9D(3).

Such a statutory instrument may:

(a) contain such incidental, supplemental, consequential and transitional provision as the Secretary of State thinks appropriate;

(b) make different provision for different cases: CDDA 1986, s 9D(4).

Interpretation

17.71 Section 54 of the Competition Act 1998 applies for the purposes of ss 9A–9D: CDDA 1986, s 9E(1).

Each of the following is a specified regulator for the purposes of a breach of competition law in relation to a matter in respect of which he or it has a function:

(a) the Director General of Telecommunications;

(b) the Gas and Electricity Markets Authority;

(c) the Director General of Water Services;

(d) the Rail Regulator;

(e) the Civil Aviation Authority: CDDA 1986, s 9E(2).

The court is the High Court or (in Scotland) the Court of Session: CDDA 1986, s 9E(3).

Conduct includes omission: CDDA 1986, s 9E(4).

Director includes shadow director: CDDA 1986, s 9E(5).

Other cases of disqualification

Participation in wrongful trading

17.72 Where the court makes a declaration under s 213 or 214 of the Insolvency Act 1986 that a person is liable to make a contribution to a company's assets, then, whether or not an application for such an order is made by any person, the court may, if it thinks fit, also make a disqualification order against the person to whom the declaration relates: CDDA 1986, s 10(1).

The maximum period of disqualification under this section is 15 years: CDDA 1986, s 10(2).

In this section 'company' includes overseas company: CDDA 1986, s 10(3) (as inserted by SBEEA 2015, Sch 7, Part 1).

Undischarged bankrupts

17.73 It is an offence for a person to act as director of a company or directly or indirectly to take part in or be concerned in the promotion, formation or management of a company, without the leave of the court, at a time when any of the circumstances mentioned in s 11(2) apply to the person: CDDA 1986, s 11(1) (as inserted by SBEEA 2015, s 113(1)).

The circumstances are:

(a) the person is an undischarged bankrupt:

  (i) in England and Wales or Scotland, or

  (ii) in Northern Ireland,

(b) a bankruptcy restrictions order or undertaking is in force in respect of the person under:

  (i) the Bankruptcy (Scotland) Act 1985 or the Insolvency Act 1986, or

  (ii) the Insolvency (Northern Ireland) Order 1989,

(c) a debt relief restrictions order or undertaking is in force in respect of the person under:

  (i) the Insolvency Act 1986, or

  (ii) the Insolvency (Northern Ireland) Order 1989,

(d) a moratorium period under a debt relief order applies in relation to the person under—

   (i) the Insolvency Act 1986, or

   (ii) the Insolvency (Northern Ireland) Order 1989: CDDA 1986, s 11(2) (as inserted by SBEEA 2015, s 113(1)).

In s 11(1) "the court" means:

(a) for the purposes of subsection (2)(a)(i):

   (i) the court by which the person was adjudged bankrupt, or

   (ii) in Scotland, the court by which sequestration of the person's estate was awarded or, if awarded other than by the court, the court which would have jurisdiction in respect of sequestration of the person's estate,

(b) for the purposes of subsection (2)(b)(i):

   (i) the court which made the order,

   (ii) in Scotland, if the order has been made other than by the court, the court to which the person may appeal against the order, or

   (iii) the court to which the person may make an application for annulment of the undertaking,

(c) for the purposes of subsection (2)(c)(i):

   (i) the court which made the order, or

   (ii) the court to which the person may make an application for annulment of the undertaking,

(d) for the purposes of subsection (2)(d)(i), the court to which the person would make an application under section 251M(1) of the Insolvency Act 1986 (if the person were dissatisfied as mentioned there),

(e) for the purposes of paragraphs (a)(ii), (b)(ii), (c)(ii) and (d)(ii) of subsection (2), the High Court of Northern Ireland: CDDA 1986, s 11(2A) (as inserted by SBEEA 2015, s 113(1))."

In England and Wales, the leave of the court shall not be given unless notice of intention to apply for it has been served on the official receiver; and it is the latter's duty, if he is of opinion that it is contrary to the public interest that the application should be granted, to attend on the hearing of the application and oppose it: CDDA 1986, s 11(3).

The term 'company' includes a company incorporated outside Great Britain that has an established place of business in Great Britain: CDDA 1986, s 11(4).

Determining unfitness etc: matters to be taken into account

17.74 Section 12C CDDA 1986 applies where a court must determine:

(a) whether a person's conduct as a director of one or more companies or overseas companies makes the person unfit to be concerned in the management of a company;

(b) whether to exercise any discretion it has to make a disqualification order under any of s 2 to 4, 5A, 8 or 10;

(c) where the court has decided to make a disqualification order under any of those sections or is required to make an order under section 6, what the period of disqualification should be: CDDA 1986, s 12C(1) (as inserted by SBEEA 2015, s 106(5)).

17.75 But this section does not apply where the court in question is one mentioned in section 2(2)(b) or (c): CDDA 1986, s 12C(2) (as inserted by SBEEA 2015, s 106(5)).

This section also applies where the Secretary of State must determine:

(a) whether a person's conduct as a director of one or more companies or overseas companies makes the person unfit to be concerned in the management of a company;

(b) whether to exercise any discretion the Secretary of State has to accept a disqualification undertaking under s 5A, 7 or 8: CDDA 1986, s 12C(3) (as inserted by SBEEA 2015, s 106(5)).

17.76 In making any such determination in relation to a person, the court or the Secretary of State must:

(a) in every case, have regard in particular to the matters set out in paragraphs 1 to 4 of Sch 1;

(b) in a case where the person concerned is or has been a director of a company or overseas company, also have regard in particular to the matters set out in paragraphs 5 to 7 of that Schedule: CDDA 1986, s 12C(4) (as inserted by SBEEA 2015, s 106(5)).

In this section 'director' includes a shadow director: CDDA 1986, s 12C(5) (as inserted by SBEEA 2015, s 106(5)).

17.77 Subsection (1A) of section 6 applies for the purposes of this section as it applies for the purposes of that section: CDDA 1986, s 12C(6) (as inserted by SBEEA 2015, s 106(5)).

The Secretary of State may by order modify Schedule 1; and such an order may contain such transitional provision as may appear to the Secretary of State to be necessary or expedient: CDDA 1986, s 12C(7) (as inserted by SBEEA 2015, s 106(5)).

The power to make an order under this section is exercisable by statutory instrument: CDDA 1986, s 12C(8) (as inserted by SBEEA 2015, s 106(5)).

Under Schedule 1 to CDDA 1986 (as inserted by SBEEA 2015, s 106(6)), in determining unfitness of directors, the following matters will be taken into account:

Matters to be taken into account in all cases

17.78

- The extent to which the person was responsible for the causes of any material contravention by a company or overseas company of any applicable legislative or other requirement.

- Where applicable, the extent to which the person was responsible for the causes of a company or overseas company becoming insolvent.
- The frequency of conduct of the person which falls within Sch 1, para 1 or 2.
- The nature and extent of any loss or harm caused, or any potential loss or harm which could have been caused, by the person's conduct in relation to a company or overseas company.

Additional matters to be taken into account where person is or has been a director

17.79

- Any misfeasance or breach of any fiduciary duty by the director in relation to a company or overseas company.
- Any material breach of any legislative or other obligation of the director which applies as a result of being a director of a company or overseas company.
- The frequency of conduct of the director which falls within para 5 or 6.

Interpretation

17.80

- Subsections (1A) to (2A) of s 6 apply for the purposes of Sch 1 as they apply for the purposes of that section.
- In Sch 1 'director' includes a shadow director.

Consequences of contravention

Criminal penalties

17.81 If a person acts in contravention of a disqualification order or disqualification undertaking or in contravention of CDDA 1986, s 12(2), 12A or 12B or is guilty of an offence under s 11, he is liable:

(a) on conviction on indictment, to imprisonment for not more than two years or a fine, or both; and

(b) on summary conviction, to imprisonment for not more than six months or a fine not exceeding the statutory maximum, or both: CDDA 1986, s 13.

Offences by body corporate

17.82 Where a body corporate is guilty of an offence of acting in contravention of a disqualification order or disqualification undertaking or in contravention of CDDA 1986, s 12A or 12B, and it is proved that the offence occurred with the consent or connivance of, or was attributable to any neglect on the part of any director, manager, secretary or other similar officer of the body corporate, or any person who was purporting to act in any such capacity he, as well as the body corporate, is guilty of the offence and liable to be proceeded against and punished accordingly: CDDA 1986, s 14(1).

Where the affairs of a body corporate are managed by its members, CDDA 1986, s 14(1) applies in relation to the acts and defaults of a member in connection with his functions of management as if he were a director of the body corporate: CDDA 1986, s 14(2).

Personal liability for company's debts where person acts while disqualified

17.83 A person is personally responsible for all the relevant debts of a company if at any time:

(a) in contravention of a disqualification order or disqualification undertaking or in contravention of CDDA 1986, s 11, 12A or 12B he is involved in the management of the company, or

(b) as a person who is involved in the management of the company, he acts or is willing to act on instructions given without the leave of the court by a person whom he knows at that time:

   (i) to be the subject of a disqualification order or disqualification undertaking or a disqualification order under the Company Directors Disqualification (Northern Ireland) Order 2002; or

   (ii) to be an undischarged bankrupt: CDDA 1986, s 15(1).

17.84 Where a person is personally responsible under CDDA 1986, s 15 for the relevant debts of a company, he is jointly and severally liable in respect of those debts with the company and any other person who, whether under this section or otherwise, is so liable: CDDA 1986, s 15(2).

For the purposes of s 15 the relevant debts of a company are:

(a) in relation to a person who is personally responsible under paragraph (a) of s 15(1), such debts and other liabilities of the company as are incurred at a time when that person was involved in the management of the company, and

(b) in relation to a person who is personally responsible under paragraph (b) of that subsection, such debts and other liabilities of the company as are incurred at a time when that person was acting or was willing to act on instructions given as mentioned in that paragraph: CDDA 1986, s 15(3).

For the purposes of s 15, a person is involved in the management of a company if he is a director of the company or if he is concerned, whether directly or indirectly, or takes part, in the management of the company: CDDA 1986, s 15(4).

17.85 For the purposes of s 15 a person who, as a person involved in the management of a company, has at any time acted on instructions given without the leave of the court by a person whom he knew at that time to be the subject of a disqualification order or disqualification undertaking or a disqualification order under Part II of the Companies (Northern Ireland) Order 1989 or to be an undischarged bankrupt is presumed, unless the contrary is shown, to have been willing at any time thereafter to act on any instructions given by that person: CDDA 1986, s 15(5).

It will be inappropriate to make a representation order which has the effect of making the liquidator the representative of all creditors of the company, because the liquidator does not have the same interest under s 15 of CDDA 1986 as creditors

In *Re Prestige Grindings Ltd, Sharma v Yardley* [2006] 1 BCLC 440, action was taken by the liquidator to recover amount of relevant debts from disqualified director. The issue was whether it was appropriate to make a representation order making the liquidator a representative of all the company's creditors.

Judge Norris QC (sitting as a High Court judge) held that it was inappropriate to make a representation order which had the effect of making the liquidator the representative of all creditors of the company, because the liquidator did not have the same interest under s 15 of the CDDA 1986 as creditors. On the true construction of s 15, the disqualified director was personally liable to creditors for all the relevant debts and was also jointly and severally liable with the company for those debts, but, aside from the company's right of contribution from the director, s 15 did not enable an order to be made that the disqualified director pay the 'relevant debts' to the company as co-debtor and did not give the company, or its liquidator, the right to sue the disqualified director for the debts owed to creditors.

While each creditor had a direct statutory right of action in respect of his debt against the disqualified director, the liquidator's only right was to claim a contribution in circumstances where the general law so allowed. A creditor's claim was immediate and unconditional and since his claim was purely for his own benefit he was entitled to keep the proceeds of his recovery for himself and did not have to share it with other creditors, whereas the liquidator's contribution claim was made on behalf of the liquidation estate and the right to claim did not arise until there had been payment of more than an equal share of the debt. Accordingly, the liquidator and the creditors did not have 'the same interest' and the liquidator could not act in a representative role.

On the facts, however, the court allowed Revenue & Customs to join in the proceedings to save cost and expense of separate proceedings.

Proceedings under CDDA 1986, s 15 were to recover tax due as debt

In *Inland Revenue Commissioners v McEntaggart* [2006] 1 BCLC 476, Patten J held that proceedings under CDDA 1986, s 15 were not proceedings of 'negligence, default, breach of duty or breach of trust against an officer of the company' within CA 2006, s 1157, but were simply proceedings to recover the tax due as a debt. The effect of CDDA 1986, s 15 was simply to impose collateral liability on the part of the actual or would-be directors for the debts of the company. Moreover the provisions of CA 2006, s 1157 applied only where the essential nature of the proceedings, whether they be brought in equity or under the provisions of the companies legislation, was to enforce, at the suit of or for the benefit of the company, the duties which the director owed to the company. The section was therefore inapplicable to the proceedings under CDDA 1986, s 15.

Compensation orders and undertakings

17.86 The court may make a compensation order against a person on the application of the Secretary of State if it is satisfied that the conditions mentioned in s 15A(3) are met: CDDA 1986, s 15A(1) (as inserted by SBEEA 2015, s 110)).

If it appears to the Secretary of State that the conditions mentioned in subsection (3) are met in respect of a person who has offered to give the Secretary of State a compensation undertaking, the Secretary of State may accept the undertaking instead of applying, or proceeding with an application, for a compensation order: CDDA 1986, s 15A(2) (as inserted by SBEEA 2015, s 110)).

17.87 The conditions are that:

(a) the person is subject to a disqualification order or disqualification undertaking under this Act, and

(b) conduct for which the person is subject to the order or undertaking has caused loss to one or more creditors of an insolvent company of which the person has at any time been a director: CDDA 1986, s 15A(3) (as inserted by SBEEA 2015, s 110)).

An 'insolvent company' is a company that is or has been insolvent and a company becomes insolvent if:

(a) the company goes into liquidation at a time when its assets are insufficient for the payment of its debts and other liabilities and the expenses of the winding up,

(b) the company enters administration, or

(c) an administrative receiver of the company is appointed: CDDA 1986, s 15A(4) (as inserted by SBEEA 2015, s 110)).

17.88 The Secretary of State may apply for a compensation order at any time before the end of the period of two years beginning with the date on which the disqualification order referred to in paragraph (a) of s 15A(3) was made, or the disqualification undertaking referred to in that paragraph was accepted: CDDA 1986, s 15A(5) (as inserted by SBEEA 2015, s 110)).

In the case of a person subject to a disqualification order under section 8ZA or 8ZD, or a disqualification undertaking under section 8ZC or 8ZE, the reference in subsection (3)(b) to conduct is a reference to the conduct of the main transgressor in relation to which the person has exercised the requisite amount of influence: CDDA 1986, s 15A(6) (as inserted by SBEEA 2015, s 110)).

In this section and ss 15B and 15C 'the court' means:

(a) in a case where a disqualification order has been made, the court that made the order,

(b) in any other case, the High Court or, in Scotland, the Court of Session: CDDA 1986, s 15A(7) (as inserted by SBEEA 2015, s 110)).

Amounts payable under compensation orders and undertakings

17.89 A compensation order is an order requiring the person against whom it is made to pay an amount specified in the order:

(a) to the Secretary of State for the benefit of:

  (i) a creditor or creditors specified in the order;

  (ii) a class or classes of creditor so specified;

(b) as a contribution to the assets of a company so specified: CDDA 1986, s 15B(1) (as inserted by SBEEA 2015, s 110)).

17.90 A compensation undertaking is an undertaking to pay an amount specified in the undertaking:

(a) to the Secretary of State for the benefit of:

  (i) a creditor or creditors specified in the undertaking;

  (ii) a class or classes of creditor so specified;

(b) as a contribution to the assets of a company so specified: CDDA 1986, s 15B(2) (as inserted by SBEEA 2015, s 110)).

17.91 When specifying an amount the court (in the case of an order) and the Secretary of State (in the case of an undertaking) must in particular have regard to:

(a) the amount of the loss caused;

(b) the nature of the conduct mentioned in s 15A(3)(b);

(c) whether the person has made any other financial contribution in recompense for the conduct (whether under a statutory provision or otherwise) : CDDA 1986, s 15B(3) (as inserted by SBEEA 2015, s 110)).

An amount payable by virtue of s 15B(2) under a compensation undertaking is recoverable as if payable under a court order: CDDA 1986, s 15B(4) (as inserted by SBEEA 2015, s 110)).

An amount payable under a compensation order or compensation undertaking is provable as a bankruptcy debt: CDDA 1986, s 15B(5) (as inserted by SBEEA 2015, s 110)).

Variation and revocation of compensation undertakings

17.92 The court may, on the application of a person who is subject to a compensation undertaking:

(a) reduce the amount payable under the undertaking, or

(b) provide for the undertaking not to have effect: CDDA 1986, s 15C(1) (as inserted by SBEEA 2015, s 110)).

On the hearing of an application under subsection (1), the Secretary of State must appear and call the attention of the court to any matters which the Secretary of State considers relevant, and may give evidence or call witnesses: CDDA 1986, s 15C(1) (as inserted by SBEEA 2015, s 110)).

Application for disqualification order

17.93 A person intending to apply for the making of a disqualification order or, in the case of an order under s 5A, the High Court shall give not less than ten days' notice of his intention to the person against whom the order is sought; and on the hearing of the application the last-mentioned person may appear and himself give evidence or call witnesses: CDDA 1986, s 16(1) (as inserted by SBEEA 2015, Sch 7, Part 1).

An application to a court , other than a court mentioned in s 2(2)(b) or (c) for the making against any person of a disqualification order under any of ss 2–4 of CDDA 1986 may be made by the Secretary of State or the official receiver, or by the liquidator or any past or present member or creditor of any company or overseas company in relation to which that person has committed or is alleged to have committed an offence or other default: CDDA 1986, s 16(2) (as inserted by SBEEA 2015, Sch 7, Part 1).

17.94 On the hearing of any application under this Act made by a person falling within CDDA 1986, s 16(4), the applicant shall appear and call the attention of the court to any matters which seem to him to be relevant, and may himself give evidence or call witnesses: CDDA 1986, s 16(3).

The persons referred to in s 16(3) are:

(a) the Secretary of State;

(b) the official receiver;

(c) the OFT;

(d) the liquidator;

(e) a specified regulator (within the meaning of CDDA 1986, s 9E): CDDA 1986, s 16(4).

The notice provision under CDDA 1986, s 16 was directory and not mandatory

With regard to the notice period under CDDA 1986, s 16, in *Secretary of State for Trade and Industry v Langridge; Re Cedac Ltd* [1991] Ch 402, the Court of Appeal in England held that the ten-day requirement was not mandatory but only directory. Subsequently, the Scottish case of *Secretary of State for Trade and Industry v Lovett* 1996 SC 32 adopted the position in *Langridge*.

In *Secretary of State for Trade and Industry v Swan* [2003] EWHC 1780 (Ch), Laddie J held that 'although failure to give 10 days' notice does not, per se, render the disqualification proceedings a nullity, taken with other factors, including the shortness of the notice, it may do so'.

Section 16 was further considered in Scotland by Sheriff Principal Lockhart in *Secretary of State of Business, Enterprise and Regulatory Reform v Smith and Smith* 2010 SLT (Sh Ct) 26.

It was contended that the directory status under CDDA 1986, s 16(1) should be reconsidered with particular reference to the Human Rights Act 1998, and that the failure to regard s 16(1) as mandatory amounted to a breach of arts 6 and 8 of Sch 1 to the 1998 Act.

Sheriff Principal Lockhart did not accept this contention, stating that he was bound by *Lovett*. Further, the directors had not been prejudiced by the failure to give no less than ten days' notice. Sheriff Principal further stated that where there was proof of the notice being sent, its receipt may be presumed unless evidence existed rebutting that presumption.

There is no requirement in the notice of disqualification proceedings to state which of the companies was the lead company

In *Re Surrey Leisure Ltd, Official Receiver v Keam* [1999] 1 BCLC 731, disqualification proceedings were commenced against a director of two companies. However, the notice of disqualification proceedings contained reference to only one company. The issue was whether the omission amounted to non-compliance and vitiated proceedings?

Jonathan Parker J held that the notice complied with CDDA 1986, s 16(1). Section 16(1) contained no specific provisions as to what the required notice was to contain. In the absence of any further specific statutory requirements as to the content of the notice, to hold that in order to comply with s 16(1) a notice must specify which was, or were, to be the lead company, or companies in the proceedings would be to write into the sub-section a requirement which Parliament had not thought fit to include. The correct approach to the issue of compliance was to consider whether, on the facts of the particular case, the respondent had received the limited protection supposed to be afforded to him by the sub-section.

On the facts, s 16 had been complied with. The Official Receiver was not required to state in the notice which was the lead company for the purposes of serving notice.

Application for leave under an order or undertaking

17.95 Where a person is subject to a disqualification order made by a court having jurisdiction to wind up companies, any application for leave for the purposes of CDDA 1986, s 1(1)(a), shall be made to that court: CDDA 1986, s 17(1).

Where:

(a) a person is subject to a disqualification order made under CDDA 1986, s 2 by a court other than a court having jurisdiction to wind up companies, or

(b) a person is subject to a disqualification order made under CDDA 1986, s 5,

any application for leave for the purposes of s 1(1)(a) shall be made to any court which, when the order was made, had jurisdiction to wind up the company (or, if there is more than one such company, any of the companies) to which the offence (or any of the offences) in question related: CDDA 1986, s 17(2).

17.96 Where a person is subject to a disqualification undertaking accepted at any time under CDDA 1986, s 5A, 7 or 8, any application for leave for the purposes of s 1A(1)(a) shall be made to any court to which, if the Secretary of State had applied for a disqualification order under the section in question at that time, his application could have been made: CDDA 1986, s 17(3) (as inserted by SBEEA 2015, Sch 7, Part 1).

Where a person is subject to a disqualification undertaking accepted at any time under s 8ZC, any application for leave for the purposes of s 1A(1)(a) must be made to any court to which, if the Secretary of State had applied for a disqualification order under section 8ZA at that time, that application could have been made: CDDA 1986, s 17(3ZA) (as inserted by SBEEA 2015, Sch 7, Part 1).

Where a person is subject to a disqualification undertaking accepted at any time under s 8ZE, any application for leave for the purposes of s 1A(1)(a) must be made to the High Court or, in Scotland, the Court of Session: CDDA 1986, s 17(3ZB) (as inserted by SBEEA 2015, Sch 7, Part 1).

17.97 Where a person is subject to a disqualification undertaking accepted at any time under CDDA 1986, s 9B, any application for leave for the purposes of s 9B(4) shall be made or (in Scotland) the Court of Session: CDDA 1986, s 17(3A).

But where a person is subject to two or more disqualification orders or undertakings (or to one or more disqualification orders and to one or more disqualification undertakings), any application for leave for the purposes of CDDA 1986, s 1(1)(a) or 1A(1)(a) shall be made to any court to which any such application relating to the latest order to be made, or undertaking to be accepted, could be made: CDDA 1986, s 17(4).

17.98 On the hearing of an application for leave for the purposes of s 1(1)(a) or 1A(1)(a), the Secretary of State shall appear and call the attention of the court to any matters which seem to him to be relevant, and may himself give evidence or call witnesses: CDDA 1986, s 17(5).

CDDA 1986, s 17(5) does not apply to an application for leave for the purposes of s 1(1)(a) if the application for the disqualification order was made under s 9A: CDDA 1986, s 17(6).

In such a case and in the case of an application for leave for the purposes of s 9B(4) on the hearing of the application whichever of the OFT or a specified regulator (within the meaning of s 9E) applied for the order or accepted the undertaking as the case may be:

(a) must appear and draw the attention of the court to any matters which appear to it or him (as the case may be) to be relevant;

(b) may give evidence or call witnesses: CDDA 1986, s 17(7).

The court has wide discretion in deciding whether to grant leave to act despite a person being disqualified

In *Re Dawes & Henderson (Agencies) Limited (No 2)* [1999] 2 BCLC 317, Sir Richard Scott held that the discretion given to the court under CDDA 1986, s 17 to grant leave was unfettered by any statutory condition or criterion and it would be wrong for the court to create any such fetters or conditions. Upon a s 17 application the court had to balance the protection of the public, considering the nature of the defects in company management that led to the disqualification order, and the need that the applicant should be able to act as a director of a particular company. Where no need had been demonstrated on the part of the company or the applicant, a small risk to the public would justify refusing the application.

In deciding whether to grant leave, the protection of the public is an important aspect for consideration

In *Re Tech Textiles Ltd, Secretary of State for Trade and Industry v Vane* [1998] 1 BCLC 259, Arden J held that there was no express guidance in the CDDA 1986 on exercise of the discretion to grant leave to act as a director. The purpose of disqualification was protective rather than penal, and that was the starting point. Leave was not to be too freely given. Legislative policy required the disqualification of unfit directors to minimise the risk of harm to the public, and the courts must not by granting leave prevent the achievement of that policy objective. 'Leave' included 'conditional leave' and accordingly the court had power to grant leave on such terms as it thought fit.

Further, the process of considering whether the public was adequately protected if leave was given involved considering a number of factors. The public for that purpose included all relevant interest groups, such as shareholders, employees, lenders, customers and other creditors. The court had to look at the grounds on which unfitness was found, the character and previous career of the applicant, his conduct since the proceedings for disqualification were begun, the circumstances of the company of which the applicant was to become a director and whether there was a potential for the matters which were held to constitute unfitness to recur. In the context, 'need' had to be interpreted as a practical need. There would be companies where the involvement of the applicant in the capacity sought was vital to customer or investor confidence, or for some other sufficient reason.

See also: *Re Majestic Recording Studios Ltd* [1989] BCLC 1; *Re Sevenoaks Stationers (Retail) Ltd* [1991] BCLC 325; and *Secretary of State for Trade and Industry v Palfreman* [1995] 2 BCLC 301.

The court will consider the protection of the public as one of the paramount considerations in deciding whether or not to disqualify a director

Similarly, in *Re Barings plc (No 4), Secretary of State for Trade and Industry v Baker* [1999] 1 BCLC 262, Sir Richard Scott V-C, decided that CDDA 1986, s 17 leave should not be granted in circumstances in which the effect of its grant would be to undermine the purpose of the disqualification order. The improprieties which had led to and required the making of a disqualification order and the need to protect the public from any repetition of the conduct in question had to be kept in mind when considering whether a grant of s 17 leave should be made.

He stated:

> 'It seems to me that the importance of protecting the public from the conduct that led to the disqualification order and the need that the applicant should be able to act as director of a particular company must be kept in balance with one another. The court in considering whether or not to grant leave should, in particular, pay attention to the nature of the defects in company management that led to the disqualification order and ask itself whether, if leave were granted, a situation might arise in which there would be a risk of recurrence of those defects'.

On the facts, the court granted a director leave to act as such owing to is invaluable advice and guidance.

17.99 If leave is granted, the court can impose conditions for the leave including role played by the person on the Board and duration of the leave: *Re Dawes & Henderson Ltd* [1999] 2 BCLC 317.

Where the court persons a person to act as a director in a company any conditions imposed by be strictly followed

In *Re Brian Sheridan Cars Ltd, Official Receiver v Sheridan* [1996] 1 BCLC 327, David Neuberger QC held that a person disqualified from acting as a director pursuant to CDDA 1986, s 1 who was then granted leave to act as a director of specified companies pursuant to CDDA 1986, s 17 was being accorded a privilege or indulgence by the court which was liable to be withdrawn if he was casual in any way in relation to his conduct as a director or with regard to any aspect of the proceedings. Where a s 17 order permitted a person to act as a director on specific terms it was of cardinal importance that those terms were strictly observed, since a failure to observe those terms meant that in acting as a director he was not acting pursuant to the leave granted to him and was contravening the Act which rendered him liable under ss 13 and 15 to criminal penalties and personal liability for the company's debts. Other persons involved with the management of a company where a disqualified person continued to act as a director of that company in breach of the terms of an order under s 17 were also potentially under personal liability for the companies' debts under s 15. Even where the court was prepared to extend a s 17 order where the person concerned had been in breach of the terms of a previous s 17 order, he (and, quite possibly, his co-directors and other officers of the company) were still vulnerable in relation to the period when he was continuing to act as a director in breach of the terms of the s 17 order.

Register of disqualification orders and undertakings

17.100 The Secretary of State may make regulations requiring officers of courts to furnish him with such particulars as the regulations may specify of cases in which:

(a) a disqualification order is made, or

(b) any action is taken by a court in consequence of which such an order or a disqualification undertaking is varied or ceases to be in force, or

(c) leave is granted by a court for a person subject to such an order to do anything which otherwise the order prohibits him from doing; or

(d) leave is granted by a court for a person subject to such an undertaking to do anything which otherwise the undertaking prohibits him from doing

and the regulations may specify the time within which, and the form and manner in which, such particulars are to be furnished: CDDA 1986, s 18(1).

17.101 The Secretary of State shall, from the particulars so furnished, continue to maintain the register of orders, and of cases in which leave has been granted as mentioned in subsection (1)(c) of CDDA 1986: CDDA 1986, s 18(2).

The Secretary of State shall include in the register such particulars as he considers appropriate of:

(a) disqualification undertakings accepted by him under s. 5A, 7, 8, 8ZC or 8ZE;

(b) disqualification undertakings accepted by the OFT or a specified regulator under s 9B;

(c) cases in which leave has been granted as mentioned in subsection (1)(d): CDDA 1986, s 18(2A).

When an order or undertaking of which entry is made in the register ceases to be in force, the Secretary of State shall delete the entry from the register and all particulars relating to it which have been furnished to him under this section or any previous corresponding provision and, in the case of a disqualification undertaking, any other particulars he has included in the register: CDDA 1986, s 18(3).

17.102 The register shall be open to inspection on payment of such fee as may be specified by the Secretary of State in regulations: CDDA 1986, s 18(4).

The Regulations in force are the *Companies (Disqualification Orders) Regulations 2009 SI 2009/2471*. The purpose of the Regulations is to require certain court officers to provide the Secretary of State with particulars of disqualification orders and grants of leave in relation to such orders or disqualification undertakings made or accepted under the CDDA 1986, and of any action taken by a court in consequence of which any such orders or undertakings are varied or cease to be in force. The instrument prescribes the particulars and form in which the particulars are to be provided by the court officers to the Secretary of State.

Legal professional privilege

17.103 In proceedings against a person for an offence under the CDDA 1986, nothing in that Act is taken to require any person to disclose any information that he is entitled to refuse to disclose on grounds of legal professional privilege (in Scotland, confidentiality of communications): CDDA 1986, s 20A.

Foreign directors' disqualification

17.104 Part 40 of the CA 2006 is concerned with company directors' foreign disqualification.

Part 40 addresses a gap that previously existed under the law. Persons who had been disqualified from being a director, or from holding an equivalent position, or engaging in the management of a company in another State, were able to form a company in the UK, to appoint themselves a director of that company and then operate that company either in the UK or in the State where they have been disqualified. The provisions in Part 40 give the Secretary of State a power to close the gap by making regulations to disqualify from being a director of a UK company, persons who have been disqualified in another State.

17.105 Part 40 is the first part which is outside the company law provisions of the Act. It does not, therefore, form part of the Companies Acts. This is due to the fact that the provisions in this part are linked with those of the Company Directors' Disqualification Act 1986. That Act is not part of the Companies Acts because it has implications beyond companies to other bodies (such as NHS foundation trusts) and extends beyond persons covered by the Companies Acts to persons such as insolvency practitioners. The fact that Part 40 is not part of the Companies Acts has the consequence that the definitions in the earlier parts of the Act do not apply – hence the need to define the term 'the court' in s 1183. Similarly, the definitions for Part 40 are not listed in Sch 8 to the Act.

Persons subject to foreign restrictions

17.106 Section 1182 of CA 2006 defines what is meant by references in Part 40 to a person being subject to 'foreign restrictions': CA 2006, s 1182(1).

A person is subject to foreign restrictions if under the law of a country or territory outside the United Kingdom:

(a) he is, by reason of misconduct or unfitness, disqualified to any extent from acting in connection with the affairs of a company,

(b) he is, by reason of misconduct or unfitness, required:

(i) to obtain permission from a court or other authority, or

(ii) to meet any other condition,

before acting in connection with the affairs of a company, or

(c) he has, by reason of misconduct or unfitness, given undertakings to a court or other authority of a country or territory outside the United Kingdom:

(i) not to act in connection with the affairs of a company, or

(ii) restricting the extent to which, or the way in which, he may do so: CA 2006, s 1182(2).

17.107 The references in s 1182(2) to acting in connection with the affairs of a company are to doing any of the following:

(a) being a director of a company;

(b) acting as receiver of a company's property; or

(c) being concerned or taking part in the promotion, formation or management of a company: CA 2006, s 1183.

Power to disqualify

Disqualification of persons subject to foreign restrictions

17.108 The Secretary of State may make provision by regulations disqualifying a person subject to foreign restrictions from:

(a) being a director of a UK company,

(b) acting as receiver of a UK company's property, or

(c) in any way, whether directly or indirectly, being concerned or taking part in the promotion, formation or management of a UK company: CA 2006, s 1184(1).

The regulations may provide that a person subject to foreign restrictions:

(a) is disqualified automatically by virtue of the regulations, or

(b) may be disqualified by order of the court on the application of the Secretary of State: CA 2006, s 1184(2).

17.109 The regulations may provide that the Secretary of State may accept an undertaking (a 'disqualification undertaking') from a person subject to foreign restrictions that he will not do anything which would be in breach of a disqualification under s 1184(1): CA 2006, s 1184(3).

Under Part 40 of the CA 2006:

(a) a person disqualified under this Part is a person:

(i) disqualified as mentioned in s 1184(2)(a) or (b), or

(ii) who has given and is subject to a disqualification undertaking;

(b) references to a breach of a disqualification include a breach of a disqualification undertaking.

17.110 The regulations may provide for applications to the court by persons disqualified under Part 40 for permission to act in a way which would otherwise be in breach of the disqualification: CA 2006, s 1184(5).

The regulations must provide that a person ceases to be disqualified under Part 40 on his ceasing to be subject to foreign restrictions: CA 2006, s 1184(6).

Disqualification regulations: supplementary

17.111 The Regulations under CA 2006, s 1184 may make different provision for different cases and may in particular distinguish between cases by reference to:

(a) the conduct on the basis of which the person became subject to foreign restrictions;

(b) the nature of the foreign restrictions;

(c) the country or territory under whose law the foreign restrictions were imposed: CA 2006, s 1185(1).

The Regulations under s 1184(2)(b) or (5) (provision for applications to the court):

(a) must specify the grounds on which an application may be made;

(b) may specify factors to which the court shall have regard in determining an application: CA 2006, s 1185(2).

17.112 The regulations may, in particular, require the court to have regard to the following factors:

(a) whether the conduct on the basis of which the person became subject to foreign restrictions would, if done in relation to a UK company, have led a court to make a disqualification order on an application under the Company Directors Disqualification Act 1986 (c 46) or the Company Directors Disqualification (Northern Ireland) Order 2002 (SI 2002/3150 (NI 4));

(b) in a case in which the conduct on the basis of which the person became subject to foreign restrictions would not be unlawful if done in relation to a UK company, the fact that the person acted unlawfully under foreign law;

(c) whether the person's activities in relation to UK companies began after he became subject to foreign restrictions;

(d) whether the person's activities (or proposed activities) in relation to UK companies are undertaken (or are proposed to be undertaken) outside the United Kingdom: CA 2006, s 1185(3).

The Regulations under s 1184(3) ('provision as to undertakings given to the Secretary of State') may include provision allowing the Secretary of State, in determining whether to accept an undertaking, to take into account matters other than criminal convictions notwithstanding that the person may be criminally liable in respect of those matters: CA 2006, s 1185(4).

17.113 The Regulations under s 1184(5) (provision for application to court for permission to act) may include provision:

(a) entitling the Secretary of State to be represented at the hearing of the application, and

(b) as to the giving of evidence or the calling of witnesses by the Secretary of State at the hearing of the application: CA 2006, s 1185(5).

Offence of breach of disqualification

17.114 The Regulations under s 1184 may provide that a person disqualified under Part 40 who acts in breach of the disqualification commits an offence: CA 2006, s 1186(1).

The regulations may provide that a person guilty of such an offence is liable:

(a) on conviction on indictment, to imprisonment for a term not exceeding two years or a fine (or both);

(b) on summary conviction:

  (i) in England and Wales, to imprisonment for a term not exceeding 12 months or to a fine not exceeding the statutory maximum (or both);

  (ii) in Scotland or Northern Ireland, to imprisonment for a term not exceeding six months, or to a fine not exceeding the statutory maximum (or both): CA 2006, s 1186(2).

In relation to an offence committed before the commencement of s 154(1) of the Criminal Justice Act 2003 (c 44), for '12 months' in subsection (2)(b)(i) substitute 'six months': CA 2006, s 1186(3).

Power to make persons liable for company's debts

Personal liability for debts of company

17.115 The Secretary of State may provide by regulations that a person who, at a time when he is subject to foreign restrictions:

(a) is a director of a UK company, or

(b) is involved in the management of a UK company,

is personally responsible for all debts and other liabilities of the company incurred during that time: CA 2006, s 1187(1).

17.116 A person who is personally responsible by virtue of this section for debts and other liabilities of a company is jointly and severally liable in respect of those debts and liabilities with:

(a) the company, and

(b) any other person who (whether by virtue of this section or otherwise) is so liable: CA 2006, s 1187(2).

For the purposes of this section a person is involved in the management of a company if he is concerned, whether directly or indirectly, or takes part, in the management of the company: CA 2006, s 1187(3).

17.117 The regulations may make different provision for different cases and may in particular distinguish between cases by reference to:

(a) the conduct on the basis of which the person became subject to foreign restrictions;

(b) the nature of the foreign restrictions;

(c) the country or territory under whose law the foreign restrictions were imposed: CA 2006, s 1187(4).

Power to require statements to be sent to the registrar of companies

Statements from persons subject to foreign restrictions

17.118 The Secretary of State may make provision by regulations requiring a person who:

(a) is subject to foreign restrictions, and

(b) is not disqualified under Part 40,

to send a statement to the registrar if he does anything that, if done by a person disqualified under this Part, would be in breach of the disqualification: CA 2006, s 1188(1).

17.119 The statement must include such information as may be specified in the regulations relating to:

(a) the person's activities in relation to UK companies, and

(b) the foreign restrictions to which the person is subject: CA 2006, s 1188(2).

The statement must be sent to the registrar within such period as may be specified in the regulations: CA 2006, s 1188(3).

The regulations may make different provision for different cases and may in particular distinguish between cases by reference to:

(a) the conduct on the basis of which the person became subject to foreign restrictions;

(b) the nature of the foreign restrictions;

(c) the country or territory under whose law the foreign restrictions were imposed: CA 2006, s 1188(4).

Statements from persons disqualified

17.120 The Secretary of State may make provision by regulations requiring a statement or notice sent to the registrar of companies under any of the provisions listed below that relates (wholly or partly) to a person who:

(a) is a person disqualified under Part 40, or

(b) is subject to a disqualification order or disqualification undertaking under the Company Directors Disqualification Act 1986 or the Company Directors Disqualification (Northern Ireland) Order 2002, SI 2002/3150 (NI 4),

to be accompanied by an additional statement: CA 2006, s 1189(1).

17.121 The provisions referred to above are:

(a) section 12 ('statement of a company's proposed officers'),

(b) section 167(2) ('notice of person having become director'), and

(c) section 276 ('notice of a person having become secretary or one of joint secretaries'): CA 2006, s 1189(2).

The additional statement is a statement that the person has obtained permission from a court, on an application under s 1184(5) or (as the case may be) for the purposes of s 1(1)(a) of the Company Directors Disqualification Act 1986 or Art 3(1) of the Company Directors Disqualification (Northern Ireland) Order 2002, SI 2002/3150 (NI 4), to act in the capacity in question: CA 2006, s 1189(3).

Statements: whether to be made public

17.122 The Regulations under ss 1188 or 1189 (statements required to be sent to registrar) may provide that a statement sent to the registrar of companies under the regulations is to be treated as a record relating to a company for the purposes of s 1080 (the companies register): CA 2006, s 1190(1).

The regulations may make provision as to the circumstances in which such a statement is to be, or may be:

(a) withheld from public inspection, or

(b) removed from the register: CA 2006, s 1190(2).

The regulations may, in particular, provide that a statement is not to be withheld from public inspection or removed from the register unless the person to whom it relates provides such information, and satisfies such other conditions, as may be specified: CA 2006, s 1190(3).

17.123 The regulations may provide that s 1081 (note of removal of material from the register) does not apply, or applies with such modifications as may be specified, in the case of material removed from the register under the regulations: CA 2006, s 1190(4).

The term 'specified' means specified in the regulations: CA 2006, s 1190(5).

Offences

17.124 The Regulations under s 1188 or 1189 may provide that it is an offence for a person:

(a) to fail to comply with a requirement under the regulations to send a statement to the registrar;

(b) knowingly or recklessly to send a statement under the regulations to the registrar that is misleading, false or deceptive in a material particular: CA 2006, s 1191(1).

17.125 The regulations may provide that a person guilty of such an offence is liable:

(a) on conviction on indictment, to imprisonment for a term not exceeding two years or a fine (or both);

(b) on summary conviction:

  (i) in England and Wales, to imprisonment for a term not exceeding 12 months or to a fine not exceeding the statutory maximum (or both);

  (ii) in Scotland or Northern Ireland, to imprisonment for a term not exceeding six months, or to a fine not exceeding the statutory maximum (or both): CA 2006, s 1191(2).

In relation to an offence committed before the commencement of s 154(1) of the Criminal Justice Act 2003, for '12 months in subsection (2)(b)(i) substitute 'six months': CA 2006, s 1191(3).

Definitions

17.126

Company:	a company incorporated or formed under the law of the country or territory in question, and
Court:	means: (a) in England and Wales, the High Court or a county court; (b) in Scotland, the Court of Session or the sheriff court; (c) in Northern Ireland, the High Court.
Director:	the holder of an office corresponding to that of director of a UK company.
Receiver:	includes any corresponding officer under the law of that country or territory.
UK company:	a company registered under the CA 2006.

18 Derivative claims

Contents

Introduction

18.1 The issue as to whether or not to bring a derivate claim is a significant question that may be faced by the board of directors or the shareholders collectively in arriving at a decision where a director(s) has breached a duty. The decision to bring a claim may be governed by a number of factors:

- **Time:** the length of time that it would take to initiate and complete legal proceedings against the director may divert the company's attention away from its main activities, and such time in litigation proceedings may not be justified.
- **Cost:** the costs of bringing a claim against the director may be substantial and may affect the company's resources, and deter any legal proceedings from taking place.
- **Reputation:** the company's reputation may be at issue and it may conclude either to bring proceedings to vindicate the company, or that its reputation would be damaged if proceedings were brought in court, and it prefers not to be dragged into litigation.

- **Best Interests:** in deciding whether or not to litigate, directors will need to take account of the best interests of the company, including the interests of the shareholders collectively.

18.2 Derivative claims usually arise where there has been a breach of duty by the director(s) and the company is being prevented (either by the directors or shareholders) from bringing an action against the directors. A shareholder, therefore, seeks to bring court proceedings to enforce a right of the company with the benefit of any action accruing to the company: *Estmanco (Kilner House) Ltd v Greater London Council* [1982] 1 WLR 2. In some situations, the wrongdoer directors may control decision making at board level and prevent the company from bringing an action against themselves, because the delinquent directors have a personal interest within the company. Decisions at board level to bring proceedings against the directors would arise where the directors have lost control of the board, or, as a result of a takeover, the previous directors have been replaced by new directors, who now wish to bring derivative proceedings after subsequent discovery of breaches of duties by the previous directors.

18.3 At the shareholder level, the decision to bring derivative proceedings may be initiated by a resolution of the shareholders conferring such power. However, if the directors are also shareholders who have majority control, they could prevent any resolution being passed, or deliberately omit to put the matter of litigation before the shareholders' meeting.

This chapter examines how a shareholder may be able to bring a derivative claim, including the causes of action and outcomes before the court. It also considers the legal and procedural aspects and the interaction between the CA 2006 and the Civil Procedure Rules that impact upon derivative claims.

18.4 This chapter addresses the following issues:

- the position of derivative actions at common law;
- an outline of the rule in *Foss v Harbottle*;
- statutory derivative claims; and
- the 'reflective loss' principle.

Derivative claims and proceedings by members

18.5 This section considers derivative actions in England and Wales or Northern Ireland from both a common law and a statutory position. It considers the rule in *Foss v Harbottle* and the procedural aspects for a shareholder to bring derivative proceedings, including some of the exceptions to the *Foss v Harbottle* principle.

The position at common law: the rule in Foss v Harbottle

18.6 Traditionally at common law, the courts demonstrated some reluctance to interfere in the internal affairs and management of the company. If the majority had decided on a particular course of action, the courts would not second-guess the decisions of the directors or shareholders. Judicial attitudes at the time were that the corporate decision makers were best qualified and experienced in management matters, and to address what was in the best interests of the company when embarking on a particular transaction. The courts favoured the majority rule approach to the effect that if the majority decided on a particular action or transaction, the minority would have to accept the majority decision. This became known as the 'rule in *Foss v Harbottle*', considered below. One of the principal issues with this rule was that it did not take proper account of the detriment, injustice, harm or injury that may be suffered by the company itself. The company's interests were not sufficiently protected unless a shareholder could come within certain exceptions to the rule in *Foss v Harbottle*. The combined effect of this rule and exceptions meant that it was legally and procedurally difficult to bring derivative claims at common law.

18.7 The position regarding derivative claims at common law was aptly summarised by Lord Denning in *Wallersteiner v Moir (No 2)* [1975] 1 All ER 849 who highlighted the plight of the company and the shareholder who were faced with obstacles in the way from bringing derivative proceedings. It was a plea to legislative authorities to find a proper mechanism for derivative proceedings to be brought.

At common law, the position regarding derivative claims was governed by the rule in *Foss v Harbottle* (1843) 2 Hare 461.

Where wrongdoer control exists, the company is the proper claimant. Where the majority decide on a particular matter, this will generally bind the minority

The rule in *Foss v Harbottle* (1843) 2 Hare 461 comprised two principles. First, where a wrong was allegedly done to a company, the proper claimant in legal proceedings was the company. Secondly, in respect of an alleged transaction which may bind the company a simple majority of the members, a shareholder may not bring any action or claim in respect of the alleged transaction.

The Law Commission Report

18.8 The Law Commissions of England and Wales and Scotland published a report in 1997 on *Shareholder Remedies*. It recommended law reform designed to make shareholder remedies more affordable and more appropriate in modern conditions.

It recommended a new procedure for derivative claims based on a cause of action. The derivative procedure would have statutory force and only available to the company's shareholders. The objective was to replace the common law derivative action with the statutory procedure. Some of the Law Commissions' recommendations were incorporated in the CA 2006.

The effect of the CA 2006 on the rule in Foss v Harbottle

18.9 The CA 2006 has effectively replaced the derivative common law derivative action by the statutory code for derivative claims under Ch 1 of Pt 11 of CA 2006.

The principles set out in the rule in *Foss v Harbottle* and subsequent common law cases on derivative actions have largely been incorporated under the CA 2006.

The procedural aspects of the derivative claim have changed and are addressed in detail under CA 2006.

18.10 In *Iesini and others v Westrip Holdings Ltd* [2011] 1 BCLC 498, Lewison J stated that: 'In the first place the statutory derivative claim has replaced the common law derivative action. A derivative claim may 'only' be brought under the Act'.

The procedural aspects of the derivative claim will therefore be governed by CA 2006 rather than the common law principles.

However, the statutory basis of the derivative claim does not mean that the rule in *Foss v Harbottle* is no longer applicable or totally abrogated particularly in respect of multiple derivative actions. In *Waddington Ltd v Chan Chun Hoo Thomas* [2009] 2 BCLC 82, the Hong Kong Court of Final Appeal commented that the rule in *Foss v Harbottle* was not displaced by the Companies Acts (see Ribiero J and Lord Millett (particularly in respect of 'multiple derivative' actions which are not addressed under the CA 2006 and therefore fall to be considered by the common law principles). See too: *Universal Project Management Services Ltd v Fort Gilkicker Ltd* [2013] Ch 551; and *Abouraya v Sigmund* [2014] All ER 208.

Statutory derivative claims – the position under the Companies Act 2006

18.11 The statutory derivative claim is governed by Chapter 1 of Part 11 of the CA 2006 and the Civil Procedure Rules Part 19, Practice Direction 19C – Derivative Claims. The Practice Direction applies to derivative claims under Chapter 1 of Part 11 CA 2006, including permission to continue or take over such claims. It does not apply to claims or order under CA 2006, s 996 (unfair prejudicial conduct) for which a separate regime applies.

Definition of a 'Derivative Claim'

18.12 The CA 2006 sets out the statutory definition of a 'derivative claim'. Part 11, Chapter 1 applies to proceedings in England and Wales or Northern Ireland by a member of a company:

(a) in respect of a cause of action vested in the company; and

(b) seeking relief on behalf of the company.

This is referred to in Pt 11, Ch 1 as a 'derivative claim': CA 2006, s 260(1).

A derivative claim may only be brought:

(a) under Chapter 1; or

(b) in pursuance of an order of the court in proceedings under CA 2006, s 994 (proceedings for protection of members against unfair prejudice): CA 2006, s 260(2).

Establishing a cause of action

18.13 A derivative claim under Part 11 of Chapter 1 may be brought only in respect of a cause of action arising from an actual or proposed act or omission involving:

- negligence,
- default,
- breach of duty, or
- breach of trust by a director of the company.

The cause of action may be against the director or another person (or both): CA 2006, s 260(3). The term 'director' includes a former director; a shadow director is treated as a director: CA 2006, s 260(5). There is no definition of 'another person' but this could include those assisting the director of the company who have caused some wrongs to the company in terms of negligence, default, breach of duty or breach of trust. They cannot arise independently of the director. The 'another person' may include a third party who may be sued rather the director.

It is immaterial whether the cause of action arose before or after the person seeking to bring or continue the derivative claim became a member of the company: CA 2006, s 260(4).

A derivative claim only applies to present members. It excludes former shareholders. The term 'a member of a company' includes a person who is not a member, but to whom shares in the company have been transferred or transmitted by operation of law: CA 2006, s 260(5) – this usually operates on death or bankruptcy of a shareholder. The term 'member' will usually refer to a minority shareholder and, very exceptionally, to a controlling shareholder. It also applies to a shareholder who is registered in the register of members.

The courts will also have regard to any fraud or abuse of power in derivative claims

In *Cinematic Finance Ltd v Ryder* [2010] EWHC 3387, Roth J was of the view that, in general, it was only the company, acting by its proper organ, that could bring proceedings for a wrong done to the company. A minority shareholder had no power to do so. A derivative claim represented an exception to the general rule whereby a minority shareholder was permitted to claim a remedy in respect of a wrong done to the company. The essential question was whether there had been a fraud on the minority, which generally involved an abuse of power by the directors and a stifling of the claim by reason of the control exercised by wrongdoers over the company.

The new statutory code in the Companies Act 2006 preserved the existing law as to the need to show 'wrongdoers control'. The new statutory rules did not formulate a substantive rule to replace the rule in *Foss v Harbottle* but provided a new procedure with more modern, flexible and accessible criteria for determining whether a shareholder could pursue an action. The Act would need radical language to displace such a well-established rule. Section 261(4) made it clear that the court had the discretion to allow a derivative action to continue. Although s 263(2) did not mention that permission was to be refused where the applicant had control of the company, it would only be in exceptional circumstances that such an application would be allowed to continue. The instant circumstances were not exceptional. The evidence indicated that one of the principal reasons for using a derivative action procedure was to save the cost of pursuing the remedy through the insolvency procedure. That was not a sufficient reason to allow a derivative action to proceed.

Application for permission to continue derivative claim

18.14 In deciding whether it is in the company's interests to bring derivative proceedings, the court will be the ultimate authority in addressing this issue. Upon issuing a claim form under the Practice Direction 19-C, a member of a company who brings a derivative claim under Part 11, Chapter 1 must apply to the court for permission (in Northern Ireland, leave) to continue it: CA 2006, s 261(1). The objective is for the shareholder to obtain a quick decision by the court on whether it is in the company's interests to bring a derivative claim; and the court being satisfied that it is in the company's best interests for such proceedings to be brought. There are various stages involved in the application for permission to continue the derivative claim.

The shareholder must complete a claim form which must be headed 'Derivative Claim'. If the claimant seeks an order that the defendant company or other body concerned indemnify the claimant against liability for costs incurred in the permission application or the claim, this should be stated in the permission application or claim form or both, as the case requires: Practice Direction 19C – Derivative Claims, paras 2(1) and 2(2). The claimant will be the shareholder and the co-defendants will be the director and the company: see 19C, para 4.

The first stage: establishing a prima facie case

18.15 At the first stage, only the shareholder will be before the court based on evidence filed to establish a *prima facie* case for permission to continue the derivative claim. The decision whether the claimant's evidence discloses a *prima facie* case will normally be made without submissions from or (in the case of an oral hearing to reconsider such a decision reached pursuant to r 19.9A(9)) attendance by the company. If without invitation from the court the company volunteers a submission or attendance, the company will not normally be allowed any costs of that submission or attendance: Practice Direction 19C, para 5.

18.16 If it appears to the court that the application and the evidence filed by the applicant in support of it do not disclose a *prima facie* case for giving permission (or leave), the court:

(a) must dismiss the application; and

(b) may make any consequential order it considers appropriate: CA 2006, s 261(2).

The potential defendants against whom a derivative claim may be brought is wide and not limited to directors

In *Iesini and Others v Westrip Holdings Ltd* [2011] 1 BCLC 498, Lewison J stated a derivative claim as defined by s 260(3) was not confined to a claim against the insiders. The cause of action may be against the director or another person (or both). The cause of action must arise from an actual or proposed act or omission involving negligence, default, breach of duty or breach of trust by a director of the company. However, since the cause of action must arise from his default (etc), a derivative claim brought under Pt 11, Ch 1 will not allow a shareholder to pursue the company's claim against a third party where that claim depends on a cause of action that has arisen independently from the director's default (etc).

The CA 2006 provides for a two-stage procedure where it is the member himself who brings the proceedings. At the first stage, the applicant is required to make a *prima facie* case for permission to continue a derivative claim, and the court considers the question on the basis of the evidence filed by the applicant only, without requiring evidence from the defendant or the company. The court must dismiss the application if the applicant cannot establish a *prima facie* case. The case to which s 261(1) refers is a *prima facie* case 'for giving permission'. This necessarily entails a decision that there is a *prima facie* case, both that the company has a good cause of action and that the cause of action arises out of a directors' default, breach of duty (etc). This is precisely the decision that the Court of Appeal required in *Prudential Assurance Co Ltd v Newman Industries Ltd (No 2)* [1982] 1 All ER 354.

However, in order for a claim to qualify under Pt 11, Ch 1 as a derivative claim (whether the cause of action is against a director, a third party or both) the court must, it seems to me, be in a position to find that the cause of action relied on in the claim arises from an act or omission involving default or breach of duty (etc) by a director. I do not consider that at the second stage this is simply a matter of establishing a *prima facie* case (at least in the case of an application under s 260) as was the case under the old law, because that forms the first stage of the procedure. At the second stage something more must be needed'.

However, it is contended that the threshold for the *prima facie* case is far higher than required under s 261. There is no requirement under the CA 2006 to show a *prima facie* case both that the company has a good cause of action and that the cause of action arises out of a directors' default, breach of duty.

The second

18.17 At the second stage, if the application is not dismissed under s 261(2), the court:

(a) may give directions as to the evidence to be provided by the company; and

(b) may adjourn the proceedings to enable the evidence to be obtained: CA 2006, s 261(3).

18.18 On hearing the application, the court may:

(a) give permission (or leave) to continue the claim on such terms as it thinks fit;

(b) refuse permission (or leave) and dismiss the claim; or

(c) adjourn the proceedings on the application and give such directions as it thinks fit: CA 2006, s 261(4).

This second stage no longer involves a consideration of a *prima facie* case. In *FanmailUK.com v Cooper* [2008] EWHC 2198 (Ch), [2008] BCC 877 Robert Englehart QC, sitting as a deputy judge, stated that on an application under CA 2006, s 261 it would be 'quite wrong … to embark on anything like a mini-trial of the action'. However, in *Iesini and Others v Westrip Holdings Ltd* [2011] 1 BCLC 498, Lewison J was of the view that the court also had to form a view on the strength of the claim in order properly to consider the requirements of CA 2006, ss 263(2)(a) and 263(3)(b). Any view could only be provisional where the action had yet to be tried; but the courts would have to make a decision based on the material before them. In *Iesini*, the proceedings were adjourned to allow a dispute as to the company's ownership to be resolved before proceeding to any derivative claim.

The first stage process of examining a prima facie case cannot be side-stepped: the court will consider all evidence presented to it in deciding whether a prima facie case has been established

In *Langley Ward Ltd v Trevor* [2011] All ER 78, the claimant company and its sole shareholder held equal stake in the second defendant's company along with the first defendant. The claimant company commenced proceedings against the first defendant in respect of various allegations and sought a continuation of action as a derivative action on behalf of the second defendant. The issue was whether the application for continuation should be allowed. It was held that, as a threshold requirement, under s 260(3) of the Act, a derivative claim might only be brought in respect of 'a cause of action arising from an … act or omission involving negligence, default, breach of duty or breach of trust by a director of a company'. A further threshold requirement was imposed by s 263(2) of the Act and stated to the effect that permission should be refused if the court was satisfied: '(a) that a person acting in accordance with section 172 (duty to promote the success of the company) would not seek to continue the claim'.

In this case, the company was deadlocked and had run its course. Further, the company was, in short, a natural candidate to be wound up on a just and equitable ground by either shareholder. Accordingly, it seemed right to proceed on the basis that the company would almost certainly go into winding up by one route or another. It was, therefore, appropriate to consider the comparative merits of leaving all or some of the disputes to be dealt with by a liquidator rather than by litigation in a derivative action, and factor those into the overall decision which the court had to reach under s 263 of the Act as regards each of the claims.

The court emphasised the need to ensure that the first stage process of examining a *prima facie* case was not side-stepped, and that the court would have regard, at the first stage, to the evidence on the documentation presented to it. This saved both time and money and ensured that only the real merits of the arguments proceeded to the next stage: see Judge David Donaldson QC's comments.

Permission to continue the derivative action may be refused where conduct complained of was authorised or ratified by the company

In *Re Singh Brothers Contractors (North West) Ltd; Singh v Singh* [2013] EWHC 2138, an action was commenced by way of a derivative claim. The claimant and the first defendant were directors and shareholders of the second defendant company. The first defendant was being paid remuneration and receiving dividends from the company which were being recorded in the company's accounts. The claimant issued a derivative claim alleging that the payments made to the first defendant were unlawful. The claimant applied for permission to continue the derivative claim. The issue was whether permission should be granted. Judge Hodge QC held that this was a clear case where permission to bring a derivative claim should be refused. In his view, the principal reason for the refusal was that the conduct on the part of the first defendant was either authorised by the company before it occurred, or had effectively since been ratified. So far as the payment of excessive dividends was concerned, these were all clearly recorded in the company's accounts. Against the background as recorded in the company's accounts, no director, acting in accordance with CA 2006, s 172, would have sought to continue the instant challenge to either the allegedly excessive dividend payments or the allegedly excessive remuneration. In any event, on the evidence, the real motivation acting upon the claimant in seeking to continue the instant derivative claim was the feeling of animosity that he entertained towards the defendant as a result of the mother's will. The real motivation of the claimant was seeking to strike at his brother rather than genuinely seeking to promote the best interests of the company. Accordingly, the discretionary ground to refuse permission to continue the claim under s 263(3)(a) of the Act was established.

18.19 The position of a shareholder in a public limited company bringing a derivative action on the company's behalf was considered in *Bridge v Daley* (17 June 2015). The shareholder complained of mismanagement by the directors in the conduct of the company's affairs. Hodge J (sitting as a High Court judge) held that it was 'extraordinary' for a shareholder of a public company to bring such derivative proceedings. He refused the shareholder permission

Although the claimant was required under CA 2006, s 261 to show a prima face case that the company has a cause of action, s 263 did not require any such test but based upon factors for court consideration

In *Hughes v Weiss* [2012] All ER (D) 197, the claimant, a barrister, and the first defendant, a solicitor, had decided to go into business together. In February 2005, they incorporated the second defendant company, (Iuvus), as the vehicle of a joint venture for the provision of commercial legal consultancy services in the field of asset finance. They had been the two directors of Iuvus, and each held one of two issued shares. They had agreed initially to draw the same small salary from Iuvus and to supplement that income by the receipt of equal dividends as were appropriate. The venture had been an equal quasi-partnership. By autumn 2006, their relationship had become strained as the first defendant felt that the claimant was 'not pulling her weight'. In June 2007, they agreed to terminate their quasi-partnership. Iuvus was dissolved in July 2011, when it failed to file an annual return. Its assets of just over £15,000 vested in the Crown as *bona vacantia.*

The claimant, with a view to bringing the instant proceedings, procured the restoration of Iuvus to the register and then advanced three claims in respect of causes of action that were vested in the company (the derivative claims). They were that the first defendant: (i) had wrongfully transferred £100,000 out of the account of Iuvus to his personal bank account, and had thereafter failed to return it or account for it; (ii) in breach of his fiduciary duty to Iuvus, he had carried on business in competition with it; and (iii) had diverted payment of invoices from Iuvus to himself and failed to account for the receipts. At the same time the claimant applied pursuant to section 261 of the Companies Act 2006 (the Act) for permission to continue those derivative claims against the first defendant. It fell to be determined whether the claimant should be granted permission to carry on those derivative claims against the first defendant.

According to Judge Keyser QC, the application to proceed with the derivative claims would be allowed.

Section 263 CA 2006 did not require a derivative claim to satisfy any particular merits test before permission to continue it would be given. However, an applicant under s 261 should establish a *prima facie* case that the company had a good cause of action which arose out of the defendant's breach of duty. In order to consider the requirements of ss 263(2)(a) and (3)(b), the court should form the best view it could, on the strength of the claim, on the material before it. There was no particular threshold or standard of proof that had to be satisfied.

The judge considered the claimant had good prospects of establishing that Iuvus had a claim against the first defendant for breach of duty. In respect of the first head of claim (relating to the £100,000) it seemed that there was a strong case for saying that the first defendant had misappropriated company monies and was trying to find ways of justifying his wrongdoing and avoiding repayment. In respect of the second head of claim (carrying on a competing business in breach of fiduciary duty), the evidence was incomplete, however, the provisional view was that the claimant's case was a strong one. In respect of the third head of claim (diverting funds), there was clear evidence of wrongdoing.

In light of s 263(2), permission would be refused if the court was satisfied that the acts or omissions complained of had been authorised by the company before they had occurred or had since been ratified by the company, but the court was not so satisfied (see paragraph 42 of the judgment).

In the instant case, the court was not so satisfied.

Section 263(2)(a) would apply only where the court was satisfied that no director acting in accordance with s 172 would seek to continue the claim. If some directors would, and others would not, have sought to continue the claim the case was one for the application of s 263(3)(b). Many of the same considerations would apply to that. It could not be said that no director acting in accordance with s 172 would seek to continue the derivative claims in the instant case.

With respect to the matters which fell to be considered under s 263(3), in the instant case, none of them constituted a bar to a derivative claim.

The court should have regard to all the factors under CA 2006, s 263 in deciding whether or not to grant permission to continue the claim as a derivative claim

In *Kiani v Cooper* [2010] All ER (D) 97, the claimant and the first defendant were the sole directors and shareholders of WPL (the company), which was formed to sell and develop a particular property in Essex. It was common ground that by a subsequent agreement another development was undertaken of other properties in Essex. On 6 November 2009, the claimant obtained interim permission on paper to commence a derivative action, as defined by s 260 on behalf of the company against the first defendant and the third defendant company (DPM), of which the first defendant was also a director and majority shareholder.

On 9 November, the claimant succeeded in obtaining an order restraining the first and third defendants from petitioning for the winding up of the company as creditors (the restraining order). The claimant subsequently applied, pursuant to s 261, for permission to continue the derivative action and the restraining order.

In support of her application, the claimant alleged that the first defendant had acted in breach of his duties in various respects, namely that: (i) he had claimed sums personally as a creditor of the company. He had demanded repayment and sought to wind the company up on the basis that the monies were due and owing. The claimant relied on what she said were the express terms of an oral agreement that those sums had been paid as member's contributions, not to be released from the company until after development and sale, but even if they were loans, the same agreement applied; (ii) although the defendant was both a director and the majority shareholder of DPM, DPM also alleged that it was a creditor of the company and sought to wind it up on that ground; and (iii) payments had been made out of the company's bank account by the first defendant to another company, CFL, whose shares were registered in the name of the first defendant's secretary. The invoices in respect of CFL called for immediate payment, but the work alleged to have been done to support them was unspecified, being described in the briefest and most general terms.

Proudman J held that the application would be allowed. In respect of the various breaches of duty allegedly committed by the first defendant, the claimant had made out a case for breach of fiduciary duty to the relevant standard to give rise to a derivative claim. The issue was then whether permission should be given to continue it. In all the circumstances of the case, it appeared that the claimant was acting in good faith within s 263(3)(a). Further, the fact that she could achieve the relief she sought in a more roundabout way did not mean that she ought not to be granted permission in the instant case – that was merely one of the factors the court had to consider. Moreover, considering all the relevant factors, a director acting in accordance with his duty would wish to continue the claim down to disclosure. It followed that the claimant's application to continue the action in the name of the company ought to be granted, and unless the court was offered undertakings in lieu, the existing restraining order would also be continued.

A range of factors set out in CA 2006, s 263 will impact upon a court's decision as to whether or not to give permission to continue a claim as a derivative claim

In *Stainer v Lee* [2011] 1 BCLC 537, Roth J stated that the mandatory bar in s 263(2)(a) would apply only where the court was satisfied that no director acting in accordance with s 172 would seek to continue the claim. If some directors would, and others would not, the case was one for the application of s 263(3)(b). Many of the same considerations would also apply to that paragraph. Section 263(3) and (4) did not prescribe a particular standard of proof that had to be satisfied but rather required consideration of a range of factors to reach an overall view.

Further, a director acting in accordance with his duties pursuant to s 172 would be likely to regard it as important to continue the claim at least beyond the instant stage. Moreover, given what was at the heart of the instant case, a derivative action was entirely appropriate, therefore the theoretical availability to the applicant of proceedings by way of an unfair prejudice petition was not a reason to refuse permission. Furthermore, the applicant was acting in good faith. It was clear that he had brought the proceedings not only in his own interests but for the benefit of a large number of minority shareholders.

Permission was therefore granted to continue the claim.

In considering whether derivative proceedings should be brought, the court will have regard to the interests of independent board members and any independent shareholders

In one of the first cases on derivative claims under CA 2006, *Airey v Cordell* [2006] All ER (D) 111, involved a claimant who was a minority shareholder in the fifth defendant company. The sixth defendant company was a wholly owned subsidiary of the fifth defendant. They both manufactured and sold vehicle licence plates and component parts. They had developed a product known as 'E-plate' whereby an electronic tag was embedded into a number plate which allowed details of vehicles and their movements to be monitored. The first to third defendants were the other shareholders and the directors in the fifth defendant.

In October 2005, the claimant was notified of a proposal whereby the fourth defendant company (of which the first to third defendants would own over 80% of the issued share capital) would acquire a licence to produce, manufacture and market E-plate technology. Unnamed investors would also subscribe to the fourth defendant's share capital. The claimant was subsequently informed that no shares had been allocated to him, but that he could subscribe as a financial investor. The claimant made attempts to obtain further information to satisfy himself as to why the venture was not being pursued through the fifth and sixth defendants but was not satisfied with the response he obtained. Over time, three further proposals were put forward for the future of E-plate. The first to third defendants were of the view that the fourth proposal satisfied the claimant's concerns. The claimant did not agree. Meanwhile, the claimant had issued proceedings alleging various breaches of fiduciary duty by the first to third defendants. That action was a derivative action and as such, under CPR 19.9(3), SI 1998 No 3132, the claimant required permission to carry on the claim on behalf of the fifth and sixth defendants. In the instant application, the claimant applied, *inter alia*, for such permission in respect of an amended particulars of claim.

The first to fourth defendants accepted that the claimant had a *prima facie* case, but contended that, at the instant stage, no independent board acting reasonably would consider it in the interests of either company to bring the claim.

An issue arose as to the test to be applied by the court in such circumstances.

Warren J ruled that in order to determine whether it was appropriate to grant permission for a derivative action to proceed, it was not for the court to assert its own view of what it would do if it was the board. The court merely had to be satisfied that a reasonable independent board could take the view that it was appropriate to bring the proceedings. Only if no reasonable board would bring proceedings should the court not sanction the bringing of a shareholder's derivative action.

It would not be right to shut out a minority shareholder on the basis of the court's possibly inadequate assessment.

In the instant case and at the instant stage, a reasonable independent board would press for some sort of benefit for the company. It might threaten proceedings, but it would withdraw proceedings if a reasonable offer was received. It could not, therefore, be said that no reasonable board would not pursue the first to third defendants using litigation. Moreover, the fourth proposal was not sufficient to protect the claimant's interests. It would, however, be appropriate to allow a period of time to see whether an agreement could be reached on a proposal which would adequately protect the claimant's interests. If such a proposal was forthcoming, the claimant would not be allowed to proceed.

Application for permission to continue claim as a derivative claim

18.20 In this section, the position of the derivative claim is considered from the company's perspective where the company has brought a claim against a director or another person.

Claim by the company

18.21 The CA 2006, s 262 applies where:

- a company has brought a claim; and
- the cause of action on which the claim is based could be pursued as a derivative claim under Part 11, Chapter 1: CA 2006, s 262(1).

Application by the member

18.22 A member of the company may apply to the court for permission (in Northern Ireland, leave) to continue the claim as a derivative claim on the ground that:

- the manner in which the company commenced or continued the claim amounts to an abuse of the process of the court;
- the company has failed to prosecute the claim diligently; and
- it is appropriate for the member to continue the claim as a derivative claim: CA 2006, s 262(2).

There is no definition of 'diligently' but the court would apply the ordinary, natural meaning to refer to persevering and all relentless efforts being used to prosecute the claim. The company would need to demonstrate that it prosecuted the claim diligently.

Possible court orders

18.23 If it appears to the court that the application and the evidence filed by the applicant in support of it do not disclose a *prima facie* case for giving permission (or leave), the court:

(a) must dismiss the application; and

(b) may make any consequential order it considers appropriate: CA 2006, s 262(3).

If the application is not dismissed under s 262(3), the court:

(a) may give directions as to the evidence to be provided by the company; and

(b) may adjourn the proceedings to enable the evidence to be obtained: CA 2006, s 262(4).

On hearing the application, the court may:

(a) give permission (or leave) to continue the claim as a derivative claim on such terms as it thinks fit;

(b) refuse permission (or leave) and dismiss the application; or

(c) adjourn the proceedings on the application and give such directions as it thinks fit.

Should permission be given?

18.24 In deciding whether to give permission to a shareholder to continue a claim as a derivative claim, the court is required to have regard to various factors in arriving at its decision. Section 263 is, therefore, key to understanding the factors involved, the importance that the court attaches to these factors and the link to ss 261 and 262. There is no threshold to be achieved under s 263. The court is not required to consider whether there is a strong or a weak case.

The court was required to dismiss any application under s 261 if it was satisfied under s 263(2)(a) that a director acting in accordance with s 172 (duty to promote the success of the company) would not seek to continue the claim

In *Franbar Holdings Limited v Patel* [2009] 1 BCLC 1, a company called Medicentres (UK) Ltd was established to provide primary healthcare and medical services. It had branches at a number of railway stations and other central London locations. Franbar Holdings Ltd had sold 75 per cent of the shares in Medicentres to Casualty Plus Ltd. Franbar and Casualty Plus entered into a shareholders' agreement under which Casualty Plus was entitled to, and did, appoint two directors of Medicentres. Those directors had *de facto* control of Medicentres' affairs. Franbar was entitled to appoint two directors under the agreement. Disputes arose between Franbar and Casualty Plus in relation to the affairs of Medicentres.

Franbar issued proceedings against Casualty Plus for breach of the shareholders' agreement. It presented a petition under s 994 of the Companies Act 2006 against Casualty Plus, seeking an order for Casualty Plus to purchase Franbar's shares in Medicentres, and made a claim against Medicentres and the two Casualty Plus directors, which it sought permission to continue as a derivative claim. Franbar's allegations in the s 994 petition, the shareholders' action and the derivative claim were similar. Franbar complained about the alleged diversion of business opportunities from Medicentres to Casualty Plus, the suspension of one of Franbar's appointed directors, an alleged failure to provide financial information, the suitability of one of the directors appointed by Casualty Plus, in the light of his previous involvement with insolvent companies, including in particular Swindon Brewing Co Ltd, and miscellaneous acts by the directors appointed by Casualty Plus. An open offer had been made to purchase Franbar's shares in Medicentres at an independent expert valuation on the assumption that everything alleged in the petition was either remedied or true. It was said that Franbar's refusal to accept that offer meant that the petition was an abuse of process.

All the parties accepted that the proper ambit of the dispute was about the terms on which Franbar could exit from its involvement in Medicentres; the case was not one in which there was any question that a remedy was required to protect the interests of a minority shareholder who wished to remain involved in Medicentres' affairs in addition to its application for permission to continue the derivative claim under s 261(1).

In relation to the question under s 263(3)(d) of whether the acts complained of could be ratified by the company, Franbar contended that, in respect of conduct which occurred under 1 October 2007, the connected person provisions in s 239 had replaced the principle that breach of duty by a director was incapable of ratification where it constituted a fraud on the minority in circumstances in which the wrongdoers were in control of the company.

It was held by William Trower QC that the court was required to dismiss any application under s 261 if it was satisfied under s 263(2)(a) that a director acting in accordance with s 172 (duty to promote the success of the company) would not seek to continue the claim. On the facts, there was sufficient material for the hypothetical director to conclude that the conduct of Medicentres' business by those in control of it had given rise to actionable breaches of duty. As it seemed likely that the directors appointed by Casualty Plus were behind much of that conduct, the court could not be satisfied that a hypothetical director acting in accordance with s 172 would conclude that the case advanced was insufficiently cogent to justify continuation of the claim.

The court, in exercising its discretion, next had to have regard to the relevant statutory considerations set out in s 263(3). It appeared that Franbar had no motive in wishing to continue the derivative claim, apart from a desire to ensure that the value it extracted from its shareholding in Medicentres was full and fair. The court could not conclude at this stage that the derivative claim was not being pursued in good faith for the purposes of s 263(3)(a).

For the purposes of s 263(3)(b), the hypothetical director acting in accordance with s 172 would take into account a wide range of considerations when assessing the importance of continuing the claim. The complaints were not yet in a form in which the hypothetical director might be expected to conclude that there were obvious breaches of duty which ought to be pursued and that the recovery to be expected in consequence of those breaches would be substantial. It was likely that the hypothetical director would be more inclined to regard pursuit of the derivative claim as less important in light of the fact that several of the complaints were more naturally to be formulated as breaches of the shareholders' agreement and acts of unfair prejudice (already the subject matter of proceedings commenced by the minority shareholder). Where, as in the present case, a buy-out of the minority by the majority had been offered, and the principal issue was one of valuation, the hypothetical director would be less likely to attach importance to continuing the derivative claim.

In relation to conduct which occurred after 1 October 2007, s 239(7) expressly preserved any rule of law as to acts that were incapable of being ratified by the company. That would include acts which were *ultra vires* the company in the strict sense, but also those which, pursuant to any rule of law, were incapable of being ratified for some other reason. The effect of s 239 was not to restrict the types of circumstance in which ratification was not possible because of wrongdoer control to those in which the connected person requirements of s 239(3) and (4) were satisfied. It followed that, where the question of ratification arose in the context of an application to continue a derivative claim, the question which the court had to ask itself was whether the ratification had the effect that the claimant was being improperly prevented from bringing the claim on behalf of the company. That might still be the case where the new connected person provisions were not satisfied, but there was still actual wrongdoer control pursuant to which there had been a diversion of assets to persons associated with the wrongdoer, albeit not connected in the sense for which provision was made by s 239(4). It was possible that Franbar would establish at trial that, in all the circumstances of the case, some of the breaches alleged would prove to be incapable of ratification: see too *North-West Transportation Co Ltd v Beatty* (1887) 12 App Cas 589; and *Smith v Croft (No 3)* [1987] BCLC 355.

There was no aspect of the derivative claim for which Franbar could not be compensated by relief granted in the s 994 petition or the shareholders' action. Section 263(3)(f) did not require the exact identity of the defendants. What was required was for the act or omission of which the complaint was made to give rise to a cause of action available to the member in its own right. Doubtless such a cause of action would sometimes be a claim against the same director defendants, but the subsection was not limited to such claims. The only limitation was that the cause of action should arise out of the same act or omission; where that act or omission gave rise to both a claim for unfair prejudice against a member and a claim for breach of duty against a director, s 263(3)(f) was engaged.

Balancing the relevant considerations justice was best achieved by refusing permission to continue the derivative claim.

In determining whether to grant permission for a derivative claim under the CA 2006, it was mandatory for the court to refuse permission under s 263(2)(a) if the relevant facts showed that a notional director, acting in accordance with his duty to promote the success of the company, would consider that it was not in the company's interest for the claim to proceed

In *Mission Capital plc v Sinclair* [2010] 1 BCLC 304, the board of directors of a company comprised the two applicants, who were the only executive directors, and three non-executive directors. The applicants were also employed by the company. At a board meeting, the non-executive directors voted to terminate the applicants' employment immediately, which had the effect under the articles that they were required to resign their directorships forthwith. The board appointed a new executive director in their place. The company commenced an action against the applicants seeking an injunction to exclude them from the company's premises and for delivery of certain documents. The applicants, who contended that their employment contracts were still subsisting and their purported resignations from the board were invalid, counterclaimed seeking injunctions reinstating them to the board and prohibiting the company and non-executive directors from preventing them from attending the company's premises and performing their duties under their service agreements.

The applicants also sought permission under s 263 to bring a derivative claim against the non-executive directors and the new directors appointed in their place.

It was held by Floyd J that the applicants' counterclaim for an injunction reinstating them as employees was, in effect, an application for the grant of specific performance of their service contracts and would normally be refused in favour of an award of damages if breach of the service contracts was proved. Although the applicants had an arguable case that their dismissal was invalid, they were unable to show the degree of mutual trust and confidence between the company as employer and themselves as employees which would bring their application within the exception to the general rule that a contract for personal services would not be specifically enforced. As it was arguable that their employment contracts were still in existence, it was also arguable that the provision in the articles requiring their automatic resignation as directors had not come into effect and that they were entitled to reinstatement as directors. However, the balance of justice came down in favour of refusing any application for injunctive relief, because restoring them to their position as directors would lead to strife as they would then be under the control of a board of directors with whom they were locked in litigation, they would be in the minority as directors, they had not shown that the company would be unable to manage satisfactorily without them, the company had given an undertaking not to make disposals without giving them notice, and the balance of justice was not sufficiently weighted in their favour to justify granting mandatory relief. The application for reinstatement as employees and/or directors would therefore be refused.

In determining whether to grant permission for a derivative action pursuant to Pt 11 of the 2006 Act, it was mandatory for the court to refuse permission under s 263(2)(a) if the relevant facts showed that a notional director, acting in accordance with his duty to promote the success of the company, would consider that it was not in the company's interest for the claim to proceed. If, as in the present case, the court could not be satisfied that the notional director would not seek to continue the claim, it then had to consider the discretionary factors set out in s 263(3) before giving permission. In that respect, the court would exercise its discretion under s 263(3)(b) and (f) by refusing the applicants permission to bring the derivative action, on the grounds that: (a) they had not shown that they would achieve any relief that they could not obtain by means of an unfair prejudice petition under s 994; or (b) that a notional director would attach much importance to the claim.

Taking account of other factors in CA 2006, s 263, if a hypothetical director, acting reasonably in the interests of its members, would decide not continue with its derivative claim, the claim cannot then be pursued by the member

In *Stimpson and Others v Southern Private Landlords Association* [2009] EWHC 2072 (Ch), the first defendant association represented the interests of private landlords who became members after paying an annual subscription. The first claimant was the president and director of the first defendant. The second to fourth defendants were statutory directors of the first defendant. A dispute arose, firstly in relation to the appointment of the fifth defendant as a director and the subsequent resolution by a quorum of the first defendant's directors affiliating the first defendant with the sixth defendant. Following the passing of the resolution, the first defendant transferred its assets to the sixth defendant who, in turn, discharged the first defendant's liabilities and provided similar services to the first defendant's subscribers. The first claimant sought permission to issue a derivative claim under s 261 of the Companies Act 2006. The other claimants supported the first claimant in his action.

The issue for determination was, *inter alia*, whether a hypothetical director would have attached great importance to the continuation of the derivative claim.

Judge Pelling held that the claim would be dismissed.

On the facts of the instant case, a hypothetical director, acting reasonably in the interests of its members, would not continue with its derivative claim. If the court was wrong in that regard it would, in the circumstances, refuse the claimant permission to continue his derivative action.

18.25 The following provisions apply where a member of a company applies for permission (in Northern Ireland, leave) under s 261 or 262: CA 2006, s 263.

Under the CA 2006, the court must refuse permission by a member to continue the claim as a derivative claim in three situations. Permission (or leave) must be refused if the court is satisfied that a person acting in accordance with s 172 (duty to promote the success of the company) would not seek to continue the claim.

This aspect is sometimes referred to as the 'hypothetical director'. The court will not consider what a reasonable director would have done in the circumstances, nor what the court would have considered that a director would have done in this regard. The court is required to have regard to the fact that a director of a company must act in the way he considers, in good faith, would be most likely to promote the success of the company for the benefit of its members as a whole, and in doing so have regard (amongst other matters) to:

(a) the likely consequences of any decision in the long term;

(b) the interests of the company's employees;

(c) the need to foster the company's business relationships with suppliers, customers and others;

(d) the impact of the company's operations on the community and the environment;

(e) the desirability of the company maintaining a reputation for high standards of business conduct; and

(f) the need to act fairly as between members of the company: CA 2006, s 172.

18.26 In *Iesini v Westrip Holdings Ltd* [2011] 1 BCLC 498, Lewison J interpreted CA 2006, s 263(2)(a) as meaning that no director would seek to pursue the claim. Section 263(2)(a) is one of the main duties of loyalty that a director owes to the company to act in the best interests of the company.

However, a distinction arises in an application for breach of s 172 and an application under s 263(2)(a). Under s 172, provided the director has acted in good faith in promoting the long term interests of the company, the courts will not second-guess directors' decisions. However, under s 263(2)(a), the courts will be required to interfere and determine whether a person acting in accordance with s 172 would not seek to continue the claim. In *Iesini*, Lewison J was of the view that this was 'essentially a commercial decision, which the court is ill-equipped to take except in a clear case'. The decision required a consideration of various factors, including that the court must refuse permission to continue the claim as a derivative claim if it is satisfied that the hypothetical director would not seek to continue the claim. In some cases, the courts have concluded that having regard to s 172, a hypothetical director would seek to continue a claim.

A hypothetical director may conclude on the facts and evidence that a claim could have been brought as a derivative claim

This was the position in *Kiani v Cooper* [2010] 2 BCLC 427 where Proudman J stated that a notional director, having regard to s 172, would conclude that disclosure of documentation was required and that there was a case to be tried owing to strong evidence of breach of fiduciary duties.

However, in *Kleanthous v Paphitis* [2011] EWHC 2287, Newey J was of the view that in the light of established authority, the court could potentially grant permission for a derivative claim to be continued without being satisfied that there was a strong case. The merits of the claim would be relevant to whether permission should be given, but there was no set threshold.

In this case, there were arguable claims against the respondents. However, the chances of them succeeding were significantly less than even. The claims against the fourth respondent were particularly weak. Applying s 263(2)(a) of the Act therefore, permission to continue the claim would be refused on the basis that 'a person acting in accordance with section 172 … would not seek to continue the claim'.

Accordingly, the court refused permission for the derivative claim to continue.

In the Scottish case of *Wishart v Castlecroft Securities Ltd* [2009 CSIH 65], the court concluded, having regard to the factors in s 263(3), that the claim should continue. In so doing, the court attached particular importance to the factors in s 268(2)(b) and (f). Under s 268(2)(b), the court was required to take into account the importance that a person acting in accordance with s 172 would attach to raising the derivative proceedings. Several factors might be relevant in that regard, including the prospects of success of the proposed proceedings. Having regard to the authorities on the fiduciary duties of company directors and the accessory liabilities of third parties, and taking into consideration the affidavits and productions, the proposed derivative proceedings were arguable. It was not apparent that there were any substantial countervailing factors which would lead a director acting in accordance with s 172 to attach little or no importance to raising them. Under s 268(2)(f), the court must take into account whether the cause of action was one which the member could pursue in his own right rather than on behalf of the company.

The issue of authorisation or ratification by the company is also important in the court deciding whether or not the claim should continue as a derivative claim. Neither the company nor the shareholder may subsequently query the act or omission once it has been ratified or authorised by the company. Authorisation or ratification will be an absolute bar to the continuation of the derivative claim. The provision does not state who should authorise or ratify – the directors or the shareholders – but in practice this will be a matter for the company's articles of association or the shareholders. The effect of authorisation is that there is no further breach of duty and ratification means that if any breach of duty existed, it has been cured. In law, shareholders cannot ratify illegal or *ultra vires* acts or acts that are in breach of the company's articles of association. The court will also have regard to the interests of disinterested shareholders in arriving at its decision.

Factors for consideration in deciding whether the derivative claim should proceed

18.27 In considering whether to give permission (or leave) to continue the derivative claim, the court must take into account six factors which are non-exhaustive, in particular:

(a) **Whether the member is acting in good faith in seeking to continue the claim:**

The shareholder has the burden of showing the court that he is acting in good faith in wishing to continue the derivative claim. Motive is therefore an important consideration. If the motive is tainted by malice or frivolous or vexatious litigation, then good faith cannot be shown. Also, where a shareholder has personal interests to be derived from the litigation.

> ***The court will have regard to the bona fides of the shareholder bringing the derivative claim***
>
> In *Stainer v Lee* [2011] 1 BCLC 537, Roth J considered that the shareholder had acted in good faith and indeed had support from 35 other shareholders in the company.

> ***There must be a 'real purpose' in bringing the derivative action***
>
> Once there is a 'real purpose' in bringing the derivative claim, the courts may accept the need for continuation of such claim: *Mission Capital plc v Sinclair* [2010] 1 BCLC 537.
>
> On the facts, Floyd J refused the shareholder permission to continue the claim as a derivative claim taking account of the factors.

The court considers the interests of the company as a whole rather than personal motives or interests of the shareholder in determining whether to agree to the continuation of the derivative claim by the shareholder: *Franbar Holdings Ltd v Patel* [2009] 1 BCLC 1; *Parry v Bartlett* [2011] EWHC 3146.

> ***The derivative claim must be brought bona fide for the company's benefit***
>
> In *Barrett v Duckett* [1995] 1 BCLC 243, Peter Gibson LJ stated that a shareholder would be allowed to bring a derivative action on behalf of a company where the action was brought bona fide for the benefit of the company for wrongs to the company, for which no other remedy was available and not for an ulterior purpose. Conversely, if the action was brought for an ulterior purpose or if another adequate remedy was available, the court would not allow the derivative action to proceed. The conduct of the shareholder and motives will be considered by the court. This aspect was previously addressed in *Nurcombe v Nurcombe* [1984] BCLC 557 by Lawton LJ.

(b) The importance that a person acting in accordance with s 172 (duty to promote the success of the company) would attach to continuing it:

Under this heading, the court will consider the position from the hypothetical director's viewpoint in the manner he considers will most likely promote the success of the company. In *Franbar Holdings Ltd v Patel* [2009] 1 BCLC 1, Judge William Trower stated that the hypothetical director acting in accordance with s 172 would take into account a wide range of considerations when assessing the importance of continuing the claim. These would include such matters as:

- the prospects of success of the claim,
- the ability of the company to make a recovery on any award of damages,
- the disruption which would be caused to the development of the company's business by having to concentrate on the proceedings,
- the costs of the proceedings and
- any damage to the company's reputation and business if the proceedings were to fail. This includes any potential claim for relief under s 994.

The court may also consider the views of independent non-executive directors as to whether or not a derivative claim should proceed: *Kleanthous v Paphitis* [2011] EWHC 2287.

(c) Where the cause of action results from an act or omission that is yet to occur, whether the act or omission could be, and in the circumstances would be likely to be: authorised by the company before it occurs, or ratified by the company after it occurs.

The acts or omissions refer to negligence, default, breach of duty or breach of trust. The court has the power to adjourn proceedings to allow for any ratification of the act or omission. The ratification will usually be by the shareholders at a general meeting. The issue is whether the effect of ratification is to improperly prevent the claimant from bringing a derivative claim on behalf of the company: see *Smith v Croft (No 2)* [1987] 3 All ER 909. The issue of authorisation may be given by board members who are not involved in the cause of action.

(d) Where the cause of action arises from an act or omission that has already occurred, whether the act or omission could be, and in the circumstances would be likely to be, ratified by the company:

The court will have regard to all applicable facts in determining whether ratification would be possible. This is not necessarily a bar to bringing the claim as a derivative claim but only one of the factors for the court's consideration.

(e) Whether the company has decided not to pursue the claim:

This decision could be taken by either the directors or the shareholders. In this situation, they decide not to bring proceedings against the director concerned but they do not ratify or authorise the act in question. If no decision has been taken then the court could adjourn the proceedings for the company to decide whether or not to pursue the claim. In *Kleanthous v Paphitis* [2011] EWHC 2287, the fact that the board of directors had established a committee which had resolved not to pursue any claim was influential for the court in refusing the shareholder leave to continue the claim as a derivative claim.

(f) Whether the act or omission in respect of which the claim is brought gives rise to a cause of action that the member could pursue in his own right rather than on behalf of the company: CA 2006, s 263(3):

Under the heading, the court considers whether there is any possible action which a shareholder can bring in his own right rather than as a derivative action which arises from the same act or omission. In such circumstances, the shareholder may be able to bring a claim for unfair prejudicial conduct by those in control of the company. Although a shareholder may pursue the claim as a derivative claim because the costs and expenses will be met by the company, the courts have shown reluctance to grant the shareholder damages owing to the reflective loss principle considered at 18.13.

> In *Franbar Holdings Ltd v Patel* [2009] 1 BCLC 1, Judge William Trower was of the view that the cause of action should arise out of the same act or omission; where that act or omission gives rise to both a claim for unfair prejudice against a member and a claim for breach of duty against a director, s 263(3)(f) is engaged. The adequacy of the remedy available to the member in his own right is, however, a matter which will go into the balance when assessing the weight of this consideration on the facts of the case. The judge decided that Franbar could pursue all its claims under s 994 as well as breach of the shareholders' agreement.
>
> See too Proudman J in *Kiani v Cooper* [2010] 2 BCLC 427.

In some of the cases before the courts where the shareholder is seeking leave to continue with the derivative claim, the courts have refused permission to continue with such claim where in effect, the shareholder was seeking a petitioner's relief for unfair prejudicial conduct under CA 2006, s 994.

In *Mission Capital plc v Sinclair* [2010] 1 BCLC 304, Floyd J decided that the appropriate action for the Sinclairs was to seek to petition for unfair prejudicial conduct under s 994. He refused permission for the shareholders to continue with the claim as a derivative claim.

In *Kleanthous v Paphitis* [2011] EWHC 2287, Newey J refused to grant the shareholder permission to continue the claim as a derivative claim on the basis that the shareholder could pursue an action under s 994, including the fact that much of the monies recovered from the respondents would be returned to them by way of a distribution.

18.28 There may be valid reasons for the shareholder not to pursue an action under s 994. First, the shareholder would have to show unfair prejudicial conduct in the affairs of the company which affects the shareholder or some part of the shareholders. Second, the shareholder may not wish to be bought out and leave the company as one of the remedies is for the shareholder's shares to be purchased by the company. Third, the shareholder may wish to continue in such capacity with the company for long-term gains to be made by the company. The shareholder therefore may not find pursuing a claim under s 994 an attractive one. He therefore tries to pursue a derivative claim in the hope that he may seek some redress for the company without the need to exit from the company.

In some circumstances, the derivative claim may be more beneficial than a claim for unfair prejudicial conduct

In *Wishart v Castlecroft Securities Ltd* [2009] CSIH 615, the Scottish Court considered whether an alternative remedy may be suitable having regard to s 263(3). The case concerned a diversion of corporate opportunity by a company director. The Court stated that proceedings under s 994 would however constitute, at best, an indirect means of achieving what could be achieved directly by derivative proceedings. Further, the complainant's case was not that the company's affairs have been mismanaged. The relief the complainant sought was to have the company restored to the position in which it ought to be, by an order for restitution or damages; not that he should be bought out. In that regard, the Court noted that an order requiring him to be bought out at the time, when the commercial property market was depressed, would not be an attractive remedy. The order sought in the proposed derivative proceedings, that the properties in question be declared to be held upon a constructive trust for the company, would in reality be a more valuable remedy, since the claimant could then benefit from any rise in the value of his shareholding over the longer term, consequent upon a recovery in the market. Furthermore, any inquiry into whether there had been mismanagement, or into the price at which the claimant should be bought out, would require the court to establish the truth or otherwise of the claimant's allegations. The Court also noted that the company did not appear to be deadlocked, and that it continued to trade. In these circumstances, the availability of an alternative remedy under s 994 did not appear be a compelling consideration.

The possibility of winding up

18.29 In some cases, the courts have considered whether the winding up of the company may be the most appropriate outcome rather than proceed by way of a derivative claim. The language under s 263(3) refers to a 'cause of action' and while such a term may not be appropriate for a shareholder to bring an action in his own right, it may be a relevant circumstance that the court may consider in deciding whether or not to continue with the derivative proceedings.

In some circumstances, winding up a company may be the most preferred option

In *Langley Ward Ltd v Trevor* [2011] All ER (D) 78, the company was a quasi-partnership and was ultimately in a deadlock position including having completed all its projects. Judge David Donaldson QC decided that the company was a natural candidate to be wound up on a just and equitable ground by either shareholder (see too *Re Yenidje Tobacco Co Ltd* [1916] 2 Ch 426; *Re Worldhams Park Golf Course Ltd, Whidbourne v Troth* [1998] 1 BCLC 554 at 556). Accordingly, it seemed right to proceed on the basis that the company would almost certainly go into winding up by one route or another. It was therefore appropriate to consider the comparative merits of leaving all or some of the disputes to be dealt with by a liquidator rather than by litigation in a derivative action, and factor those into the overall decision which the court had to reach under s 263 as regards each of the claims.

18.30 The list set out in s 263(3) is not exhaustive. Although it must have regard 'in particular' to the factors set out, the court may consider other aspects that may be relevant to a decision on whether or not a shareholder may continue with the derivative claim. This aspect incorporates one strand of the rule in *Foss v Harbottle*, that where independent shareholders did not wish to bring proceedings, then the courts would take this into account in deciding the derivative claim: *Smith v Croft (No 2)* [1988] Ch 114. The following additional aspects have been considered by the courts:

(1) **Costs and expenses of continuing the derivative claim**. In *Iesini v Westrip Holdings Limited* [2011] 1 BCLC 498, Lewison J considered that the potential liability for costs was a relevant consideration.

(2) **The interests of the company's employees**. In *Stimpson v Southern Private Landlords Association* [2010] BCC 387, Judge Pelling QC considered that the position of the remaining employees in the company remained bleak and that this was a matter which the court should take into account: 'The significance of a point such as this is very fact sensitive, but it is nonetheless one that is relevant here at least when considering whether to give permission because s 263(3) is not exhaustive and here a relatively small number of employees are at risk …'

(3) **Any monies recovered from the defendants would ultimately be returned to them by way of a distribution as they were the company's majority shareholders**: *Kleanthous v Paphitis* [2011] EWHC 2287 where the principal director/shareholder held 72% of the company's shares.

(4) **The court may also have regard to the merits of the claim**: *Wishart v Castlecroft Securities Limited* [2009] CSIH 615; and *Kleanthous v Paphitis* [2011] EWHC 2287.

In considering whether to give permission (or leave) the court shall have particular regard to any evidence before it as to the views of members of the company who have no personal interest, direct or indirect, in the matter: CA 2006, s 263(4).

In this regard, the court will consider the views of disinterested shareholders as to whether the derivative action should be continued. In *Steiner v Lee* [2011] 1 BCLC 537, Roth J considered the interests of independent shareholders as important to the derivative claim proceedings.

The difficulty in practice is to identify who are the disinterested shareholders 'who have no personal interest, direct or indirect, in the matter' and then to ascertain how their views are to be obtained.

Disinterested shareholders will be those who do not stand to benefit from the derivative claim

According to Lewison J in *Iesini v Westrip Holdings Ltd* [2011] 1 BCLC 498 disinterested shareholders will be those who do not have a financial interest in the outcome beyond their interests as shareholders in the company.

18.31 Once the court takes account of the views of disinterested members, the court thereafter has the power to grant permission for the continuation of the derivative claim. The court has, in some cases, had regard to costs that may be incurred of proceeding with the derivative claim. In other cases, the courts have granted permission to a shareholder to continue with the derivative claim on a limited basis only such as disclosure of certain documentation that would provide a better picture of the merits of the case: *Steiner v Lee* [2011] 1 BCLC 537; and *Kiani v Cooper* [2010] 2 BCLC 427.

The court also has power to refuse permission or to adjourn proceedings and give such directions as it thinks fit.

In a derivative claim, the court will have regard to the views of the independent shareholders: *Smith v Croft (No 3)* [1987] BCLC 355.

'Wrongdoer control' of a company was not an absolute preclusive condition for bringing a derivative claim

In *Bamford v Harvey* [2012] EWHC 2858 (Ch); [2012] WLR (D) 298, the court was required to consider whether a derivative action by a shareholder seeking permission to continue an action against a fellow shareholder and the company as a derivative claim. The issue before the Court was whether the concept of 'wrongdoer control' was an absolute preclusive condition for bringing a derivative claim. In so doing, the Court had regard to CA 2006, ss 263(2)–(4).

Roth J held that 'wrongdoer control' of a company was not an absolute preclusive condition for the bringing of a derivative claim. However, where proceedings clearly could have been brought in the name of the company and no objection was raised on that ground, they should be so brought.

See too: *In Cinematic Finance Ltd v Ryder and Others* [2010] EWHC 3387.

The issue of costs in derivative proceedings

18.32 Where the court hears a derivative claim, it may make an indemnity order requiring the company to indemnify the claimants for costs incurred in bringing the proceedings. Part 11 of the CA 2006 makes no reference to the issue of costs in respect of derivative claims. However, under 'Practice Direction 19C – Derivative Claims', if the claimant seeks an order that the defendant company or other body concerned indemnify the claimant against liability for costs incurred in the permission application or the claim, this should be stated in the permission application or claim form or both, as the case requires: para 2(2).

This may be a matter to which the court will have regard particularly taking account of the expenses involved, and whether the expense involved would justify continuation of the claim. It may also be an issue for the shareholder who may not have the financial means to commence litigation.

In *Wallersteiner v Moir (No 2)* [1975] 1 All ER 849, the Court of Appeal stated that it was open to the court in a minority shareholder's action to order that the company should indemnify the claimant against the costs incurred in the action. Where the wrongdoers themselves controlled the company, a minority shareholder's action brought to obtain redress, whether brought in the claimant's own name or on behalf of himself and the other minority shareholders, and even though brought without the company's authority, was, in substance, a representative action on behalf of the company to obtain redress for the wrongs done to the company. Accordingly, provided that it was reasonable and prudent in the company's interest for the claimant to bring the action and it was brought by him in good faith, it was a proper exercise of judicial discretion or in accordance with the principles of equity, that the court should order the company to pay the claimant's costs down to judgment whether the action succeeded or not.

Normally a shareholder should be indemnified for his costs in bringing a derivative claim

In *Stainer v Lee* [2011] 1 BCLC 537, Roth J agreed with the principle set out in *Wallersteiner v Moir (No 2)* that a shareholder who received the sanction of the court to proceed with a derivative action, should normally be indemnified as to his reasonable costs by the company for the benefit of which the action would accrue. However, where the amount of likely recovery was presently uncertain, there was concern that his costs could become disproportionate. Accordingly,

Roth J placed a ceiling on the costs for which he granted an indemnity for the future (ie excluding the costs of the present application) at £40,000 (exclusive of VAT). There would be liberty to apply to extend the scope of that indemnity.

The claimant to derivative proceedings should also accept the rise of costs in such claims

In *Kiani v Cooper* [2010] 2 BCLC 427, Proudman J was of the view that the claimant should also take part of the risks of costs associated with the derivative claim. While Proudman J was prepared to make an order that the claimant's costs should be borne by the company, he was not prepared to grant her an indemnity in respect of any adverse costs order: 'It seems to me that [the claimant] should be required to assume part of the risk of the litigation.'

The provisions in the articles of association were limited to costs and expenses reasonably incurred by the director in the performance of his duties and did not extend to costs in pursuing the derivative claim

In *Carlisle & Cumbria United Independent Supporters' Society Ltd v CUFC Holdings Ltd* [2010] All ER (D) 25 (May), the derivative claim had already been settled and the case before the Court of Appeal concerned the claimant's costs of the proceedings, and whether he was entitled to claim these from the company. Arden LJ spoke of 'an expectation of [the Claimant] receiving its proper costs from the Companies on an indemnity basis if the action had gone forward'. The defendant director in question argued that he should be indemnified by the company for his costs in bringing the derivative claim pursuant to the company's articles of association which provided that a director had a right of indemnity for acts done in the course of acting as a director. The Court of Appeal rejected the director's contention. According to Arden LJ, the provision in the articles of association was limited to expenditure reasonably and properly incurred by the director.

The possibility of bringing multiple derivative claims and claims against overseas companies

18.33 One issue that has not been addressed under Part 11 is whether there is scope for bringing multiple derivative claims under the CA 2006 where, for example, a parent company brings proceedings in respect of wrongs done to a subsidiary company. Multiple derivative actions have their origins under the common law.

Multiple derivative actions may be brought under common law by a parent company which was a member of its subsidiary

In *Waddington Ltd v Chan Chun Hoo Thomas* [2009] 2 BCLC 82, the Hong Kong Court of Final Appeal held that a shareholder could maintain a multiple derivative action at common law on behalf of a subsidiary of the company of which he was a member, since any depletion of the subsidiary's assets caused indirect loss to its parent company and its shareholders, which gave him a legitimate interest in the relief claimed sufficient to justify him in bringing proceedings to recover the loss. Accordingly, where a wrongdoer defrauded a subsidiary or sub-subsidiary of a parent company and his control of the parent company precluded an action by the subsidiary in which the cause of action was vested, a shareholder in the parent company could bring a multiple derivative action against him.

See too *Renova Resources Private Equity Ltd v Gilbertson* [2009] CILR 268.

18.34 Part 11 of CA 2006 does not specify whether or not multiple derivative claims could be brought.

Multiple derivative actions can still be brought under common law but not under the CA 2006

In *Universal Project Management Services Ltd v Fort Gilkicker Ltd* [2013] Ch 551, the claimant and the second defendant were participants in a property development joint venture carried on through a limited liability partnership ('LLP') in which they were the only members with equal shares.

The LLP owned all the shares in the first defendant, a company incorporated as a special purpose vehicle to carry out one of the development projects ('the development') identified by the joint venture. The claimant was not a shareholder in the company in which the cause of action was alleged to be vested. Rather, it was a member of the LLP which owned all the shares in that company.

A disagreement arose in relation to the development. The second defendant incorporated the third defendant, a company wholly owned and controlled by him, and secured the purchase of the development on the same terms which had previously been available to the first defendant.

The claimant brought proceedings, alleging that the second defendant had pretended that the third defendant was another joint venture entity and had thereby misappropriated a valuable business opportunity of the first defendant for his personal benefit, in breach of his fiduciary duty to the first defendant. Since that claim was solely vested in the first defendant, the claimant applied under s 260 of the Companies Act 2006 for permission to continue the proceedings as a double derivative action (a sub-species of the multiple derivative action) on the first defendant's behalf against the second and third defendants.

It was common ground that, prior to the coming into force of the Companies Act 2006, derivative actions relating to companies were creatures of the common law and that the ordinary derivative action (by which a member of a company was exceptionally permitted to litigate a cause of action vested in the company when the company was unable to do so) had been wholly replaced by the statutory derivative claim provided in Ch 1 of Pt 11 of the 2006 Act, which conferred locus standi only upon a member of the relevant company.

It was held that the shareholder would be granted permission for the proceedings to continue. According to Briggs J, the derivative action was a procedural device designed by the common law to enable justice to be done where the wrongdoer was in control of the entity in which the cause of action was vested. The device was a single piece of procedural ingenuity, which did not distinguish between ordinary, multiple or double derivative actions, and was sufficiently flexible to accommodate as the legal champion or representative of a company in wrongdoer control a would-be claimant who was either (and usually) a member of that company or (exceptionally) a member of its parent company where that parent company was in the same wrongdoer control.

Briggs J stated that CA 2006, s 260, which had replaced the ordinary derivative action by a member of the allegedly wronged company with the statutory derivative claim provided in Ch 1 of Pt 11 of that Act, had not abolished the whole of the common law derivative action in relation to companies and had left other instances of the application of the procedural device unaffected. Therefore, the common law multiple derivative action remained available as a means of dealing with wrongs done to the company. The precise nature of the corporate body which owned the wronged company's shares was of no legal relevance, provided that it was itself in wrongdoer control and had some members who were interested in seeing the wrong done to the company put right. Further, the second defendant's status as an equal owner of the LLP and as one of the only two directors of the first defendant meant that there was wrongdoer control, that, accordingly, the court would grant permission for the continuation of the multiple derivative action, but that, in all the circumstances, the proceedings would be temporarily stayed for negotiations to take place.

Briggs J further held that the provisions of CA 2006, Pt 11 did not apply to double derivative actions and had not implicitly or otherwise abolished the common law jurisdiction of the courts to entertain such actions.

See too *Halle v Trax BW Ltd* [2000] BCC 1020; *Trumann Investment Group v Societe Generale SA* [2002] EWHC 2621; and *Airey v Cordell* [2007] Bus LR 391.

As the multiple derivative action could not be brought under the CA 2006, the common law principles therefore applied and need to be satisfied

In *Abouraya v Sigmund* [2014] EWHC 277, the claimant and the first defendant (S) were the only members of the second defendant company. Each of them held one share in the second defendant. The third defendant company (Triangle UK) was incorporated in England and was a wholly-owned subsidiary of the second defendant. A dispute arose relating to alleged misappropriations of funds belonging to Triangle UK and the alleged diversion of a business opportunity available to it. It was alleged that S had procured the misappropriations and diversion of the business opportunity, but that the party to gain from those actions was not S herself, but another company.

The claimant claimed to be a creditor of Triangle UK. He commenced proceedings in the High Court, seeking to recover the payments and benefit of the contract for Triangle UK. A further issue arose as to whether the claimant held his share in the second defendant absolutely, or whether S had a right to the share. It was very unlikely that the court would give permission for a nominee shareholder to proceed with a derivative action against the beneficial owner of the share. In such circumstances, a nominee shareholder would have no legitimate interest in the proceedings. The claimant sought permission to continue the action against S as a derivative claim on behalf of and for the benefit of the second and third defendants.

First, the claimant needed to demonstrate a *prima facie* case that Triangle UK was entitled to the relief claimed. Secondly, the claimant needed to establish a prima facie case that the proposed derivative action fell within the exception to the rule in *Foss v Harbottle* (1843) 67 ER 189 (the exception).

Richards J held that the application would be dismissed and refused permission to the claimant to continue the claim as a derivative action. He decided that on the evidence, the claimant had demonstrated a *prima facie* case that, viewed solely from the point of view of Triangle UK, Triangle UK had a claim for relief. However, on the basis of all the authorities, the claimant had failed to establish a *prima facie* case that the proposed derivative action fell within the exception of the rule in *Foss v Harbottle*. The claimant was unable to demonstrate that he had suffered any loss as a shareholder in Triangle UK and had made no attempt to do so. Further, the claimant was unable to show a prima facie case that S had benefited personally from the alleged breaches of duty. The claimant's real motive was to advance his interests as a creditor of Triangle UK.

In *Bhullar v Bhullar* [2015] All ER 130, Morgan J held that it was settled law that the common law did provide for the possibility of a double (or multiple) derivative claim and that the court's jurisdiction in that respect had not been taken away by ss 260 to 264 of the 2006 Act. Accordingly, applying settled law, the court had jurisdiction to permit a double derivative claim.

18.35 Another aspect for consideration is whether a derivative claim may be brought against overseas companies. However, s 1 excludes overseas companies from the definition of 'company'. It may be argued that although s 260(2) merely sets out the procedure for derivative claims that fall within s 260, it has not abolished the ability to bring derivative proceedings at common law.

The Secretary of State may by regulations:

(a) amend s 263(2) so as to alter or add to the circumstances in which permission (or leave) is to be refused;

(b) amend s 263(3) so as to alter or add to the matters that the court is required to take into account in considering whether to give permission (or leave): CA 2006, s 263(5).

Before making any such regulations, the Secretary of State shall consult such persons as he considers appropriate: CA 2006, s 263(6).

Application for permission to continue derivative claim brought by another member

18.36 Section 264 applies where a member of a company ('the claimant'):

(a) has brought a derivative claim;

(b) has continued as a derivative claim a claim brought by the company; or

(c) has continued a derivative claim under this section: CA 2006, s 264(1).

Another member of the company ('the applicant') may apply to the court for permission (in Northern Ireland, leave) to continue the claim on the ground that:

(a) the manner in which the proceedings have been commenced or continued by the claimant amounts to an abuse of the process of the court;

(b) the claimant has failed to prosecute the claim diligently; and

(c) it is appropriate for the applicant to continue the claim as a derivative claim: CA 2006, s 264(2).

18.37 If it appears to the court that the application and the evidence filed by the applicant in support of it do not disclose a *prima facie* case for giving permission (or leave), the court:

(a) must dismiss the application; and

(b) may make any consequential order it considers appropriate: CA 2006, s 264(3).

If the application is not dismissed under s 264(3), the court:

(a) may give directions as to the evidence to be provided by the company; and

(b) may adjourn the proceedings to enable the evidence to be obtained: CA 2006, s 264(4).

On hearing the application, the court may:

(a) give permission (or leave) to continue the claim on such terms as it thinks fit;

(b) refuse permission (or leave) and dismiss the application; or

(c) adjourn the proceedings on the application and give such directions as it thinks fit: CA 2006, s 264(5).

Derivative proceedings in Scotland

18.38 In Scotland, a member of a company may raise proceedings in respect of an act or omission specified in s 265(3) in order to protect the interests of the company and obtain a remedy on its behalf: CA 2006, s 265(1).

A member of a company may raise such proceedings only under s 265(1): CA 2006, s 265(2).

The act or omission referred to in s 265(1) is any actual or proposed act or omission involving negligence, default, breach of duty or breach of trust by a director of the company: CA 2006, s 265(3).

Proceedings may be raised under s 265(1) against (either or both):

(a) the director referred to in s 265(3); or

(b) another person: CA 2006, s 265(4).

18.39 It is immaterial whether the act or omission in respect of which the proceedings are to be raised or, in the case of continuing proceedings under s 267 or 269, are raised, arose before or after the person seeking to raise or continue them became a member of the company: CA 2006, s 265(5).

Section 265 does not affect:

(a) any right of a member of a company to raise proceedings in respect of an act or omission specified in s 265(3) in order to protect his own interests and obtain a remedy on his own behalf; or

(b) the court's power to make an order under s 996(2)(c) or anything done under such an order: CA 2006, s 265(6).

Under this Chapter 2, the following terms apply:

(a) proceedings raised under s 265(1) are referred to as 'derivative proceedings';

(b) the act or omission in respect of which they are raised is referred to as the 'cause of action';

(c) 'director' includes a former director;

(d) references to a director include a shadow director; and

(e) references to a member of a company include a person who is not a member but to whom shares in the company have been transferred or transmitted by operation of law: CA 2006, s 265(7).

Requirement for leave and notice

18.40 Derivative proceedings may be raised by a member of a company only with the leave of the court: CA 2006, s 266(1).

An application for leave must:

(a) specify the cause of action; and

(b) summarise the facts on which the derivative proceedings are to be based: CA 2006, s 266(2).

If it appears to the court that the application and the evidence produced by the applicant in support of it do not disclose a *prima facie* case for granting it, the court:

(a) must refuse the application; and

(b) may make any consequential order it considers appropriate: CA 2006, s 266(3).

If the application is not refused under s 266(3):

(a) the applicant must serve the application on the company;

(b) the court:

- may make an order requiring evidence to be produced by the company; and
- may adjourn the proceedings on the application to enable the evidence to be obtained; and

(c) the company is entitled to take part in the further proceedings on the application: CA 2006, s 266(4).

On hearing the application, the court may:

(a) grant the application on such terms as it thinks fit;

(b) refuse the application; or

(c) adjourn the proceedings on the application and make such order as to further procedure as it thinks fit: CA 2006, s 266(5).

Application to continue proceedings as derivative proceedings

18.41 Section 267 applies where:

(a) a company has raised proceedings; and

(b) the proceedings are in respect of an act or omission which could be the basis for derivative proceedings: CA 2006, s 267(1).

A member of the company may apply to the court to be substituted for the company in the proceedings, and for the proceedings to continue in consequence as derivative proceedings, on the ground that:

(a) the manner in which the company commenced or continued the proceedings amounts to an abuse of the process of the court;

(b) the company has failed to prosecute the proceedings diligently; and

(c) it is appropriate for the member to be substituted for the company in the proceedings: CA 2006, s 267(2).

18.42 If it appears to the court that the application and the evidence produced by the applicant in support of it do not disclose a *prima facie* case for granting it, the court:

(a) must refuse the application; and

(b) may make any consequential order it considers appropriate: CA 2006, s 267(3).

If the application is not refused under s 267(3):

(a) the applicant must serve the application on the company;

(b) the court:

(i) may make an order requiring evidence to be produced by the company; and

(ii) may adjourn the proceedings on the application to enable the evidence to be obtained, and

(c) the company is entitled to take part in the further proceedings on the application: CA 2006, s 267(4).

18.43 On hearing the application, the court may:

(a) grant the application on such terms as it thinks fit;

(b) refuse the application; or

(c) adjourn the proceedings on the application and make such order as to further procedure as it thinks fit: CA 2006, s 267(5).

Granting of leave

18.44 The court must refuse leave to raise derivative proceedings or an application under s 267 if satisfied:

(a) that a person acting in accordance with s 172 (duty to promote the success of the company) would not seek to raise or continue the proceedings (as the case may be); or

(b) where the cause of action is an act or omission that is yet to occur, that the act or omission has been authorised by the company; or

(c) where the cause of action is an act or omission that has already occurred, that the act or omission:

(i) was authorised by the company before it occurred, or

(ii) has been ratified by the company since it occurred: CA 2006, s 268(1).

18.45 In considering whether to grant leave to raise derivative proceedings or an application under s 267, the court must take into account, in particular:

(a) whether the member is acting in good faith in seeking to raise or continue the proceedings (as the case may be);

(b) the importance that a person acting in accordance with s 172 (duty to promote the success of the company) would attach to raising or continuing them (as the case may be);

(c) where the cause of action is an act or omission that is yet to occur, whether the act or omission could be, and in the circumstances would be likely to be:

(i) authorised by the company before it occurs; or

(ii) ratified by the company after it occurs;

(d) where the cause of action is an act or omission that has already occurred, whether the act or omission could be, and in the circumstances would be likely to be, ratified by the company;

(e) whether the company has decided not to raise proceedings in respect of the same cause of action or to persist in the proceedings (as the case may be);

(f) whether the cause of action is one which the member could pursue in his own right rather than on behalf of the company: CA 2006, s 268(2).

18.46 In considering whether to grant leave to raise derivative proceedings or an application under s 267, the court shall have particular regard to any evidence before it as to the views of members of the company who have no personal interest, direct or indirect, in the matter: CA 2006, s 268(3).

The Secretary of State may by regulations:

(a) amend s 268(1) so as to alter or add to the circumstances in which leave or an application is to be refused;

(b) amend s 268(2) so as to alter or add to the matters that the court is required to take into account in considering whether to grant leave or an application: CA 2004, s 268(4).

Before making any such regulations the Secretary of State shall consult such persons as he considers appropriate: CA 2006, s 268(5).

Application by a member to be substituted for member pursuing derivative proceedings

18.47 Section 268 applies where a member of a company ('the claimant'):

(a) has raised derivative proceedings;

(b) has continued as derivative proceedings raised by the company; or

(c) has continued derivative proceedings under this section: CA 2006, s 269(1).

Another member of the company ('the applicant') may apply to the court to be substituted for the claimant in the action on the ground that:

(a) the manner in which the proceedings have been commenced or continued by the claimant amounts to an abuse of the process of the court,

(b) the claimant has failed to prosecute the proceedings diligently; and

(c) it is appropriate for the applicant to be substituted for the claimant in the proceedings: CA 2006, s 269(2).

18.48 If it appears to the court that the application and the evidence produced by the applicant in support of it do not disclose a *prima facie* case for granting it, the court:

(a) must refuse the application; and

(b) may make any consequential order it considers appropriate: CA 2006, s 269(3).

If the application is not refused under s 269(3):

(a) the applicant must serve the application on the company;

(b) the court:

  (i) may make an order requiring evidence to be produced by the company;

  (ii) may adjourn the proceedings on the application to enable the evidence to be obtained, and

(c) the company is entitled to take part in the further proceedings on the application: CA 2006, s 269(4).

18.49 On hearing the application, the court may:

(a) grant the application on such terms as it thinks fit;

(b) refuse the application; or

(c) adjourn the proceedings on the application and make such order as to further procedure as it thinks fit: CA 2006, s 269(5).

The reflective loss principle

18.50 In connection with derivative proceedings, on occasions the courts have also addressed the 'reflective loss' principle. In corporate terms, this applies where the losses of individual shareholders are inseparable from the general losses of the company (eg where a company suffers a loss owing to a breach of duty owed to it by a director). It arises where the company and the shareholder have rights against the director arising from the same set of facts and circumstances. The 'reflective principle' is based on the concept that the losses suffered by the company should also be reflected in the losses suffered by the shareholder.

It is based on the premise that a shareholder may also have suffered loss in terms of a diminution in the value of his shareholding as a result of the loss suffered by the company. Accordingly, the shareholder's loss is reflected in that of the company's loss. A company may bring proceedings against the wrongdoer to recover its loss. However, the issue has been whether a shareholder could also bring proceedings for any loss it may have suffered, owing to the breach of duty by the wrongdoer as well as a breach of duty to the shareholder.

Although a shareholder has locus standi to bring proceedings under the reflective loss principle, a person in his capacity other than a shareholder may also be able to bring proceedings under this principle such as a creditor: *Gardner v Parker* [2004] 2 BCLC 554.

Where a shareholder only suffers a diminution in value of his shares owing to losses suffered by the company, this is a wrong to the company preventing the shareholder from claiming any losses

In *Prudential Assurance Co Ltd v Newman Industries Limited (No 2)* [1982] 1 All ER 354, the Court of Appeal stated:

> '... It is also correct that, if directors convene a meeting on the basis of a fraudulent circular, a shareholder will have a right of action to recover any loss which he has been personally caused in consequence of the fraudulent circular; this might include the expense of attending the meeting. But what he cannot do is to recover damages merely because the company in which he is interested has suffered damage. He cannot recover a sum equal to the diminution in the market value of his shares,

> or equal to the likely diminution in dividend, because such a 'loss' is merely a reflection of the loss suffered by the company. The shareholder does not suffer any personal loss. His only "loss" is through the company, in the diminution in the value of the net assets of the company.

Accordingly, the shareholder could not claim for any reflective loss.

As the director's act or omission is a wrong done to the company, only the company can properly recover for losses

In *Stein v Blake* [1998] 1 All ER 724, the Court of Appeal followed the *Prudential* case and held that the loss sustained by a shareholder by a diminution in the value of his shares by reason of the misappropriation of the company's assets was a loss recoverable only by the company and not by the shareholder, who had suffered no loss distinct from that suffered by the company. Accordingly, in this case only the companies concerned, and not the claimant, could bring an action for recovery of the loss.

A shareholder cannot recover a loss that is reflective of the company loss

The leading case on the 'no reflective loss' principle is *Johnson v Gore Wood & Co* [2001] 1 BCLC 313. The Supreme Court held that it was necessary to scrutinise the pleadings closely in order to ascertain whether the loss claimed appeared to be or was one which would be made good if the company had enforced its full rights against the party responsible, and whether the loss claimed was merely a reflection of the loss suffered by the company. Any reasonable doubt would have to be resolved in favour of the claimant. In carrying out that exercise, as in determining at trial whether the shareholder's claim should be upheld on the facts, the court was required, on the one hand, to respect the principle of company autonomy, ensure that the company's creditors were not prejudiced by the action of individual shareholders, and ensure that a party did not recover compensation for a loss which another party had suffered. On the other hand, the court had to be astute to ensure that the party who had in fact suffered loss was not arbitrarily denied fair compensation.

In this case, the claim for the diminution in the value of J's pension and majority shareholding in the company was merely a reflection of the company's loss, and would therefore be struck out, in so far as it related to payments which the company would have made into a pension fund for J. However, that claim was not objectionable in principle in so far as it related to enhancement in the value of J's pension if the payments had been duly made. As regards the other heads of claim, the claim for aggravated damages failed on the pleaded facts, while the claim for mental distress and anxiety (Lord Cooke dissenting) fell foul of the principle that damages for such loss were not generally recoverable in respect of a breach of contract.

Lord Bingham stated the following principles that were derived from cases addressing the no-reflective loss principle:

(1) Where a company suffers loss caused by a breach of duty owed to it, only the company may sue in respect of that loss. No action lies at the suit of a shareholder suing in that capacity and no other to make good a diminution in the value of the shareholder's shareholding where that merely reflects the loss suffered by the company. A claim will not lie by a shareholder to make good a loss which would be made good if the company's assets were replenished through action against the party responsible for the loss, even if the company, acting through its constitutional organs, has declined or failed to make good that loss. So much is clear from *Prudential Assurance Co Ltd v Newman Industries Ltd (No 2)* [1982] 1 All ER 354 at 366–367, [1982] Ch 204 at 222–223; *Heron International Ltd v Lord Grade* [1983] BCLC 244 at 261–262, *Fischer (George) (GB) Ltd* v *Multi-Construction Ltd* [1995] 1 BCLC 260 at 266 and 270–271, *Gerber Garment Technology Inc v Lectra Systems Ltd* [1997] RPC 443;and *Stein v Blake* [1998] 1 All ER 724 esp at 726–729.

(2) Where a company suffers loss but has no cause of action to sue to recover that loss, the shareholder in the company may sue in respect of it (if the shareholder has a cause of action to do so), even though the loss is a diminution in the value of the shareholding. This is supported by *Lee v Sheard* [1955] 3 All ER 777 at 778, [1956] 1 QB 192 at 195–196, the *Fischer* case and the *Gerber* case.

(3) Where a company suffers loss caused by a breach of duty to it, and a shareholder suffers a loss separate and distinct from that suffered by the company caused by breach of a duty independently owed to the shareholder, each may sue to recover the loss caused to it by breach of the duty owed to it but neither may recover loss caused to the other by breach of the duty owed to that other. I take this to be the effect of *Lee v Sheard* [1955] 3 All ER 777 at 778, [1956] 1 QB 192 at 195–196; *Heron International Ltd v Lord Grade* [1983] BCLC 244 at 262; *Howard (RP) Ltd & Richard Alan Witchell v Woodman Matthews and Co (a firm)* [1983] BCLC 117 at 123, the *Gerber* case and *Stein v Blake* [1998] 1 All ER 724 at 726.

18.51 The rationale behind the rule against recovery of reflective loss is that there should be no double recovery, so a shareholder can only bring a derivative action for losses of the company, and may not allege she has suffered a loss in her personal capacity for a personal right. To this extent, the rights of the shareholder are subservient to those of the company. The objective is that the defendant should not have to compensate twice for the same loss. However, the reflective loss principle may apply where the company cannot for some reason enforce its claim or its claim is weak against the defendant, but that the shareholder may have a good claim and seek compensation for losses sustained.

Subject to certain limitations, if the company's claim is not pursued or there is some defence to the company's claim, the shareholder could pursue his claim

In *Day v Cook* [2002] EWCA 592, [2002] 1 BCLC 1, Mr Day was the principal shareholder in TL. He carried on his business through TL and other companies. It was a case brought against a solicitor for breach of duty where it was difficult to ascertain whether any breach of duty was a breach of the duty owed to a corporate entity rather than the individual. It was not a case where there was any suggestion that the breach of duty to the individual involved the destruction of the corporate entity thus preventing the corporate entity bringing its own claim. Nor was it a case where it was argued that the diminution in value of the shareholding contained different elements one of which could be categorised as a purely personal loss. Arden LJ, having analysed *Johnson v Gore Wood*, said this ([2002] 1 BCLC 1 at [38]):

> 'It will thus be seen from the speeches in *Johnson v Gore Wood* that where there is a breach of duty to both the shareholder and the company and the loss which the shareholder suffers is merely a reflection of the company's loss there is now a clear rule that the shareholder cannot recover. That follows from the graphic example of the shareholder who is led to part with the key to the company's money box and the theft of the company's money from that box. It is not simply the case that double recovery will not be allowed, so that, for instance if the company's claim is not pursued or there is some defence to the company's claim, the shareholder can pursue his claim. The company's claim, if it exists, will always trump that of the shareholder.'

Arden LJ however recognised there were limits when she said:

> 'However, it is apparent that there are limits to the application of the no reflective loss principle. The principal limit is that the no reflective loss principle does not apply where the company has no claim and hence the only duty is the duty owed to the shareholder (Lord Bingham's proposition (2)). Likewise it does not apply where the loss which the shareholder suffers is additional to and different from that which the company suffers and a duty is also owed to the shareholder: see Lord Bingham's proposition (3) and see *Heron International Ltd v Lord Grade* [1983] BCLC 244, as explained by Lord Millett in *Johnson v Gore Wood*. There may well be other limits.'

18.52 However, the position is different where the company itself has failed to recover its loss or part of the loss because it does not take any action or settles a claim; and the company is unable to compensate some or all the shareholders for their reflective loss.

The 'no-reflective' principle will not apply where the wrongful act of the director placed the company in a position that it could not bring a claim. A separate cause of action in these circumstances may entitle the shareholder to claim reflective losses and compensation

Subsequently, in *Giles v Rhind* [2003] 1 BCLC 1, the company claimed against its former director/shareholder for breach of contractual duty of confidence as he had diverted a contract from the company. The company went into liquidation and discontinued the action because of lack of funds. The shareholder brought proceedings for loss of remuneration and loss of value of shares and share conversion rights. The issue before the court was whether the shareholder was entitled to pursue his claim because defendant director/shareholder had, by his own wrongdoing, destroyed or disabled the company thereby preventing it from pursuing its claim.

The Court of Appeal considered the 'no-reflective loss' principle and distinguished *Johnson v Gore, Wood & Co* by holding that the principle of no reflective loss which barred a shareholder from recovering in respect of loss suffered by the company as the result of a breach of duty owed to it, did not apply where the defendant had, by his own wrongdoing, destroyed or disabled the company so that, by reason of the wrong done to it, it was unable to pursue its claim against the defendant. Accordingly, given that the object of the covenants broken by the defendant was to protect the claimant's investment in, loan to, and remuneration from, the company, and that the defendant's breaches and use of confidential information to poach the company's major customer had caused the claimant's investment to be seriously damaged, his loan to become irrecoverable and his remuneration and employment to be discontinued as a result of the company's business being destroyed, the claimant was entitled to pursue his claim that his shares had become valueless and he had lost his loan as a result of the defendant's actions. In any event, his claim for loss of remuneration and other benefits was not a claim for reflective loss; therefore he was also entitled to pursue those claims.

An action for reflective losses could be brought by a person other than a shareholder (eg a creditor)

In *Gardner v Parker* [2004] 2 BCLC 554, there was a breach of duty by a director which caused loss to the shareholder who was also the creditor of the company. The Court of Appeal held that the rule against reflective loss was not concerned with barring causes of action as such, but with barring recovery of certain types of loss; therefore whether the cause of action lay in common law or equity and whether the remedy lay in damages or restitution made no difference as to its applicability. Furthermore, since the foundation of the rule against reflective loss was the need to avoid double recovery, there was a powerful case for saying that it should be applied in a case where, in its absence, both the beneficiary and the company would be able to recover effectively the same damages from the defaulting trustee/director. Accordingly, the fact that a claim was brought for breach of fiduciary duty did not prevent the claim being barred by the application of the rule against reflective loss: see *Shaker v Al-Bedrawi* [2003] 1 BCLC 157.

Although the rule against reflective loss did not apply where the wrongdoer had disabled the company from pursuing its claim against him, the mere fact that the company chose not to claim against the defendant, or settled with him on comparatively generous terms, did not, without more, justify disapplying the rule. Accordingly, the rule against reflective loss would not be disapplied as a result of the settlement.

Further, the rule against reflective loss was not limited to claims brought by a shareholder in his capacity as such, but also applied to him in his capacity as an employee of the company with a right or even an expectation of receiving contributions to his pension fund. There was, therefore, no logical reason why it should not apply to a shareholder in his capacity as a creditor of the company expecting repayment of his debt. Accordingly the claim based on the loan was barred by the rule against reflective loss.

Neuberger LJ stated:

> 'I think that the effect of the speeches in *Johnson's* case can be taken as accurately summarised by Blackburne J at first instance in *Giles v Rhind* [2001] 2 BCLC 582 at [27], subject to the qualifications expressed in the judgment of Chadwick LJ in the Court of Appeal (see [2003] 1 BCLC 1 at [61] and [62], [2003] Ch 618 at [61] and [62]). As amended by those two qualifications, it seems to me that Blackburne J's formulation was approved by this court (Keene LJ having agreed with Chadwick LJ) in the following terms, so far as relevant:
>
> "(1) a loss claimed by a shareholder which is merely reflective of a loss suffered by the company – ie a loss which would be made good if the company had enforced in full its rights against the defendant wrongdoer – is not recoverable by the shareholder [save in a case where, by reason of the wrong done to it, the company is unable to pursue its claim against the wrongdoer]; (2) where there is no reasonable doubt that that is the case, the court can properly act, in advance of trial, to strike out the offending heads of claim; (3) the irrecoverable loss (being merely reflective of the company's loss) is not confined to the individual claimant's loss of dividends on his shares or diminution in the value of his shareholding in the company but extends ... to 'all other payments which the shareholder might have obtained from the company if it had not been deprived of its funds' and also ... 'to other payments which the company would have made if it had had the necessary funds even if the plaintiff would have received them qua employee and not qua shareholder' [save that this does not apply to the loss of future benefits to which the claimant had an expectation but no contractual entitlement]; (4) the principle is not rooted simply in the avoidance of double recovery in fact; it extends to heads of loss which the company could have claimed but has chosen not to and therefore includes the case where the company has settled for less than it might ...; (5) provided the loss claimed by the shareholder is merely reflective of the company's loss and provided the defendant wrongdoer owed duties both to the company and to the shareholder, it is irrelevant that the duties so owed may be different in content."'

A claim for reflective loss does not necessarily bar a claimant from claiming other damages

In *Parry v Day* [2005] 2 BCLC 542, Judge Rich QC held that the loss claimed by the claimants was reflective loss for which, ordinarily, only the company could sue, since at the time the mistake was discovered and the defendant and his wife refused or failed to remedy it gratuitously, the company had causes of action against the defendant for breach of fiduciary duty as a director and for rectification.

However, the company had been disabled from bringing a rectification claim by the defendant who had by his own conduct stifled such a claim, not only by insisting that a clause be inserted in the agreement for the transfer of the ransom strip to the effect that the agreement was in full and final settlement of the company's claims against the defendant and his wife, but also by actively encouraging the purchaser of the development land to put pressure on the company to complete the sale thereby causing the company to pay a further £110,000 to the defendant and his wife for the ransom strip.

In those circumstances the defendant could not be permitted to assert that even though he had prevented the company from bringing its rectification claim the fact that it was not able to meant that he, although the wrongdoer, did not have to pay anybody. Accordingly, even though the claimants were claiming for reflected loss they were not barred from succeeding in their claim for damages. The defendant would therefore be ordered to pay the claimants respectively 51% and 14% of the outstanding loss suffered by the company after payment of damages by the company's solicitors.

Under the reflective loss principle, a shareholder should not be entitled to claim losses for his own benefit as the company should be the party that benefits: retreat from Giles v Rhind

The cases of *Giles v Rhind* and *Parker v Day* were criticised by Lord Millett in *Waddington v Chan Chun Hoo Thomas* [2009] 2 BCLC 82, who stated:

> '... it could not be right to allow the shareholder to bring an action for its own benefit; this would entail recovery by the wrong party to the prejudice of the company and its creditors. It would produce precisely the result which I identified as unacceptable in *Johnson v Gore Wood & Co* [2001] 1 BCLC 313 at 367, [2002] 2 AC 1 at 64; it would allow the plaintiff to obtain by a judgment of the court the very same extraction of value from the company at the expense of its creditors that it alleged the defendant had obtained by fraud. The Court of Appeal vouchsafed no explanation to justify this result, an explanation which might be thought to be particularly necessary given that the company was in administrative receivership.
>
> Some way needed to be found in *Giles v Rhind* which would allow the company to recover damages despite the discontinuance of its own

> proceedings. If the company had not been in administrative receivership, the simplest course would have been to allow the shareholder to bring a derivative action. As it was, this course would not have been open, for the company was no longer under the control of the wrongdoer. But the court could have given the shareholder leave to apply to direct the administrative receiver to bring the action if the shareholder was willing to fund it. The discontinuance should not have been an obstacle to either course. There is no logic in allowing such an action where the wrongdoers are in a position to stifle any proceedings by the company, and disallowing it where they have succeeded in doing so.
>
> The Court of Appeal may have assumed that the principle established in *Johnson v Gore Wood & Co* is not engaged where the company has lost the right to sue. But the House of Lords expressly applied the principle not only where the company had the right to sue but also where it had declined or failed to sue. There was nothing new in this. In *Prudential v Newman (No 2)* it had been submitted that a personal action at the suit of the shareholder will lie to recover reflective loss if the company's remedy is for some reason not pursued. The Court of Appeal countered the argument by posing the rhetorical question: "How can the failure of the company to pursue its remedy against the robber entitle the shareholder to recover for himself?"'

Lord Millett considered that *Giles v Rhind* and *Perry v Day* had been wrongly decided.

The principles on reflective loss set out in Giles v Rhind and Gardner v Parker applied

However, in *Webster v Sanderson* [2009] 2 BCLC 542, the claimant sued a firm of solicitors for failing to lodge a claim in time against another law firm. He claimed for loss of a failed investment and loss for solicitors' breach of duty. The Court of Appeal decided that *Giles v Rhind* was binding upon it and applied in *Gardner v Parker.* The court stated that the present case was not one where the company had been prevented from suing the wrongdoer by the wrongdoer's own acts. In the present case, the company could have mounted a claim through its liquidator, or such a claim could have been asserted by an assignee from the liquidator. The company was not disabled from bringing the claim, unlike the position in *Giles v Rhind.*

In *Sukhoruchkin and Others v Van Bekestein* [2013] All ER (D) 150 (Jul), Morgan J following the *Webster* case, stated that it was settled law that a loss claimed by a shareholder which was merely reflective of a loss suffered by the company was not recoverable by the shareholder, save in a case where, by reason of the wrong done to it, the company was unable to pursue its claim against the wrongdoer (the 'no reflective loss' principle).

A shareholder could claim independent damages separate from the company

In *Heron International Limited v Lord Grade* (1 March 1982), the Court of Appeal distinguished between the losses that are suffered by the company and those by the shareholder. It was of the opinion that the no-reflective loss principle was not a bar to a shareholder claiming independent damages separate from the losses suffered by the company.

Checklist: derivative actions at common law

18.53 *This checklist sets out the position of derivative actions at common law and the situations when such actions may be brought. It should be noted that much of the common law on derivative actions has been replaced by the statutory derivative claim under the CA 2006; and remnants of the common law principles may apply, for example, to 'multiple derivative actions' at common law*

No	Issue	Reference
1	Traditionally, the courts were reluctant to interfere in the company's internal management decisions – directors were best placed to decide corporate matters	*Burland v Earle* [1902] AC 83
2	Where a wrong is allegedly done to a company, the proper claimant in legal proceedings is the company	*Foss v Harbottle* (1843) 2 Hare 461
3	Where a majority decide on a particular transaction, this will bind the minority	*Foss v Harbottle* (1843) 2 Hare 461
4	The nature of the derivative action brought by a member must enable the company to enforce rights against the wrongdoers and claim remedies for the benefit of the company	
5	The company must establish a *prima facie* case that: the company is entitled to the relief claimed; and the action falls within the proper boundaries of the rule restricting members'' actions on behalf of the company	*Prudential Assurance Co Limited Co Limited v Newman Industries Ltd (No 2)* [1982] 1 All ER 354
6	Exceptions to the rule in *Foss v Harbottle* allowing the claimant to bring an action include: • fraud on the minority • misuse or abuse of power	*Edwards v Halliwell [1950]* 2 All ER 1064 *Estmanco (Kilner House) Ltd v Greater London Council* [1982] 1 All ER 437
7	The court will take account of the views of independent shareholders as to whether or not the derivative action should proceed	*Smith v Croft (No 2)* [1987] 3 All ER 909

No	Issue	Reference
8	The common law position on multiple derivative actions has not been replaced by the CA 2006 and the common law principles will therefore apply The court will take account of the conduct of the claimant in bringing the action on behalf of the company	*Waddington Ltd v Chan Chun Hoo Thomas* [2005] 2 BCLC 8 *Universal Project Management Services Ltd v Fort Gilkicker Ltd* [2013] Ch 551 *Abouraya v Sigmund* [2014] All ER 208 *Nurcombe v Nurcombe* [1984] BCLC 557

Checklist: practice and procedure of statutory derivative claims

18.54 *This checklist sets out the practice and procedure for commencing a derivative claim under CA 2006, Pt 11, Ch 1. It is essentially based on the CPR Rules.*

No	Issue	Reference
1	Only a member of a company may bring proceedings by way of a derivative claim	CA 2006, s 260(4) CA 2006, s 260(3)
2	There must be a 'cause of action'	
3	The cause of action must arise from actual or proposed act or omission involving: Negligence Default Breach of duty Breach of trust By a director or another person	CA 2006, s 260(3)
4	A claimant member completes a Claim Form headed 'Derivative Claim'	Practice Direction 19C para 2(1)
5	The company (including the director or another person) must be made a defendant to the claim	CPR 19.9(2)
6	Claimant must also file with the Claim Form: Application notice under Part 23 CPR for permission to continue the claim; and The written evidence on which the claimant relies in support of the permission application	CPR 19.9A(2)
7	The claimant must not make the company a respondent to the permission application	CPR 19.9A(3)

No	Issue	Reference
8	Claimant must notify the company of the claim and permission application by sending to the company as soon as reasonably practicable after the claim form is issued: • A notice in the form set out in PD 19C • Attach a copy of the provisions of the CA 2006 required by that form • The application notice • Copy of evidence filed by the claimant in support of the permission application	CPR 19.9A(4)
9	Claimant must thereafter send the notice and documents to the company under Part 6 CPR by way of service on the company	CPR 19.9A(5)
10	Claimant must file a witness statement confirming that claimant has notified the compan	CPR 19.9A(6)
11	After issuance of the claim, the claimant must not take any further step in the proceedings without the court's permission other than: • A step permitted or required by rule 19.9A or 19.9C; or • Making an urgent application for interim relief	CPR 19.9 r (4)
12	At the first stage, the claimant must establish a *prima facie* case for application to continue the derivative claim	CA 2006, s 261(2)
13	The company's attendance will not be required at this hearing – but the court may take account of any voluntary submissions by the company of any evidence of documents	PD 19C r 5
14	Where an application is made to the High Court, it will be assigned to the Chancery Division and decided by a High Court judge	PD 19C r 6(1)
15	If the application is made to the county court, it will be decided by a circuit judge	PD 19C r 6(2)
16	At the second stage, if the application is not dismissed, the court will proceed to give directions on the evidence to be obtained by the company	CA 2006, s 261(4)
17	As an alternative to the s 261 derivative claim, the CA 2006 sets out a procedure for an application by a member to continue a claim as a derivative claim and the factors to which the courts will have regard in arriving at its decision	CA 2006, ss 262, 263

Definitions

18.55

Derivative Claim:	CA 2006, Pt 11, Ch 1 applies to proceedings in England and Wales or Northern Ireland by a member of a company: (a) in respect of a cause of action vested in the company; and (b) seeking relief on behalf of the company.

19 Unfair prejudicial conduct

Contents

Introduction

19.1 A shareholder who is aggrieved about the management of a company's affairs, which are being conducted in an unfair prejudicial manner, may have a potential remedy to apply to the court and seek an appropriate statutory order. However, the scope of unfair prejudicial conduct is wide-ranging, and the task of the courts has been to consider the circumstances of its application in demonstrating whether or not the test for unfair prejudicial conduct has been met and for the aggrieved shareholder to seek a remedy.

19.2 Over the years, judicial attitudes have varied in connection with the general concept of unfair prejudicial conduct. This is because the courts have been required to adjudicate and determine the scope of conduct and behaviour that may be tolerable or acceptable within the confines of the company's management, function and operations. While a particular form of conduct within the company may be considered as acceptable to management, the courts have been required to declare whether such conduct is illegal, unethical or of such a nature, that it cannot manifestly be acceptable to the aggrieved shareholder. In other words, the courts are required to intervene in corporate affairs. Other judicial attitudes have preferred a policy of non-intervention into the company's affairs on the basis that the courts will not second-guess management decisions, and that management is best placed to decide the affairs of the company.

19.3 The unfair prejudicial conduct position becomes more acute in small companies, which operate as 'quasi-partnerships' with loose, informal arrangements akin in some circumstances, to a 'gentleman's agreement' on the operation, functioning and management of the company. Of course, such arrangements or agreements between the parties may not be expressly set out in a formal agreement, other than the company's articles of association, which provide a limited boundary and a starting point within which shareholders and directors may operate, but does not include other 'arrangements' to which the parties have agreed, whether verbally or through conduct. Such arrangements may give rise to legitimate expectations on the part of the member that his rights, interests, considerations, actions and motivations may be exercised in a particular manner that satisfy the member's objectives within the company. The shareholder also joins the company based on certain assumptions: that the company will be operated in accordance with its constitution; that the directors will exercise their fiduciary, common law and general statutory duties in accordance with the law; that the company will operate in an ethical and proper manner in accordance with applicable laws and regulations; and that the majority will exercise their powers in a proper manner. These legitimate expectations and assumptions may arise at the outset before joining the company or subsequently over a period of time once a person becomes a shareholder in the company. The shareholder has expectations that his contributions and efforts will be rewarded within the company, that he will be treated fairly and equitably in the performance of his duties, particularly in a managerial capacity or a senior position that equates with his desire to fulfil his own objectives and which align with the corporate objectives. Any wrongful exclusion or non-participation in the company's management destroys the trust and confidence and the agreed informal arrangements between the parties and which formed the basis upon which the shareholder joined as a member. It was the ticket to his entry into the company. He joined on the basis of agreed informal rules. Acrimony, bitterness and shattered dreams lead the aggrieved shareholder to seek to reinforce the informal but fundamental understanding or arrangement that was previously reached. The shareholder pleads 'unfairness' in the treatment that he receives from the company's management, and despite attempts at any reconciliation, the ultimate end may be an exit from the company, or seeking to regulate the company's affairs for the future. Clearly, the shareholder's legitimate expectations give rise to equitable considerations, which may make it unjust for a party to act unfairly or in a prejudicial manner towards the other. The shareholder will need to persuade the court that factually, taking account of various circumstances and arrangements and understandings previously reached and which have been breached, he seeks to petition to the court for relief. In this way, the scene is set for the courts to adjudicate on the unfair prejudicial conduct, and the appropriate remedy for the aggrieved shareholder in the circumstances.

19.4 This Chapter addresses the following aspects:

- The grounds for petitioning to the court.
- What constitutes 'unfair prejudicial conduct'?
- Who may petition to the court?
- The possible statutory orders that the court may make.

Petition by company member for unfair prejudice

19.5 The CA 2006, Pt 30 sets out an important and frequently used remedy for a shareholder who may be aggrieved about the functioning and operation of the company's affairs. A member of a company may apply to the court by petition for an order on the ground:

(a) that the company's affairs are being or have been conducted in a manner that is unfairly prejudicial to the interests of members generally or of some part of its members (including at least himself); or

(b) that an actual or proposed act or omission of the company (including an act or omission on its behalf) is or would be so prejudicial: CA 2006, s 994(1).

19.6 Typically, it is the minority shareholder who will present the petition before the court for unfair prejudicial conduct. The issue usually arises where there is a deadlock situation and one shareholder wishes to leave the company, or where the shareholder believed that he had a legitimate expectation to participate in the company's management, but has been so excluded from participation, or the shareholder may wish to exit from the company and disputes arise over valuation of the shares and at what price the exiting shareholder will get for the sale shares. Many disputes are usually settled where a fair offer is made for the shares without the need to proceed towards a hearing of the petition, or proceedings may be stayed if the parties are minded to reach an amicable settlement.

In other circumstances, the position of settlement of disputes may be governed by the shareholders' agreement setting out the dispute settlement mechanism which may be by way of arbitration. An issue has arisen before the courts as to whether parties to a dispute can contract out of the statutory right to petition for unfair prejudicial conduct under s 994.

Disputes between shareholders may be the subject of arbitration proceedings

In *Fulham Football Club (1987) Ltd v Richards* [2012] 1 All ER 414, the Court of Appeal held that disputes between shareholders can be subject to reference to arbitration. Patten LJ stated that the statutory provisions about unfair prejudice contained in s 994, gave to a shareholder an optional right to invoke the assistance of the court in cases of unfair prejudice. The court was not concerned with the possible winding up of the company and there was nothing in the scheme of those provisions which made the resolution of the underlying dispute inherently unsuitable for determination by arbitration on the grounds of public policy. The only restriction placed upon the arbitrator was in respect of the kind of relief which could be granted. There was no authority which suggested that an agreement to resolve a dispute between shareholders which might justify a winding-up order on just and equitable grounds would either infringe the statute or be void on grounds of public policy. The Arbitration Act 1996 sets out the principle that parties should be free to agree how their disputes were resolved, subject only to such safeguards as were necessary in the public interest; it was not necessary in the public interest that agreements to refer disputes about the internal management of a company should in general be prohibited or necessary to prohibit arbitration agreements, to the extent that they applied to disputes as to whether a company's affairs were being conducted in an unfairly prejudicial manner to the interests of its members.

Shareholders considering entering into shareholders' agreements should consider retaining the right to petition to the court for unfair prejudicial conduct.

Who can petition?

19.7 Section 994 provides that only a member of the company may petition to the court – usually known as the petitioner. The provisions of Part 30 also apply to a person who is not a member of a company, but to whom shares in the company have been transferred or transmitted by operation of law: CA 2006, s 994(2): *Re a Company (No 007828 of 1985)* (1986) 2 BCCC 98951. An agreement to transfer or transmit is not sufficient. The transferor must execute a proper instrument of transfer and have this delivered to the transferee: *Re a Company (No 003160 of 1986)* (1986) BCLC 99276. A person must have proper standing to bring a petition under s 994. A proper instrument of transfer is required to be executed in respect of the transfer or transmission. A blank transfer form is insufficient as well as an agreement to transfer: see Mervyn J in *Re Quickdome Ltd* [1988] BCLC 370.

19.8 A petition may also be brought by a trustee in bankruptcy or a personal representative of the trustee: *Re McCarthy Surfacing Ltd* [2006] All ER 193. A person may still be able to petition despite the fact that the directors have refused to register the petitioner's shares.

A nominee shareholder may also petition under s 994: *Atlasview Ltd v Brightview Ltd* [2004] 2 BCLC 191.

It is also possible for a petitioner to bring proceedings under s 994 where the company may be insolvent: *Gamlestaden Fastigheter AB v Baltic Partners Ltd* [2008] 1 BCLC 468. Section 994 did not prevent the court from granting a remedy even though there may be no financial benefit to the petitioner.

19.9 Where the company is subject to an administration order, para 74 of Schedule B1 to the Insolvency Act 1986 is concerned with challenging the administrator's conduct of the company. This provides that:

> '74 (1) A creditor or member of a company in administration may apply to the court claiming that:
>
> (a) the administrator is acting or has acted so as unfairly to harm the interests of the applicant (whether alone or in common with some or all other members or creditors); or
>
> (b) the administrator proposes to act in a way which would unfairly harm the interests of the applicant (whether alone or in common with some or all other members or creditors). [para 74(1).]
>
> (2) A creditor or member of a company in administration may apply to the court claiming that the administrator is not performing his functions as quickly or as efficiently as is reasonably practicable. [para 74(2).]
>
> (3) The court may:
>
> (a) grant relief;
>
> (b) dismiss the application;
>
> (c) adjourn the hearing conditionally or unconditionally;
>
> (d) make an interim order;

(e) make any other order it thinks appropriate. [para 74(3).]

(4) In particular, an order under this paragraph may:

(a) regulate the administrator's exercise of his functions;

(b) require the administrator to do or not do a specified thing;

(c) require a decision of the company's creditors to be sought on the matter;

(d) provide for the appointment of an administrator to cease to have effect;

(e) make consequential provision'. [para 74(4).]

The petitioner's conduct may be a relevant factor for the court in considering a petition for unfair prejudicial conduct

In *Richardson v Blackmore* [2006] All ER 345, Lloyd LJ stated that the petitioner's conduct in relation to a forged letter was neither sufficiently serious nor sufficiently closely related to the respondents' unfairly prejudicial conduct to make it appropriate for the court to exercise its discretion so as to refuse to grant the petitioner a remedy under s 994 which it would otherwise grant.

In *Re London School of Electronics Ltd* [1985] 2 BCLC 273, Nourse J held that s 994 empowered the court to grant such relief as it thought fit, provided that it was satisfied that the company's affairs were being, or had been, conducted in a manner unfairly prejudicial to the interests of some part of the members; that the section had to be construed as it stood, without importing any other test such as whether it was just and equitable and therefore although the conduct of the petitioner could affect the relief which the court thought fit to grant under s 994, there was no independent or overriding requirement that it should be just and equitable to grant relief or that the petitioner should come to court with clean hands.

Further, in *R A Noble & Sons (Clothing) Ltd* [1983] BCLC 273, Nourse J was of the view that there was no need for a petitioner to show that the persons controlling the company acted either in bad faith or with a conscious intent to treat the petitioner unfairly.

19.10 In most cases, the petitioner will be a minority shareholder. However, there is nothing to prevent a majority or controlling shareholder from bringing an action under s 994, although in such situations it may be difficult for the controlling shareholder to show that the affairs of the company were unfairly prejudicial as such shareholder may elect to use his voting power to control the company's affairs.

A controlling shareholder may petition for unfair prejudicial conduct

In *Re Legal Costs Negotiators Limited* [1999] 2 BCLC 171, the Court of Appeal were required to consider, *inter alia*, whether a majority shareholder could bring proceedings for unfair prejudicial conduct. It held that s 994 was concerned with the company's affairs and not with the affairs of individuals. The section was concerned with acts done by the company or those authorised to act as its organs. Where a petitioner was able to control the conduct which allegedly constituted unfairly prejudicial conduct within the terms of s 994 the court would normally expect the petitioner to exercise its control to terminate the allegedly unfairly prejudicial conduct. On the facts, the respondent was not by exercising his right as a shareholder conducting the affairs of the company, and in any event, the petitioners had control of the company which enabled them to put an end to the unfairly prejudicial conduct.

See too *Parkinson v Eurofinance Group Ltd* [2001] 1 BCLC 720.

Nature of the conduct involved

19.11 In some cases, the courts have refused to grant the petitioner standing to bring proceedings or order relief for the petitioner on the ground of the petitioner's conduct in bringing the proceedings.

A petitioner's conduct may be an appropriate consideration for the court in considering unfair prejudicial conduct

In *Grace v Biagioli* [2006] 2 BCLC 70, a minority shareholder was removed from office as a director. However, he had been secretly negotiating to buy out a potential competitor. One issue before the court was whether the majority directors entitled to dismiss the minority director from office.

It was held by the Court of Appeal that applying the principle that ordinarily it was not unfair for the affairs of a company to be conducted in accordance with its articles or any other relevant and legally enforceable agreement unless it would be inequitable for such an agreement to be enforced. The majority shareholders' use of the powers and voting rights conferred by the articles could not be regarded as contrary to good faith if they were invoked to protect the company from conduct which was itself either in breach of a relevant agreement or otherwise detrimental to the well-being of the company and its assets. However, the appellant's conduct in attempting to negotiate the purchase of a potential competitor which would have placed him in a position of conflict with his duties as a director, and his willingness to embark on such negotiations without any prior disclosure or discussion with his fellow directors and shareholders, and his subsequent attempts to conceal his actions, all justified his dismissal as a director.

19.12 Section 994 refers to the conduct of the company's affairs that will be the subject of the petition. Alternatively, it can relate to an actual or proposed act or omission of the company (including an act or omission on its behalf). A dispute between shareholders, for example a shareholder not selling his shares, was not conduct in connection with the company's affairs: *Re Legal Costs Negotiators Limited* [1999] 2 BCLC 171.

The scope of s 994 is wide to include the company's controllers, namely directors or shareholders or both. It also includes the control of a subsidiary by its parent company, and the conduct of the subsidiary's business may be treated as that of its parent company.

The nature of control exercised by a parent over its subsidiary in such a way may be unfair prejudicial conduct

In *Nicholas v Soundcraft Electronics Ltd* [1993] BCLC 360, the company was incorporated in 1977 by three shareholders and the issued share capital of the company at the material time was 4,000 ordinary shares of which 75 per cent were held by Soundcraft Electronics Ltd (Electronics) and the remainder were divided equally between the claimant and another person. The company was to be a 75 per cent subsidiary of Electronics with a board of four – the claimant and another person who were to be executive directors and two others who represented Electronics, the parent company. Electronics was to support the company financially until it was financially viable but the extent of the support was not discussed or defined.

The claimant submitted that Electronics breached its obligation by withholding financial support for the company between 1980 and 1981 and further, during the period 1984 to 1985 when Electronics was in severe financial difficulties it again withheld sums due to the company. The claimant applied for relief under CA 2006, s 994 (previously CA 1985, s 459).

The Court of Appeal held that Electronics exercised detailed control over the affairs of the company and when it withheld payments to the company it was doing so as part of the general control that it exercised over the affairs of the company. Accordingly, the non-payment of the debts due to the company did relate to the manner in which the affairs of the company were conducted. However, the reason why Electronics delayed payment was to try to keep the group, which was in financial difficulties, afloat, something which was in the interests of the company, and accordingly this could not constitute unfair prejudice in the conduct of the company's affairs.

See too *Scottish Co-operative Wholesale Society Ltd v Meyer* [1959] AC 324.

The 'affairs of a company' may include those of its subsidiary

In *Gross v Rackind* [2005] 1 WLR 3505, the Court of Appeal held that the conduct of the affairs of one company could also be conduct of the affairs of another, where for example, a holding company had been held to have been conducting the affairs of a subsidiary. The expression 'the affairs of the company' was one of the widest import which could include the affairs of a subsidiary of that company. Equally, however, the affairs of a subsidiary could also be the affairs of its holding company, especially where the directors of the holding company, which necessarily controlled the affairs of the subsidiary, also represented a majority of the directors of the subsidiary.

See too *Re Dominion International Group (No 2)* [1996] 1 BCLC 634.

A person may only petition to the court in his capacity as a member of the company and not in any other capacity

In *Arrow Nominees Inc v Blackledge* [2000] 2 BCLC 167, the Court of Appeal decided that the allegations made in the petition by the petitioner were allegations of oppressive conduct by the shareholder in its capacity as supplier or as lender, and not as majority shareholder.

The term 'affairs of the company' should be liberally interpreted

In *Hawkes v Cuddy* [2009] 2 BCLC 427, the Court of Appeal stated that although deadlock and the inability of the company to conduct its business might be inherent in a breakdown of the trust and confidence which the parties had in each other when the business was initially contemplated, they did not satisfy the requirements for the exercise of the jurisdiction under s 994 to grant relief on the grounds of unfair prejudice. Further, the 'affairs of a company' were to be liberally interpreted for the purposes of s 994 and could extend to matters which were capable of coming before the board for its consideration, and were not restricted merely to those that actually came before the board.

In *Oak Investment Partners XII v Broughtwood* [2010] 2 BCLC 459, mismanagement of the affairs of a company and conduct by one party to a quasi-partnership arrangement in respect of a jointly owned company that caused an irrevocable breakdown in the relationship of trust and confidence inherent in the arrangement were both capable of being unfairly prejudicial conduct. Since the constitutional arrangements relating to the structure of the companies in the group were central to the way that the parties as quasi-partners agreed that their joint venture was to be implemented, and since those arrangements imposed mutual duties of good faith, trust, disclosure and co-operation on them both, the appellant's conduct in seeking, and for a short period achieving, practical control of the business so that he could run it in his own way and in reneging on his agreement with his quasi-partner was underhand and unconstitutional, damaging to the business, and destroyed any element of continuing trust and confidence that might have existed between the quasi-partners. That serious misconduct was by itself sufficient to justify an order that the appellant sell his shares, but in addition his conduct in interfering with management outside his specific duties was seriously destructive of the group's well-being and amounted to unfairly prejudicial conduct for the purposes of s 994.

19.13 The court will not entertain a petition by the petitioner when the conduct complained of has not materialised.

The conduct complained of must have materialised for the petitioner to petition for unfair prejudicial conduct

In *Astec (BSR) plc* [1998] 2 BCLC 556, Jonathan Parker J decided that although the meaning of the expression 'conduct of the affairs of the company' was wide enough to include what went on in the boardroom prior to the moment when a collective decision was taken, the stance taken by a dissentient minority in the stages leading up to the taking of that decision could not amount to conduct of the company's affairs, since the views of that minority were not reflected in the ensuing collective decision. Accordingly the mere voicing of dissentient views by a minority on the board could not found a petition under s 994.

What are the interests of the members?

19.14 Section 994(1) states that the conduct must be unfairly prejudicial to the 'interests of members generally or of some part of its members…' There is no statutory definition of 'interests'. The interests must be in connection with the company's affairs and not personal or other interests of the shareholder: *Gamlestaden Fastigheter AB v Batlic Partners Ltd* [2008] 1 BCLC 468.

The interests must apply to the members in their capacity as shareholders and not any other interest

In *Re A Company (No 00314 of 1989), ex parte Estate Acquisition & Development Limited* [1991] BCLC 154, Mummery J was of the view that s 994 applied to conduct which was unfairly prejudicial to the interests of the member qua member. It did not extend to conduct which was prejudicial to other interests of persons who happened to be members of the company (see *Re a company* [1983] BCLC 126 at 135, [1983] 2 All ER 36 at 44, [1983] Ch 178 at 189 and *Re a company* [1986] BCLC 376 at 378). The interests of the member(s) referred to in the section were not, however, necessarily limited to his strict legal rights under the constitution of the company. The concept of 'unfair prejudice' to 'interests' embraced a wider range of complaints than infringement of a member's legal rights under the articles and under the Companies Acts.

19.15 The category as to what constitutes the interests of the members is not closed: but it is extremely wide. In *O'Neill v Phillips* [1999] 2 BCLC 1, Lord Hoffmann stated that 'the requirement that prejudice must be suffered as a member should not be too narrowly or technically construed'.

Similarly, in *Shepherd v Williamson* [2010] All ER 142, Proudman J held that the court might make an order pursuant to s 994 if, but only if, a member could show that the affairs of the company had been conducted in a manner unfairly prejudicial to his interests, as a member, or of the members generally. This requirement should not be too narrowly construed. Further, the conduct complained of had to be both unfair and prejudicial to the petitioner. The use of the word 'unfairly' enabled the court to have a regard to wider equitable considerations. Furthermore, a petitioner's own misconduct might be relevant to the grant of relief. The court had a very wide discretion as to the relief it granted pursuant to s 994.

In some circumstances the courts have been willing to grant the petitioner relief where the petitioner could show that there was some close connection between the member's interests and those of the company, for example, where the shareholder is also a creditor of the company: *R & H Electrical Limited v Haden Bill Electrical Limited* [1995] 2 BCLC 280; see too Richards J in *Re Woven Rugs Limited* [2010] All ER 41.

What constitutes 'unfairly prejudicial'?

19.16 The conduct complained of must be 'unfairly prejudicial'. There is no statutory definition of this term and much falls on case law to consider circumstances in which this may arise. Many of the cases on unfair prejudicial conduct have been concerned with small companies where management is in the hands of a few key officers. These companies are considered to be similar to 'quasi-partnerships' because apart from their articles of association, their management functions and operations are sometimes governed by loose arrangements and informal agreements on the management of a company's affairs. These 'informal' agreements or arrangements may be verbal or arising through conduct. These can give rise to some legitimate expectations on the part of either the shareholder as his participation in the company. Issues tend to arise when such expectations are not met or disputed by the other party, which creates a conflict as to what exactly was agreed between the parties including their understanding.

The aspect of legitimate expectations may arise at the moment that the company is formed or it may arise subsequently: *Tay Bok Choon v Tahanson Sdn Bhd* [1987] 1 WLR 413; *Strahan v Wilcock* [2006] 2 BCLC 555.

If a company's board of directors make a bona fide decision not to effect a reduction of capital but to retain it within the company, the fact that this financially affects a shareholder does not mean that it is necessarily unfairly prejudicial: *Re a Company* [1986] BCC 990.

'Unfairly prejudicial' are flexible terms to meet various circumstances that could be faced by a petitioner

According to Neill LJ in *Re Saul D Harrison and Sons plc* [1995] 1 BCLC 14, the words 'unfairly prejudicial' were general words and they should be applied flexibly to meet the circumstances of the particular case. Further, the conduct must be both prejudicial (in the sense of causing prejudice or harm to the relevant interest) and also unfairly so: conduct may be unfair without being prejudicial or prejudicial without being unfair, and it is not sufficient if the conduct satisfies only one of these tests. In construing the word 'unfairly' in this context it will be necessary to take account not only of the legal rights of the petitioner, but also whether there are any equitable considerations such as the petitioner's legitimate expectations to be weighed in the balance.

According to Neill LJ in order to establish unfairness it was not enough to show that some managerial decision may have prejudiced the petitioner's interest. A shareholder on joining a company will be deemed to have accepted the risk that in the wider interests of the company decisions may be taken which will prejudice his own interests. Thus it may be necessary for the directors to take steps which are prejudicial to some of the members in order to secure the future prosperity of the company or even its survival: cf *Nicholas v Soundcraft Electronics Ltd* [1993] BCLC 360 at 372 per Ralph Gibson LJ. Although it was open to the court to find that serious mismanagement of a company's business constituted conduct that was unfairly prejudicial to the interests of the shareholders, the court would normally be very reluctant to accept that managerial decisions could amount to unfairly prejudicial conduct: see *Re Elgindata Ltd* [1991] BCLC 959 at 993. He stated:

> 'A shareholder can legitimately complain, however, if the directors exceed the powers vested in them or exercise their powers for some illegitimate or ulterior purpose.
>
> Though in general members of a company have no legitimate expectations going beyond the legal rights conferred on them by the constitution of the company, additional legitimate expectations may be superimposed in certain circumstances. These may arise from agreements or understandings between the members or between the members and the directors.'

The test for determining unfairness is objective. According to Hoffmann LJ, in deciding what is fair or unfair for the purposes of s 994, it was important to bear in mind that fairness was being used in the context of a 'commercial relationship'. The articles of association were the contractual terms governing the relationships of the shareholders with the company and each other. They determine the powers of the board and the company in general meeting and everyone who becomes a member of a company is taken to have agreed to them. Since keeping promises and honouring agreements is probably the most important element of commercial fairness, the starting point in any case under s 994 will be to ask whether the conduct of which the shareholder complains was in accordance with the articles of association. The powers which the shareholders have entrusted to the board are fiduciary powers, which must be exercised for the benefit of the company as a whole. If the board act for some ulterior purpose, they step outside the terms of the bargain between the shareholders and the company. As a matter of ordinary company law, this may or may not entitle the individual shareholder to a remedy.'

Trivial or technical infringements of the articles were not intended to give rise to petitions under s 994. Hoffmann LJ stated that the very minimum required to make out a case of unfairness was that the powers of management have been used for an unlawful purpose or the articles otherwise infringed.

CA 2006, s 994 requires the petitioner to show both prejudice and unfairness

In *Re Sunrise Radio Limited, Kohli v Lit* [2010] 1 BCLC 367, Judge Purle QC stated there must be both prejudice and unfairness. Prejudice will most often be established by reference to conduct having a depressive effect (actual or threatened) on the value of the petitioner's shareholding, which will in most cases be a minority holding, typically in a private company with restrictions on transfer. Unfairness, in turn, most often connoted some breach of the articles, statute, or general principles of company law. However, the operation of the section was not necessarily limited to such cases. The test was an objective one. There may be mutual understandings between shareholders giving rise to special rights of a quasi-partnership kind. Even without that, the conduct of the company's directors may, whether by reason of malevolence, crass stupidity, or something in between, fall so far short of the standards to be expected of them as to lead to the conclusion that the petitioning shareholder cannot reasonably be expected to have the minimum of trust and confidence in the integrity or basic competence of the board that any shareholder is entitled ordinarily to expect. This is so irrespective of any impact on the value of his or her shares, and irrespective of whether any specific breach of the articles, statute, or the general principles of company law was involved.

A member may be able to rely on equitable considerations might make it unfair for those conducting the affairs of the company to rely on their strict legal powers

In the leading case of *O'Neill v Phillips* [1999] 2 BCLC 1, the House of Lords considered the issue as to what constituted unfair prejudicial conduct and decided that for the purposes of s 994, although a member of a company would not ordinarily be entitled to complain of unfairness unless there had been some breach of the terms on which he had agreed that the company's affairs should be conducted, equitable considerations might make it unfair for those conducting the affairs of the company to rely on their strict legal powers. That would be so where the exercise of the power in question would conflict with the promises the parties had exchanged, and it was not necessary that such promises should be independently enforceable as a matter of contract. A promise may be binding as a matter of justice and equity although for one reason or another (eg because in favour of a third party) it would not be enforceable in law.

In the only speech in the House of Lords, Lord Hoffmann stated that:

> 'In s [994 CA 2006] Parliament has chosen fairness as the criterion by which the court must decide whether it has jurisdiction to grant relief. It is clear … that it chose this concept to free the court from technical considerations of legal right and to confer a wide power to do what appeared just and equitable. But this does not mean that the court can do whatever the individual judge happens to think fair. The concept of

> fairness must be applied judicially and the content which it is given by the courts must be based upon rational principles.
>
> Although fairness is a notion which can be applied to all kinds of activities, its content will depend upon the context in which it is being used. Conduct which is perfectly fair between competing businessmen may not be fair between members of a family. In some sports it may require, at best, observance of the rules, in others ("it's not cricket") it may be unfair in some circumstances to take advantage of them. All is said to be fair in love and war. So the context and background are very important.
>
> In the case of s 994, the background has the following two features. First, a company is an association of persons for an economic purpose, usually entered into with legal advice and some degree of formality. The terms of the association are contained in the articles of association and sometimes in collateral agreements between the shareholders. Thus the manner in which the affairs of the company may be conducted is closely regulated by rules to which the shareholders have agreed. Secondly, company law has developed seamlessly from the law of partnership, which was treated by equity, like the Roman societas, as a contract of good faith. One of the traditional roles of equity, as a separate jurisdiction, was to restrain the exercise of strict legal rights in certain relationships in which it considered that this would be contrary to good faith. These principles have, with appropriate modification, been carried over into company law.
>
> The first of these two features leads to the conclusion that a member of a company will not ordinarily be entitled to complain of unfairness unless there has been some breach of the terms on which he agreed that the affairs of the company should be conducted. But the second leads to the conclusion that there will be cases in which equitable considerations make it unfair for those conducting the affairs of the company to rely upon their strict legal powers. Thus unfairness may consist in a breach of the rules or in using the rules in a manner which equity would regard as contrary to good faith.'

Therefore, unfairness may only be shown in either of the following two situations:

(a) a breach of agreed terms between the parties on how the company should be conducted; or

(b) establishing a complaint by reference to equitable considerations.

Lord Hoffmann rejected the test of 'legitimate expectations' as inappropriate to unfairness. This previously applied where a shareholder considered that he had a legitimate expectation to participate in the company's management and was excluded from such participation.

Interpreting 'unfairly prejudicial'

19.17 The CA 2006 does not set out any guidance on the concept of 'unfairly prejudicial'. The term has been interpreted judicially in a variety of situations. In *Re Saul D Harrison and Sons plc* [1995] 1 BCLC 14, Hoffmann LJ stated: '"Unfairly prejudicial" is deliberately imprecise language which was chosen by Parliament.' He further stated:

> 'In deciding what is fair or unfair for the purposes of s 994 CA 2006, it is important to have in mind that fairness is being used in the context of a commercial relationship. The articles of association are just what their name implies: the contractual terms which govern the relationships of the shareholders with the company and each other. They determine the powers of the board and the company in general meeting and everyone who becomes a member of a company is taken to have agreed to them. Since keeping promises and honouring agreements is probably the most important element of commercial fairness, the starting point in any case under s 994 CA 2006 will be to ask whether the conduct of which the shareholder complains was in accordance with the articles of association.
>
> The answer to this question often turns on the fact that the powers which the shareholders have entrusted to the board are fiduciary powers, which must be exercised for the benefit of the company as a whole. If the board act for some ulterior purpose, they step outside the terms of the bargain between the shareholders and the company. As a matter of ordinary company law, this may or may not entitle the individual shareholder to a remedy.
>
> Although one begins with the articles and the powers of the board, a finding that conduct was not in accordance with the articles does not necessarily mean that it was unfair, still less that the court will exercise its discretion to grant relief.
>
> So trivial or technical infringements of the articles were not intended to give rise to petitions under s 459.'

Neill LJ was of the following opinion:

> '(1) The words "unfairly prejudicial" are general words and they should be applied flexibly to meet the circumstances of the particular case. I have in mind the warning which Lord Wilberforce gave in *Ebrahimi v Westbourne Galleries Ltd* [1972] 2 All ER 492 at 496, [1973] AC 360 at 374 in relation to the words "just and equitable":
>
> "Illustrations may be used, but general words should remain general and not be reduced to the sum of particular instances."
>
> It is also relevant to bear in mind that whereas a winding-up order on just and equitable grounds will terminate the existence of the company a wider range of remedies is available under section 461. In Re a Company (No 00314 of 1989), ex parte Estate Acquisition and Development Ltd [1991] BCLC 154 at 161 Mummery J put the matter as follows:

"Under ss 459 to 461 the court is not, therefore, faced with a death sentence decision dependent on establishing just and equitable grounds for such a decision. The court is more in the position of a medical practitioner presented with a patient who is alleged to be suffering from one or more ailments which can be treated by an appropriate remedy applied during the course of the continuing life of the company."

(2) On the other hand, as Hoffmann J pointed out in *Re a Company (No 007623 of 1984)* [1986] BCLC 362 at 367 in relation to a s 459 petition:

"... the very width of the jurisdiction means that unless carefully controlled it can become a means of oppression".

These words have been echoed in later cases.

(3) The relevant conduct (of commission or omission) must relate to the affairs of the company of which the petitioner is a member: see Peter Gibson J in *Re a Company (No 005685 of 1988), ex parte Schwarcz (No 2)* [1989] BCLC 427 at 437.

(4) The conduct must be both prejudicial (in the sense of causing prejudice or harm to the relevant interest) and also unfairly so: conduct may be unfair without being prejudicial or prejudicial without being unfair, and it is not sufficient if the conduct satisfies only one of these tests: see Peter Gibson J [1989] BCLC 427 at 437.

(5) In construing the word "unfairly" in this context it will be necessary to take account not only of the legal rights of the petitioner, but also consider whether there are any equitable considerations such as the petitioner's legitimate expectations to be weighed in the balance.

(6) For the purpose of determining the legal rights of the petitioner one turns to the memorandum and articles of the company because the articles constitute the contract between the company and the member in respect of his rights and liabilities as a shareholder. Furthermore, it is to be remembered that the management of a company is entrusted to the directors, who have to exercise their powers in the interests of the company as a whole.

(7) In order to establish unfairness it is clearly not enough to show that some managerial decisions may have prejudiced the petitioner's interest. A shareholder on joining a company will be deemed to have accepted the risk that in the wider interests of the company decisions may be taken which will prejudice his own interests. Thus it may be necessary for the directors to take steps which are prejudicial to some of the members in order to secure the future prosperity of the company or even its survival: cf *Nicholas v Soundcraft Electronics Ltd* [1993] BCLC 360 at 372 per Ralph Gibson LJ. Though it is open to the court to find that serious mismanagement of a company's business constitutes conduct that is unfairly prejudicial to the interests of the shareholders, the court will normally be very reluctant to accept that managerial decisions can amount to unfairly prejudicial conduct: see *Re Elgindata Ltd* [1991] BCLC 959 at 993.

In one of the leading cases on "unfairly prejudicial", Lord Hoffmann in *O'Neill v Phillips* [1999] 1 WLR 1092 stated that the principle of fairness must be applied in an equitable context depending upon the situation in which it is being used. His Lordship stated that a company was an association of persons for an economic purpose, usually entered into with legal advice and some degree of formality. The terms of the association were contained in the articles of association and sometimes in collateral agreements between the shareholders. The manner in which the affairs of the company may be conducted was closely regulated by rules to which the shareholders had agreed. For the purposes of s 994, although a member of a company would not ordinarily be entitled to complain of unfairness unless there had been some breach of the terms on which he had agreed that the company's affairs should be conducted, equitable considerations might make it unfair for those conducting the affairs of the company to rely on their strict legal powers. That would be the case where the exercise of the power in question would conflict with the promises the parties had exchanged, and it was not necessary that such promises should be independently enforceable as a matter of contract. A promise may be binding as a matter of justice and equity although for one reason or another (eg because in favour of a third party) it would not be enforceable in law.

In *Re Guidezone Ltd* [2000] 2 BCLC 321, Jonathan Parker J was of the view that Lord Hoffmann in *O'Neill v Phillips* had established that unfairness for the purposes of s 994 CA 2006 was not to be judged by reference to subjective notions of fairness, but rather by testing whether, applying established equitable principles, the majority had acted, or was proposing to act, in a manner which equity would regard as contrary to good faith. In the case of a quasi-partnership company, exclusion of the minority from participation in the management of the company, contrary to the agreement or understanding on the basis of which the company was formed, provided a clear example of conduct by the majority which equity regarded as contrary to good faith. Similarly, unfairness might arise from agreements or promises made, or understandings reached, during the life of the company which it would be unfair to allow the majority to ignore. Applying traditional equitable principles, equity would not hold the majority to an agreement, promise or understanding which was not enforceable at law unless and until the minority had acted in reliance on it. Unfairness for the purposes of s 994 might also arise where an event occurred which put an end to the basis upon which the parties entered into association with each other, making it unfair that one shareholder should insist upon the continuance of the association. The unfairness in such a case would arise from the conduct of the majority in insisting upon the continuance of the association in the changed circumstances, not in the changed circumstances themselves.

A petition under s 994 may be based on the fact that a shareholder had a legitimate expectation that the company's affairs would be conducted in the company's interests. This is the position in "quasi-partnership" companies where members may allege they had a legitimate expectation to participate in the company's affairs and decision-making processes. Alternatively, the company's articles may restrict the rights of directors or shareholders from removal. In such cases, the member may have a legitimate expectation not to be removed as a shareholder or director. The term "legitimate expectation" was considered by Lord Hoffmann in *O'Neill v Phillips* as 'the "correlative right" to which a relationship between company members may give rise in a case when, on equitable principles, it would be regarded as unfair for a majority to exercise a power conferred upon them by the articles to the prejudice of another member.'

19.18 In *Re Astec (BSR) plc* [1988] 2 BCLC 556, Jonathan Parker J stated that in order to give rise to an equitable constraint based on 'legitimate expectation' what was required was a personal relationship or personal dealings of some kind between the party seeking to exercise the legal right and the party seeking to restrain such exercise, such as will affect the conscience of the former. In the absence of a personal relationship, or personal dealings of that kind, a shareholder could reasonably and legitimately expect no more than that the board of the company would act in accordance with its fiduciary duties and that the affairs of the company would be conducted in accordance with its articles of association and with the Act. Such expectations merely affirmed the existence of the shareholders' legal rights. They did not constrain the exercise of those rights.

In some situations, the exercise of legal rights may be subject to equitable considerations of a personal character

In *Ebrahimi v Westbourne Galleries Limited* [1972] 2 All ER 492, Lord Wilberforce addressed the issue of quasi-partnerships and the equitable considerations that should be taken into account. In that case, he was addressing the position of 'just and equitable' winding up of a company under s 112(1)(g) of the Insolvency Act 1986 and stated:

> 'The words [just and equitable] are a recognition of the fact that a limited company is more than a mere legal entity, with a personality in law of its own: that there is room in company law for recognition of the fact that behind it, or amongst it, there are individuals, with rights, expectations and obligations inter se which are not necessarily submerged in the company structure. That structure is defined by the Companies Act [2006] and by the articles of association by which shareholders agree to be bound. In most companies and in most contexts, this definition is sufficient and exhaustive, equally so whether the company is large or small. The "just and equitable" provision does not, as the respondents [the company] suggest, entitle one party to disregard the obligation he assumes by entering a company, nor the court to dispense him from it. It does, as equity always does, enable the court to subject the exercise of legal rights to equitable considerations; considerations, that is, of a personal character arising between one individual and another, which may make it unjust, or inequitable, to insist on legal rights, or to exercise them in a particular way.'

19.19 Lord Wilberforce was not intending to set out an exhaustive list of factors concerning shareholders in a company becoming subject to equitable considerations between themselves in the exercise of their rights as members. Further, the term 'quasi-partnership' is only intended as a useful shorthand label, which should not in itself govern the answer to be given to the underlying question, whether the circumstances surrounding the conduct of the affairs of a particular company are such as to give rise to equitable constraints upon the behaviour of other members going beyond the strict rights and obligations set out in the Companies Act and the articles of association.

The issue of 'equitable considerations' may arise where the relationship of the parties may have changed over a period of time from that of an employer–employee to where the employee becomes a director and shareholder in the company. This arises particularly in a quasi-partnership situation.

See too: *Re BC & G Care Homes Ltd* [2015] All ER 115 (removal of a director by majority shareholders was contrary to informal arrangement in a quasi partnership); and *Arbuthnott v Bonnyman* [2015] EWCA Civ 536.

The conduct must be both prejudicial and unfair to the member's interests

In *Croly v Good* [2010] 2 BCLC 569, Cooke J stated that in order to succeed on a petition under s 994 of the 2006 Act the petitioner had to establish that the conduct complained of was both prejudicial to his interests and unfair to him in his capacity as a shareholder of the company, and not in any other capacity such as that of employee. The element of unfairness would generally be established by reference to a breach of the basis on which the petitioner agreed that the affairs of the company would be conducted, which would normally be according to the constitution of the company, in particular the articles of association since that formed the basis of the contract between the members. However, in the case of a quasi-partnership company, where additional equitable considerations arose by virtue of the nature of the relationship which the parties had entered into with a view to carrying on business through the company, the court was more likely to conclude that it would be unfair not to give effect to, or bring to an end, the parties' informal arrangements even though they did not give rise to legal entitlements, or that it would be unfair to exclude a participator from the management or conduct of the company's business.

19.20 Further, the quasi-partnership relationship depends upon mutual trust and confidence, which if breached, would result in equitable considerations being taken into account to determine unfairness. The parties in such circumstances may not have recorded the terms of their agreement in writing as to how the affairs of the company should be conducted – instead relying upon the understandings of the parties within the company.

A breach of mutual trust and confidence in a quasi-partnership may lead to unfair prejudicial conduct

In *Re Astec (BSR) plc* [1998] 2 BCLC 556, Jonathan Parker J stated:

> '... in order to give rise to an equitable constraint based on "legitimate expectation" what is required is a personal relationship or personal dealings of some kind between the party seeking to exercise the legal right and the party seeking to restrain such exercise, such as will affect the conscience of the former.'

In *O'Neill v Phillips* [1999] 2 BCLC 1, Lord Hoffmann considered the concept of unwritten agreements between the parties including the reference to 'conscience' as used in *Re Astec* and stated:

> 'This is putting the matter in very traditional language, reflecting in the word "conscience" the ecclesiastical origins of the long-departed Court of Chancery. As I have said, I have no difficulty with this formulation. But I think that one useful cross-check in a case like this is to ask whether the exercise of the power in question would be contrary to what the parties, by words or conduct, have actually agreed. Would it conflict with the promises which they appear to have exchanged? In *Blisset v Daniel* the limits were found in the "general meaning" of the partnership articles themselves. In a quasi-partnership company, they will usually be found in the understandings between the members at the time they entered into association. But there may be later promises, by words or conduct, which it would be unfair to allow a member to ignore. Nor is it necessary that such promises should be independently enforceable as a matter of contract. A promise may be binding as a matter of justice and equity although for one reason or another (eg because in favour of a third party) it would not be enforceable in law.'

19.21 The understanding of the parties may not necessarily be in written form, but rather through promises or by conduct usually connected with participation within the company. These aspects are likely to be taken into account by the courts in addressing equitable considerations. In *Strahan v Wilcock* [2006] 2 BCLC 555, Arden LJ stated that, in determining what equitable obligations arose between the parties, the court must look at all the circumstances, including the company's constitution, any written agreement between the shareholders and the conduct of the parties.

The test for unfair prejudicial conduct is objective – that of a reasonable bystander

The nature of a quasi-partnership and equitable considerations arose in *Fisher v Cadman* [2006] 1 BCLC 499. The father ran the business in an informal manner without any meetings or AGMs. Following the father's death, the sons operated the business paying themselves remuneration and, as alleged by the brothers' sister, departing from the company's articles of association in not holding meetings. The petitioner sister petitioned to the court under s 994 alleging unfair prejudicial conduct.

Sales J decided that when a dispute arose between shareholders of a company which was effectively run as a 'quasi-partnership', the underlying question was whether the circumstances surrounding the conduct of the affairs of the company were such as to give rise to equitable constraints on the behaviour of those who had *de facto* control of the company which went beyond the strict rights and obligations set out in the CA 2006 and the articles of association. The test of unfair prejudice to a minority shareholder's interests in such a situation was whether a reasonable bystander, observing the consequences of the conduct of those who had *de facto* control, would regard that conduct as having unfairly prejudiced the minority shareholder's interests. However, a corollary of the test of unfairness was that the court would take into account any agreement, understanding or clearly established pattern of acquiescence on the part of the minority shareholder which could have led those in control of the company to depart from strict adherence to the articles. If that was the case, the minority shareholder was entitled to give notice that he would no longer acquiesce in a departure from the terms of the articles, in which case those in control of the company were thereafter required to adhere to the articles.

The relationship between the petitioner and the respondents as shareholders amounted to a quasi-partnership in which the family relationship was as important as the relationship defined by the articles of association. There was no agreement that the petitioner would have a role in the management of the company, she had not provided any capital, having been given or inherited her shareholding from her parents; after her father's death the company had continued to be managed as he had run it, namely as a small family company run on a very informal basis. This showed that there was a common understanding on all sides that the articles were not a complete and exhaustive statement of how the relationship between the members and between the members and management should be conducted. It followed that there were wider equitable constraints on the way in which the respondents could behave in relation to the company and the petitioner was going beyond the simple terms of the articles of association.

Sales J concluded that the payment of directors' remuneration was also excessive.

19.22 There are some cases where lack of participation in management has been held to be unfairly prejudicial conduct.

A legitimate expectation for participation in the company's management may lead to unfair prejudicial conduct

In *Brownlow v G H Marshall Limited* [2000] 2 BCLC 655, a family-run business operated as a quasi-partnership, where brothers and sisters participated in the company's decision-making process. Following acrimonious relationship between the parties, the sister was excluded from the board as a director. She petitioned under s 994 for unfair prejudicial conduct.

McCombe QC decided that the concept of fairness was the criterion by which to judge whether relief should be granted under s 994 and conduct which was fair between competing businessmen might not always be fair between members of a family. In the circumstances of the instant case, having regard to the fact that the company was one in which considerations of a personal character arose out of the relationships between the family shareholders, equitable considerations might disentitle the majority from removing a minority shareholder from office without making a reasonable offer, if asked, for the purchase of the minority member's shares. The existence of service agreements did not change the position. It had never been suggested that the separate agreements between the company and the individual directors were intended to affect the rights or expectations, as shareholders, of those directors who held shares. No agreement had been reached between the shareholders as to what would happen to the shares of person dismissed from employment under the agreements. In the absence of such agreement or some contrary understanding, the terms of the service agreements did not override the equitable considerations.

Accordingly, the sister's claims for an order that her shares should be purchased by one or more of the respondents succeeded.

See too *Apex Global Management Ltd v FI Call Ltd* [2015] EWHC 3269, where the court decided that in respect of a 'quasi-partnership', unfair prejudicial conduct must be shown where there had been a breach of a legal right or some equitable constraint in respect of conduct of the company's affairs.

Case law examples of successful claims for unfair prejudicial conduct

19.23

Case	*Nature of conduct*
Grace v Biagioli [2006] 2 BCLC 70	Failure to pay dividend once declared.
Lloyd v Casey [2002] 1 BCLC 454	Director engaging in transactions for his personal gain to the company's detriment.
Irvine v Irvine (No 1) [2007] 1 BCLC 349	Director awarding himself excessive remuneration without board or shareholder approval to the minority shareholder's detriment as less dividends received.
Re Woven Rugs Limited [2010] All ER 41	A refinancing of the company resulted in benefit to the majority shareholders to the detriment of minority shareholders.
Re Little Olympian Each-Ways Ltd (No 3) [1995] 1 BCLC 636	Director transferring the company's assets to another company at an undervalue. The assets were subsequently sold to a third party for a gain.

Case	*Nature of conduct*
Re Brenfield Squash Racquets Club Limited [1996] 2 BCLC 184	Company's assets were used to secure the debts of the majority shareholders.
Re McCarthy Surfacing Limited, Hequet v McCarthy [2009] 1 BCLC 622	A bonus agreement prevented minority shareholders from receiving dividends on a project.
Allmark v Burnham [2006] 2 BCLC 437	Majority shareholders establishing a business in competition with company to the minority shareholder's detriment.

19.24 For the purposes of s 994(1)(a), a removal of the company's auditor from office:

(a) on grounds of divergence of opinions on accounting treatments or audit procedures; or

(b) on any other improper grounds,

shall be treated as being unfairly prejudicial to the interests of some part of the company's members: CA 2006, s 994(1A) (as inserted by the Statutory Auditors and Third Country Auditors Regulations 2007, SI 2007 No 3494, reg 42).

19.25 Under s 994 and so far as applicable for the purposes of this section in the other provisions of Part 30, 'company' means:

(a) a company within the meaning of this Act; or

(b) a company that is not such a company but is a statutory water company within the meaning of the Statutory Water Companies Act 1991 (c 58): CA 2006, s 994(3). See *Re a Company (No 00314 of 1989)* [1991] BCLC 154.

Petition by Secretary of State

19.26 Section 995 applies to a company in respect of which:

- the Secretary of State has received a report under s 437 of the Companies Act 1985 (c 6) (inspector's report);
- the Secretary of State has exercised his powers under ss 447 or 448 (powers to require documents and information or to enter and search premises);
- the Secretary of State or the Financial Services Authority has exercised his or its powers under Part 11 of the Financial Services and Markets Act 2000 (c 8) (information gathering and investigations); or
- the Secretary of State has received a report from an investigator appointed by him or the Financial Services Authority under that Part: CA 2006, s 995(1).

19.27 If it appears to the Secretary of State that in the case of such a company:

- the company's affairs are being or have been conducted in a manner that is unfairly prejudicial to the interests of members generally or of some part of its members, or
- an actual or proposed act or omission of the company (including an act or omission on its behalf) is or would be so prejudicial,

he may apply to the court by petition for an order under this Part: CA 2006, s 995(2).

The Secretary of State may do this in addition to, or instead of, presenting a petition for the winding up of the company: CA 2006, s 995(3).

Under s 995, and so far as applicable for the purposes of this section in the other provisions of this Part, the term 'company' means any body corporate that is liable to be wound up under the Insolvency Act 1986 (c 45) or the Insolvency (Northern Ireland) Order 1989, SI 1989/2405 (NI 19): CA 2006, s 995(4).

Powers of the court under Part 30

19.28 Section 996 sets out important remedies for a shareholder once it has been demonstrated that there has been unfair prejudicial conduct under s 994. If the court is satisfied that a petition under Part 30 is well founded, it may make such order as it thinks fit for giving relief in respect of the matters complained of: CA 2006, s 996(1). The remedial orders are not granted by the court as of right and are discretionary, but the orders are wide-ranging. According to Patten J in *Grace v Biagioli* [2006] 2 BCLC 70, the court is 'entitled to look at the realities and practicalities of the overall situation, past, present and future'. The nature of the court's powers could include other remedies such as damages: *Gamlestaden Fastigheter AB v Baltic Partners Limited* [2008] 1 BCLC 468.

At times, the courts have also considered granting interim orders.

An interim order may be granted under the remedial orders of the court set out in CA 2006, s 996

In *Pringle v Callard* [2008] 2 BCLC 505, Arden LJ stated that when considering the grant of interim remedies on a s 994 petition, the court must consider first whether there was a serious issue to be tried on the petition and, if there was, then to consider whether there was an adequate remedy for the petitioner at the end of the day. The Court of Appeal stated *per curium* that, in essence, it was contrary to principle to impose a director on a company. In any event, it was highly impractical so to do where there were disputes between the directors or indeed allegations of improper conduct. Accordingly, the court would have to be extraordinarily cautious before imposing a director on a company by way of an interim remedy.

19.29 Without prejudice to the generality of s 996(1), the court's order may:

- regulate the conduct of the company's affairs in the future (eg see *Re Harmer* [1958] 3 All ER 689, where the court ordered the father to be removed as chairman of the company to allow his sons to participate in the company's management. The father was considered dictatorial and refused to entertain any interference in the company's management by his sons);
- require the company:
  - to refrain from doing or continuing an act complained of, or
  - to do an act that the petitioner has complained it has omitted to do;
- authorise civil proceedings to be brought in the name and on behalf of the company by such person or persons and on such terms as the court may direct;
- require the company not to make any, or any specified, alterations in its articles without the leave of the court; and
- provide for the purchase of the shares of any members of the company by other members or by the company itself and, in the case of a purchase by the company itself, the reduction of the company's capital accordingly: CA 2006, s 996(2).

This remedy is one of most common orders sought by many petitioners petitioning under s 994. There is a preference for a detachment from the company so that the petitioner is brought out and the company continues with the management of its business.

In some cases, the court may order a 'clean break' from participation in the company's management

In *Petition of (1) Thomas Orr and (2) James Orr Petitioner for orders under section 996 of the Companies Act 2006 in respect of D S Orr & Sons (Holdings) Limited and DS Orr & Sons Limited* [2013] CSOH 116, the Scottish court was required to consider the position of unfair prejudicial conduct under s 994. In this case, the family had, for many years, carried on the business of farming which later followed a reorganisation of the business. Disputes arose within the family as to the company's management resulting in deadlock as it was impossible to appoint a chairman. Lord Doherty held that the affairs of the company had been conducted unfairly prejudicially to the interests of the petitioners. The imposition of an independent chairman was considered, but was not a viable option because of the cost of hiring such a person and the drain this would place on the company's resources. Given that the petitioners were innocent parties and would discharge their duties to the companies and the shareholders, Lord Doherty took account of the need not only to redress the unfairly prejudicial conduct but also to put right and cure matters for the future. He granted the petitioners control of the company for a period of two years; no further meetings were to take place until proper notice had been served; a director was to be removed from the company; a limit was to be placed on the number of directors of the company including quorum at meetings; a chairman was appointed from among the petitioners; and accountants and a law firm were to be put in place to assist in the administration of the company's affairs.

The court may have regard to the long-term interests of the company in granting an appropriate remedy

In *Grace v Biagioli* [2006] 2 BCLC 70, the case concerned the refusal of the majority shareholders to pay a dividend to the minority shareholder. Instead, the dividends were paid as management fees to the directors. Patten J in the Court of Appeal stated that the most appropriate remedy would be to buy out the petitioner. He was of the view that in most cases, the usual order would be to require the respondents to buy out the petitioning shareholder at a price to be fixed by the court. This was normally the most appropriate order to deal with intra-company disputes involving small private companies. The reasons for making such an order would free the petitioner from the company and enable him to extract his share of the value of its business and assets in return for foregoing any future right to dividends. The company and its business would be preserved for the benefit of the respondent shareholders, free from his claims and the possibility of future difficulties between shareholders would be removed. In cases of serious prejudice and conflict between shareholders, it was unlikely that any regime or safeguards which the court could impose would be as effective to preserve the peace and to safeguard the rights of the minority. Although, as Lord Hoffmann emphasised in *O'Neill v Phillips*, there was no room within this jurisdiction for the equivalent of no-fault divorce, nothing less than a clean break was likely in most cases of proven fault to satisfy the objectives of the court's power to intervene.

In some situations a buy-out of the minority shareholder may be the only appropriate remedy

In *Re Coloursource Limited, Dalby v Bodilly* [2005] BCC 627, the two shareholders established a company on a 50–50 basis. The relationship between the parties deteriorated. The respondent allotted further shares to himself which had the effect of diluting the petitioner's shareholding to 5%. The petitioner contended that the buy-out was the only appropriate remedy. Blackburne J decided that the first respondent's actions in causing the allotment and issue of the shares unquestionably amounted to unfairly prejudicial conduct. The first respondent had no real prospect of success in contending otherwise at trial. Moreover, it was unlikely that the first respondent would be successful in persuading a court that a different conclusion as to remedy was more appropriate.

19.30 Some issues tend to revolve around the valuation of shares where the court has ordered a buy out of the petitioner's shares.

Certain principles should be applied in the valuation of the exiting minority's shares

The starting point on valuation of shares is *Re Bird Precision Bellows Limited* [1985] 1 BCC 99. Bird Precision Bellows Ltd ('Company') was incorporated in 1975. The petitioners, who held 26% of the issued share capital of the company, alleged that the company was a quasi-partnership and that from the date of its incorporation there was an agreement or understanding that they would participate in the conduct of the company's affairs. This was challenged by the respondents, who held the remaining 74% of the company's issued share capital. The petitioners were removed from office as directors and wrongfully excluded from the company's business. The petitioners presented a petition under s 994 alleging that the affairs of the company had been conducted in a manner unfairly prejudicial to their interests as members and sought an order under s 996 that the respondents purchase their shares. At the first hearing of the petition before Vinelott J, it was ordered by agreement that the respondents purchase the shares of the petitioners 'at such a price as the court shall hereafter determine'. The petition came before Nourse J for determination of the price.

Nourse J established the following principles on valuation of shares which was affirmed by the Court of Appeal ((1985) 1 BCC 99467):

1. The price should be fixed pro rata according to the value of the shares as a whole without any discount to reflect the fact that the shares constituted a minority holding.
2. The price fixed by the court under s 996 at which shares were to be purchased should be fair.
3. Although general guidelines could be given as to what constituted a fair price in cases of common occurrence, the issue could not, however, be conclusively determined until the facts in a particular case had been examined. There was no rule of universal application either that the price of a minority shareholding in a small private company should be fixed on a pro rata basis according to the value of the shares as a whole or, alternatively, that the price should be discounted to reflect the fact that the shares were a minority holding. Where the sale was being forced on the holder because of the unfairly prejudicial manner in which the affairs of the company were being conducted by the majority, and the shares to be valued had been acquired on the incorporation of a quasi-partnership company and it was thus expected that the holder would participate in the conduct of the company's affairs, as a general rule it was only fair that the price should be fixed pro rata without any discount. That general rule applied not only where there had been unfairly prejudicial conduct on the part of the majority but also where, as in the present case, there had been an agreement for the price to be determined by the court without any admission as to such conduct. Equally, as a general rule, if the order was for the purchase of the shares of a delinquent majority, the price should not contain a premium to reflect their majority control. However, in the exceptional case where a shareholder had so acted as to deserve his exclusion, the price could be appropriately discounted since he could be treated as if he had elected to sell his shares, and such a sale would be at a discount.

On the facts, the company was a quasi-partnership since it had been set up on the understanding that the petitioners would participate in the conduct of its affairs and, although their conduct was not beyond reproach, they had not in the circumstances acted so as to deserve their exclusion. Accordingly it was appropriate that the price to be paid for their shares should be fixed on a pro rata basis without any discount to reflect the fact that the shares constituted a minority holding.

Since the agreement between the parties that the shares be purchased at a fair value to be determined by the court did not contain any provision that the price should bear interest from some date prior to its determination, or that the petitioners should receive damages for the loss of the use of the purchase moneys, there was no basis for the award of interest before judgment.

Where shares in a quasi-partnership company had been acquired at a price which was discounted because they were a minority holding and the purchaser had acquired them as an investment without any intention of participating in the company's affairs, it might well be fair that the shares should be bought out on the same basis where an order for their purchase is made under s 75(4)(d).

19.31 A large part of the cases tend to be in connection with quasi-management partnerships where the courts have stated the valuation must be on a *pro rata* basis.

Some established bases for valuation of the shares could be applied where a minority shareholder was bought out

In *CVC/Opportunity Equity Partners Ltd v Denarco Almeida* [2002] 2 BCLC 108, the Privy Council stated that the valuation should be based as a sale of the total business to a third party interested in purchasing the shares.

According to Lord Millett, there were essentially three possible bases on which a minority holding of shares in an unquoted company could be valued. In descending order, these were: (i) as a rateable proportion of the total value of the company as a going concern without any discount for the fact that the holding in question is a minority holding; (ii) as before but with such a discount; and (iii) as a rateable proportion of the net assets of the company at their break up or liquidation value. Which of these should be adopted as the appropriate basis of valuation depended on all the circumstances. The choice must be fair to both parties. Further it was difficult to see any justification for adopting the break up or liquidation basis of valuation, where the purchaser intended to continue to carry on the business of the company as a going concern. This would give the purchaser a windfall at the expense of the seller.

According to Lord Millett, if the going concern value was adopted, a further question arose: whether a discount should be applied to reflect the fact that the holding was a minority one. An outsider would normally be unwilling to pay a significant price for a minority holding in a private company, and a fair price as between a willing seller and a willing purchaser might be expected to reflect this fact. It would seem to be unreasonable for the seller to demand a higher price from an unwilling purchaser than he could obtain from a willing one. Small private companies commonly had articles which restricted the transfer of shares by requiring a shareholder who was desirous of disposing of his shares to offer them first to the other shareholders at a price fixed by the company's auditors. It was the common practice of auditors in such circumstances to value the shares as between a willing seller and a willing buyer and to apply a substantial discount to reflect the fact that the shares represent a minority holding.

Lord Millett further stated:

> 'The context in which the shares fall to be valued in a case such as the present is, however, very different. Mr Demarco is not desirous of disposing of his shares; he would rather keep them and continue to participate in the management of the company. It is Opportunity's conduct in excluding him from management that has driven him, however reluctantly, to seek to realise the value of his investment. In this situation the case law in England is that normally the shares should be valued without any discount (see eg *Re Bird Precision Bellows Ltd* [1985] BCLC 493, [1986] Ch 658, *Virdi v Abbey Leisure Ltd, Re Abbey Leisure Ltd* [1990] BCLC 342 and *O'Neill v Phillips* [1999] 2 BCLC 1).
>
> ... The rationale for denying a discount to reflect the fact that the holding in question is a minority holding lies in the analogy between a quasi-partnership company and a true partnership. On the dissolution of a partnership, the ordinary course is for the court to direct a sale of the partnership business as a going concern with liberty for any of the former partners who wish to bid for the business to do so. But the court has power to ascertain the value of a former partner's interest without a sale if it can be done by valuation, and frequently does so where his interest is relatively small: see *Syers v Syers* (1876) 1 App Cas 174. But the valuation is not based on a notional sale of the outgoing partner's share to the continuing partners who, being the only possible purchasers, would offer relatively little. It is based on a notional sale of the business as a whole to an outside purchaser.'

A non-discount basis of valuation of shares may be applied to an exiting minority shareholder where the company is a quasi-partnership

In *Strahan v Wilcox* [2006] 2 BCLC 555, the Court of Appeal was required to determine whether the company in question was a quasi-partnership and the basis of valuation of the minority shareholder's shares.

The Court of Appeal decided that the question of whether the company was a quasi-partnership was to be answered by considering whether if the company had been incorporated at the time it was alleged to have become a quasi-partnership (ie at the time when the minority shareholder acquired his shares, the company would have been formed on the basis of a personal relationship involving mutual confidence; whether, under the arrangements agreed between the parties, all the parties, other than those who were to be sleeping members, would be entitled to participate in the conduct of the business; and whether there was a restriction on the transfer of the members' interests in the company: *Ebrahimi v Westbourne Galleries Ltd* [1973] AC 360).

Once it had been determined that a quasi-partnership existed, the next stage would be to consider the basis of valuation of the shares. It was found that there were equitable considerations which bound the appellant to purchase the minority shareholder's shares on a non-discounted basis. Accordingly, the appellant's failure to buy out on a non-discounted basis constituted unfair prejudice.

The court has to fix a price for the shares that is fair

In *Attwood v Maidment* [2013] 2 BCLC 46, the respondent, M, was ordered to purchase shares in AH Ltd following a successful petition brought by the petitioner, A, for relief for unfair prejudice under CA 2006, s 994.

M and A had been 50:50 shareholders in AH Ltd. The petition succeeded principally on the ground that M as sole director had procured AH Ltd to transfer its entire portfolio of 46 properties to him at an undervalue.

At first instance, the judge gave valuation directions for ascertaining the fair value of the shares in AH Ltd. M appealed against certain of those directions, namely: (i) that AH Ltd's business should be valued on a going concern basis and not on a liquidation basis; (ii) that the contingent liability for corporation tax payable on the disposal of AH Ltd's properties should be valued at the amount actually paid as tax by AH Ltd on the disposal at an undervalue to M; (iii) that there should be no discount for the likely reduction in the proceeds of sale if the AH Ltd's properties were sold as a single portfolio; (iv) that there should be no deduction for the costs of selling the properties; and (v) that the rate for quasi-interest should be 2 per cent over Bank of England base rate (BBR) from 1 October 2005 to 31 October 2008 and 3 per cent over BBR for the period from 31 October 2008 to 16 July 2012.

One of the issues was whether the valuation of AH Ltd as a going concern was inconsistent with the judge's previous holding that, failing agreement with A, M should have put AH Ltd into liquidation rather than procure the transfer of properties to himself at an undervalue.

The Court of Appeal held that the judge had to fix a price which was fair. There was no inflexible rule that only in a quasi-partnership case could the court order a valuation on a going concern basis. If AH Ltd was valued on a liquidation basis, M (the purchasing member) would receive the difference between the going concern value of the entire company and its break up value. He would therefore receive a windfall at the expense of the outgoing member, A. There was therefore no inconsistency. The judge had to decide whether that resulted in a fair value being fixed for A's shares. A valuation on a break up basis would ignore the fact that M had acquired the assets.

19.32 If the company is not a quasi-partnership, the courts will value the minority shareholder's shares on a discounted basis because the minority shareholder held the shares as an investment in the company.

Where the company is not a quasi-partnership, a discounted basis for valuing the shares could be applied

Some cases have demonstrated the court's application of a discounted basis where there is no quasi-partnership.

In *Irvine v Irvine (No 2)* [2007] 1 BCLC 445, the company was not a quasi-partnership. The issue was whether the valuation should be on a *pro rata* basis or at a discount. Blackburn J held that a minority shareholding was to be valued as such (namely as a minority interest in the company) unless some good reason existed to attribute to it a *pro rata* share of the overall value of the company. Short of a quasi-partnership or some other exceptional circumstance, there was no reason to accord to it a quality which it lacked. In the instant case, there were no circumstances which could be described as exceptional. Accordingly, the minority shareholding should be valued on a discounted basis.

In *Strahan v Wilcock* [2006] 2 BCLC 555 Arden LJ stated that shares were generally ordered to be purchased on the basis of their valuation on a non-discounted basis where the party against whom the order was made had acted in breach of the obligation of good faith applicable to the parties' relationship by analogy with partnership law, that is to say where a 'quasi-partnership' relationship had been found to exist. It was difficult to conceive of circumstances in which a non-discounted basis of valuation would be appropriate where there was unfair prejudice for the purposes of the CA 2006.A discounted basis also applied in *Re Planet Organic Limited* [2000] 1 BCLC 366, where an order was made by the court directing the sale of shares held by an ordinary shareholder and certain preference shareholders at a fair price. The issue was whether the preference shareholders were to be regarded as quasi-partners such that no discount would be applied to the valuation of ordinary shares in arriving at valuation of preference shares. As regards the ordinary shareholder, the *pro rata* valuation would apply. With regard to the preference shareholders, they were merely investors who had not taken any active part in the company's management. Accordingly, the discount basis of valuation would apply. According to Jacob J, the preference shareholders had not undertaken anywhere near as much risk as the ordinary shareholders as regards their participation in the company. As a practical matter, the preference shareholders were not really expecting to be concerned with the management of the company. They were essentially investors in the enterprise and not partners in it. The order that the preference shares be sold merely provided that the sale should be at a fair price. The preference shareholders were not quasi-partners.

However, in *Re Sunrise Radio Ltd, Kohli v Lit* [2010] 1 BCLC 367, even though the company was not a quasi-partnership, the court ordered the valuation of the shares on a *pro rata* valuation basis. HHJ Purle QC stated that there was no rule of universal application excluding an undiscounted valuation where there was no quasi-partnership. The court had a very wide discretion to do what was considered fair and equitable in all the circumstances of the case, in order to put right and cure for the future the unfair prejudice which the petitioner had suffered at the hands of the other shareholders of the company.

In that regard, it was unreal to treat the petitioner as a willing seller, selling on any basis which involved a discounted price. Another relevant factor in any given case might be to consider whether the facts would justify a winding up on the just and equitable ground, in which event the shareholder would receive a rateable proportion of the realised assets. In the winding-up context, the just and equitable ground was not limited to cases of quasi-partnership. A minority in an unfair prejudice petition should not ordinarily be worse off than in a winding up. That did not mean that winding up should routinely be sought as an alternative in s 994 cases. Rather, the potential availability of relief through the winding-up process should in an appropriate case be taken into account in fashioning the remedy. Furthermore, the value of the shares in the hands of the respondents to a petition might be a very material factor, for the respondents might be unjustly enriched by the acquisition of shares at a discount where the acquisition had been triggered by their wrongful conduct, especially if there was reason to suspect or believe that their conduct, or some material part of it, might have been influenced by a desire to buy out or worsen the position of the minority. In the instant case, the petitioner was not a quasi-partner in any relevant sense at the material time. However, the fair course in the circumstances was to require the petitioner's shares to be valued on an undiscounted basis: she would receive a rateable proportion of the value of the shares of the company as a whole.

19.33 There may be circumstances where the petitioner seeks an order for the respondent to purchase his shares, and the issue arises whether the respondent has the financial means to purchase the petitioner's shares, or whether the court may invoke an 'escape clause' and order another remedy under CA 2006, s 996.

The court will not include an 'escape clause' in considering the appropriate remedy to be granted under CA 2006, s 996

In *Re Cumana Ltd* [1986] BCLC 430, it was contended by the respondent company that the order to purchase the petitioner's shares should have contained an 'escape clause' to enable the court to order alternative relief should the company be unable to raise the money to buy the shares. The Court of Appeal rejected this view.

According to Lawton LJ, the fact that a wrongdoer was impecunious was no reason why judgment should not be given against him for the amount of compensation due to his victim. See too *Scottish Co-operative Wholesale Society Ltd v Meyer* [1958] 3 All ER 66 at 89, [1959] AC 324 at 369, per Lord Denning. Nicholls LJ stated that the 'difficulties in formulating and implementing an appropriate escape clause were such as to make this proposal impracticable and unsatisfactory'.

An escape clause was not an appropriate where it was conceded by the company that unfair prejudicial conduct had occurred

In *Re Scitec Group Ltd* [2011] 1 BCLC 277, Newey J was of the view that an escape clause should not be included in the appropriate relief to be granted, particularly where the company had conceded that there had been unfair prejudicial conduct which affected the petitioner. The petitioner further required the certainty of a purchase of shares by the company, particularly where the petitioner had not committed a wrong and where his conduct was not open to any serious criticism.

Supplementary provisions

Application of general rule-making powers

19.34 The power to make rules under s 411 of the Insolvency Act 1986 (c 45) or Article 359 of the Insolvency (Northern Ireland) Order 1989 (SI 1989 No 2405 (NI 19)), so far as relating to a winding-up petition, applies for the purposes of a petition under this Part: CA 2006, s 997.

Copy of order affecting company's constitution to be delivered to registrar

19.35 Where an order of the court under Part 30:

(a) alters the company's constitution; or

(b) gives leave for the company to make any, or any specified, alterations to its constitution,

the company must deliver a copy of the order to the registrar: CA 2006, s 998(1).

It must do so within 14 days from the making of the order or such longer period as the court may allow: CA 2006, s 998(2).

19.36 If a company makes default in complying with this section, an offence is committed by:

(a) the company; and

(b) every officer of the company who is in default: CA 2006, s 998(3).

A person guilty of an offence under this section is liable on summary conviction to a fine not exceeding level 3 on the standard scale and, for continued contravention, a daily default fine not exceeding one-tenth of level 3 on the standard scale: CA 2006, s 998(4).

Supplementary provisions where company's constitution altered

19.37 Section 999 applies where an order under Part 30 alters a company's constitution: CA 2006, s 999(1).

If the order amends:

(a) a company's articles; or

(b) any resolution or agreement to which Chapter 3 of Part 3 applies (resolution or agreement affecting a company's constitution), the copy of the order delivered to the registrar by the company under s 998 must be accompanied by a copy of the company's articles, or the resolution or agreement in question, as amended: CA 2006, s 999(2).

19.38 Every copy of a company's articles issued by the company after the order is made must be accompanied by a copy of the order, unless the effect of the order has been incorporated into the articles by amendment: CA 2006, s 999(3).

If a company makes default in complying with s 999 an offence is committed by:

(a) the company; and

(b) every officer of the company who is in default: CA 2006, s 999(4).

A person guilty of an offence under this section is liable on summary conviction to a fine not exceeding level 3 on the standard scale: CA 2006, s 999(5).

Checklist: unfair prejudice applications

19.39 *This checklist sets out the procedural aspects governing the application for unfair prejudice applications. The Companies (Unfair Prejudice Applications) Proceedings Rules 2009 SI 2009/2469 ('Rules'), apply in relation to petitions presented to the court under Pt 30 of the CA 2006 (protection of company's members against unfair prejudice) by a member of a company under s 994(1), by a person treated as a member under s 994(2) or by the Secretary of State under s 995.*

Except so far as inconsistent with the CA 2006 and these Rules, the Civil Procedure Rules 1998 also apply to proceedings under Pt 30 of the CA 2006 with any necessary modifications.

No	Issue	Reference
1	The provisions concerning the applications for unfair prejudicial conduct are set out in further detail by way of Statutory Instrument	The Companies (Unfair Prejudice Applications) Proceedings Rules 2009 SI 2009/2469
2	**Presentation of petition** • The petition shall be in the form set out in the Schedule to these Rules, with such variations, if any, as the circumstances may require. • The petition shall specify the grounds on which it is presented and the nature of the relief which is sought by the petitioner, and shall be delivered to the court for filing with sufficient copies for service under Rule 4.	Paragraph 3

No	Issue	Reference
	• The court shall fix a hearing for a day ('the return day') on which, unless the court otherwise directs, the petitioner and any respondent (including the company) shall attend before the registrar or District Judge for directions to be given in relation to the procedure on the petition. • On fixing the return day, the court shall return to the petitioner sealed copies of the petition for service, each endorsed with the return day and the time of hearing.	
3	**Service of petition** • The petitioner shall, at least 14 days before the return day, serve a sealed copy of the petition on the company. • In the case of a petition based upon s 994 CA 2006, the petitioner shall also, at least 14 days before the return day, serve a sealed copy of the petition on every respondent named in the petition.	Paragraph 4
4	**Return of petition** On the return day, or at any time after it, the court shall give such directions as it thinks appropriate with respect to the following matters: (a) service of the petition on any person, whether in connection with the time, date and place of a further hearing, or for any other purpose; (b) whether points of claim and defence are to be delivered; (c) whether, and if so by what means, the petition is to be advertised; (d) the manner in which any evidence is to be adduced at any hearing before the judge and in particular (but without prejudice to the generality of the above) as to: (i) the taking of evidence wholly or in part by witness statement or orally; (ii) the cross-examination of any persons making a witness statement; (iii) the matters to be dealt with in evidence;	Paragraph 5

No	Issue	Reference
	(e) any other matter affecting the procedure on the petition or in connection with the hearing and disposal of the petition; and (f) such orders, if any, including a stay for any period, as the court thinks fit, with a view to mediation or other alternative dispute resolution.	
5	**Advertisement of the order** If the court considers that the order should be advertised, it shall give directions as to the manner and time of advertisement.	Paragraph 6

20 Company secretaries

Contents

Introduction

20.1 The role of company secretaries was previously limited to simple administration with few assigned responsibilities and duties within the corporate governance framework. The secretary's tasks were largely confined to ordering company stationery and acting on the instructions of company officers for specific delegated functions, and some filing requirements at Companies House.

However, the modern perception of company secretaries has changed, particularly with regard to public and listed companies, where the company secretarial role in discharging corporate governance duties within the company has become increasingly significant.

20.2 This chapter considers the role and function of the company secretary under the Companies Act 2006 and the UK Corporate Governance Code 2012, the circumstances when a company secretary may be appointed, including the important role of the company secretary in public companies.

This chapter addresses the following issues:

- whether a company secretary is required to be appointed by a private company;
- the requirements and qualifications for the appointment of a company secretary for public companies;
- the role and function of the company secretary;
- the applicability of the UK Corporate Governance Code to company secretaries;

The chapter also includes checklists on the appointment and dismissal of a company secretary.

Private company exemption

20.3 Under CA 2006, s 270(1), private companies are not required to have a secretary. If a secretary was appointed before 6 April 2008, the secretary may resign or his or her appointment terminated. As from 6 April 2008, it is optional for a private company as to whether it appoints a company secretary. If it chooses not to do so, the company and its officers must continue to discharge their obligations in compliance with the Companies Act 2006. It a private company chooses to have a company secretary, his or her status will be the same as previously.

CA 2006 defines a private company 'without a secretary' as a company which has taken advantage of the exemption under s 270: CA 2006, s 270(2). Any references to a private company 'with a secretary' should be construed accordingly.

For private companies without a secretary:

(a) anything authorised or required to be given or sent to, or served on, the company by being sent to its secretary:

  (i) may be given or sent to, or served on, the company itself; and

  (ii) if addressed to the secretary will be treated as addressed to the company; and

(b) anything else required or authorised to be done by or to the secretary of the company may be done by or to:

  (i) a director; or

  (ii) a person authorised generally or specifically in that behalf by the directors: CA 2006, s 270(3).

20.4 Where a private company's articles of association immediately before 6 April 2008 expressly required it to have a secretary, it is treated as a company 'with a secretary' for the purposes of CA 2006, s 270(2), until its articles are amended to remove the requirement. In this regard, a provision:

(a) requiring or authorising things to be done by or in relation to a secretary; or

(b) as to the manner in which, or terms on which, a secretary is to be appointed or removed,

is not a provision expressly requiring the company to have a secretary: *Companies Act 2006 (Commencement No 5, Transitional Provisions and Savings) Order 2007, SI 2007/3495, Sch 4, para 4.*

Public companies

20.5 Under CA 2006, s 271, a public company must appoint a company secretary. The secretary must be qualified to act as such under CA 2006, s 273.

In respect of both a private company and a public company, a secretary cannot act as the statutory auditor of the company: CA 2006, s 1214. Further, on the company's incorporation, if a company secretary is to be appointed, details of the secretary (or joint secretaries) should be notified to Registrar at Companies House: CA 2006, s 12(1)(b). Form INO1 should be used. For subsequent appointments, Forms APO3 (Appointment of Secretary) or APO4 should be used. Form TMO2 is used for termination of the secretary's appointment. Forms CHO3 (Change of Secretary's Details) and CHO4 (Change of Corporate Secretary's Details) should be used.

Qualifications of secretaries of public companies

20.6 A secretary of a public company must be a qualified person to act in that capacity. It is the duty of the directors of a public company to take all reasonable steps to secure that the secretary (or each joint secretary) of the company:

(a) is a person who appears to them to have the requisite knowledge and experience to discharge the functions of secretary of the company; and

(b) has one or more stipulated qualifications: CA 2006, s 273(1).

20.7 Thus, a person seeking the position of company secretary in a public company must satisfy one or more of the following qualifications:

(a) he has held the office of secretary of a public company for at least three of the five years immediately preceding his appointment as secretary;

(b) he is a member of any of the bodies specified in s 273(3);

(c) he is a barrister, advocate or solicitor called or admitted in any part of the UK;

(d) he is a person who, by virtue of his holding or having held any other position or his being a member of any other body, appears to the directors to be capable of discharging the functions of secretary of the company.

20.8 The bodies referred to (in (b) above) are:

(a) the Institute of Chartered Accountants in England and Wales;

(b) the Institute of Chartered Accountants of Scotland;

(c) the Association of Chartered Certified Accountants;

(d) the Institute of Chartered Accountants in Ireland;

(e) the Institute of Chartered Secretaries and Administrators;

(f) the Chartered Institute of Management Accountants;

(g) the Chartered Institute of Public Finance and Accountancy: CA 2006, s 273(3).

Direction requiring public company to appoint secretary

20.9 Where it appears to the Secretary of State that a public company is in breach of s 271 (requirement to have a secretary), the Secretary of State may give the company a direction: CA 2006, s 272(1).

Such direction must state that the company appears to be in breach of that section and specify:

(a) what the company must do in order to comply with the direction; and

(b) the period within which it must do so.

That period must be not less than one month or more than three months after the date on which the direction is given: CA 2006, s 272(2). The direction must also inform the company of the consequences of failing to comply: CA 2006, s 272(3).

20.10 Under s 272(4), where the company is in breach of s 271 it must comply with the direction by:

(a) making the necessary appointment; and

(b) giving notice of it under s 276,

before the end of the period specified in the direction.

20.11 If the company has already made the necessary appointment, it must comply with the direction by giving notice of it under s 276 before the end of the period specified in the direction: CA 2006, s 272(5). If it fails to comply with a direction under this section, an offence is committed by:

(a) the company; and

(b) every officer of the company who is in default.

For this purpose, a shadow director is treated as an officer of the company: CA 2006, s 272(6).

A person guilty of an offence under this section is liable on summary conviction to a fine not exceeding level 5 on the standard scale and, for continued contravention, a daily default fine not exceeding one-tenth of level 5 on the standard scale: CA 2006, s 272(7).

Discharge of function where office vacant or secretary unable to act

20.12 Where in the case of any company, the office of secretary is vacant, or there is for any other reason no secretary capable of acting, anything required or authorised to be done by or to the secretary may be done:

(a) by or to an assistant or deputy secretary (if any); or

(b) if there is no assistant or deputy secretary or none capable of acting, by or to any person authorised generally or specifically in that behalf by the directors: CA 2006, s 274.

Duty to keep register of secretaries

20.13 Under CA 2006, s 275(1), a company must keep a register of its secretaries and this must contain the required particulars (see ss 277–279) of the person or persons who are the secretary or joint secretaries of the company: CA 2006, s 275(2). The register must be kept available for inspection:

(a) at the company's registered office; or

(b) at a place specified in regulations under s 1136: CA 2006, s 275(3).

The company must give notice to the registrar of the place at which the register is kept available for inspection and of any change in that place, unless it has at all times been kept at the company's registered office: CA 2006, s 275(4).

20.14 The register must be open to the inspection:

(a) of any member of the company without charge; and

(b) of any other person on payment of such fee as may be prescribed: CA 2006, s 275(5).

20.15 If default is made in complying with s 275(1), (2) or (3), or default is made for 14 days in complying with s 275(4), or an inspection required under s 275(5) is refused, an offence is committed by:

(a) the company; and

(b) every officer of the company who is in default.

For this purpose, a shadow director is treated as an officer of the company: CA 2006, s 275(6).

A person guilty of an offence under this section is liable on summary conviction to a fine not exceeding level 5 on the standard scale and, for continued contravention, a daily default fine not exceeding one-tenth of level 5 on the standard scale: CA 2006, s 275(7).

In the event of a refusal of inspection of the register, the court may by order compel an immediate inspection of it: CA 2006, s 275(8).

Duty to notify registrar of changes

20.16 A company must, within a period of 14 days from:

(a) a person becoming or ceasing to be its secretary or one of its joint secretaries; or

(b) the occurrence of any change in the particulars contained in its register of secretaries;

give notice to the registrar of the change and of the date on which it occurred: CA 2006, s 276(1). Form CHO3 (Change of Secretary's Details) or Form CHO4 (Change of Corporate Secretary's details) should be used.

20.17 Notice of a person having become secretary, or one of joint secretaries, of the company must be accompanied by a statement by the company that the person has consented to act in the relevant capacity: CA 2006, s 276(2) (as inserted by SBEEA 2015, s 100(5)).

If default is made in complying with this section, an offence is committed by every officer of the company who is in default, and for this purpose, a shadow director is treated as an officer of the company: s 276(3) CA 2006.

A person guilty of an offence under this section is liable on summary conviction to a fine not exceeding level 5 on the standard scale and, for continued contravention, a daily default fine not exceeding one-tenth of level 5 on the standard scale: CA 2006, s 276(4).

Particulars of secretaries to be registered: individuals

20.18 A company's register of secretaries must contain the following particulars in the case of an individual:

(a) name and any former name;

(b) address: CA 2006, s 277(1).

20.19 For the purposes of this section 'name' means a person's Christian name (or other forename) and surname, except that in the case of:

(a) a peer; or

(b) an individual usually known by a title,

the title may be stated instead of his Christian name (or other forename) and surname or in addition to either or both of them: CA 2006, s 277(2).

20.20 A 'former name' means a name by which the individual was formerly known for business purposes. Where a person is or was formerly known by more than one such name, each of them must be stated: CA 2006, s 277(3).
It is not necessary for the register to contain particulars of a former name in the following cases:

(a) in the case of a peer or an individual normally known by a British title, where the name is one by which the person was known previous to the adoption of or succession to the title;

(b) in the case of any person, where the former name:

  (i) was changed or disused before the person attained the age of 16 years; or

  (ii) has been changed or disused for 20 years or more: CA 2006, s 277(4).

20.21 The address required to be stated in the register is a service address. This may be stated to be 'The company's registered office': CA 2006, s 277(5). There is no requirement to provide the residential address of the secretary.

Once the company is incorporated, the person(s) who are named are deemed to be appointed: CA 2006, s 16(6).

Particulars of secretaries to be registered: corporate secretaries and firms

20.22 A company's register of secretaries must contain the following particulars in the case of a body corporate, or a firm that is a legal person under the law by which it is governed:

(a) corporate or firm name;

(b) registered or principal office;

(c) in the case of an EEA company to which the First Company Law Directive (68/151/EEC) applies, particulars of:

 (i) the register in which the company file mentioned in Article 3 of that Directive is kept (including details of the relevant state); and

 (ii) the registration number in that register;

(d) in any other case, particulars of:

 (i) the legal form of the company or firm and the law by which it is governed; and

 (ii) if applicable, the register in which it is entered (including details of the state) and its registration number in that register: CA 2006, s 278(1).

If all the partners in a firm are joint secretaries, it is sufficient to state the particulars that would be required if the firm were a legal person and the firm had been appointed secretary: CA 2006, s 278(2).

Particulars of secretaries to be registered: power to make regulations

20.23 Under CA 2006, s 279(2) the Secretary of State may make provision by regulations amending:

(a) s 277 (particulars of secretaries to be registered: individuals); or

(b) s 278 (particulars of secretaries to be registered: corporate secretaries and firms),

so as to add to or remove items from the particulars required to be contained in a company's register of secretaries: CA 2006, s 279.

Acts done by person in dual capacity

20.24 Under CA 2006, s 280 a provision requiring or authorising a thing to be done by or to a director and the secretary of a company, is not satisfied by its being done by or to the same person acting both as director and as, or in place of, the secretary.

Duties and functions of a company secretary

20.25 The duties and functions of a company secretary are varied and wide-ranging under the Companies Act 2006, and generally under common law and the law of contract, include authority to bind the company. Some of the essential duties and functions include the following:

- ensuring compliance with the company's articles of association and memorandum of association;
- preparing background reports and research papers for board/shareholders' meetings;
- completing the statutory registers including register of members (CA 2006, s 114); secretaries (CA 2006, s 265); directors (CA 2006, s 162); debenture holders (CA 2006, s 743); and company charges (CA 2006, ss 877 and 892);
- compliance with the statutory returns including company's reports and financial accounts; annual returns; appointment and removal of directors/secretary/auditor; filing amendments to the company's articles of association;
- ensuring compliance with the UK Corporate Governance Code as applicable to listed companies including independent advice to the board on governance aspects;
- ensuring good communication flow between directors and shareholders within the corporate governance structure;
- assisting in ensuring that directors receive induction and training on their duties, functions and liabilities;
- organising and convening board and shareholders' meetings which includes sending notices of meetings;
- preparing minutes of board and shareholders' meetings;
- where appropriate, ensuring that the company's website contains accurate and true information including details of any forthcoming meetings;
- ensuring that all proper and correct procedures are followed in connection with convening meetings and matters to be attended to after the meetings;
- maintaining good shareholder communications generally and attending to their queries on any corporate matters arising.

Significant cases on company secretaries

20.26

A secretary does not have authority to make representations on the company's behalf

In *Barnet, Hoares & Co v South London Tramway Co* (1887) 18 QB D 815, the Court of Appeal held that a secretary did not have authority to make any representations on behalf of the company. Lord Esher MR considered that a secretary is a mere servant of the company; his position was that he was to do what he was told, and no person could assume that he had any authority to represent anything at all; nor could anyone assume that statements made by him were necessarily to be accepted as trustworthy without further inquiry.

Fry LJ also agreed that the company secretary could not bind the company as the secretary had no authority to make any representations to bind the company.

According to Lopes LJ, it would be unreasonable to make an inference that the secretary had authority to make any representation on the company's behalf such as to bind the company.

The duties of a secretary are limited to purely administrative matters

The *Barnet, Hoares & Co v South London Tramway Co* decision was followed in *George Whitechurch Ltd v Cavanagh* [1902] AC 117. In this case, transfer of shares in a company having been lodged with the company's secretary without the certificates for the shares, the secretary fraudulently certified upon the transfers that the certificates for the shares were in the company's office. The proposed transferee brought an action against the company for refusing to register him as the owner. It was held by the House of Lords that in permitting its secretary to certify transfers of shares, a company did not authorise the secretary to do more than give a receipt for certificates of shares which were actually lodged in the office. If the secretary gave a receipt or an acknowledgment for certificates which had not been lodged, the company was not estopped from setting up the true facts.

Lord Macnaghten stated: 'Now, the duties of a company's secretary are well understood. They are of a limited and of a somewhat humble character'.

See too: *Ruben v Great Fingall Consolidated* [1906] AC 439 (secretary had no authority to act for the company in the transaction).

A company secretary has wider responsibilities and duties, which are not limited to administrative matters

However, the modern position of company secretaries was examined by the Court of Appeal in *Panorama Developments (Guildford) Ltd v Fidelis Furnishing*

Fabrics Ltd [1971] 2 QB 711 in which the Court of Appeal decided that Lord Esher's dicta that a company secretary was a mere servant could no longer be accepted. According to Lord Denning:

> 'But times have changed. A company secretary is a much more important person nowadays than he was in 1887. He is an officer of the company with extensive duties and responsibilities. This appears not only in the modern Companies Acts, but also by the role which he plays in the day-to-day business of companies. He is no longer a mere clerk. He regularly makes representations on behalf of the company and enters into contracts on its behalf which come within the day-to-day running of the company's business. So much so that he may be regarded as held out as having authority to do such things on behalf of the company. He is certainly entitled to sign contracts connected with the administrative side of a company's affairs, such as employing staff, and ordering cars, and so forth. All such matters now come within the ostensible authority of a company's secretary'.

Lord Denning decided that on the facts, the company secretary had ostensible authority to enter into contracts for the hire of these cars and, therefore, the company was required to pay for them: 'Mr. Bayne was a fraud. But it was the company which put him in the position in which he, as company secretary, was able to commit the frauds'. The company was therefore held liable to pay for the hire of the cars.

Salmon LJ noted that the company secretary's position had changed since 1887. The 'humble position' previously occupied by the secretary had given way to a person who had an enhanced authority, status and responsibility within the company. The secretary was now considered as the chief administrative officer of the company. As regards matters concerned with administration, the secretary had ostensible authority to sign contracts on the company's behalf.

In undertaking his functions as a company secretary, he was not concerned with carrying on the company's business under the CA 2006

In *Re Maidstone Buildings Provisions Ltd* [1971] 1 WLR 1085, Mr Penny (P') was the secretary of a company, Maidstone Buildings Provisions Limited ('M Limited'), a position which he held from March 1960 until his resignation on 21 November 1962. He was re-appointed secretary on 13 December 1962 but resigned again in April 1965. M Limited went into voluntary liquidation in June 1965. At all material times P was a partner in a firm of chartered accountants who were the company's auditors. Liquidator brought proceedings against the directors of M Limited, and also, on different grounds, against P, alleging *inter alia* that M Limited was insolvent, and that, since March 1961, the directors and P, knowing that the company was trading at a loss and was insolvent, had regularly caused the company to purchase goods company on credit and to incur debts in respect of wages, salaries and other outgoings. So far as P was concerned, it was alleged that as secretary and financial adviser, he had failed to advise the directors that the company was insolvent and should cease to trade, and thus was 'knowingly [a party] to the carrying on of the business' of M Limited in a fraudulent manner, within the provisions of the Companies Act dealing with fraudulent trading. P applied for the proceedings against him to be struck out on the ground that they disclosed no reasonable cause of action.

Pennycuick V-C held that P was entitled to the relief sought. In performing the duties appropriate to the office of secretary, he was not concerned in carrying on the business of the company. Furthermore, in order to be a party to the carrying on of the business of a company within the Companies Act, a person must have taken some positive steps, mere inertia was not enough. Accordingly, on the assumption that, in addition to being secretary, P had also acted as financial adviser to the company and that, as such, he was under a duty to give advice to the directors, the failure to give that advice was not sufficient to render him a party to the carrying on of the company's business. With regard to a company secretary, Pennycuick was of the view that while merely performing the duties appropriate to the office of secretary, the company secretary was not concerned in the management in the company. Further, the company secretary was not concerned in carrying on the business of the company. However, in other situations, a person who held the office of secretary may in some other capacity be concerned in the management of the company's business.

Under CA 2006, s 1173, an 'officer' in relation to a body corporate, includes a director, manager or secretary. The effect of this definition is that for certain purposes of the CA 2006, the secretary may be liable for certain penalties set out in various provisions of the CA 2006.

Applicability of the UK Corporate Governance Code to company secretaries

20.27 According to the Cadbury Committee's 'Report on the Financial Aspects of Corporate Governance' (1992), the company secretary was perceived as a person providing impartial advice to the company's Board of Directors on their duties and responsibilities. The Committee stated:

> 'The company secretary has a key role to play in ensuring that board procedures are both followed and regularly reviewed. The chairman and the board will look to the company secretary for guidance on what their responsibilities are under the rules and regulations to which they are subject and on how those responsibilities should be discharged. All directors should have access to the advice and services of the company secretary and should recognise that the chairman is entitled to the strong and positive support of the company secretary in ensuring the effective functioning of the board. It should be standard practice for the company secretary to administer, attend and prepare minutes of board proceedings.

Under the Companies Act the directors have a duty to appoint as secretary someone who is capable of carrying out the duties which the post entails. The responsibility for ensuring that the secretary remains capable, and any question of the secretary's removal, should be a matter for the board as a whole.

The Committee expects that the company secretary will be a source of advice to the chairman and to the board on the implementation of the Code of Best Practice.' (para 4.25)

Checklist of provisions governing the role and function of company secretaries

20.28 *The UK Corporate Governance Code 2012 contains some provisions governing the role and function of company secretaries for a premium listed company. The following checklist applies:*

No	Issue	Reference
1	**Main principle** The board should be supplied in a timely manner with information in a form and of a quality appropriate to enable it to discharge its duties.	B.5: Information and Support
2	**Supporting principles** The chairman is responsible for ensuring that the directors receive accurate, timely and clear information. Management has an obligation to provide such information but directors should seek clarification or amplification where necessary. Under the direction of the chairman, the company secretary's responsibilities include ensuring good information flows within the board and its committees and between senior management and non-executive directors, as well as facilitating induction and assisting with professional development as required. The company secretary should be responsible for advising the board through the chairman on all governance matters.	
3	**Code provisions** The board should ensure that directors, especially non-executive directors, have access to independent professional advice at the company's expense where they judge it necessary to discharge their responsibilities as directors. Committees should be provided with sufficient resources to undertake their duties.	B.5.1.

No	Issue	Reference
	All directors should have access to the advice and services of the company secretary, who is responsible to the board for ensuring that board procedures are complied with. Both the appointment and removal of the company secretary should be a matter for the board as a whole.	B.5.2.

Checklist for appointing a company secretary

20.29 *Note: A company secretary is not required for a private company limited by shares. The following checklist only applies if one is appointed and it sets out the steps and procedures for appointment. The checklist also applies to the appointment of a company secretary in a public company. The appointment may be governed by a company's articles of association. If the company has adopted Table A 1985, regulation 99 provides for the appointment by the directors. However, the Model Articles for private and public companies do not set any provisions for the appointment of a company secretary. Companies established after 1 October 2009 may either need to amend their articles to include a provision for the appointment of a company secretary or modify the Model Articles to include such provision.*

A suggested provision would be:

> *'Subject to the provisions of the Companies Act 2006, the secretary shall be appointed by the directors for such term, at such remuneration and upon such conditions as they may think fit; and any secretary so appointed may be removed by them'.*

The checklist set out below on the procedure will need to be adapted depending upon the procedures set out in the company's articles of association on convening a board meeting.

No	Issue	Reference
1	Prospective secretary to write to the company's board of directors of interest in acting as the company secretary. The company's auditor cannot act as the company's secretary. The secretary of a public company must be qualified to act as a secretary of such company. A person must consent to being appointed as the company's secretary.	CA 2006, s 1214 CA 2006, s 276(2) (as inserted by SBEEA 2015, s 100(5))
2	Prepare a Board Agenda setting out details of the proposed appointment and terms upon which employment will be made. Board to convene a meeting on reasonable notice. Notice to state date, time and place of the meeting.	Articles of association. Employment contract or written particulars: Employment Rights Act 1996, s 1
3	Ensure quorum available at the board meeting.	Articles of association

No	Issue	Reference
4	Directors vote by simple majority at the board meeting on the appointment of the company secretary. Consider whether the company secretary will be remunerated and terms of remuneration and any employment contract or written particulars of employment. Also, whether the company secretary will be a signatory to any of the company's bank accounts and financial authority limits? Will any professional liability indemnity insurance be taken out in respect of the company secretary?	Employment Rights Act 1996, s 1
5	Consider dispensing with a board meeting if directors can pass a written resolution for the appointment of the company secretary.	Articles of Association
6	After the board meeting, prepare minutes of the meeting recording appointment of the company secretary.	Minutes
7	Update the company's statutory books. Complete the Register of Secretaries.	CA 2006, s 275
8	Secretary to also provide a service address which need not be the residential address. File at Companies House on the appointment of the company secretary.	CA 2006, s 277(1)
	Details required for a non-corporate secretary are: • company number; • company name; • date of appointment; • date of birth; • full name of secretary; • full service address; • the signature of the new secretary.	Within 14 days, use Form IN01 (Application to register a company) for the first appointment upon incorporation of the company.
	Details required for a corporate secretary are: • whether the company is being appointed within the EEA; • country of registration; • registration number; • governing law (Non EEA companies); • legal form (Non EEA companies).	For subsequent appointments use Form APO3 (Appointment of a non-corporate secretary) or AP04 (Appointment of a corporate secretary): CA 2006, s 276
	Consider a change to bank mandate forms and secretary as signatory to company bank account	Bank mandate forms

Checklist for company secretary's dismissal

20.30 *This checklist applies where a company secretary is to be dismissed from office. The matter is considered at the board meeting and not at a shareholders' meeting. The CA 2006 does not address the position of removal of a secretary. Therefore, this aspect is considered to be within the authority of the directors.*

No	Issue	Reference
1	Prepare a Board Agenda setting out details of the proposed termination. Board to ensure it has considered applicable employment law issues on termination of the contract of employment and followed appropriate procedures for termination. Board to convene on reasonable notice. Notice to state date, time and place of meeting.	Articles of association Employment Rights Act 1996 and/or other employment legislation
2	Ensure quorum available at the board meeting.	Articles of association
3	Directors to consider the grounds for dismissal and whether a fair dismissal including carrying out proper steps and procedures of an investigative nature in connection with the performance or conduct of the company secretary. HR report should be obtained and any other supporting evidence of proposed dismissal.	HR report Employment/service contract Settlement agreement
4	Consider also terms of the employment/service contract including any restrictive covenants and restraint of trade/non-solicitation clauses.	
5	Consider also whether a settlement agreement may be appropriate in the circumstances.	
6	Directors vote by simple majority on a show of hands at the board meeting on the dismissal of the company secretary.	
7	Consider dispensing with a board meeting if directors can pass a written resolution for the dismissal of the company secretary.	Articles of Association
8	After the board meeting, prepare minutes of the meeting recording dismissal of the company secretary.	Minutes
9	Update the company's statutory books.	Register of Secretaries

No	Issue	Reference
10	File at Companies House on the termination of the company secretary. This will also apply on the company secretary's resignation. Note: In respect of public companies, if a public company does not appoint a company secretary, the Secretary of State can issue a direction requiring such appointment and the date within which the appointment must be made (within one to three months from the date of the Secretary of State's direction)	Within 14 days, use Form TM02 (Termination of Appointment of Secretary) CA 2006, s 272

Prescribed forms for secretaries

20.31 The following are the prescribed forms for secretaries, which are required to be registered at Companies House as appropriate.

Form No:	Details
INO1:	Application to register a company (upon incorporation)
APO3:	Appointment of Secretary
APO4:	Appointment of Corporate Secretary
TMO2:	Terminating appointment as secretary
AR01:	Annual return for returns made up to a date on or after 1 October 2011
CHO3:	Change of particulars for secretary
CHO4:	Change of particulars of corporate secretary

Definitions

20.32

Former Name: A name by which the individual was formerly known for business purposes. Where a person is or was formerly known by more than one such name, each of them must be stated: CA 2006, s 277(3).

Name: A person's Christian name (or other forename) and surname except that in the case of:

(a) a peer; or

(b) an individual usually known by a title,

the title may be stated instead of his Christian name (or other forename) and surname or in addition to either or both of them: CA 2006, s 277(2).

Officer: in relation to a body corporate, includes a director, manager or secretary.

21 Resolutions and meetings

Contents

Introduction

21.1 UK company law and the CA 2006 establish a demarcation in the responsibilities of directors and shareholders in the corporate governance structure. Company directors are accountable to the shareholders for their actions with shareholders having residual authority over governance issues. This aspect is reflected in the division of responsibilities of directors and shareholders in convening meetings to consider specific aspects of the company's operations and business.

This Chapter addresses the following aspects taking account of the amendments under SBEEA 2015 and the DA 2015:

- The different forms of resolutions.
- The practice and procedure for convening meetings.
- The circumstances where meetings may be dispensed with.
- The concept of informal unanimous consent of shareholders.

Resolutions

21.2 A distinction is made under the CA 2006 between resolutions passed by a private company and those passed by a public company. A resolution of the members (or of a class of members) of a *private* company must be passed:

(a) as a written resolution in accordance with CA 2006, Pt 13, Ch 2; or

(b) at a meeting of the members (to which the provisions of CA 2006, Pt 13, Ch 3 apply): CA 2006, s 281(1).

A resolution of the members (or of a class of members) of a *public* company must be passed at a meeting of the members (to which the provisions of CA 2006, Pt 13, Ch 3 and, where relevant, Ch 4 apply): CA 2006, s 281(2).

21.3 Where a provision of the Companies Acts:

(a) requires a resolution of a company, or of the members (or a class of members) of a company; and

(b) does not specify what kind of resolution is required,

what is required is an ordinary resolution unless the company's articles require a higher majority (or unanimity): CA 2006, s 281(3).

21.4 Part 13 of the CA 2006 does not affect any enactment or rule of law as to:

(a) things done otherwise than by passing a resolution;

(b) circumstances in which a resolution is or is not treated as having been passed; or

(c) cases in which a person is precluded from alleging that a resolution has not been duly passed: CA 2006, s 281(4).

Ordinary resolutions

21.5 An ordinary resolution of the members (or of a class of members) of a company means a resolution that is passed by a simple majority: CA 2006, s 282(1).

A written resolution is passed by a simple majority if it is passed by members representing a simple majority of the total voting rights of eligible members (see CA 2006, Pt 13, Ch 2): CA 2006, s 282(2).

A resolution passed at a meeting on a show of hands is passed by a simple majority if it is passed by a simple majority of the votes cast by those entitled to vote: CA 2006, s 282(3).

A resolution passed on a poll taken at a meeting is passed by a simple majority if it is passed by members representing a simple majority of the total voting rights of members who (being entitled to do so) vote in person, by proxy or in advance (see CA 2006, s 322A) on the resolution: CA 2006, s 282(4).

Anything that may be done by ordinary resolution may also be done by special resolution: CA 2006, s 282(5).

Special resolutions

21.6 A special resolution of the members (or of a class of members) of a company means a resolution passed by a majority of not less than 75%: CA 2006, s 283(1).

A written resolution is passed by a majority of not less than 75% if it is passed by members representing not less than 75% of the total voting rights of eligible members (see CA 2006, Pt 13, Ch 2): CA 2006, s 283(2).

21.7 Where a resolution of a private company is passed as a written resolution:

(a) the resolution is not a special resolution unless it stated that it was proposed as a special resolution; and

(b) if the resolution so stated, it may only be passed as a special resolution: CA 2006, s 283(3).

A resolution passed at a meeting on a show of hands is passed by a majority of not less than 75% if it is passed by not less than 75% of the votes cast by those entitled to vote: CA 2006, s 283(4).

A resolution passed on a poll taken at a meeting is passed by a majority of not less than 75% if it is passed by members representing not less than 75% of the total voting rights of the members who (being entitled to do so) vote in person, by proxy or in advance (see CA 2006, s 322A) on the resolution: CA 2006, s 283(5).

21.8 Where a resolution is passed at a meeting:

(a) the resolution is not a special resolution unless the notice of the meeting included the text of the resolution and specified the intention to propose the resolution as a special resolution; and

(b) if the notice of the meeting so specified, the resolution may only be passed as a special resolution: CA 2006, s 283(6).

The text of the resolution must state that it is a special resolution to ensure its validity

In *Moorgate Mercantile Holdings Limited* [1980] 1 All ER 40, the court was required to determine the validity of the special resolution for reduction of capital. The issue was whether the resolution as passed was substantially the same as that proposed.

Slade J held that a notice of intention to propose a special resolution was valid for the purpose only if it identified the intended resolution by specifying either the text or the entire substance of the resolution which it was intended to propose. Further, a special resolution was validly passed in accordance with CA 2006 only if it was the same resolution as that identified in the preceding notice. In deciding whether there was complete identity between the substance of the resolution as passed and the substance of the intended resolution as notified there was no room for the application of the *de minimis* principle. If, however, the resolution as passed either departed in some respects from the text of the resolution set out in the preceding notice (eg on account of the correction of grammatical or clerical errors or the use of more formal language) or was reduced into the form of a new text which was not included in the notice, it could properly be regarded as 'the resolution' identified in the notice provided there had been no departure from the substance of the circulated text.

Votes: general rules

21.9 On a vote on a written resolution:

(a) in the case of a company having a share capital, every member has one vote in respect of each share or each £10 of stock held by him; and

(b) in any other case, every member has one vote: CA 2006, s 284(1).

On a vote on a resolution on a show of hands at a meeting, each member present in person has one vote: CA 2006, s 284(2).

21.10 On a vote on a resolution on a poll taken at a meeting:

(a) in the case of a company having a share capital, every member has one vote in respect of each share or each £10 of stock held by him; and

(b) in any other case, every member has one vote: CA 2006, s 284(3).

The provisions of CA 2006, s 284 have effect subject to any provision of the company's articles: CA 2006, s 284(4).

21.11 Nothing in CA 2006, s 284 is to be read as restricting the effect of:

(1) s 152 (exercise of rights by nominees);

(2) s 285 (voting by proxy);

(3) s 322 (exercise of voting rights on poll);

(4) s 322A (voting on a poll: votes cast in advance); or

(5) s 323 (representation of corporations at meetings): CA 2006, s 284(5).

Voting by proxy

21.12 On a vote on a resolution on a show of hands at a meeting, every proxy present who has been duly appointed by one or more members entitled to vote on the resolution has one vote. This is subject to s 285(2): CA 2006, s 285(1).

On a vote on a resolution on a show of hands at a meeting, a proxy has one vote for and one vote against the resolution if:

(a) the proxy has been duly appointed by more than one member entitled to vote on the resolution; and

(b) the proxy has been instructed by one or more of those members to vote for the resolution and by one or more other of those members to vote against it: CA 2006, s 285(2).

On a poll taken at a meeting of a company all or any of the voting rights of a member may be exercised by one or more duly appointed proxies: CA 2006, s 285(3).

Where a member appoints more than one proxy, sub-s (3) does not authorise the exercise by the proxies taken together of more extensive voting rights than could be exercised by the member in person: s 285(4).

Section 285(1) and (2) have effect subject to any provision of the company's articles: CA 2006, s 285(5).

Voting rights on poll or written resolution

21.13 In relation to a resolution required or authorised by an enactment, if a private company's articles provide that a member has a different number of votes in relation to a resolution when it is passed as a written resolution and when it is passed on a poll taken at a meeting:

(a) the provision about how many votes a member has in relation to the resolution passed on a poll is void; and

(b) a member has the same number of votes in relation to the resolution when it is passed on a poll as the member has when it is passed as a written resolution.

Votes of joint holders of shares

21.14 In the case of joint holders of shares of a company, only the vote of the senior holder who votes (and any proxies duly authorised by him) may be counted by the company: CA 2006, s 286(1).

For the purposes of this section, the senior holder of a share is determined by the order in which the names of the joint holders appear in the register of members or, if an election under s 128B is in force in respect of the company, in the register kept by the registrar under s 1080): CA 2006, s 286(2) (as inserted by SBEEA 2015, Sch 5, Pt 2).

Section 286(1) and (2) have effect subject to any provision of the company's articles: CA 2006, s 286(3).

Saving for provisions of articles as a determination of entitlement to vote

21.15 Nothing in this CA 2006, Pt 13, Ch 1 affects:

(a) any provision of a company's articles:

  (i) requiring an objection to a person's entitlement to vote on a resolution to be made in accordance with the articles; and

  (ii) for the determination of any such objection to be final and conclusive, or

(b) the grounds on which such a determination may be questioned in legal proceedings: CA 2006, s 287.

Written resolution of private companies

21.16 In the Companies Acts a 'written resolution' means a resolution of a private company proposed and passed in accordance with Pt 13, Ch 2: CA 2006, s 288(1).

The following may not be passed as a written resolution:

(a) a resolution under s 168 removing a director before the expiration of his period of office;

(b) a resolution under s 510 removing an auditor before the expiration of his term of office: CA 2006, s 288(2).

21.17 A resolution may be proposed as a written resolution:

(a) by the directors of a private company (see s 291), or

(b) by the members of a private company (see ss 292–295): CA 2006, s 288(3).

21.18 References in enactments passed or made before Ch 2 comes into force to:

(a) a resolution of a company in general meeting; or

(b) a resolution of a meeting of a class of members of the company,

have effect as if they included references to a written resolution of the members, or of a class of members, of a private company (as appropriate): CA 2006, s 288(4).

21.19 A written resolution of a private company has effect as if passed (as the case may be):

(a) by the company in general meeting; or

(b) by a meeting of a class of members of the company,

and references in enactments passed or made before this section comes into force to a meeting at which a resolution is passed or to members voting in favour of a resolution shall be construed accordingly: CA 2006, s 288(5).

Eligible members

21.20 In relation to a resolution proposed as a written resolution of a private company, the eligible members are the members who would have been entitled to vote on the resolution on the circulation date of the resolution (see CA 2006, s 290): CA 2006, s 289(1).

If the persons entitled to vote on a written resolution change during the course of the day that is the circulation date of the resolution, the eligible members are the persons entitled to vote on the resolution at the time that the first copy of the resolution is sent or submitted to a member for his agreement: CA 2006, s 289(2).

Circulation date

21.21 References in CA 2006, Pt 13 to the circulation date of a written resolution are to the date on which copies of it are sent or submitted to members in accordance with Ch 2 (or if copies are sent or submitted to members on different days, to the first of those days): CA 2006, s 290.

Circulation of written resolutions proposed by directors

21.22 CA 2006, s 291 applies to a resolution proposed as a written resolution by the directors of the company: CA 2006, s 291(1). Under s 291(2), the company must send or submit a copy of the resolution to every eligible member.

The company must do so:

(a) by sending copies at the same time (so far as reasonably practicable) to all eligible members in hard copy form, in electronic form or by means of a website; or

(b) if it is possible to do so without undue delay, by submitting the same copy to each eligible member in turn (or different copies to each of a number of eligible members in turn),

or by sending copies to some members in accordance with paragraph (a) and submitting a copy or copies to other members in accordance with paragraph (b): CA 2006, s 292(3).

21.23 The copy of the resolution must be accompanied by a statement informing the member:

(a) how to signify agreement to the resolution (see s 296); and

(b) as to the date by which the resolution must be passed if it is not to lapse (see s 297): CA 2006, s 291(4).

21.24 In the event of default in complying with this section, an offence is committed by every officer of the company who is in default: CA 2006, s 291(5).

A person guilty of an offence under this section is liable:

(a) on conviction on indictment, to a fine;

(b) on summary conviction, to a fine not exceeding the statutory maximum: CA 2006, s 291(6).

The validity of the resolution, if passed, is not affected by a failure to comply with this section: CA 2006, s 291(7).

Members' power to require circulation of written resolution

21.25 The members of a private company may require the company to circulate a resolution that may properly be moved and is proposed to be moved as a written resolution: CA 2006, s 292(1).

Any resolution may properly be moved as a written resolution unless:

(a) it would, if passed, be ineffective (whether by reason of inconsistency with any enactment or the company's constitution or otherwise);

(b) it is defamatory of any person; or

(c) it is frivolous or vexatious: CA 2006, s 292(2).

21.26 Where the members require a company to circulate a resolution they may require the company to circulate with it a statement of not more than 1,000 words on the subject matter of the resolution: CA 2006, s 292(3).

A company is required to circulate the resolution and any accompanying statement once it has received requests that it do so from members representing not less than the requisite percentage of the total voting rights of all members entitled to vote on the resolution: CA 2006, s 292(4).

The 'requisite percentage' is 5% or such lower percentage as is specified for this purpose in the company's articles: CA 2006, s 292(5).

21.27 A request:

(a) may be in hard copy form or in electronic form;

(b) must identify the resolution and any accompanying statement; and

(c) must be authenticated by the person or persons making it: CA 2006, s 292(6).

Circulation of written resolution proposed by members

21.28 A company that is required under CA 2006, s 292 to circulate a resolution must send or submit to every eligible member:

(a) a copy of the resolution; and

(b) a copy of any accompanying statement.

This is subject to s 294(2) (deposit or tender of sum in respect of expenses of circulation) and s 295 (application not to circulate members' statement): CA 2006, s 293(1).

21.29 The company must do so:

(a) by sending copies at the same time (so far as reasonably practicable) to all eligible members in hard copy form, in electronic form or by means of a website; or

(b) if it is possible to do so without undue delay, by submitting the same copy to each eligible member in turn (or different copies to each of a number of eligible members in turn),

or by sending copies to some members in accordance with paragraph (a) and submitting a copy or copies to other members in accordance with paragraph (b): CA 2006, s 293(2).

21.30 The company must send or submit the copies (or, if copies are sent or submitted to members on different days, the first of those copies) not more than 21 days after it becomes subject to the requirement under CA 2006, s 292 to circulate the resolution: CA 2006, s 293(3).

The copy of the resolution must be accompanied by guidance as to:

(a) how to signify agreement to the resolution (see s 296); and

(b) the date by which the resolution must be passed if it is not to lapse (see s 297): CA 2006, s 293(4).

21.31 In the event of default in complying with this section, an offence is committed by every officer of the company who is in default: CA 2006, s 293(5).

A person guilty of an offence under this section is liable:

(a) on conviction on indictment, to a fine;

(b) on summary conviction, to a fine not exceeding the statutory maximum: CA 2006, s 293(6).

The validity of the resolution, if passed, is not affected by a failure to comply with this section: CA 2006, s 293(7).

Expenses of circulation

21.32 The expenses of the company in complying with CA 2006, s 293 must be paid by the members who requested the circulation of the resolution unless the company resolves otherwise: CA 2006, s 294(1).

Unless the company has previously so resolved, it is not bound to comply with that section unless there is deposited with or tendered to it a sum reasonably sufficient to meet its expenses in doing so: CA 2006, s 294(2).

Application not to circulate members' statements

21.33 A company is not required to circulate a members' statement under CA 2006, s 293 if, on an application by the company or another person who claims to be aggrieved, the court is satisfied that the rights conferred by s 292 and that section are being abused: CA 2006, s 295(1).

The court may order the members who requested the circulation of the statement to pay the whole or part of the company's costs (in Scotland, expenses) on such an application, even if they are not parties to the application: CA 2006, s 295(2).

Procedure for signifying agreement to written resolution

21.34 A member signifies his agreement to a proposed written resolution when the company receives from him (or from someone acting on his behalf) an authenticated document:

(a) identifying the resolution to which it relates; and

(b) indicating his agreement to the resolution: CA 2006, s 296(1).

The document must be sent to the company in hard copy form or in electronic form: CA 2006, s 296(2).

A member's agreement to a written resolution, once signified, may not be revoked: CA 2006, s 296(3).

A written resolution is passed when the required majority of eligible members have signified their agreement to it: CA 2006, s 296(4).

Period for agreeing to written resolution

21.35 A proposed written resolution lapses if it is not passed before the end of:

(a) the period specified for this purpose in the company's articles; or

(b) if none is specified, the period of 28 days beginning with the circulation date: CA 2006, s 297(1).

The agreement of a member to a written resolution is ineffective if signified after the expiry of that period: CA 2006, s 297(2).

Sending documents relating to written resolution by electronic means

21.36 Where a company has given an electronic address in any document containing or accompanying a proposed written resolution, it is deemed to have agreed that any document or information relating to that resolution may be sent by electronic means to that address (subject to any conditions or limitations specified in the document): CA 2006, s 298(1).

In this section 'electronic address' means any address or number used for the purposes of sending or receiving documents or information by electronic means: CA 2006, s 298(2).

Publication of written resolution on website

21.37 CA 2006, s 299 applies where a company sends:

(a) a written resolution; or

(b) a statement relating to a written resolution,

to a person by means of a website: CA 2006, s 299(1).

The resolution or statement is not validly sent for the purposes of Ch 2 unless the resolution is available on the website throughout the period beginning with the circulation date and ending on the date on which the resolution lapses under s 297: CA 2006, s 299(2).

Relationship between Companies Act 2006, Ch 2, Pt 13 and provisions of company's articles

21.38 A provision of the articles of a private company is void in so far as it would have the effect that a resolution that is required by or otherwise provided for in an enactment could not be proposed and passed as a written resolution: CA 2006, s 300.

Resolutions at meetings

Resolutions at general meetings

21.39 A resolution of the members of a company is validly passed at a general meeting if:

(a) notice of the meeting and of the resolution is given; and

(b) the meeting is held and conducted,

in accordance with the provisions of Ch 3 (and, where relevant, Ch 4 of Pt 13 of the CA 2006) and the company's articles: CA 2006, s 301.

The term 'meeting' in the context of company law is not defined by CA 2006. However, the ordinary meaning of the word 'meeting' denotes 'a coming together of two or more persons': *Re Altitude Scaffolding Ltd, Re T & N Limited* [2007] 1 BCLC 199 per David Richards J.

The rationale for meetings is to allow those attending to give informed consent (where possible) on company matters

In *Byng v London Life Association Ltd* [1989] BCLC 400, Sir Nicholas Browne-Wilkinson set out the rationale for meetings:

> 'The rationale behind the requirement for meetings in the [CA 2006] is that the members shall be able to attend in person so as to debate and vote on matters affecting the company. Until recently this could only be achieved by everyone being physically present in the same room face to face. Given modern technological advances, the same result can now be achieved without all the members coming face to face; without being physically in the same room they can be electronically in each other's presence so as to hear and be heard and to see and be seen. The fact that such a meeting could not have been foreseen at the time the first statutory requirements for meetings were laid down, does not require us to hold that such a meeting is not within the meaning of the word "meeting" in the 1985 Act. Thus, communication by telephone has been held to be a "telegraph" within the meaning of the Telegraph Acts 1863 and 1869, notwithstanding that the telephone had not been invented or contemplated when those Acts were passed: see *A-G v Edison Telephone Co of London Ltd* (1880) 6 QBD 244.'

Directors' power to call general meetings

21.40 The directors of a company may call a general meeting of the company: CA 2006, s 302.

Members' power to require directors to call general meeting

21.41 The members of a company may require the directors to call a general meeting of the company: CA 2006, s 303(1).

The directors are required to call a general meeting once the company has received requests to do so from:

(a) members representing at least 5% of such of the paid-up capital of the company as carries the right of voting at general meetings of the company (excluding any paid-up capital held as treasury shares); or

(b) in the case of a company not having a share capital, members who represent at least 5% of the total voting rights of all the members having a right to vote at general meetings: CA 2006, s 303(2).

21.42 A request:

(a) must state the general nature of the business to be dealt with at the meeting; and

(b) may include the text of a resolution that may properly be moved and is intended to be moved at the meeting: CA 2006, s 303(4).

The request must be a valid one by the shareholders representing 5% of the total voting rights if directors are to call the EGM: *Rose v McGivern* [1998] 2 BCLC 593; *Ball v Metal Industries Ltd* 1957 SC 315.

21.43 A resolution may properly be moved at a meeting unless:

(a) it would, if passed, be ineffective (whether by reason of inconsistency with any enactment or the company's constitution or otherwise);

(b) it is defamatory of any person; or

(c) it is frivolous or vexatious: CA 2006, s 303(5).

21.44 A request:

(a) may be in hard copy form or in electronic form; and

(b) must be authenticated by the person or persons making it: CA 2006, s 303(6).

Directors' duty to call meetings required by members

21.45 Directors required under CA 2006, s 303 to call a general meeting of the company must call a meeting:

(a) within 21 days from the date on which they become subject to the requirement; and

(b) to be held on a date not more than 28 days after the date of the notice convening the meeting: CA 2006, s 304(1).

If the requests received by the company identify a resolution intended to be moved at the meeting, the notice of the meeting must include notice of the resolution: CA 2006, s 304(2).

The business that may be dealt with at the meeting includes a resolution of which notice is given in accordance with this section: CA 2006, s 304(3).

If the resolution is to be proposed as a special resolution, the directors are treated as not having duly called the meeting if they do not give the required notice of the resolution in accordance with s 283: CA 2006, s 304(4).

Power of members to call meeting at company's expense

21.46 If the directors:

(a) are required under CA 2006, s 303 to call a meeting; and

(b) do not do so in accordance with s 304,

the members who requested the meeting, or any of them representing more than one half of the total voting rights of all of them, may themselves call a general meeting: CA 2006, s 305(1).

21.47 Where the requests received by the company included the text of a resolution intended to be moved at the meeting, the notice of the meeting must include notice of the resolution: CA 2006, s 305(2).

The meeting must be called for a date not more than three months after the date on which the directors become subject to the requirement to call a meeting: CA 2006, s 305(3).

The meeting must be called in the same manner, as nearly as possible, as that in which meetings are required to be called by directors of the company: CA 2006, s 305(4).

The business which may be dealt with at the meeting includes a resolution of which notice is given in accordance with this section: CA 2006, s 305(5).

21.48 Any reasonable expenses incurred by the members requesting the meeting by reason of the failure of the directors duly to call a meeting must be reimbursed by the company: CA 2006, s 305(6).

Any sum so reimbursed shall be retained by the company out of any sums due or to become due from the company by way of fees or other remuneration in respect of the services of such of the directors as were in default: CA 2006, s 305(7).

Power of court to order meeting

21.49 It is possible for the court to order a general meeting to be held and this is at the discretion of the court.

CA 2006, s 306 applies if for any reason it is impracticable:

(a) to call a meeting of a company in any manner in which meetings of that company may be called; or

(b) to conduct the meeting in the manner prescribed by the company's articles or this Act: CA 2006, s 306(1).

21.50 The court may, either of its own motion or on the application:

(a) of a director of the company; or

(b) of a member of the company who would be entitled to vote at the meeting,

order a meeting to be called, held and conducted in any manner the court thinks fit: CA 2006, s 306(2).

Where such an order is made, the court may give such ancillary or consequential directions as it thinks expedient: CA 2006, s 306(3).

Such directions may include a direction that one member of the company present at the meeting be deemed to constitute a quorum: CA 2006, s 303(4).

A meeting called, held and conducted in accordance with an order under this section is deemed for all purposes to be a meeting of the company duly called, held and conducted: CA 2006, s 306(5).

21.51 Some of the cases under s 306 have been concerned with the quorum requirements at general meetings, particularly where there is no requisite quorum at such meetings, and the applicant is seeking the court's permission to pass certain resolutions at an inquorate meeting, or where there is a deadlock at these meetings and there is no provision in the articles of association or any shareholders' agreement to resolve such deadlock.

The fact that a petition for unfair prejudicial conduct under s 994 has been presented, does not necessarily prevent the court from considering applications under s 306; but it will be a factor that the court will consider particularly where class rights are involved as set out in a shareholders' agreement:

The court will take account of class rights of shareholders in respect of shareholder meetings

In *Harman v BML Group Ltd* [1994] 2 BCLC 674, Dillon LJ stated that CA 2006, s 306 was not intended to override any class rights of shareholders. He considered that the wording of s 306 was wide and would include circumstances where a company with a large number of shareholders or members had failed to comply with the provisions of the articles as to the retirement of directors by rotation and found that it had no directors and it was necessary to have directors appointed. Other circumstances would be where the company's share register and records of its membership had been destroyed in a fire, and a meeting was necessary to resurrect the membership of the company and carry out the necessary formalities until that could be done. Another situation would be where under the articles, notices of meetings had to be given to overseas shareholders and there were hostilities in foreign parts which prevented that being done and that could have prevented meetings being validly convened. The court can therefore give directions as to the meetings to be held.

The court may have regard to the interests of minority shareholders in respect of shareholder meetings

In *Re Sticky Fingers Restaurant Limited* [1992] BCLC 84, Mervyn Davies J granted an order under CA 2006, s 306 the effect of which restrained the majority shareholder from using his voting rights to exclude the minority shareholder, a director of the company, pending outcome of the s 994 petition for unfair prejudicial conduct.

The fiduciary position of a director of the company did not prevent him assuming the position of chairman of a general meeting of the company regardless of any conflict of interest that may exist

In *Might SA v Redbus Interhouse plc* [2004] 2 BCLC 449, the applicant applied under s 306 on the basis that the chairman to be appointed for the general meeting would be one of the directors whom the shareholders proposed to remove from office; and if the director was to be appointed as chairman he would have a conflict of interest and vested interest not to be removed. The issue was whether it was impracticable to hold a meeting.

Lindsay J refused the applicant's application under s 306 and decided that the fiduciary position of a director of the company did not prevent him assuming the position of chairman of a general meeting of the company, even though that might put him in a position of conflict between his individual position and his fiduciary duty, since there was no requirement in the CA 2006 or the articles that the chairman of a general meeting had to be neutral. Further, the fact that there might be such a conflict between duty and interest was not sufficient to render it 'impracticable' to call a meeting of the company.

In *Monnington v Easier plc* [2006] 2 BCLC 283, Rimer J stated that the court had jurisdiction to make an order under s 306 only where it was impracticable to call or conduct a meeting.

21.52 Section 306 does not define 'impracticable'. Each case will be decided on its facts as to what is impracticable. The objective of s 306 is to allow for the continuity of the company's functioning and operations without unnecessary hindrance.

The court may make an order validating resolutions at a shareholders' meeting

Vectone Entertainment Holding Limited v South Entertainment Ltd [2004] 2 BCLC 224, concerned the refusal of a minority shareholder to attend a general meeting so that the meeting became inquorate without him; and any resolutions passed were invalid. The majority shareholder sought an order from the court for the convening of a general meeting to enable invalidly passed resolutions to be put to, and passed by, a properly constituted meeting. The issue was whether the court would grant such order.

Richard Sheldon QC sitting as a Deputy Judge of the High Court summarised the following principles that would be applicable by the court when exercising its discretion to grant relief under s 306:

(i) Although s 306 was a procedural section intended to enable company business which needed to be conducted at a general meeting to be so conducted, the court would not allow the procedure to be used to override class rights or substantive rights conferred on a shareholder.

(ii) Where there was a majority shareholder and no class rights attaching to particular classes of shares which the convening of a general meeting was designed to override, the court in exercising its discretion under s 306 would consider whether the company was in a position to manage its affairs properly and would also take into account the ordinary right of the majority shareholder to remove or appoint a director in exercise of his majority voting power.

(iii) The fact that quorum provisions in the articles of association required two members' attendance was not in itself sufficient to prevent the court making an order under s 306 to break a deadlock in favour of a majority shareholder who was seeking a proper order, such as the appointment of a director, which he had the right to procure in ordinary circumstances.

(iv) Section 306 was not designed to affect substantive voting rights or to shift the balance of power between shareholders in a case where they had agreed that power should be shared equally and where the potential deadlock was something which must be taken to have been agreed for the protection of each shareholder but a quorum provision was not of itself sufficient to constitute such an agreement.

On the facts, the claimant obtained a court order to validate the resolutions passed at the general meeting.

21.53 On occasions, the court has been involved under CA 2006, s 306 where violence may be involved:

The court may dispense with a meeting where there is actual violence or a risk of threatened violence

Re British Union for the Abolition of Vivisection [1995] 2 BCLC 1, concerned the impossibility of holding a meeting owing to factionalised sections within the group causing disruption and intervention of the police. The applicants also sought an order that the voting on a resolution by the other members of BUAV should be by way of postal ballot and that the requirement of personal attendance as provided for in BUAV's articles should accordingly be dispensed with.

The court granted the order under s 306. Rimmer J decided that it was clear from the requirement of the BUAV constitution that members should personally attend meetings in order to vote that they should feel free to attend to vote and not be deterred from doing so by the fear of the extremism of a radical minority. The conduct of the minority at the annual general meeting of BUAV had been disgraceful and intolerable and would have the effect of frightening away many of BUAV's peaceful majority. There was a legitimate fear that this conduct would be repeated at any meeting of BUAV. Accordingly, on the facts, it was clear that it was impracticable to summon a meeting as provided for in the company's constitution.

The concept of 'impracticable' signifies that there must be regard to all the circumstances to determine the practicability of holding a meeting

Where shareholders hold shares in different proportions, the principle of majority rule may apply to circumvent the quorum requirements. However, where the parties have deliberately established the quorum requirements because they have equal shareholdings, then s 306 may not be used to resolve such deadlock.

Re El Sombrero Ltd [1958] Ch 900, involved the refusal of directors to hold meetings leading to an application by a shareholder to compel the holding of such meeting. Wynn-Parry J was required to consider whether such a meeting was 'impracticable' and held that that the question raised by the word 'impracticable' was merely whether in the particular circumstances of the case, the desired meeting of the company could as a practical matter be conducted.

On the true construction of s 306, there was nothing to prevent the court intervening in a proper case and where the application before it was opposed by other shareholders. He stated that the term 'if for any reason' was wide in scope. Also the term 'impracticable' was not synonymous with impossible. In determining impracticability, it was necessary to examine the circumstances of the particular case and answer the question whether, as a practical matter, the desired meeting of the company could be conducted, there being no doubt, of course, that it could be convened and held.

21.54 There have been occasions where shareholders have been absent from meetings or simply refuse to attend meetings. In such cases the courts have intervened to allow meetings to be held.

The court may order a meeting to be held where it is inquorate

In *Re Opera Photographic Limited* [1989] BCLC 763, the company's articles of association required two members for a quorum at a meeting. The director refused to attend, so that the quorate meeting could not be held.

Morritt J held that the quorum requirements in the company's articles of association could not be treated as conferring on the defendant a form of veto to prevent the holding of a shareholders' meeting to consider removing him from office as director. Accordingly, since the applicant held a majority of the shares and possessed a statutory right to remove the defendant from office but it was impracticable to hold a meeting because of the quorum requirements, the court would make the order sought under s 306.

A petition presented to the court for unfair prejudicial conduct under CA 2006, s 994 did not prevent the court from exercising its powers to convene a meeting

In *Re Whitchurch Insurance Consultants Limited* [1993] BCLC 1359, the husband and wife business eventually succumbed to a deterioration in business relationships.

The husband tried to remove his wife as a director by requisitioning a meeting but the wife refused to attend meetings convened. She also petitioned under CA 2006, s 994 on grounds of unfair prejudicial conduct.

Harman J held that the mere existence of a s 994 petition at the date of the hearing of an application under s 306 was not an inevitable bar to the court making an order under that section but was something which the court would take into account in considering whether to exercise its discretion to make such an order. On the facts, it was impracticable to hold a meeting and the order sought would be made to allow a board of directors which would be quorate to be appointed.

21.55 In some situations, the court has not exercised its discretion to make an order under s 306.

Section 306 was a procedural section and was not designed to affect substantive voting rights or to shift the balance of power between shareholders particularly in a deadlock situation: it had no application to a board meeting

In *Ross v Telford* [1998] 1 BCLC 82, the husband and wife were the two directors of two companies. They were also equal shareholders of one of the companies. The quorum for board and general meetings of both companies was two with the result that both companies were potentially deadlocked at both board and general meeting levels. In the course of an acrimonious divorce and ancillary relief proceedings the husband claimed that the wife had fraudulently amassed undisclosed assets at the expense of one of the companies, L Ltd, and himself by causing a supplier of goods to the company to raise bogus invoices for fictitious goods which were never delivered and that she had added her husband's signature to cheques withdrawing funds from L Ltd.

The husband applied to the court for an order under s 306 requiring a meeting of L Ltd to be called in order that L Ltd's action against the bank could be ratified. The judge ordered that L Ltd, on the husband's requisition, could convene a meeting of its shareholders for the purpose of considering and voting on a resolution for the appointment of a representative of the husband's solicitors as a third director of the company for one year and that a representative of the husband's solicitors could attend at that meeting and vote. The wife appealed against the order.

The Court of Appeal allowed the wife's appeal. Nourse LJ stated that s 306 was not an appropriate vehicle for resolving deadlock between two equal shareholders since this provision did not empower the court to break a deadlock at either a board or general meeting of a company and in fact had nothing to do with board meetings. Section 306 was a procedural section and was not designed to affect substantive voting rights or to shift the balance of power between shareholders by permitting a 50% shareholder to override the wishes of the other 50% shareholder where they had agreed that power would be shared equally and where a potential deadlock was a matter which must be taken to have been agreed on with the consent and for the protection of each of them. It followed that the judge had no jurisdiction to regulate the affairs of the company by ordering that a meeting of its shareholders be called and that a representative of the husband's solicitors be permitted to attend a general meeting of L Ltd as an additional director.

In any event, even if there had been jurisdiction the judge had exercised his discretion incorrectly, since (i) the application was in substance an attempt by the husband to relitigate an issue which had been fully investigated and decided against him in the ancillary relief proceedings, (ii) the district judge had ruled that the wife, who opposed the action, was beneficially entitled to half the assets of both companies and (iii) an inquiry into whether the husband could fund the action was pending.

Accordingly, no order under s 306 was granted.

Section 306 was merely a procedural device enabling the company's business to be conducted at general meetings

Union Music Ltd v Watson [2003] 1 BCLC 453, concerned a minority shareholder's refusal to attend a company meeting leading to a deadlock. The quorum provisions in the articles required the attendance of two members. The issue was whether the court should exercise discretion to order a meeting.

The Court of Appeal held that s 306 was a procedural section plainly intended to enable company business which needed to be conducted at a general meeting to be so conducted so that the company could manage its affairs without being frustrated by the impracticability of calling or conducting a general meeting in the manner prescribed by the articles and the Act.

Where there was a majority shareholder and no class rights attaching to particular classes of shares which the convening of a general meeting was designed to override, the court in exercising its discretion under s 306 would consider whether the company was in a position to manage its affairs properly and would also take into account the ordinary right of the majority shareholder to remove or appoint a director in exercise of his majority voting power. The fact that quorum provisions in the articles required two members' attendance was not in itself sufficient to prevent the court making an order under s 306 to break a deadlock in favour of a majority shareholder who was seeking a proper order, such as the appointment of a director, which he had the right to procure in ordinary circumstances.

Further, one of the clauses in the shareholders' agreement was a quorum provision rather than a provision for a class right or a substantive right, and although the first claimant would be acting in contravention of that clause if it exercised its voting rights at a meeting not attended by the shareholder or his proxy, that did not prevent the court making an order under s 306 convening a meeting for the single act of enabling the appointment of a new director to be considered and voted on even though only one member would be present at that meeting.

The cases of *Harman v BML Group Ltd* [1994] 2 BCLC 674 and *Ross v Telford* [1998] 1 BCLC 82 were distinguished.

Notice required of general meeting

21.56 CA 2006, s 307 applies to:

(a) a general meeting of a company that is not a traded company; and

(b) a general meeting of a traded company that is an opted-in company (as defined by s 971(1)), where:

  (i) the meeting is held to decide whether to take any action that might result in the frustration of a takeover bid for the company; or

  (ii) the meeting is held by virtue of s 969 (power of offeror to require general meeting to be held): CA 2006, s 307(A1).

For corresponding provision(s) in relation to general meetings of traded companies (other than meetings within sub-s (A1)(b)), see s 307A: CA 2006, s 307(A2).

21.57 A general meeting of a private company (other than an adjourned meeting) must be called by notice of at least 14 days: CA 2006, s 307(1).

A general meeting of a public company (other than an adjourned meeting) must be called by notice of:

(a) in the case of an annual general meeting, at least 21 days; and

(b) in any other case, at least 14 days: CA 2006, s 307(2).

The company's articles may require a longer period of notice than that specified in s 307(1) or (2): CA 2006, s 307(3).

In *Smyth v Darley* (1849) 2 HL Cas 789, the court stated that failure to give notice in a timely manner would render a meeting void.

21.58 A general meeting may be called by shorter notice than that otherwise required if shorter notice is agreed by the members: CA 2006, s 307(4). The shorter notice must be agreed to by a majority in number of the members having a right to attend and vote at the meeting, being a majority who:

(a) together hold not less than the requisite percentage in nominal value of the shares giving a right to attend and vote at the meeting (excluding any shares in the company held as treasury shares); or

(b) in the case of a company not having a share capital, together represent not less than the requisite percentage of the total voting rights at that meeting of all the members: CA 2006, s 307(5).

21.59 The requisite percentage is:

(a) in the case of a private company, 90% or such higher percentage (not exceeding 95%) as may be specified in the company's articles;

(b) in the case of a public company, 95%: CA 2006, s 307(6).

Sections 307(5) and (6) of CA 2006 do not apply to an annual general meeting of a public company (see instead s 337(2)): CA 2006, s 307(7).

Notice required of general meeting: certain meetings of traded companies

21.60 A general meeting of a traded company must be called by notice of:

(a) in a case where conditions A to C (set out below) are met, at least 14 days;

(b) in any other case, at least 21 days: CA 2006, s 307A(1).

21.61 Condition A is that the general meeting is not an annual general meeting: CA 2006, s 307A(2).

Condition B is that the company offers the facility for members to vote by electronic means accessible to all members who hold shares that carry rights to vote at general meetings. This condition is met if there is a facility, offered by the company and accessible to all such members, to appoint a proxy by means of a website: CA 2006, s 307A(3).

Condition C is that a special resolution reducing the period of notice to not less than 14 days has been passed:

(a) at the immediately preceding annual general meeting; or

(b) at a general meeting held since that annual general meeting: CA 2006, s 307A(4).

In the case of a company which has not yet held an annual general meeting, condition C is that a special resolution reducing the period of notice to not less than 14 days has been passed at a general meeting: CA 2006, s 307A(5).

The company's articles may require a longer period of notice than that specified in s 308(1): CA 2006, s 307A(6).

21.62 Where a general meeting is adjourned, the adjourned meeting may be called by shorter notice than required by s 307A(1). But in the case of an adjournment for lack of a quorum this subsection applies only if:

(a) no business is to be dealt with at the adjourned meeting the general nature of which was not stated in the notice of the original meeting; and

(b) the adjourned meeting is to be held at least 10 days after the original meeting: CA 2006, s 307A(7).

Nothing in this section applies in relation to a general meeting of a kind mentioned in s 307(A1)(b) (certain meetings regarding takeover of opted-in company): CA 2006, s 307A(8).

The chairman has authority to adjourn a meeting but the decision to adjourn must be taken in good faith in the interests of all the shareholders: any aspect of bad faith may nullify the adjournment.

The chairman has no general right to adjourn a meeting of his own motion at common law unless expressly stated otherwise

At common law, where there is no document expressly regulating the powers of adjournment, the chairman has no general right to adjourn a meeting at his own will and pleasure, there being no circumstance preventing the effective continuation of the proceedings: see *National Dwellings Society v Sykes* [1894] 3 Ch 159 at 162.

However, a chairman has such power where unruly conduct prevents the continuation of business: see *John v Rees* [1970] Ch 345 at 379–383.

It is also established that when in an orderly meeting a poll is demanded on a motion to adjourn and such poll cannot be taken forthwith, the chairman has the power to suspend the meeting with a view to its continuance at a later date after the result of the poll is known: *Jackson v Hamlyn* [1953] Ch 577. In that case Upjohn J expressly held that the chairman was not 'adjourning' the meeting within the meaning of the article there in question. He held that the chairman had power to stand over the proceedings to another time, since some such power had to exist in order to give effect to the provisions as to polls in the articles. There was a residual power in the chairman to take such steps as would, in the ordinary usage of the word, amount to an adjournment.

In *R v D'Oyly* (1840) 12 Ad & El 139 at 159, it was stated that:

> 'Setting aside the inconvenience that might arise if a majority of the parishioners could determine the point of adjournment, we think that the person who presides at the meeting is the proper individual to decide this. It is on him that it devolves, both to preserve order in the meeting, and to regulate the proceedings so as to give all persons entitled a reasonable opportunity of voting. He is to do the acts necessary for those purposes on his own responsibility, and subject to being called upon to answer for his conduct if he has done anything improperly.'

At meetings, the chairman must act in good faith and within the scope of his authority

In *Salisbury Gold Mining Co Ltd v Hathorn* [1897] AC 268, Lord Herschell stated that the chairman must not abuse his authority and act in the interests of a particular group of shareholders or act in bad faith when considering an adjournment of a meeting:

> 'It is true that it vests in the chairman large powers which might conceivably be used improperly by him; but, on the other hand, if there were no check upon the power of those present at a meeting to adjourn it to a future date, it is equally conceivable that a small minority of the shareholders might seriously prejudice the interests of the company and defy the wishes of the majority of its members.'

The chairman is required to regulate and preside over the proper functioning of meetings

In *Byng v London Life Association Ltd* [1989] BCLC 400, the Court of Appeal stated that the chairman of a meeting had at common law a duty to regulate proceedings so as to enable those attending to be heard and to vote and this conferred, *inter alia*, a power to adjourn any meeting. On the facts, since the chairman was unable to ascertain the views of the members at the morning meeting he had a residual power to adjourn it. The chairman's decision to adjourn would be invalid not only if taken in bad faith but also if he failed to take into account relevant factors, or took into account irrelevant factors, or reached a conclusion which no reasonable chairman could have reached having regard to the purpose of his power to adjourn.

On the facts of the case, the chairman failed to take into account the following relevant factors: the attempts by the members to adjourn the meeting *sine die*, their objections to the adjournment of the meeting until the afternoon, that the members present at the morning meeting who could not attend the adjourned meeting would be unable to vote since it was too late for them to deposit proxies, and finally that it would have been possible to terminate the meeting and reconvene it at a later date.

The Court of Appeal held that since the morning meeting was not validly adjourned, and the proceedings at the afternoon meeting were therefore invalid.

Manner in which notice to be given

21.63 Notice of a general meeting of a company must be given:

(a) in hard copy form;

(b) in electronic form; or

(c) by means of a website (see s 309),

or partly by one such means and partly by another: CA 2006, s 308.

Publication of notice of meeting on website

21.64 Notice of a meeting is not validly given by a company by means of a website unless it is given in accordance with s 309: CA 2006, s 309(1).

When the company notifies a member of the presence of the notice on the website the notification must:

(a) state that it concerns a notice of a company meeting;

(b) specify the place, date and time of the meeting; and

(c) in the case of a public company, state whether the meeting will be an annual general meeting: CA 2006, s 309(2).

The notice must be available on the website throughout the period beginning with the date of that notification and ending with the conclusion of the meeting: CA 2006, s 309(3).

Persons entitled to receive notice of meetings

21.65 Notice of a general meeting of a company must be sent to:

(a) every member of the company; and

(b) every director: CA 2006, s 310(1).

21.66 In s 310(1), the reference to members includes any person who is entitled to a share in consequence of the death or bankruptcy of a member, if the company has been notified of their entitlement: CA 2006, s 310(2).

In s 310(2), the reference to the bankruptcy of a member includes:

(a) the sequestration of the estate of a member;

(b) a member's estate being the subject of a protected trust deed (within the meaning of the Bankruptcy (Scotland) Act 1985 (c 66)): CA 2006, s 310(3).

21.67 Section 310 of the CA 2006 subject to:

(a) any enactment; and

(b) any provision of the company's articles: CA 2006, s 310(4).

Contents of notices of meetings

21.68 Notice of a general meeting of a company must state:

(a) the time and date of the meeting; and

(b) the place of the meeting: CA 2006, s 311(1).

Notice of a general meeting of a company must state the general nature of the business to be dealt with at the meeting: CA 2006, s 311(2).

In relation to a company other than a traded company, this subsection has effect subject to any provision of the company's articles.

21.69 Notice of a general meeting of a traded company must also include:

(a) a statement giving the address of the website on which the information required by s 311A (traded companies: publication of information in advance of general meeting) is published;

(b) a statement:

    (i) that the right to vote at the meeting is determined by reference to the register of members or, if an election under s 128B is in force in respect of the company, in the register kept by the registrar under s 1080; and

(ii) of the time when that right will be determined in accordance with s 360B(2) (traded companies: share dealings before general meetings);

(c) a statement of the procedures with which members must comply in order to be able to attend and vote at the meeting (including the date by which they must comply);

(d) a statement giving details of any forms to be used for the appointment of a proxy;

(e) where the company offers the facility for members to vote in advance (see s 322A) or by electronic means (see s 360A), a statement of the procedure for doing so (including the date by which it must be done, and details of any forms to be used); and

(f) a statement of the right of members to ask questions in accordance with s 319A (traded companies: questions at meetings): CA 2006, s 311(3) (as inserted by SBEEA 2015, Sch 5, Pt 2).

There is no requirement for all shareholders to be physically present at the same place for a meeting to be validly convened

In respect of venues for the meetings, the Court of Appeal in *Byng v London Life Association Ltd* [1989] BCLC 400, stated that in order for a meeting of members to be validly constituted it was not necessary for all the members to be physically present in the same room. A valid meeting could take place if the shareholders were in different places provided all steps were taken to direct shareholders to the places other than the main venue where the meeting was to be held and that there were adequate audio visual links to enable those in all the locations to see and hear what was going on in the other rooms.

Traded companies: publication of information in advance of general meeting

21.70 A traded company must ensure that the following information relating to a general meeting of the company is made available on a website:

(a) the matters set out in the notice of the meeting;

(b) the total numbers of:

(i) shares in the company; and

(iii) shares of each class,

in respect of which members are entitled to exercise voting rights at the meeting;

(c) the totals of the voting rights that members are entitled to exercise at the meeting in respect of the shares of each class;

(d) members' statements, members' resolutions and members' matters of business received by the company after the first date on which notice of the meeting is given: CA 2006, s 311A(1).

21.71 The information must be made available on a website that:

(a) is maintained by or on behalf of the company; and

(b) identifies the company: CA 2006, s 311A(2).

Access to the information on the website, and the ability to obtain a hard copy of the information from the website, must not be conditional on payment of a fee or otherwise restricted: CA 2006, s 311A(3).

21.72 The information:

(a) must be made available:

  (i) in the case of information required by sub-s (1)(a)–(c), on or before the first date on which notice of the meeting is given; and

  (ii) in the case of information required by sub-s (1)(d), as soon as reasonably practicable, and

(b) must be kept available throughout the period of two years beginning with the date on which it is first made available on a website in accordance with this section: CA 2006, s 311A(4).

21.73 A failure to make information available throughout the period specified in s (4)(b) is disregarded if:

(a) the information is made available on the website for part of that period; and

(b) the failure is wholly attributable to circumstances that it would not be reasonable to have expected the company to prevent or avoid: CA 2006, s 311A(5).

The amounts mentioned in sub-s (1)(b) and (c) must be ascertained at the latest practicable time before the first date on which notice of the meeting is given: CA 2006, s 311A(6).

21.74 Failure to comply with this section does not affect the validity of the meeting or of anything done at the meeting: CA 2006, s 311A(7).

If CA 2006, s 311A is not complied with as respects any meeting, an offence is committed by every officer of the company who is in default: CA 2006, s 311A(8).

A person guilty of an offence under this section is liable on summary conviction to a fine not exceeding level 3 on the standard scale: CA 2006, s 311A(9).

Resolution requiring special notice

21.75 Where by any provision of the Companies Acts special notice is required of a resolution, the resolution is not effective unless notice of the intention to move it has been given to the company at least 28 days before the meeting at which it is moved: CA 2006, s 312(1).

The company must, where practicable, give its members notice of any such resolution in the same manner and at the same time as it gives notice of the meeting: CA 2006, s 312(2).

21.76 Where that is not practicable, the company must give its members notice at least 14 days before the meeting:

(a) by advertisement in a newspaper having an appropriate circulation; or

(b) in any other manner allowed by the company's articles: CA 2006, s 312(3).

If, after notice of the intention to move such a resolution has been given to the company, a meeting is called for a date 28 days or less after the notice has been given, the notice is deemed to have been properly given, though not given within the time required: CA 2006, s 312(4).

Accidental failure to give notice of resolution or meeting

21.77 Where a company gives notice of:

(a) a general meeting; or

(b) a resolution intended to be moved at a general meeting,

any accidental failure to give notice to one or more persons shall be disregarded for the purpose of determining whether notice of the meeting or resolution (as the case may be) is duly given: CA 2006, s 313(1).

21.78 Except in relation to notice given under:

(a) s 304 (notice of meetings required by members)

(b) s 305 (notice of meetings called by members); or

(c) s 339 (notice of resolutions at AGMs proposed by members),

sub-s (1) has effect subject to any provision of the company's articles: CA 2006, s 313(2).

An accidental omission is distinguished from an omission. In the latter situation, proceedings at meetings will be declared void.

> ***An omission to give notice of a meeting will invalidate proceedings at that meeting***
>
> In *Musselwhite v C H Musselwhite & Son Ltd* [1962] Ch 964, there was an omission to serve notice arising from an error as to legal position of a shareholder's membership within the company.
>
> Russell J held that that the omission to give notice of a meeting to the claimants prima facie invalidated the meeting, and that an omission arising from an error was not accidental. The meeting was therefore a nullity.

Members' power to require circulation of statements

21.79 The members of a company may require the company to circulate, to members of the company entitled to receive notice of a general meeting, a statement of not more than 1,000 words with respect to:

(a) a matter referred to in a proposed resolution to be dealt with at that meeting; or

(b) other business to be dealt with at that meeting: CA 2006, s 314(1).

21.80 A company is required to circulate a statement once it has received requests to do so from:

(a) members representing at least 5% of the total voting rights of all the members who have a relevant right to vote (excluding any voting rights attached to any shares in the company held as treasury shares); or

(b) at least 100 members who have a relevant right to vote and hold shares in the company on which there has been paid up an average sum, per member, of at least £100.

See also CA 2006, s 153 (exercise of rights where shares held on behalf of others): CA 2006, s 314(2).

21.81 In CA 2006, s 314(2), a 'relevant right to vote' means:

(a) in relation to a statement with respect to a matter referred to in a proposed resolution, a right to vote on that resolution at the meeting to which the requests relate; and

(b) in relation to any other statement, a right to vote at the meeting to which the requests relate: CA 2006, s 314(3).

21.82 A request:

(a) may be in hard copy form or in electronic form;

(b) must identify the statement to be circulated;

(c) must be authenticated by the person or persons making it; and

(d) must be received by the company at least one week before the meeting to which it relates: CA 2006, s 314(4).

Company's duty to circulate members' statement

21.83 A company that is required under CA 2006, s 314, to circulate a statement must send a copy of it to each member of the company entitled to receive notice of the meeting:

(a) in the same manner as the notice of the meeting; and

(b) at the same time as, or as soon as reasonably practicable after, it gives notice of the meeting: CA 2006, s 315(1).

Section 315(1) of CA 2006 applies subject to s 316(2) (deposit or tender of sum in respect of expenses of circulation) and s 317 (application not to circulate members' statement): CA 2006, s 315(2).

21.84 In the event of default in complying with this section, an offence is committed by every officer of the company who is in default: CA 2006, s 315(3).

A person guilty of an offence under this section is liable:

(a) on conviction on indictment, to a fine;

(b) on summary conviction, to a fine not exceeding the statutory maximum: CA 2006, s 315(4).

Expenses of circulating members' statement

21.85 The expenses of the company in complying with CA 2006, s 315 need not be paid by the members who requested the circulation of the statement if:

(a) the meeting to which the requests relate is an annual general meeting of a public company; and

(b) requests sufficient to require the company to circulate the statement are received before the end of the financial year preceding the meeting: CA 2006, s 316(1).

21.86 Otherwise:

(a) the expenses of the company in complying with that section must be paid by the members who requested the circulation of the statement unless the company resolves otherwise; and

(b) unless the company has previously so resolved, it is not bound to comply with that section unless there is deposited with or tendered to it, not later than one week before the meeting, a sum reasonably sufficient to meet its expenses in doing so: CA 2006, s 316(2).

Application not to circulate members' statement

21.87 A company is not required to circulate a members' statement under CA 2006, s 315 if, on an application by the company or another person who claims to be aggrieved, the court is satisfied that the rights conferred by s 314 and that section are being abused: CA 2006, s 317(1).

The court may order the members who requested the circulation of the statement to pay the whole or part of the company's costs (in Scotland, expenses) on such an application, even if they are not parties to the application: CA 2006, s 317(2).

Quorum at meetings

21.88 In the case of a company limited by shares or guarantee and having only one member, one qualifying person present at a meeting is a quorum: CA 2006, s 318(1). In any other case, subject to the provisions of the company's articles, two qualifying persons present at a meeting are a quorum, unless:

(a) each is a qualifying person only because he is authorised under s 323 to act as the representative of a corporation in relation to the meeting, and they are representatives of the same corporation; or

(b) each is a qualifying person only because he is appointed as proxy of a member in relation to the meeting, and they are proxies of the same member: CA 2006, s 318(2).

21.89 For the purposes of this section a 'qualifying person' means:

(a) an individual who is a member of the company;

(b) a person authorised under s 323 (representation of corporations at meetings) to act as the representative of a corporation in relation to the meeting; or

(c) a person appointed as proxy of a member in relation to the meeting: CA 2006, s 318(3).

Where a resolution is passed at a meeting which does not have the requisite quorum, it is void: see *Re Romford Canal Co, Pocock's Claims* (1883) 24 Ch D 85.

Chairman of meeting

21.90 A member may be elected to be the chairman of a general meeting by a resolution of the company passed at the meeting: CA 2006, s 319(1).

Section 319(1) is subject to any provision of the company's articles that states who may or may not be chairman: CA 2006, s 319(2).

At common law, a chairman has a duty to ensure proper conduct of meetings and that those attending meetings had a right to be heard and vote at properly held meetings: *Byng v London Life Association Limited* [1989] BCLC 400.

> ***A chairman has a duty to properly conduct meetings***
>
> In *National Dwelling Society v Sykes* [1894] 3 Ch 159, Chitty J held that it was the duty of a chairman to preserve order, conduct proceedings regularly, and take care that the sense of the meeting was properly ascertained with regard to any question before it.

Traded companies: questions at meetings

21.91 At a general meeting of a traded company, the company must cause to be answered any question relating to the business being dealt with at the meeting put by a member attending the meeting: CA 2006, s 319A(1).

No such answer need be given:

(a) if to do so would:

  (i) interfere unduly with the preparation for the meeting; or

  (ii) involve the disclosure of confidential information;

(b) if the answer has already been given on a website in the form of an answer to a question; or

(c) if it is undesirable in the interests of the company or the good order of the meeting that the question be answered: CA 2006, s 319A(2).

Declaration by chairman on a show of hands

21.92 On a vote on a resolution at a meeting on a show of hands, a declaration by the chairman that the resolution:

(a) has or has not been passed; or

(b) passed with a particular majority,

is conclusive evidence of that fact without proof of the number or proportion of the votes recorded in favour of or against the resolution: CA 2006, s 320(1).

An entry in respect of such a declaration in minutes of the meeting recorded in accordance with s 355 is also conclusive evidence of that fact without such proof: CA 2006, s 320(2). Section 320 does not have effect if a poll is demanded in respect of the resolution (and the demand is not subsequently withdrawn): CA 2006, s 320(3).

Right to demand a poll

21.93 A provision of a company's articles is void in so far as it would have the effect of excluding the right to demand a poll at a general meeting on any question other than:

(a) the election of the chairman of the meeting; or

(b) the adjournment of the meeting: CA 2006, s 321(1).

21.94 A provision of a company's articles is void in so far as it would have the effect of making ineffective a demand for a poll on any such question which is made:

(a) by not less than five members having the right to vote on the resolution; or

(b) by a member or members representing not less than 10% of the total voting rights of all the members having the right to vote on the resolution (excluding any voting rights attached to any shares in the company held as treasury shares); or

(c) by a member or members holding shares in the company conferring a right to vote on the resolution, being shares on which an aggregate sum has been paid up equal to not less than 10% of the total sum paid up on all the shares conferring that right (excluding shares in the company conferring a right to vote on the resolution which are held as treasury shares): CA 2006, s 321(2).

Voting on a poll

21.95 On a poll taken at a general meeting of a company, a member entitled to more than one vote need not, if he votes, use all his votes or cast all the votes he uses in the same way: CA 2006, s 322.

Voting on a poll: votes cast in advance

21.96 A company's articles may contain provision to the effect that on a vote on a resolution on a poll taken at a meeting, the votes may include votes cast in advance: CA 2006, s 322A(1).

In the case of a traded company any such provision in relation to voting at a general meeting may be made subject only to such requirements and restrictions as are:

(a) necessary to ensure the identification of the person voting; and

(b) proportionate to the achievement of that objective.

Nothing in this subsection affects any power of a company to require reasonable evidence of the entitlement of any person who is not a member to vote: CA 2006, s 322A(2).

21.97 Any provision of a company's articles is void in so far as it would have the effect of requiring any document casting a vote in advance to be received by the company or another person earlier than the following time:

(a) in the case of a poll taken more than 48 hours after it was demanded, 24 hours before the time appointed for the taking of the poll;

(b) in the case of any other poll, 48 hours before the time for holding the meeting or adjourned meeting: CA 2006, s 322A(3).

Representation of corporations at meetings

21.98 If a corporation (whether or not a company within the meaning of this Act) is a member of a company, it may by resolution of its directors or other governing body authorise a person or persons to act as its representative or representatives at any meeting of the company: CA 2006, s 323(1).

A person authorised by a corporation is entitled to exercise (on behalf of the corporation) the same powers as the corporation could exercise if it were an individual member of the company. Where a corporation authorises more than one person, this subsection is subject to sub-ss (3) and (4): CA 2006, s 323(2).

On a vote on a resolution on a show of hands at a meeting of the company, each authorised person has the same voting rights as the corporation would be entitled to: CA 2006, s 323(3).

21.99 Where s 323(3) does not apply and more than one authorised person purport to exercise a power under s 323(2) in respect of the same shares:

(a) if they purport to exercise the power in the same way as each other, the power is treated as exercised in that way;

(b) if they do not purport to exercise the power in the same way as each other, the power is treated as not exercised: CA 2006, s 323(3).

Rights to appoint proxies

21.100 A member of a company is entitled to appoint another person as his proxy to exercise all or any of his rights to attend and to speak and vote at a meeting of the company: CA 2006, s 324(1).

In the case of a company having a share capital, a member may appoint more than one proxy in relation to a meeting, provided that each proxy is appointed to exercise the rights attached to a different share or shares held by him, or (as the case may be) to a different £10, or multiple of £10, of stock held by him: CA 2006, s 324(2).

Obligation of proxy to vote in accordance with instructions

21.101 A proxy must vote in accordance with any instructions given by the member by whom the proxy is appointed: CA 2006, s 324A.

Notice of meeting to contain statement of rights

21.102 In every notice calling a meeting of a company there must appear, with reasonable prominence, a statement informing the member of:

(a) his rights under s 324, and

(b) any more extensive rights conferred by the company's articles to appoint more than one proxy: CA 2006, s 325(1).

Failure to comply with this section does not affect the validity of the meeting or of anything done at the meeting: CA 2006, s 325(2).

21.103 If s 325 is not complied with as respects any meeting, an offence is committed by every officer of the company who is in default: CA 2006, s 325(3). A person guilty of an offence under this section is liable on summary conviction to a fine not exceeding level 3 on the standard scale: CA 2006, s 325(4).

Company-sponsored invitations to appoint proxies

21.104 If for the purposes of a meeting there are issued at the company's expense invitations to members to appoint as proxy a specified person or a number of specified persons, the invitations must be issued to all members entitled to vote at the meeting: CA 2006, s 326(1).

Section 326(1) is not contravened if:

(a) there is issued to a member at his request a form of appointment naming the proxy or a list of persons willing to act as proxy; and

(b) the form or list is available on request to all members entitled to vote at the meeting: CA 2006, s 326(2).

If s 326(1) is contravened as respects a meeting, an offence is committed by every officer of the company who is in default: CA 2006, s 326(3).

A person guilty of an offence under this section is liable on summary conviction to a fine not exceeding level 3 on the standard scale: CA 2006, s 326(4).

Notice required of appointment of proxy etc

21.105 In the case of a traded company:

(a) the appointment of a person as proxy for a member must be notified to the company in writing;

(b) where such an appointment is made, the company may require reasonable evidence of:

 (i) the identity of the member and of the proxy;

 (ii) the member's instructions (if any) as to how the proxy is to vote; and

 (iii) where the proxy is appointed by a person acting on behalf of the member, authority of that person to make the appointment;

but may not require to be provided with anything else relating to the appointment: CA 2006, s 327(A1).

21.106 The following provisions apply in the case of traded companies and other companies as regards:

(a) the appointment of a proxy; and

(b) any document necessary to show the validity of, or otherwise relating to, the appointment of a proxy: CA 2006, s 327(1).

21.107 Any provision of the company's articles is void in so far as it would have the effect of requiring any such appointment or document to be received by the company or another person earlier than the following time:

(a) in the case of a meeting or adjourned meeting, 48 hours before the time for holding the meeting or adjourned meeting;

(b) in the case of a poll taken more than 48 hours after it was demanded, 24 hours before the time appointed for the taking of the poll.

In calculating the periods mentioned in sub-s (2) no account shall be taken of any part of a day that is not a working day: CA 2006, s 327(3) (as inserted by DA 2006 Sch 6, Pt 8).

Chairing meetings

21.108 A proxy may be elected to be the chairman of a general meeting by a resolution of the company passed at the meeting: CA 2006, s 328(1). Section 327(1) is subject to any provision of the company's articles that states who may or who may not be chairman: CA 2006, s 327(2).

Right of proxy to demand a poll

21.109 The appointment of a proxy to vote on a matter at a meeting of a company authorises the proxy to demand, or join in demanding, a poll on that matter: CA 2006, s 328(1).

In applying the provisions of CA 2006, s 321(2) (requirements for effective demand), a demand by a proxy counts:

(a) for the purposes of paragraph (a), as a demand by the member;

(b) for the purposes of paragraph (b), as a demand by a member representing the voting rights that the proxy is authorised to exercise;

(c) for the purposes of paragraph (c), as a demand by a member holding the shares to which those rights are attached: CA 2006, s 328(2).

Notice required of termination of proxy's authority

21.110 In the case of a traded company the termination of the authority of a person to act as proxy must be notified to the company in writing: CA 2006, s 330(A1).

The following provisions apply in the case of traded companies and other companies as regards notice that the authority of a person to act as proxy is terminated ('notice of termination'): CA 2006, s 330(1).

The termination of the authority of a person to act as proxy does not affect:

(a) whether he counts in deciding whether there is a quorum at a meeting;

(b) the validity of anything he does as chairman of a meeting; or

(c) the validity of a poll demanded by him at a meeting,

unless the company receives notice of the termination before the commencement of the meeting: CA 2006, s 330(2).

21.111 The termination of the authority of a person to act as proxy does not affect the validity of a vote given by that person unless the company receives notice of the termination:

(a) before the commencement of the meeting or adjourned meeting at which the vote is given; or

(b) in the case of a poll taken more than 48 hours after it is demanded, before the time appointed for taking the poll: CA 2006, s 320(3).

If the company's articles require or permit members to give notice of termination to a person other than the company, the references above to the company receiving notice have effect as if they were or (as the case may be) included a reference to that person: CA 2006, s 330(4).

21.112 Sections 330(2) and (3) have effect subject to any provision of the company's articles which has the effect of requiring notice of termination to be received by the company or another person at a time earlier than that specified in those subsections.

This is subject to s 330(6): CA 2006, s 330(5). Under s 330(6), any provision of the company's articles is void in so far as it would have the effect of requiring notice of termination to be received by the company or another person earlier than the following time:

(a) in the case of a meeting or adjourned meeting, 48 hours before the time for holding the meeting or adjourned meeting;

(b) in the case of a poll taken more than 48 hours after it was demanded, 24 hours before the time appointed for the taking of the poll: CA 2006, s 330(6) (as inserted by DA 2006, Sch 6, Pt 8).

In calculating the periods mentioned in s 330(3)(b) and (6) no account shall be taken of any part of a day that is not a working day: CA 2006, s 330(7).

Saving for more extensive rights conferred by articles

21.113 Nothing in ss 324–330 (proxies) prevents a company's articles from conferring more extensive rights on members or proxies than are conferred by those sections.

Resolution passed at adjourned meeting

21.114 Where a resolution is passed at an adjourned meeting of a company, the resolution is for all purposes to be treated as having been passed on the date on which it was in fact passed, and is not to be deemed passed on any earlier date: CA 2006, s 332.

Sending documents relating to meetings etc in electronic form

21.115 Where a company has given an electronic address in a notice calling a meeting, it is deemed to have agreed that any document or information relating to proceedings at the meeting may be sent by electronic means to that address (subject to any conditions or limitations specified in the notice): CA 2006, s 333(1).

Where a company has given an electronic address:

(a) in an instrument of proxy sent out by the company in relation to the meeting, or

(b) in an invitation to appoint a proxy issued by the company in relation to the meeting,

it is deemed to have agreed that any document or information relating to proxies for that meeting may be sent by electronic means to that address (subject to any conditions or limitations specified in the notice): CA 2006, s 333(2).

21.116 In s 333(2), documents relating to proxies include:

(a) the appointment of a proxy in relation to a meeting;

(b) any document necessary to show the validity of, or otherwise relating to, the appointment of a proxy; and

(c) notice of the termination of the authority of a proxy: CA 2006, s 333(3).

The term 'electronic address' means any address or number used for the purposes of sending or receiving documents or information by electronic means: CA 2006, s 333(4).

Traded company: duty to provide electronic address for receipt of proxies etc

21.117 A traded company must provide an electronic address for the receipt of any document or information relating to proxies for a general meeting: CA 2006, s 333A(1).

The company must provide the address either:

(a) by giving it when sending out an instrument of proxy for the purposes of the meeting or issuing an invitation to appoint a proxy for those purposes; or

(b) by ensuring that it is made available, throughout the period beginning with the first date on which notice of the meeting is given and ending with the conclusion of the meeting, on the website on which the information required by s 311A(1) is made available: CA 2006, s 333A(2).

The company is deemed to have agreed that any document or information relating to proxies for the meeting may be sent by electronic means to the address provided (subject to any limitations specified by the company when providing the address): CA 2006, s 333A(3).

21.118 In s 333A:

(a) documents relating to proxies include:

  (i) the appointment of a proxy for a meeting;

  (ii) any document necessary to show the validity of, or otherwise relating to, the appointment of a proxy; and

  (iii) notice of the termination of the authority of a proxy;

(b) 'electronic address' has the meaning given by s 333(4): CA 2006, s 333A(4).

Application to class meetings

21.119 The provisions of CA 2006, Ch 3 apply (with necessary modifications) in relation to a meeting of holders of a class of shares as they apply in relation to a general meeting. This is subject to s 334(2)–(3): CA 2006, s 334(1).

The following provisions of Ch 3 do not apply in relation to a meeting of holders of a class of shares:

(a) ss 303–305 (members' power to require directors to call general meeting);

(b) s 306 (power of court to order meeting); and

(c) ss 311(3), 311A, 319A, 327(A1), 330(A1) and 333A (additional requirements relating to traded companies): CA 2006, s 334(2).

CA 2006, s 307(1)–(6) apply in relation to a meeting of holders of a class of shares in a traded company as they apply in relation to a meeting of holders of a class of shares in a company other than a traded company (and, accordingly, CA 2006, s 307A does not apply in relation to such a meeting): CA 2006, s 334(2A).

21.120 The following provisions (in addition to those mentioned in s 334(2)) do not apply in relation to a meeting in connection with the variation of rights attached to a class of shares (a 'variation of class rights meeting'):

(a) s 318 (quorum); and

(b) s 321 (right to demand a poll): CA 2006, s 334(3).

21.121 The quorum for a variation of class rights meeting is:

(a) for a meeting other than an adjourned meeting, two persons present holding at least one-third in nominal value of the issued shares of the class in question (excluding any shares of that class held as treasury shares);

(b) for an adjourned meeting, one person present holding shares of the class in question: CA 2006, s 334(4).

For the purposes of CA 2006, s 334(4), where a person is present by proxy or proxies, he is treated as holding only the shares in respect of which those proxies are authorised to exercise voting rights: CA 2006, s 334(5).

At a variation of class rights meeting, any holder of shares of the class in question present may demand a poll: CA 2006, s 334(6).

21.122 For the purposes of s 334:

(a) any amendment of a provision contained in a company's articles for the variation of the rights attached to a class of shares, or the insertion of any such provision into the articles, is itself to be treated as a variation of those rights; and

(b) references to the variation of rights attached to a class of shares include references to their abrogation: CA 2006, s 334(7).

Application to class meetings: companies without a share capital

21.123 The provisions of CA 2006, Pt 13, Ch 3 apply (with necessary modifications) in relation to a meeting of a class of members of a company without a share capital as they apply in relation to a general meeting.

This is subject to s 335(2) and (3): CA 2006, s 335(1).

The following provisions of this Ch 3 do not apply in relation to a meeting of a class of members:

(a) ss 303–305 (members' power to require directors to call general meeting); and

(b) s 306 (power of court to order meeting): CA 2006, s 335(2).

21.124 The following provisions (in addition to those mentioned in sub-s (2)) do not apply in relation to a meeting in connection with the variation of the rights of a class of members (a 'variation of class rights meeting'):

(a) s 318 (quorum); and

(b) s 321 (right to demand a poll): CA 2006, s 335(3).

21.125 The quorum for a variation of class rights meeting is:

(a) for a meeting other than an adjourned meeting, two members of the class present (in person or by proxy) who together represent at least one-third of the voting rights of the class;

(b) for an adjourned meeting, one member of the class present (in person or by proxy): CA 2006, s 335(4).

At a variation of class rights meeting, any member present (in person or by proxy) may demand a poll: CA 2006, s 335(5).

21.126 For the purposes of s 335:

(a) any amendment of a provision contained in a company's articles for the variation of the rights of a class of members, or the insertion of any such provision into the articles, is itself to be treated as a variation of those rights; and

(b) references to the variation of rights of a class of members include references to their abrogation: CA 2006, s 335(6).

Public companies and traded companies: additional requirements for AGMs

Public companies and traded companies: annual general meeting

21.127 Every public company must hold a general meeting as its annual general meeting in each period of six months beginning with the day following its accounting reference date (in addition to any other meetings held during that period): CA 2006, s 336(1).

Every private company that is a traded company must hold a general meeting as its annual general meeting in each period of nine months beginning with the day following its accounting reference date (in addition to any other meetings held during that period): CA 2006, s 336(1A). Otherwise, private companies that are not traded companies are not required to hold AGMs unless its articles provide that such meetings be held.

A notice to the shareholders must give full and frank details of the matters to be considered at the general meeting

In *Baillie v Oriental Telephone and Electric Co Ltd* [1915] 1 Ch 503, the issue concerned the sufficiency of a notice of an AGM which omitted certain aspects for consideration by the members, namely the amount of remuneration that had been paid to the directors. It was contended by the claimant that the notice provided by the company for the AGM did not provide sufficient details of the resolutions to be passed.

The Court of Appeal held that the notice did not give a sufficiently full and frank disclosure to the shareholders of the facts upon which they were asked to vote; and that the resolutions were invalid and not binding upon the company.

There must be full and frank disclosure to the shareholders to allow them to make informed decisions at the AGMs.

The contents of the notice of a general meeting must not mislead shareholders and must properly set out issues for consideration

In *Kaye v Croydon Tramways Company* [1898] 1 Ch 358, the Court of Appeal held that the notice, by reason of its certain omissions did not fairly disclose the purpose for which the meeting was convened as required under the Companies Acts.

According to Lindley LJ:

> '… this notice has been most artfully framed to mislead the shareholders. It is a tricky notice, and it is to my mind playing with words to tell shareholders that they are convened for the purpose of considering a contract for the sale of their undertaking, and to conceal from them that a large portion of that purchase-money is not to be paid to the vendors who sell that undertaking. I am perfectly alive to the danger of putting into notices, especially notices by advertisement, more than the Act of Parliament requires, and I agree that all that the Act of Parliament requires is that the purpose shall be stated. But it must be stated fairly: it must not be stated so as to mislead; and one of the main purposes of this agreement, so far as the directors care about it, is that they shall get a large sum of money without disclosing the fact to their shareholders. I do not think that this notice discloses the purpose for which the meeting is convened. It is not a notice disclosing that purpose fairly, and in a sense not to mislead those to whom it is addressed.'

The notice of the general meeting must disclose all facts to the shareholders

In *Tiessen v Henderson* [1899] 1 Ch 861, Kekewich J held that the notice of an extraordinary general meeting must disclose all facts necessary to enable the shareholder receiving it to determine in his interest whether or not he ought to attend the meeting; and pecuniary interest of a director in the matter of a special resolution to be proposed at the meeting is a material fact for this purpose.

He stated:

> 'The question is merely whether each shareholder as and when he received the notice of the meeting, in which I include the circular of the same date, had fair warning of what was to be submitted to the meeting. A shareholder may properly and prudently leave matters in which he

> takes no personal interest to the decision of the majority. But in that case he is content to be bound by the vote of the majority; because he knows the matter about which the majority are to vote at the meeting. If he does not know that, he has not a fair chance of determining in his own interest whether he ought to attend the meeting, make further inquiries, or leave others to determine the matter for him.'

21.128 A company that fails to comply with CA 2006, s 336(1) or (1A) as a result of giving notice under s 392 (alteration of accounting reference date):

(a) specifying a new accounting reference date; and

(b) stating that the current accounting reference period or the previous accounting reference period is to be shortened,

shall be treated as if it had complied with s 336(1) if it holds a general meeting as its annual general meeting within three months of giving that notice: CA 2006, s 336(2).

21.129 If a company fails to comply with s 336(1) or (1A), an offence is committed by every officer of the company who is in default: CA 2006, s 336(3).

A person guilty of an offence under s 336 is liable:

(a) on conviction on indictment, to a fine;

(b) on summary conviction, to a fine not exceeding the statutory maximum: CA 2006, s 336(4).

Continuous failure to hold annual general meetings may constitute unfair prejudicial conduct.

> ***Repeated failures to hold AGMs may be unfairly prejudicial conduct***
>
> In *Re a company (No 00789 of 1987), ex parte Shooter*, and in *Re a company (No 3017 of 1987), ex parte Broadhurst* [1990] BCLC 384, there were repeated failures to hold AGM's and lay accounts at the meeting.
>
> Harman J held that the repeated failure to hold annual general meetings and lay accounts before the members depriving the members of their right to know and consider the state of the company, was conduct unfairly prejudicial to the interests of all the members and not some part of the members.

Public companies and traded companies: notice of AGM

21.130 A notice calling an annual general meeting of a public company or a private company that is a traded company must state that the meeting is an annual general meeting: CA 2006, s 337(1).

An annual general meeting of a public company that is not a traded company may be called by shorter notice than that required by s 307(2) or by the company's articles (as the case may be), if all the members entitled to attend and vote at the meeting agree to the shorter notice: CA 2006, s 337(2).

Where a notice calling an annual general meeting of a traded company is given more than six weeks before the meeting, the notice must include:

(a) if the company is a public company, a statement of the right under s 338 to require the company to give notice of a resolution to be moved at the meeting, and

(b) whether or not the company is a public company, a statement of the right under s 338A to require the company to include a matter in the business to be dealt with at the meeting: CA 2006, s 337(3).

Public companies: members' power to require circulation of resolutions for AGMs

21.131 The members of a public company may require the company to give, to members of the company entitled to receive notice of the next annual general meeting, notice of a resolution which may properly be moved and is intended to be moved at that meeting: CA 2006, s 338(1).

A resolution may properly be moved at an annual general meeting unless:

(a) it would, if passed, be ineffective (whether by reason of inconsistency with any enactment or the company's constitution or otherwise);

(b) it is defamatory of any person; or

(c) it is frivolous or vexatious: CA 2006, s 338(2).

21.132 A company is required to give notice of a resolution once it has received requests that it do so from:

(a) members representing at least 5% of the total voting rights of all the members who have a right to vote on the resolution at the annual general meeting to which the requests relate (excluding any voting rights attached to any shares in the company held as treasury shares); or

(b) at least 100 members who have a right to vote on the resolution at the annual general meeting to which the requests relate and hold shares in the company on which there has been paid up an average sum, per member, of at least £100.

See also CA 2006, s 153 (exercise of rights where shares held on behalf of others): CA 2006, s 338(3).

21.133 A request:

(a) may be in hard copy form or in electronic form;

(b) must identify the resolution of which notice is to be given;

(c) must be authenticated by the person or persons making it; and

(d) must be received by the company not later than:

(i) six weeks before the annual general meeting to which the requests relate; or

(ii) if later, the time at which notice is given of that meeting: CA 2006, s 338(4).

Traded companies: members' power to include other matters in business dealt with at AGM

21.134 The members of a traded company may request the company to include in the business to be dealt with at an annual general meeting any matter (other than a proposed resolution) which may properly be included in the business: CA 2006, s 339A(1).

A matter may properly be included in the business at an annual general meeting unless:

(a) it is defamatory of any person; or

(b) it is frivolous or vexatious: CA 2006, s 339A(2).

21.135 A company is required to include such a matter once it has received requests that it do so from:

(a) members representing at least 5% of the total voting rights of all the members who have a right to vote at the meeting; or

(b) at least 100 members who have a right to vote at the meeting and hold shares in the company on which there has been paid up an average sum, per member, of at least £100.

See also CA 2006, s 153 (exercise of rights where shares held on behalf of others): CA 2006, s 339A(3).

21.136 A request:

(a) may be in hard copy form or electronic form;

(b) must identify the matter to be included in the business;

(c) must be accompanied by a statement setting out the grounds for the request; and

(d) must be authenticated by the person or persons making it: CA 2006, s 339A(4).

21.137 A request must be received by the company not later than:

(a) six weeks before the meeting; or

(b) if later, the time at which notice is given of the meeting: CA 2006, s 339A(5).

Public companies: company's duty to circulate members' resolutions for AGMs

21.138 A company that is required under CA 2006, s 338 to give notice of a resolution must send a copy of it to each member of the company entitled to receive notice of the annual general meeting:

(a) in the same manner as notice of the meeting; and

(b) at the same time as, or as soon as reasonably practicable after, it gives notice of the meeting: CA 2006, s 339(1).

Section 339(1) applies subject to s 340(2) (deposit or tender of sum in respect of expenses of circulation): CA 2006, s 339(2).

The business which may be dealt with at an annual general meeting includes a resolution of which notice is given in accordance with this section: CA 2006, s 339(3).

21.139 In the event of default in complying with this section, an offence is committed by every officer of the company who is in default: CA 2006, s 339(4).

A person guilty of an offence under this section is liable:

(a) on conviction on indictment, to a fine;

(b) on summary conviction, to a fine not exceeding the statutory maximum: CA 2006, s 339(5).

Public companies: expenses of circulating members' resolutions for AGMs

21.140 The expenses of the company in complying with s 339 need not be paid by the members who requested the circulation of the resolution if requests sufficient to require the company to circulate it are received before the end of the financial year preceding the meeting: CA 2006, s 340(1). Otherwise:

(a) the expenses of the company in complying with that section must be paid by the members who requested the circulation of the resolution unless the company resolves otherwise, and

(b) unless the company has previously so resolved, it is not bound to comply with that section unless there is deposited with or tendered to it, not later than:

  (i) six weeks before the annual general meeting to which the requests relate; or

  (ii) if later, the time at which notice is given of that meeting,

a sum reasonably sufficient to meet its expenses in complying with that section: CA 2006, s 340(2).

Traded companies: duty to circulate members' matters for AGM

21.141 A company that is required under s 338A to include any matter in the business to be dealt with at an annual general meeting must:

(a) give notice of it to each member of the company entitled to receive notice of the annual general meeting:

  (i) in the same manner as notice of the meeting; and

  (ii) at the same time as, or as soon as reasonably practicable after, it gives notice of the meeting; and

(b) publish it on the same website as that on which the company published the information required by CA 2006, s 311A: CA 2006, s 340A(1).

Section 340A(1) applies subject to s 340B(2) (deposit or tender of sum in respect of expenses of circulation): CA 2006, s 340A(2).

21.142 In the event of default in complying with s 340, an offence is committed by every officer of the company who is in default: CA 2006, s 340A(3). A person guilty of an offence under the section is liable:

(a) on conviction on indictment, to a fine;

(b) on summary conviction, to a fine not exceeding the statutory maximum: CA 2006, s 340A(4).

Traded companies: expenses of circulating members' matters to be dealt with at AGM

21.143 The expenses of the company in complying with s 340A need not be paid by the members who requested the inclusion of the matter in the business to be dealt with at the annual general meeting if requests sufficient to require the company to include the matter are received before the end of the financial year preceding the meeting: CA 2006, s 340B(1). Otherwise:

(a) the expenses of the company in complying with that section must be paid by the members who requested the inclusion of the matter unless the company resolves otherwise; and

(b) unless the company has previously so resolved, it is not bound to comply with that section unless there is deposited with or tendered to it, not later than:

  (i) six weeks before the annual general meeting to which the requests relate; or

  (ii) if later, the time at which notice is given of that meeting,

a sum reasonably sufficient to meet its expenses in complying with that section: CA 2006, s 340B.

Additional requirements for quoted companies and traded companies

Results of poll to be made available on website

21.144 Where a poll is taken at a general meeting of a quoted company that is not a traded company, the company must ensure that the following information is made available on a website:

(a) the date of the meeting;

(b) the text of the resolution or, as the case may be, a description of the subject matter of the poll;

(c) the number of votes cast in favour; and

(d) the number of votes cast against: CA 2006, s 341(1).

21.145 Where a poll is taken at a general meeting of a traded company, the company must ensure that the following information is made available on a website:

(a) the date of the meeting;

(b) the text of the resolution or, as the case may be, a description of the subject matter of the poll;

(c) the number of votes validly cast;

(d) the proportion of the company's issued share capital (determined at the time at which the right to vote is determined under s 360B(2)) represented by those votes;

(e) the number of votes cast in favour;

(f) the number of votes cast against; and

(g) the number of abstentions (if counted): CA 2006, s 341(1A).

21.146 A traded company must comply with s 341(1A) by:

(a) the end of 16 days beginning with the day of the meeting; or

(b) if later, the end of the first working day after the day on which the result of the poll is declared: CA 2006, s 341(1B).

The provisions of s 353 (requirements as to website availability) apply: CA 2006, s 341(2).

In the event of default in complying with this section (or with the requirements of s 353 as it applies for the purposes of this section), an offence is committed by every officer of the company who is in default: CA 2006, s 341(3).

A person guilty of an offence under sub-s (3) is liable on summary conviction to a fine not exceeding level 3 on the standard scale: CA 2006, s 341(4).

21.147 Failure to comply with this section (or the requirements of s 353) does not affect the validity of:

(a) the poll; or

(b) the resolution or other business (if passed or agreed to) to which the poll relates: CA 2006, s 341(5).

Section 341 only applies to polls taken after this section comes into force: CA 2006, s 341(6).

Members' power to require independent report on poll

21.148 The members of a quoted company may require the directors to obtain an independent report on any poll taken, or to be taken, at a general meeting of the company: CA 2006, s 342(1).

The directors are required to obtain an independent report if they receive requests to do so from:

(a) members representing not less than 5% of the total voting rights of all the members who have a right to vote on the matter to which the poll relates (excluding any voting rights attached to any shares in the company held as treasury shares), or

(b) not less than 100 members who have a right to vote on the matter to which the poll relates and hold shares in the company on which there has been paid up an average sum, per member, of not less than £100.

See also CA 2006, s 153 (exercise of rights where shares held on behalf of others): CA 2006, s 342(2).

Where the requests relate to more than one poll, s 342(2) must be satisfied in relation to each of them: CA 2006, s 342(3).

21.149 A request:

(a) may be in hard copy form or in electronic form;

(b) must identify the poll or polls to which it relates;

(c) must be authenticated by the person or persons making it; and

(d) must be received by the company not later than one week after the date on which the poll is taken: CA 2006, s 342(4).

Appointment of independent assessor

21.150 Directors who are required under CA 2006, s 342 to obtain an independent report on a poll or polls must appoint a person they consider to be appropriate (an 'independent assessor') to prepare a report for the company on it or them: CA 2006, s 343(1). The appointment must be made within one week after the company being required to obtain the report: CA 2006, s 343(2).

The directors must not appoint a person who:

(a) does not meet the independence requirement in CA 2006, s 344; or

(b) has another role in relation to any poll on which he is to report (including, in particular, a role in connection with collecting or counting votes or with the appointment of proxies): CA 2006, s 343(3).

In the event of default in complying with this section, an offence is committed by every officer of the company who is in default: CA 2006, s 343(4).

A person guilty of an offence under this section is liable on summary conviction to a fine not exceeding level 5 on the standard scale: CA 2006, s 343(5).

21.151 If at the meeting no poll on which a report is required is taken:

(a) the directors are not required to obtain a report from the independent assessor; and

(b) his appointment ceases (but without prejudice to any right to be paid for work done before the appointment ceased): CA 2006, s 343(6).

Rights of independent assessor: right to information

21.152 A person may not be appointed as an independent assessor:

(a) if he is:

  (i) an officer or employee of the company; or

  (iii) a partner or employee of such a person, or a partnership of which such a person is a partner;

(b) if he is:

  (i) an officer or employee of an associated undertaking of the company; or

  (iii) a partner or employee of such a person, or a partnership of which such a person is a partner;

(c) if there exists between:

  (i) the person or an associate of his; and

  (iii) the company or an associated undertaking of the company,

a connection of any such description as may be specified by regulations made by the Secretary of State: CA 2006, s 344(1).

An auditor of the company is not regarded as an officer or employee of the company for this purpose: CA 2006, s 344(2).

21.153 In s 344:

'associated undertaking' means:

(a) a parent undertaking or subsidiary undertaking of the company; or

(b) a subsidiary undertaking of a parent undertaking of the company; and

'associate' has the meaning given by s 345: CA 2006, s 344(3).

Meaning of 'associate'

21.154 CA 2006, s 345 defines 'associate' for the purposes of CA 2006, s 344 (independence requirement): s 345(1).

In relation to an individual, 'associate' means:

(a) that individual's spouse or civil partner or minor child or step-child;

(b) any body corporate of which that individual is a director; and

(c) any employee or partner of that individual: CA 2006, s 345(2).

21.155 In relation to a body corporate, 'associate' means:

(a) any body corporate of which that body is a director;

(b) any body corporate in the same group as that body; and

(c) any employee or partner of that body or of any body corporate in the same group: CA 2006, s 345(3).

21.156 In relation to a partnership that is a legal person under the law by which it is governed, 'associate' means:

(a) any body corporate of which that partnership is a director;

(b) any employee of or partner in that partnership; and

(c) any person who is an associate of a partner in that partnership: CA 2006, s 345(4).

21.157 In relation to a partnership that is not a legal person under the law by which it is governed, 'associate' means any person who is an associate of any of the partners: CA 2006, s 345(5).

In s 345, in relation to a limited liability partnership, for 'director' read 'member': CA 2006, s 345(6).

Effect of appointment of a partnership

21.158 CA 2006, s 346 applies where a partnership that is not a legal person under the law by which it is governed is appointed as an independent assessor: CA 2006, s 346(1).

Unless a contrary intention appears, the appointment is of the partnership as such and not of the partners: CA 2006, s 346(2).

Where the partnership ceases, the appointment is to be treated as extending to:

(a) any partnership that succeeds to the practice of that partnership; or

(b) any other person who succeeds to that practice having previously carried it on in partnership: CA 2006, s 346(3).

21.159 For the purposes of s 346(3):

(a) a partnership is regarded as succeeding to the practice of another partnership only if the members of the successor partnership are substantially the same as those of the former partnership; and

(b) a partnership or other person is regarded as succeeding to the practice of a partnership only if it or he succeeds to the whole or substantially the whole of the business of the former partnership: CA 2006, s 346(4).

21.160 Where the partnership ceases and the appointment is not treated under s 346(3) as extending to any partnership or other person, the appointment may with the consent of the company be treated as extending to a partnership, or other person, who succeeds to:

(a) the business of the former partnership; or

(b) such part of it as is agreed by the company is to be treated as comprising the appointment: CA 2006, s 346(5).

The independent assessor's report

21.161 The report of the independent assessor must state his opinion whether:

(a) the procedures adopted in connection with the poll or polls were adequate;

(b) the votes cast (including proxy votes) were fairly and accurately recorded and counted;

(c) the validity of members' appointments of proxies was fairly assessed;

(d) the notice of the meeting complied with s 325 (notice of meeting to contain statement of rights to appoint proxy);

(e) s 326 (company-sponsored invitations to appoint proxies) was complied with in relation to the meeting: CA 2006, s 347(1).

The report must give his reasons for the opinions stated: CA 2006, s 347(2).

If he is unable to form an opinion on any of those matters, the report must record that fact and state the reasons for it: CA 2006, s 347(3).

The report must state the name of the independent assessor: CA 2006, s 347(4).

Rights of independent assessor: right to attend meeting etc

21.162 Where an independent assessor has been appointed to report on a poll, he is entitled to attend:

(a) the meeting at which the poll may be taken; and

(b) any subsequent proceedings in connection with the poll: CA 2006, s 348(1).

21.163 He is also entitled to be provided by the company with a copy of:

(a) the notice of the meeting; and

(b) any other communication provided by the company in connection with the meeting to persons who have a right to vote on the matter to which the poll relates: CA 2006, s 348(2).

The rights conferred by this section are only to be exercised to the extent that the independent assessor considers necessary for the preparation of his report: CA 2006, s 348(3).

If the independent assessor is a firm, the right under s 348(1) to attend the meeting and any subsequent proceedings in connection with the poll is exercisable by an individual authorised by the firm in writing to act as its representative for that purpose: CA 2006, s 348(4).

Rights of independent assessor: right to information

21.164 The independent assessor is entitled to access to the company's records relating to:

(a) any poll on which he is to report;

(b) the meeting at which the poll or polls may be, or were, taken: CA 2006, s 349(1).

21.165 The independent assessor may require anyone who at any material time was:

(a) a director or secretary of the company;

(b) an employee of the company;

(c) a person holding or accountable for any of the company's records;

(d) a member of the company; or

(e) an agent of the company,

to provide him with information or explanations for the purpose of preparing his report: CA 2006, s 349(2).

For this purpose 'agent' includes the company's bankers, solicitors and auditor: CA 2006, s 349(3).

21.166 A statement made by a person in response to a requirement under this section may not be used in evidence against him in criminal proceedings except proceedings for an offence under s 350 (offences relating to provision of information): CA 2006, s 349(4).

A person is not required by this section to disclose information in respect of which a claim to legal professional privilege (in Scotland, to confidentiality of communications) could be maintained in legal proceedings: CA 2006, s 349(5).

Offences relating to provision of information

21.167 A person who fails to comply with a requirement under s 349 without delay commits an offence unless it was not reasonably practicable for him to provide the required information or explanation: CA 2006, s 350(1).

A person guilty of an offence under s 350(1) is liable on summary conviction to a fine not exceeding level 3 on the standard scale: CA 2006, s 350(2).

A person commits an offence who knowingly or recklessly makes to an independent assessor a statement (oral or written) that:

(a) conveys or purports to convey any information or explanations which the independent assessor requires, or is entitled to require, under s 349; and

(b) is misleading, false or deceptive in a material particular: CA 2006, s 350(3).

21.168 A person guilty of an offence under s 350(3) is liable:

(a) on conviction on indictment, to imprisonment for a term not exceeding two years or a fine (or both);

(b) on summary conviction:

  (i) in England and Wales, to imprisonment for a term not exceeding 12 months or to a fine not exceeding the statutory maximum (or both);

  (ii) in Scotland or Northern Ireland, to imprisonment for a term not exceeding six months, or to a fine not exceeding the statutory maximum (or both): CA 2006, s 350(4).

Nothing in s 350 affects any right of an independent assessor to apply for an injunction (in Scotland, an interdict or an order for specific performance) to enforce any of his rights under ss 348 or 349: CA 2006, s 350(5).

Information to be made available on website

21.169 Where an independent assessor has been appointed to report on a poll, the company must ensure that the following information is made available on a website:

(a) the fact of his appointment;

(b) his identity;

(c) the text of the resolution or, as the case may be, a description of the subject matter of the poll to which his appointment relates; and

(d) a copy of a report by him which complies with s 347: CA 2006, s 351(1).

The provisions of s 353 (requirements as to website availability) apply: CA 2006, s 351(2).

In the event of default in complying with s 351 (or with the requirements of s 353 as it applies for the purposes of this section), an offence is committed by every officer of the company who is in default: CA 2006, s 351(3).

A person guilty of an offence under s 351(3) is liable on summary conviction to a fine not exceeding level 3 on the standard scale: CA 2006, s 351(4).

21.170 Failure to comply with this section (or the requirements of s 353) does not affect the validity of:

(a) the poll; or

(b) the resolution or other business (if passed or agreed to) to which the poll relates: CA 2006, s 351(5).

Application of provisions to class meetings

21.171 The provisions of CA 2006, s 341 (results of poll to be made available on website) apply (with any necessary modifications) in relation to a meeting of holders of a class of shares of a quoted company or traded company in connection with the variation of the rights attached to such shares as they apply in relation to a general meeting of the company: CA 2006, s 352(1).

The provisions of ss 342–351 (independent report on poll) apply (with any necessary modifications) in relation to a meeting of holders of a class of shares of a quoted company in connection with the variation of the rights attached to such shares as they apply in relation to a general meeting of the company: CA 2006, s 352(1A).

21.172 For the purposes of s 352:

(a) any amendment of a provision contained in a company's articles for the variation of the rights attached to a class of shares, or the insertion of any such provision into the articles, is itself to be treated as a variation of those rights; and

(b) references to the variation of rights attached to a class of shares include references to their abrogation: CA 2006, s 352(2).

Requirements as to website availability

21.173 The following provisions apply for the purposes of:

(a) s 341 of the CA 2006 (results of poll to be made available on website); and

(b) s 351 of the CA 2006 (report of independent observer to be made available on website): CA 2006, s 353(1).

21.174 The information must be made available on a website that:

(a) is maintained by or on behalf of the company; and

(b) identifies the company in question: CA 2006, s 353(2).

Access to the information on the website, and the ability to obtain a hard copy of the information from the website, must not be conditional on the payment of a fee or otherwise restricted: CA 2006, s 353(3).

21.175 The information:

(a) must be made available as soon as reasonably practicable; and

(b) must be kept available throughout the period of two years beginning with the date on which it is first made available on a website in accordance with this section: CA 2006, s 353(4).

21.176 A failure to make information available on a website throughout the period specified in s 353(4)(b) is disregarded if:

(a) the information is made available on the website for part of that period; and

(b) the failure is wholly attributable to circumstances that it would not be reasonable to have expected the company to prevent or avoid: CA 2006, s 353(5).

Records of resolutions and meetings

Records

21.177 Every company must keep records comprising:

(a) copies of all resolutions of members passed otherwise than at general meetings;

(b) minutes of all proceedings of general meetings; and

(c) details provided to the company in accordance with CA 2006, s 357 (decisions of sole member): CA 2006, s 355(1).

The records must be kept for at least ten years from the date of the resolution, meeting or decision (as appropriate): CA 2006, s 355(2).

If a company fails to comply with s 355, an offence is committed by every officer of the company who is in default: CA 2006, s 355(3).

A person guilty of an offence under this section is liable on summary conviction to a fine not exceeding level 3 on the standard scale and, for continued contravention, a daily default fine not exceeding one-tenth of level 3 on the standard scale: CA 2006, s 355(4).

Records as evidence of resolutions

21.178 CA 2006, s 356 applies to the records kept in accordance with s 355: CA 2006, s 356(1).

The record of a resolution passed otherwise than at a general meeting, if purporting to be signed by a director of the company or by the company secretary, is evidence (in Scotland, sufficient evidence) of the passing of the resolution: CA 2006, s 356(2).

Where there is a record of a written resolution of a private company, the requirements of this Act with respect to the passing of the resolution are deemed to be complied with unless the contrary is proved: CA 2006, s 356(3).

The minutes of proceedings of a general meeting, if purporting to be signed by the chairman of that meeting or by the chairman of the next general meeting, are evidence (in Scotland, sufficient evidence) of the proceedings at the meeting: CA 2006, s 356(4).

21.179 Where there is a record of proceedings of a general meeting of a company, then, until the contrary is proved:

(a) the meeting is deemed duly held and convened;

(b) all proceedings at the meeting are deemed to have duly taken place; and

(c) all appointments at the meeting are deemed valid: CA 2006, s 356(5).

Records of decisions by sole member

21.180 CA 2006, s 357 applies to a company limited by shares or by guarantee that has only one member: CA 2006, s 357(1).

Where the member takes any decision that:

(a) may be taken by the company in general meeting; and

(b) has effect as if agreed by the company in general meeting,

he must (unless that decision is taken by way of a written resolution) provide the company with details of that decision: CA 2006, s 357(2).

If a person fails to comply with this section he commits an offence: CA 2006, s 357(3), and a person found guilty of such offence is liable on summary conviction to a fine not exceeding level 2 on the standard scale: CA 2006, s 357(4).

Failure to comply with this section does not affect the validity of any decision referred to in CA 2006, s 357(2): CA 2006, s 357(5).

Inspection of records of resolutions and meetings

21.181 The records referred to in CA 2006, s 355 (records of resolutions etc) relating to the previous ten years must be kept available for inspection:

(a) at the company's registered office; or

(b) at a place specified in regulations under CA 2006, s 1136: CA 2006, s 358(1).

21.182 The company must give notice to the registrar:

(a) of the place at which the records are kept available for inspection; and

(b) of any change in that place,

unless they have at all times been kept at the company's registered office: CA 2006, s 358(2).

21.183 The records must be open to the inspection of any member of the company without charge: s 358(3).

Any member may require a copy of any of the records on payment of such fee as may be prescribed: CA 2006, s 358(4).

If default is made for 14 days in complying with s 358(2) or an inspection required under s 358(3) is refused, or a copy requested under sub-s (4) is not sent, an offence is committed by every officer of the company who is in default: CA 2006, s 358(5).

A person guilty of an offence under this section is liable on summary conviction to a fine not exceeding level 3 on the standard scale and, for continued contravention, a daily default fine not exceeding one-tenth of level 3 on the standard scale: CA 2006, s 358(6).

In a case in which an inspection required under s 358(3) is refused or a copy requested under s 358(4) is not sent, the court may by order compel an immediate inspection of the records or direct that the copies required be sent to the persons who requested them: CA 2006, s 358(7).

Records of resolutions and meetings of class of members

21.184 The provisions of CA 2006, Pt 13, Ch 6 apply (with necessary modifications) in relation to resolutions and meetings of:

(a) holders of a class of shares; and

(b) in the case of a company without a share capital, a class of members,

as they apply in relation to resolutions of members generally and to general meetings: CA 2006, s 359.

Supplementary aspects

Computation of periods of notice etc: clear day

21.185 Section 360 of the CA 2006 applies for the purposes of the following provisions set out in Pt 13:

(a) s 307(1) and (2) (notice required of general meeting);

(b) s 307A(1), (4), (5) and (7)(b) (notice required of general meeting of traded company);

(c) s 312(1) and (3) (resolution requiring special notice);

(d) s 314(4)(d) (request to circulate members' statement);

(e) s 316(2)(b) (expenses of circulating statement to be deposited or tendered before meeting);

(f) s 337(3) (contents of notice of AGM of traded company);

(g) s 338(4)(d)(i) (request to circulate member's resolution at AGM of public company);

(h) s 338A(5) (request to include matter in the business to be dealt with at AGM of traded company);

(i) s 340(2)(b)(i) (expenses of circulating statement to be deposited or tendered before meeting); and

(j) s 340B(2)(b) (traded companies: duty to circulate members' matters for AGM): s 360(1).

21.186 Any reference in those provisions to a period of notice, or to a period before a meeting by which a request must be received or sum deposited or tendered, is to a period of the specified length excluding:

(a) the day of the meeting; and

(b) the day on which the notice is given, the request received or the sum deposited or tendered: CA 2006, s 360(2).

Electronic meetings and voting

21.187 Nothing in CA 2006, Pt 13 is to be taken to preclude the holding and conducting of a meeting in such a way that persons who are not present together at the same place may by electronic means attend and speak and vote at it: CA 2006, s 360A(1).

In the case of a traded company the use of electronic means for the purpose of enabling members to participate in a general meeting may be made subject only to such requirements and restrictions as are:

(a) necessary to ensure the identification of those taking part and the security of the electronic communication; and

(b) proportionate to the achievement of those objectives: CA 2006, s 360A(2).

Nothing in s 360A(2) affects any power of a company to require reasonable evidence of the entitlement of any person who is not a member to participate in the meeting: CA 2006, s 360A(3).

Traded companies: requirements for participating in and voting at general meetings

21.188 Any provision of a traded company's articles is void in so far as it would have the effect of:

(a) imposing a restriction on a right of a member to participate in and vote at a general meeting of the company unless the member's shares have (after having been acquired by the member and before the meeting) been deposited with, or transferred to, or registered in the name of another person; or

(b) imposing a restriction on the right of a member to transfer shares in the company during the period of 48 hours before the time for the holding of a general meeting of the company if that right would not otherwise be subject to that restriction: CA 2006, s 360B(1).

A traded company must determine the right to vote at a general meeting of the company by reference to the register of members as at a time (determined by the company) that is not more than 48 hours before the time for the holding of the meeting: CA 2006, s 360B(2).

In calculating the period mentioned in s 360B(1)(b) or (2), no account is to be taken of any part of a day that is not a working day: CA 2006, s 360B(3).

21.189 Nothing in this section affects:

(a) the operation of:

  (i) CA 2006, Pt 22 (information about interests in a company's shares);

  (ii) CA 1985, Pt 15 (orders imposing restrictions on shares); or

  (iii) any provision in a company's articles relating to the application of any provision of either of those Parts; or

(b) the validity of articles prescribed, or to the same effect as articles prescribed, under CA 2006, s 19 (power of Secretary of State to prescribe model articles): CA 2006, s 360B(4).

If an election is in force under s 128B in respect of a company, the reference in sub-s (2) to the register of members is to be read as a reference to the register kept by the registrar under s 1080: CA 2006, s 360B(5) (as inserted by SBEEA 2015, Sch 5, Pt 2).

Meaning of 'traded company'

21.190 The term 'traded company' means a company any shares of which:

(a) carry rights to vote at general meetings; and

(b) are admitted to trading on a regulated market in an EEA State by or with the consent of the company: CA 2006, s 360C.

Meaning of 'quoted company'

21.191 The term 'quoted company' has the same meaning as in CA 2006, Pt 15.

Informal unanimous consent of shareholders

21.192 Although CA 2006 sets out the law including rules and procedures for meetings to be convened and held, there has also at times been a recognition by the courts that not all the formalities may need to be complied with if the shareholders unanimously assent informally to the passing of resolutions. The courts have held that such informal assent, provided it is unanimous, is equivalent to a validly convened meeting at which a resolution is passed. This has become known as the *'Duomatic principle'* based on the case below. The common law principle is enshrined under the CA 2006, s 281(4)(a) states that '... nothing in this Part affects any enactment of rule of law as to things done otherwise than by passing a resolution'. Section 281(4)(c) states that 'nothing in this Part affects any enactment or rule of law as to ... cases in which a person is precluded from alleging that a resolution has not been duly passed.'

21.193 The *Duomatic* principle applies to both public and private companies but may have less application to private companies who may now use the written resolution procedure to pass certain resolutions. The principle is based on the rationale that as all members have validly and competently agreed on a matter affecting the company, the company should not be denied the free-will and decision making of all the shareholders: *Baroness Wenlock v River Dee Co* (1883) 36 Ch D 675; *Re New Cedos Engineering Co Ltd* [1994] 1 BCLC 797; and *Euro Brokers Holdings Ltd v Monecor (London) Ltd* [2003] 1 BCLC 506. The principle operates as a mechanism that waives the formal requirements for convening meetings.

The *Duomatic* principle does not permit shareholders to do informally what they could not have done formally by way of a written resolution or at a meeting: *Re New Cedos Engineering Co Ltd* [1994] 1 BCLC 797; *Atlas Wright (Europe) Ltd v Wright* [1999] BCC 163.

Unanimous informal agreement of shareholders is equivalent to a validly convened meeting

As long ago as 1920, in *Re Express Engineering Works Ltd* [1920] 1 Ch 466, the Court of Appeal considered the resolution to approve a debenture at a meeting which had not been convened in compliance with the Companies Acts, and held that as there was no suggestion of fraud involved, the company was bound in a matter *intra vires* by the unanimous agreement of its shareholders. Although the meeting was styled a directors' meeting, all the five shareholders were present, and they might well have turned it into a general meeting, and transacted the same business. In these circumstances the issue of the debentures was not invalid.

All shareholders must assent albeit in an informal manner

In *Parker & Cooper v Reading* [1926] Ch 975, Astbury J held that a company was bound in a matter *intra vires* the company by the unanimous agreement of all its corporators. If all the individual shareholders in fact assent to a transaction that is *intra vires* the company, though *ultra vires* the board, it was not necessary that they should hold a meeting in one room or one place to express that assent simultaneously.

21.194 This has become known as the *'Duomatic'* principle, which has given rise to subject of much case law in this area.

There is no procedural requirement to hold a formal meeting as an informal unanimous agreement may suffice subject to exceptions under CA 2006

In *Re Duomatic Ltd* [1969] 1 All ER 161, Buckley J was of the view that although the shareholders did not take the formal step of formally convening a general meeting of the company and passing a formal resolution approving the payment of directors' salaries, they had at the time of passing the accounts applied their minds as to whether their drawings as directors should be approved as being on account of remuneration payable to them as directors. Accordingly, their consent should be regarded as tantamount to a resolution of a general meeting. Only those shareholders who are entitled to vote at meetings can informally consent: shareholders who have no voting rights cannot assent.

The Duomatic principle has also been applied where there was no formal compliance with the CA 2006 for a meeting to be convened, particularly in respect of approval of long-term service contracts under s 188

In *Wright v Atlas Wright (Europe) Limited* [1999] 2 BCLC 301, Potter LJ in the Court of Appeal held that although the agreement between the claimant and the defendant did not comply with the requirements of s 188, the agreement was not rendered void under that provision. This was because the agreement was rendered enforceable by application of the principle in *Re Duomatic Ltd* [1969] 1 All ER 161, namely that the unanimous consent of all shareholders who have a right to attend and vote at a general meeting of the company can override formal, including statutory, requirements in relation to the passing of resolutions at such meetings.

Further, in determining whether to apply the *Re Duomatic Ltd* principle the court must examine the underlying purpose of the statutory provision.

The underlying purpose of s 188 was limited and did not exclude or render inappropriate the application of the *Re Duomatic Ltd* principle. Section 188 was for the benefit and protection of shareholders. It was to ensure that a company should not be bound by an obligation to employ a director for more than five years unless its members had considered and approved the relevant term. The underlying intention of the section was to require unequivocal approval of the shareholders regarding a long-term contract in respect of which there had been proper opportunity for the shareholders to consider the terms of the agreement approved.

Although s 188 set out the formality required as a precondition to the passing of the resolution, it was no more than a formality in the nature of a notice provision designed to ensure the opportunity for fully informed consent by the shareholders. It was thus amenable to waiver by the class for whose protection it was designed.

The Duomatic principle may apply to substantial property transactions

In *NBH Limited v Hoare* [2006] 2 BCLC 649, the court was required to consider whether the *Duomatic* principle also applied to substantial property transactions under CA 2006, s 190.

Park J held that the principle of informal shareholder approval being as binding as a resolution in general meeting applied to transactions affected by s 190 and therefore the shareholders' prior approval sufficed to meet the requirement of s 190.

21.195 In *Multinational Gas v Multinational Services* [1983] Ch 258, Lawton LJ stated that where approval was given to acts of directors by the shareholders even though informally, the approval precluded the company asserting any liability against the director because the adoption of the director's acts by the shareholders in agreement with each other made the directors' acts the acts of the company itself.

However, there have been some situations where the court has not accepted the application of the *Duomatic* principle.

For the Duomatic principle to apply, there must be unqualified agreement by the shareholders

In *Schofield v Schofield* [2011] 2 BCLC 319, the Court of Appeal held that although assent could have been express or implied, verbal or by conduct, given at the time of the informal meeting or later, however, nothing short of unqualified agreement, objectively established, would suffice to establish assent within the *Duomatic* principle.

Before the Duomatic principle can apply, the shareholders must be properly appraised of all the facts

In *EIC Services Ltd v Phipps* [2004] 2 BCLC 589, the issue was whether the issue of shares and bonus shares had been assented to by all the shareholders at an informal meeting, where some shareholders were not fully appraised of all relevant facts to provide an informed assent.

Neuberger J held that the *Duomatic* principle could not apply in such situations. He stated that the essence of the *Duomatic* principle was that, where the articles of a company required a course to be approved by a group of shareholders at a general meeting, that requirement could be avoided if all members of the group, being aware of the relevant facts, either gave their approval to that course, or so conducted themselves as to make it inequitable for them to deny that they had given their approval.

Whether the approval was given in advance or after the event, whether it was characterised as agreement, ratification, waiver, or estoppel, and whether members of the group gave their consent in different ways at different times, was irrelevant. However, before the *Duomatic* principle could be applied, the shareholders who were said to have assented or waived their objection had to have had the appropriate, or 'full', knowledge. Accordingly, where the directors merely informed shareholders of an intended (or past) action on the part of the directors, in circumstances in which neither the directors nor the shareholders were aware that the consent of the shareholders was required to that action, the shareholders could not be said, as a matter both of ordinary language and legal concept, to have 'assented' to that action for *Duomatic* purposes.

Quite apart from the fact that a shareholder could not be said to assent to a matter if he was merely told of it, he could not have the necessary full knowledge to enable him to assent if he was not even aware that his assent was being sought in relation to the matter, let alone that the obtaining of his consent was a significant factor in relation to it.

Although the shareholders might well have been aware of the projected bonus issue their consent to the issue was neither sought nor given and nor were they informed that the bonus issue would involve capitalisation of part of the company's share premium account.

The consent of the shareholders must be objectively established: *Schofield v Schofield* [2011] 2 BCLC 319. This may include agreement by the shareholder or some other mechanism that constitutes consent: *Re Bailey Hay & Co* [1971] 1 WLR 1357.

The Duomatic principle is subject to some limitations

In *Secretary of State for Business, Innovation and Skills v Doffman (No 2)* [2011] 2 BCLC 541, Newey J stated that the principle of ratification by informal shareholder approval or conduct of a course of action requiring a resolution at a general meeting was subject to the limitations that:

(a) unless it was inequitable for the shareholders to deny that they had given their approval, the principle did not apply if the shareholders had not addressed their minds to the matter in question;

(b) the principle did not apply if there was an unlawful distribution to shareholders; and

(c) the application of the principle was precluded if the company's financial circumstances were such that the creditors were at risk and their interests overrode those of the shareholders.

Where the acts of other shareholders are required to effect the assent, the Duomatic principle cannot then apply

There must be competence by the shareholder to assent to the meeting. The *Duomatic* principle cannot apply where the acts of other shareholders are required to affect the assent. In *Re New Cedos Engineering Co Ltd* [1994] 1 BCLC 797, Oliver J held that the *Duomatic* principle would not apply where a shareholder had knowledge of the facts giving rise to any previous invalidity of meetings. Further, the principle would not apply where all the shareholders entitled to attend and vote, assented to something *intra vires*, the company would be bound by that assent even though it was not given at a properly constituted meeting because the act of other shareholders was also required to assent.

The *Duomatic* principle cannot apply to relieve directors of liability in respect of transactions which are ultra vires the company (in the narrow or wider sense): *Rolled Steel Products* [1986] Ch 246.

The principle would not apply to unlawful distribution of capital or unlawful payment of dividends: Re *Aveling Barford Ltd* [1989] 1 WLR 360; *Secretary of State for Business Innovation and Skills v Doffman* [2011] 2 BCLC 541.

The Duomatic principle applied where breaches of duty by directors were ratified by the unanimous approval of the shareholders

The application of the *Duomatic* principle was considered in *Madoff Securities International Ltd v Raven* [2013] EWHC 3147. Popplewell J was of the view that the principle was applicable if the directors honestly and reasonably believed the company to be solvent, notwithstanding that with the benefit of hindsight it could be shown to be insolvent or of doubtful solvency. The solvency of the company must however be objectively ascertained: *Lexi v Luqman (No 1)* [2007] EWHC 2652; *Tradepower (Holdings) Ltd v Tradepower (Hong Kong) Ltd* [2010] 1 HKC 380.

Popplewell J further stated that in order to rely on the *Duomatic* principle and for the shareholders to ratify a transaction, the transaction must be bone fide and honest: see *Re Bowthorpe Holdings Ltd* [2003] 1 BCLC 226. This involved a consideration of the legal and factual issues. On the facts, he found that directors had acted honestly and in good faith. According to Popplewell J:

> 'The legal issue is therefore whether the *Duomatic* principle is inapplicable where the directors are acting honestly but the shareholders approve the transaction acting in bad faith, in this case for the dishonest purposes of furthering a fraud. The factual issues depend upon the state of mind and intentions of the voting shareholders.'

On the facts, insofar as the transactions and payments involved a breach by the directors to act in what they perceived to be the interests of the company, or a failure to exercise reasonable care, skill and diligence, they were ratified by the shareholders unanimously. Accordingly, such ratification made such acts the acts of the company.

22 Control of political donations and expenditure

Contents

Introduction

22.1 Part IV to the Political Parties, Elections and Referendums Act 2000 (c 41) (PPERA 2000) is concerned with the control of donations to registered parties and their members, and sets out obligations on such parties and members to disclose the nature and source of funds received, and the persons from whom they receive donations: see ss 50–71. The CA 2006 interacts with PPERA 2000 in the regulation and control or corporate political donations and expenditure.

Donations by companies is addressed under Pt 14 of the CA 2006 which concerns the control of political donations and expenditure made by companies to various political parties, political organisations and independent election candidates: CA 2006, s 362. It is interrelated with Pt IV of PPERA in respect of donations that can be given by a permissible donor and the value of the donation.

This Chapter addresses the following essential concepts that are applicable to corporate donations and expenditures:

- The definition of 'political parties'.
- The nature of 'political organisations' (other than political parties).
- Identifying 'independent election candidates' at any election to public office.
- The meaning of 'political donations' and 'political expenditure' made by companies.

These definitions are essential towards understanding how corporate donations and expenditures are regulated under the CA 2006.

22.2 In particular, consideration is given to the following questions:

- In what circumstances will a political donation or political expenditure require authorisation?
- What form of authorisation is required?
- What is the liability of directors for unauthorised donations or expenditure?
- What powers of enforcement against directors are available to the company or the shareholders?
- What are the circumstances in which companies will be exempt from CA 2006, Pt 14 requirements.

The position before the Companies Act 2006

Early case law

22.3 Before the Companies Act 2006, the regulation of corporate donations for political purposes was largely fragmented, comprising partly legislation (previously CA 1985) and partly case law. In respect of case law, judicial attitudes were concerned with the interpretation of a company's objects clause in its memorandum of association and the distinction between objects and powers in the objects clause, in determining whether or not the corporate activity or the donation was *ultra vires* the company.

A company must have an express objects clause permitting political donations

One of the earliest cases on corporate political donations was *Simmonds v Heffer* [1983] BCLC 298. The main objects of the League Against Cruel Sports Limited ('the League') were to prevent and oppose cruelty to animals, and in particular cruelty resulting from hunting with hounds of deer, foxes and otters, the digging of badgers, and the coursing of hares and rabbits.

In the 1979 General Election, the Labour Party committed itself, if elected, to introduce legislation banning hare coursing and stag hunting and because of this, the executive committee of the League contributed £80,000 to the Labour Party which was in two parts: the first part, £50,000, was paid over for the funding of the Labour Party election campaign. The second part, £30,000, was paid on the understanding that it would be used to help the Labour Party meet the substantial cost of the work and campaigning to give public support for the commitment in its manifesto to the cause of animal welfare generally, and in particular that part of it within the objects and purposes of the League.

A League member challenged the payments on the grounds that they were *ultra vires* the company. The issue arising in this case was whether or not some donations made by the League in 1979 were within the capacity of the League under the terms of its memorandum of association.

Mervyn Davies J considered that in deciding to give effect to its aims by paying out money to the Labour Party General Election Campaign Committee for its general purposes, the League also decided that the money paid out might be spent, not only on its own aims, but also on the aims of the Labour Party; those aims extended far beyond the League's aims. He decided that the payment of £50,000 was ultra vires, as it could be used for purposes unconnected with the League's objects and it was recoverable by the League. The objects of the League were specific and accordingly the donation of £50,000 might not have been spent by the Labour Party for the League's objects, but for other purposes. The League did not have the capacity to provide such payment to the Labour Party.

However, the donation of £30,000 was valid in that it could only be used for purposes which were clearly within and consistent with the League's objects. See too *Re Horsley and Weight Ltd* [1982] Ch 442 at 448.

The position under the Political Parties, Elections and Referendums Act 2000

22.4 PPERA 2000 regulates the registration of political parties including donations to such parties and accounting requirements. Part IV of PPERA 2000 imposes restrictions on the sources of donations by prohibiting foreign and anonymous donations to political parties and makes registered parties subject to reporting requirements in respect of donations above a certain value. CA 2006 makes reference to specific provisions of PPERA 2000 in respect of donations by companies to political parties. This section sets out the key provisions under PPERA 2000 that impact on CA 2006.

22.5 Under s 50 of Pt IV of PPERA 2000, a donation, in relation to a registered party, means (subject to PPERA 2000, s 52):

'(a) any gift to the party of money or other property – a gift includes a bequest;

(b) any sponsorship provided in relation to the party (as defined by PPERA 2000, s 51);

(c) any subscription or other fee paid for affiliation to, or membership of, the party;

(d) any money spent (otherwise than by or on behalf of the party) in paying any expenses incurred directly or indirectly by the party;

(e) …

(f) the provision otherwise than on commercial terms of any property, services or facilities for the use or benefit of the party (including the services of any person).'

Therefore, under s 50, the term 'donation' refers to gifts of money and property (including money or property transferred to a party for consideration which is less than its value); the provision of any sponsorship in relation to the party; subscriptions and affiliation fees; money spent (other than by or on behalf of the party) to meet expenses incurred by the party; and loans, property, services and other facilities provided to the party on other than commercial terms. Anything given or transferred to an officer, agent, trustee or member of the party in that capacity will be regarded as having been given or transferred to the party, unless it is given solely for his own use or benefit. A donation to a member or officer of a party for use otherwise than on the business of the party as such – for example, in assisting him in standing for an internal election – is subject to the separate controls under PPERA 2000, s 71 and Sch 7. The definition of a 'donation' applies to anything given or transferred to the party either directly or indirectly through a third person.

22.6 Section 51 defines 'sponsorship' for the purpose of Pt IV. The definition covers any money or other property transferred to a party for the purpose of helping the party with meeting any defined expenses. The term 'defined expenses' refers to expenses incurred in connection with:

(a) any conference, meeting or other event organised by or on behalf of the party;

(b) the preparation, production or dissemination of any publication; or

(c) any study or research: PPERA 2000, s 51(2).

However, the payment of an admission charge to any conference, meeting or other event, or the purchase price of any publication, does not constitute sponsorship: PPERA 2000, s 51(3).

22.7 Under PPERA 2000, s 52 the following are not regarded as a donation:

'(a) …

(b) any grant under s 170 of the Criminal Justice and Public Order Act 1994 (security costs at party conferences);

(c) any payment made by or on behalf of the European Parliament for the purpose of assisting members of the Parliament to perform their functions as such members;

(d) the transmission by a broadcaster, free of charge, of a party political broadcast or a referendum campaign broadcast (within the meaning of s 127);

(e) any other facilities provided in pursuance of any right conferred on candidates or a party at an election or a referendum by any enactment;

(f) the provision of assistance by a person appointed under s 9 of the Local Government and Housing Act 1989;

(g) the provision by any individual of his own services which he provides voluntarily in his own time and free of charge;

(h) any interest accruing to a registered party in respect of any donation which is dealt with by the party in accordance with s 56(2)(a) or (b)': PPERA 2000, s 52(1).

The following are also disregarded as donations:

(a) any donation which (in accordance with any enactment) falls to be included in a return as to election expenses in respect of a candidate or candidates at a particular election; and

(b) any donation whose value (as determined in accordance with s 53) is not more than £500: PPERA 2000, s 52(2).

22.8 Section 53 of PPERA 2000 deals with the valuation of donations. Gifts of property are required to be valued at their market value, that is at the price they would fetch on their sale in the open market (see PPERA 2000, s 160(1)). Where money or property is transferred to a party for a consideration less than the market value of the property, the value of the donation is the difference between the value of the money or the market value of the property and the consideration provided by the party: PPERA 2000, s 53(2). Similarly, where loans, property, services and other facilities are provided on other than commercial terms, their value will be taken to be the difference between their actual cost to the party and the cost which the party would have incurred if they had been provided on commercial terms: PPERA 2000, s 53(4). In the case of any sponsorship, the value of the donation is to be taken to be the value of the money or property transferred to the party; the value of any benefit conferred on the sponsor is to be disregarded: PPERA 2000, s 53(3).

The next section considers the donations made by companies under the CA 2006 regime.

Political parties, organisations to which CA 2006, Pt 14 applies

22.9 Part 14 of the CA 2006 sets out definitions of terms that apply in respect of corporate donations. It addresses three particular types of situation:

- donations to political parties;
- donations to political organisations;
- donations to independent election candidates.

Political party'

22.10 Part 14 of the CA 2006 applies to a *political party* in the following circumstances:

(a) it is registered under Pt 2 of the Political Parties, Elections and Referendums Act 2000 (c 41); or

(b) it carries on, or proposes to carry on, activities for the purposes of or in connection with the participation of the party in any election or elections to public office held in a member state other than the UK: CA 2006, s 363(1).

'Political organisation'

22.11 Part 14 of the CA 2006 applies to an organisation (a 'political organisation') if it carries on, or proposes to carry on, activities that are capable of being reasonably regarded as intended:

(a) to affect public support for a political party to which, or an independent election candidate to whom, the part applies; or

(b) to influence voters in relation to any national or regional referendum held under the law of the UK or another member state: CA 2006, s 363(2).

However, trade unions (CA 2006, s 374(2)) and all-party parliamentary groups (CA 2006, s 376) are not considered as political organisations.

Independent election candidate'

22.12 Part 14 applies to an independent election candidate at any election to public office held in the UK or another member state: CA 2006, s 363(3).

Any reference in Pt 14 to a political party, political organisation or independent election candidate, or to political expenditure, is to a party, organisation, independent candidate or expenditure to which Pt 14 applies: CA 2006, s 363(4).

Meaning of 'political donation'

22.13 The CA 2006, s 364 sets out the definition of 'political donation' for the purposes of Pt 14. In relation to a *political party* or other *political organisation*:

(a) 'political donation' means anything that in accordance with ss 50–52 of the PPERA 2000:

  (i) constitutes a donation for the purposes of Ch 1 of Pt 4 of the PPERA 2000 (control of donations to registered parties); or

  (ii) would constitute such a donation reading references in those sections to a registered party as references to any political party or other political organisation, and

(b) s 53 of PPERA 2000 applies, in the same way, for the purpose of determining the value of a donation: CA 2006, s 364(2).

22.14 In relation to an *independent election candidate*:

(a) 'political donation' means anything that, in accordance with PPERA 2000, ss 50–52 would constitute a donation for the purposes of Ch 1 of Pt 4 of that Act (control of donations to registered parties) reading references in those sections to a registered party as references to the independent election candidate; and

(b) PPERA 2000, s 53 applies, in the same way, for the purpose of determining the value of a donation: CA 2006, s 364(3).

For the purposes of CA 2006, s 364, ss 50 and 53 of PPERA 2000 (c 41) (definition of 'donation' and value of donations) are treated as if the amendments to those sections made by the Electoral Administration Act 2006 (which remove from the definition of 'donation' loans made otherwise than on commercial terms) had not been made: CA 2006, s 364(4).

Meaning of 'political expenditure'

22.15 In Pt 14 of the CA 2006, 'political expenditure', in relation to a company, means expenditure incurred by the company on:

(a) the preparation, publication or dissemination of advertising or other promotional or publicity material:

  (i) of whatever nature; and

  (ii) however published or otherwise disseminated,

  that, at the time of publication or dissemination, is capable of being reasonably regarded as intended to affect public support for a political party or other political organisation, or an independent election candidate; or

(b) activities on the part of the company that are capable of being reasonably regarded as intended:

  (i) to affect public support for a political party or other political organisation, or an independent election candidate; or

  (ii) to influence voters in relation to any national or regional referendum held under the law of a member State: CA 2006, s 365(1).

For the purposes of Pt 14 of the CA 2006, a political donation does not count as political expenditure: CA 2006, s 365(2).

22.16 The Companies (Political Expenditure Exemption) Order 2007, SI 2007/2081 exempts companies whose ordinary business includes the publication of news (such as newspapers, and other publishing or media-related companies) from having to seek shareholder authorisation in order to prepare, publish, or disseminate material of a political nature. This is because it would be impractical for them to have to comply with the provisions on political expenditure in Pt 14 of the CA 2006 for something which is within the ordinary course of their business. It applies to political expenditure incurred in respect of the preparation, publication or dissemination of news material, where that material contains matter which would render that preparation, publication or dissemination on the part of the company an activity on the part of the company that is capable of being reasonably regarded as intended:

(a) to affect public support for a political party or other political organisation, or an independent election candidate; or

(b) to influence voters in relation to any national or regional referendum held under the law of a member state: reg 3.

22.17 The Order applies to any company whose ordinary course of business includes, or is proposed to include, the publication or dissemination to the public, or any part of the public, of news material, or the preparation of such material for publication or dissemination to the public, or any part of the public.

It is irrelevant:

(a) by which means or modes the news material is to be prepared, published or disseminated; or

(b) where the public, or any part of the public, to which such material is published or disseminated is located or the identity or description of the public or any part of it: reg 4.

Authorisation required for donations or expenditure

22.18 Under the CA 2006, s 366, a company must not:

(a) make a political donation to a political party or other political organisation, or to an independent election candidate; or

(b) incur any political expenditure,

unless the donation or expenditure is authorised in accordance with the following provisions: CA 2006, s 366(1).

22.19 The donation or expenditure must be authorised:

(a) in the case of a company that is not a subsidiary of another company, by a resolution of the members of the company;

(b) in the case of a company that is a subsidiary of another company by:

  (i) a resolution of the members of the company; and

  (ii) a resolution of the members of any relevant holding company: CA 2006, s 366(2).

No resolution is required on the part of a company that is a wholly-owned subsidiary of a UK-registered company: CA 2006, s 366(3).

22.20 For the purposes of CA 2006, s 366(2)(b)(ii) a 'relevant holding company' means a company that, at the time the donation was made or the expenditure was incurred:

(a) was a holding company of the company by which the donation was made or the expenditure was incurred;

(b) was a UK-registered company; and

(c) was not a subsidiary of another UK-registered company: CA 2006, s 366(4).

22.21 The resolution or resolutions required by CA 2006, s 366:

(a) must comply with s 367 (form of authorising resolution); and

(b) must be passed before the donation is made or the expenditure incurred: CA 2006, s 366(5).

Nothing in s 367 enables a company to be authorised to do anything that it could not lawfully do apart from this section: CA 2006, s 366(6).

Form of authorising resolution

22.22 A resolution conferring authorisation for the purposes of CA 2006, Pt 14 may relate to:

(a) the company passing the resolution;

(b) one or more subsidiaries of that company; or

(c) the company passing the resolution and one or more subsidiaries of that company: CA 2006, s 367(1).

22.23 A resolution may be expressed to relate to all companies that are subsidiaries of the company passing the resolution:

(a) at the time the resolution is passed; or

(b) at any time during the period for which the resolution has effect,

without identifying them individually: CA 2006, s 367(2).

22.24 The resolution may authorise donations or expenditure under one or more of the following heads:

(a) donations to political parties or independent election candidates;

(b) donations to political organisations other than political parties;

(c) political expenditure: CA 2006, s 367(3).

22.25 The resolution must specify a head or heads:

(a) in the case of a resolution under s 367(2), for all of the companies to which it relates taken together;

(b) in the case of any other resolution, for each company to which it relates: CA 2006, s 367(4).

The resolution must be expressed in general terms conforming with s 367(3) and must not purport to authorise particular donations or expenditure: CA 2006, s 367(5).

For each of the specified heads the resolution must authorise donations or, as the case may be, expenditure up to a specified amount in the period for which the resolution has effect (see s 368): CA 2006, s 367(6).

22.26 The resolution must specify such amounts:

(a) in the case of a resolution under s 367(2) for all of the companies to which it relates taken together;

(b) in the case of any other resolution, for each company to which it relates: CA 2006, s 367(7).

Period for which resolution has effect

22.27 A resolution conferring authorisation for the purposes of Pt 14 has effect for a period of four years beginning with the date on which it is passed unless the directors determine, or the articles require, that it is to have effect for a shorter period beginning with that date: CA 2006, s 368(1).

The power of the directors to make a determination under CA 2006, s 368 is subject to any provision of the articles that operates to prevent them from doing so: CA 2006, s 368(2).

Liability of directors in case of unauthorised donation or expenditure

22.28 The CA 2006, s 369 applies where a company has made a political donation or incurred political expenditure without the authorisation required by Pt 14: CA 2006, s 369(1).

The 'directors in default' are jointly and severally liable:

(a) to make good to the company the amount of the unauthorised donation or expenditure, with interest; and

(b) to compensate the company for any loss or damage sustained by it as a result of the unauthorised donation or expenditure having been made: CA 2006, s 369(2).

The term 'director' includes a shadow director: CA 2006, s 379(1).

22.29 The 'directors in default' are:

(a) those who, at the time the unauthorised donation was made or the unauthorised expenditure was incurred, were directors of the company by which the donation was made or the expenditure was incurred; and

(b) where:

  (i) that company was a subsidiary of a relevant holding company; and

  (ii) the directors of the relevant holding company failed to take all reasonable steps to prevent the donation being made or the expenditure being incurred,

the directors of the relevant holding company: CA 2006, s 369(3).

22.30 For the purposes of CA 2006 s 369(3)(b), a 'relevant holding company' means a company that, at the time the donation was made or the expenditure was incurred:

(a) was a holding company of the company by which the donation was made or the expenditure was incurred;

(b) was a UK-registered company; and

(c) was not a subsidiary of another UK-registered company: CA 2006, s 369(4).

22.31 The interest referred to in s 369(2)(a) is interest on the amount of the unauthorised donation or expenditure, so far as not made good to the company:

(a) in respect of the period beginning with the date when the donation was made or the expenditure was incurred; and

(b) at such rate as the Secretary of State may prescribe by regulations.

Section 379(2) of CA 2006 (construction of references to date when donation made or expenditure incurred) does not apply for the purposes of this CA 2006, s 369(5).

Where only part of a donation or expenditure was unauthorised, then s 369 applies only to so much of it as was unauthorised: CA 2006, s 369(6).

Enforcement of directors' liability by shareholder action

22.32 Any liability of a director under the CA 2006, s 369 is enforceable:

(a) in the case of a liability of a director of a company to that company, by proceedings brought in the name of the company by an 'authorised group' of its members;

(b) in the case of a liability of a director of a holding company to a subsidiary, by proceedings brought in the name of the subsidiary by:

 (i) an authorised group of members of the subsidiary; or

 (ii) an authorised group of members of the holding company: CA 2006, s 370(1).

This is in addition to the right of the company to which the liability is owed to bring proceedings itself to enforce the liability: CA 2006, s 370(2).

22.33 An 'authorised group' of members of a company means:

(a) the holders of not less than 5% in nominal value of the company's issued share capital;

(b) if the company is not limited by shares, not less than 5% of its members; or

(c) not less than 50 of the company's members: CA 2006, s 370(3).

The right to bring proceedings under s 370 is subject to the provisions of s 371: CA 2006, s 370(4).

Nothing in CA 2006, s 370 affects any right of a member of a company to bring or continue proceedings under Pt 11 (derivative claims or proceedings): CA 2006, s 370(5). Therefore, a shareholder is not barred from bringing a derivative action.

Enforcement of directors' liability by shareholder action: supplementary

22.34 A group of members may not bring proceedings under CA 2006, s 370 in the name of a company unless:

(a) the group has given written notice to the company stating:

 (i) the cause of action and a summary of the facts on which the proceedings are to be based;

(ii) the names and addresses of the members comprising the group; and

(iii) the grounds on which it is alleged that those members constitute an authorised group; and

(b) not less than 28 days have elapsed between the date of the giving of the notice to the company and the bringing of the proceedings: CA 2006, s 371(1).

The right to bring proceedings is not conferred on an individual shareholder, but a group of shareholders. This could be attributed to bad faith or *male fide* intentions of individual shareholders and may allow for better success if legal proceedings are brought by a group of shareholders in the best interests of shareholders as a whole.

22.35 Where such a notice is given to a company, any director of the company may apply to the court within the period of 28 days beginning with the date of the giving of the notice for an order directing that the proposed proceedings shall not be brought, on one or more of the following grounds:

(a) that the unauthorised amount has been made good to the company;

(b) that proceedings to enforce the liability have been brought, and are being pursued with due diligence, by the company;

(c) that the members proposing to bring proceedings under this section do not constitute an authorised group: CA 2006, s 371(2).

22.36 Where an application is made on the ground mentioned in CA 2006, sub-s 371(2)(b) the court may as an alternative to directing that the proposed proceedings under s 370 are not to be brought, direct:

(a) that such proceedings may be brought on such terms and conditions as the court thinks fit; and

(b) that the proceedings brought by the company:

(i) shall be discontinued; or

(ii) may be continued on such terms and conditions as the court thinks fit: CA 2006, s 371(3).

22.37 The members by whom proceedings are brought under s 370 owe to the company in whose name they are brought the same duties in relation to the proceedings as would be owed by the company's directors if the proceedings were being brought by the company. These include the duties of care and loyalty.

But proceedings to enforce any such duty may be brought by the company only with the permission of the court: CA 2006, s 371(4). Here, the court will wish to ensure that the interests of the shareholders are actually being protected.

Proceedings brought under s 370 may not be discontinued or settled by the group except with the permission of the court, which may be given on such terms as the court thinks fit: CA 2006, s 371(5). This allows the court to ensure that the group of shareholders do not personally gain a personal benefit from the proceedings but that such proceedings have taken account of the best interests of the shareholders.

Costs of shareholder action

22.38 The CA 2006, s 372 applies in relation to proceedings brought under s 370 in the name of a company ('the company') by an authorised group ('the group'): CA 2006, s 372(1).

The group may apply to the court for an order directing the company to indemnify the group in respect of costs incurred or to be incurred by the group in connection with the proceedings: CA 2006, s 372(2). This provision is designed to ensure that the costs of such derivative proceedings are borne by the company, as it will be the company that will benefit from the derivative proceedings and not the shareholders.

The court may make such an order on such terms as it thinks fit: CA 2006, s 372(3).

The group is not entitled to be paid any such costs out of the assets of the company except by virtue of such an order: CA 2006, s 372(3).

22.39 If no such order has been made with respect to the proceedings, then:

(a) if the company is awarded costs in connection with the proceedings, or it is agreed that costs incurred by the company in connection with the proceedings should be paid by any defendant, the costs shall be paid to the group; and

(b) if any defendant is awarded costs in connection with the proceedings, or it is agreed that any defendant should be paid costs incurred by him in connection with the proceedings, the costs shall be paid by the group: CA 2006, s 372(4).

In the application of s 372 to Scotland, the term 'costs' is substituted for 'expenses' and for 'defendant' the term 'defender' applies: CA 2006, s 372(5).

Information for purposes of shareholder action

22.40 Where proceedings have been brought under the CA 2006, s 370 in the name of a company by an authorised group, the group is entitled to require the company to provide it with all information relating to the subject matter of the proceedings that is in the company's possession or under its control or which is reasonably obtainable by it: CA 2006, s 373(1). The objective of this provision is to allow the group of shareholders to determine (and seek professional advice) as to whether to bring any proceedings.

If the company, having been required by the group to do so, refuses to provide the group with all or any of that information, the court may, on an application made by the group, make an order directing:

(a) the company; and

(b) any of its officers or employees specified in the application,

to provide the group with the information in question in such form and by such means as the court may direct: CA 2006, s 373(2).

Trade unions

22.41 A donation to a trade union, other than a contribution to the union's political fund, is not a political donation for the purposes of Pt 14: CA 2006, s 374(1). A trade union is not a political organisation for the purposes of s 365 (meaning of 'political expenditure'): CA 2006, s 374(2).

In CA 2006 s 374, the following are defined terms:

- *'trade union'* has the meaning given by s 1 of the Trade Union and Labour Relations (Consolidation) Act 1992 or Art 3 of the Industrial Relations (Northern Ireland) Order 1992, SI 1992/807 (NI 5);
- *'political fund'* means the fund from which payments by a trade union in the furtherance of political objects are required to be made by virtue of s 82(1)(a) of that Act or Art 57(2)(a) of that order: CA 2006, s 374(3).

Subscription for membership of trade association

22.42 A subscription paid to a trade association for membership of the association is not a political donation for the purposes of Pt 14: CA 2006, s 375(1). For this purpose:

- *'trade association'* means an organisation formed for the purpose of furthering the trade interests of its members, or of persons represented by its members; and
- *'subscription'* does not include a payment to the association to the extent that it is made for the purpose of financing any particular activity of the association: CA 2006, s 375(2).

All-party parliamentary group

22.43 An all-party parliamentary group is not a political organisation for the purposes of Pt 14: CA 2006, s 376(1). As set out in s 376(2), 'all-party parliamentary group' means an all-party group composed of members of one or both of the Houses of Parliament (or of such members and other persons).

Political expenditure exempted by order

22.44 Authorisation under CA 2006, Pt 14 is not needed for political expenditure that is exempt by virtue of an order of the Secretary of State under this section: CA 2006, s 377(1). An order may confer an exemption in relation to:

(a) companies of any description or category specified in the order; or

(b) expenditure of any description or category so specified (whether framed by reference to goods, services or other matters in respect of which such expenditure is incurred or otherwise),

or both: CA 2006, s 377(2).

If or to the extent that expenditure is exempt from the requirement of authorisation under Pt 14 by virtue of an order under s 377, it shall be disregarded in determining what donations are authorised by any resolution of the company passed for the purposes of this Part: CA 2006, s 377(3).

See the Companies (Political Expenditure Exemption) Order 2007, SI 2007/2081.

Donations not amounting to more than £5,000 in any 12-month period

22.45 Authorisation under CA 2006, Pt 14 is not needed for a donation except to the extent that the total amount of:

(a) that donation; and

(b) other relevant donations made in the period of 12 months ending with the date on which that donation is made,

exceeds £5,000: CA 2006, s 378(1).

22.46 The following are defined terms:

- *'donation'* means a donation to a political party or other political organisation or to an independent election candidate; and
- *'other relevant donations'* means:
  (a) in relation to a donation made by a company that is not a subsidiary, any other donations made by that company or by any of its subsidiaries;
  (b) in relation to a donation made by a company that is a subsidiary, any other donations made by that company, by any holding company of that company or by any other subsidiary of any such holding company: CA 2006, s 378(2).

If or to the extent that a donation is exempt by virtue of s 378 from the requirement of authorisation under Pt 14, it is disregarded in determining what donations are authorised by any resolution passed for the purposes of this Part: CA 2006, s 378(3).

Acceptance of donations by political parties

22.47 Sections 54–61 of PPERA 2000 regulate donations made to political parties. Section 54 introduces the concept of a 'permissible donor', as a means of prohibiting the foreign funding of political parties. It provides that a party may accept a donation only from a permissible donor and where the identity of the donor is known: PPERA 2000, s 54(1). The latter requirement is intended to cover not only cases where a donation is made anonymously, but also where an identity has been given but is clearly fictional (and it is therefore impossible to establish that the donor is a permissible donor).

The sources of funding that are regarded as permissible include individuals registered in an electoral register; a company registered in the UK under CA 2006 or incorporated in a member state of the EU and which carries on business in the UK; a registered political party; a trade union; a building society; a limited liability partnership; a friendly society or industrial and provident society and any other unincorporated association which is carrying on business or other activities, and has its main office, in the UK: PPERA 2000, s 54(2).

Under s 55, special provision is made in respect of donations from certain specified sources. Where a political party receives a donation, for example, from a company, to meet the reasonable travel and subsistence expenses of a member or officer of the party for the purpose of undertaking an overseas visit, such a donation is to be regarded as being from a permissible donor, irrespective of whether the donor is one of those listed in s 54(2).

Checklist for political donations and expenditure by companies

22.48 *This checklist sets out the essential framework for consideration where companies contemplate engaging in political donations and political expenditure.*

No	Issue	Reference
1	Is it a 'donation'? Is the donation or expenditure made to a *'political party'*? Does it fall within the definition of a 'political parties'? Consider the interaction between PPERA 2000 and CA 2006, Pt 14.	PPERA 2000, s 50; CA 2006, s 363(1)
2	Is the donation made to a *'political organisation'*?	CA 2006, s 363(2)
3	Is the donation to an *'independent election candidate'*?	CA 2006, s 363(3)
4	Is it a *'political donation'*?	CA 2006, s 364(1)
5	Is the company engaging in any *'political expenditure'*?	CA 2006, s 365
6	Has the company obtained authorisation to make the political donation or expenditure? Does it comply with the form of authorisation under the CA 2006? Is the authorisation within the period specified under the CA 2006? Is it a general authorisation?	CA 2006, s 366 CA 2006, s 367 CA 2006, s 368
7	Is there any prohibition on making political donations or expenditures in the company's articles of association?	Articles of association
8	Consider the duties of directors as part of their general duties and conflict between their personal interests and interests of shareholders in respect of donations:	
	• Duty to act within powers	CA 2006, s 171
	• Duty to promote the company's success	CA 2006, s 172
	• Duty to exercise independent judgement	CA 2006, s 173
	• Duty to exercise reasonable care, skill and diligence	CA 2006, s 174
	• Duty to avoid conflicts of interest	CA 2006, s 175
9	Consider the liability of directors for unauthorised donation or expenditure. Liability is joint and several. This does not prejudice individual shareholder from bringing an action under the general derivative proceedings.	CA 2006, ss 369, 370–374

No	Issue	Reference
10	Consider enforcement of directors' liability by group of shareholders as part of a derivative action.	CA 2006, s 375
11	Consider exemptions to Pt 14 for political donations and political expenditures:	CA 2006, s 376
	• Trade unions	
	• Subscription for membership of trade association	
	• All-party parliamentary group	CA 2006, s 377
	• Political expenditure exempted by order	The Companies (Political Expenditure Exemption) Order 2007, SI 2007/2081
	• Donations not amounting to more than £5,000 in any 12-month period	CA 2006, s 378
12	A company is a 'permissible donor' for the purposes of acceptance of donations by political parties.	PPERA 2000, s 54

Definitions

22.49

All-party parliamentary group: An all-party group composed of members of one or both of the Houses of Parliament (or of such members or other persons).

Organisation: Includes any body corporate or unincorporated association or any combination of persons: CA 2006, s 379(1).

Political donation: See CA 2006, s 364.

Political expenditure: See CA 2006, s 365.

Political fund: The fund from which payments by a trade union in the furtherance of political objects are required to be made by virtue of s 82(1)(a) of the Trade Union and Labour Relations (Consolidation) Act 1992.

Political organisation: An organisation that carries on, or proposes to carry on, activities that are capable of being reasonably regarded as intended:

(i) to affect public support for a political party to which, or an independent election candidate to whom, CA 2006, Pt 14 applies; or

	(ii) to influence voters in relation to any national or regional referendum held under the law of the UK or another member state: CA 2006, s 363(2).
Political party:	A party that is registered under Pt 2 of the Political Parties, Elections and Referendums Act 2000 (c 41); or carries on, or proposes to carry on, activities for the purposes of or in connection with the participation of the party in any election or elections to public office held in a member state other than the UK: CA 2006, s 363(1).
Time of donation or expenditure:	Except as otherwise provided, any reference in Pt 14 to the CA 2006 to the time at which a donation is made or expenditure is incurred is, in a case where the donation is made or expenditure incurred in pursuance of a contract, any earlier time at which that contract is entered into by the company: CA 2006, s 379(2).
Trade association:	An organisation formed for the purpose of furthering the trade interests of its members, or of persons represented by its members: CA 2006, s 375(2).
Trade union:	As defined by s 1 of the Trade Union and Labour Relations (Consolidation) Act 1992 or Art 3 of the Industrial Relations (Northern Ireland) Order 1992, SI 1992/807 (NI 5).

23 Accounts and reports

Contents

Introduction

23.1 One of the fundamental principles of company law is disclosure of information dating back to the first Companies Act and subsequent government committees were established to consider company law reform including the Greene Committee, Cohen Committee and the Jenkins Committee. Many of the provisions of the CA 2006 are based on ensuring there is proper dissemination of information to enable shareholders to make informed decisions on corporate matters. Directors are accountable to the company for ensuring the long-term prosperity and success of the company. One of their primary objectives of commercial companies is to maximize profits for the shareholders. Shareholders who contribute capital into the company and invest have a legitimate expectation that the directors will use corporate funds for proper purposes and not to deplete the funds for other purposes unrelated to the company's business.

23.2 The fortunes of the company are largely in the hands of the directors who have been delegated a degree of authority from the shareholders to manage the company. Directors are also accountable for the financial affairs of the company and to report certain disclosures under the CA 2006. This allows shareholders to monitor their investment and to know the actual position of the company at a certain point of time through the company's profit and loss and balance sheet mechanisms. Ultimately, shareholders owe no duty or loyalty to the company from a financial or other perspective and may exit at any time depending upon the circumstances. However, a mutual understanding develops when a shareholder contributes capital: the shareholder understands that he takes a financial risk in his investment but at the same time, he informs the company whether impliedly or expressly that he has a legitimate expectation (but not a right) to dividends in the company. The company understands this message and acting through its directors tries to ensure that corporate funds are used judiciously as necessarily and properly required for the effective functioning of the company. The company strives to retain the investor for as long as possible through a financial reward on almost an annual basis. Creditors also have an interest in ensuring the company's success in the facilities and securities they provide the company. In return, they expect to receive regular financial information on the company's performance as a measure of its success or failure. Employees' fortunes may also be linked to the financial performance of the company. If the company makes healthy profits, they have an expectation in receiving an annual financial reward and particularly so in relation to directors' remuneration.

23.3 This Chapter is concerned with the company's accounts and reports as set out in Pt 15 of the CA 2006, and addresses the following key areas:

- The small companies regime on disclosure of financial information.
- Quoted and unquoted companies.
- A company's accounting record and financial year.
- Aspects of Annual accounts.
- The strategic report.
- The directors' report.
- Filing obligations.

This Chapter takes account of the Companies, Partnerships and Groups (Accounts and Reports) Regulations 2015, SI 2015/980 (in force 6 April 2015).

Scheme of Companies Act 2006, Pt 15

23.4 Under the scheme of Pt 15, the requirements as to accounts and reports apply in relation to each financial year of a company: CA 2006, s 380(1).

In certain respects, different provisions apply to different kinds of company: CA 2006, s 380(2). These are divided into small, medium-sized and large companies.

Companies subject to the small companies regime

23.5 The small companies regime applies to a company for a financial year in relation to which the company:

(a) qualifies as small (see ss 382 and 383); and

(b) is not excluded from the regime (see s 384): CA 2006, s 381.

Companies qualifying as small: general

23.6 The CA 2006 provides a definition of a 'small' company for the purposes of preparation of financial accounts and certain exemptions.

A company qualifies as small in relation to its first financial year if the qualifying conditions are met in that year: CA 2006, s 382(1).

Subject to sub-s (2), a company qualifies as small in relation to a subsequent financial year if the qualifying conditions are met in that year: CA 2006, s 382(1A).

In relation to a subsequent financial year, where on its balance sheet date a company meets or ceases to meet the qualifying conditions, that affects its qualification as a small company only if it occurs in two consecutive financial years: CA 2006, s 382(2).

23.7 The qualifying conditions are met by a company in a year in which it satisfies two or more of the following requirements:

Turnover:	Not more than £10.2 million
Balance sheet total:	Not more than £5.1 million
Number of employees:	Not more than 50

For a period that is a company's financial year but not in fact a year, the maximum figures for turnover must be proportionately adjusted: CA 2006, s 382(4).

The term 'balance sheet total' means the aggregate of the amounts shown as assets in the company's balance sheet: CA 2006, s 382(5).

The number of employees means the average number of persons employed by the company in the year, determined as follows:

(a) find for each month in the financial year the number of persons employed under contracts of service by the company in that month (whether throughout the month or not);

(b) add together the monthly totals; and

(c) divide by the number of months in the financial year: CA 2006, s 382(6).

Section 382 is subject to s 383 (companies qualifying as small: parent companies): CA 2006, s 382(7).

Companies qualifying as small: parent companies

23.8 A parent company qualifies as a small company in relation to a financial year only if the group headed by it qualifies as a small group: CA 2006, s 383(1).

A group qualifies as small in relation to the parent company's first financial year if the qualifying conditions are met in that year: CA 2006, s 383(2).

Subject to sub-s (3), a group qualifies as small in relation to a subsequent financial year of the parent company if the qualifying conditions are met in that year: CA 2006, s 383(2A).

In relation to a subsequent financial year of the parent company, where on the parent company's balance sheet date the group meets or ceases to meet the qualifying conditions, that affects the group's qualification as a small group only if it occurs in two consecutive financial years: CA 2006, s 383(3).

23.9 The qualifying conditions are met by a group in a year in which it satisfies two or more of the following requirements:

Aggregate turnover	Not more than £10.2 million net (or £12.2 million gross)
Aggregate balance sheet total	Not more than £5.1 million net (or £6.1 million gross)
Aggregate number of employees	Not more than 50

The aggregate figures are ascertained by aggregating the relevant figures determined in accordance with s 382 for each member of the group: CA 2006, s 383(5).

In relation to the aggregate figures for turnover and balance sheet total, 'net' means after any set-offs and other adjustments made to eliminate group transactions:

(a) in the case of Companies Act accounts, in accordance with regulations under s 404; and

(b) in the case of IAS accounts, in accordance with international accounting standards.

'Gross' means without those set-offs and other adjustments: CA 2006, s 383(6).

A company may satisfy any relevant requirement on the basis of either the net or the gross figure: CA 2006, s 383(7).

23.10 The figures for each subsidiary undertaking shall be those included in its individual accounts for the relevant financial year, that is:

(a) if its financial year ends with that of the parent company, that financial year; and

(b) if not, its financial year ending last before the end of the financial year of the parent company.

If those figures cannot be obtained without disproportionate expense or undue delay, the latest available figures shall be taken: CA 2006, s 383(7).

Companies excluded from the small companies regime

23.11 Section 384 provides exemptions from the small company regime. The small companies regime does not apply to a company that was at any time within the financial year to which the accounts relate to:

(a) a public company;

(b) a company that:

  (i) is an authorised insurance company, a banking company, an e-money issuer, a MiFID investment firm or a UCITS management company; or

  (ii) carries on insurance market activity; or

(c) a member of an ineligible group: CA 2006, s 384(1).

23.12 A group is ineligible if any of its members is:

(a) a traded company;

(b) a body corporate (other than a company) whose shares are admitted to trading on a regulated market in an EEA State;

(c) a person (other than a small company) who has permission under Pt 4 of the Financial Services and Markets Act 2000 (c 8) to carry on a regulated activity;

(d) a small company that is an authorised insurance company, a banking company, an e-money issuer, a MiFID investment firm or a UCITS management company; or

(e) a person who carries on insurance market activity: CA 2006, s 384(2).

A company is a small company for the purposes of sub-s (2) if it qualified as small in relation to its last financial year ending on or before the end of the financial year to which the accounts relate: CA 2006, s 384(3).

Companies qualifying as micro-entities

23.13 A company qualifies as a micro-entity in relation to its first financial year if the qualifying conditions are met in that year: CA 2006, s 384A(1).

Subject to sub-s (3), a company qualifies as a micro-entity in relation to a subsequent financial year if the qualifying conditions are met in that year: CA 2006, s 384A(2).

In relation to a subsequent financial year, where on its balance sheet date a company meets or ceases to meet the qualifying conditions, that affects its qualification as a micro-entity only if it occurs in two consecutive financial years: CA 2006, s 384A(3).

23.14 The qualifying conditions are met by a company in a year in which it satisfies two or more of the following requirements: (CA 2006, s 384A(4):

1. Turnover	Not more than £632,000
2. Balance sheet total	Not more than £316,000
3. Number of employees	Not more than 10

For a period that is a company's financial year but not in fact a year the maximum figures for turnover must be proportionately adjusted: CA 2006, s 384A(5).

The balance sheet total means the aggregate of the amounts shown as assets in the company's balance sheet: CA 2006, s 384A(6).

The number of employees means the average number of persons employed by the company in the year, determined as follows:

(a) find for each month in the financial year the number of persons employed under contracts of service by the company in that month (whether throughout the month or not);

(b) add together the monthly totals; and

(c) divide by the number of months in the financial year: CA 2006, s 384A(7).

23.15 In the case of a company which is a parent company, the company qualifies as a micro-entity in relation to a financial year only if:

(a) the company qualifies as a micro-entity in relation to that year, as determined by sub-ss (1)–(7); and

(b) the group headed by the company qualifies as a small group, as determined by s 383(2)–(7): CA 2006, s 384A(8).

Companies excluded from being treated as micro-entities

23.16 The micro-entity provisions do not apply in relation to a company's accounts for a particular financial year if the company was at any time within that year:

(a) a company excluded from the small companies regime by virtue of s 384;

(b) an investment undertaking as defined in Article 2(14) of Directive 2013/34/EU of 26 June 2013 on the annual financial statements etc of certain types of undertakings;

(c) a financial holding undertaking as defined in Article 2(15) of that Directive;

(d) a credit institution as defined in Article 4 of Directive 2006/48/EC of the European Parliament and of the Council of 14 June 2006 relating to the taking up and pursuit of the business of credit institutions, other than one referred to in Article 2 of that Directive;

(e) an insurance undertaking as defined in Article 2(1) of Council Directive 91/674/EEC of 19 December 1991 on the annual accounts of insurance undertakings; or

(f) a charity: CA 2006, s 384B(1).

23.17 The micro-entity provisions also do not apply in relation to a company's accounts for a financial year if:

(a) the company is a parent company which prepares group accounts for that year as permitted by s 398, or

(b) the company is not a parent company but its accounts are included in consolidated group accounts for that year: CA 2006, s 384B(2).

Quoted and unquoted companies

23.18 For the purposes of Pt 15, a company is a quoted company in relation to a financial year if it is a quoted company immediately before the end of the accounting reference period by reference to which that financial year was determined: CA 2006, s 385(1).

A 'quoted company' means a company whose equity share capital:

(a) has been included in the official list in accordance with the provisions of Pt 6 of the Financial Services and Markets Act 2000 (c 8); or

(b) is officially listed in an EEA State; or

(c) is admitted to dealing on either the New York Stock Exchange or the exchange known as Nasdaq.

In paragraph (a) 'the official list' has the meaning given by s 103(1) of the Financial Services and Markets Act 2000: CA 2006, s 385(2). An 'unquoted company' means a company that is not a quoted company: CA 2006, s 385(3).

23.19 The Secretary of State may, by regulations, amend or replace the provisions of sub-ss (1)–(2) so as to limit or extend the application of some or all of the provisions of this Part that are expressed to apply to quoted companies: CA 2006, s 385(4).

Regulations under s 385 extending the application of any such provision of CA 2006, Pt 15 are subject to affirmative resolution procedure: CA 2006, s 385(5).

Accounting records

23.20 Chapter 2, Pt 15 of the CA 2006 sets out the obligations required to keep accounting records by companies and penalties for default.

Duty to keep accounting records

23.21 Every company must keep adequate accounting records: CA 2006, s 386(1). Adequate accounting records means records that are sufficient:

(a) to show and explain the company's transactions;

(b) to disclose with reasonable accuracy, at any time, the financial position of the company at that time; and

(c) to enable the directors to ensure that any accounts required to be prepared comply with the requirements of CA 2006 (and, where applicable, of Art 4 of the IAS Regulation): CA 2006, s 386(2).

23.22 Accounting records must, in particular, contain:

(a) entries from day to day of all sums of money received and expended by the company and the matters in respect of which the receipt and expenditure takes place; and

(b) a record of the assets and liabilities of the company: CA 2006, s 386(3).

23.23 If the company's business involves dealing in goods, the accounting records must contain:

(a) statements of stock held by the company at the end of each financial year of the company;

(b) all statements of stock takings from which any statement of stock as is mentioned in para (a) has been or is to be prepared; and

(c) except in the case of goods sold by way of ordinary retail trade, statements of all goods sold and purchased, showing the goods and the buyers and sellers in sufficient detail to enable all these to be identified: CA 2006, s 386(4).

A parent company that has a subsidiary undertaking in relation to which the above requirements do not apply must take reasonable steps to secure that the undertaking keeps such accounting records as to enable the directors of the parent company to ensure that any accounts required to be prepared under CA 2006, Pt 15 comply with the requirements of the Act (and, where applicable, of Art 4 of the IAS Regulation): CA 2006, s 386(5).

Duty to keep accounting records: offence

23.24 If a company fails to comply with any provision of s 386 (duty to keep accounting records), an offence is committed by every officer of the company who is in default: CA 2006, s 387(1). It is a defence for a person charged with such an offence to show that he acted honestly and that in the circumstances in which the company's business was carried on the default was excusable: CA 2006, s 387(2).

A person guilty of an offence under s 387 is liable:

(a) on conviction on indictment, to imprisonment for a term not exceeding two years or a fine (or both);

(b) on summary conviction:

  (i) in England and Wales, to imprisonment for a term not exceeding 12 months or to a fine not exceeding the statutory maximum (or both),

  (ii) in Scotland or Northern Ireland, to imprisonment for a term not exceeding six months, or to a fine not exceeding the statutory maximum (or both: CA 2006, s 387(3)).

Where and for how long are records to be kept?

23.25 A company's accounting records:

(a) must be kept at its registered office or such other place as the directors think fit; and

(b) must at all times be open to inspection by the company's officers: CA 2006, s 388(1).

In *DTC (CNC) Ltd v Gary Sargeant & Co* [1996] 1 BCLC 529, the court held that accountants could not establish a lien for any unpaid fees in respect of the accounting records.

23.26 If accounting records are kept at a place outside the UK, accounts and returns with respect to the business dealt with in the accounting records so kept must be sent to, and kept at, a place in the UK, and must at all times be open to such inspection: CA 2006, s 388(2).

The accounts and returns to be sent to the UK must be such as to:

(a) disclose with reasonable accuracy the financial position of the business in question at intervals of not more than six months; and

(b) enable the directors to ensure that the accounts required to be prepared under CA 2006, Pt 15 comply with the requirements of the Act (and, where applicable, of Art 4 of the IAS Regulation): CA 2006, s 388(3).

23.27 Accounting records that a company is required by s 386 to keep must be preserved by it:

(a) in the case of a private company, for three years from the date on which they are made;

(b) in the case of a public company, for six years from the date on which they are made: CA 2006, s 388(4).

Section 388(4) is subject to any provision contained in rules made under s 411 of the Insolvency Act 1986 (c 45) (company insolvency rules) or Art 359 of the Insolvency (Northern Ireland) Order 1989, SI 1989/2405 (NI 19): CA 2006, s 388(5).

Where and for how long records are to be kept: offences

23.28 If a company fails to comply with any provision of ss 388(1)–(3) (requirements as to keeping of accounting records), an offence is committed by every officer of the company who is in default: CA 2006, s 389(1). It is a defence for a person charged with such an offence to show that he acted honestly and that in the circumstances in which the company's business was carried on the default was excusable: CA 2006, s 389(2).

An officer of a company commits an offence if he:

(a) fails to take all reasonable steps for securing compliance by the company with sub-s (4) of that section (period for which records to be preserved); or

(b) intentionally causes any default by the company under that subs: CA 2006, s 389(3).

23.29 A person guilty of an offence under s 389 is liable:

(a) on conviction on indictment, to imprisonment for a term not exceeding two years or a fine (or both);

(b) on summary conviction:

    (i) in England and Wales, to imprisonment for a term not exceeding 12 months or to a fine not exceeding the statutory maximum (or both),

    (ii) in Scotland or Northern Ireland, to imprisonment for a term not exceeding six months, or to a fine not exceeding the statutory maximum (or both): CA 2006, s 389(4).

A company's financial year

23.30 Chapter 3 of Pt 15 considers provisions dealing with a company's financial year, including accounting reference date.

A company's financial year is determined as follows: CA 2006, s 390(1).

Its first financial year:

(a) begins with the first day of its first accounting reference period; and

(b) ends with the last day of that period or such other date, not more than seven days before or after the end of that period, as the directors may determine: CA 2006, s 390(2).

Subsequent financial years:

(a) begin with the day immediately following the end of the company's previous financial year; and

(b) end with the last day of its next accounting reference period or such other date, not more than seven days before or after the end of that period, as the directors may determine: CA 2006, s 390(3).

23.31 In relation to an undertaking that is not a company, references in CA 2006 to its financial year are to any period in respect of which a profit and loss account of the undertaking is required to be made up (by its constitution or by the law under which it is established), whether that period is a year or not: CA 2006, s 390(4).

The directors of a parent company must secure that, except where in their opinion there are good reasons against it, the financial year of each of its subsidiary undertakings coincides with the company's own financial year: CA 2006, s 390(5).

Accounting reference periods and accounting reference date

23.32 A company's accounting reference periods are determined according to its accounting reference date in each calendar year: CA 2006, s 391(1).

The accounting reference date of a company incorporated in Great Britain before 1 April 1996 is:

(a) the date specified by notice to the registrar in accordance with s 224(2) of CA 1985 (c 6) (notice specifying accounting reference date given within nine months of incorporation); or

(b) failing such notice:

  (i) in the case of a company incorporated before 1 April 1990, 31 March; and

  (ii) in the case of a company incorporated on or after 1 April 1990, the last day of the month in which the anniversary of its incorporation falls: CA 2006, s 391(2).

23.33 The accounting reference date of a company incorporated in Northern Ireland before 22 August 1997 is:

(a) the date specified by notice to the registrar in accordance with Art 232(2) of the Companies (Northern Ireland) Order 1986, SI 1986/1032 (NI 6) (notice specifying accounting reference date given within nine months of incorporation); or

(b) failing such notice:

  (i) in the case of a company incorporated before the coming into operation of Art 5 of the Companies (Northern Ireland) Order 1990, SI 1990/593 (NI 5), 31 March; and

  (ii) in the case of a company incorporated after the coming into operation of that article, the last day of the month in which the anniversary of its incorporation falls: CA 2006, s 391(3).

23.34 The accounting reference date of a company incorporated:

(a) in Great Britain on or after 1 April 1996 and before the commencement of CA 2006;

(b) in Northern Ireland on or after 22 August 1997 and before the commencement of CA 2006; or

(c) after the commencement of CA 2006,

is the last day of the month in which the anniversary of its incorporation falls: CA 2006, s 391(4).

23.35 A company's first accounting reference period is the period of more than six months, but not more than 18 months, beginning with the date of its incorporation and ending with its accounting reference date: CA 2006, s 391(5).

Its subsequent accounting reference periods are successive periods of 12 months beginning immediately after the end of the previous accounting reference period and ending with its accounting reference date: CA 2006, s 391(6).

Section 391 applies subject to the provisions of s 392 (alteration of accounting reference date): CA 2006, s 391(7).

Alteration of accounting reference date

23.36 A company may by notice given to the registrar specify a new accounting reference date having effect in relation to:

(a) the company's current accounting reference period and subsequent periods; or

(b) the company's previous accounting reference period and subsequent periods.

A company's 'previous accounting reference period' means the one immediately preceding its current accounting reference period: CA 2006, s 392(1).

23.37 The notice must state whether the current or previous accounting reference period:

(a) is to be shortened, so as to come to an end on the first occasion on which the new accounting reference date falls or fell after the beginning of the period; or

(b) is to be extended, so as to come to an end on the second occasion on which that date falls or fell after the beginning of the period: CA 2006, s 392(2).

23.38 A notice extending a company's current or previous accounting reference period is not effective if it was given less than five years after the end of an earlier accounting reference period of the company that was extended under s 392.

This does not apply:

(a) to a notice given by a company that is a subsidiary undertaking or parent undertaking of another EEA undertaking if the new accounting reference date coincides with that of the other EEA undertaking or, where that undertaking is not a company, with the last day of its financial year;

(b) where the company is in administration under Pt 2 of the Insolvency Act 1986 or Pt 3 of the Insolvency (Northern Ireland) Order 1989, SI 1989/2405 (NI 19); or

(c) where the Secretary of State directs that it should not apply, which he may do with respect to a notice that has been given or that may be given: CA 2006, s 392(3).

23.39 A notice under s 392 may not be given in respect of a previous accounting reference period if the period for filing accounts and reports for the financial year determined by reference to that accounting reference period has already expired: CA 2006, s 392(4).

An accounting reference period may not be extended so as to exceed 18 months and a notice under this section is ineffective if the current or previous accounting reference period as extended in accordance with the notice would exceed that limit.

This does not apply where the company is in administration under Pt 2 of the Insolvency Act 1986 (c 45) or Pt 3 of the Insolvency (Northern Ireland) Order 1989 (SI 1989 No 2405 (NI 19)): CA 2006, s 392(5).

In s 392, the term 'EEA undertaking' means an undertaking established under the law of any part of the UK or the law of any other EEA State: CA 2006, s 392(6).

Annual accounts

23.40 Chapter 4 of Pt 15 sets out the requirements on annual accounts of a company.

Accounts to give true and fair view

23.41 The directors of a company must not approve accounts for the purposes of Ch 4, Pt 15 of the CA 2006, unless they are satisfied that they give a true and fair view of the assets, liabilities, financial position and profit or loss:

(a) in the case of the company's individual accounts, of the company; and

(b) in the case of the company's group accounts, of the undertakings included in the consolidation as a whole, so far as concerns members of the company: CA 2006, s 393(1).

23.42 The following provisions apply to the directors of a company which qualifies as a micro-entity in relation to a financial year (see ss 384A and 384B) in their consideration of whether the Companies Act individual accounts of the company for that year give a true and fair view as required by sub-s (1)(a):

(a) where the accounts comprise only micro-entity minimum accounting items, the directors must disregard any provision of an accounting standard which would require the accounts to contain information additional to those items;

(b) in relation to a micro-entity minimum accounting item contained in the accounts, the directors must disregard any provision of an accounting standard which would require the accounts to contain further information in relation to that item; and

(c) where the accounts contain an item of information additional to the micro-entity minimum accounting items, the directors must have regard to any provision of an accounting standard which relates to that item: CA 2006, s 393(1A).

The auditor of a company in carrying out his functions under CA 2006 in relation to the company's annual accounts must have regard to the directors' duty under s 393(1): CA 2006, s 393(2).

Duty to prepare individual accounts

23.43 The directors of every company must prepare accounts for the company for each of its financial years unless the company is exempt from that requirement under s 394A.

Those accounts are referred to as the company's 'individual accounts': CA 2006, s 394. This duty also applies to small companies but with an abbreviated form of accounts.

Individual accounts: exemption for dormant subsidiaries

23.44 A company is exempt from the requirement to prepare individual accounts for a financial year if:

(a) it is itself a subsidiary undertaking;

(b) it has been dormant throughout the whole of that year; and

(c) its parent undertaking is established under the law of an EEA State: CA 2006, s 394A(1).

23.45 Exemption is conditional upon compliance with all of the following conditions:

(a) all members of the company must agree to the exemption in respect of the financial year in question;

(b) the parent undertaking must give a guarantee under s 394C in respect of that year;

(c) the company must be included in the consolidated accounts drawn up for that year or to an earlier date in that year by the parent undertaking in accordance with:

(i) the provisions of Directive 2013/34/EU of the European Parliament and of the Council on the annual financial statements, consolidated financial statements and related reports of certain types of undertakings; or

(ii) international accounting standards;

(d) the parent undertaking must disclose in the notes to the consolidated accounts that the company is exempt from the requirement to prepare individual accounts by virtue of s 392; and

(e) the directors of the company must deliver to the registrar within the period for filing the company's accounts and reports for that year:

(i) a written notice of the agreement referred to in sub-s (2)(a);

(ii) the statement referred to in s 394C(1);

(iii) a copy of the consolidated accounts referred to in sub-s (2)(c);

(iv) a copy of the auditor's report on those accounts; and

(v) a copy of the consolidated annual report drawn up by the parent undertaking: CA 2006, s 394A(2).

Companies excluded from the dormant subsidiaries exemption

23.46 A company is not entitled to the exemption conferred by s 394A (dormant subsidiaries) if it was at any time within the financial year in question:

(a) a traded company as defined in s 385(2);

(b) a company that:

(i) is an authorised insurance company, a banking company, an e-money issuer, a MiFID investment firm or a UCITS management company; or

(ii) carries on insurance market activity; or

(c) a special register body as defined in s 117(1) of the Trade Union and Labour Relations (Consolidation) Act 1992 or an employers' association as defined in s 122 of that Act or Art 4 of the Industrial Relations (Northern Ireland) Order 1992, SI 1992/807 (NI 5): CA 2006, s 394B.

Dormant subsidiaries exemption: parent undertaking declaration of guarantee

23.47 A guarantee is given by a parent undertaking under CA 2006, s 394 when the directors of the subsidiary company deliver to the registrar a statement by the parent undertaking that it guarantees the subsidiary company under this section: CA 2006, s 394C(1).

The statement under s 394C(1) must be authenticated by the parent undertaking and must specify:

(a) the name of the parent undertaking;

(b) if the parent undertaking is incorporated in the UK, its registered number (if any);

(c) if the parent undertaking is incorporated outside the UK and registered in the country in which it is incorporated, the identity of the register on which it is registered and the number with which it is so registered;

(d) the name and registered number of the subsidiary company in respect of which the guarantee is being given;

(e) the date of the statement; and

(f) the financial year to which the guarantee relates: CA 2006, s 394C(2).

23.48 A guarantee given under s 394 has the effect that:

(a) the parent undertaking guarantees all outstanding liabilities to which the subsidiary company is subject at the end of the financial year to which the guarantee relates, until they are satisfied in full; and

(b) the guarantee is enforceable against the parent undertaking by any person to whom the subsidiary company is liable in respect of those liabilities: CA 2006, s 394C(3).

Individual accounts: applicable accounting framework

23.49 Under s 395(1), a company's individual accounts may be prepared:

(a) in accordance with s 396 ('Companies Act individual accounts'); or

(b) in accordance with international accounting standards ('IAS individual accounts').

This is subject to the provisions of ss 395 and 407 (consistency of financial reporting within group): CA 2006, s 395(1).

The individual accounts of a company that is a charity must be Companies Act individual accounts: CA 2006, s 395(2).

After the first financial year in which the directors of a company prepare IAS individual accounts ('the first IAS year'), all subsequent individual accounts of the company must be prepared in accordance with international accounting standards unless there is a relevant change of circumstance. This is subject to s 395(4A): CA 2006, s 395(3).

23.50 There is a relevant change of circumstance if, at any time during or after the first IAS year:

(a) the company becomes a subsidiary undertaking of another undertaking that does not prepare IAS individual accounts,

(aa) the company ceases to be a subsidiary undertaking,

(b) the company ceases to be a company with securities admitted to trading on a regulated market in an EEA State, or

(c) a parent undertaking of the company ceases to be an undertaking with securities admitted to trading on a regulated market in an EEA State: CA 2006, s 395(4).

23.51 After a financial year in which the directors of a company prepare IAS individual accounts for the company, the directors may change to preparing

Companies Act individual accounts for a reason other than a relevant change of circumstance provided they have not changed to Companies Act individual accounts in the period of five years preceding the first day of that financial year: CA 2006, s 395(4A).

In calculating the five-year period for the purpose of s 395(4A), no account should be taken of a change due to a relevant change of circumstance: CA 2006, s 395(4B).

If, having changed to preparing Companies Act individual accounts, the directors again prepare IAS individual accounts for the company ss 395(3) and (4) apply again as if the first financial year for which such accounts are again prepared were the first IAS year: CA 2006, s 395(5).

Companies Act individual accounts

23.52 Companies Act individual accounts must state:

(a) the part of the United Kingdom in which the company is registered;

(b) the company's registered number;

(c) whether the company is a public or a private company and whether it is limited by shares or by guarantee;

(d) the address of the company's registered office; and

(e) where appropriate, the fact that the company is being wound-up: CA 2006, s 395B(A1).

23.53 Companies Act individual accounts must comprise:

(a) a balance sheet as at the last day of the financial year; and

(b) a profit and loss account: CA 2006, s 396(1).

23.54 The accounts must:

(a) in the case of the balance sheet, give a true and fair view of the state of affairs of the company as at the end of the financial year; and

(b) in the case of the profit and loss account, give a true and fair view of the profit or loss of the company for the financial year: CA 2006, s 396(2).

In the case of the individual accounts of a company which qualifies as a micro-entity in relation to the financial year (see ss 384A and 384B), the micro-entity minimum accounting items included in the company's accounts for the year are presumed to give the true and fair view required by sub-s (2): CA 2006, s 396(2A).

23.55 The accounts must comply with provision made by the Secretary of State by regulations as to:

(a) the form and content of the balance sheet and profit and loss account; and

(b) additional information to be provided by way of notes to the accounts: CA 2006, s 396(3).

23.56 If compliance with the regulations, and any other provision made by or under CA 2006 as to the matters to be included in a company's individual accounts or in notes to those accounts, would not be sufficient to give a true and fair view, the necessary additional information must be given in the accounts or in a note to them: CA 2006, s 396(4).

If in special circumstances compliance with any of those provisions is inconsistent with the requirement to give a true and fair view, the directors must depart from that provision to the extent necessary to give a true and fair view.

Particulars of any such departure, the reasons for it and its effect must be given in a note to the accounts: CA 2006, s 396(5).

Subsections (4) and (5) do not apply in relation to the micro-entity minimum accounting items included in the individual accounts of a company for a financial year in relation to which the company qualifies as a micro-entity: CA 2006, s 396(6).

IAS individual accounts

23.57 IAS individual accounts must state:

(a) the part of the United Kingdom in which the company is registered;

(b) the company's registered number;

(c) whether the company is a public or a private company and whether it is limited by shares or by guarantee;

(d) the address of the company's registered office; and

(e) where appropriate, the fact that the company is being wound-up: CA 2006, s 397(1).

The notes to the accounts must state that the accounts have been prepared in accordance with international accounting standards: CA 2006, s 397(2).

Option to prepare group accounts

23.58 If at the end of a financial year a company subject to the small companies regime is a parent company, the directors, as well as preparing individual accounts for the year, may prepare group accounts for the year: CA 2006, s 398.

Duty to prepare group accounts

23.59 Section 399 applies to companies that are not subject to the small companies regime: CA 2006, s 399(1).

If at the end of a financial year the company is a parent company, the directors, as well as preparing individual accounts for the year, must prepare group accounts for the year unless the company is exempt from that requirement: CA 2006, s 399(2).

A company is exempt from the requirement to prepare group accounts if:

(a) it would be subject to the small companies regime but for being a public company; and

(b) it is not a traded company: CA 2006, s 399(2A).

23.60 There are further exemptions under:

- s 400 (company included in EEA accounts of larger group);
- s 401 (company included in non-EEA accounts of larger group); and
- s 402 (company none of whose subsidiary undertakings need be included in the consolidation): CA 2006, s 399(3).

A company to which s 399 applies but which is exempt from the requirement to prepare group accounts may do so: CA 2006, s 399(4).

Exemptions for company included in EEA group accounts of larger company

23.61 A company is exempt from the requirement to prepare group accounts if it is itself a subsidiary undertaking and its immediate parent undertaking is established under the law of an EEA State, in the following cases:

(a) where the company is a wholly owned subsidiary of that parent undertaking;

(b) where that parent undertaking holds 90% or more of the allotted shares in the company and the remaining shareholders have approved the exemption;

(c) where that parent undertaking holds more than 50% (but less than 90%) of the allotted shares in the company and notice requesting the preparation of group accounts has not been served on the company by the shareholders holding in aggregate at least 5% of the allotted shares in the company.

Such notice must be served at least six months before the end of the financial year to which it relates: CA 2006, s 400(1).

23.62 Exemption is conditional upon compliance with all of the following conditions:

(a) the company must be included in consolidated accounts for a larger group drawn up to the same date, or to an earlier date in the same financial year, by a parent undertaking established under the law of an EEA State;

(b) those accounts must be drawn up and audited, and that parent undertaking's annual report must be drawn up, according to that law:

   (i) in accordance with the provisions of Directive 2013/34/EU of the European Parliament and of the Council on the annual financial statements, consolidated financial statements and related reports of certain types of undertakings; or

   (ii) in accordance with international accounting standards;

(c) the company must disclose in the notes to its individual accounts that it is exempt from the obligation to prepare and deliver group accounts;

(d) the company must state in its individual accounts the name of the parent undertaking that draws up the group accounts referred to above and:

  (i) the address of the undertaking's registered office (whether in or outside the United Kingdom); or

  (ii) if it is unincorporated, the address of its principal place of business;

(e) the company must deliver to the registrar, within the period for filing its accounts and reports for the financial year in question, copies of:

  (i) those group accounts; and

  (ii) the parent undertaking's annual report,

  together with the auditor's report on them;

(f) any requirement of Pt 35 of the CA 2006 as to the delivery to the registrar of a certified translation into English must be met in relation to any document comprised in the accounts and reports delivered in accordance with para (e): CA 2006, s 400(2).

23.63 For the purposes of s 400(1)(b) and (c), shares held by a wholly owned subsidiary of the parent undertaking, or held on behalf of the parent undertaking or a wholly owned subsidiary, will be attributed to the parent undertaking: CA 2006, s 400(3).

The exemption does not apply to a company which is a traded company: CA 2006, s 400(4).

Shares held by directors of a company for the purpose of complying with any share qualification requirement shall be disregarded in determining for the purposes of s 400 whether the company is a wholly owned subsidiary: CA 2006, s 400(5).

Exemptions for company included in non-EEA group accounts of larger group

23.64 A company is exempt from the requirement to prepare group accounts if it is itself a subsidiary undertaking and its parent undertaking is not established under the law of an EEA State, in the following cases:

(a) where the company is a wholly owned subsidiary of that parent undertaking;

(b) where that parent undertaking holds 90% or more of the allotted shares in the company and the remaining shareholders have approved the exemption; or

(c) where that parent undertaking holds more than 50% (but less than 90%) of the allotted shares in the company and notice requesting the preparation of group accounts has not been served on the company by the shareholders holding in aggregate at least 5% of the allotted shares in the company.

Such notice must be served at least six months before the end of the financial year to which it relates: CA 2006, s 401(1).

23.65 Exemption is conditional upon compliance with all of the following conditions:

(a) the company and all of its subsidiary undertakings must be included in consolidated accounts for a larger group drawn up to the same date, or to an earlier date in the same financial year, by a parent undertaking;

(b) those accounts and, where appropriate, the group's annual report, must be drawn up:

   (i) in accordance with the provisions of Directive 2013/34/EU of the European Parliament and of the Council of 26 June 2013 on the annual financial statements, consolidated financial statements and related reports of certain types of undertakings;

   (ii) in a manner equivalent to consolidated accounts and consolidated reports so drawn up;

   (iii) in accordance with international accounting standards adopted pursuant to the IAS Regulation; or

   (iv) in accordance with accounting standards which are equivalent to such international accounting standards, as determined pursuant to Commission Regulation (EC) No 1569/2007 of 21 December 2007 establishing a mechanism for the determination of equivalence of accounting standards applied by third country issuers of securities pursuant to Directives 2003/71/EC and 2004/109/EC of the European Parliament and of the Council;

(c) the group accounts must be audited by one or more persons authorised to audit accounts under the law under which the parent undertaking which draws them up is established;

(d) the company must disclose in its individual accounts that it is exempt from the obligation to prepare and deliver group accounts;

(e) the company must state in its individual accounts the name of the parent undertaking which draws up the group accounts referred to above and:

   (i) the address of the undertaking's registered office (whether in or outside the United Kingdom); or

   (ii) if it is unincorporated, the address of its principal place of business;

(f) the company must deliver to the registrar, within the period for filing its accounts and reports for the financial year in question, copies of:

   (i) the group accounts; and

   (ii) where appropriate, the consolidated annual report,

   together with the auditor's report on them;

(g) any requirement of CA 2006, Pt 35 as to the delivery to the registrar of a certified translation into English must be met in relation to any document comprised in the accounts and reports delivered in accordance with para (f): CA 2006, s 401(2).

23.66 For the purposes of s 401(1)(b) and (c), shares held by a wholly owned subsidiary of the parent undertaking, or held on behalf of the parent undertaking or a wholly owned subsidiary, are attributed to the parent undertaking: CA 2006, s 401(3).

The exemption does not apply to a company which is a traded company: CA 2006, s 401(4).

Shares held by directors of a company for the purpose of complying with any share qualification requirement shall be disregarded in determining for the purposes of s 401 whether the company is a wholly owned subsidiary: CA 2006, s 401(5).

Exemptions if no subsidiary undertakings need to be included in the consolidation

23.67 A parent company is exempt from the requirement to prepare group accounts if under s 405, all of its subsidiary undertakings could be excluded from consolidation in Companies Act group accounts: CA 2006, s 402.

Group accounts: applicable accounting framework

23.68 The group accounts of certain parent companies are required by Art 4 of the IAS Regulation to be prepared in accordance with international accounting standards ('IAS group accounts'): CA 2006, s 403(1).

The group accounts of other companies may be prepared:

(a) in accordance with s 404 ('Companies Act group accounts'); or

(b) in accordance with international accounting standards ('IAS group accounts').

This is subject to the following provisions of s 403: CA 2006, s 403(2).

The group accounts of a parent company that is a charity must be Companies Act group accounts: CA 2006, s 403(3).

23.69 After the first financial year in which the directors of a parent company prepare IAS group accounts ('the first IAS year'), all subsequent group accounts of the company must be prepared in accordance with international accounting standards unless there is a relevant change of circumstance. This is subject to s 403(5A): CA 2006: s 403(4).

There is a relevant change of circumstance if, at any time during or after the first IAS year:

(a) the company becomes a subsidiary undertaking of another undertaking that does not prepare IAS group accounts;

(b) the company ceases to be a company with securities admitted to trading on a regulated market in an EEA State; or

(c) a parent undertaking of the company ceases to be an undertaking with securities admitted to trading on a regulated market in an EEA State: CA 2006, s 403(5).

23.70 After a financial year in which the directors of a parent company prepare IAS group accounts for the company, the directors may change to preparing Companies Act group accounts for a reason other than a relevant change of circumstance provided they have not changed to Companies Act group accounts in the period of five years preceding the first day of that financial year: CA 2006, s 403(5A).

In calculating the five-year period for the purpose of s 403(5A), no account should be taken of a change due to a relevant change of circumstance: CA 2006, s 403(5B).

If, having changed to preparing Companies Act group accounts, the directors again prepare IAS group accounts for the company, ss 403(4) and (5) apply again as if the first financial year for which such accounts are again prepared were the first IAS year: CA 2006, s 403(5C).

Companies act group accounts

23.71 Companies Act group accounts must state, in respect of the parent company:

(a) the part of the United Kingdom in which the company is registered;

(b) the company's registered number;

(c) whether the company is a public or a private company and whether it is limited by shares or by guarantee;

(d) the address of the company's registered office; and

(e) where appropriate, the fact that the company is being wound-up: CA 2006, s 404(A1).

23.72 Companies Act group accounts must comprise:

(a) a consolidated balance sheet dealing with the state of affairs of the parent company and its subsidiary undertakings; and

(b) a consolidated profit and loss account dealing with the profit or loss of the parent company and its subsidiary undertakings: CA 2006, s 404(1).

The accounts must give a true and fair view of the state of affairs as at the end of the financial year, and the profit or loss for the financial year, of the undertakings included in the consolidation as a whole, so far as concerns members of the company: CA 2006, s 404(2).

23.73 The accounts must comply with provision made by the Secretary of State by regulations as to:

(a) the form and content of the consolidated balance sheet and consolidated profit and loss account; and

(b) additional information to be provided by way of notes to the accounts: CA 2006, s 404(3).

23.74 If compliance with the regulations, and any other provision made by or under CA 2006 as to the matters to be included in a company's group accounts or in notes to those accounts, would not be sufficient to give a true and fair view, the necessary additional information must be given in the accounts or in a note to them: CA 2006, s 404(4).

If in special circumstances compliance with any of those provisions is inconsistent with the requirement to give a true and fair view, the directors must depart from that provision to the extent necessary to give a true and fair view.

Particulars of any such departure, the reasons for it and its effect must be given in a note to the accounts: CA 2006, s 404(5).

Companies Act group accounts: subsidiary undertakings included in the consolidation

23.75 Where a parent company prepares Companies Act group accounts, all the subsidiary undertakings of the company must be included in the consolidation, subject to the following exceptions: CA 2006, s 405(1).

A subsidiary undertaking may be excluded from consolidation if its inclusion is not material for the purpose of giving a true and fair view (but two or more undertakings may be excluded only if they are not material taken together): CA 2006, s 405(2).

23.76 A subsidiary undertaking may be excluded from consolidation where:

(a) severe long-term restrictions substantially hinder the exercise of the rights of the parent company over the assets or management of that undertaking; or

(b) extremely rare circumstances mean that the information necessary for the preparation of group accounts cannot be obtained without disproportionate expense or undue delay; or

(c) the interest of the parent company is held exclusively with a view to subsequent resale: CA 2006, s 405(3); and

(d) the reference in s 405(3)(a) to the rights of the parent company and the reference in s 405(3)(c) to the interest of the parent company are, respectively, to rights and interests held by or attributed to the company for the purposes of the definition of 'parent undertaking' (see s 1162) in the absence of which it would not be the parent company: CA 2006, s 405(4).

IAS group accounts

23.77 IAS group accounts must state:

(a) the part of the United Kingdom in which the company is registered;

(b) the company's registered number;

(c) whether the company is a public or a private company and whether it is limited by shares or by guarantee;

(d) the address of the company's registered office; and

(e) where appropriate, the fact that the company is being wound-up: CA 2006, s 406(1).

The notes to the accounts must state that the accounts have been prepared in accordance with international accounting standards: CA 2006, s 406(2).

Consistency of financial reporting within group

23.78 The directors of a parent company must secure that the individual accounts of –

(a) the parent company; and

(b) each of its subsidiary undertakings,

are all prepared using the same financial reporting framework, except to the extent that in their opinion there are good reasons for not doing so: CA 2006, s 407(1).

Section 407(1) does not apply if the directors do not prepare group accounts for the parent company: CA 2006, s 407(2).

Section 407(1) only applies to accounts of subsidiary undertakings that are required to be prepared under this Part: CA 2006, s 407(3).

Section 407(1) does not require accounts of undertakings that are charities to be prepared using the same financial reporting framework as accounts of undertakings which are not charities: CA 2006, s 407(4).

Section 407(1)(a) does not apply where the directors of a parent company prepare IAS group accounts and IAS individual accounts: CA 2006, s 407(5).

Individual profit and loss account where group accounts prepared

23.79 Section 408 applies where:

(a) a company prepares group accounts in accordance with CA 2006; and

(b) the company's individual balance sheet shows the company's profit and loss for the financial year determined in accordance with this Act: CA 2006, s 408(1).

23.80 If the accounts are prepared in accordance with the small companies regime, the balance sheet must contain, in a prominent position above the signature:

(a) in the case of individual accounts prepared in accordance with the micro-entity provisions, a statement to that effect; or

(b) in the case of accounts not prepared as mentioned in para (a), a statement to the effect that the accounts have been prepared in accordance with the provisions applicable to companies subject to the small companies regime: CA 2006, s 408(3).

The exemption conferred by s 408 is conditional upon its being disclosed in the company's annual accounts that the exemption applies: CA 2006, s 408(4).

Information about related undertakings

23.81 The Secretary of State may make provision by regulations requiring information about related undertakings to be given in notes to a company's annual accounts: CA 2006, s 409(1).

The regulations:

(a) may make different provision according to whether or not the company prepares group accounts; and

(b) may specify the descriptions of undertaking in relation to which they apply, and make different provision in relation to different descriptions of related undertaking: CA 2006, s 409(2).

23.82 The regulations may provide that information need not be disclosed with respect to an undertaking that:

(a) is established under the law of a country outside the UK; or

(b) carries on business outside the UK,

if the following conditions are met: CA 2006, s 409(3).

23.83 The conditions are:

(a) that in the opinion of the directors of the company the disclosure would be seriously prejudicial to the business of:

 (i) that undertaking;

 (ii) the company;

 (iii) any of the company's subsidiary undertakings; or

 (iv) any other undertaking which is included in the consolidation;

(b) that the Secretary of State agrees that the information need not be disclosed: CA 2006, s 409(4).

Where advantage is taken of any such exemption, that fact must be stated in a note to the company's annual accounts: CA 2006, s 409(5).

Information about off-balance sheet arrangements

23.84 If in any financial year:

(a) a company is or has been party to arrangements that are not reflected in its balance sheet; and

(b) at the balance sheet date the risks or benefits arising from those arrangements are material,

the information required by this section must be given in the notes to the company's annual accounts: CA 2006, s 410A(1).

23.85 The information required is:

(a) the nature and business purpose of the arrangements; and

(b) the financial impact of the arrangements on the company: CA 2006, s 410A(2).

The information need only be given to the extent necessary for enabling the financial position of the company to be assessed: CA 2006, s 410A(3).

23.86 If the company is subject to the small companies regime in relation to the financial year (see s 381), it need not comply with sub-s (2)(b): CA 2006, s 410A(4).

Section 410A applies in relation to group accounts as if the undertakings included in the consolidation were a single company: CA 2006, s 410A(5).

Information about employee numbers and costs

23.87 The notes to a company's annual accounts must disclose the average number of persons employed by the company in the financial year: CA 2006, s 411(1).

In the case of a company not subject to the small companies regime, the notes to the company's accounts must also disclose the average number of persons within each category of persons so employed: CA 2006, s 411(1A).

The categories by reference to which the number required to be disclosed by s 411(1A) is to be determined must be such as the directors may select having regard to the manner in which the company's activities are organised: CA 2006, s 411(2).

23.88 The average number required by s 411(1) or (1A) is determined by dividing the relevant annual number by the number of months in the financial year: CA 2006, s 411(3).

The relevant annual number is determined by ascertaining for each month in the financial year:

(a) for the purposes of s 411(1), the number of persons employed under contracts of service by the company in that month (whether throughout the month or not); and

(b) for the purposes of s 411(1A), the number of persons in the category in question of persons so employed;

and adding together all the monthly numbers: CA 2006, s 411(4).

23.89 Except in the case of a company subject to the small companies regime, the notes to the company's annual accounts or the profit and loss account must disclose, with reference to all persons employed by the company during the financial year, the total staff costs of the company relating to the financial year broken down between:

(a) wages and salaries paid or payable in respect of that year to those persons;

(b) social security costs incurred by the company on their behalf; and

(c) other pension costs so incurred: CA 2006, s 411(5).

23.90 Under s 411(5), the term 'pension costs' includes any costs incurred by the company in respect of:

(a) any pension scheme established for the purpose of providing pensions for persons currently or formerly employed by the company;

(b) any sums set aside for the future payment of pensions directly by the company to current or former employees; and

(c) any pensions paid directly to such persons without having first been set aside.

'Social security costs' means any contributions by the company to any state social security or pension scheme, fund or arrangement: CA 2006, s 411(6).

Section 411 applies in relation to group accounts as if the undertakings included in the consolidation were a single company: CA 2006, s 411(7).

Information about directors' benefits: remuneration

23.91 The Secretary of State may make provision by regulations requiring information to be given in notes to a company's annual accounts about directors' remuneration: CA 2006, s 412(1).

The matters about which information may be required include:

(a) gains made by directors on the exercise of share options;

(b) benefits received or receivable by directors under long-term incentive schemes;

(c) payments for loss of office (as defined in s 215);

(d) benefits receivable, and contributions for the purpose of providing benefits, in respect of past services of a person as director or in any other capacity while director; and

(e) consideration paid to or receivable by third parties for making available the services of a person as director or in any other capacity while director: CA 2006, s 412(2).

Without prejudice to the generality of s 412(1), regulations under s 412 may make any such provision as was made immediately before the commencement of this Part by Pt 1 of Sch 6 to the Companies Act 1985 (c 6): CA 2006, s 412(3).

23.92 For the purposes of s 412 and regulations made under it, amounts paid to or receivable by:

(a) a person connected with a director; or

(b) a body corporate controlled by a director,

are treated as paid to or receivable by the director.

The expressions 'connected with' and 'controlled by' in s 412 have the same meaning as in Pt 10 of the CA 2006 (company directors): CA 2006, s 412(4).

23.93 It is the duty of:

(a) any director of a company; and

(b) any person who is or has at any time in the preceding five years been a director of the company,

to give notice to the company of such matters relating to himself as may be necessary for the purposes of regulations under s 412: CA 2006, s 412(5).

A person who makes default in complying with s 412(5) commits an offence and will be liable on summary conviction to a fine not exceeding level 3 on the standard scale: CA 2006, s 412(6).

Information about directors' benefits: advances, credit and guarantees

23.94 In the case of a company that does not prepare group accounts, details of:

(a) advances and credits granted by the company to its directors; and

(b) guarantees of any kind entered into by the company on behalf of its directors,

must be shown in the notes to its individual accounts: CA 2006, s 413(1).

23.95 In the case of a parent company that prepares group accounts, details of:

(a) advances and credits granted to the directors of the parent company, by that company or by any of its subsidiary undertakings; and

(b) guarantees of any kind entered into on behalf of the directors of the parent company, by that company or by any of its subsidiary undertakings,

must be shown in the notes to the group accounts: CA 2006, s 413(2).

23.96 The details required of an advance or credit are:

(a) its amount;

(b) an indication of the interest rate;

(c) its main conditions;

(d) any amounts repaid;

(e) any amounts written off; and

(f) any amounts waived: CA 2006, s 413(3).

23.97 The details required of a guarantee are:

(a) its main terms;

(b) the amount of the maximum liability that may be incurred by the company (or its subsidiary); and

(c) any amount paid and any liability incurred by the company (or its subsidiary) for the purpose of fulfilling the guarantee (including any loss incurred by reason of enforcement of the guarantee): CA 2006, s 413(4).

23.98 There must also be stated in the notes to the accounts the totals:

(a) of amounts stated under s 413(3)(a);

(b) of amounts stated under s 413(3)(d);

(ba) of amounts stated under s 413(3)(e);

(bb) of amounts stated under s 413(3)(f);

(c) of amounts stated under s 413(4)(b); and

(d) of amounts stated under s 413(4)(c): CA 2006, s 413(5).

23.99 References in s 413 to the directors of a company are to the persons who were directors at any time in the financial year to which the accounts relate: CA 2006, s 413(6).

The requirements of s 413 apply in relation to every advance, credit or guarantee subsisting at any time in the financial year to which the accounts relate:

(a) whenever it was entered into;

(b) whether or not the person concerned was a director of the company in question at the time it was entered into; and

(c) in the case of an advance, credit or guarantee involving a subsidiary undertaking of that company, whether or not that undertaking was such a subsidiary undertaking at the time it was entered into: CA 2006, s 413(7).

Banking companies and the holding companies of credit institutions need only state the details required by s 413(5)(a) and (c): CA 2006, s 413(8).

Approval and signing of accounts

23.100 A company's annual accounts must be approved by the board of directors and signed on behalf of the board by a director of the company: CA 2006, s 414(1).

The signature must be on the company's balance sheet: CA 2006, s 414(2).

If the accounts are prepared in accordance with the provisions applicable to companies subject to the small companies regime, the balance sheet must contain a statement to that effect in a prominent position above the signature: CA 2006, s 414(3).

23.101 If annual accounts are approved that do not comply with the requirements of CA 2006 (and, where applicable, of Art 4 of the IAS Regulation), every director of the company who:

(a) knew that they did not comply, or was reckless as to whether they complied; and

(b) failed to take reasonable steps to secure compliance with those requirements or, as the case may be, to prevent the accounts from being approved,

commits an offence: CA 2006, s 414(4).

23.102 A person guilty of an offence under s 414 is liable:

(a) on conviction on indictment, to a fine; and

(b) on summary conviction, to a fine not exceeding the statutory maximum: CA 2006, s 414(5).

Duty to prepare strategic report

23.103 Chapter 4A of Pt 15 is concerned with the strategic report. It is made pursuant to the *Companies Act 2006 (Strategic Report and Directors' Report) Regulations 2013, SI 2013/1970*. Chapter 4A requires companies (other than those eligible for the small companies regime for accounts) to prepare a strategic report. It also prescribes the content of that report, including a requirement to provide information regarding the employment of people of each sex within the company. The strategic report must be approved by the directors and signed by one of them. The 2013 Regulations will apply to financial years ending on or after 30 September 2013. The strategic report replaces the business review and will be presented as a separate section of the annual report, outside of the directors' report.

23.104 The FRC has produced an *Exposure Draft: Guidance on the Strategic Report* (2013) which highlights the following guidance:

- It is applicable to all entities preparing strategic reports, although the FRC notes that the guidance has been written 'with quoted companies in mind'.
- Only information that is material to shareholders should be included in the strategic report.
- Strategic reports should include information that:
  - is fair, balanced and understandable;
  - is concise;
  - is forward looking;
  - is specific to the entity in question; and
  - that links to other information included within the annual report. The FRC provides supplementary guidance which provides suggested examples where information should be linked within the annual report.

Duty to prepare strategic report

23.105 The directors of a company must prepare a strategic report for each financial year of the company: CA 2006, s 414A.

Section 414A(1) does not apply if the company is entitled to the small companies exemption: CA 2006, s 414A(2).

For a financial year in which:

(a) the company is a parent company; and

(b) the directors of the company prepare group accounts,

the strategic report must be a consolidated report (a 'group strategic report') relating to the undertakings included in the consolidation: CA 2006, s 414A(3).

A group strategic report may, where appropriate, give greater emphasis to the matters that are significant to the undertakings included in the consolidation, taken as a whole: CA 2006, s 414A(4).

23.106 In the case of failure to comply with the requirement to prepare a strategic report, an offence is committed by every person who:

(a) was a director of the company immediately before the end of the period for filing accounts and reports for the financial year in question; and

(b) failed to take all reasonable steps for securing compliance with that requirement: CA 2006, s 414A(5).

23.107 A person guilty of an offence under s 414A is liable:

(a) on conviction on indictment, to a fine; or

(b) on summary conviction, to a fine not exceeding the statutory maximum: CA 2006, s 414A(6).

Strategic report: small companies exemption

23.108 A company is entitled to the small companies exemption in relation to the strategic report for a financial year if:

(a) it is entitled to prepare accounts for the year in accordance with the small companies regime; or

(b) it would be so entitled but for being or having been a member of an ineligible group: CA 2006, s 414B.

Contents of strategic report

23.109 The purpose of the strategic report is to inform members of the company and help them assess how the directors have performed their duty under s 172 (duty to promote the success of the company): CA 2006, s 414C(1).

In assessing whether directors have performed their duty under s 172, it is submitted that in the event an issue arises as to a breach of s 172, the courts may also have regard to the strategic report prepared by the directors in assessing whether they actually did promote the company's success having regard to the statements set out in the strategic report and the position in reality and practice.

23.110 The strategic report must contain:

(a) a fair review of the company's business; and

(b) a description of the principal risks and uncertainties facing the company: CA 2006, s 414C(2).

23.111 The review required is a balanced and comprehensive analysis of:

(a) the development and performance of the company's business during the financial year; and

(b) the position of the company's business at the end of that year,

consistent with the size and complexity of the business: CA 2006, s 414C(3).

23.112 The review must, to the extent necessary for an understanding of the development, performance or position of the company's business, include:

(a) analysis using financial key performance indicators; and

(b) where appropriate, analysis using other key performance indicators, including information relating to environmental and employee matters: CA 2006, s 414C(4).

Under s 414C(4), the term 'key performance indicators' means factors by reference to which the development, performance or position of the company's business can be measured effectively: CA 2006, s 414C(5).

Where a company qualifies as medium-sized in relation to a financial year (see ss 465–467), the review for the year need not comply with the requirements of s 414C(4) so far as they relate to non-financial information: CA 2006, s 414C(6).

23.113 In the case of a quoted company the strategic report must, to the extent necessary for an understanding of the development, performance or position of the company's business, include:

(a) the main trends and factors likely to affect the future development, performance and position of the company's business; and

(b) information about:

  (i) environmental matters (including the impact of the company's business on the environment);

  (ii) the company's employees; and

  (iii) social, community and human rights issues,

including information about any policies of the company in relation to those matters and the effectiveness of those policies.

If the report does not contain information of each kind mentioned in paragraphs (b)(i), (ii) and (iii), it must state which of those kinds of information it does not contain: CA 2006, s 414C(7).

23.114 In the case of a quoted company the strategic report must include:

(a) a description of the company's strategy;

(b) a description of the company's business model;

(c) a breakdown showing at the end of the financial year:

  (i) the number of persons of each sex who were directors of the company;

  (ii) the number of persons of each sex who were senior managers of the company (other than persons falling within sub-paragraph (i)); and

  (iii) the number of persons of each sex who were employees of the company: CA 2006, s 414C(8).

23.115 In s 414C(8), the term 'senior manager' means a person who:

(a) has responsibility for planning, directing or controlling the activities of the company, or a strategically significant part of the company; and

(b) is an employee of the company: CA 2006, s 414C(9).

23.116 In relation to a group strategic report:

(a) the reference to the company in s 414C(8)(c)(i) is to the parent company; and

(b) the breakdown required by s 414C(8)(c)(ii) must include the number of persons of each sex who were the directors of the undertakings included in the consolidation: CA 2006, s 414C(10).

The strategic report may also contain any matters that the directors consider are of strategic importance to the company required by regulations made under s 416(4): CA 2006, s 414C(11).

The report must, where appropriate, include references to, and additional explanations of, amounts included in the company's annual accounts: CA 2006, s 414C(12).

Subject to sub-s (10), in relation to a group strategic report s 414C has effect as if the references to the company were references to the undertakings included in the consolidation: CA 2006, s 414C(13).

Nothing in s 414C requires the disclosure of information about impending developments or matters in the course of negotiation if the disclosure would, in the opinion of the directors, be seriously prejudicial to the interests of the company: CA 2006, s 414C.

Approval and signing of strategic report

23.117 The strategic report must be approved by the board of directors and signed on behalf of the board by a director or the secretary of the company: CA 2006, s 414D(1).

If a strategic report is approved that does not comply with the requirements of the CA 2006, every director of the company who:

(a) knew that it did not comply, or was reckless as to whether it complied; and

(b) failed to take reasonable steps to secure compliance with those requirements or, as the case may be, to prevent the report from being approved,

commits an offence: CA 2006, s 414D(2).

23.118 A person guilty of an offence under s 414D will be liable:

(a) on conviction on indictment, to a fine;

(b) on summary conviction, to a fine not exceeding the statutory maximum: CA 2006, s 414D(3).

Directors' report

23.119 Chapter 4 of Pt 15 addresses aspects concerning the directors' report.

Duty to prepare directors' report

23.120 The directors of a company must prepare a directors' report for each financial year of the company: CA 2006, s 415(1).

Subsection (1) does not apply if the company qualifies as a micro-entity (see ss 384A and 384B): CA 2006, s 415(1A).

For a financial year in which:

(a) the company is a parent company; and

(b) the directors of the company prepare group accounts,

the directors' report must be a consolidated report (a 'group directors' report') relating to the undertakings included in the consolidation: CA 2006, s 415(2).

A group directors' report may, where appropriate, give greater emphasis to the matters that are significant to the undertakings included in the consolidation, taken as a whole: CA 2006, s 415(3).

23.121 In the case of failure to comply with the requirement to prepare a directors' report, an offence is committed by every person who:

(a) was a director of the company immediately before the end of the period for filing accounts and reports for the financial year in question; and

(b) failed to take all reasonable steps for securing compliance with that requirement: CA 2006, s 415(4).

23.122 A person guilty of an offence under s 415 is liable:

(a) on conviction on indictment, to a fine;

(b) on summary conviction, to a fine not exceeding the statutory maximum: CA 2006, s 415(5).

Directors' report: small companies exemption

23.123 A company is entitled to small companies exemption in relation to the directors' report for a financial year if:

(a) it is entitled to prepare accounts for the year in accordance with the small companies regime; or

(b) it would be so entitled but for being, or having been, a member of an ineligible group: CA 2006, s 415A(1).

23.124 The exemption is relevant to:

(a) s 416(3) (contents of report: statement of amount recommended by way of dividend); and

(b) ss 444–446 (filing obligations of different descriptions of company): CA 2006, s 415A(2) .

Content of directors' report: general

23.125 The directors' report for a financial year must state the names of the persons who, at any time during the financial year, were directors of the company: CA 2006, s 416(1).

Except in the case of a company entitled to the small companies exemption, the report must state the amount (if any) that the directors recommend should be paid by way of dividend: CA 2006, s 416(3).

The Secretary of State may make provision by regulations as to other matters that must be disclosed in a directors' report.

Without prejudice to the generality of this power, the regulations may make any such provision as was formerly made by Sch 7 to the CA 1985: CA 2006, s 416(4).

23.126 Under the Companies Act 2006 (Strategic Report and Directors' Report) Regulations 2013 (SI 2013/1970), where the company is a quoted company, there is a duty to provide disclosures concerning greenhouse gas emissions: reg 15.

Paragraphs 15–20 of the 2013 Regulations applies to the directors' report for a financial year if the company is a quoted company: reg 15(1).

The report must state the annual quantity of emissions in tonnes of carbon dioxide equivalent from activities for which that company is responsible including:

(a) the combustion of fuel; and

(b) the operation of any facility: reg 15(2).

The report must state the annual quantity of emissions in tonnes of carbon dioxide equivalent resulting from the purchase of electricity, heat, steam or cooling by the company for its own use: reg: 15(3).

Paragraphs 15(2) and (3) of the 2013 Regulations apply only to the extent that it is practical for the company to obtain the information in question; but where it is not practical for the company to obtain some or all of that information, the report must state what information is not included and why: reg 15(4).

23.127 The directors' report must state the methodologies used to calculate the information disclosed under para 15(2) and (3): reg 16.

The directors' report must state at least one ratio which expresses the quoted company's annual emissions in relation to a quantifiable factor associated with the company's activities: reg 17.

With the exception of the first year for which the directors' report contains the information required by paras 15(2) and (3) and 17, the report must state not only the information required by paras 15(2) and (3) and 17, but also that information as disclosed in the report for the preceding financial year: reg 18.

The directors' report must state if the period for which it is reporting the information required by paragraph 15(2) and (3) is different to the period in respect of which the directors' report is prepared: reg 19.

23.128 The following definitions apply for the purposes of paras 15–19:

- 'emissions' means emissions into the atmosphere of a greenhouse gas as defined in s 92 of the Climate Change Act 2008 which are attributable to human activity;
- 'tonne of carbon dioxide equivalent' has the meaning given in s 93(2) of the Climate Change Act 2008.

Content of directors' report: statement as to disclosure to auditors

23.129 Section 418 applies to a company unless:

(a) it is exempt for the financial year in question from the requirements of Pt 16 as to audit of accounts; and

(b) the directors take advantage of that exemption: CA 2006, s 418(1).

23.130 The directors' report must contain a statement to the effect that, in the case of each of the persons who are directors at the time the report is approved:

(a) so far as the director is aware, there is no relevant audit information of which the company's auditor is unaware; and

(b) he has taken all the steps that he ought to have taken as a director in order to make himself aware of any relevant audit information and to establish that the company's auditor is aware of that information: CA 2006, s 418(2).

'Relevant audit information' means information needed by the company's auditor in connection with preparing his report: CA 2006, s 418(3).

23.131 A director is regarded as having taken all the steps that he ought to have taken as a director to do the things mentioned in s 418(2)(b) if he has:

(a) made such enquiries of his fellow directors and of the company's auditors for that purpose; and

(b) taken such other steps (if any) for that purpose,

as are required by his duty as a director of the company to exercise reasonable care, skill and diligence: CA 2006, s 418(4).

23.132 Where a directors' report containing the statement required by s 418 is approved but the statement is false, every director of the company who:

(a) knew that the statement was false, or was reckless as to whether it was false; and

(b) failed to take reasonable steps to prevent the report from being approved,

commits an offence: CA 2006, s 418(5).

23.133 A person guilty of an offence under s 418(5) is liable:

(a) on conviction on indictment, to imprisonment for a term not exceeding two years or a fine (or both);

(b) on summary conviction:

(i) in England and Wales, to imprisonment for a term not exceeding 12 months or to a fine not exceeding the statutory maximum (or both); and

(ii) in Scotland or Northern Ireland, to imprisonment for a term not exceeding six months, or to a fine not exceeding the statutory maximum (or both): CA 2006, s 418(6).

Approval and signing of directors' report

23.134 The directors' report must be approved by the board of directors and signed on behalf of the board by a director or the secretary of the company: CA 2006, s 419(1).

If in preparing the report advantage is taken of the small companies exemption, it must contain a statement to that effect in a prominent position above the signature: CA 2006, s 419(2).

23.135 If a directors' report is approved that does not comply with the requirements of CA 2006, every director of the company who:

(a) knew that it did not comply, or was reckless as to whether it complied; and

(b) failed to take reasonable steps to secure compliance with those requirements or, as the case may be, to prevent the report from being approved,

commits an offence: CA 2006, s 419(3).

23.136 A person guilty of an offence under s 419 will be liable:

(a) on conviction on indictment, to a fine; or

(b) on summary conviction, to a fine not exceeding the statutory maximum: CA 2006, s 419(4).

Approval and signing of separate governance statement

23.137 Any separate corporate governance statement must be approved by the board of directors and signed on behalf of the board by a director or the secretary of the company: CA 2006, s 419A.

Quoted companies: directors' remuneration report

Duty to prepare directors' remuneration report

23.138 The directors of a quoted company must prepare a directors' remuneration report for each financial year of the company: CA 2006, s 420(1). In the case of failure to comply with the requirement to prepare a directors' remuneration report, every person who:

(a) was a director of the company immediately before the end of the period for filing accounts and reports for the financial year in question; and

(b) failed to take all reasonable steps for securing compliance with that requirement,

commits an offence: CA 2006, s 420(2).

23.139 A person guilty of an offence under s 420 will be liable:

(a) on conviction on indictment, to a fine; or

(b) on summary conviction, to a fine not exceeding the statutory maximum: CA 2006, s 420(3).

Contents of directors' remuneration report

23.140 The Secretary of State may make provision by regulations as to:

(a) the information that must be contained in a directors' remuneration report;

(b) how information is to be set out in the report; and

(c) what is to be the auditable part of the report: CA 2006, s 421(1).

Without prejudice to the generality of this power, the regulations may make any such provision as was made, immediately before the commencement of CA 2006, Pt 15, by Sch 7A to the CA 1985 (c 6): CA 2006, s 421(2).

23.141 It is the duty of:

(a) any director of a company; and

(b) any person who is or has at any time in the preceding five years been a director of the company,

to give notice to the company of such matters relating to himself as may be necessary for the purposes of regulations under s 421: CA 2006, s 421(3).

A person who makes default in complying with s 421(3) commits an offence and is liable on summary conviction to a fine not exceeding level 3 on the standard scale: CA 2006, s 421(4).

Approval and signing of contents of directors' remuneration report

23.142 The directors' remuneration report must be approved by the board of directors and signed on behalf of the board by a director or the secretary of the company: CA 2006, s 422(1). If a directors' remuneration report is approved that does not comply with the requirements of CA 2006, every director of the company who:

(a) knew that it did not comply, or was reckless as to whether it complied; and

(b) failed to take reasonable steps to secure compliance with those requirements or, as the case may be, to prevent the report from being approved,

commits an offence: CA 2006, s 422(2).

23.143 A person guilty of an offence under s 422 is liable:

(a) on conviction on indictment, to a fine; or

(b) on summary conviction, to a fine not exceeding the statutory maximum: CA 2006, s 422(3).

Publication of accounts and reports

Duty to circulate copies of annual accounts and reports

23.144 Every company must send a copy of its annual accounts and reports for each financial year to:

(a) every member of the company;

(b) every holder of the company's debentures; and

(c) every person who is entitled to receive notice of general meetings: CA 2006, s 423(1).

23.145 Copies need not be sent to a person for whom the company does not have a current address: CA 2006, s 423(2).

A company has a 'current address' for a person if:

(a) an address has been notified to the company by the person as one at which documents may be sent to him; and

(b) the company has no reason to believe that documents sent to him at that address will not reach him: CA 2006, s 423(3).

23.146 In the case of a company not having a share capital, copies need not be sent to anyone who is not entitled to receive notices of general meetings of the company: CA 2006, s 423(4).

Where copies are sent out over a period of days, references in the Companies Acts to the day on which copies are sent out shall be read as references to the last day of that period: CA 2006, s 423(5).

Section 423 applies subject to s 426 (option to provide strategic report with supplementary material): CA 2006, s 423(6).

Time allowed for sending out copies of accounts and reports

23.147 The time allowed for sending out copies of the company's annual accounts and reports is as follows: CA 2006, s 424(1). A private company must comply with s 423 not later than:

(a) the end of the period for filing accounts and reports; or

(b) if earlier, the date on which it actually delivers its accounts and reports to the registrar: CA 2006, s 424(2).

A public company must comply with s 423 at least 21 days before the date of the relevant accounts meeting: CA 2006, s 424(3).

If, in the case of a public company, copies are sent out later than is required by s 424(3), they shall, despite that, be deemed to have been duly sent if it is so agreed by all the members entitled to attend and vote at the relevant accounts meeting: CA 2006, s 424(4).

23.148 Whether the time allowed is that for a private company or a public company is determined by reference to the company's status immediately before the end of the accounting reference period by reference to which the financial year for the accounts in question was determined: CA 2006, s 424(5).

Under s 423 the 'relevant accounts meeting' means the accounts meeting of the company at which the accounts and reports in question are to be laid: CA 2006, s 424(6).

Default in sending out copies of accounts and reports: offences

23.149 If default is made in complying with ss 423 or 424, an offence is committed by:

(a) the company; and

(b) every officer of the company who is in default: CA 2006, s 425(1).

23.150 A person guilty of an offence under s 425 is liable:

(a) on conviction on indictment, to a fine; or

(b) on summary conviction, to a fine not exceeding the statutory maximum: CA 2006, s 425(2).

Option to provide strategic report with supplementary material

23.151 A company may:

(a) in such cases as may be specified by regulations made by the Secretary of State; and

(b) provided any conditions so specified are complied with,

provide a copy of the strategic report together with the supplementary material described in s 426A instead of copies of the accounts and reports required to be sent out in accordance with s 423: CA 2006, s 426(1).

23.152 Copies of those accounts and reports must, however, be sent to any person entitled to be sent them in accordance with that section and who wishes to receive them: CA 2006, s 426(2).

The Secretary of State may make provision by regulations as to the manner in which it is to be ascertained, whether before or after a person becomes entitled to be sent a copy of those accounts and reports, whether he wishes to receive them: CA 2006, s 426(3).

Section 426 applies to copies of accounts and reports required to be sent out by virtue of s 146 to a person nominated to enjoy information rights as it applies to copies of accounts and reports required to be sent out in accordance with s 423 to a member of the company: CA 2006, s 426(5).

23.153 The Companies (Receipt of Accounts and Reports) Regulations 2013, SI 2013/1973, applies to the strategic report with supplementary material ('the Regulations').

Subject to the Regulations, a company may send a copy of its strategic report with supplementary material instead of a copy of its full accounts and reports to:

(a) a person specified in s 423(1) (duty to circulate copies of annual accounts and reports); and

(b) a person nominated to enjoy information rights under s 146 (traded companies: nomination of persons to enjoy information rights): reg 4.

23.154 However there will be specific cases in which the sending of the strategic report with supplementary material will be prohibited. In the following cases a company may not send a copy of its strategic report with supplementary material to a person specified in reg 4:

(a) in the case of any such person, where it is prohibited from doing so by any relevant provision of its constitution;

(b) in the case of any such person who is the holder of a debenture, where it is prohibited from doing so by a relevant provision in any instrument constituting or otherwise governing any of the company's debentures of which that person is a holder; or

(c) in the case of any such person (whether or not the holder of a debenture) where it is prohibited from sending a summary financial statement to any such person by any relevant provision of its constitution: reg 5(1).

23.155 In the following cases a company may not send a copy of its strategic report with supplementary material to a person specified in reg 4 in relation to any financial year:

(a) where, in relation to that year, no auditor's report has been made in respect of the annual accounts of the company, or the strategic report, or the directors' report, or the auditable part of the directors' remuneration report, where relevant, under ss 495 (auditor's report on company's annual accounts), 496 (auditor's report on strategic report and directors' report) and 497 (auditor's report on auditable part of directors' remuneration report) of the 2006 Act respectively;

(b) where the period for filing accounts and reports for that year under s 442 of the 2006 Act (period for filing accounts) has expired; and

(c) where the strategic report in respect of that financial year has not been approved by the board of directors and has not been signed on behalf of the board by a director of the company: reg 5(2).

For the purposes of reg 5(l) any provision (however expressed) which requires copies of the full accounts and reports to be sent to a person specified in reg 4, or which forbids the sending of a copy of the strategic report with supplementary material under s 426 of the 2006 Act (option to provide strategic report with supplementary material), is a relevant provision: reg 5(3).

23.156 Paragraph 6 deals with the ascertainment of the wishes of a person specified in reg 4. A company may not send a copy of the strategic report with supplementary material to a person specified in reg 4 unless the company has ascertained that the person does not wish to receive copies of its full accounts and reports, and paras (2) and (3) apply for the ascertainment of whether or not such a person wishes to receive copies of the full accounts and reports for a financial year: reg 6(1).

Where a person specified in reg 4 has expressly notified the company either that the person wishes to receive copies of the full accounts and reports or that the person wishes, instead of copies of those documents, to receive a copy of the strategic report with supplementary material, the company must send copies of the full accounts and reports or strategic report with supplementary material, as appropriate, to that person in respect of the financial years to which the notification applies: reg 6(2).

23.157 Where there has been no such express notification to the company by such a person, that person may be taken to have elected to receive a strategic report with supplementary material if the person fails to respond to an opportunity to elect to receive copies of the full accounts and reports given to the person either:

(a) by a consultation notice under reg 7, or

(b) as part of a relevant consultation of that person's wishes by the company under reg 8: reg 6(3).

For the purposes of reg 6(2), a notification has effect in relation to a financial year if it relates to that year (whether or not it has been given at the invitation of the company) and if it has been received by the company not later than 28 days before the first date on which copies of the full accounts and reports for that year are sent to the persons specified in reg 4 in accordance with s 423: reg 6(4).

23.158 Regulation 7 deals with consultation by notice. A consultation notice under this regulation is notice given by a company to a person specified in reg 4 which:

(a) states that for the future, so long as the person is a person so specified, the person will be sent a copy of the strategic report with supplementary material for each financial year instead of a copy of the company's full accounts and reports, unless the person notifies the company that the person wishes to receive full accounts and reports;

(b) states that the card or form accompanying the notice in accordance with reg 9(3) must be returned by a date specified in the notice, being a date at least 21 days after service of the notice and not less than 28 days before the first date on which copies of the full accounts and reports for the next financial year for which that person is entitled to receive them are sent out to persons specified in reg 4 in accordance with s 423;

(c) includes a statement in a prominent position to the effect that the strategic report and supplementary material will not contain sufficient information to allow as full an understanding of the results and state of affairs of the company or group as would be provided by the full annual accounts and reports and that persons specified in reg 4 requiring more detailed information have the right to obtain, free of charge, a copy of the company's last full accounts and reports.

23.159 Regulation 8 is concerned with relevant consultation. A company may conduct a relevant consultation to ascertain the wishes of a person specified in reg 4: reg 8(1).

For the purposes of reg 8, a relevant consultation of the wishes of such a person is a notice given to that person which:

(a) states that for the future, so long as the person is a person specified in reg 4, the person will be sent a strategic report with supplementary material instead of the full accounts and reports of the company, unless the person notifies the company that the person wishes to continue to receive full accounts and reports;

(b) accompanies a copy of the full accounts and reports; and

(c) accompanies a copy of a strategic report with supplementary material, with respect to the financial year covered by those full accounts and reports and which is identified in the notice as an example of the documents which that person will receive for the future, so long as the person is a person specified in reg 4, unless the person notifies the company to the contrary: reg 8(2).

Supplementary material

23.160 The supplementary material referred to in s 426 must be prepared in accordance with s 426A.

The supplementary material must:

(a) contain a statement that the strategic report is only part of the company's annual accounts and reports;

(b) state how a person entitled to them can obtain a full copy of the company's annual accounts and reports;

(c) state whether the auditor's report on the annual accounts was unqualified or qualified and, if it was qualified, set out the report in full together with any further material needed to understand the qualification;

(d) state whether, in that report, the auditor's statement under s 496 (whether strategic report and directors' report consistent with the accounts) was unqualified or qualified and, if it was qualified, set out the qualified statement in full together with any further material needed to understand the qualification;

(e) in the case of a quoted company, contain a copy of that part of the directors' remuneration report which sets out the single total figure table in respect of the company's directors' remuneration in accordance with the requirements of Sch 8 to the Large and Medium-sized Companies (Accounts and Reports) Regulations 2008, SI 2008/410: CA 2006, s 426A(2) (as inserted by the Companies Act 2013 (Strategic Report and Directors' Report) Regulations 2013, SI 2013/1970).

Quoted companies: annual accounts and reports to be made available on website

23.161 A quoted company must ensure that its annual accounts and reports:

(a) are made available on a website; and

(b) remain so available until the annual accounts and reports for the company's next financial year are made available in accordance with s 430: CA 2006, s 430(1).

23.162 The annual accounts and reports must be made available on a website that:

(a) is maintained by or on behalf of the company; and

(b) identifies the company in question: CA 2006, s 430(2).

23.163 Access to the annual accounts and reports on the website, and the ability to obtain a hard copy of the annual accounts and reports from the website, must not be:

(a) conditional on the payment of a fee; or

(b) otherwise restricted, except so far as necessary to comply with any enactment or regulatory requirement (in the UK or elsewhere): CA 2006, s 430(3).

23.164 The annual accounts and reports:

(a) must be made available as soon as reasonably practicable; and

(b) must be kept available throughout the period specified in s 430(1)(b): CA 2006, s 430(4).

23.165 A failure to make the annual accounts and reports available on a website throughout that period is disregarded if:

(a) the annual accounts and reports are made available on the website for part of that period; and

(b) the failure is wholly attributable to circumstances that it would not be reasonable to have expected the company to prevent or avoid: CA 2006, s 430(5).

In the event of default in complying with s 430, an offence is committed by every officer of the company who is in default: CA 2006, s 430(6).

A person guilty of an offence under s 430(6) is liable on summary conviction to a fine not exceeding level 3 on the standard scale: CA 2006, s 430(7).

Right of member or debenture holder to copies of accounts and reports: unquoted companies

23.166 A member of, or holder of debentures of, an unquoted company is entitled to be provided, on demand and without charge, with a copy of:

(a) the company's last annual accounts;

(aa) the strategic report (if any) for the last financial year;

(b) the last directors' report; and

(c) the auditor's report on those accounts (including the statement on that report and (where applicable) on the strategic report): CA 2006, s 431(1).

The entitlement under s 431 is to a single copy of those documents, but that is in addition to any copy to which a person may be entitled under s 423: CA 2006, s 431(2).

23.167 If a demand made under s 431 is not complied with within seven days of receipt by the company, an offence is committed by:

(a) the company; and

(b) every officer of the company who is in default: CA 2006, s 431(3).

A person guilty of an offence under s 431 is liable on summary conviction to a fine not exceeding level 3 on the standard scale and, for continued contravention, a daily default fine not exceeding one-tenth of level 3 on the standard scale: CA 2006, s 431(4).

Right of member or debenture holder to copies of accounts and reports: quoted companies

23.168 A member of, or holder of debentures of, a quoted company is entitled to be provided, on demand and without charge, with a copy of:

(a) the company's last annual accounts;

(b) the last directors' remuneration report;

(ba) the strategic report (if any) for the last financial year;

(c) the last directors' report; and

(d) the auditor's report on those accounts (including the report on the directors' remuneration report, on the strategic report (where this is covered by the auditor's report and on the directors' report): CA 2006, s 432(1).

23.169 The entitlement under s 432 is to a single copy of those documents, but that is in addition to any copy to which a person may be entitled under s 423: CA 2006, s 432(2). If a demand made under s 432 is not complied with within seven days of receipt by the company, an offence is committed by:

(a) the company; and

(b) every officer of the company who is in default: CA 2006, s 432(3).

A person guilty of an offence under s 432 will be liable on summary conviction to a fine not exceeding level 3 on the standard scale and, for continued contravention, a daily default fine not exceeding one-tenth of level 3 on the standard scale: CA 2006, s 432(4).

Name of signatory to be stated in published copies of accounts and reports

23.170 Every copy of a document to which s 433 applies that is published by or on behalf of the company must state the name of the person who signed it on behalf of the board: CA 2006, s 433(1).

In the case of an unquoted company, s 433 applies to copies of:

(a) the company's balance sheet;

(aa) the strategic report; and

(b) the directors' report: CA 2006, s 433(2).

23.171 In the case of a quoted company, s 433 applies to copies of:

(a) the company's balance sheet;

(b) the directors' remuneration report;

(ba) the strategic report; and

(c) the directors' report: CA 2006, s 433(3).

23.172 If a copy is published without the required statement of the signatory's name, an offence is committed by:

(a) the company; and

(b) every officer of the company who is in default: CA 2006, s 433(4).

A person guilty of an offence under s 433 is liable on summary conviction to a fine not exceeding level 3 on the standard scale: CA 2006, s 433(5).

Requirements in connection with publication of statutory accounts

23.173 If a company publishes any of its statutory accounts, they must be accompanied by the auditor's report on those accounts (unless the company is exempt from audit and the directors have taken advantage of that exemption): CA 2006, s 434(1).

A company that prepares statutory group accounts for a financial year must not publish its statutory individual accounts for that year without also publishing with them its statutory group accounts: CA 2006, s 434(2).

A company's 'statutory accounts' are its accounts for a financial year as required to be delivered to the registrar under s 441: CA 2006, s 434(3).

23.174 If a company contravenes any provision of s 434, an offence is committed by:

(a) the company; and

(b) every officer of the company who is in default: CA 2006, s 434(4).

A person guilty of an offence under s 434 is liable on summary conviction to a fine not exceeding level 3 on the standard scale: CA 2006, s 434(5).

Requirements in connection with publication of non-statutory accounts

23.175 If a company publishes non-statutory accounts, it must publish with them a statement indicating:

(a) that they are not the company's statutory accounts;

(b) whether statutory accounts dealing with any financial year with which the non-statutory accounts purport to deal have been delivered to the registrar; and

(c) whether an auditor's report has been made on the company's statutory accounts for any such financial year, and if so whether the report:

    (i) was qualified or unqualified, or included a reference to any matters to which the auditor drew attention by way of emphasis without qualifying the report; or

    (ii) contained a statement under s 498(2) (accounting records or returns inadequate or accounts or directors' remuneration report not agreeing with records and returns), or s 498(3) (failure to obtain necessary information and explanations): CA 2006, s 435(1).

The company must not publish with non-statutory accounts the auditor's report on the company's statutory accounts: CA 2006, s 435(2).

23.176 References in s 435 to the publication by a company of 'non-statutory accounts' are to the publication of:

(a) any balance sheet or profit and loss account relating to, or purporting to deal with, a financial year of the company; or

(b) an account in any form purporting to be a balance sheet or profit and loss account for a group headed by the company relating to, or purporting to deal with, a financial year of the company,

otherwise than as part of the company's statutory accounts: CA 2006, s 435(3).

In s 435(3)(b), 'a group headed by the company' means a group consisting of the company and any other undertaking (regardless of whether it is a subsidiary undertaking of the company) other than a parent undertaking of the company: CA 2006, 435(4).

23.177 If a company contravenes any provision of s 435, an offence is committed by:

(a) the company; and

(b) every officer of the company who is in default: CA 2006, s 435(5).

A person guilty of an offence under s 435 is liable on summary conviction to a fine not exceeding level 3 on the standard scale: CA 2006, s 435(6).

Meaning of publication in relation to accounts and reports

23.178 Section 436 applies for the purposes of:

(a) s 433 (name of signatory to be stated in published copies of accounts and reports);

(b) s 434 (requirements in connection with publication of statutory accounts); and

(c) s 435 (requirements in connection with publication of non-statutory accounts): CA 2006, s 436(1).

For the purposes of those sections a company is regarded as publishing a document if it publishes, issues or circulates it or otherwise makes it available for public inspection in a manner calculated to invite members of the public generally, or any class of members of the public, to read it: CA 2006, s 436(2).

Public companies laying of accounts and reports before general meeting

23.179 The directors of a public company must lay before the company in general meeting copies of its annual accounts and reports: CA 2006, s 437(1). Section 437 must be complied with not later than the end of the period for filing the accounts and reports in question: CA 2006, s 437(2). In the Companies Acts, 'accounts meeting' in relation to a public company, means a general meeting of the company at which the company's annual accounts and reports are (or are to be) laid in accordance with this section: CA 2006, s 437(3).

Public companies: offence of failure to law accounts and reports

23.180 If the requirements of s 437 are not complied with before the end of the period allowed, every person who immediately before the end of that period was a director of the company commits an offence: CA 2006, s 438(1).

It is a defence for a person charged with such an offence to prove that he took all reasonable steps for securing that those requirements would be complied with before the end of that period: CA 2006, s 438(2). It is not a defence to prove that the documents in question were not in fact prepared as required by this Part: CA 2006, s 438(3).

A person guilty of an offence under s 438 is liable on summary conviction to a fine not exceeding level 5 on the standard scale and, for continued contravention, a daily default fine not exceeding one-tenth of level 5 on the standard scale: CA 2006, s 438(4).

Quoted companies: members' approval of directors' remuneration report

23.181 A quoted company must, prior to the accounts meeting, give to the members of the company entitled to be sent notice of the meeting notice of the intention to move at the meeting, as an ordinary resolution, a resolution approving the directors' remuneration report for the financial year: CA 2006, s 439(1).

The notice may be given in any manner permitted for the service on the member of notice of the meeting: CA 2006, s 439(2).

The business that may be dealt with at the accounts meeting includes the resolution. This is so notwithstanding any default in complying with s 439(1) or (2): CA 2006, s 439(3). The existing directors must ensure that the resolution is put to the vote of the meeting: CA 2006, s 439(4).

No entitlement of a person to remuneration is made conditional on the resolution being passed by reason only of the provision made by s 439: CA 2006, s 439(5).

23.182 Under s 439:

(a) 'the accounts meeting' means the general meeting of the company before which the company's annual accounts for the financial year are to be laid; and

(b) 'existing director' means a person who is a director of the company immediately before that meeting: CA 2006, s 439(6).

Quoted companies: offences in connection with procedure for approval

23.183 In the event of default in complying with s 439(1) (notice to be given of resolution for approval of directors' remuneration report), an offence is committed by every officer of the company who is in default: CA 2006, s 440(1).

If the resolution is not put to the vote of the accounts meeting, an offence is committed by each existing director: CA 2006, s 440(2).

It is a defence for a person charged with an offence under s 440(2) to prove that he took all reasonable steps for securing that the resolution was put to the vote of the meeting: CA 2006, s 440(3).

A person guilty of an offence under s 440 is liable on summary conviction to a fine not exceeding level 3 on the standard scale: CA 2006, s 440(4).

23.184 Under s 440:

(a) 'the accounts meeting' means the general meeting of the company before which the company's annual accounts for the financial year are to be laid; and

(b) 'existing director' means a person who is a director of the company immediately before that meeting: CA 2006, s 440(4).

Filing of accounts and report

23.185 Chapter 10 of Pt 15 addresses the obligations to file accounts and report.

Duty to file accounts and reports with the registrar

23.186 The directors of a company must deliver to the registrar for each financial year the accounts and reports required by:

(a) s 444 (filing obligations of companies subject to small companies regime);

(b) s 444A (filing obligations of companies entitled to small companies exemption in relation to directors' report);

(c) s 445 (filing obligations of medium-sized companies);

(d) s 446 (filing obligations of unquoted companies); or

(e) s 447 (filing obligations of quoted companies): CA 2006, s 441(1).

23.187 This is subject to:

(a) s 448 (unlimited companies exempt from filing obligations); and

(b) s 448A (dormant subsidiaries exempt from filing obligations): CA 2006, s 441(2).

Period allowed for filing accounts

23.188 Section 442 specifies the period allowed for the directors of a company to comply with their obligation under s 441 to deliver accounts and reports for a financial year to the registrar. This is referred to in the Companies Acts as the 'period for filing' those accounts and reports: CA 2006, s 442(1).

The period is:

(a) for a private company, nine months after the end of the relevant accounting reference period; and

(b) for a public company, six months after the end of that period.

This is subject to the following provisions of s 442: CA 2006, s 442(2).

23.189 If the relevant accounting reference period is the company's first and is a period of more than 12 months, the period is:

(a) nine months or six months, as the case may be, from the first anniversary of the incorporation of the company, or

(b) three months after the end of the accounting reference period,

whichever last expires: CA 2006, s 442(3).

23.190 If the relevant accounting reference period is treated as shortened by virtue of a notice given by the company under s 392 (alteration of accounting reference date), the period is:

(a) that applicable in accordance with the above provisions; or

(b) three months from the date of the notice under that section,

whichever last expires: CA 2006, s 442(4).

23.191 Subject to sub-s (5A), if for any special reason the Secretary of State thinks fit he may, on an application made before the expiry of the period otherwise allowed, by notice in writing to a company, extend that period by such further period as may be specified in the notice: CA 2006, s 442(5).

Any such extension must not have the effect of extending the period for filing to more than twelve months after the end of the relevant accounting reference period: CA 2006, s 442(5A).

Whether the period allowed is that for a private company or a public company is determined by reference to the company's status immediately before the end of the relevant accounting reference period: CA 2006, s 442(6).

Under s 442, 'the relevant accounting reference period' means the accounting reference period by reference to which the financial year for the accounts in question was determined: CA 2006, s 442(6).

Calculation of period allowed

23.192 Section 443 applies for the purposes of calculating the period for filing a company's accounts and reports which is expressed as a specified number of months from a specified date or after the end of a specified previous period: CA 2006, s 443(1).

Subject to the following provisions, the period ends with the date in the appropriate month corresponding to the specified date or the last day of the specified previous period: CA 2006, s 443(2).

23.193 If the specified date, or the last day of the specified previous period, is the last day of a month, the period ends with the last day of the appropriate month (whether or not that is the corresponding date): CA 2006, s 443(3).

If:

(a) the specified date, or the last day of the specified previous period, is not the last day of a month but is the 29th or 30th, and

(b) the appropriate month is February,

the period ends with the last day of February: CA 2006, s 443(4).

'The appropriate month' means the month that is the specified number of months after the month in which the specified date, or the end of the specified previous period, falls: CA 2006, s 443(5).

Filing obligations of different descriptions of company

Filing obligations of companies subject to the small companies regime

23.194 The directors of a company subject to the small companies regime:

(a) must deliver to the registrar for each financial year a copy of the balance sheet drawn up as at the last day of that year; and

(b) may also deliver to the registrar:

   (i) a copy of the company's profit and loss account for that year; and

   (ii) a copy of the directors' report for that year: CA 2006, s 444(1).

Where the directors deliver to the registrar a copy of the company's profit and loss account under sub-s (1)(b)(i), the directors must also deliver to the registrar a copy of the auditor's report on the accounts (and any directors' report) that it delivers.

This does not apply if the company is exempt from audit and the directors have taken advantage of that exemption: CA 2006, s 444(2).

Where the balance sheet or profit and loss account is abridged pursuant to para 1A of Sch 1 to the Small Companies and Groups (Accounts and Directors' Report) Regulations (SI 2008/409), the directors must also deliver to the registrar a statement by the company that all the members of the company have consented to the abridgement: CA 2006, s.442(2A).

23.195 The copies of accounts and reports delivered to the registrar must be copies of the company's annual accounts and reports, except that where the company prepares Companies Act accounts:

(a) the directors may deliver to the registrar a copy of a balance sheet drawn up in accordance with regulations made by the Secretary of State; and

(b) there may be omitted from the copy profit and loss account delivered to the registrar such items as may be specified by the regulations.

These are referred to in CA 2006, Pt 15 as 'abbreviated accounts': CA 2006, s 444(3).

23.196 Where the directors of a company subject to the small companies regime:

(a) do not deliver to the registrar a copy of the company's profit and loss account; or

(b) do not deliver to the registrar a copy of the directors' report;

the copy of the balance sheet delivered to the registrar must contain in a prominent position a statement that the company's annual accounts and reports have been delivered in accordance with the provisions applicable to companies subject to the small companies regime: CA 2006, s 444(5).

23.197 Subject to sub-s (5C), where the directors of a company subject to the small companies regime do not deliver to the registrar a copy of the company's profit and loss account:

(a) the copy of the balance sheet delivered to the registrar must disclose that fact; and

(b) unless the company is exempt from audit and the directors have taken advantage of that exemption, the notes to the balance sheet delivered must satisfy the requirements in sub-s (5B): CA 2006, s 444(5A).

23.198 Those requirements are that the notes to the balance sheet must:

(a) state whether the auditor's report was qualified or unqualified;

(b) where that report was qualified, disclose the basis of the qualification (reproducing any statement under s 498(2)(a) or (b) or s 498(3), if applicable);

(c) where that report was unqualified, include a reference to any matters to which the auditor drew attention by way of emphasis; and

(d) state:

   (i) the name of the auditor and (where the auditor is a firm) the name of the person who signed the auditor's report as senior statutory auditor; or

   (ii) if the conditions in s 506 (circumstances in which names may be omitted) are met, that a resolution has been passed and notified to the Secretary of State in accordance with that section: CA 2006, s 444(5B).

23.199 Subsection (5A) does not apply in relation to a company if:

(a) the company qualifies as a micro-entity (see ss 384A and 384B) in relation to a financial year; and

(b) the company's accounts are prepared for that year in accordance with any of the micro-entity provisions: CA 2006, s 444(5C).

The copies of the balance sheet and any directors' report delivered to the registrar under s 433 must state the name of the person who signed it on behalf of the board: CA 2006, s 444(6).

23.200 The copy of the auditor's report delivered to the registrar under s 444 must:

(a) state the name of the auditor and (where the auditor is a firm) the name of the person who signed it as senior statutory auditor; or

(b) if the conditions in s 506 (circumstances in which names may be omitted) are met, state that a resolution has been passed and notified to the Secretary of State in accordance with that section: CA 2006, s 444(7).

Filing obligations of medium-sized companies

23.201 The directors of a company that qualifies as a medium-sized company in relation to a financial year (see ss 465–467) must deliver to the registrar a copy of:

(a) the company's annual accounts;

(aa) the strategic report; and

(b) the directors' report: CA 2006, s 445(1).

They must also deliver to the registrar a copy of the auditor's report on those accounts (and on the strategic report and the directors' report).

This does not apply if the company is exempt from audit and the directors have taken advantage of that exemption: CA 2006, s 445(2).

The copies of the balance sheet strategic report and directors' report delivered to the registrar under s 445 must state the name of the person who signed it on behalf of the board: CA 2006, s 445(5).

23.202 The copy of the auditor's report delivered to the registrar under s 445 must:

(a) state the name of the auditor and (where the auditor is a firm) the name of the person who signed it as senior statutory auditor; or

(b) if the conditions in s 506 (circumstances in which names may be omitted) are met, state that a resolution has been passed and notified to the Secretary of State in accordance with that section: CA 2006, s 445(6).

23.203 Section 445 does not apply to companies within:

(a) s 444 (filing obligations of companies subject to the small companies regime); or

(b) s 444A (filing obligations of companies entitled to small companies exemption in relation to directors' report): CA 2006, s 445(7).

Filing obligations of unquoted companies

23.204 The directors of an unquoted company must deliver to the registrar for each financial year of the company a copy of:

(a) the company's annual accounts;

(aa) the strategic report;

(b) the directors' report; and

(c) any separate corporate governance statement: CA 2006, s 446(1).

The directors must also deliver to the registrar a copy of the auditor's report on those accounts (strategic report and the directors' report and any separate corporate governance statement).

This does not apply if the company is exempt from audit and the directors have taken advantage of that exemption: CA 2006, s 446(2).

The copies of the balance sheet, directors' report and any separate corporate governance statement delivered to the registrar under s 446 must state the name of the person who signed it on behalf of the board: CA 2006, s 446(3).

23.205 The copy of the auditor's report delivered to the registrar under s 446 must:

(a) state the name of the auditor and (where the auditor is a firm) the name of the person who signed it as senior statutory auditor; or

(b) if the conditions in s 506 (circumstances in which names may be omitted) are met, state that a resolution has been passed and notified to the Secretary of State in accordance with that section: CA 2006, s 446(4).

23.206 Section 446 does not apply to companies within:

(a) s 444 (filing obligations of companies subject to the small companies regime);

(aa) section 444A (filing obligations of companies entitled to small companies exemption in relation to directors' report); or

(b) s 445 (filing obligations of medium-sized companies): CA 2006, s 446(5).

Filing obligations of quoted companies

23.207 The directors of a quoted company must deliver to the registrar for each financial year of the company a copy of:

(a) the company's annual accounts;

(b) the directors' remuneration report;

(ba) the strategic report;

(c) the directors' report; and

(d) any separate corporate governance statement: CA 2006, s 447(1).

They must also deliver a copy of the auditor's report on those accounts (and on the directors' remuneration report, the strategic report (where this is covered by the auditor's report) and the directors' report and any separate corporate governance statement): CA 2006, s 447(2).

The copies of the balance sheet, the directors' remuneration report, the strategic report, the directors' report and any separate corporate governance statement delivered to the registrar under s 447 must state the name of the person who signed it on behalf of the board: CA 2006, s 447(3).

23.208 The copy of the auditor's report delivered to the registrar under s 447 must:

(a) state the name of the auditor and (where the auditor is a firm) the name of the person who signed it as senior statutory auditor; or

(b) if the conditions in s 506 (circumstances in which names may be omitted) are met, state that a resolution has been passed and notified to the Secretary of State in accordance with that section: CA 2006, s 447(4).

Unlimited companies exempt from obligation to file accounts

23.209 The directors of an unlimited company are not required to deliver accounts and reports to the registrar in respect of a financial year if the following conditions are met: CA 2006, s 448(1).

The conditions are that at no time during the relevant accounting reference period:

(a) has the company been, to its knowledge, a subsidiary undertaking of an undertaking which was then limited;

(b) have there been, to its knowledge, exercisable by or on behalf of two or more undertakings which were then limited, rights which if exercisable by one of them would have made the company a subsidiary undertaking of it; or

(c) has the company been a parent company of an undertaking which was then limited.

The references above to an undertaking being limited at a particular time are to an undertaking (under whatever law established) the liability of whose members is at that time limited: CA 2006, s 448(2).

23.210 The exemption conferred by s 448 does not apply if:

(a) the company is a banking or insurance company or the parent company of a banking or insurance group; or

(b) each of the members of the company is:

  (i) a limited company;

  (ii) another unlimited company each of whose members is a limited company; or

  (iii) a Scottish partnership each of whose members is a limited company.

The references in para (b) to a limited company, another unlimited company or a Scottish partnership include a comparable undertaking incorporated in or formed under the law of a country or territory outside the UK: CA 2006, s 448(3).

23.211 Where a company is exempt by virtue of s 448 from the obligation to deliver accounts:

(a) s 434(3) (requirements in connection with publication of statutory accounts: meaning of 'statutory accounts') has effect with the substitution for the words 'as required to be delivered to the registrar under section 441' of the words 'as prepared in accordance with this Part and approved by the board of directors'; and

(b) s 435(1)(b) (requirements in connection with publication of non-statutory accounts: statement whether statutory accounts delivered) has effect with the substitution for the words from 'whether statutory accounts' to 'have been delivered to the registrar' of the words 'that the company is exempt from the requirement to deliver statutory accounts': CA 2006, s 448(4).

Under s 448, the 'relevant accounting reference period', in relation to a financial year, means the accounting reference period by reference to which that financial year was determined: CA 2006, s 448(5).

Dormant subsidiaries exempt from obligation to file accounts

23.212 The directors of a company are not required to deliver a copy of the company's individual accounts to the registrar in respect of a financial year if:

(a) the company is a subsidiary undertaking;

(b) it has been dormant throughout the whole of that year; and

(c) its parent undertaking is established under the law of an EEA State: CA 2006, s 448A(1).

23.213 Exemption is conditional upon compliance with all of the following conditions:

(a) all members of the company must agree to the exemption in respect of the financial year in question;

(b) the parent undertaking must give a guarantee under s 448C in respect of that year;

(c) the company must be included in the consolidated accounts drawn up for that year or to an earlier date in that year by the parent undertaking in accordance with:

   (i) the provisions of Directive 2013/34/EU of the European Parliament and of the Council on the annual financial statements, consolidated financial statements and related reports of certain types of undertakings; or

   (ii) international accounting standards;

(d) the parent undertaking must disclose in the notes to the consolidated accounts that the directors of the company are exempt from the requirement to deliver a copy of the company's individual accounts to the registrar by virtue of s 448A; and

(e) the directors of the company must deliver to the registrar within the period for filing the company's accounts and reports for that year:

   (i) a written notice of the agreement referred to in s 448A(2)(a);

   (ii) the statement referred to in s 448C(1);

   (iii) a copy of the consolidated accounts referred to in s 448A(2)(c);

   (iv) a copy of the auditor's report on those accounts; and

   (v) a copy of the consolidated annual report drawn up by the parent undertaking: CA 2006, s 448A(2).

Companies excluded from the dormant subsidiaries exemption

23.214 The directors of a company are not entitled to the exemption conferred by s 448A (dormant subsidiaries) if the company was at any time within the financial year in question:

(a) a traded company as defined in s 385(2);

(b) a company that:

(i) is an authorised insurance company, a banking company, an e-Money issuer, a MiFID investment firm or a UCITS management company; or

(ii) carries on insurance market activity; or

(c) a special register body as defined in s 117(1) of the Trade Union and Labour Relations (Consolidation) Act 1992 or an employers' association as defined in s 122 of that Act or Art 4 of the Industrial Relations (Northern Ireland) Order 1992, SI 1992/807 (NI 5): CA 2006, s 448B.

Dormant subsidiaries filing exemption: parent undertaking declaration of guarantee

23.215 A guarantee is given by a parent undertaking under s 448 when the directors of the subsidiary company deliver to the registrar a statement by the parent undertaking that it guarantees the subsidiary company under s 448: CA 2006, s 448C(1).

The statement under s 448(1) must be authenticated by the parent undertaking and must specify:

(a) the name of the parent undertaking;

(b) if the parent undertaking is incorporated in the UK, its registered number (if any);

(c) if the parent undertaking is incorporated outside the UK and registered in the country in which it is incorporated, the identity of the register on which it is registered and the number with which it is so registered;

(d) the name and registered number of the subsidiary company in respect of which the guarantee is being given;

(e) the date of the statement; and

(f) the financial year to which the guarantee relates: CA 2006, s 448C(2).

23.216 A guarantee given under s 448C has the effect that:

(a) the parent undertaking guarantees all outstanding liabilities to which the subsidiary company is subject at the end of the financial year to which the guarantee relates, until they are satisfied in full; and

(b) the guarantee is enforceable against the parent undertaking by any person to whom the subsidiary company is liable in respect of those liabilities: CA 2006, s 448C(3).

Approval and signing of abbreviated accounts

23.217 Abbreviated accounts must be approved by the board of directors and signed on behalf of the board by a director of the company: CA 2006, s 450(1). The signature must be on the balance sheet: CA 2006, s 450(2).

The balance sheet must contain in a prominent position above the signature a statement to the effect that it is prepared in accordance with the special provisions of CA 2006 relating (as the case may be) to companies subject to the small companies regime or to medium-sized companies: CA 2006, s 450(3).

23.218 If abbreviated accounts are approved that do not comply with the requirements of regulations under the relevant section, every director of the company who:

(a) knew that they did not comply, or was reckless as to whether they complied; and

(b) failed to take reasonable steps to prevent them from being approved,

commits an offence: CA 2006, s 450(4).

23.219 A person guilty of an offence under s 450(4) is liable:

(a) on conviction on indictment, to a fine;

(b) on summary conviction, to a fine not exceeding the statutory maximum: CA 2006, s 450(5).

Default in filing accounts and reports: offences

23.220 If the requirements of s 441 (duty to file accounts and reports) are not complied with in relation to a company's accounts and reports for a financial year before the end of the period for filing those accounts and reports, every person who immediately before the end of that period was a director of the company commits an offence: CA 2006, s 451(1).

It is a defence for a person charged with such an offence to prove that he took all reasonable steps to secure that those requirements would be complied with before the end of that period: CA 2006, s 451(2).

It is not a defence to prove that the documents in question were not in fact prepared as required by CA 2006, Pt 15: CA 2006, s 451(3).

A person guilty of an offence under s 451 is liable on summary conviction to a fine not exceeding level 5 on the standard scale and, for continued contravention, a daily default fine not exceeding one-tenth of level 5 on the standard scale: CA 2006, s 451(4).

Default in filing accounts and reports: court order

23.221 If:

(a) the requirements of s 441 (duty to file accounts and reports) are not complied with in relation to a company's accounts and reports for a financial year before the end of the period for filing those accounts and reports; and

(b) the directors of the company fail to make good the default within 14 days after the service of a notice on them requiring compliance,

the court may, on the application of any member or creditor of the company or of the registrar, make an order directing the directors (or any of them) to make good the default within such time as may be specified in the order: CA 2006, s 452(1).

The court's order may provide that all costs (in Scotland, expenses) of and incidental to the application are to be borne by the directors: CA 2006, s 452(2).

Civil penalty for failure to file accounts and reports

23.222 Where the requirements of s 441 are not complied with in relation to a company's accounts and reports for a financial year before the end of the period for filing those accounts and reports, the company is liable to a civil penalty.

This is in addition to any liability of the directors under s 451: CA 2006, s 453(1).

The amount of the penalty shall be determined in accordance with regulations made by the Secretary of State by reference to:

(a) the length of the period between the end of the period for filing the accounts and reports in question and the day on which the requirements are complied with; and

(b) whether the company is a private or public company: CA 2006, s 453(2).

The penalty may be recovered by the registrar and is to be paid into the Consolidated Fund: CA 2006, s 453(3). It is not a defence in proceedings under s 453 to prove that the documents in question were not in fact prepared as required by this Part: CA 2006, s 453(4).

Revision of defective accounts and reports

23.223 Chapter 11 of Pt 15 deals with revision of defective accounts and reports.

Voluntary revision of accounts

23.224 If it appears to the directors of a company that:

(a) the company's annual accounts;

(b) the directors' remuneration report or the directors' report; or

(c) a strategic report of the company,

did not comply with the requirements of CA 2006 (or, where applicable, of Art 4 of the IAS Regulation), they may prepare revised accounts or a revised report or statement: CA 2006, s 454(1).

23.225 Where copies of the previous accounts or report have been sent out to members, delivered to the registrar or (in the case of a public company) laid before the company in general meeting, the revisions must be confined to:

(a) the correction of those respects in which the previous accounts or report did not comply with the requirements of CA 2006 (or, where applicable, of Art 4 of the IAS Regulation); and

(b) the making of any necessary consequential alterations: CA 2006, s 454(2).

23.226 The Secretary of State may make provision by regulations as to the application of the provisions of CA 2006 in relation to:

(a) revised annual accounts;

(b) a revised directors' remuneration report or directors' report; or

(c) a revised strategic report of the company: CA 2006, s 454(3).

23.227 The regulations may, in particular:

(a) make different provision according to whether the previous accounts or report are replaced or are supplemented by a document indicating the corrections to be made;

(b) make provision with respect to the functions of the company's auditor in relation to the revised accounts or report;

(c) require the directors to take such steps as may be specified in the regulations where the previous accounts or report have been:

  (i) sent out to members and others under s 423;

  (ii) laid before the company in general meeting; or

  (iii) delivered to the registrar;

or where a strategic report and supplementary material containing information derived from the previous accounts or report have been sent to members under s 426;

(d) apply the provisions of CA 2006 (including those creating criminal offences) subject to such additions, exceptions and modifications as are specified in the regulations: CA 2006, s 454(4).

23.228 The Secretary of State has enacted the Companies (Revision of Defective Accounts and Reports) Regulations 2008 (SI 2008 No 373) which has been amended by the Companies (Revision of Defective Accounts and Reports) Regulations 2013 (SI 2013 No 1971).

With regard to the content of the revised accounts, Companies (Revision of Defective Accounts and Reports) Regulations 2008, SI 2008/373 as amended by the Companies (Revision of Defective Accounts and Reports) Regulations 2013, SI 2013/1971, the provisions of CA 2006 and, where applicable, Art 4 of the IAS Regulation as to the matters to be included in the annual accounts of a company, apply to revised accounts as if the revised accounts were prepared and approved by the directors as at the date of the original annual accounts: reg 3(1).

In particular:

(a) in the case of Companies Act accounts:

   (i) s 393 of the 2006 Act (accounts to give true and fair view);

   (ii) s 396(2) of that Act (Companies Act individual accounts: true and fair view); and

   (iii) s 404(2) of that Act (Companies Act group accounts: true and fair view); and

(b) in the case of IAS accounts, s 393 of the 2006 Act and international accounting standards,

apply so as to require a true and fair view to be shown in the revised accounts of the matters referred to in those accounts, viewed as at the date of the original annual accounts: reg 3(2).

23.229 The provisions of the 2006 Act as to the matters to be included in a strategic report, directors' report, directors' remuneration report or revised directors' remuneration policy apply to a revised report or policy as if the revised report or policy were prepared and approved by the directors of the company as at the date of the original strategic report, directors' report, directors' remuneration report or revised directors' remuneration policy: reg 3(4).

With regard to approval and signature to the revised accounts, the procedure for approving and signing of accounts under s 414 applies equally to revision accounts, except that in the case of revision by supplementary note, it applies as if it required a signature on the supplementary note instead of on the company's balance sheet. Where copies of the original annual accounts have been sent out to members under s 423(1) (duty to circulate copies of annual accounts and reports), laid before the company in general meeting under s 437(1) (public companies: laying of accounts and reports before general meeting) in the case of a public company, or delivered to the registrar under s 441(1) (duty to file accounts and reports with the registrar), the directors must, before approving the revised accounts under s 414, cause statements as to the following matters to be made in a prominent position in the revised accounts (in the case of a revision by supplementary note, in that note):

(a) in the case of a revision by replacement:

   (i) that the revised accounts replace the original annual accounts for the financial year (specifying it);

   (ii) that they are now the statutory accounts of the company for that financial year;

   (iii) that they have been prepared as at the date of the original annual accounts and not as at the date of revision and accordingly do not deal with events between those dates;

   (iv) the respects in which the original annual accounts did not comply with the requirements of the 2006 Act; and

   (v) any significant amendments made consequential upon the remedying of those defects;

(b) in the case of a revision by supplementary note:

(i) that the note revises in certain respects the original annual accounts of the company and is to be treated as forming part of those accounts; and

(ii) that the annual accounts have been revised as at the date of the original annual accounts and not as at the date of revision and accordingly do not deal with events between those dates,

and must, when approving the revised accounts, cause the date on which the approval is given to be stated in them (in the case of revision by supplementary note, in that note). Section 414(4) and (5) applies, with respect to a failure to comply with this paragraph, as if the requirements of this paragraph were requirements of CA 2006, Pt 15.

Approval and signature of revised strategic report

23.230 Regulation 4A of the Companies (Revision of Defective Accounts and Reports) Regulations 2008, SI 2008/373 as amended by the Companies (Revision of Defective Accounts and Reports) Regulations 2013, SI 2013/1971 is concerned with the approval and signature of a revised strategic report.

Section 414D(1) and (2) of the 2006 Act applies to a revised strategic report, except that in the case of revision by supplementary note, they shall apply as if they required the signature to be on the supplementary note: reg 4A(1).

23.231 Where the original strategic report has been sent out to members under s 423(1), laid before the company in general meeting under s 437(1) in the case of a public company, or delivered to the registrar under s 441(1), the directors shall, before approving the revised report under s 414E(1), cause statements as to the following matters to be made in a prominent position in the revised report (in the case of a revision by supplementary note, in that note):

(a) in the case of a revision by replacement:

(i) that the revised report replaces the original report for the financial year (specifying it);

(ii) that it has been prepared as at the date of the original strategic report and not as at the date of revision and accordingly does not deal with any events between those dates;

(iv) the respects in which the original strategic report did not comply with the requirements of the 2006 Act; and

(iv) any significant amendments made consequential upon the remedying of those defects,

(b) in the case of revision by a supplementary note:

(i) that the note revises in certain respects the original strategic report of the company and is to be treated as forming part of that report; and

(ii) that the strategic report has been revised as at the date of the original strategic report and not as at the date of the revision and accordingly does not deal with events between those dates, and shall, when approving the revised report, cause the date on which the approval is given to be stated in it (in the case of a revision by supplementary note, in that note). Section 414A(5)(2) applies, with respect to a failure to comply with this paragraph, as if the requirements of this paragraph were requirements of CA 2006, Pt 15: reg 4A(2).

Effect of revision and publication of accounts

23.232 Upon the directors approving revised accounts under reg 4, the provisions of CA 2006 have effect as if the revised accounts were, as from the date of their approval, the annual accounts of the company in place of the original annual accounts: reg 10(1).

In particular, the revised accounts shall as from that date be the company's annual accounts for the relevant financial year for the purposes of the following provisions of CA 2006:

(a) s 431 (right of member or debenture holder to copies of accounts and reports: unquoted companies);

(b) s 432 (right of member or debenture holder to copies of accounts and reports: quoted companies);

(c) s 434(3) (requirements in connection with publication of statutory accounts); and

(d) s 423 (duty to circulate copies of annual accounts and reports), s 437 (public companies; laying of accounts and reports before general meeting) and s 441 (duty to file accounts and reports with the registrar), if the requirements of those sections have not been complied with prior to the date of revision.

23.233 Where the directors have prepared revised accounts or a revised report under s 454 and copies of the original annual accounts or report have been sent to any person under ss 146 or 423, the directors must send to any such person:

(a) in the case of a revision by replacement, a copy of the revised accounts, or (as the case may be) the revised report, together with a copy of the auditor's report on those accounts, or (as the case may be) on that report; or

(b) in the case of a revision by supplementary note, a copy of that note together with a copy of the auditor's report on the revised accounts, or (as the case may be) on the revised report,

not more than 28 days after the date of revision: reg 12(2).

23.234 The directors must also, not more than 28 days after the revision, send a copy of the revised accounts or (as the case may be) revised report, together with a copy of the auditor's report on those accounts or (as the case may be) on that report, to any person who is not a person entitled to receive a copy under reg 12(2) but who is, as at the date of revision:

(a) a member of the company;

(b) a holder of the company's debentures; or

(c) a person who is entitled to receive notice of general meetings, unless the company would be entitled at that date to send to that person a summary financial statement under s 426 (option to provide summary financial statement). Section 423(2)–(4) applies to this paragraph as it applies to s 423(1): reg 12(3).

23.235 Section 425 (default in sending out copies of accounts and reports: offences) applies to a default in complying with this regulation as if the provisions of this regulation were provisions of s 423 and as if the references in that section to 'the company' and 'every officer of the company who is in default' were a reference to each of the directors who approved the revised accounts under reg 4 or revised report under regs 5 or 6: reg 12(4).

Where, prior to the date of revision of the original annual accounts, the company had completed sending out copies of those accounts under s 423, references in that Act to the day on which accounts are sent out under s 423 are to be construed as referring to the day on which the original accounts were sent out (applying s 423(5) as necessary) notwithstanding that those accounts have been revised; where the company had not completed, prior to the date of revision, the sending out of copies of those accounts under that section, such references are to the day, or the last day, on which the revised accounts are sent out: reg 12(5).

Laying of revised accounts or a revised report

23.236 Where the directors of a public company have prepared revised accounts or a revised report under s 454 and copies of the original annual accounts or report have been laid before a general meeting under s 437, a copy of the revised accounts or (as the case may be) the revised report, together with a copy of the auditor's report on those accounts, or (as the case may be) on that report, must be laid before the next general meeting of the company held after the date of revision at which any annual accounts for a financial year are laid, unless the revised accounts, or (as the case may be) the revised report, have already been laid before an earlier general meeting: reg 13(2).

23.237 Section 438 (public companies: offence of failure to lay accounts and reports) applies with respect to a failure to comply with the requirements of this regulation as it has effect with respect to a failure to comply with the requirements of s 437 but as if:

(a) the reference in s 438(1) to 'the period allowed' was a reference to the period between the date of revision of the revised accounts or (as the case may be) the revised report and the date of the next general meeting of the company held after the date of revision at which any annual accounts for a financial year are laid; references in s 438(1) and (2) to 'that period' are to be construed accordingly; and

(b) the references in s 438(3) to 'the documents in question' and 'this Part' were, respectively, a reference to the documents referred to in para (2) and the provisions of CA 2006, Pt 15 as applied by the Regulations: reg 13(3).

Delivery of revised accounts

23.238 Where the directors have prepared revised accounts or a revised report under s 454 and a copy of the original annual accounts or report has been delivered to the registrar under s 441(1), the directors of the company must, within 28 days of the date of revision, deliver to the registrar:

(a) in the case of a revision by replacement, a copy of the revised accounts or (as the case may be) the revised report, together with a copy of the auditor's report on those accounts or (as the case may be) on that report; or

(b) in the case of a revision by supplementary note, a copy of that note, together with a copy of the auditor's report on the revised accounts or (as the case may be) on the revised report: reg 14(2).

23.239 Sections 451 (default in filing accounts and reports: offences) and 452 (default in filing accounts: court order) apply with respect to a failure to comply with the requirements of this regulation as they apply with respect to a failure to comply with the requirements of s 441 but as if:

(a) the references in s 451(1) and in s 452(1)(a) to 'the period for filing those accounts and reports' were references to the period of 28 days referred to in para (2); the references in s 451(1) and (2) to 'that period' are to be construed accordingly; and

(b) the references in s 451(3) to 'the documents in question' and 'this Part' were, respectively, a reference to the documents referred to in para (2) and the provisions of CA 2006, Pt 15 as applied by the Regulations: reg 13(3).

Small and medium-sized companies

23.240 Regulation 15 applies (subject to reg 19(2)) where the directors have prepared revised accounts under s 454 and the company has, prior to the date of revision, delivered to the registrar accounts which are abbreviated accounts within the meaning of s 444(3) and (4) (filing obligations of companies subject to small companies regime) or 445(3) and (4) (filing obligations of medium-sized companies) of that Act: reg 15(1).

Where the abbreviated accounts so delivered to the registrar would, if they had been prepared by reference to the revised accounts, not comply with the provisions of the CA 2006 (whether because the company would not have qualified as a small or (as the case may be) medium-sized company in the light of the revised accounts or because the accounts have been revised in a manner which affects the content of the abbreviated accounts), the directors of the company shall cause the company either:

(a) to deliver to the registrar a copy of the revised accounts, together with a copy of the directors' report and the auditor's report on the revised accounts; or

(b) (if on the basis of the revised accounts they would be entitled under CA 2006 to do so) to prepare further abbreviated accounts drawn up in accordance with the provisions of that Act and deliver them to the registrar together with a statement as to the effect of the revisions made: reg 15(2).

23.241 Where the abbreviated accounts would, if they had been prepared by reference to the revised accounts, comply with the requirements of the CA 2006, the directors of the company shall cause the company to deliver to the registrar:

(a) a note stating that the annual accounts of the company for the relevant financial year (specifying it) have been revised in a respect which has no bearing on the abbreviated accounts delivered for that year, together with

(b) a copy of any auditor's report on the revised accounts: reg 15(3).

Revised abbreviated accounts or a note under this regulation must be delivered to the registrar within 28 days after the date of revision of the revised accounts: reg 15(4).

23.242 Sections 451 (default in filing accounts and reports: offences) and 452 (default in filing accounts: court order) apply with respect to a failure to comply with the requirements of this regulation as they apply with respect to a failure to comply with the requirements of s 441 but as if:

(a) the references in s 451(1) and in s 452(1)(a) to 'the period for filing those accounts and reports' were references to the period of 28 days referred to in para (4); the references in s 451(1) and (2) to 'that period' are to be construed accordingly; and

(b) the references in s 451(3) to 'the documents in question' and 'this Part' were, respectively, a reference to the documents referred to in paragraph (4) and the provisions of CA 2006, Pt 15 as applied by the Regulations: reg 15(5).

23.243 Where the directors have delivered to the registrar abbreviated accounts which do not comply with the provisions of the 2006 Act for reasons other than those specified in reg 15(2), the directors of the company shall cause the company:

(a) to prepare further abbreviated accounts in accordance with the provisions of ss 444(3) and (4) or 445(3) and (4) (as the case may be); and

(b) to deliver those accounts to the registrar within 28 days after the date of revision together with a statement as to the effect of the revisions made: reg 16(2).

23.244 Where the provisions of ss 444(3) and (4) and 445(3) and (4) as to the matters to be included in abbreviated accounts have been amended after the date of delivery of the original abbreviated accounts but prior to the date of revision of the revised accounts or report, references in regs 15 and 16 to the provisions of CA 2006 or to any particular provisions of that Act are to be construed as references to the provisions of that Act, or to the particular provision, as in force at the date of the delivery of the original abbreviated accounts: reg 19(2).

Secretary of State's notice in respect of accounts or reports

23.245 Section 455 applies where:

(a) copies of a company's annual accounts or strategic report or directors' report have been sent out under s 423; or

(b) a copy of a company's annual accounts or strategic report or directors' report has been delivered to the registrar or (in the case of a public company) laid before the company in general meeting,

and it appears to the Secretary of State that there is, or may be, a question whether the accounts or report comply with the requirements of CA 2006 (or, where applicable, of Art 4 of the IAS Regulation): CA 2006, s 455(1).

23.246 The Secretary of State may give notice to the directors of the company indicating the respects in which it appears that such a question arises or may arise: CA 2006, s 455(2).

The notice must specify a period of not less than one month for the directors to give an explanation of the accounts or report or prepare revised accounts or a revised report: CA 2006, s 455(3).

If at the end of the specified period, or such longer period as the Secretary of State may allow, it appears to the Secretary of State that the directors have not:

(a) given a satisfactory explanation of the accounts or report; or

(b) revised the accounts or report so as to comply with the requirements of CA 2006 (or, where applicable, of Art 4 of the IAS Regulation),

the Secretary of State may apply to the court: CA 2006, s 455(4).

The provisions of s 455 apply equally to revised annual accounts and revised strategic reports and revised directors' reports, in which case they have effect as if the references to revised accounts or reports were references to further revised accounts or reports: CA 2006, s 455(5).

Application to court in respect of defective accounts or reports

23.247 An application may be made to the court:

(a) by the Secretary of State, after having complied with s 455; or

(b) by a person authorised by the Secretary of State for the purposes of s 456,

for a declaration (in Scotland, a declarator) that the annual accounts of a company do not comply, or a strategic report or a directors' report does not comply, with the requirements of CA 2006 (or, where applicable, of Art 4 of the IAS Regulation) and for an order requiring the directors of the company to prepare revised accounts or a revised report: CA 2006, s 456(1).

Notice of the application, together with a general statement of the matters at issue in the proceedings, must be given by the applicant to the registrar for registration: CA 2006, s 456(2).

23.248 If the court orders the preparation of revised accounts, it may give directions as to:

(a) the auditing of the accounts;

(b) the revision of any directors' remuneration report, strategic report and supplementary material directors' report;

(c) the taking of steps by the directors to bring the making of the order to the notice of persons likely to rely on the previous accounts,

and such other matters as the court thinks fit: CA 2006, s 456(3).

23.249 If the court orders the preparation of a strategic report or revised directors' report it may give directions as to:

(a) the review of the report by the auditors;

(b) the revision of any summary financial statement;

(c) the taking of steps by the directors to bring the making of the order to the notice of persons likely to rely on the previous report; and

(d) such other matters as the court thinks fit: CA 2006, s 456(4).

23.250 If the court finds that the accounts or report did not comply with the requirements of CA 2006 (or, where applicable, of Art 4 of the IAS Regulation) it may order that all or part of:

(a) the costs (in Scotland, expenses) of and incidental to the application; and

(b) any reasonable expenses incurred by the company in connection with or in consequence of the preparation of revised accounts or a revised report,

are to be borne by such of the directors as were party to the approval of the defective accounts or report.

For this purpose every director of the company at the time of the approval of the accounts or report shall be taken to have been a party to the approval unless he shows that he took all reasonable steps to prevent that approval: CA 2006, s 456(5).

23.251 Where the court makes an order under s 456(5), it shall have regard to whether the directors party to the approval of the defective accounts or report either knew or ought to have known that the accounts or report did not comply with the requirements of CA 2006 (or, where applicable, of Art 4 of the IAS Regulation) and it may exclude one or more directors from the order or order the payment of different amounts by different directors: CA 2006, s 456(6).

On the conclusion of proceedings on an application under s 456, the applicant must send to the registrar for registration a copy of the court order or, as the case may be, give notice to the registrar that the application has failed or been withdrawn: CA 2006, s 456(7).

The provisions of s 456 apply equally to revised annual accounts and revised strategic reports and revised directors' reports, in which case they have effect as if the references to revised accounts or reports were references to further revised accounts or reports: CA 2006, s 456(8).

Other persons authorised to apply to the court

23.252 The Secretary of State may by order (an 'authorisation order') authorise for the purposes of s 456 any person appearing to him:

(a) to have an interest in, and to have satisfactory procedures directed to securing, compliance by companies with the requirements of CA 2006 (or, where applicable, of Art 4 of the IAS Regulation) relating to accounts and strategic reports and directors' reports;

(b) to have satisfactory procedures for receiving and investigating complaints about companies' annual accounts and strategic reports and directors' reports; and

(c) otherwise to be a fit and proper person to be authorised: CA 2006, s 457(1).

A person may be authorised generally or in respect of particular classes of case, and different persons may be authorised in respect of different classes of case: CA 2006, s 457(2).

23.253 The Secretary of State may refuse to authorise a person if he considers that his authorisation is unnecessary having regard to the fact that there are one or more other persons who have been or are likely to be authorised: CA 2006, s 457(3).

If the authorised person is an unincorporated association, proceedings brought in, or in connection with, the exercise of any function by the association as an authorised person may be brought by or against the association in the name of a body corporate whose constitution provides for the establishment of the association: CA 2006, s 457(4).

23.254 An authorisation order may contain such requirements or other provisions relating to the exercise of functions by the authorised person as appear to the Secretary of State to be appropriate.

No such order is to be made unless it appears to the Secretary of State that the person would, if authorised, exercise his functions as an authorised person in accordance with the provisions proposed: CA 2006, s 457(5).

Where authorisation is revoked, the revoking order may make such provision as the Secretary of State thinks fit with respect to pending proceedings: CA 2006, s 457(6).

Disclosure of information by tax authorities

23.255 The Commissioners for Her Majesty's Revenue and Customs may disclose information to a person authorised under s 457 for the purpose of facilitating:

(a) the taking of steps by that person to discover whether there are grounds for an application to the court under s 456 (application in respect of defective accounts etc); or

(b) a decision by the authorised person whether to make such an application: CA 2006, s 458(1).

23.256 Section 458 applies despite any statutory or other restriction on the disclosure of information provided that, in the case of personal data within the meaning of the Data Protection Act 1998 (c 29), information is not to be disclosed in contravention of that Act: CA 2006, s 458(2).

Information disclosed to an authorised person under s 458:

(a) may not be used except in or in connection with:

  (i) taking steps to discover whether there are grounds for an application to the court under s 456, or

  (ii) deciding whether or not to make such an application,

  or in, or in connection with, proceedings on such an application; and

(b) must not be further disclosed except:

  (i) to the person to whom the information relates; or

  (ii) in, or in connection with, proceedings on any such application to the court: CA 2006, s 458(3).

23.257 A person who contravenes s 458(3) commits an offence unless:

(a) he did not know, and had no reason to suspect, that the information had been disclosed under s 458; or

(b) he took all reasonable steps and exercised all due diligence to avoid the commission of the offence: CA 2006, s 458(4).

23.258 A person guilty of an offence under s 458(4) is liable:

(a) on conviction on indictment, to imprisonment for a term not exceeding two years or a fine (or both);

(b) on summary conviction:

  (i) in England and Wales, to imprisonment for a term not exceeding 12 months or to a fine not exceeding the statutory maximum (or both);

  (ii) in Scotland or Northern Ireland, to imprisonment for a term not exceeding six months, or to a fine not exceeding the statutory maximum (or both): CA 2006, s 458(5).

23.259 Where an offence under s 458 is committed by a body corporate, every officer of the body who is in default also commits the offence. For this purpose:

(a) any person who purports to act as director, manager or secretary of the body is treated as an officer of the body; and

(b) if the body is a company, any shadow director is treated as an officer of the company: CA 2006, s 458(6).

Power of authorised person to require documents, information and explanations

23.260 Section 459 applies where it appears to a person who is authorised under s 457 that there is, or may be, a question whether a company's annual accounts or strategic report or directors' report comply with the requirements of CA 2006 (or, where applicable, of Art 4 of the IAS Regulation): CA 2006, s 459(1).

The authorised person may require any of the persons mentioned in s 459(3) to produce any document, or to provide him with any information or explanations, that he may reasonably require for the purpose of:

(a) discovering whether there are grounds for an application to the court under s 456; or

(b) deciding whether to make such an application: CA 2006, s 459(2).

23.261 Those persons are:

(a) the company;

(b) any officer, employee, or auditor of the company; and

(c) any persons who fell within para (b) at a time to which the document or information required by the authorised person relates: CA 2006, s 459(3).

If a person fails to comply with such a requirement, the authorised person may apply to the court: CA 2006, s 459(4).

23.262 If it appears to the court that the person has failed to comply with a requirement under s 459(2), it may order the person to take such steps as it directs for securing that the documents are produced or the information or explanations are provided: CA 2006, s 459(5).

A statement made by a person in response to a requirement under s 459(2) or an order under s 459(5) may not be used in evidence against him in any criminal proceedings: CA 2006, s 459(6).

Nothing in s 459 compels any person to disclose documents or information in respect of which a claim to legal professional privilege (in Scotland, to confidentiality of communications) could be maintained in legal proceedings: CA 2006, s 459(7).

Under s 459, 'document' includes information recorded in any form: CA 2006, s 459(8).

Restrictions on disclosure of information obtained under compulsory powers

23.263 Section 460 applies to information (in whatever form) obtained in pursuance of a requirement or order under s 459 (power of authorised person to require documents etc) that relates to the private affairs of an individual or to any particular business: CA 2006, s 460(1).

No such information may, during the lifetime of that individual or so long as that business continues to be carried on, be disclosed without the consent of that individual or the person for the time being carrying on that business: CA 2006, s 460(2).

This does not apply:

(a) to disclosure permitted by s 461 (permitted disclosure of information obtained under compulsory powers); or

(b) to the disclosure of information that is or has been available to the public from another source: CA 2006, s 460(3).

23.264 A person who discloses information in contravention of s 460 commits an offence, unless:

(a) he did not know, and had no reason to suspect, that the information had been disclosed under CA 2006, s 459; or

(b) he took all reasonable steps and exercised all due diligence to avoid the commission of the offence: CA 2006, s 460(4).

23.265 A person guilty of an offence under s 460 is liable:

(a) on conviction on indictment, to imprisonment for a term not exceeding two years or a fine (or both);

(b) on summary conviction:

(i) in England and Wales, to imprisonment for a term not exceeding 12 months or to a fine not exceeding the statutory maximum (or both);

(ii) in Scotland or Northern Ireland, to imprisonment for a term not exceeding six months, or to a fine not exceeding the statutory maximum (or both): CA 2006, s 460(5).

23.266 Where an offence under s 460 is committed by a body corporate, every officer of the body who is in default also commits the offence. For this purpose:

(a) any person who purports to act as director, manager or secretary of the body is treated as an officer of the body; and

(b) if the body is a company, any shadow director is treated as an officer of the company: CA 2006, s 460(6).

Permitted disclosure of information obtained under compulsory powers

23.267 The prohibition in s 460 of the disclosure of information obtained in pursuance of a requirement or order under s 459 (power of authorised person to require documents etc) that relates to the private affairs of an individual or to any particular business has effect subject to the following exceptions: CA 2006, s 461(1).

It does not apply to the disclosure of information for the purpose of facilitating the carrying out by the authorised person of his functions under s 456: CA 2006, s 461(2).

23.268 It does not apply to disclosure to:

(a) the Secretary of State;

(b) the Department of Enterprise, Trade and Investment for Northern Ireland;

(c) the Treasury;

(d) the Bank of England;

(e) the Financial Services Authority; or

(f) the Commissioners for Her Majesty's Revenue and Customs: CA 2006, s 461(3).

23.269 It does not apply to disclosure:

(a) for the purpose of assisting the Financial Reporting Council Limited to exercise its functions under CA 2006, Pt 42;

(aa) for the purpose of facilitating the carrying out of inspections under para 23 of Sch 10 (arrangements for independent monitoring of audits of listed companies and other major bodies);

(b) with a view to the institution of, or otherwise for the purposes of, disciplinary proceedings relating to the performance by an accountant or auditor of his professional duties;

(c) for the purpose of enabling or assisting the Secretary of State or the Treasury to exercise any of their functions under any of the following:

  (i) the Companies Acts,

  (ii) Pt 5 of the Criminal Justice Act 1993 (c 36) (insider dealing),

  (iii) the Insolvency Act 1986 or the Insolvency (Northern Ireland) Order 1989, SI 1989/2405 (NI 19),

  (iv) the Company Directors' Disqualification Act 1986 or the Company Directors' Disqualification (Northern Ireland) Order 2002, SI 2002/3150 (NI 4),

  (v) the Financial Services and Markets Act 2000 (c 8);

(d) for the purpose of enabling or assisting the Department of Enterprise, Trade and Investment for Northern Ireland to exercise any powers conferred on it by the enactments relating to companies, directors' disqualification or insolvency;

(e) for the purpose of enabling or assisting the Bank of England to exercise its functions;

(f) for the purpose of enabling or assisting the Commissioners for Her Majesty's Revenue and Customs to exercise their function;

(g) for the purpose of enabling or assisting the Financial Services Authority to exercise its functions under any of the following:

  (i) the legislation relating to friendly societies or to industrial and provident societies;

  (ii) the Building Societies Act 1986 (c 53);

  (iii) Pt 7 of the Companies Act 1989 (c 40);

  (iv) the Financial Services and Markets Act 2000; or

(h) in pursuance of any EU obligation: CA 2006, s 461(4).

It does not apply to disclosure to a body exercising functions of a public nature under legislation in any country or territory outside the UK that appear to the authorised person to be similar to his functions under s 456 for the purpose of enabling or assisting that body to exercise those functions: CA 2006, s 461(5).

23.270 In determining whether to disclose information to a body in accordance with s 461(5), the authorised person must have regard to the following considerations:

(a) whether the use which the body is likely to make of the information is sufficiently important to justify making the disclosure;

(b) whether the body has adequate arrangements to prevent the information from being used or further disclosed other than:

  (i) for the purposes of carrying out the functions mentioned in that subsection, or

(ii) for other purposes substantially similar to those for which information disclosed to the authorised person could be used or further disclosed: CA 2006, s 461(6).

Nothing in s 461 authorises the making of a disclosure in contravention of the Data Protection Act 1998 (c 29): CA 2006, s 461(7).

Power to amend categories of permitted disclosure

23.271 The Secretary of State may by order amend s 461(3), (4) and (5): CA 2006, s 462(1).

An order under s 462 must not amend:

(a) s 462(3) (UK public authorities) by specifying a person unless the person exercises functions of a public nature (whether or not he exercises any other function);

(b) s 462(4) (purposes for which disclosure permitted) by adding or modifying a description of disclosure unless the purpose for which the disclosure is permitted is likely to facilitate the exercise of a function of a public nature; or

(c) s 462(5) (overseas regulatory authorities) so as to have the effect of permitting disclosures to be made to a body other than one that exercises functions of a public nature in a country or territory outside the UK: CA 2006, s 462(2).

Supplementary provisions

Liability for false or misleading statements in reports

23.272 The reports to which s 463 applies are:

(a) the strategic report;

(b) the directors' report; and

(c) the directors' remuneration report: CA 2006, s 463(1).

23.273 A director of a company is liable to compensate the company for any loss suffered by it as a result of:

(a) any untrue or misleading statement in a report to which s 463 applies; or

(b) the omission from a report to which s 463 applies of anything required to be included in it: CA 2006, s 463(2).

23.274 He is so liable only if:

(a) he knew the statement to be untrue or misleading or was reckless as to whether it was untrue or misleading; or

(b) he knew the omission to be dishonest concealment of a material fact: CA 2006, s 463(3).

No person shall be subject to any liability to a person other than the company resulting from reliance, by that person or another, on information in a report to which s 463 applies: CA 2006, s 463(4).

23.275 The reference in s 463(4) to a person being subject to a liability includes a reference to another person being entitled as against him to be granted any civil remedy or to rescind or repudiate an agreement: CA 2006, s 463(5).

Section 463 does not affect:

(a) liability for a civil penalty; or

(b) liability for a criminal offence: CA 2006, s 463(6).

Accounting standards

23.276 Under Pt 15, the term 'accounting standards' means statements of standard accounting practice issued by such body or bodies as may be prescribed by regulations: CA 2006, s 464(1).

The references in Pt 15 to accounting standards applicable to a company's annual accounts are to such standards as are, in accordance with their terms, relevant to the company's circumstances and to the accounts: CA 2006, s 464(2).

Regulations under s 464 may contain such transitional and other supplementary and incidental provisions as appear to the Secretary of State to be appropriate: CA 2006, s 464(3).

Companies qualifying as medium-sized: general

23.277 A company qualifies as medium-sized in relation to its first financial year if the qualifying conditions are met in that year: CA 2006, s 465(1).

A company qualifies as medium-sized in relation to a subsequent financial year:

(a) if the qualifying conditions are met in that year and the preceding financial year;

(b) if the qualifying conditions are met in that year and the company qualified as medium-sized in relation to the preceding financial year; or

(c) if the qualifying conditions were met in the preceding financial year and the company qualified as medium-sized in relation to that year: CA 2006, s 465(2).

23.278 The qualifying conditions are met by a company in a year in which it satisfies two or more of the following requirements: CA 2006, s 465(3).

• Turnover	Not more than £36 million
• Balance sheet total	Not more than £18 million
• Number of employees	Not more than 250

23.279 For a period that is a company's financial year but not in fact a year the maximum figures for turnover must be proportionately adjusted: CA 2006, s 465(4).

The balance sheet total means the aggregate of the amounts shown as assets in the company's balance sheet: CA 2006, s 465(5).

The number of employees means the average number of persons employed by the company in the year, determined as follows:

(a) find for each month in the financial year the number of persons employed under contracts of service by the company in that month (whether throughout the month or not);

(b) add together the monthly totals; and

(c) divide by the number of months in the financial year: CA 2006, s 465(6).

Section 465 is subject to s 466 (companies qualifying as medium-sized: parent companies): CA 2006, s 465(7).

Companies qualifying as medium-sized: parent companies

23.280 A parent company qualifies as a medium-sized company in relation to a financial year only if the group headed by it qualifies as a medium-sized group: CA 2006, s 466(1). A group qualifies as medium-sized in relation to the parent company's first financial year if the qualifying conditions are met in that year: CA 2006, s 466(2).

A group qualifies as medium-sized in relation to a subsequent financial year of the parent company:

(a) if the qualifying conditions are met in that year and the preceding financial year;

(b) if the qualifying conditions are met in that year and the group qualified as medium-sized in relation to the preceding financial year; and

(c) if the qualifying conditions were met in the preceding financial year and the group qualified as medium-sized in relation to that year: CA 2006, s 466(3).

23.281 The qualifying conditions are met by a group in a year in which it satisfies two or more of the following requirements: CA 2006, s 466(4).

Aggregate turnover	Not more than £36 million net (or £43.2 million gross)
Aggregate balance sheet total	Not more than £18 million net (or £21.6 million gross)
Aggregate number of employees	Not more than 250

23.282 The aggregate figures are ascertained by aggregating the relevant figures determined in accordance with s 465 for each member of the group: CA 2006, s 466(5).

In relation to the aggregate figures for turnover and balance sheet total:

'net' means after any set-offs and other adjustments made to eliminate group transactions:

(a) in the case of Companies Act accounts, in accordance with regulations under s 404;

(b) in the case of IAS accounts, in accordance with international accounting standards; and

'gross' means without those set-offs and other adjustments: CA 2006, s 466(6).

A company may satisfy any relevant requirement on the basis of either the net or the gross figure.

23.283 The figures for each subsidiary undertaking shall be those included in its individual accounts for the relevant financial year, that is:

(a) if its financial year ends with that of the parent company, that financial year; and

(b) if not, its financial year ending last before the end of the financial year of the parent company.

If those figures cannot be obtained without disproportionate expense or undue delay, the latest available figures shall be taken: CA 2006, s 466(7).

Companies excluded from being treated as medium-sized companies

23.284 A company is not entitled to take advantage of any of the provisions of Pt 15 relating to companies qualifying as medium-sized if it was at any time within the financial year in question:

(a) a public company;

(b) a company that:

  (i) has permission under Pt 4 of the Financial Services and Markets Act 2000 (c 8) to carry on a regulated activity; or

  (ii) carries on insurance market activity; or

(c) a member of an ineligible group: CA 2006, s 467(1).

23.285 A group is ineligible if any of its members is:

(a) a traded company;

(b) a body corporate (other than a company) whose shares are admitted to trading on a regulated market;

(c) a person (other than a small company) who has permission under Pt 4 of the Financial Services and Markets Act 2000 to carry on a regulated activity;

(d) a small company that is an authorised insurance company, a banking company, an e-money issuer, a MiFID investment firm] or a UCITS management company; or

(e) a person who carries on insurance market activity: CA 2006, s 467(2).

A company is a small company for the purposes of s 467(2) if it qualified as small in relation to its last financial year ending on or before the end of the financial year in question: CA 2006, s 467(3).

Section 467 does not prevent a company from taking advantage of s 417(7) (business review: non-financial information) by reason only of its having been a member of an ineligible group at any time within the financial year in question: CA 2006, s 467(4).

General power to make further provision about accounts and reports

23.286 The Secretary of State may make provision by regulations about:

(a) the accounts and reports that companies are required to prepare;

(b) the categories of companies required to prepare accounts and reports of any description;

(c) the form and content of the accounts and reports that companies are required to prepare;

(d) the obligations of companies and others as regards:

- (i) the approval of accounts and reports;
- (ii) the sending of accounts and reports to members and others;
- (iii) the laying of accounts and reports before the company in general meeting;
- (iv) the delivery of copies of accounts and reports to the registrar; and
- (v) the publication of accounts and reports: CA 2006, s 468(1).

23.287 The regulations may amend CA 2006, Pt 15 by adding, altering or repealing provisions: CA 2006, s 468(2). However, they must not amend (other than consequentially):

(a) s 393 (accounts to give true and fair view); or

(b) the provisions of Ch 11 (revision of defective accounts and reports): CA 2006, s 468(3).

The regulations may create criminal offences in cases corresponding to those in which an offence is created by an existing provision of CA 2006, Pt 15.

The maximum penalty for any such offence may not be greater than is provided in relation to an offence under the existing provision.

The regulations may provide for civil penalties in circumstances corresponding to those within s 453(1) (civil penalty for failure to file accounts and reports.

The provisions of ss 453(2)–(5) apply in relation to any such penalty: CA 2006, s 469(5).

Preparation and filing of accounts in Euros

23.288 The amounts set out in the annual accounts of a company may also be shown in the same accounts translated into Euros: CA 2006, s 469(1).

When complying with s 441 (duty to file accounts and reports), the directors of a company may deliver to the registrar an additional copy of the company's annual accounts in which the amounts have been translated into Euros: CA 2006, s 469(2).

In both cases:

(a) the amounts must have been translated at the exchange rate prevailing on the date to which the balance sheet is made up; and

(b) that rate must be disclosed in the notes to the accounts: CA 2006, s 469(3).

Subsection (3)(b) does not apply to the Companies Act individual accounts of a company for a financial year in which the company qualifies as a micro-entity (see ss 384A and 384B): CA 2006, s 469(3A).

23.289 For the purposes of ss 434 and 435 (requirements in connection with published accounts) any additional copy of the company's annual accounts delivered to the registrar under s 469(2) above shall be treated as statutory accounts of the company.

In the case of such a copy, references in those sections to the auditor's report on the company's annual accounts shall be read as references to the auditor's report on the annual accounts of which it is a copy: CA 2006, s 469(4).

Power to apply provisions to banking partnerships

23.290 The Secretary of State may by regulations apply to banking partnerships, subject to such exceptions, adaptations and modifications as he considers appropriate, the provisions of CA 2006, Pt 15 (and of regulations made under Pt 15) applying to banking companies: CA 2006, s 470(1).

A 'banking partnership' means a partnership which has permission under Pt 4 of the Financial Services and Markets Act 2000 (c 8).

But a partnership is not a banking partnership if it has permission to accept deposits only for the purpose of carrying on another regulated activity in accordance with that permission: CA 2006, s 470(2).

Expressions used in s 470 that are also used in the provisions regulating activities under the Financial Services and Markets Act 2000 have the same meaning here as they do in those provisions.

See s 22 of that Act, orders made under that section and Sch 2 to that Act: CA 2006, s 470(3).

Meaning of 'annual accounts' and related expressions

23.291 Under Pt 15, a company's 'annual accounts', in relation to a financial year, means:

(a) any individual accounts prepared by the company for that year (see s 394); and

(b) any notes to the individual balance sheet accounts prepared by the company for that year (see ss 398 and 399).

This is subject to s 408 (option to omit individual profit and loss account from annual accounts where information given in notes to the individual balance sheet accounts): CA 2006, s 471(1).

23.292 In the case of an unquoted company, its 'annual accounts and reports' for a financial year are:

(a) its annual accounts;

(aa) the strategic report (if any);

(b) the directors' report; and

(c) the auditor's report on those accounts, the strategic report (where this is covered by the auditor's report) and the directors' report (unless the company is exempt from audit): CA 2006, s 471(2).

23.293 In the case of a quoted company, its 'annual accounts and reports' for a financial year are:

(a) its annual accounts;

(b) the directors' remuneration report;

(c) the directors' report; and

(d) the auditor's report on those accounts, on the auditable part of the directors' remuneration report and on the directors' report: CA 2006, s 471(3).

Notes to the accounts

23.294 In the case of a company which qualifies as a micro-entity in relation to a financial year (see ss 384A and 384B), the notes to the accounts for that year required by s 413 of this Act and reg 5A of, and para 57 of Pt 3 of Sch 1 to, the Small Companies and Groups (Accounts and Directors' Report) Regulations 2008 (SI 2008/409) must be included at the foot of the balance sheet: CA 2006, s 472(1A).

The references in Pt 15 to a company's annual accounts, or to a balance sheet or profit and loss account, include notes to the accounts giving information which is required by any provision of CA 2006 or international accounting standards, and required or allowed by any such provision to be given in a note to company accounts: CA 2006, s 472(2).

Meaning of 'corporate governance statement'

23.295 Under Pt 15, the term 'corporate governance statement' means the statement required by rules 7.2.1 to 7.2.11 in the Disclosure Rules and Transparency Rules sourcebook issued by the Financial Services Authority: CA 2006, s 472A(1).

Those rules were inserted by Annex C of the Disclosure Rules and Transparency Rules Sourcebook (Corporate Governance Rules) Instrument 2008 made by the Authority on 26 June 2008 (FSA 2008/32): CA 2006, s 472A(2).

A 'separate' corporate governance statement means one that is not included in the directors' report: CA 2006, s 472(3).

Parliamentary procedures for certain regulations under CA 2006, Pt 15

23.296 Section 473 applies to regulations under the following provisions of Pt 15:

(a) s 396 (Companies Act individual accounts);

(b) s 404 (Companies Act group accounts);

(c) s 409 (information about related undertakings);

(d) s 412 (information about directors' benefits: remuneration, pensions and compensation for loss of office);

(e) s 416 (contents of directors' report: general);

(f) s 421 (contents of directors' remuneration report);

(g) s 444 (filing obligations of companies subject to small companies regime);

(h) s 445 (filing obligations of medium-sized companies); and

(i) s 468 (general power to make further provision about accounts and reports): CA 2006, s 473(1).

Any such regulations may make consequential amendments or repeals in other provisions of CA 2006, or in other enactments: CA 2006, s 473(2).

23.297 Regulations that:

(a) restrict the classes of company which have the benefit of any exemption, exception or special provision;

(b) require additional matter to be included in a document of any class; or

(c) otherwise render the requirements of this Part more onerous,

are subject to affirmative resolution procedure: CA 2006, s 473(3).

Otherwise, the regulations are subject to negative resolution procedure: CA 2006, s 473(4).

Definitions

23.298

e-money issuer:	means a person who has permission under Pt 4 of the Financial Services and Markets Act 2000 (c 8) to carry on the activity of issuing electronic money within the meaning of Art 9B of the Financial Services and Markets Act 2000 (Regulated Activities) Order 2001 (SI 2001 No 544).
Group:	means a parent undertaking and its subsidiary undertakings.

IAS Regulation: EC Regulation No 1606/2002 of the European Parliament and of the Council of 19 July 2002 on the application of international accounting standards.

Included in the consolidation: in relation to group accounts, or 'included in consolidated group accounts', means that the undertaking is included in the accounts by the method of full (and not proportional) consolidation, and references to an undertaking excluded from consolidation shall be construed accordingly.

International accounting standards: the international accounting standards, within the meaning of the IAS Regulation, adopted from time to time by the European Commission in accordance with that Regulation.

Micro-entity minimum accounting item: an item of information required by this Part or by regulations under this Part to be contained in the Companies Act individual accounts of a company for a financial year in relation to which it qualifies as a micro-entity (see sections 384A and 384B).

Micro-entity provisions: any provisions of this Part, Part 16 or regulations under this Part relating specifically to the individual accounts of a company which qualifies as a micro-entity.

MiFID investment firm: an investment firm within the meaning of Art 4.1.1 of Directive 2004/39/EC of the European Parliament and of the Council of 21 April 2004 on markets in financial instruments, other than:

(a) a company to which that Directive does not apply by virtue of Art 2 of that Directive;

(b) a company which is an exempt investment firm within the meaning of reg 4A(3) of the Financial Services and Markets Act 2000 (Markets in Financial Instruments) Regulations 2007; and

(c) any other company which fulfils all the requirements set out in reg 4C(3) of those Regulations.

Profit and loss account: in relation to a company that prepares IAS accounts, includes an income statement or other equivalent financial statement required to be prepared by international accounting standards.

Qualified: in relation to an auditor's report, means that the report does not state the auditor's unqualified opinion that the accounts have been properly prepared in accordance with this Act.

Regulated activity: has the meaning given in s 22 of the Financial Services and Markets Act 2000, except that it does not include activities of the kind specified in any of the following provisions of the Financial Services and Markets Act 2000 (Regulated Activities) Order 2001 (SI 2001 No 544):

(a) Art 25A (arranging regulated mortgage contracts);

(b) Art 25B (arranging regulated home reversion plans);

(c) Art 25C (arranging regulated home purchase plans);

(ca) Art 25E (arranging regulated sale and rent back agreements);

(d) Art 39A (assisting administration and performance of a contract of insurance);

(e) Art 53A (advising on regulated mortgage contracts);

(f) Art 53B (advising on regulated home reversion plans);

(g) Art 53C (advising on regulated home purchase plans);

(ga) Art 53D (advising on regulated sale and rent back agreements);

(h) Art 21 (dealing as agent), Art 25 (arranging deals in investments) or Art 53 (advising on investments) where the activity concerns relevant investments that are not contractually based investments (within the meaning of Art 3 of that Order); or

(i) Art 64 (agreeing to carry on a regulated activity of the kind mentioned in paras (a)–(h)).

Turnover: in relation to a company, means the amounts derived from the provision of goods and services, after deduction of:

(a) trade discounts;

(b) value added tax; and

(c) any other taxes based on the amounts so derived.

Traded company: a company any of whose transferable securities are admitted to trading on a regulated market.

UCITS management company: has the meaning given by the Glossary forming part of the Handbook made by the Financial Services Authority under the Financial Services and Markets Act 2000 (c 8): CA 2006, s 474(1).

In the case of an undertaking not trading for profit, any reference in Pt 15 to a profit and loss account is to an income and expenditure account.

References to profit and loss and, in relation to group accounts, to a consolidated profit and loss account shall be construed accordingly: CA 2006, s 474(2).

24 Audits and auditors

Contents

Introduction

24.1 Part 16 of the Companies Act 2006 (as amended by the Deregulation Act 2015 and the Companies, Partnerships and Groups (Accounts and Reports)

Regulations 2015, SI 2015/980 (in force 6 April 2015) concerns the audited accounts and reports of a company. One objective is to demonstrate to the shareholders the financial position of the company and the nature of the investments made by the shareholders in the company. Another objective is transparency of the information provided to enable shareholders to make an informed decision on the company's financial status. It also provides a mechanism for directors' accountability towards the shareholders on the company's financial affairs. In this regard, auditors perform an essential function in auditing the company's accounts.

This Chapter addresses the following aspects:

- The requirement for audited accounts and exemptions.
- Appointment of auditors.
- Functions of auditors.
- Removal and resignation of auditors.
- Auditors' liability.

Requirement for audited accounts

24.2 A company's annual accounts for a financial year must be audited in accordance with CA 2006, Pt 16 unless the company:

(a) is exempt from audit under:

- CA 2006, s 477 (small companies);
- CA 2006, s 479A (subsidiary companies); or
- CA 2006, s 480 (dormant companies);

or

(b) is exempt from the requirements of Pt 16 under s 482 (non-profit-making companies subject to public sector audit): CA 2006, s 475(1).

A company is not entitled to any such exemption unless its balance sheet contains a statement by the directors to that effect: CA 2006, s 475(2).

24.3 A company is not entitled to exemption under any of the provisions mentioned in s 475(1)(a), unless its balance sheet contains a statement by the directors to the effect that:

(a) the members have not required the company to obtain an audit of its accounts for the year in question in accordance with s 476; and

(b) the directors acknowledge their responsibilities for complying with the requirements of this Act with respect to accounting records and the preparation of accounts: CA 2006, s 475(3).

The statement required by ss 475(2) or (3) must appear on the balance sheet above the signature required by s 414: CA 2006, s 475(4).

Right of members to require audit

24.4 The members of a company that would otherwise be entitled to exemption from audit under any of the provisions mentioned in CA 2006, s 475(1)(a) may by notice under s 476 require it to obtain an audit of its accounts for a financial year: CA 2006, s 476(1).

The notice must be given by:

(a) members representing not less in total than 10% in nominal value of the company's issued share capital, or any class of it; or

(b) if the company does not have a share capital, not less than 10% in number of the members of the company: CA 2006, s 476(2).

The notice may not be given before the financial year to which it relates and must be given not later than one month before the end of that year: CA 2006, s 476(3).

Small companies: conditions for exemption from audit

24.5 A company that qualifies as a small company in relation to a financial year is exempt from the requirements of this Act relating to the audit of accounts for that year: CA 2006, s 477(1).

For the purposes of s 477 whether a company qualifies as a small company will be determined in accordance with CA 2006, ss 382(1)–(6): CA 2006, s 477(4).

24.6 Section 477 of the CA 2006 applies subject to:

- s 475(2) and (3) (requirements as to statements to be contained in balance sheet);
- s 476 (right of members to require audit);
- s 478 (companies excluded from small companies exemption); and
- s 479 (availability of small companies exemption in case of group company): CA 2006, s 477(5).

Companies excluded from small companies exemption

24.7 A company is not entitled to the exemption conferred by CA 2006, s 477 (small companies) if it was at any time within the financial year in question:

(a) a public company;

(b) a company that:

  (i) is an authorised insurance company, a banking company, an e-money issuer, a MiFID investment firm, or a UCITS management company; or

  (ii) carries on insurance market activity; or

(c) a special register body as defined in s 117(1) of the Trade Union and Labour Relations (Consolidation) Act 1992 (c 52) or an employers' association as defined in s 122 of that Act or Article 4 of the Industrial Relations (Northern Ireland) Order 1992 (SI 1992 No 807 (NI 5)): CA 2006, s 478.

Availability of small companies exemption in case of group company

24.8 A company is not entitled to the exemption conferred by s 477 (small companies) in respect of a financial year during any part of which it was a group company unless:

(a) the group:

(i) qualifies as a small group in relation to that financial year; and

(ii) was not at any time in that year an ineligible group; or

(b) sub-s (3) applies: CA 2006, s 479(1).

A company is not excluded by sub-s (1) if, throughout the whole of the period or periods during the financial year when it was a group company, it was both a subsidiary undertaking and dormant: CA 2006, s 479(3).

24.9 The following terms apply under s 479:

(a) 'group company' means a company that is a parent company or a subsidiary undertaking; and

(b) 'the group', in relation to a group company, means that company together with all its associated undertakings.

For this purpose undertakings are associated if one is a subsidiary undertaking of the other or both are subsidiary undertakings of a third undertaking: CA 2006, s 479(4).

24.10 For the purposes of s 479:

(a) whether a group qualifies as small shall be determined in accordance with s 383 (companies qualifying as small: parent companies);

(b) 'ineligible group' has the meaning given by s 384(2) and (3): CA 2006, s 479(5).

The provisions mentioned in s 479(5) apply for the purposes of the section as if all the bodies corporate in the group were companies: CA 2006, s 479(6).

Subsidiary companies: conditions for exemption from audit

24.11 A company is exempt from the requirements of the Act relating to the audit of individual accounts for a financial year if:

(a) it is itself a subsidiary undertaking; and

(b) its parent undertaking is established under the law of an EEA State: CA 2006, s 479A(1).

24.12 Exemption is conditional upon compliance with all of the following conditions:

(a) all members of the company must agree to the exemption in respect of the financial year in question;

(b) the parent undertaking must give a guarantee under s 479C in respect of that year;

(c) the company must be included in the consolidated accounts drawn up for that year or to an earlier date in that year by the parent undertaking in accordance with:

  (i) the provisions of Directive 2013/34/EU of the European Parliament and of the Council on the annual financial statements, consolidated statements and related reports of certain types of undertakings; or

  (ii) international accounting standards;

(d) the parent undertaking must disclose in the notes to the consolidated accounts that the company is exempt from the requirements of the Act relating to the audit of individual accounts by virtue of s 479A; and

(e) the directors of the company must deliver to the registrar on or before the date that they file the accounts for that year:

  (i) a written notice of the agreement referred to in sub-s (2)(a);

  (ii) the statement referred to in s 479C(1);

  (iii) a copy of the consolidated accounts referred to in sub-s (2)(c);

  (iv) a copy of the auditor's report on those accounts; and

  (v) a copy of the consolidated annual report drawn up by the parent undertaking: CA 2006, s 479A(2).

24.13 Section 479A applies subject to:

(a) s 475(2) and (3) (requirements as to statements contained in balance sheet); and

(b) s 476 (right of members to require audit): CA 2006, s 479A(3).

Companies excluded from the subsidiary companies audit exemption

24.14 A company is not entitled to the exemption conferred by CA 2006, s 479A (subsidiary companies) if it was at any time within the financial year in question:

(a) a traded company as defined in CA 2006, s 474(1);

(b) a company that:

  (i) is an authorised insurance company, a banking company, an e-money issuer, a MiFID investment firm or a UCITS management company; or

  (ii) carries on insurance market activity; or

(c) a special register body as defined in s 117(1) of the Trade Union and Labour Relations (Consolidation) Act 1992 or an employers' association as defined in s 122 of that Act or Art 4 of the Industrial Relations (Northern Ireland) Order 1992, SI 1992/807 (NI 5): CA 2006, s 479B.

Subsidiary companies audit exemption: parent undertaking declaration of guarantee

24.15 A guarantee is given by a parent undertaking under s 479C when the directors of the subsidiary company deliver to the registrar a statement by the parent undertaking that it guarantees the subsidiary company under this section: CA 2006, s 479C(1). Such statement under, s 479C(1) must be authenticated by the parent undertaking and must specify:

(a) the name of the parent undertaking;

(b) if the parent undertaking is incorporated in the UK, its registered number (if any);

(c) if the parent undertaking is incorporated outside the UK and registered in the country in which it is incorporated, the identity of the register on which it is registered and the number with which it is so registered;

(d) the name and registered number of the subsidiary company in respect of which the guarantee is being given;

(e) the date of the statement; and

(f) the financial year to which the guarantee relates: CA 2006, s 479C(2).

24.16 A guarantee given under s 479C has the effect that:

(a) the parent undertaking guarantees all outstanding liabilities to which the subsidiary company is subject at the end of the financial year to which the guarantee relates, until they are satisfied in full; and

(b) the guarantee is enforceable against the parent undertaking by any person to whom the subsidiary company is liable in respect of those liabilities: CA 2006, s 479C(3).

Dormant companies: conditions for exemption from audit

24.17 A company is exempt from the requirements of the CA 2006 relating to the audit of accounts in respect of a financial year if:

(a) it has been dormant since its formation; or

(b) it has been dormant since the end of the previous financial year and certain conditions are met: CA 2006, s 480(1).

24.18 The conditions are that the company:

(a) as regards its individual accounts for the financial year in question:

 (i) is entitled to prepare accounts in accordance with the small companies regime (see CA 2006, ss 381–384); or

(ii) would be so entitled but for having been a public company or a member of an ineligible group; and

(b) is not required to prepare group accounts for that year: CA 2006, s 480(2).

24.19 Section 480 applies subject to:

(a) s 475(2) and (3) (requirements as to statements to be contained in balance sheet);

(b) s 476 (right of members to require audit); and

(c) s 481 (companies excluded from dormant companies exemption): CA 2006, s 486(3).

Companies excluded from dormant companies exemption

24.20 A company is not entitled to the exemption conferred by s 480 (dormant companies) if it was at any time within the financial year in question a company that:

(za) is a traded company as defined in CA 2006, s 474(1);

(a) is an authorised insurance company, a banking company, an e-money issuer, a MiFID investment firm or a UCITS management company; or

(b) carries on insurance market activity: CA 2006, s 481.

Non-profit-making companies subject to public sector audit

24.21 The requirements of CA 2006, Pt 15 as to audit of accounts do not apply to a company for a financial year if it is non-profit-making and its accounts:

(a) are subject to audit by the Comptroller and Auditor General by virtue of an order under s 25(6) of the Government Resources and Accounts Act 2000;

(ab) are subject to audit by the Auditor General for Wales by virtue of:

(i) an order under s 144 of the Government of Wales Act 1998; or

(ii) paragraph 18 of Sch 8 to the Government of Wales Act 2006;

(b) are accounts:

(i) in relation to which s 21 of the Public Finance and Accountability (Scotland) Act 2000 (asp 1) (audit of accounts: Auditor General for Scotland) applies; or

(ii) that are subject to audit by the Auditor General for Scotland by virtue of an order under s 483 (Scottish public sector companies: audit by Auditor General for Scotland); or

(c) are subject to audit by the Comptroller and Auditor General for Northern Ireland by virtue of an order under Art 5(3) of the Audit and Accountability (Northern Ireland) Order 2003, SI 2003/418 (NI 5): CA 2006, s 482(1).

In the case of a company that is a parent company or a subsidiary undertaking, s 482(1) applies only if every group undertaking is non-profit-making: CA 2006, s 482(2).

In s 482, 'non-profit-making' has the same meaning as in Article 54 of the Treaty on the Functioning of the European Union: CA 2006, s 482(3).

The section has effect subject to s 475(2) (balance sheet to contain statement that company entitled to exemption under this section): CA 2006, s 482(4).

Scottish public sector companies: audit by Auditor General for Scotland

24.22 The Scottish Ministers may by order provide for the accounts of a company having its registered office in Scotland to be audited by the Auditor General for Scotland: CA 2006, s 483(1). Such an order under CA 2006, s 483(1) may be made in relation to a company only if it appears to the Scottish Ministers that the company:

(a) exercises in or as regards Scotland functions of a public nature none of which relate to reserved matters (within the meaning of the Scotland Act 1998 (c 46)); or

(b) is entirely or substantially funded from a body having accounts falling within paragraph (a) or (b) of sub-s (3): CA 2006, s 483(2).

24.23 Those accounts are:

(a) accounts in relation to which s 21 of the Public Finance and Accountability (Scotland) Act 2000 (asp 1) (audit of accounts: Auditor General for Scotland) applies;

(b) accounts which are subject to audit by the Auditor General for Scotland by virtue of an order under s 483: CA 2006, s 483(3).

24.24 An order under CA 2006, s 483(1) may make such supplementary or consequential provision (including provision amending an enactment) as the Scottish Ministers think expedient: CA 2006, s 483(4).

An order under s 483(1) shall not be made unless a draft of the statutory instrument containing it has been laid before, and approved by resolution of, the Scottish Parliament: CA 2006, s 483(5).

General power of amendment by regulations

24.25 The Secretary of State may by regulations amend Pt 16, Ch 1 or s 539 (minor definitions) so far as applying to that chapter by adding, altering or repealing provisions: CA 2006, s 484(1).

The regulations may make consequential amendments or repeals in other provisions of CA 2006, or in other enactments: CA 2006, s 484(2).

Regulations under s 484 imposing new requirements, or rendering existing requirements more onerous, are subject to affirmative resolution procedure: CA 2006, s 484(3).

Appointment of auditors

24.26 This section addresses the appointment, functions and role of auditors in companies. It also addresses their dismissal and resignation.

Appointment of auditors of private companies: general

24.27 An auditor or auditors of a private company must be appointed for each financial year of the company, unless the directors reasonably resolve otherwise on the ground that audited accounts are unlikely to be required: CA 2006, s 485(1).

For each financial year for which an auditor or auditors is or are to be appointed (other than the company's first financial year), the appointment must be made before the end of the period of 28 days beginning with:

(a) the end of the time allowed for sending out copies of the company's annual accounts and reports for the previous financial year (see CA 2006, s 424); or

(b) if earlier, the day on which copies of the company's annual accounts and reports for the previous financial year are sent out under CA 2006, s 423.

This is the 'period for appointing auditors': CA 2006, s 485(2).

24.28 The directors may appoint an auditor or auditors of the company:

(a) at any time before the company's first period for appointing auditors;

(b) following a period during which the company (being exempt from audit) did not have any auditor, at any time before the company's next period for appointing auditors; or

(c) to fill a casual vacancy in the office of auditor: CA 2006, s 485(3).

24.29 The members may appoint an auditor or auditors by ordinary resolution:

(a) during a period for appointing auditors;

(b) if the company should have appointed an auditor or auditors during a period for appointing auditors but failed to do so; or

(c) where the directors had power to appoint under sub-s (3) but have failed to make an appointment: s 485(4): CA 2006, s 485(4).

24.30 An auditor or auditors of a private company may only be appointed:

(a) in accordance with this section; or

(b) in accordance with s 486 (default power of Secretary of State).

This is without prejudice to any deemed re-appointment under s 487: CA 2006, s 485(5).

In some situations auditors may be considered as officers of the company. In *Re London and General Bank* [1895] 2 Ch 166, the Court of Appeal held that the bank's auditors were officers of the company. Lindley LJ said: '… it seems to me impossible to deny that for some purposes and to some extent an auditor is an officer of the company'.

The Court of Appeal rejected the argument that an officer must be a person who is concerned with the management of the company or has at least some measure of control over the assets of the company.

In *Re Kingston Cotton Mill Co* [1896] 1 Ch 6, the Court of Appeal held that *London and General Bank* was of general application. The distinction drawn by Kay LJ in the earlier case between auditors appointed by the company to report upon the balance sheet and accounts presented to them by the officers of the company and persons asked, ad hoc, to carry out a particular audit exercise, was referred to. This distinction was specifically picked up in *Re Western Counties Steam Bakeries and Milling Co* [1897] 1 Ch 617. The earlier cases were distinguished. Lindley LJ said (at 627):

> 'An auditor may or may not be an officer of a company. So may anybody else – eg, a banker or solicitor. Prima facie such persons are not officers. See as to bankers, *Re Imperial Land Co of Marseilles* ((1870) LR 10 Eq 298); as to solicitors *Re Carter's Case* ((1886) 31 Ch D 496). But if appointed to an office under the company, and if they act in that office as officers of the company, they will be officers … That was decided in the case of *Re Liberator Permanent Benefit Building Society* ((1894) 71 LT 406), and no irregularity in their appointment would, I conceive, avail them. But to be an officer there must be an office, and an office imports a recognised position with rights and duties annexed to it, and it would be an abuse of words to call a person an officer who fills no such position either de jure or de facto, but who happens to do some of the work which he would have to do if he were an officer in the proper sense of the word.'

Accordingly in that case, because the relevant persons had never been appointed as auditors of the company, they were held not to be officers of the company.

> Finally, in *R v Shacter* [1960] 1 All ER 61, a criminal case, the Court of Appeal again followed the earlier cases. The relevant offences were statutory offences which could only be committed by an officer of a company. The Court of Appeal considered that the question was answered by ascertaining in what capacity the person had been appointed. If the person had been appointed to hold 'the office of auditor … it can well be asked what office an auditor is being appointed to unless it is an office in the company and what officer he becomes unless it be an officer of the company' (See [1960] 1 All ER 61 at 63, per Lord Parker CJ).

In *Mutual Reinsurance Co Ltd v Peat Marwick Mitchell & Co* [1997] 1 BCLC 1, the Court of Appeal held that auditors are officers of the company when appointed under the Companies Act 1985, s 384.

Appointment of auditors of private companies: default power of Secretary of State

24.31 If a private company fails to appoint an auditor or auditors in accordance with s 485, the Secretary of State may appoint one or more persons to fill the vacancy: CA 2006, s 486(1).

Where s 485(2) applies and the company fails to make the necessary appointment before the end of the period for appointing auditors, the company must within one week of the end of that period give notice to the Secretary of State of his power having become exercisable: CA 2006, s 486(2).

24.32 If a company fails to give the notice required by s 486, an offence is committed by:

(a) the company; and

(b) every officer of the company who is in default: CA 2006, s 486(3).

A person guilty of an offence under this section will be liable on summary conviction to a fine not exceeding level 3 on the standard scale and, for continued contravention, a daily default fine not exceeding one-tenth of level 3 on the standard scale: CA 2006, s 486(4).

Term of office of auditors of a private company

24.33 An auditor or auditors of a private company hold office in accordance with the terms of their appointment, subject to the requirements that:

(a) they do not take office until any previous auditor or auditors cease to hold office; and

(b) they cease to hold office at the end of the next period for appointing auditors unless re-appointed: CA 2006, s 487(1).

24.34 Where no auditor has been appointed by the end of the next period for appointing auditors, any auditor in office immediately before that time is deemed to be re-appointed at that time, unless:

(a) he was appointed by the directors; or

(b) the company's articles require actual re-appointment; or

(c) the deemed re-appointment is prevented by the members under s 488; or

(d) the members have resolved that he should not be re-appointed; or

(e) the directors have resolved that no auditor or auditors should be appointed for the financial year in question: CA 2006, s 487(2).

This is without prejudice to the provisions of Pt 16 as to removal and resignation of auditors: CA 2006, s 487(3).

No account shall be taken of any loss of the opportunity of deemed re-appointment under s 487 in ascertaining the amount of any compensation or damages payable to an auditor on his ceasing to hold office for any reason: CA 2006, s 487(4).

Prevention by members of deemed re-appointment of auditor

24.35 An auditor of a private company is not deemed to be re-appointed under CA 2006, s 487(2) if the company has received notices under this section from members representing at least the requisite percentage of the total voting rights of all members who would be entitled to vote on a resolution that the auditor should not be re-appointed: CA 2006, s 488(1).

The 'requisite percentage' is 5%, or such lower percentage as is specified for this purpose in the company's articles: CA 2006, s 488(2).

A notice:

(a) may be in hard copy or electronic form;

(b) must be authenticated by the person or persons giving it; and

(c) must be received by the company before the end of the accounting reference period immediately preceding the time when the deemed re-appointment would have effect: CA 2006, s 488(3).

Appointment of auditors of a public company

Appointment of auditors of a public company: general

24.36 An auditor or auditors of a public company must be appointed for each financial year of the company, unless the directors reasonably resolve otherwise on the ground that audited accounts are unlikely to be required: CA 2006, s 489(1).

For each financial year for which an auditor or auditors is or are to be appointed (other than the company's first financial year), the appointment must be made before the end of the accounts meeting of the company at which the company's annual accounts and reports for the previous financial year are laid: CA 2006, s 489(2).

The directors may appoint an auditor or auditors of the company:

(a) at any time before the company's first accounts meeting;

(b) following a period during which the company (being exempt from audit) did not have any auditor, at any time before the company's next accounts meeting;

(c) to fill a casual vacancy in the office of auditor: CA 2006, s 489(3).

24.37 The members may appoint an auditor or auditors by ordinary resolution:

(a) at an accounts meeting;

(b) if the company should have appointed an auditor or auditors at an accounts meeting but failed to do so;

(c) where the directors had power to appoint under s 489(3) but have failed to make an appointment: CA 2006, s 489(4).

24.38 An auditor or auditors of a public company may only be appointed:

(a) in accordance with s 489; or

(b) in accordance with s 490 (default power of Secretary of State): CA 2006, s 489(5).

Appointment of auditors of a public company: default power of Secretary of State

24.39 If a public company fails to appoint an auditor or auditors in accordance with s 489, the Secretary of State may appoint one or more persons to fill the vacancy: CA 2006, s 490(1).

Where s 489(2) applies and the company fails to make the necessary appointment before the end of the accounts meeting, the company must within one week of the end of that meeting give notice to the Secretary of State of his power having become exercisable: CA 2006, s 490(2).

24.40 If a company fails to give the notice required by this section, an offence is committed by:

(a) the company; and

(b) every officer of the company who is in default: CA 2006, s 490(3).

A person guilty of an offence under this section will be liable on summary conviction to a fine not exceeding level 3 on the standard scale and, for continued contravention, a daily default fine not exceeding one-tenth of level 3 on the standard scale: CA 2006, s 490(4).

Term of office of auditors of a public company

24.41 The auditor or auditors of a public company hold office in accordance with the terms of their appointment, subject to the requirements that:

(a) they do not take office until the previous auditor or auditors have ceased to hold office; and

(b) they cease to hold office at the conclusion of the accounts meeting next following their appointment, unless re-appointed: CA 2006, s 490(1).

This is without prejudice to the provisions of Pt 16 as to removal and resignation of auditors: CA 2006, s 490(2).

Fixing of auditor's remuneration

24.42 The remuneration of an auditor appointed by the members of a company must be fixed by the members by ordinary resolution or in such manner as the members may by ordinary resolution determine: CA 2006, s 492(1).

The remuneration of an auditor appointed by the directors of a company must be fixed by the directors: CA 2006, s 492(2).

The remuneration of an auditor appointed by the Secretary of State must be fixed by the Secretary of State: CA 2006, s 492(3).

For the purposes of s 492 'remuneration' includes sums paid in respect of expenses: CA 2006, s 492(4).

Section 492 applies in relation to benefits in kind as to payments of money: CA 2006, s 492(5).

Disclosure of terms of audit appointment

24.43 The Secretary of State may make provision by regulations for securing the disclosure of the terms on which a company's auditor is appointed, remunerated or performs his duties.

Nothing in the following provisions of s 493 affects the generality of this power: CA 2006, s 493(1).

The regulations may:

(a) require disclosure of:

  (i) a copy of any terms that are in writing; and

  (ii) a written memorandum setting out any terms that are not in writing;

(b) require disclosure to be at such times, in such places and by such means as are specified in the regulations;

(c) require the place and means of disclosure to be stated:

  (i) in a note to the company's annual accounts (in the case of its individual accounts) or in such manner as is specified in the regulations (in the case of group accounts);

  (ii) in the directors' report; or

  (iii) in the auditor's report on the company's annual accounts: CA 2006, s 493(2).

The provisions of s 493 apply to a variation of the terms mentioned in s 493(1) as they apply to the original terms: CA 2006, s 493(3).

Disclosure of services provided by auditor or associates and related remuneration

24.44 The Secretary of State may make provision by regulations for securing the disclosure of:

(a) the nature of any services provided for a company by the company's auditor (whether in his capacity as auditor or otherwise) or by his associates;

(b) the amount of any remuneration received or receivable by a company's auditor, or his associates, in respect of any such services.

Nothing in the following provisions of s 494 affects the generality of this power: CA 2006, s 494(1).

24.45 The regulations may provide:

(a) for disclosure of the nature of any services provided to be made by reference to any class or description of services specified in the regulations (or any combination of services, however described);

(b) for the disclosure of amounts of remuneration received or receivable in respect of services of any class or description specified in the regulations (or any combination of services, however described);

(c) for the disclosure of separate amounts so received or receivable by the company's auditor or any of his associates, or of aggregate amounts so received or receivable by all or any of those persons: CA 2006, s 494(2).

24.46 The regulations may:

(a) provide that 'remuneration' includes sums paid in respect of expenses;

(b) apply to benefits in kind as well as to payments of money, and require the disclosure of the nature of any such benefits and their estimated money value;

(c) apply to services provided for associates of a company as well as to those provided for a company;

(d) define 'associate' in relation to an auditor and a company respectively: CA 2006, s 494(3).

24.47 The regulations may provide that any disclosure required by the regulations is to be made:

(a) in a note to the company's annual accounts (in the case of its individual accounts) or in such manner as is specified in the regulations (in the case of group accounts);

(b) in the directors' report; or

(c) in the auditor's report on the company's annual accounts: CA 2006, s 494(4).

If the regulations provide that any such disclosure is to be made as mentioned in s 494(4)(a) or (b), the regulations may require the auditor to supply the directors of the company with any information necessary to enable the disclosure to be made: CA 2006, s 494(5).

Functions of the auditor

Auditor's report on company's annual accounts

24.48 A company's auditor must make a report to the company's members on all annual accounts of the company of which copies are, during his tenure of office:

(a) in the case of a private company, to be sent out to members under CA 2006, s 423;

(b) in the case of a public company, to be laid before the company in general meeting under s 437: CA 2006, s 495(1).

24.49 The auditor's report must include:

(a) an introduction identifying the annual accounts that are the subject of the audit and the financial reporting framework that has been applied in their preparation; and

(b) a description of the scope of the audit identifying the auditing standards in accordance with which the audit was conducted: CA 2006, s 495(2).

24.50 The report must state clearly whether, in the auditor's opinion, the annual accounts:

(a) give a true and fair view:

  (i) in the case of an individual balance sheet, of the state of affairs of the company as at the end of the financial year;

  (ii) in the case of an individual profit and loss account, of the profit or loss of the company for the financial year;

  (iii) in the case of group accounts, of the state of affairs as at the end of the financial year and of the profit or loss for the financial year of the undertakings included in the consolidation as a whole, so far as concerns members of the company;

(b) have been properly prepared in accordance with the relevant financial reporting framework; and

(c) have been prepared in accordance with the requirements of this Act (and, where applicable, Article 4 of the IAS Regulation).

Expressions used in this subsection or sub-s (3A) that are defined for the purposes of Pt 16 (see ss 464, 471 and 474) have the same meaning as in that Part: CA 2006, s 495(3).

24.51 The following provisions apply to the auditors of a company which qualifies as a micro-entity in relation to a financial year (see ss 384A and 384B) in their consideration of whether the Companies Act individual accounts of the company for that year give a true and fair view as mentioned in sub-s (3)(a):

(a) where the accounts comprise only micro-entity minimum accounting items, the auditors must disregard any provision of an accounting standard which would require the accounts to contain information additional to those items;

(b) in relation to a micro-entity minimum accounting item contained in the accounts, the auditors must disregard any provision of an accounting standard which would require the accounts to contain further information in relation to that item; and

(c) where the accounts contain an item of information additional to the micro-entity minimum accounting items, the auditors must have regard to any provision of an accounting standard which relates to that item: CA 2006, s 495(3A).

24.52 The auditor's report:

(a) must be either unqualified or qualified; and

(b) must include a reference to any matters to which the auditor wishes to draw attention by way of emphasis without qualifying the report: CA 2006, s 495(4).

The objective of the auditor's report demonstrates transparency and accountability of directors towards their shareholders

In respect of the auditor's report, Lord Oliver in *Caparo Industries plc v Dickman* [1990] 1 All ER 583, stated:

> '... the primary purpose of the statutory requirement that a company's accounts shall be audited annually is almost self-evident. The structure of the corporate trading entity, at least in the case of public companies whose shares are dealt with on an authorised stock exchange, involves the concept of a more or less widely distributed holding of shares rendering the personal involvement of each individual shareholder in the day-to-day management of the enterprise impracticable, with the result that management is necessarily separated from ownership. The management is confided to a board of directors which operates in a fiduciary capacity and is answerable to and removable by the shareholders who can act, if they act at all, only collectively and only through the medium of a general meeting. Hence the legislative provisions requiring the board annually to give an account of its stewardship to a general meeting of the shareholders.'

24.53 The board's task is to demonstrate accountability towards its stakeholders. As shareholders do not have the time to watch and tower over their directors or monitor their every move, auditors are entrusted to scrutinise the company's accounts which provides some reassurance, independence and comfort that directors are acting in the company's best interests and truly guarding the shareholders' interests.

Auditor's report on directors' report

24.54 In his report on the company's annual accounts, the auditor must:

(a) state whether, in his opinion, based on the work undertaken in the course of the audit:

  (i) the information given in the strategic report (if any) and the directors' report for the financial year for which the accounts are prepared is consistent with those accounts; and

  (ii) any such strategic report and the directors' report have been prepared in accordance with applicable legal requirements;

(b) state whether, in the light of the knowledge and understanding of the company and its environment obtained in the course of the audit, he has identified material misstatements in the strategic report (if any) and the directors' report; and

(c) if applicable, give an indication of the nature of each of the misstatements referred to in paragraph (b): CA 2006, s 496.

Auditor's report on auditable part of directors' remuneration report

24.55 If the company is a quoted company, the auditor, in his report on the company's annual accounts for the financial year, must:

(a) report to the company's members on the auditable part of the directors' remuneration report; and

(b) state whether in his opinion that part of the directors' remuneration report has been properly prepared in accordance with this Act: CA 2006, s 497(1).

For the purposes of Pt 16, 'the auditable part' of a directors' remuneration report is the part identified as such by regulations under s 421: CA 2006, s 497(2).

Auditor's report on separate corporate governance statement

24.56 Where the company prepares a separate corporate governance statement in respect of a financial year, the auditor must, in his report of the company's annual accounts for that year:

(a) state whether, in his opinion, based on the work undertaken in the course of the audit, the information given in the statement in compliance with rules 7.2.5 and 7.2.6 in the Disclosure Rules and Transparency Rules sourcebook made by the Financial Conduct Authority (information about internal control and risk management systems in relation to financial reporting processes and about share capital structures):

  (i) is consistent with those accounts; and

  (ii) has been prepared in accordance with applicable legal requirements;

(b) state whether, in the light of the knowledge and understanding of the company and its environment obtained in the course of the audit, he has identified material misstatements in the information in the statement referred to in paragraph (a);

(c) if applicable, give an indication of the nature of each of the misstatements referred to in paragraph (b); and

(d) state whether, in his opinion, based on the work undertaken in the course of the audit, rules 7.2.2, 7.2.3 and 7.2.7 in the Disclosure Rules and Transparency Rules sourcebook made by the Financial Conduct Authority (information about the company's corporate governance code and practices and about its administrative, management and supervisory bodies and their committees) have been complied with, if applicable: CA 2006, s 497A(1).

The rules referred to above were inserted by Annex C of the Disclosure Rules and Transparency Rules Sourcebook (Corporate Governance Rules) Instrument 2008 made by the Authority on 26 June 2008 (FSA 2008/32): CA 2006, s 497A(2).

Duties and rights of auditors

24.57 One of the principal purposes for conducting an audit is to obtain evidence and verify details of the disclosures made in the company's financial statements, and ensure that such financial statements are free from misstatements, misrepresentations and error or fraud: In *Barings plc v Coopers & Lybrand* [1997] 1 BCLC 427, the Court of Appeal stated that auditors were required to conduct their audit in such a way as to make it probable that material misstatements in financial documents would be detected.

Previous case law demonstrated that a low standard of diligence, skill and care in preparing the audit was required of an auditor. However, a much higher standard of duty is now required of an auditor particularly in respect of an audit client Early case law was particularly concerned with the extent to which the auditor could rely on management information that was being provided to the auditor, and limited the auditor's duties towards detecting any 'suspicious circumstances' in connection with the company's financial affairs. The auditor was only required to exercise reasonable skill and care in the performance of his duties for the client. The auditors were given much flexibility in connection with the information provided by management.

Auditors were not required to advise the company's management on transactional matters

In *Re London and General Bank Limited (No 2)* [1895] 2 Ch 673, the Court of Appeal stated that it is no part of the duty of an auditor of a company to give advice, either to directors or shareholders, as to what they ought to do. He had nothing to do with the prudence or imprudence of making loans with or without security or whether the business of the company is being conducted prudently or imprudently, profitably or unprofitably. It is nothing to him whether dividends are properly or improperly declared, provided he discharges his own duty to the shareholders which is to ascertain and state the true financial position of the company at the time of the audit.

To ascertain the true position of the company the auditor must examine the books of the company, taking reasonable care to ascertain that they do show the true position. Assuming the books to be so kept as to show the true position, the auditor has to frame a balance sheet showing that position according to the books and to certify that the balance sheet presented is correct in that sense.

Lindley LJ depicted a low standard of care and skill required of an auditor in the performance of his duties:

> 'But an auditor is not bound to do more than exercise reasonable care and skill in making inquiries and investigations. He is not an insurer. He does not guarantee that the books do correctly show the true position of the company's affairs. He does not even guarantee that his balance sheet is accurate according to the books of the company, for that would render him responsible for error on his part even if he were deceived without any want of reasonable care on his part, eg, by the fraudulent concealment from him of a book. Even in the case of suspicion he is not bound to exercise more than reasonable care and skill. What is reasonable care in any particular case must depend on the circumstances of that case. An auditor is justified in acting on the opinion of an expert where special knowledge is required'.

An auditor may rely upon statements made by the company's trusted employee in auditing the accounts

In *Re Kingston Cotton Mill Co (No 2)* [1896] 2 Ch 279, the Court of Appeal was of the view that the auditor was justified in placing reliance on the statements made by a company's employee who was trusted by the company, unless the auditor had grounds for suspicion. It stated that it was not part of the duty of the auditors to take stock; they were justified in relying on the certificates of the manager, a person of acknowledged competence and high reputation, and were not bound to check his certificates in the absence of anything to raise suspicion, and that they were not liable for the dividends wrongfully paid.

An auditor was not bound to be suspicious where there were no circumstances to arouse suspicion; he was only bound to exercise a reasonable amount of care and skill.

An auditor must employ an 'inquiring mind' in the provision of audit services

In *Fomento (Sterling Area) Ltd v Selsdon Foundation Pen Co Ltd* [1958] 1 WLR 45, Lord Denning stated that an auditor has a duty to work with an 'inquiring mind':

> 'What is the proper function of an auditor? It is said that he is bound only to verify the sum, the arithmetical conclusion, by reference to the books and all necessary vouching material and oral explanations; and that it is no part of his function to inquire whether an article is covered by patents or not. I think this is too narrow a view. An auditor is not to be confined to the mechanics of checking vouchers and making arithmetical computations. He is not to be written off as a professional "adder-upper and subtractor". His vital task is to take care to see that errors are not made, be they errors of computation, or errors of omission or commission, or downright untruths. To perform this task properly, he must come to it with an inquiring mind – not suspicious of dishonesty, I agree – but suspecting that someone may have made a mistake somewhere and that a check must be made to ensure that there has been none. I would not have it thought that *Re Kingston Cotton Mill Co (No 2)* ([1896] 2 Ch 279) relieved an auditor of his responsibility for making a proper check. But the check, to be effective, may require some legal knowledge, or some knowledge of patents or other specialty. What is he then to do? Take, for instance, a point of law arising in the course of auditing a company's accounts. He may come on a payment which, it appears to him, may be unlawful, in that it may not be within the powers of the corporation, or improper in that it may have no warrant or justification. He is, then, not only entitled but bound to inquire into it and, if need be, to disallow it; see *Roberts v Hopwood* ([1925] AC 578 at p 605), *Re Ridsdel, Ridsdel v Rawlinson* ([1947] 2 All ER 312 at p 316). It may be, of course, that he has sufficient legal knowledge to deal with it himself, as many accountants have, but, if it is beyond him, he is entitled to take legal advice on the principle stated in *Bevan v Webb*

([1901] 2 Ch 59 at p 75), that "permission to a man to do an act, which he cannot do effectually without the help of an agent, carries with it the right to employ an agent".

So, also, with an auditor who is employed for the purpose of checking the royalties payable. It is part of his duty to use reasonable care to see that none has been omitted which ought to be included. He is not bound to accept the ipse dixit of the licensee that there are no other articles which attract royalty. He is entitled to check the accuracy of that assertion by inquiring the nature of any other articles, which, it appears to him, may come within the patented field. If he cannot be sure, of his own knowledge, whether they attract royalty or not, he can take the advice of a patent agent, just as, within the legal sphere, he can take the advice of a lawyer. This is, however, subject to the seal of confidence …'

Modernly, the courts take a strict view on the duties of auditors to be put on enquiry in connection with altered invoices and to act of their own volition

In *Re Thomas Gerrard & Son Ltd* [1967] 2 All ER 525, Pennycuick J was of the view that the discovery of the altered invoices put the auditors on enquiry, and, they were therefore bound to examine further (eg by examining the suppliers' statements and communicating with the suppliers if necessary) into the purchases of stock at the end of each current accounting period and the attribution of price to the succeeding period of account. In this regard, the auditors had failed in their duty to exercise reasonable care and skill.

The courts may also have regard to auditing and accounting standards both nationally and internationally in determining the common law duties of directors: *Lloyd Cheyham & Co Ltd v Littlejohn & Co* [1987] BCLC 303.

The liability of auditors towards their client is likely to arise where there has been a breach of the auditor's duty under the scope of services in the engagement letter. This can arise where the auditor has omitted to consider a material matter which could have prevented further mismanagement or which could have required management to take positive action to prevent the issue from arising again: *Leeds Estate, Building and Investment Co v Shepherd* (1887) 36 Ch D 787; *Baring plc (in liquidation) v Coopers & Lybrand (No 1)* [2002] 2 BCLC 364; and *Equitable Life Assurance Society v Ernst & Young* [2003] 2 BCLC 603.

Auditors have a duty to report any fraud involving the company

In *Sesea Finance Limited v KPMG* [2000] 1 BCLC 236, the company which was the subject of an audit from KPMG claimed that it had suffered losses because of fraud and theft committed by a dominant figure within the company's group. The company claimed that the auditors were under duty to warn of fraud discovered in the course of the audit. The issue before the court was whether the auditors had such a duty.

The Court of Appeal held that where a company's auditors discovered that a senior employee had been defrauding the company on a massive scale, and that employee was in a position to continue doing so, the auditors would normally have a duty to report the discovery to the management immediately, not merely when rendering their report. Moreover, if the auditors suspected that the management might be involved in, or was condoning fraud or other irregularities, the duty to report overrode the duty of confidentiality, and the auditors would have to report directly to a third party without the management's knowledge or consent. The relevant considerations would include the extent to which the fraud or other irregularity was likely to result in material gain or loss for any person or was likely to affect a large number of persons, and the extent to which non-disclosure would enable the fraud or irregularity to be repeated in the future.

In the course of his judgment, Kennedy LJ stated that when a firm of accountants accepts instructions to audit the accounts of a company for a fiscal year, its primary obligation is within a reasonable time to exercise an appropriate level of skill and care in reporting to the company's members on the accounts of the company, stating, in their opinion, whether the accounts of the company give a true and fair view of the company's financial affairs. An auditor may be able to limit liability for negligence towards an audit client by raising the defence of contributory negligence under the Law Reform (Contributory Negligence) Act 1945. The auditor will allege that the company's management are partially to blame for the auditor's actions. This has the effect that the claimant's damages are reduced by such amount as the court considers just and equitable under the circumstances.

In some cases, auditors also make use of 'representation letters' which require companies that are being audited to represent a certain financial state of affairs to the best of their knowledge and belief. If this is not subsequently found to be the case, then auditors have tended to rely on such letters as partial defence to a negligence action: *Barings plc (in liquidation) v Coopers & Lybrand* [2002] 2 BCLC 410.

An internal wrongdoing by the sole director and shareholder provided a defence to auditors for negligently failing to detect the wrongdoing

In *Stone & Rolls Ltd (in liquidation) v Moore Stephens (a firm)* [2009] 2 BCLC 563, the Supreme Court was required to consider the extent of an auditor's duty for internal wrongdoing by the company.

S was a shadow director of the claimant company and its beneficial owner. By means of a power of attorney he had complete managerial control of every aspect of its affairs and was effectively its sole directing mind and will. He used the company to perpetrate a fraud on a number of banks which were induced to make payments to the company on the presentation of false invoices and documents against letters of credit issued by the banks for the purchase of large quantities of non-existent agricultural products. The letters of credit were not reimbursed and the monies paid over to the company were paid away to participants in the fraud and could not be traced. The banks defrauded in that manner included K Bank, which paid out $US94.5 million on the worthless invoices and documents. K Bank brought an action in deceit against both the company and s in the High Court and was awarded damages of more than $94 million. The company was unable to satisfy the judgment and was put into liquidation by the bank. The liquidators brought an action against the defendants, who were the company's auditors, seeking to recover damages for the benefit of the company's creditors (the defrauded banks) on the grounds that the defendants were liable in both contract and tort in negligently failing to detect the fraud in the course of their audit. The defendants applied to have the claim struck out on the grounds that it was barred by the principle of *ex turpi causa non oritur actio* because the essence of the company's action was a claim that it was entitled to be indemnified by the defendants in respect of liabilities it had incurred by its own fraud.

The judge refused to strike out the claim but on appeal the Court of Appeal held that it ought to be struck out on the grounds that a company could be directly liable for a dishonest act if the dishonesty of its directing mind and will was attributed to it, S's fraud was to be attributed to the company as he was not just the company's agent but its sole directing mind and will, and he had procured the company to enter into the fraudulent transactions with the bank.

The liquidators appealed to the House of Lords, contending that the company was entitled to rely on the principle of non-attribution, namely that the law did not attribute knowledge of a deception to the person who was being deceived, so that knowledge of the fraud was not to be attributed to the company because the fraud was practised on the company itself, and the defendants ought not to be permitted to rely on the *ex turpi causa* because detection of dishonesty in the operation of the company's affairs was the very thing that the defendants, as auditors, were retained to do.

The House of Lords held (Lords Scott and Mance dissenting) that where a fraud was perpetrated by a company whose directing mind and will was its sole shareholder and he was solely responsible for its actions, the fraud was to be attributed to the company and any claim by it against its auditors for not detecting the fraud was barred by the *ex turpi causa* principle. The principle of non-attribution did not apply in such circumstances because the company was primarily liable to the persons defrauded (the banks), it was relying on its own fraud, rather than fraud for which it was only vicariously liable, in order to found its claim, and there were no innocent participators in the company. Since s and the company were effectively one and the same person and S's fraud was to be attributed to the company, it was precluded by the *ex turpi causa* principle from obtaining damages from the defendants for the amount it owed its creditors. (*Dicta* of Lord Mansfield CJ in *Holman v Johnson* (1775) 1 Cowp 341 at 343 applied. *Tinsley v Milligan* [1993] 3 All ER 65 and *Caparo Industries plc v Dickman* [1990] BCLC 273 considered. *Re Hampshire Land Co* [1896] 2 Ch 743 not applied.)

The fact that the company's illegal conduct was the very thing that the defendant was under a duty to prevent did not exclude the *ex turpi causa* defence. If the very thing from which the defendant owed a duty to save the claimant from being harmed was, or included, the commission of a criminal offence, as a matter of public policy, the claim was barred by the *ex turpi causa* principle. The circumstances were also such that in order to recover damages the liquidators would have to establish that the scope of the duty undertaken by the defendant auditors extended to taking reasonable care to ensure that the company was not used as a vehicle for fraud and that it owed that duty to those whom the company might defraud, which the company would be unable to do.

The House of Lords while not deciding on the issue raised the issue as to whether the *ex turpi causa* principle will bar a claim by a company with independent shareholders where those shareholders were unaware that the directing mind and will of the company had involved the company in fraud.

Lord Phillips considered the duties of auditors and stated that such duties were founded in contract and the extent of the duties undertaken by contract must be interpreted in the light of the relevant statutory provisions and the relevant auditing standards. The duties are duties of reasonable care in carrying out the audit of the company's accounts. They are owed to the company in the interests of its shareholders. No duty is owed directly to the individual shareholders. This is because the shareholders' interests are protected by the duty owed to the company. No duty is owed to the creditors: *Al Saudi Banque v Clark Pixley (a firm)* [1990] BCLC 46. The auditing standards require auditors who have reason to suspect that the directors of a company are behaving fraudulently to draw this to the attention of the proper authority.

His Lordship next considered the following issues in analysing the duty of care owed by auditors:

Doctrine of ex turpi causa

This was a principle which prevented a claimant from using the court to obtain benefits from his own illegal conduct and held that the principle applied to the present case owing to the fraud and wrongdoing conducted internally by the company's director. The court would not assist a claimant to recover compensation for his own illegal conduct.

Principle of attribution and Re Hampshire Land

The principle of attribution did not apply as the company was primarily liable for the fraud perpetrated. The *Re Hampshire Land* principle also had no application to this case.

The very thing

It was argued on behalf of the company that the auditors had a duty to protect the company from the fraudulent acts of its director. This argument was rejected on the grounds that it was not the duty of auditors to prevent the perpetration of fraud by the company's directing mind and will. To do so would be to extend the scope of the auditors' reasonable duty of care.

Lord Walker

Lord Walker was of the view that no one could found a cause of action based on his own criminal conduct. Further, the company was primarily and not vicariously liable for frauds perpetrated on the bank. The director of the company was the company's persona: he was its directing mind and will – the very ego and centre of the personality of the corporation. He agreed with the reasoning of Lords Phillips and Lord Brown.

Lord Brown

The principle of *ex turpi causa* applied to bar a claim where a company was involved in fraud or wrongdoing.

Stone & Rolls Limited was considered by the Supreme Court in *Jetivia SA v Bilta (UK) Ltd* [2015] UKSC 23. The Supreme Court did not consider the *Jetivia* case as an appropriate forum to address fully the illegality defence and stated the urgency in reviewing this defence in any forthcoming case on this issue. Many of their Lordships comments were therefore obiter with differing perspectives as to the proper application of this defence. According to Lords Toulson and Hodge, the defence of illegality was a rule of public policy dependent upon the nature of the particular claim brought by the claimant and the relationship between the parties. Owing to the fiduciary duties of directors towards an insolvent company, directors must have proper regard to creditors' interests: a position addressed under the CA 2006, s 172 and at common law and equity: *Kinsella v Russell Kinsela Pty Ltd (in liquidation)* (1986) 4 NSWR 722; and *West Mercia Safetywear v Dodd* [1988] BCLC 250. The significant feature of the illegality defence was based on public policy grounds, and directors could not escape liability for breach of their fiduciary duty on the ground that they were in control of the company. Another different perspective put forward by Lord Sumption was that the defence of illegality was a rule of law independent of any judicial value judgment about the balance of equities in each case. However, Lord Sumption did not agree with Lords Toulson and Hodge on the 'statutory policy' argument defeating the claim of Illegality defence. The Supreme Court was also divided in the proper analysis to be attributed to *Stone & Rolls Limited v Moore Stephens* [2009] 1 AC 1391. In *Stone & Rolls*, the majority of the law Lords reached different conclusions as to how the illegality defence should be applied, including the difficulty of identifying the ratio of the case. However, there was agreement that *Stone & Rolls* was particular to its facts and should be confined to such particular facts and not looked at again. See also *Safeway Stores Ltd v Twigger* [2010] EWCA Civ 1472. *Stone & Rolls* will most probably be left to gather dust as confined to its particular facts with no pertinent ratio that serves any useful purpose.

Duties of auditor

24.58 A company's auditor, in preparing his report, must carry out such investigations as will enable him to form an opinion as to:

(a) whether adequate accounting records have been kept by the company and returns adequate for their audit have been received from branches not visited by him; and

(b) whether the company's individual accounts are in agreement with the accounting records and returns; and

(c) in the case of a quoted company, whether the auditable part of the company's directors' remuneration report is in agreement with the accounting records and returns: CA 2006, s 498(1).

24.59 If the auditor is of the opinion:

(a) that adequate accounting records have not been kept, or that returns adequate for their audit have not been received from branches not visited by him; or

(b) that the company's individual accounts are not in agreement with the accounting records and returns; or

(c) in the case of a quoted company, that the auditable part of its directors' remuneration report is not in agreement with the accounting records and returns,

the auditor shall state that fact in his report: CA 2006, s 498(2).

If the auditor fails to obtain all the information and explanations which, to the best of his knowledge and belief, are necessary for the purposes of his audit, he shall state that fact in his report: CA 2006, s 498(3).

24.60 If:

(a) the requirements of regulations under s 412 (disclosure of directors' benefits: remuneration, pensions and compensation for loss of office) are not complied with in the annual accounts; or

(b) in the case of a quoted company, the requirements of regulations under s 421 as to information forming the auditable part of the directors' remuneration report are not complied with in that report,

the auditor must include in his report, so far as he is reasonably able to do so, a statement giving the required particulars: CA 2006, s 498(4).

24.61 If the directors of the company:

(a) have prepared accounts in accordance with the small companies regime; or

(b) have taken advantage of small companies exemption in preparing the directors' report,

and in the auditor's opinion they were not entitled to do so, the auditor shall state that fact in his report: CA 2006, s 498(5).

Auditor's duties in relation to separate corporate governance statement

24.62 Where the company is required to prepare a corporate governance statement in respect of a financial year and no such statement is included in the directors' report:

(a) the company's auditor, in preparing his report on the company's annual accounts for that year, must ascertain whether a corporate governance statement has been prepared; and

(b) if it appears to the auditor that no such statement has been prepared, he must state that fact in his report: CA 2006, s 498A.

Auditor's general right to information

24.63 An auditor of a company:

(a) has a right of access at all times to the company's books, accounts and vouchers (in whatever form they are held); and

(b) may require any of the following persons to provide him with such information or explanations as he thinks necessary for the performance of his duties as auditor: CA 2006, s 499(1).

24.64 Those persons are:

(a) any officer or employee of the company;

(b) any person holding or accountable for any of the company's books, accounts or vouchers;

(c) any subsidiary undertaking of the company which is a body corporate incorporated in the UK;

(d) any officer, employee or auditor of any such subsidiary undertaking or any person holding or accountable for any books, accounts or vouchers of any such subsidiary undertaking;

(e) any person who fell within any of paragraphs (a)–(d) at a time to which the information or explanations required by the auditor relates or relate: CA 2006, s 499(2).

24.65 A statement made by a person in response to a requirement under this s 499 may not be used in evidence against him in criminal proceedings except proceedings for an offence under s 501: CA 2006, s 499(3).

Nothing in s 499 compels a person to disclose information in respect of which a claim to legal professional privilege (in Scotland, to confidentiality of communications) could be maintained in legal proceedings: CA 2006, s 499(4).

Auditor's right to information from overseas subsidiaries

24.66 Where a parent company has a subsidiary undertaking that is not a body corporate incorporated in the UK, the auditor of the parent company may require it to obtain from any of the following persons such information or explanations as he may reasonably require for the purposes of his duties as auditor: CA 2006, s 500(1).

Those persons are:

(a) the undertaking;

(b) any officer, employee or auditor of the undertaking;

(c) any person holding or accountable for any of the undertaking's books, accounts or vouchers;

(d) any person who fell within paragraph (b) or (c) at a time to which the information or explanations relates or relate: CA 2006, s 500(2).

24.67 If so required, the parent company must take all such steps as are reasonably open to it to obtain the information or explanations from the person concerned: CA 2006, s 500(3).

A statement made by a person in response to a requirement under s 500 may not be used in evidence against him in criminal proceedings except proceedings for an offence under s 501: CA 2006, s 500(4).

Nothing in s 500 compels a person to disclose information in respect of which a claim to legal professional privilege (in Scotland, to confidentiality of communications) could be maintained in legal proceedings: CA 2006, s 500(5).

Auditor's right to information: offences

24.68 A person commits an offence if they knowingly or recklessly make to an auditor of a company a statement (oral or written) that:

(a) conveys or purports to convey any information or explanations which the auditor requires, or is entitled to require, under CA 2006, s 499; and

(b) is misleading, false or deceptive in a material particular: CA 2006, s 501(1).

24.69 A person guilty of an offence under s 501(1) will be liable:

(a) on conviction on indictment, to imprisonment for a term not exceeding two years or a fine (or both);

(b) on summary conviction:

  (i) in England and Wales, to imprisonment for a term not exceeding 12 months or to a fine not exceeding the statutory maximum (or both);

  (ii) in Scotland or Northern Ireland, to imprisonment for a term not exceeding six months or to a fine not exceeding the statutory maximum (or both): CA 2006, s 501(2).

A person who fails to comply with a requirement under s 499 without delay commits an offence unless it was not reasonably practicable for him to provide the required information or explanations: CA 2006, s 501(3).

24.70 If a parent company fails to comply with s 500, an offence is committed by:

(a) the company; and

(b) every officer of the company who is in default: CA 2006, s 501(4).

A person guilty of an offence under sub-ss (3) or (4) will be liable on summary conviction to a fine not exceeding level 3 on the standard scale: CA 2006, s 501(5).

Nothing in s 501 affects any right of an auditor to apply for an injunction (in Scotland, an interdict or an order for specific performance) to enforce any of his rights under ss 499 or 500: CA 2006, s 501(6).

Auditor's right in relation to resolutions and meetings

24.71 In relation to a written resolution proposed to be agreed to by a private company, the company's auditor is entitled to receive all such communications relating to the resolution as, by virtue of any provision of CA 2006, Pt 13, Ch 2, are required to be supplied to a member of the company: CA 2006, s 502(1).

A company's auditor is entitled:

(a) to receive all notices of, and other communications relating to, any general meeting which a member of the company is entitled to receive;

(b) to attend any general meeting of the company; and

(c) to be heard at any general meeting which he attends on any part of the business of the meeting which concerns him as auditor: CA 2006, s 502(2).

Where the auditor is a firm, the right to attend or be heard at a meeting is exercisable by an individual authorised by the firm in writing to act as its representative at the meeting: CA 2006, s 502(3).

Signature of auditor's report

24.72 The auditor's report must state the name of the auditor and be signed and dated: CA 2006, s 503(1). Where the auditor is an individual, the report must be signed by him: CA 2006, s 503(2). Where the auditor is a firm, the report must be signed by the senior statutory auditor in his own name, for and on behalf of the auditor: CA 2006, s 503(3).

Senior statutory auditor

24.73 The senior statutory auditor means the individual identified by the firm as senior statutory auditor in relation to the audit in accordance with:

(a) standards issued by the European Commission; or

(b) if there is no applicable standard so issued, any relevant guidance issued by:

 (i) the Secretary of State; or

 (ii) a body appointed by order of the Secretary of State: CA 2006, s 504(1).

The person identified as senior statutory auditor must be eligible for appointment as auditor of the company in question (see CA 2006, Pt 42, Ch 2): CA 2006, s 504(2).

The senior statutory auditor is not, by reason of being named or identified as senior statutory auditor or by reason of his having signed the auditor's report, subject to any civil liability to which he would not otherwise be subject: CA 2006, s 504(3).

Names to be stated in published copies in auditor's report

24.74 Every copy of the auditor's report that is published by or on behalf of the company must:

(a) state the name of the auditor and (where the auditor is a firm) the name of the person who signed it as senior statutory auditor; or

(b) if the conditions in CA 2006, s 506 (circumstances in which names may be omitted) are met, state that a resolution has been passed and notified to the Secretary of State in accordance with that section: CA 2006, s 505(1).

For the purposes of s 505 a company is regarded as publishing the report if it publishes, issues or circulates it or otherwise makes it available for public inspection in a manner calculated to invite members of the public generally, or any class of members of the public, to read it: CA 2006, s 505(2).

24.75 If a copy of the auditor's report is published without the statement required by s 505, an offence will be committed by:

(a) the company; and

(b) every officer of the company who is in default: CA 2006, s 505(3).

A person guilty of an offence under s 505 will be liable on summary conviction to a fine not exceeding level 3 on the standard scale: CA 2006, s 505(4).

Circumstances in which names may be omitted

24.76 The auditor's name and, where the auditor is a firm, the name of the person who signed the report as senior statutory auditor, may be omitted from:

(a) published copies of the report; and

(b) the copy of the report delivered to the registrar under Ch 10 of Pt 15 (filing of accounts and reports),

if certain conditions are met: CA 2006, s 506(1).

24.77 The conditions are that the company:

(a) considering on reasonable grounds that statement of the name would create or be likely to create a serious risk that the auditor or senior statutory auditor, or any other person, would be subject to violence or intimidation, has resolved that the name should not be stated; and

(b) has given notice of the resolution to the Secretary of State, stating:

 (i) the name and registered number of the company;

 (ii) the financial year of the company to which the report relates; and

 (iii) the name of the auditor and (where the auditor is a firm) the name of the person who signed the report as senior statutory auditor: CA 2006, s 506(2).

Offences in connection with auditor's report

24.78 A person to whom this section applies commits an offence if he knowingly or recklessly causes a report under CA 2006, s 495 (auditor's report on company's annual accounts) to include any matter that is misleading, false or deceptive in a material particular: CA 2006, s 507(1).

A person to whom s 507 applies commits an offence if he knowingly or recklessly causes such a report to omit a statement required by:

(a) s 498(2)(b) (statement that company's accounts do not agree with accounting records and returns);

(b) s 498(3) (statement that necessary information and explanations not obtained); or

(c) s 498(5) (statement that directors wrongly took advantage of exemption from obligation to prepare group accounts): CA 2006, s 507(2).

24.79 Section 507 applies to:

(a) where the auditor is an individual, that individual and any employee or agent of his who is eligible for appointment as auditor of the company;

(b) where the auditor is a firm, any director, member, employee or agent of the firm who is eligible for appointment as auditor of the company: CA 2006, s 507(3).

24.80 A person guilty of an offence under s 507 will be liable:

(a) on conviction on indictment, to a fine;

(b) on summary conviction, to a fine not exceeding the statutory maximum: CA 2006, s 507(4).

Guidance for regulatory and prosecuting authorities: England, Wales and Northern Ireland

24.81 The Secretary of State may issue guidance for the purpose of helping relevant regulatory and prosecuting authorities to determine how they should carry out their functions in cases where behaviour occurs that:

(a) appears to involve the commission of an offence under s 507 (offences in connection with auditor's report); and

(b) has been, is being or may be investigated pursuant to arrangements:

   (i) under para 15 of Sch 10 (investigation of complaints against auditors and supervisory bodies); or

   (ii) of a kind mentioned in para 24 of that Schedule (independent investigation for disciplinary purposes of public interest cases): CA 2006, s 508(1).

The Secretary of State must obtain the consent of the Attorney General before issuing any such guidance: CA 2006, s 508(2).

24.82 In s 508, 'relevant regulatory and prosecuting authorities' means:

(a) supervisory bodies within the meaning of Pt 42 of the Act;

(b) bodies to which the Secretary of State may make grants under s 16(1) of the Companies (Audit, Investigations and Community Enterprise) Act 2004 (c 27) (bodies concerned with accounting standards etc);

(c) the Director of the Serious Fraud Office;

(d) the Director of Public Prosecutions or the Director of Public Prosecutions for Northern Ireland; and

(e) the Secretary of State.

Section 508 does not apply to Scotland.

Guidance for regulatory authorities: Scotland

24.83 The Lord Advocate may issue guidance for the purpose of helping relevant regulatory authorities to determine how they should carry out their functions in cases where behaviour occurs that:

(a) appears to involve the commission of an offence under s 507 (offences in connection with auditor's report); and

(b) has been, is being or may be investigated pursuant to arrangements:

  (i) under para 15 of Sch 10 (investigation of complaints against auditors and supervisory bodies); or

  (ii) of a kind mentioned in para 24 of that Schedule (independent investigation for disciplinary purposes of public interest cases): CA 2006, s 509(1).

The Lord Advocate must consult the Secretary of State before issuing any such guidance: CA 2006, s 509(2).

24.84 Under s 509, 'relevant regulatory authorities' means:

(a) supervisory bodies within the meaning of CA 2006, Pt 42;

(b) bodies to which the Secretary of State may make grants under s 16(1) of the Companies (Audit, Investigations and Community Enterprise) Act 2004 (c 27) (bodies concerned with accounting standards etc); and

(c) the Secretary of State: CA 2006, s 509(3).

Section 509 applies only to Scotland: CA 2006, s 509(4).

Removal and resignation of auditors

Resolution removing auditor from office

24.85 The members of a company may remove an auditor from office at any time: CA 2006, s 510(1).

This power is exercisable only:

(a) by ordinary resolution at a meeting; and

(b) in accordance with s 511 (special notice of resolution to remove auditor): CA 2006, s 510(2).

24.86 Nothing in s 510 is to be taken as depriving the person removed of compensation or damages payable to him in respect of the termination:

(a) of his appointment as auditor; or

(b) of any appointment terminating with that as auditor: CA 2006, s 510(3).

An auditor may not be removed from office before the expiration of his term of office except by resolution under s 510: CA 2006, s 510(4).

The removal of an auditor on improper grounds may constitute unfair prejudicial conduct on the part of some of the company's shareholders

In *Re Sunrise Radio Limited v Kohli* [2010] 1 BCLC 367, Judge Purle QC stated:

> 'Thus, there can (and, in the case specified in s 994(1A), must) be a finding of unfair prejudice even though the effect of the conduct complained of has no necessary impact on the value of the complaining shareholders' investment. Moreover, a board acting in good faith may genuinely, and correctly, disagree with (say) the accounting treatments, but removal of the auditor on those grounds will be unfairly prejudicial, reflecting the importance the law attaches to absolute standards of behaviour in the accounting process.'

Special notice required for resolution removing auditor from office

24.87 Special notice is required for a resolution at a general meeting of a company removing an auditor from office: CA 2006, s 511(1).

On receipt of notice of such an intended resolution the company must immediately send a copy of it to the auditor proposed to be removed: CA 2006, s 511(2).

The auditor proposed to be removed may, with respect to the intended resolution, make representations in writing to the company (not exceeding a reasonable length) and request their notification to members of the company: CA 2006, s 511(3).

The company must (unless the representations are received by it too late for it to do so):

(a) in any notice of the resolution given to members of the company, state the fact of the representations having been made; and

(b) send a copy of the representations to every member of the company to whom notice of the meeting is or has been sent: CA 2006, s 511(4).

24.88 If a copy of any such representations is not sent out as required because received too late or because of the company's default, the auditor may (without prejudice to his right to be heard orally) require that the representations be read out at the meeting: CA 2006, s 511(5).

Copies of the representations need not be sent out and the representations need not be read at the meeting if, on the application either of the company or of any other person claiming to be aggrieved, the court is satisfied that the auditor is using the provisions of s 511 to secure needless publicity for defamatory matter.

The court may order the company's costs (in Scotland, expenses) on the application to be paid in whole or in part by the auditor, notwithstanding that he is not a party to the application: CA 2006, s 511(6).

Rights of auditor who has been removed from office

24.89 An auditor who has been removed by resolution under s 510 has, notwithstanding his removal, the rights conferred by s 502(2) in relation to any general meeting of the company:

(a) at which his term of office would otherwise have expired; or

(b) at which it is proposed to fill the vacancy caused by his removal: CA 2006, s 513(1).

In such a case the references in that section to matters concerning the auditor as auditor shall be construed as references to matters concerning him as a former auditor: CA 2006, s 513(2).

Failure to re-appoint auditor: special procedure required for written resolution

24.90 The CA 2006, s 514 applies where a resolution is proposed as a written resolution of a private company whose effect would be to appoint a person as auditor in place of a person (the 'outgoing auditor') who, at the time the resolution is proposed, is an auditor of the company and who is to cease to hold office at the end of a period for appointing auditors.

But this section does not apply if the auditor is to cease to hold office by virtue of ss 510 or 516: CA 2006, s 514(1) (as inserted by DA 2015, Sch 5, Pt 2).

This section also applies where a resolution is proposed as a written resolution of a private company whose effect would be to appoint a person as auditor where, at the time the resolution is proposed, the company does not have an auditor and the person proposed to be appointed is not a person (the 'outgoing auditor') who was an auditor of the company when the company last had an auditor.

But this is subject to sub-s (2A): CA 2006, s 514(2) (as inserted by DA 2015, Sch 5, Pt 2).

24.91 This section does not apply (by virtue of s 514(2)) if:

(a) a period for appointing auditors has ended since the outgoing auditor ceased to hold office;

(b) the outgoing auditor ceased to hold office by virtue of ss 510 or 516, or

(c) the outgoing auditor has previously had the opportunity to make representations with respect to a proposed resolution under sub-s (4) of this section or an intended resolution under s 515(4): CA 2006, s 514(2A) (as inserted by DA 2015, Sch 5, Pt 2).

Where this section applies, the company must send a copy of the proposed resolution to the person proposed to be appointed and to the outgoing auditor: CA 2006, s 514(3) (as inserted by DA 2015, Sch 5, Pt 2).

24.92 The outgoing auditor may, within 14 days after receiving the notice, make with respect to the proposed resolution representations in writing to the company (not exceeding a reasonable length) and request their circulation to members of the company: CA 2006, s 514(4).

The company must circulate the representations together with the copy or copies of the resolution circulated in accordance with CA 2006, s 291 (resolution proposed by directors) or s 293 (resolution proposed by members): CA 2006, s 514(5).

24.93 Where s 514(5) applies:

(a) the period allowed under s 293(3) for service of copies of the proposed resolution is 28 days instead of 21 days; and

(b) the provisions of s 293(5) and (6) (offences) apply in relation to a failure to comply with that subsection as in relation to a default in complying with that section: CA 2006, s 514(6).

Copies of the representations need not be circulated if, on the application either of the company or of any other person claiming to be aggrieved, the court is satisfied that the auditor is using the provisions of s 514 to secure needless publicity for defamatory matter.

The court may order the company's costs (in Scotland, expenses) on the application to be paid in whole or in part by the auditor, notwithstanding that he is not a party to the application: CA 2006, s 514(7).

If any requirement of s 514 is not complied with, the resolution is ineffective: CA 2006, s 514(8).

Failure to re-appoint auditor: special notice required for resolution at general meeting

24.94 Special notice is required for a resolution at a general meeting of a private company whose effect would be to appoint a person as auditor in place of a person (the 'outgoing auditor') who, at the time the notice is given, is an auditor of the company and who is to cease to hold office at the end of a period for appointing auditors.

But special notice is not required under this subsection if the auditor is to cease to hold office by virtue of ss 510 or 516: CA 2006, s 515(1) (as inserted by DA 2015, Sch 5, Pt 2).

24.95 Special notice is required for a resolution at a general meeting of a public company whose effect would be to appoint a person as auditor in place of a person (the 'outgoing auditor') who, at the time the notice is given, is an auditor of the company and who is to cease to hold office at the end of an accounts meeting.

But special notice is not required under this subsection if the auditor is to cease to hold office by virtue of ss 510 or 516: CA 2006, s 515(1A) (as inserted by DA 2015, Sch 5, Pt 2).

24.96 Special notice is required for a resolution at a general meeting of a company whose effect would be to appoint a person as auditor where, at the time the notice is given, the company does not have an auditor and the person proposed to be appointed is not a person (the 'outgoing auditor') who was an auditor of the company when the company last had an auditor.

But this is subject to sub-s (2A): CA 2006, s 515(2) (as inserted by DA 2015, Sch 5, Pt 2).

24.97 Special notice is not required under s 515(2) if:

(a) a period for appointing auditors has ended or (as the case may be) an accounts meeting of the company has been held since the outgoing auditor ceased to hold office;

(b) the outgoing auditor ceased to hold office by virtue of s 510 or 516; or

(c) the outgoing auditor has previously had the opportunity to make representations with respect to an intended resolution under sub-s (4) of this section or a proposed resolution under s 514(4): CA 2006, s 515(2A) (as inserted by DA 2015, Sch 5, Pt 2).

24.98 On receipt of notice of an intended resolution mentioned in sub-s (1), (1A) or (2), the company shall forthwith send a copy of it to the person proposed to be appointed and to the outgoing auditor: CA 2006, s 515(3) (as inserted by DA 2015, Sch 5, Pt 2).

The outgoing auditor may make with respect to the intended resolution representations in writing to the company (not exceeding a reasonable length) and request their notification to members of the company: CA 2006, s 515(4).

24.99 The company must (unless the representations are received by it too late for it to do so):

(a) in any notice of the resolution given to members of the company, state the fact of the representations having been made; and

(b) send a copy of the representations to every member of the company to whom notice of the meeting is or has been sent: CA 2006, s 515(5).

If a copy of any such representations is not sent out as required because received too late or because of the company's default, the outgoing auditor may (without prejudice to his right to be heard orally) require that the representations be read out at the meeting: CA 2006, s 515(6).

Copies of the representations need not be sent out and the representations need not be read at the meeting if, on the application either of the company or of any other person claiming to be aggrieved, the court is satisfied that the auditor is using the provisions of s 515 to secure needless publicity for defamatory matter.

The court may order the company's costs (in Scotland, expenses) on the application to be paid in whole or in part by the outgoing auditor, notwithstanding that he is not a party to the application: CA 2006, s 515(7).

Resignation of auditor

24.100 An auditor of a company may resign office by sending a notice to that effect to the company: CA 2006, s 516(1) (as inserted by DA 2015, Sch 5, Pt 2). Where the company is a public interest company, the notice is not effective unless it is accompanied by the statement required by s 519: CA 2006, s 516(2) (as inserted by DA 2015, Sch 5, Pt 1).

An effective notice of resignation operates to bring the auditor's term of office to an end as of the date on which the notice is received or on such later date as may be specified in it: CA 2006, s 516(3).

Rights of resigning auditor

24.101 Section 518 of the CA 2006 applies where an auditor's (A's) notice of resignation is accompanied by a statement under s 519 except where:

(a) the company is a non-public interest company; and

(b) the statement includes a statement to the effect that A considers that none of the reasons for A's ceasing to hold office, and no matters (if any) connected with A's ceasing to hold office, need to be brought to the attention of members or creditors of the company (as required by s 519(3B)): CA 2006, s 518(1) (as inserted by DA 2015, Sch 5, Pt 1).

A may send with the notice an authenticated requisition calling on the directors of the company forthwith duly to convene a general meeting of the company for the purpose of receiving and considering such explanation of the reasons for, and matters connected with A's resignation as A may wish to place before the meeting: CA 2006, s 518(2) (as inserted by DA 2015, Sch 5, Pts 1 and 2).

24.102 A may request the company to circulate to its members:

(a) before the meeting convened on A's requisition; or

(b) before any general meeting at which A's term of office would otherwise have expired or at which it is proposed to fill the vacancy caused by A's resignation,

a statement in writing (not exceeding a reasonable length) of the reasons for, and matters connected with A's resignation: CA 2006, s 518(3) (as inserted by DA 2015, Sch 5, Pt 1).

24.103 The company must (unless the statement is received too late for it to comply):

(a) in any notice of the meeting given to members of the company, state the fact of the statement having been made; and

(b) send a copy of the statement to every member of the company to whom notice of the meeting is or has been sent: CA 2006, s 518(4).

The directors must within 21 days from the date on which the company receives a requisition under s 518 proceed duly to convene a meeting for a day not more than 28 days after the date on which the notice convening the meeting is given: CA 2006, s 518(5) (as inserted by DA 2015, Sch 5, Pt 2).

24.104 If default is made in complying with sub-s (5), every director who failed to take all reasonable steps to secure that a meeting was convened commits an offence: CA 2006, s 518(6).

A person guilty of an offence under s 518 will be liable:

(a) on conviction on indictment, to a fine;

(b) on summary conviction to a fine not exceeding the statutory maximum: CA 2006, s 518(7).

24.105 If a copy of the statement mentioned above is not sent out as required because received too late or because of the company's default, the auditor may (without prejudice to his right to be heard orally) require that the statement be read out at the meeting: CA 2006, s 518(8).

Copies of a statement need not be sent out and the statement need not be read out at the meeting if, on the application either of the company or of any other person who claims to be aggrieved, the court is satisfied that the auditor is using the provisions of s 518 to secure needless publicity for defamatory matter.

The court may order the company's costs (in Scotland, expenses) on such an application to be paid in whole or in part by the auditor, notwithstanding that he is not a party to the application: CA 2006, s 518(9).

An auditor who has resigned has, notwithstanding his resignation, the rights conferred by s 502(2) in relation to any such general meeting of the company as is mentioned in sub-ss 518(3)(a) or (b).

In such a case the references in s 518 to matters concerning the auditor as auditor shall be construed as references to matters concerning him as a former auditor: CA 2006, s 518(10).

Statement by auditor to be sent to company

24.106 An auditor of a public interest company who is ceasing to hold office (at any time and for any reason) must send to the company a statement of the reasons for doing so: CA 2006, s 519(1) (as inserted by DA 2015, s 18(2)).

An auditor ('A') of a non-public interest company who is ceasing to hold office must send to the company a statement of the reasons for doing so unless A satisfies the first or second condition: CA 2006, s 519(2) (as inserted by DA 2015, s 18(2)).

The first condition is that A is ceasing to hold office:

(a) in the case of a private company, at the end of a period for appointing auditors;

(b) in the case of a public company, at the end of an accounts meeting: CA 2006, s 519(2A) (as inserted by DA 2015, s 18(2)).

The second condition is that:

(a) A's reasons for ceasing to hold office are all exempt reasons (as to which see s 519A(3)); and

(b) there are no matters connected with A's ceasing to hold office that A considers need to be brought to the attention of members or creditors of the company: CA 2006, s 519(2B) (as inserted by DA 2015, s 18(2)).

24.107 A statement under this section must include:

(a) the auditor's name and address;

(b) the number allocated to the auditor on being entered in the register of auditors kept under s 1239;

(c) the company's name and registered number: CA 2006, s 519(3) (as inserted by DA 2015, s 18(2)).

Where there are matters connected with an auditor's ceasing to hold office that the auditor considers need to be brought to the attention of members or creditors of the company, the statement under this section must include details of those matters: CA 2006, s 519(3A) (as inserted by DA 2015, s 18(2)).

24.108 Where:

(a) an auditor ('A') of a non-public interest company is required by sub-s (2) to send a statement; and

(b) A considers that none of the reasons for A's ceasing to hold office, and no matters (if any) connected with A's ceasing to hold office, need to be brought to the attention of members or creditors of the company,

A's statement under this section must include a statement to that effect: CA 2006, s 519(3B) (as inserted by DA 2015, s 18(2)).

24.109 A statement under s 519 must be sent:

(a) in the case of resignation, along with the notice of resignation;

(b) in the case of failure to seek re-appointment, not less than 14 days before the end of the time allowed for next appointing an auditor;

(c) in any other case, not later than the end of the period of 14 days beginning with the date on which he ceases to hold office: CA 2006, s 519(4) (as inserted by DA 2015, Sch 5, Pts 1 and 2).

A person ceasing to hold office as auditor who fails to comply with s 519 commits an offence: CA 2006, s 519(5).

24.110 In proceedings for such an offence it is a defence for the person charged to show that he took all reasonable steps and exercised all due diligence to avoid the commission of the offence: CA 2006,s 519(6).

A person guilty of an offence under s 519 will be liable:

(a) on conviction on indictment, to a fine;

(b) on summary conviction, to a fine not exceeding the statutory maximum: CA 2006, s 519(7).

24.111 Where an offence under this section is committed by a body corporate, every officer of the body who is in default also commits the offence. For this purpose:

(a) any person who purports to act as director, manager or secretary of the body is treated as an officer of the body; and

(b) if the body is a company, any shadow director is treated as an officer of the company: CA 2006, s 519(8).

Meaning of 'public interest company', 'non-public interest company' and 'exempt reasons'

24.112 In this Chapter 4 of the CA 2006, Pt 16 the following terms apply:

'public interest company' means a company:

(a) any of whose transferable securities are included in the official list (within the meaning of Pt 6 of the Financial Services and Markets Act 2000); or

(b) any of whose equity share capital is officially listed in an EEA state;

'non-public interest company' means a company that is not a public interest company: CA 2006, s 519A(1) (as inserted by DA 2015, s 18(3)).

For the purposes of the definition of 'public interest company', 'transferable securities' means anything which is a transferable security for the purposes of Directive 2004/39/EC of the European Parliament and of the Council on markets in financial instruments: CA 2006, s 519A(2) (as inserted by DA 2015, s 18(3)).

24.113 In the application of this Chapter to an auditor ('A') of a company ceasing to hold office, the following are 'exempt reasons':

(a) A is no longer to carry out statutory audit work within the meaning of Pt 42 (see s 1210(1));

(b) the company is, or is to become, exempt from audit under ss 477, 479A or 480, or from the requirements of this Part under s 482, and intends to include in its balance sheet a statement of the type described in s 475(2);

(c) the company is a subsidiary undertaking of a parent undertaking that is incorporated in the United Kingdom and:

(i) the parent undertaking prepares group accounts; and

(ii) A is being replaced as auditor of the company by the auditor who is conducting, or is to conduct, an audit of the group accounts;

(d) the company is being wound up under Pt 4 of the Insolvency Act 1986 or Pt 5 of the Insolvency (Northern Ireland) Order 1989 (SI 1989/2405 (NI 19)), whether voluntarily or by the court, or a petition under Pt 4 of that Act or Pt 5 of that Order for the winding up of the company has been presented and not finally dealt with or withdrawn: CA 2006, s 519A(3) (as inserted by DA 2015, s 18(3)).

But the reason described in sub-s (3)(c) is only an exempt reason if the auditor who is conducting, or is to conduct, an audit of the group accounts is also conducting, or is also to conduct, the audit (if any) of the accounts of each of the subsidiary undertakings (of the parent undertaking) that is incorporated in the United Kingdom and included in the consolidation: CA 2006, s 519A(4) (as inserted by DA 2015, s 18(3)).

The Secretary of State may by order amend the definition of 'public interest company' in sub-s (1): CA 2006, s 519A(5) (as inserted by DA 2015, s 18(3)).

Company's duties in relation to statement

24.114 Section 520 of CA 2006 applies where a company receives from an auditor ('A') who is ceasing to hold office a statement under s 519 except where:

(a) the company is a non-public interest company; and

(b) the statement includes a statement to the effect that A considers that none of the reasons for A's ceasing to hold office, and no matters (if any) connected with A's ceasing to hold office, need to be brought to the attention of members or creditors of the company (as required by s 519(3B)): CA 2006, s 520(1) (as inserted by DA 2015, Sch 5, Pt 1).

24.115 Where this section applies, the company must within 14 days of the receipt of the statement either:

(a) send a copy of it to every person who under s 423 is entitled to be sent copies of the accounts; or

(b) apply to the court: CA 2006, s 520(2) (as inserted by DA 2015, Sch 5, Pt 2).

If it applies to the court, the company must notify the auditor of the application: CA 2006, s 520(3).

24.116 If the court is satisfied that the auditor is using the provisions of s 519 to secure needless publicity for defamatory matter:

(a) it shall direct that copies of the statement need not be sent out; and

(b) it may further order the company's costs (in Scotland, expenses) on the application to be paid in whole or in part by the auditor, even if he is not a party to the application.

The company must within 14 days of the court's decision send to the persons mentioned in sub-s (2)(a) a statement setting out the effect of the order: CA 2006, s 520(4).

If no such direction is made the company must send copies of the statement to the persons mentioned in sub-s (2)(a) within 14 days of the court's decision or, as the case may be, of the discontinuance of the proceedings: CA 2006, s 520(5).

24.117 In the event of default in complying with s 520 an offence is committed by every officer of the company who is in default: CA 2006, s 520(6).

In proceedings for such an offence it is a defence for the person charged to show that he took all reasonable steps and exercised all due diligence to avoid the commission of the offence: CA 2006, s 520(7).

A person guilty of an offence under s 520 will be liable:

(a) on conviction on indictment, to a fine;

(b) on summary conviction, to a fine not exceeding the statutory maximum: CA 2006, s 520(8).

Special considerations applied to proceedings under CA 2006, s 520(3) in respect of auditors

In *Jarvis plc v PricewaterhouseCoopers* [2000] 2 BCLC 368, the auditors had provided audit work for Jarvis and dispute arose between the parties on audit fees and additional work required. The auditors resigned and made a statement of the circumstances connected with their ceasing to hold office. Jarvis brought proceedings alleging use by the auditors of statement to secure needless publicity for defamatory matter.

The court held that CA 2006, s 520 anticipated that, whatever the outcome of proceedings under s 520(3), there would be a decision of the court. If the court upheld the charge of impropriety against the auditor there plainly had to be a court order in the terms set out in s 520(6)(a). There did not have to be any positive decision of the court that it was 'not satisfied' under s 520(7). All that s 520(7) contemplated was that the proceedings were brought to an end without the court being 'so satisfied'. It was sufficient that the proceedings were brought to an end by final judgment, striking out or discontinuance.

Three special considerations applied to proceedings under s 520(3): first, the auditor (unless the court held otherwise) acted for the benefit of the members and creditors and should not be out of pocket if the company increased the costs of the discharge of his duty by commencing proceedings under the section which failed. Secondly the company in proceedings under s 520 had to allege that the auditor acted in bad faith. When such an allegation was made and not substantiated, the court had long shown itself ready to respond by ordering payment of costs on an indemnity basis. Thirdly, the opportunity afforded by s 520(3) to companies to delay the dissemination of statements by commencing proceedings was susceptible of abuse by the unscrupulous. In this case Jarvis made serious allegations against PwC which had to be withdrawn and PwC acted with total propriety. The proceedings were bound to fail and Jarvis would be ordered to pay the costs of PwC on an indemnity basis. It was unnecessary to decide whether Jarvis acted in good faith.

Lightman J stated:

> 'Section [519 CA 2006] imposes upon auditors an important duty, in the public interest and in the interest of the persons interested and indirectly of creditors and the investing public, to make a statement. Indeed it is a duty of such importance that a failure to comply constitutes

> a criminal offence. The auditor is the judge of whether there are relevant circumstances: he must exercise his judgment and, uninfluenced by any collateral considerations, make up his own mind and state whether he considers that there are circumstances which ought to be brought to the attention of the persons interested to whom for this purpose he must owe a duty of care. He is uniquely placed to judge. The requirement is not designed to protect the auditors or give the auditors an opportunity to say something which protects their goodwill or reputation when they cease to be the auditors, and the court will presume that the auditors who make a statement under s [519(1)] are acting in faithful discharge of their duty and not in pursuit of any private or collateral interest, unless the contrary is shown.'

Copy of statement to be sent to registrar

24.118 The CA 2006, s 521(A1) applies where an auditor ('A') of a company sends a statement to the company under s 519 except where:

(a) the company is a non-public interest company; and

(b) the statement includes a statement to the effect that A considers that none of the reasons for A's ceasing to hold office, and no matters (if any) connected with A's ceasing to hold office, need to be brought to the attention of members or creditors of the company (as required by s 519(3B)): CA 2006, s 521(A1) (as inserted by DA 2015, Sch 5, Pt 1).

Where the section applies, unless within 21 days beginning with the day on which he sent the statement under s 519 the auditor receives notice of an application to the court under s 520, he must within a further seven days send a copy of the statement to the registrar: CA 2006, s 521(1) (as inserted by DA 2015, Sch 5, Pts 1 and 2).

If an application to the court is made under s 520 and the auditor subsequently receives notice under sub-s (5) of that section, he must within seven days of receiving the notice send a copy of the statement to the registrar: CA 2006, s 521(2).

An auditor who fails to comply with sub-ss (1) or (2) commits an offence: CA 2006, s 521(3).

In proceedings for such an offence it is a defence for the person charged to show that he took all reasonable steps and exercised all due diligence to avoid the commission of the offence: CA 2006, s 521(4).

24.119 A person guilty of an offence under this section will be liable:

(a) on conviction on indictment, to a fine;

(b) on summary conviction, to a fine not exceeding the statutory maximum: CA 2006, s 521(5).

24.120 Where an offence under s 521 is committed by a body corporate, every officer of the body who is in default also commits the offence. For this purpose:

(a) any person who purports to act as director, manager or secretary of the body is treated as an officer of the body; and

(b) if the body is a company, any shadow director is treated as an officer of the company: CA 2006, s 521(6).

Duty of auditor to send statement to appropriate audit authority

24.121 Where an auditor of a company sends a statement under s 519, the auditor must at the same time send a copy of the statement to the appropriate audit authority: CA 2006, s 522(1) (as inserted by DA 2015, Sch 5, Pt 1).

A person ceasing to hold office as auditor who fails to comply with this section commits an offence: CA 2006, s 522(5).

If that person is a firm an offence is committed by:

(a) the firm; and

(b) every officer of the firm who is in default: CA 2006, s 522(6).

In proceedings for an offence under s 522 it is a defence for the person charged to show that he took all reasonable steps and exercised all due diligence to avoid the commission of the offence: CA 2006, s 522(7).

24.122 A person guilty of an offence under s 522 will be liable:

(a) on conviction on indictment, to a fine;

(b) on summary conviction, to a fine not exceeding the statutory maximum: CA 2006, s 522(8).

Duty of company to notify appropriate audit authority

24.123 The CA 2006, s 523 applies if an auditor is ceasing to hold office:

(a) in the case of a private company, at any time other than at the end of a period for appointing auditors;

(b) in the case of a public company, at any time other than at the end of an accounts meeting: CA 2006, s 523(1) (as inserted by DA 2015, s 18(4)).

But this section does not apply if the company reasonably believes that the only reasons for the auditor's ceasing to hold office are exempt reasons (as to which see s 519A(3)): CA 2006, s 523(1A) (as inserted by DA 2015, s 18(4)).

24.124 Where this section applies, the company must give notice to the appropriate audit authority that the auditor is ceasing to hold office: CA 2006, s 523(2) (as inserted by DA 2015, s 18(4)).

The notice is to take the form of a statement by the company of what the company believes to be the reasons for the auditor's ceasing to hold office and must include the information listed in s 519(3).

This is subject to sub-s (2C): CA 2006, s 523(2A) (as inserted by DA 2015, s 18(4)).

Subsection (2C) applies where:

(a) the company receives a statement from the auditor under s 519;

(b) the statement is sent at the time required by s 519(4); and

(c) the company agrees with the contents of the statement: CA 2006, s 523(2B) (as inserted by DA 2015, s 18(4)).

Where this subsection applies, the notice may instead take the form of a copy of the statement endorsed by the company to the effect that it agrees with the contents of the statement: CA 2006, s 523(2C) (as inserted by DA 2015, s 18(4)).

24.125 A notice under this section must be given within the period of 28 days beginning with the day on which the auditor ceases to hold office: CA 2006, s 523(3) (as inserted by DA 2015, s 18(4)).

The DA 2015, Sch 5 (auditors ceasing to hold office) makes provision about the following matters:

(a) the notification requirements that apply on an auditor ceasing to hold office;

(b) the requirements that apply if there is a failure to re-appoint an auditor;

(c) the replacement of references to documents being deposited at a company's registered office: CA 2006, DA 2015, s18(5).

24.126 If a company fails to comply with this section, an offence will be committed by:

(a) the company; and

(b) every officer of the company who is in default: CA 2006, s 523(4).

In proceedings for such an offence it is a defence for the person charged to show that he took all reasonable steps and exercised all due diligence to avoid the commission of the offence: CA 2006, s 523(5).

24.127 A person guilty of an offence under this section will be liable:

(a) on conviction on indictment, to a fine;

(b) on summary conviction, to a fine not exceeding the statutory maximum: CA 2006, s 523(6).

Provision of information to accounting authorities

24.128 Where the appropriate audit authority receives a statement under s 522 or a notice under s 523, the authority may forward to the accounting authorities:

(a) a copy of the statement or notice; and

(b) any other information the authority has received from the auditor or the company concerned in connection with the auditor's ceasing to hold office: CA 2006, s 524(1) (as inserted by DA 2015, Sch 5, Pt 1).

24.129 The accounting authorities are:

(a) the Secretary of State; and

(b) any person authorised by the Secretary of State for the purposes of CA 2006, s 456 (revision of defective accounts: persons authorised to apply to court): CA 2006, s 524(2).

If the court has made an order under s 520(4) directing that copies of the statement need not be sent out by the company, ss 460 and 461 (restriction on further disclosure) apply in relation to the copies sent to the accounting authorities as they apply to information obtained under s 459 (power to require documents etc): CA 2006, s 524(4).

Meaning of 'appropriate audit authority'

24.130 In CA 2006, ss 522, 523 and 524 'appropriate audit authority' means:

(a) in relation to an auditor of a public interest company (other than one conducted by an Auditor General), the Financial Reporting Council Limited;

(b) in relation to an auditor of a non-public interest company (other than an Auditor General), the relevant supervisory body;

(c) in relation to an Auditor General, the Independent Supervisor.

'Supervisory body' and 'Independent Supervisor' have the same meaning as in Pt 42 (statutory auditors) (see CA 2006, ss 1217 and 1228): CA 2006, s 525(1) (as inserted by DA 2015, Sch 5, Pt 1).

Effect of casual vacancies

24.131 If an auditor ceases to hold office for any reason, any surviving or continuing auditor or auditors may continue to act: CA 2006, s 526.

Quoted companies: rights of members to raise audit concerns at accounts meeting

Members' power to require website publications of audit concerns

24.132 The members of a quoted company may require the company to publish on a website a statement setting out any matter relating to:

(a) the audit of the company's accounts (including the auditor's report and the conduct of the audit) that are to be laid before the next accounts meeting; or

(b) any circumstances connected with an auditor of the company ceasing to hold office since the previous accounts meeting,

that the members propose to raise at the next accounts meeting of the company: CA 2006, s 527(1).

24.133 A company is required to do so once it has received requests to that effect from:

(a) members representing at least 5% of the total voting rights of all the members who have a relevant right to vote (excluding any voting rights attached to any shares in the company held as treasury shares); or

(b) at least 100 members who have a relevant right to vote and hold shares in the company on which there has been paid up an average sum, per member, of at least £100.

See also s 153 (exercise of rights where shares held on behalf of others): CA 2006, s 527(2).

In s 527(2) of CA 2006, a 'relevant right to vote' means a right to vote at the accounts meeting: CA 2006, s 527(3).

24.134 A request:

(a) may be sent to the company in hard copy or electronic form;

(b) must identify the statement to which it relates;

(c) must be authenticated by the person or persons making it; and

(d) must be received by the company at least one week before the meeting to which it relates: CA 2006, s 527(4).

24.135 A quoted company is not required to place on a website a statement under s 527 if, on an application by the company or another person who claims to be aggrieved, the court is satisfied that the rights conferred by the section are being abused: CA 2006, s 527(5).

The court may order the members requesting website publication to pay the whole or part of the company's costs (in Scotland, expenses) on such an application, even if they are not parties to the application: CA 2006, s 527(6).

Requirements as to website availability

24.136 The following provisions apply for the purposes of s 527 (website publication of members' statement of audit concerns): CA 2006, s 528(1).

The information must be made available on a website that:

(a) is maintained by or on behalf of the company; and

(b) identifies the company in question: CA 2006, s 528(2).

Access to the information on the website, and the ability to obtain a hard copy of the information from the website, must not be conditional on the payment of a fee or otherwise restricted: CA 2006, s 528(3).

24.137 The statement:

(a) must be made available within three working days of the company being required to publish it on a website; and

(b) must be kept available until after the meeting to which it relates: CA 2006, s 528(4).

24.138 A failure to make information available on a website throughout the period specified in sub-s (4)(b) is disregarded if:

(a) the information is made available on the website for part of that period; and

(b) the failure is wholly attributable to circumstances that it would not be reasonable to have expected the company to prevent or avoid: CA 2006, s 528(5).

Website publication: company's supplementary duties

24.139 A quoted company must in the notice it gives of the accounts meeting draw attention to:

(a) the possibility of a statement being placed on a website in pursuance of members' requests under CA 2006, s 527; and

(b) the effect of the following provisions of this section: CA 2006, s 529(1).

A company may not require the members requesting website publication to pay its expenses in complying with that section or s 528 of the CA 2006 (requirements in connection with website publication): CA 2006, s 529(2).

24.140 Where a company is required to place a statement on a website under s 527 it must forward the statement to the company's auditor not later than the time when it makes the statement available on the website: CA 2006, s 528(3).

The business which may be dealt with at the accounts meeting includes any statement that the company has been required under CA 2006, s 527 to publish on a website: CA 2006, s 528(4).

Website publication: offences

24.141 In the event of default in complying with:

(a) CA 2006, s 528 (requirements as to website publication); or

(b) CA 2006, s 529 (companies' supplementary duties in relation to request for website publication),

an offence is committed by every officer of the company who is in default: CA 2006, s 530(1).

24.142 A person guilty of an offence under s 530 will be liable:

(a) on conviction on indictment, to a fine;

(b) on summary conviction, to a fine not exceeding the statutory maximum: CA 2006, s 530(2).

Meaning of 'quoted company'

24.143 For the purposes of CA 2006, Pt 16, Ch 5 a company is a quoted company if it is a quoted company in accordance with CA 2006, s 385 (quoted and unquoted companies for the purposes of Pt 15) in relation to the financial year to which the accounts to be laid at the next accounts meeting relate: CA 2006, s 531(1).

The provisions of s 531(4)–(6) CA 2006 (power to amend definition by regulations) apply in relation to the provisions of Ch 5 as in relation to the provisions of that Part: CA 2006, s 531(2).

Auditors' liability

24.144 Like other professionals, auditors owe a duty of care in the performance of their work. There are various types of claims that may arise against auditors:

A contractual claim – in this case, the client alleges a breach of contractual duty by the auditor in the scope of work or services performed (eg failure to complete the deliverables within a fixed time period).

A tortious claim – here the client may allege negligence, misleading, inaccurate or gross negligence in the performance of services by the auditor which has caused loss to the client. In this situation, the client may be able to sue the auditors for damages.

A tortious claim by a third party against auditors – in this case there is no direct relationship between the third party and the auditors, but the third party's alleged reliance placed on the audited accounts prepared by the auditors, with a claim for damages. The claim can arise on the basis of an 'assumption of responsibility' in giving advice to the third party for example, or meeting the tests set out in *Caparo Industries plc v Dickman* [1990] 1 All ER 568 of foreseeability, proximity and fairness. However, there is no one single test in determining the liability of auditors. In *Customs and Excise Commissioners v Barclays Bank* [2006] 4 All ER 256, Lord Bingham stated that the emphasis should be on 'the detailed circumstances of the particular case and the particular relationship between the parties in the context of their legal and factual situation as a whole'. See too, *Standard Chartered Bank v Ceylon Petroleum* [2011] EWCH 1785.

24.145 There has been much case law illustrating the standard of care required by an auditor in the performance of an audit.

An auditor must perform his duties with skill, care and caution

In *Re Kingston Cotton Mill Co (No 2)* [1896] 2 Ch 279, Lopes LJ stated:

> 'It is the duty of an auditor to bring to bear on the work he has to perform that skill, care, and caution which a reasonably competent, careful, and cautious auditor would use. What is reasonable skill, care, and caution must depend on the particular circumstances of each case. An auditor is not bound to be a detective, or, as was said, to approach his work with suspicion or with a foregone conclusion that there is

> something wrong. He is a watch-dog, but not a bloodhound. He is justified in believing tried servants of the company in whom confidence is placed by the company. He is entitled to assume that they are honest, and to rely upon their representations, provided he takes reasonable care. If there is anything calculated to excite suspicion he should probe it to the bottom; but in the absence of anything of that kind he is only bound to be reasonably cautious and careful.'

An auditor must ensure that errors are not made in the course of providing services

In *Fomento (Sterling Area) Ltd v Selsdon Fountain Pen Co* Ltd [1958] 1 All ER 11, Lord Denning was of the view that:

> 'An auditor is not to be confined to the mechanics of checking vouchers and making arithmetical computations. He is not to be written off as a professional "adder-upper and subtractor". His vital task is to take care to see that errors are not made, be they errors of computation, or errors of omission or commission, or downright untruths. To perform this task properly, he must come to it with an inquiring mind – not suspicious of dishonesty, I agree – but suspecting that someone may have made a mistake somewhere and that a check must be made to ensure that there has been none.'

An auditor's task is to conduct the audit as to make it probable that material misstatements in financial documents will be detected

In *Barings plc v Coopers and Lybrand* [1997] 1 BCLC 427, Leggatt LJ stated:

> 'The primary responsibility for safeguarding a company's assets and preventing errors and defalcations rests with the directors. But material irregularities, and a fortiori fraud, will normally be brought to light by sound audit procedures, one of which is the practice of pointing out weaknesses in internal controls. An auditor's task is so to conduct the audit as to make it probable that material misstatements in financial documents will be detected.'

Claims by third parties

Many of the cases in respect of auditors' liability have concerned claims by third parties against auditors based on a sufficient proximate relationship between the two parties giving rise to a duty of care. The issue has been to determine what is the standard of duty of care owed by the auditors towards third parties who claim negligence against the auditors? In this regard, the courts applied the common law principles of the tort of deceit to impose liability: it was necessary to show that the statement was falsely made and reliance was placed by the third party on the false statement: *Derry v Peek* (1889) 14 App Cas 337. In an action of deceit, the claimant must prove actual fraud. Fraud is proved when it is shown that a false representation has been made knowingly, or without belief in its truth, or recklessly, without caring whether it be true or false. A false statement, made through carelessness and without reasonable ground for believing it to be true, may be evidence of fraud, but it does not necessarily amount to fraud. Such a statement, if made in the honest belief that it is true, is not fraudulent and does not render the person making it liable to an action of deceit.

Subsequently, the courts considered the application to auditors of the common law rules on negligent misstatements which caused economic loss to the third party based on the principles in *Hedley Byrne & Co Ltd v Heller & Partners Ltd* [1964] AC 465, where the House of Lords held that a negligent, though honest, misrepresentation, spoken or written, may give rise to an action for damages for financial loss caused thereby, apart from any contract or fiduciary relationship. This was because the law would imply a duty of care when a party seeking information from a party who had special skill, trusted him to exercise due care, and that party knew or ought to have known that reliance was being placed on his skill and judgment.

In order to demonstrate a duty of care owed by auditors towards third parties, three criteria were essential The foreseeability of damage, proximity of relationship and the reasonableness or otherwise of imposing a duty

The leading case in this area is *Caparo Industries plc v Dickman* [1990] 1 All ER 568.

In this case, the respondents owned shares in a public company, F plc, whose accounts for the year ended 31 March 1984 showed profits far short of the predicted figure which resulted in a dramatic drop in the quoted share price. After receipt of the audited accounts for the year ended 31 March 1984 the respondents purchased more shares in F plc and later that year made a successful takeover bid for the company. Following the takeover, the respondents brought an action against the auditors of the company, alleging that the accounts of F plc were inaccurate and misleading in that they showed a pre-tax profit of some £1.432 million for the year ended 31 March 1984 when in fact there had been a loss of over £400,000, that the auditors had been negligent in auditing the accounts, that the respondents had purchased further shares and made their takeover bid in reliance on the audited accounts, and that the auditors owed them a duty of care either as potential bidders for F plc because they ought to have foreseen that the 1984 results made F plc vulnerable to a takeover bid or as an existing shareholder of F plc interested in buying more shares.

On the trial of a preliminary issue whether the auditors owed a duty of care to the respondents, the judge held that the auditors did not.

The respondents appealed to the Court of Appeal, which allowed their appeal in part on the ground that the auditors owed the respondents a duty of care as shareholders but not as potential investors.

The auditors appealed to the House of Lords and the respondents cross-appealed against the Court of Appeal's decision that they could not claim as potential investors.

The House of Lords held that for a duty of care to arise, three aspects were required to be present:

- foreseeability of damage;
- proximity of relationship; and
- the reasonableness or otherwise of imposing a duty.

In determining whether there was a relationship of proximity between the parties the court, guided by situations in which the existence, scope and limits of a duty of care had previously been held to exist rather than by a single general principle, would determine whether the particular damage suffered was the kind of damage which the defendant was under a duty to prevent and whether there were circumstances from which the court could pragmatically conclude that a duty of care existed. See too Brennan J in *Sutherland Shire Council v Heyman* (1985) 60 ALR 1 at 43–44.

Where a statement put into more or less general circulation might foreseeably be relied on by strangers for any one of a variety of different purposes which the maker of the statement had no specific reason to anticipate there was no relationship of proximity between the maker of the statement and any person relying on it unless it was shown that the maker knew that his statement would be communicated to the person relying on it, either as an individual or as a member of an identifiable class, specifically in connection with a particular transaction or a transaction of a particular kind and that that person would be very likely to rely on it for the purpose of deciding whether to enter into that transaction. See too: *Cann v Willson* (1888) 39 Ch D 39; the *dictum* of Denning LJ in *Candler v Crane Christmas & Co* [1951] 1 All ER 426 at 433–436; *Hedley Byrne & Co Ltd v Heller & Partners Ltd* [1963] 2 All ER 575; and *Smith v Eric s Bush (a firm), Harris v Wyre Forest DC* [1989] 2 All ER 514.

The auditor of a public company's accounts owed no duty of care to a member of the public at large who relied on the accounts to buy shares in the company because the court would not deduce a relationship of proximity between the auditor and a member of the public when to do so would give rise to unlimited liability on the part of the auditor. Furthermore, an auditor owed no duty of care to an individual shareholder in the company who wished to buy more shares in the company, since an individual shareholder was in no better position than a member of the public at large and the auditor's statutory duty to prepare accounts was owed to the body of shareholders as a whole, the purpose for which accounts were prepared and audited being to enable the shareholders as a body to exercise informed control of the company and not to enable individual shareholders to buy shares with a view to profit. It followed that the auditors did not owe a duty of care to the respondents either as shareholders or as potential investors in the company. See too, the *dictum* of Richmond P in *Scott Group Ltd v McFarlane* [1978] 1 NZLR 553 at 566–567.

Lord Oliver was of the view that the provisions under the Companies Act on audits and auditors required directors to be responsible for preparation of the company's accounts and for the auditors to audit them. The audit is primarily for the company's benefit but may at times be relied upon by other class of persons other than the company's shareholders. The company was entitled to rely upon them owing to the fiduciary relationship of directors towards the company; and the employment of auditors to prepare the accounts was based on a contractual relationship between the auditors and the company.

The provisions under the Companies Act concerning audits and auditors did not establish a formal relationship of a duty of care by auditors towards third parties who required a copy of the audited reports or towards those who inspected the accounts at Companies House. A duty of care by the auditors under the Companies Act was only owed to the company's shareholders, but did not extend to a shareholder's decision to buy further shares in the company.

According to Lord Bridge, in order to establish a duty of care by the auditors towards other persons, there was a requirement to show a "special relationship" with the third party who suffered loss. In this regard, the claimant was required to demonstrate that the auditors considered that the accounts and report:

> '... would be communicated to the plaintiff, either as an individual or as a member of an identifiable class, specifically in connection with a particular transaction or transactions of a particular kind (eg in a prospectus inviting investment) and that the plaintiff would be very likely to rely on it for the purpose of deciding whether or not to enter upon that transaction or upon a transaction of that kind.'

The House of Lords disapproved of Woolf J's reasoning in *JEB Fasteners Ltd v Marks Bloom & Co* [1981] 3 All ER 289; and *Twomax Ltd v Dickson, McFarlane & Robinson* 1982 SC 113.

Some of the issues surrounding negligence of auditors have concentrated on the issue of proximity, foreseeability and causation aspects.

Although the auditors were at fault for failure to provide a qualified report but they were not liable as no reliance has been placed on the unqualified report

In *Berg Sons and Co Ltd v Adams* [1993] BCLC 1045, the issue was whether the auditors had acted negligently in failing to qualify the company's accounts; and as a result whether the company was misled by the accounts. Another issue was whether the knowledge of the sole executive director and beneficial owner of company should be attributed to the company.

Hobhouse J held that the auditors should not have provided an unqualified report given the circumstances and they were therefore at fault. However, the company was only entitled to nominal damages for breach of contract since G (the only shareholder in the company), who was the directing mind and will of the company and whose knowledge was the company's knowledge, had not relied upon nor been misled by the unqualified certificate.

The company's submission that G's knowledge should not be imputed to the company would be rejected as G was not guilty of any criminal conduct, fraud, or breach of trust or duty. In particular, G was not in breach of the duty which arose once a company was insolvent to preserve its assets in the interests of creditors, since the company was not insolvent or approaching insolvency at the time of the audit for the accounts.

Further, the company had not proved that the defendants' failure to qualify the accounts had any relevance to the eventual failure of the company or that it was reasonably foreseeable/within the contemplation of the parties that an unqualified certificate would cause the company or its members any loss.

The auditors owed no duty of care in tort to the defendants, as the purpose of the statutory audit was to provide a mechanism to enable those having a proprietary interest in the company or being concerned in its management or control to have accurate financial information. Further it was not foreseeable that defendants would place any material reliance on the accounts.

In order for the auditors to be liable in relation to a breach of duty in contract or in tort, it must first be proven that the alleged wrong was the effective or dominant cause of the claimants' loss

In *Galoo Ltd v Bright Grahame Murray* [1994] 1 WLR 1360, it was alleged that the auditors were negligent in not spotting that the company was in fact insolvent: the account showed that the company was in fact solvent at the time. If the accounts had shown that the company was insolvent, it would have ceased trading immediately.

The Court of Appeal held that for the auditors to be liable in relation to a breach of duty imposed on a defendant in contract or in tort in a situation analogous to a breach of contract, it must first be proven that the alleged wrong was the effective or dominant cause of the claimants' loss. In determining whether the loss of the claimants was caused by a breach of duty, or was merely the occasion for the loss, the court applied its common sense to the issue. Applying this test to the facts, the breach of duty by the auditors gave Galoo the opportunity to continue to incur loss, but it did not cause such loss in the sense that cause was used in law. See too *Haugesund Kommune v Depfa ACS Bank* [2012] QB 549.

24.146 As regards an auditor's liability for negligent misstatement, according to the dissenting judgment of Lord Denning in *Candler v Crane, Christmas & Co* [1951] 2 KB 164 (which was approved in *Caparo Industries plc v Dickman* [1990] 2 AC 605), 'accountants owe a duty of care not only to their own clients, but also to all those whom they know will rely on their accounts in the transactions for which those accounts are prepared'. According to Lord Denning, accountants, exercising a calling which required knowledge and skill, owed a duty to use care in the work, which resulted in their accounts and reports, and also in the rendering of their accounts and reports. They owed that duty not only to their clients with whom they had contracted, but to any third person to whom they showed their accounts and reports or to whom they knew that their clients were going to show them, when, to the knowledge of the accountants that person would consider their accounts and reports with a view to the investment of money or taking other action to his gain or detriment. The duty only extended in respect of those transactions for which the accountants knew that their accounts were required. Lord Denning held that accountants would be liable for negligent misstatements even though there was no contractual relationship between the auditors and the third parties:

> 'First, what persons are under such duty? My answer is those persons such as accountants, surveyors, valuers and analysts, whose profession and occupation it is to examine books, accounts, and other things, and to make reports on which other people – other than their clients – rely in the ordinary course of business. Their duty is not merely a duty to use care in their reports. They have also a duty to use care in their work which results in their reports. Herein lies the difference between these professional men and other persons who have been held to be under no duty to use care in their statements, such as promoters who issue a prospectus and trustees who answer inquiries about the trust funds … Those persons do not bring, and are not expected to bring, any professional knowledge or skill into the preparation of their statements: they can only be made responsible by the law affecting persons generally, such as contract, estoppel, innocent misrepresentation or fraud. But it is very different with persons who engage in a calling which requires special knowledge and skill. From very early times it has been held that they owe a duty of care to those who are closely and directly affected by their work, apart altogether from any contract or undertaking in that behalf.'

With specific regard to accountants, he stated:

> 'They owe the duty, of course, to their employer or client; and also I think to any third person to whom they themselves show the accounts, or to whom they know their employer is going to show the accounts, so as to induce him to invest money or take some other action on them. But I do not think the duty can be extended still further so as to include strangers of whom they have heard nothing and to whom their employer without their knowledge may choose to show their accounts. Once the accountants have handed their accounts to their employer they are not, as a rule, responsible for what he does with them without their knowledge or consent.'

The principles concerning negligent misstatements established in *Hedley Byrne & Co Ltd v Heller & Partners Ltd* were further elucidated by Lord Bridge in *Caparo Industries plc v Dickman* [1990] 2 AC 605, where he stated that:

> '… that the defendant knew that his statement would be communicated to the plaintiff, either as an individual or as a member of an identifiable class,

specifically in connection with a particular transaction or transactions of a particular kind (eg in a prospectus inviting investment) and that the plaintiff would be very likely to rely on it for the purpose of deciding whether or not to enter upon that transaction or upon a transaction of that kind.'

24.147 In this regard, the test is objective. Lord Oliver set out the following test in establishing the necessary relationship between the maker of a statement or giver of advice ('the adviser') and the recipient who acts in reliance upon it ('the advisee'):

(1) the advice is required for a purpose, whether particularly specified or generally described, which is made known, either actually or inferentially, to the adviser at the time when the advice is given;

(2) the adviser knows, either actually or inferentially, that his advice will be communicated to the advisee, either specifically or as a member of an ascertainable class, in order that it should be used by the advisee for that purpose;

(3) it is known either actually or inferentially, that the advice so communicated is likely to be acted upon by the advisee for that purpose without independent inquiry, and

(4) it is so acted upon by the advisee to his detriment.

Modern approaches towards auditors' negligence towards clients

24.148 A modern approach to auditors' negligence is to look at the scope of the duty of care in the sense of responsibility for the claimant's loss.

The courts will have regard to the scope of duty and services that the auditors were required to provide the client

This was illustrated in *Johnson v Gore Wood & Co* [2003] EWCA Civ 1728, which concerned the alleged negligence of a law firm to its client. According to the Court of Appeal, the court was required to address the question: whether the loss claimed was the kind of loss in respect of which the duty was owed? According to Arden LJ:

> 'Starting with *Caparo v Dickman*, the courts have moved away from characterising questions as to the measure of damages for the tort of negligence as questions of causation and remoteness. The path that once led in that direction now leads in a new direction. The courts now analyse such questions by enquiring whether the duty which the tortfeasor owed was a duty in respect of the kind of loss of which the victim complains. Duty is no longer determined in abstraction from the consequences or vice-versa. The same test applies whether the duty of care is contractual or tortious. To determine the scope of the duty the court must examine carefully the purpose for which advice was being given and generally the surrounding circumstances. The determination

of the scope of the duty thus involves an intensely fact-sensitive exercise. The final result turns on the facts, and it is likely to be only the general principles rather than the solution in any individual case that are of assistance in later cases.'

This requires the court to look at the primary facts of the advice given. Further, the court has to ask simply whether the loss that occurred was 'the kind of loss in respect of which the duty was owed'. The court must, therefore, ask for what purpose the advice was given. In some cases, depending on the facts, it will be sufficient that the purpose can be generally described.

As Lord Bridge said in *Caparo v Dickman* at page 627, '[i]t is never sufficient to ask whether A owes B a duty of care. It is always necessary to determine the scope of the duty by reference to the kind of damage from which A must take care to save B harmless'. Ultimately, that decision turns on the court's principled assessment of the primary facts.

24.149 What is the position where auditors are required to prepare specially commissioned reports?

Where reports are specially commissioned for auditors to prepare, there may be liability for negligent misstatements

In *JEB Fasteners Ltd v Marks, Bloom & Co* [1983] 1 All ER 583, the claimant took over a company but its accounts were incorrect. The incorrectness had not been identified by the company's auditor. However, the auditors were held not to be liable because the main reason for taking over the company was to obtain the services of the company's directors. It was known that the company's financial position was poor at the time. The Court of Appeal held that the terms 'reliance' and 'relied on' were capable of bearing either a narrow and precise meaning of 'induced' or 'wholly dependent on', or a wider meaning of 'being encouraged or supported in' taking a decision by subsidiary factors which if untrue would be a matter of disappointment but would not affect the taking of the decision. Furthermore (per Stephenson LJ), in the context of negligent misrepresentation the false misrepresentation had to play a real and substantial, although not necessarily decisive, part in inducing the claimant to act if it was to be a cause of the loss because the claimant 'relied on' it (in the narrow sense of that term). The judge had been ambiguous in using the term 'rely on' to mean 'encouraged' rather than 'induced' and he had been wrong to separate out as different issues the question whether the claimants relied on the accounts and the question whether the claimants had suffered loss by relying on the accounts: both were merely different ways of stating the issue of causation. Nevertheless, it was clear that the judge's underlying reasoning had been that although the claimants had been aware of and had considered the accounts they had not to any material degree affected the claimants' judgment in deciding to take over the company, and, on the facts, there was ample evidence to support that conclusion.

There was no relationship of proximity between the claimants and auditors as to establish a duty of care and damages

In *James McNaughton Paper Group Ltd v Hicks, Anderson and Co* [1991] 2 QB 113, while negotiations were taking place for the takeover of a group of companies by the claimant company, the group instructed the defendants, their accountants, to prepare accounts for the group. The defendants submitted the accounts as 'final drafts' showing a net loss for the year of £48,094 and, in reply to a question put by the claimants, said that the group were 'breaking even or doing marginally worse' Subsequently, the claimants completed the takeover and discovered a number of errors in the accounts. The claimants claimed in negligence against the defendants for loss and damage suffered as a result of the takeover.

The judge at first instance, gave judgment for the claimants and held that the defendants' answer to the claimants was a misrepresentation, and that the defendants were in breach of a duty of care they had owed to the claimants in respect of the accounts and the answer.

The Court of Appeal held that that there was not such a relationship of proximity between the claimants and defendants as to establish a duty of care; that the defendants could not have been expected to foresee the damage which the claimants alleged they had suffered in reliance upon the draft accounts and the answer given by the defendants in general terms; and that, accordingly it was not fair, just and reasonable to impose on the defendants a duty of care to the claimants in relation to the accounts and the answer.

According to Neill LJ:

> '... in England a restrictive approach is now adopted to any extension of the scope of the duty of care beyond the person directly intended by the maker of the statement to act upon it; and (b) that in deciding whether a duty of care exists in any particular case it is necessary to take all the circumstances into account; but (c) that, notwithstanding (b), it is possible to identify certain matters which are likely to be of importance in most cases in reaching a decision as to whether or not a duty exists. I propose to examine these matters under a series of headings, though the headings involve a substantial measure of overlap.'

The headings included: (1) the purpose for which the statement was made; (2) the purpose for which the statement was communicated; (3) the relationship between the adviser, the advisee and any relevant third party; (4) the state of knowledge of the adviser; and (5) reliance by the advisee.

Assumption of responsibility

24.150 Subsequent to *Caparo*, the cases have highlighted the issue of assumption of responsibility by the auditors towards third parties as a basis of a 'special relationship' existing between the parties.

Auditors are not required consciously to assume responsibility for preparation of the audited accounts towards third parties

In *Electra Private Equity Partners v KPMG Peat Marwick* [2001] 1 BCLC 589, the Court of Appeal held that there was no requirement that auditors should 'consciously' assume responsibility for the preparation of audit reports for third parties, based on an objective test and as factually determined by the courts as to whether the auditors had assumed such responsibility.

Auditors did not assume any responsibility to a third party in the preparation of certain representations made in their letter to the company

In *Abbott v Strong* [1998] 2 BCLC 420, the court considered the issue of assumption of responsibility.

The claimants were more than 200 shareholders in a public company who subscribed for a £20 million rights issue of new shares. The circular inviting shareholders to subscribe was accompanied by a forecast by the directors that the company's profits in the forthcoming year would be at least £6 million and a letter from the fifth defendants, a firm of accountants, to the directors stating that they had reviewed the accounting policies and calculations on which the profits forecast was based and that in their opinion the forecast had been properly compiled and was consistent with the company's accounting policies. The company subsequently collapsed and its shares became worthless. The claimants brought an action against the directors and the accountants seeking to recover the amounts subscribed for the rights issue. The claimants alleged that the circular inviting shareholders to subscribe for the rights issue contained false information and that the accountants' letter was misleading as the result of fraudulent misrepresentations made and forged documents presented to the accountants by the company's managing director (who was subsequently convicted of fraud and forgery). As against the accountants the claimants applied to amend the statement of claim to allege, *inter alia*, that in addition to any duty of care specifically arising out of representations made in the accountants' letter, under the law relating to negligent misstatements the accountants owed the claimants the same duty of care as that owed to the company to investigate and verify the profits forecast and ensure that its advice regarding the profits forecast was correct since they must have known that the substance of their advice to the directors would be passed on to the shareholders when they were invited to subscribe to the rights issue. The question arose whether it was arguable that the accountants owed a duty of care to the claimants in respect of the accuracy of the profits forecast stated in the circular beyond the duty of care, if any, which the accountants owed to the claimants by reason of the representations in their letter attached to the circular.

Ferris J held that a person who made a statement or gave advice to another for the purpose of assisting that person to make representations to a third party did not owe a duty of care to the third party if the third party was unaware of his participation in the preparation of the representations, since the third party in receiving and acting on the representations in ignorance of the first party's role in their preparation could not be said to have relied on the first party. Accordingly, the first party could not be said to have assumed any responsibility to the third party in assisting in the preparation of the representations. It followed that it was not arguable that the accountants owed a duty of care to the claimants in respect of the accuracy of the profits forecast stated in the circular beyond the duty of care, if any, which the accountants owed to the claimants by reason of the representations in their letter attached to the circular.

Auditors had not assumed any responsibility to a third party for certain statements made at a completion meeting

In *Peach Publishing Ltd v Slater and Co* [1998] BCC 139, the Court of Appeal was required to consider the position of accountants who gave verbal assurances and statements to the purchasers at a meeting that the accounts they had prepared were accurate. It held that there was no assumption of responsibility in making such statements. According to Morritt LJ: 'The circumstances in which the statement was made must also be considered in order to evaluate the significance of the facts that the statement was both voluntary and direct.' The accountant who made the representation did so as an adviser to the seller as client and not to the purchaser. The accountant was not acting as an independent expert. The objective of the statement was to request the seller to warrant the accuracy of the accounts and not for the purchaser to rely on the statement.

However, in *ADT Ltd v BDO Binder Hamlyn* [1996] BCC 808, the issue was whether the accountants assumed responsibility to the purchaser for the accuracy of the accounts at a meeting. May J concluded that the accountants were liable for the negligent misstatement:

> 'Binders undoubtedly professed accounting and specifically auditing skills and Mr Bishop attended the meeting in his capacity as an accountant audit partner. He was, in my judgment, fully aware of the nature of the very transaction which ADT had in contemplation, viz: the acquisition of BSG, the Company whose Group accounts his firm audited. He took it upon himself to give information or advice directly to ADT, viz: that he stood by the accounts by which he meant that within the limits of Binders' professional competence the accounts gave a true and fair view of the state of affairs of the company. He knew the purpose for which ADT required this information and advice, viz: as an ingredient to help them finally to decide whether to make the contemplated bid or not. He knew that ADT would place reliance on what he said without further inquiry since he knew that it was "the final hurdle". These ingredients of a duty of care are therefore all present in this case and I have to consider whether objectively and in fairness Binders through Mr Bishop are to be taken to have assumed responsibility to ADT for the reliability of the advice or information which he gave.'

It was held there was assumption of responsibility and damages were assessed against the accountants.

It is not sufficient to merely show an assumption of responsibility to the person being advised

In *Phelps v Hillingdon London Borough Council* [2001] 2 AC 619. In that case the House of Lords held that a person exercising a particular skill or profession might owe a duty of care in its performance to those who might foreseeably be injured if due care and skill were not exercised; that such duty did not depend on the existence of a contractual relationship between the person causing and the person suffering the damage. In the course of his judgment, Lord Slynn said:

> 'It is sometimes said that there has to be an assumption of responsibility by the person concerned. That phrase can be misleading in that it can suggest that the professional person must knowingly and deliberately accept responsibility. It is, however, clear that the test is an objective one: *Henderson v Merrett Syndicates Ltd* [1995] 2 AC 145, 181. The phrase means simply that the law recognises that there is a duty of care. It is not so much that responsibility is assumed as that it is recognised or imposed by the law.'

However, in *Williams v Natural Life Health Foods Limited* [1998] 1 WLR 830, Lord Steyn emphasised the importance of establishing assumption of responsibility. In that case, the House of Lords decided that a director of a limited company would only be personally liable to claimants for loss which they suffered as a result of negligent advice given to them by the company, if he had assumed personal responsibility for that advice and the claimants had relied on that assumption of responsibility. Whether there had been such an assumption of responsibility was to be determined objectively, so that the primary focus had to be on exchanges (including statements and conduct) between the parties. Moreover, the test of reliance was not simply reliance in fact, but whether the claimants could reasonably rely on the assumption of responsibility.

In preparing their audit, auditors only owed duties to the company's shareholders as a whole and not to any individual shareholders or the wider public

An illustration of this is in *Barings plc v Coopers & Lybrand (No 1)* [2002] 2 BCLC 364, where it was alleged that the auditors had failed to detect the employee's fraud in the company which in turn caused the collapse of the parent company. An action in contract and tort was commenced. It was claimed that had the audits been conducted properly, the wrongdoing would have been uncovered.

According to Evans-Lombe J, where a claimant claimed damages in tort flowing from a negligent misstatement, he was required to plead and prove not only that the loss for which compensation was claimed was caused by the defendant's breach of duty to the claimant and was foreseeable, but also that the claim arose from a transaction or class of transactions that was within the contemplation of the defendant at the time he undertook the relevant duty and for the purpose of which, *inter alia*, he provided his services, and, further, that the claimant relied on those services for the purpose of that transaction.

Accordingly, the claimant had to establish that the defendant had in contemplation the transaction by which the claimant suffered loss in order for the defendant to have assumed a duty to exercise due care and skill to protect the claimant from the loss resulting from it, either because the defendant had been directly informed that the claimant either would or was likely to embark on the transaction in reliance on his advice or other statement or that, from the surrounding circumstances of the case, it could be inferred that he knew of the transaction and the reliance.

'Knowledge' on the part of the defendant embraced not only actual knowledge but such knowledge as would be attributed to a reasonable person placed in the defendant's position but in both cases the claimant was required to plead the circumstances on the basis of which he alleged that the defendant knew of the intended transaction of the claimant and his reliance on the defendant for the purpose of it.

Accordingly, in the case of a claim in tort against an auditor the claimant had to plead and prove, in addition to a relationship between the auditor and the claimant capable of giving rise to a duty of care and that the loss flowing from the auditor's breach of that duty was caused by the auditor's negligent report and was foreseeable, that, at the time he undertook those services, the auditor had in contemplation that they would be relied on by the claimant for the purpose of a particular transaction or class of transactions that was likely to result and that the claimant had, in fact, relied on the auditor's report when embarking on such transaction which resulted in the loss for which compensation was claimed.

The claims were struck out on the basis that the auditors did not have in contemplation other companies in the group that would place reliance on the audit reports.

24.151 It may however be possible to show liability that in conducting an audit for a subsidiary, the auditors also assumed responsibility towards the parent company in providing a true and fair view of the company's accounts, particularly where the parent copany would be placing reliance on the audited accounts of the subsidiary: *Barings plc (in administration) v Coopers & Lybrand* [1997] 1 BCLC 427.

Auditors should be made aware of the purpose and the audience for which the audited accounts are being prepared

In *Andrew v Kounnis Freeman* [1999] 2 BCLC 641, the Court of Appeal held that in determining whether the auditors had assumed a responsibility to the claimants, the court had to take the facts alleged by the claimants to be proved. While the fact that an auditor repeated his statutory report to a third party did not necessarily imply an assumption of responsibility for it, in determining whether responsibility had been so assumed, it was not correct to concentrate attention on the terms of the request for information alone, instead of asking whether the purpose of the request would be apparent to a reasonable person in the position of the requested party. It was also necessary to ask whether such a person would be aware that his skill and judgment were very likely to be relied on, unless the statements he made were conditional or otherwise qualified to show that reliance should not be placed on them.

Voidness of provisions protecting auditors from liability

24.152 Section 532 of CA 2006 applies to any provision:

(a) for exempting an auditor of a company (to any extent) from any liability that would otherwise attach to him in connection with any negligence, default, breach of duty or breach of trust in relation to the company occurring in the course of the audit of accounts; or

(b) by which a company directly or indirectly provides an indemnity (to any extent) for an auditor of the company, or of an associated company, against any liability attaching to him in connection with any negligence, default, breach of duty or breach of trust in relation to the company of which he is auditor occurring in the course of the audit of accounts: CA 2006, s 532(1).

24.153 Any such provision is void, except as permitted by:

(a) CA 2006, s 533 (indemnity for costs of successfully defending proceedings); or

(b) CA 2006, ss 534–536 (liability limitation agreements): CA 2006, s 532(2).

Section 532 applies to any provision, whether contained in a company's articles or in any contract with the company or otherwise: CA 2006, s 532(3). For the purposes of the section companies are associated if one is a subsidiary of the other or both are subsidiaries of the same body corporate: CA 2006, s 532(4).

Indemnity for costs of successfully defending proceedings

24.154 Section 532 of the CA 2006 (general voidness of provisions protecting auditors from liability) does not prevent a company from indemnifying an auditor against any liability incurred by him:

(a) in defending proceedings (whether civil or criminal) in which judgment is given in his favour or he is acquitted, or

(b) in connection with an application under CA 2006, s 1157 (power of court to grant relief in case of honest and reasonable conduct) in which relief is granted to him by the court: CA 2006, s 533.

Liability limitation agreements

24.155 A 'liability limitation agreement' is an agreement that purports to limit the amount of a liability owed to a company by its auditor in respect of any negligence, default, breach of duty or breach of trust, occurring in the course of the audit of accounts, of which the auditor may be guilty in relation to the company: CA 2006, s 534(1).

Section 532 (general voidness of provisions protecting auditors from liability) does not affect the validity of a liability limitation agreement that:

(a) complies with s 535 (terms of liability limitation agreement) and of any regulations under that section; and

(b) is authorised by the members of the company (see s 536): CA 2006, s 534(2).

24.156 Such an agreement:

(a) is effective to the extent provided by s 537, and

(b) is not subject:

   (i) in England and Wales or Northern Ireland, to ss 2(2) or 3(2)(a) of the Unfair Contract Terms Act 1977 (c 50);

   (ii) in Scotland, to ss 16(1)(b) or 17(1)(a) of that Act: CA 2006, s 534(3).

Terms of liability limitation agreement

24.157 A liability limitation agreement:

(a) must not apply in respect of acts or omissions occurring in the course of the audit of accounts for more than one financial year; and

(b) must specify the financial year in relation to which it applies: CA 2006, s 535(1).

24.158 The Secretary of State may by regulations:

(a) require liability limitation agreements to contain specified provisions or provisions of a specified description;

(b) prohibit liability limitation agreements from containing specified provisions or provisions of a specified description: CA 2006, s 535(2).

'Specified' here means specified in the regulations.

Without prejudice to the generality of the power conferred by CA 2006, s 535(2), that power may be exercised with a view to preventing adverse effects on competition.

Subject to the preceding provisions of s 535 section, it is immaterial how a liability limitation agreement is framed. In particular, the limit on the amount of the auditor's liability need not be a sum of money, or a formula, specified in the agreement: CA 2006, s 535(3).

Authorisation of agreement by members of the company

24.159 A liability limitation agreement is authorised by the members of the company if it has been authorised under s 536 and that authorisation has not been withdrawn: CA 2006, s 536(1).

A liability limitation agreement between a private company and its auditor may be authorised:

(a) by the company passing a resolution, before it enters into the agreement, waiving the need for approval;

(b) by the company passing a resolution, before it enters into the agreement, approving the agreement's principal terms; or

(c) by the company passing a resolution, after it enters into the agreement, approving the agreement: CA 2006, s 536(2).

24.160 A liability limitation agreement between a public company and its auditor may be authorised:

(a) by the company passing a resolution in general meeting, before it enters into the agreement, approving the agreement's principal terms; or

(b) by the company passing a resolution in general meeting, after it enters into the agreement, approving the agreement: CA 2006, s 536(3).

24.161 The 'principal terms' of an agreement are terms specifying, or relevant to the determination of:

(a) the kind (or kinds) of acts or omissions covered;

(b) the financial year to which the agreement relates; or

(c) the limit to which the auditor's liability is subject: CA 2006, s 536(4).

24.162 Authorisation under s 536 may be withdrawn by the company passing an ordinary resolution to that effect:

(a) at any time before the company enters into the agreement; or

(b) if the company has already entered into the agreement, before the beginning of the financial year to which the agreement relates.

Paragraph (b) has effect notwithstanding anything in the agreement: s 536(5) CA 2006.

Effect of liability limitation agreement

24.163 A liability limitation agreement is not effective to limit the auditor's liability to less than such amount as is fair and reasonable in all the circumstances of the case having regard (in particular) to:

(a) the auditor's responsibilities under CA 2006, Pt 16;

(b) the nature and purpose of the auditor's contractual obligations to the company; and

(c) the professional standards expected of him: CA 2006, s 537(1).

A liability limitation agreement that purports to limit the auditor's liability to less than the amount mentioned in s 537(1) shall have effect as if it limited his liability to that amount: CA 2006, s 537(2).

24.164 In determining what is fair and reasonable in all the circumstances of the case no account is to be taken of:

(a) matters arising after the loss or damage in question has been incurred; or

(b) matters (whenever arising) affecting the possibility of recovering compensation from other persons liable in respect of the same loss or damage: CA 2006, s 537(3).

Disclosure of agreement by company

24.165 A company which has entered into a liability limitation agreement must make such disclosure in connection with the agreement as the Secretary of State may require by regulations: CA 2006, s 538(1).

The regulations may provide, in particular, that any disclosure required by the regulations shall be made:

(a) in a note to the company's annual accounts (in the case of its individual accounts) or in such manner as is specified in the regulations (in the case of group accounts); or

(b) in the directors' report: CA 2006, s 538(2).

Meaning of 'corporate governance statement'

24.166 The term 'corporate governance statement' means the statement required by rules 7.2.1 to 7.2.11 in the Disclosure Rules and Transparency Rules sourcebook issued by the Financial Services Authority: CA 2006, s 538A(1).

Those rules were inserted by Annex C of the Disclosure Rules and Transparency Rules Sourcebook (Corporate Governance Rules) Instrument 2008 made by the Authority on 26 June 2008 (FSA 2008/32): CA 2006, s 538A(2).

A 'separate' corporate governance statement means one that is not included in the directors' report: CA 2006, s 538A(3).

Definitions

24.167

'e-money issuer': means a person who has permission under Pt 4 of the Financial Services and Markets Act 2000 (c 8) to carry on the activity of issuing electronic money within the meaning of Art 9B of the Financial Services and Markets Act 2000 (Regulated Activities) Order 2001 (SI 2001 No 544).

'MiFID investment firm': means an investment firm within the meaning of Art 4.1.1 of Directive 2004/39/EC of the European Parliament and of the Council of 21 April 2004 on markets in financial instruments, other than:

(a) a company to which that Directive does not apply by virtue of Article 2 of that Directive;

(b) a company which is an exempt investment firm within the meaning of reg 4A(3) of the Financial Services and Markets Act 2000 (Markets in Financial Instruments) Regulations 2007; and

(c) any other company which fulfils all the requirements set out in reg 4C(3) of those Regulations.

'qualified', in relation to an auditor's report (or a statement contained in an auditor's report): means that the report or statement does not state the auditor's unqualified opinion that the accounts have been properly prepared in accordance with this Act or, in the case of an undertaking not required to prepare accounts in accordance with this Act, under any corresponding legislation under which it is required to prepare accounts.

'turnover', in relation to a company: means the amounts derived from the provision of goods and services falling within the company's ordinary activities, after deduction of:

(a) trade discounts

(b) value added tax; and

(c) any other taxes based on the amounts so derived.

'UCITS management company': has the meaning given by the Glossary forming part of the Handbook made by the Financial Services Authority under the Financial Services and Markets Act 2000.

25 Company share capital

Contents

Introduction

25.1 Part 17 of the CA 2006 contains provisions dealing with a company's share capital. Part 17 comprises ten chapters. Chapter 1 is concerned with shares and share capital of a company; Ch 2 contains general provisions on allotment of shares; Ch 3 deals with allotment of equity securities containing existing shareholders' right of pre-emption; Ch 4 addresses public companies allotment where the issue is not fully subscribed; Ch 5 deals with payment for shares; Ch 6 is concerned with independent valuation of non-cash consideration of public companies; Ch 7 addresses share premiums; Ch 8 applies to alteration of share capital; Ch 9 deals with classes of shares and class rights; and Ch 10 applies to reduction of share capital. This Chapter takes account of changes under the Small Business, Enterprise and Employment Act 2015 (SBEEA 2015).

Shares and share capital of a company

25.2 Chapter 1 addresses the issue of shares and share capital of a company. It comprises nine sections, providing definitions on terms used and clarification of some of the concepts used in Pt 17 of the CA 2006.

Shares

25.3 Section 540 of the CA 2006 is concerned with definitional aspects of the term 'shares'. In the Companies Acts, the term 'share', in relation to a company, means share in the company's share capital: CA 2006, s 540(1). A company's shares may no longer be converted into stock: CA 2006, s 540(2).

Stock created before the commencement of Pt 17 of the CA 2006 may be reconverted into shares in accordance with CA 2006, ss 540(3) and 620.

In the Companies Acts, references to shares include stock except where a distinction between share and stock is express or implied; and references to a number of shares include an amount of stock where the context admits of the reference to shares being read as including stock: CA 2006, s 540(4).

Nature of shares

25.4 Section 541 governs the nature of shares. The shares or other interest of a member in a company are personal property (or, in Scotland, moveable property) and are not in the nature of real estate (or heritage).

Nominal value of shares

25.5 Shares in a limited company having a share capital must each have a fixed nominal value: CA 2006, s 542(1). An allotment of a share that does not have a fixed nominal value is void: CA 2006, s 542(2).

Shares in a limited company having a share capital may be denominated in any currency, and different classes of shares may be denominated in different currencies. But see s 765 (initial authorised minimum share capital requirement for public company to be met by reference to share capital denominated in sterling or euros): CA 2006, s 542(3).

If a company purports to allot shares in contravention of s 542, an offence is committed by every officer of the company who is in default: CA 2006, s 542(4).

25.6 A person guilty of an offence under s 542 is liable on conviction on indictment, to a fine; on summary conviction, to a fine not exceeding the statutory maximum: CA 2006, s 542(5).

Section 542 should be read together with s 9, which requires the application for registration of a company that is to be formed with a share capital, to include a 'statement of capital and initial shareholdings'. The contents of this statement are prescribed in s 10, and this includes a requirement to set out a total number of shares, and the aggregate nominal value of the shares, which are to be taken by the subscribers to the memorandum on formation.

Numbering of shares

25.7 Section 543 states that each share in a company having a share capital must be distinguished by its appropriate number, except in the following circumstances: CA 2006, s 543(1).

If at any time all the issued shares in a company are fully paid up and rank *pari passu* for all purposes; or all the issued shares of a particular class in a company are fully paid up and rank *pari passu* for all purposes, none of those shares need thereafter have a distinguishing number so long as it remains fully paid up and ranks *pari passu* for all purposes with all shares of the same class for the time being issued and fully paid up: CA 2006, s 543(2).

Transferability of shares

25.8 The shares or other interest of any member in a company are transferable in accordance with the company's articles: CA 2006, s 544(1).

This is subject to the Stock Transfer Act 1963 (c 18) or the Stock Transfer Act (Northern Ireland) 1963 (c 24 (NI)) (which enables securities of certain descriptions to be transferred by a simplified process); and regulations under Ch 2 of Pt 21 of this Act (which enable title to securities to be evidenced and transferred without a written instrument): CA 2006, s 544(2). See Pt 21 of this Act generally as regards share transfers: CA 2006, s 544(3).

Companies having a share capital

25.9 Section 545 provides that references in the Companies Acts to a company having a share capital are to a company that has power under its constitution to issue shares

Issued and allotted share capital

25.10 Section 546 states that the references in the Companies Acts to 'issued share capital' are to shares of a company that have been issued; and to 'allotted share capital' are to shares of a company that have been allotted: CA 2006, s 546(1). Issuance and allotment are two different aspects under the CA 2006: *Clarke's Case* (1878) 8 Ch D 635.

In *National Westminster Bank plc v Inland Revenue Commissioners* [1994] 3 All ER 1, the House of Lords considered the distinction between 'issue of shares' and 'allotment' and held that shares were 'issued' when an application had been followed by allotment and notification and completed by entry on the register. The term 'issue' in relation to shares meant something distinct from allotment and imported that some subsequent act had been done whereby the title of the allottee had become complete. The Companies Acts preserved the distinction in English law between an enforceable contract for the issue of shares (which contract was constituted by an allotment) and the issue of shares, which was completed by registration. Accordingly, the word 'issue' under the previous Income and Corporation Taxes Act 1988 was appropriate to indicate the whole process whereby unissued shares were applied for, allotted and finally registered.

References in the Companies Acts to issued or allotted shares, or to issued or allotted share capital, include shares taken on the formation of the company by the subscribers to the company's memorandum: CA 2006, s 546(2).

Share capital

Called-up share capital

25.11 Section 547 defines a company's called-up share capital. In the Companies Acts 'called-up share capital', in relation to a company, means so much of its share capital as equals the aggregate amount of the calls made on its shares (whether or not those calls have been paid), together with any share capital paid up without being called; any share capital to be paid on a specified future date under the articles, the terms of allotment of the relevant shares or any other arrangements for payment of those shares; and 'uncalled share capital' is to be construed accordingly.

Equity share capital

25.12 Section 547 defines equity share capital. In the Companies Acts 'equity share capital' in relation to a company, means its issued share capital excluding any part of that capital that, neither as respects dividends nor as respects capital, carries any right to participate beyond a specified amount in a distribution.

Allotment of shares: general provisions

25.13 Companies Act 2006, Ch 2 sets out the provisions on allotment of shares. It comprises 11 sections.

Power of directors to allot shares

Exercise by directors of power to allot shares

25.14 Section 549 states that the directors of a company must not exercise any power of the company to allot shares in the company; or to grant rights to subscribe for, or to convert any security into, shares in the company, except in accordance with s 550 (private company with single class of shares) or s 551 (authorisation by company): CA 2006, s 549(1).

Section 549(1) does not apply to the allotment of shares in pursuance of an employees' share scheme; or to the grant of a right to subscribe for, or to convert any security into, shares so allotted: CA 2006, s 549(2).

In the event s 549 applies in relation to the grant of a right to subscribe for, or to convert any security into, shares, it does not apply in relation to the allotment of shares pursuant to that right: CA 2006, s 549(3).

25.15 A director who knowingly contravenes, or permits or authorises a contravention of s 549 commits an offence: CA 2006, s 549(4). A person who is guilty of an offence under s 549 will be liable on conviction on indictment, to a fine; and on summary conviction, to a fine not exceeding the statutory maximum: CA 2006, s 549(5).

Nothing in s 549 affects the validity of an allotment or other transaction: CA 2006, s 549(6).

Power of directors to allot shares etc: private company with only one class of shares

25.16 Where a private company has only one class of shares, the directors may exercise any power of the company to allot shares of that class, or to grant rights to subscribe for or to convert any security into such shares, except to the extent that they are prohibited from doing so by the company's articles: CA 2006, s 550.

Section 550 empowers the directors to allot shares (or to grant rights to subscribe for or convert any security into shares) where the company is a private company which will have only one class after the proposed allotment. There is no requirement for the directors to have prior authority from the company's members for such an allotment of shares In addition, the members may, if they wish, restrict or prohibit this power through the articles of association. The definition of 'classes of shares' is contained in s 808.

Power of directors to allot shares etc: authorisation by company

25.17 The directors of a company may exercise a power of the company to allot shares in the company, or to grant rights to subscribe for or to convert any security into shares in the company, if they are authorised to do so by the company's articles or by resolution of the company: CA 2006, s 551(1).

Authorisation may be given for a particular exercise of the power or for its exercise generally, and may be unconditional or subject to conditions: CA 2006, s 551(2).

The authorisation must state the maximum amount of shares that may be allotted under it, and specify the date on which it will expire, which must be not more than five years from: (i) in the case of authorisation contained in the company's articles at the time of its original incorporation, the date of that incorporation; and (ii) in any other case, the date on which the resolution is passed by virtue of which the authorisation is given: CA 2006, s 551(3).

25.18 The authorisation may be renewed or further renewed by resolution of the company for a further period not exceeding five years, and be revoked or varied at any time by resolution of the company: CA 2006, s 551(4).

A resolution renewing authorisation must state (or restate) the maximum amount of shares that may be allotted under the authorisation or, as the case may be, the amount remaining to be allotted under it, and specify the date on which the renewed authorisation will expire: CA 2006, s 551(5).

In relation to rights to subscribe for or to convert any security into shares in the company, references in s 551 to the maximum amount of shares that may be allotted under the authorisation are to the maximum amount of shares that may be allotted pursuant to the rights: CA 2006, s 551(6).

25.19 The directors may allot shares, or grant rights to subscribe for or to convert any security into shares, after authorisation has expired if the shares are allotted, or the rights are granted, in pursuance of an offer or agreement made by the company before the authorisation expired, and the authorisation allowed the company to make an offer or agreement which would or might require shares to be allotted, or rights to be granted, after the authorisation had expired: CA 2006, s 551(7).

A resolution of a company to give, vary, revoke or renew authorisation under s 551 may be an ordinary resolution, even though it amends the company's articles: CA 2006, s 551(8).

Chapter 3 of Pt 3 of the CA 2006 (resolutions affecting a company's constitution) applies to a resolution under s 551: CA 2006, s 551(9).

Prohibition of commissions, discounts and allowances

General prohibition of commissions, discounts and allowances

25.20 Section 552 sets out the general prohibition of commissions, discounts and allowance. Except as permitted by s 553 (permitted commission), a company must not apply any of its shares or capital money, either directly or indirectly, in payment of any commission, discount or allowance to any person in consideration of his subscribing or agreeing to subscribe (whether absolutely or conditionally) for shares in the company, or procuring or agreeing to procure subscriptions (whether absolute or conditional) for shares in the company: CA 2006, s 552(1).

It is immaterial how the shares or money are so applied, whether by being added to the purchase money of property acquired by the company or to the contract price of work to be executed for the company, or being paid out of the nominal purchase money or contract price, or otherwise: CA 2006, s 552(2).

Nothing in s 552 affects the payment of such brokerage as has previously been lawful: CA 2006, s 552(3).

Permitted commission

25.21 Section 553 states that a company may, if the following conditions are satisfied, pay a commission to a person in consideration of his subscribing or agreeing to subscribe (whether absolutely or conditionally) for shares in the company, or procuring or agreeing to procure subscriptions (whether absolute or conditional) for shares in the company: CA 2006, s 553(1).

The conditions are that the payment of the commission is authorised by the company's articles; and the commission paid or agreed to be paid does not exceed (i) 10% of the price at which the shares are issued, or (ii) the amount or rate authorised by the articles, whichever is the less: CA 2006, s 553(2).

A vendor to, or promoter of, or other person who receives payment in money or shares from, a company may apply any part of the money or shares so received in payment of any commission the payment of which directly by the company would be permitted by s 553: CA 2006, s 553(3).

Registration of allotment

25.22 A company must register an allotment of shares as soon as practicable and in any event within two months after the date of the allotment: CA 2006, s 554(1).

This does not apply if the company has issued a share warrant in respect of the shares (see s 779): CA 2006, s 554(2).

If an election is in force under Pt 8, Ch 2A, the obligation under sub-s (1) to register the allotment of shares is replaced by an obligation to deliver particulars of the allotment of shares to the registrar in accordance with that Chapter: CA 2006, s 554(2A) (as inserted by SBEEA 2015, Sch 5, Pt 2).

25.23 If a company fails to comply with s 544, an offence is committed by the company, and every officer of the company who is in default: CA 2006, s 554(3).

A person guilty of an offence under s 554 is liable on summary conviction to a fine not exceeding level 3 on the standard scale and, for continued contravention, a daily default fine not exceeding one-tenth of level 3 on the standard scale: CA 2006, s 554(4).

For the company's duties as to the issue of share certificates etc, see Pt 21 (certification and transfer of securities): CA 2006, s 554(5).

Return of allotment

25.24 Sections 555–557 are concerned with provisions dealing with return of allotment.

Return of allotment by limited company

25.25 Section 555 applies to a company limited by shares and to a company limited by guarantee and having a share capital: CA 2006, s 551(1). The company must, within one month of making an allotment of shares, deliver to the registrar for registration a return of the allotment: CA 2006, s 551(2). This return must contain the prescribed information, and be accompanied by a statement of capital: CA 2006, s 551(3).

The statement of capital must state with respect to the company's share capital at the date to which the return is made up the total number of shares of the company, the aggregate nominal value of those shares; the aggregate amount (if any) unpaid on those shares (whether on account of their nominal value or by way of premium), and for each class of shares (i) prescribed particulars of the rights attached to the shares, (ii) the total number of shares of that class, and (iii) the aggregate nominal value of shares of that class: CA 2006, s 555(4) (as amended by SBEEA 2015, Sch 6).

25.26 A return of allotments made under this section must be accompanied by a statement of capital. A statement of capital is in essence a 'snapshot' of a company's total subscribed capital at a particular point in time (in this context, the date to which the return of allotments is made up).

The requirement for a statement of capital when an allotment of new shares is made implements a requirement in the Second Company Law Directive (77/91/EEC) which states:

> '… the statutes or instruments of incorporation of the company shall always give at least the following information … (e) when the company has no authorized capital, the amount of the subscribed capital …'

'Statutes' and 'instruments of incorporation' equate to the articles and memorandum and the need to disclose information pertaining to the aggregate of a company's subscribed capital flows from the abolition of the requirement for a company to have an authorised share capital.

25.27 Whilst this Directive only applies to public companies, the requirement to provide a statement of capital, here and elsewhere in the CA 2006, extends to private companies limited by shares (and in certain cases to unlimited companies having a share capital, for example, where such companies make their annual return to the registrar). The public register will contain up-to-date information on a company's share capital.

Return of allotment by unlimited company allotting new class of shares

25.28 Section 556 applies to an unlimited company that allots shares of a class with rights that are not in all respects uniform with shares previously allotted: CA 2006, s 556(1).

The company must, within one month of making such an allotment, deliver to the registrar for registration a return of the allotment: CA 2006, s 556(2).

The return must contain the prescribed particulars of the rights attached to the shares: CA 2006, s 556(3).

For the purposes of s 556, shares are not to be treated as different from shares previously allotted by reason only that the former do not carry the same rights to dividends as the latter during the 12 months immediately following the former's allotment: CA 2006, s 556(4).

Offence of failure to make return

25.29 If a company makes default in complying with s 555 (return of allotment of shares by limited company), or s 556 (return of allotment of new class of shares by unlimited company), an offence is committed by every officer of the company who is in default: CA 2006, s 557(1).

A person guilty of an offence under s 557 will be liable on conviction on indictment, to a fine; and on summary conviction, to a fine not exceeding the statutory maximum and, for continued contravention, a daily default fine not exceeding one-tenth of the statutory maximum: CA 2006, s 557(2).

In the case of default in delivering to the registrar within one month after the allotment the return required by ss 555 or 556, any person liable for the default may apply to the court for relief, and the court, if satisfied (i) that the omission to deliver the document was accidental or due to inadvertence, or (ii) that it is just and equitable to grant relief, may make an order extending the time for delivery of the document for such period as the court thinks proper: CA 2006, s 557(3).

Supplementary provisions

When shares are allotted

25.30 For the purposes of the Companies Acts, shares in a company are taken to be allotted when a person acquires the unconditional right to be included in the company's register of members (or, as the case may be, to have the person's name and other particulars delivered to the registrar under Pt 8, Ch 2A and registered by the registrar) in respect of the shares: CA 2006, s 558 (as inserted by SBEEA 2015, Sch 5, Pt 2).

Provisions about allotment not applicable to shares taken on formation

25.31 The provisions of CA 2006, Pt 17, Ch 2 have no application in relation to the taking of shares by the subscribers to the memorandum on the formation of the company: CA 2006, s 559.

Allotment of equity securities: existing shareholders' right of pre-emption

25.32 Chapter 3 to Pt 17 of the CA 2006 is concerned with allotment of equity securities with reference to existing shareholders' rights of pre-emption.

Meaning of 'equity securities' and related expressions

25.33 The term 'equity securities' means ordinary shares in the company, or rights to subscribe for, or to convert securities into, ordinary shares in the company; the term 'ordinary shares' means shares other than shares that as respects dividends and capital carry a right to participate only up to a specified amount in a distribution: CA 2006, s 560(1).

The references to the allotment of equity securities in CA 2006, Pt 17, Ch 3 include the grant of a right to subscribe for, or to convert any securities into, ordinary shares in the company, and the sale of ordinary shares in the company that immediately before the sale are held by the company as treasury shares: CA 2006, s 560(2).

Existing shareholders' right of pre-emption

25.34 A company must not allot equity securities to a person on any terms unless it has made an offer to each person who holds ordinary shares in the company to allot to him on the same or more favourable terms a proportion of those securities that is as nearly as practicable equal to the proportion in nominal value held by him of the ordinary share capital of the company, and the period during which any such offer may be accepted has expired or the company has received notice of the acceptance or refusal of every offer so made: CA 2006, s 561(1).

Securities that a company has offered to allot to a holder of ordinary shares may be allotted to him, or anyone in whose favour he has renounced his right to their allotment, without contravening s 561(1)(b): CA 2006, s 561(2).

If s 561(1) applies in relation to the grant of such a right, it does not apply in relation to the allotment of shares in pursuance of that right: CA 2006, s 561(3).

25.35 Shares held by the company as treasury shares are disregarded for the purposes of s 561, so that the company is not treated as a person who holds ordinary shares, and the shares are not treated as forming part of the ordinary share capital of the company: CA 2006, s 561(4).

Section 561 is subject to ss 564–566 (exceptions to pre-emption right), ss 567 and 568 (exclusion of rights of pre-emption), ss 569–573 (disapplication of pre-emption rights), and s 576 (saving for certain older pre-emption procedures): CA 2006, s 561(5).

Communication of pre-emption offers to shareholders

25.36 Section 562 applies as to the manner in which offers required by s 561 are to be made to holders of a company's shares: CA 2006, s 562(1). Such offers may be made in hard copy or electronic form: CA 2006, s 562(2).

If the holder has no registered address in an EEA state and has not given to the company an address in an EEA state for the service of notices on him, or is the holder of a share warrant, the offer may be made by causing it, or a notice specifying where a copy of it can be obtained or inspected, to be published in the Gazette: CA 2006, s 562(3).

25.37 The offer must state a period during which it may be accepted and the offer shall not be withdrawn before the end of that period: CA 2006, s 562(4).

The period must be at least 21 days beginning, in the case of an offer made in hard copy, with the date on which the offer is sent or supplied; in the case of an offer made in electronic form, with the date on which the offer is sent; or in the case of an offer made by publication in the *Gazette*, with the date of publication: CA 2006, s 562(5).

The Secretary of State may, by regulations made by statutory instrument, reduce the period specified in s 562(5) (but not to less than 14 days), or increase that period: CA 2006, s 562(6).

Liability of company and officers in case of contravention

25.38 Section 563 concerns liability of company and officers in case of contravention. It applies where there is a contravention of s 561 (existing shareholders' right of pre-emption), or s 562 (communication of pre-emption offers to shareholders): CA 2006, s 563(1).

The company and every one of its officers who knowingly authorised or permitted the contravention, are jointly and severally liable to compensate any person to whom an offer should have been made in accordance with those provisions for any loss, damage, costs or expenses which the person has sustained or incurred by reason of the contravention: CA 2006, s 563(2).

No proceedings to recover any such loss, damage, costs or expenses shall be commenced after the expiration of two years from the delivery to the registrar of companies of the return of allotment, or where equity securities other than shares are granted, from the date of the grant: CA 2006, s 563(3).

Exceptions to right of pre-emption

Exception to pre-emption right: bonus shares

25.39 Section 564 deals with exceptions to right of pre-emption in respect of bonus shares. It states that s 561(1) (existing shareholders' right of pre-emption) does not apply in relation to the allotment of bonus shares: CA 2006, s 564.

Exception to pre-emption right: issue for non-cash consideration

25.40 Section 565 states that s 561(1) (existing shareholders' right of pre-emption) does not apply to a particular allotment of equity securities if these are, or are to be, wholly or partly paid up otherwise than in cash: CA 2006, s 565.

Exception to pre-emption right: securities held under employees' share scheme

25.41 Section 566 states that s 561 (existing shareholders' right of pre-emption) does not apply to the allotment of securities that would, apart from any renunciation or assignment of the right to their allotment, be held under an employees' share scheme: CA 2006, s 566.

Exclusion of right of pre-emption

Exclusion of requirements by private companies

25.42 All or any of the requirements of s 561 (existing shareholders' right of pre-emption), or s 562 (communication of pre-emption offers to shareholders) may be excluded by provision contained in the articles of a private company: CA 2006, s 567(1).

They may be excluded generally in relation to the allotment by the company of equity securities, or in relation to allotments of a particular description: CA 2006, s 567(2).

25.43 Any requirement or authorisation contained in the articles of a private company that is inconsistent with either of those sections is treated for the purposes of this section as a provision excluding that section: CA 2006, s 567(3).

A provision to which s 568 applies (exclusion of pre-emption right: corresponding right conferred by articles) is not to be treated as inconsistent with s 561: CA 2006, s 567(4).

Exclusion of pre-emption right: articles conferring corresponding right

25.44 Section 568 deals with exclusion of pre-emption right with reference to articles conferring corresponding right. The provisions of this section apply where, in a case in which s 561 (existing shareholders' right of pre-emption) would otherwise apply a company's articles contain provision ('pre-emption provision') prohibiting the company from allotting ordinary shares of a particular class unless it has complied with the condition that it makes such an offer as is described in s 561(1) to each person who holds ordinary shares of that class, and in accordance with that provision (i) the company makes an offer to allot shares to such a holder, and (ii) he or anyone in whose favour he has renounced his right to their allotment accepts the offer: CA 2006, s 568(1).

In that case, s 561 does not apply to the allotment of those shares and the company may allot them accordingly: CA 2006, s 568(2).

25.45 The provisions of s 562 (communication of pre-emption offers to shareholders) apply in relation to offers made in pursuance of the pre-emption provision of the company's articles: CA 2006, s 568(3). This is subject to s 567 (exclusion of requirements by private companies).

If there is a contravention of the pre-emption provision of the company's articles, the company, and every officer of it who knowingly authorised or permitted the contravention, are jointly and severally liable to compensate any person to whom an offer should have been made under the provision for any loss, damage, costs or expenses which the person has sustained or incurred by reason of the contravention: CA 2006, s 568(4).

No proceedings to recover any such loss, damage, costs or expenses may be commenced after the expiration of two years from the delivery to the registrar of companies of the return of allotment, or where equity securities other than shares are granted, from the date of the grant: CA 2006, s 568(5).

Disapplication of pre-emption rights

Disapplication of pre-emption rights: private company with only one class of shares

25.46 Section 569 states that the directors of a private company that has only one class of shares may be given power by the articles, or by a special resolution of the company, to allot equity securities of that class as if s 561 (existing shareholders' right of pre-emption) did not apply to the allotment, or applied to the allotment with such modifications as the directors may determine: CA 2006, s 569(1).

Where the directors make an allotment under s 569, the provisions of Ch 3 to Pt 17 apply accordingly: CA 2006, s 569(2).

Disapplication of pre-emption rights: directors acting under general authorisation

25.47 Section 570 states that where the directors of a company are generally authorised for the purposes of s 551 (power of directors to allot shares etc: authorisation by company), they may be given power by the articles, or by a special resolution of the company, to allot equity securities pursuant to that authorisation as if s 561 (existing shareholders' right of pre-emption) did not apply to the allotment, or applied to the allotment with such modifications as the directors may determine: CA 2006, s 570(1).

Where the directors make an allotment under s 570, the provisions of Ch 3 have effect accordingly: CA 2006, s 570(2).

25.48 The power conferred by s 570 ceases to have effect when the authorisation to which it relates is revoked, or would (if not renewed) expire. But if the authorisation is renewed the power may also be renewed, for a period not longer than that for which the authorisation is renewed, by a special resolution of the company: CA 2006, s 570(3).

Notwithstanding that the power conferred by s 570 has expired, the directors may allot equity securities in pursuance of an offer or agreement previously made by the company if the power enabled the company to make an offer or agreement that would or might require equity securities to be allotted after it expired: CA 2006, s 570(4).

Disapplication of pre-emption rights by special resolution

25.49 Where the directors of a company are authorised for the purposes of s 551 (power of directors to allot shares etc: authorisation by company), whether generally or otherwise, the company may by special resolution resolve that s 561 (existing shareholders' right of pre-emption) does not apply to a specified allotment of equity securities to be made pursuant to that authorisation, or applies to such an allotment with such modifications as may be specified in the resolution: CA 2006, s 571(1).

Where such a resolution is passed, the provisions of Ch 3 have effect accordingly: CA 2006, s 571(2).

25.50 A special resolution under s 571 ceases to have effect when the authorisation to which it relates is either revoked or would expire if not renewed: CA 2006, s 571(3). But if the authorisation is renewed the resolution may also be renewed, for a period not longer than that for which the authorisation is renewed, by a special resolution of the company.

Notwithstanding that any such resolution has expired, the directors may allot equity securities in pursuance of an offer or agreement previously made by the company if the resolution enabled the company to make an offer or agreement that would or might require equity securities to be allotted after it expired: CA 2006, s 571(4).

25.51 A special resolution under s 571, or a special resolution to renew such a resolution, must not be proposed unless it is recommended by the directors, and the directors have complied with the following provisions: CA 2006, s 571(5).

Before such a resolution is proposed, the directors must make a written statement setting out their reasons for making the recommendation, the amount to be paid to the company in respect of the equity securities to be allotted, and the directors' justification of that amount: CA 2006, s 571(6).

The directors' statement must, if the resolution is proposed as a written resolution, be sent or submitted to every eligible member at or before the time at which the proposed resolution is sent or submitted to him; or if the resolution is proposed at a general meeting, be circulated to the members entitled to notice of the meeting with that notice: CA 2006, s 571(7).

Liability for false statement in the directors' statement

25.52 Section 572 deals with liability for false statement in the directors' statement. It applies in relation to a directors' statement under s 571 (special resolution disapplying pre-emption rights) that is sent, submitted or circulated under s 571(7): CA 2006, s 572(1).

A person who knowingly or recklessly authorises or permits the inclusion of any matter that is misleading, false or deceptive in a material particular in such a statement commits an offence: CA 2006, s 572(2).

A person found guilty of an offence under s 572 will be liable, on conviction or indictment, to imprisonment for a term not exceeding two years or a fine (or both); on summary conviction (i) in England and Wales, to imprisonment for a term not exceeding 12 months or to a fine not exceeding the statutory maximum (or both); (ii) in Scotland or Northern Ireland, to imprisonment for a term not exceeding six months, or to a fine not exceeding the statutory maximum (or both): CA 2006, s 572(3).

Disapplication of pre-emption rights: sale of treasury shares

25.53 Section 573 applies in relation to a sale of shares that is an allotment of equity securities by virtue of s 560(2)(b) (sale of shares held by company as treasury shares): CA 2006, s 573(1).

The directors of a company may be given power by the articles, or by a special resolution of the company, to allot equity securities as if s 561 (existing shareholders' right of pre-emption) did not apply to the allotment, or applied to the allotment with such modifications as the directors may determine: CA 2006, s 573(2).

The provisions of s 570(2) and (4) apply in that case as they apply to a case within sub-s (1) of that section: CA 2006, s 573(3).

25.54 The company may by special resolution resolve that s 561 shall not apply to a specified allotment of securities, or shall apply to the allotment with such modifications as may be specified in the resolution: CA 2006, s 573(4).

The provisions of s 571(2) and (4)–(7) apply in that case as they apply to a case within sub-s (1) of that section: CA 2006, s 573(5).

Supplementary provisions

References to holder of shares in relation to offer

25.55 Section 574 states that in Ch 3 to Pt 17 of the CA 2006, in relation to an offer to allot securities required by s 561 (existing shareholders' right of pre-emption), or any provision to which s 568 applies (articles conferring corresponding right), a reference (however expressed) to the holder of shares of any description is to whoever was the holder of shares of that description at the close of business on a date to be specified in the offer: CA 2006, s 574(1).

The specified date must fall within the period of 28 days immediately before the date of the offer: CA 2006, s 574(2).

Saving for other restrictions on offer or allotment

25.56 Section 575 states that the provisions of Ch 3 to Pt 17 of the CA 2006 are without prejudice to any other enactment by virtue of which a company is prohibited (whether generally or in specified circumstances) from offering or allotting equity securities to any person: CA 2006, s 575(1).

Where a company cannot by virtue of such an enactment offer or allot equity securities to a holder of ordinary shares of the company, those shares are disregarded for the purposes of s 561 (existing shareholders' right of pre-emption), so that the person is not treated as a person who holds ordinary shares, and the shares are not treated as forming part of the ordinary share capital of the company: CA 2006, s 575(2).

Public companies: allotment where issue not fully subscribed

25.57 Chapter 4 to Pt 17 of the CA 2006 is concerned with public companies with regard to allotment where issue not fully subscribed.

Public companies: allotment where issue not fully subscribed

25.58 Section 578 states that no allotment shall be made of shares of a public company offered for subscription unless the issue is subscribed for in full, or the offer is made on terms that the shares subscribed for may be allotted (i) in any event, or (ii) if specified conditions are met (and those conditions are met): CA 2006, s 578(1).

If shares are prohibited from being allotted by s 578(1) and 40 days have elapsed after the first making of the offer, all money received from applicants for shares must be repaid to them forthwith, without interest: s 578(2).

If any of the money is not repaid within 48 days after the first making of the offer, the directors of the company are jointly and severally liable to repay it, with interest at the rate for the time being specified under s 17 of the Judgments Act 1838 (c 110) from the expiration of the 48th day: CA 2006, s 578(3).

A director is not so liable if he proves that the default in the repayment of the money was not due to any misconduct or negligence on his part.

25.59 Section 578 applies in the case of shares offered as wholly or partly payable otherwise than in cash as it applies in the case of shares offered for subscription: CA 2006, s 578(4).

In that case the references in s 578(1) to subscription are to be construed accordingly; references in s 578(2) and (3) to the repayment of money received from applicants for shares include (i) the return of any other consideration so received (including, if the case so requires, the release of the applicant from any undertaking), or (ii) if it is not reasonably practicable to return the consideration, the payment of money equal to its value at the time it was so received; and references to interest apply accordingly: CA 2006, s 578(5).

Any condition requiring or binding an applicant for shares to waive compliance with any requirement of s 578 is void: CA 2006, s 578(6).

Public companies: effect of irregular allotment where issue not fully subscribed

25.60 An allotment made by a public company to an applicant in contravention of s 578 (public companies: allotment where issue not fully subscribed) is voidable at the instance of the applicant within one month after the date of the allotment, and not later: CA 2006, s 579(1).

It is so voidable even if the company is in the course of being wound up: CA 2006, s 579(2).

A director of a public company who knowingly contravenes, or permits or authorises the contravention of, any provision of s 578 with respect to allotment is liable to compensate the company and the allottee respectively for any loss, damages, costs or expenses that the company or allottee may have sustained or incurred by the contravention: CA 2006, s 579(3).

Proceedings to recover any such loss, damages, costs or expenses may not be brought more than two years after the date of the allotment: CA 2006, s 579(4).

Payment for shares

25.61 CA 2006, Pt 17, Ch 5 is concerned with the provisions dealing with payment for shares. It contains 13 provisions.

General rules

Shares not to be allotted at a discount

25.62 Section 580 addresses the rules that shares must not be allotted at a discount.

A company's shares must not be allotted at a discount: CA 2006, s 580(1). The allotment must not be less than the nominal value or par value of the shares.

If shares are allotted in contravention of s 580, the allottee is liable to pay the company an amount equal to the amount of the discount, with interest at the appropriate rate: CA 2006, s 580(2).

Shares cannot be allotted at a discount

In *Ooregum Gold Mining Co of India v Roper* [1892] AC 125, the House of Lords held that a company had no power to issue shares as fully paid up, for a money consideration less than their nominal value.

According to Vaughan Williams LJ in *Re Innes & Co Ltd* [1903] 2 Ch 254, each transaction must be considered on its facts to see if there is any basis for a colourable transaction:

> 'It cannot be suggested that mere inadequacy of price was sufficient of itself to invalidate the contract. You must show that, these shares not

> having been paid for at all, the contract for purchase was a colourable transaction, and that in truth and in fact, qua value, these shares were not part of the consideration, but were a gift.'
>
> In *Re White Star Line Ltd* [1938] 1 Ch 458, the Court of Appeal held that the consideration payable for the shares in money's worth by way of deferred creditors' certificates which were less than the nominal value of the shares, was 'illusory' and did not amount to a payment under the Companies Acts
>
> See too, *Welton v Saffery* [1897] AC 299; and *Re Eddystone Marine Insurance Co* [1893] 3 Ch 9.

Provision for different amounts to be paid on shares

25.63 A company, if so authorised by its articles, may make arrangements on the issue of shares for a difference between the shareholders in the amounts and times of payment of calls on their shares; accept from any member the whole or part of the amount remaining unpaid on any shares held by him, although no part of that amount has been called up; or pay a dividend in proportion to the amount paid up on each share where a larger amount is paid up on some shares than on others: CA 2006, s 581(1).

General rule as to means of payment

25.64 Shares allotted by a company, and any premium on them, may be paid up in money or money's worth (including goodwill and know-how): CA 2006, s 582(1).

Section 582 does not prevent a company from allotting bonus shares to its members, or from paying up, with sums available for the purpose, any amounts for the time being unpaid on any of its shares (whether on account of the nominal value of the shares or by way of premium): CA 2006, s 582(2).

Section 581 applies subject to the following provisions of CA 2006, Pt 17, Ch 5 (additional rules for public companies): CA 2006, s 582(3).

Meaning of payment in cash

25.65 The following provisions apply for the purposes of the Companies Acts: CA 2006, s 583(1).

A share in a company is deemed paid up (as to its nominal value or any premium on it) in cash, or allotted for cash, if the consideration received for the allotment or payment up is a cash consideration: CA 2006, s 583(2).

The term 'cash consideration' means cash received by the company, or a cheque received by the company in good faith that the directors have no reason for suspecting will not be paid, or a release of a liability of the company for a liquidated sum, or an undertaking to pay cash to the company at a future date, or payment by any other means giving rise to a present or future entitlement (of the company or a person acting on the company's behalf) to a payment, or credit equivalent to payment, in cash: CA 2006, s 583(3).

In relation to 'a release of a liability of the company for a liquidated sum', in *Re Harmony and Montague Tin and Copper Mining Co, Spargo's Case* (1873) 8 Ch App 407, James LJ was of the opinion that a set-off between allotment of shares to a shareholder and release of a liability of the company for a liquidated sum amounted to payment in 'cash' for the shares without any physical movement of the cash.

25.66 The Secretary of State may by order provide that particular means of payment specified in the order are to be regarded as falling within s 583(3)(e): CA 2006, s 583(4).

In relation to the allotment or payment up of shares in a company the payment of cash to a person other than the company, or an undertaking to pay cash to a person other than the company, counts as consideration other than cash: CA 2006, s 583(5).

This does not apply for the purposes of Ch 3 to Pt 17 of the CA 2006 (allotment of equity securities: existing shareholders' right of pre-emption). For the purpose of determining whether a share is or is to be allotted for cash, or paid up in cash, 'cash' includes foreign currency: CA 2006, s 583(6).

In *Wragg Ltd* [1897] 1 Ch 796, the Court of Appeal stated that in respect of a company limited by shares, the court will not enquire into the adequacy of the consideration for the shares unless tainted by aspects such as fraud. The court stated that the liability of a shareholder to pay the company the price of his shares was a statutory liability. Provided that a company acted honestly and not colourably and provided that it had not been so imposed upon as to be entitled to be relieved from its bargain, an agreement by the company to pay for property or services in fully paid-up shares was valid and binding on the company and its creditors. Unless the transaction was impeached eg, on the ground of fraud – the value of the property or services paid for in shares could not be inquired into; the value of what was acquired by the company was measured by the price at which the company agreed to buy for the asset or services.

Additional rules for public companies

Public companies: shares taken by subscribers of memorandum

25.67 Shares taken by a subscriber to the memorandum of a public company in pursuance of an undertaking of his in the memorandum, and any premium on the shares, must be paid up in cash: CA 2006, s 584.

Public companies: must not accept undertakings to do work or perform services

25.68 A public company must not accept at any time, in payment up of its shares or any premium on them, an undertaking given by any person that he or another should do work or perform services for the company or any other person: CA 2006, s 585(1).

If a public company accepts such an undertaking in payment up of its shares or any premium on them, the holder of the shares when they or the premium are treated as paid up (in whole or in part) by the undertaking is liable: (a) to pay the company in respect of those shares an amount equal to their nominal value, together with the whole of any premium or, if the case so requires, such proportion of that amount as is treated as paid up by the undertaking; and (b) to pay interest at the appropriate rate on the amount payable under paragraph (a): CA 2006, s 585(2).

The reference in s 585(2) to the holder of shares includes a person who has an unconditional right to be included in the company's register of members in respect of those shares, or to have an instrument of transfer of them executed in his favour: CA 2006, s 585(3).

Public companies: shares must be at least one-quarter paid up

25.69 A public company must not allot a share except as paid up at least as to one-quarter of its nominal value and the whole of any premium on it: CA 2006, s 586(1).

This does not apply to shares allotted in pursuance of an employees' share scheme: CA 2006, s 586(2).

If a company allots a share in contravention of s 586, the share is to be treated as if one-quarter of its nominal value, together with the whole of any premium on it, had been received, and the allottee is liable to pay the company the minimum amount which should have been received in respect of the share under s 586(1) (less the value of any consideration actually applied in payment up, to any extent, of the share and any premium on it), with interest at the appropriate rate: CA 2006, s 586(3).

Section 586(3) does not apply to the allotment of bonus shares, unless the allottee knew or ought to have known the shares were allotted in contravention of this section: CA 2006, s 586(4).

Public companies: payment by long-term undertaking

25.70 A public company must not allot shares as fully or partly paid up (as to their nominal value or any premium on them) otherwise than in cash if the consideration for the allotment is or includes an undertaking which is to be, or may be, performed more than five years after the date of the allotment: CA 2006, s 587(1).

If a company allots shares in contravention of s 587(1), the allottee is liable to pay the company an amount equal to the aggregate of their nominal value and the whole of any premium (or, if the case so requires, so much of that aggregate as is treated as paid up by the undertaking), with interest at the appropriate rate: CA 2006, s 587(2).

Where a contract for the allotment of shares does not contravene s 587(1), any variation of the contract that has the effect that the contract would have contravened the subsection, if the terms of the contract as varied had been its original terms, is void: CA 2006, s 587(3).

This applies also to the variation by a public company of the terms of a contract entered into before the company was re-registered as a public company.

25.71 Where a public company allots shares for a consideration which consists of or includes (in accordance with sub-s (1)) an undertaking that is to be performed within five years of the allotment, and the undertaking is not performed within the period allowed by the contract for the allotment of the shares, the allottee is liable to pay the company, at the end of the period so allowed, an amount equal to the aggregate of the nominal value of the shares and the whole of any premium (or, if the case so requires, so much of that aggregate as is treated as paid up by the undertaking), with interest at the appropriate rate: CA 2006, s 587(4).

The references in s 587 to a contract for the allotment of shares include an ancillary contract relating to payment in respect of them: CA 2006, s 587(5).

Supplementary provisions

Liability of subsequent holders of shares

25.72 If a person becomes a holder of shares in respect of which there has been a contravention of any provision of Ch 5 to Pt 17 of the CA 2006, and by virtue of that contravention another is liable to pay any amount under the provision contravened, that person is also liable to pay that amount (jointly and severally with any other person so liable), subject as follows: CA 2006, s 588(1).

A person otherwise liable under s 587(1) is exempted from that liability if either he is a purchaser for value and, at the time of the purchase, he did not have actual notice of the contravention concerned, or he derived title to the shares (directly or indirectly) from a person who became a holder of them after the contravention and was not liable under s 588(1): CA 2006, s 588(2).

25.73 The references in s 588 to a holder, in relation to shares in a company, include any person who has an unconditional right to be included in the company's register of members (or, as the case may be, to have the person's name and other particulars delivered to the registrar under Pt 8, Ch 2A and registered by the registrar) in respect of those shares, or to have an instrument of transfer of the shares executed in his favour: CA 2006, s 588(3) (as inserted by SBEEA 2015, Sch 5, Pt 2).

Section 588 applies in relation to a failure to carry out a term of a contract as mentioned in s 587(4) (public companies: payment by long-term undertaking) as it applies in relation to a contravention of a provision of Ch 5 to Pt 17 of the CA 2006: CA 2006, s 588(4).

Power of court to grant relief

25.74 Section 589 applies in relation to liability under s 585(2) (liability of allottee in case of breach by public company of prohibition on accepting undertaking to do work or perform services), s 587(2) or (4) (liability of allottee in case of breach by public company of prohibition on payment by long-term undertaking), or s 588 (liability of subsequent holders of shares) as it applies in relation to a contravention of those sections: CA 2006, s 589(1).

A person who is subject to any such liability to a company in relation to payment in respect of shares in the company, or is subject to any such liability to a company by virtue of an undertaking given to it in, or in connection with, payment for shares in the company, may apply to the court to be exempted in whole or in part from the liability: CA 2006, s 589(2).

25.75 In the case of a liability within s 589(2)(a), the court may exempt the applicant from the liability only if and to the extent that it appears to the court just and equitable to do so having regard to:

(a) whether the applicant has paid, or is liable to pay, any amount in respect of:

   (i) any other liability arising in relation to those shares under any provision of Ch 5 or Ch 6 to Pt 17 of the CA 2006; or

   (ii) any liability arising by virtue of any undertaking given in or in connection with payment for those shares;

(b) whether any person other than the applicant has paid or is likely to pay, whether in pursuance of any order of the court or otherwise, any such amount;

(c) whether the applicant or any other person:

   (i) has performed in whole or in part, or is likely so to perform any such undertaking; or

   (ii) has done or is likely to do any other thing in payment or part payment for the shares: CA 2006, s 589(3).

In the case of a liability within CA 2006, s 589(2)(b), the court may exempt the applicant from the liability only if and to the extent that it appears to the court just and equitable to do so having regard to whether the applicant has paid or is liable to pay any amount in respect of liability arising in relation to the shares under any provision of Chapters 5 or 6 of the CA 2006; or whether any person other than the applicant has paid or is likely to pay, whether in pursuance of any order of the court or otherwise, any such amount: CA 2006, s 589(4).

25.76 In determining whether it should exempt the applicant in whole or in part from any liability, the court must have regard to the following overriding principles: (a) a company that has allotted shares should receive money or money's worth at least equal in value to the aggregate of the nominal value of those shares and the whole of any premium or, if the case so requires, so much of that aggregate as is treated as paid up; (b) subject to that, where a company would, if the court did not grant the exemption, have more than one remedy against a particular person, it should be for the company to decide which remedy it should remain entitled to pursue: CA 2006, s 589(5).

If a person brings proceedings against another ('the contributor') for a contribution in respect of liability to a company arising under any provision of Chapters 5 or 6 of the CA 2006 and it appears to the court that the contributor is liable to make such a contribution, the court may, if and to the extent that it appears to it just and equitable to do so having regard to the respective culpability (in respect of the liability to the company) of the contributor and the person bringing the proceedings, exempt the contributor in whole or in part from his liability to make such a contribution, or order the contributor to make a larger contribution than, but for this subsection, he would be liable to make: CA 2006, s 589(6).

Penalty for contravention of CA 2006, Pt 17, Ch 5

25.77 Section 590 sets out the penalty for contravention of Ch 5. If a company contravenes any of the provisions of Ch 5, an offence is committed by the company, and every officer of the company who is in default: CA 2006, s 590(1). A person found guilty of an offence will be liable on conviction on indictment, to a fine; on summary conviction, to a fine not exceeding the statutory maximum: CA 2006, s 590(2).

Enforceability of undertakings to do work etc

25.78 An undertaking given by any person, in or in connection with payment for shares in a company, to do work or perform services or to do any other thing, if it is enforceable by the company apart from Ch 5, is so enforceable notwithstanding that there has been a contravention in relation to it of a provision of Chs 5 or 6 to Pt 17 of the CA 2006: CA 2006, s 591(1). This is without prejudice to s 589 (power of court to grant relief etc in respect of liabilities): CA 2006, s 591(2).

The appropriate rate of interest

25.79 For the purposes of Ch 5 to Pt 17 of the CA 2006, the 'appropriate rate' of interest is 5% per annum, or such other rate as may be specified by order made by the Secretary of State: CA 2006, s 592(1).

Public companies: independent valuation of non-cash consideration

Non-cash consideration for shares

25.80 Chapter 6 to Pt 17 of the CA 2006 addresses the issue of independent valuation of non-cash consideration in respect of public companies.

Public company: valuation of non-cash consideration for shares

25.81 Section 593 considers the public company valuation of non-cash consideration for shares. A public company must not allot shares as fully or partly paid up (as to their nominal value or any premium on them) otherwise than in cash unless the consideration for the allotment has been independently valued in accordance with the provisions of this Chapter, the valuer's report has been made to the company during the six months immediately preceding the allotment of the shares, and a copy of the report has been sent to the proposed allottee: CA 2006, s 593(1).

For this purpose the application of an amount standing to the credit of any of a company's reserve accounts, or its profit and loss account, in paying up (to any extent) shares allotted to members of the company, or premiums on shares so allotted, does not count as consideration for the allotment: CA 2006, s 593(2).

Accordingly, s 593(1) does not apply in that case.

25.82 If a company allots shares in contravention of s 593(1) and either the allottee has not received the valuer's report required to be sent to him, or there has been some other contravention of the requirements of this section or s 596 that the allottee knew or ought to have known amounted to a contravention, the allottee is liable to pay the company an amount equal to the aggregate of the nominal value of the shares and the whole of any premium (or, if the case so requires, so much of that aggregate as is treated as paid up by the consideration), with interest at the appropriate rate: CA 2006, s 593(3).

Section 593 applies subject to s 594 (exception to valuation requirement: arrangement with another company), and s 595 (exception to valuation requirement: merger): CA 2006, s 593(4).

In *Re Bradford Investments Limited* [1991] BCLC 224, shares were allotted for non-cash consideration without a valuation report. What was the liability of the allottees in these circumstances?

Hoffmann J held that as allottees of the shares, the ordinary shareholders were liable under the Companies Acts to the company for the nominal value of the shares. That sum became due and payable immediately upon the shares being allotted.

In *Ossory Estates plc* [1988] BCLC 213, a public company purchased property for non-cash consideration without a valuation report. The CA 2006 sets out some exemptions to the need for a valuation report. Harman J stated that, in considering whether to grant an exemption order, the court was required by the Companies Acts to have regard to the overriding principle that a company which allotted shares should receive money or money's worth at least equal in value to the aggregate of the nominal value of the shares and any premium.

On the facts, this was ultimately satisfied and a valuation report had been subsequently prepared.

In *Bradford Investments plc (No 2)* [1991] BCLC 688, Hoffmann J held that relief under s 606 could not apply as the overriding principle under the Companies Acts was that the company should receive assets worth at least the nominal value of the allotted shares and any premium. On the facts, this was not the case and the exemption was not granted.

Similarly, in *System Control plc v Munro Corporate plc* [1990] BCLC 659, a valuation report had not been prepared as required under the CA 2006. Hoffmann J held that exemption could not be granted as there was no evidence on the facts demonstrating that the company had received at least the nominal amount on the sale of the shares.

Exception to valuation requirement: arrangement with another company

25.83 Section 594 states that s 593 (valuation of non-cash consideration) does not apply to the allotment of shares by a company ('company A') in connection with an arrangement to which this section applies: CA 2006, s 594(1).

Section 594 applies to an arrangement for the allotment of shares in company A on terms that the whole or part of the consideration for the shares allotted is to be provided by the transfer to that company, or the cancellation, of all or some of the shares, or of all or some of the shares of a particular class, in another company ('company B'): CA 2006, s 594(2). It is immaterial whether the arrangement provides for the issue to company A of shares, or shares of any particular class, in company B: CA 2006, s 594(3). The section applies to an arrangement only if under the arrangement it is open to all the holders of the shares in company B (or, where the arrangement applies only to shares of a particular class, to all the holders of shares of that class) to take part in the arrangement: CA 2006, s 594(4).

In determining whether that is the case, the following will be disregarded: (a) shares held by or by a nominee of company A; (b) shares held by or by a nominee of a company which is (i) the holding company, or a subsidiary, of company A, or (ii) a subsidiary of such a holding company; (c) shares held as treasury shares by company B: CA 2006, s 594(5).

25.84 In s 594, the term 'arrangement' means any agreement, scheme or arrangement (including an arrangement sanctioned in accordance with Pt 26 (arrangements and reconstructions), or s 110 of the Insolvency Act 1986 (c 45) or Art 96 of the Insolvency (Northern Ireland) Order 1989 (SI 1989 No 2405 (NI 19)) (liquidator in winding up accepting shares as consideration for sale of company property)). The term 'company', except in reference to company A, includes any body corporate: CA 2006, s 594(6).

Exception to valuation requirement: merger

25.85 It states that s 593 (valuation of non-cash consideration) does not apply to the allotment of shares by a company in connection with a proposed merger with another company: CA 2006, s 595(1).

A proposed merger is where one of the companies proposes to acquire all the assets and liabilities of the other in exchange for the issue of shares or other securities of that one to shareholders of the other, with or without any cash payment to shareholders: CA 2006, s 595(2).

The term 'company', in reference to the other company, includes any body corporate: CA 2006, s 595(3).

Non-cash consideration for shares: requirements as to valuation and report

25.86 Section 596 applies to non-consideration for shares and requirements as to valuation and report. The provisions of ss 1150–1153 (general provisions as to independent valuation and report) apply to the valuation and report required by s 593 (public company: valuation of non-cash consideration for shares): CA 2006, s 596(1).

The valuer's report must state the nominal value of the shares to be wholly or partly paid for by the consideration in question; the amount of any premium payable on the shares; the description of the consideration and, as respects so much of the consideration as he himself has valued, a description of that part of the consideration, the method used to value it and the date of the valuation; the extent to which the nominal value of the shares and any premium are to be treated as paid up: (i) by the consideration; (ii) in cash: CA 2006, s 596(2).

The valuer's report must contain or be accompanied by a note by him in the case of a valuation made by a person other than himself, that it appeared to himself reasonable to arrange for it to be so made or to accept a valuation so made, whoever made the valuation, that the method of valuation was reasonable in all the circumstances, that it appears to the valuer that there has been no material change in the value of the consideration in question since the valuation, and that, on the basis of the valuation, the value of the consideration, together with any cash by which the nominal value of the shares or any premium payable on them is to be paid up, is not less than so much of the aggregate of the nominal value and the whole of any such premium as is treated as paid up by the consideration and any such cash: CA 2006, s 596(3).

25.87 Where the consideration to be valued is accepted partly in payment up of the nominal value of the shares and any premium and partly for some other consideration given by the company, s 593 and the preceding provisions of this section apply as if references to the consideration accepted by the company included the proportion of that consideration that is properly attributable to the payment up of that value and any premium: CA 2006, s 596(4).

In such a case the valuer must carry out, or arrange for, such other valuations as will enable him to determine that proportion, and his report must state what valuations have been made under this subsection and also the reason for, and method and date of, any such valuation and any other matters which may be relevant to that determination: CA 2006, s 596(5).

Copy of report to be delivered to registrar

25.88 Section 597 provides for a copy of the report to be delivered to the registrar. A company to which a report is made under s 593 as to the value of any consideration for which, or partly for which, it proposes to allot shares must deliver a copy of the report to the registrar for registration.

The copy must be delivered at the same time that the company files the return of the allotment of those shares under s 555 (return of allotment by limited company): CA 2006, s 597(1).

25.89 If default is made in complying with s 597(1) or (2), an offence is committed by every officer of the company who is in default: CA 2006, s 597(3). A person found guilty of an offence under this section will be liable on conviction on indictment, to a fine; on summary conviction, to a fine not exceeding the statutory maximum and, for continued contravention, a daily default fine not exceeding one-tenth of the statutory maximum: CA 2006, s 597(4).

In the case of default in delivering to the registrar any document as required by s 597, any person liable for the default may apply to the court for relief: CA 2006, s 597(5).

The court, if satisfied that the omission to deliver the document was accidental or due to inadvertence, or that it is just and equitable to grant relief, may make an order extending the time for delivery of the document for such period as the court thinks proper: CA 2006, s 597(6).

Transfer of non-cash asset in initial period

Public company: agreement for transfer of non-cash asset in initial period

25.90 A public company formed as such must not enter into an agreement with a person who is a subscriber to the company's memorandum, for the transfer by him to the company, or another, before the end of the company's initial period of one or more non-cash assets, and under which the consideration for the transfer to be given by the company is at the time of the agreement equal in value to one-tenth or more of the company's issued share capital, unless the conditions referred to below have been complied with: CA 2006, s 598(1).

The company's 'initial period' means the period of two years beginning with the date of the company being issued with a certificate under s 761 (trading certificate): CA 2006, s 598(2).

The conditions are those specified in s 599 (requirement of independent valuation), and s 601 (requirement of approval by members): CA 2006, s 598(3).

25.91 Section 598 does not apply where it is part of the company's ordinary business to acquire, or arrange for other persons to acquire, assets of a particular description, and the agreement is entered into by the company in the ordinary course of that business: CA 2006, s 598(4).

Section 598 does not apply to an agreement entered into by the company under the supervision of the court or of an officer authorised by the court for the purpose: CA 2006, s 598(5).

Agreement for transfer of non-cash asset: requirement of independent valuation

25.92 Section 599 deals with agreement for transfer of non-cash asset and the requirement of independent valuation. The following conditions must have been complied with: the consideration to be received by the company, and any consideration other than cash to be given by the company, must have been independently valued in accordance with the provisions of Ch 6 to Pt 17 of the CA 2006; the valuer's report must have been made to the company during the six months immediately preceding the date of the agreement, and a copy of the report must have been sent to the other party to the proposed agreement not later than the date on which copies have to be circulated to members under s 601(3): CA 2006, s 599(1).

25.93 The reference in s 599(1)(a) to the consideration to be received by the company is to the asset to be transferred to it or, as the case may be, to the advantage to the company of the asset's transfer to another person: CA 2006, s 599(2).

The reference in s 599(1)(c) to the other party to the proposed agreement is to the person referred to in s 598(1)(a): CA 2006, s 599(3).

If he has received a copy of the report under s 601 in his capacity as a member of the company, it is not necessary to send another copy under s 599.

Section 599 does not affect any requirement to value any consideration for purposes of s 593 (valuation of non-cash consideration for shares): CA 2006, s 599(4).

Agreement for transfer of non-cash asset: requirements as to valuation and report

25.94 The provisions of ss 1150–1153 (general provisions as to independent valuation and report) apply to the valuation and report required by s 599 (public company: transfer of non-cash asset): CA 2006, s 600(1).

The valuer's report must state the consideration to be received by the company, describing the asset in question (specifying the amount to be received in cash) and the consideration to be given by the company (specifying the amount to be given in cash), and the method and date of valuation: CA 2006, s 600(2).

The valuer's report must contain or be accompanied by a note by him in the case of a valuation made by a person other than himself, that it appeared to himself reasonable to arrange for it to be so made or to accept a valuation so made, whoever made the valuation, that the method of valuation was reasonable in all the circumstances, that it appears to the valuer that there has been no material change in the value of the consideration in question since the valuation, and that, on the basis of the valuation, the value of the consideration to be received by the company is not less than the value of the consideration to be given by it: CA 2006, s 600(3).

25.95 Any reference in s 599 or s 600 to consideration given for the transfer of an asset includes consideration given partly for its transfer: CA 2006, s 600(4).

In such a case the value of any consideration partly so given is to be taken as the proportion of the consideration properly attributable to its transfer, the valuer must carry out or arrange for such valuations of anything else as will enable him to determine that proportion, and his report must state what valuations have been made for that purpose and also the reason for and method and date of any such valuation and any other matters which may be relevant to that determination: CA 2006, s 600(5).

Agreement for transfer of non-cash asset: requirement of approval by members

25.96 The following conditions must have been complied with, namely: the terms of the agreement must have been approved by an ordinary resolution of the company, the requirements of s 601 must have been complied with as respects the circulation to members of copies of the valuer's report under s 599 and a copy of the proposed resolution must have been sent to the other party to the proposed agreement: CA 2006, s 601(1).

The reference in s 601(1)(c) to the other party to the proposed agreement is to the person referred to in s 598(1)(a): CA 2006, s 601(2).

The requirements of s 601 as to circulation of copies of the valuer's report are as follows: if the resolution is proposed as a written resolution, copies of the valuer's report must be sent or submitted to every eligible member at or before the time at which the proposed resolution is sent or submitted to him; if the resolution is proposed at a general meeting, copies of the valuer's report must be circulated to the members entitled to notice of the meeting not later than the date on which notice of the meeting is given: CA 2006, s 601(3).

Copy of resolution to be delivered to registrar

25.97 Section 602 applies to a copy of the resolution to be delivered to the registrar. A company that has passed a resolution under s 601 with respect to the transfer of an asset must, within 15 days of doing so, deliver to the registrar a copy of the resolution together with the valuer's report required by that section: CA 2006, s 602(1).

If a company fails to comply with s 602(1), an offence is committed by the company, and every officer of the company who is in default: CA 2006, s 602(2).

A person guilty of an offence under s 602 is liable on summary conviction to a fine not exceeding level 3 on the standard scale and, for continued contravention, to a daily default fine not exceeding one-tenth of level 3 on the standard scale: CA 2006, s 602(3).

Adaptation of provisions in relation to company re-registering as public

25.98 Section 603 deals with adaptation for provisions in relation to company re-registering as public. The provisions of ss 598–602 (public companies: transfer of non-cash assets) apply with the following adaptations in relation to a company re-registered as a public company the reference in s 598(1)(a) to a person who is a subscriber to the company's memorandum shall be read as a reference to a person who is a member of the company on the date of re-registration; the reference in s 598(2) to the date of the company being issued with a certificate under s 761 (trading certificate) shall be read as a reference to the date of re-registration: CA 2006, s 603.

Agreement for transfer of non-cash asset: effect of contravention

25.99 Section 604 addresses the effect of contravention in respect of an agreement to transfer of non-cash asset. It applies where a public company enters into an agreement in contravention of s 598 and either the other party to the agreement has not received the valuer's report required to be sent to him, or there has been some other contravention of the requirements of Ch 6 to Pt 17 that the other party to the agreement knew or ought to have known amounted to a contravention: CA 2006, s 604(1).

In those circumstances the company is entitled to recover from that person any consideration given by it under the agreement, or an amount equal to the value of the consideration at the time of the agreement, and the agreement, so far as not carried out, is void: CA 2006, s 604(2).

25.100 If the agreement is or includes an agreement for the allotment of shares in the company, then whether or not the agreement also contravenes s 593 (valuation of non-cash consideration for shares), s 604 does not apply to it in so far as it is for the allotment of shares, and the allottee is liable to pay the company an amount equal to the aggregate of the nominal value of the shares and the whole of any premium (or, if the case so requires, so much of that aggregate as is treated as paid up by the consideration), with interest at the appropriate rate: CA 2006, s 604(3).

Supplementary provisions

Liability of subsequent holders of shares

25.101 Section 605 deals with liability of subsequent holders of shares. If a person becomes a holder of shares in respect of which there has been a contravention of s 593 (public company: valuation of non-cash consideration for shares) and by virtue of that contravention another is liable to pay any amount under the provision contravened, that person is also liable to pay that amount (jointly and severally with any other person so liable) unless he is exempted from liability under s 605(3) below: CA 2006, s 605(1).

25.102 If a company enters into an agreement in contravention of s 598 (public company: agreement for transfer of non-cash asset in initial period) and the agreement is or includes an agreement for the allotment of shares in the company, a person becomes a holder of shares allotted under the agreement, and by virtue of the agreement and allotment under it another person is liable to pay an amount under s 604, the person who becomes the holder of the shares is also liable to pay that amount (jointly and severally with any other person so liable), unless he is exempted from liability under s 605(3): CA 2006, s 605(2). This applies whether or not the agreement also contravenes s 593.

25.103 A person otherwise liable under s 605(1) or (2) is exempt from that liability if either he is a purchaser for value and, at the time of the purchase, he did not have actual notice of the contravention concerned, or he derived title to the shares (directly or indirectly) from a person who became a holder of them after the contravention and was not liable under s 605(1) or (2): CA 2006, s 605(3).

The references in s 605 to a holder, in relation to shares in a company, include any person who has an unconditional right to be included in the company's register of members (or, as the case may be, to have the person's name and other particulars delivered to the registrar under Pt 8, Ch 2A and registered by the registrar) in respect of those shares, or to have an instrument of transfer of the shares executed in his favour: CA 2006, s 605(4) (as inserted by SBEEA 2015, Sch 5, Pt 2).

Power of court to grant relief

25.104 Section 606 applies to the power of the court to grant relief. A person who is liable to a company under any provision of Pt 17, Ch 6 in relation to payment in respect of any shares in the company, or is liable to a company by virtue of an undertaking given to it in, or in connection with, payment for any shares in the company, may apply to the court to be exempted in whole or in part from the liability: CA 2006, s 606(1).

25.105 In the case of a liability within s 606(1)(a), the court may exempt the applicant from the liability only if and to the extent that it appears to the court just and equitable to do so having regard to (a) whether the applicant has paid, or is liable to pay, any amount in respect of (i) any other liability arising in relation to those shares under any provision of Ch 6 or Ch 5, or (ii) any liability arising by virtue of any undertaking given in, or in connection with, payment for those shares; (b) whether any person other than the applicant has paid or is likely to pay, whether in pursuance of any order of the court or otherwise, any such amount; (c) whether the applicant or any other person (i) has performed in whole or in part, or is likely so to perform any such undertaking, or (ii) has done or is likely to do any other thing in payment or part payment for the shares: CA 2006, s 606(2).

In the case of a liability within s 606(1)(b), the court may exempt the applicant from the liability only if and to the extent that it appears to the court just and equitable to do so having regard to whether the applicant has paid or is liable to pay any amount in respect of liability arising in relation to the shares under any provision of Ch 6 or Ch 5; whether any person other than the applicant has paid or is likely to pay, whether in pursuance of any order of the court or otherwise, any such amount: CA 2006, s 606(3).

25.106 In determining whether it should exempt the applicant in whole or in part from any liability, the court must have regard to the certain overriding principles, namely: that a company that has allotted shares should receive money or money's worth at least equal in value to the aggregate of the nominal value of those shares and the whole of any premium or, if the case so requires, so much of that aggregate as is treated as paid up; subject to this, that where such a company would, if the court did not grant the exemption, have more than one remedy against a particular person, it should be for the company to decide which remedy it should remain entitled to pursue: CA 2006, s 606(4).

25.107 If a person brings proceedings against another ('the contributor') for a contribution in respect of liability to a company arising under any provision of Ch 6 or Ch 5 and it appears to the court that the contributor is liable to make such a contribution, the court may, if and to the extent that it appears to it just and equitable to do so having regard to the respective culpability (in respect of the liability to the company) of the contributor and the person bringing the proceedings, exempt the contributor in whole or in part from his liability to make such a contribution, or order the contributor to make a larger contribution than, but for s 606(5), he would be liable to make: CA 2006, s 606(5).

Where a person is liable to a company under s 604(2) (agreement for transfer of non-cash asset: effect of contravention), the court may, on application, exempt him in whole or in part from that liability if and to the extent that it appears to the court to be just and equitable to do so having regard to any benefit accruing to the company by virtue of anything done by him towards the carrying out of the agreement mentioned in that subsection: CA 2006, s 606(6).

Penalty for contravention of CA 2006, Pt 17, Ch 6

25.108 Section 607 sets out the penalty for contravention of Ch 6 to Pt 17 of the CA 2006. It applies where a company contravenes s 593 (public company allotting shares for non-cash consideration), or s 598 (public company entering into agreement for transfer of non-cash asset): CA 2006, s 607(1).

An offence is committed by the company, and every officer of the company who is in default: CA 2006, s 607(2). A person found guilty of an offence under s 607 will be liable on conviction on indictment, to a fine; on summary conviction, to a fine not exceeding the statutory maximum: CA 2006, s 607(3).

Enforceability of undertakings to do work etc

25.109 Section 608 applies to enforceability of undertakings to do work. An undertaking given by any person, in or in connection with payment for shares in a company, to do work or perform services or to do any other thing, if it is enforceable by the company apart from Ch 6, is so enforceable notwithstanding that there has been a contravention in relation to it of a provision of this Ch 6 or Ch 5: CA 2006, s 608(1).

This is without prejudice to s 606 (power of court to grant relief etc in respect of liabilities): CA 2006, s 608(2).

The appropriate rate of interest

25.110 Section 609 states that, for the purposes of CA 2006, Pt 17, Ch 6, the 'appropriate rate' of interest is 5% per annum, or such other rate as may be specified by order made by the Secretary of State: CA 2006, s 609(1).

Share premiums

25.111 Chapter 7 to Pt 17 of the CA 2006 contains provisions on share premiums.

The share premium account

Application of share premiums

25.112 Section 610 deals with the application of share premiums

If a company issues shares at a premium, whether for cash or otherwise, a sum equal to the aggregate amount or value of the premiums on those shares must be transferred to an account called 'the share premium account': CA 2006, s 610(1).

Where, on issuing shares, a company has transferred a sum to the share premium account, it may use that sum to write off the expenses of the issue of those shares; any commission paid on the issue of those shares: CA 2006, s 610(2).

The company may use the share premium account to pay up new shares to be allotted to members as fully paid bonus shares: CA 2006, s 610(3).

Subject to s 610(2) and (3), the provisions of the Companies Acts relating to the reduction of a company's share capital apply as if the share premium account were part of its paid up share capital: CA 2006, s 610(4).

Section 610 applies subject to s 611 (group reconstruction relief); s 612 (merger relief); and s 614 (power to make further provisions by regulations): CA 2006, s 610(5).

In Ch 7, the term 'the issuing company' means the company issuing shares as mentioned in s 610(1) above: CA 2006, s 610(6).

> In *Henry-Head & Co Ltd v Ropner Holdings Ltd* [1951] 2 All ER 994, a holding company was formed to acquire shares of two associated companies and to effect amalgamation. A £1 share of the new company was issued for each £1 share in the two associated companies The company's assets were undervalued and were worth more than the nominal value of the shares.
>
> Harman J held that the excess amount was rightly transferred to the share premium account under s 610.

Similarly, in *Shearer (Inspector of Taxes) v Bercain Ltd* [1980] 3 All ER 295, Walton J held that where shares were issued at a premium, whether for cash or otherwise than for cash, s 610 required the premium to be carried into a share premium account in the books of the company issuing the shares; the premium could only be distributed if the procedure for reduction of capital was carried through.

Judge Purle QC in *Re Sunrise Radio Ltd, Kohli v Lit* [2010] 1 BCLC 367 held that there had been a breach of directors' duties (by improper use of their powers) by issuing shares at par value when they could have considered alternatives, such as issuing shares at a premium. This was unfairly prejudicial conduct to the minority shareholder.

Relief from requirements as to share premiums

Group reconstruction relief

25.113 Section 611 deals with group reconstruction relief. It applies where the issuing company: (a) is a wholly owned subsidiary of another company ('the holding company'), and (b) allots shares (i) to the holding company, or (ii) to another wholly owned subsidiary of the holding company, in consideration for the transfer to the issuing company of non-cash assets of a company ('the transferor company') which is a member of the group of companies that comprises the holding company and all its wholly owned subsidiaries: CA 2006, s 611(1).

Where the shares in the issuing company allotted in consideration for the transfer are issued at a premium, the issuing company is not required by s 610 to transfer any amount in excess of the minimum premium value to the share premium account: CA 2006, s 611(2).

25.114 The minimum premium value means the amount (if any) by which the base value of the consideration for the shares allotted exceeds the aggregate nominal value of the shares: CA 2006, s 611(3).

The base value of the consideration for the shares allotted is the amount by which the base value of the assets transferred exceeds the base value of any liabilities of the transferor company assumed by the issuing company as part of the consideration for the assets transferred: CA 2006, s 611(4).

For the purposes of s 611: (a) the base value of assets transferred is taken as (i) the cost of those assets to the transferor company, or (ii) if less, the amount at which those assets are stated in the transferor company's accounting records immediately before the transfer; (b) the base value of the liabilities assumed is taken as the amount at which they are stated in the transferor company's accounting records immediately before the transfer: CA 2006, s 611(5).

Merger relief

25.115 Section 612 applies where the issuing company has secured at least a 90% equity holding in another company in pursuance of an arrangement providing for the allotment of equity shares in the issuing company on terms that the consideration for the shares allotted is to be provided by the issue or transfer to the issuing company of equity shares in the other company, or by the cancellation of any such shares not held by the issuing company: CA 2006, s 612(1).

If the equity shares in the issuing company allotted in pursuance of the arrangement in consideration for the acquisition or cancellation of equity shares in the other company are issued at a premium, s 610 does not apply to the premiums on those shares: CA 2006, s 612(2).

25.116 Where the arrangement also provides for the allotment of any shares in the issuing company on terms that the consideration for those shares is to be provided by the issue or transfer to the issuing company of non-equity shares in the other company, or by the cancellation of any such shares in that company not held by the issuing company, relief under s 612(2) extends to any shares in the issuing company allotted on those terms in pursuance of the arrangement: CA 2006, s 612(3).

Section 612 does not apply in a case falling within s 611 (group reconstruction relief): CA 2006, s 612(4).

Merger relief: meaning of 90% equity holding

25.117 Section 613 states that the following provisions have effect to determine for the purposes of s 612 (merger relief) whether a company ('company A') has secured at least a 90% equity holding in another company ('company B') in pursuance of such an arrangement as is mentioned in s 612(1): CA 2006, s 613(1).

Company A has secured at least a 90% equity holding in company B if in consequence of an acquisition or cancellation of equity shares in company B (in pursuance of that arrangement) it holds equity shares in company B of an aggregate amount equal to 90% or more of the nominal value of that company's equity share capital: CA 2006, s 613(2).

For this purpose it is immaterial whether any of those shares were acquired in pursuance of the arrangement; and shares in company B held by the company as treasury shares are excluded in determining the nominal value of company B's share capital: CA 2006, s 613(3).

25.118 Where the equity share capital of company B is divided into different classes of shares, company A is not regarded as having secured at least a 90% equity holding in company B unless the requirements of s 613(2) are met in relation to each of those classes of shares taken separately: CA 2006, s 613(4).

For the purposes of s 613, shares held by a company that is company A's holding company or subsidiary, or a subsidiary of company A's holding company, or its or their nominees, are treated as held by company A: CA 2006, s 613(5).

Power to make further provision by regulations

25.119 Section 614 considers the power to make further provisions by regulations. The Secretary of State may, by regulations, make such provision as he thinks appropriate for relieving companies from the requirements of s 610 (application of share premiums) in relation to premiums other than cash premiums for restricting or otherwise modifying any relief from those requirements provided by this Chapter: CA 2006, s 614(1).

Relief may be reflected in the company's balance sheet

25.120 Section 615 states that an amount corresponding to the amount representing the premiums, or part of the premiums, on shares issued by a company that by virtue of any relief under CA 2006, Pt 17, Ch 7 is not included in the company's share premium account may also be disregarded in determining the amount at which any shares or other consideration provided for the shares issued is to be included in the company's balance sheet.

25.121 The following definitions apply for the purposes of CA 2006, Pt 17, Ch 7.

The term 'arrangement' means any agreement, scheme or arrangement (including an arrangement sanctioned in accordance with:

(a) Part 26 (arrangements and reconstructions); or

(b) the Insolvency Act 1986 (c 45), s 110 or the Insolvency (Northern Ireland) Order 1989 (SI 1989/2405 (NI 19)), art 96 (liquidator in winding up accepting shares as consideration for sale of company property)).

'Company', except in reference to the issuing company, includes any body corporate.

'Equity shares' means shares comprised in a company's equity share capital, and 'non-equity shares' means shares (of any class) that are not so comprised.

'The issuing company' has the meaning given by s 610(6): CA 2006, s 616(1).

References in Ch 7 (however expressed) to:

(a) the acquisition by a company of shares in another company; and

(b) the issue or allotment of shares to, or the transfer of shares to or by, a company,

include (respectively) the acquisition of shares by, and the issue or allotment or transfer of shares to or by, a nominee of that company: CA 2006, s 616(2).

The reference in s 611 to the transferor company shall be read accordingly.

References in Ch 7 to the transfer of shares in a company include the transfer of a right to be included in the company's register of members (or, as the case may be, have your name and other particulars delivered to the registrar under Pt 8, Ch 2A and registered by the registrar) in respect of those shares: CA 2006, s 616(3) (as inserted by SBEEA 2015, Sch 5, Pt 2).

Alteration of share capital

25.122 Chapter 8 to Pt 17 of the CA 2006 applies to alteration of share capital.

How share capital may be altered

Alteration of share capital of limited company

25.123 A limited company having a share capital may not alter its share capital except in the following ways: CA 2006, s 617(1). The company may increase its share capital by:

(a) allotting new shares in accordance with Pt 17; or

(b) reducing its share capital in accordance with Ch 10: CA 2006, s 617(2).

The company may sub-divide or consolidate all or any of its share capital in accordance with s 618, or reconvert stock into shares in accordance with s 620: CA 2006, s 617(3).

The company may redenominate all or any of its shares in accordance with s 622, and may reduce its share capital in accordance with s 626 in connection with such a redenomination: CA 2006, s 617(4).

25.124 Section 617 does not affect the power of a company to purchase its own shares, or to redeem shares, in accordance with Pt 18; or the power of a company to purchase its own shares in pursuance of an order of the court under s 98 (application to court to cancel resolution for re-registration as a private company), s 721(6) (powers of court on objection to redemption or purchase of shares out of capital), s 759 (remedial order in case of breach of prohibition of public offers by private company), or Pt 30 (protection of members against unfair prejudice); the forfeiture of shares, or the acceptance of shares surrendered in lieu, in pursuance of the company's articles, for failure to pay any sum payable in respect of the shares; the cancellation of shares under s 662 (duty to cancel shares held by or for a public company); the power of a company to enter into a compromise or arrangement in accordance with Pt 26 (arrangements and reconstructions), or to do anything required to comply with an order of the court on an application under that Part: CA 2006, s 617(5). Further, CA 2006, s 617(5) does not affect:

- the cancellation of a share warrant issued by the company and of the shares specified in it by a cancellation order or suspended cancellation order made under para 6 of Schedule 4 to the Small Business, Enterprise and Employment Act 2015 (cancellation where share warrants not surrendered in accordance with that Schedule): CA 2006, s 617(5)(f) (as inserted by SBEEA 2015, Sch 4);
- the cancellation of a share warrant issued by the company and of the shares specified in it pursuant to ss 1028A(2) or 1032A(2) (cancellation of share warrants on restoration of a company): CA 2006, s 617(5)(g) (as inserted by SBEEA 2015, Sch 4).

Sub-division or consolidation of shares

Sub-division or consolidation of shares

25.125 Section 618 applies to subdivision or consolidation of shares.

A limited company having a share capital may sub-divide its shares, or any of them, into shares of a smaller nominal amount than its existing shares, or consolidate and divide all or any of its share capital into shares of a larger nominal amount than its existing shares: CA 2006, s 618(1).

In any sub-division, consolidation or division of shares under this section, the proportion between the amount paid and the amount (if any) unpaid on each resulting share must be the same as it was in the case of the share from which that share is derived: CA 2006, s 618(2).

25.126 A company may exercise a power conferred by s 618 only if its members have passed a resolution authorising it to do so: CA 2006, s 618(3).

A resolution under s 618(3) may authorise a company to exercise more than one of the powers conferred by this section; to exercise a power on more than one occasion; to exercise a power at a specified time or in specified circumstances: CA 2006, s 618(4). The company's articles may exclude or restrict the exercise of any power conferred by this section: CA 2006, s 618(5).

25.127 Consolidation of a company's share capital involves combining a number of shares into a new share of commensurate nominal value: for example, ten £1 shares may be combined to make one £10 share. Sub-division of a company's share capital involves dividing a share into a number of new shares with a smaller nominal value: for example, a £10 share may be sub-divided into ten £1 shares.

Section 618 sets out the circumstances and manner in which a limited company may consolidate or sub-divide its share capital. Where shares in a company are sub-divided or consolidated, the proportion between the amount paid and the amount unpaid (if any) on the original share(s) must remain the same in relation to the share(s) resulting from the sub-division or consolidation. If, for example, £2 is unpaid on a £10 share that is subsequently sub-divided into ten £1 shares, there will now be 20p unpaid on each of those ten shares.

25.128 A company may exercise a power conferred on it under this section only if the members have passed a resolution authorising it to do so, which may be an ordinary resolution or a resolution requiring a higher majority (as the articles may require). Such a resolution may authorise a company to exercise more than one of the powers conferred on it under this section, for example, the resolution may authorise a sub-division of one class of the company's shares and a consolidation of another. It may also authorise the company to exercise a power conferred on it under this section on more than one occasion or at a specified time or in specified circumstances. This avoids the directors having to obtain authorisation from the company's members on each and every occasion that a company alters its share capital under this section (which may be inconvenient to the directors and members alike or impractical due to timing constraints).

Notice to registrar of sub-division or consolidation

25.129 Section 619 deals with notice to the registrar of sub-division or consolidation. If a company exercises the power conferred by s 618 (sub-division or consolidation of shares), it must within one month after doing so give notice to the registrar, specifying the shares affected: CA 2006, s 619(1).

The notice must be accompanied by a statement of capital: CA 2006, s 619(2).

25.130 Immediately following the exercise of the power, the statement of capital must state with respect to the company's share capital: (a) the total number of shares of the company; (b) the aggregate nominal value of those shares; (c) for each class of shares (i) prescribed particulars of the rights attached to the shares, (ii) the total number of shares of that class, and (iii) the aggregate nominal value of shares of that class; and (d) the aggregate amount (if any) unpaid on those shares (whether on account of their nominal value or by way of premium),: CA 2006, s 619(3) (as inserted by SBEEA 2015, Sch 6).

25.131 If default is made in complying with s 619, an offence is committed by the company, and every officer of the company who is in default: CA 2006, s 619(4).

A person found guilty of an offence under this section will be liable on summary conviction to a fine not exceeding level 3 on the standard scale and, for continued contravention, a daily default fine not exceeding one-tenth of level 3 on the standard scale: CA 2006, s 619(5).

Reconversion of stock into shares

Reconversion of stock into shares

25.132 Section 620 applies to reconversion of stock into shares. A limited company that has converted paid-up shares into stock (before the repeal by this Act of the power to do so) may reconvert that stock into paid-up shares of any nominal value: CA 2006, s 620(1).

A company may exercise the power conferred by s 620 only if its members have passed an ordinary resolution authorising it to do so: CA 2006, s 620(2). A resolution under s 620(2) may authorise a company to exercise the power conferred by this section on more than one occasion; at a specified time or in specified circumstances: CA 2006, s 620(3).

Notice to registrar of reconversion of stock into shares

25.133 If a company exercises a power conferred by s 620 (reconversion of stock into shares) it must within one month after doing so give notice to the registrar, specifying the stock affected: CA 2006, s 621(1). Such notice must be accompanied by a statement of capital: CA 2006, s 621(2).

The statement of capital must state with respect to the company's share capital immediately following the exercise of the power (a) the total number of shares of the company, (b) the aggregate nominal value of those shares, (c) for each class of shares (i) prescribed particulars of the rights attached to the shares, (ii) the total number of shares of that class, and (iii) the aggregate nominal value of shares of that class; and (d) the aggregate amount (if any) unpaid on those shares (whether on account of their nominal value or by way of premium) : CA 2006, s 621(3) (as inserted by SBEEA 2015, Sch 6).

25.134 If default is made in complying with s 621, an offence is committed by the company, and every officer of the company who is in default: CA 2006, s 621(4).

A person who is found guilty of an offence under this section will be liable on summary conviction to a fine not exceeding level 3 on the standard scale and, for continued contravention, a daily default fine not exceeding one-tenth of level 3 on the standard scale: CA 2006, s 621(5).

Redenomination of share capital

Redenomination of share capital

25.135 A limited company having a share capital may by resolution redenominate its share capital or any class of its share capital: CA 2006, s 622(1). The term 'redenominate' means convert shares from having a fixed nominal value in one currency to having a fixed nominal value in another currency. The conversion must be made at an appropriate spot rate of exchange specified in the resolution: CA 2006, s 622(2).

The rate must be either a rate prevailing on a day specified in the resolution, or a rate determined by taking the average of rates prevailing on each consecutive day of a period specified in the resolution: CA 2006, s 622(3).

The day or period specified for the purposes of paragraph (a) or (b) must be within the period of 28 days ending on the day before the resolution is passed.

25.136 A resolution under s 622 may specify conditions which must be met before the redenomination takes effect: CA 2006, s 622(4). Redenomination in accordance with a resolution under this section takes effect on the day on which the resolution is passed, or on such later day as may be determined in accordance with the resolution: CA 2006, s 622(5). A resolution under this section lapses if the redenomination for which it provides has not taken effect at the end of the period of 28 days beginning on the date on which it is passed: CA 2006, s 622(6).

A company's articles may prohibit or restrict the exercise of the power conferred by the section: CA 2006, s 622(7).

Chapter 3 of Pt 3 of the CA 2006 (resolutions affecting a company's constitution) applies to a resolution under s 622: CA 2006, s 622(8).

Calculation of new nominal values

25.137 For each class of share the new nominal value of each share is calculated as follows:

Step one

Take the aggregate of the old nominal values of all the shares of that class.

Step two

Translate that amount into the new currency at the rate of exchange specified in the resolution.

Step three

Divide that amount by the number of shares in the class: CA 2006, s 623.

Effect of redenomination

25.138 The redenomination of shares does not affect any rights or obligations of members under the company's constitution, nor any restrictions affecting members under the company's constitution.

In particular, it does not affect entitlement to dividends (including entitlement to dividends in a particular currency), voting rights or any liability in respect of amounts unpaid on shares: CA 2006, s 624(1).

For this purpose, the company's constitution includes the terms on which any shares of the company are allotted or held: CA 2006, s 624(2).

Subject to s 624(1), references to the old nominal value of the shares in any agreement or statement, or in any deed, instrument or document, shall (unless the context otherwise requires) be read after the resolution takes effect as references to the new nominal value of the shares: CA 2006, s 624(3).

Notice to registrar of redenomination

25.139 If a limited company having a share capital redenominates any of its share capital, it must within one month after doing so give notice to the registrar, specifying the shares redenominated: CA 2006, s 625(1).

The notice must state the date on which the resolution was passed, and be accompanied by a statement of capital: CA 2006, s 625(2).

The statement of capital must state with respect to the company's share capital as redenominated by the resolution: (a) the total number of shares of the company; (b) the aggregate nominal value of those shares; (c) for each class of shares (i) prescribed particulars of the rights attached to the shares, (ii) the total number of shares of that class, and (iii) the aggregate nominal value of shares of that class; and (d) the aggregate amount (if any) unpaid on those shares (whether on account of their nominal value or by way of premium): CA 2006, s 625(3) (as inserted by SBEEA 2015, Sch 6).

25.140 If default is made in complying with s 625, an offence is committed by the company, and every officer of the company who is in default: CA 2006, s 625(4).

A person who is found guilty of an offence under this section will be liable on summary conviction to a fine not exceeding level 3 on the standard scale and, for continued contravention, a daily default fine not exceeding one-tenth of level 3 on the standard scale: CA 2006, s 625(5).

Reduction of capital in connection with redenomination

25.141 Under s 626, a limited company that passes a resolution redenominating some or all of its shares may, for the purpose of adjusting the nominal values of the redenominated shares to obtain values that are, in the opinion of the company, more suitable, reduce its share capital: CA 2006, s 626(1). A reduction of capital under this section requires a special resolution of the company: CA 2006, s 626(2).

Any such resolution must be passed within three months of the resolution effecting the redenomination: CA 2006, s 626(3).

25.142 The amount by which a company's share capital is reduced under s 626 must not exceed 10% of the nominal value of the company's allotted share capital immediately after the reduction: CA 2006, s 626(4). A reduction of capital under this section does not extinguish or reduce any liability in respect of share capital not paid up: CA 2006, s 626(5).

Nothing in Ch 10 applies to a reduction of capital under s 626: CA 2006, s 626(6).

Notice to registrar of reduction of capital in connection with redenomination

25.143 A company that passes a resolution under s 626 (reduction of capital in connection with redenomination) must, within 15 days after the resolution is passed, give notice to the registrar stating the date of the resolution, and the date of the resolution under s 622 in connection with which it was passed: CA 2006, s 627(1). This is in addition to the copies of the resolutions themselves that are required to be delivered to the registrar under Ch 3, Ch 3 of the CA 2006. The notice must be accompanied by a statement of capital: CA 2006, s 627(2).

The statement of capital must state with respect to the company's share capital as reduced by the resolution (a) the total number of shares of the company, (b) the aggregate nominal value of those shares, (c) for each class of shares (i) prescribed particulars of the rights attached to the shares, (ii) the total number of shares of that class, and (iii) the aggregate nominal value of shares of that class; and (d) the aggregate amount (if any) unpaid on those shares (whether on account of their nominal value or by way of premium): CA 2006, s 627(3) (as inserted by SBEEA 2015, Sch 6).

25.144 The registrar must register the notice and the statement on receipt: CA 2006, s 627(4).

The reduction of capital is not effective until those documents are registered: CA 2006, s 627(5).

The company must also deliver to the registrar, within 15 days after the resolution is passed, a statement by the directors confirming that the reduction in share capital is in accordance with s 626(4) (reduction of capital not to exceed 10% of nominal value of allotted shares immediately after reduction): CA 2006, s 627(6).

25.145 If default is made in complying with s 627, an offence is committed by the company, and every officer of the company who is in default: CA 2006, s 627(7).

A person who is found guilty of an offence under this section will be liable on conviction on indictment to a fine and, on summary conviction, to a fine not exceeding the statutory maximum: CA 2006, s 627(8).

Redenomination reserve

25.146 The amount by which a company's share capital is reduced under s 626 (reduction of capital in connection with redenomination) must be transferred to a reserve, called 'the redenomination reserve': CA 2006, s 628(1).

This reserve may be applied by the company in paying up shares to be allotted to members as fully paid bonus shares: CA 2006, s 628(2).

Subject to that, the provisions of the Companies Acts relating to the reduction of a company's share capital apply as if the redenomination reserve were paid-up share capital of the company: CA 2006, s 628(3).

Classes of share and class rights

25.147 At common law, the term 'Classes of shares' (or 'class rights') is normally used where the rights that attach to a particular share relate to matters such as voting rights, a right to dividends and a right to a return of capital when a company is wound up. Rights attach to a particular class of shares if the holders of shares in that class enjoy rights that are not enjoyed by the holders of shares in another class.

Introduction to Pt 17, Ch 9

Classes of shares

25.148 For the purposes of the Companies Acts, shares are of one class if the rights attached to them are in all respects uniform: CA 2006, s 629(1).

For this purpose the rights attached to shares are not regarded as different from those attached to other shares by reason only that they do not carry the same rights to dividends in the 12 months immediately following their allotment: CA 2006, s 629(2).

Variation of class rights

Variation of class rights: companies having a share capital

25.149 Section 630 is concerned with the variation of the rights attached to a class of shares in a company having a share capital: CA 2006, s 630(1).

Rights attached to a class of a company's shares may only be varied:

(a) in accordance with provision in the company's articles for the variation of those rights; or

(b) where the company's articles contain no such provision, if the holders of shares of that class consent to the variation in accordance with this section: CA 2006, s 630(2).

This is without prejudice to any other restrictions on the variation of the rights: CA 2006, s 630(3).

25.150 The consent required for the purposes of s 630 on the part of the holders of a class of a company's shares is:

(a) consent in writing from the holders of at least three-quarters in nominal value of the issued shares of that class (excluding any shares held as treasury shares); or

(b) a special resolution passed at a separate general meeting of the holders of that class sanctioning the variation: CA 2006, 630(4).

Any amendment of a provision contained in a company's articles for the variation of the rights attached to a class of shares, or the insertion of any such provision into the articles, is itself to be treated as a variation of those rights: CA 2006, s 630(5).

25.151 Under s 630 and (except where the context otherwise requires) in any provision in a company's articles for the variation of the rights attached to a class of shares, references to the variation of those rights include references to their abrogation: CA 2006, s 630(6).

Variation of class rights: companies without a share capital

25.152 Section 631 is concerned with the variation of the rights of a class of members of a company where the company does not have a share capital: CA 2006, s 631(1).

Rights of a class of members may only be varied:

(a) in accordance with provision in the company's articles for the variation of those rights; or

(b) where the company's articles contain no such provision, if the members of that class consent to the variation in accordance with this section: CA 2006, s 631(2).

This is without prejudice to any other restrictions on the variation of the rights: CA 2006, s 631(3).

25.153 The consent required for the purposes of s 631 on the part of the members of a class is:

(a) consent in writing from at least three-quarters of the members of the class; or

(b) a special resolution passed at a separate general meeting of the members of that class sanctioning the variation: CA 2006, s 631(4).

Any amendment of a provision contained in a company's articles for the variation of the rights of a class of members, or the insertion of any such provision into the articles, is itself to be treated as a variation of those rights: CA 2006, s 631(5).

25.154 Under s 631, and (except where the context otherwise requires) in any provision in a company's articles for the variation of the rights of a class of members, references to the variation of those rights include references to their abrogation: CA 2006, s 631(6).

Variation of class rights: saving for court's powers under other provisions

25.155 Nothing in ss 630 or 631 (variation of class rights) affects the power of the court under:

- s 98 (application to cancel resolution for public company to be re-registered as private);
- Part 26 (arrangements and reconstructions); or
- Part 30 (protection of members against unfair prejudice): CA 2006, s 632.

Right to object to variation: companies having a share capital

25.156 Section 633 deals with the procedure or right to object to variation in respect of companies having a share capital. It applies where the rights attached to any class of shares in a company are varied under s 630 (variation of class rights: companies having a share capital): CA 2006, s 633(1).

The holders of not less in the aggregate than 15% of the issued shares of the class in question (being persons who did not consent to or vote in favour of the resolution for the variation) may apply to the court to have the variation cancelled: CA 2006, s 633(2). For this purpose any of the company's share capital held as treasury shares is disregarded.

If such an application is made, the variation has no effect unless and until it is confirmed by the court: CA 2006, s 633(3).

25.157 Application to the court:

(a) must be made within 21 days after the date on which the consent was given or the resolution was passed (as the case may be); and

(b) may be made on behalf of the shareholders entitled to make the application by such one or more of their number as they may appoint in writing for the purpose: CA 2006, s 633(4).

25.158 The court, after hearing the applicant and any other persons who apply to the court to be heard and appear to the court to be interested in the application, may, if satisfied having regard to all the circumstances of the case that the variation would unfairly prejudice the shareholders of the class represented by the applicant, disallow the variation, and shall if not so satisfied confirm it.

The decision of the court on any such application is final: CA 2006, s 633(5).

References in s 633 to the variation of the rights of holders of a class of shares include references to their abrogation: CA 2006, s 633(6).

Right to object to variation: companies without a share capital

25.159 Section 634 applies where the rights of any class of members of a company are varied under s 631 (variation of class rights: companies without a share capital): CA 2006, s 634(1).

Members amounting to not less than 15% of the members of the class in question (being persons who did not consent to or vote in favour of the resolution for the variation) may apply to the court to have the variation cancelled: CA 2006, s 634(2). If such an application is made, the variation has no effect unless and until it is confirmed by the court: CA 2006, s 634(3).

25.160 Application to the court must be made within 21 days after the date on which the consent was given or the resolution was passed (as the case may be) and may be made on behalf of the members entitled to make the application by such one or more of their number as they may appoint in writing for the purpose: CA 2006, s 634(4).

The court, after hearing the applicant and any other persons who apply to the court to be heard and appear to the court to be interested in the application, may, if satisfied having regard to all the circumstances of the case that the variation would unfairly prejudice the members of the class represented by the applicant, disallow the variation, and shall if not so satisfied confirm it.

The decision of the court on any such application is final: CA 2006, s 634(5).

References in s 634 to the variation of the rights of a class of members include references to their abrogation: CA 2006, s 634(6).

Copy of court order to be forwarded to the registrar

25.161 The company must within 15 days after the making of an order by the court on an application under ss 633 or 634 (objection to variation of class rights) forward a copy of the order to the registrar: CA 2006, s 635(1).

If default is made in complying with s 635 an offence is committed by:

(a) the company; and

(b) every officer of the company who is in default: CA 2006, s 635(2).

A person found guilty of an offence under s 635 will be liable on summary conviction to a fine not exceeding level 3 on the standard scale and, for continued contravention, a daily default fine not exceeding one-tenth of level 3 on the standard scale: CA 2006, s 635(3).

Matters to be notified to the registrar

Notice of name or other designation of class of shares

25.162 Where a company assigns a name or other designation, or a new name or other designation, to any class or description of its shares, it must within one month from doing so deliver to the registrar a notice giving particulars of the name or designation so assigned: CA 2006, s 636(1).

If default is made in complying with s 636, an offence is committed by:

(a) the company; and

(b) every officer of the company who is in default: CA 2006, s 636(2).

A person who is found guilty of an offence under this section will be liable on summary conviction to a fine not exceeding level 3 on the standard scale and, for continued contravention, a daily default fine not exceeding one-tenth of level 3 on the standard scale: CA 2006, s 636(3).

Notice of particulars of variation of rights attached to shares

25.163 Where the rights attached to any shares of a company are varied, the company must within one month from the date on which the variation is made deliver to the registrar a notice giving particulars of the variation: CA 2006, s 637(1).

If default is made in complying with this section, an offence is committed by:

(a) the company; and

(b) every officer of the company who is in default: CA 2006, s 637(2).

A person guilty of an offence under this section will be liable on summary conviction to a fine not exceeding level 3 on the standard scale and, for continued contravention, a daily default fine not exceeding one-tenth of level 3 on the standard scale: CA 2006, s 637(3).

Notice of new class of members

25.164 If a company not having a share capital creates a new class of members, the company must within one month from the date on which the new class is created deliver to the registrar a notice containing particulars of the rights attached to that class: CA 2006, s 638(1).

If default is made in complying with s 638, an offence is committed by:

(a) the company; and

(b) every officer of the company who is in default: CA 2006, s 638(2).

A person guilty of an offence under this section will be liable on summary conviction to a fine not exceeding level 3 on the standard scale and, for continued contravention, a daily default fine not exceeding one-tenth of level 3 on the standard scale: CA 2006, s 638(3).

Notice of name or other designation of class of members

25.165 Where a company not having a share capital assigns a name or other designation, or a new name or other designation, to any class of its members, it must within one month from doing so deliver to the registrar a notice giving particulars of the name or designation so assigned: CA 2006, s 639(1).

If default is made in complying with s 639, an offence is committed by:

(a) the company; and

(b) every officer of the company who is in default: CA 2006, s 639(2).

A person found guilty of an offence under this section will be liable on summary conviction to a fine not exceeding level 3 on the standard scale and, for continued contravention, a daily default fine not exceeding one-tenth of level 3 on the standard scale: CA 2006, s 639(3).

Notice of particulars of variation of class rights

25.166 If the rights of any class of members of a company not having a share capital are varied, the company must within one month from the date on which the variation is made deliver to the registrar a notice containing particulars of the variation: CA 2006, s 640(1).

If default is made in complying with s 640, an offence is committed by:

(a) the company; and

(b) every officer of the company who is in default: CA 2006, s 640(2).

A person guilty of an offence under this section is liable on summary conviction to a fine not exceeding level 3 on the standard scale and, for continued contravention, a daily default fine not exceeding one-tenth of level 3 on the standard scale: CA 2006, s 640(3).

Reduction of share capital

25.167 Chapter 10 of Pt 17 is concerned with reduction of capital.

Introduction to Pt 17, Ch 1

Circumstances in which a company may reduce its share capital

25.168 A limited company having a share capital may reduce its share capital:

(a) in the case of a private company limited by shares, by special resolution supported by a solvency statement (ss 642–644);

(b) in any case, by special resolution confirmed by the court (ss 645 to 651): CA 2006, s 641(1).

A company may not reduce its capital under s 641(1)(a) if as a result of the reduction there would no longer be any member of the company holding shares other than redeemable shares: CA 2006, s 641(2).

A company may not reduce its share capital under s 641(1)(a) or (b) CA 2006 as part of a scheme by virtue of which a person, or a person together with its associates, is to acquire all the shares in the company or (where there is more than one class of shares in a company) all the shares of one or more classes, in each case other than shares that are already held by that person or its associates: CA 2006, s 641(2A) (as inserted by the Companies Act 2006 (Amendment of Part 17) Regulations 2015, SI 2015/472, para 3).

25.169 Section 641(2A) does not apply to a scheme under which:

(a) the company is to have a new parent undertaking;

(b) all or substantially all of the members of the company become members of the parent undertaking; and

(c) the members of the company are to hold proportions of the equity share capital of the parent undertaking in the same or substantially the same proportions as they hold the equity share capital of the company: CA 2006, s 641(2B) (as inserted by the Companies Act 2006 (Amendment of Part 17) Regulations 2015, SI 2015/472, para 3).

25.170 In this section:

'associate' has the meaning given by s 988 (meaning of 'associate'), reading references in that section to an offeror as references to the person acquiring the shares in the company;

'scheme' means a scheme of a kind described in s 900(1)(a) and (b) (powers of court to facilitate reconstruction or amalgamation): CA 2006, s 641(2C) (as inserted by the Companies Act 2006 (Amendment of Part 17) Regulations 2015, SI 2015/472, para 3).

25.171 Subject to CA 2006, s 641(2)–(2B), a company may reduce its share capital under this section in any way: CA 2006, s 641(3).

The 2015 Regulations (SI 2015/472) do not apply in relation to a scheme that:

(a) gives effect to, or is proposed in connection with, a takeover announcement made in relation to a company before the day on which these Regulations come into force; or

(b) gives effect to, or is proposed in connection with, a pre-commencement offer to acquire all the shares in a company that is not subject to the rules or (where there is more than one class of shares in a company) all the shares of one or more classes, in each case other than shares that on the date that the terms of the offer were agreed were already held by the person making the offer or its associates: reg 2(2).

25.172 Under SI 2015/472, the following terms apply:

'pre-commencement offer' means an offer the terms of which (including the fact that the offer will be implemented by a scheme) have been agreed between the company concerned and the person making the offer before the day on which these Regulations come into force; and

'takeover announcement' means a public announcement that:

(a) concerns a firm intention to acquire all the shares in a company or (where there is more than one class of shares in a company) all the shares of one or more classes, in each case other than shares that on the date of the announcement were already held by the person making the announcement or its associates; and
(b) on the date of the announcement, was made under rules made by the Panel: reg 2(3).

25.173 The effect of SI 2015/472 is to prohibit a company from reducing its share capital as part of a scheme of arrangement where the purpose of the scheme is to acquire all the shares of the company, except where the acquisition amounts to a restructuring which inserts a new holding company into the group structure. The effect of reg 2 (transitional provision) is to ensure that the prohibition does not affect takeovers where the announcement concerning a firm intention to make an offer has been made before the regulation comes into force, or the terms of the offer have been agreed in the case of a company that is not subject to the rules.

25.174 In particular, a company may:

(a) extinguish or reduce the liability on any of its shares in respect of share capital not paid up; or

(b) either with or without extinguishing or reducing liability on any of its shares:

   (i) cancel any paid-up share capital that is lost or unrepresented by available assets; or

   (ii) repay any paid-up share capital in excess of the company's wants: CA 2006, s 641(4).

A special resolution under s 641 may not provide for a reduction of share capital to take effect later than the date on which the resolution has effect in accordance with Pt 17, Ch 10: CA 2006, s 641(5).

CA 2006, Pt 17, Ch 10 (apart from s 641(5) above) has effect subject to any provision of the company's articles restricting or prohibiting the reduction of the company's share capital: CA 2006, s 641(6).

Private companies: reduction of capital supported by solvency statement

Reduction of capital supported by solvency statement

25.175 A resolution for reducing share capital of a private company limited by shares is supported by a solvency statement if:

(a) the directors of the company make a statement of the solvency of the company in accordance with s 643 (a 'solvency statement') not more than 15 days before the date on which the resolution is passed; and

(b) the resolution and solvency statement are registered in accordance with s 644: CA 2006, s 642(1).

25.176 Where the resolution is proposed as a written resolution, a copy of the solvency statement must be sent or submitted to every eligible member at or before the time at which the proposed resolution is sent or submitted to him: CA 2006, s 642(2).

Where the resolution is proposed at a general meeting, a copy of the solvency statement must be made available for inspection by members of the company throughout that meeting: CA 2006, s 642(3).

The validity of a resolution is not affected by a failure to comply with ss 642(2) or (3): CA 2006, s 642(4).

Solvency statement

25.177 A solvency statement is a statement that each of the directors:

(a) has formed the opinion, as regards the company's situation at the date of the statement, that there is no ground on which the company could then be found to be unable to pay (or otherwise discharge) its debts; and

(b) has also formed the opinion:

  (i) if it is intended to commence the winding up of the company within 12 months of that date, that the company will be able to pay (or otherwise discharge) its debts in full within 12 months of the commencement of the winding up; or

  (ii) in any other case, that the company will be able to pay (or otherwise discharge) its debts as they fall due during the year immediately following that date: CA 2006, s 643(1).

25.178 In forming those opinions, the directors must take into account all of the company's liabilities (including any contingent or prospective liabilities): CA 2006, s 643(2).

The solvency statement must be in the prescribed form and must state:

(a) the date on which it is made; and

(b) the name of each director of the company: CA 2006, s 643(3).

25.179 If the directors make a solvency statement without having reasonable grounds for the opinions expressed in it, and the statement is delivered to the registrar, an offence is committed by every director who is in default: CA 2006, s 643(4).

A person guilty of an offence under s 643(4) is liable:

(a) on conviction on indictment, to imprisonment for a term not exceeding two years or a fine (or both);

(b) on summary conviction:

(i) in England and Wales, to imprisonment for a term not exceeding 12 months or to a fine not exceeding the statutory maximum (or both);

(ii) in Scotland or Northern Ireland, to imprisonment for a term not exceeding six months, or to a fine not exceeding the statutory maximum (or both): CA 2006, s 643(5).

Registration of resolution and supporting documents

25.180 Within 15 days after the resolution for reducing share capital is passed the company must deliver to the registrar:

(a) a copy of the solvency statement; and

(b) a statement of capital.

This is in addition to the copy of the resolution itself that is required to be delivered to the registrar under Ch 3 of Pt 3: CA 2006, s 644(1).

25.181 The statement of capital must state with respect to the company's share capital as reduced by the resolution:

(a) the total number of shares of the company;

(b) the aggregate nominal value of those shares;

(ba) the aggregate amount (if any) unpaid on those shares (whether on account of their nominal value or by way of premium); and

(c) for each class of shares:

   (i) prescribed particulars of the rights attached to the shares;

   (ii) the total number of shares of that class; and

   (iii) the aggregate nominal value of shares of that class: CA 2006, s 644(2) (as inserted by SBEEA 2015, Sch 6).

The registrar must register the documents delivered to him under s 644(1) on receipt: CA 2006, s 644(3). The resolution does not take effect until those documents are registered: CA 2006, s 644(4).

25.182 The company must also deliver to the registrar, within 15 days after the resolution is passed, a statement by the directors confirming that the solvency statement was:

(a) made not more than 15 days before the date on which the resolution was passed; and

(b) provided to members in accordance with s 642(2) or (3): CA 2006, s 644(5).

25.183 The validity of a resolution is not affected by:

(a) a failure to deliver the documents required to be delivered to the registrar under s 644(1) within the time specified in that subsection; or

(b) a failure to comply with s 644(5): CA 2006, s 644(6).

25.184 If the company delivers to the registrar a solvency statement that was not provided to members in accordance with s 642(2) or (3), an offence is committed by every officer of the company who is in default: CA 2006, s 644(7).

If default is made in complying with s 644, an offence is committed by:

(a) the company; and

(b) every officer of the company who is in default: CA 2006, s 644(8).

25.185 A person found guilty of an offence under s 644(7) or (8) will be liable:

(a) on conviction on indictment, to a fine;

(b) on summary conviction, to a fine not exceeding the statutory maximum: CA 2006, s 644(9).

Reduction of capital confirmed by the court

Application to court for order of confirmation

25.186 Where a company has passed a resolution for reducing share capital, it may apply to the court for an order confirming the reduction: CA 2006, s 645(1).

If the proposed reduction of capital involves either:

(a) diminution of liability in respect of unpaid share capital; or

(b) the payment to a shareholder of any paid-up share capital,

s 646 (creditors entitled to object to reduction) applies unless the court directs otherwise: CA 2006, s 645(2).

25.187 The court may, if having regard to any special circumstances of the case it thinks proper to do so, direct that s 646 is not to apply as regards any class or classes of creditors: CA 2006, s 645(3).

The court may direct that s 646 is to apply in any other case: CA 2006, s 645(4).

Creditors entitled to object to reduction

25.188 Where s 646 applies (see ss 645(2) and (4)), every creditor of the company who at the date fixed by the court is entitled to any debt or claim that, if that date were the commencement of the winding up of the company would be admissible in proof against the company, is entitled to object to the reduction of capital: CA 2006, s 646(1).

The court shall settle a list of creditors entitled to object: CA 2006, s 646(2).

For that purpose the court:

(a) shall ascertain, as far as possible without requiring an application from any creditor, the names of those creditors and the nature and amount of their debts or claims; and

(b) may publish notices fixing a day or days within which creditors not entered on the list are to claim to be so entered or are to be excluded from the right of objecting to the reduction of capital: CA 2006, s 646(3).

25.189 If a creditor entered on the list whose debt or claim is not discharged or has not determined does not consent to the reduction, the court may, if it thinks fit, dispense with the consent of that creditor on the company securing payment of his debt or claim: CA 2006, s 646(4).

For this purpose the debt or claim must be secured by appropriating (as the court may direct) the following amount:

(a) if the company admits the full amount of the debt or claim or, though not admitting it, is willing to provide for it, the full amount of the debt or claim;

(b) if the company does not admit, and is not willing to provide for, the full amount of the debt or claim, or if the amount is contingent or not ascertained, an amount fixed by the court after the like enquiry and adjudication as if the company were being wound up by the court: CA 2006, s 646(5).

Offences in connection with list of creditors

25.190 If an officer of the company:

(a) intentionally or recklessly:

  (i) conceals the name of a creditor entitled to object to the reduction of capital; or

  (ii) misrepresents the nature or amount of the debt or claim of a creditor, or

(b) is knowingly concerned in any such concealment or misrepresentation,

he commits an offence: CA 2006, s 647(1).

25.191 A person guilty of an offence under s 647 will be liable:

(a) on conviction on indictment, to a fine;

(b) on summary conviction, to a fine not exceeding the statutory maximum: CA 2006, s 647(2).

Court order confirming reduction

25.192 The court may make an order confirming the reduction of capital on such terms and conditions as it thinks fit: CA 2006, s 648(1). The court must not confirm the reduction unless it is satisfied, with respect to every creditor of the company who is entitled to object to the reduction of capital that either:

(a) his consent to the reduction has been obtained; or

(b) his debt or claim has been discharged, or has determined or has been secured: CA 2006, s 648(2).

25.193 Where the court confirms the reduction, it may order the company to publish (as the court directs) the reasons for reduction of capital, or such other information in regard to it as the court thinks expedient with a view to giving proper information to the public, and (if the court thinks fit) the causes that led to the reduction: CA 2006, s 648(3).

The court may, if for any special reason it thinks proper to do so, make an order directing that the company must, during such period (commencing on or at any time after the date of the order) as is specified in the order, add to its name as its last words the words 'and reduced'.

If such an order is made, those words are, until the end of the period specified in the order, deemed to be part of the company's name: CA 2006, s 648(4).

Registration of order and statement of capital

25.194 The registrar, on production of an order of the court confirming the reduction of a company's share capital and the delivery of a copy of the order and of a statement of capital (approved by the court), shall register the order and statement.

This is subject to s 650 (public company reducing capital below authorised minimum): CA 2006, s 649(1).

25.195 The statement of capital must state with respect to the company's share capital as altered by the order:

(a) the total number of shares of the company;

(b) the aggregate nominal value of those shares;

(ba) the aggregate amount (if any) unpaid on those shares (whether on account of their nominal value or by way of premium); and

(c) for each class of shares:

  (i) prescribed particulars of the rights attached to the shares;

  (ii) the total number of shares of that class; and

  (iii) the aggregate nominal value of shares of that class: CA 2006, s 649(2) (as inserted by SBEEA 2015, Sch 6).

25.196 The resolution for reducing share capital, as confirmed by the court's order, takes effect:

(a) in the case of a reduction of share capital that forms part of a compromise or arrangement sanctioned by the court under Pt 26 (arrangements and reconstructions):

  (i) on delivery of the order and statement of capital to the registrar; or

  (ii) if the court so orders, on the registration of the order and statement of capital;

(b) in any other case, on the registration of the order and statement of capital: CA 2006, s 649(3).

25.197 Notice of the registration of the order and statement of capital must be published in such manner as the court may direct: CA 2006, s 649(4). The registrar must certify the registration of the order and statement of capital: CA 2006, s 649(5). The certificate:

(a) must be signed by the registrar or authenticated by the registrar's official seal; and

(b) is conclusive evidence:

   (i) that the requirements of this Act with respect to the reduction of share capital have been complied with; and

   (ii) that the company's share capital is as stated in the statement of capital: CA 2006, s 649(6).

Public company reducing capital below authorised minimum

Public company reducing capital below authorised minimum

25.198 Section 650 applies where the court makes an order confirming a reduction of a public company's capital that has the effect of bringing the nominal value of its allotted share capital below the authorised minimum: CA 2006, s 650(1).

The registrar must not register the order unless either:

(a) the court so directs; or

(b) the company is first re-registered as a private company: CA 2006, s 650(2).

Section 651 provides an expedited procedure for re-registration in these circumstances: CA 2006, s 650(3).

Expedited procedure for re-registration as a private company

25.199 The court may authorise the company to be re-registered as a private company without its having passed the special resolution required by s 97: CA 2006, s 651(1).

If it does so, the court must specify in the order the changes to the company's name and articles to be made in connection with the re-registration: CA 2006, s 651(2).

The company may then be re-registered as a private company if an application to that effect is delivered to the registrar together with:

(a) a copy of the court's order; and

(b) notice of the company's name, and a copy of the company's articles, as altered by the court's order: CA 2006, s 651(3).

25.200 On receipt of such an application the registrar must issue a certificate of incorporation altered to meet the circumstances of the case: CA 2006, s 651(4).

The certificate must state that it is issued on re-registration and the date on which it is issued: CA 2006, s 651(5).

On the issue of the certificate:

(a) the company by virtue of the issue of the certificate becomes a private company; and

(b) the changes in the company's name and articles take effect: CA 2006, s 651(6).

The certificate is conclusive evidence that the requirements of this Act as to re-registration have been complied with: CA 2006, s 651(7).

Effect of reduction of capital

Liability of members following reduction of capital

25.201 Where a company's share capital is reduced a member of the company (past or present) is not liable in respect of any share to any call or contribution exceeding in amount the difference (if any) between:

(a) the nominal amount of the share as notified to the registrar in the statement of capital delivered under ss 644, 649, 1028A or 1032A of this Act or para 7 of Sch 4 to the Small Business, Enterprise and Employment Act 2015; and

(b) the amount paid on the share or the reduced amount (if any) which is deemed to have been paid on it, as the case may be: CA 2006, s 652(1) (as inserted by SBEEA 2015, Sch 4).

This is subject to s 653 (liability to creditor in case of omission from list): CA 2006, s 652(2).

Nothing in s 653 affects the rights of the contributories among themselves: CA 2006, s 652(3).

Liability to creditor in case of omission from list of creditors

25.202 Section 653 applies where, in the case of a reduction of capital confirmed by the court:

(a) a creditor entitled to object to the reduction of share capital is by reason of his ignorance:

  (i) of the proceedings for reduction of share capital; or

  (ii) of their nature and effect with respect to his debt or claim,

not entered on the list of creditors; and

(b) after the reduction of capital the company is unable to pay the amount of his debt or claim: CA 2006, s 653(1).

25.203 Every person who was a member of the company at the date on which the resolution for reducing capital took effect under s 649(3) is liable to contribute for the payment of the debt or claim an amount not exceeding that which he would have been liable to contribute if the company had commenced to be wound up on the day before that date: CA 2006, s 653(2).

If the company is wound up, the court on the application of the creditor in question, and proof of ignorance as mentioned in s 653(1)(a), may if it thinks fit:

(a) settle accordingly a list of persons liable to contribute under s 653; and

(b) make and enforce calls and orders on them as if they were ordinary contributories in a winding up: CA 2006, s 653(3).

The reference in s 653(1)(b) to a company being unable to pay the amount of a debt or claim has the same meaning as in s 123 of the Insolvency Act 1986 (c 45) or Art 103 of the Insolvency (Northern Ireland) Order 1989 (SI 1989/2405 (NI 19)): CA 2006, s 653(4).

Miscellaneous and supplementary provisions

25.204 Chapter 11 of Pt 17 is concerned with miscellaneous and supplementary provisions

Treatment of reserve arising from reduction of capital

25.205 A reserve arising from the reduction of a company's share capital is not distributable, subject to any provision made by order under s 654: CA 2006, s 654(1).

The Secretary of State may by order specify cases in which:

(a) the prohibition in s 654(1) does not apply; and

(b) the reserve is to be treated for the purposes of Pt 23 (distributions) as a realised profit: CA 2006, s 654(2).

Shares no bar to damages against company

25.206 A person is not debarred from obtaining damages or other compensation from a company by reason only of his holding or having held shares in the company or any right to apply or subscribe for shares or to be included in the company's register of members (or have his name and other particulars delivered to the registrar under Ch 2A of Pt 8 and registered by the registrar).in respect of shares: CA 2006, s 655.

Public companies: duty of directors to call meeting on serious loss of capital

25.207 Where the net assets of a public company are half or less of its called-up share capital, the directors must call a general meeting of the company to consider whether any, and if so what, steps should be taken to deal with the situation: CA 2006, s 656(1).

They must do so not later than 28 days from the earliest day on which that fact is known to a director of the company: CA 2006, s 656(2).

The meeting must be convened for a date not later than 56 days from that day: CA 2006, s 656(3).

25.208 If there is a failure to convene a meeting as required by s 656, each of the directors of the company who:

(a) knowingly authorises or permits the failure; or

(b) after the period during which the meeting should have been convened, knowingly authorises or permits the failure to continue,

commits an offence: CA 2006, s 656(4).

25.209 A person guilty of an offence under s 656 is liable:

(a) on conviction on indictment, to a fine;

(b) on summary conviction, to a fine not exceeding the statutory maximum: CA 2006, s 656(5).

Nothing in s 656 authorises the consideration at a meeting convened in pursuance of s 656(1) of any matter that could not have been considered at that meeting apart from s 656: CA 2006, s 656(6).

Checklist: application and allotment of shares and pre-emption rights

25.210 *This checklist sets out the practice and procedure for an application and allotment of shares to a shareholder including pre-emption rights. It should be adapted depending upon the company's articles of association governing procedural meetings. It is concerned with a private company limited by shares.*

No	Issue	Reference
1	Some preliminary issues in connection with an application and allotment of shares include: ● Before the company issues further shares, will alternative source of funding be considered? ● Is the purpose of issuing shares to raise further funds? ● Will the company need to increase its share capital to issue shares?	
2	The company's directors cannot allot shares unless there is authority to do so.	CA 2006, s 549
3	The authority to allot shares may either be: (a) in the articles of association; or (b) by an ordinary resolution	CA 2006, s 551
4	Check the private limited company's articles of association to see if there is authority for directors to allot shares	
5	Assuming that the private company limited by shares requires an ordinary resolution to be passed requiring authorisation to issue shares, the following procedure would apply:	

No	Issue	Reference
	Before the Board meeting	
	• Call a Board meeting. Either a director or a secretary (if there is one) may call a Board meeting. Reasonable notice is required.	
	• Prepare an Agenda setting out the terms and manner of redemption:	
	At the Board meeting:	
	• Ensure that a quorum is present	
	• Consider whether any directors' interests need to be declared	
	• Chairman presides at the Board meeting	
	• Voting will be on a show of hands	
	• The directors will vote to put the ordinary resolution to the EGM for authority to allot shares. The authority for allotment of the shares may be either specific relating to particular allotment of shares or general, or it may be unconditional or subject to conditions. The authority must be for a fixed duration not exceeding 5 years and must state the date on which it expires and the maximum number of shares involved. The authority may be revoked, varied or renewed at any time by ordinary resolution of the EGM	CA 2006, s 551(2), (3) and (4)
	• Consider if a Board meeting can be dispensed with by a written resolution procedure	
	• In respect of pre-emption rights:	
	– Consider any pre-emption rights of shareholders before issuing shares to the shareholders	CA 2006, s 561–571
	– Consider whether any pre-emption rights of shareholders may be disapplied	
	– Consider disapplication of pre-emption rights by special resolution proposed at the Board meeting and the EGM	
	• Adjourn the Board meeting	
	After the Board meeting:	
	• Prepare minutes of the Board meeting	
	• Call the EGM	
	• Notice of EGM to state:	
	– date of the EGM	
	– time	

No	Issue	Reference
	– place	
	– a note on proxy	
	– the text of the ordinary resolution (allotment) and/or special resolution (disapplication of pre-emption rights)	
	– consider whether the EGM can be dispensed with by written resolution	
	• At the EGM:	
	– Ensure quorum is present	CA 2006, s 570
	– Chairman presides at the meeting	
	– Voting will be on a show of hands unless a poll is demanded to pass the ordinary resolution and/or the special resolution	
	• After the EGM:	
	– Prepare minutes of the EGM	
	• Reconvene the Board meeting:	
	– Issue the shares	
	– Issue the share certificates	
	– Entry of shareholder in the register of members	
	– File the resolutions at Companies House	
	– File SH01 (return of allotments of shares) within one month at Companies House	CA 2006, s 551(2)

Definitions

25.211

Allotted share capital:	shares of a company that have been allotted
Equity securities:	ordinary shares in the company, or rights to subscribe for, or to convert securities into, ordinary shares in the company
Issued share capital:	shares of a company that have been issued
Ordinary shares:	shares other than shares that as respects dividends and capital carry a right to participate only up to a specified amount in a distribution
Share:	in relation to a company, means share in the company's share capital

26 Acquisition by limited company of its own shares

Contents

Introduction

26.1 A traditional rule has existed at common law that a company must maintain its capital in what has become known as the 'capital maintenance' doctrine. The legal and practical effect of this doctrine is to protect the interests of shareholders from an unlawful depletion of a company's capital, and to prevent any disguised gifts out of capital, such as payments by way of directors' remuneration; including an unlawful reduction of capital. The creditors' interests also intrude in such circumstances, by establishing particular safeguards for various financial transactions contemplated by the CA 2006. This Chapter takes account of changes under SBEEA 2015.

This Chapter considers the following aspects:

- Acquisition of own shares.
- Financial assistance for the acquisition of shares.
- Redeemable shares.
- Purchase of own shares.

General provisions: introduction

General rule against limited company acquiring its own shares

26.2 Part 18 of the CA 2006 is concerned with acquisition by a limited company of its own shares. It is supplemented by the Companies Act 2006 (Amendment of Part 18) Regulations 2015, SI 2015/532.

There is a general prohibition that a limited company must not acquire its own shares, whether by purchase, subscription or otherwise, except in accordance with the provisions of Pt 18: CA 2006, s 658(1).

26.3 If a company purports to act in contravention of s 658 an offence is committed by:

(a) the company, and

(b) every officer of the company who is in default,

and the purported acquisition is void: CA 2006, s 658(2).

26.4 A person guilty of an offence under this s 658 will be liable on conviction on indictment, to imprisonment for a term not exceeding two years or a fine (or both); on summary conviction in England and Wales, to imprisonment for a term not exceeding 12 months or a fine not exceeding the statutory maximum (or both); in Scotland or Northern Ireland, to imprisonment for a term not exceeding six months or a fine not exceeding the statutory maximum (or both): CA 2006, s 658(3).

At common law, the courts emphasised the need to protect the shareholders and the company's creditors through the doctrine of maintenance of the company's capital, to ensure that the company had sufficient capital for the needs of the business. The capital could not be withdrawn until the company's winding up when the shareholders would receive the capital upon payment of all creditors. The doctrine of maintenance of a company's capital ensured that the company's capital was not unlawfully reduced, otherwise such reduction would be considered ultra vires and beyond the company's capacity.

A company may not acquire its own shares as this would amount to a reduction of its capital

The doctrine of maintenance of capital was established in *Trevor v Whitworth* (1887) 12 App Cas 409. Here, the House of Lords held that capital of the company could only be returned through effecting a reduction under the Companies Acts or on liquidation. It decided that the company could not acquire its own shares even where authorised under its articles of association. The protection of creditors was considered by the House of Lords as an important aspect of the maintenance of capital doctrine. Lord Watson stated:

> 'One of the main objects contemplated by the legislature, in restricting the power of limited companies to reduce the amount of their capital as set forth in the memorandum, is to protect the interests of the outside public who may become their creditors. In my opinion the effect of these statutory restrictions is to prohibit every transaction between a company and a shareholder, by means of which the money already paid to the company in respect of his shares is returned to him, unless the Court has sanctioned the transaction. Paid-up capital may be diminished or lost in the course of the company's trading; that is a result which no legislation can prevent; but persons who deal with, and give credit to a limited company, naturally rely upon the fact that the company is trading with a certain amount of capital already paid, as well as upon the responsibility of its members for the capital remaining at call; and they are entitled to assume that no part of the capital which has been paid into the coffers of the company has been subsequently paid out, except in the legitimate course of its business.'

Lord Herschell cited Cotton LJ in *Guinness v Land Corp of Ireland* (1882) 22 Ch 349 at 375, and adopted the test then propounded:

> '… whatever has been paid by a member cannot be returned to him. In my opinion … the capital cannot be diverted from the objects of the society. It is, of course, liable to be spent or lost in carrying on the business of the company, but no part of it can be returned to a member …'

Lord Macnaughten, stated that the question involved:

> '… the broader question whether it is competent for a limited company under any circumstances to invest any portion of its capital in the purchase of a share of its own capital stock, or to return any portion of its capital to any shareholder …'

The common law rule established in *Trevor v Whitworth* was consolidated under s 658 of the CA 2006.

Capital may only be returned to the company if sanctioned by the court

In *Barclays Bank plc v British & Commonwealth Holdings plc* [1996] 1 BCLC 1 (affirmed by the CA on other aspects [1996] 1 BCLC 27), Harman J stated that the principle established by *Trevor v Whitworth* was that a company could not return capital to its members except by a reduction of capital sanctioned by the court. This principle applied even if the company's memorandum of association expressly provided for such a return. The principle was based upon 'grounds of public policy': see *MacDougall v Jersey Imperial Hotel Co Ltd* (1864) 2 Hem & M 528 at 535, 71 ER 568 at 571 per Page-Wood VC.

The capital maintenance doctrine is also associated with the rule that the company must not deplete its assets through a disguised gift out of capital or through gratuitous payments: see *Re Halt Garage (1964) Ltd* [1982] 3 All ER 1016; *Brady v Brady* [1988] BCLC 20 (at first instance).

Exceptions to general rule

26.5 There are, however, exceptions to the general prohibition. A limited company may acquire any of its own fully paid shares otherwise than for valuable consideration: CA 2006, s 659(1): see *Re Castiglione's Will Trust* [1958] Ch 549.

Section 658 does not prohibit the following:

(a) the acquisition of shares in a reduction of capital duly made;

(b) the purchase of shares in pursuance of an order of the court under:

   (i) s 98 (application to court to cancel resolution for re-registration as a private company);

   (ii) s 721(6) (powers of court on objection to redemption or purchase of shares out of capital);

   (iii) s 759 (remedial order in case of breach of prohibition of public offers by private company); or

   (iv) Part 30 (protection of members against unfair prejudice);

(c) the forfeiture of shares, or the acceptance of shares surrendered in lieu, in pursuance of the company's articles, for failure to pay any sum payable in respect of the shares: CA 2006, s 659(3).

Shares held by company's nominee

Treatment of shares held by nominee

26.6 The general prohibition under CA 2006, s 658 does not apply where the company acquired the shares through a nominee. Section 660 applies where shares in a limited company:

(a) are taken by a subscriber to the memorandum as nominee of the company;

(b) are issued to a nominee of the company; or

(c) are acquired by a nominee of the company, partly paid up, from a third person: CA 2006, s 660(1).

For all purposes, the shares are to be treated as held by the nominee on his own account, and the company is to be regarded as having no beneficial interest in them: CA 2006, s 660(2).

26.7 Section 660 does not apply:

(a) to shares acquired otherwise than by subscription by a nominee of a public company, where:

  (i) a person acquires shares in the company with financial assistance given to him, directly or indirectly, by the company for the purpose of or in connection with the acquisition; and

  (ii) the company has a beneficial interest in the shares;

(b) to shares acquired by a nominee of the company when the company has no beneficial interest in the shares: CA 2006, s 660(3).

Liability of others where nominee fails to make payment in respect of shares

26.8 Section 661 applies where shares in a limited company:

(a) are taken by a subscriber to the memorandum as nominee of the company;

(b) are issued to a nominee of the company; or

(c) are acquired by a nominee of the company, partly paid up, from a third person: CA 2006, s 661(1).

26.9 If the nominee, having been called on to pay any amount for the purposes of paying up, or paying any premium on, the shares, fails to pay that amount within 21 days from being called on to do so, then:

(a) in the case of shares that he agreed to take as subscriber to the memorandum, the other subscribers to the memorandum; and

(b) in any other case, the directors of the company when the shares were issued to or acquired by him,

are jointly and severally liable with him to pay that amount: CA 2006, s 661(2).

26.10 If in proceedings for the recovery of an amount under s 661(2) it appears to the court that the subscriber or director has acted honestly and reasonably, and having regard to all the circumstances of the case, ought fairly to be relieved from liability, the court may relieve him, either wholly or in part, from his liability on such terms as the court thinks fit: CA 2006, s 661(3).

26.11 If a subscriber to a company's memorandum or a director of a company has reason to apprehend that a claim will or might be made for the recovery of any such amount from him:

(a) he may apply to the court for relief; and

(b) the court has the same power to relieve him as it would have had in proceedings for recovery of that amount: CA 2006, s 661(4).

Section 661 does not apply to shares acquired by a nominee of the company when the company has no beneficial interest in the shares: CA 2006, s 661(5).

Shares held by or for public company

Duty to cancel shares in public company held by or for the company

26.12 Section 662 applies in the case of a public company:

(a) where shares in the company are forfeited, or surrendered to the company in lieu of forfeiture, in pursuance of the articles, for failure to pay any sum payable in respect of the shares;

(b) where shares in the company are surrendered to the company in pursuance of s 102C(1)(b) of the Building Societies Act 1986 (c 53);

(c) where shares in the company are acquired by it (otherwise than in accordance with Pts 18 or 30 of the CA 2006 (protection of members against unfair prejudice)) and the company has a beneficial interest in the shares;

(d) where a nominee of the company acquires shares in the company from a third party without financial assistance being given directly or indirectly by the company and the company has a beneficial interest in the shares; or

(e) where a person acquires shares in the company, with financial assistance given to him, directly or indirectly, by the company for the purpose of or in connection with the acquisition, and the company has a beneficial interest in the shares: CA 2006, s 662(1).

26.13 Unless the shares or any interest of the company in them are previously disposed of, the company must:

(a) cancel the shares and diminish the amount of the company's share capital by the nominal value of the shares cancelled; and

(b) where the effect is that the nominal value of the company's allotted share capital is brought below the authorised minimum, apply for re-registration as a private company, stating the effect of the cancellation: CA 2006, s 662(2).

26.14 It must do so no later than:

(a) in a case within s 662(1)(a) or (b), three years from the date of the forfeiture or surrender;

(b) in a case within s 662(1)(c) or (d), three years from the date of the acquisition; and

(c) in a case within s 662(1)(e), one year from the date of the acquisition: CA 2006, s 662(3).

The directors of the company may take any steps necessary to enable the company to comply with s 662 and may do so without complying with the provisions of Ch 10 of Pt 17 (reduction of capital). See also s 664 (re-registration as private company in consequence of cancellation): CA 2006, s 662(4).

Neither the company nor, in a case within s 662(1)(d) or (e), the nominee or other shareholder may exercise any voting rights in respect of the shares: CA 2006, s 662(5).

Any purported exercise of those rights is void: CA 2006, s 662(6).

Notice of cancellation of shares

26.15 Where a company cancels shares in order to comply with s 662, it must within one month after the shares are cancelled give notice to the registrar, specifying the shares cancelled: CA 2006, s 663(1).

The notice must be accompanied by a statement of capital: CA 2006, s 663(2). The statement of capital must state with respect to the company's share capital immediately following the cancellation:

(a) the total number of shares of the company;

(b) the aggregate nominal value of those shares;

(ba) the aggregate amount (if any) unpaid on those shares (whether on account of their nominal value or by way of premium); and

(c) for each class of shares:

  (i) prescribed particulars of the rights attached to the shares,

  (ii) the total number of shares of that class; and

  (iii) the aggregate nominal value of shares of that class: CA 2006, s 663(3) (as inserted by SBEEA 2015, Sch 6).

26.16 If default is made in complying with s 663, an offence is committed by the company, and every officer of the company who is in default: CA 2006, s 663(4). A person guilty of an offence under this section will be liable on summary conviction to a fine not exceeding level 3 on the standard scale and, for continued contravention, a daily default fine not exceeding one-tenth of level 3 on the standard scale: CA 2006, s 663(5).

Re-registration as private company in consequence of cancellation

26.17 Where a company is obliged to re-register as a private company to comply with s 662, the directors may resolve that the company should be so re-registered. Ch 3 of Pt 3 (resolutions affecting a company's constitution) applies to any such resolution: CA 2006, s 664(1).

The resolution may make such changes in the company's name, and in the company's articles, as are necessary in connection with its becoming a private company: CA 2006, s 664(2).

26.18 The application for re-registration must contain a statement of the company's proposed name on re-registration: CA 2006, s 664(3). The application must be accompanied by:

(a) a copy of the resolution (unless a copy has already been forwarded under Ch 3 of Pt 3);

(b) a copy of the company's articles as amended by the resolution; and

(c) a statement of compliance: CA 2006, s 664(4).

The statement of compliance required is a statement that the requirements of s 664 as to re-registration as a private company have been complied with: CA 2006, s 664(5).

The registrar may accept the statement of compliance as sufficient evidence that the company is entitled to be re-registered as a private company: CA 2006, s 664(6).

Issue of certificate of incorporation on re-registration

26.19 If, on an application under s 664, the registrar is satisfied that the company is entitled to be re-registered as a private company, the company shall be re-registered accordingly: CA 2006, s 665(1).

The registrar must issue a certificate of incorporation altered to meet the circumstances of the case: CA 2006, s 665(2). The certificate must state that it is issued on re-registration and the date on which it is issued: CA 2006, s 665(3).

On the issue of the certificate the company by virtue of the issue of the certificate becomes a private company, and the changes in the company's name and articles take effect: CA 2006, s 665(4).

The certificate is conclusive evidence that the requirements of the CA 2006 as to re-registration have been complied with: CA 2006, s 665(5).

Effect of failure to re-register

26.20 If a public company that is required by s 662 to apply to be re-registered as a private company fails to do so before the end of the period specified in s 662(3), Ch 1 of Pt 20 (prohibition of public offers by private company) applies as if it were a private company: CA 2006, s 666(1).

Subject to that, the company continues to be treated as a public company until it is so re-registered: CA 2006, s 666(2).

Offence in case of failure to cancel shares or re-register

26.21 Section 667 applies where a company, when required to do by s 662 fails to cancel any shares, or fails to make an application for re-registration as a private company, within the time specified in s 662(3): CA 2006, s 667(1).

An offence is committed by the company, and every officer of the company who is in default: CA 2006, s 667(2). A person guilty of an offence under s 667 will be liable on summary conviction to a fine not exceeding level 3 on the standard scale and, for continued contravention, a daily default fine not exceeding one-tenth of level 3 on the standard scale: CA 2006, s 667(3).

Application of provisions to company re-registering as public company

26.22 Section 668 applies where, after shares in a private company:

(a) are forfeited in pursuance of the company's articles or are surrendered to the company in lieu of forfeiture;

(b) are acquired by the company (otherwise than by any of the methods permitted by Pts 18 or 30 (protection of members against unfair prejudice)), the company having a beneficial interest in the shares;

(c) are acquired by a nominee of the company from a third party without financial assistance being given directly or indirectly by the company, the company having a beneficial interest in the shares; or

(d) are acquired by a person with financial assistance given to him, directly or indirectly, by the company for the purpose of or in connection with the acquisition, the company having a beneficial interest in the shares;

the company is re-registered as a public company: CA 2006, s 668(1).

26.23 In that case the provisions of ss 662–667 apply to the company as if it had been a public company at the time of the forfeiture, surrender or acquisition, subject to the following modification: CA 2006, s 668(2).

The modification is that the period specified in s 662(3)(a), (b) or (c) (period for complying with obligations under that section) runs from the date of the re-registration of the company as a public company: CA 2006, s 668(3).

Transfer to reserve on acquisition of shares by public company or nominee

26.24 Where:

(a) a public company, or a nominee of a public company, acquires shares in the company; and

(b) those shares are shown in a balance sheet of the company as an asset,

an amount equal to the value of the shares must be transferred out of profits available for dividend to a reserve fund and is not then available for distribution: CA 2006, s 669(1).

Section 669(1) applies to an interest in shares as it applies to shares. As it so applies the reference to the value of the shares shall be read as a reference to the value to the company of its interest in the shares: CA 2006, s 669(2).

Charges of public company on own shares

Public companies: general rule against lien or charge on own shares

26.25 A lien or other charge of a public company on its own shares (whether taken expressly or otherwise) is void, except as permitted by s 670: CA 2006, s 670(1). In the case of any description of company, a charge is permitted if the shares are not fully paid up and the charge is for an amount payable in respect of the shares: CA 2006, s 670(2). In the case of a company whose ordinary business:

(a) includes the lending of money; or

(b) consists of the provision of credit or the bailment (in Scotland, hiring) of goods under a hire-purchase agreement, or both,

a charge is permitted (whether the shares are fully paid or not) if it arises in connection with a transaction entered into by the company in the ordinary course of that business: CA 2006, s 670(3).

In the case of a company that has been re-registered as a public company, a charge is permitted if it was in existence immediately before the application for re-registration: CA 2006, s 670(4).

Supplementary provisions

Interests to be disregarded in determining whether company has beneficial interest

26.26 Section 671 states that in determining whether a company has a beneficial interest in shares for the purposes of Ch 1, Pt 22, any such interest as is mentioned in ss 672 (residual interest under pension scheme or employees' share scheme), 673 (employer's charges and other rights of recovery), or 674 (rights as personal representative or trustee) must be disregarded.

Residual interest under pension scheme or employees' share scheme

26.27 Where the shares are held on trust for the purposes of a pension scheme or employees' share scheme, there shall be disregarded any residual interest of the company that has not vested in possession: CA 2006, s 672.

The term 'residual interest' means a right of the company to receive any of the trust property in the event of:

(a) all the liabilities arising under the scheme having been satisfied or provided for; or

(b) the company ceasing to participate in the scheme; or

(c) the trust property at any time exceeding what is necessary for satisfying the liabilities arising or expected to arise under the scheme: CA 2006, s 672(2).

In s 672(2), the reference to a right includes a right dependent on the exercise of a discretion vested by the scheme in the trustee or another person and the reference to liabilities arising under a scheme includes liabilities that have resulted, or may result, from the exercise of any such discretion: CA 2006, s 672(3).

26.28 For the purposes of s 672 a residual interest vests in possession in a case within s 672(2)(a), on the occurrence of the event mentioned there (whether or not the amount of the property receivable pursuant to the right is ascertained); or in a case within s 672(2)(b) or (c), when the company becomes entitled to require the trustee to transfer to it any of the property receivable pursuant to that right: CA 2006, s 672(4).

26.29 Where by virtue of s 672 shares are exempt from ss 660 or 661 (shares held by company's nominee) at the time they are taken, issued or acquired but the residual interest in question vests in possession before they are disposed of or fully paid up, those sections apply to the shares as if they had been taken, issued or acquired on the date on which that interest vests in possession: CA 2006, s 672(5).

Where by virtue of s 672 shares are exempt from ss 662–668 (shares held by or for public company) at the time they are acquired but the residual interest in question vests in possession before they are disposed of, those sections apply to the shares as if they had been acquired on the date on which the interest vests in possession: CA 2006, s 672(6).

Employer's charges and other rights of recovery

26.30 Where the shares are held on trust for the purposes of a pension scheme there shall be disregarded:

(a) any charge or lien on, or set-off against, any benefit or other right or interest under the scheme for the purpose of enabling the employer or former employer of a member of the scheme to obtain the discharge of a monetary obligation due to him from the member;

(b) any right to receive from the trustee of the scheme, or as trustee of the scheme to retain, an amount that can be recovered or retained:

   (i) under s 61 of the Pension Schemes Act 1993 (c 48), or otherwise, as reimbursement or partial reimbursement for any contributions equivalent premium paid in connection with the scheme under Pt 3 of that Act, or

   (ii) under s 57 of the Pension Schemes (Northern Ireland) Act 1993 (c 49), or otherwise, as reimbursement or partial reimbursement for any contributions equivalent premium paid in connection with the scheme under Pt 3 of that Act: CA 2006, s 673(1).

26.31 Where the shares are held on trust for the purposes of an employees' share scheme, there shall be disregarded any charge or lien on, or set-off against, any benefit or other right or interest under the scheme for the purpose of enabling the employer or former employer of a member of the scheme to obtain the discharge of a monetary obligation due to him from the member: CA 2006, s 673(2).

Rights as personal representative or trustee

26.32 Section 674 deals with the rights as personal representative or trustee. Where the company is a personal representative or trustee, there shall be disregarded any rights that the company has in that capacity including, in particular any right to recover its expenses or be remunerated out of the estate or trust property, and any right to be indemnified out of that property for any liability incurred by reason of any act or omission of the company in the performance of its duties as personal representative or trustee.

Meaning of 'pension scheme'

26.33 Section 675 defines the term pension scheme as a scheme for the provision of benefits consisting of or including relevant benefits for or in respect of employees or former employees: CA 2006, s 675(1).

In s 675(1), the term 'relevant benefits' means any pension, lump sum, gratuity or other like benefit either given, or to be given on retirement or on death or in anticipation of retirement or, in connection with past service, after retirement or death: CA 2006, s 657(2).

Application of provisions to directors

26.34 Section 676 states that for the purposes of Ch 1 of Pt 18 references to 'employer' and 'employee', in the context of a pension scheme or employees' share scheme, shall be read as if a director of a company were employed by the scheme.

Financial assistance for purchase of own shares

Origins of financial assistance

26.35 The provisions on financial assistance are intended to protect against the general mischief that the resources of the target company and its subsidiaries must not be used directly or indirectly to assist the purchaser financially to make the acquisition. This may prejudice the interests of the creditors of the target or its group, and the interests of the shareholders who do not accept the offer to acquire their shares or to whom the offer was not made: *Chaston v SWP Group plc* [2003] 1 BCLC 675. The main objective of the provisions of Pt 18 have been to primarily protect the interests of shareholders and creditors from unlawful financial assistance transactions: punitive sanctions are secondary to this objective.

Previously, a common practice grew of purchasing the shares of a company having a substantial cash balance or realisable assets – the effect of which was to arrange for the purchase monies to be lent to the purchaser by the company. This position was the subject of consideration in *Re VGM Holdings Ltd [1942]* 1 All ER 224.

The Greene Committee

26.36 Historically, the provisions on financial assistance owe much of their origin to the Greene Committee's. The Greene Committee was of the view that providing financial assistance for the acquisition of own shares was 'highly improper' and was open to abuse.

It recommended that companies should be prohibited from directly or indirectly providing any financial assistance in connection with a purchase (made or to be made) of their own shares by third persons, whether such assistance took the form of a loan, guarantee, provision of security, or otherwise. As an exception, the Greene Committee stated that the prohibition should not apply in the case of companies whose ordinary business included the lending of money, to money let in the ordinary course of such business, or to scheme by which a company puts up money in the hands of trustees for purchasing shares of the company to be held for the benefit of employees or to loans direct to employees for the same purpose.

Companies Act 1929

26.37 Some of Greene's recommendations were incorporated into the CA 1929. Section 45 made it unlawful

> '… for a company to give, whether directly or indirectly, and whether by means of a loan, guarantee, the provision of security or otherwise, any financial assistance for the purpose of or in connection with a purchase made or to be made by any person of any shares in the company.'

Previously, a common practice grew of purchasing the shares of a company having a substantial cash balance or realisable assets – the effect of which was to arrange for the purchase monies to be lent to the purchaser by the company. This position was the subject of consideration in *Re VGM Holdings Limited* [1942] 1 All ER 224, where the Court of Appeal held that in interpreting CA 1929, s 45, the word 'purchase' in this section did not include the acquisition of shares by subscription or allotment. According to Lord Greene:

> '… it seems to me that the word "purchase" cannot, with propriety, be applied to the legal transaction under which a person, by the machinery of application and allotment, becomes a shareholder in the company; he does not purchase anything when he does that.'

Companies Act 1945

26.38 Section 54 of the CA 1948 gave rise to some concerns in some of the subsequent cases as to the broad scope of that section and innocuous transactions that could be caught within this section.

In *Belmont Finance Corp v Williams Furniture Limited (No 2)* [1980] 1 All ER 393, the Court of Appeal held that a breach of CA 1948, s 54 occurred if a company, without regard to its own commercial interests, bought something from a third party with the sole purpose of putting the third party in funds to acquire shares in the company, notwithstanding that the price paid was a fair price.

In *Armour Hick Northern Ltd v Whitehouse* [1980] 1 WLR 1520, Mervyn Davies J held that on the true construction of CA 1948, s 54(1), the prohibition against the provision of financial assistance for the purchase of shares was not confined to assistance given to a purchaser, but extended to assistance given to the vendor of the shares.

Jenkins Committee

26.39 In 1962, the Jenkins Committee in its 'Report of the Company Law Committee' stated that it would be unwise to attempt a precise definition of the term "financial assistance". It recommended that it should be unlawful for a company to give financial assistance for the acquisition of its shares or those of its holding company unless the transaction whereby such assistance is given has been approved by a special resolution of the company and there has been filed with the Registrar of Companies a declaration or solvency. It also recommended an imposition of a substantial penalty for making a declaration of solvency without reasonable grounds, with a presumption that a declaration has been made without reasonable grounds if within 12 months of the filing of the declaration the company was wound up and its debts were not paid in full within 12 months of the commencement of the winding up.

Companies Act 1981

26.40 The Companies Act 1981, *inter alia*, introduced a mechanism to buy back and redeem shares including a procedure allowing private companies limited by shares to provide financial assistance for the purchase of their shares out of capital.

Reformulation under CA 1985

26.41 The CA 1985 reformulated the provisions on financial assistance which were set out under ss 155–159, and gave rise to some significant cases on the breadth and scope of the definition of 'financial assistance'.

Company Law Review

26.42 As part of the reform of company law in the UK, the Government embarked on a series of reviews on modernising company law. It also addressed the position on financial assistance in 'Modern Law for a Competitive Economy: Final Report' (July 2001) and concluded that private companies should not have to comply with the complex rules prohibiting a company from giving any form of financial assistance to assist in the sale and purchase of its shares so that the 'whitewash' procedure would no longer apply. Further, public companies should have exemptions from the rules restricting them from giving any form of financial assistance to assist in the sale and purchase of their shares.

Companies Act 2006

26.43 The present provisions on financial assistance are set out in Ch 2 of Pt 18 which addresses the financial assistance for purchase of own shares.

As recommended by the Company Law Review Group (*Final Report*, paragraph 10.6), CA 2006 abolished the prohibition on the giving of financial assistance by a private company for the purchase of shares in itself and, as a consequence, the relaxations for private company for the purchase of shares in itself. The relaxations for private companies (sometimes referred to as the 'whitewash' procedure) are no longer required.

The prohibitions on the rules on financial assistance by a company for the acquisition of its own shares are paramount for the protection of the interests of creditors and shareholders: *Chaston v SWP Group plc* [2003] 1 BCLC 675.

Introductory

Meaning of 'financial assistance'

26.44 The starting point in determining whether financial assistance has been given is to consider the statutory definition of the term. Section 677 sets out the definition of financial assistance. In Ch 2 of Pt 18, the term 'financial assistance' means:

(a) financial assistance given by way of gift;

(b) financial assistance given:

  (i) by way of guarantee, security or indemnity (other than an indemnity in respect of the indemnifier's own neglect or default); or

  (ii) by way of release or waiver,

(c) financial assistance given:

  (i) by way of a loan or any other agreement under which any of the obligations of the person giving the assistance are to be fulfilled at a time when in accordance with the agreement any obligation of another party to the agreement remains unfulfilled; or

  (ii) by way of the novation of, or the assignment (in Scotland, assignation) of rights arising under, a loan or such other agreement; or

(d) any other financial assistance given by a company where:

  (i) the net assets of the company are reduced to a material extent by the giving of the assistance; or

  (ii) the company has no net assets: CA 2006, s 677(1).

The term 'net assets' here means the aggregate amount of the company's assets less the aggregate amount of its liabilities: CA 2006, s 677(2).

For this purpose a company's liabilities include (where it draws up Companies Act individual accounts) any provision of a kind specified for the purposes of this subsection by regulations under s 396; and (where it draws up IAS individual accounts) any provision made in those accounts: CA 2006, s 677(3).

Early definitions of 'indemnity'

Holroyd Pearce LJ in *Yeoman Credit Ltd v Latter* [1961] 2 All ER 294 at 296, referred to the term indemnity and stated:

> 'An indemnity is a contract by one party to keep the other harmless against loss, but a contract of guarantee is a contract to answer for the debt, default or miscarriage of another who is to be primarily liable to the promisee.'

In determining what constitutes financial assistance, the courts will look at the commercial realities of the transaction

This was reinforced by Hoffmann J in *Charterhouse Investment Trust Ltd v Tempest Diesels Ltd* [1986] BCLC 1. He said:

> 'There are two elements in the commission of offence under the [CA 2006]. The first is the giving of financial assistance and the second is that it should have been given "for the purpose of or in connection with" in this case, a purchase of shares ... There is no definition of giving financial assistance in the section, although some examples are given. The words have no technical meaning and their frame of reference is in my judgment the language of ordinary commerce. One must examine the commercial realities of the transaction and decide whether it can properly be described as the giving of financial assistance by the company, bearing in mind that the section is a penal one and should not be strained to cover transactions which are not fairly within it.'

According to Hoffmann J, the term 'financial assistance' should be given its normal commercial meaning. The section required that there should be assistance or help for the purpose of acquiring the shares and that that assistance should be financial.

The term 'financial assistance' should be given its natural meaning

In *Barclays Bank plc v British & Commonwealth Holdings plc* [1996] 1 BCLC 1, there was a gratuitous distribution of the company's assets and financial assistance for the purchase of its shares. The Court of Appeal first addressed the maintenance of capital doctrine and stated that under the rule in *Trevor v Whitworth* (1887) 12 App Cas 409 a transaction which involved a return of capital to a company's members in whatever form and under whatever label and whether directly or indirectly was void.

Second the terms used to define financial assistance under s 677 were to be given their normal meaning. The term 'indemnity' in the context of s 677(1)(b)(i) bore a technical meaning and entailed a contract by one party to keep the other party harmless against loss. The Court of Appeal approved Hoffmann J's decision in *Charterhouse*.

'Financial assistance' is essentially a commercial concept

In *McNiven (Inspector of Taxes) v Westmoreland Investments Ltd* [2001] STC 237, Lord Hoffmann set out a distinction between the term 'financial assistance' which was essentially a commercial concept and other words used in CA 2006, s 677 which have a legal meaning:

> 'The distinction between commercial and legal concepts has also been drawn in other areas of legislation. So, for example, the term "financial assistance" in s 151 of the Companies Act 1985 has been construed as a commercial concept, involving an inquiry into the commercial realities of the transaction (see *Burton v Palmer* [1980] 2 NSWLR 878 at 889–890 and *Charterhouse Investment Trust Ltd v Tempest Diesels Ltd* [1986] BCLC 1). But the same is not necessarily true of other terms used in the same section, such as "indemnity". As Aldous LJ said in *Barclays Bank plc v British & Commonwealth Holdings plc* [1996] 1 BCLC 1 at 39, [1996] 1 WLR 1 at 14: "It was submitted that as the words 'financial assistance' had no technical meaning and their frame of reference was the language of ordinary commerce, the word 'indemnity' should be similarly construed. The fallacy in that submission is clear. The words 'financial assistance' are not words which have any recognised legal significance whereas the word 'indemnity' does. It is used in the section as one of a number of words having a recognised legal meaning." I would only add by way of caution that although a word may have a "recognised legal meaning", the legislative context may show that it is in fact being used to refer to a broader commercial concept.'

Financial assistance is a commercial concept based on a fact-sensitive analysis

In *Chaston v SWP Group plc* [2003] 1 BCLC 675, the Court of Appeal was required to consider whether payment of professional fees by a subsidiary of a target amounted to financial assistance. It held that it did. The mischief to which the CA 2006 was directed was the use, directly or indirectly, of the resources of the target company and its subsidiaries to assist the purchaser financially to make the acquisition. What mattered was the commercial substance of the transaction.

Arden LJ stated:

> '… the term "financial assistance" is clearly established to be a commercial concept. Accordingly, the question whether financial assistance exists in any given case may be fact-sensitive and not one which can be answered simply by applying a legal definition. The question is whether from a commercial point of view the transaction impugned amounts to financial assistance. If the company's participation in the transaction meets that test, no straining of the statutory language occurs.'

According to Arden LJ, s 677 only prescribed a number of forms of financial assistance. It did not, however, define the term 'financial assistance'.

There was no requirement to show any detriment to constitute financial assistance. See too *Belmont Finance Corp Ltd v Williams Furniture Ltd* [1980] 1 All ER 393. The detrimental aspect may, however, arise in relation to any other financial assistance given by a company where:

(i) the net assets of the company are reduced to a material extent by the giving of the assistance; or

(ii) the company has no net assets: CA 2006, s 677(1)(d).

The court will have regard to the commercial realities of the transaction in determining whether financial assistance was provided

MT Realisations Ltd v Digital Equipments Co Ltd [2003] 2 BCLC 117, concerned purchase of shares with financial assistance of the company with respect to the sale of a loss-making subsidiary. Debts owed by other subsidiaries to the purchaser of the company were set off against the purchase price. The issue was whether the set-off arrangement amounted to the provision of financial assistance to allow the acquisition of the company. The Court of Appeal had regard to the commercial realities of the transaction and concluded that the subsidiary was not giving any financial assistance to the parent company for the acquisition of its own shares.

26.45 Section 677(1)(d) is wide in its scope and catches any other financial assistance other than those set out in s 677(1)(a)–(c).

A security provided for a loan was not financial assistance under the CA 2006

In *Anglo Petroleum Ltd v TFB (Mortgages) Ltd* [2008] 1 BCLC 185, the Court of Appeal stated that where a company provided security in return for a loan, this could not be financial assistance. The absence of a clear definition of financial assistance meant that (s 677) could give rise to uncertainties and had the potential to catch transactions which might be considered innocuous. In cases where its application was doubtful, it was important to remember its central purpose: to examine the commercial realities of the transaction and to bear in mind that it was a penal statute.

26.46 If a company merely discharges a debt which it owes, this cannot amount to financial assistance: *Armour Hick Northern Limited v Armour Trust Ltd* [1980] 3 All ER 833.

In *Re Uniq plc* [2012] 1 BCLC 783, Richards J held that payment of a debt owed by a company did not amount to financial assistance. In this case the exception under s 678(2) applied.

Circumstances in which financial assistance is prohibited

Assistance for acquisition of shares in a public company

26.47 Section 678 sets out the principal prohibition on the giving of financial assistance and the timing of such assistance. It deals with the issue of assistance for the acquisition of shares in a public company. Where a person is acquiring, or proposing to acquire, shares in a public company, it is not lawful either for that company, or one of its subsidiaries, to give financial assistance directly or indirectly for the purpose of the acquisition before or at the same time as the acquisition takes place: CA 2006, s 678(1): See *Parlett v Guppys (Bridport) Ltd* [1996] 2 BCLC 34.

26.48 Section 678(1) does not prohibit a company from giving financial assistance for the acquisition of shares in it or its holding company if:

(a) the company's principal purpose in giving the assistance is not to give it for the purpose of any such acquisition; or

(b) the giving of the assistance for that purpose is only an incidental part of some larger purpose of the company, and the assistance is given in good faith in the interests of the company: CA 2006, s 678(2).

26.49 Where:

(a) a person has acquired shares in a company; and

(b) a liability has been incurred (by that or another person) for the purpose of the acquisition,

it is not lawful for that company, or a subsidiary, to give financial assistance directly or indirectly for the purpose of reducing or discharging the liability if, at the time the assistance is given, the company in which the shares were acquired is a public company: CA 2006, s 678(3): *Arab Bank plc v Mercantile Holdings Limited* [1994] Ch 755.

26.50 There is, however, an exception to the general prohibition. Section 678(3) does not prohibit a company from giving financial assistance if:

(a) the company's principal purpose in giving the assistance is not to reduce or discharge any liability incurred by a person for the purpose of the acquisition of shares in the company or its holding company; or

(b) the reduction or discharge of any such liability is only an incidental part of some larger purpose of the company,

and the assistance is given in good faith in the interests of the company: CA 2006, s 678(4).

26.51 Section 678 applies subject to ss 681 and 682 (unconditional and conditional exceptions to prohibition): CA 2006, s 678(5).

Once the financial assistance definition has been satisfied, it will be necessary to show that the exceptions to financial assistance set out in s 678 apply: *Charterhouse Investment Trust Ltd v Tempest Diesels Ltd* [1986] BCLC 1.

Payment of excessive rent could not be said to be linked to the acquisition of shares in the company

In *Dyment v Boyden* [2005] 1 BCLC 163, a shareholder agreed to buy out other shareholders by accepting a lease from them at an excessive rent. The payment of this rent materially reduced the company's net assets. The issue was whether the payment of excessive rent amounted to 'financial assistance' and whether this was given by the company directly or indirectly for purposes of acquiring shares. Was the company in fact discharging liabilities incurred by a shareholder for the purpose of acquiring shares?

The Court of Appeal held that although it was obvious that the respondents' object in asking for and obtaining an excessive rent was compensation for loss of earnings, that could not be deemed to be the purpose of the applicant and the company, since it could not be inferred that the respondents' purpose was also the purpose of the applicant and the company. Their purpose was to acquire the premises to keep the business going. In order to do that they had (a) undertaken the obligation of procuring the company's entry into the lease and (b) discharged that obligation by entering into the lease. In those circumstances the excessive rent demanded by the respondents could not be said to be linked to the acquisition of the shares. Accordingly, although the company's entry into the lease was 'in connection with' the acquisition of the respondents' shares by the applicant, it was not 'for the purpose of' that acquisition under s 678(2).

26.52 The exceptions to financial assistance set out in s 678(2) were considered by the House of Lords in *Brady v Brady* [1988] 2 All ER 617.

The exception to the prohibition on financial assistance is that the transaction itself must be incidental to a larger purpose and must be given in 'good faith'

In *Brady v Brady* [1988] 2 All ER 617, the House of Lords was required to consider whether the financial assistance in question from B Ltd to M Ltd was provided in the interests of the company and as an incidental part of some larger purpose. It concerned a transfer of assets in return for fully paid up shares in a new company and loan stock owing to a corporate reorganisation of the family company because of disputes between directors. The company transferred assets to a new company which in turn used the assets to pay off loan stock. The issue was whether the company provided financial assistance to a subsidiary to reduce the subsidiary's liability to company; and if so, whether the financial assistance was given in the interests of company and as an incidental part of some larger purpose.

The House of Lords took a narrow approach to the exceptions. It held that although the transaction involved the provision by B Ltd of financial assistance to M Ltd to reduce M Ltd's liability, the assistance had been provided 'in good faith in the interests of the company', within s 678(2)(b) as not only was the proposed transfer calculated to advance B Ltd's corporate and commercial interests and the interests of its employees, but it was also in the interest of the company and its creditors that it should continue under proper management with the differences between the directors resolved.

However, the financial assistance had not been provided by B Ltd as 'an incidental part of some larger purpose of the company' and therefore the transaction was not saved by s 678(2)(b) from being prohibited by s 678(1), since a 'larger purpose' was not the same as a 'more important reason' and therefore the financial or commercial advantages flowing from the transaction, although possibly the most important reason for providing the assistance, could not constitute part of the larger purpose of the company. In the circumstances, the benefits accruing from the proposed transaction in the form of breaking the management deadlock were not part of the larger purpose of the financial assistance but were the essence of the scheme itself. Accordingly, the financial assistance was *prima facie* unlawful.

However, the transaction was saved as it was a private company which could give financial assistance out of capital (previously CA 1985, s 155).

26.53 Although *Brady v Brady* interpreted narrowly the exceptions where financial assistance would be permissible, there have been situations where the court has been prepared to admit the exception under s 678(2).

Payments made by a company so as to obtain release of its actual and prospective liabilities was not financial assistance: it was incidental to a larger purpose and given in good faith

In *Re Uniq plc* [2012] 1 BCLC 783, a scheme of arrangement was proposed in connection with the company's pension fund liability of more than £235 million. The company's shareholders agreed to give up 90.2% of their shares in exchange for the company being discharged from obligations under the pension scheme. The issues before the court were whether there was sufficient benefit to members under the scheme to amount to compromise or arrangement; and whether this constituted unlawful financial assistance provided by a subsidiary for acquisition of the company's shares.

Richards J held that although the payment that was to be made would be provision of financial assistance by a subsidiary to enable another company to purchase the 90.2% shareholding in the company, the payment fell within the exception in s 678(2) and was not unlawful under s 678(1). The purpose of the payment was to obtain the release of the company's actual and prospective liabilities under the salary-related pension scheme and, as such, would be overwhelmingly in the interests of the company and made in good faith.

Furthermore, if the company's payment of administrative and professional fees and provision of indemnities for the other company amounted to the giving of financial assistance for the acquisition of shares, those actions would not be unlawful under s 678(1) because they were commercially necessary for the restructuring, they were in the interests of both creditors and members and they would be done in pursuance of an order of the court sanctioning a scheme of arrangement. They would thus be exempt under s 681(2)(e) from the prohibition on giving financial assistance for the acquisition of shares.

Assistance by public company for acquisition of shares in its private holding company

26.54 Section 679 states that where a person is acquiring or proposing to acquire shares in a private company, it is not lawful for a public company that is a subsidiary of that company to give financial assistance directly or indirectly for the purpose of the acquisition before or at the same time as the acquisition takes place: CA 2006, s 679(1).

Section 679(1) does not prohibit a company from giving financial assistance for the acquisition of shares in its holding company if:

(a) the company's principal purpose in giving the assistance is not to give it for the purpose of any such acquisition; or

(b) the giving of the assistance for that purpose is only an incidental part of some larger purpose of the company, and

the assistance is given in good faith in the interests of the company: CA 2006, s 679(2).

26.55 Where:

(a) a person has acquired shares in a private company; and

(b) a liability has been incurred (by that or another person) for the purpose of the acquisition,

it is not lawful for a public company that is a subsidiary of that company to give financial assistance directly or indirectly for the purpose of reducing or discharging the liability: CA 2006, s 679(3).

26.56 Section 679(3) does not prohibit a company from giving financial assistance if:

(a) the company's principal purpose in giving the assistance is not to reduce or discharge any liability incurred by a person for the purpose of the acquisition of shares in its holding company, or

(b) the reduction or discharge of any such liability is only an incidental part of some larger purpose of the company, and

the assistance is given in good faith in the interests of the company: CA 2006, s 679(4).

Section 679 applies subject to ss 681 and 682 (unconditional and conditional exceptions to prohibition): CA 2006, s 679(5).

Prohibited financial assistance an offence

26.57 Section 680 creates a criminal offence for unlawful financial assistance. If a company contravenes either s 678(1) or (3) or s 679(1) or (3) (prohibited financial assistance) an offence is committed by the company, and every officer of the company who is in default: CA 2006, s 680(1).

A person guilty of an offence under s 680 will be liable on conviction on indictment, to imprisonment for a term not exceeding two years or a fine (or both); on summary conviction in England and Wales, to imprisonment for a term not exceeding 12 months or to a fine not exceeding the statutory maximum (or both); in Scotland or Northern Ireland, to imprisonment for a term not exceeding six months, or to a fine not exceeding the statutory maximum (or both): CA 2006, s 680(2).

26.58 In *Victor Battery Co Ltd v Curry's Limited* [1946] Ch 242, Roxburgh J was of the view that the object of CA 2006, s 680 was to punish the company and its officers through the imposition of fines; and that the section was not designed for the protection of the company. This position was followed in *Curtis Furnishing Stores Ltd v Freedman* [1966] 1 WLR 1219 per Cross J (and cf: *S. Western Mineral Water Co Ltd v Ashmore* [1967] 1 WLR 1110. However, the English courts subsequently rejected these previous decisions and restored the principal philosophy and objective of the sanctions, namely to uphold the protection of shareholders and the creditors: *Selangor Rubber Estates Ltd v Cradock (No 3)* [1968] 1 WLR 1555.

26.59 Similarly, in *Heald v O'Connor* [1971] 1 WLR 497, Fisher J stated that on the assumption that the giving of the debenture was to secure the repayment of the loan in order to enable the defendant to pay for shares, and that without such security the claimants would not have been willing to make the loan, the defendants had put forward a good defence and thus would be given leave to defend for the following reasons:

(i) the company had given financial assistance within the meaning of CA 2006, s 677 (previously CA 1948, s 54) since some meaning had to be given to the words 'give … financial assistance' by means of 'the provision of security' in that subsection, and the meaning must be such as to cover some matter not already covered by the other words 'loan' and 'guarantee'; the usual and possibly the only way in which a company could give financial assistance was by means of the provision of a security;

(ii) in the circumstances of the case the company had undoubtedly given financial assistance to the defendant as the purchaser of the shares by the provision of a security and it was not open to the claimants to argue that, if the security was invalid, no financial assistance could have been given by the provision of a security; all that was necessary to make the financial assistance effective was that the plaintiffs believed that the security was valid and on the strength of it made the loan.

26.60 In *Wallersteiner v Moir* [1974] 3 All ER 217, the Court of Appeal found financial assistance had been given for the acquisition of shares contrary to CA 2006, s 677 (previously CA 1948, s 54) and decided that any director who was a party to a breach of s 677 was guilty of misfeasance and liable to recoup to the company any loss occasioned by the default.

26.61 The modern view is now reflected in *Arab Bank plc v Mercantile Holdings Limited* [1994] Ch 71.

The claimant bank granted a loan facility of £15.4 million to the second defendant, a company incorporated in England, for the express purpose of enabling it to acquire the entire share capital of Q Ltd, also incorporated in England. Q Ltd was the parent company of the first defendant and owned its entire share capital. The first defendant was incorporated in Gibraltar but maintained a place of business in Great Britain and was the owner of a leasehold property which it charged in favour of the plaintiff bank to secure the moneys advanced to the second defendant under the loan facility. At the time that the charge was granted both defendants entered into the transaction honestly and in good faith in reliance on legal advice that, the first defendant being a foreign subsidiary, the transaction was not caught by s 677 of the CA 2006 (previously s 151 of the CA 1985), which made it unlawful for a company or one of its subsidiaries to give financial assistance for the purpose of acquiring its shares. The leasehold property was held by the first defendant on a ground rental of £580,000 per annum. It was sublet to a firm of solicitors for a term expiring in the year 2012, with a mutual break option in 2007, at a rent of £2 million per annum with five-yearly reviews. The claimant bank wished to realise its security by selling the property for 12 million, but the defendants contended that the bank's power of sale was not exercisable because the security was void, having been granted in contravention of s 677. The intended purchaser, knowing of the defendants' contentions, refused to enter into the contract to purchase until the claimant bank should obtain a court order for sale which would confirm the bank's title.

The bank sought a declaration that its power of sale was exercisable, and for an order pursuant to s 91(2) of the Law of Property Act 1925 for sale of the property. It was held by Millett J that the words 'any of its subsidiaries' in s 677 (previously s 151 of the CA 1985) were to be construed as limited to such subsidiaries as were companies incorporated in England; that s 677 therefore did not prohibit a foreign subsidiary of an English parent company giving financial assistance for the acquisition of the latter's shares. Accordingly, the security was valid and the bank's power of sale had arisen and was exercisable.

Exceptions from prohibition

Unconditional exceptions

26.62 The financial assistance prohibitions do not apply to the following types of situations (s 681(1)):

(a) a distribution of the company's assets by way of:

  (i) dividend lawfully made; or

  (ii) distribution in the course of a company's winding up;

(b) an allotment of bonus shares;

(c) a reduction of capital under Ch 10 of Pt 17;

(d) a redemption of shares under Ch 3 to Pt 18 or a purchase of shares under Ch 4 to Pt 18;

(e) anything done in pursuance of an order of the court under Pt 26 (order sanctioning compromise or arrangement with members or creditors);

(f) anything done under an arrangement made in pursuance of s 110 of the Insolvency Act 1986 or Art 96 of the Insolvency (Northern Ireland) Order 1989, SI 1989/2405 (NI 19) (liquidator in winding up accepting shares as consideration for sale of company's property);

(g) anything done under an arrangement made between a company and its creditors that is binding on the creditors by virtue of Pt 1 of the Insolvency Act 1986 or Pt 2 of the Insolvency (Northern Ireland) Order 1989, SI 1989/2405 (NI 19): CA 2006 s 680(2).

Conditional exceptions

26.63 Section 682 states that the financial assistance prohibitions do not apply in the following circumstances:

(a) if the company giving the assistance is a private company; or

(b) if the company giving the assistance is a public company and:

  (i) the company has net assets that are not reduced by the giving of the assistance; or

  (ii) to the extent that those assets are so reduced, the assistance is provided out of distributable profits: CA 2006, s 682(1).

26.64 The transactions to which s 682 applies are:

(a) where the lending of money is part of the ordinary business of the company, the lending of money in the ordinary course of the company's business;

(b) the provision by the company, in good faith in the interests of the company or its holding company, of financial assistance for the purposes of an employees' share scheme;

(c) the provision of financial assistance by the company for the purposes of or in connection with anything done by the company (or another company in the same group) for the purpose of enabling or facilitating transactions in shares in the first-mentioned company or its holding company between, and involving the acquisition of beneficial ownership of those shares by:

  (i) bona fide employees or former employees of that company (or another company in the same group); or

  (ii) spouses or civil partners, widows, widowers or surviving civil partners, or minor children or step-children of any such employees or former employees;

(d) the making by the company of loans to persons (other than directors) employed in good faith by the company with a view to enabling those persons to acquire fully paid shares in the company or its holding company to be held by them by way of beneficial ownership: CA 2006, s 682(2).

The term 'net assets' refers to the amount by which the aggregate of the company's assets exceeds the aggregate of its liabilities: CA 2006, s 682(3).

26.65 For this purpose:

(a) the amount of both assets and liabilities shall be taken to be as stated in the company's accounting records immediately before the financial assistance is given; and

(b) 'liabilities' includes any amount retained as reasonably necessary for the purpose of providing for a liability the nature of which is clearly defined and that is either likely to be incurred or certain to be incurred but uncertain as to amount or as to the date on which it will arise: CA 2006, s 682(4).

For the purposes of s 679(2)(c), a company is in the same group if it is a holding company or subsidiary of that company or a subsidiary of a holding company of that company: CA 2006, s 682(5).

Civil consequences of giving prohibited financial assistance

26.66 One civil consequence flowing from the prohibition on giving financial assistance is that as between the parties, the transaction is unenforceable and void at common law: *Brady v Brady* [1988] 2 All ER 617.

Another civil consequence flowing from the unlawful financial assistance is that there may have been a breach of directors' duties in giving such assistance. The company has the ability to bring an action against the directors in the circumstances: *Steen v Law* [1964] AC 287.

The company may also be able to bring an action against third parties for the unlawful financial assistance: *Belmont Finance v Williams Furniture* [1979] Ch 250.

Sometimes the courts have resorted to severing the illegal aspect of the transaction so as to save the agreement to the extent possible.

In *Carney v Herbert* [1985] 1 All ER 438, Lord Brightman considered that the illegal provisions could be severed from the agreement thereby making the agreement enforceable.

The giving of financial assistance in breach of s 668 may constitute a breach of a director's duties to the company under Pt 10, Ch 2 (General Duties).

In *In A Flap Envelope Co Ltd* [2004] 1 BCLC 64, the director in question made an improper statutory declaration for the purposes of giving financial assistance out of capital. Jonathan Crow (sitting as a Deputy Judge in the High Court) considered there to be a breach of a director's duty to act in the best interests of the company in failing to make proper enquiries as to the company's financial position.

Any misapplication of assets or property of the company may result in breach of trust and an account to the company for profits made by the director: *JJ Harrison (Properties) Ltd v Harrison* [2002] 1 BCLC 162.

Redeemable shares

Introduction

26.67 Chapter 3 to Pt 18 is concerned with redeemable shares.

Power of limited company to issue redeemable shares

26.68 Section 684 states that a limited company having a share capital may issue shares that are to be redeemed or are liable to be redeemed at the option of the company or the shareholder ('redeemable shares'), subject to the following provisions: CA 2006, s 684(1).

The articles of a private limited company may exclude or restrict the issue of redeemable shares: s 684(2). For private companies only, it removes the requirement for prior authorisation in the company's articles for a proposed allotment of redeemable shares. If they wish, the members may, however, restrict or prohibit the authority given to a company by s 684, by including a provision to this effect in the company's articles.

A public limited company may only issue redeemable shares if it is authorised to do so by its articles: CA 2006, s 684(3). No redeemable shares may be issued at a time when there are no issued shares of the company that are not redeemable: CA 2006, s 684(4).

Terms and manner of redemption

26.69 The directors of a limited company may determine the terms, conditions and manner of redemption of shares if they are authorised to do so by the company's articles, or by a resolution of the company: CA 2006, s 685(1).

A resolution under s 685(1)(b) may be an ordinary resolution, even though it amends the company's articles: CA 2006, s 685(2).

26.70 Where the directors are authorised under s 685(1) to determine the terms, conditions and manner of redemption of shares:

(a) they must do so before the shares are allotted; and

(b) any obligation of the company to state in a statement of capital the rights attached to the shares extends to the terms, conditions and manner of redemption: CA 2006, s 685(3).

Where the directors are not so authorised, the terms, conditions and manner of redemption of any redeemable shares must be stated in the company's articles: CA 2006, s 685(4).

Payment for redeemable shares

26.71 Section 686 states that redeemable shares in a limited company may not be redeemed unless they are fully paid: CA 2006, s 686(1).

The terms of redemption of shares in a limited company may provide that the amount payable on redemption may, by agreement between the company and the holder of the shares, be paid on a date later than the redemption date: CA 2006, s 686(2). Unless redeemed in accordance with a provision authorised by CA 2006, s 686(2), the shares must be paid for on redemption: CA 2006, s 686(3).

Financing of redemption

26.72 A private limited company may redeem redeemable shares out of capital in accordance with Ch 5 to Pt 18: CA 2006, s 687(1). Subject to that, redeemable shares in a limited company may only be redeemed out of distributable profits of the company, or the proceeds of a fresh issue of shares made for the purposes of the redemption: CA 2006, s 687(2).

Any premium payable on redemption of shares in a limited company must be paid out of distributable profits of the company, subject to the following provision: CA 2006, s 687(3).

26.73 If the redeemable shares were issued at a premium, any premium payable on their redemption may be paid out of the proceeds of a fresh issue of shares made for the purposes of the redemption, up to an amount equal to:

(a) the aggregate of the premiums received by the company on the issue of the shares redeemed; or

(b) the current amount of the company's share premium account (including any sum transferred to that account in respect of premiums on the new shares),

whichever is less: CA 2006, s 687(4).

The amount of the company's share premium account is reduced by a sum corresponding (or by sums in the aggregate corresponding) to the amount of any payment made under s 687(4): CA 2006, s 687(5). Section 687 is subject to s 735(4) (terms of redemption enforceable in a winding up): CA 2006, s 687(6).

Redeemed shares treated as cancelled

26.74 Where shares in a limited company are redeemed the shares are treated as cancelled, and the amount of the company's issued share capital is diminished accordingly by the nominal value of the shares redeemed: CA 2006, s 688.

Notice to registrar of redemption

26.75 If a limited company redeems any redeemable shares it must within one month after doing so give notice to the registrar, specifying the shares redeemed: CA 2006, s 689(1).

The notice must be accompanied by a statement of capital: CA 2006, s 689(2).

26.76 The statement of capital must state with respect to the company's share capital immediately following the redemption:

(a) the total number of shares of the company;

(b) the aggregate nominal value of those shares;

(ba) the aggregate amount (if any) unpaid on those shares (whether on account of their nominal value or by way of premium); and

(c) for each class of shares:

(i) prescribed particulars of the rights attached to the shares;

(ii) the total number of shares of that class; and

(iii) the aggregate nominal value of shares of that class: CA 2006, s 689(3) (as inserted by SBEEA 2015, Sch 6).

26.77 If default is made in complying with s 689, an offence is committed by the company, and every officer of the company who is in default: CA 2006, s 689(4). A person guilty of an offence under this section will be liable on summary conviction to a fine not exceeding level 3 on the standard scale and, for continued contravention, a daily default fine not exceeding one-tenth of level 3 on the standard scale: CA 2006, s 689(5).

Chapter 4 to Pt 18 of the CA 2006 is concerned with purchase of own shares.

General provisions

Power of limited company to purchase own shares

26.78 Section 690 is concerned with power of a limited company to purchase own shares. A limited company having a share capital may purchase its own shares (including any redeemable shares), subject to the following provisions of Ch 5 to Pt 18 and any restriction or prohibition in the company's articles: CA 2006, s 690(1).

A limited company may not purchase its own shares if as a result of the purchase there would no longer be any issued shares of the company other than redeemable shares or shares held as treasury shares: CA 2006, s 690(2).

Payment for purchase of own shares

26.79 A limited company may not purchase its own shares unless they are fully paid: CA 2006, s 691(1). Where a limited company purchases its own shares, the shares must be paid for on purchase: CA 2006, s 691(2).

But s 691(2) does not apply in a case where a private limited company is purchasing shares for the purposes of or pursuant to an employees' share scheme: CA 2006, s 691(3).

Financing of purchase of own shares

26.80 A private limited company may purchase its own shares out of capital in accordance with Ch 5 to Pt 18: CA 2006, s 692(1).

If authorised to do so by its articles, a private limited company may purchase its own shares out of capital otherwise than in accordance with Ch 5, up to an aggregate purchase price in a financial year of the lower of:

(a) £15,000; or

(b) the nominal value of 5% of its fully paid share capital as at the beginning of the financial year: CA 2006, s 692(1ZA) (as inserted by the Companies Act 2006 (Amendment of Part 18) Regulations 2015, SI 2015/532, reg 3(2)).

26.81 If the share capital of the company is not denominated in sterling, the value in sterling of the share capital shall be calculated for the purposes of sub-s (1ZA)(b) at an appropriate spot rate of exchange: CA 2006, s 692(1A) (as inserted by the Companies Act 2006 (Amendment of Part 18) Regulations 2015, SI 2015/532, reg 3(3)).

The rate must be a rate prevailing on a day specified in the resolution authorising the purchase of the shares: CA 2006, s 692(1B).

26.82 Subject to sub-ss (1) and (1ZA):

(a) a limited company may only purchase its own shares out of:

(i) distributable profits of the company; or

(ii) the proceeds of a fresh issue of shares made for the purpose of financing the purchase; and

(b) any premium payable on the purchase by a limited company of its own shares must be paid out of distributable profits of the company, subject to s 693(3): CA 2006, s 692(2) (as inserted by the Companies Act 2006 (Amendment of Part 18) Regulations 2015, SI 2015/532, reg 3(4)).

26.83 If the shares to be purchased were issued at a premium, any premium payable on their purchase by the company may be paid out of the proceeds of a fresh issue of shares made for the purpose of financing the purchase, up to an amount equal to:

(a) the aggregate of the premiums received by the company on the issue of the shares purchased; or

(b) the current amount of the company's share premium account (including any sum transferred to that account in respect of premiums on the new shares),

whichever is the less: CA 2006, s 692(3).

26.84 The amount of the company's share premium account is reduced by a sum corresponding (or by sums in the aggregate corresponding) to the amount of any payment made under s 692(3): CA 2006, s 692(4). Section 692 applies subject to s 735(4) (terms of purchase enforceable in a winding up): CA 2006, s 692(5).

It is not necessary for the financing for own shares purchase to be from cash consideration.

The effect of reg 3 under the Companies Act 2006 (Amendment of Part 18) Regulations 2015, SI 2015/532 is that a company that buys back its own shares may finance the purchase in accordance with Ch 5 or, without Ch 5 applying under CA 2006, s 692(1ZA).

> ***The terms of purchase of own shares must set out the payment provisions***
>
> In *BDG Roof-Bond Ltd v Douglas* [2000] 1 BCLC 401, Park J held that the own-share purchase was not invalidated by the Companies Acts which required the terms of the purchase to provide for payment on the purchase. In the same way as a dividend could be paid in cash or in kind, a company could pay for the own-share purchase by a transfer of assets.

Authority for purchase of own shares

Authority for purchase of own shares

26.85 Section 701 distinguishes between two types of purchase of own shares.

A limited company may only purchase its own shares:

(a) by an off-market purchase authorised in accordance with s 693A or in pursuance of a contract approved in advance in accordance with s 694; or

(b) by a market purchase, authorised in accordance with s 701: CA 2006, s 693(1).

26.86 A purchase is 'off-market' if the shares:

(a) are purchased otherwise than on a recognised investment exchange; or

(b) are purchased on a recognised investment exchange but are not subject to a marketing arrangement on the exchange: CA 2006, s 693(2).

26.87 For this purpose a company's shares are subject to a marketing arrangement on a recognised investment exchange if:

(a) they are listed under Pt 6 of the Financial Services and Markets Act 2000 (c 8); or

(b) the company has been afforded facilities for dealings in the shares to take place on the exchange:

  (i) without prior permission for individual transactions from the authority governing that investment exchange; and

  (ii) without limit as to the time during which those facilities are to be available: CA 2006, s 693(3).

26.88 A purchase is a 'market purchase' if it is made on a recognised investment exchange and is not an off-market purchase by virtue of s 693(2)(b): CA 2006, s 693(4).

The term 'recognised investment exchange' means a recognised investment exchange (within the meaning of Pt 18 of the Financial Services and Markets Act 2000) other than an overseas exchange (within the meaning of that Part): CA 2006, s 693(5).

Authority for off-market purchase for the purposes of or pursuant to an employees' share scheme

26.89 A company may make an off-market purchase of its own shares for the purposes of or pursuant to an employees' share scheme if the purchase has first been authorised by a resolution of the company under this section: CA 2006, s 693A(1).

That authority:

(a) may be general or limited to the purchase of shares of a particular class or description; and

(b) may be unconditional or subject to conditions: CA 2006, s 693A(2).

26.90 The authority must:

(a) specify the maximum number of shares authorised to be acquired; and

(b) determine both the maximum and minimum prices that may be paid for the shares: CA 2006, s 693A(3).

26.91 The authority may be varied, revoked or from time to time renewed by a resolution of the company: CA 2006, s 693A(4).

A resolution conferring, varying or renewing authority must specify a date on which it is to expire, which must not be later than five years after the date on which the resolution is passed: CA 2006, s 693A(5).

26.92 A company may make a purchase of its own shares after the expiry of the time limit specified if:

(a) the contract of purchase was concluded before the authority expired; and

(b) the terms of the authority permitted the company to make a contract of purchase that would or might be executed wholly or partly after its expiration: CA 2006, s 693A(6).

26.93 A resolution to confer or vary authority under this section may determine the maximum or minimum price for purchase by:

(a) specifying a particular sum; or

(b) providing a basis or formula for calculating the amount of the price (but without reference to any person's discretion or opinion): CA 2006, s 693A(7).

Part 3, Ch 3 (resolutions affecting a company's constitution) applies to a resolution under this section: CA 2006, s 693A(8).

Authority for off-market purchase

Authority for off-market purchase

26.94 Subject to s 693A, a company may only make an off-market purchase of its own shares in pursuance of a contract approved prior to the purchase in accordance with s 694: CA 2006, s 694(1).

Either:

(a) the terms of the contract must be authorised by a resolution of the company before the contract is entered into; or

(b) the contract must provide that no shares may be purchased in pursuance of the contract until its terms have been authorised by a resolution of the company: CA 2006, s 694(2).

The contract may be a contract, entered into by the company and relating to shares in the company, that does not amount to a contract to purchase the shares but under which the company may (subject to any conditions) become entitled or obliged to purchase the shares: CA 2006, s 694(3).

26.95 The authority conferred by a resolution under s 694 may be varied, revoked or from time to time renewed by a special resolution of the company: CA 2006, s 694(4). In the case of a public company a resolution conferring, varying or renewing authority must specify a date on which the authority is to expire, which must not be later than five years after the date on which the resolution is passed: CA 2006, s 694(5).

A resolution conferring, varying, revoking or renewing authority under s 694 is subject to s 695 (exercise of voting rights), and s 696 (disclosure of details of contract): CA 2006, s 694(6).

Resolution authorising off-market purchase: exercise of voting rights

26.96 Section 695 applies to a resolution to confer, vary, revoke or renew authority for the purposes of s 694 (authority for off-market purchase of own shares): CA 2006, s 695(1).

Where the resolution is proposed as a written resolution, a member who holds shares to which the resolution relates is not an eligible member: CA 2006, s 695(2).

Where the resolution is proposed at a meeting of the company, it is not effective if:

(a) any member of the company holding shares to which the resolution relates exercises the voting rights carried by any of those shares in voting on the resolution; and

(b) the resolution would not have been passed if he had not done so: CA 2006, s 695(3).

26.97 For this purpose:

(a) a member who holds shares to which the resolution relates is regarded as exercising the voting rights carried by those shares not only if he votes in respect of them on a poll on the question whether the resolution shall be passed, but also if he votes on the resolution otherwise than on a poll;

(b) any member of the company may demand a poll on that question; a vote and a demand for a poll by a person as proxy for a member are the same respectively as a vote and a demand by the member: CA 2006, s 695(4).

Resolution authorising off-market purchase: disclosure of details of contract

26.98 Section 696 applies in relation to a resolution to confer, vary, revoke or renew authority for the purposes of s 694 (authority for off-market purchase of own shares): CA 2006, s 696(1).

A copy of the contract (if it is in writing) or a memorandum setting out its terms (if it is not) must be made available to members:

(a) in the case of a written resolution, by being sent or submitted to every eligible member at or before the time at which the proposed resolution is sent or submitted to him;

(b) in the case of a resolution at a meeting, by being made available for inspection by members of the company both:

  (i) at the company's registered office for not less than 15 days ending with the date of the meeting; and

  (ii) at the meeting itself: CA 2006, s 696(2).

26.99 A memorandum of contract terms so made available must include the names of the members holding shares to which the contract relates: CA 2006, s 696(3).

A copy of the contract so made available must have annexed to it a written memorandum specifying those names that do not appear in the contract itself: CA 2006, s 696(4).

The resolution is not validly passed if the requirements of s 696 are not complied with: CA 2006, s 696(5).

Variation of contract for off-market purchase

26.100 A company may only agree to a variation of a contract authorised under s 694 (authority for off-market purchase) if the variation is approved in advance in accordance with s 687: CA 2006, s 687(1).

The terms of the variation must be authorised by a resolution of the company before it is agreed to: CA 2006, s 697(2). That authority may be varied, revoked, or from time to time renewed by a resolution of the company: CA 2006, s 697(3).

In the case of a public company a resolution conferring, varying or renewing authority must specify a date on which the authority is to expire. This must be no later than five years after the date on which the resolution is passed: CA 2006, s 697(4).

A resolution conferring, varying, revoking or renewing authority under s 697 is subject to s 698 (exercise of voting rights) and 699 (disclosure of details of variation): CA 2006, s 697(5).

Resolution authorising variation: exercise of voting rights

26.101 Section 698 applies to a resolution to confer, vary, revoke or renew authority for the purposes of s 697 (variation of contract for off-market purchase of own shares): CA 2006, s 698(1).

Where the resolution is proposed as a written resolution, a member who holds shares to which the resolution relates is not an eligible member: CA 2006, s 698(2). Where the resolution is proposed at a meeting of the company, it is not effective if:

(a) any member of the company holding shares to which the resolution relates exercises the voting rights carried by any of those shares in voting on the resolution; and

(b) the resolution would not have been passed if he had not done so: CA 2006, s 698(3).

26.102 For this purpose:

(a) a member who holds shares to which the resolution relates is regarded as exercising the voting rights carried by those shares not only if he votes in respect of them on a poll on the question whether the resolution shall be passed, but also if he votes on the resolution otherwise than on a poll;

(b) any member of the company may demand a poll on that question; and

(c) a vote and a demand for a poll by a person as proxy for a member are the same respectively as a vote and a demand by the member: CA 2006, s 698(4).

Resolution authorising variation: disclosure of details of variation

26.103 Section 699 applies in relation to a resolution under s 697 (variation of contract for off-market purchase of own shares): CA 2006, s 699(1). A copy of the proposed variation (if it is in writing) or a written memorandum giving details of the proposed variation (if it is not) must be made available to members:

(a) in the case of a written resolution, by being sent or submitted to every eligible member at or before the time at which the proposed resolution is sent or submitted to him;

(b) in the case of a resolution at a meeting, by being made available for inspection by members of the company both:

  (i) at the company's registered office for not less than 15 days ending with the date of the meeting; and

  (ii) at the meeting itself: CA 2006, s 699(2).

26.104 As mentioned in s 699(2), a copy of the original contract must be made available or, as the case may be, a memorandum of its terms, together with any variations previously made: CA 2006, s 699(3).

A memorandum of the proposed variation so made available must include the names of the members holding shares to which the variation relates: CA 2006, s 699(4).

A copy of the proposed variation so made available must have annexed to it a written memorandum specifying such of those names as do not appear in the variation itself: CA 2006, s 699(5). The resolution is not validly passed if the requirements of s 699 are not complied with: CA 2006, s 699(6).

Release of company's rights under contract for off-market purchase

26.105 An agreement by a company to release its rights under a contract approved under s 694 (authorisation of off-market purchase) is void unless the terms of the release agreement are approved in advance in accordance with s 700: CA 2006, s 700(1).

The terms of the proposed agreement must be authorised by a l resolution of the company before the agreement is entered into: CA 2006, s 700(2). That authority may be varied, revoked or from time to time renewed by a resolution of the company: CA 2006, s 700(3).

In the case of a public company a resolution conferring, varying or renewing authority must specify a date on which the authority is to expire, which must not be later than five years after the date on which the resolution is passed: CA 2006, s 700(4).

The provisions of ss 698 (exercise of voting rights) and 699 (disclosure of details of variation) apply to a resolution authorising a proposed release agreement as they apply to a resolution authorising a proposed variation: CA 2006, s 700(5).

Authority for market purchase

Authority for market purchase

26.106 A company may only make a market purchase of its own shares if the purchase has first been authorised by a resolution of the company: CA 2006, s 701(1). That authority may be general or limited to the purchase of shares of a particular class or description, and may be unconditional or subject to conditions: CA 2006, s 701(2).

The authority must specify the maximum number of shares authorised to be acquired, and determine both the maximum and minimum prices that may be paid for the shares: CA 2006, s 701(3).

The authority may be varied, revoked or from time to time renewed by a resolution of the company: CA 2006, s 701(4). A resolution conferring, varying or renewing authority must specify a date on which it is to expire, which must not be later than five years after the date on which the resolution is passed: CA 2006, s 701(5).

26.107 A company may make a purchase of its own shares after the expiry of the time limit specified if:

(a) the contract of purchase was concluded before the authority expired; and

(b) the terms of the authority permitted the company to make a contract of purchase that would or might be executed wholly or partly after its expiration: CA 2006, s 701(6).

26.108 A resolution to confer or vary authority under s 701 may determine either or both the maximum and minimum price for purchase by:

(a) specifying a particular sum; or

(b) providing a basis or formula for calculating the amount of the price (but without reference to any person's discretion or opinion): CA 2006, s 701(7).

Chapter 3 of Pt 3 (resolutions affecting a company's constitution) applies to a resolution under s 701: CA 2006, s 701(8).

Supplementary provisions

Copy of contract or memorandum to be available for inspection

26.109 Section 702 applies where a company has entered into:

(a) a contract approved under s 694 (authorisation of contract for off-market purchase); or

(b) a contract for a purchase authorised under s 701 (authorisation of market purchase): CA 2006, s 702(1).

The company must keep available for inspection a copy of the contract or, if the contract is not in writing, a written memorandum setting out its terms: CA 2006, s 702(2).

26.110 The copy or memorandum must be kept available for inspection from the conclusion of the contract until the end of the period of ten years beginning with:

(a) the date on which the purchase of all the shares in pursuance of the contract is completed; or

(b) the date on which the contract otherwise determines: CA 2006, s 702(3).

The copy or memorandum must be kept available for inspection at the company's registered office, or at a place specified in regulations under s 1136: CA 2006, s 702(4).

26.111 The company must give notice to the registrar of the place at which the copy or memorandum is kept available for inspection, and of any change in that place, unless it has at all times been kept at the company's registered office: CA 2006, s 702(5).

Every copy or memorandum required to be kept under s 702 must be kept open to inspection without charge by any member of the company, and in the case of a public company, by any other person: CA 2006, s 702(6). The provisions of this section apply to a variation of a contract as they apply to the original contract: CA 2006, s 702(7).

Enforcement of right to inspect copy or memorandum

26.112 If default is made in complying with s 702(2), (3) or (4), or default is made for 14 days in complying with s 702(5), or an inspection required under s 702(6) is refused, an offence is committed by the company, and every officer of the company who is in default: CA 2006, s 703(1). A person guilty of an offence under this section will be liable on summary conviction to a fine not exceeding level 3 on the standard scale and, for continued contravention, a daily default fine not exceeding one-tenth of level 3 on the standard scale: CA 2006, s 703(2).

In the case of refusal of an inspection required under s 702(6) the court may by order compel an immediate inspection: CA 2006, s 703(3).

No assignment of company's right to purchase own shares

26.113 The rights of a company under a contract authorised under s 693A (authority for off-market purchase for the purposes of or pursuant to an employees' share scheme), s 694 (authority for off-market purchase), or s 701 (authority for market purchase) are not capable of being assigned: CA 2006, s 704.

Payments apart from purchase price to be made out of distributable profits

26.114 A payment made by a company in consideration of:

(a) acquiring any right with respect to the purchase of its own shares in pursuance of a contingent purchase contract approved under s 694 (authorisation of off-market purchase);

(b) the variation of any contract approved under that section; or

(c) the release of any of the company's obligations with respect to the purchase of any of its own shares under a contract:

(i) approved under s 694; or

(ii) authorised under s 701 (authorisation of market purchase),

must be made out of the company's distributable profits: CA 2006, s 705(1).

26.115 If this requirement is not met in relation to a contract, then:

(a) in a case within s 705(1)(a), no purchase by the company of its own shares in pursuance of that contract may be made under this CA 2006, Pt 18, Ch 4;

(b) in a case within s 705(1)(b), no such purchase following the variation may be made under CA 2006, Pt 18, Ch 4;

(c) in a case within s 705(1)(c), the purported release is void: CA 2006, s 705(2).

Treatment of shares purchased

26.116 Where a limited company makes a purchase of its own shares in accordance with CA 2006, Pt 18, Ch 4, then:

(a) if s 724 (treasury shares) applies, the shares may be held and dealt with in accordance with Ch 6;

(b) if that section does not apply:

(i) the shares are treated as cancelled; and

(ii) the amount of the company's issued share capital is diminished accordingly by the nominal value of the shares cancelled: CA 2006, s 706.

Return to registrar of purchase of own shares

26.117 Where a company purchases shares under CA 2006, Pt 18, Ch 4, it must deliver a return to the registrar within the period of 28 days beginning with the date on which the shares are delivered to it: CA 2006, s 707(1).

The return must distinguish:

(a) shares in relation to which s 724 (treasury shares) applies and shares in relation to which that section does not apply; and

(b) shares in relation to which that section applies:

 (i) that are cancelled forthwith (under s 729 (cancellation of treasury shares); and

 (ii) that are not so cancelled: CA 2006, s 707(2).

26.118 The return must state, with respect to shares of each class purchased the number and nominal value of the shares, and the date on which they were delivered to the company: CA 2006, s 707(3).

In the case of a public company the return must also state the aggregate amount paid by the company for the shares and the maximum and minimum prices paid in respect of shares of each class purchased: CA 2006, s 707(4).

Particulars of shares delivered to the company on different dates and under different contracts may be included in a single return: CA 2006, s 707(5). In such a case the amount required to be stated under s 707(4)(a) is the aggregate amount paid by the company for all the shares to which the return relates.

26.119 If default is made in complying with s 707, an offence is committed by every officer of the company who is in default: CA 2006, s 707(6). A person guilty of an offence under this section will be liable on conviction on indictment, to a fine; on summary conviction to a fine not exceeding the statutory maximum; and for continued contravention, a daily default fine not exceeding one-tenth of the statutory maximum: CA 2006, s 707(7).

Notice to registrar of cancellation of shares

26.120 If on the purchase by a company of any of its own shares in accordance with CA 2006, Pt 18:

(a) section 724 (treasury shares) does not apply (so that the shares are treated as cancelled), or

(b) that section applies, but the shares are cancelled forthwith (under s 729 (cancellation of treasury shares),

the company must give notice of cancellation to the registrar, within the period of 28 days beginning with the date on which the shares are delivered to it, specifying the shares cancelled: CA 2006, s 708(1).

26.121 The notice must be accompanied by a statement of capital, except where the statement of capital would be the same as a statement of capital that is required to be delivered to the registrar under s 720B(1): CA 2006, s 708(2) (as inserted by the Companies Act 2006 (Amendment of Part 18) Regulations 2015, SI 2025/532, reg 4). The effect of reg 4 is to remove the requirement to deliver a statement of capital to the registrar when shares are cancelled under CA 2006, s 708(2) following a purchase by a company of its own shares for the purposes of an employees' share scheme, if the statement of capital would be identical to that delivered under CA 2006, s 720B(1) (registration of documents for purchase of own shares for the purpose of or pursuant to an employees' share scheme). The statement of capital must state with respect to the company's share capital immediately following the cancellation:

(a) the total number of shares of the company;

(b) the aggregate nominal value of those shares;

(ba) the aggregate amount (if any) unpaid on those shares (whether on account of their nominal value or by way of premium); and

(c) for each class of shares:

  (i) prescribed particulars of the rights attached to the shares;

  (ii) the total number of shares of that class;

  (iii) the aggregate nominal value of shares of that class: CA 2006, s 708(3) (as inserted by SBEEA 2015, Sch 6).

26.122 If default is made in complying with s 708, an offence is committed by the company, and every officer of the company who is in default: CA 2006, s 708(4). A person guilty of an offence under this section will be liable on summary conviction to a fine not exceeding level 3 on the standard scale and, for continued contravention, a daily default fine not exceeding one-tenth of level 3 on the standard scale: CA 2006, s 708(5).

Redemption or purchase by private company out of capital

26.123 CA 2006, Pt 18, Ch 5 is concerned with the redemption or purchase by private company out of capital.

Power of private limited company to redeem or purchase own shares out of capital

26.124 A private limited company may, in accordance with CA 2006, Pt 18, Ch 5 but subject to any restriction or prohibition in the company's articles, make a payment in respect of the redemption or purchase of its own shares otherwise than out of distributable profits or the proceeds of a fresh issue of shares: CA 2006, s 709(1).

The references in Ch 5 to payment out of capital are to any payment so made, whether or not it would be regarded apart from s 709 as a payment out of capital: CA 2006, s 709(2).

This Chapter is subject to s 692(1ZA) (purchase of own shares up to annual limit): CA 2006, s 709(3) (as inserted by the Companies Act 2006 (Amendment of Part 18) Regulations 2015, SI 2025/532, reg 5). This ensures that there is no conflict.

The permissible capital payment

26.125 The payment that may, in accordance with Ch 5, be made by a company out of capital in respect of the redemption or purchase of its own shares is such amount as, after applying for that purpose:

(a) any available profits of the company; and

(b) the proceeds of any fresh issue of shares made for the purposes of the redemption or purchase,

is required to meet the price of redemption or purchase: CA 2006, s 710(1).

That is referred to in Ch 5 as 'the permissible capital payment' for the shares: CA 2006, s 710(2).

Available profits

26.126 For the purposes of Ch 5, the available profits of the company, in relation to the redemption or purchase of any shares, are the profits of the company that are available for distribution (within the meaning of Pt 23): CA 2006, s 711(1). But the question whether a company has any profits so available, and the amount of any such profits, are determined in accordance with s 712 instead of in accordance with ss 836–842 in that Part: CA 2006, s 711(2).

Determination of available profits

26.127 The available profits of the company are determined as follows: CA 2006, s 712(1).

First, determine the profits of the company by reference to the following items as stated in the relevant accounts:

(a) profits, losses, assets and liabilities;

(b) provisions of the following kinds:

  (i) where the relevant accounts are Companies Act accounts, provisions of a kind specified for the purposes of this subsection by regulations under s 396;

  (ii) where the relevant accounts are IAS accounts, provisions of any kind,

(c) share capital and reserves (including undistributable reserves): CA 2006, s 712(2).

26.128 Second, reduce the amount so determined by the amount of:

(a) any distribution lawfully made by the company; and

(b) any other relevant payment lawfully made by the company out of distributable profits,

after the date of the relevant accounts and before the end of the relevant period: CA 2006, s 712(3).

26.129 The term 'other relevant payment lawfully made' includes:

(a) financial assistance lawfully given out of distributable profits in accordance with Ch 2;

(b) payments lawfully made out of distributable profits in respect of the purchase by the company of any shares in the company; and

(c) payments of any description specified in s 705 (payments other than purchase price to be made out of distributable profits) lawfully made by the company: CA 2006, s 712(4).

The resulting figure is the amount of available profits: CA 2006, s 712(5).

26.130 The term 'the relevant accounts' are any accounts that are prepared as at a date within the relevant period, and are such as to enable a reasonable judgment to be made as to the amounts of the items mentioned in s 712(2): CA 2006, s 712(6).

The term 'the relevant period' means the period of three months ending with the date on which the solvency statement is made in accordance with s 720A or the directors' statement is made in accordance with s 714: CA 2006, s 712(7).

Requirements for payment out of capital

26.131 A payment out of capital by a private company for the redemption or purchase of its own shares is not lawful unless the requirements of the following sections are met, namely:

- s 714 (directors' statement and auditor's report);
- s 716 (approval by special resolution);
- s 719 (public notice of proposed payment); and
- s 720 (directors' statement and auditor's report to be available for inspection): CA 2006, s 713(1).

This is subject to s 720A and to any order of the court under s 721 (power of court to extend period for compliance on application by persons objecting to payment): CA 2006, s 713(2).

Directors' statement and auditor's report

26.132 The company's directors must make a statement in accordance with s 714: CA 2006, s 714(1). This must specify the amount of the permissible capital payment for the shares in question: CA 2006, s 714(2).

It must state that, having made full inquiry into the affairs and prospects of the company, the directors have formed the opinion:

(a) as regards its initial situation immediately following the date on which the payment out of capital is proposed to be made, that there will be no grounds on which the company could then be found unable to pay its debts; and

(b) as regards its prospects for the year immediately following that date, that having regard to:

  (i) their intentions with respect to the management of the company's business during that year; and

  (ii) the amount and character of the financial resources that will in their view be available to the company during that year,

the company will be able to continue to carry on business as a going concern (and will accordingly be able to pay its debts as they fall due) throughout that year: CA 2006, s 714(3).

26.133 In forming their opinion for the purposes of s 714(3)(a), the directors must take into account all of the company's liabilities (including any contingent or prospective liabilities): CA 2006, s 714(4).

The directors' statement must be in the prescribed form and must contain such information with respect to the nature of the company's business as may be prescribed: CA 2006, s 714(5).

It must, in addition, have annexed to it a report addressed to the directors by the company's auditor stating that:

(a) he has inquired into the company's state of affairs;

(b) the amount specified in the statement as the permissible capital payment for the shares in question is in his view properly determined in accordance with ss 710–712; and

(c) he is not aware of anything to indicate that the opinion expressed by the directors in their statement as to any of the matters mentioned in s 714(3) above is unreasonable in all the circumstances: CA 2006, s 714(6).

Directors' statement: offence if no reasonable grounds for opinion

26.134 If the directors make a statement under s 714 without having reasonable grounds for the opinion expressed in it, an offence is committed by every director who is in default: CA 2006, s 715(1).

A person guilty of an offence under s 715 will be liable, on conviction on indictment, to imprisonment for a term not exceeding two years or a fine (or both); on summary conviction in England and Wales, to imprisonment for a term not exceeding 12 months or a fine not exceeding the statutory maximum (or both); in Scotland or Northern Ireland, to imprisonment for a term not exceeding six months or a fine not exceeding the statutory maximum (or both): CA 2006, s 715(2).

Payment to be approved by special resolution

26.135 The payment out of capital must be approved by a special resolution of the company: CA 2006, s 716(1). This must be passed on, or within the week immediately following, the date on which the directors make the statement required by s 714: CA 2006, s 716(2).

A resolution under s 716 is subject to s 717 (exercise of voting rights) and s 718 (disclosure of directors' statement and auditors' report): CA 2006, s 716(3).

Resolution authorising payment: exercise of voting rights

26.136 Section 717 applies to a resolution under s 716 (authority for payment out of capital for redemption or purchase of own shares): CA 2006, s 717(1). Where the resolution is proposed as a written resolution, a member who holds shares to which the resolution relates is not an eligible member: CA 2006, s 717(2).

Where the resolution is proposed at a meeting of the company, it is not effective if:

(a) any member of the company holding shares to which the resolution relates exercises the voting rights carried by any of those shares in voting on the resolution; and

(b) the resolution would not have been passed if he had not done so: CA 2006, s 717(3).

26.137 For this purpose:

(a) a member who holds shares to which the resolution relates is regarded as exercising the voting rights carried by those shares not only if he votes in respect of them on a poll on the question whether the resolution shall be passed, but also if he votes on the resolution otherwise than on a poll;

(b) any member of the company may demand a poll on that question; and

(c) a vote and a demand for a poll by a person as proxy for a member are the same respectively as a vote and a demand by the member: CA 2006, s 717(4).

Resolution authorising payment: disclosure of directors' statement and auditor's report

26.138 Section 718 applies to a resolution under s 716 (resolution authorising payment out of capital for redemption or purchase of own shares): CA 2006, s 718(1).

A copy of the directors' statement and auditor's report under s 714 must be made available to members:

(a) in the case of a written resolution, by being sent or submitted to every eligible member at or before the time at which the proposed resolution is sent or submitted to him;

(b) in the case of a resolution at a meeting, by being made available for inspection by members of the company at the meeting: CA 2006, s 718(2).

The resolution is ineffective if this requirement is not complied with: CA 2006, s 718(3).

Public notice of proposed payment

26.139 Within the week immediately following the date of the resolution under s 716 the company must publish a notice in the Gazette:

(a) stating that the company has approved a payment out of capital for the purpose of acquiring its own shares by redemption or purchase or both (as the case may be);

(b) specifying:

  (i) the amount of the permissible capital payment for the shares in question, and

  (ii) the date of the resolution,

(c) stating where the directors' statement and auditor's report required by s 714 are available for inspection; and

(d) stating that any creditor of the company may at any time within the five weeks immediately following the date of the resolution apply to the court under s 721 for an order preventing the payment: CA 2006, s 719(1).

26.140 Within the week immediately following the date of the resolution the company must also either cause a notice to the same effect as that required by s 719(1) to be published in an appropriate national newspaper, or give notice in writing to that effect to each of its creditors: CA 2006, s 719(2).

The term 'an appropriate national newspaper' means a newspaper circulating throughout the part of the UK in which the company is registered: CA 2006, s 719(3).

Not later than the day on which the company first publishes the notice required by s 719(1), or if earlier, first publishes or gives the notice required by s 719(2), the company must deliver to the registrar a copy of the directors' statement and auditor's report required by s 714: CA 2006, s 719(4).

Directors' statement and auditor's report to be available for inspection

26.141 The directors' statement and auditor's report must be kept available for inspection throughout the period:

(a) beginning with the day on which the company:

  (i) first publishes the notice required by s 719(1); or

  (ii) if earlier, first publishes or gives the notice required by s 719(2); and

(b) ending five weeks after the date of the resolution for payment out of capital: CA 2006, s 720(1).

26.142 They must be kept available for inspection at the company's registered office, or at a place specified in regulations under s 1136: CA 2006, s 720(2).

The company must give notice to the registrar of the place at which the statement and report are kept available for inspection, and of any change in that place, unless they have at all times been kept at the company's registered office: CA 2006, s 720(3). They must be open to the inspection of any member or creditor of the company without charge: CA 2006, s 720(4).

26.143 If default is made for 14 days in complying with s 720(3), or an inspection under s 720(4) is refused, an offence is committed by the company and every officer of the company who is in default: CA 2006, s 720(5). A person guilty of an offence under this section will be liable on summary conviction to a fine not exceeding level 3 on the standard scale and, for continued contravention, a daily default fine not exceeding one-tenth of level 3 on the standard scale: CA 2006, s 720(6).

In the case of a refusal of an inspection required by sub-s (4), the court may by order compel an immediate inspection: CA 2006, s 720(7).

Requirements for payment out of capital: employees' share schemes

Reduced requirements for payment out of capital for purchase of own shares for the purposes of or pursuant to an employees' share scheme

26.144 The CA 2006, s 713(1) does not apply to the purchase out of capital by a private company of its own shares for the purposes of or pursuant to an employees' share scheme when approved by special resolution supported by a solvency statement: CA 2006, s 720A(1).

For the purposes of CA 2006, s 720A, a resolution is supported by a solvency statement if:

(a) the directors of the company make a solvency statement (see s 643) not more than 15 days before the date on which the resolution is passed; and

(b) the resolution and solvency statement are registered in accordance with s 720B: CA 2006, s 720A(2).

26.145 Where the resolution is proposed as a written resolution, a copy of the solvency statement must be sent or submitted to every eligible member at or before the time at which the proposed resolution is sent or submitted to the member: CA 2006, s 720A(3).

Where the resolution is proposed at a general meeting, a copy of the solvency statement must be made available for inspection by members of the company throughout that meeting: CA 2006, s 720A(4).

The validity of a resolution is not affected by a failure to comply with s 720A(3) or (4): CA 2006, s 720A(5).

Section 717 (resolution authorising payment: exercise of voting rights) applies to a resolution under this section as it applies to a resolution under s 716: CA 2006, s 720A(6).

Registration of resolution and supporting documents for purchase of own shares for the purposes of or pursuant to an employees' share scheme

26.146 Within 15 days after the passing of the resolution for a payment out of capital by a private company for the purchase of its own shares for the purposes of or pursuant to an employee' share scheme the company must deliver to the registrar:

(a) a copy of the solvency statement;

(b) a copy of the resolution; and

(c) a statement of capital: CA 2006, s 720B(1).

26.147 The statement of capital must state with respect to the company's share capital as reduced by the resolution:

(a) the total number of shares of the company;

(b) the aggregate nominal value of those shares;

(ba) the aggregate amount (if any) unpaid on those shares (whether on account of their nominal value or by way of premium); and

(c) for each class of shares:

  (i) prescribed particulars of the rights attached to the shares;

  (ii) the total number of shares of that class; and

  (iii) the aggregate nominal value of shares of that class: CA 2006, s 720B(2).

The registrar must register the documents delivered to him under s 720B(1) on receipt: CA 2006, s 720B(3).

The resolution does not take effect until those documents are registered: CA 2006, s 720B(4).

26.148 The company must also deliver to the registrar, within 15 days after the resolution is passed, a statement by the directors confirming that the solvency statement was:

(a) made not more than 15 days before the date on which the resolution was passed; and

(b) provided to members in accordance with s 720A(3) or (4): CA 2006, s 720B(5).

26.149 The validity of a resolution is not affected by:

(a) a failure to deliver the documents required to be delivered to the registrar under sub-s (1) within the time specified in that subsection; or

(b) a failure to comply with s 720B(5): CA 2006, s 720B(6).

If the company delivers to the registrar a solvency statement that was not provided to members in accordance with s 720A(3) or (4), an offence is committed by every officer of the company who is in default: CA 2006, s 720B(7).

26.150 If default is made in complying with this section, an offence is committed by:

(a) the company; and

(b) every officer of the company who is in default: CA 2006, s 720B(8).

26.151 A person guilty of an offence under s 720B(7) or (8) is liable:

(a) on conviction on indictment, to a fine;

(b) on summary conviction, to a fine not exceeding the statutory maximum: CA 2006, s 720B(9).

Objection to payment by members or creditors

Application to court to cancel resolution

26.152 Where a private company passes a special resolution approving a payment out of capital for the redemption or purchase of any of its shares any member of the company (other than one who consented to or voted in favour of the resolution), and any creditor of the company, may apply to the court for the cancellation of the resolution: CA 2006, s 721(1).

The application must be made within five weeks after the passing of the resolution, and may be made on behalf of the persons entitled to make it by such one or more of their number as they may appoint in writing for the purpose: CA 2006, s 721(2).

26.153 On an application under s 721 the court may if it thinks fit:

(a) adjourn the proceedings so that an arrangement may be made to the satisfaction of the court:

   (i) for the purchase of the interests of dissentient members; or

   (ii) for the protection of dissentient creditors, and

(b) give such directions and make such orders as it thinks expedient for facilitating or carrying into effect any such arrangement: CA 2006, s 721(3).

26.154 Subject to that, the court must make an order either cancelling or confirming the resolution and may do so on such terms and conditions as it thinks fit: CA 2006, s 721(4).

If the court confirms the resolution, it may by order alter or extend any date or period of time specified in the resolution, or in any provision of CA 2006, Pt 18, Ch 5 applying to the redemption or purchase to which the resolution relates: CA 2006, s 721(5).

The court's order may, if the court thinks fit, provide for the purchase by the company of the shares of any of its members and for the reduction accordingly of the company's capital, and make any alteration in the company's articles that may be required in consequence of that provision: CA 2006, s 721(6).

The court's order may, if the court thinks fit, require the company not to make any, or any specified, amendments of its articles without the leave of the court: CA 2006, s 721(7).

Notice to registrar of court application or order

26.155 Under s 722, on making an application under s 721 (application to court to cancel resolution) the applicants, or the person making the application on their behalf, must immediately give notice to the registrar: CA 2006, s 722(1). This is without prejudice to any provision of rules of court as to service of notice of the application.

On being served with notice of any such application, the company must immediately give notice to the registrar: CA 2006, s 722(2).

Within 15 days of the making of the court's order on the application, or such longer period as the court may at any time direct, the company must deliver to the registrar a copy of the order: CA 2006, s 722(3).

26.156 If a company fails to comply with s 722(2) or (3), an offence is committed by the company, and every officer of the company who is in default: CA 2006, s 722(4).

A person guilty of an offence under s 722 will be liable on summary conviction to a fine not exceeding level 3 on the standard scale and, for continued contravention, a daily default fine not exceeding one-tenth of level 3 on the standard scale: CA 2006, s 722(5).

Supplementary provisions

Time when payment out of capital to be made or shares to be surrendered

26.157 The payment out of capital, if made in accordance with a resolution under s 716 must be made:

(a) no earlier than five weeks after the date on which the resolution under s 716 is passed; and

(b) no more than seven weeks after that date: CA 2006, s 723(1).

26.158 Shares to be purchased in accordance with a resolution under s 720A must be surrendered:

(a) no earlier than five weeks after the date on which the resolution under s 720A is passed; and

(b) no later than seven weeks after that date: CA 2006, s 723(1A) (as inserted by the Companies Act 2006 (Amendment of Part 18) Regulations 2015, SI 2015/532, reg 6).

This is subject to any exercise of the court's powers under s 721(5) (power to alter or extend time where resolution confirmed after objection): CA 2006, s 723(2).

The effect of reg 6 is that where a company buys back its own shares under CA 2006, s 720A for the purposes of or pursuant to an employees' share scheme, the time limit for the return of the shares to the company such that the obligation to pay arises is specified in relation to the date the resolution approving such buy back is passed. This is to allow a company to take advantage of the option of deferred payment in CA 2006, s 691(3).

Treasury shares

26.159 Chapter 6 to Pt 18 is concerned with treasury shares.

Where a company buys back its own shares, it is normally required to cancel those shares. Certain companies (principally those which are listed or those which are traded on the Alternative Investment Market (AIM) and equivalent companies in the EEA) may elect not to cancel shares which have been bought back, but instead hold them 'in treasury'. A share which is held in treasury may be sold at a future point in time. As the directors do not have to obtain prior authority from the company's members before selling treasury shares, this facility enables companies to raise capital more quickly than they would otherwise be able to.

Concept of Treasury shares

26.160 The CA 2006, s 724 applies where:

(a) a limited company makes a purchase of its own shares in accordance with Ch 4; and

(b) the purchase is made out of distributable profits; or

(c) with cash under section 692(1)(b) : CA 2006, s 724(1) (as inserted by the Companies Act 2006 (Amendment of Part 18) Regulations 2015, SI 2015/532, reg 7).

26.161 Where s 724 applies, the company may hold the shares (or any of them) or deal with any of them, at any time, in accordance with ss 727 or 729: CA 2006, s 724(3).

Where shares are held by the company, the company must be entered in its register of members (or have his name and other particulars delivered to the registrar under Ch 2A of Pt 8 and registered by the registrar) as the member holding the shares: CA 2006, s 724(4).

26.162 In the Companies Acts references to a company holding shares as treasury shares are to the company holding shares that:

(a) were (or are treated as having been) purchased by it in circumstances in which s 724 applies; and

(b) have been held by the company continuously since they were so purchased (or treated as purchased): CA 2006, s 724(5).

Treasury shares: exercise of rights

26.163 Section 726 applies where shares are held by a company as treasury shares: CA 2006, s 726(1).

The company must not exercise any right in respect of the treasury shares, and any purported exercise of such a right is void: CA 2006, s 726(2). This applies, in particular, to any right to attend or vote at meetings.

No dividend may be paid, and no other distribution (whether in cash or otherwise) of the company's assets (including any distribution of assets to members on a winding up) may be made to the company, in respect of the treasury shares: CA 2006, s 726(3).

26.164 Nothing in s 726 prevents an allotment of shares as fully paid bonus shares in respect of the treasury shares, or the payment of any amount payable on the redemption of the treasury shares (if they are redeemable shares): CA 2006, s 726(4).

Shares allotted as fully paid bonus shares in respect of the treasury shares are treated as if purchased by the company, at the time they were allotted, in circumstances in which s 724(1) (treasury shares) applied: CA 2006, s 726(5).

Treasury shares: disposal

26.165 Where shares are held as treasury shares, the company may at any time sell the shares (or any of them) for a cash consideration, or transfer the shares (or any of them) for the purposes of or pursuant to an employees' share scheme: CA 2006, s 727(1).

In s 727(1)(a) 'cash consideration' means:

(a) cash received by the company; or

(b) a cheque received by the company in good faith that the directors have no reason for suspecting will not be paid; or

(c) a release of a liability of the company for a liquidated sum; or

(d) an undertaking to pay cash to the company on or before a date not more than 90 days after the date on which the company agrees to sell the shares; or

(e) payment by any other means giving rise to a present or future entitlement (of the company or a person acting on the company's behalf) to a payment, or credit equivalent to payment, in cash: CA 2006, s 727(2).

For this purpose, the term 'cash' includes foreign currency.

26.166 The Secretary of State may by order provide that particular means of payment specified in the order are to be regarded as falling within s 727(2)(e): CA 2006, s 727(3).

If the company receives a notice under s 979 (takeover offers: right of offeror to buy out minority shareholders) that a person desires to acquire shares held by the company as treasury shares, the company must not sell or transfer the shares to which the notice relates except to that person: CA 2006, s 727(4).

Treasury shares: notice of disposal

26.167 Where shares held by a company as treasury shares are sold, or are transferred for the purposes of an employees' share scheme, the company must deliver a return to the registrar not later than 28 days after the shares are disposed of: CA 2006, s 728(1).

The return must state with respect to shares of each class disposed of the number and nominal value of the shares, and the date on which they were disposed of: CA 2006, s 728(2).

Particulars of shares disposed of on different dates may be included in a single return: CA 2006, s 728(3).

26.168 If default is made in complying with s 728 an offence is committed by every officer of the company who is in default: CA 2006, s 728(4). A person guilty of an offence under this section will be liable on conviction on indictment, to a fine; and on summary conviction, to a fine not exceeding the statutory maximum and, for continued contravention, a daily default fine not exceeding one-tenth of the statutory maximum: CA 2006, s 728(5).

Treasury shares: cancellation

26.169 Where shares are held as treasury shares, the company may at any time cancel the shares: CA 2006, s 729(1).

If a company cancels shares held as treasury shares, the amount of the company's share capital is reduced accordingly by the nominal amount of the shares cancelled: CA 2006, s 729(4). The directors may take any steps required to enable the company to cancel its shares under this section without complying with the provisions of Ch 10 of Pt 17 (reduction of share capital): CA 2006, s 729(5).

Treasury shares: notice of cancellation

26.170 Where shares held by a company as treasury shares are cancelled, the company must deliver a return to the registrar not later than 28 days after the shares are cancelled. This does not apply to shares that are cancelled forthwith on their acquisition by the company (see s 708): CA 2006, s 730(1).

The return must state with respect to shares of each class cancelled the number and nominal value of the shares, and the date on which they were cancelled: CA 2006, s 730(2).

Particulars of shares cancelled on different dates may be included in a single return: CA 2006, s 730(3).

The notice must be accompanied by a statement of capital: CA 2006, s 730(4).

26.171 The statement of capital must state with respect to the company's share capital immediately following the cancellation:

(a) the total number of shares of the company;

(b) the aggregate nominal value of those shares;

(ba) the aggregate amount (if any) unpaid on those shares (whether on account of their nominal value or by way of premium); and

(c) for each class of shares:

  (i) prescribed particulars of the rights attached to the shares;

  (ii) the total number of shares of that class; and

  (iii) the aggregate nominal value of shares of that class: CA 2006, s 730(5) (as inserted by SBEEA, Sch 6).

26.172 If default is made in complying with s 730, an offence is committed by the company, and every officer of the company who is in default: CA 2006, s 730(6). A person guilty of an offence under this section will be liable on summary conviction to a fine not exceeding level 3 on the standard scale and, for continued contravention, a daily default fine not exceeding one-tenth of level 3 on the standard scale: CA 2006, s 730(7).

Treasury shares: treatment of proceeds of sale

26.173 Where shares held as treasury shares are sold, the proceeds of sale must be dealt with in accordance with s 731: CA 2006, s 731(1).

If the proceeds of sale are equal to or less than the purchase price paid by the company for the shares, the proceeds are treated for the purposes of Pt 23 (distributions) as a realised profit of the company: CA 2006, s 731(2).

If the proceeds of sale exceed the purchase price paid by the company an amount equal to the purchase price paid is treated as a realised profit of the company for the purposes of that Part, and the excess must be transferred to the company's share premium account: CA 2006, s 731(3).

For the purposes of s 731, the purchase price paid by the company must be determined by the application of a weighted average price method, and if the shares were allotted to the company as fully paid bonus shares, the purchase price paid for them is treated as nil: CA 2006, s 731(4).

Treasury shares: offences

26.174 If a company contravenes any of the provisions of CA 2006, Pt 18, Ch 6 (except s 730 (notice of cancellation)), an offence is committed by the company, and every officer of the company who is in default: CA 2006, s 732(1). A person guilty of an offence under this section will be liable on conviction on indictment, to a fine; on summary conviction to a fine not exceeding the statutory maximum: CA 2006, s 732(2).

Supplementary provisions

26.175 Chapter 7 to Pt 18 sets out the supplementary provisions.

The capital redemption reserve

26.176 In the following circumstances a company must transfer amounts to a reserve, called the 'capital redemption reserve': CA 2006, s 733(1).

Where under CA 2006, Pt 18 shares of a limited company are redeemed or purchased wholly out of the company's profits, the amount by which the company's issued share capital is diminished in accordance with s 688(b) (on the cancellation of shares redeemed), or s 706(b)(ii) (on the cancellation of shares purchased), must be transferred to the capital redemption reserve: CA 2006, s 733(2).

26.177 If the shares are redeemed or purchased wholly or partly out of the proceeds of a fresh issue, and the aggregate amount of the proceeds is less than the aggregate nominal value of the shares redeemed or purchased, the amount of the difference must be transferred to the capital redemption reserve. This does not apply in the case of a private company if, in addition to the proceeds of the fresh issue, the company applies a payment out of capital under Ch 5 or under CA 2006, s 692(1ZA) in making the redemption or purchase: CA 2006, s 733(3) (as inserted by the Companies Act 2006 (Amendment of Part 18) Regulations 2015, SI 2015/532, reg 7).

26.178 The amount by which a company's share capital is diminished in accordance with s 729(4) (on the cancellation of shares held as treasury shares) must be transferred to the capital redemption reserve: CA 2006, s 733(4).

The company may use the capital redemption reserve to pay up new shares to be allotted to members as fully paid bonus shares: CA 2006, s 733(5).

Subject to that, the provisions of the Companies Acts relating to the reduction of a company's share capital apply as if the capital redemption reserve were part of its paid up share capital: CA 2006, s 733(6).

Accounting consequences of payment out of capital

26.179 Section 734 applies where a payment out of capital is made in accordance with Ch 5 or s 692(1ZA) (redemption or purchase of own shares by private company out of capital): CA 2006, s 734(1) (as inserted by the Companies Act 2006 (Amendment of Part 18) Regulations 2015, SI 2015/532, reg 9).

In relation to a payment under s 692(1ZA) references to the permissible capital payment are to the purchase price of the shares or (if less) the part of it met out of the payment under s 692(1ZA) and any proceeds of a fresh issue used to make the purchase: CA 2006, s 734(1A) (as inserted by the Companies Act 2006 (Amendment of Part 18) Regulations 2015, SI 2015/532, reg 9).

26.180 If the permissible capital payment is less than the nominal amount of the shares redeemed or purchased, the amount of the difference must be transferred to the company's capital redemption reserve: CA 2006, s 734(2).

If the permissible capital payment is greater than the nominal amount of the shares redeemed or purchased the amount of any capital redemption reserve, share premium account or fully paid share capital of the company, and any amount representing unrealised profits of the company for the time being standing to the credit of any revaluation reserve maintained by the company, may be reduced by a sum not exceeding (or by sums not in total exceeding) the amount by which the permissible capital payment exceeds the nominal amount of the shares: CA 2006, s 734(3).

Where the proceeds of a fresh issue are applied by the company in making a redemption or purchase of its own shares in addition to a payment out of capital under CA 2006, Pt 18, Ch 5 the references in s 734(2) and (3) to the permissible capital payment are to be read as referring to the aggregate of that payment and those proceeds: CA 2006, s 734(4).

Effect of company's failure to redeem or purchase

26.181 Section 735 applies where a company issues shares on terms that they are or are liable to be redeemed, or agrees to purchase any of its shares: CA 2006, s 735(1).

The company is not liable in damages in respect of any failure on its part to redeem or purchase any of the shares: CA 2006, s 735(2). This is without prejudice to any right of the holder of the shares other than his right to sue the company for damages in respect of its failure.

The court will not grant an order for specific performance of the terms of redemption or purchase if the company shows that it is unable to meet the costs of redeeming or purchasing the shares in question out of distributable profits: CA 2006, s 735(3).

If the company is wound up and at the commencement of the winding up any of the shares have not been redeemed or purchased, the terms of redemption or purchase may be enforced against the company: CA 2006, s 735(4). When shares are redeemed or purchased under s 735(4), they are treated as cancelled.

26.182 Section 735(4) does not apply if:

(a) the terms provided for the redemption or purchase to take place at a date later than that of the commencement of the winding up; or

(b) during the period:

   (i) beginning with the date on which the redemption or purchase was to have taken place, and

   (ii) ending with the commencement of the winding up,

the company could not at any time have lawfully made a distribution equal in value to the price at which the shares were to have been redeemed or purchased: CA 2006, s 735(5).

26.183 There shall be paid in priority to any amount that the company is liable under CA 2006, s 735(4) to pay in respect of any shares:

(a) all other debts and liabilities of the company (other than any due to members in their character as such); and

(b) if other shares carry rights (whether as to capital or as to income) that are preferred to the rights as to capital attaching to the first-mentioned shares, any amount due in satisfaction of those preferred rights.

Subject to that, any such amount shall be paid in priority to any amounts due to members in satisfaction of their rights (whether as to capital or income) as members: CA 2006, s 735(6).

Checklist: issuing redeemable shares

26.184 *This checklist sets out the practice and procedure for a company issuing redeemable shares. It is covered by the regime under Ch 3 of Pt 18 of the CA 2006. It should be adapted depending upon the company's articles of association governing meetings*

No	Issue	Reference
1	Must be a limited company having a share capital.	CA 2006, s 684(1)
2	The company may issue shares that are redeemed or liable to be redeemed at the option of the company or the shareholder.	CA 2006, s 684
3	Check the private limited company's articles of association to see if they exclude or restrict the issuance of redeemable shares.	CA 2006, s 684(2)
4	A public company may only issue shares if expressly provided for in its Articles of Association.	CA 2006, s 684(3)
5	A company may not issue redeemable shares at a time when there are no issued shares of the company that are not redeemed.	CA 2006, s 684(4)
6	Check the Articles of Association of a limited company to see if the directors are authorised to determine the terms, conditions and manner of redemption.	CA 2006, s 685(1)
7	If the directors are not so authorised, call a Board meeting. Either a director or a secretary (if there is one) may call a Board meeting. Reasonable notice is required.	
8	Prepare an Agenda setting out the terms and manner of redemption: At the Board meeting: • Ensure that a quorum is present • Consider whether any directors' interests need to be declared • Chairman presides at the Board meeting • Voting will be on a show of hands • The directors will vote to put the ordinary resolution to the EGM to approve the terms and manner of redemption • Consider if a Board meeting can be dispensed with by a written resolution procedure. After the Board meeting: • Prepare minutes of the Board meeting • Call the EGM • Notice of EGM to state: – date of the EGM – time – place – a note on proxy	

No	Issue	Reference
	– the text of the ordinary resolution – consider whether the EGM can be dispensed with by written resolution attaching the manner and terms of redemption. ● At the EGM: – Ensure quorum is present – Chairman presides at the meeting – Voting will be on a show of hands unless a poll is demanded to pass the ordinary resolution. ● After the EGM: – Prepare minutes of the EGM.	
9	Ensure that shares in a limited company are not redeemed unless they are fully paid.	
10	Where shares in a limited company are redeemed the shares are treated as cancelled, and the amount of the company's issued share capital is diminished accordingly by the nominal value of the shares redeemed.	
11	If a limited company redeems any redeemable shares it must within one month after doing so give notice to the registrar, specifying the shares redeemed. The notice must be accompanied by a statement of capital. The statement of capital must state with respect to the company's share capital immediately following the redemption:	CA 2006, s 689(1)
	(a) the total number of shares of the company; (b) the aggregate nominal value of those shares; (c) for each class of shares: (i) prescribed particulars of the rights attached to the shares; (ii) the total number of shares of that class; and (iii) the aggregate nominal value of shares of that class; and	CA 2006, s 689(2)
	(d) the amount paid up and the amount (if any) unpaid on each share (whether on account of the nominal value of the share or by way of premium.	CA 2006, s 689(3)

Definitions

26.185

'Distributable profits':	In relation to the giving of any financial assistance this means (a) those profits out of which the company could lawfully make a distribution equal in value to that assistance, and (b) includes – in a case where the financial assistance consists of or includes, or is treated as arising in consequence of the sale, transfer or other disposition of a non-cash asset – any profit that, if the company were to make a distribution of that character would be available for that purpose (see s 846). In Pt 18 (except in Ch 2 (financial assistance): see s 683 'distributable profits', in relation to the making of any payment by a company, means profits out of which the company could lawfully make a distribution (within the meaning given by s 830) equal in value to the payment: CA 2006, s 736.
'Distribution':	'Distribution' has the same meaning as in Pt 23 (distributions) (see s 829): CA 2006, s 683.
'Person incurring a liability':	This includes his changing his financial position by making an agreement or arrangement (whether enforceable or unenforceable, and whether on his own account or with any other person) or by any other means, and a reference to a company giving financial assistance for the purposes of reducing or discharging a liability incurred by a person for the purpose of the acquisition of shares including its giving such assistance for the purpose of wholly or partly restoring his financial position to what it was before the acquisition took place: CA 2006, s 683(2).

27 Debentures

Contents

Introduction

27.1 Part 19 of the CA 2006 sets out the provisions on debentures and regulates the definition of the term including the register of debenture holders.

This Chapter addresses the following aspects:

- The statutory concept of 'debentures'.
- Case law on the interpretation of 'debentures'.
- The register of debenture holders.

General provisions

Meaning of 'debenture'

27.2 Section 738 of the CA 2006 refers to the term 'debenture'. It states that in the Companies Acts, the term 'debenture' includes debenture stock, bonds and any other securities of a company, whether or not they constitute a charge on the assets of the company. The section does not, however, fully define a debenture and the term described is non-exhaustive. It is not necessary for the debenture to be secured on the company's assets for it to constitute a debenture.

As early as 1887, at common law, the courts found difficulty in defining the term 'debenture'. Chitty J in *Edmonds v Blaina Furnaces Co* (1887) 36 Ch D 215 at 219 stated that the word 'debenture' had no precise legal definition, but always imported an acknowledgment of a debt and generally, if not always, a covenant or an agreement to pay. A debenture was 'a memorandum of agreement, which contained a covenant by a company to pay to … persons, who were mentioned in the agreement as lenders, the sum of money set opposite his name, pari passu, and which charged all the property of the company as security for the payment thereof …'

27.3 In *Levy v Abercorris Slate & Slab Co* (1887) 37 Ch 260, Chitty J referred to the difficulty of defining the term: 'I cannot find any precise definition of the term, it is not either in law or commerce a strictly technical term, or what is called a term of art.' He stated that 'any document which either creates a debt or acknowledges it, is a debenture'. See also Sir Nathaniel Lindley who had previously stated simply: 'What the correct meaning of "debenture" is I do not know': *British India Steam Navigation Co v Inland Revenue Commissioners* (1887) 37 Ch D 260, 264. He also stated: 'We know that there are various kinds of instruments commonly called debentures. You may have mortgage debentures, which are charges of some kind on property. You may have debentures which are bonds; and, if this instrument were under seal, it would be a debenture of that kind. You may have a debenture which is nothing more than an acknowledgment of indebtedness.'

Chitty J was of the view that the term debenture meant a document which either created a debt or acknowledged it, and any document which fulfilled either of these conditions was a 'debenture'.

The debenture document should also refer to an acknowledgment of a debt and generally, if not always, a covenant or an agreement to pay: *Topham v Greenside Fire-Brick Co* (1887) 37 Ch D 281.

The label attached to a document describing it as a debenture was not conclusive evidence of the nature of a debenture

In *Lemon v Austin Friars Investment Trust, Ltd* (1881) 7 QBD 165, 172 Pollock MR made the point that the name ascribed to the document by the parties was not conclusive as to whether or not the document was properly described as a 'debenture' (the document was there called an 'income stock certificate'). Further, he also referred to the fact that the 'primary qualification of a debenture' had been fulfilled – 'namely that it is an acknowledgement of the indebtedness'. The objective of a debenture was to record indebtedness.

Warrington LJ also considered a debenture as an acknowledgement of indebtedness.

An acknowledgement of a debt may take the characteristics of a debenture

In the Court of Appeal case of *R v Findlater* [1939] 1 KB 594, it was held that the undertaking by the company to pay the insurance premiums constituted an acknowledgment of an existing debt and, consequently, the certificates were debentures. See too *R v Naiman Soskin and Wilson* per Goddard J (29 April 1938, unreported).

In *MV Slavenburg's Bank v Intercontinental Natural Resources Ltd* [1980] All ER 955 at 976, Lloyd J (*obiter*) considered a general credit agreement by which a bank was to provide a company with credit facilities could constitute a debenture.

A mortgage was a form of debenture

In *Knightsbridge Estates Trust Ltd v Byrne* [1940] AC 613, a mortgage of freehold land contained a covenant to repay the secured loan by half-yearly instalments over a period of 40 years. The mortgagors sought early redemption arguing that the contractual postponement of repayment over a 40 year period was void in equity. The respondents relied upon the mortgage constituting a debenture as defined by the previous s 380 of the Companies Act 1929 so that s 74 applied to prevent the condition for postponement becoming invalid in equity on grounds of the length of the period. The House of Lords held that it was a debenture.

Section 380 defined a 'debenture' as including: 'debenture stock, bonds and any other securities of a company whether constituting a charge on the assets of the company or not'.

Viscount Maugham was of the view that there was no one unifying definition of the term 'debenture' and relied on *Levy v Abercorris Slate and Slab Co*, to the effect that a debenture meant a document which either created a debt or acknowledged it, and any document which fulfilled either of these conditions was a debenture.

The term 'debenture' applied to any document which created or acknowledged a debt

In *Fons HF (in Liquidation) and another v Pillar Securitisation Sàrl* [2014] All ER 215, in October 2007 and February 2008, under two shareholder loan agreements ('SLAs'), the claimant (Fons) made unsecured loans to the first defendant company (Corporal) in which it held both ordinary and preference shares.

In September 2008, Fons as chargor and another company (Kaupthing) as chargee entered into a legal charge (the charge). The case concerned the interpretation of the definition of the word '*Shares*' contained in clause 1.1 of a legal charge ('the Charge') entered into between Fons as Chargor, and Kaupthing as Lender/ Chargee. Under clause 3.1 of the Charge (headed 'Grant of security'), the legal charge provided that:

> 'The Chargor, as a continuing security for the payment, discharge and performance of the Secured Obligations, charges and agrees to charge in favour of the Lender:
>
> 3.1.1 by way of first legal mortgage, the Shares;
>
> 3.1.2 by way of first equitable mortgage, the Distribution Rights from time to time accruing to or on the Shares; and
>
> 3.1.3 to the extent not validly and effectively charged by way of mortgage pursuant to clauses 3.1.1 or 3.1.2, by way of first fixed charge, the Secured Property and all the Chargor's interest in the Secured Property.'

The charge defined shares as:

> '... all shares (if any) specified in Schedule 1 (*Shares*), and also all other stocks, shares, debentures, bonds, warrants, coupons or other securities now or in the future owned by the Chargor in Corporal from time to time or any in which it has an interest.'

The parties disputed whether 'shares' in the definition clause encompassed the rights of Fons under the SLAs.

The Court of Appeal was required to determine whether the definition of shares in the definition clause encompassed the rights of Fons under the SLAs. It held that the term 'debenture' had a wider and less specific meaning than 'bonds, warrants and coupons' and, context apart, was not limited to an instrument which was transmissible or of a bearer nature. As a matter of language, the term could apply to any document which created or acknowledged a debt; did not have to include some form of charge; and could be a single instrument, rather than one in a series.

According to the Court of Appeal, the definition of shares in the charge had intended to extend beyond ordinary and preference shares held by Fons in Corporal. The inclusion of the reference to 'debentures, bonds, warrants, coupons or other securities' clearly indicated that the charge had been to cover a much wider range of assets or investments than stocks and shares in their conventional sense. Further, the phrase 'or other securities' was not to be read as limited to some form of security in the sense of a charge over property. Additionally, the asset in question had to be one which Fons either owned or in which it had an interest. On the basis of the proper definition of debentures, the SLAs were debentures. They comprised, in each case, a written instrument, which created and thereby acknowledged the relevant debts owed by Corporal. Accordingly, there was no reason why the reasonable observer should regard the reference to other securities as limiting debentures to a meaning which would exclude the SLAs in the instant case. Once it had been clear from a reading of the charge that that they had not had to include a charge over Corporal's assets, he would have read debentures as having its ordinary meaning of an acknowledgement of debt recorded in a written document.

Perpetual debentures

27.4 Section 739 states that a condition contained in debentures, or in a deed for securing debentures, is not invalid by reason only that the debentures are made:

(a) irredeemable; or

(b) redeemable only:

  (i) on the happening of a contingency (however remote); or

  (ii) on the expiration of a period (however long),

any rule of equity to the contrary notwithstanding: CA 2006, s 739(1).

Section 739(1) applies to debentures whenever issued and to deeds whenever executed: CA 2006, s 739(2).

There must be provision in the company's articles of association to issue irredeemable debentures. The company must be a going concern where irredeemable debentures have been issued.

Irredeemable debentures may only be issued where there is power in the company's articles to do so

In *Southern Brazilian Rio Grande do Sul Railway Co Ltd* [1905] 2 Ch 78, by its memorandum of association, one of the objects of the company was stated to be to borrow money by the issue of any mortgages, debentures, debenture stock, bonds, or obligations. Under the articles, the board was authorised to issue debenture stock to be secured upon the property of the company and to be irredeemable or redeemable as the board should determine. The company issued irredeemable debenture stock charged upon its assets as a floating charge. The undertaking of the company had been sold and the company was being wound up voluntarily. The liquidators proposed to pay off the debenture stock at par but a shareholder took out a summons to determine whether they were entitled to do so.

Buckley J held that the company had no power under the memorandum of association to issue irredeemable debenture stock, which was really equivalent to a perpetual annuity; that the articles might be referred to explain the borrowing powers of the company, but that the granting of perpetual annuities was not a borrowing within those powers; and that the stockholder was only entitled to a return of his money paid to the company and interest. He further held that the debenture stock should not be repayable as long as the company was a going concern. Where the company was in liquidation, the shareholder was only entitled to a return of his money paid to the company with interest.

Enforcement of contract to subscribe for debentures

27.5 A contract with a company to take up and pay for debentures of the company may be enforced by an order for specific performance: CA 2006, s 740.

Registration of allotment of debentures

27.6 A company must register an allotment of debentures as soon as practicable and in any event within two months after the date of the allotment: CA 2006, s 741(1).

If a company fails to comply with s 741, an offence is committed by:

(a) the company; and

(b) every officer of the company who is in default: CA 2006, s 741(2).

27.7 A person guilty of an offence under this section is liable on summary conviction to a fine not exceeding level 3 on the standard scale and, for continued contravention, to a daily default fine not exceeding one-tenth of level 3 on the standard scale: CA 2006, s 741(3).

For the duties of the company as to the issue of the debentures, or certificates of debenture stock, see CA 2006, Pt 21 (certification and transfer of securities): CA 2006, s 741(4).

Debentures to bearer (Scotland)

27.8 Section 742 deals with debentures to bearer (Scotland). It provides that, notwithstanding anything in the statute of the Scots Parliament of 1696, Ch 25, debentures to bearer issued in Scotland are valid and binding according to their terms.

Register of debenture holders

Register of debenture holders

27.9 Any register of debenture holders of a company that is kept by the company must be kept available for inspection at the company's registered office, or at a place specified in regulations under s 1136: CA 2006, s 743(1).

A company must give notice to the registrar of the place where any such register is kept available for inspection and of any change in that place: CA 2006, s 743(2). No such notice is required if the register has, at all times since it came into existence, been kept available for inspection at the company's registered office: CA 2006, s 743(3).

27.10 If a company defaults for 14 days in complying with s 743(2), an offence is committed by:

(a) the company; and

(b) every officer of the company who is in default: CA 2006, s 743(4).

A person guilty of an offence under this section will be liable on summary conviction to a fine not exceeding level 3 on the standard scale and, for continued contravention, a daily default fine not exceeding one-tenth of level 3 on the standard scale: CA 2006, s 743(5).

27.11 References in s 743 to a register of debenture holders includes a duplicate register of debenture holders kept outside the UK, or any part of such a register: CA 2006, s 743(6).

Accordingly, under s 743, there is no requirement for a company to keep a register of debenture holders but, if such a register is kept, then it (or any duplicate) must be kept available for inspection at either the company's registered office or a place permitted under regulations made under s 1136. (This is the same as for the obligatory registers of members, see s 114.)

Register of debenture holders: right to inspect and require copy

27.12 Every register of debenture holders of a company must, except when duly closed, be open to the inspection of the registered holder of any such debentures, or any holder of shares in the company, without charge, and of any other person on payment of such fee as may be prescribed: CA 2006, s 744(1).

Any person may require a copy of the register, or any part of it, on payment of such fee as may be prescribed: CA 2006, s 744(2).

27.13 A person seeking to exercise either of the rights conferred by this s 744 must make a request to the company to that effect: CA 2006, s 744(3).

The request must contain the following information:

(a) in the case of an individual, his name and address;

(b) in the case of an organisation, the name and address of an individual responsible for making the request on behalf of the organisation;

(c) the purpose for which the information is to be used; and

(d) whether the information will be disclosed to any other person, and if so:

  (i) where that person is an individual, his name and address;

  (ii) where that person is an organisation, the name and address of an individual responsible for receiving the information on its behalf; and

  (iii) the purpose for which the information is to be used by that person: CA 2006, s 744(4).

27.14 Under s 744, a register is 'duly closed' if it is closed in accordance with provision contained:

(a) in the articles or in the debentures; or

(b) in the case of debenture stock in the stock certificates; or

(c) in the trust deed or other document securing the debentures or debenture stock: CA 2006, s 744(5).

The total period for which a register is closed in any year must not exceed 30 days.

The references in s 744 to a register of debenture holders include a duplicate of a register of debenture holders that is kept outside the UK, or of any part of such a register: CA 2006, s 744(6).

Register of debenture holders: response to request for inspection or copy

27.15 Where a company receives a request under s 744 (register of debenture holders: right to inspect and require copy), it must within five working days either comply with the request, or apply to the court: CA 2006, s 745(1).

If it applies to the court it must notify the person making the request: CA 2006, s 745(2).

27.16 If on an application under s 745 the court is satisfied that the inspection or copy is not sought for a proper purpose:

(a) it shall direct the company not to comply with the request; and

(b) it may further order that the company's costs (in Scotland, expenses) on the application be paid in whole or in part by the person who made the request, even if he is not a party to the application: CA 2006, s 745(3).

27.17 If the court makes such a direction and it appears to the court that the company is or may be subject to other requests made for a similar purpose (whether made by the same person or different persons) it may direct that the company is not to comply with any such request: CA 2006, s 745(4).

The order must contain such provision as appears to the court appropriate to identify the requests to which it applies.

If, on an application under s 745, the court does not direct the company not to comply with the request, the company must comply with the request immediately upon the court giving its decision or, as the case may be, the proceedings being discontinued: CA 2006, s 745(5).

Register of debenture holders: refusal of inspection or default in providing copy

27.18 If an inspection required under s 744 (register of debenture holders: right to inspect and require copy) is refused or default is made in providing a copy required under that section, otherwise than in accordance with an order of the court, an offence is committed by:

(a) the company; and

(b) every officer of the company who is in default: CA 2006, s 746(1).

27.19 A person guilty of an offence under s 746 will be liable on summary conviction to a fine not exceeding level 3 on the standard scale and, for continued contravention, to a daily default fine not exceeding one-tenth of level 3 on the standard scale: CA 2006, s 746(2).

In the case of any such refusal or default the court may by order compel an immediate inspection or, as the case may be, direct that the copy required be sent to the person requesting it: CA 2006, s 746(3).

Register of debenture holders: offences in connection with request for or disclosure of information

27.20 It is an offence for a person knowingly or recklessly to make in a request under s 744 (register of debenture holders: right to inspect and require copy) a statement that is misleading, false or deceptive in a material particular: CA 2006, s 747(1).

It is an offence for a person in possession of information obtained by exercise of either of the rights conferred by that section:

(a) to do anything that results in the information being disclosed to another person; or

(b) to fail to do anything with the result that the information is disclosed to another person,

knowing, or having reason to suspect, that person may use the information for a purpose that is not a proper purpose: CA 2006, s 747(2).

27.21 A person guilty of an offence under s 747 is liable on conviction on indictment, to imprisonment for a term not exceeding two years or a fine (or both); or on summary conviction in England and Wales, to imprisonment for a term not exceeding 12 months or to a fine not exceeding the statutory maximum (or both); in Scotland or Northern Ireland, to imprisonment for a term not exceeding six months, or to a fine not exceeding the statutory maximum (or both): CA 2006, s 747(3).

27.22 Section 747 creates two offences. First, in relation to the requirement in s 744 to provide information in a request for access, it is an offence knowingly or recklessly to make a statement that is misleading, false or deceptive in a material particular. Second, it is an offence for a person having obtained information pursuant to an exercise of the rights in s 744 to do anything or fail to do anything which results in that information being disclosed to another person knowing or having reason to suspect that the other person may use the information for a purpose that is not a proper purpose.

Time limit for claims arising from entry in the register

27.23 Section 748 sets out the time limit for claims arising from entry in the register. Liability incurred by a company:

(a) from the making or deletion of an entry in the register of debenture holders; or

(b) from a failure to make or delete any such entry,

is not enforceable more than ten years after the date on which the entry was made or deleted or, as the case may be, the failure first occurred: CA 2006, s 748(1).

This is without prejudice to any lesser period of limitation (and, in Scotland, to any rule that the obligation giving rise to the liability prescribes before the expiry of that period): CA 2006, s 748(2).

Supplementary provisions

Right of debenture holder to copy of the deed

27.24 Any holder of debentures of a company is entitled, on request and on payment of such fee as may be prescribed, to be provided with a copy of any trust deed for securing the debentures: CA 2006, s 749(1).

If default occurs in complying with this section, an offence is committed by every officer of the company who is in default: CA 2006, s 749(2). A person guilty of an offence under this section will be liable on summary conviction to a fine not exceeding level 3 on the standard scale and, for continued contravention, a daily default fine not exceeding one-tenth of level 3 on the standard scale: CA 2006, s 749(3).

In the case of any such default the court may direct that the copy required be sent to the person requiring it: CA 2006, s 749(4).

Liability of trustees of debentures

27.25 Any provision contained in:

(a) a trust deed for securing an issue of debentures; or

(b) any contract with the holders of debentures secured by a trust deed,

is void in so far as it would have the effect of exempting a trustee of the deed from, or indemnifying him against, liability for breach of trust where he fails to show the degree of care and diligence required of him as trustee, having regard to the provisions of the trust deed conferring on him any powers, authorities or discretions: CA 2006, s 750(1).

27.26 Section 750(1) does not invalidate:

(a) a release otherwise validly given in respect of anything done or omitted to be done by a trustee before the giving of the release;

(b) any provision enabling such a release to be given:

  (i) on being agreed to by a majority of not less than 75% in value of the debenture holders present and voting in person or, where proxies are permitted, by proxy at a meeting summoned for the purpose; and

  (ii) either with respect to specific acts or omissions or on the trustee dying or ceasing to act: CA 2006, s 750(2).

Section 750 is subject to s 751 (saving for certain older provisions): CA 2006, s 750(3).

Liability of trustees of debentures: saving for certain older provisions

27.27 Section 751 states that s 750 (liability of trustees of debentures) does not operate:

(a) to invalidate any provision in force on the relevant date so long as any person:

  (i) then entitled to the benefit of the provision; or

  (ii) afterwards given the benefit of the provision under s 751(3) below, remains a trustee of the deed in question; or

(b) to deprive any person of any exemption or right to be indemnified in respect of anything done or omitted to be done by him while any such provision was in force: CA 2006, s 751(1).

27.28 The relevant date for this purpose is:

(a) 1 July 1948 in a case where s 192 of the Companies Act 1985 (c 6) applied immediately before the commencement of this section; or

(b) 1 July 1961 in a case where Art 201 of the Companies (Northern Ireland) Order 1986, SI 1986/1032 (NI 6) then applied: CA 2006, s 751(2).

27.29 While any trustee of a trust deed remains entitled to the benefit of a provision saved by s 751(1) above, the benefit of that provision may be given either:

(a) to all trustees of the deed, present and future; or

(b) to any named trustees or proposed trustees of it,

by a resolution passed by a majority of not less than 75% in value of the debenture holders present in person or, where proxies are permitted, by proxy at a meeting summoned for the purpose: CA 2006, s 751(3).

A meeting for that purpose must be summoned in accordance with the provisions of the deed or, if the deed makes no provision for summoning meetings, in a manner approved by the court: CA 2006, s 751(4).

Power to reissue redeemed debentures

27.30 Where a company has redeemed debentures previously issued, then unless:

(a) provision to the contrary (express or implied) is contained in the company's articles or in any contract made by the company; or

(b) the company has, by passing a resolution to that effect or by some other act, manifested its intention that the debentures shall be cancelled,

the company may reissue the debentures, either by reissuing the same debentures or by issuing new debentures in their place: CA 2006, s 752(1). Section 752(1) is deemed always to have had effect.

27.31 On a reissue of redeemed debentures, the person entitled to the debentures has (and is deemed always to have had) the same priorities as if the debentures had never been redeemed: CA 2006, s 752(2).

The reissue of a debenture or the issue of another debenture in its place under s 752 is treated as the issue of a new debenture for the purposes of stamp duty: CA 2006, s 752(3).

It is not so treated for the purposes of any provision limiting the amount or number of debentures to be issued.

27.32 A person lending money on the security of a debenture reissued under s 752 which appears to be duly stamped may give the debenture in evidence in any proceedings for enforcing his security without payment of the stamp duty or any penalty in respect of it, unless he had notice (or, but for his negligence, might have discovered) that the debenture was not duly stamped: CA 2006, s 752(4). In that case the company is liable to pay the proper stamp duty and penalty.

Deposit of debentures to secure advances

27.33 Section 753 states that where a company has deposited any of its debentures to secure advances from time to time on current account or otherwise, the debentures are not treated as redeemed by reason only of the company's account having ceased to be in debit while the debentures remained so deposited.

Priorities where debentures are secured by floating charge

27.34 Section 754 applies where debentures of a company registered in England and Wales or Northern Ireland are secured by a charge that, as created, was a floating charge: CA 2006, s 754(1).

If possession is taken, by or on behalf of the holders of the debentures, of any property comprised in or subject to the charge, and the company is not at that time in the course of being wound up, the company's preferential debts shall be paid out of assets coming to the hands of the persons taking possession in priority to any claims for principal or interest in respect of the debentures: CA 2006, s 754(2).

27.35 The term 'preferential debts' means the categories of debts listed in Schedule 6 to the Insolvency Act 1986 (c 45) or Schedule 4 to the Insolvency (Northern Ireland) Order 1989 (SI 1989 No 2405 (NI 19)). For the purposes of those schedules 'the relevant date' is the date of possession being taken as mentioned in s 754(2): CA 2006, s 754(3).

Payments under s 754 must be recouped, as far as may be, out of the assets of the company available for payment of general creditors: CA 2006, s 754(4).

Checklist: debentures

27.36 *This Checklist sets out an overview of the regulatory framework governing debentures.*

No	Issue	Act reference
1	The statutory term 'debenture' includes debenture stock, bonds and any other securities of a company, whether or not they constitute a charge on the assets of the company.	CA 2006, s 738
2	The definition of debenture is not-exhaustive and does not have any precise legal definition but typically refers to an acknowledgement of debt.	*Edmonds v Blaina Furnaces* (1887) 36 Ch D 215; *Levy v Abercorris Slate & Slab Co* (1887) 37 Ch 260
3	The label that the parties attach to a debenture deed is not conclusive evidence of a debenture.	*Lemon v Austin Friars Investment Trust Limited* (1881) 7 QBD 172

No	Issue	Act reference
4	A mortgage was a form of debenture.	*Knightsbridge Estates Trust Ltd v Byrne* [1940] AC 613
5	The term 'debenture' had a wider and less specific meaning than 'bonds, warrants and coupons' and, context apart, was not limited to an instrument which was transmissible or of a bearer nature. As a matter of language, the term could apply to any document which created or acknowledged a debt; did not have to include some form of charge; and could be a single instrument, rather than one in a series.	*Fons HF (in Liquidation) and another v Pillar Securitisation Sàrl* [2014] All ER 215
6	A company may issue redeemable or irredeemable debentures.	CA 2006, s 739; *Southern Brazil Rio Grande do Sul Railway Co Ltd* [1905] 2 Ch 78
7	A contract with a company to take up and pay for debentures of the company may be enforced by an order for specific performance.	CA 2006, s 740
8	A company must register an allotment of debentures as soon as practicable and in any event within two months after the date of the allotment.	CA 2006, s 741
9	Any register of debenture holders of a company that is kept by the company must be kept available for inspection at the company's registered office, or at a place specified in regulations under s 1136.	CA 2006, s 743(1)
10	Every register of debenture holders of a company must, except when duly closed, be open to the inspection of the registered holder of any such debentures, or any holder of shares in the company, without charge, and of any other person on payment of such fee as may be prescribed and right to take a copy. Failure to do so may lead to criminal penalties.	CA 2006, s 744(1); s 747

Definitions

27.37

Preferential debts: The categories of debts listed in Schedule 6 to the Insolvency Act 1986 (c 45) or Schedule 4 to the Insolvency (Northern Ireland) Order 1989, SI 1989/2405 (NI 19).

28 Certification, transfer of securities and people with significant control

Contents

Introduction

28.1 Part 21 of the CA 2006 concerns the certification and transfer of securities. The principal objective of Pt 21 is to set out the legal effect of certification to the securities and a requirement for directors to issue shares on allotment.

This Chapter also considers Pt 21A (information about people with significant control) as inserted by the Small Business, Enterprise and Employment Act 2015 (SBEEA 2015), s 81 and Sch 3) which requires companies to keep a register of people with significant control over the company, supplemented by the draft of the Register of People with Significant Control Regulations 2015 (expected to come into force on 1 January 2016). This is in line with one of the objectives of the SBEEA 2015 towards ensuring company transparency, and to make it easier to see who owns or controls the company, and who might be making decisions about how they operate.

28.2 This Chapter addresses the following aspects:

- The legal nature of a share certificate.
- Requirement for directors to register shares on allotment and effect.
- Transfer of securities.
- Share warrants.
- The requirements and the meaning of a 'person with significant control' and the maintenance of a public register under the CA 2006, Pt 21A.

Share certificate to be evidence of title

28.3 In the case of a company registered in England and Wales or Northern Ireland, a certificate under the common seal of the company specifying any shares held by a member is prima facie evidence of his title to the shares: CA 2006, s 768(1).

In the case of a company registered in Scotland:

(a) a certificate under the common seal of the company specifying any shares held by a member; or

(b) a certificate specifying any shares held by a member and subscribed by the company in accordance with the Requirements of Writing (Scotland) Act 1995 (c 7),

is sufficient evidence, unless the contrary is shown, of his title to the shares: CA 2006, s 768(2).

Issue of certificates etc on allotment

Duty of company as to issue of certificates etc on allotment

28.4 A company must, within two months after the allotment of any of its shares, debentures or debenture stock, complete and have ready for delivery:

(a) the certificates of the shares allotted;

(b) the debentures allotted; or

(c) the certificates of the debenture stock allotted: CA 2006, s 769(1).

28.5 Section 769(1) does not apply:

(a) if the conditions of issue of the shares, debentures or debenture stock provide otherwise;

(b) in the case of allotment to a financial institution (see s 778); or

(c) in the case of an allotment of shares if, following the allotment, the company has issued a share warrant in respect of the shares (see s 779): CA 2006, s 769(2).

28.6 If default is made in complying with s 769(1) an offence is committed by every officer of the company who is in default: CA 2006, s 769(3).

A person guilty of an offence under s 769(3) is liable on summary conviction to a fine not exceeding level 3 on the standard scale and, for continued contravention, a daily default fine not exceeding one-tenth of level 3 on the standard scale: CA 2006, s 769(4).

Transfer of securities

Registration of transfer

28.7 A company may not register a transfer of shares in or debentures of the company unless:

(a) a proper instrument of transfer has been delivered to it, or

(b) the transfer:

  (i) is an exempt transfer within the Stock Transfer Act 1982 (c 41); or

  (ii) is in accordance with regulations under Ch 2 of Pt 21: CA 2006, s 770(1).

Section 770(1) of CA 2006 does not affect any power of the company to register as shareholder or debenture holder a person to whom the right to any shares in or debentures of the company has been transmitted by operation of law: CA 2006, s 770(2).

Procedure on transfer being lodged

28.8 When a transfer of shares in or debentures of a company has been lodged with the company, the company must either:

(a) register the transfer; or

(b) give the transferee notice of refusal to register the transfer, together with its reasons for the refusal,

as soon as practicable and in any event within two months after the date on which the transfer is lodged with it: CA 2006, s 771(1).

If the company refuses to register the transfer, it must provide the transferee with such further information about the reasons for the refusal as the transferee may reasonably request. This does not include copies of minutes of meetings of directors: CA 2006, s 771(2).

28.9 If a company fails to comply with CA 2006, s 771 an offence is committed by:

(a) the company; and

(b) every officer of the company who is in default: CA 2006, s 771(3).

A person guilty of an offence under s 771 will be liable on summary conviction to a fine not exceeding level 3 on the standard scale and, for continued contravention, a daily default fine not exceeding one-tenth of level 3 on the standard scale: CA 2006, s 771(4).

28.10 Section 771 of the CA 2006 does not apply:

(a) in relation to a transfer of shares if the company has issued a share warrant in respect of the shares (see CA 2006, s 779);

(b) in relation to the transmission of shares or debentures by operation of law: CA 2006, s 771(5).

The Board's right of declining registration of shares was required to be actively exercised by a vote of the Board

In *Re Hackney Pavilion Ltd* [1924] 1 Ch 276, under an article, the executrix of a deceased member of a company had the right to be registered as a member, subject to the directors' absolute discretionary right to decline such registration.

At a Board meeting of the two directors to consider the executrix's application for registration, one director proposed and the other opposed registration.

The Board being equally divided, and there being no casting vote, the proposal was not carried, and the secretary was instructed to write to the executrix's solicitors accordingly and to return all the documents – namely, a transfer by the executrix to herself, certificates and registration fee.

It was held by Astbury J that the Board's right of declining registration was required to be actively exercised by a vote of the Board *ad hoc*. The mere failure to pass the proposed resolution for registration was not a formal active exercise of the right to decline. The executrix's absolute right to registration therefore remained intact, and the register was required to be rectified accordingly.

A failure by directors to exercise the right to refuse transfer of shares may result in rectification of the register in favour of the applicant

In *Moodie v Shepherd (Bookbinders) Limited* [1949] 2 All ER 1044, the company's articles of association provided for a right of refusal by directors to register a transfer of shares by passing a resolution. The company's directors could not agree on the decision whether or not to refuse registration of the applicant executor's shares.

The House of Lords held that the directors could exercise their right to decline registration under the articles of association only by passing a resolution to that effect. However, mere failure to pass a resolution was not a formal active exercise of the right to decline; and, therefore, as the right had not been exercised, the executors were entitled to be registered as members of the company.

The powers conferred by the company's articles of association on the directors to refuse to register the transfer must be exercised within a reasonable time

In *Re Swaledale Cleaners Ltd* [1968] 3 All ER 619, the articles of association of the company provided that 'If the directors refuse to register a transfer of any shares, they shall within two months after the date on which the transfer was lodged with the company send to the transferee notice of the refusal.' There was also a similar statutory provision to s 771 of the CA 2006. The directors took four months to decide owing to quorum issues and ultimately refused to register the shares.

The Court of Appeal held (ordering rectification of the register of shares) that the powers conferred by the articles of association on the directors to refuse to register the transfer must be exercised within a reasonable time and, a reasonable time having expired before the purported refusal, the right of refusal had been lost.

According to Harman LJ: other things being equal, a reasonable time within which directors must make up their minds either to accept a transfer or to refuse it must be the two months within which they have to make an answer under s 771(1) of the CA 2006.

Provided the decision to refuse registration was taken with a reasonable time, failure to comply with the statutory notice period did not render directors' decision invalid

In *Popley v Planarrive Ltd* [1997] 1 BCLC 8, P submitted shares for registration in his name, which, if registered, would have given him control of the company as a shareholder. If P obtained such control he would use his power to obtain control of the board. The articles of association provided that the directors of the company had an absolute discretion to refuse to register a transfer of shares. The articles (Art 25 of Table A of the Companies Act 1985) also provided that, if the directors refused to register a transfer of shares, they should send to the transferee, within two months after the date on which the transfer was lodged, notice of their refusal to register the transfer. The directors refused to register the ten shares in P's name but did not inform P of their decision as they were obliged to do under Art 25.

Laddie J held that the court was willing to proceed on the basis that the directors' refusal to register the shares in P's name was taken within two months of his request having been submitted to the company. Accordingly, there were no grounds for applying the principle in *Re Swaledale Cleaners Ltd* [1968] 3 All ER 619. All that the principle in *Re Swaledale Cleaners Ltd* decided was that if the directors failed to exercise their discretion within a reasonable time they lost their power to refuse registration. However, different considerations applied where the decision was taken within a reasonable time but there was a failure to inform the transferee of the decision. Such a failure may well expose the directors to civil or criminal liability but could not relate back to turn the proper exercise of the directors' powers into a nullity. Accordingly, on the facts, the failure to comply with Art 25 could not result in the directors' refusal to register being ineffective.

Laddie J also held that in exercising their power to refuse to register a transfer of shares the directors had to act bona fide in the interests of the company. The onus was on P to show that they had not done so.

Transfer of shares on application of transferor

28.11 On the application of the transferor of any share or interest in a company, the company shall enter in its register of members the name of the transferee (or, as the case may be, deliver the name of the transferee to the registrar under Ch 2A of Pt 8),in the same manner and subject to the same conditions as if the application for the entry (or delivery) were made by the transferee: CA 2006, s 772 (as inserted by the SBEEA 2015, Sch 5, Pt 2).

Execution of share transfer by personal representative

28.12 An instrument of transfer of the share or other interest of a deceased member of a company:

(a) may be made by his personal representative although the personal representative is not himself a member of the company; and

(b) is as effective as if the personal representative had been such a member at the time of the execution of the instrument: CA 2006, s 773.

This is known as transmission by operation of law and it may apply on death of the shareholder. There is no requirement for a proper instrument of transfer before registration can be effected. The next further process is for the personal representative of the deceased to be registered as a member.

Evidence of grant of probate

28.13 The production to a company of any document that is by law sufficient evidence of the grant of:

(a) probate of the will of a deceased person;

(b) letters of administration of the estate of a deceased person; or

(c) confirmation as executor of a deceased person,

shall be accepted by the company as sufficient evidence of the grant: CA 2006, s 774.

Certification of instrument of transfer

28.14 The certification by a company of an instrument of transfer of any shares in, or debentures of, the company is to be taken as a representation by the company to any person acting on the faith of the certification that there have been produced to the company such documents as on their face show a *prima facie* title to the shares or debentures in the transferor named in the instrument: CA 2006, s 775(1).

The certification is not to be taken as a representation that the transferor has any title to the shares or debentures: CA 2006, s 775(2).

Where a person acts on the faith of a false certification by a company made negligently, the company is under the same liability to him as if the certification had been made fraudulently: CA 2006, s 775(3).

28.15 For the purposes of CA 2006, s 775:

(a) an instrument of transfer is certificated if it bears the words 'certificate lodged' (or words to the like effect);

(b) the certification of an instrument of transfer is made by a company if:

(i) the person issuing the instrument is a person authorised to issue certificated instruments of transfer on the company's behalf; and

(ii) the certification is signed by a person authorised to certificate transfers on the company's behalf or by an officer or employee either of the company or of a body corporate so authorised;

(c) a certification is treated as signed by a person if:

(i) it purports to be authenticated by his signature or initials (whether handwritten or not); and

(ii) it is not shown that the signature or initials was or were placed there neither by himself nor by a person authorised to use the signature or initials for the purpose of certificating transfers on the company's behalf: CA 2006, s 775(4).

Issue of certificates etc on transfer

Duty of company as to issue of certificates etc on transfer

28.16 A company must, within two months after the date on which a transfer of any of its shares, debentures or debenture stock is lodged with the company, complete and have ready for delivery:

(a) the certificates of the shares transferred;

(b) the debentures transferred; or

(c) the certificates of the debenture stock transferred: CA 2006, s 776(1).

28.17 For this purpose a 'transfer' means:

(a) a transfer duly stamped and otherwise valid; or

(b) an exempt transfer within the Stock Transfer Act 1982 (c 41),

but does not include a transfer that the company is for any reason entitled to refuse to register and does not register: CA 2006, s 776(2).

28.18 Section 776(1) CA 2006 does not apply:

(a) if the conditions of issue of the shares, debentures or debenture stock provide otherwise;

(b) in the case of a transfer to a financial institution (see CA 2006, s 778); or

(c) in the case of a transfer of shares if, following the transfer, the company has issued a share warrant in respect of the shares (see CA 2006, s 779): CA 2006, s 776(3).

28.19 Section 776(1) of CA 2006 applies subject to s 777 (cases where the Stock Transfer Act 1982 applies): CA 2006, s 776(4). If default is made in complying with s 776(1) an offence is committed by every officer of the company who is in default: CA 2006, s 776(5).

A person guilty of an offence under CA 2006, s 776 is liable on summary conviction to a fine not exceeding level 3 on the standard scale and, for continued contravention, a daily default fine not exceeding one-tenth of level 3 on the standard scale: CA 2006, s 776(6).

Issue of certificates etc: cases within the Stock Transfer Act 1982

28.20 Section 776(1) of CA 2006 (duty of company as to issue of certificates etc on transfer) does not apply in the case of a transfer to a person where, by virtue of regulations under s 3 of the Stock Transfer Act 1982, he is not entitled to a certificate or other document of or evidencing title in respect of the securities transferred: CA 2006, s 777(1).

But if in such a case the transferee:

(a) subsequently becomes entitled to such a certificate or other document by virtue of any provision of those regulations; and

(b) gives notice in writing of that fact to the company,

s 776 (duty to company as to issue of certificates etc) has effect as if the reference in s 776(1) to the date of the lodging of the transfer were a reference to the date of the notice: CA 2006, s 777(2).

Issue of certificates etc on allotment or transfer to financial institution

Issue of certificates etc: allotment or transfer to financial institution

28.21 A company:

(a) of which shares or debentures are allotted to a financial institution;

(b) of which debenture stock is allotted to a financial institution; or

(c) with which a transfer for transferring shares, debentures or debenture stock to a financial institution is lodged,

is not required in consequence of that allotment or transfer to comply with CA 2006, ss 769(1) or 776(1) (duty of company as to issue of certificates etc): CA 2006, s 778(1).

28.22 A 'financial institution' means:

(a) a recognised clearing house acting in relation to a recognised investment exchange; or

(b) a nominee of:

(i) a recognised clearing house acting in that way; or

(ii) a recognised investment exchange,

designated for the purposes of s 778 in the rules of the recognised investment exchange in question.

Expressions used in s 778(2) have the same meaning as in Pt 18 of the Financial Services and Markets Act 2000 (c 8): CA 2006, s 778(2).

Share warrants

Prohibition on issue of new share warrants and effect of existing share warrants

28.23 Section 779 of the CA 2006 (as amended by the SBEEA 2015, s 84) addresses abolition of share warrants to the bearer. It also makes provision for arrangements by which share warrants issued before the SBEEA 2015, s 84 comes into force are to be converted into registered shares or cancelled. As of 26 May 2015, share warrants to bearer (known as 'bearer shares') were abolished. Any existing share warrants must be surrendered within nine months.

A company limited by shares may, if so authorised by its articles, issue with respect to any fully paid shares a warrant (a 'share warrant') stating that the bearer of the warrant is entitled to the shares specified in it: CA 2006, s 779(1).

28.24 A share warrant issued under the company's common seal or (in the case of a company registered in Scotland) subscribed in accordance with the Requirements of Writing (Scotland) Act 1995 (c 7) entitles the bearer to the shares specified in it and the shares may be transferred by delivery of the warrant: CA 2006, s 779(2).

A company that issues a share warrant may, if so authorised by its articles, provide (by coupons or otherwise) for the payment of the future dividends on the shares included in the warrant: CA 2006, s 779(3).

No share warrant may be issued by a company (irrespective of whether its articles purport to authorise it to do so) on or after the day on which s 84 of the SBEEA 2015 comes into force: CA 2006, s 779(4) (as inserted by the SBEEA 2015, s 84).

The SBEEA 2015, Sch 4 sets out the arrangements for conversion and cancellation of existing share warrants: SBEEA 2015, s 84(3). There are detailed rules setting out the rights of surrender during the surrender period; consequences of failure to surrender; cancellation orders and suspended cancellation orders; payment into court in connection with the cancellation; and offences.

Amendment of company's articles to reflect abolition of share warrants

28.25 Section 85 of the SBEEA 2015 applies in the case of a company limited by shares if, immediately before the day on which s 84 comes into force, the company's articles contain provision authorising the company to issue share warrants ('the offending provision'): SBEEA 2015, s 85(1).

The company may amend its articles for the purpose of removing the offending provision:

(a) without having passed a special resolution as required by s 21 of the CA 2006;

(b) without complying with any provision for entrenchment which is relevant to the offending provision (see s 22 of that Act): SBEEA 2015, s 85(2).

28.26 Section 26 of the CA 2006 sets out the duty of a company to send the registrar a copy of its articles where they have been amended: SBEEA 2015, s 85(3).

Expressions defined for the purposes of the CA 2006 have the same meaning in this section as in that Act: SBEEA 2015, s 85(4).

The Secretary of State is required to review the provisions of SBEEA 2015, s 84 no later than five years after these provisions come into force. See too the government's publication: Better Regulation Framework Manual (July 2013).

Right of surrender during surrender period

28.27 Paragraph 1(1) to Sch 4 of the SBEEA 2015 applies in relation to a company which has issued a share warrant which has not been surrendered for cancellation before the day on which the SBEEA 2015, s 84 comes into force (the 'commencement date'): SBEEA 2015, Sch 4, para 1(1).

During the period of nine months beginning with the commencement date (the 'surrender period') the bearer of the share warrant has a right of surrender in relation to the warrant: SBEEA 2015, Sch 4, para 1(2).

28.28 For the purposes of the SBEEA 2015, Sch 4, if the bearer of a share warrant has a right of surrender in relation to the warrant, the bearer is entitled on surrendering the warrant for cancellation:

(a) to have the bearer's name entered as a member in the register of members of the company concerned; or

(b) where an election is in force under the CA 2006, s 128B (option to keep membership information on central register) in respect of the company, to have the bearer's name and other particulars delivered to the registrar, and the document containing that information registered by the registrar and the date recorded, as if the information were information required to be delivered under s 128E of that Act: SBEEA 2015, Sch 4, para 1(3).

28.29 A company must, as soon as reasonably practicable and in any event before the end of the period of two months beginning with the day on which a share warrant is surrendered for cancellation pursuant to a right of surrender, complete and have ready for delivery the certificates of the shares specified in the warrant: SBEEA 2015, Sch 4, para 1(4).

If a company fails to comply with the SBEEA 2015, para 1(4) an offence is committed by every officer of the company who is in default: SBEEA 2015, Sch 5, para 1(5).

28.30 A company must, as soon as reasonably practicable and in any event before the end of the period of one month beginning with the commencement date, give notice to the bearer of a share warrant issued by the company of:

(a) the bearer's right of surrender;

(b) the consequences of not exercising that right before the end of the period of seven months beginning with the commencement date (see para 3);

(c) the fact that the right will cease to be exercisable at the end of the surrender period; and

(d) the consequences of not exercising the right before the end of that period (see in particular paras 5, 6 and 9 to 12): SBEEA 2015, Sch 4, para 2(1).

If a company fails to comply with this paragraph an offence is committed by every officer of the company who is in default: SBEEA 2015, Sch 4, para 2(2).

Consequences of failure to surrender during first seven months of surrender period

28.31 Paragraph 3(1) to Sch 4 to the SBEEA 2015 applies in relation to a share warrant of a company which has not been surrendered by the bearer for cancellation before the end of the period of seven months beginning with the commencement date: SBEEA 2015, Sch 4, para 3(1).

Any transfer of, or agreement to transfer, the share warrant made after the end of that period is void: SBEEA 2015, Sch 4, para 3(2).

With effect from the end of that period, all rights which are attached to the shares specified in the warrant are suspended (including any voting rights and any right to receive a dividend or other distribution): SBEEA 2015, Sch 4, para 3(3).

28.32 The company must pay into a separate bank account that complies with para 3(5) any dividend or other distribution which the bearer of the share warrant would, but for the suspension, have been entitled to receive: SBEEA 2015, Sch 4, para 3(4).

A bank account complies with this sub-paragraph if the balance of the account:

(a) bears interest at an appropriate rate; and

(b) can be withdrawn by such notice (if any) as is appropriate: SBEEA 2015, Sch 4, para 3(5).

28.33 If the share warrant is subsequently surrendered in accordance with the SBEEA 2015, Sch 4:

(a) the suspension ceases to have effect on surrender; and

(b) the suspension period amount must be paid to the bearer by the company: SBEEA 2015, Sch 4, para 3(6).

28.34 The 'suspension period amount', in relation to a share warrant, is:

(a) the aggregate amount of any dividends or other distributions which the bearer of the warrant would, but for the suspension, have been entitled to receive; plus

(b) any interest accrued on that amount: SBEEA 2015, Sch 4, para 3(7).

Second notice of right to surrender

28.35 A company must, before the end of the period of eight months beginning with the commencement date, give further notice to the bearer of a share warrant of the company of:

(a) the bearer's right of surrender;

(b) the consequences of not having exercised the right of surrender before the end of the period of seven months beginning with the commencement date (see para 3); and

(c) the matters referred to in para 2(1)(c) and (d): SBEEA 2015, Sch 4, para 4(1).

If a company fails to comply with this paragraph an offence is committed by every officer of the company who is in default: SBEEA 2015, Sch 4, para 4(2).

Expiry of right to surrender and applications for cancellation of outstanding share warrants

28.36 Paragraph 5(1) applies in relation to a company which has issued a share warrant which has not been surrendered for cancellation before the end of the surrender period: SBEEA 2015, Sch 4, para 5(1).

The company must, as soon as reasonably practicable and in any event before the end of the period of three months beginning with the day after the end of the surrender period, apply to the court for an order (referred to in this Schedule as a 'cancellation order') cancelling with effect from the date of the order:

(a) the share warrant; and

(b) the shares specified in it: SBEEA 2015, Sch 4, para 5(2).

The company must give notice to the bearer of the share warrant of the fact that an application has been made under this paragraph before the end of the period of 14 days beginning with the day on which it is made; and the notice must include a copy of the application: SBEEA 2015, Sch 4, para 5(3).

28.37 If a company fails to comply with sub-paragraph (2) or (3) an offence is committed by every officer of the company who is in default: SBEEA 2015, Sch 4, para 5(4).

A company must, on making an application for a cancellation order, immediately give notice to the registrar: SBEEA 2015, Sch 4, para 5(5).

If a company fails to comply with sub-paragraph (5) an offence is committed by:

(a) the company; and

(b) every officer of the company who is in default: SBEEA 2015, Sch 4, para 5(6).

Cancellation orders and suspended cancellation orders

28.38 The court must make a cancellation order in respect of a share warrant if, on an application under para 5, it is satisfied that:

(a) the company has given notice to the bearer of the share warrant as required by paras 2 and 4; or

(b) the bearer had actual notice by other means of the matters mentioned in para 2(1): SBEEA 2015, Sch 4, para 6(1).

28.39 If, on such an application, the court is not so satisfied, it must instead make a suspended cancellation order in respect of the share warrant: SBEEA 2015, Sch 4, para 6(2).

A 'suspended cancellation order' is an order:

(a) requiring the company to give notice to the bearer of the share warrant containing the information set out in sub-paragraph (4) before the end of the period of five working days beginning with the day the order is made;

(b) providing that the bearer of the share warrant has a right of surrender during the period of two months beginning with the day the order is made (referred to in this Schedule as 'the grace period'); and

(c) if the share warrant is not so surrendered, cancelling it and the shares specified in it with effect from the end of the grace period: SBEEA 2015, Sch 4, para 6(3).

28.40 A notice required to be given by a suspended cancellation order must:

(a) inform the bearer of the share warrant of the fact that the bearer has a right of surrender during the grace period;

(b) inform the bearer of the consequences of not having exercised that right before the end of the period of seven months beginning with the commencement date (see para 3); and

(c) explain that the share warrant will be cancelled with effect from the end of the grace period if it is not surrendered before then: SBEEA 2015, Sch 4, para 6(4).

28.41 Where a share warrant is cancelled by an order under this paragraph, the company concerned must, as soon as reasonably practicable:

(a) enter the cancellation date in its register of members; or

(b) where an election is in force under the CA 2006, s 128B (option to keep membership information on central register) in respect of the company, deliver that information to the registrar as if it were information required to be delivered under s 128E of that Act: SBEEA 2015, Sch 4, para 6(5).

In the SBEEA 2015, Sch 4, 'the cancellation date', in relation to a share warrant, means the day its cancellation by a cancellation order or suspended cancellation order takes effect: SBEEA 2015, Sch 4, para 6(6).

Registration of reduction of share capital

28.42 The SBEEA 2015, Sch 4, para 7(1) applies in relation to a company if a share warrant of the company and the shares specified in it are cancelled by a cancellation order or a suspended cancellation order: SBEEA 2015, Sch 4, para 7(1).

The company must, before the end of the period of 15 days beginning with the cancellation date, deliver to the registrar:

(a) a copy of the order;

(b) in the case of a suspended cancellation order, a statement confirming that the share warrant and the shares specified in it have been cancelled by the order with effect from the cancellation date; and

(c) a statement of capital: SBEEA 2015, Sch 4, para 7(2).

28.43 The statement of capital must state with respect to the company's share capital as reduced by the cancellation of the share warrant and the shares specified in it:

(a) the total number of shares of the company;

(b) the aggregate nominal value of those shares;

(c) the aggregate amount (if any) unpaid on those shares (whether on account of their nominal value or by way of premium); and

(d) for each class of shares:

  (i) such particulars of the rights attached to the shares as are prescribed by the Secretary of State under the CA 2006, s 644(2)(c)(i);

  (ii) the total number of shares of that class; and

  (iii) the aggregate nominal value of shares of that class: SBEEA 2015, Sch 4, para 7(3).

28.44 If the company fails to comply with this paragraph an offence is committed by:

(a) the company; and

(b) every officer of the company who is in default: SBEEA 2015, Sch 4, para 7(4).

In the case of a public company, a statement of capital delivered under this paragraph is to be treated as a document subject to the Directive disclosure requirements for the purposes of the CA 2006 (see CA 2006, s 1078): SBEEA 2015, Sch 4, para 7(5).

Reduction of share capital below authorised minimum in case of public company

28.45 The SBEEA 2015, Sch 4, para 8(1) applies where the court makes a cancellation order or a suspended cancellation order in relation to a public company and:

(a) in the case of a cancellation order, the order has the effect of bringing the nominal value of its allotted share capital below the authorised minimum; or

(b) in the case of a suspended cancellation order, the order may have that effect from the end of the grace period: SBEEA 2015, Sch 4, para 8(1).

28.46 The registrar must not register the cancellation order or (as the case may be) the suspended cancellation order if it has that effect from the end of the grace period unless:

(a) the court so directs in the order concerned; or

(b) the company is first re-registered as a private company: SBEEA 2015, Sch 4, para 8(2).

28.47 The expedited procedure for re-registration provided by the CA 2006, s 651 applies for the purposes of this paragraph as it applies for the purposes of s 650 of that Act: SBEEA 2015, Sch 4, para 8(3).

Where the court makes an order under the CA 2006, s 651 in connection with a suspended cancellation order, the order under s 651 must be conditional on the suspended cancellation order having the effect mentioned in sub-paragraph (1)(b) from the end of the grace period: SBEEA 2015, Sch 4, para 8(4).

Payment into court in connection with cancellation

28.48 Where a share warrant is cancelled by a cancellation order or suspended cancellation order, the company concerned must, before the end of the period of 14 days beginning with the cancellation date, make a payment into court of an amount equal to:

(a) the aggregate nominal value of the shares specified in the warrant and the whole of any premium paid on them; plus

(b) the suspension period amount: SBEEA 2015, Sch 4, para 9(1).

If a company fails to comply with sub-paragraph (1) an offence is committed by every officer of the company who is in default: SBEEA 2015, Sch 4, para 9(2).

28.49 A person who, at the end of the period of seven months beginning with the commencement date, was the bearer of a share warrant which has been cancelled by a cancellation order or a suspended cancellation order may apply to the court for the sum paid into court under para 9(1) in respect of the shares specified in the warrant to be paid to that person: SBEEA 2015, Sch 4, para 10(1).

Such an application may only be made during the period:

(a) beginning with the day which is six months after the cancellation date; and

(b) ending with the day which is three years after the cancellation date: SBEEA 2015, Sch 4, para 10(2).

28.50 The court may grant an application under sub-paragraph (1) only if it is satisfied that there are exceptional circumstances justifying the failure of the bearer of the share warrant to exercise the right of surrender:

(a) in the case of a warrant cancelled by a cancellation order, before the end of the surrender period; or

(b) in the case of a warrant cancelled by a suspended cancellation order, before the end of the grace period: SBEEA 2015, Sch 4, para 10(3).

28.51 The SBEEA 2015, Sch 4, para 11(1) applies in relation to a company in respect of which a cancellation order or suspended cancellation order has been made if any of the following is appointed in relation to the company after the cancellation date:

(a) an administrator;

(b) an administrative receiver;

(c) a liquidator;

and that person is referred to in this paragraph as the 'office-holder': SBEEA 2015, Sch 4, para 10(1).

28.52 The office-holder may apply to the court for the sum paid into court under para 9(1)(a) to be paid to the office-holder by way of a contribution to the company's assets: SBEEA 2015, Sch 4, para 10(2).

Such an application may only be made during the period:

(a) beginning with the cancellation date; and

(b) ending with the day which is three years after that date: SBEEA 2015, Sch 4, para 10(2).

Anything left of a sum paid into court under para 9(1) immediately after the end of the period mentioned in para 11(3) must be paid into the Consolidated Fund: SBEEA 2015, Sch 4, para 12(1).

28.53 Paragraph 12(1) does not apply to any amount in respect of which an application under para 10(1) or 11(2) has been made but not yet determined before the end of that period unless and until the application is dismissed and either:

(a) the period for bringing an appeal against the dismissal has expired; or

(b) in a case where an appeal is brought before the end of that period, the appeal is dismissed, abandoned or otherwise ceases to have effect: SBEEA 2015, Sch 4, para 12(2).

Company with outstanding share warrants: prohibition on striking off

28.54 An application under the CA 2006, s 1003 (application for voluntary striking off) on behalf of a company must not be made at a time when there is a share warrant issued by the company: SBEEA 2015, Sch 4, para 13(1).

It is an offence for a person to make an application in contravention of this section: SBEEA 2015, Sch 4, para 13(2).

In proceedings for such an offence it is a defence for the accused to prove that the accused did not know, and could not reasonably have known, of the existence of the share warrant: SBEEA 2015, Sch 4, para 13(3).

Notices

28.55 A notice required by virtue of any provision of Sch 4 to be given to the bearer of a share warrant must be:

(a) published in the Gazette;

(b) communicated to that person in the same way (if any) as the company concerned normally communicates with that person for other purposes relating to the shares specified in the warrant; and

(c) made available in a prominent position on the company's website (if it has one) during the period mentioned in sub-paragraph (2) (and see sub-paragraph (3)): SBEEA 2015, Sch 4, para 14(1).

28.56 That period is the period beginning with the day on which the notice is published in the Gazette and ending with:

(a) in the case of a notice required by para 2, the day on which a notice required by para 4 is made available on the company's website;

(b) in the case of a notice required by para 4, the day on which a notice required by para 5(3) is made available on the company's website;

(c) in the case of a notice required by para 5(3), the day on which the court makes a cancellation order or (as the case may be) suspended cancellation order in respect of the share warrant;

(d) in the case of a notice required by virtue of para 6(3)(a), the end of the grace period: SBEEA 2015, Sch 4, para 14(2).

Nothing in this paragraph requires a notice to be made available on the company's website after the day on which the last of the share warrants issued by the company to be surrendered is surrendered: SBEEA 2015, Sch 4, para 14(3).

The CA 2006, ss 1143–1148 (company communications provisions) apply for the purposes of this Part of this Schedule as they apply for the purposes of the Companies Acts: SBEEA 2015, Sch 4, para 14(4).

Company filings: language requirements

28.57 The CA 2006, ss 1103, 1104 and 1107 (language requirements) apply to all documents required to be delivered to the registrar under this Part of this Schedule: SBEEA 2015, Sch 4, para 15.

Application of the CA 2006, ss 1112 and 1113

28.58 Sections 1112 (general false statement offence) and 1113 (enforcement of company's filing obligations) of the CA 2006 apply for the purposes of this Part of this Schedule as they apply for the purposes of the Companies Acts: SBEEA 2015, Sch 4, para 16.

Offences

28.59 For the purposes of any offence under this Part of Sch 4, a shadow director is treated as an officer of the company: SBEEA 2015, Sch 4, para 17.

A person guilty of an offence under Sch 4, para 1(5) is liable on summary conviction to a fine not exceeding level 3 on the standard scale and, for continued contravention, a daily default fine not exceeding one-tenth of level 3 on the standard scale: SBEEA 2015, Sch 4, para 18(1).

28.60 A person guilty of an offence under any other provision of Sch 4 is liable:

(a) on conviction on indictment, to a fine;

(b) on summary conviction:

  (i) in England and Wales, to a fine;

  (ii) in Scotland or Northern Ireland, to a fine not exceeding the statutory maximum: SBEEA 2015, Sch 4, para 18(2).

28.61 The following sections of the CA 2006 apply for the purposes of this Part of this Schedule as they apply for the purposes of the Companies Acts:

(a) ss 1121 and 1122 (liability of officer in default);

(b) s 1125 (meaning of 'daily default fine');

(c) ss 1127 and 1128 (general provision about summary proceedings);

(d) s 1129 (legal professional privilege);

(e) s 1132 (production and inspection of documents): SBEEA 2015, Sch 4, para 19.

Offences in connection with share warrants (Scotland)

28.62 If in Scotland a person:

(a) with intent to defraud, forges or alters, or offers, utters, disposes of, or puts off, knowing the same to be forged or altered, any share warrant or coupon, or any document purporting to be a share warrant or coupon issued in pursuance of CA 2006; or

(b) by means of any such forged or altered share warrant, coupon or document:

  (i) demands or endeavours to obtain or receive any share or interest in a company under CA 2006; or

(ii) demands or endeavours to receive any dividend or money payment in respect of any such share or interest,

knowing the warrant, coupon or document to be forged or altered, he commits an offence: CA 2006, s 781(1).

28.63 If in Scotland a person without lawful authority or excuse (of which proof lies on him):

(a) engraves or makes on any plate, wood, stone, or other material, any share warrant or coupon purporting to be –

  (i) a share warrant or coupon issued or made by any particular company in pursuance of CA 2006; or

  (ii) a blank share warrant or coupon so issued or made; or

  (iii) a part of such a share warrant or coupon; or

(b) uses any such plate, wood, stone, or other material, for the making or printing of any such share warrant or coupon, or of any such blank share warrant or coupon or of any part of such a share warrant or coupon; or

(c) knowingly has in his custody or possession any such plate, wood, stone, or other material,

he commits an offence: CA 2006, s 781(2).

28.64 A person guilty of an offence under CA 2006, s 781(1) will be liable on summary conviction to imprisonment for a term not exceeding six months or to a fine not exceeding level 5 on the standard scale (or both): CA 2006, s 781(3).

A person guilty of an offence under s 781(2) is liable:

(a) on conviction on indictment, to imprisonment for a term not exceeding seven years or a fine (or both);

(b) on summary conviction, to imprisonment for a term not exceeding six months or a fine not exceeding the statutory maximum (or both): CA 2006, s 781(3).

Supplementary provisions

Issue of certificates etc: court order to make good default

28.65 If a company on which a notice has been served requiring it to make good any default in complying with:

(a) CA 2006, s 769(1) (duty of company as to issue of certificates etc on allotment);

(b) s 776(1) (duty of company as to issue of certificates etc on transfer); or

(c) s 780(1) (duty of company as to issue of certificates etc on surrender of share warrant),

fails to make good the default within ten days after service of the notice, the person entitled to have the certificates or the debentures delivered to him may apply to the court: CA 2006, s 782(1).

28.66 The court may on such an application make an order directing the company and any officer of it to make good the default within such time as may be specified in the order: CA 2006, s 782(2).

The order may provide that all costs (in Scotland, expenses) of and incidental to the application are to be borne by the company or by an officer of it responsible for the default: CA 2006, s 782(3).

Evidencing and transfer of title to securities without written instrument

Scope of Ch 2

28.67 In Ch 2:

(a) 'securities' means shares, debentures, debenture stock, loan stock, bonds, units of a collective investment scheme within the meaning of the Financial Services and Markets Act 2000 (c 8) and other securities of any description;

(b) references to title to securities include any legal or equitable interest in securities;

(c) references to a transfer of title include a transfer by way of security;

(d) references to transfer without a written instrument include, in relation to bearer securities, transfer without delivery: CA 2006, s 783.

Power to make regulations

28.68 The power to make regulations under Ch 2 is exercisable by the Treasury and the Secretary of State, either jointly or concurrently: CA 2006, s 784(1).

References in Ch 2 to the authority having power to make regulations shall accordingly be read as references to both or either of them, as the case may require: CA 2006, s 784(2).

Powers exercisable

Provision enabling procedures for evidencing and transferring title

28.69 Provision may be made by regulations for enabling title to securities to be evidenced and transferred without a written instrument: CA 2006, s 785(1).

The regulations may make provision:

(a) for procedures for recording and transferring title to securities; and

(b) for the regulation of those procedures and the persons responsible for or involved in their operation: CA 2006, s 785(2).

The regulations must contain such safeguards as appear to the authority making the regulations appropriate for the protection of investors and for ensuring that competition is not restricted, distorted or prevented: CA 2006, s 785(3).

The regulations may, for the purpose of enabling or facilitating the operation of the procedures provided for by the regulations, make provision with respect to the rights and obligations of persons in relation to securities dealt with under the procedures: CA 2006, s 785(4).

28.70 The regulations may include provision for the purpose of giving effect to:

(a) the transmission of title to securities by operation of law;

(b) any restriction on the transfer of title to securities arising by virtue of the provisions of any enactment or instrument, court order or agreement;

(c) any power conferred by any such provision on a person to deal with securities on behalf of the person entitled: CA 2006, s 785(5).

28.71 The regulations may make provision with respect to the persons responsible for the operation of the procedures provided for by the regulations:

(a) as to the consequences of their insolvency or incapacity; or

(b) as to the transfer from them to other persons of their functions in relation to those procedures: CA 2006, s 785(6).

Provision enabling or requiring arrangements to be adopted

28.72 Regulations under Ch 2 may make provision:

(a) enabling the members of a company or of any designated class of companies to adopt, by ordinary resolution, arrangements under which title to securities is required to be evidenced or transferred (or both) without a written instrument; or

(b) requiring companies, or any designated class of companies, to adopt such arrangements: CA 2006, s 786(1).

28.73 The regulations may make such provision:

(a) in respect of all securities issued by a company; or

(b) in respect of all securities of a specified description: CA 2006, s 786(2).

28.74 The arrangements provided for by regulations making such provision as is mentioned in CA 2006, s 786(1):

(a) must not be such that a person who but for the arrangements would be entitled to have his name entered in the company's register of members (or, as the case may be, delivered to the registrar under Ch 2A of Pt 8) ceases to be so entitled; and

(b) must be such that a person who but for the arrangements would be entitled to exercise any rights in respect of the securities continues to be able effectively to control the exercise of those rights: CA 2006, s 786(3).

28.75 The regulations may:

(a) prohibit the issue of any certificate by the company in respect of the issue or transfer of securities;

(b) require the provision by the company to holders of securities of statements (at specified intervals or on specified occasions) of the securities held in their name; and

(c) make provision as to the matters of which any such certificate or statement is, or is not, evidence: CA 2006, s 786(4).

28.76 Under CA 2006, s 786:

(a) references to a designated class of companies are to a class designated in the regulations or by order under s 787; and

(b) 'specified' means specified in the regulations: CA 2006, s 786(5).

Provision enabling or requiring arrangements to be adopted: order-making powers

28.77 The authority having power to make regulations under Ch 2 may by order:

(a) designate classes of companies for the purposes of CA 2006, s 786 (provision enabling or requiring arrangements to be adopted);

(b) provide that, in relation to securities of a specified description:

  (i) in a designated class of companies; or

  (ii) in a specified company or class of companies,

specified provisions of regulations made under Ch 2 by virtue of that section either do not apply or apply subject to specified modifications: CA 2006, s 787(1).

Under CA 2006, s 786(2), the term 'specified' means specified in the order: CA 2006, s 787(2).

Information about people with significant control

Introduction

28.78 The SBEEA 2015 (by inserting Pt 21A into the CA 2006), introduced a number of measures to increase the accountability of companies by facilitating the process of seeing who owns or controls companies, and the persons who may make decisions on the operation and functioning of companies. This is achieved principally through the establishment of a central register of people with significant control ('PSC'). The effect of this register is to capture and see who owns the shares in the company and also who influences or controls a company discretely. Companies will still need to keep their own register of people with significant control. The objective is to increase trust and encourage investment in the UK. As from January 2016, companies will be required to keep information about who owns and controls them in their own register. From April 2016, they should send the information to Companies House with their confirmation statement or as part of the incorporation package (for companies incorporating after 6 April 2016). The central register will contain a full set of data on all UK companies by April 2017. Companies House will make all information from companies available for free, in a central, searchable register of people with significant control. Not all companies will need to record the people with significant control information as there are certain exemptions for such companies set out in the SBEEA 2015.

28.79 Part 21A is supplemented by a draft of the Register of People with Significant Control Regulations 2015 (draft regulations have been prepared and are due to come into force in January 2016). The draft Regulations set out details of the applicability of the register to specific persons and to the protection regime to ensure that the information on the register is not misused.

Schedule 1A of the CA 2006 defines what is meant by 'a person with significant control' ('PSC') and sets out a company's requirements to obtain required information on such people and hold it in a register kept available for public inspection (the 'PSC register'). Schedule 1A also sets out the obligations that apply to people with significant control and certain legal entities; and the requirement for companies to provide information in the PSC register to the registrar in the context of their confirmation statement under Pt 24 of the CA 2006. The registrar will make the information public with limited exceptions.

28.80 The objective of s 790A (as inserted by the SBEEA 2015, s 81 and Sch 3) is to provide an overview of the operation and function of the CA 2006, Pt 21A for ease of navigation of the various sections, including the purpose and objective of the Part and its interrelationship with other sections of the CA 2006. Part 21A is arranged as follows:

(a) the remaining provisions of Ch 1 to Pt 21A of the CA 2006 identify the companies to which P 21A applies, and explain some key terms, including what it means to have 'significant control' over a company;

(b) Ch 2 to Pt 21A of the CA 2006 imposes duties on companies to gather information, and on others to supply information, to enable companies to keep the register required by Ch 3 to Pt 21A;

(c) Ch 3 to Pt 21A requires companies to keep a register, referred to as a 'register of people with significant control over the company' and to make the register available to the public;

(d) Ch 4 to Pt 21A gives private companies the option of using an alternative method of record-keeping; and

(e) Ch 5 to Pt 21A makes provision for excluding certain material from the information available to the public.

Companies to which Pt 21A applies

28.81 Part 21A of the CA 2006 applies to companies other than:

(a) DTR5 issuers; and

(b) companies of any description specified by the Secretary of State by regulations: CA 2006, s 790B(1). Under draft reg 3 of the Register of People with Significant Control Regulations 2015, a company that has voting shares admitted to trading on a regulated market in an EEA state other than the United Kingdom is specified for the purpose of s 790B(1)(b) of the Act. As many companies are already required to provide substantial information about their major owners, the effect of draft reg 3 is to exempt companies who are required to comply with Ch 5 of the Financial Conduct Authority's Disclosure Rules and Transparency Rules sourcebook (DTR5 issuers) from having to keep a register of people with significant control to avoid duplication of effort. Draft reg 3 will add an exemption for companies from having to keep a register of people with significant control.

28.82 In deciding whether to specify a description of the company, the Secretary of State is to have regard to the extent to which companies of that description are bound by disclosure and transparency rules (in the UK or elsewhere) broadly similar to the ones applying to DTR5 issuers: CA 2006, s 790B(2).

A 'DTR5 issuer' is an issuer to which Ch 5 of the Disclosure Rules and Transparency Rules sourcebook made by the Financial Conduct Authority (as amended or replaced from time to time) applies: CA 2006, s 790B(3).

Key terms

28.83 Section 790C of the CA 2006 explains some key terms used in Pt 21A: CA 2006, s 790C(1).

References to a person with (or having) 'significant control' over a company are to an individual who meets one or more of the specified conditions in relation to the company: CA 2006, s 790C(2).

The 'specified conditions' are those specified in Pt 1 of Sch 1A: CA 2006, s 790C(3). This provides that a person with significant control over a company is an individual (X) who meets one or more of the 'specified conditions' in relation to the company.

The Specified Conditions (SCHEDULE 1A)

References to People with Significant Control over a Company

Introduction

1. This Part of this Schedule specifies the conditions at least one of which must be met by an individual ('X') in relation to a company ('company Y') in order for the individual to be a person with 'significant control' over the company.

Ownership of shares

2. The first condition is that X holds, directly or indirectly, more than 25% of the shares in company Y.

Ownership of voting rights

3. The second condition is that X holds, directly or indirectly, more than 25% of the voting rights in company Y.

Ownership of right to appoint or remove directors

4. The third condition is that X holds the right, directly or indirectly, to appoint or remove a majority of the board of directors of company Y.

Significant influence or control

5. The fourth condition is that X has the right to exercise, or actually exercises, significant influence or control over company Y.

Trusts, partnerships etc

6. The fifth condition is that:

   (a) the trustees of a trust or the members of a firm that, under the law by which it is governed, is not a legal person meet any of the other specified conditions (in their capacity as such) in relation to company Y, or would do so if they were individuals, and

   (b) X has the right to exercise, or actually exercises, significant influence or control over the activities of that trust or firm.

Part 2 concerns holding an interest in a company. Part 3 deals with power to amend thresholds.

28.84 Individuals with significant control over a company are either 'registrable' or 'non-registrable' in relation to the company:

(a) they are 'non-registrable' if they do not hold any interest in the company except through one or more other legal entities over each of which they have significant control and each of which is a 'relevant legal entity' ('RLE') in relation to the company;

(b) otherwise, they are 'registrable',

and references to a 'registrable person' in relation to a company are to an individual with significant control over the company who is registrable in relation to that company: CA 2006, s 790C(4).

28.85 A 'legal entity' is a body corporate or a firm that is a legal person under the law by which it is governed: CA 2006, s 790C(5).

In relation to a company, a legal entity is a 'relevant legal entity' if:

(a) it would have come within the definition of a person with significant control over the company if it had been an individual; and

(b) it is subject to its own disclosure requirements: CA 2006, s 790C(6).

28.86 A legal entity is 'subject to its own disclosure requirements' if:

(a) Part 21A of the CA 2006 applies to it (whether by virtue of s 790B or another enactment that extends the application of this Part);

(b) it is a DTR5 issuer;

(c) it is of a description specified in regulations under CA 2006, s 790B (or that section as extended); or

(d) it is of a description specified by the Secretary of State by regulations made under this paragraph: CA 2006, s 790C(7). Under draft reg 4 of the Register of People with Significant Control Regulations 2015, a legal entity that has voting shares admitted to trading on a regulated market in an EEA state other than the UK is specified for the purposes of CA 2006, s 790C(7)(d). Therefore, companies may be added by regulations to the list of entities that are considered to be subject to their own disclosure requirements.

28.87 A relevant legal entity is either 'registrable' or 'non-registrable' in relation to a company:

(a) it is 'non-registrable' if it does not hold any interest in the company except through one or more other legal entities over each of which it has significant control and each of which is also a relevant legal entity in relation to the company;

(b) otherwise, it is 'registrable',

and references to a 'registrable relevant legal entity' in relation to a company are to a relevant legal entity which is registrable in relation to that company: CA 2006, s 790C(8). The effect of the terminology is to determine whether or not the individual's or RLE's details must be entered or noted in the company's PSC register.

28.88 For the purposes of s 790C(4) and (8):

(a) whether someone:

  (i) holds an interest in a company; or

  (ii) holds that interest through another legal entity,

  is to be determined in accordance with Pt 2 of Sch 1A;

(b) whether someone has significant control over that other legal entity is to be determined in accordance with s 790C(2) and (3) and Pt 1 of Sch 1A, reading references in those provisions to the company as references to that other entity: CA 2006, s 790C(9).

28.89 The effect of provisions in respect of RLE's is that, if for example, company A is owned by company B and company B maintains a PSC register under Part 21A, a person ('P') with significant control over both B and A as a result of the same shareholding (held through B) need not be registered as a PSC in relation to A, provided that P has no other interest in the company through any other means. Instead, B will be noted in A's PSC register as an RLE. Those looking at A's register will be able then to look at B's register to identify P. The objective is to avoid, where appropriate ownership disclosure arrangements are in place, duplicative reporting.

Example of Relevant Legal Entities required to keep information on the register of PSC

Relevant Legal Entity X

↓

Relevant Legal Entity Y

↓

Company Z

In some cases, a legal entity rather than a person may fulfil one or more of the conditions above. Entities that fulfil one of the conditions and that are required to hold a PSC register or disclose information for example as a DTR5 issuer, are referred to as 'relevant legal entities'. Not all relevant legal entities should be recorded on the register. By not requiring all entities to look through their ownership chain in these circumstances makes it easier for an entity to maintain its own register, whilst still ensuring that information on all people with significant control will be available on the public register.

In the above example, three UK registered companies are involved. Company Z is fully owned by Company Y, and Company Y is fully owned by Company X. Companies X and Y are both relevant legal entities (they both keep a PSC register) who own more than 25% of the share capital of Z (Y directly and X indirectly). In order to avoid duplication of information on the register, Company Z would include only the first relevant legal entity (here Company Y) in its PSC register, and should not include Company X. Any person who is interested to look further would need to search Company Y's PSC register which would identify Company X. In this example, the first relevant legal entity in the chain is Company Y which will be a registerable relevant legal entity. Company X will be a non-registerable relevant legal entity and should not be included in Company Z's PSC register.

28.90 The register that a company is required to keep under s 790M (register of people with significant control over a company) is referred to as the company's 'PSC register': CA 2006, s 790C(10).

In deciding whether to specify a description of legal entity under para (d) of the CA 2006, s 790C(7), the Secretary of State is to have regard to the extent to which entities of that description are' bound by disclosure and transparency rules (in the United Kingdom or elsewhere) broadly similar to the ones applying to an entity falling within any other paragraph of that subsection: CA 2006, s 790C(11).

28.91 Subject to express provision in Pt 21A of the CA 2006 and to any modification prescribed by regulations under this subsection, this Part is to be read and have effect as if each of the following were an individual, even if they are legal persons under the laws by which they are governed:

(a) a corporation sole;

(b) a government or government department of a country or territory or a part of a country or territory;

(c) an international organisation whose members include two or more countries or territories (or their governments);

(d) a local authority or local government body in the UK or elsewhere: CA 2006, s 790C(12).

Chapter 2 of Pt 21A of the CA 2006 deals with information gathering.

Company's duty to investigate and obtain information

28.92 Certain duties are imposed on companies and PSCs. A company to which Pt 21A applies must take reasonable steps:

(a) to find out if there is anyone who is a registrable person or a registrable relevant legal entity in relation to the company; and

(b) if so, to identify them: CA 2006, s 790D(1).

Without limiting s 790D(1), a company to which Pt 21A applies must give notice to anyone whom it knows or has reasonable cause to believe to be a registrable person or a registrable relevant legal entity in relation to it: CA 2006, s 790D(2).

28.93 The notice, if addressed to an individual, must require the addressee:

(a) to state whether or not he or she is a registrable person in relation to the company (within the meaning of Pt 21A); and

(b) if so, to confirm or correct any particulars of his or hers that are included in the notice, and supply any that are missing: CA 2006, s 790D(3).

28.94 The notice, if addressed to a legal entity, must require the addressee:

(a) to state whether or not it is a registrable relevant legal entity in relation to the company (within the meaning of Pt 21A); and

(b) if so, to confirm or correct any of its particulars that are included in the notice, and supply any that are missing: CA 2006, s 790D(4).

28.95 A company to which Pt 21A applies may also give notice to a person under this section if it knows or has reasonable cause to believe that the person:

(a) knows the identity of someone who falls within s 790D(6); or

(b) knows the identity of someone likely to have that knowledge: CA 2006, s 790D(5). The aim of this section is to provide the company with the means to obtain information on registerable persons and RLE's where it does not itself know their identity, including where there are entities in the ownership chain which are not RLE's but which might know the identity of a registerable person or RLE. For example, a company may know that a person (X) is acting on behalf of PSC (P), but may not know any of P's details. The company may serve notice on X in order to obtain information on P.

It would be possible for a company to serve notice on a lawyer under s 790D(5) to obtain information and the issue would be whether the information held by a lawyer about PSC's or RLE's would be subject to legal professional privilege. If so, the lawyer would be exempt from providing such information under s 790D(12).

28.96 The persons who fall within s 790D(6) are:

(a) any registrable person in relation to the company;

(b) any relevant legal entity in relation to the company;

(c) any entity which would be a relevant legal entity in relation to the company but for the fact that s 790C(6)(b) does not apply in respect of it: CA 2006, s 790D(6).

28.97 A notice under s 790D(5) may require the addressee:

(a) to state whether or not the addressee knows the identity of:

  (i) any person who falls within s 790D(6); or

  (ii) any person likely to have that knowledge, and

(b) if so, to supply any particulars of theirs that are within the addressee's knowledge, and state whether or not the particulars are being supplied with the knowledge of each of the persons concerned: CA 2006, s 790D(7).

A notice under this section must state that the addressee is to comply with the notice by no later than the end of the period of one month beginning with the date of the notice: CA 2006, s 790D(8).

As the company's duty to provide information under s 790D is on-going and continuous, there is no defined period within which steps must be taken or notice given.

28.98 The Secretary of State may by regulations make further provision about the giving of notices under this section, including the form and content of any such notices and the manner in which they must be given: CA 2006, s 790D(9). This is set out under draft reg 9 of the Register of People with Significant Control Regulations 2015 which provides that a warning notice given under Sch 1B, para 1 to the Act must:

(a) specify the date on which the warning notice is given;

(b) be accompanied by a copy of the notice given under ss 790D or 790E of the Act to which the warning notice relates;

(c) identify the addressee's relevant interest in the company by reference to the shares or right in question; and

(d) state that the company will consider reasons provided to it as to why the addressee failed to comply with the notice given under ss 790D or 790E of the Act.

This will tell them that the company will issue them with a restriction notice. The effect of a restriction notice is to freeze the person or entity's interest in the company until the company obtains the information it needs and lifts the restrictions. Further, the holder of the interest in the shares will not be able to sell, transfer or receive any benefit from the rights, or exercise the rights attached to them.

28.99 A restrictions notice issued under Sch 1B, para 1 to the Act must:

(a) specify the date on which the restrictions notice is issued;

(b) be accompanied by a copy of the warning notice which preceded the restrictions notice;

(c) identify the addressee's relevant interest in the company by reference to the shares or right in question;

(d) explain the effect of the restrictions notice;

(e) state that, by virtue of the restrictions notice, certain acts or failures to act may constitute an offence; and

(f) state that an aggrieved person may apply to the court for an order directing that the relevant interest cease to be subject to restrictions: reg 10.

28.100 Regulations 12 and 13 address the withdrawal and effect of withdrawal of the restrictions notice.

Under draft reg 11, a company must take account of any incapacity of the addressee in deciding what counts as 'valid reason' sufficient to justify the addressee's failure to comply with the notice.

A company is not required to take steps or give notice under s 790D(11) with respect to a registrable person or registrable relevant legal entity if:

(a) the company has already been informed of the person's status as a registrable person or registrable relevant legal entity in relation to it, and been supplied with all the particulars; and

(b) in the case of a registrable person, the information and particulars were provided either by the person concerned or with his or her knowledge: CA 2006, s 790D(11). The objective of s 790D(11) is to ensure that individuals are in all cases aware of their entry in the company's PSC register. This is important for example in the event that the individual wants to apply for their information to be protected from disclosure, and to ensure that the individual knows to update the company should their personal details change.

28.101 A person to whom a notice under s 790D(5) is given is not required by that notice to disclose any information in respect of which a claim to legal professional privilege (in Scotland, to confidentiality of communications) could be maintained in legal proceedings: CA 2006, s 790D(12).

A reference to knowing the identity of a person includes knowing information from which that person can be identified.

The term 'particulars' means:

(i) in the case of a registrable person or a registrable relevant legal entity, the required particulars (see s 790K), and

(ii) in any other case, any particulars that will allow the person to be contacted by the company: CA 2006, s 790D(13).

Company's duty to keep information up-to-date

28.102 Section 790E applies if particulars of a registrable person or registrable relevant legal entity are stated in a company's PSC register: CA 2006, s 790E(1).

The company must give notice to the person or entity if the company knows or has reasonable cause to believe that a relevant change has occurred: CA 2006, s 790E(2).

In the case of a registrable person, a 'relevant change' occurs if:

(a) the person ceases to be a registrable person in relation to the company; or

(b) any other change occurs as a result of which the particulars stated for the person in the PSC register are incorrect or incomplete: CA 2006, s 790E(3).

28.103 In the case of a registrable relevant legal entity, a 'relevant change' occurs if:

(a) the entity ceases to be a registrable relevant legal entity in relation to the company; or

(b) any other change occurs as a result of which the particulars stated for the entity in the PSC register are incorrect or incomplete: CA 2006, s 790E(4).

28.104 The company must give the notice as soon as reasonably practicable after it learns of the change or first has reasonable cause to believe that the change has occurred: CA 2006, s 790E(5).

The notice must require the addressee:

(a) to confirm whether or not the change has occurred; and

(b) if so:

   (i) to state the date of the change; and

   (ii) to confirm or correct the particulars included in the notice, and supply any that are missing from the notice: CA 2006, s 790E(6).

Sections 790D (8)–(10) apply to notices under s 790E as to notices under that section: CA 2006, s 790E(7).

28.105 A company is not required to give notice under s 790E if:

(a) the company has already been informed of the relevant change; and

(b) in the case of a registrable person, that information was provided either by the person concerned or with his or her knowledge: CA 2006, s 790E(8).

Failure by company to comply with information duties

28.106 If a company fails to comply with a duty under the CA 2006, ss 790D or 790E to take steps or give notice, an offence is committed by:

(a) the company; and

(b) every officer of the company who is in default: CA 2006, s 790F(1).

28.107 A person guilty of an offence under s 790F is liable:

(a) on conviction on indictment, to imprisonment for a term not exceeding two years or a fine (or both);

(b) on summary conviction:

 (i) in England and Wales, to imprisonment for a term not exceeding twelve months or a fine (or both);

 (ii) in Scotland, to imprisonment for a term not exceeding twelve months or to a fine not exceeding the statutory maximum (or both);

 (iii) in Northern Ireland, to imprisonment for a term not exceeding six months or to a fine not exceeding the statutory maximum (or both): CA 2006, s 790F(2).

Sections 790G and 790H of the CA 2006 apply to duty on others on information gathering.

Duty to supply information

28.108 The CA 2006, s 790G complements s 790D with the aim of ensuring that registerable persons and RLE's who are not known to or identified by the company under s 790D are nevertheless entered in the company's PSC. The duty to supply information under s 790G is partly based on the regulations under the Financial Services and Markets Act 2000 (implementing the Transparency Directive 2013/50/EU) which places a disclosure obligation on investors in certain public listed companies.

Section 790G of the CA 2006 applies to a person if:

(a) the person is a registrable person or a registrable relevant legal entity in relation to a company;

(b) the person knows that to be the case or ought reasonably to do so;

(c) the required particulars of the person are not stated in the company's PSC register;

(d) the person has not received notice from the company under s 790D(2); and

(e) the circumstances described in paras (a) to (d) have continued for a period of at least one month: CA 2006, s 790G(1).

28.109 The person must:

(a) notify the company of the person's status (as a registrable person or registrable relevant legal entity) in relation to the company;

(b) state the date, to the best of the person's knowledge, on which the person acquired that status; and

(c) give the company the required particulars (see s 790K): CA 2006, s 790G(2).

The duty under s 790G(2) must be complied with by the end of the period of one month beginning with the day on which all the conditions in sub-s (1)(a)–(e) were first met with respect to the person: CA 2006, s 790G(3).

Duty to update information

28.110 Section 790H complements s 790E in connection with a registerable person or RLE to notify the company of relevant changes to information in the PSC register. The objective is to ensure that changes to information in the PSC register that are not known to or identified by the company are nevertheless recorded which will support the accuracy of the company's PSC register.

Section 790H applies to a person if:

(a) the required particulars of the person (whether a registrable person or a registrable relevant legal entity) are stated in a company's PSC register;

(b) a relevant change occurs;

(c) the person knows of the change or ought reasonably to do so;

(d) the company's PSC register has not been altered to reflect the change; and

(e) the person has not received notice from the company under s 790E by the end of the period of one month beginning with the day on which the change occurred: CA 2006, s 790H(1).

28.111 The person must:

(a) notify the company of the change;

(b) state the date on which it occurred; and

(c) give the company any information needed to update the PSC register: CA 2006, s 790H(2).

28.112 The duty under s 790H(2) must be complied with by the later of:

(a) the end of the period of two months beginning with the day on which the change occurred; and

(b) the end of the period of one month beginning with the day on which the person discovered the change: CA 2006, s 790H(3).

The term 'relevant change' has the same meaning as in s 790E: CA 2006, s 790H(4).

Compliance

Enforcement of disclosure requirements

28.113 Schedule 1B contains provisions for when a person (whether an individual or a legal entity) fails to comply with a notice under ss 790D or 790E or a duty under ss 790G or 790H: CA 2006, s 790I.

Exemption from information and registration requirements

Power to make exemptions

28.114 The Secretary of State may exempt a person (whether an individual or a legal entity) under s 790J: CA 2006, s 790J(1).

The effect of an exemption is:

(a) the person is not required to comply with any notice under ss 790D(2) or 790E (but if a notice is received, the person must bring the existence of the exemption to the attention of the company that sent it);

(b) companies are not obliged to take steps or give notice under those sections to or with respect to that person;

(c) notices under s 790D(5) do not require anyone else to give any information about that person;

(d) the duties imposed by ss 790G and 790H do not apply to that person; and

(e) the person does not count for the purposes of s 790M as a registrable person or, as the case may be, a registrable relevant legal entity in relation to any company: CA 2006, s 790J(2).

The Secretary of State must not grant an exemption under s 790J unless the Secretary of State is satisfied that, having regard to any undertaking given by the person to be exempted, there are special reasons why that person should be exempted: CA 2006, s 790J(3).

Required particulars

28.115 Section 790K sets out the information that must be held by the company in respect of registerable persons (both individuals and legal entities) and RLE's, and sets out what should be recorded on the register. The information set out below should provide for a unique identification of individuals registered.

The 'required particulars' of an individual who is a registrable person are:

(a) name;

(b) a service address;

(c) the country or state (or part of the United Kingdom) in which the individual is usually resident;

(d) nationality;

(e) date of birth;

(f) usual residential address;

(g) the date on which the individual became a registrable person in relation to the company in question;

(h) the nature of his or her control over that company (see Sch 1A); and

(i) if, in relation to that company, restrictions on using or disclosing any of the individual's PSC particulars are in force under regulations under s 790ZG, that fact: CA 2006, s 790K(1). This will enable the register available for public inspection to indicate that information has been withheld from public disclosure.

28.116 Under reg 7 of the Register of People with Significant Control Regulations 2015, the particulars required by ss 790K(1)(h), 790K(2)(e) and 790K(3)(f) of the Act (particulars as to nature of control over the company) are every statement listed in Sch 1 that is true in relation to the person in question. Regulation 7 and Sch 1 require the register to show which of the five conditions the PSC satisfies. The five conditions are set out at para **28.86** above.

Where appropriate the draft Regulations also require an indication of the extent of control exercised into three broad bands: (i) whether the PSC owns more than 25% up to 50%; (ii) more than 50% up to 75%; and (iii) 75% or more of the share capital.

28.117 In the case of a person in relation to which Pt 21A has effect by virtue of s 790C(12) as if the person were an individual, the 'required particulars' are:

(a) name;

(b) principal office;

(c) the legal form of the person and the law by which it is governed;

(d) the date on which it became a registrable person in relation to the company in question; and

(e) the nature of its control over the company (see Sch 1A): CA 2006, s 790K(2).

28.118 The 'required particulars' of a registrable relevant legal entity are:

(a) corporate or firm name;

(b) registered or principal office;

(c) the legal form of the entity and the law by which it is governed;

(d) if applicable, the register of companies in which it is entered (including details of the state) and its registration number in that register;

(e) the date on which it became a registrable relevant legal entity in relation to the company in question; and

(f) the nature of its control over that company (see Sch 1A): CA 2006, s 790K(3).

Section 163(2) (particulars of directors to be registered: individuals) applies for the purposes of s 790K(1): CA 2006, s 790K(4).

28.119 The Secretary of State may by regulations make further provision about the particulars required by s 790K(1)(h), (2)(e) and (3)(f): CA 2006, s 790K(5). These are set out in the draft Register of People with Significant Control Regulations 2015. It should be noted that there will be situations where a company has no PSC or does not yet have details confirmed. Draft reg 8 sets out the information that companies should put in their register of people with significant control in such situations. The draft

Regulations require companies to make a note in their register about the following circumstances if they arise:

- when a company has established that it does not have any people with significant control or registrable relevant legal entities;
- when a company has reason to believe there are PSCs but has not been able to identify them or to get their details confirmed;
- when the company has issued a formal request for information and the addressee has not complied within the set timescale;
- when a company has placed restrictions on the interest in it held by a person or entity that has not complied with a formal request for information;
- when a company does not possess information that can be placed on the register and cannot make any other note as to the progress of its investigation.

When any statements on the register no longer apply, companies will be obliged to state that fact on the register and set out the date when the circumstances changed. Companies should not make any other note other than the ones required by legislation.

Power to amend required particulars

28.120 The Secretary of State may by regulations amend s 790K so as to add to or remove from any of the lists of required particulars: CA 2006, s 790L.

Register of people with significant control

28.121 Chapter 3 to Pt 21A of the CA 2006 is concerned with the register of people with significant control. The SBEEA 2015, Sch 3 amends the CA 2006 to require companies to keep a register of people who have significant control over the company as part of transparency within the company: SBEEA 2015, s 81. The requirements and meaning of a 'person with significant control' are set out in that Schedule. The Secretary of State must carry out a review of Pt 21A and related provisions of CA 2006 inserted by the SBEEA 2015 within three years of the SBEEA 2015, s 92 coming into force. Section 92 makes provision for information in the PSC register to be delivered to the registrar of companies ('registrar'). It is considered appropriate for the review to take account of both the company's requirement to maintain a register (Pt 21A) and the requirement to provide this information to the registrar and to make it publicly available: SBEEA 2015, s 82.

Duty to keep register

28.122 A company to which Pt 21A applies must keep a register of people with significant control over the company: CA 2006, s 790M(1). This will be one of the registers that companies are required to keep under the CA 2006 together with others including the register of members and directors (CA 2006, ss113 and 162 respectively).

These registers wil provide publicly available information on the management, ownership and control arrangements of the company.

The required particulars of any individual with significant control over the company who is 'registrable' in relation to the company must be entered in the register once all the required particulars of that individual have been confirmed: CA 2006, s 790M(2).

The company must not enter any of the individual's particulars in the register until they have all been confirmed: CA 2006, s 790M(3). The objective is to avoid the inclusion of partial data in the PSC register which may make it more difficult to identify where a company or individual has failed to comply with its duty under Ch 2 to Pt 21A of the CA 2006.

28.123 Particulars of any individual with significant control over the company who is 'non-registrable' in relation to the company must not be entered in the register: CA 2006, s 790M(4).

But the required particulars of any entity that is a registrable relevant legal entity in relation to the company must be noted in the register once the company becomes aware of the entity's status as such: CA 2006, s 790M(5).

If the company becomes aware of a relevant change (within the meaning of s 790E) with respect to a registrable person or registrable relevant legal entity whose particulars are stated in the register:

(a) details of the change and the date on which it occurred must be entered in the register; but

(b) in the case of a registrable person, the details and date must not be entered there until they have all been confirmed: CA 2006, s 790M(6).

The Secretary of State may by regulations require additional matters to be noted in a company's PSC register: CA 2006, s 790M(7). This would ensure clarity for those searching the register.

28.124 A person's required particulars, and the details and date of any relevant change with respect to a person, are considered for the purposes of s 790M(8) to have been 'confirmed' if:

(a) the person supplied or confirmed them to the company (whether voluntarily, pursuant to a duty imposed by Pt 21A or otherwise);

(b) another person did so but with that person's knowledge; or

(c) they were included in a statement of initial significant control delivered to the registrar under s 9 by subscribers wishing to form the company: CA 2006, s 790M(9). This will ensure that individuals are aware of their inclusion in the register particularly if they want to apply for their information to be protected from disclosure.

28.125 In the case of someone who was a registrable person or a registrable relevant legal entity in relation to the company on its incorporation:

(a) the date to be entered in the register as the date on which the individual became a registrable person, or the entity became a registrable relevant legal entity, is to be the date of incorporation; and

(b) in the case of a registrable person, that particular is deemed to have been 'confirmed': CA 2006, s 790M(10).

28.126 For the purposes of s 790(11):

(a) if a person's usual residential address is the same as his or her service address, the entry for him or her in the register may state that fact instead of repeating the address (but this does not apply in a case where the service address is stated to be 'The company's registered office');

(b) nothing in s 126 (trusts not to be entered on register) affects what may be entered in a company's PSC register or is receivable by the registrar in relation to people with significant control over a company (even if they are members of the company);

(c) see s 790J (exemptions) for cases where a person does not count as a registrable person or a registrable relevant legal entity: CA 2006, s 790M(11).

28.127 If a company makes default in complying with s 790M, an offence is committed by:

(a) the company; and

(b) every officer of the company who is in default: CA 2006, s 790M(12).

A person guilty of an offence under s 790M is liable on summary conviction to a fine not exceeding level 3 on the standard scale and, for continued contravention, a daily default fine not exceeding one-tenth of level 3 on the standard scale: CA 2006, s 790M(13).

A company to which Pt 21A applies is not by virtue of anything done for the purposes of this section affected with notice of, or put upon inquiry as to, the rights of any person in relation to any shares or rights in or with respect to the company: CA 2006, s 790M(14).

Register to be kept available for inspection

28.128 Sections 790N to 790V provide how a company must maintain and make the PSC register available. These provisions are based on CA 2006, ss 114 to 121 and 125 which make similar provisions to a company's register of members. These two registers will then provide a complete picture of the company's ownership and control.

A company's PSC register must be kept available for inspection:

(a) at its registered office; or

(b) at a place specified in regulations under s 1136: CA 2006, s 790N(1).

This is based on CA 2006, s 114 (register to be kept available for inspection).

28.129 A company must give notice to the registrar of the place where its PSC register is kept available for inspection and of any change in that place: CA 2006, s 790N(2).

No such notice is required if the register has, at all times since it came into existence, been kept available for inspection at the company's registered office: CA 2006, s 790N(3).

28.130 If a company makes default for 14 days in complying with s 790N(2), an offence is committed by:

(a) the company; and

(b) every officer of the company who is in default: CA 2006, s 790N(3).

A person guilty of an offence under the CA 2006, s 790N is liable on summary conviction to a fine not exceeding level 3 on the standard scale and, for continued contravention, a daily default fine not exceeding one-tenth of level 3 on the standard scale: CA 2006, s 790N(3).

Rights to inspect and require copies

28.131 The CA 2006, s 790O applies to companies that hold their own PSC register (as they have not elected to hold their own PSC register at Companies House). A company's PSC register must be open to the inspection of any person without charge: CA 2006, s 790O(1). Section 790O is based on CA 2006, s 114 (register to be kept available for inspection).

Any person may require a copy of a company's PSC register, or any part of it, on payment of such fee as may be prescribed: CA 2006, s 790O(2). The draft of the Register of People with Significant Control Regulations 2015 sets the fee at £12.00: see reg 5(1). The following is considered a 'part' of the PSC register:

(a) the required particulars of a registerable person;

(b) the required particulars of a registerable relevant legal entity;

(c) any one additional matter that is required to be noted in the register under reg 8 (additional matters to be noted on the register): see reg 5(3).

28.132 A person seeking to exercise either of the rights conferred by this section must make a request to the company to that effect: CA 2006, s 790O(3).

The request must contain the following information:

(a) in the case of an individual, his or her name and address;

(b) in the case of an organisation, the name and address of an individual responsible for making the request on behalf of the organisation; and

(c) the purpose for which the information is to be used: CA 2006. s 790O(3).

28.133 The request must be for a proper purpose. There is no definition of 'proper purpose' but the term is intended to have and wide interpretation and application. The purpose of the register is to provide transparency of company ownership and control, and a person may inspect the register in the interests of finding out that information. This could, for example, arise in the context of investigative journalism.

Section 790O is based on the CA 2006, s 116 (right to inspect and take copies). However, unlike the register of members, it is considered important that any person may inspect the register free of charge due to the scope of those who may be registerable persons of RLE's in respect of a company and may therefore wish to inspect a company's register.

PSC register – response to request for inspection or copy

28.134 Section 790P is based on the CA 2006, s 117 (register of members: response to request for inspection or copy). It sets out how a company must respond to a request made under s 790O.

Where a company receives a request under s 790O, it must within five working days either:

(a) comply with the request; or

(b) apply to the court: CA 2006, s 790P(1).

If it applies to the court, it must notify the person making the request: CA 2006, s 790P(2).

28.135 If on an application under this section the court is satisfied that the inspection or copy is not sought for a proper purpose:

(a) it must direct the company not to comply with the request; and

(b) it may further order that the company's costs (in Scotland, expenses) on the application be paid in whole or in part by the person who made the request, even if that person is not a party to the application: CA 2006, s 790P(3). The term 'proper purpose' is not defined but this may be read in light of the fact that the purpose of the PSC register is to provide public information about a company's ownership and control.

28.136 If the court makes such a direction and it appears to the court that the company is or may be subject to other requests made for a similar purpose (whether made by the same person or different persons), it may direct that the company is not to comply with any such request.

The order must contain such provision as appears to the court appropriate to identify the requests to which it applies: CA 2006, s 790P(4).

If on an application under s 790P the court does not direct the company not to comply with the request, the company must comply with the request immediately upon the court giving its decision or, as the case may be, the proceedings being discontinued: CA 2006, s 790P(5).

PSC register – refusal of inspection or default in providing copy

28.137 Section 790Q is based on the CA 2006, s 118 (register of members: refusal of inspection or default in providing copy).

If an inspection required under s 790O is refused or default is made in providing a copy required under that section, otherwise than in accordance with an order of the court, an offence is committed by:

(a) the company; and

(b) every officer of the company who is in default: CA 2006, s 790Q(1).

A person guilty of an offence under this section is liable on summary conviction to a fine not exceeding level 3 on the standard scale and, for continued contravention, a daily default fine not exceeding one-tenth of level 3 on the standard scale: CA 2006, s 790Q(2).

In the case of any such refusal or default the court may by order compel an immediate inspection or, as the case may be, direct that the copy required be sent to the person requesting it: CA 2006, s 790Q(3).

PSC register – offences in connection with request for or disclosure of information

28.138 It is an offence for a person knowingly or recklessly to make in a request under s 790O a statement that is misleading, false or deceptive in a material particular: CA 2006, s 790R(1).

It is an offence for a person in possession of information obtained by exercise of either of the rights conferred by that section:

(a) to do anything that results in the information being disclosed to another person; or

(b) to fail to do anything with the result that the information is disclosed to another person,

knowing, or having reason to suspect, that person may use the information for a purpose that is not a proper purpose: CA 2006, s 790R(2).

28.139 A person guilty of an offence under the CA 2006, s 790R is liable:

(a) on conviction on indictment, to imprisonment for a term not exceeding two years or a fine (or both);

(b) on summary conviction:

    (i) in England and Wales, to imprisonment for a term not exceeding twelve months or to a fine (or both);

    (ii) in Scotland, to imprisonment for a term not exceeding twelve months or to a fine not exceeding the statutory maximum (or both);

    (iii) in Northern Ireland, to imprisonment for a term not exceeding six months or to a fine not exceeding the statutory maximum (or both): CA 2006, s 790R(3).

Section 790R is based on the CA 2006, s 119 (register of members: offences in connection with request for or disclosure of information).

Information as to state of register

28.140 This is based on the CA 2006, s 120 (information as to state of register and index).

Where a person inspects the PSC register, or the company provides a person with a copy of the register or any part of it, the company must inform the person of the most recent date (if any) on which alterations were made to the register and whether there are further alterations to be made: CA 2006, s 790S(1).

If a company fails to provide the information required under s 790S(1), an offence is committed by:

(a) the company; and

(b) every officer of the company who is in default: CA 2006, s 790S(2).

A person guilty of an offence under the CA 2006, s 790S is liable on summary conviction to a fine not exceeding level 3 on the standard scale: CA 2006, s 790S(3).

Protected information

28.141 The objective of s 790T is to make clear that a company is under a duty to keep its PSC register available for inspection and does not extend to information protected from public disclosure under regulations made under Ch 5 to Pt 21A of the CA 2006.

Sections 790N and 790O(1) and (2) are subject to:

(a) s 790ZF (protection of information as to usual residential address); and

(b) any provision of regulations made under s 790ZG (protection of material): CA 2006, s 790T(1).

Section 790T(1) is not to be taken to affect the generality of the power conferred by virtue of s 790ZG(3)(f): CA 2006, s 790T(2).

Removal of entries from the register

28.142 An entry relating to an individual who used to be a registrable person may be removed from the company's PSC register after the expiration of ten years from the date on which the individual ceased to be a registrable person in relation to the company: CA 2006, s 790U(1).

An entry relating to an entity that used to be a registrable relevant legal entity may be removed from the company's PSC register after the expiration of ten years from the date on which the entity ceased to be a registrable relevant legal entity in relation to the company: CA 2006, s 790U(2).

Power of court to rectify register

28.143 The CA 2006, s 790V is based on the CA 2006, s 125 (power of court to rectify register).

If:

(a) the name of any person is, without sufficient cause, entered in or omitted from a company's PSC register as a registrable person or registrable relevant legal entity; or

(b) is made or unnecessary delay takes place in entering on the PSC register the fact that a person has ceased to be a registrable person or registrable relevant legal entity,

the person aggrieved or any other interested party may apply to the court for rectification of the register: CA 2006, s 790V(1).

The court may either refuse the application or may order rectification of the register and payment by the company of any damages sustained by any party aggrieved: CA 2006, s 790V(2).

28.144 On such an application, the court may:

(a) decide any question as to whether the name of any person who is a party to the application should or should not be entered in or omitted from the register; and

(b) more generally, decide any question necessary or expedient to be decided for rectification of the register: CA 2006, s 790V(3).

In the case of a company required by this Act to send information stated in its PSC register to the registrar of companies, the court, when making an order for rectification of the register, must by its order direct notice of the rectification to be given to the registrar: CA 2006, s 790V(4).

28.145 The reference in s 790V to 'any other interested party' is to:

(a) any member of the company; and

(b) any other person who is a registrable person or a registrable relevant legal entity in relation to the company: CA 2006, s 790V(5).

Alternative method of record-keeping

28.146 Chapter 4 to Pt 21A is concerned with alternative methods of record keeping.

Chapter 4 sets out rules allowing private companies to keep information on the register kept by the registrar instead of entering it in their PSC register: CA 2006, s 790W(1).

The register kept by the registrar (see s 1080) is referred to in Ch 4 as 'the central register': CA 2006, s 790W(2).

Chapter 3 must be read with Ch 4: CA 2006, s 790W(3).

Nothing in Ch 4 affects the duties imposed by Ch 2: CA 2006, s 790W(4).

Where an election under s 790X is in force in respect of a company, references in Ch 2 to the company's PSC register are to be read as references to the central register: CA 2006, s 790W(4).

Right to make an election

28.147 A private company may elect to keep its PSC register on the central register.

An election may be made under s 790X:

(a) by the subscribers wishing to form a private company under this Act; or

(b) by the private company itself once it is formed and registered: CA 2006, s 790X(1).

28.148 The election is of no effect unless:

(a) notice of the intention to make the election was given to each eligible person at least 14 days before the day on which the election was made; and

(b) no objection was received by the subscribers or, as the case may be, the company from any eligible person within that notice period: CA 2006, s 790X(2).

28.149 A person is an 'eligible person' if:

(a) in a case of an election by the subscribers wishing to form a private company, the person's particulars would, but for the election, be required to be entered in the company's PSC register on its incorporation; and

(b) in the case of an election by the company itself:

(i) the person is a registrable person or a registrable relevant legal entity in relation to the company; and

(ii) the person's particulars are stated in the company's PSC register: CA 2006, s 790X(3).

An election under this section is made by giving notice of election to the registrar: CA 2006, s 790X(4).

28.150 If the notice is given by subscribers wishing to form a private company:

(a) it must be given when the documents required to be delivered under s 9 are delivered to the registrar; and

(b) it must be accompanied by a statement confirming that no objection was received as mentioned in s 790X(2): CA 2006, s 790X(5).

28.151 If the notice is given by the company, it must be accompanied by:

(a) a statement confirming that no objection was received as mentioned in s 790X(2); and

(b) a statement containing all the information that is required to be contained in the company's PSC register as at the date of the notice in respect of matters that are current as at that date: CA 2006, s 790X(6).

28.152 The company must where necessary update the statement sent under s 790X(6)(b) to ensure that the final version delivered to the registrar contains all the information that is required to be contained in the company's PSC register as at the time immediately before the election takes effect (see s 790Y) in respect of matters that are current as at that time: CA 2006, s 790X(7).

The obligation in s 790X(7) to update the statement includes an obligation to rectify it (where necessary) in consequence of the company's PSC register being rectified (whether before or after the election takes effect) : CA 2006, s 790X(8).

28.153 If default is made in complying with s 790X(7), an offence is committed by:

(a) the company; and

(b) every officer of the company who is in default.

For this purpose a shadow director is treated as an officer of the company: CA 2006, s 790X(9).

A person guilty of an offence under this section is liable on summary conviction to a fine not exceeding level 3 on the standard scale and, for continued contravention, a daily default fine not exceeding one-tenth of level 3 on the standard scale: CA 2006, s 790X(10).

28.154 A reference in Ch 4 to Pt 21A of the CA 2006 to matters that are current as at a given date or time is a reference to:

(a) persons who are a registrable person or registrable relevant legal entity in relation to the company as at that date or time and whose particulars are required to be contained in the company's PSC register as at that date or time; and

(b) any other matters that are current as at that date or time: CA 2006, s 790X(11).

Effective date of election

28.155 An election made under s 790X takes effect when the notice of election is registered by the registrar: CA 2006, s 790Y(1).

The election remains in force until either:

(a) the company ceases to be a private company; or

(b) a notice of withdrawal sent by the company under s 790ZD is registered by the registrar,

whichever occurs first: CA 2006, s 790Y(2).

Effect of election on obligations under Ch 3

28.156 The effect of an election under s 790X on a company's obligations under Ch 3 is as follows: CA 2006, s 790Z(1).

The company's obligation to maintain a PSC register does not apply with respect to the period when the election is in force: CA 2006, s 790Z(2).

This means that, during that period:

(a) the company must continue to keep a PSC register in accordance with Ch 3 (an 'historic' register) containing all the information that was required to be stated in that register as at the time immediately before the election took effect; but

(b) the company does not have to update that register to reflect any changes that occur after that time: CA 2006, s 790Z(3).

The provisions of Ch 3 (including the rights to inspect or require copies of the PSC register) continue to apply to the historic register during the period when the election is in force: CA 2006, s 790Z(4).

28.157 The company must place a note in its historic register:

(a) stating that an election under s 790X is in force;

(b) recording when that election took effect; and

(c) indicating that up-to-date information about people with significant control over the company is available for public inspection on the central register: CA 2006, s 790Z(5).

Section 790M(12) and (13) apply if a company makes default in complying with s 790Z(5) as they apply if a company makes default in complying with that section: CA 2006, s 790Z(6).

The obligations under s 790Z with respect to an historic register do not apply in a case where the election was made by subscribers wishing to form a private company: CA 2006, s 790Z(7).

Duty to notify registrar of changes

28.158 The duty under s 790ZA(2) applies during the period when an election under s 790X is in force: CA 2006, s 790ZA(1).

The company must deliver to the registrar any information that the company would during that period have been obliged under Ch 3 to enter in its PSC register, had the election not been in force: CA 2006, s 790ZA(2).

The information must be delivered as soon as reasonably practicable after the company becomes aware of it and, in any event, no later than the time by which the company would have been required to enter the information in its PSC register: CA 2006, s 790ZA(3).

28.159 If default is made in complying with this section, an offence is committed by:

(a) the company; and

(b) every officer of the company who is in default.

For this purpose a shadow director is treated as an officer of the company: CA 2006, s 790ZA(4).

A person guilty of an offence under s 790ZA is liable on summary conviction to a fine not exceeding level 3 on the standard scale and, for continued contravention, a daily default fine not exceeding one-tenth of level 3 on the standard scale: CA 2006, s 790ZA(5).

Information as to state of central register

28.160 When a person inspects or requests a copy of material on the central register relating to a company in respect of which an election under s 790X is in force, the person may ask the company to confirm that all information that the company is required to deliver to the registrar under this Chapter has been delivered: CA 2006, s 790ZB(1).

If a company fails to respond to a request under s 790ZB(1), an offence is committed by:

(a) the company; and

(b) every officer of the company who is in default: CA 2006, s 790ZB(2).

A person guilty of an offence under s 790ZB is liable on summary conviction to a fine not exceeding level 3 on the standard scale: CA 2006, s 790ZB(3).

Power of court to order company to remedy default or delay

28.161 Section 790ZC applies if:

(a) the name of a person is without sufficient cause included in, or omitted from, information that a company delivers to the registrar under this Chapter concerning persons who are a registrable person or a registrable relevant legal entity in relation to the company; or

(b) default is made or unnecessary delay takes place in informing the registrar under this Chapter that a person:

  (i) has become a registrable person or a registrable relevant legal entity in relation to the company; or

  (ii) has ceased to be a registrable person or a registrable relevant legal entity in relation to it: CA 2006, s 790ZC(1).

The person aggrieved, or any other interested party, may apply to the court for an order requiring the company to deliver to the registrar the information (or statements) necessary to rectify the position: CA 2006, s 790ZC(2).

The court may either refuse the application or may make the order and order the company to pay any damages sustained by any party aggrieved: CA 2006, s 790ZC(3).

28.162 On such an application the court may decide:

(a) any question as to whether the name of any person who is a party to the application should or should not be included in or omitted from information delivered to the registrar under this Chapter about persons who are a registrable person or a registrable relevant legal entity in relation to the company; and

(b) any question necessary or expedient to be decided for rectifying the position: CA 2006, s 790ZC(4).

Nothing in s 790ZC affects a person's rights under ss 1095 or 1096 (rectification of register on application to registrar or under court order): CA 2006, s 790ZC(5).

28.163 The reference in s 790ZC to 'any other interested party' is to:

(a) any member of the company; and

(b) any other person who is a registrable person or a registrable relevant legal entity in relation to the company): CA 2006, s 790ZC(6).

Withdrawing the election

28.164 A company may withdraw an election made by or in respect of it under s 790X: CA 2006, s 790ZD(1).

Withdrawal is achieved by giving notice of withdrawal to the registrar: CA 2006, s 790ZD(2).

The withdrawal takes effect when the notice is registered by the registrar: CA 2006, s 790ZD(3).

The effect of withdrawal is that the company's obligation under Ch 3 to maintain a PSC register applies from then on with respect to the period going forward: CA 2006, s 790ZD(4).

28.165 This means that, when the withdrawal takes effect:

(a) the company must enter in its PSC register all the information that is required to be contained in that register in respect of matters that are current as at that time;

(b) the company must also retain in its register all the information that it was required under s 790Z(3)(a) to keep in an historic register while the election was in force; but

(c) the company is not required to enter in its register information relating to the period when the election was in force that is no longer current: CA 2006, s 790ZD(5).

28.166 The company must place a note in its PSC register:

(a) stating that the election under s 790X has been withdrawn;

(b) recording when that withdrawal took effect; and

(c) indicating that information about people with significant control over the company relating to the period when the election was in force that is no longer current is available for public inspection on the central register: CA 2006, s 790ZD(6).

Section 790M(12) and (13) apply if a company makes default in complying with s 790ZD(6) as they apply if a company makes default in complying with that section: CA 2006, s 790ZD(7).

Power to extend option to public companies

28.167 The Secretary of State may by regulations amend this Act:

(a) to extend this Chapter (with or without modification) to public companies or public companies of a class specified in the regulations; and

(b) to make such other amendments as the Secretary of State thinks fit in consequence of that extension: CA 2006, s 790ZE(1).

Chapter 5 to Pt 21A of the CA 2006 deals with protection from disclosure.

Protection of information as to usual residential address

28.168 The provisions of ss 240–244 (directors' residential addresses: protection from disclosure) apply to information within s 790F(2) as to protected information within the meaning of those sections: CA 2006, s 790ZF(1).

The information within s 790ZF(2) is:

(a) information as to the usual residential address of a person with significant control over a company; and

(b) the information that such a person's service address is his or her usual residential address: CA 2006, s 790ZF(2).

Section 790ZF(1) does not apply to information relating to a person if an application under regulations made under s 790ZG has been granted with respect to that information and not been revoked: CA 2006, s 790ZF(3).

Power to make regulations protecting material

28.169 The Secretary of State may by regulations make provision requiring the registrar and the company to refrain from using or disclosing PSC particulars of a prescribed kind (or to refrain from doing so except in prescribed circumstances) where an application is made to the registrar requesting them to refrain from so doing: CA 2006, s 790ZG(1). This aspect is set out in the Register of People with Significant Control Regulations 2015.

'PSC particulars' are particulars of a person with significant control over the company:

(a) including a person who used to be such a person; but

(b) excluding any person in relation to which this Part has effect by virtue of s 790C(12) as if the person were an individual: CA 2006, s 790ZG(2).

28.170 Regulations under s 790ZG may make provision as to:

(a) who may make an application;

(b) the grounds on which an application may be made;

(c) the information to be included in and documents to accompany an application;

(d) how an application is to be determined;

(e) the duration of and procedures for revoking the restrictions on use and disclosure;

(f) the operation of ss 790N–790S in cases where an application is made, and

(g) the charging of fees by the registrar for disclosing PSC particulars where the regulations permit disclosure, by way of exception, in prescribed circumstances: CA 2006, s 790ZG(3).

28.171 Provision under s 790ZG(3)(d) and (e) may in particular:

(a) confer a discretion on the registrar;

(b) provide for a question to be referred to a person other than the registrar for the purposes of determining the application or revoking the restrictions: CA 2006, s 790ZG(4).

Nothing in s 790ZG or in regulations made under it affects the use or disclosure of particulars of a person in any other capacity (for example, the use or disclosure of particulars of a person in that person's capacity as a member or director of the company): CA 2006, s 790ZG(6).

28.172 This section concerns the regime to protect information about people in exceptional circumstances. The provisions in the SBEEA 2015, Sch 3 together with draft regs 14–36 of the Register of People with Significant Control Regulations 2015 establish a regime that will provide the following protections:

- the residential address of all people with significant control will be kept by the company but will never appear on the registers that companies make available to the public or the central public register. This information would only be accessible by specified public authorities and credit reference agencies (CRAs) which satisfy the conditions specified in Sch 3 to the Regulations: see draft regs 14 and 15 and 17–19;
- a company's own PSC register will show the full date of birth of a person with significant control, but the day of the date of birth will not appear on the central register. It will only do so where a company has specifically chosen to keep its PSC information solely at Companies House: see draft reg 25;
- some people may feel that they or somebody they live with would be at serious risk of violence or intimidation due to the activities of a company they are involved with. Although a PSC's residential address will not be on a public register, these people will be able to apply to Companies House to prevent their residential address from being disclosed to CRAs. Company directors are currently able to apply for this level of protection also;
- the draft Regulations also make provision for a second type of protection available to PSC's who feel that if their wider PSC information was on a public register they or somebody they live with would be at serious risk of violence or intimidation due to the activities of a company they are involved with. Alternatively they may feel at risk as a result of a particular characteristic or attribute specific to themselves taken together with the company they are involved with. These PSCs will be able to apply to Companies House to stop all of their PSC information from appearing on any public register: see draft regs 27–29;
- people will be able to apply to Companies House for these protections from January 2016. Their details will be suppressed from the register until the outcome of their application and any appeal. If the application is granted, the details will continue to be suppressed: see draft reg 32;
- if an application for protection is not granted the decision can be appealed on specified grounds, including that the decision is unlawful, irrational or unreasonable: see draft regs 31 and 35.

Checklist: certification and transfer of securities

28.173 *This Checklist sets out an overview of the regulatory framework governing certification and transfer of securities.*

No	Issue	Act reference
1	The certificate prepared by the company setting out shares held by a shareholder is prima facie evidence of his title to the shares, unless the contrary is shown.	CA 2006, s 768
2	A company must, within two months after the allotment of any of its shares, debentures or debenture stock, complete and have ready for delivery: (a) the certificates of the shares allotted; (b) the debentures allotted; or (c) the certificates of the debenture stock allotted	CA 2006, s 769
3	A company may not register a transfer of shares in or debentures of the company unless: (a) a proper instrument of transfer has been delivered to it, or (b) the transfer: (i) is an exempt transfer within the Stock Transfer Act 1982 (c 41); or (ii) is in accordance with regulations under Ch 2 of Pt 21.	CA 2006, s 770
4	When a transfer of shares in or debentures of a company has been lodged with the company, the company must either: (a) register the transfer; or (b) give the transferee notice of refusal to register the transfer, together with its reasons for the refusal, as soon as practicable and in any event within two months after the date on which the transfer is lodged with it. Failure to comply may lead to criminal penalties.	CA 2006, s 771 *Moodie v Shepherd (Bookbinders) Limited* [1949] 2 All ER 1044; *Popley v Planarrive Ltd* [1997] 1 BCLC 8
5	On an application for transfer of shares by the transferor, the company must register in the register of members the same interest for the transferee.	CA 2006, s 772
6	On a transmission of shares on death, a personal representative may apply to be registered as a member and upon evidence of probate.	CA 2006, s 773

No	Issue	Act reference
7	The certification of instrument of transfer evidence prima facie title to the shares or debentures, but not a representation that the transferor has any title to the shares or debentures.	CA 2006, s 775
8	A company must issue a certificate for shares/debentures within two months after the date on which the transfer is made.	CA 2006, s 776

Definitions

28.174

Securities: Shares, debentures, debenture stock, loan stock, bonds, units of a collective investment scheme within the meaning of the Financial Services and Markets Act 2000 (c 8) and other securities of any description.

Transfer:

(a) a transfer duly stamped and otherwise valid; or

(b) an exempt transfer within the Stock Transfer Act 1982 (c 41).

29 Information about interests in a company's shares

Contents

Introduction

29.1 Part 22 of the CA 2006 is concerned with information about interest in a company's shares. The provisions of this Part concern a public company's right to investigate who has an interest in its shares. This may be important for various reasons such as knowing the true identity of the person holding the shares as in some cases, shares may be held by a nominee. Another factor may be that the person in question is progressively building up a shareholding in the company that may ultimately have the effect of launching a takeover bid for the company, or to build up a sizeable percentage to block the passing of resolutions that are not in the interests of the individual concerned. The provisions set out in Pt 22 do not apply automatically but are triggered off where the company requires particular information about the shareholding acquired by a person. To some extent, Pt 22 mechanisms are protective of public companies by giving them an opportunity to engage in identity, investigation and information verification. The provisions create a series of criminal offences to emphasise the seriousness with which the provisions should be treated and complied. These are purely domestic provisions, and are not required by European Community law.

29.2 The obligation to disclose interests in the shares of a company are subject to the following:

- CA 2006, Pt 22, ss 793–828 concerning the right to investigate who has an interest in the public company's shares; and
- the Disclosure and Transparency Rules (DTRs) (implementing the European Transparency Obligations Directive (Directive 2004/109/EC). The DTRs apply to all companies listed on a regulated security exchange.

29.3 This Chapter considers the following:

- The legal aspects, practice and procedure enabling a company to seek information from person about interests in its shares.
- The Supreme Court decision in *Eclairs Group Ltd v JKX Oil & Gas plc; Glengary Overseas Ltd v Oil & Gas plc* [2015] UKSC 71.
- Application for seeking a court order imposing restrictions on a person's shares.
- How the shareholders can require the company to act in connection with information about interests in the company's shares.

Companies to which Pt 22 applies

29.4 Part 22 of the CA 2006 applies only to public companies: CA 2006, s 791.

Shares to which Pt 22 applies

29.5 The references in CA 2006, Pt 22 to a 'company's shares' are to the company's issued shares of a class carrying rights to vote in all circumstances at general meetings of the company (including any shares held as treasury shares): CA 2006, s 792(1).

The temporary suspension of voting rights in respect of any shares does not affect the application of Pt 22 in relation to interests in those or any other shares: CA 2006, s 792(2).

Section 792 of the CA 2006 addresses the type of shares for which a CA 2006, s 793 notice may be issued, namely shares carrying the rights to vote in all circumstances at general meetings. However, shares held by a company 'in treasury' following a purchase of its own shares, (as an alternative to cancelling such shares on purchase) are included in the definition.

Notice requiring information about interests in shares

Notice by company requiring information about interests in its shares

29.6 A public company may give notice to any person whom the company knows or has reasonable cause to believe:

(a) to be interested in the company's shares;

(b) or to have been so interested at any time during the three years immediately preceding the date on which the notice is issued: CA 2006, s 793(1).

29.7 The notice may require the person:

(a) to confirm that fact or (as the case may be) to state whether or not it is the case; and

(b) if he holds, or has during that time held, any such interest, to give such further information as may be required in accordance with the following provisions of s 793: CA 2006, s 793(2).

29.8 The notice may require the person to whom it is addressed to give particulars of his own present or past interest in the company's shares (held by him at any time during the three-year period mentioned in CA 2006, s 793(1)(b)).

The notice may require the person:

(a) to confirm that fact or (as the case may be) to state whether or not it is the case, and

(b) if he holds, or has during that time held, any such interest, to give such further information as may be required in accordance with the following provisions of s 793: CA 2006, s 793(2).

29.9 The notice may require the person to whom it is addressed to give particulars of his own present or past interest in the company's shares (held by him at any time during the three-year period mentioned in s 793(1)(b)): CA 2006, s 793(3)

The notice may require the person to whom it is addressed, where:

(a) his interest is a present interest and another interest in the shares subsists; or

(b) another interest in the shares subsisted during that three-year period at a time when his interest subsisted,

to give, so far as lies within his knowledge, such particulars with respect to that other interest as may be required by the notice: CA 2006, s 793(4).

29.10 The particulars referred to in sub-ss (3) and (4) include:

(a) the identity of persons interested in the shares in question; and

(b) whether persons interested in the same shares are or were parties to:

  (i) an agreement to which CA 2006, s 824 applies (certain share acquisition agreements); or

  (ii) an agreement or arrangement relating to the exercise of any rights conferred by the holding of the shares: CA 2006, s 793(5).

29.11 The notice may require the person to whom it is addressed, where his interest is a past interest, to give (so far as lies within his knowledge) particulars of the identity of the person who held that interest immediately upon his ceasing to hold it: CA 2006, s 793(6).

The objective of s 793 of the CA 2006 is to seek information about a person's 'interest' in the company's shares, whether past or present

In *Re TR Technology Investment Trust plc* [1988] BCLC 256, Hoffmann J stated that the objective of s 793 enabled the company to require any person who was reasonably believed to have an interest in the company's shares to give particulars of the interests of any other persons whom he knew to be interested in the same shares.

Another issue arose as to how much information the company could require the other party to be prima facie, s 793 allows the company to ask for whatever particulars it thinks fit, provided that they are 'with respect to that other interest'. There were two safeguards against abuse by the company. First, the company's only remedy for failure to comply was an application for restrictions under Pt 22 of the CA 2006; and the grant of that remedy was within the discretion of the court. Second, it was a defence to any criminal proceedings that the requirement was frivolous or vexatious.

29.12 The information required by the notice must be given within such reasonable time as may be specified in the notice: CA 2006, s 793(7).

The concept of 'reasonable time' should allow the person sufficient time to seek advice and assistance in connection with notice served by the company

The issue of 'reasonable time' was addressed in *Re Lonrho plc (no 2)* [1989] BCLC 309. The issue before the court was whether the persons to whom notices were served and were abroad had been given reasonable time to respond as set out in the notices (namely two days) including time to seek legal advice from English lawyers. The information provided was three days out of time during which time Lonhro had obtained a freezing order on the interested persons' shares and claimed costs for the court and legal fees application. According to Vinelott J, Lonrho should pay the respondents' costs. Where a widely framed notice under [s 793 of the 2006 Act] was served on a person resident and carrying on business outside the UK, the addressee should be given time to consult with English lawyers to ascertain the extent of the information that can properly be sought and to answer any points of difficulty relating to the formulation of an answer. On the facts, the time given by Lonrho to the respondents to reply to its notice was not reasonable and therefore it was not a valid notice. Accordingly Lonrho was required to pay the respondents costs.

29.13 The company has power under s 793 to send notices to persons domiciled in another jurisdiction even where there is no link with the UK: *Re F H Lloyd Holdings plc* [1985] BCLC 293 per Nourse J.

The objective of CA 2006, s 793 is that it allows a public company to issue a notice requiring a person who it knows, or has reasonable cause to believe, has an interest in its shares (or to have had an interests in the previous three years) to confirm or deny the fact, and if the former, to disclose certain information about the interest, including information about any other person with an interest in the shares.

Section 783(3) and (4) of CA 2006 enable the company to require details to be given of a person's past or present interest and to provide details of any other interest subsisting in the shares of which he is aware. This provision allows the company to pursue information through a chain of nominees by requiring each in the chain to disclose the person for whom they are acting. Under s 783(6), where the addressee's interest is a past one, a company can ask for information concerning any person by whom the interest was acquired immediately subsequent to their interest. Particulars may also be required of any share acquisition agreements, or any agreement or arrangement as to how the rights attaching to those shares should be exercised (CA 2006, ss 824 and 825).

29.14 Section 783 enables companies to discover the identity of those with voting rights (direct or indirect) that fall below the thresholds for automatic disclosure, and it also enables companies (and members of the company) to ascertain the underlying beneficial owners of shares.

The notice is not required to be in hard copy (under the general provisions on sending or supplying documents or information in CA 2006, Pt 37). Notices, and responses thereto, may be given in electronic form. A response must be given in reasonable time. What is reasonable has not been defined so as to allow flexibility according to the circumstances, but if the time given is not reasonable, the company will not have served a valid notice.

The objective of the CA 2006, s 793 notices is for the company to obtain information which the company does not have and in circumstances of which the company is not entirely cognisant. The restrictions under CA 2006, Part 22 are set out as a sanction to compel the provision of information to which the company is entitled. Accordingly, any the power to restrict the rights attaching to shares in the articles of association was wholly ancillary to the statutory power to call for information under CA 2006, s 793.

In the leading case on s.793 CA 2006, *Eclairs Group Limited v JKX Oil & Gas plc; Glengary Overseas Ltd v JKX Oil and Gas plc* [2015] UKSC 71, JKX was a public company with shares listed on the London Stock Exchange. The company also had a Ukrainian subsidiary with interests in oil and gas. Eclairs and Glengary were claimants who through nominee companies, held a beneficial interest in JKX of 39%.

Eclairs required JKX to convene an EGM under CA 2006, s 303 to consider resolutions to remove two executive directors and replace them with three new ones. JKX's Board was concerned that the effect of the EGM was an attempt to conduct a raid and gain control of JKX by the Ukrainian and Russian individuals.

In such event, JKX served notices pursuant to a power contained in its articles of association (Article 42), seeking information about the share ownerships and arrangements between the two shareholders including details about:

- number of shares held;
- nature of interest in the shares; and
- whether they were parties to any agreement or arrangement relating to the acquisition of shares in JKX or the exercise of voting rights.

Once JKX received responses to its notices, it considered them materially inaccurate and subsequently served restriction notices under its articles of association the effect of which was to prevent the voting and transfer of Eclairs' and Glengary's shares. The claimants brought proceedings challenging the restriction notices. The claimants contended that the notices requiring information about their shares were invalid for non-compliance with the CA 2006 and articles of association. Further, the directors were not entitled to impose restrictions as they did not have reasonable cause to believe that the responses to the notices were inadequate; and that the directors had acted for an improper purpose in imposing the restrictions.

At first instance, Mann J was required to consider: (1) the effect of the s 793 notices; and (2) whether the directors had acted for an improper purpose contrary to CA 2006, s 171 and held that the restrictions were ineffective because the directors had, in imposing them, been motivated by an improper purpose.

The Court of Appeal considered both the effect of the CA 2006, s 793 and directors' improper motives. The latter issue is considered in connection with the proper purposes doctrine with Longmore LJ and Sir Robin Jacob providing the majority view with Briggs LJ supporting Mann J's view.

The issue before the Supreme Court was whether the proper purpose rule applied to Article 42 and the scope of the rule in its application to directors' duties including the impact of s 793 notices. On the issue of s 793 of the CA 2006, the Supreme Court held that the objective of the s 793 of the CA 2006 notices was for the company to obtain information which the company did not have and in circumstances of which the company was not entirely cognisant. The restrictions under Part 22 of the CA 2006 were set out as a sanction to compel the provision of information to which the company was entitled. Accordingly, any the power to restrict the rights attaching to shares in the articles of association (Article 42) was wholly ancillary to the statutory power to call for information under s 793 of the CA 2006.

Notice requiring information: order imposing restrictions on shares

29.15 Where a notice under CA 2006, s 793 (notice requiring information about interests in company's shares) is served by a company on a person who is or was interested in shares in the company, and that person fails to give the company the information required by the notice within the time specified in it, the company may apply to the court for an order directing that the shares in question be subject to restrictions.

For the effect of such an order see s 797: CA 2006, s 794(1).

If the court is satisfied that such an order may unfairly affect the rights of third parties in respect of the shares, it may, for the purpose of protecting those rights and subject to such terms as it thinks fit, direct that such acts by such persons or descriptions of persons and for such purposes as may be set out in the order shall not constitute a breach of the restrictions: CA 2006, s 794(2).

The interests of third parties should be considered before the court makes an order under s 794 of the CA 2006

In *Lonhro plc (No 4)* [1990] BCLC 151, Peter Gibson J stated that in exercising its jurisdiction to make an order under CA 2006, s 794, the court would take into consideration the interests of innocent third parties in deciding whether or not such an order should be made. However, once the court determined that an order should be made, the order had to take the form set out in CA 2006, s 797 and the court had no jurisdiction to make a modified order which would qualify the restrictions set out in that section.

29.16 On an application under s 794 the court may make an interim order. Any such order may be made unconditionally or on such terms as the court thinks fit: CA 2006, s 794(3).

Sections 798–802 of the CA 2006 make further provision about orders under s 794: CA 2006, s 794(4).

The effect of s 794 is to allow the court to make a 'freezing order' in respect of the shares.

A person to whom notice is served must give full and truthful responses

In *Re TR Technology Investment Trust plc* [1988] BCLC 256, Hoffmann J stated that a person 'fails to give the company any information required by the notice' within the meaning of [s 794(1)] if he does not give a full and truthful answer. The company was entitled under [s 793] to ask the party on whom it served a notice for particulars of the nature of the interest in its shares of any person known to that party as having an interest in the shares. Accordingly, since the information supplied in response to the [s 793] notices did not enable the company to identify the real owner of the shares, the judge was entitled to make the order freezing the shares. Since a public company had an unqualified right to know the identity of the real owner of the shares, where it was shown that sufficient information was not provided under a [s 793] notice, the company was entitled to a restriction order and there was no need to show that damages would not be an adequate remedy or that the company would suffer loss if the information were not provided. In addition, it was no objection to the granting of an order freezing its shares that the board of the company was seeking the information to ward off a take-over bid. On the facts, taking into consideration the facts supplied both before and after the restriction order was made, there was still a triable issue as to whether the respondents had fully disclosed the nature of their interests in the company's shares. The respondents could not argue that the company had in its possession all the information from which it could garner who was interested in its shares, as the company could only enter in the register to be maintained under [s 808] such information as was supplied to it by persons on whom a [s 793] order had been served. However, the consequences of continuing the restriction must also be taken into account. As the respondent was willing to give a satisfactory undertaking not to dispose of the shares pending trial, the order made with respect to the shares would be discharged.

29.17 The courts are of the view that an application for restriction orders should not be considered as a fertile ground for applicants to seek further information of persons for the purposes of gaining further advantage over them.

Once information required by the company is provided, the restriction order is no longer effective

In *Re Ricardo Group plc* [1989] BCLC 566, Millett J was required to consider an application to the court for relief under the predecessor to CA 2006, s 793. On the facts, he refused relief and stated the effect and purpose of restriction orders: an order imposing Pt 22 restrictions on shares had a much wider effect than an ordinary interlocutory injunction. Far from preserving the status quo, they interfered with it. They were granted as a sanction to compel the provision of information to which the company was entitled. Once the information was supplied, any further justification for the continuance of the sanction disappeared. The restriction orders were not to be used as weapons to gain a temporary advantage over an opponent in a contested takeover bid. Their only legitimate purpose was to coerce a recalcitrant respondent into providing the requisite information.

Notice requiring information: offences

29.18 A person who:

(a) fails to comply with a notice under CA 2006, s 793 (notice requiring information about interests in company's shares);

(b) in purported compliance with such a notice:

   (i) makes a statement that he knows to be false in a material particular; or

   (ii) recklessly makes a statement that is false in a material particular, commits an offence: CA 2006, s 795(1).

A person does not commit an offence under s 795(1)(a) if he proves that the requirement to give information was frivolous or vexatious: CA 2006, s 795(2).

29.19 A person guilty of an offence under s 795 is liable on conviction on indictment, to imprisonment for a term not exceeding two years or a fine (or both); on summary conviction in England and Wales, to imprisonment for a term not exceeding 12 months or to a fine not exceeding the statutory maximum (or both); in Scotland or Northern Ireland, to imprisonment for a term not exceeding six months, or to a fine not exceeding the statutory maximum (or both): CA 2006, s 795(3).

Notice requiring information: persons exempted from obligation to comply

29.20 A person is not obliged to comply with a notice under CA 2006, s 793 (notice requiring information about interests in company's shares) if he is for the time being exempted by the Secretary of State from the operation of that section: CA 2006, s 796(1).

The Secretary of State must not grant any such exemption unless he has consulted the Governor of the Bank of England, and he (the Secretary of State) is satisfied that, having regard to any undertaking given by the person in question with respect to any interest held or to be held by him in any shares, there are special reasons why that person should not be subject to the obligations imposed by that section: CA 2006, s 796(2).

Orders imposing restrictions on shares

Consequences of order imposing restrictions

29.21 The effect of an order under CA 2006, s 794 that shares are subject to restrictions is as follows, namely:

(a) any transfer of the shares is void;

(b) no voting rights are exercisable in respect of the shares;

(c) no further shares may be issued in right of the shares or in pursuance of an offer made to their holder;

(d) except in a liquidation, no payment may be made of sums due from the company on the shares, whether in respect of capital or otherwise: CA 2006, s 797(1).

29.22 Where shares are subject to the restriction in s 797(1)(a), an agreement to transfer the shares is void. This does not apply to an agreement to transfer the shares on the making of an order under CA 2006, s 800 made by virtue of CA 2006, s 979(3)(b) (removal of restrictions in case of court-approved transfer): CA 2006, s 797(2).

Where shares are subject to the restriction in s 797(1)(c) or (d), an agreement to transfer any right to be issued with other shares in right of those shares, or to receive any payment on them (otherwise than in a liquidation), is void. This does not apply to an agreement to transfer any such right on the making of an order under CA 2006, s 800 made by virtue of CA 2006, s 797(3)(b) (removal of restrictions in case of court-approved transfer): CA 2006, s 797(3).

Penalty for attempted evasion of restrictions

29.23 Section 798 of the CA 2006 applies where shares are subject to restrictions by virtue of an order under s 794: CA 2006, s 798(1).

A person commits an offence if he:

(a) exercises or purports to exercise any right:

  (i) to dispose of shares that to his knowledge, are for the time being subject to restrictions; or

  (ii) to dispose of any right to be issued with any such shares; or

(b) votes in respect of any such shares (whether as holder or proxy), or appoints a proxy to vote in respect of them,

(c) being the holder of any such shares, fails to notify of their being subject to those restrictions a person whom he does not know to be aware of that fact but does know to be entitled (apart from the restrictions) to vote in respect of those shares whether as holder or as proxy, or

(d) being the holder of any such shares, or being entitled to a right to be issued with other shares in right of them, or to receive any payment on them (otherwise than in a liquidation), enters into an agreement which is void under s 797(2) or (3): CA 2006, s 798(2).

29.24 If shares in a company are issued in contravention of the restrictions, an offence is committed by:

(a) the company;

(b) and every officer of the company who is in default: CA 2006, s 798(3).

29.25 A person guilty of an offence under s 798 will be liable:

(a) on conviction on indictment, to a fine;

(b) on summary conviction, to a fine not exceeding the statutory maximum: CA 2006, s 798(4).

The provisions of CA 2006, s 798 are subject to any directions under s 794(2) (directions for protection of third parties); or ss 799 or 800 of the CA 2006 (relaxation or removal of restrictions), and in the case of an interim order under s 794(3) CA 2006, to the terms of the order: CA 2006, s 798(5).

Relaxation of restrictions

29.26 An application may be made to the court on the ground that an order directing that shares shall be subject to restrictions unfairly affects the rights of third parties in respect of the shares: CA 2006, s 799(1).

An application for an order under s 799 may be made by the company or by any person aggrieved: CA 2006, s 799(2).

If the court is satisfied that the application is well-founded, it may, for the purpose of protecting the rights of third parties in respect of the shares, and subject to such terms as it thinks fit, direct that such acts by such persons or descriptions of persons and for such purposes as may be set out in the order do not constitute a breach of the restrictions: CA 2006, s 799(3).

Removal of restrictions

29.27 An application may be made to the court for an order directing that the shares shall cease to be subject to restrictions: CA 2006, s 800(1).

An application for an order under s 800 may be made by the company or by any person aggrieved: CA 2006, s 800(2).

The court must not make an order under this section unless:

(a) it is satisfied that the relevant facts about the shares have been disclosed to the company and no unfair advantage has accrued to any person as a result of the earlier failure to make that disclosure, or

(b) the shares are to be transferred for valuable consideration and the court approves the transfer: CA 2006, s 800(3).

29.28 An order under this section made by virtue of s 800(3)(b) may continue, in whole or in part, the restrictions mentioned in s 797(1)(c) and (d) CA 2006 (restrictions on issue of further shares or making of payments) so far as they relate to a right acquired or offer made before the transfer: CA 2006, s 800(4).

Where any restrictions continue in force under CA 2006, s 800(4):

(a) an application may be made under s 800 for an order directing that the shares shall cease to be subject to those restrictions, and

(b) s 800(3) does not apply in relation to the making of such an order: CA 2006, s 800(5).

Order for sale of shares

29.29 The court may order that the shares subject to restrictions be sold, subject to the court's approval as to the sale: CA 2006, s 801(1).

An application for an order under s 801 may only be made by the company: CA 2006, s 801(2).

Where the court has made an order under this section, it may make such further order relating to the sale or transfer of the shares as it thinks fit: CA 2006, s 801(3).

An application for an order under s 801(3) may be made by the company, by the person appointed by or in pursuance of the order to effect the sale, or by any person interested in the shares: CA 2006, s 801(4).

On making an order under s 801(1) or (3), the court may order that the applicant's costs (in Scotland, expenses) be paid out of the proceeds of sale: CA 2006, s 801(5).

Application of proceeds of sale under court order

29.30 Where shares are sold in pursuance of an order of the court under CA 2006, s 801 the proceeds of the sale, less the costs of the sale, must be paid into court for the benefit of the persons who are beneficially interested in the shares: s 802(1) CA 2006.

A person who is beneficially interested in the shares may apply to the court for the whole or part of those proceeds to be paid to him: CA 2006, s 802(2).

29.31 On such an application the court shall order the payment to the applicant of the whole of the proceeds of sale together with any interest on them, or if another person had a beneficial interest in the shares at the time of their sale, such proportion of the proceeds and interest as the value of the applicant's interest in the shares bears to the total value of the shares. This is subject to the following qualification: CA 2006, s 802(3).

If the court has ordered under s 801(5) that the costs (in Scotland, expenses) of an applicant under that section are to be paid out of the proceeds of sale, the applicant is entitled to payment of his costs (or expenses) out of those proceeds before any person interested in the shares receives any part of those proceeds: CA 2006, s 802(4).

Power of members to require company to act

Power of members

29.32 The members of a company may require it to exercise its powers under CA 2006, s 793 (notice requiring information about interests in shares): CA 2006, s 803(1).

A company is required to do so once it has received requests (to the same effect) from members of the company holding at least 10% of such of the paid-up capital of the company as carries a right to vote at general meetings of the company (excluding any voting rights attached to any shares in the company held as treasury shares): CA 2006, s 803(2).

A request:

(a) may be in hard copy form or in electronic form;

(b) must:

  (i) state that the company is requested to exercise its powers under CA 2006, s 793;

  (ii) specify the manner in which the company is requested to act; and

  (iii) give reasonable grounds for requiring the company to exercise those powers in the manner specified; and

(c) must be authenticated by the person or persons making it: CA 2006, s 803(3).

29.33 Section 803 of the CA 2006 requires a company to exercise its powers under s 793 on the request of members holding at least 10% of such of the paid up capital of the company as carries the right to vote at general meetings (other than voting rights attached to shares held in treasury). This provision recognises that members of a company may have a legitimate reason for wanting the company to exercise its statutory powers to demand information even if the management does not want to. For example, the members might want to act where they suspect that the directors are involved in building a holding from behind the shelter of nominees.

Provision is made as to the form and the procedure in relation to requests. The 10% threshold may be met from a series of requests from members that the company act, rather than one collective request. Those making a request must not only specify the manner in which they require the powers to be exercised, but must also give reasonable grounds for requiring the company to exercise the powers in the manner specified (CA 2006, s 803(3)(b)(ii) and (iii)).

Duty of company to comply with requirement

29.34 A company that is required under CA 2006, s 803 to exercise its powers under s 793 (notice requiring information about interests in company's shares) must exercise those powers in the manner specified in the requests: CA 2006, s 804(1).

If default is made in complying with s 804(1), an offence is committed by every officer of the company who is in default: CA 2006, s 804(2).

A person guilty of an offence under s 804 will be liable on conviction on indictment, to a fine; and on summary conviction, to a fine not exceeding the statutory maximum: CA 2006, s 804(3).

Report to members on outcome of investigation

29.35 On the conclusion of an investigation carried out by a company in pursuance of a requirement under CA 2006, s 803, the company must cause a report of the information received in pursuance of the investigation to be prepared.

The report must be made available for inspection within a reasonable period (not more than 15 days) after the conclusion of the investigation: CA 2006, s 805(1).

Where a company undertakes an investigation in pursuance of a requirement under s 803, and the investigation is not concluded within three months after the date on which the company became subject to the requirement, the company must cause to be prepared in respect of that period, and in respect of each succeeding period of three months ending before the conclusion of the investigation, an interim report of the information received during that period in pursuance of the investigation: CA 2006, s 805(2).

Each such report must be made available for inspection within a reasonable period (not more than 15 days) after the end of the period to which it relates: CA 2006, s 805(3).

29.36 The reports must be retained by the company for at least six years from the date on which they are first made available for inspection and must be kept available for inspection during that time at the company's registered office, or at a place specified in regulations under CA 2006, s 1136: CA 2006, s 805(4).

The company must give notice to the registrar of the place at which the reports are kept available for inspection, and of any change in that place, unless they have at all times been kept at the company's registered office: CA 2006, s 805(5).

The company must within three days of making any report prepared under s 805 available for inspection, notify the members who made the requests under s 803 where the report is so available: CA 2006, s 805(6).

An investigation carried out by a company in pursuance of a requirement under s 803 is concluded when (a) the company has made all such inquiries as are necessary or expedient for the purposes of the requirement, and (b) in the case of each such inquiry (i) a response has been received by the company, or (ii) the time allowed for a response has elapsed: CA 2006, s 805(7).

Report to members: offences

29.37 If default is made for 14 days in complying with CA 2006, s 805(5) (notice to registrar of place at which reports made available for inspection) an offence is committed by the company, and every officer of the company who is in default: CA 2006, s 806(1).

A person guilty of an offence under s 806(1) is liable on summary conviction to a fine not exceeding level 3 on the standard scale and, for continued contravention, a daily default fine not exceeding one-tenth of level 3 on the standard scale: CA 2006, s 806(2).

29.38 If default is made in complying with any other provision of s 805 (report to members on outcome of investigation), an offence is committed by every officer of the company who is in default: CA 2006, s 806(3).

A person guilty of an offence under s 806(3) is liable on conviction on indictment, to a fine; on summary conviction, to a fine not exceeding the statutory maximum: CA 2006, s 806(4).

Right to inspect and request copy of reports

29.39 Any report prepared under CA 2006, s 805 must be open to inspection by any person without charge: CA 2006, s 807(1).

Any person is entitled, on request and on payment of such fee as may be prescribed, to be provided with a copy of any such report or any part of it. The copy must be provided within ten days after the request is received by the company: CA 2006, s 807(2).

29.40 If an inspection required under s 807(1) is refused, or default is made in complying with s 807(2), an offence is committed by the company, and every officer of the company who is in default: CA 2006, s 807(3).

A person guilty of an offence under s 807 will be liable on summary conviction to a fine not exceeding level 3 on the standard scale and, for continued contravention, a daily default fine not exceeding one-tenth of level 3 on the standard scale: CA 2006, s 807(4).

In the case of any such refusal or default the court may by order compel an immediate inspection or, as the case may be, direct that the copy required be sent to the person requiring it: CA 2006, s 807(5).

Register

Register of interests disclosed

29.41 The company must keep a register of information received by it in pursuance of a requirement imposed under CA 2006, s 793 (notice requiring information about interests in company's shares): CA 2006, s 808(1).

A company which receives any such information must, within three days of the receipt, enter in the register the fact that the requirement was imposed and the date on which it was imposed, and the information received in pursuance of the requirement: CA 2006, s 808(2).

The information must be entered against the name of the present holder of the shares in question or, if there is no present holder or the present holder is not known, against the name of the person holding the interest: CA 2006, s 808(3).

The register must be made up so that the entries against the names entered in it appear in chronological order: CA 2006, s 808(4).

29.42 If default is made in complying with s 808 an offence is committed by the company and every officer of the company who is in default: CA 2006, s 808(5). A person guilty of an offence under this section will be liable on summary conviction to a fine not exceeding level 3 on the standard scale and, for continued contravention, a daily default fine not exceeding one-tenth of level 3 on the standard scale: CA 2006, s 808(6).

29.43 The company is not by virtue of anything done for the purposes of s 808 affected with notice of, or put upon inquiry as to, the rights of any person in relation to any shares: CA 2006, s 808(7).

Section 808 provides that if, as a result of a s 793 investigation, the company receives information relating to the present interests held by any person in relevant shares, it must within three days enter in a register of interests disclosed the fact that the requirement (to disclose information under the notice) was imposed and the date on which it was imposed; and the information received in response to the notice under CA 2006, s 793.

The information must be entered against the name of the present holder of the shares in question (as under the CA 1985), or if the present holder is not known or there is no present holder, then against the name of the person holding the interest. Section 808(6) and (7) provide for criminal penalties for any default in complying with this clause. Section 808(8) makes it clear that information that a company receives under this part does not mean that the company needs to be concerned with the existence of any trust over the shares.

Register to be kept available for inspection

29.44 The register kept under CA 2006, s 808 (register of interests disclosed) must be kept available for inspection at the company's registered office, or at a place specified in regulations under s 1136: CA 2006, s 809(1).

A company must give notice to the registrar of companies of the place where the register is kept available for inspection and of any change in that place: CA 2006, s 809(2). However, no such notice is required if the register has at all times been kept available for inspection at the company's registered office: CA 2006, s 809(3).

29.45 If default is made in complying with s 809(1), or a company makes default for 14 days in complying with s 809(2), an offence is committed by the company, and every officer of the company who is in default: CA 2006, s 809(4).

A person guilty of an offence under s 809 is liable on summary conviction to a fine not exceeding level 3 on the standard scale and, for continued contravention, a daily default fine not exceeding one-tenth of level 3 on the standard scale: CA 2006, s 809(5).

Associated index

29.46 Unless the register kept under CA 2006, s 808 (register of interests disclosed) is kept in such a form as itself to constitute an index, the company must keep an index of the names entered in it: CA 2006, s 810(1).

The company must make any necessary entry or alteration in the index within ten days after the date on which any entry or alteration is made in the register: CA 2006, s 810(2).

The index must contain, in respect of each name, a sufficient indication to enable the information entered against it to be readily found: CA 2006, s 810(3).

The index must be at all times kept available for inspection at the same place as the register: CA 2006, s 810(4).

29.47 If default is made in complying with s 810, an offence is committed by the company, and every officer of the company who is in default: CA 2006, s 810(5). A person guilty of an offence under this section will be liable on summary conviction to a fine not exceeding level 3 on the standard scale and, for continued contravention, a daily default fine not exceeding one-tenth of level 3 on the standard scale: CA 2006, s 810(6).

Rights to inspect and require copy of entries

29.48 The register required to be kept under CA 2006, s 808 (register of interests disclosed), and any associated index must be open to inspection by any person without charge: CA 2006, s 811(1).

Any person is entitled, on request and on payment of such fee as may be prescribed, to be provided with a copy of any entry in the register: CA 2006, s 811(2). A person seeking to exercise either of the rights conferred by s 811 must make a request to the company to that effect: CA 2006, s 811(3).

29.49 The request must contain the following information:

(a) in the case of an individual, his name and address;

(b) in the case of an organisation, the name and address of an individual responsible for making the request on behalf of the organisation;

(c) the purpose for which the information is to be used; and

(d) whether the information will be disclosed to any other person, and if so:

   (i) where that person is an individual, his name and address,

   (ii) where that person is an organisation, the name and address of an individual responsible for receiving the information on its behalf, and

(iii) the purpose for which the information is to be used by that person: CA 2006, s 811(4).

Under s 811, the register and index must be open to inspection by any person without charge. For a prescribed fee, any person is entitled to a copy of any entry on the register. A person seeking access to the register under this clause must provide the information specified in s 811(4), including his name and address and the purpose for which the information is to be used.

Court supervision of purpose for which rights may be exercised

29.50 Where a company receives a request under CA 2006, s 811 (register of interests disclosed: right to inspect and require copy), it must comply with the request if it is satisfied that it is made for a proper purpose, and refuse the request if it is not so satisfied: CA 2006, s 812(1). If the company refuses the request, it must inform the person making the request, stating the reason why it is not satisfied: CA 2006, s 812(2). A person whose request is refused may apply to the court: CA 2006, s 812(3).

If an application is made to the court, the person who made the request must notify the company and the company must use its best endeavours to notify any persons whose details would be disclosed if the company were required to comply with the request: CA 2006, s 812(4).

29.51 If the court is not satisfied that the inspection or copy is sought for a proper purpose, it shall direct the company not to comply with the request: CA 2006, s 812(5).

If the court makes such a direction and it appears to the court that the company is or may be subject to other requests made for a similar purpose (whether made by the same person or different persons), it may direct that the company is not to comply with any such request.

The order must contain such provision as appears to the court appropriate to identify the requests to which it applies: CA 2006, s 812(6).

29.52 If the court does not direct the company not to comply with the request, the company must comply with the request immediately upon the court giving its decision or, as the case may be, the proceedings being discontinued: CA 2006, s 812(7).

Section 812 of the CA 2006 provides that the company must only allow the inspection of the register or the copy requested if satisfied that it is for a proper purpose. If it refuses, the person concerned may apply to the court for it to allow the inspection. If an application to the court is made, the person must notify the company, and the company must use its best endeavors to notify any persons whose details might be disclosed.

Register of interests disclosed: refusal of inspection or default in providing copy

29.53 If an inspection required under CA 2006, s 811 (register of interests disclosed: right to inspect and require copy) is refused or default is made in providing a copy required under that section, otherwise than in accordance with the CA 2006, s 812, an offence is committed by the company, and every officer of the company who is in default: CA 2006, s 813(1) (as inserted by SBEEA 2015, s 83). A person guilty of an offence under s 813 will be liable on summary conviction to a fine not exceeding level 3 on the standard scale and, for continued contravention, a daily default fine not exceeding one-tenth of level 3 on the standard scale: CA 2006, s 813(2).

In the case of any such refusal or default the court may by order compel an immediate inspection or, as the case may be, direct that the copy required be sent to the person requesting it: CA 2006, s 813(3).

Section 813 provides for court enforcement and criminal penalties for any default in complying with s 811.

Register of interests disclosed: offences in connection with request for or disclosure of information

29.54 It is an offence for a person knowingly or recklessly to make in a request under CA 2006, s 811 (register of interests disclosed: right to inspect or require copy) a statement that is misleading, false or deceptive in a material particular: CA 2006, s 814(1).

It is an offence for a person in possession of information obtained by exercise of either of the rights conferred by that section to do anything that results in the information being disclosed to another person, or to fail to do anything with the result that the information is disclosed to another person, knowing, or having reason to suspect, that person may use the information for a purpose that is not a proper purpose: CA 2006, s 814(2).

29.55 A person guilty of an offence under s 814 is liable on conviction on indictment, to imprisonment for a term not exceeding two years or a fine (or both); and on summary conviction in England and Wales, to imprisonment for a term not exceeding 12 months or to a fine not exceeding the statutory maximum (or both); in Scotland or Northern Ireland, to imprisonment for a term not exceeding six months, or to a fine not exceeding the statutory maximum (or both): CA 2006, s 814(3).

Section 814 provides for criminal penalties for misleading, false or deceptive statements given when making a request under CA 2006, s 811. It also makes it a criminal offence for the person who receives information under s 811 to disclose it to another person, if he knows or has reason to suspect that it may be used for an improper purpose.

Entries not to be removed from the register

29.56 Entries in the register kept under CA 2006, s 808 (register of interests disclosed) must not be deleted except in accordance with s 816 (old entries), or s 817 (incorrect entry relating to third party): CA 2006, s 815(1). If an entry is deleted in contravention of s 815(1), the company must restore it as soon as reasonably practicable: CA 2006, s 815(2).

If default is made in complying with s 815(1) or (2), an offence is committed by the company, and every officer of the company who is in default: CA 2006, s 815(3). A person guilty of an offence under s 815 will be liable on summary conviction to a fine not exceeding level 3 on the standard scale and, for continued contravention of s 815(2), a daily default fine not exceeding one-tenth of level 3 on the standard scale: CA 2006, s 815(4).

Under s 815, entries can only be removed from the register in accordance with ss 816 and 817, and if wrongly deleted must be restored as soon as reasonably practicable. Section 815(3) and (4) provide for criminal penalties for any default in complying with s 815.

Removal of entries from register: old entries

29.57 A company may remove an entry from the register kept under CA 2006, s 808 (register of interests disclosed) if more than six years have elapsed since the entry was made: CA 2006, s 816.

Removal of entries from the register: incorrect entry relating to third party

29.58 Section 817 of the CA 2006 applies where in pursuance of an obligation imposed by a notice under s 793 (notice requiring information about interests in company's shares) a person gives to a company the name and address of another person as being interested in shares in the company: CA 2006, s 817(1). That other person may apply to the company for the removal of the entry from the register: CA 2006, s 817(2).

If the company is satisfied that the information in pursuance of which the entry was made is incorrect, it must remove the entry: CA 2006, s 817(3).

If an application under CA 2006, s 817(3) is refused, the applicant may apply to the court for an order directing the company to remove the entry in question from the register, and the court may make such an order if it thinks fit: CA 2006, s 817(3).

Adjustment of entry relating to share acquisition agreement

29.59 If a person who is identified in the register kept by a company under CA 2006, s 808 (register of interests disclosed) as being a party to an agreement to which s 824 applies (certain share acquisition agreements) ceases to be a party to the agreement, he may apply to the company for the inclusion of that information in the register: CA 2006, s 818(1).

If the company is satisfied that he has ceased to be a party to the agreement, it shall record that information (if not already recorded) in every place where his name appears in the register as a party to the agreement: CA 2006, s 818(2).

If an application under s 818 is refused (otherwise than on the ground that the information has already been recorded), the applicant may apply to the court for an order directing the company to include the information in question in the register. The court may make such an order if it thinks fit: CA 2006, s 818(3).

29.60 Section 818 provides that a person identified in the register as being party to a s 824 share acquisition agreement (this may include a concert party agreement) may when he ceases to be party to the agreement, request that the register should be amended to record that information. Such entries may appear in several places on the register, as each member of the concert party is required in their individual notification to identify the other members of the concert party. If the company refuses an application, the court may order the company to comply if it thinks fit.

Duty of company ceasing to be a public company

29.61 If a company ceases to be a public company, it must continue to keep any register kept under s 808 (register of interests disclosed), and any associated index, until the end of the period of six years after it ceased to be such a company: CA 2006, s 819(1).

If default is made in complying with s 819, an offence is committed by the company, and every officer of the company who is in default: CA 2006, s 819(2). A person guilty of an offence under this section will be liable on summary conviction to a fine not exceeding level 3 on the standard scale and, for continued contravention, a daily default fine not exceeding one-tenth of level 3 on the standard scale: CA 2006, s 819(3).

Meaning of interest in shares

Interest in shares: general

29.62 Section 820 of the CA 2006 applies to determine for the purposes of Pt 22 of the Act whether a person has an interest in shares: CA 2006, s 820(1).

In Pt 22, a reference to an interest in shares includes an interest of any kind whatsoever in the shares, and any restraints or restrictions to which the exercise of any right attached to the interest is or may be subject shall be disregarded: CA 2006, s 820(2).

Where an interest in shares is comprised in property held on trust, every beneficiary of the trust is treated as having an interest in the shares: CA 2006, s 820(3).

29.63 A person is treated as having an interest in shares if (a) he enters into a contract to acquire them, or (b) not being the registered holder, he is entitled (i) to exercise any right conferred by the holding of the shares, or (ii) to control the exercise of any such right: CA 2006, s 820(4).

For the purposes of s 820(4)(b) a person is entitled to exercise or control the exercise of a right conferred by the holding of shares if he has a right (whether subject to conditions or not) the exercise of which would make him so entitled, or is under an obligation (whether subject to conditions or not) the fulfillment of which would make him so entitled: CA 2006, s 820(5).

A person is treated as having an interest in shares if he has a right to call for delivery of the shares to himself or to his order, or he has a right to acquire an interest in shares or is under an obligation to take an interest in shares. This applies whether the right or obligation is conditional or absolute: CA 2006, s 820(6).

Persons having a joint interest are treated as each having that interest: CA 2006, s 820(7). It is immaterial that shares in which a person has an interest are unidentifiable: CA 2006, s 820(8).

The concept of 'interest in shares' is widely defined

The term 'interest in shares' is widely defined as an interest of any kind whatsoever in the shares and includes beneficial ownership as well as direct ownership. The courts have described this wide definition as being designed 'to counter the limitless ingenuity of persons who prefer to conceal their interest behind trusts and corporate entities': *Re TR Technology Investment Trust plc* [1988] BCLC 256 at 261. Hoffman J stated:

> 'In my view the purpose of [s 793 of the CA 2006] would be defeated if the company could not ask for particulars of the nature of the interest of any person known to the respondent as having an interest in the shares. Part [22] deliberately defines "interest" very broadly indeed. It casts a net so wide and finely meshed that in a case like this in which a complicated structure of trusts and companies has been created, a request for the identity of all persons interested will trawl in a large number of parties ... A list of names would not enable the company to discover who was "the real owner of the shares" unless it could ask who were the sharks and who were the minnows: see *Re Geers Gross plc* [1988] BCLC 140, [1988] 1 All ER 224.'

According to Nourse LJ in *Re Geers Gross plc* [1988] BCLC 140 at 143:

> '... the clear purpose of [Pt 22 of the 2006 Act] is to give a public company, and ultimately the public at large, a prima facie unqualified right to know who are the real owners of its voting shares.'

Interest in shares: right to subscribe for shares

29.64 Section 793 of the CA 2006 (notice by company requiring information about interests in its shares) applies in relation to a person who has, or previously had, or is or was entitled to acquire, a right to subscribe for shares in the company as it applies in relation to a person who is or was interested in shares in that company: CA 2006, s 821(1).

The references in that section to an interest in shares shall be read accordingly: CA 2006, s 821(2).

Interest in shares: family interests

29.65 For the purposes of CA 2006, Pt 22 a person is taken to be interested in shares in which his spouse or civil partner, or any infant child or step-child of his, is interested: CA 2006, s 822(1).

In relation to Scotland 'infant' means a person under the age of 18 years: CA 2006, s 822(2).

Interest in shares: corporate interests

29.66 For the purposes of CA 2006, Pt 22 a person is taken to be interested in shares if a body corporate is interested in them and the body or its directors are accustomed to act in accordance with his directions or instructions, or he is entitled to exercise or control the exercise of one-third or more of the voting power at general meetings of the body: CA 2006, s 823(1).

A person is treated as entitled to exercise or control the exercise of voting power if another body corporate is entitled to exercise or control the exercise of that voting power, and he is entitled to exercise or control the exercise of one-third or more of the voting power at general meetings of that body corporate: CA 2006, s 823(2).

A person is treated as entitled to exercise or control the exercise of voting power if he has a right (whether or not subject to conditions) the exercise of which would make him so entitled, or he is under an obligation (whether or not subject to conditions) the fulfillment of which would make him so entitled: CA 2006, s 823(3).

Interest in shares: agreement to acquire interests in a particular company

29.67 This aspect is concerned with the concert party arrangement. For the purposes of CA 2006, Pt 22 an interest in shares may arise from an agreement between two or more persons that includes provision for the acquisition by any one or more of them of interests in shares of a particular public company (the 'target company' for that agreement): CA 2006, s 824(1).

Section 824 applies to such an agreement if the agreement includes provision imposing obligations or restrictions on any one or more of the parties to it with respect to their use, retention or disposal of their interests in the shares of the target company acquired in pursuance of the agreement (whether or not together with any other interests of theirs in the company's shares to which the agreement relates), and an interest in the target company's shares is in fact acquired by any of the parties in pursuance of the agreement: CA 2006, s 824(2).

The reference in s 824(2) to the use of interests in shares in the target company is to the exercise of any rights or of any control or influence arising from those interests (including the right to enter into an agreement for the exercise, or for control of the exercise, of any of those rights by another person): CA 2006, s 824(3).

29.68 Once an interest in shares in the target company has been acquired in pursuance of the agreement, s 824 continues to apply to the agreement so long as the agreement continues to include provisions of any description mentioned in CA 2006, s 824(2).

This applies irrespective of: (a) whether or not any further acquisitions of interests in the company's shares take place in pursuance of the agreement; (b) any change in the persons who are for the time being parties to it; (c) any variation of the agreement.

The references in this s 824(4) to the agreement include any agreement having effect (whether directly or indirectly) in substitution for the original agreement.

Under s 824, the term 'agreement' includes any agreement or arrangement; and references to provisions of an agreement include undertakings, expectations or understandings operative under an arrangement; and any provision whether express or implied and whether absolute or not. The references elsewhere in Pt 22 to an agreement to which s 824 applies have a corresponding meaning: CA 2006, s 824(5).

29.69 Section 824 does not apply to an agreement that is not legally binding unless it involves mutuality in the undertakings, expectations or understandings of the parties to it; or to an agreement to underwrite or sub-underwrite an offer of shares in a company, provided the agreement is confined to that purpose and any matters incidental to it: CA 2006, s 824(6).

This section concerns the obligation to give details of certain share acquisition arrangements in response to a notice under CA 2006, s 793. It covers any agreement or arrangement, whether or not legally binding, which involves undertakings, expectations or understandings that interests in shares will be acquired and that they will be subject to relevant restrictions while the agreement subsists. This may include groups of persons acting in concerts to prepare the way for a takeover offer for the company or to support a pending takeover offer.

Extent of obligation in case of share acquisition agreement

29.70 For the purposes of CA 2006, Pt 22 each party to an agreement to which CA 2006, s 824 applies is treated as interested in all shares in the target company in which any other party to the agreement is interested apart from the agreement (whether or not the interest of the other party was acquired, or includes any interest that was acquired, in pursuance of the agreement): CA 2006, s 825(1).

For those purposes an interest of a party to such an agreement in shares in the target company is an interest apart from the agreement if he is interested in those shares otherwise than by virtue of the application of s 824 (and s 825) in relation to the agreement: CA 2006, s 825(2).

Accordingly, any such interest of the person (apart from the agreement) includes for those purposes any interest treated as his under ss 822 or 823 (family or corporate interests) or by the application of s 824 of the CA 2006 (and s 825) in relation to any other agreement with respect to shares in the target company to which he is a party: CA 2006, s 825(3).

29.71 A notification with respect to his interest in shares in the target company made to the company under Pt 22 by a person who is for the time being a party to an agreement to which s 824 applies must state that the person making the notification is a party to such an agreement, and include the names and (so far as known to him) the addresses of the other parties to the agreement, identifying them as such, and state whether or not any of the shares to which the notification relates are shares in which he is interested by virtue of s 824 (and s 825) and, if so, the number of those shares: CA 2006, s 825(4).

Section 825(1) CA 2006 provides that one person's interest in a concert party agreement is to be attributed to another. Section 825(2) and (3) explain what an interest apart from the concert party is, and s 825(4) concerns the mechanics of notification of an interest in a concert party agreement.

Other supplementary provisions

Information protected from wider disclosure

29.72 Information in respect of which a company is for the time being entitled to any exemption conferred by regulations under CA 2006, s 409(3) (information about related undertakings to be given in notes to accounts: exemption where disclosure harmful to company's business) must not be included in a report under s 805 (report to members on outcome of investigation), and must not be made available under s 811 (right to inspect and request copy of entries): CA 2006, s 826(1).

Where any such information is omitted from a report under s 805, that fact must be stated in the report: CA 2006, s 826(2).

Under s 409 the Secretary of State may make regulations exempting a company from the need to disclose information relating to related undertakings in notes to its accounts. The Secretary of State must agree that the information need not be disclosed. Where advantage is taken of this exemption, the fact must be stated in the company's annual accounts. Section 826 provides that this name information must not be included in a s 805 report, (though its omission must be noted in the report), and must not be available for inspection under s 811.

Reckoning of periods for fulfilling obligations

29.73 Where the period allowed by any provision of CA 2006, Pt 22 for fulfilling an obligation is expressed as a number of days, any day that is not a working day shall be disregarded in reckoning that period: CA 2006, s 827.

Power to make further provision by regulations

29.74 The Secretary of State may by regulations amend the definition of shares to which Pt 22 of the CA 2006 applies (CA 2006, s 792), the provisions as to notice by a company requiring information about interests in its shares (CA 2006, s 793), and the provisions as to what is taken to be an interest in shares (CA 2006, ss 820 and 821): CA 2006, s 828(1).

The regulations may amend, repeal or replace those provisions and make such other consequential amendments or repeals of provisions of Pt 22 of the CA 2006 as appear to the Secretary of State to be appropriate: CA 2006, s 828(2).

Section 828 confers power on the Secretary of State to make regulations to amend the definition of shares to which Pt 22 of the CA 2006 applies (CA 2006, s 828(1)(a) re-enacting s 210A(1)(a) of CA 1985). Power is also conferred to amend the provisions in CA 2006, s 793 as to notice by a company requiring information about interests in its shares, (CA 2006, s 828(1)(b) re-enacting s 210A(1)(e)) CA 1985, and the provisions as to what is to be taken to be an interest in shares (CA 2006, s 828(1)(c)).

Checklist

29.75 *This checklist sets out the regulatory framework concerning information about interests in a company's shares with particular reference to Pt 22 of the CA 2006 where a company serves notice on a person and the consequences ensuing from such notice.*

No	Issue	Act reference
1	The provisions concerning information about interests in a company's shares are only applicable to public companies.	Part 22, CA 2006, s 791
2	A company may serve notice requiring interests in its shares where it knows or has reasonable cause to believe that a person is interested in its shares; or has been so interested at any time during the three years before the notice was served.	CA 2006, s 793
3	The s 793 notice may require the person to confirm whether or not he has interest in the shares; and to give information as to his own present and past interest in the company's shares.	CA 2006, s 793
4	The person to whom notice is served is not required to give details of interests he has in shares in other companies. Consider the nature of questions that may be asked and ensure they relate solely to the person's interest in the shares.	*Eclairs Group Ltd v JKX Oil and Gas plc* [2014] EWCA Civ 640
5	The term 'interest' in shares has a wide meaning and should not be interpreted narrowly.	*Re TR Technology Investment Trust plc* [1988] BCLC 256
6	The information required by the notice must be given within such reasonable time as specified in the notice.	CA 2006, s 793; *Re Lonhro plc (no 2)* [1989] BCLC 309
7	An application may be made to the court by the company for an order imposing restrictions on the person's shares where that person fails to give information under the notice within a reasonable time.	CA 2006, s 794
8	In considering whether to make a restriction order, the court must take account of interests of third parties.	*Re Lonhro plc (no 2)* [1989] BCLC 309
9	The effect of the application by the company to the court is to obtain a 'freezing order' in respect of the person's shares.	*Re TR Technology Investment Trust plc* [1988] BCLC 256

No	Issue	Act reference
10	Failure to comply with the notice requiring information or making a false or reckless statement is a criminal offence.	CA 2006, s 795
11	The effect of an order imposing restrictions on shares is that any transfer of shares is void; no voting rights are exercisable in respect of the shares; no further shares may be issued to the person.	CA 2006, s 797
12	Criminal penalties apply for attempted evasion of restrictions by a person any exercising any right to dispose of shares that are the subject of restrictions or failure to notify that the shares are subject to restrictions.	CA 2006, s 798
13	An application may be made to the court by the company or an aggrieved person on the ground that the order directing that the shares be subject to restrictions unfairly affects the rights of third parties in respect of the shares.	CA 2006, s 799(1) and (2)
14	The court has power to make such order as it thinks fit in connection with the relaxation of the restrictions imposed, including protecting the rights of third parties in respect of the shares and direct that the acts of such persons set out in the order do not constitute a breach of restrictions.	CA 2006, s 799(3)
15	The court has power to order that the shares subject to restrictions be sold subject to the court's approval as to the sale including such other order that they court may think fit – the court has a wide discretion.	CA 2006, s 801
16	Any proceeds from sale of the shares must be paid into court for the benefit of the persons beneficially interested in the shares.	

Definitions

29.76

Infant: a person under the age of 18 years (Scotland).

Interest in Shares: includes an interest of any kind whatsoever in the shares, and any restraints or restrictions to which the exercise of any right attached to the interest is or may be subject shall be disregarded.

30 Distributions

Contents

Introduction

30.1 Part 23 of the CA 2006 is concerned with distributions. It comprises three chapters. Chapter 1 addresses the restrictions on when distributions may be made. It sets out the meaning of distributions and some general rules. Chapter 2 sets out the justification of distribution by reference to accounts. Chapter 3 contains the supplementary provisions.

This Chapter addresses the following aspects:

- What constitutes a 'distribution'.
- Aspects concerning 'disguised gifts' out of capital.
- Circumstances when a transaction will not be a distribution.
- Remedies where an unlawful distribution is found to exist.

Distributions also are a form of dividends which are declared by directors and approved by shareholders. The definition of a distribution under Pt 23 is however much wider and includes cash and other forms of distributions but not from capital.

Restrictions on when distributions may be made

30.2 Chapter 1 sets out the restrictions on when distributions may be made with some introductory and general rules including definitions.

Meaning of 'distribution'

30.3 The term 'distribution' is widely defined and means every description of distribution of a company's assets to its members, whether in cash or otherwise, subject to the following exceptions: CA 2006, s 829(1). The term is not limited to cash but includes other forms of distribution including non-cash dividends. An equity payment may also be considered as a distribution if the conditions in Pt 23 of the CA 2006 are met: *TXU Europe Group plc* [2004] 1 BCLC 519.

The definition has at times caught 'disguised distributions' whereby the company enters into a transaction with the shareholder which is not at arm's length. The value of the transaction is transferred to the shareholder by the company is larger and disproportionate. In some cases, the courts have held that the label attached by the parties to a 'distribution' was in practice not a distribution, but a disguised gift out of capital. Most cases in this area have relied on the common law in what has become known as 'disguised gifts' out of capital. In other cases, there has been less reliance on the common law principles and more on insolvency provisions of the IA 1986 to address misfeasance, preferences and transactions at an undervalue. At common law, the courts have particularly considered the value of the transactions passing between the company and the shareholder and whether or not the considerations was at arm's length; and addressed the issue of good faith in respect of the transaction.

Any return of corporate assets to the shareholders must be in compliance with CA 2006 and the common law – otherwise it will be unlawful and ultra vires

At common law, Pennycuick J observed in *Ridge Securities Ltd v IRC* [1964] 1 All ER 275 at 288:

> 'A company can only lawfully deal with its assets in furtherance of its objects. The corporators may take assets out of the company by way of dividend or, with leave of the court, by way of reduction of capital, or in a winding up. They may of course acquire them for full consideration. They cannot take assets out of the company by way of voluntary disposition, however described, and, if they attempt to do so, the disposition is ultra vires the company.'

In *MacPherson v European Strategic Bureau Ltd* [2000] 2 BCLC 683, the Court of Appeal stated that it was a breach of the duties owed by directors to the company or alternatively an act which was *ultra vires* the company for them to enter into an arrangement which sought to achieve a distribution of assets, as if on a winding up, without making proper provision for creditors, since to do so amounted to an attempt to circumvent the protection which the Companies Act aimed to provide to those giving credit to businesses carried on with the benefit of limited liability. Such an arrangement failed the test of validity of a distribution of assets because it could not be described as being either for the benefit and to promote the prosperity of the company or reasonably incidental to the carrying on of the company's business. Since the distribution of assets as if on a winding up but without making proper provision for creditors was not permitted by Pt 23 of the CA 2006, it was also an act outside the directors' powers: see too *Re Lee, Behrens and Co Ltd*.

Chadwick LJ in *MacPherson v European Strategic Bureau Ltd* stated that to enter into an arrangement which sought to achieve a distribution of assets, as if on a winding up, without making proper provision for creditors was, itself, a breach of the duties which directors owed to the company; alternatively, it was *ultra vires* the company.

See too: *Barclays Bank plc v British and Commonwealth Holdings plc* [1996] BCLC 1.

30.4 This common law principle established in *Ridge* appears to be broader than the statutory principle on distributions in that at common law, any return of assets to a shareholder whether or not a distribution may be considered unlawful without observance of the objects and powers of the company. Therefore, any distribution of corporate assets to the company's shareholders must be in accordance with the company's objects or the statutory provisions of the CA 2006. The principle of 'disguised gifts' usually arises where a transaction is entered into between the company and the shareholder which is not, in reality, a distribution but is disguised as one. This can include excessive distributions or disproportionate amounts being provided to the shareholder. Alternatively, in exchange for the distribution by the company, the shareholder provides no consideration or value to justify such distribution.

Provided directors have exercised their powers for a proper purpose and within the company's objects, the court will not inquire into whether the distribution was for the company's benefit

In *Re Halt Garage (1964) Ltd* [1982] 3 All ER 1016, Oliver J stated that where payments to a director were made under the authority of the company acting in general meeting pursuant to an express power in its articles to award director's remuneration (and there was no question of fraud on the company's creditors or on minority shareholders) the competence of the company to award the remuneration depended on whether the payments were genuinely director's remuneration (as opposed to a disguised gift out of capital) and not an abstract test of benefit to the company. The amount of remuneration awarded in such circumstances was a matter of company management and, provided there had been a genuine exercise of the company's power to award remuneration, it was not for the court to determine if, or to what extent, the remuneration awarded was reasonable.

There was no evidence that, having regard to the company's turnover, the husband's drawings were patently excessive or unreasonable as director's remuneration, or that they were disguised gifts of capital rather than genuine awards of remuneration. Accordingly, the court would not inquire into whether it would have been more beneficial to the company to have made lesser awards of remuneration to him, since that was a matter for the company.

With regard to the wife's drawings, although the company's articles included the power to award remuneration for the mere assumption of the office of director – even where the director was not active in the conduct of the company's business

– that power predicated that a director would receive remuneration for services either rendered or to be rendered. The mere fact that the label of 'director's remuneration' was attached to the drawings did not preclude the court from examining their true nature. With regard to the wife's inactivity during the period in question, it could not be said that all of the amounts drawn by the wife in that period were genuine awards of remuneration to her for holding office as a director. The part of her drawings in excess of what would have been a reasonable award of remuneration for holding office as a director amounted to a disguised gift of capital or payment of dividends in recognition of her co-proprietorship of the business. It was *ultra vires* the company and repayable to the liquidator.

Accordingly, Oliver J decided that payment to the wife where no services had been rendered was a disguised gift out of capital, even though the parties may have acted in good faith and in honesty in connection with the transaction.

An unlawful distribution of capital was a breach of fiduciary duty and improper exercise of power

Aveling Barford Ltd v Perion Ltd [1989] BCLC 626, concerned an intra-group transfer where an unlawful return of capital included a breach of fiduciary duty in respect of a sale of the company's property at an alleged undervalue to a company controlled by the same person who controlled the seller's company. Hoffmann J held that the sale to the defendant was not a genuine exercise of the power of the claimant to sell its property. It was a sale at an undervalue for the purpose of enabling the director, the sole beneficial owner of the claimant company, to obtain an unauthorised return of capital. It was *ultra vires* and could not be ratified.

According to Hoffmann J:

> 'Whether or not the transaction is a distribution to shareholders does not depend exclusively on what the parties choose to call it. The court looks at the substance rather than the outward appearance.'

See also s 846 of the CA 2006.

30.5 In some cases, the distribution was, in reality, a disguised gift out of capital.

A disguised gift out of capital will be unlawful and ultra vires

In *Secretary of State for Business, Innovation and Skills v Doffman (No 2)* [2011] 2 BCLC 541, the defendant directors were using companies to buy properties with the potential for residential development. They used valuations based on development potential to obtain bank loans considerably higher than the purchase price. They also applied for loans for other investments. One of the companies paid £1.2 million to its affiliate for an option to buy property. It was held by

Newey J that the option granted could not be regarded as bona fide, since in the circumstances, £1.2 million was a very large sum for an 18-month option. Further, the amount was irregular and simply represented the surplus funds which the company had available at the time. There was no attempt to exercise the option. The payment for the option was considered as a disguised gift out of capital, particularly as the company had no profits available for distribution. The option was merely a scheme to transfer the money out of the company.

30.6 The court looks at the context and substance of the transaction to identify whether it is a distribution or an unlawful return of capital.

Where appropriate, the court may take account of the subjective intentions of the parties to a distribution transaction

In the leading case of *Progress Property Co Ltd v Moorgarth* [2011] 2 BCLC 332, the case concerned a sale of shares which was negotiated by a director in the genuine belief that the transaction was a commercial sale at market value. Was it a sale at undervalue, an unlawful distribution of assets and therefore *ultra vires*?

The Supreme Court decided that whether or not a transaction infringed the common law rule of unlawful return of capital to a shareholder was a matter of substance, not form. The label attached to the transaction by the parties was not decisive, since the essential issue was how a sale was to be characterised.

The court's real task was to inquire into the true purpose and substance of the impugned transaction. That called for an investigation of all the relevant facts, including sometimes the state of mind of the persons who orchestrated the corporate activity. A distribution described as a dividend but actually paid out of capital was unlawful, however technical the error and however well-meaning the directors who paid it. A transaction which was an improper attempt to extract value by the pretence of an arm's-length sale was also unlawful, but if the transaction with a shareholder was genuinely at arm's length it would stand, even if it appeared with hindsight to have been a bad bargain.

A mere arithmetical difference between the consideration given for an asset and its retrospective valuation in subsequent proceedings did not of itself mean that there was a distribution of capital, and in assessing the adequacy of the consideration a margin of appreciation could properly be allowed.

A relentlessly objective rule that there was an unlawful return of capital whenever the company entered into a transaction with a shareholder which resulted in a transfer of value not covered by distributable profits regardless of the purpose of the transaction, would be oppressive and unworkable and would tend to cast doubt on any transaction between a company and a shareholder, even if negotiated at arm's length and in perfect good faith, whenever the company proved with hindsight that it had got significantly the worse of the transaction.

On the facts, the Supreme Court held that the sale of shares was a genuine sale and not a dressed-up return of capital and therefore *intra vires* the company.

> Lord Walker considered that the participants' subjective intentions were however sometimes relevant, and a distribution disguised as an arm's length commercial transaction was the paradigm example. If a company sells to a shareholder at a low value assets which are difficult to value precisely, but which are potentially very valuable, the transaction may call for close scrutiny, and the company's financial position, and the actual motives and intentions of the directors, will be highly relevant. There may be questions to be asked as to whether the company was under financial pressure compelling it to sell at an inopportune time, as to what advice was taken, how the market was tested, and how the terms of the deal were negotiated. If the conclusion is that it was a genuine arm's length transaction then it will stand, even if it may, with hindsight, appear to have been a bad bargain. If it was an improper attempt to extract value by the pretence of an arm's length sale, it will be held unlawful. But either conclusion will depend on a realistic assessment of all the relevant facts, not simply a retrospective valuation exercise in isolation from all other inquiries.

Exceptions

30.7 The CA 2006 provides certain exceptions where the transaction is not caught as a distribution. The following are not distributions for the purposes of Pt 23, namely:

(a) an issue of shares as fully or partly paid bonus shares;

(b) the reduction of share capital;

  (i) by extinguishing or reducing the liability of any of the members on any of the company's shares in respect of share capital not paid up, or

  (ii) by repaying paid-up share capital;

(c) the redemption or purchase of any of the company's own shares out of capital (including the proceeds of any fresh issue of shares) or out of unrealised profits in accordance with Chs 3, 4 or 5 of Pt 18;

(d) a distribution of assets to members of the company on its winding up: CA 2006, s 829(2).

General rules

30.8 Sections 830–831 set out the general rules applicable to distributions.

Distributions to be made only out of profits available for the purpose

30.9 A company may only make a distribution out of profits available for the purpose: CA 2006, s 830(1).

A company's profits available for distribution are its accumulated, realised profits, (as long as they have not previously been utilised by distribution or capitalisation) less its accumulated, realised losses (as long as they have not previously been written off in a reduction or reorganisation of capital duly made): CA 2006, s 830(2).

Section 830(2) applies subject to ss 832 and 835 (Investment companies etc: Distributions out of accumulated revenue profits).

Net asset restriction on distributions by public companies

30.10 Section 831 states that a public company may only make a distribution:

(a) if the amount of its net assets is not less than the aggregate of its called-up share capital and undistributable reserves; and

(b) if, and to the extent that, the distribution does not reduce the amount of those assets to less than that aggregate: CA 2006, s 831(1).

30.11 The term a company's 'net assets' means the aggregate of the company's assets less the aggregate of its liabilities: CA 2006, s 831(2).

The term 'liabilities' includes:

(a) where the relevant accounts are Companies Act accounts, provisions of a kind specified for the purposes of s 831(3) by regulations under s 396;

(b) where the relevant accounts are IAS accounts, provisions of any kind: CA 2006, s 831(3).

30.12 A company's undistributable reserves are:

(a) its share premium account;

(b) its capital redemption reserve;

(c) the amount by which its accumulated, unrealised profits (as long as they have not previously been utilised by capitalisation) exceed its accumulated, unrealised losses (as long as they have not previously been written off in a reduction or reorganisation of capital duly made);

(d) any other reserve that the company is prohibited from distributing:

   (i) by any enactment (other than one contained in Pt 23), or

   (ii) by its articles: CA 2006, s 831(4).

30.13 The reference in paragraph (c) to 'capitalisation' does not include a transfer of profits of the company to its capital redemption reserve.

A public company must not include any uncalled share capital as an asset in any accounts relevant for purposes of s 831: CA 2006, s 831(5).

Section 831(1) applies subject to ss 832 and 835 (Investment companies etc: Distributions out of accumulated revenue profits): CA 2006, s 831(6).

Distributions by investment companies

Distributions by investment companies out of accumulated revenue profits

30.14 Section 832 sets out the distributions by investment companies out of accumulated revenue profits. An investment company may make a distribution out of its accumulated, realised revenue profits if the following conditions are met: CA 2006, s 832(1).

It may make such a distribution only if, and to the extent that, its accumulated, realised revenue profits, as long as they have not previously been utilised by a distribution or capitalisation, exceed its accumulated revenue losses (whether realised or unrealised), as long as they have not previously been written off in a reduction or reorganisation of capital duly made: CA 2006, s 832(2).

It may make such a distribution only if the amount of its assets is at least equal to one-and-a-half times the aggregate of its liabilities to creditors, and if, and to the extent that, the distribution does not reduce that amount to less than one-and-a-half times that aggregate: CA 2006, s 832(3).

For this purpose a company's liabilities to creditors include in the case of Companies Act accounts, provisions of a kind specified for the purposes of s 832(4) by regulations under s 396; in the case of IAS accounts, provisions for liabilities to creditors: CA 2006, s 832(4).

30.15 The following conditions must also be met, namely:

(a) the company's shares must be listed on a recognised UK investment exchange;

(b) during the relevant period it must not have:

  (i) distributed any capital profits otherwise than by way of the redemption or purchase of any of the company's own shares in accordance with Chs 3 or 4 of Pt 18, or

  (ii) applied any unrealised profits or any capital profits (realised or unrealised) in paying up debentures or amounts unpaid on its issued shares;

(c) it must have given notice to the registrar under s 833(1) (notice of intention to carry on business as an investment company):

  (i) before the beginning of the relevant period, or

  (ii) as soon as reasonably practicable after the date of its incorporation: CA 2006, s 832(5).

30.16 For the purposes of s 832, the term 'recognised UK investment exchange' means a recognised investment exchange within the meaning of Pt 18 of the Financial Services and Markets Act 2000 (c 8), other than an overseas investment exchange within the meaning of that Part; the 'relevant period' is the period beginning with (i) the first day of the accounting reference period immediately preceding that in which the proposed distribution is to be made, or (ii) where the distribution is to be made in the company's first accounting reference period, the first day of that period, and ending with the date of the distribution: CA 2006, s 832(6).

The company must not include any uncalled share capital as an asset in any accounts relevant for purposes of s 832: CA 2006, s 832(7).

Meaning of 'investment company'

30.17 Section 833 sets out the meaning of 'investment company'. Under Pt 23 an 'investment company' means a public company that has given notice (which has not been revoked) to the registrar of its intention to carry on business as an investment company, and since the date of that notice has complied with the following requirements: CA 2006, s 833(1).

Those requirements are:

(a) that the business of the company consists of investing its funds mainly in securities, with the aim of spreading investment risk and giving members of the company the benefit of the results of the management of its funds;

(b) that the condition in s 834 is met as regards holdings in other companies;

(c) that distribution of the company's capital profits is prohibited by its articles;

(d) that the company has not retained, otherwise than in compliance with Pt 23, in respect of any accounting reference period more than 15% of the income it derives from securities: CA 2006, s 833(2).

30.18 Section 833(2)(c) does not require an investment company to be prohibited by its articles from redeeming or purchasing its own shares in accordance with Chs 3 or 4 of Pt 18 out of its capital profits: CA 2006, s 833(3).

Notice to the registrar under s 833 may be revoked at any time by the company on giving notice to the registrar that it no longer wishes to be an investment company within the meaning of this section: CA 2006, s 833(4).

On giving such a notice, the company ceases to be such a company: CA 2006, s 833(5).

Investment company: condition as to holdings in other companies

30.19 Section 834 deals with the investment company with reference to holdings in other companies. The condition referred to in s 833(2)(b) (requirements to be complied with by investment company) is that none of the company's holdings in companies (other than those that are for the time being investment companies) represents more than 15% by value of the company's investments: CA 2006, s 834(1).

For this purpose:

(a) holdings in companies that:

   (i) are members of a group (whether or not including the investing company); and

   (ii) are not for the time being investment companies,

   are treated as holdings in a single company; and

(b) where the investing company is a member of a group, money owed to it by another member of the group (i) is treated as a security of the latter held by the investing company, and (ii) is accordingly treated as, or as part of, the holding of the investing company in the company owing the money: CA 2006, s 834(2).

30.20 The condition does not apply to a holding in a company acquired before 6 April 1965 that on that date represented not more than 25% by value of the investing company's investments, or to a holding in a company that, when it was acquired, represented not more than 15% by value of the investing company's investments, so long as no addition is made to the holding: CA 2006, s 834(3).

For the purposes of s 834(3):

(a) the term 'holding' means the shares or securities (whether of one class or more than one class) held in any one company;

(b) an addition is made to a holding whenever the investing company acquires shares or securities of that one company, otherwise than by being allotted shares or securities without becoming liable to give any consideration, and if an addition is made to a holding that holding is acquired when the addition or latest addition is made to the holding; and

(c) where, in connection with a scheme of reconstruction, a company issues shares or securities to persons holding shares or securities in a second company in respect of and in proportion to (or as nearly as may be in proportion to) their holdings in the second company, without those persons becoming liable to give any consideration, a holding of the shares or securities in the second company and a corresponding holding of the shares or securities so issued shall be regarded as the same holding: CA 2006, s 834(4).

30.21 Under s 834, the term 'company' and 'shares' is to be construed in accordance with ss 99 and 288 of the Taxation of Chargeable Gains Act 1992 (c 12); the term 'group' means a company and all companies that are its 51% subsidiaries (within the meaning of s 838 of the Income and Corporation Taxes Act 1988 (c 1)); and the term 'scheme of reconstruction' has the same meaning as in s136 of the Taxation of Chargeable Gains Act 1992: CA 2006, s 834(5).

Power to extend provisions relating to investment companies

30.22 The Secretary of State may by regulations extend the provisions of ss 832–834 (distributions by investment companies out of accumulated profits), with or without modifications, to other companies whose principal business consists of investing their funds in securities, land or other assets with the aim of spreading investment risk and giving their members the benefit of the results of the management of the assets: CA 2006, s 835(1).

Justification of distribution by reference to accounts

30.23 Chapter 2 applies to justification of distribution by reference to accounts.

Section 836 states that whether a distribution may be made by a company without contravening Pt 23 is determined by reference to the following items as stated in the relevant accounts:

(a) profits, losses, assets and liabilities;

(b) provisions of the following kinds:

(i) where the relevant accounts are Companies Act accounts, provisions of a kind specified for the purposes of this subsection by regulations under s 396;

(ii) where the relevant accounts are IAS accounts, provisions of any kind;

(c) share capital and reserves (including undistributable reserves): CA 2006, s 836(1) CA 2006.

30.24 The relevant accounts are the company's last annual accounts, except that where the distribution would be found to contravene Pt 23 by reference to the company's last annual accounts, it may be justified by reference to interim accounts. Where the distribution is proposed to be declared during the company's first accounting reference period, or before any accounts have been circulated in respect of that period, it may be justified by reference to initial accounts: CA 2006, s 836(2).

The section makes reference to individual accounts of a company and not accounts of a group of companies that are relevant for distribution purposes: *Inn Spirit Ltd v Burns* [2002] 2 BCLC 780.

30.25 The requirements of s 837 (as regards the company's last annual accounts), s 838 (as regards interim accounts) and s 839 (as regards initial accounts) must be complied with, as and where applicable: CA 2006, s 836(3).

If any applicable requirement of those sections is not complied with, the accounts may not be relied on for the purposes of Pt 23 and the distribution is accordingly treated as contravening this Part: CA 2006, s 836(4).

The importance of reference to the accounts cannot be overstated in determining whether or not a distribution should be made.

A company's power to pay dividends or make other distributions out of profits available for the purpose was linked to and controlled by the very detailed codes for accounts laid down in the CA 2006

In *Bairstow v Queens Moat Houses plc* [2001] 2 BCLC 531, the directors had declared dividends based on the company's accounts, which gave the misleading impression that the company had made profits that were available for distribution. The directors contended that although the parent company did not have distributable profits, its wholly owned subsidiaries could make these distributions available to the parent company for distribution, and that any breach of the parent company's accounts or accounting treatment was merely technical in nature. Further, any contravention of Pt 23 only applied where the company was insolvent, which was not the case here.

The Court of Appeal held, reinforcing the significance of the company's accounts to provide a true and fair view of the company's financial position. According to the Court of Appeal, the strict and mandatory character of the provisions of s 836 ensured that a company's power to pay dividends or make other distributions out of profits available for the purpose was linked to and controlled by the very detailed codes for accounts laid down in the Companies Act. The requirement in s 836 that any distribution could be made only in accordance with a company's financial statements, drawn up in the proper format and laid before the company in general meeting could not be regarded as a mere procedural technicality. It followed that the former directors could not go behind the figures for the company's distributable profits disclosed by the accounts which they had prepared, signed and laid before the company in general meeting when deciding the dividends to be declared: *Precision Dippings Ltd v Precision Dippings Marketing Ltd* [1985] BCLC 385; *Re Duomatic Ltd* [1969] 2 Ch 365. See also *Allied Carpets Group plc v Nethercott* [2001] BCC 81.

The principle that directors were accountable to the company for unlawful dividends paid in contravention of the provisions of Pt 23, whether or not the dividends were demonstrably paid out of capital, applied regardless of whether the company was solvent or insolvent. On the principle that a corporation was a legal person separate from the persons who were from time to time its members or shareholders, the right to reclaim dividends unlawfully paid belonged to the company for the protection of both creditors and shareholders and if directors caused a company to pay a dividend which was *ultra vires* and unlawful, the fact that the company was still solvent was not a defence to a claim against the directors to make good the unlawful distribution: *Re Exchange Banking Co, Flitcroft's Case* (1882) 21 Ch D 519.

30.26 In considering the lawfulness of the distributions, the courts may also have regard to s 1157, which provides a defence for the directors if they acted honestly and reasonably and ought fairly to be excused, or by making such order as the court thinks fit in respect of misfeasance under IA 1986, s 212.

The court may have regard to the defence under CA 2006, s 1157 as to whether the directors acted honestly in the circumstances

This issue arose in *Bairstow v Queens Moat Houses plc*, where Robert Walker LJ stated that since it was an absolute precondition to the grant of relief under s 1157 that the officer of the company seeking relief had acted 'honestly and reasonably', the judge's finding that the former directors were guilty of dishonestly preparing false accounts for 1991, in order to deceive the market into the belief that the company and the group were much more profitable than they actually were, meant that it was not open to the trial to find that they had acted honestly and reasonably in paying dividends on the strength of those accounts.

It will be a breach of directors' duty for failure to make proper provision in the accounts for tax liability

In *Loquitur Ltd, IRC v Richmond* [2003] BCLC 442, the directors of a company failed to make appropriate provision in the company's accounts for tax liability. The company paid a dividend of £5.9 million to the parent company. This was successfully challenged by HMRC on grounds of misfeasance under s 212 of the Insolvency Act 1986. Etherton J found that the directors had acted in breach of their duty and were guilty of misfeasance for failure to make proper provision in the accounts for the HMRC tax liability, which resulted in the improper preparation of the company's accounts.

According to Etherton J, the directors had failed to demonstrate that they had acted reasonably in failing to make provision in the interim accounts, and in authorising and procuring payment of the dividend. In paying the dividend the directors had not exercised proper skill and care in the best interests of the company, which included the interests of the creditors. In the circumstances the court had no jurisdiction to grant them relief from liability under s 1157(1) of the Companies Act 2006. However, although the court was unable to grant relief under that section, it was appropriate in the present case for the court to exercise its further discretion under s 212(3) of the Insolvency Act 1986, by limiting the amount which should be paid by the directors to the company to the amount of the corporation tax liability on the sale of the business.

Even though a company may declare dividends in excess of its contemplated distribution, the declaration may still be lawful provided the dividends that are declared are made from profits available for the purpose: *Re Marini Ltd, Liquidator of Marini Ltd v Dickenson* [2004] BCC 172.

Requirements applicable in relation to relevant accounts

Requirements where last annual accounts used

30.27 Section 837 provides that the company's last annual accounts means the company's individual accounts that were last circulated to members in accordance with s 423 (duty to circulate copies of annual accounts and reports), or if in accordance with s 426 the company provided a summary financial statement instead, that formed the basis of that statement: CA 2006, s 837(1).

The accounts must have been properly prepared in accordance with the CA 2006, or have been so prepared subject only to matters that are not material for determining (by reference to the items mentioned in s 836(1)) whether the distribution would contravene Pt 23: CA 2006, s 837(2).

30.28 Unless the company is exempt from audit and the directors take advantage of that exemption, the auditor must have made his report on the accounts: CA 2006, s 837(3).

If that report was qualified:

(a) the auditor must have stated in writing (either at the time of his report or subsequently) whether in his opinion the matters in respect of which his report is qualified are material for determining whether a distribution would contravene Pt 23; and

(b) a copy of that statement must:

 (i) in the case of a private company, have been circulated to members in accordance with s 423, or

 (ii) in the case of a public company, have been laid before the company in general meeting: s 837(4).

An auditor's statement is sufficient for the purposes of a distribution if it relates to distributions of a description that includes the distribution in question, even if at the time of the statement it had not been proposed: CA 2006, s 837(5).

The importance of the auditor's statement has been the subject of case law.

The effect of CA 2006, s 837 was to protect the company's creditors

In *Precision Dippings Ltd v Precision Dippings Marketing Ltd* [1985] BCLC 385, Precision Dippings Ltd (the Company) in September 1982 paid a cash dividend of £60,000 to Precision Dippings Marketing Ltd (Marketing) which held the vast majority of the shares in the Company, the remainder being held jointly by Marketing and two directors of the Company. At the time the dividend was paid the auditors of the Company had issued a qualified report on its accounts for the year ending 1982, but had failed to state in writing whether the qualification caused any payment of a dividend to be in contravention of the statutory provisions regulating the distribution of a company's assets as was required by the Companies Act. The directors of the Company were unaware of that provision, and it was accepted that they were advised by the Company's auditors that £60,000 could be paid by way of dividend. In April 1984, after the Company had become insolvent and had gone into liquidation, the auditors issued a written declaration to the effect that the qualification in their report did not affect the validity of the dividend payment. The shareholders held a meeting and accepted the report. The liquidator sought to restore an order whereby judgment was awarded to the Company to recover the £60,000 dividend payment made to Marketing.

The Court of Appeal held that since s 837(3) was designed for the protection of creditors, compliance with its requirements was not a procedural matter which could be waived with the unanimous agreement of all members of the company entitled to vote at meetings of the company.

Nor did the resolution of the shareholders accepting the statement of the auditors after the Company had gone into liquidation have the effect of ratifying the payment of the dividend since once the Company went into liquidation the members had no power to ratify to the detriment of the creditors anything done previously by the directors.

Therefore, the payment of the dividend was an *ultra vires* act. Accordingly, since Marketing was a volunteer and had received the money with notice of all the facts, Marketing held the £60,000 on constructive trust for the company.

Requirements where interim accounts used

30.29 Section 838 provides that interim accounts must be accounts that enable a reasonable judgment to be made as to the amounts of the items mentioned in s 836(1): CA 2006, s 838(1).

Where interim accounts are prepared for a proposed distribution by a public company, the following requirements apply: CA 2006, s 838(2).

The accounts must have been properly prepared, or have been so prepared subject to matters that are not material for determining (by reference to the items mentioned in s 836(1)) whether the distribution would contravene Pt 23: CA 2006, s 838(3).

30.30 The term 'properly prepared' means prepared in accordance with ss 395–397 (requirements for company individual accounts), applying those requirements with such modifications as are necessary because the accounts are prepared otherwise than in respect of an accounting reference period: CA 2006, s 838(4).

The balance sheet comprised in the accounts must have been signed in accordance with s 414: CA 2006, s 838(5).

A copy of the accounts must have been delivered to the registrar. Any requirement of Pt 35 as to the delivery of a certified translation into English of any document forming part of the accounts must also have been met: CA 2006, s 838(6).

Requirements where initial accounts used

30.31 Section 839 sets out the requirements where initial accounts are used. Initial accounts must be accounts that enable a reasonable judgment to be made as to the amounts of the items mentioned in s 836(1): CA 2006, s 839(1).

Where initial accounts are prepared for a proposed distribution by a public company, the following requirements apply: CA 2006, s 839(2).

The accounts must have been properly prepared, or have been so prepared subject to matters that are not material for determining (by reference to the items mentioned in s 836(1)) whether the distribution would contravene Pt 23: CA 2006, s 839(3).

The term 'properly prepared' means prepared in accordance with ss 395–397 (requirements for company individual accounts), applying those requirements with such modifications as are necessary because the accounts are prepared otherwise than in respect of an accounting reference period: CA 2006, s 839(4).

30.32 The company's auditor must have made a report stating whether, in his opinion, the accounts have been properly prepared: CA 2006, s 839(5).

If that report was qualified:

(a) the auditor must have stated in writing (either at the time of his report or subsequently) whether in his opinion the matters in respect of which his report is qualified are material for determining whether a distribution would contravene Pt 23; and

(b) a copy of that statement must:

 (i) in the case of a private company, have been circulated to members in accordance with s 423, or

 (ii) in the case of a public company, have been laid before the company in general meeting: CA 2006, s 839(6).

A copy of the accounts, of the auditor's report and of any auditor's statement must have been delivered to the registrar.

Any requirement of Pt 35 as to the delivery of a certified translation into English of any of those documents must also have been met: CA 2006, s 839(7).

Application of provisions to successive distributions etc

Successive distributions etc by reference to the same accounts

30.33 Section 840 states that in determining whether a proposed distribution may be made by a company in a case where:

(a) one or more previous distributions have been made in pursuance of a determination made by reference to the same relevant accounts, or

(b) relevant financial assistance has been given, or other relevant payments have been made, since those accounts were prepared,

the provisions of Pt 23 apply as if the amount of the proposed distribution was increased by the amount of the previous distributions, financial assistance and other payments: CA 2006, s 840(1).

30.34 The financial assistance and other payments that are relevant for this purpose are:

(a) financial assistance lawfully given by the company out of its distributable profits;

(b) financial assistance given by the company in contravention of ss 678 or 679 (prohibited financial assistance) in a case where the giving of that assistance reduces the company's net assets or increases its net liabilities;

(c) payments made by the company in respect of the purchase by it of shares in the company, except a payment lawfully made otherwise than out of distributable profits; and

(d) payments of any description specified in s 705 (payments apart from purchase price of shares to be made out of distributable profits): CA 2006, s 840(2).

The term 'financial assistance' has the same meaning as in Ch 2 of Pt 18 (see s 677): CA 2006, s 840(3).

30.35 For the purpose of applying s 840(2)(b) in relation to any financial assistance, the term 'net assets' means the amount by which the aggregate amount of the 'company's assets exceeds the aggregate amount of its liabilities, and 'net liabilities' means the amount by which the aggregate amount of the company's liabilities exceeds the aggregate amount of its assets, taking the amount of the assets and liabilities to be as stated in the company's accounting records immediately before the financial assistance is given: CA 2006, s 840(4).

For this purpose, a company's liabilities include any amount retained as reasonably necessary for the purposes of providing for any liability:

(a) the nature of which is clearly defined, and which is either likely to be incurred; or

(b) certain to be incurred but uncertain as to amount or as to the date on which it will arise: CA 2006, s 840(5).

Supplementary provisions

30.36 Chapter 3 to Pt 23 sets out supplementary provisions governing distributions.

Accounting matters

Realised losses and profits and revaluation of fixed assets

30.37 Section 841 states that the following provisions have effect for the purposes of Pt 23: CA 2006, s 841(1).

The following are treated as realised losses, namely:

(a) in the case of Companies Act accounts, provisions of a kind specified for the purposes of this paragraph by regulations under s 396 (except revaluation provisions); and

(b) in the case of IAS accounts, provisions of any kind (except revaluation provisions): CA 2006, s 841(2).

The term a 'revaluation provision' means a provision in respect of a diminution in value of a fixed asset appearing on a revaluation of all the fixed assets of the company, or of all of its fixed assets other than goodwill: CA 2006, s 841(3).

30.38 For the purpose of s 841(2) and (3), any consideration by the directors of the value at a particular time of a fixed asset is treated as a revaluation provided:

(a) the directors are satisfied that the aggregate value at that time of the fixed assets of the company that have not actually been revalued is not less than the aggregate amount at which they are then stated in the company's accounts; and

(b) it is stated in a note to the accounts:

  (i) that the directors have considered the value of some or all of the fixed assets of the company without actually revaluing them;

  (ii) that they are satisfied that the aggregate value of those assets at the time of their consideration was not less than the aggregate amount at which they were then stated in the company's accounts; and

  (iii) that accordingly, by virtue of s 841(4), amounts are stated in the accounts on the basis that a revaluation of fixed assets of the company is treated as having taken place at that time: CA 2006, s 841(4).

30.39 Where:

(a) on the revaluation of a fixed asset, an unrealised profit is shown to have been made, and

(b) on or after the revaluation, a sum is written off or retained for depreciation of that asset over a period,

an amount equal to the amount by which that sum exceeds the sum which would have been so written off or retained for the depreciation of that asset over that period, if that profit had not been made, is treated as a realised profit made over that period: CA 2006, s 841(5).

Determination of profit or loss in respect of asset where records incomplete

30.40 In determining for the purposes of Pt 23 whether a company has made a profit or loss in respect of an asset where:

(a) there is no record of the original cost of the asset; or

(b) a record cannot be obtained without unreasonable expense or delay,

its cost is taken to be the value ascribed to it in the earliest available record of its value made on or after its acquisition by the company: CA 2006, s 842.

Realised profits and losses of long-term insurance business

30.41 Section 843 states that the provisions of this section apply for the purposes of Pt 23 as it applies in relation to an authorised insurance company carrying on long-term business: CA 2006, s 843(1).

An amount included in the relevant part of the company's balance sheet that:

(a) represents a surplus in the fund or funds maintained by it in respect of its long-term business; and

(b) has not been allocated to policy holders or, as the case may be, carried forward unappropriated in accordance with asset identification rules made under s 142(2) of the Financial Services and Markets Act 2000 (c 8),

is treated as a realised profit: CA 2006, s 843(2).

30.42 For the purposes of s 843(2):

(a) the relevant part of the balance sheet is that part of the balance sheet that represents accumulated profit or loss;

(b) a surplus in the fund or funds maintained by the company in respect of its long-term business means an excess of the assets representing that fund or those funds over the liabilities of the company attributable to its long-term business, as shown by an actuarial investigation: CA 2006, s 843(3).

30.43 A deficit in the fund or funds maintained by the company in respect of its long-term business is treated as a realised loss: CA 2006, s 843(4).

For this purpose a deficit in any such fund or funds means an excess of the liabilities of the company attributable to its long-term business over the assets representing that fund or those funds, as shown by an actuarial investigation: CA 2006, s 843(5).

Subject to s 843(2) and (4), any profit or loss arising in the company's long-term business is to be left out of account: CA 2006, s 843(6).

30.44 The term an 'actuarial investigation' means an investigation made into the financial condition of an authorised insurance company in respect of its long-term business:

(a) carried out once in every period of 12 months in accordance with rules made under Pt 10 of the Financial Services and Markets Act 2000; or

(b) carried out in accordance with a requirement imposed under s 166 of that Act, by an actuary appointed as actuary to the company: CA 2006, s 843(6).

The term 'long-term business' means business that consists of effecting or carrying out contracts of long-term insurance. This definition must be read with s 22 of the Financial Services and Markets Act 2000 any relevant order under that section and Schedule 2 to that Act: CA 2006, s 843(7).

Treatment of development costs

30.45 Where development costs are shown or included as an asset in a company's accounts, any amount shown or included in respect of those costs is treated:

(a) for the purposes of s 830 (distributions to be made out of profits available for the purpose) as a realised loss; and

(b) for the purposes of s 832 (distributions by investment companies out of accumulated revenue profits) as a realised revenue loss: CA 2006, s 844(1).

30.46 This is subject to the following exceptions.

Section 844(1) does not apply to any part of that amount representing an unrealised profit made on revaluation of those costs: CA 2006, s 844(2).

Section 844(1) does not apply if:

(a) there are special circumstances in the company's case justifying the directors in deciding that the amount there mentioned is not to be treated as required by s 844(1);

(b) it is stated:

  (i) in the case of Companies Act accounts, in the note required by regulations under s 396 as to the reasons for showing development costs as an asset, or

  (ii) in the case of IAS accounts, in any note to the accounts, that the amount is not to be so treated; and

(c) the note explains the circumstances relied upon to justify the decision of the directors to that effect: CA 2006, s 844(3).

Distributions in kind

Distributions in kind: determination of amount

30.47 Section 845 applies for determining the amount of a distribution consisting of, or including, or treated as arising in consequence of, the sale, transfer or other disposition by a company of a non-cash asset where:

(a) at the time of the distribution the company has profits available for distribution; and

(b) if the amount of the distribution were to be determined in accordance with s 845, the company could make the distribution without contravening Pt 23: CA 2006, s 845(1).

30.48 The amount of the distribution (or the relevant part of it) is taken to be:

(a) in a case where the amount or value of the consideration for the disposition is not less than the book value of the asset, zero;

(b) in any other case, the amount by which the book value of the asset exceeds the amount or value of any consideration for the disposition: CA 2006, s 845(2).

30.49 For the purposes of s 845(1)(a), the company's profits available for distribution are treated as increased by the amount (if any) by which the amount or value of any consideration for the disposition exceeds the book value of the asset: CA 2006, s 845(3).

The term 'book value', in relation to an asset, means:

(a) the amount at which the asset is stated in the relevant accounts; or

(b) where the asset is not stated in those accounts at any amount, zero: CA 2006, s 845(4).

The provisions of Ch 2 of Pt 23 (justification of distribution by reference to accounts) apply subject to s 845(5).

Distributions in kind: treatment of unrealised profits

30.50 Section 846 applies where:

(a) a company makes a distribution consisting of or including, or treated as arising in consequence of, the sale, transfer or other disposition by the company of a non-cash asset; and

(b) any part of the amount at which that asset is stated in the relevant accounts represents an unrealised profit: CA 2006, s 846(1).

30.51 That profit is treated as a realised profit:

(a) for the purpose of determining the lawfulness of the distribution in accordance with this Pt (whether before or after the distribution takes place), and

(b) for the purpose of the application, in relation to anything done with a view to, or in connection with, the making of the distribution, of any provision of regulations under s 396 under which only realised profits are to be included in or transferred to the profit and loss account: CA 2006, s 846(2).

30.52 In *Capital Maintenance: Other Issues*, the Company Law Review Group explored the difficulties created by the decision in *Aveling Barford Ltd v Perion Ltd* [1989] BCLC 626 and made a number of suggestions as to how these difficulties might be overcome. Section 845 removes doubts to which the decision in this case has given rise, in particular when a transfer of an asset to a member amounts to a distribution. The concern behind this section is that, following the decision in *Aveling Barford*, it is unclear when intra-group transfers of assets can be conducted by reference to the 'asset's book value' rather than its market value (which will frequently be higher than the book value).

The decision in *Aveling Barford* concerned the sale of a property by a company (which had no distributable profits) at a considerable undervalue to another company controlled by the 'company's ultimate sole beneficial shareholder. The transaction was held to be void as an unauthorised return of capital. Whilst this case decided nothing about the situation where a company that has distributable profits makes an intra-group transfer of assets at book value, there was a concern that, as such a transfer may have an element of undervalue, the transaction would constitute a distribution thereby requiring the company to have distributable profits sufficient to cover the difference in value. The result has been that companies are often required either to abandon a transfer or to structure it in a more complex way (eg having the assets revalued and then sold (or distributed under s 276 of the CA 1985) so that the distributable reserves are increased by the 'realised profit' arising on the sale/distribution followed by a capital contribution of the asset to the relevant group member).

30.53 Section 845 does not disturb the position in *Aveling Barford* such that where a company which does not have distributable profits makes a distribution by way of a transfer of assets at an undervalue, this will be an unlawful distribution contrary to Pt 23.

It clarifies, however, the position where a company does have distributable profits and provides that where the conditions referred to in s 845(1)(a) and (b) are amounts of any distribution consisting of, or arising from the sale, transfer or other disposition by a company of a non-cash asset to a member of the company should be calculated by reference to the value at which that asset is included in the company's accounts (ie its 'book value'). Thus, if an asset is transferred for a consideration not less than its book value, the amount of the distribution is zero, but if the asset is transferred for a consideration less than its book value, the amount of the distribution is equal to that shortfall (which will therefore need to be covered by distributable profits) – see s 845(2)(a) and (b). This avoids the potential need for many companies to carry out asset revaluations requiring professional advice and incurring fees to advisors prior to making a distribution of a non-cash asset.

The conditions that must be satisfied for s 845(2)(a) and (b) to apply are that at the time of the disposition of the asset, the company must have profits available for distribution and that if the amount of such a distribution were to be determined in accordance with this section, it could be made without contravening any of the provisions of Pt 23 (eg ss 830 and 831).

30.54 Under s 845(3), in determining whether it has profits available for distribution (as defined in s 830) a company may treat any profit that would arise on the proposed disposition of the non-cash asset (ie the amount (if any) by which the consideration received exceeds the book value of the asset) as increasing its distributable profits.

Section 846 applies where a company 'makes a distribution of or including a non-cash asset' and allows a company which has revalued assets showing an unrealised profit in the accounts, to treat that profit as a realised profit where the distribution is a one off, or includes a non-cash asset. Section 846 tracks the drafting of s 845 so that it applies not only where the company makes a distribution consisting of or including a non-cash asset, but also where a company makes a distribution arising from the sale, transfer or other disposition by it of a non-cash asset, in other words in the same circumstances that are described in s 845.

Consequences of unlawful distribution

30.55 Section 847 applies where a distribution or part of one, made by a company to one of its members is made in contravention of Pt 23: CA 2006, s 847(1).

If at the time of the distribution the member knows or has reasonable grounds for believing that it is so made, he is liable:

(a) to repay it (or that part of it, as the case may be) to the company; or

(b) in the case of a distribution made otherwise than in cash, to pay the company a sum equal to the value of the distribution (or part) at that time: CA 2006, s 847(2).

This is without prejudice to any obligation imposed apart from s 847 on a member of a company to repay a distribution unlawfully made to him: CA 2006, s 847(3).

30.56 Section 847 does not apply in relation to:

(a) financial assistance given by a company in contravention of ss 678 or 679; or

(b) any payment made by a company in respect of the redemption or purchase by the company of shares in itself: CA 2006, s 847(4).

30.57 The issue before the courts has been in respect of the wording where a shareholder 'knows or has reasonable grounds for believing' that the distribution was made in contravention of Pt 23. This applies where a shareholder becomes aware of, or is put on notice that the distribution is contrary to CA 2006. In *Precision Dippings*, the Court of Appeal highlighted that Marketing had notice of receipt of payment which was in contravention of CA 2006 and, accordingly, it held the payment on constructive trust for the company (see also *Moxham v Grant* [1900] 1 QB 88 and *Allied Carpets Group plc v Nethercott* [2001] BCC 81).

The CA 2006 does not impose any criminal sanctions for breach of the distributions provisions. It also lacks much reference to the civil consequences where such a breach is found to have occurred save for CA 2006, s 847 which requires the person who has received the distribution in contravention of CA, to be liable to repay it back. It requires knowledge by the person concerned that was made in breach of the statutory provisions. However, the transaction is neither void nor voidable.

A shareholder was liable to return a distribution if he either knew, or could not have been unaware that it was paid in circumstances which amounted to a contravention of the restrictions on distributions

In *It's a Wrap (UK) Limited v Gala* [2006] 2 BCLC 634, the defendants, a husband and wife, set up a company in 2000 to run shops selling cards, gifts and candles. The business was their livelihood; they were employed by the company and were its only directors and shareholders. Even though the company made a loss in the years ended 31 December 2001 and 31 December 2002 and there were no profits available for distribution, the defendants paid themselves dividends of £14,000 each in lieu of salary in those years, having been advised that to do so was a tax-efficient way of drawing a salary. The company traded unsuccessfully and went into insolvent liquidation in January 2004. The liquidator brought a claim against the defendants alleging that the dividend payments for 2001 and 2002 were made in breach of the Companies Act, which provided that a company could not make a distribution except out of profits available for the purpose. The defendants were liable to repay the dividends because they knew, or ought to have known, that the distribution was made when the company had no profits out of which to pay dividends.

According to the defendants, the CA 2006 did not apply because they were unaware that payment of the dividends was prohibited. The deputy judge dismissed the claim, holding that the CA 2006 required knowledge or reasonable grounds for belief that a distribution contravened the Act before liability to repay could be imposed and therefore no liability arose if the shareholder receiving the distribution was unaware that the payment of a dividend would contravene the Act. The liquidator appealed.

The Court of Appeal held that a shareholder was liable to return a distribution if he either knew, or could not have been unaware that it was paid in circumstances which amounted to a contravention of the restrictions on distributions in the EEC Second Directive. Therefore, a shareholder was liable under CA 2006 to repay a distribution if he knew, or ought reasonably to have known of the facts which constituted a contravention of the Act, regardless of whether or not he knew about the legal rules which restricted distributions. Accordingly, it was not open to a shareholder to claim that he was not liable to return a distribution because he did not know of the restrictions on the making of distributions in the Act. Since the defendants knew that the company had no profits, they were to be taken as having known that the dividend payments for 2001 and 2002 were made in contravention of CA 2006.

30.58 Although CA 2006 sets out the liability of the recipient where a distribution is in contravention of Pt 23, it does not address the statutory liability of directors. The common law will apply in such cases and imposes liability on directors on the basis of constructive trusteeship and the joint and several liability of directors, who are considered as trustees of the company.

An unlawful distribution is not subject to ratification by the shareholders

In *Re Exchange Banking Co, Flitcroft's Case* (1882) 21 Ch D 518, the directors of a limited company for several years presented reports and balance sheets to the general meetings of shareholders in which various debts known by the directors to be bad were entered as assets, An apparent profit was shown though, in fact, there was none. The shareholders, relying on these documents, passed resolutions declaring dividends, which the directors accordingly paid. An order having been made to wind up the company, the liquidator applied for an order on the directors to replace the amount of dividends paid out of capital.

The Court of Appeal held that that even if the shareholders had known the true facts, so that their ratification of the payment of dividends would have bound themselves individually, they could not bind the company as the payment of dividends out of corpus was *ultra vires* the company, and was incapable of ratification by the shareholders:

Further, the fact that the capital thus improperly applied was distributed pro-rata among the whole body of shareholders did not protect the directors, as the shareholders were not the corporation, and payment to them would not prevent the corporation (before winding up) or the liquidator (after winding up) from compelling the directors to replace the money so that it might be applied to proper purposes.

Bacon VC considered directors as trustees of the money which may be collected by subscriptions, and of all the property that may be acquired; they have the direction and management of that property, and at the same time they have incurred direct obligation to the persons who have so entrusted them with their money.

Jessel MR was of the view that if directors who are quasi trustees for the company improperly pay away the assets to the shareholders, they are liable to replace them.

30.59 At common law, the effect of the decision in *Filtcroft's* case is that directors who are involved in unlawful distribution may be required to restore back to the company the distribution made, even though they have not received any dividends themselves. This principle applies to both insolvent and solvent companies.

In some situations, the court may impose a constructive trust where a distribution has been made

By the courts imposing the constructive trusteeship principle, the company may recover the whole amount of the unlawful distribution. It does not matter whether the distribution could have been lawfully made. In *JJ Harrison (Properties) Ltd v Harrison* [2002] 1 BCLC 162, Chadwick LJ likened the directors to constructive trustees who held assets for the benefit of the company. He stated that a director, on appointment to that office, assumed the duties of a trustee in relation to the company's property. If, thereafter, he took possession of that property, his possession 'is coloured from the first by the trust and confidence by means of which he obtained it'. His obligations as a trustee in relation to that property did not arise out of the transaction by which he obtained it for himself. The true analysis was that his obligations as a trustee in relation to the property predated the transaction by which it was conveyed to him. The conveyance of the property to himself by the exercise of his powers in breach of trust did not release him from those obligations. He was trustee of the property because it had become vested in him; his obligations to deal with the property as a trustee arose out of his pre-existing duties as a director, not out of the circumstances in which the property was conveyed.

30.60 Similarly, in *Re Lands Allotment Co* [1894] 1 Ch 616, the Court of Appeal held that directors of a company were trustees as to monies of the company which either came to their hands or were under their control. According to Lindley LJ:

> 'Although directors are not properly speaking trustees, yet they have always been considered and treated as trustees of money which comes to their hands or which is actually under their control; and ever since joint stock companies were invented directors have been held liable to make good moneys which they have misapplied upon the same footing as if they were trustees.'

Kay LJ stated:

> 'Now, case after case has decided that directors of trading companies are not for all purposes trustees or in the position of trustees, or quasi trustees, or to be treated as trustees in every sense; but if they deal with the funds of a company, although those funds are not absolutely vested in them, but funds which are under their control, and deal with those funds in a manner which is beyond their powers, then as to that dealing they are treated as having committed a breach of trust.'

Liability on directors in connection with unlawful distributions arises on the basis that they failed to exercise the degree of care and skill required of a director. It can also arise in respect of actual knowledge of improper distribution. At common law, the standard of care and skill was much lower. In *Dovey v Corey* [1901] AC 477, the directors were not in breach of their duty of care and skill in making improper payments: see too, *Kingston Cotton Mill (No 2)* [1896] 1 Ch 331.

A debate arises whether unlawful distributions are one of strict liability or fault-based?

The issue of unlawful declaration of dividends arose in *Re Paycheck Services 3 Ltd, Revenue and Customs Commissioners v Holland* [2011] 1 BCLC 141. Lord Hope addressed the issue as to whether this aspect was subject to strict liability or a fault-based approach. According to Lord Hope, there were two lines of authority on this issue. On the one hand, there were cases in which it has been said without qualification that directors were under a duty not to cause an unlawful and *ultra vires* payment of a dividend: *Re Exchange Banking Co, Flitcroft's Case* (1882) 21 Ch D 519; *Re Lands Allotment Co* [1894] 1 Ch 616 at 638; *Selangor United Rubber Estates Ltd v Cradock (a bankrupt) (No 3)* [1968] 2 All ER 1073 at 1092; *Belmont Finance Corp Ltd v Williams Furniture Ltd (No 2)* [1980] 1 All ER 393 at 404 and *Re Loquitar Ltd, IRC v Richmond* [2003] EWHC 999 (Ch) at [135]–[137].

On the other hand, there was a line of authority to the effect that a director was only liable if he made a misapplication of a company's assets if he knew, or ought reasonably to have known, that it was a misapplication: *Re County Marine Insurance Co, Rance's Case* (1870) 6 Ch App 104 at 118; *Re Kingston Cotton Mill Co (No 2)* [1896] 1 Ch 331 at 345–348; *Dovey v Cory* [1901] AC 477 at 489–490; *Re City Equitable Fire Insurance Co Ltd* [1925] Ch 407 at 426 per Romer J.

However, Lord Hope considered that the trend of modern authority supported the view that a director who caused a misapplication of a company's assets was, in principle, strictly liable to make good the misapplication, subject to his right to make good, if he could, a claim to relief under s 1157 of the CA 2006. The authorities that favoured the contrary view came to an end with *Dovey v Cory* [1901] AC 477, as the later judgment of Romer J in *Re City Equitable Fire Insurance Co Ltd* [1925] Ch 407 can be read, at least in relation to dividends, as supporting strict liability. Furthermore, the whole point of introducing the right to claim relief under s 1157 was to enable the court to mitigate the potentially harsh effect of being held strictly liable.

Lord Hope also stated (*obiter*) that in respect of unlawful distributions, the remedy was the obligation to restore the moneys wrongfully paid out and not equitable compensation or damages for loss sustained. Where dividends had been paid unlawfully, the directors' obligation was to account to the company for the full amount of those dividends owing to the trusteeship duties of directors: see *Bairstow v Queens Moat Houses plc* [2001] EWCA Civ 712 at [54], [2001] 2 BCLC 531 at [54] per Robert Walker LJ.

However, there was discretion under s 212 of the Insolvency Act 1986 for the judge to limit the award to what was required to make up the deficiency of a particular creditor where the claim was made by a party other than the liquidator.

The remedy for unlawful distribution is restoration of the assets

In *Madoff Securities International Limited v Raven* [2013] All ER 216, Popplewell J was required, *inter alia*, to address the issue of unlawful distributions made by the company. He accepted that the appropriate remedy would be restoration of the loss caused by the payments, subject to relief from sanctions in appropriate cases, without an inquiry into the counterfactual hypothesis of what would have happened had the duty been fulfilled. A counterfactual hypothesis would only be necessary for the purposes of a claim for breach of duty to exercise reasonable care, skill and diligence.

Popplewell J decided on the facts that the Madoff brothers were in breach of their duty to exercise reasonable care and skill by failing to address their minds to the question whether the payments made were in the interests of the company. However, this was not causative of any loss. Had the brothers done so, they would have concluded that the payments were in the company's interests, and the payments would still have been made. He concluded that collectively, the directors would have made a decision not to make or permit any payments in question.

Popplewell J also considered the issue of the directors' no loss defence. In this case, the directors contended that no loss was suffered in making payments and therefore no sums were recoverable for any actionable breached of duty established against them. The Claimants contended that the payments were made from the company's own assets and the obligation of a delinquent director was to restore such assets. On the issue of no loss defence, Popplewell J concluded the directors succeeded on the no loss defence.

Other matters

Saving for certain older provisions in articles

30.61 Where immediately before the relevant date a company was authorised by a provision of its articles to apply its unrealised profits in paying up in full or in part unissued shares to be allotted to members of the company as fully or partly paid bonus shares, that provision continues (subject to any alteration of the articles) as authority for those profits to be so applied after that date: CA 2006, s 848(1).

For this purpose the relevant date is:

(a) for companies registered in Great Britain, 22 December 1980; and

(b) for companies registered in Northern Ireland, 1 July 1983: CA 2006, s 848(2).

Restriction on application of unrealised profits

30.62 A company must not apply an unrealised profit in paying up debentures or any amounts unpaid on its issued shares: CA 2006, s 849.

Treatment of certain older profits or losses

30.63 Where the directors of a company, after making all reasonable enquiries, are unable to determine whether a particular profit made before the relevant date is realised or unrealised, they may treat the profit as realised: CA 2006, s 850(1).

Where the directors of a company, after making all reasonable enquiries, are unable to determine whether a particular loss made before the relevant date is realised or unrealised, they may treat the loss as unrealised: CA 2006, s 850(2).

For this purpose the relevant date is:

(a) for companies registered in Great Britain, 22 December 1980; and

(b) for companies registered in Northern Ireland, 1 July 1983: CA 2006, s 850(3).

Application of rules of law restricting distributions

30.64 Except as provided in s 851, the provisions of Pt 23 are without prejudice to any rule of law restricting the sums out of which, or the cases in which, a distribution may be made: CA 2006, s 851(1).

For the purposes of any rule of law requiring distributions to be paid out of profits or restricting the return of capital to members:

(a) section 845 (distributions in kind: determination of amount) applies to determine the amount of any distribution or return of capital consisting of or including, or treated as arising in consequence of the sale, transfer or other disposition by a company of a non-cash asset; and

(b) section 846 (distributions in kind: treatment of unrealised profits) applies as it applies for the purposes of Pt 23: CA 2006, s 851(2).

30.65 The references to distributions are to amounts regarded as distributions for the purposes of any such rule of law referred to in s 851(1): CA 2006, s 851(3).

Section 851 preserves the existing common law rules on unlawful distributions (see s 851(1)) which continue to be an essential component in determining what amounts to an unlawful distribution.

Section 851(2) makes an exception to this: in particular, it provides that the lawfulness and amount of distributions in kind are established by the statutory rules in ss 845 and 846 and not by any applicable common law rules.

Saving for other restrictions on distributions

30.66 The provisions of Pt 23 are without prejudice to any enactment or any provision of a company's articles, restricting the sums out of which, or the cases in which, a distribution may be made: CA 2006, s 852.

Checklist

30.67 *This Checklist sets out the key regulatory framework governing distributions including the position at common law.*

No	Issue	Reference
1	The term 'distribution' is widely defined and catches a distribution of a company's assets to its shareholders – whether cash or otherwise	CA 2006, s 829
2	Any return of corporate assets must be in compliance with the CA 2006 and common law – otherwise it will be unlawful and ultra vires	*Ridge Securities Ltd v IRC* [1964] 1 All ER 275
3	In some cases, the distribution may take the form of a 'disguised gift' out of capital which will be contrary to CA 2006 and the powers of directors	*Re Halt Garage* [1982] 3 All ER 1016
4	Where appropriate, the court may take into account the subjective intentions of the parties to a distribution transaction	*Progress Property Ltd v Moorgarth* [2011] 2 BCLC 332
5	There are certain exceptions where a transaction will not be considered as a distribution and includes the issue of shares as fully or partly paid bonus shares; or reduction of capital	CA 2006, s 829
6	Distributions may only be made from profits available for the purpose	CA 2006, s 830
7	Special rules apply to distributions by investment companies	CA 2006, s 832
8	The consequences of unlawful distribution are that a person is liable to repay it if at the time of the distribution, the person knows or has reasonable grounds for believing that it was made in contravention of the CA 2006	CA 2006, s 847; It's a *Wrap (UK) Ltd v Gala* [2006] 2 BCLC 634

No	Issue	Reference
9	An unlawful distribution is not subject to ratification by the shareholders	*Re Exchange Banking Co, Filtcroft's Case* (1882) 21 Ch D 518
10	Where appropriate, the court may impose a constructive trust where an unlawful distribution has been made	*JJ Harrison (Properties) Ltd* [2002] 1 BCLC 162
11	A debate arises whether the act of unlawful distribution is one of strict liability or fault-based?	*Re Paycheck Services 3 Ltd* [2011] 1 BCLC 141; *Madoff Securities International Limited v Raven* [2013] All ER 216

Definitions

30.68

'Profit or losses of any description':	Profits or losses of that description made at any time and, except where the context otherwise requires, are to profits or losses of a revenue or capital character.
'Capitalisation':	In relation to a company's profits, means any of the following operations (whenever carried out) applying the profits in wholly or partly paying up unissued shares in the company to be allotted to members of the company as fully or partly paid bonus shares; or transferring the profits to capital redemption reserve.
'Realised profits' and 'realised losses':	In relation to a company's accounts, are to such profits or losses of the company as fall to be treated as realised in accordance with principles generally accepted at the time when the accounts are prepared, with respect to the determination for accounting purposes of realised profits or losses.
'Fixed assets':	Assets of a company that are intended for use on a continuing basis in the company's activities.

31 Annual confirmation

Contents

Introduction

31.1 Part 24 of the CA 2006 (as amended by the SBEEA 2015) governs the company's annual confirmation of accuracy of the information on the register at Companies House. There is no longer a requirement for companies to deliver an annual return, but to deliver to the registrar an annual confirmation statement.

Annual confirmation of accuracy of information on register

31.2 Section 853A of the CA 2006 (as amended by the SBEEA 2015, s 92) deals with the duty to deliver confirmation statements. Every company must, before the end of the period of 14 days after the end of each review period, deliver to the registrar:

(a) such information as is necessary to ensure that the company is able to make the statement referred to in paragraph (b); and

(b) a statement (a 'confirmation statement') confirming that all information required to be delivered by the company to the registrar in relation to the confirmation period concerned under any duty mentioned in the CA 2006, s 853A(2) either:

   (i) has been delivered; or

   (ii) is being delivered at the same time as the confirmation statement: CA 2006, s 853A(1).

31.3 The duties are:

(a) any duty to notify a relevant event (see s 853B);

(b) any duty under ss 853C to 853I: CA 2006, s 853A(2).

31.4 The term 'confirmation period':

(a) in relation to a company's first confirmation statement, means the period beginning with the day of the company's incorporation and ending with the date specified in the statement ('the confirmation date');

(b) in relation to any other confirmation statement of a company, means the period beginning with the day after the confirmation date of the last such statement and ending with the confirmation date of the confirmation statement concerned: CA 2006, s 853A(3).

The confirmation date of a confirmation statement must be no later than the last day of the review period concerned: CA 2006, s 853A(4).

31.5 Each of the following is a review period for the purposes of Pt 24:

(a) the period of 12 months beginning with the day of the company's incorporation;

(b) each period of 12 months beginning with the day after the end of the previous review period: CA 2006, s 853A(5).

A company, however, has the ability to submit a confirmation statement at any point in the review period. But where a company delivers a confirmation statement with a confirmation date which is earlier than the last day of the review period concerned, the next review period is the period of 12 months beginning with the day after the confirmation date: CA 2006, s 853A(6).

31.6 For the purpose of making a confirmation statement, a company is entitled to assume that any information has been properly delivered to the registrar if it has been delivered within the period of five days ending with the date on which the statement is delivered: CA 2006, s 853A(7). This allows the company to make the confirmation statement in good faith when delivering Information to the registrar which has been accepted by the registrar. However, a company may not make such an assumption under the CA 2006, s 853A(7) if it has had notification from the registrar that such information has not been properly delivered: CA 2006, s 853A(8).

But it does not apply in a case where the company has received notice from the registrar.

Duties to notify a relevant event

31.7 The following duties are duties to notify a relevant event:

(a) the duty to give notice of a change in the address of the company's registered office (see s 87);

(b) in the case of a company in respect of which an election is in force under s 128B (election to keep membership information on central register), the duty to deliver anything as mentioned in s 128E;

(c) the duty to give notice of a change as mentioned in s 167 (change in directors or in particulars required to be included in register of directors or register of directors' residential addresses);

(d) in the case of a company in respect of which an election is in force under s 167A (election to keep information in register of directors or register of directors' residential addresses on central register), the duty to deliver anything as mentioned in s 167D;

(e) in the case of a private company with a secretary or a public company, the duty to give notice of a change as mentioned in s 276 (change in secretary or joint secretaries or in particulars required to be included in register of secretaries);

(f) in the case of a private company with a secretary in respect of which an election is in force under s 279A (election to keep information in register of secretaries on central register), the duty to deliver anything as mentioned in s 279D;

(g) in the case of a company in respect of which an election is in force under s 790X (election to keep information in PSC register on central register), the duty to deliver anything as mentioned in s 790ZA;

(h) in the case of a company which, in accordance with regulations under s 1136, keeps any company records at a place other than its registered office, any duty under the regulations to give notice of a change in the address of that place: CA 2006, s 853B.

Duty to notify a change in company's principal business activities

31.8 Section 853C of the CA 2006 applies where:

(a) a company makes a confirmation statement; and

(b) there has been a change in the company's principal business activities during the confirmation period concerned: CA 2006, s 853C(1).

The company must give notice to the registrar of the change at the same time as it delivers the confirmation statement: CA 2006, s 853C(2).

The information as to the company's new principal business activities may be given by reference to one or more categories of any prescribed system of classifying business activities: CA 2006, s 853C(3).

Duty to deliver statement of capital

31.9 Section 853D of the CA 2006 applies where a company having a share capital makes a confirmation statement: CA 2006, s 853D(1).

The company must deliver a statement of capital to the registrar at the same time as it delivers the confirmation statement: CA 2006, s 853D(2).

Section 853D(2) does not apply if there has been no change in any of the matters required to be dealt with by the statement of capital since the last such statement was delivered to the registrar: CA 2006, s 853D(3).

31.10 The statement of capital must state with respect to the company's share capital at the confirmation date:

(a) the total number of shares of the company;

(b) the aggregate nominal value of those shares;

(c) the aggregate amount (if any) unpaid on those shares (whether on account of their nominal value or by way of premium); and

(d) for each class of shares:

(i) prescribed particulars of the rights attached to the shares;

(ii) the total number of shares of that class; and

(iii) the aggregate nominal value of shares of that class: CA 2006, s 853D(4).

Duty to notify trading status of shares

31.11 Section 853E of the CA 2006 applies where a company having a share capital makes a confirmation statement: CA 2006, s 853E(1).

The company must deliver to the registrar a statement dealing with the matters mentioned in s 853E(4) at the same time as it delivers the confirmation statement: CA 2006, s 853E(2).

Section 853E(2) does not apply if and to the extent that the last statement delivered to the registrar under this section applies equally to the confirmation period concerned: CA 2006, s 853E(3).

31.12 The matters are:

(a) whether any of the company's shares were, at any time during the confirmation period concerned, shares admitted to trading on a relevant market or on any other market which is outside the United Kingdom; and

(b) if so, whether both of the conditions mentioned in s 853E(5) were satisfied throughout the confirmation period concerned: CA 2006, s 853E(4).

31.13 The conditions are that:

(a) there were shares of the company which were shares admitted to trading on a relevant market;

(b) the company was a DTR5 issuer: CA 2006, s 853E(5).

31.14 The term 'DTR5 issuer' means an issuer to which Chapter 5 of the Disclosure Rules and Transparency Rules sourcebook made by the Financial Conduct Authority (as amended or replaced from time to time) applies.

The term 'relevant market' means any of the markets mentioned in the Financial Services and Markets Act 2000 (Prescribed Markets and Qualifying Investments) Order 2001, art 4(1): CA 2006, s 853E(6).

Duty to deliver shareholder information: non-traded companies

31.15 Section 853F of the CA 2006 applies where:

(a) a non-traded company makes a confirmation statement; and

(b) there is no election in force under s 128B in respect of the company: CA 2006, s 853F(1).

A 'non-traded company' is a company none of whose shares were, at any time during the confirmation period concerned, shares admitted to trading on a relevant market or on any other market which is outside the United Kingdom: CA 2006, s 853F(2).

The company must deliver the information falling within s 853F(5) to the registrar at the same time as it delivers the confirmation statement: CA 2006, s 853F(3).

31.16 Section 853F(3) does not apply if and to the extent that the information most recently delivered to the registrar under this section applies equally to the confirmation period concerned: CA 2006, s 853F(4).

The information is:

(a) the name (as it appears in the company's register of members) of every person who was at any time during the confirmation period a member of the company;

(b) the number of shares of each class held at the end of the confirmation date concerned by each person who was a member of the company at that time;

(c) the number of shares of each class transferred during the confirmation period concerned by or to each person who was a member of the company at any time during that period; and

(d) the dates of registration of those transfers: CA 2006, s 853F(5).

The registrar may impose requirements about the form in which information of the kind mentioned in s 853F(5)(a) is delivered for the purpose of enabling the entries on the register relating to any given person to be easily found: CA 2006, s 853F(1).

Duty to deliver shareholder information: certain traded companies

31.17 Section 853G of the CA 2006 applies where a traded company makes a confirmation statement: CA 2006, s 853G(1).

A 'traded company' is a company any of whose shares were, at any time during the confirmation period concerned, shares admitted to trading on a relevant market or on any other market which is outside the United Kingdom: CA 2006, s 853G(2).

But a company is not a traded company if throughout the confirmation period concerned:

(a) there were shares of the company which were shares admitted to trading on a relevant market; and

(b) the company was a DTR5 issuer: CA 2006, s 853G(3).

The company must deliver the information falling within s 853G(6) to the registrar at the same time as it delivers the confirmation statement: CA 2006, s 853G(4).

31.18 Section 853G(4) does not apply if and to the extent the information most recently delivered to the registrar under this section applies equally to the confirmation period concerned: CA 2006, s 853G(5).

The information is:

(a) the name and address (as they appear in the company's register of members) of each person who, at the end of the confirmation date concerned, held at least 5% of the issued shares of any class of the company; and

(b) the number of shares of each class held by each such person at that time: CA 2006, s 853G(6).

Duty to deliver information about exemption from Pt 21A

31.19 Section 853H of the CA 2006 applies where a company:

(a) which is not a DTR5 issuer; and

(b) to which Pt 21A does not apply (information about people with significant control, see s 790B),

makes a confirmation statement: CA 2006, s 853H(1).

The company must deliver to the registrar a statement of the fact that it is a company to which Pt 21A does not apply at the same time as it delivers the confirmation statement: CA 2006, s 853H(2).

Section 853H(2) does not apply if the last statement delivered to the registrar under this section applies equally to the confirmation period concerned: CA 2006, s 853H(3).

Duty to deliver information about people with significant control

31.20 Section 853I of the CA 2006 applies where:

(a) a company to which Pt 21A (information about people with significant control) applies makes a confirmation statement; and

(b) there is no election in force under s 790X in respect of the company: CA 2006, s 853I(1).

The company must deliver the information stated in its PSC register to the registrar at the same time as it delivers the confirmation statement: CA 2006, s 853I(2).

31.21 Section 853I(2) does not apply if and to the extent that the information most recently delivered to the registrar under this section applies equally to the confirmation period concerned: CA 2006, s 853I(3).

The term 'PSC register' has the same meaning as in Pt 21A (see s 790C): CA 2006, s 853I(4).

Power to amend duties to deliver certain information

31.22 The Secretary of State may by regulations make provision about the duties on a company in relation to the delivery of information falling within ss 853E(4), 853F(5),

853G(6), 853H(2) or 853I(2) (referred to in this section as 'relevant information'): CA 2006, s 853J(1).

The regulations may, in particular, make provision requiring relevant information to be delivered:

(a) on such occasions as may be prescribed;

(b) at such intervals as may be prescribed: CA 2006, s 853J(2).

The regulations may amend or repeal the provisions of ss 853A, 853B and 853E to 853I: CA 2006, s 853J(3).

31.23 The regulations may provide:

(a) that where a company fails to comply with any duty to deliver relevant information an offence is committed by:

   (i) the company;

   (ii) every director of the company;

   (iii) in the case of a private company with a secretary or a public company, every secretary of the company; and

   (iv) every other officer of the company who is in default;

(b) that a person guilty of such an offence is liable on summary conviction:

   (i) in England and Wales, to a fine and, for continued contravention, a daily default fine not exceeding the greater of £500 and one-tenth of level 4 on the standard scale;

   (ii) in Scotland or Northern Ireland, to a fine not exceeding level 5 on the standard scale and, for continued contravention, a daily default fine not exceeding one-tenth of level 5 on the standard scale;

(c) that, in the case of continued contravention, an offence is also committed by every officer of the company who did not commit an offence under provision made under paragraph (a) in relation to the initial contravention but who is in default in relation to the continued contravention;

(d) that a person guilty of such an offence is liable on summary conviction:

   (i) in England and Wales, to a fine not exceeding the greater of £500 and one-tenth of level 4 on the standard scale for each day on which the contravention continues and the person is in default;

   (ii) in Scotland or Northern Ireland, to a fine not exceeding one-tenth of level 5 on the standard scale for each day on which the contravention continues and the person is in default: CA 2006, s 853J(4).

The regulations may provide that, for the purposes of any provision made under s 853J(4), a shadow director is to be treated as a director: CA 2006, s 853J(5).

Confirmation statements: power to make further provision by regulations

31.24 The Secretary of State may by regulations make further provision as to the duties to deliver information to the registrar to which a confirmation statement is to relate: CA 2006, s 853K(1).

The regulations may:

(a) amend or repeal the provisions of ss 853A to 853I; and

(b) provide for exceptions from the requirements of those sections as they have effect from time to time: CA 2006, s 853K(2).

Regulations under this section which provide that a confirmation statement must relate to a duty to deliver information not for the time being mentioned in s 853A(2) are subject to affirmative resolution procedure: CA 2006, s 853K(3).

Failure to deliver confirmation statement

31.25 If a company fails to deliver a confirmation statement before the end of the period of 14 days after the end of a review period an offence is committed by:

(a) the company;

(b) every director of the company;

(c) in the case of a private company with a secretary or a public company, every secretary of the company; and

(d) every other officer of the company who is in default.

For this purpose a shadow director is treated as a director: CA 2006, s 853L(1).

31.26 A person guilty of an offence under s 853L(1) is liable on summary conviction:

(a) in England and Wales to a fine, and, for continued contravention, a daily default fine not exceeding the greater of £500 and one-tenth of level 4 on the standard scale;

(b) in Scotland or Northern Ireland, to a fine not exceeding level 5 on the standard scale and, for continued contravention, a daily default fine not exceeding one-tenth of level 5 on the standard scale: CA 2006, s 853L(2);

The contravention continues until such time as a confirmation statement specifying a confirmation date no later than the last day of the review period concerned is delivered by the company to the registrar: CA 2006, s 853L(3).

31.27 It is a defence for a director or secretary charged with an offence under s 853L(1)(b) or (c) to prove that the person took all reasonable steps to avoid the commission or continuation of the offence: CA 2006, s 853L(4).

In the case of continued contravention, an offence is also committed by every officer of the company who did not commit an offence under s 853L(1) in relation to the initial contravention but who is in default in relation to the continued contravention: CA 2006, s 853L(5).

31.28 A person guilty of an offence under s 853L(5) is liable on summary conviction:

(a) in England and Wales, to a fine not exceeding the greater of £500 and one-tenth of level 4 on the standard scale for each day on which the contravention continues and the person is in default;

(b) in Scotland or Northern Ireland, to a fine not exceeding one-tenth of level 5 on the standard scale for each day on which the contravention continues and the person is in default: CA 2006, s 853L(6).

32 Company charges

Contents

Introduction

32.1 Part 25 of the CA 2006 is concerned with company charges. Part 25 provides a scheme for the registration of charges created by a company. The aim of the registration is not only to set out all of the company's charges but more fundamentally 'to warn unsuspecting creditors that the debtor company has charged its assets': *Re Welsh Irish Ferries Limited* [1985] BCLC 327, per Nourse J.

Part 25 comprises three chapters. Chapter 1 is concerned with companies registered in England and Wales or in Northern Ireland. Chapter 2 addresses company charges in Scotland. Chapter 3 deals with the powers of the Secretary of State.

This Chapter considers the following aspects:

- The concept of a fixed and floating charge.
- Requirement to register charges.
- The register of charges.

Fixed and floating charges

32.2 In English company law, a distinction is made between a fixed and floating charge. A fixed charge is a charge over for example, a tangible asset or a charge over book debt. It evidences a debt due by the debtor to the creditor over a security interest such as the debtor's property. The relationship between the debtor and creditor is contractual which sets out the responsibilities and obligations of the parties. The fixed charge will typically restrict the debtor's right to dispose of the asset while the charge is secured. On the debtor's insolvency, the asset may be sold to realise funds for the creditor and discharge the loan made to the debtor.

A floating charge is a charge that is secured over assets but which has the flexibility that the debtor is free to deal with the assets in the ordinary course of business until an event occurs (such as 'crystallisation' for example on the company's winding up), the effect of which is that the assets subject to the floating charge will be identified and becomes a fixed charge and a particular point in time with the objective of realising funds for the creditor. The assets may take the form of stock in trade. A classic definition of a floating charge was set out by Romer LJ in *Re Yorkshire Woolcombers Association Ltd* [1903] 2 Ch 284 as comprising three characteristics:

- there must be an intention to create a charge on a class of assets both present and future;
- the assets are such that are changing in the ordinary course of business; and
- the company has flexibility to deal with the assets that are charged in the ordinary course of business.

See too: *Ilingworth v Houldsworth* [1904] AC 355.

32.3 The modern judicial attitudes towards floating charges is that the principal characteristic of a floating charge is the flexibility for the company to deal with the charged assets in the ordinary course of business.

The fact that a charge is described as a 'fixed' charge is not conclusive. The court will construe the document giving rise to the charge to determine the nature of the charge.

32.4 In *Agnew v Commissioner for Inland Revenue* [2001] AC 710, in the Privy Council, Lord Millet stated that the critical feature which distinguished a floating from a fixed charge lay in the chargor's ability, freely and without the chargee's consent, to control and manage the charged assets and withdraw them from the security. He set out the distinctive feature between a fixed and floating charge. He considered that in deciding whether a charge is a fixed charge or a floating charge, the court is engaged in a two-stage process. At the first stage it must construe the instrument of charge and seek to gather the intentions of the parties from the language they have used. But the object at this stage of the process is not to discover whether the parties intended to create a fixed or a floating charge – it is to ascertain the nature of the rights and obligations which the parties intended to grant each other in respect of the charged assets. Once these have been ascertained, the court can then embark on the second stage of the process, which is one of categorisation. This is a matter of law. It does not depend on the intention of the parties. If their intention, properly gathered from the language of the instrument, is to grant the company rights in respect of the charged assets which are inconsistent with the nature of a fixed charge, then the charge cannot be a fixed charge however they may have chosen to describe it.

A floating charge is distinguished from a fixed charge by its flexibility in allowing a debtor to deal freely with assets in the ordinary course of business

The *Agnew* approach was followed in In *Re Spectrum Plus Limited* [2005] 2 BCLC 269, where the House of Lords held that the essential characteristic of a floating charge, distinguishing it from a fixed charge, was that the asset subject to the charge was not finally appropriated as a security for the payment of the debt until the occurrence of some future event. In the meantime, the chargor was left free to use the charged asset and to remove it from the security. Thus there could be no difference in categorisation between the grant of a fixed charge expressed to come into existence on a future event in relation to a specified class of assets owned by the chargor at that time and the grant of a floating charge over the specified class of assets with crystallisation taking place on the occurrence of that event. Nor, in principle, could there be any difference in categorisation between such grants and the grant of a charge over the specified assets expressed to be a fixed charge but where the chargor was permitted until the occurrence of the specified event to remove the charged assets from the security.

Companies registered in England and Wales or in Northern Ireland – requirement to register company charges

Charges created by a company

32.5 Chapter 1 is concerned with companies registered in England and Wales and Northern Ireland.

A company that creates a charge must deliver the prescribed particulars of the charge, together with the instrument (if any) by which the charge is created or evidenced, to the registrar for registration before the end of the period allowed for registration: CA 2006, s 860(1).

Registration of a charge may instead be effected on the application of a person interested in it: CA 2006, s 860(2).

Where registration is effected on the application of some person other than the company, that person is entitled to recover from the company the amount of any fees properly paid by him to the registrar on registration: CA 2006, s 860(3).

32.6 If a company fails to comply with s 860(1), an offence is committed by the company, and every officer of it who is in default: CA 2006, s 860(4). A person guilty of an offence under s 860 will be liable on conviction on indictment, to a fine; on summary conviction, to a fine not exceeding the statutory maximum: CA 2006, s 860(5).

Section 860(4) does not apply if registration of the charge has been effected on the application of some other person: CA 2006, s 860(6).

32.7 Not all types of charges (such as a retention of title agreement or seller's lien: *London and Cheshire Insurance Co Ltd v Laplagrene Property Co Ltd* [1971] Ch 499) are registerable. Under s 860, only the following charges are to be registered at Companies House:

(a) a charge on land or any interest in land, other than a charge for any rent or other periodical sum issuing out of land;

(b) a charge created or evidenced by an instrument which, if executed by an individual, would require registration as a bill of sale;

(c) a charge for the purposes of securing any issue of debentures;

(d) a charge on uncalled share capital of the company;

(e) a charge on calls made but not paid;

(f) a charge on book debts of the company;

(g) a floating charge on the company's property or undertaking;

(h) a charge on a ship or aircraft, or any share in a ship; and

(i) a charge on goodwill or on any intellectual property: CA 2006, s 860(7).

Charges which have to be registered: supplementary

32.8 Section 861 states that the holding of debentures entitling the holder to a charge on land is not, for the purposes of s 860(7)(a), an interest in the land: CA 2006, s 861(1).

It is immaterial for the purposes of Ch 1 to Pt 25 where land subject to a charge is situated: CA 2006, s 861(2).

The deposit by way of security of a negotiable instrument given to secure the payment of book debts is not, for the purposes of s 860(7)(f), a charge on those book debts: CA 2006, s 861(3).

32.9 For the purposes of s 860(7)(i), the term 'intellectual property' means any patent, trade mark, registered design, copyright or design right; any licence under or in respect of any such right: CA 2006, s 861(4).

In Ch 1 to Pt 25, the term 'charge' includes a mortgage and 'company' means a company registered in England and Wales or in Northern Ireland: CA 2006, s 861(5).

Charges existing on property acquired

32.10 Section 862 applies where a company acquires property which is subject to a charge of a kind which would, if it had been created by the company after the acquisition of the property, have been required to be registered under Ch 1 to Pt 25: CA 2006, s 862(1).

The company must deliver the prescribed particulars of the charge, together with a certified copy of the instrument (if any) by which the charge is created or evidenced, to the registrar for registration: CA 2006, s 862(2).

Section 862(2) must be complied with before the end of the period allowed for registration: CA 2006, s 862(3). If default is made in complying with this section, an offence is committed by the company, and every officer of it who is in default:

CA 2006, s 862(4). A person guilty of an offence under this section will be liable on conviction on indictment, to a fine; on summary conviction, to a fine not exceeding the statutory maximum: CA 2006, s 862(5).

Special rules about debentures

32.11 Sections 863–865 of the CA 2006 deal with special rules applicable to debentures.

Charge in series of debentures

32.12 Where a series of debentures containing, or giving by reference to another instrument, any charge to the benefit of which debenture holders of that series are entitled *pari passu* is created by a company, it is for the purposes of s 860(1) sufficient if the required particulars, together with the deed containing the charge (or, if there is no such deed, one of the debentures of the series), are delivered to the registrar before the end of the period allowed for registration: CA 2006, s 863(1).

The following are the required particulars:

(a) the total amount secured by the whole series;

(b) the dates of the resolutions authorising the issue of the series and the date of the covering deed (if any) by which the series is created or defined;

(c) a general description of the property charged; and

(d) the names of the trustees (if any) for the debenture holders: CA 2006, s 863(2).

Particulars of the date and amount of each issue of debentures of a series of the kind mentioned in s 863(1) must be sent to the registrar for entry in the register of charges: CA 2006, s 863(3).

32.13 Failure to comply with s 863(3) does not affect the validity of the debentures issued: CA 2006, s 863(4).

Section 860(2)–(6) applies for the purposes of s 863 as they apply for the purposes of that section, but as if references to the registration of a charge were references to the registration of a series of debentures: CA 2006, s 863(5).

Additional registration requirement for commission etc in relation to debentures

32.14 Where any commission, allowance or discount has been paid or made either directly or indirectly by a company to a person in consideration of his subscribing or agreeing to subscribe, whether absolutely or conditionally, for debentures in a company, or procuring or agreeing to procure subscriptions, whether absolute or conditional, for such debentures, the particulars required to be sent for registration under s 860 shall include particulars as to the amount or rate per cent of the commission, discount or allowance so paid or made: CA 2006, s 864(1).

The deposit of debentures as security for a debt of the company is not, for the purposes of s 864, treated as the issue of debentures at a discount: CA 2006, s 864(2). Failure to comply with this section does not affect the validity of the debentures issued: CA 2006, s 864(3).

Endorsement of certificate on debentures

32.15 The company must cause a copy of every certificate of registration given under s 869 to be endorsed on every debenture or certificate of debenture stock which is issued by the company, and the payment of which is secured by the charge so registered: CA 2006, s 865(1).

But this does not require a company to cause a certificate of registration of any charge so given to be endorsed on any debenture or certificate of debenture stock issued by the company before the charge was created: CA 2006, s 865(2).

If a person knowingly and wilfully authorises or permits the delivery of a debenture or certificate of debenture stock which under s 865 is required to have endorsed on it a copy of a certificate of registration, without the copy being so endorsed upon it, he commits an offence: CA 2006, s 865(3). A person guilty of an offence under this section is liable on summary conviction to a fine not exceeding level 3 on the standard scale: CA 2006, s 865(4).

Charges in other jurisdictions

32.16 Sections 866–867 of the CA 2006 deal with charges in other jurisdictions.

Charges created in, or over property in, jurisdictions outside the UK

32.17 Where a charge is created outside the UK comprising property situated outside the UK, the delivery to the registrar of a verified copy of the instrument by which the charge is created or evidenced has the same effect for the purposes of this chapter as the delivery of the instrument itself: CA 2006, s 866(1).

Where a charge is created in the UK but comprises property outside the UK, the instrument creating or purporting to create the charge may be sent for registration under s 860 even if further proceedings may be necessary to make the charge valid or effectual according to the law of the country in which the property is situated: CA 2006, s 866(2).

Charges created in, or over property in, another UK jurisdiction

32.18 Section 867 states that s 867(2) applies where a charge comprises property situated in a part of the UK other than the part in which the company is registered. Registration in that other part is necessary to make the charge valid or effectual under the law of that part of the UK: CA 2006, s 867(1).

The delivery to the registrar of a verified copy of the instrument by which the charge is created or evidenced, together with a certificate stating that the charge was presented for registration in that other part of the UK on the date on which it was so presented has, for the purposes of Pt 25, Ch 1, the same effect as the delivery of the instrument itself: CA 2006, s 867(2).

Orders charging land: Northern Ireland

Northern Ireland: registration of certain charges etc affecting land

32.19 Where a charge imposed by an order under Art 46 of the Judgments Enforcement (Northern Ireland) Order 1981 (SI 1981 No 226) or notice of such a charge is registered in the Land Registry against registered land or any estate in registered land of a company, the Registrar of Titles shall, as soon as may be, cause two copies of the order made under Art 46 of that Order or of any notice under Art 48 of that Order to be delivered to the registrar: CA 2006, s 868(1).

Where a charge imposed by an order under Art 46 of the 1981 Order is registered in the Registry of Deeds against any unregistered land or estate in land of a company, the Registrar of Deeds shall as soon as may be cause two copies of the order to be delivered to the registrar: CA 2006, s 868(2).

32.20 On delivery of copies under s 863, the registrar shall register one of them in accordance with s 869, and not later than seven days from that date of delivery, cause the other copy together with a certificate of registration under s 869(5) to be sent to the company against which judgment was given: CA 2006, s 868(3).

Where a charge to which s 868(1) or (2) applies is vacated, the Registrar of Titles or, as the case may be, the Registrar of Deeds shall cause a certified copy of the certificate of satisfaction lodged under Art 132(1) of the 1981 Order to be delivered to the registrar for entry of a memorandum of satisfaction in accordance with s 872: CA 2006, s 868(4).

The register of charges

32.21 Sections 869–873 of the CA 2006 govern the register of charges.

Register of charges to be kept by registrar

32.22 The registrar must keep, with respect to each company, a register of all the charges requiring registration under Ch 1 to Pt 25: CA 2006, s 869(1).

In the case of a charge to the benefit of which holders of a series of debentures are entitled, the registrar shall enter in the register the required particulars specified in s 863(2): CA 2006, s 869(2).

In the case of a charge imposed by the Enforcement of Judgments Office under Art 46 of the 1981 Order, the registrar shall enter in the register the date on which the charge became effective: CA 2006, s 869(3).

32.23 In the case of any other charge, the registrar shall enter in the register the following particulars:

(a) if it is a charge created by a company, the date of its creation and, if it is a charge which was existing on property acquired by the company, the date of the acquisition;

(b) the amount secured by the charge;

(c) short particulars of the property charged; and

(d) the persons entitled to the charge: CA 2006, s 869(4).

The registrar will give a certificate of the registration of any charge registered in pursuance of this Chapter, stating the amount secured by the charge: CA 2006, s 869(5).

32.24 The certificate must be signed by the registrar or authenticated by the registrar's official seal, and is conclusive evidence that the requirements of Pt 25, Ch 1 as to registration have been satisfied: CA 2006, s 869(6). The registrar's certificate is conclusive even where the certificate was issued by mistake or error by the registrar or that the charge was not validly registered: *Ali v Top Marques Car Rental Ltd* [2006] EWHC 109; and must be accepted by all who have notice of the charge, including liquidators: *National Provincial and Union Bank of England v Charnley* [1924] 1 KB 431.

The Registrar's certificate is conclusive evidence of registration of a charge

In *Re C L Nye Ltd* [1971] Ch 442, Harman LJ stated that the certificate was conclusive evidence of registration of a charge. The hub point of creating the register under s 869 was to give security to persons relying on the certificate.

The issue of a certificate by the Registrar was conclusive as to registration of the charge

In *Cunard Steamship Co Ltd v Hopwood* [1908] 2 Ch 564, the particulars filed were defective in that the date of the resolution creating the debenture stock was omitted by the company. However, the certificate of the registrar was held conclusive as to this and the security was valid against the liquidator and other creditors.

See too *Re Yolland, Husson & Birkett Ltd* [1908] 1 Ch 152 at 158, per Cozens-Hardy MR.

In *National Provincial and Union Bank of England v Charnley* [1924] 1 KB 431, the instrument of charge covered land and movable plant. The chargee, in presenting particulars for registration, stated the property charged as being land only and indeed struck out from the list on the then prescribed form that description of the instrument which would be appropriate to a charge on movable plant. The entry on the register similarly omitted all reference to any charge on chattels. However, the certificate was conclusive evidence that the requirements of the Act had been complied with. The instrument of charge was held to be effective security against a judgment creditor of the company seeking to enforce his judgment against the movable plant. Scrutton and Atkin LJJ were of the view that once a certificate has been given by the Registrar in respect to a particular specified document which created a mortgage or charge, it was conclusive that the mortgage or charge so created was properly registered, even though the particulars put forward by the person applying for registration were incomplete, and the entry in the register by the registrar was defective.

In *Re Mechanisations (Eaglescliffe) Ltd* [1966] Ch 20, the particulars delivered by the chargee did not correctly state the payments secured by the charge; nor did the consequent entries on the register; nor did the certificate. The liquidator did not seek to avoid the whole security, but only to the extent of understatement of the payments secured, arguing that the certificate bound the chargee and so made his incorrect particulars the truth. Buckley J followed the *Charnley* case and held that the certificate was conclusive evidence not of the correctness of the particulars stated in the certificate itself, but of compliance with the requirements of the statute.

In *Re Eric Holmes (Property) Ltd* [1965] Ch 1052 Pennycuick J held that the certificate was conclusive as to delivery of particulars within the 21-day period after the creation of the charge, an incorrect date having been inserted in the charge, in the particulars delivered, and in the register – though, in fact, the charge had been created more than 21 days before the particulars were delivered.

Challenging the registrar's certificate?

32.25 Once the registrar grants a certificate under s 869, can his decision be the subject of a challenge by judicial review? The court will not entertain judicial review proceedings owing to the conclusivity of the certificate. This will be the case even where the charge was registered in error or that the charge contains errors or is inaccurate: *Ali v Top Marques Car Rental Ltd* [2006] EWHC 109; and *National Provincial and Union Bank v Charnley* [1924] 1 KB 431. The registrar is unlikely to be subject to an action for damages despite the conclusivity particularly where third parties may be misled: *Ministry of Housing and Local Government v Sharp* [1970] 2 QB 223; and *Davis v Radcliffe* [1990] 1 WLR 821.

However, there may be some exceptions to this rule such as fraud.

Where fraud is apparent, it may vitiate the conclusivity of the Registrar's certificate

In *R v Registrar of Companies ex parte Central Bank of India* [1986] QB 1114, Slade LJ considered that the Registrar at Companies House had certain functions entrusted to him by Parliament in issuing the conclusivity certificate. The registrar would be required to ask himself a number of questions (being a mixture of fact and law) before issuing the certificate. This could include the true date for creation of the charge. The registrar would be required to answer this question to the best of his ability for the purpose of determining whether or not the charge was eligible for registration. The registrar was also required to consider some special cases before issuing the certificate. First, where a purported certificate given by the registrar under s 869 of the CA 2006 disclosed an error on the face of it. In such situation, the registrar may not be able to correct the error. The second special situation might arise where the certificate had been obtained by fraud. Even in that case a direct attack on the certificate would, at least prima facie, be ruled out (see *Re Eric Holmes (Property) Ltd* [1965] Ch 1052, 1072 per Pennycuick J) though the court may act in personam against the fraudulent party so as to prevent him taking advantage of the fraudulently obtained certificate (see, for example, *Lazarus Estates Ltd v Beasley* [1956] 1 QB 702); and, furthermore, a creditor personally damaged by the fraud might be able to take proceedings for damages: see *Re C L Nye Ltd* [1971] Ch 442, 474, per Russell LJ.

The register kept in pursuance of s 869 must be open to inspection by any person: CA 2006, s 869(7).

The period allowed for registration

32.26 The period allowed for registration of a charge created by a company is:

(a) 21 days beginning with the day after the day on which the charge is created; or

(b) if the charge is created outside the UK, 21 days beginning with the day after the day on which the instrument by which the charge is created or evidenced (or a copy of it) could, in due course of post (and if despatched with due diligence) have been received in the UK: CA 2006, s 870(1).

32.27 The period allowed for registration of a charge to which property acquired by a company is subject is:

(a) 21 days beginning with the day after the day on which the acquisition is completed; or

(b) if the property is situated and the charge was created outside the UK, 21 days beginning with the day after the day on which the instrument by which the charge is created or evidenced (or a copy of it) could, in due course of post (and if dispatched with due diligence) have been received in the UK: CA 2006, s 870(2).

The period allowed for registration of particulars of a series of debentures as a result of s 863 is if there is a deed containing the charge mentioned in s 863(1), 21 days beginning with the day after the day on which that deed is executed, or if there is no such deed, 21 days beginning with the day after the day on which the first debenture of the series is executed: CA 2006, s 870(3).

Registration of enforcement of security

32.28 If a person obtains an order for the appointment of a receiver or manager of a company's property, or appoints such a receiver or manager under powers contained in an instrument, he shall within seven days of the order or of the appointment under those powers, give notice of the fact to the registrar: CA 2006, s 871(1).

Where a person appointed receiver or manager of a company's property under powers contained in an instrument ceases to act as such receiver or manager, he shall, on so ceasing, give the registrar notice to that effect: CA 2006, s 871(2).

The registrar must enter a fact of which he is given notice under this section in the register of charges: CA 2006, s 871(3).

A person who makes default in complying with the requirements of s 871 commits an offence: CA 2006, s 871(4). A person guilty of an offence under this section is liable on summary conviction to a fine not exceeding level 3 on the standard scale and, for continued contravention, a daily default fine not exceeding one-tenth of level 3 on the standard scale: CA 2006, s 871(5).

Entries of satisfaction and release

32.29 Section 872(2) applies if a statement is delivered to the registrar verifying with respect to a registered charge:

(a) that the debt for which the charge was given has been paid or satisfied in whole or in part; or

(b) that part of the property or undertaking charged has been released from the charge or has ceased to form part of the company's property or undertaking: CA 2006, s 872(1).

The registrar may enter on the register a memorandum of satisfaction in whole or in part, or of the fact part of the property or undertaking has been released from the charge or has ceased to form part of the company's property or undertaking (as the case may be): CA 2006, s 872(2).

Where the registrar enters a memorandum of satisfaction in whole, the registrar shall if required send the company a copy of it: CA 2006, s 872(3).

Rectification of register of charges

32.30 Section 873 states that s 873(2) applies if the court is satisfied:

(a) that the failure to register a charge before the end of the period allowed for registration, or the omission or mis-statement of any particular with respect to any such charge or in a memorandum of satisfaction:

  (i) was accidental or due to inadvertence or to some other sufficient cause; or

  (ii) is not of a nature to prejudice the position of creditors or shareholders of the company; or

(b) that on other grounds it is just and equitable to grant relief: CA 2006, s 873(1).

32.31 The court may, on the application of the company or a person interested and on such terms and conditions as seem to the court just and expedient, order that the period allowed for registration shall be extended or, as the case may be, that the omission or mis-statement shall be rectified: CA 2006, s 873(2). The court requires the applicant, however, to act quickly in effecting the charge: *Re Teleomatic Ltd* [1994] 1 BCLC 30. In respect of omissions or mis-statements, the court does not have power to remove an entry nor the removal of information volunteered by the company which was not required to be provided: *Exeter Trust Ltd v Screenways Ltd* [1991] BCLC 888; and *Igroup Ltd v Ocwen* [2004] 1 WLR 451.

This is a discretionary power which the courts may exercise and full details must be provided as to the reasons for non-registration or as to mistaken registration and not merely that it was due to inadvertence. In *Re Kris Cruisers Ltd* [1949] Ch 138, the court stated that the term 'some other sufficient cause' were words which would be satisfied if it were proved that the secretary of a company had been wrongly advised by his solicitor or counsel that registration need not be sought. Vaisey J considered this section to be 'a benevolent section in this sense, that it appears to give the mortgagee or the chargee a complete and unfettered opportunity for repentance and really to place him in the same position exactly as if he had been careful and not careless, diligent and not negligent'.

The court also considered other grounds where it would be 'just and equitable to grant relief'. This arose in *Re Braemar Investments Limited* [1989] Ch 54. These include situations where on quickly learning of the failure to register, the charge is registered but the overriding consideration is whether it is just and equitable to extend the period for registration (per Hoffmann J).

32.32 The power of rectification given to the court includes the correction of certain omissions or misstatements. The court does not have power to delete the whole registration: *Exeter Trust Ltd v Screenways Ltd* [1991] BCLC 888 (per Nourse LJ).

Normally, the court will not make an order for rectification once liquidation commences or the company is insolvent: *Re s Abrahams and Sons* [1902] 1 Ch 695; and *Re Ashpurton Estates Ltd* [1983] Ch 110. However, in exceptional circumstances, the court may grant such an order: *Barclays Bank plc v Stuart London Ltd* [2001] 2 BCLC 316; and *RM Arnold & Co Ltd* [1984] BCLC 535.

The power of rectification was limited to correcting mistakes or omissions

In *Igroup Ltd v Owen* [2004] 2 BCLC 61, Lightman J stated that the power of rectification granted to the court was limited to correcting mistakes of omission or commission in the entry of any particulars with respect to a mortgage or charge or in a memorandum of satisfaction made by the registrar on the register of charges maintained by the registrar under the Companies Acts. It did not extend to mistakes otherwise than in a particular entered on the register, and accordingly did not extend to the information particulars entered on prescribed mortgage or charge forms submitted to Companies House by an applicant. Accordingly, the court had no power to grant the relief claimed . Nor did the court have any inherent power of rectification since there was binding authority that such a power was wholly inconsistent with the limited statutory jurisdiction to order rectification under the Companies Acts.

Avoidance of certain charges

Consequence of failure to register charges created by a company

32.33 If a company creates a charge to which s 860 applies, the charge is void (so far as any security on the company's property or undertaking is conferred by it) against:

(a) a liquidator of the company;

(b) an administrator of the company; and

(c) a creditor of the company,

unless that section is complied with: CA 2006, s 874(1).

In *Smith v Bridgend County Borough Council* [2002] 1 AC 336, the Supreme Court held that the term 'void against the liquidator', meant void against a company acting by its liquidator.

32.34 If a creditor has a registered charge which is subject to an unregistered charge, that creditor has a priority to the unregistered charge regardless of whether the company is in liquidation or administration and even where he had knowledge that the unregistered charge existed: *Re Monolithic Building Co* [1915] 1 Ch 643.

Section 874(1) is subject to the provisions of Ch 1 to Pt 25: CA 2006, s 874(2).

Section 874(1) is without prejudice to any contract or obligation for repayment of the money secured by the charge; when a charge becomes void under this section, the money secured by it immediately becomes payable: CA 2006, s 874(3).

Companies' records and registers

Companies to keep copies of instruments creating charges

32.35 A company must keep available for inspection a copy of every instrument creating a charge requiring registration under Pt 25, Ch 1, including any document delivered to the company under s 868(3)(b) (Northern Ireland: Orders imposing charges affecting land): CA 2006, s 875(1).

In the case of a series of uniform debentures, a copy of one of the debentures of the series is sufficient: CA 2006, s 875(2).

Company's register of charges

32.36 Every limited company must keep available for inspection a register of charges and enter in it:

(a) all charges specifically affecting property of the company; and

(b) all floating charges on the whole or part of the company's property or undertaking: CA 2006, s 876(1).

The entry shall, in each case, give a short description of the property charged, the amount of the charge and, except in the cases of securities to bearer, the names of the persons entitled to it: CA 2006, s 876(2).

If an officer of the company knowingly and wilfully authorises or permits the omission of an entry required to be made in pursuance of s 876, he commits an offence: CA 2006, s 876(3). A person guilty of an offence under this section will be liable on conviction on indictment, to a fine; on summary conviction, to a fine not exceeding the statutory maximum: CA 2006, s 876(4).

Instruments creating charges and register of charges to be available for inspection

32.37 Section 877 applies to:

(a) documents required to be kept available for inspection under s 875 (copies of instruments creating charges); and

(b) a company's register of charges kept in pursuance of s 876: CA 2006, s 877(1).

The documents and register must be kept available for inspection at the company's registered office, or at a place specified in regulations under s 1136: CA 2006, s 877(2).

The company must give notice to the registrar of the place at which the documents and register are kept available for inspection, and of any change in that place, unless they have at all times been kept at the company's registered office: CA 2006, s 877(3).

The documents and register shall be open to the inspection of any creditor or member of the company without charge, and of any other person on payment of such fee as may be prescribed: CA 2006, s 877(4).

32.38 If default is made for 14 days in complying with s 877(3) or an inspection required under s 877(4) is refused, an offence is committed by the company, and every officer of the company who is in default: CA 2006, s 877(5). A person guilty of an offence under this section will be liable on summary conviction to a fine not exceeding level 3 on the standard scale and, for continued contravention, a daily default fine not exceeding one-tenth of level 3 on the standard scale: CA 2006, s 877(6).

If an inspection required under s 877(4) is refused, the court may, by order, compel an immediate inspection: CA 2006, s 877(7).

Companies registered in Scotland

32.39 Chapter 2 to Pt 25 is concerned with companies registered in Scotland.

Charges requiring registration

32.40 Charges created by a company

A company that creates a charge to which s 878 applies must deliver the prescribed particulars of the charge, together with a copy certified as a correct copy of the instrument (if any) by which the charge is created or evidenced, to the registrar for registration before the end of the period allowed for registration: CA 2006, s 878(1). Registration of a charge to which this section applies may instead be effected on the application of a person interested in it: CA 2006, s 878(2).

Where registration is effected on the application of some person other than the company, that person is entitled to recover from the company the amount of any fees properly paid by him to the registrar on the registration: CA 2006, s 878(3).

32.41 If a company fails to comply with s 878(1), an offence is committed by the company, and every officer of the company who is in default: CA 2006, s 878(4). A person guilty of an offence under this section will be liable on conviction on indictment, to a fine; on summary conviction, to a fine not exceeding the statutory maximum: CA 2006, s 878(5).

Section 878(4) does not apply if registration of the charge has been effected on the application of some other person: CA 2006, s 878(6).

Section 878 applies to the following charges:

(a) a charge on land or any interest in such land, other than a charge for any rent or other periodical sum payable in respect of the land;

(b) a security over incorporeal moveable property of any of the following categories:

  (i) goodwill;

  (ii) a patent or a licence under a patent;

  (iii) a trademark;

  (iv) a copyright or a licence under a copyright;

  (v) a registered design or a licence in respect of such a design;

  (vi) a design right or a licence under a design right;

  (vii) the book debts (whether book debts of the company or assigned to it); and

  (viii) uncalled share capital of the company or calls made but not paid,

(c) a security over a ship or aircraft or any share in a ship; and

(d) a floating charge: CA 2006, s 878(7).

Charges which have to be registered: supplementary

32.42 A charge on land, for the purposes of s 878(7)(a) includes a charge created by a heritable security within the meaning of s 9(8) of the Conveyancing and Feudal Reform (Scotland) Act 1970 (c 35): CA 2006, s 879(1).

The holding of debentures entitling the holder to a charge on land is not, for the purposes of s 878(7)(a), deemed to be an interest in land: CA 2006, s 879(2).

It is immaterial for the purposes of Ch 2 to Pt 25 where land subject to a charge is situated: CA 2006, s 879(3).

32.43 The deposit by way of security of a negotiable instrument given to secure the payment of book debts is not, for the purposes of s 878(7)(b)(vii), to be treated as a charge on those book debts: CA 2006, s 879(4).

The references in Ch 2 to Pt 25 to the date of the creation of a charge are, in the case of a floating charge, the date on which the instrument creating the floating charge was executed by the company creating the charge and in any other case, the date on which the right of the person entitled to the benefit of the charge was constituted as a real right: CA 2006, s 879(5).

In Ch 2, the term 'company' means an incorporated company registered in Scotland: CA 2006, s 879(3).

Duty to register charges existing on property acquired

32.44 Section 880 states that s 880(2) applies where a company acquires any property which is subject to a charge of any kind as would, if it had been created by the company after the acquisition of the property, have been required to be registered under Pt 25, Ch 2: CA 2006, s 880(1).

The company must deliver the prescribed particulars of the charge, together with a copy (certified to be a correct copy) of the instrument (if any) by which the charge was created or is evidenced, to the registrar for registration before the end of the period allowed for registration: CA 2006, s 880(2).

If default is made in complying with s 880, an offence is committed by the company and every officer of it who is in default: CA 2006, s 880(3). A person guilty of an offence under this section is liable on conviction on indictment, to a fine; on summary conviction, to a fine not exceeding the statutory maximum: CA 2006, s 880(4).

Charge by way of ex facie absolute disposition, etc

32.45 Section 881 states that for the avoidance of doubt, it is hereby declared that, in the case of a charge created by way of an *ex facie* absolute disposition or assignation qualified by a back letter or other agreement, or by a standard security qualified by an agreement, compliance with s 878(1) does not of itself render the charge unavailable as security for indebtedness incurred after the date of compliance: CA 2006, s 881(1).

Where the amount secured by a charge so created is purported to be increased by a further back letter or agreement, a further charge is held to have been created by the *ex facie* absolute disposition or assignation or (as the case may be) by the standard security, as qualified by the further back letter or agreement: CA 2006, s 881(2).

In that case, the provisions of Ch 2 to Pt 25 apply to the further charge as if references in this Chapter (other than in s 881) to a charge were references to the further charge and references to the date of the creation of a charge were references to the date on which the further back letter or agreement was executed: CA 2006, s 881(3).

Special rules about debentures

Charge in series of debentures

32.46 Where a series of debentures containing, or giving by reference to any other instrument, any charge to the benefit of which the debenture holders of that series are entitled *pari passu*, is created by a company, it is sufficient for purposes of s 878 if the required particulars, together with a copy of the deed containing the charge (or, if there is no such deed, of one of the debentures of the series) are delivered to the registrar before the end of the period allowed for registration: CA 2006, s 882(1).

The following are the required particulars:

(a) the total amount secured by the whole series;

(b) the dates of the resolutions authorising the issue of the series and the date of the covering deed (if any) by which the security is created or defined;

(c) a general description of the property charged;

(d) the names of the trustees (if any) for the debenture holders; and

(e) in the case of a floating charge, a statement of any provisions of the charge and of any instrument relating to it which prohibit or restrict or regulate the power of the company to grant further securities ranking in priority to, or *pari passu* with, the floating charge, or which vary or otherwise regulate the order of ranking of the floating charge in relation to subsisting securities: CA 2006, s 882(2).

Where more than one issue is made of debentures in the series, particulars of the date and amount of each issue of debentures of the series must be sent to the registrar for entry in the register of charges: CA 2006, s 882(3).

32.47 Failure to comply with s 882(3) does not affect the validity of any of those debentures: CA 2006, s 882(4).

Section 878(2)–(6) applies for the purposes of s 882 as it applies for the purposes of that section, but as if a reference to the registration of the series of debentures has been substituted for the reference to the registration of the charge: CA 2006, s 882(5).

Additional registration requirement for commission etc in relation to debentures

32.48 Where any commission, allowance or discount has been paid or made either directly or indirectly by a company to a person in consideration of his subscribing or agreeing to subscribe, whether absolutely or conditionally, for debentures in a company, or procuring or agreeing to procure subscriptions, whether absolute or conditional, for such debentures, the particulars required to be sent for registration under s 878 must include particulars as to the amount or rate per cent of the commission, discount or allowance so paid or made: CA 2006, s 883(1).

The deposit of debentures as security for a debt of the company is not, for the purposes of s 883, treated as the issue of debentures at a discount: CA 2006, s 883(2). Failure to comply with this section does not affect the validity of the debentures issued: CA 2006, s 883(3).

Charges on property outside the UK

32.49 Where a charge is created in the UK but comprises property outside the UK, a copy of the instrument creating or purporting to create the charge may be sent for registration under s 878 even if further proceedings may be necessary to make the charge valid or effectual according to the law of the country in which the property is situated: CA 2006, s 884.

The register of charges

Register of charges to be kept by registrar

32.50 The registrar must keep, with respect to each company, a register of all the charges requiring registration under Pt 25, Ch 2: CA 2006, s 885(1).

In the case of a charge to the benefit of which holders of a series of debentures are entitled, the registrar shall enter in the register the required particulars specified in s 882(2): CA 2006, s 885(2).

32.51 In the case of any other charge, the registrar must enter in the register the following particulars:

(a) if it is a charge created by a company, the date of its creation and, if it is a charge which was existing on property acquired by the company, the date of the acquisition;

(b) the amount secured by the charge;

(c) short particulars of the property charged;

(d) the persons entitled to the charge; and

(e) in the case of a floating charge, a statement of any of the provisions of the charge and of any instrument relating to it which prohibit, restrict or regulate the company's power to grant further securities ranking in priority to, or *pari passu* with, the floating charge, or which vary or otherwise regulate the order of ranking of the floating charge in relation to subsisting securities: CA 2006, s 885(3).

32.52 The registrar must give a certificate of the registration of any charge registered in pursuance of Ch 2 to Pt 25, stating the name of the company and the person first-named in the charge among those entitled to the benefit of the charge (or, in the case of a series of debentures, the name of the holder of the first such debenture issued) and the amount secured by the charge: CA 2006, s 885(4).

The certificate must be signed by the registrar or authenticated by the registrar's official seal. This is conclusive evidence that the requirements of Ch 2 to Pt 25 as to registration have been satisfied: CA 2006, s 885(5). The register kept in pursuance of s 885 must be open to inspection by any individual: CA 2006, s 885(6).

The period allowed for registration

32.53 The period allowed for registration of a charge created by a company is 21 days beginning with the day after the day on which the charge is created, or if the charge is created outside the UK, 21 days beginning with the day after the day on which a copy of the instrument by which the charge is created or evidenced could, in due course of post (and if despatched with due diligence) have been received in the UK: CA 2006, s 886(1).

The period allowed for registration of a charge to which property acquired by a company is subject is 21 days beginning with the day after the day on which the transaction is settled. If the property is situated and the charge was created outside the UK, this is 21 days beginning with the day after the day on which a copy of the instrument by which the charge is created or evidenced could, in due course of post (and if despatched with due diligence) have been received in the UK: CA 2006, s 886(2).

The period allowed for registration of particulars of a series of debentures as a result of s 882 is if there is a deed containing the charge mentioned in s 882(1), 21 days beginning with the day after the day on which that deed is executed, or if there is no such deed, 21 days beginning with the day after the day on which the first debenture of the series is executed: CA 2006, s 886(2).

Entries of satisfaction and relief

32.54 Section 887 states that s 887(2) applies if a statement is delivered to the registrar verifying (with respect to any registered charge) that the debt for which the charge was given has been paid or satisfied in whole or in part, or that part of the property charged has been released from the charge or has ceased to form part of the company's property: CA 2006, s 887(1).

If the charge is a floating charge, the statement must be accompanied by either (a) a statement by the creditor entitled to the benefit of the charge, or a person authorised by him for the purpose, verifying that the statement mentioned in s 887(1) is correct; or (b) a direction obtained from the court, on the ground that the statement by the creditor mentioned in paragraph (a) could not be readily obtained, dispensing with the need for that statement: CA 2006, s 887(2).

32.55 The registrar may enter on the register a memorandum of satisfaction (in whole or in part) regarding the fact contained in the statement mentioned in s 887(1): CA 2006, s 887(3).

Where the registrar enters a memorandum of satisfaction in whole, he shall, if required, furnish the company with a copy of the memorandum: CA 2006, s 887(4).

Nothing in s 887 requires the company to submit particulars with respect to the entry in the register of a memorandum of satisfaction where the company, having created a floating charge over all or any part of its property, disposes of part of the property subject to the floating charge: CA 2006, s 887(5).

Rectification of register of charges

32.56 Section 888 states that s 888(2) applies if the court is satisfied:

(a) that the failure to register a charge before the end of the period allowed for registration, or the omission or mis-statement of any particular with respect to any such charge or in a memorandum of satisfaction:

(i) was accidental or due to inadvertence or to some other sufficient cause; or

(ii) is not of a nature to prejudice the position of creditors or shareholders of the company, or

(b) that on other grounds it is just and equitable to grant relief: CA 2006, s 888(1).

The court may, on the application of the company or a person interested, and on such terms and conditions as seem to the court just and expedient, order that the period allowed for registration shall be extended or, as the case may be, that the omission or mis-statement shall be rectified: CA 2006, s 888(2).

Avoidance of certain charges

Charges void unless registered

32.57 If a company creates a charge to which CA 2006, s 878 applies, the charge is void (so far as any security on the company's property or any part of it is conferred by the charge) against:

(a) the liquidator of the company;

(b) an administrator of the company; and

(c) any creditor of the company unless that section is complied with: CA 2006, s 889(1).

Section 889(1) is without prejudice to any contract or obligation for repayment of the money secured by the charge; and when a charge becomes void under s 889 the money secured by it immediately becomes payable: CA 2006, s 889(2).

Companies' records and registers

Copies of instruments creating charges to be kept by company

32.58 Every company must cause a copy of every instrument creating a charge requiring registration under Pt 25, Ch 2 to be kept available for inspection: CA 2006, s 890(1).

In the case of a series of uniform debentures, a copy of one debenture of the series is sufficient: CA 2006, s 890(2).

Company's register of charges

32.59 Every company must keep available for inspection a register of charges and enter in it all charges specifically affecting property of the company, and all floating charges on any property of the company: CA 2006, s 891(1).

There shall be given in each case a short description of the property charged, the amount of the charge and, except in the case of securities to bearer, the names of the persons entitled to it: CA 2006, s 891(2).

If an officer of the company knowingly and wilfully authorises or permits the omission of an entry required to be made in pursuance of s 891, he commits an offence: CA 2006, s 891(3). A person guilty of an offence under this section will be liable on conviction on indictment to a fine and on summary conviction, to a fine not exceeding the statutory maximum: CA 2006, s 891(4).

Instruments creating charges and register of charges to be available for inspection

32.60 Section 892 applies to documents required to be kept available for inspection under s 890 (copies of instruments creating charges) and a company's register of charges kept in pursuance of s 891: CA 2006, s 892(1).

The documents and register must be kept available for inspection at the company's registered office, or at a place specified in regulations under s 1136: CA 2006, s 892(2).

The company must give notice to the registrar of the place at which the documents and register are kept available for inspection, and of any change in that place, unless they have at all times been kept at the company's registered office: CA 2006, s 892(3).

The documents and register shall be open to the inspection of any creditor or member of the company without charge and of any other person on payment of such fee as may be prescribed: CA 2006, s 892(4).

32.61 If default is made for 14 days in complying with s 892(3) or an inspection required under s 892(4) is refused, an offence is committed by the company and every officer of the company who is in default: CA 2006, s 892(5). A person guilty of an offence under this section will be liable on summary conviction to a fine not exceeding level 3 on the standard scale and, for continued contravention, a daily default fine not exceeding one-tenth of level 3 on the standard scale: CA 2006, s 892(6).

If an inspection required under s 892(4) is refused, the court may by order compel an immediate inspection: CA 2006, s 892(7).

Powers of the Secretary of State

32.62 Chapter 3 to Pt 25 sets out the powers of the Secretary of State in respect of company charges.

Power to make provision for effect of registration in special register

32.63 Under s 893, the term a 'special register' means a register, other than the register of charges kept under Pt 25, in which a charge to which Ch 1 or Ch 2 to Pt 25 applies is required or authorised to be registered: CA 2006, s 893(1).

The Secretary of State may by order make provision for facilitating the making of information-sharing arrangements between the person responsible for maintaining a special register ('the responsible person') and the registrar that meet the requirement in s 893(4). 'Information-sharing arrangements' are arrangements to share and make use of information held by the registrar or by the responsible person: CA 2006, s 893(2).

32.64 If the Secretary of State is satisfied that appropriate information-sharing arrangements have been made, he may by order provide that:

(a) the registrar is authorised not to register a charge of a specified description under Ch 1 or Ch 2 to Pt 25;

(b) a charge of a specified description that is registered in the special register within a specified period is to be treated as if it had been registered (and certified by the registrar as registered) in accordance with the requirements of Ch 1 or, as the case may be, Ch 2 to Pt 25; and

(c) the other provisions of Ch 1 or, as the case may be, Ch 2 to Pt 25 apply to a charge so treated with specified modifications: CA 2006, s 893(3).

The information-sharing arrangements must ensure that persons inspecting the register of charges are made aware, in a manner appropriate to the inspection, of the existence of charges in the special register which are treated in accordance with provision so made, and are able to obtain information from the special register about any such charge: CA 2006, s 893(4).

32.65 An order under s 893 may:

(a) modify any enactment or rule of law which would otherwise restrict or prevent the responsible person from entering into or giving effect to information-sharing arrangements;

(b) authorise the responsible person to require information to be provided to him for the purposes of the arrangements;

(c) make provision about:

(i) the charging by the responsible person of fees in connection with the arrangements and the destination of such fees (including provision modifying any enactment which would otherwise apply in relation to fees payable to the responsible person); and

(ii) the making of payments under the arrangements by the registrar to the responsible person; and

(d) require the registrar to make copies of the arrangements available to the public (in hard copy or electronic form): CA 2006, s 893(5).

The term 'specified' means specified in an order under this section: CA 2006, s 893(6).

32.66 A description of the charge may be specified, in particular, by reference to one or more of the following:

(a) the type of company by which it is created;

(b) the form of charge;

(c) the description of assets over which it is granted;

(d) the length of the period between the date of its registration in the special register and the date of its creation: CA 2006, s 893(7).

Provision may be made under s 893 relating to registers maintained under the law of a country or territory outside the United Kingdom: CA 2006, s 893(8). This section therefore gives power for the Secretary of State to make an order providing that, if a charge is registered in another register (eg the register of floating charges under the Bankruptcy and Diligence etc (Scotland) Act 2007), then the registrar may not register it, but it will be treated as if it had been registered in accordance with the requirements of Pt 25. The power may only be exercised if appropriate information-sharing arrangements have been made between the registrar and the person responsible for the other register. This is to ensure that a person searching the register will have access to information about charges registered in that other register.

General power to make amendments to Pt 25

32.67 Under s 894, the Secretary of State may by regulations amend Pt 25 by altering, adding or repealing provisions, make consequential amendments or repeals in this Act or any other enactment (whether passed or made before or after this Act): CA 2006, s 894(1).

Checklist – board approval to a charge

32.68 *This checklist provides procedural aspects for approval to a charge by the company's Board of Directors. This checklist should be adapted depending on the company's articles of associations on procedural aspects.*

No	Issue	Reference
1	Consider the type of charge that is being created and the terms of the charge (including negative pledge clauses and crystallisation).	CA 2006, s 860
2	The essential characteristic of a floating charge is its ability for flexibility and freedom of movement of assets.	*Re Spectrum Plus Limited* [2005] 2 BCLC 269
3	Prepare an Agenda for the Board Meeting.	Agenda
4	Call a Board meeting – on reasonable notice setting out date, time and place of meeting.	Notice
5	Consider if Board Meeting may be dispensed with by a written resolution procedure?	Written resolution
6	Directors to declare any interest in the charge.	CA 2006, ss 177, 182
7	Ensure quorum present and consider whether Chairman has a casting vote in the event of a deadlock.	
8	Directors vote on a show of hands by simple majority to approve the charge.	
9	Prepare minutes of the Board meeting.	Minutes
10	Lodge the charge at Companies House using prescribed form and fee.	
11	Obtain certificate of registration from Registrar.	
12	Update register of charges/director's interests.	Statutory register

Companies House prescribed mortgage forms

32.69

Mortgage No	*Type of charge*	*Fee*	*CA 2006 reference*
MR01	Particulars of a charge	£13	859A and 859J
MR02	Particulars of a charge subject to which property or undertaking has been acquired	£13	859C and 859J
MR03	Particulars for the registration of a charge to secure a series of debentures	£13	859B and 859J
MR06	Statement of company acting as a trustee		859J
MR08	Particulars of a charge where there is no instrument	£13	859A and 859J
MR09	Particulars of a charge subject to which property or undertaking has been acquired where there is no instrument	£13	859C and 859J
MR10	Particulars for the registration of a charge to secure a series of debentures where there is no instrument	£13	859B and 859J

Definitions

32.70

The 1981 Order:	The Judgments Enforcement (Northern Ireland) Order 1981, SI 1981/226 (NI 6).
Registrar of Deeds:	The registrar appointed under the Registration of Deeds Act (Northern Ireland) 1970 (c 25).
Registry of Deeds:	Has the same meaning as in the Registration of Deeds Acts.
Registration of Deeds Acts:	The Registration of Deeds Act (Northern Ireland) 1970 and every statutory provision for the time being in force amending that Act or otherwise relating to the registry of deeds, or the registration of deeds, orders or other instruments or documents in such registry.
Land Registry and the Registrar of Titles:	These are to be construed in accordance with s 1 of the Land Registration Act (Northern Ireland) 1970 (c 18).
Registered land and Unregistered land:	Has the same meaning as in Pt 3 of the Land Registration Act (Northern Ireland) 1970.

33 Dissolution and restoration to the register

Contents

Introduction

33.1 Part 31 of the CA 2006 addresses dissolution and restoration to the register of a company. It comprises three chapters. Chapter 1 is concerned with striking off, the registrar's power to strike off a defunct company as well as voluntary striking off. Chapter 2 addresses what happens to the property of a dissolved company including vesting as *bona vacantia* and effect of Crown disclaimer. Chapter 3 contains provisions on restoration to the register including administrative restoration to the register, and restoration to the register by the court. This Chapter also takes account of the changes under the SBEEA 2015, on administrative aspects of restoration or by the court, of a company with bearer share warrants in issue at the time of strike-off or dissolution.

This chapter addresses the following issues:

- the procedure for striking off a company from the register;
- how the concept of voluntary striking off operates;
- the position regarding property of the dissolved company; and
- the different forms of restoration and the effect of restoration.

Dissolution and restoration to the register – striking off

33.2 Chapter 1 is concerned with striking off. It examines the registrar's role in striking off a defunct company as well as voluntary striking off. In practice, this can be a useful mechanism for the Registrar to remove the company from the list of companies maintained at Companies House, and allows for a speedier process from an administrative viewpoint rather than for companies to proceed towards liquidation, which may take time including costs involved. The registrar's power to strike off a company gives the company an opportunity to file its accounts and rectify its filing obligations with Companies House.

Registrar's power to strike off a defunct company

Power to strike off a company not carrying on business or in operation

33.3 This provision gives the registrar power to effect an accelerated procedure for striking off defunct companies. If the registrar has reasonable cause to believe that a company is not carrying on business or is not in operation, the registrar may send a letter to the company inquiring whether it is carrying on business or is in operation: CA 2006, s 1000(1).

There is no statutory definition of 'not carrying on business' or 'in operation'. In practice, the registrar may take into account all facts and circumstances including failure to lodge accounts or to respond to letters or failure by the company to communicate with the registrar in response to any requests made the by the registrar. The registrar may take this view if, for example:

- he has not received documents from a company that should have sent them to him
- mail that the registrar has sent to a company's registered office is returned undelivered
- the company has no directors.

33.4 Before striking the company off the register, the registrar is required to write two formal letters and send notice to the company's registered office to ascertain whether the company is still carrying on business or in operation.

If the registrar does not within 14 days of sending the letter receive any answer, the registrar must, within 14 days after the expiration of that period, send to the company by post a registered letter referring to the first letter, and stating:

(a) that no answer to it has been received; and

(b) that if an answer is not received to the second letter within 14 days from its date, a notice will be published in the *Gazette* with a view to striking the company's name off the register: CA 2006, s 1000(2) (as inserted by the SBEEA 2015, s 103(2)(a)).

33.5 If the registrar receives an answer to the effect that the company is not carrying on business or in operation, or does not within 14 days after sending the second letter receive any answer, the registrar may publish in the *Gazette*, and send to the company by post, a notice that at the expiration of two months from the date of the notice the name of the company mentioned in it will, unless cause is shown to the contrary, be struck off the register and the company will be dissolved: CA 2006, s 1000(3) (as inserted by the SBEEA 2015, s 103(2)(b)).

At the expiration of the time mentioned in the notice the registrar may, unless cause to the contrary is previously shown by the company, strike its name off the register: CA 2006, s 1000(4).

The registrar must publish a notice in the *Gazette* stating that the company's name has been struck off the register: CA 2006, s 1000(5).

On the publication of the notice in the *Gazette*, the company is dissolved.

33.6 However, the liability (if any) of every director, managing officer and member of the company continues and may be enforced as if the company had not been dissolved. Nothing in s 1000 affects the power of the court to wind up a company which has been struck off the register: CA 2006, s 1000(7).

It is, therefore, advisable for the company's officers to promptly reply to any formal inquiry by the Registrar and deliver any outstanding documents at Companies House.

As to the application to LLPs, see the Limited Liability Partnerships (Application of Companies Act 2006) Regulations 2009, SI 2009/1804, as amended by the Companies and Limited Liability Partnerships (Filing Requirements) Regulations 2015, SI 2015/1695.

Duty to act in case of the company being wound up

33.7 Section 1001 applies to situations where there is a duty to act in case of a company being wound up. If, in such circumstances:

(a) the registrar has reasonable cause to believe:

 (i) that no liquidator is acting; or

 (ii) that the affairs of the company are fully wound up; and

(b) the returns required to be made by the liquidator have not been made for a period of six consecutive months,

the registrar must publish in the *Gazette* and send to the company or the liquidator (if any) a notice that at the expiration of two months from the date of the notice the name of the company mentioned in it will, unless cause is shown to the contrary, be struck off the register and the company will be dissolved: CA 2006, s 1001(1) (as inserted by the SBEEA 2015, s 103(3)).

33.8 At the expiration of the time mentioned in the notice the registrar may, unless cause to the contrary is previously shown by the company, strike its name off the register: CA 2006, s 1001(2).

The registrar must publish notice in the *Gazette* of the company's name having been struck off the register: CA 2006, s 1001(3). On the publication of the notice in the *Gazette*, the company is dissolved: CA 2006, s 1001(4).

However, the liability (if any) of every director, managing officer and member in CA 2006, s 1001 affects the power of the court to wind up a company the name of which has been struck off the register: CA 2006, s 1001(5).

Supplementary provisions as to service of letter or notice

33.9 A letter or notice to be sent under ss 1000 or 1001 to a company may be addressed to the company at its registered office or, if no office has been registered, to the care of some officer of the company: CA 2006, s 1002(1).

If there is no officer of the company whose name and address are known to the registrar, the letter or notice may be sent to each of the persons who subscribed the memorandum (if their addresses are known to the registrar): CA 2006, s 1002(2).

A notice to be sent to a liquidator under s 1001 may be addressed to him at his last known place of business: CA 2006, s 1002(3).

Voluntary striking off

Striking off on application by a company

33.10 An alternative to the registrar striking off a company from the register is the voluntary striking off by the company as the applicant. This provides another speedy and effective mechanism to terminate the company's existence, subject to certain procedures being followed.

A company may apply to the registrar to be struck off the register and dissolved. The company can do this if it is no longer needed. For example, the directors may wish to retire and there is no one to take over from them; or it is a subsidiary whose name is no longer needed; or it was set up to exploit an idea that turned out not to be feasible. Some companies who are dormant or non-trading choose to apply for strike off. Where a decision is taken by the company's directors that no longer want to retain the company and wish to have it struck off, the registrar will not normally pursue any outstanding late filing penalties unless the company is restored to the register at a later stage.

This procedure is not an alternative to formal insolvency proceedings where these are appropriate. Even if the company is struck off and dissolved, creditors and others could apply for the company to be restored to the register.

Section 1003 applies to striking off on application by a company, also known as 'voluntary striking off'. On application by a company, the registrar of companies may strike the company's name off the register: CA 2006, s 1003(1).

33.11 The application must be made on the company's behalf by its directors or by a majority of them and must contain the prescribed information: CA 2006, s 1003(2). The applicant must complete Form DS01 'Striking off application by a company'. The form must be signed and dated by:

- the sole director, if there is only one;

- by both, if there are two;
- by all, or the majority of directors, if there are more than two.

The registrar may not strike a company off under s 1003 until after the expiration of two months from the publication by the registrar in the *Gazette* of a notice stating that the registrar may exercise the power under this section in relation to the company and inviting any person to show cause why that should not be done: CA 2006, s 1003(3) (as inserted by the SBEEA 2015, s 103(4)).

33.12 The registrar must publish a notice in the *Gazette* of the company's name having been struck off: CA 2006, s 1003(4). On the publication of the notice in the *Gazette*, the company is dissolved: CA 2006, s 1003(4).

However the liability (if any) of every director, managing officer and member of the company continues and may be enforced as if the company had not been dissolved. Nothing in s 1003 affects the power of the court to wind up a company the name of which has been struck off the register: CA 2006, s 1003(6). Therefore, liability issues are still preserved despite the company no longer existing.

Circumstances in which an application is not to be made: activities of company

33.13 Section 1004 deals with the circumstances in which the application for striking off may not be made.

An application under s 1003 (application for voluntary striking off) on behalf of a company must not be made if, at any time in the previous three months, the company has:

(a) changed its name;

(b) traded or otherwise carried on business;

(c) made a disposal for value of property or rights that, immediately before ceasing to trade or otherwise carry on business, it held for the purpose of disposal for gain in the normal course of trading or otherwise carrying on business; or

(d) engaged in any other activity, except one which is:

  (i) necessary or expedient for the purpose of making an application under that section, or deciding whether to do so;

  (ii) necessary or expedient for the purpose of concluding the affairs of the company;

  (iii) necessary or expedient for the purpose of complying with any statutory requirement; and

  (iv) specified by the Secretary of State by order for the purposes of this sub-para: CA 2006, s 1004(1).

For the purposes of s 1004, a company is not to be treated as trading or otherwise carrying on a business by virtue only of the fact that it makes a payment in respect of a liability incurred in the course of trading or otherwise carrying on business: CA 2006, s 1004(2).

33.14 The Secretary of State may by order amend s 1004(1) for the purpose of altering the period in relation to which the doing of the things mentioned in paras (a)–(d) of that subsection is relevant: CA 2006, s 1004(3). It is an offence for a person to make an application in contravention of this section: CA 2006, s 1004(5). In proceedings for such an offence it is a defence for the accused to prove that he did not know, and could not reasonably have known, of the existence of the facts that led to the contravention: CA 2006, s 1004(6).

A person guilty of an offence under s 1004 will be liable on conviction on indictment, to a fine; and on summary conviction, to a fine not exceeding the statutory maximum: CA 2006, s 1004(7).

Circumstances in which an application is not to be made: other proceedings not concluded

33.15 An application under s 1003 (application for voluntary striking off) on behalf of a company must not be made at a time when:

(a) an application to the court under Pt 26 has been made on behalf of the company for the sanctioning of a compromise or arrangement and the matter has not been finally concluded;

(b) a voluntary arrangement in relation to the company has been proposed under Pt 1 of the Insolvency Act 1986 (c 45) or Pt 2 of the Insolvency (Northern Ireland) Order 1989 (SI 1989 No 2405 (NI 19)) and the matter has not been finally concluded;

(c) the company is in administration under Pt 2 of that Act or Pt 3 of that Order;

(d) para 44 of Sch B1 to that Act or para 45 of Sch B1 to that Order applies (*interim moratorium* on proceedings where an application to the court for an administration order has been made or notice of intention to appoint administrator has been filed);

(e) the company is being wound up under Pt 4 of that Act or Pt 5 of that Order, whether voluntarily or by the court, or a petition under that Part for winding up of the company by the court has been presented and not finally dealt with or withdrawn;

(f) there is a receiver or manager of the company's property; and

(g) the company's estate is being administered by a judicial factor: CA 2006, s 1005(1).

33.16 For the purposes of s 1005(1)(a), the matter is finally concluded if:

(a) the application has been withdrawn;

(b) the application has been finally dealt with without a compromise or arrangement being sanctioned by the court; or

(c) a compromise or arrangement has been sanctioned by the court and has, together with anything required to be done under any provision made in relation to the matter by order of the court, been fully carried out: CA 2006, s 1005(2).

33.17 For the purposes of s 1005(1)(b), the matter is finally concluded if:

(a) no meetings are to be summoned under s 3 of the Insolvency Act 1986 (c 45) or Art 16 of the Insolvency (Northern Ireland) Order 1989;

(b) meetings summoned under that section or article fail to approve the arrangement with no, or the same, modifications;

(c) an arrangement approved by meetings summoned under that section, or in consequence of a direction under s 6(4)(b) of that Act or Art 19(4)(b) of that Order, has been fully implemented; or

(d) the court makes an order under s 6(5) of that Act or Art 19(5) of that Order revoking approval given at previous meetings and, if the court gives any directions under s 6(6) of that Act or Art 19(6) of that Order, the company has done whatever it is required to do under those directions: CA 2006, s 1005(3).

33.18 It is an offence for a person to make an application in contravention of s 1005: CA 2006, s 1005(4). In proceedings for such an offence it is a defence for the accused to prove that he did not know, and could not reasonably have known, of the existence of the facts that led to the contravention: CA 2006, s 1005(6).

A person guilty of an offence under s 1005 will be liable on conviction on indictment, to a fine; and on summary conviction, to a fine not exceeding the statutory maximum: CA 2006, s 1005(6).

Copy of application to be given to members, employees, etc

33.19 The CA 2006 sets out some safeguards for those likely to be affected by a company's dissolution. The persons listed below should be warned before applying, as any of them may object to the company being struck off. A company may notify any other organisation or party who may have an interest in the company's affairs, otherwise they might later object to the application. Examples include Her Majesty's Revenue and Customs, local authorities, especially if the company is under any obligation involving planning permission or health and safety issues, training and enterprise councils and government agencies.

Section 1006 deals with the copy of the application to be given to a certain person.

33.20 A person who makes an application under s 1003 (application for voluntary striking off) on behalf of a company must secure that, within seven days from the day on which the application is made, a copy of it is given to every person who at any time on that day is:

(a) a member of the company;

(b) an employee of the company;

(c) a creditor of the company;

(d) a director of the company;

(e) a manager or trustee of any pension fund established for the benefit of employees of the company; or

(f) a person of a description specified for the purposes of this paragraph by regulations made by the Secretary of State: CA 2006, s 1006(1).

33.21 Section 1006(1) does not require a copy of the application to be given to a director who is a party to the application: CA 2006, s 1006(2).

The duty imposed by s 1006 ceases to apply if the application is withdrawn before the end of the period for giving the copy application: CA 2006, s 1006(3).

A person who fails to perform the duty imposed on him by s 1006 commits an offence. If he does so with the intention of concealing the making of the application from the person concerned, he commits an aggravated offence: CA 2006, s 1006(4).

In proceedings for an offence under s 1006 it is a defence for the accused to prove that he took all reasonable steps to perform the duty: CA 2006, s 1006(5).

33.22 A person guilty of an offence under s 1006 (other than an aggravated offence) is liable on conviction on indictment, to a fine; on summary conviction, to a fine not exceeding the statutory maximum: CA 2006, s 1006(6). A person guilty of an aggravated offence under this section will be liable on conviction on indictment, to imprisonment for a term not exceeding seven years or a fine (or both) and on summary conviction:

(i) in England and Wales, to imprisonment for a term not exceeding 12 months or to a fine not exceeding the statutory maximum (or both); and

(ii) in Scotland or Northern Ireland, to imprisonment for a term not exceeding six months, or to a fine not exceeding the statutory maximum (or both): CA 2006, s 1006(7).

Copy of application to be given to new members, employees, etc

33.23 Section 1007 requires a copy of the application for striking off to be given to new members. It applies any time after the day on which a company makes an application under s 1003 (application for voluntary striking off) and before the day on which the application is finally dealt with or withdrawn: CA 2006, s 1007(1).

A person who is a director of the company at the end of a day on which a person (other than himself) becomes:

(a) a member of the company;

(b) an employee of the company;

(c) a creditor of the company;

(d) a director of the company;

(e) a manager or trustee of any pension fund established for the benefit of employees of the company; or

(f) a person of a description specified for the purposes of this paragraph by regulations made by the Secretary of State,

must secure that a copy of the application is given to that person within seven days from that day: CA 2006, s 1007(2).

The duty imposed by s 1007 ceases to apply if the application is finally dealt with or withdrawn before the end of the period for giving the copy application: CA 2006, s 1007(3).

33.24 A person who fails to perform the duty imposed on him by s 1007 commits an offence. If he does so with the intention of concealing the making of the application from the person concerned, he commits an aggravated offence: CA 2006, s 1007(4).

In proceedings for an offence under s 1007 it is a defence for the accused to prove that at the time of the failure he was not aware of the fact that the company had made an application under s 1003 of the CA 2006, or that he took all reasonable steps to perform the duty: CA 2006, s 1007(5).

A person guilty of an offence under s 1007 (other than an aggravated offence) will be liable on conviction on indictment, to a fine; and on summary conviction, to a fine not exceeding the statutory maximum. A person guilty of an aggravated offence under s 1007 is liable on conviction on indictment, to imprisonment for a term not exceeding seven years or a fine (or both); on summary conviction in England and Wales, to imprisonment for a term not exceeding 12 months or to a fine not exceeding the statutory maximum (or both); in Scotland or Northern Ireland, to imprisonment for a term not exceeding six months, or to a fine not exceeding the statutory maximum (or both): CA 2006, s 1007(6).

Copy of application: provisions as to service of documents

33.25 The following provisions apply for the purposes of s 1006 (copy of application to be given to members, employees, etc), and s 1007 (copy of application to be given to new members, employees, etc): CA 2006, s 1008(1).

A document is treated as having been given to a person if it is delivered to him, left at his proper address or sent by post to him at that address: CA 2006, s 1008(2).

For the purposes of s 1008(2) and s 7 of the Interpretation Act 1978 (c 30) (service of documents by post) as it applies in relation to that subsection, the proper address of a person is:

(a) in the case of a firm incorporated or formed in the UK, its registered or principal office;

(b) in the case of a firm incorporated or formed outside the UK:

  (i) if it has a place of business in the UK, its principal office in the UK; or

  (ii) if it does not have a place of business in the UK, its registered or principal office;

(c) in the case of an individual, his last known address: CA 2006, s 1008(3).

In the case of a creditor of the company, a document is treated as having been given to him if it is left at, or sent by post to the place of business with which the company has had dealings by virtue of which he is a creditor of the company, or if there is more than one such place of business, at each of them: CA 2006, s 1008(4).

Circumstances in which an application is to be withdrawn

33.26 Section 1009 applies where, at any time on or after the day on which a company makes an application under s 1003 (application for voluntary striking off) and before the day on which the application is finally dealt with or withdrawn:

(a) the company:

  (i) changes its name;

  (ii) trades or otherwise carries on business;

  (iii) makes a disposal for value of any property or rights other than those which it was necessary or expedient for it to hold for the purpose of making, or proceeding with, an application under that section; or

  (iv) engages in any activity, except one to which s 1009(4) applies;

(b) an application is made to the court under Pt 26 on behalf of the company for the sanctioning of a compromise or arrangement;

(c) a voluntary arrangement in relation to the company is proposed under Pt 1 of the Insolvency Act 1986 (c 45) or Pt 2 of the Insolvency (Northern Ireland) Order 1989 (SI 1989 No 2405 (NI 19));

(d) an application to the court for an administration order in respect of the company is made under para 12 of Sch B1 to that Act or para 13 of Sch B1 to that Order;

(e) an administrator is appointed in respect of the company under paras 14 or 22 of Sch B1 to that Act, or paras 15 or 23 of Sch B1 to that Order, or a copy of notice of intention to appoint an administrator of the company under any of those provisions is filed with the court;

(f) there arise any of the circumstances in which, under s 84(1) of that Act or Art 70 of that Order, the company may be voluntarily wound up;

(g) a petition is presented for the winding up of the company by the court under Pt 4 of that Act or Pt 5 of that Order;

(h) a receiver or manager of the company's property is appointed; or

(i) a judicial factor is appointed to administer the company's estate: CA 2006, s 1009(1).

33.27 Form DS02 should be used to withdraw the application if directors change their mind or the company ceases to be eligible for striking off. An interested party may object to the dissolution by making objections or complaints in writing to the Registrar with any supporting evidence, such as copies of invoices that may prove that the company is trading. Other reasons could include:

- if the company has broken any of the conditions of its application for example, it has traded, changed its name or become subject to insolvency proceedings during the three-month period before the application, or afterwards
- if the directors have not informed interested parties
- if any of the declarations on the form are false

- if some form of action is being taken, or is pending, to recover any money owed (such as a winding-up petition or action in a small claims court)
- if other legal action is being taken against the company
- if the directors have wrongfully traded or committed a tax fraud or some other offence.

33.28 A person who is a director of the company at the end of a day on which any of the events mentioned in s 1009(1) occurs must secure that the company's application is withdrawn forthwith: CA 2006, s 1009(2).

For the purposes of s 1009(1)(a), a company is not treated as trading or otherwise carrying on business by virtue only of the fact that it makes a payment in respect of a liability incurred in the course of trading or otherwise carrying on business: CA 2006, s 1009(3).

33.29 The excepted activities referred to in s 1009(1)(a)(iv) are:

(a) any activity necessary or expedient for the purposes of:

  (i) making, or proceeding with, an application under s 1003 (application for voluntary striking off);

  (ii) concluding affairs of the company that are outstanding because of what has been necessary or expedient for the purpose of making, or proceeding with, such an application; or

  (iii) complying with any statutory requirement;

(b) any activity specified by the Secretary of State by order for the purposes of this subsection: CA 2006, s 1009(4).

33.30 A person who fails to perform the duty imposed on him by s 1009 commits an offence: CA 2006, s 1009(5). In proceedings for an offence under this section it is a defence for the accused to prove that at the time of the failure he was not aware of the fact that the company had made an application under s 1003, or that he had taken all reasonable steps to perform the duty: CA 2006, s 1009(6). A person guilty of an offence under s 1009 will be liable on conviction on indictment, to a fine; and on summary conviction, to a fine not exceeding the statutory maximum: CA 2006, s 1009(7).

Withdrawal of application

33.31 An application under s 1003 is withdrawn by notice to the registrar: CA 2006, s 1010.

Meaning of 'creditor'

33.32 A 'creditor' is defined as including a contingent or prospective creditor: CA 2006, s 1011.

Property of dissolved company

33.33 Chapter 2 of Pt 31 is concerned with the property of the dissolved company once the company has been struck off.

Property of dissolved company to be bona vacantia

33.34 When a company is dissolved, all property and rights whatsoever vested in or held on trust for the company immediately before its dissolution (including leasehold property, but not including property held by the company on trust for another person) are deemed to be *bona vacantia* and:

(a) accordingly belong to the Crown, or to the Duchy of Lancaster or to the Duke of Cornwall for the time being (as the case may be); and

(b) vest and may be dealt with in the same manner as other *bona vacantia* accruing to the Crown, to the Duchy of Lancaster or to the Duke of Cornwall: CA 2006, s 1012(1).

Section 1012(1) applies subject to the possible restoration of the company to the register under Ch 3 to Pt 31 (see s 1034): CA 2006, s 1012(2).

Therefore, all property, cash and other assets owned by a company when it is dissolved automatically pass to the Crown. However, liabilities do not pass to the Crown on dissolution and they are normally extinguished.

33.35 Dealing with dissolved companies' assets depends on:

- the last registered office address;
- where the asset is situated.

If the company's last registered office and the asset was in England or Wales, but not in the Duchies of Lancaster or Cornwall, its assets are dealt with by the Treasury Solicitor.

If the company's last registered office and the asset was in Scotland its assets are dealt with by the Queen's and Lord Treasurer's Remembrancer.

If the company's last registered office and the asset was in Northern Ireland its assets are dealt with by the Crown Solicitor's Office.

If the company's last registered office and the asset was in the Duchies of Cornwall or Lancaster, its assets fall to be dealt with by the Duchies' solicitors.

The Duchy of Cornwall comprises the County of Cornwall. The Duchy of Lancaster comprises the Counties of Lancashire, Merseyside and parts of Greater Manchester, Cheshire and Cumbria. Further details as to the precise boundaries of the Duchy can be obtained from the Duchy Office.

Duchy Office
1 Lancaster Place
Strand
London WC2E 7ED
Tel: 020 7836 8277

33.36 If the last registered office and the asset are in different jurisdictions, the location of the last registered office will usually determine who deals with the asset.

The asset types include:

- land and interests in land in England and Wales
- bank accounts
- other forms of cash (such as insurance policies, tax refunds or sums paid into court)
- copyrights
- trademarks
- patents and other intellectual property
- the benefit of mortgages where sums are owed to a dissolved company
- the benefit of other assets or agreements that the company entered into

The government's Bona Vacantia Division does not deal with assets which are held by a dissolved company as a trustee for someone else.

33.37 The Treasury Solicitor cannot undertake the following:

- pay the liabilities of dissolved companies
- manage or insure property or assets
- take formal possession of assets before selling them
- sell assets for less than market value
- sell where it is not cost effective to do so
- give any form of title guarantee when selling – the risk of buying a *bona vacantia* asset is with the purchaser
- provide any legal advice
- help resolve problems where there is no value for the Crown or where it would not be cost effective to do so

Crown disclaimer of property vesting as bona vacantia

33.38 Where property vests in the Crown under s 1012, the Crown's title to it under that section may be disclaimed by a notice signed by the Crown representative (ie the Treasury Solicitor or, in relation to property in Scotland, the Queen's and Lord Treasurer's Remembrancer): CA 2006, s 1013(1).

The right to execute a notice of disclaimer under s 1013 may be waived by or on behalf of the Crown either expressly or by taking possession: CA 2006, s 1013(2).

33.39 A notice of disclaimer must be executed within three years after:

(a) the date on which the fact that the property may have vested in the Crown under s 1012 first comes to the notice of the Crown representative; or

(b) if ownership of the property is not established at that date, the end of the period reasonably necessary for the Crown representative to establish the ownership of the property: CA 2006, s 1013(3).

If an application in writing is made to the Crown representative by a person interested in the property requiring him to decide whether he will or will not disclaim, any notice of disclaimer must be executed within 12 months after the making of the application, or such further period as may be allowed by the court: CA 2006, s 1013(4).

33.40 A notice of disclaimer under s 1013 is of no effect if it is shown to have been executed after the end of the period specified by s 1013(3) or (4): CA 2006, s 1013(5). A notice of disclaimer under this section must be delivered to the registrar and retained and registered by him: CA 2006, s 1013(6). Copies of it must be published in the *Gazette* and sent to any persons who have given the Crown representative notice that they claim to be interested in the property: CA 2006, s 1013(7).

Section 1013 applies to property vested in the Duchy of Lancaster or the Duke of Cornwall under s 1012 as if for references to the Crown and the Crown representative there were respectively substituted references to the Duchy of Lancaster and to the Solicitor to that Duchy, or to the Duke of Cornwall and to the Solicitor to the Duchy of Cornwall, as the case may be: CA 2006, s 1013(8).

The Crown, therefore, has a statutory power to disclaim (give up) its interest in *bona vacantia*.

33.41 If Bona Vacantia Division disclaim an asset, it means that a particular asset is treated as never having passed to the Crown as *bona vacantia*. It can disclaim any kind of asset, at any time and without prior notice to anyone. The power to disclaim is frequently used in relation to difficult or problematic land, land which has limited value or where it would not be cost effective to dispose of it.

As soon as Bona Vacantia Division have evidence that an asset has vested in the Crown they will consider whether it should be disclaimed before taking further steps. They will continue to consider whether the asset should be disclaimed as the case progresses.

33.42 The Bona Vacantia Division usually disclaim the following:

- land used in common, such as private roads, service yards, amenity land, or the common parts of an estate or a block of flats;
- property subject to onerous covenants or other potential liabilities;
- property which is contaminated or has buildings, trees, or other items which are in a dangerous state and condition;
- property in negative equity;
- property subject to a dispute or competing claims;
- low value property;
- commercial leases that pass to the Crown as bona vacantia;
- assets which are the subject of dispute or litigation.

If the Bona Vacantia Division decide to disclaim an asset they will issue a notice of disclaimer. A copy of the disclaimer notice will be published in the London Gazette and a copy sent to the Registrar of Companies and anyone who has given Bona Vacantia Division notice that they claim to be interested in the asset. The effect of disclaimer is that the property or asset is deemed not to have vested in the Crown as *bona vacantia*. The Leasehold title is extinguished on disclaimer. If the property disclaimed is freehold land, the freehold title will be extinguished and the property will 'escheat' to the Crown Estate.

Effect of Crown disclaimer

33.43 Where notice of disclaimer is executed under s 1013 as respects any property, that property is deemed not to have vested in the Crown under s 1012: CA 2006, s 1014(1).

The following sections contain provisions as to the effect of the Crown disclaimer:

- ss 1015–1019 apply in relation to property in England and Wales or Northern Ireland; or
- ss 1020–1022 apply in relation to property in Scotland: CA 2006, s 1014(2).

Effect of Crown disclaimer: England and Wales and Northern Ireland

General effect of disclaimer

33.44 The Crown's disclaimer operates so as to terminate, as from the date of the disclaimer, the rights, interests and liabilities of the company in or in respect of the property disclaimed: CA 2006, s 1015(1).

It does not, except so far as is necessary for the purpose of releasing the company from any liability, affect the rights or liabilities of any other person: CA 2006, s 1015(2).

Disclaimer of leaseholds

33.45 The disclaimer of any property of a leasehold character does not take effect unless a copy of the disclaimer has been served (so far as the Crown representative is aware of their addresses) on every person claiming under the company as an underlessee or mortgagee, and either:

(a) no application under s 1017 (power of court to make vesting order) is made with respect to that property before the end of the period of 14 days beginning with the day on which the last notice under this paragraph was served; or

(b) where such an application has been made, the court directs that the disclaimer shall take effect: CA 2006, s 1016(1).

Where the court gives a direction under s 1016(1)(b) it may also, instead of or in addition to any order it makes under s 1017, make such order as it thinks fit with respect to fixtures, tenant's improvements and other matters arising out of the lease: CA 2006, s 1016(2).

33.46 The term 'Crown representative' means:

(a) in relation to property vested in the Duchy of Lancaster, the Solicitor to that Duchy;

(b) in relation to property vested in the Duke of Cornwall, the Solicitor to the Duchy of Cornwall;

(c) in relation to property in Scotland, the Queen's and Lord Treasurer's Remembrancer;

(d) in relation to other property, the Treasury Solicitor: CA 2006, s 1016(3).

Power of the court to make vesting order

33.47 The court may on application by a person who:

(a) claims an interest in the disclaimed property, or

(b) is under a liability in respect of the disclaimed property that is not discharged by the disclaimer,

make an order under s 1017 in respect of the property: CA 2006, s 1017(1).

33.48 An order under s 1017 is an order for the vesting of the disclaimed property in, or its delivery to:

(a) a person entitled to it (or a trustee for such a person); or

(b) a person subject to such a liability as is mentioned in s 1017(1)(b) (or a trustee for such a person): CA 2006, s 1017(2).

An order under s 1017(2)(b) may only be made where it appears to the court that it would be just to do so for the purpose of compensating the person subject to the liability in respect of the disclaimer: CA 2006, s 1017(3). An order under this section may be made on such terms as the court thinks fit: CA 2006, s 1017(4).

On a vesting order being made under s 1017, the property comprised in it vests in the person named in that behalf in the order without conveyance, assignment or transfer: CA 2006, s 1017(5).

Protection of persons holding under a lease

33.49 The court must not make an order under s 1017 vesting property of a leasehold nature in a person claiming under the company as underlessee or mortgagee except on terms making that person:

(a) subject to the same liabilities and obligations as those to which the company was subject under the lease; or

(b) if the court thinks fit, subject to the same liabilities and obligations as if the lease had been assigned to him: CA 2006, s 1018(1).

Where the order relates to only part of the property comprised in the lease, s 1018(1) applies as if the lease had comprised only the property comprised in the vesting order: CA 2006, s 1018(2).

33.50 A person claiming under the company as underlessee or mortgagee who declines to accept a vesting order on such terms is excluded from all interest in the property: CA 2006, s 1018(3).

If there is no person claiming under the company who is willing to accept an order on such terms, the court has power to vest the company's estate and interest in the property in any person who is liable (whether personally or in a representative character and whether alone or jointly with the company) to perform the lessee's covenants in the lease: CA 2006, s 1018(4).

The court may vest that estate and interest in such a person freed and discharged from all estates, encumbrances and interests created by the company: CA 2006, s 1018(5).

Land subject to rentcharge

33.51 Where in consequence of the disclaimer land that is subject to a rentcharge vests in any person, neither he nor his successors in title are subject to any personal liability in respect of sums becoming due under the rentcharge, except sums becoming due after he, or some person claiming under or through him, has taken possession or control of the land or has entered into occupation of it: CA 2006, s 1019.

Effect of Crown disclaimer: Scotland

General effect of disclaimer

33.52 The Crown's disclaimer operates to determine, as from the date of the disclaimer, the rights, interests and liabilities of the company, and the property of the company, in or in respect of the property disclaimed: CA 2006, s 1020(1).

It does not (except so far as is necessary for the purpose of releasing the company and its property from liability) affect the rights or liabilities of any other person: CA 2006, s 1020(2).

Power of the court to make a vesting order

33.53 The court may:

(a) on application by a person who either claims an interest in disclaimed property or is under a liability not discharged by CA 2006 in respect of disclaimed property; and

(b) on hearing such persons as it thinks fit, make an order for the vesting of the property in or its delivery to any persons entitled to it, or to whom it may seem just that the property should be delivered by way of compensation for such liability, or a trustee for him: CA 2006, s 1021(1).

The order may be made on such terms as the court thinks fit: CA 2006, s 1021(2).

On a vesting order being made under s 1021, the property comprised in it vests accordingly in the person named in that behalf in the order, without conveyance or assignation for that purpose: CA 2006, s 1021(3).

Protection of persons holding under a lease

33.54 Where the property disclaimed is held under a lease the court must not make a vesting order in favour of a person claiming under the company, whether:

(a) as sub-lessee; or

(b) as creditor in a duly registered or (as the case may be) recorded heritable security over a lease,

except on the following terms: CA 2006, s 1022(1).

33.55 The person must by the order be made subject:

(a) to the same liabilities and obligations as those to which the company was subject under the lease in respect of the property; or

(b) if the court thinks fit, only to the same liabilities and obligations as if the lease had been assigned to him.

33.56 In either event (if the case so requires) the liabilities and obligations must be as if the lease had comprised only the property comprised in the vesting order: CA 2006, s 1022(2).

A sub-lessee or creditor declining to accept a vesting order on such terms is excluded from all interest in and security over the property: CA 2006, s 1022(3).

33.57 If there is no person claiming under the company who is willing to accept an order on such terms, the court has power to vest the company's estate and interest in the property in any person liable (either personally or in a representative character, and either alone or jointly with the company) to perform the lessee's obligations under the lease: CA 2006, s 1022(4).

The court may vest that estate and interest in such a person freed and discharged from all interests, rights and obligations created by the company in the lease or in relation to the lease: CA 2006, s 1022(5).

For the purposes of s 1022 a heritable security is duly recorded if it is recorded in the Register of Sasines, and is duly registered if registered in accordance with the Land Registration (Scotland) Act 1979 (c 33): CA 2006, s 1022(6).

Supplementary provisions

Liability for rentcharge on company's land after dissolution

33.58 Section 1023 applies where on the dissolution of a company land in England and Wales or Northern Ireland that is subject to a rentcharge vests by operation of law in the Crown or any other person ('the proprietor'): CA 2006, s 1023(1).

Neither the proprietor nor his successors in title are subject to any personal liability in respect of sums becoming due under the rentcharge, except sums becoming due after the proprietor, or some person claiming under or through him, has taken possession or control of the land or has entered into occupation of it: CA 2006, s 1023(2).

The term 'company' includes any body corporate: CA 2006, s 1023(3).

Restoration to the register

33.59 The CA 2006, Pt 31, Ch 3 (ss 1024–1028) addresses issues concerned with the restoration of the register.

Application for administrative restoration to the register

33.60 Under certain conditions, where a company was dissolved because it appeared to be no longer carrying on business or in operation, a former director or member may apply to the registrar to have the company restored. This is called 'administrative restoration'. If the registrar restores the company it is deemed to have continued in existence as if it had not been dissolved and struck off the register.

An application may be made to the registrar to restore to the register a company that has been struck off the register under s 1000 or s 1001 (power of registrar to strike off defunct company): CA 2006, s 1024(1).

33.61 An application under s 1024 may be made whether or not the company has in consequence been dissolved: CA 2006, s 1024(2). Such application may only be made by a former director or former member of the company: CA 2006, s 1024(3). It may not be made after the end of the period of six years from the date of the dissolution of the company.

For this purpose an application is made when it is received by the registrar: CA 2006, s 1024(4).

Requirements for administrative restoration

33.62 On an application under s 1024, the registrar shall restore the company to the register if, and only if, the following conditions are met: CA 2006, s 1025(1).

The first condition is that the company was carrying on business or in operation at the time of its striking off: CA 2006, s 1025(2).

The second condition is that, if any property or right previously vested in or held on trust for the company has vested as *bona vacantia*, the Crown representative has signified to the registrar in writing consent to the company's restoration to the register: CA 2006, s 1025(3).

It is the applicant's responsibility to obtain that consent and to pay any costs (in Scotland, expenses) of the Crown representative in dealing with the property during the period of dissolution, or in connection with the proceedings on the application, that may be demanded as a condition of giving consent: CA 2006, s 1025(4).

The third condition is that the applicant has delivered to the registrar such documents relating to the company as are necessary to bring up to date the records kept by the registrar, and paid any penalties under s 453 or corresponding earlier provisions (civil penalty for failure to deliver accounts) that were outstanding at the date of dissolution or striking off: CA 2006, s 1025(5).

33.63 The term 'Crown representative' means: (a) in relation to property vested in the Duchy of Lancaster, the Solicitor to that Duchy; (b) in relation to property vested in the Duke of Cornwall, the Solicitor to the Duchy of Cornwall; (c) in relation to property in Scotland, the Queen's and Lord Treasurer's Remembrancer; (d) in relation to other property, the Treasury Solicitor: CA 2006, s 1025(6).

Application to be accompanied by statement of compliance

33.64 An application under s 1024 (application for administrative restoration to the register) must be accompanied by a statement of compliance: CA 2006, s 1026(1).

The statement of compliance required is a statement that the person making the application has standing to apply (see s 1024(3)), and that the requirements for administrative restoration (see s 1025) are met: CA 2006, s 1026(2).

The registrar may accept the statement of compliance as sufficient evidence of those matters: CA 2006, s 1026(3).

Form RT01 (Application for Administrative Restoration) should be used to make an application to the Registrar accompanied by the statement of compliance and a fee of £100.

33.65 The applicant must meet the Crown representative's costs or expenses (if demanded). The company must pay any statutory penalties for late filing of accounts delivered to the registrar outside the period allowed for filing. The penalties that may be due are:

- unpaid penalties outstanding on accounts delivered late before the company was dissolved
- penalties due for accounts delivered on restoration, if the accounts were overdue at the date the company was dissolved.

The company must also pay the appropriate filing fee on submission of any outstanding documents.

33.66 The level of any late filing penalty depends on how late the accounts are when Companies House receives them. In the case of accounts delivered on restoration, the registrar will normally disregard the period during which the company was dissolved. For example, a set of accounts that should have been delivered two months before a private company was dissolved are normally regarded as two months late if they are delivered on restoration and the company must pay the relevant penalty before the restoration of the company.

The company is not liable for late filing penalties for accounts received on restoration but which became due while the company was dissolved.

Registrar's decision on application for administrative restoration

33.67 The registrar must give notice to the applicant of the decision on an application under s 1024 (application for administrative restoration to the register): CA 2006, s 1027(1).

If the decision is that the company should be restored to the register, the restoration takes effect as from the date that notice is sent: CA 2006, s 1027(2).

In the case of such a decision, the registrar must enter on the register a note of the date as from which the company's restoration to the register takes effect, and cause notice of the restoration to be published in the *Gazette*: CA 2006, s 1027(3).

The notice under s1027(3)(b) must state the name of the company or, if the company is restored to the register under a different name (see s 1033), that name and its former name, the company's registered number, and the date as from which the restoration of the company to the register takes effect: CA 2006, s 1027(4).

Effect of administrative restoration

33.68 The general effect of administrative restoration to the register is that the company is deemed to have continued in existence as if it had not been dissolved or struck off the register: CA 2006, s 1028(1).

The company is not liable to a penalty under s 453 or any corresponding earlier provision (civil penalty for failure to deliver accounts) for a financial year in relation to which the period for filing accounts and reports ended after the date of dissolution or striking off, and before the restoration of the company to the register: CA 2006, s 1028(2).

33.69 The court may give such directions and make such provision as seems just for placing the company and all other persons in the same position (as nearly as may be) as if the company had not been dissolved or struck off the register: CA 2006, s 1028(3).

An application to the court for such directions or provision may be made any time within three years after the date of restoration of the company to the register: CA 2006, s 1028(4).

Administrative restoration of company with share warrants

33.70 Section 1028A of the CA 2006 (as inserted by the SBEEA 2015, Sch 4) applies in relation to a company which has been struck off the register under ss 1000 or 1001 and which, at the time it was struck off, had any share warrant in issue: CA 2006, s 1028A(1) (as inserted by the SBEEA 2015, Sch 4).

If the registrar restores the company to the register under s 1025, the share warrant and the shares specified in it are cancelled with effect from the date the restoration takes effect: CA 2006, s 1028A(2) (as inserted by the SBEEA 2015, Sch 4).

If as a result of s 1028A(2) the company has no issued share capital, the company must, before the end of the period of one month beginning with the date the restoration takes effect, allot at least one share in the company; and s 549(1) does not apply to such an allotment: CA 2006, s 1028A(3) (as inserted by the SBEEA 2015, Sch 4).

33.71 The company must, before the end of the period of 15 days beginning with the date the restoration takes effect, deliver a statement of capital to the registrar: CA 2006, s 1028A(1) (as inserted by the SBEEA 2015, Sch 4).

Section 1028A(4) does not apply in a case where the company is required under s 1028A(3) to make an allotment (because in such a case s 555 will apply): CA 2006, s 1028A(5) (as inserted by the SBEEA 2015, Sch 4).

The statement of capital must state with respect to the company's share capital as reduced by the cancellation of the share warrant and the shares specified in it:

(a) the total number of shares of the company;

(b) the aggregate nominal value of those shares;

(c) the aggregate amount (if any) unpaid on those shares (whether on account of their nominal value or by way of premium); and

(d) for each class of shares:

   (i) prescribed particulars of the rights attached to the shares;

   (ii) the total number of shares of that class; and

   (iii) the aggregate nominal value of shares of that class: CA 2006, s 1028A(6) (as inserted by the SBEEA 2015, Sch 4).

33.72 Where a share warrant is cancelled in accordance with s 1028A(2), the company must, as soon as reasonably practicable:

(a) enter the date the cancellation takes effect in its register of members; or

(b) where an election is in force under s 128B of the CA 2006 (option to keep membership information on central register) in respect of the company, deliver that information to the registrar as if it were information required to be delivered under s 128E of that Act: CA 2006, s 1028A(7) (as inserted by the SBEEA 2015, Sch 4).

33.73 Section 1028A(9) applies where:

(a) any property or right previously vested in or held on trust for the company in respect of any share specified in a share warrant has vested as *bona vacantia* (see s 1012); and

(b) the warrant and the share are cancelled on the restoration of the company in accordance with this section: CA 2006, s 1028A(8) (as inserted by the SBEEA 2015, Sch 4).

33.74 On restoration of the company, that property or right:

(a) may not be returned to the company; and

(b) accordingly, remains vested as *bona vacantia*: CA 2006, s 1028A(9) (as inserted by the SBEEA 2015, Sch 4).

33.75 If default is made in complying with s 1028A(3) or (4), an offence is committed by:

(a) the company; and

(b) every officer of the company who is in default.

For this purpose a shadow director is treated as an officer of the company: CA 2006, s 1028A(10) (as inserted by the SBEEA 2015, Sch 4).

33.76 A person guilty of an offence under this section is liable:

(a) on conviction on indictment, to a fine;

(b) on summary conviction:

  (i) in England and Wales, to a fine;

  (ii) in Scotland or Northern Ireland, to a fine not exceeding the statutory maximum: CA 2006, s 1028A(11) (as inserted by the SBEEA 2015, Sch 4).

33.77 Until the SBEEA 2015, s 97 (contents of statements of capital) comes into force, the s 1028A inserted by sub-para (1) has effect as if in sub-para (6):

(a) para (c) were omitted; and

(b) after para (d) there were inserted 'and'

(e) the amount paid up and the amount (if any) unpaid on each share (whether on account of the nominal value of the share or by way of premium): SBEEA 2015, Sch 4.

Until the SBEEA 2015, s 94 (option to keep information on central register) comes into force, s 1028A inserted by sub-para (1) has effect as if, in s 1028A(7), para (b) (and the 'or' preceding it) were omitted: SBEEA 2015, Sch 4.

Restoration to the register by the court

33.78 This is governed by ss 1029–1032 of the CA 2006.

Application to the court for restoration to the register

33.79 An application may be made to the court to restore to the register a company:

(a) that has been dissolved under Ch 9 of Pt 4 of the Insolvency Act 1986 (c 45) or Ch 9 of Pt 5 of the Insolvency (Northern Ireland) Order 1989 (SI 1989 No 2405 (NI 19)) (dissolution of company after winding up);

(b) that is deemed to have been dissolved under para 84(6) of Sch B1 to that Act or para 85(6) of Sch B1 to that Order (dissolution of company following administration); or

(c) that has been struck off the register:

(i) under ss 1000 or 1001 (power of registrar to strike off defunct company); or

(ii) under s 1003 (voluntary striking off);

whether or not the company has in consequence been dissolved: CA 2006, s 1029(1).

33.80 An application under s 1029 may be made by:

(a) the Secretary of State;

(b) any former director of the company;

(c) any person having an interest in land in which the company had a superior or derivative interest;

(d) any person having an interest in land or other property:

(i) that was subject to rights vested in the company; or

(ii) that was benefited by obligations owed by the company;

(e) any person who but for the company's dissolution would have been in a contractual relationship with it;

(f) any person with a potential legal claim against the company;

(g) any manager or trustee of a pension fund established for the benefit of employees of the company;

(h) any former member of the company (or the personal representatives of such a person);

(i) any person who was a creditor of the company at the time of its striking off or dissolution;

(j) any former liquidator of the company;

(k) where the company was struck off the register under s 1003 (voluntary striking off), any person of a description specified by regulations under s 1006(1)(f) or 1007(2)(f) (persons entitled to notice of application for voluntary striking off);

or by any other person appearing to the court to have an interest in the matter: CA 2006, s 1029(2).

When an application to the court may be made

33.81 An application to the court for restoration of a company to the register may be made at any time for the purpose of bringing proceedings against the company for damages for personal injury: CA 2006, s 1030(1).

No order shall be made on such an application if it appears to the court that the proceedings would fail by virtue of any enactment as to the time within which proceedings must be brought: CA 2006, s 1030(2).

In making that decision the court must have regard to its power under s 1032(3) (power to give consequential directions etc) to direct that the period between the dissolution (or striking off) of the company and the making of the order is not to count for the purposes of any such enactment: CA 2006, s 1030(3).

In any other case an application to the court for restoration of a company to the register may not be made after the end of the period of six years from the date of the dissolution of the company, subject as follows: CA 2006, s 1030(4).

33.82 Where the company has been struck off the register under ss 1000 or 1001 (power of registrar to strike off defunct company), an application to the registrar has been made under s 1024 (application for administrative restoration to the register) within the time allowed for making such an application and the registrar has refused the application, an application to the court under s 1030 may be made within 28 days of notice of the registrar's decision being issued by the registrar, even if the period of six years mentioned in s 1030(4) above has expired: CA 2006, s 1030(5).

For the purposes of s 1030:

(a) 'personal injury' includes any disease and any impairment of a person's physical or mental condition; and

(b) references to damages for personal injury include:

  (i) any sum claimed by virtue of s 1(2)(c) of the Law Reform (Miscellaneous Provisions) Act 1934 (c 41) or s 14(2)(c) of the Law Reform (Miscellaneous Provisions) Act (Northern Ireland) 1937 (1937 c 9 (NI)) (funeral expenses)); and

  (ii) damages under the Fatal Accidents Act 1976 (c 30), the Damages (Scotland) Act 1976 (c 13) or the Fatal Accidents (Northern Ireland) Order 1977 (SI 1977 No 1251 (NI 18)): CA 2006, s 1030(6).

33.83 The application is made to the court by completing a Pt 8 claim form. The Registrar at the Companies Court in London usually hears restoration cases in chambers once a week. Cases are also heard at the District Registries. Alternatively, an application may be made to the County Court that has authority to wind up the company.

The Court will require:

- evidence that the originating document was served
- written confirmation that the solicitor dealing with the *bona vacantia* assets has no objection to the restoration of the company (there should be attached a copy of the solicitor's letter to the affidavit or witness statement this does not apply in Scotland)
- when the company was incorporated and the nature of its objects (there should be attached a copy of the certificate of incorporation and the memorandum of association and, if appropriate, the articles of association)
- its membership and officers
- its trading activity and, if applicable, when it stopped trading
- an explanation of any failure to deliver accounts, annual returns or notices to the registrar
- details of the striking-off and dissolution
- comments on the company's solvency
- any other information that explains the reason for the application.

33.84 In England and Wales and in Northern Ireland the above information must be provided in an affidavit or witness statement. In Scotland this information can be provided in the petition to restore.

The registrar will provide information to assist in an application to the Court. Before the Court hearing, the registrar will normally require the delivery of any statutory documents to bring the company's public file up to date. These documents should be sent at least five working days before the hearing, to allow the registrar sufficient time to process or return them for amendment.

Decision on application for restoration by the court

33.85 On an application under s 1029 the court may order the restoration of the company to the register:

(a) if the company was struck off the register under ss 1000 or 1001 (power of registrar to strike off defunct companies) and the company was, at the time of the striking off, carrying on business or in operation; or

(b) if the company was struck off the register under s 1003 (voluntary striking off) and any of the requirements of ss 1004–1009 were not complied with; or

(c) if, in any other case, the court considers it just to do so: CA 2006, s 1031(1).

If the court orders restoration of the company to the register, the restoration takes effect on a copy of the court's order being delivered to the registrar: CA 2006, s 1031(2).

The registrar must cause to be published in the *Gazette* notice of the restoration of the company to the register: CA 2006, s 1031(3).

The notice must state the name of the company or, if the company is restored to the register under a different name (see s 1033), that name and its former name, the company's registered number, and the date on which the restoration took effect: CA 2006, s 1031(3).

Effect of court order for restoration to the register

33.86 Under the CA 2006, the general effect of an order by the court for restoration to the register is that the company is deemed to have continued to exist as if it had not been dissolved or struck off the register: CA 2006, s 1032(1).

The company is not liable to a penalty under s 453 or any corresponding earlier provision (civil penalty for failure to deliver accounts) for a financial year in relation to which the period for filing accounts and reports ended after the date of dissolution or striking off, and before the restoration of the company to the register: CA 2006, s 1032(2).

33.87 The court may give such directions and make such provision as seems just for placing the company and all other persons in the same position (as nearly as may be) as if the company had not been dissolved or struck off the register: CA 2006, s 1032(3).

The court may also give directions as to:

(a) the delivery to the registrar of such documents relating to the company as are necessary to bring up to date the records kept by the registrar;

(b) the payment of the costs (in Scotland, expenses) of the registrar in connection with the proceedings for the restoration of the company to the register; and

(c) where any property or right previously vested in or held on trust for the company has vested as *bona vacantia*, the payment of the costs (in Scotland, expenses) of the Crown representative:

   (i) in dealing with the property during the period of dissolution; or

   (ii) in connection with the proceedings on the application: CA 2006, s 1032(4).

The term 'Crown representative' means (a) in relation to property vested in the Duchy of Lancaster, the Solicitor to that Duchy; (b) in relation to property vested in the Duke of Cornwall, the Solicitor to the Duchy of Cornwall; (c) in relation to property in Scotland, the Queen's and Lord Treasurer's Remembrancer; (d) in relation to other property, the Treasury Solicitor: CA 2006, s 1032(5).

33.88 The registrar will normally restore a company with the name it had before it was struck off and dissolved. However, if at the date of restoration the company's former name is the same as another name on the registrar's index of company names, he cannot restore the company with its former name. A check should be mase as to whether the company's name is the same as another on the register by using the WebCheck service.

If the name is no longer available, the court order may state another name by which the company is to be restored. On restoration, Companies House will issue a change of name certificate as if the company had changed its name.

Alternatively, the company may be restored to the register as if its registered company number is also its name. The company then has 14 days from the date of restoration to pass a resolution to change the name of the company. There must be delivered a copy of the resolution and a 'notice of change of name by resolution of directors' (Form NM05) to Companies House with the appropriate fee. Companies House will then issue a change of name certificate. It is an offence if the company does not change its name within 14 days of being restored with the number as its name. The change of name does not take effect until we have issued the certificate.

33.89 There are also costs or penalties involved. Where property has become *bona vacantia*, the Court may direct that the claimant meets costs of the Crown representative in dealing with the property during the period of dissolution or in connection with the proceedings. The Court may also direct that the claimant meets the registrar's costs in connection with the proceedings for the restoration.

The company must normally pay any statutory penalties for late filing of accounts delivered to the registrar outside the period allowed for filing. The penalties that may be due are:

- unpaid penalties outstanding on accounts delivered late before the company was dissolved

- penalties due for accounts delivered on restoration, if the accounts were overdue at the date the company was dissolved.

The appropriate filing fee must also be paid on submission of outstanding documents.

The level of any late filing penalty depends on how late the accounts are when Companies House receives them. For example, a set of accounts that should have been delivered two months before a private company was dissolved are normally regarded as two months late if they are delivered on restoration and the relevant penalty must be paid. The company is not liable for late filing penalties for accounts received on restoration but which became due while the company was dissolved.

A court order under s 1032 of the CA 2006 was retrospective

In an earlier case of *Tyman's Limited v Craven* [1952] 2 QB 100, an application to the county court for a new tenancy was made on 23 July 1951 on behalf of a company which had been struck off the register in November 1950.

The company was subsequently restored to the register pursuant to s 353 of the CA 1948 on 15 October 1951. The application was set for hearing on 31 October 1951 and was dismissed by the county court judge on the basis that the restoration order was not retrospective.

The Court of Appeal by a majority (Sir Raymond Evershed MR and Hodson LJ, Jenkins LJ dissenting) allowed the company's appeal. Having referred extensively to *Morris v Harris*, the court held that an order under s 353 declaring that 'the company shall be deemed to have continued in existence as if its name had not been struck off', was effective to validate retrospectively all acts done in the name or on behalf of the company during the period between its dissolution and the restoration of its name to the register. Therefore, the company was to be regarded as never having been dissolved and it was not open to the landlord to object that no application had been made on behalf of the company on 23 July 1951, merely by reason of the company's having been struck off the register.

The effect of CA 2006, s 1032 is that the court order for restoration has retrospective effect

In *RLoans v The Registrar of Companies* [2013] All ER 180, on 3 January 2007, joint administrators were appointed by directors of the company pursuant to para 22 of Sch B1 to the Insolvency Act 1986 (the 1986 Act). The joint administrators sent a notice to the registrar of companies that they thought the company had no property which might permit a distribution to creditors. The joint administrators' notice was registered by the registrar, with the result that, at that time, the appointment of the joint administrators ceased to have effect. On 24 September 2010, the company was deemed to be dissolved pursuant to para 84(6) of Sch B1 to the 1986 Act.

The petitioner, a major creditor of the company, presented a petition to the court for, inter alia, the restoration of the company to the register of companies and an order that the winding-up of the company take effect retrospectively from 24

June 2010. The petitioner, in its claim against the company, contended that the repayment of a loan of over £4m to a director and shareholder was a preference, pursuant to s 239 of the 1986 Act. Section 240(3)(d) of the 1986 Act provided that, where a preference applied by reason of a liquidation commencing at the time when the appointment of an administrator ceased to have effect, the date of the onset of insolvency was the date the company entered administration. In the present case, however, if the commencement of the winding up was 1 November 2012, it would not commence at the time when the appointment of an administrator ceased to have effect, namely 24 June 2010.

Accordingly, an issue arose in that, after the company was dissolved, if it was restored to the register, it would be deemed to have continued in existence as if it had not been dissolved. Its liquidation upon the petition would commence on 1 November 2012 and there would be a gap of over 16 months since the registration of the joint administrators' notice on 24 June 2010. That gap would lead to a potential difficulty for the potential preference claim because of the expiry of statutory time limits unless the liquidation's commencement date was backdated to the day the appointment of the joint administrators ceased.

The petitioner submitted that if a winding up order were made on the petition then there would be no dovetailing of the cessation of the administration and the entry into liquidation. There would be a gap of over two years. As such s 240(3)(d) of the 1986 Act would not apply and so the preference claim would not be capable of succeeding as the preference would not have been within a relevant time. For that reason an order was sought extending the administration to the instant day until a winding up order was made.

The issue for consideration was whether, as contended by the petitioner, on the true construction of para 84 of Sch B1 to the 1986 Act, either statute extended the period of administration or the court had the power to extend the period of administration to the commencement of the winding-up with the result that s 240(3)(d) of the 1986 Act would apply. The issue was whether it was right to extend the administration until the date of liquidation in reliance upon the powers conferred by s 1032(3) of the Companies Act 2006 (the 2006 Act). The petitioner submitted that para 84(7) of Sch B1 to the 1986 Act provided an express power applicable to the cessation of the administration because the suspension or disapplication applied to 'the period of three months beginning with the date of registration'.

It was held by Mr Registrar Jones that the court's power to order restoration was plainly discretionary but in the absence of special circumstances restoration should normally follow. The general effect of an order by the court for restoration to the register was that the company was deemed to have continued in existence as if it had not been dissolved or struck off the register. The company was not liable to a civil penalty for failure to deliver accounts for a financial year in relation to which the period for filing accounts and reports ended: (i) after the date of dissolution or striking off, and (ii) before the restoration of the company to the register. The court might give such directions and make such provision as seems just for placing the company and all other persons in the same position as if the company had not been dissolved or struck off the register.

In all the circumstances, the company would be restored to the register and an order would be made for the compulsory winding up of the company. No order would be made appointing a liquidator as the court only had power to make such appointment if a winding up order was made immediately upon the appointment of an administrator ceasing to have effect, and that had not occurred.

Where an application to restore a dissolved company to the register is successful, such restoration operates retrospectively, so that any court proceedings previously issued against the company whilst it was dissolved are deemed validly issued

In *Peaktone Limited v Joddrell* [2013] 1 All ER 13, Joddrell ('J') was a former employee of company Peaktone Limited ('Peaktone'). He issued proceedings in August 2009 in respect of a personal injury he had allegedly suffered whilst working for P. At the time, P was a dissolved company.

In June 2010, sometime after issuing the proceedings, J obtained an order from the Companies Court under s 1029 of the Companies Act 2006 ('CA 2006') to restore P to the register. In applying for that order, J did not mention that he had already commenced proceedings against P. P successfully applied to the County Court to strike out J's claim as an abuse of process under CPR, r 3.4(2)(b). The order striking out J's claim was subsequently set aside on appeal. P then appealed that decision. Permission was granted and the Court of Appeal ("CA") gave a final ruling in July 2012.

The key issue on appeal was whether an order made pursuant to CA 2006, s 1029 had the effect of retrospectively validating an action purportedly commenced against a company whilst it was dissolved. In order to determine the issue, the CA had to consider the meaning and effect of CA 2006, s 1032(1) (which states that 'the general effect of an order by the court for restoration to the register is that the company is deemed to have continued in existence as if it had not been dissolved or struck off the register').

The CA dismissed P's appeal and held that the effect of CA 2006, s 1032 was retrospectively to validate an action purportedly commenced by or against a company during the period of its dissolution. Section 1032 incorporated exactly the same language as had appeared in previous versions of CA 2006.

Historic jurisprudence in relation to the wording now in the section was therefore relevant and determinative. The effect of s 1032(1) of the CA 2006 was retrospectively to validate an action purportedly commenced by or against a company during the period of its dissolution. A clear distinction emerged from the jurisprudence between the consequences of the order depending upon whether the order was made pursuant to s 651 of the 1985 Act or its statutory predecessors or pursuant to s 653 of the 1985 Act or its statutory predecessors. In the first case, the order had no retrospective effect except to restore the company's corporate existence. It did not validate any actions or activities that had taken place during the period of dissolution. In particular it did not restore to life an action which, having been commenced before the company was dissolved, had abated on the company's dissolution, nor did it bring to life an action which, purportedly commenced while the company was dissolved, was a nullity. In the other case, by contrast, the effect of the deeming provision was to validate retrospectively what had happened while the company was dissolved, so that once the restoration order was made the company was to be regarded as never having been dissolved. Prior to the 2006 Act, there had been two different procedures in place.

The 2006 Act had assimilated those procedures into a single composite procedure found in s 1032(1). The fact that in all material respects Parliament had chosen to use precisely the same language in s 1032(1) of the 2006 Act as had previously appeared in s 653 of the 1985 Act and its predecessors could not have been fortuitous. Parliament had plainly been seeking to carry forward, albeit with a wider application, the principle which had, in a narrower context, been repeatedly used in successive Companies Acts. Accordingly, there had been no reason for thinking that the previous jurisprudence should not have applied to s 1032(1) of the CA 2006. That jurisprudence applied to elucidate and explain the meaning and effect of s 1032(1) of the 2006 Act in just the same way as it had elucidated and explained the meaning and effect of s 353 of the 1948 Act and s 653 of the 1985 Act. Accordingly, the appeal was dismissed.

See too: *Morris v Harris* [1927] AC 252; I *Re C W Dixon Limited* [1947] Ch 251; *Re Lewis & Smart Ltd* [1954] 1 WLR 755; *Re Workvale Ltd (In Dissolution)* [1992] 1 WLR 416; *Re Mixhurst Limited* [1993] BCC 748, *Steanes Fashions Limited v Legal and General Assurance Society Limited* [1995] 1 BCLC 332; and *Smith v White Knight Laundry Limited* [2002] 1 WLR 616.

Section 1032 of the CA 2006 was only of 'general effect' and was subject to more specific provisions concerning dissolution and restoration under the CA 2006

In *ELB Securities Ltd v Love* [2015] CSIH 67, a company had been dissolved and struck off the register on 14 June 2013. Under the CA 2006, s 1012, the rights which the company had enjoyed under a lease, vested in the Crown as *bona vacantia*. However, on 15 July 2013, the Crown disclaimed the lease under the CA 2006, s 1013. Subsequently after a short period, the company was restored to the register. The issue before the Scottish Court of Session (Inner House) concerned the position of the previous disclaimer, and whether under the CA 2006, s 1032, the company retained an interest in the lease as if the disclaimer had not occurred. According to Lady Paton, on a proper construction of the CA 2006, 'the general effect' of the restoration of the company as provided for by s 1032, merely provided for the general approach which was to be adopted in such circumstances. However, this general approach must give way to the specific and detailed provisions concerning the company's property as set out in the CA 2006, ss 1012–1014 and 1020–1022. As a result, the company's rights in the lease came to an end on 15 July 2013.

Restoration by court of company with share warrants

33.90 Section 1032A of the CA 2006 applies in relation to a company falling within s 1029(1) if, at the time it was dissolved, deemed to be dissolved or (as the case may be) struck off, it had any share warrant in issue: CA 2006, s 1032A (1) (as inserted by the SBEEA 2015, Sch 4).

If the court orders the restoration of the company to the register, the order must also cancel the share warrant and the shares specified in it with effect from the date the restoration takes effect: CA 2006, s 1032A(2) (as inserted by the SBEEA 2015, Sch 4).

If as a result of s 1032A(2) the company has no issued share capital, the company must, before the end of the period of one month beginning with the date the restoration takes effect, allot at least one share in the company; and s 549(1) does not apply to such an allotment: CA 2006, s 1032A(3) (as inserted by the SBEEA 2015, Sch 4).

33.91 Section 1032A(6) applies in a case where:

(a) the application under s 1029 was made by a person mentioned in sub-s (2)(b) or (h) of that section; or

(b) the court order specifies that it applies: CA 2006, s 1032A(4) (as inserted by the SBEEA 2015, Sch 4).

But s 1032A(6) does not apply in any case where the company is required under s 1032A(3) to make an allotment (because in such a case s 555 will apply): CA 2006, s 1032A(5) (as inserted by the SBEEA 2015, Sch 4).

In a case where this subsection applies, the company must, before the end of the period of 15 days beginning with the date the restoration takes effect, deliver a statement of capital to the registrar: CA 2006, s 1032A(6) (as inserted by the SBEEA 2015, Sch 4).

33.92 The statement of capital must state with respect to the company's share capital as reduced by the cancellation of the share warrant and the shares specified in it:

(a) the total number of shares of the company;

(b) the aggregate nominal value of those shares;

(c) the aggregate amount (if any) unpaid on those shares (whether on account of their nominal value or by way of premium); and

(d) for each class of shares:

  (i) prescribed particulars of the rights attached to the shares;

  (ii) the total number of shares of that class; and

  (iii) the aggregate nominal value of shares of that class: CA 2006, s 1032A(7) (as inserted by the SBEEA 2015, Sch 4).

33.93 Where a share warrant is cancelled by an order as mentioned in s 1032A(2), the company must, as soon as reasonably practicable:

(a) enter the date the cancellation takes effect in its register of members; or

(b) where an election is in force under s 128B of the Companies Act 2006 (option to keep membership information on central register) in respect of the company, deliver that information to the registrar as if it were information required to be delivered under s 128E of that Act: CA 2006, s 1032A(8) (as inserted by the SBEEA 2015, Sch 4).

33.94 Section 1032A(10) applies where:

(a) any property or right previously vested in or held on trust for the company in respect of any share specified in a share warrant has vested as *bona vacantia* (see s 1012); and

(b) the warrant and the share are cancelled on the restoration of the company in accordance with this section: CA 2006, s 1032A(9) (as inserted by the SBEEA 2015, Sch 4).

33.95 On restoration of the company, that property or right:

(a) may not be returned to the company; and

(b) accordingly, remains vested as *bona vacantia*: CA 2006, s 1032A(10) (as inserted by the SBEEA 2015, Sch 4).

33.96 If default is made in complying with s 1032A(3) or (6), an offence is committed by:

(a) the company; and

(b) every officer of the company who is in default: CA 2006, s 1032A(11) (as inserted by the SBEEA 2015, Sch 4).

For this purpose a shadow director is treated as an officer of the company.

33.97 A person guilty of an offence under the CA 2006, s 1032A is liable:

(a) on conviction on indictment, to a fine;

(b) on summary conviction:

  (i) in England and Wales, to a fine;

  (ii) in Scotland or Northern Ireland, to a fine not exceeding the statutory maximum: CA 2006, s 1032A(12) (as inserted by the SBEEA 2015, Sch 4).

33.98 Until s 97 of the SBEEA 2015 (contents of statements of capital) comes into force, s 1032A inserted by sub-para (1) has effect as if in s 1032A(7):

(a) para (c) were omitted; and

(b) after para (d) there were inserted 'and';

(e) the amount paid up and the amount (if any) unpaid on each share (whether on account of the nominal value of the share or by way of premium): SBEEA 2015, Sch 4.

Until s 94 of the SBEEA 2015 (option to keep information on central register) comes into force, s 1032A inserted by sub-para (1) has effect as if, in s 1032A(8), para (b) (and the 'or' preceding it) were omitted: SBEEA 2015, Sch 4.

Supplementary provisions

Company's name on restoration

33.99 A company is restored to the register with the name it had before it was dissolved or struck off the register, subject to the following provisions: CA 2006, s 1033(1).

If at the date of restoration the company could not be registered under its former name without contravening s 66 (name not to be the same as another in the registrar's index of company names), it must be restored to the register:

(a) under another name specified:

  (i) in the case of administrative restoration, in the application to the registrar; or

  (ii) in the case of restoration under a court order, in the court's order; or

(b) as if its registered number was also its name.

References to a company's being registered in a name, and to registration in that context, shall be read as including the company's being restored to the register: CA 2006, s 1033(2).

33.100 If a company is restored to the register under a name specified in the application to the registrar, the provisions of s 80 (change of name: registration and issue of new certificate of incorporation), and s 81 (change of name: effect) apply as if the application to the registrar were notice of a change of name: CA 2006, s 1033(3).

If a company is restored to the register under a name specified in the court's order, the provisions of s 80 (change of name: registration and issue of new certificate of incorporation) and s 81 (change of name: effect) apply as if the copy of the court order delivered to the registrar were notice of a change of name: CA 2006, s 1033(4).

If the company is restored to the register as if its registered number was also its name:

(a) the company must change its name within 14 days after the date of the restoration;

(b) the change may be made by resolution of the directors (without prejudice to any other method of changing the company's name);

(c) the company must give notice to the registrar of the change; and

(d) ss 80 and 81 apply as regards the registration and effect of the change: CA 2006, s 1033(5).

33.101 If the company fails to comply with s 1033(5)(a) or (c), an offence is committed by the company and every officer of the company who is in default: CA 2006, s 1033(6).

A person guilty of an offence under s 1032(6) is liable on summary conviction to a fine not exceeding level 5 on the standard scale and, for continued contravention, a daily default fine not exceeding one-tenth of level 5 on the standard scale: CA 2006, s 1033(7).

Effect of restoration to the register where property has vested as bona vacantia

33.102 The person in whom any property or right is vested by s 1012 (property of dissolved company to be *bona vacantia*) may dispose of, or of an interest in, that property or right despite the fact that the company may be restored to the register under Ch 3: CA 2006, s 1034(1).

If the company is restored to the register:

(a) the restoration does not affect the disposition (but without prejudice to its effect in relation to any other property or right previously vested in or held on trust for the company); and

(b) the Crown or, as the case may be, the Duke of Cornwall, shall pay to the company an amount equal to:

  (i) the amount of any consideration received for the property or right or, as the case may be, the interest in it; or

  (ii) the value of any such consideration at the time of the disposition; or

if no consideration was received, an amount equal to the value of the property, right or interest disposed of, as at the date of the disposition: CA 2006, s 1034(3).

33.103 There may be deducted from the amount payable under s 1034(2)(b) the reasonable costs of the Crown representative in connection with the disposition (to the extent that they have not been paid as a condition of administrative restoration or pursuant to a court order for restoration): CA 2006, s 1034(3).

Where a liability accrues under CA 2006, s 1033(2) in respect of any property or right which before the restoration of the company to the register had accrued as *bona vacantia* to the Duchy of Lancaster, the Attorney General of that Duchy shall represent Her Majesty in any proceedings arising in connection with that liability: CA 2006, s 1034(4).

Where a liability accrues under s 1033(2) in respect of any property or right which before the restoration of the company to the register had accrued as *bona vacantia* to the Duchy of Cornwall, such persons as the Duke of Cornwall (or other possessor for the time being of the Duchy) may appoint, shall represent the Duke (or other possessor) in any proceedings arising out of that liability: CA 2006, s 1034(5).

The term 'Crown representative' means: (a) in relation to property vested in the Duchy of Lancaster, the Solicitor to that Duchy; (b) in relation to property vested in the Duke of Cornwall, the Solicitor to the Duchy of Cornwall; (c) in relation to property in Scotland, the Queen's and Lord Treasurer's Remembrancer; (d) in relation to other property, the Treasury Solicitor: CA 2006, s 1034(6).

Checklist: regulatory structure for dissolution and restoration of a company

33.104 *This checklist provides an overview of the regulatory structure governing dissolution and restoration of a company. It considers the different methods of removing a company from the register at Companies House and the different forms of seeking company restoration.*

No	Issue	Reference
1	The Registrar of Companies House has power to strike off a defunct company. This applies where the company is no longer carrying on business or in operation. Examples include where the company has no directors or where the Registrar has not received documents back from the company.	CA 2006, s 1000(1)
2	Alternatively, a voluntary striking off may be applied for. The proper applicant will be the company. It usually applies where the company is no longer needed or all directors wish to retire. The removal of the company will be by the Registrar. Form DS01 'Striking off application by a company'.	CA 2006, s 1003(1)
3	The court can order restoration to the register in certain circumstances. An application is made to the court. The effect is that the company is deemed to have continued to exist as if it had not been dissolved or struck off.	CA 2006, ss 1029(1) and 1032; *RLoans v The Registrar of Companies* [2013] All ER 180
4	Restoration may also take place by administrative restoration provided certain conditions are satisfied. This allows a former director or member to apply to the Registrar to have the company restored. Form RT01 is used for the Administrative Restoration.	CA 2006, s 1024(1)
5	The assets and property of the company goes to the Crown *bona vacantia* except any of the company's liabilities	CA 2006, s 1012(1)
6	The Crown can disclaim property vesting as *bona vacantia*. Typical examples including disclaiming onerous property covenants, property in negative equity, assets which are the subject of litigation	CA 2006, s 1011(1)

Definitions

33.105

Creditor: includes a contingent or prospective creditor.

Crown Representative: (a) in relation to property vested in the Duchy of Lancaster, the Solicitor to that Duchy;

(b) in relation to property vested in the Duke of Cornwall, the Solicitor to the Duchy of Cornwall;

(c) in relation to property in Scotland, the Queen's and Lord Treasurer's Remembrancer;

(d) in relation to other property, the Treasury Solicitor: CA 2006, s 1016(3).

Personal injury: includes any disease and any impairment of a person's physical or mental condition.

34 Company investigations

Contents

Introduction

34.1 Although the system of corporate governance relies to some extent on self-regulation by companies in ensuring that there are effective and proper systems in place to monitor directors' actions and their accountability towards shareholders, self-regulation mechanisms alone cannot be the basis of an effective governance system. The maintenance of a high standard of corporate governance and the need to prevent an abuse of directors' powers and duties requires, in some cases, the need for legislation to intervene in corporate affairs supplemented by self-regulation. Shareholders cannot continuously monitor directors' activities and, they may not have the resources or the time to undertake a detailed investigation into the company's affairs. In the UK, company law legislation adds another dimension to the corporate governance system by empowering some governmental and regulatory authorities to conduct company investigations where there may be evidence of abuse of power or suspected criminal activity. This may require the interaction and coordination between the Secretary of State for Department for Business Innovation & Skills, the Serious Fraud Office, the Crown Prosecution Service and the police and other regulatory authorities.

34.2 Company investigations involve a process of intervention into the company's affairs. It may involve the appointment of investigation officers and inspectors by BIS, to determine whether or not a company under investigation may be involved in any unscrupulous activities and to prevent such activities from taking place. The process of investigation can be rigorous and encroaches on the boundaries of civil and criminal law. It may involve principles of justice and fair play in ensuring inspectors act with the utmost fairness towards those under investigation. The nature of the investigation and its outcome may have an adverse effect on the company's reputation and the reputation of its directors and key officers including the chairman and chief executive. It could lead to civil or criminal sanctions against these officers concerned. The trust and confidence which the shareholders had in their company may be eroded quickly leading to a major collapse of the company. Increasingly, company investigations involve human rights issues invoking the European Convention of Human Rights and the Human Rights Act 1998, owing to the exercise of wide powers vested in inspectors the exercise of which could contravene the human rights legislation.

34.3 At the heart of the debate on company investigations thereby maintaining an effective corporate governance system, is the need to protect the public. One of the objectives of company investigations is to protect investors, suppliers, creditors, consumers and the wider public from misconduct and the unscrupulous practices of corporations. The Secretary of State for the BIS has wide powers of investigation where such practices are suspected; depending upon the outcome of the investigation, the Secretary of State can prosecute offenders or take other appropriate action, where necessary, to ensure that those who need protection are, in fact, protected. Although the Secretary of State has the discretion to decide whether or not an investigation is appropriate, he will look at the following aspects:

- the possibility of a practical outcome from the use of BIS powers;
- the possibility of documents being available to support the complaint; and
- the wider public interest in the matter complained of.

The powers contained in the CA 1985 are used to investigate alleged complaints against companies. However, under the Financial Services and Markets Act 2000, the Secretary of State also has power to investigate partnerships, companies and individuals. The investigations are usually carried out by officials from the Companies Investigation ('CI') (its predecessor was the Companies Investigation Branch) or by private sector lawyers, accountants and other specialists.

34.4 This Chapter considers the BIS process in company investigations by considering some of the legislative provisions regulating this area. It addresses the main grounds upon which an investigation may take place. Depending upon the nature of the ground that may be invoked, the Secretary of State for the BIS may appoint inspectors to undertake the investigation. The inspectors' powers are considered and as well as the issue of whether they can be challenged on the basis that they have exceeded the powers given to them. An analysis of the concept of natural justice is considered with particular reference to case law. Human rights legislation is also at the heart of company investigations and various cases are considered with particular regard to Art 6 of the European Convention on Human Rights.

This section specifically addresses the following aspects:

- The regulatory framework governing company investigations.
- Some key reasons for company investigations.
- Formal investigations by government appointed inspectors.
- Informal investigations.
- The powers of officers in the conduct of company investigations.

- The application of 'natural justice' and human rights.
- Sanctions for non-compliance the company investigations.

Regulatory framework of company investigations

34.5 Company investigations are regulated by the following regime:

- **Part XIV of the Companies Act 1985** – the principal provisions governing company investigations are still retained under the CA 1985 which has been amended from time to time.
- **Companies Act 1989** – amended the CA 1985 to add further powers concerning search warrants.
- **Companies (Audit, Investigations and Community Enterprise) Act 2004** – amended the CA 1985 to add further powers on right of entry.
- **Criminal Justice and Police Act 2001** – amended the CA 1985 to take account of decisions of the European Court of Human Rights on subsequent use of material and documents obtained following the investigation.
- **Human Rights Act 1988** and the European Convention of Human Rights – addresses aspects of fairness of a trial of an individual and which impacts on the powers of inspectors and officers under CA 1985.
- **Insolvency Act 1986, s 124A** – allows the Secretary to petition for the company's winding up where having obtained a report following the investigation of a company, it appears expedient to wind up the company in the public interest.
- **Company Directors Disqualification Act 1986, s 8** – allows the Secretary of State to petition on the grounds of unfitness of a director subsequent to the follow up investigation into the company's affairs.

Some key reasons for company investigations

34.6 Company investigations are empowered to be undertaken by the Secretary of State for BIS through its Companies Investigation ('CI'), which is part of the Insolvency Service Agency of BIS. Whilst the vast majority of enquiries conducted by Companies Investigation are confidential enquiries under CA 1985, s 447, over the years the Secretary of State for BIS has appointed Inspectors under other sections of the Act (or earlier legislation) that allow for the publication of a report.

Inspections are normally carried out where the company involved is a major plc and the matters subject to enquiry are of significant public interest. The CI's investigations are confidential. It can neither confirm nor deny that an investigation is taking place, and by law, the CI cannot provide a person with any details of what the CI finds. It will however take action or make the information available to other regulators and enforcement agencies if it has any concerns.

34.7 CI assess all complaints made to BIS which are capable of being addressed by its powers, and decide whether or not it is in the public interest to investigate the companies against which they have been made. As part of that process, it may obtain further information from the complainants and carry out our own background research. It does not approach the companies at that stage.

It may then decide that there is no basis for an investigation.

However, if CI is satisfied that there is sufficient 'good reason' and that it is in the public interest to do so, it will normally conduct an investigation. The decision to investigate is entirely at CI's discretion.

If CI does not investigate the matter itself, it may pass the information provided to another public body that may be in a better position to investigate or act on the concerns that have been raised.

The CI's investigations are fact-finding in nature and largely inquisitorial. They are not criminal investigations as such, although they may address conduct which could amount to criminal behaviour. The CI does not have to restrict its enquiries solely to what was in the original complaint. It also issues press releases when follow up action is successfully completed.

Matters on which the CI cannot assist

34.8 The CI cannot assist with the following aspects:

- investigate unincorporated partnerships or sole traders.
- investigate companies which do not carry on business in either England, Wales or Scotland
- investigate companies which have been dissolved or in compulsory liquidation.
- resolve any differences a person may have with a company, such as a dispute over the quality of goods or services provided.
- recover any money that is owed to a person.
- intervene in any dispute between a company and its shareholders. In particular, the fact that some shareholders are unhappy with decisions made by the directors is not a basis for an enquiry.
- intervene in any dispute between the company's directors.
- give any advice or guidance on what course of action a person could or should take if he is in dispute with a company.
- comment on whether or not a company is reputable, or provide references (credit, or otherwise) for a particular company.

CI's Investigation Procedure

34.9 When the CI receives a complaint, it first sees whether or not the organisation complained about is one which the CI can investigate. Thereafter, it will see what other information it can obtain about the company, both from the person who has complained and from other sources, and assess the extent to which the activities of the company may pose a threat to the public in general. This process is known as 'vetting'. Where the CI decides that there is sufficient good reason to investigate, and that an investigation is in the wider public interest, it will appoint investigators.

Although this appointment is made by the Secretary of State for BIS, the appointment document will be signed by a Departmental official who has the authority to do so. Investigations are usually carried out by CI staff. They may however be carried out by other professionals with the necessary expertise, but under the supervision of CI. The investigators will, if required, produce copies of their authorities and identity cards.

34.10 The investigator(s) will then call at the company's premises (often unannounced) and talk to the company's officers. They will ask questions of those who appear to be in charge and require sight of documents which they feel will be useful in the enquiry, taking photocopies of anything they consider to be important. The investigator also has the facility to obtain electronic copies of information held on computers.

Investigators can demand detailed information not only from the company's directors, but also from other company employees and third parties who may be in possession of relevant documents and information.

34.11 The time taken to investigate will depend on many factors, but in particular the complexity of the issues and the extent of co-operation received. The CI's published target is to complete 90% of investigations within six months, but in practice the majority are completed much sooner than this. Once its investigators are satisfied that all the necessary information has been obtained, they will consider it with a view to recommending whether or not the Department needs to take follow up action. If necessary they will obtain legal advice. Any appropriate follow up action is then identified and agreed will be taken.

Possible outcomes following CI investigations

34.12 The CI may decide that there is insufficient good reason or that it is not in the wider public interest to investigate. However, it may decide to investigate:

- Where the investigation shows that the company's business is being operated contrary to the public interest (eg in a manner likely to cause harm, detriment or loss to third party consumers, investors and traders), the CI can ask the Court to make a winding up order. This will put the company into compulsory liquidation and thereby prevent it from further trading. This is the follow up action that the CI is most likely to take.

  However, this does not stop the individuals involved with the company from trading through another company, or on their own. The objective is to stop the immediate mischief or undesirable trading activities as soon as possible.

- If the behaviour of the directors is such that they appear 'unfit' to be directors, the CI can apply to the Court for them to be disqualified from acting as company directors, or provide information to colleagues in the Insolvency Service (who investigate companies that have become insolvent) to assist with their disqualification effort.

The objective is to stop individuals running companies in the future, but this will not stop them trading on their own or in partnership. However, they will lose the privilege of 'limited liability' and will be personally responsible for the debts they incur.

- The information that the CI obtains may be passed to BIS Prosecution Lawyers, police or other investigation agencies, with a view to them carrying out a criminal investigation, where it appears that criminal offences have been committed by the company or its officers. Where appropriate, a formal warning letter may be sent instead of prosecution.

  This is more likely where breaches are capable of being remedied and there has been no obvious harm. For example, failure to record the required company details on business correspondence. However, the decision not to prosecute will be reconsidered if the same or further offences come to the CI's attention.

- The investigation may provide the CI with information which it can pass on to another regulatory organisation which has powers to deal with what the CI have found.

- Exceptionally, where the CI has concerns about a company's trading activities or the administration of its affairs, but there is no basis for formal action or the management appear capable of remedying the position, the CI may take some other action such as an 'informal warning' letter. This will set out its concerns and the improvement expected. The CI may ask for proof that appropriate action is being taken.

However, it is not the CI's role to monitor the affairs of any company or to provide feedback to a company following an enquiry. This exceptional step will be taken only if it is the appropriate outcome in the wider public interest. The CI may have a 'second look' to confirm that improvements have been made, particularly if further complaints are received.

The investigation may show that the original concerns were unfounded, and no other concerns have arisen, in which case no further action will be taken.

Reasons for company investigations

34.13 From a consideration of past inspectors' reports on company investigations, the following key reasons typically give rise to company investigations:

- Where fraudulent trading may be involved.
- Where there is any information to suggest that the company may be involved in a pattern of misconduct.
- The nature of investigations may ensure that directors and other officers are accountable for their actions given the wide powers available to the inspectors.
- Inspections serve to indirectly protect the interests of various 'stakeholders' within the corporation including creditors, shareholders and employees against corporate misconduct.

- Inspections may serve as a deterrent effect in demonstrating to other companies and organisations of the penalties that may be imposed on them including the adverse publicity that disclosure may bring.
- The reputation of directors and key officers may be seriously affected and in some cases may lead to a disqualification under the CDDA 1986. In other cases, directors and other key officers as well as non-executive officers may go to jail.
- Inspections must be conducted with the utmost fairness and impartiality: a failure to do so may compel an applicant to invoke the European Convention of Human Rights.

An overview of the investigation powers

Complaint

34.14

Fraud? Public interest? Shareholder interest? Policy holder interest? Other wrongdoing?	No ———		
Yes ↓			
Does another regulator have an interest? Is information available?			
↓			
Is any other investigatory body making inquiries?	Yes ⟶	Do they want assistance?	No ⟶
No ↓	Yes		
Information to support allegations?	No ⟶	Is there other cause for concern?	No ⟶
Yes ↓	Yes		
Is there a civil remedy available to complainant?	Yes ⟶	A matter of great public interest?	No ⟶
↓	Yes		
Acceptable for inquiry		Not acceptable for inquiry	

The scope of investigation of companies

34.15 The CA 1985 establishes a mechanism for allowing company investigations to be carried out, depending upon the ground being invoked and the corporate abuse that may have taken place. It will be seen that the most frequently invoked powers are under ss 432 and 447 of the CA1985 depending on the nature and complexity of the investigation involved. Applications under ss 431 and 432 are relatively rare in practice.

Application of s 431: formal investigations

Appointment

34.16 Section 431 allows the Secretary of State for Business Information and Skills to appoint one or more competent inspectors to investigate a company's affairs, and to report on the result of their investigations to him: CA 1985, s 431(1). This is a formal investigation by the inspectors. It is an investigation of a company on its own application or that of its members.

Inspectors do not sit in public and their conduct of inspections are in public. In *Hearts of Oak Assurance Co Ltd v Attorney-General* [1932] AC 392, the House of Lords held that an inspector appointed (under another Act) for the purpose of examining into and reporting on the affairs of an industrial assurance company, was not entitled to conduct the inspection in public, but this did not prevent him from admitting from time to time any persons such as witnesses, the presence of whom was reasonably necessary to enable him to carry out his duty under the statute.

Potential applicants

34.17 In order to invoke s 431 appointment of inspectors, the following persons may be the potential applicants:

(a) in the case of a company having a share capital, on the application either of:

   (i) not less than 200 members; or

   (ii) members holding not less than one-tenth of the shares issued (excluding any shares held as treasury shares);

(b) in the case of a company not having a share capital, on the application of not less than one-fifth in number of the persons on the company's register of members; and

(c) in any case, on the application of the company: CA 1985, s 431(2).

Security for costs

34.18 In the above cases however, the Secretary of State may, before appointing inspectors, require the applicant(s) to give security, to an amount not exceeding £5,000, or such other sum as he may by order specify, for payment of the investigation costs: CA 1985, s 431(4).

Supporting application

34.19 The application by the above applicants must be supported by such evidence as the Secretary of State may require, for the purpose of showing that the applicant(s) has a good reason for requiring the investigation: CA 1985, s 431(3).

Those complainants requesting an investigation must satisfy the Secretary of State that there is a good reason for an investigation and they may have to pay all or some of the costs of the investigation. This provision is rarely used in practice owing to the standing of persons who can apply and the sanction of costs and expenses involved becomes counter-productive for the potential applicants.

Application of s 432 – other company investigations

34.20 This is one of the main provisions used to initiate the investigation and the appointment of inspectors to look into a company's activities. The appointment will normally be as a result of some adverse publicity surrounding the company, which is likely to involve a complex investigation.

Appointment

34.21 Under s 432, the Secretary of State must appoint one or more competent inspectors to investigate the company's affairs; inspectors must report the result of their investigations to him, if the court by order declares that its affairs ought to be so investigated: CA 1985, s 432(1).

> ***A company's 'affairs' includes all aspects concerning the company and the term is widely construed***
>
> In *R v Board of Trade Ex parte St Martins Preserving Co* [1965] 1 QB 603, the court was required to consider the definition of company's 'affairs' and the scope this covered. The court held that a company's 'affairs' were unambiguous and must be given their natural meaning of the business affairs of the company. This included its goodwill, its profit and loss, its contracts and investments and assets, including its shareholding in and ability to control a subsidiary or sub-subsidiary.
>
> Further, the affairs of a company did not cease to be its affairs upon the appointment of a receiver and manager, and the fact that the actions of a receiver and manager might primarily be designed to serve the interest of the debenture holder, and to that extent were his affairs, did not prevent them from being the 'affairs' of the company whose future might depend on such actions carried out in its name.

Grounds

34.22 The Secretary of State may make such an appointment if it appears to him that there are circumstances suggesting that:

(a) the company's affairs are being or have been conducted with intent to defraud its creditors, or the creditors of any other person, or otherwise for a fraudulent or unlawful purpose, or in a manner which is unfairly prejudicial to some part of its members. In this case, reference to a company's 'members' includes any person who is not a member but to whom shares in a company have been transferred by operation of law;

(b) any actual or proposed act or omission of the company (including an act or omission on its behalf) is or would be so prejudicial, or that the company was formed for any fraudulent or unlawful purpose – grounds (a) and (b) above are similar to the unfair prejudicial ground under CA 2006, s 994;

(c) persons concerned with the company's formation or the management of its affairs have in connection therewith been guilty of fraud, misfeasance or other misconduct towards it or towards its members; or

(d) the company's members have not been given all the information with respect to its affairs which they might reasonably expect: CA 1985, s 432(2). This section does not entitle the Secretary of State to appoint inspectors merely because the directors may have breached their duties of skill, care and diligence: *SBA Properties Ltd v Cradock* [1967] 1 WLR 716.

Inspectors may be appointed under s 432(2) of the CA 1985 on terms that any report they may make is not to be published (CA 1985, s 432A); and in such a case, s 437(3) of the CA 1985 (availability and publication of inspectors' reports) does not apply (CA 1985, s 432(2A)).

Sections 432(1) and (2) of the CA 1985 are without prejudice to the powers of the Secretary of State under s 431 of the CA 1985; and the power conferred by s 432(2) of the CA 1985 is exercisable with respect to a body corporate notwithstanding that it is in course of being voluntarily wound up: (CA 1985, s 432(3)).

Inspectors' powers during investigation

34.23 Inspectors who are appointed to investigate the company's affairs can also, where they believe it is necessary to do so, investigate a connected body corporate, such as the subsidiary or the holding company. They can report on the affairs of the connected body corporate so far as the affairs are relevant to the company's investigation which the DTI inspectors were first investigating: CA 1985, s 433. The investigation powers may also extend to unincorporated associations if they are in any way associated with the corporate body.

Publication of documents and evidence to inspectors

34.24 The DTI inspectors have wide powers to require the company's officers or agents:

(a) to produce all documents of or relating to the company which are in their custody or power;

(b) to attend before the inspectors when required to do so; and

(c) to give inspectors all assistance in connection with the investigation as they are reasonably able to give: CA 1985, s 434(1).

Inspectors were not entitled to require a person to sign a confidentiality undertaking, which went further than was either reasonable or necessary in the circumstances

In *Re An Inquiry into Mirror Group Newspapers plc* [1999] 1 BCLC 690, the court was required to consider the 'reasonableness' of assistance that could be given to inspectors under s 434(1) of the CA 1985. Kevin Maxwell ('M'), an ex-director, refused to give a confidentiality undertaking sought by the inspectors or to answer questions. The issue was whether the inspectors were entitled to require a confidentiality undertaking; whether the ex-director was justified in refusing to answer the questions; and whether there were any limits on the right of inspectors to require assistance.

Sir Richard Scott V-C held that inspectors appointed under Pt XIV of the 1985 Act owed no duty to those from whom they had obtained information or documents that might inhibit them in the use of that information or those documents for the purposes of their statutory inquiry. Nor did they have any legal obligation to such persons to insist on confidentiality undertakings being given by others before whom, for the purposes of their inquiry, they wished to put the material, since confidentiality could be protected simply by making the confidential character of the information and documents known. It followed that in the absence of any express statutory power to do so, the inspectors had not been entitled to require M to sign the confidentiality undertaking, which in any event went further than was either reasonable or necessary. Accordingly, M's refusal to sign the undertaking did not represent a failure on his part to give the inspectors any assistance he was reasonably able to give.

The purpose of Pt XIV inspections, where there were grounds that suggested some irregularity or impropriety in the conduct of the affairs of a company had occurred, was to discover what had happened. However, inspectors could not place demands on persons that were unreasonable, whether as to the time they had to expend or the expense they had to incur in preparation for the questions or in any other respect. In the instant case, having regard to the extent of the interrogations that M had already undergone, the potential burden that the questioning might place on him risked going beyond that which an unrepresented individual could reasonably be required to accept. Accordingly, until steps were taken by the inspectors to reduce that burden, M's refusal to answer questions did not constitute a breach of his statutory obligations under s 434.

34.25 If the inspectors consider that an officer or agent of the company or other body corporate, or any other person, is or may be in possession of information relating to a matter which they believe to be relevant to the investigation, they may require him:

(a) to produce to them any documents in his custody or power relating to that matter;

(b) to attend before them;

(c) otherwise to give them all assistance in connection with the investigation which he is reasonably able to give, and it is that person's duty to comply with the requirement: CA 1985, s 434(2).

It is the duty of the company's officer or agent to comply with the above requirements. The references to 'officers' or 'agents' include those past as well as present. 'Agents' in relation to a company or other body corporate include its bankers and solicitors and persons employed by it as auditors whether these persons are or are not officers of the company or other body corporate: CA 1985, s 434(4).

An inspector may, for the purposes of the investigation, examine any person on oath, and may also administer an oath: CA 1985, s 434(3).

An answer given by a person to a question put to him in exercise of the powers conferred upon the (then) DTI inspectors, may be used in evidence against him: CA 1985, s 434(5).

Unless certain documents were excluded from disclosure on the ground that they were confidential documents which the public interest required to be protected from disclosure, they would under the general law, be admissible in evidence

In practice, inspectors will usually put questions to a person under investigation. The answers may then be used in evidence against him: CA 1985, s 434(5). The evidence given by a person to inspectors in the course of an investigation may be admissible in civil proceedings. In *London & County Securities Ltd v Nicholson* [1980] 3 All ER 861, the DTI appointed inspectors pursuant to the Companies Act to investigate the company's affairs. In the course of their investigations, the inspectors took oral evidence from the company's auditors. Transcripts were made of the evidence, which was amplified in correspondence between the inspectors and the solicitors for the firm of accountants. There was no express assurance given to the witnesses that their evidence would be treated as confidential. The transcripts were later made available to the company's liquidator upon the liquidator undertaking to the court that the documents would be treated as confidential. In subsequent legal proceedings, the liquidator brought an action against the accountants alleging negligence in the conduct of the company's audits. The liquidator sought to adduce as evidence in the action the transcripts of the evidence given to the inspectors and the correspondence amplifying it on the ground that those documents were admissible under the general law. According to the defendants, the documents were not admissible because the evidence given to the inspectors was to be treated as confidential and it was in the public interest that such evidence should be protected from disclosure.

Browne-Wilkinson J (as he was then) decided that, in general, evidence given to inspectors appointed pursuant to the Companies Acts was admissible against a person subsequently in both criminal and civil proceedings. Unless the documents were excluded from disclosure on the ground that they were confidential documents which the public interest required to be protected from disclosure, they would under the general law, be admissible in evidence: *R v Scott* (1856) Dears & B 47 (unsworn evidence given by a bankrupt on his examination was admissible against him on a subsequent criminal charge): *Re Rolls Razor Ltd* [1968] 3 All ER 698; and *Karak Rubber Co Ltd v Burden* [1971] 3 All ER 1118 (Brightman J decided that only sworn evidence given to inspectors was admissible in subsequent proceedings and he excluded unsworn evidence). In *R v Harris* [1970] 3 All ER 746, Mackenna J decided that sworn evidence given by a witness to inspectors appointed under the Companies Acts was admissible against that witness in subsequent criminal proceedings.

Transcripts of evidence given by the witnesses should be disclosed but only after prior notification to the witnesses

Soden v Burns [1996] 3 All ER 967 concerned an application by the company's administrators for the production of transcripts taken by government inspectors as part of the Companies Act 1985, s 432 inquiry into the company's affairs. The transcripts comprised oral evidence given by witnesses to inspectors. The court decided that the transcripts of evidence given by the witnesses should be disclosed but only after prior notification to the witnesses, and subject to any application by the witnesses to set aside the order to disclose.

In *Re London United Investments plc* [1992] there was an appeal by the company director against a decision that the appellant had no right to remain silent on grounds of self-incrimination when required to answer questions put to him by inspectors appointed under s 432 of CA 1985 for the purpose of investigating the company's affairs. The Court of Appeal held that under the authority of *Hammond v Commonwealth of Australia* 42 ALR 327, that Parliament might take away the privilege of remaining silent. A person was bound to answer questions put by inspectors as the right to remain silent had been removed by necessary implication as it was necessary in the public interest to bring civil proceedings in the company's name. A line might be drawn where a person had been charged with a criminal offence and it might be that the court had power under s 463(2), after enquiring into a case, to refuse to punish someone for refusing to answer questions if the court felt at that stage the questioning was oppressive and therefore unfair, but this was not the case here. By reason of ss 434, 436 and 452(1) the appellant's refusal to answer was unjustified. Further, there was no evidence to suggest that the Secretary of State, in making the appointment of inspectors under CA 1985, was motivated by improper considerations. Also as a matter of law, it was not improper to appoint inspectors to investigate matters that were the subject matter of an allegation of fraud. It was clear from ss 437(1B), 449 and 451A that criminal proceedings could be initiated at the same time as inspectors were carrying out their investigations. Accordingly, there was no basis for finding that the Secretary of State had acted improperly in appointing inspectors.

Application of natural justice to company investigations

34.26 Although the concept of natural justice does not feature in the CA 1985 provisions dealing with company investigations, it has been addressed by the courts in connection with some of the procedural aspects of corporate investigations. The term 'natural justice' has been used in a variety of legal contexts, but generally refers to 'fair play' – the opportunity to be heard; the right to make representations; the fact that the judge will not perform the combined role of judge, jury and executioner; that there will be no bias in arriving at a decision that is fair and properly applies the applicable laws to the facts under consideration.

Although the proceedings before the inspectors were only administrative and inquisitorial in nature, and not judicial or quasi-judicial, yet the characteristics of the proceedings required the inspectors to act fairly

Re Pergamon Press [1971] Ch 388

One of the first cases to apply the concept of natural justice was in *Re Pergamon Press* where the Court of Appeal was required to address the procedural fairness of the powers of the inspectors in conducting their investigation balanced against the interests of the individual(s) under investigation.

In September 1969, the Board of Trade ordered an investigation under s 165 of the Companies Act 1948 (now s 432 of the CA 1985) into the affairs of Pergamon Press Limited ('P Ltd') and appointed inspectors. It was important in the public interest that the investigation should be completed speedily.

In October 1969, the L corporation (which had a sufficient holding in P Ltd for the purpose) removed Robert Maxwell ('M') and other directors from the board of P Ltd and in November 1969, began proceedings in the United States of America against M charging fraud and deceit in connection with the sale of shares in P Ltd and claiming $22,000,000. M and the other directors were apprehensive that the inspectors might make an interim report which could be used against them in the United States litigation, and that allegations might be made reflecting on their conduct. The inspectors wished to hear evidence in private from the directors who at the outset of the investigation asked for assurances that, if allegations were made against them, they should be allowed to read transcripts of the evidence adverse to them, to look at documents used against them, and to cross-examine witnesses. The inspectors were not prepared to allow the directors a right to peruse the transcripts of evidence but made it clear that no one would be criticised in any report without first being afforded the opportunity to give an explanation, that this involved that the person concerned should be told in general terms of the allegation against him, and that the inspectors would provide him with the purport of the relevant evidence and documents. The directors were not satisfied with these assurances and when called on to give evidence to the inspectors they refused to do so. An inspector's report might lead to judicial proceedings or the winding-up of the company, and the report had to be put before the company and might, at the discretion of the board, be published to the public at large. The inspectors certified the directors' refusal to give evidence to the court, and the court having inquired into the case held that the directors were not justified in their refusal.

At first instance, Plowman J held, *inter alia*, that the directors were not entitled to insist on the assurances before answering the inspectors' questions. The directors appealed to the Court of Appeal against Plowman J's decision on the grounds of natural justice.

On appeal by the directors, the Court of Appeal held that although the proceedings before the inspectors were only administrative, and not judicial or quasi-judicial, yet the characteristics of the proceedings required the inspectors to act fairly, in that if they were disposed to condemn or criticise anyone in a report they must first give him a fair opportunity to correct or contradict the allegation, for which purpose an outline of the charge would usually suffice.

Except for the requirement to act fairly, the inspectors should not be subject to any set rules of procedure and should be free to act at their own discretion. Accordingly, as the inspectors had shown that they intended to act fairly and had given every assurance that could reasonably be required, the directors' refusal to give evidence was unjustified: *R v Gaming Board for Great Britain, ex parte Benaim* [1970] 2 All ER 528.

The Court of Appeal further stated that the inspectors (who were under a duty to act fairly and to give anyone whom they proposed to condemn or criticise in their report a fair opportunity to answer what was alleged against him) had acted perfectly properly and the directors had no right to demand further assurances: see dicta of Lord Reid in *Ridge v Baldwin* [1964] AC 40, 65; and *Reg v Gaming Board for Great Britain, Ex parte Benaim and Khaida* [1970] 2 QB 417.

The Court of Appeal considered *per curiam* that although the inspectors' function under s 432 of the CA 1985 was investigatory and not judicial, they must, in view of the consequences which may follow from their report act fairly. Subject to that they must be masters of their own procedures.

According to Lord Denning, inspectors were not a court of law nor were their proceedings quasi-judicial: see In *re Grosvenor & West-End Railway Terminus Hotel Co Ltd* (1897) 76 LT 337. Inspectors nevertheless had a significant task to perform. They have to make a report which may have wide repercussions. They may, if they think fit, make findings of fact which are very damaging to those whom they name. They may accuse some; they may condemn others; they may ruin reputations or careers. Their report may lead to judicial proceedings. It may expose persons to criminal prosecutions or to civil actions. It may bring about the winding up of the company, and be used itself as material for the winding up: see In *Re SBA Properties Ltd* [1967] 1 WLR 799. The inspectors must, however, act fairly. This is a duty which rests on them, as on many other bodies, even though they are not judicial, nor quasi-judicial, but only administrative: see *Reg v Gaming Board for Great Britain, Ex parte Benaim and Khaida* [1970] 2 QB 417. The inspectors can obtain information in any way they think best, but before they condemn or criticise a man, they must give him a fair opportunity for correcting or contradicting what is said against him. They need not quote chapter and verse. An outline of the charge will usually suffice.

Sachs LJ stated:

> 'To conclude that there must be an appropriate measure of natural justice, or as it is often nowadays styled "fair play in action", in the present case is thus easy. That was, indeed, something which was well recognised by the inspectors, who expressly so stated more than once in the course of the proceedings. The real issue, however, is whether

that measure should in relation to s 432 of the CA 1985 investigations generally, or, alternatively, as regards this particular investigation, be reduced by the courts to some set of rules, or whether it should be left to the inspectors, who are men of high professional qualifications, in their discretion to proceed with that fairness of procedure that is appropriate to the particular circumstances of the case as it may develop.

In the application of the concept of fair play, there must be real flexibility, so that very different situations may be met without producing procedures unsuitable to the object in hand. That need for flexibility has been emphasised in a number of authoritative passages in the judgments cited to this court. In the forefront was that of Tucker LJ in *Russell v Duke of Norfolk* [1949] 1 All ER 109, 118, and the general effect of his views has been once again echoed recently by Lord Guest, Lord Donovan and Lord Wilberforce in *Wiseman v Borneman* [1971] AC 297, 311, 314, 320.

34.27 Subsequent cases have highlighted that natural justice does have a part to play in company investigations particularly the procedural aspects.

Where inspectors are holding an inquiry under s 432 of the CA 1985, it was sufficient for them to put to the witnesses what had been said against them by other persons, or in documents, to enable them to deal with those criticisms in the course of the inquiry

In *Maxwell v Department of Trade and Industry [1971 M No 2901]* [1974] QB 523, in September 1969 the Board of Trade appointed two inspectors under s 165 of the CA 1948 (now s 432 of the CA 1985) to investigate and report on the affairs of two limited companies following a statement by the City Panel on Takeovers that the shareholders of one of the companies might not be getting all the information about its affairs which they might reasonably expect.

The claimant, Robert Maxwell, who was at the material time chairman and chief executive of the companies, gave evidence at the inquiry and was recalled on a number of occasions so that the inspectors might put to him criticisms of him made by other witnesses or contained in documents and give him the opportunity of dealing with them.

In June 1971, the inspectors signed their first interim report which contained conclusions highly critical of the claimant. Maxwell issued writs against the department and the inspectors, seeking declarations that the inspectors had conducted the inquiry and made their report without regard to the rules of natural justice, and asking for injunctions to restrain the inspectors from proceeding with the inquiry. He also sought an injunction.

At first instance, Forbes J, while making no order, expressed his view that the inspectors had failed to observe the rules of natural justice because they had not formulated their own tentative criticisms of the plaintiff nor given him an opportunity to deal with them before making their report, and also that having said they would follow that procedure the inspectors had failed to do so.

On the trial of the consolidated actions Wien J refused the relief asked for, holding, contrary to Forbes J, that the inspectors had been eminently fair by giving the claimant proper notice of what was said against him and a fair opportunity of meeting such criticisms; and that their duty to act fairly did not require them to put their proposed conclusions to the person criticised and consider his answers before making their report. He also found that the inspectors had not undertaken to follow that procedure.

Maxwell thereafter appealed to the Court of Appeal.

The Court of Appeal held that when inspectors were holding an inquiry under s 432 of the CA 1985, it was sufficient for them to put to the witnesses what had been said against them by other persons, or in documents, to enable them to deal with those criticisms in the course of the inquiry.

Further, it was not necessary for the inspectors to put their tentative conclusions to the witnesses in order to give them an opportunity to refute them, and that the inspectors had not given any undertaking to do so in the present case. The inspectors had acted with conspicuous fairness in their conduct of the investigation as a whole and had put to the claimant all the matters which appeared to call for an answer; and that as they had acted honestly and fairly their report was not to be impugned.

The Court of Appeal considered *per curiam* that though the court had jurisdiction to make, and might in the exercise of its discretion grant, bare declarations that natural justice had not been observed in the conduct of an inquiry, the circumstances which would justify the grant of such relief in the context of an investigation under s 432 of the CA 1985 would have to be of an exceptional kind.

According to Lord Denning, inspectors were undertaking a public duty in the public interest. They must do what is fair to the best of their ability.

34.28 For further application of the 'natural justice' principles see: *F Hoffmann-La Roche & Co AG and others v Secretary of State for Trade and Industry* [1974] 2 All ER 1128.

The decision of the Secretary of State to appoint inspectors under s 432 of the CA 1985 was no more than an administrative decision, and a full application of natural justice did not apply

In some cases, rather than challenge the conduct and procedural aspects of the inspectors' investigations into the company, the issue has centered around the conduct of the Secretary of State in instigating the investigations. It is alleged that the Secretary of State acted *ultra vires* in not informing a company in advance that a corporate investigation would be carried out.

In *Norwest Holst Ltd v Department of Trade* [1978] 3 All ER 280, the claimant was a public company engaged in construction and engineering in England and internationally. Its paid up capital was some £2.432 million and it had numerous subsidiary companies. On 29 November 1976 the Secretary of State for Trade acting under s 432 of the CA 1985 authorised officers of his department to look at certain books and papers of the company and two of its subsidiaries. There was no evidence to show that the solvency of the company was in question, or that any shareholder had made a complaint, or that there had been any adverse comment on the company's affairs in the press. The certificate of the company's auditors had never been qualified. On 11 March 1977, the Secretary of State appointed two inspectors to investigate the affairs of the company under s 432 of the CA 1985. In subsequent correspondence with the Secretary of State, the company claimed that it knew of no facts or circumstances on which the Secretary of State could justify ordering an inquiry into its affairs, and asked him to disclose the circumstances and the evidence on which he relied in exercising his discretion. The Secretary of State refused to give that information but stated that the appointment had been made under s 432 of the CA 1985.

The company brought an action against the Department of Trade and the inspectors claiming (i) a declaration that the appointment of the inspectors was ultra vires and of no effect, and (ii) an injunction to restrain the inspectors from beginning their investigation. The company contended that the Secretary of State had not acted fairly or in accordance with the rules of natural justice in refusing to give the company an opportunity to answer the complaints against it before the inspectors had been appointed. The defendants applied to have the action struck out as being frivolous, vexatious and an abuse of the process of the court.

The Court of Appeal decided that the decision of the Secretary of State to appoint inspectors under s 432 of the CA 1985 was no more than an administrative decision the effect of which was to set in train an investigation at which those involved would have an opportunity of stating their case. There was therefore nothing in the rules of natural justice which required him to give the company an opportunity of stating its case before he made his decision to set up the investigation. The only requirement was that he should make his decision in good faith and there was no evidence to suggest that he had not done so. Accordingly the company's action was struck out: See dicta of Lord Reid in *Wiseman v Borneman* [1969] 3 All ER at 277–278 and of Salmon LJ in *R v Barnet and Camden Rent Tribunal, ex parte Frey Investments Ltd* [1972] 1 All ER at 1192.

Lord Denning:

> 'It is important to know the background to the legislation. It sometimes happens that public companies are conducted in a way which is beyond the control of the ordinary shareholders. The majority of the shares are in the hands of two or three individuals. These have control of the company's affairs. The other shareholders know little and are told little. They receive the glossy annual reports. Most of them throw them into the wastepaper basket. There is an annual general meeting but few of the shareholders attend. The whole management and control is in the hands of the directors. They are a self-perpetuating oligarchy; and are

virtually unaccountable. Seeing that the directors are the guardians of the company, the question is asked: *quis custodiet ipsos custodes?* who will guard the guards themselves? (see for example: *Wallersteiner v Moir* ([1974] 3 All ER 217 at 241, [1974]).

It is because companies are beyond the reach of ordinary individuals that this legislation has been passed so as to enable the Department of Trade to appoint inspectors to investigate the affairs of a company. Counsel for the company drew our attention to the practice of the Board of Trade from 1948 to 1962. It was given in evidence to Lord Jenkins's Committee on Company Law (Report of the Committee on Company Law Amendment (1962), Cmnd 1749, presided over by Lord Jenkins Cmnd 1749, para 213). The Board of Trade said that it was:

> "... very necessary to hear both sides before deciding whether or not an inspector should be appointed. By so doing it is often possible in cases in which no fraud is alleged to bring the parties together or for them to reach a mutually satisfactory arrangement so that an investigation is not necessary."

That was the practice before 1962. Counsel for the company submitted that that practice was required by the common law. He said that the principles of natural justice are to be applied; and, accordingly, both sides should be heard before an inspector is appointed.

That may have been the practice of the Board of Trade in those years; but I do not think that it was required by the common law. There are many cases where an inquiry is held, not as a judicial or quasi-judicial inquiry, but simply as a matter of good administration. In these circumstances there is no need for any preliminary notice of any charge, or anything of that sort. Take the case where a police officer is suspected of misconduct. The practice is to suspend him pending enquiries. He is not given notice of any charge at that stage, nor any opportunity of being heard. The rules of natural justice do not apply unless and until it is decided to take proceedings. Other instances can be given in other fields. For instance, the Stock Exchange may suspend dealings in a company's shares. They go by what they know, without warning the company beforehand.

When the officers of the Department of Trade are appointed to examine the books, there is no need for the rules of natural justice to be applied. If the company was forewarned and told that the officers were coming, what is to happen to the books? In a wicked world, it is not unknown for books or papers to be destroyed or lost. So also with the appointment of inspectors, under s 432 of the CA 1985. The inspectors are not to decide rights or wrongs. They are to investigate and report. This inquiry is a good administrative arrangement for the good conduct of companies and their affairs. It is not a case to which the rules of natural justice apply. There is no need for them to be given notice of a charge, or a fair opportunity of meeting it.'

Ormrod LJ:

'The phrase "the requirements of natural justice" seems to be mesmerising people at the moment. This must, I think, be due to the apposition of the words "natural" and "justice". It has been pointed out many times that the word "natural" adds nothing except perhaps a hint of nostalgia for the good old days when nasty things did not happen. If, instead, we omit it and put the question in the form stated in *Fisher v Keane*: have the ordinary principles of justice been complied with? It at once becomes much more realistic and even mundane. It is just possible that the pleader in the present case might have hesitated a little longer if he had been deprived of the use of that romantic word "natural". Another source of confusion is the automatic identification of the phrase "natural justice" with giving the person concerned an opportunity of stating his side of the story, and so on. In many cases, of course, the two are synonymous but not by any means in all.

In the present case we are concerned with the making of a decision by the Secretary of State to appoint inspectors under s 432 of the CA 1985. The purpose of the appointment is to investigate the company in order to find out what has been going on, in other words, to find the facts. At such an inquiry the company and its officers will be asked to answer the allegations or complaints against them, if there are any, and give any explanation which they wish to give. So in this case what we are concerned with is only the preliminary stage: the decision of the Secretary of State to appoint inspectors. It is said that such an appointment is likely to damage the company whose affairs are to be investigated; therefore the Secretary of State must act in accordance with the ordinary principles of justice, which means notifying the company of the basis on which the investigation is to proceed and giving it an opportunity, in advance, of being heard.

In my judgment the ordinary principles of justice do not require anything of the kind. At this stage the Secretary of State is not required to notify the company or seek its comments before ordering an investigation. It is only necessary to refer very shortly to a passage in Lord Reid's speech in *Wiseman v Borneman* ([1969] 3 All ER 275 at 277, 278, [1971] AC 297 at 308), which is conveniently cited in Sachs LJ's judgment in *Re Pergamon Press Ltd* ([1970] 3 All ER 535 at 542, [1971] Ch 388 at 403). The passage reads:

> "Every public officer who has to decide whether to prosecute or raise proceedings ought first to decide whether there is a prima facie case but no one supposes that justice requires that he should first seek the comments of the accused or the defendant on the material before him. So there is nothing inherently unjust in reaching such a decision in the absence of the other party."

To my mind that passage applies precisely to the present case.'

Geoffrey Lane LJ:

> 'First, dealing with the argument based on what is called "natural justice", it is important to remember that natural justice and the principle *audi alteram partem* are not synonymous because there are occasions, and very many occasions, when natural justice does not demand that the other side should be heard on the question.
>
> In every investigation or allegation of fraud or misfeasance there are, it seems to me, by and large three different phases. First of all, the administrative phase; next, the judicial phase; and, finally, the executive phase when the orders of the court or the tribunal are, if necessary, executed or promulgated. Quite plainly, fairness to the suspect (if one may call him that) demands that he should be given a chance of stating his case before the final period: the execution. That is set out plainly in *Cooper v Wandsworth Board of Works* and also in *Durayappah v Fernando*. Equally fairness demands that the suspect shall be given a chance of putting his side of the case before the judicial inquiry is over. That scarcely needs illustration, but if it does it is to found in *Re Pergamon Press Ltd* in 1971. But on the other side, and the other side are entitled to fairness just as the suspect is, fairness to the inquirer demands that during the administrative period he should be able to investigate without having at every stage to inquire from the suspect what his side of the matter may be. Of course it may be difficult to find out the particular point at which the administrative phase ends and the judicial phase begins. In other words, when do the judicial proceedings start? Having heard the argument of counsel for the company, put forward so forcibly in this court, it seems to me quite plain, first of all, that the s 109 investigation was still administrative; and that indeed is not called into question by the company here. It seems to me equally plain that the inquiry by the inspectors is a judicial inquiry, but how can it be argued that anything judicial is taking place before the inception of that inquiry? I do not think it can. It seems to me quite plain that the first moment at which it can be said natural justice demands that the suspect be given an opportunity to state his case is at the beginning or during the inquiry by the two inspectors appointed under s 165(b).'

Under Pt XIV of the CA 1985, company investigations should be conducted in private and that the inspectors should not make public information disclosed to them in the course of the investigation

In *Re An Inquiry Into Mirror Group Newspapers* [2000] Ch 194, an application was made by inspectors appointed by the Secretary of State for DTI under s 432 of the CA 1985 to investigate the affairs of Mirror Group Newspapers for referral to the court under s 436 of the CA 1985 the refusal of the ex-director Kevin Maxwell to answer their questions. Also, his refusal to enter into a confidentiality undertaking not to disclose information which, in the course of their questioning, they put to him. Maxwell had already undergone extensive questioning in respect of criminal proceedings, in which he was acquitted, and other civil inquiries and investigations. He was no longer in receipt of legal aid and was not legally represented, despite requests to the DTI. He submitted that the particular circumstances of the case rendered the questioning of him by the inspectors unfair and oppressive, that the inspectors had no right to require him to give the confidentiality undertaking, and that his refusal to co-operate with the inspectors was justified and should not be visited by any sanction.

The two main issues before the court were: (i) whether inspectors who had been appointed under Pt XIV of the CA 1985 were entitled to demand, of a person who was placed under a statutory obligation to attend before them and answer their question, that the person enter into an undertaking of confidentiality, and if so, the extent of this. The inspectors' case was that such a signing represented 'assistance in connection with the investigation which (the respondent was) reasonably able to give': s 434(1)(c) and s 434(2)(c) of the CA 1985; and (ii) the correct limits, if any, on the right of inspectors to require officers and agents of a company under investigation to attend before them and assist them in their investigation. An underlying issue was whether it was unfair to require the respondent to answer the inspectors' questions without the benefit of legal representation.

The court held that under Pt XIV of the Companies Act 1985, company investigations should be conducted in private and that the inspectors should not make public information disclosed to them in the course of the investigation: *Hearts of Oak Assurance Co Ltd v Attorney General* [1932] AC 392. However, this case had not imposed any other limitation on the way in which inspectors, sitting in private, conducted their investigation.

The court also stated that the signing by a proposed witness of a confidentiality undertaking was not a pre-requisite for the protection of confidential material placed before him by inspectors, provided always that he was put on notice of its confidential character. Whether material placed before a witness did in fact have a confidential character could not be answered in the abstract. However, telling the witness that it did could not elevate material that was not confidential into material that was. In the present case, the confidentiality undertaking that the inspectors required Maxwell to sign went a good deal further than was reasonable or necessary, but it did not represent a failure on his part to give the inspectors any assistance he was reasonably able to give; and that, accordingly, no question arose of the respondent's refusal being dealt with as a contempt.

Sir Richard Scott V-C also held that that the assistance that those on whom an obligation was placed by s 434 of the Act of 1985 to give was not unlimited, but extended only to that which they were reasonably able to give; that where the demands of the inspectors went beyond the assistance that the witness was reasonably able to give, whether as to the time he would have to expend or the expense he would have to incur in preparation for the questions or in any other respect, a failure to comply would not amount to a breach of statutory duty which would be treated as a contempt; that there was nothing unreasonable in the inspectors' or the department's refusal to give an assurance that the respondent's answers would not be used as the basis of any future civil or criminal proceedings; that the possibility of self-incrimination was not a justification for refusing to answer the inspectors' questions; that the refusal of the Secretary of State to give an assurance that disqualification proceedings would not be brought against a former director could not justify a refusal to answer inspectors' questions; that lack of legal representation was not in itself a ground of complaint but was to be considered and weighed with other complaints; but that, in the highly unusual circumstances, the court would not make the order sought.

The Application of Human Rights to Company Investigations

34.29 An issue that has arisen in respect of the powers of the inspectors to obtain documents and raise questions to the person concerned could self-incriminate that person in subsequent proceedings? Further, whether any responses to the inspectors would be a breach of Article 6 of the European Convention of Human Rights? Article 6 provides:

> '1. In the determination of his civil rights and obligations or of any criminal charge against him, everyone is entitled to a fair and public hearing within a reasonable time by an independent and impartial tribunal established by law. Judgment shall be pronounced publicly but the press and public may be excluded from all or part of the trial in the interest of morals, public order or national security in a democratic society, where the interests of juveniles or the protection of the private life of the parties so require, or the extent strictly necessary in the opinion of the court in special circumstances where publicity would prejudice the interests of justice.
>
> 2. Everyone charged with a criminal offence shall be presumed innocent until proved guilty according to law.
>
> 3. Everyone charged with a criminal offence has the following minimum rights:
>
> (a) to be informed promptly, in a language which he understands and in detail, of the nature and cause of the accusation against him;
>
> (b) to have adequate time and the facilities for the preparation of his defence;
>
> (c) to defend himself in person or through legal assistance of his own choosing or, if he has not sufficient means to pay for legal assistance, to be given it free when the interests of justice so require;
>
> (d) to examine or have examined witnesses against him and to obtain the attendance and examination of witnesses on his behalf under the same conditions as witnesses against him;
>
> (e) to have the free assistance of an interpreter if he cannot understand or speak the language used in court.'

The European Court of Human Rights has established various jurisprudential principles with regard to the application of human rights and its application to company investigations.

The right of an individual not to incriminate himself, which was central to the notion of a fair procedure inherent in Art 6(1) of the EHRC, was primarily concerned with the right of an accused to remain silent and was not therefore confined to statements of admission of wrongdoing or to remarks which were directly incriminating

In *Saunders v United Kingdom* [1998] 1 BCLC 362, G plc was involved in a successful takeover bid of another company. However, G plc's share price rose dramatically during the takeover bid as a result of an unlawful share support operation. The Secretary of State for Trade and Industry appointed inspectors to investigate the matter pursuant to s 432 of the Companies Act 1985. Under ss 434 and 436 of the 1985 Act, answers given by a person in the course of such inquiries could be used in evidence against him, and a refusal to co-operate with the inspectors could result in a finding of contempt of court.

The inspectors found evidence that criminal offences had been committed, and it was decided that they should continue their inquiries and pass the transcripts of their interviews to the Crown Prosecution Service. The applicant was interviewed by the inspectors and was subsequently charged with offences relating to the share support operation. In the course of the applicant's trial, transcripts of those interviews were used by the prosecution to establish his involvement in the share support operation and to refute his own evidence, and he was convicted on 12 counts of conspiracy, false accounting and theft.

The Court of Appeal rejected the applicant's contention that the use of those transcripts automatically rendered the proceedings unfair and denied him leave to appeal to the House of Lords. Thereafter the applicant lodged an application with the European Commission of Human Rights, complaining that the use at his trial of statements he had made to the inspectors under their compulsory powers had deprived him of a fair hearing in violation of Article 6(1) of the Convention for the Protection of Human Rights and Fundamental Freedoms 1950 which provides that:

> 'In the determination of … any criminal charge … everyone is entitled to a fair … hearing … by an independent and impartial tribunal …'

The Commission referred the complaint to the European Court of Human Rights.

It was held by the European Court of Human Rights that the right of an individual not to incriminate himself, which was central to the notion of a fair procedure inherent in Article 6(1) of the European Human Rights Convention, was primarily concerned with the right of an accused to remain silent and was not therefore confined to statements of admission of wrongdoing or to remarks which were directly incriminating. In particular, testimony obtained under compulsion which appeared to be of a non-incriminating nature, such as exculpatory remarks or mere information on questions of fact, could later be used by the prosecution in criminal proceedings to contradict or cast doubt upon other statements of the accused or otherwise to undermine his credibility. Accordingly, the question whether the applicant's right to a fair hearing had been infringed depended not on the nature of his statements but on the use made of them by the prosecution during the trial. It was clear, in the instant case, that the transcripts at issue had been used extensively by the prosecution to cast doubt upon the applicant's honesty and to establish his involvement in the share support operation. Such an infringement of the applicant's right not to incriminate himself could not be justified either by the complexity of corporate fraud or by the vital public interest in the investigation thereof, and it followed that there had been a violation of his rights under Article 6(1).

A third party seeking disclosure of a witness statement given to inspectors in the course of an investigation under s 432(2) of the CA 1985 must first tell the witness

In *British & Commonwealth Holdings plc v Barclays De Zoete Wedd Ltd* [1998] ALL ER 491, an application was made by the administrators of a company for disclosure of 54 witness statements taken by the DTI in the investigation of the collapse of another company under s 432(2) of the CA 1985.

The administrators of the collapsed company contended that documents in their possession were privileged from production on the grounds of confidentiality or public interest.

The court held (Neuberger J) that a third party seeking disclosure of a witness statement given to inspectors in the course of an investigation under s 432(2) of the CA 1985 must first tell the witness. Accordingly, transcripts of the collapsed company's witnesses, even edited transcripts, should not be disclosed. However, the court ordered disclosure of the chief executive's statement as to what he had previously stated during the acquisition of the collapsed company.

The functions of Inspectors is administrative and inquisitorial in nature; and the right of access to a court was not absolute but may be subject to implied limitations

Fayed v United Kingdom (1994) 16 EHRR 393 concerned the making and publication of a report by Inspectors appointed by the Secretary of State for Trade and Industry under the CA 1985, about the applicants' take-over of a company, through their company. The Inspector's report made certain criticisms of the applicants.

The applicants complained that the report determined their civil right to honour and reputation and denied them effective access to a court in the determination of this civil right. They also complained of the absence of effective remedies to challenge the findings of the Inspectors.

With regard to the investigation by the Inspectors, the European Court of Human Rights held that the Inspectors did not adjudicate, either in form or in substance, that their functions were essentially investigative. Their enquiry did not 'determine' the applicants' civil right to a good reputation, nor was its result directly decisive for that right. Article 6-1 ECHR (under its 'civil' head) was not applicable.

In connection with the proceedings to contest the Inspectors' findings the ECHR held that the right of access to a court was not absolute but may be subject to implied limitations. Whilst the national authorities enjoyed a certain margin of appreciation, the limitations applied must not impair the very essence of the right and must pursue a legitimate aim and must respect the principle of proportionality.

With respect to the limitations on the applicants' ability to take legal proceedings, whether by way of defamation action or by way of judicial review, to challenge the findings and conclusions in the Inspectors' report which were damaging to their reputation, the ECHR had regard in particular to the national authorities' responsibility to regulate the conduct of the affairs of public companies and to the safeguards that existed in relation to the impugned investigation. The limitations were not found to involve an unjustified denial of the applicants' 'right to a court'. The ECHR held that there was no violation of Art 6-1.

A person has a right not to incriminate himself

In *IJL v United Kingdom* (2001) 33 EHRR 11, the applicants were suspected of artificially inflating the price of Guinness shares to assist in the Guinness take-over of another company by means that were contrary to domestic law. The Department of Trade and Industry (DTI) (as it was then) inspectors interviewed the applicants who were required by law to answer the questions.

A department solicitor recorded that there was evidence that criminal offences had been committed and the DTI and the Crown Prosecution Service agreed a date for the inspectors' enquiries to be completed and the criminal investigation to commence. Subsequently, the inspectors passed the transcripts of their interviews with the applicants and other documents to the Crown Prosecution Service and police.

At trial, the transcripts were admitted on the basis that they were confessions, and so admissible under domestic law. The transcripts of the interviews were read to the jury over three days and were used to establish the applicants' state of knowledge. The applicants made an unsuccessful appeal against conviction to the Court of Appeal; it was now three years and eight months after the applicants were charged. Subsequently, the applicants became aware of material available to the crown prior to trial which had not previously been disclosed and sought disclosure then. They asked the Home Secretary to refer the case back to the Court of Appeal. Three years and seven months after the Court of Appeal first dismissed the case, the Home Secretary referred the case back to it. After eleven months, the Court of Appeal dismissed the appeals for the most part. The Court of Appeal denied leave to appeal to the House of Lords.

The applicants appealed to the European Court of Human Rights of claiming violations of Art 6, of the European Convention on Human Rights.

The European Court of Human Rights held that the applicants were tried together and a significant part of the Crown's case were the transcripts of the interviews, which they gave to the DTI inspectors as compelled to do under domestic law. The respondent did not contest that the transcripts, which were read out over three days, were used to incriminate each of the applicants. There had been an infringement of the right not to incriminate oneself; and therefore had been an infringement of Art 6 of the Convention in respect of that ground.

The Court further held that the applicants asserted that during the interviews the inspectors were determining a criminal charge. The domestic legislation provided that the DTI inspectors had investigative powers rather than powers to adjudicate. Moreover, a requirement to subject a preparatory interview to the guarantees of judicial procedure would unduly hamper the effective regulation in the public interest of complex financial and commercial activities. There should not be any speculation as to whether the Crown might have not brought criminal proceedings without the interviews. On these grounds, there had not been a violation of Art 6 of the Convention.

The Court stated that in principle, it was a fundamental aspect of the right to a fair trial that there should be equality of arms and that the applicants and respondent had an opportunity to have knowledge and comment on the observations filed by the other side. The Crown should disclose all material evidence in their possession for or against the accused. In the instant case, the applicants had all the material disclosed to them by the appeal proceedings stage and therefore had the opportunity to persuade the court that their convictions were unsafe on the basis of non-disclosure. The domestic appeal proceedings had remedied the defect of non-disclosure: therefore there had not been a violation of Art 6 on that ground.

34.30 However, in criminal proceedings where that person is charged with an offence to which s 434(5A) applies:

(a) no evidence relating to the answer may be adduced; and

(b) no question relating to it may be asked,

by or on behalf of the prosecution, unless evidence relating to it is adduced, or a question relating to it is asked, in the proceedings by or on behalf of that person.

34.31 Section 434(5A) applies to any offence other than:

(a) an offence under ss 2 or 5 of the Perjury Act 1911 (false statements made on oath otherwise than in judicial proceedings or made otherwise than on oath); or

(b) an offence under s 44(1) or (2) of the Criminal Law (Consolidation) (Scotland) Act 1995 (false statements made on oath or otherwise than on oath); or

(c) an offence under arts 7 or 10 of the Perjury (Northern Ireland) Order 1979 (false statements made on oath otherwise than in judicial proceedings or made otherwise than on oath): CA 1985, s 434(5B).

34.32 The term 'document' includes information recorded in any form: CA 1985, s 434(6).

The power under s 434 to require production of a document includes power, in the case of a document not in hard copy form, to require the production of a copy of the document:

(a) in hard copy form; or

(b) in a form from which a hard copy can be readily obtained: CA 1985, s 434(7).

An inspector may take copies of or extracts from a document produced in pursuance of s 434: CA 1985, s 434(8).

Obstruction of inspectors treated as contempt of court

34.33 If any person:

(a) fails to comply with the production of documents and assist inspectors with evidence in connection with the company's affairs under s 434(1)(a) or (c);

(b) refuses to comply with a requirement under s 434(1)(b) or (2); or

(c) refuses to answer any question put to him by the inspectors for the purposes of the investigation,

the inspectors may certify that fact in writing to the court: CA 1985, s 436(1).

The court can then enquire into the case; and after hearing any witnesses who may be against or on behalf of the alleged offender, and after hearing any statement which may be offered in defence, the court may punish the offender in like manner as if he had been guilty of contempt of the court: CA 1985, s 436(2).

Inspectors' reports

34.34 The inspector may, but if so directed by the Secretary of the State must, make interim reports to the Secretary of State. On conclusion of the investigation, the inspector must make a final report to the Secretary of State: CA 1985, s 437(1).

Any persons who have been appointed under ss 431 or 432 may at any time and, if the Secretary of State directs them to do so, shall inform him of any matters coming to their knowledge as a result of their investigations: CA 1985, s 437(1A).

If the inspectors were appointed under s 432 in pursuance of an order of the court, the Secretary of State shall furnish a copy of any report of theirs to the court: CA 1985, s 437(2).

If the company is registered under the Companies Act 2006 in Northern Ireland, the Secretary of State must send a copy of any interim or final report by the inspectors to the Department of Enterprise, Trade and Investment in Northern Ireland: CA 1985, s 437(2A).

34.35 In any case the Secretary of State may, if he thinks fit:

(a) forward a copy of any report made by the inspectors to the company's registered office;

(b) furnish a copy on request and on payment of the prescribed fee to:

- (i) any member of the company or other body corporate which is the subject of the report;
- (ii) any person whose conduct is referred to in the report;
- (iii) the auditors of that company or body corporate;
- (iv) the applicants for the investigation;
- (v) any other person whose financial interests appear to the Secretary of State to be affected by the matters dealt with in the report, whether as a creditor of the company or body corporate, or otherwise; and

(c) cause any such report to be printed and published: CA 1985, s 437(3).

In exercising the discretion conferred on him by s 437(3)(c) of the CA 1985 the Secretary of State was required to act in the public interest

In *Lonrho plc v Secretary of State for Trade and Industry* [1989] 2 All ER 609, the appellant made a takeover bid for a public company (Fraser) which was referred to the Monopolies and Mergers Commission. It found that the merger would operate against the public interest. The appellant then entered into negotiations to sell its holding in Fraser to the Fayed brothers, who through AIT, a company controlled by them, announced a full bid for the share capital of Fraser. As a result of its bid, AIT acquired the entire share capital of Fraser. The Secretary of State for the (then) DTI later appointed inspectors to inquire into AIT's affairs pursuant to s 432(2), following allegations by the appellant that the statements and assurances given by the Fayed brothers were false and had been fraudulently made and that they and their company were not suitable persons to control Fraser. The inspectors submitted their report to the (then) DTI having conducted their investigations, who sent a copy to the Serious Fraud Office (SFO) and the Director General of Fair Trading. The Secretary of State assured the appellant that he intended to publish the report as soon as possible, but the DTI subsequently announced in a press release that because the SFO required further time for investigation and consideration of the case, publication of the report would be deferred. The same press release announced that the Director General of Fair Trading would be considering whether to advise the Secretary of State to refer the merger to the Commission. The Secretary of State later confirmed his intention not to publish the report. The appellant sought judicial review of the Secretary of State's decision not to publish the report.

The House of Lords held that in exercising the discretion conferred on him by s 437(3)(c) of CA 1985 the Secretary of State was required to act in the public interest after taking such advice as he considered appropriate. In the circumstances, the Secretary of State had properly exercised his discretion in deciding to defer publication of the report on the ground that early publication might be prejudicial to the SFO's investigation and to a fair trial. Since arriving at his decision he had acted independently and had only confirmed his decision after careful consideration of the appellant's arguments.

Expenses of investigating a company's affairs

34.36 These investigations by the BIS inspectors will inevitably involve expense and costs to the state. The expenses of an investigation will be defrayed in the first instance by the Secretary of State. However, he will recover those expenses from the persons liable. Expenses of the investigation include such reasonable sums as the Secretary of State may determine in respect of general staff costs and overheads: CA 1985, s 439(1).

A person who is convicted on a prosecution instituted as a result of the investigation may in the same proceedings be ordered to pay those expenses to such extent as may be specified in the order: CA 1985, s 439(2).

A body corporate dealt with by an inspectors' report, where the inspectors were appointed otherwise than of the Secretary of State's own motion, is liable except where it was the applicant for the investigation, and except so far as the Secretary of State otherwise directs: CA 1985, s 439(4).

34.37 Where inspectors were appointed:

(a) under s 431 of CA 1985; or

(b) on an application under s 442(3) of CA 1985,

the applicant or applicants for the investigation is or are liable to such extent (if any) as the Secretary of State may direct: CA 1985, s 439(5).

The report of inspectors appointed otherwise than of the Secretary of State's own motion may, if they think fit, and shall if the Secretary of State so directs, include a recommendation as to the directions (if any) which they think appropriate, in the light of their investigation, to be given under s 439(4) or (5): CA 1985, s 439(6).

Any liability to repay the Secretary of State imposed by s 439(2) above is (subject to satisfaction of his right to repayment) a liability also to indemnify all persons against liability under s 439(4) and (5): CA 1985, s 439(8).

A person liable under any one of those subsections is entitled to a contribution from any other person liable under the same subsection, according to the amount of their respective liabilities under it: CA 1985, s 439(9).

Expenses to be defrayed by the Secretary of State under s 439 shall, so far as not recovered under it, be paid out of money provided by Parliament: CA 1985, s 439(10).

Inspectors' report to be evidence

34.38 A copy of any report of inspectors certified by the Secretary of State to be a true copy, is admissible in any legal proceedings as evidence of the opinion of the inspectors in relation to any matter contained in the report and, in proceedings on an application under s 8 of the Company Directors' Disqualification Act 1986 or Art 11 of the Company Directors' Disqualification (Northern Ireland) Order 2002, as evidence of any fact stated therein: CA 1985, s 441(1).

A document purporting to be a certificate as set out above shall be received in evidence and be deemed to be such a certificate, unless the contrary is proved: CA 1985, s 441(2).

The BIS investigative powers under s 432 are wider than those under s 447. Whereas under s 432 the investigation is undertaken where there is suspected malpractice and there are complex issues involved, thereby requiring BIS to probe further into the company and require persons to attend to the inspection to answer questions, s 447 does not require such attendance and is limited to document production and a search of premises for documents as well as an explanation of the documentation. Both ss 432 and 437 have, as their objective, to allow the BIS to investigate the facts and determine the nature of the allegations made against the company.

Power to investigate company ownership

34.39 This enables the Secretary of State to appoint inspectors to investigate the company's ownership, where the position is unclear. Usually this is undertaken at the request of shareholders or of the companies themselves. Companies have a legal right to know who owns the shares.

Where it appears to the Secretary of State that there is good reason to do so, he may appoint one or more competent inspectors to investigate and report on the membership of any company, and otherwise with respect to the company, for the purpose of determining the true persons who are or have been financially interested in the success or failure (real or apparent) of the company or able to control or materially to influence its policy: CA 1985, s 442(1).

34.40 If an application for investigation under s 442 with respect to particular shares or debentures of a company is made to the Secretary of State by members of the company, and the number of applicants or the amount of shares held by them is not less than that required for an application for the appointment of inspectors under s 431(2)(a) or (b), then, subject to the following provisions, the Secretary of State shall appoint inspectors to conduct the investigation applied for: CA 1985, s 442(3).

The Secretary of State shall not appoint inspectors if he is satisfied that the application is vexatious; where inspectors are appointed, their terms of appointment shall exclude any matter in so far as the Secretary of State is satisfied that it is unreasonable for it to be investigated: CA 1985, s 442(3A).

34.41 The Secretary of State may, before appointing inspectors, require the applicant or applicants to give security, to an amount not exceeding £5,000, or such other sum as he may by order specify, for payment of the costs of the investigation.

An order under s 442(3B) shall be made by statutory instrument which shall be subject to annulment in pursuance of a resolution of either House of Parliament: CA 1985, s 442(3B).

If on an application under s 442(3) it appears to the Secretary of State that the powers conferred by s 444 are sufficient for the purposes of investigating the matters which inspectors would be appointed to investigate, he may instead conduct the investigation under that section: CA 1985, s 442(3C).

Subject to the terms of their appointment, the inspectors' powers extend to the investigation of any circumstances suggesting the existence of an arrangement or understanding which, though not legally binding, is or was observed or likely to be observed in practice and which is relevant to the purposes of the investigation: CA 1985, s 442(4).

Provisions applicable on investigation under s 442

34.42 For purposes of an investigation under s 442, ss 433(1), 434, 436 and 437 apply with the necessary modifications of references to the affairs of the company or to those of any other body corporate, subject however to the following subsections: CA 1985, s 443(1).

Those sections apply to:

(a) all persons who are or have been, or whom the inspector has reasonable cause to believe to be or have been, financially interested in the success or failure or the apparent success or failure of the company or any other body corporate whose membership is investigated with that of the company, or able to control or materially influence its policy (including persons concerned only on behalf of others); and

(b) any other person whom the inspector has reasonable cause to believe possesses information relevant to the investigation,

as they apply in relation to officers and agents of the company or the other body corporate (as the case may be): CA 1985, s 443(2).

If the Secretary of State is of the opinion that there is good reason for not divulging any part of a report made by virtue of s 442 and s 443(3), he may under s 437 disclose the report with the omission of that part; he may cause to be kept by the registrar of companies a copy of the report with that part omitted or, in the case of any other such report, a copy of the whole report: CA 1985, s 443(3).

Power to obtain information as to those interested in shares

34.43 If it appears to the Secretary of State that there is good reason to investigate the ownership of any shares in or debentures of a company and that it is unnecessary to appoint inspectors for the purpose, he may require any person whom he has reasonable cause to believe to have or to be able to obtain any information as to the present and past interests in those shares or debentures and the names and addresses of the persons interested and of any persons who act or have acted on their behalf in relation to the shares or debentures to give any such information to the Secretary of State: CA 1985, s 444(1).

For this purpose a person is deemed to have an interest in shares or debentures if he has any right to acquire or dispose of them or of any interest in them, or to vote in respect of them, or if his consent is necessary for the exercise of any of the rights of other persons interested in them, or if other persons interested in them can be required, or are accustomed, to exercise their rights in accordance with his instructions: CA 1985, s 444(2).

34.44 A person who fails to give information required of him under s 444, or who in giving such information makes any statement which he knows to be false in a material particular, or recklessly makes any statement which is false in a material particular, commits an offence: CA 1985, s 444(3).

A person guilty of an offence under s 444 will be liable:

(a) on conviction on indictment, to imprisonment for a term not exceeding two years or a fine (or both);

(b) on summary conviction:

(i) in England and Wales, to imprisonment for a term not exceeding 12 months or to a fine not exceeding the statutory maximum (or both) and, for continued contravention, a daily default fine not exceeding one-fiftieth of the statutory maximum; and

(ii) in Scotland or Northern Ireland, to imprisonment for a term not exceeding six months, or to a fine not exceeding the statutory maximum (or both) and, for continued contravention, a daily default fine not exceeding one-fiftieth of the statutory maximum: CA 1985, s 444(4).

Power to impose restrictions on shares and debentures

34.45 If in connection with an investigation under either s 442 or 444, it appears to the Secretary of State that there is difficulty in finding out the relevant facts about any shares (whether issued or to be issued), he may by order that the shares shall, until further order, be subject to the restrictions of CA 1985, Pt XV: CA 1985, s 445(1).

If the Secretary of State is satisfied that an order under s 445(1) may unfairly affect the rights of third parties in respect of shares then the Secretary of State, for the purpose of protecting such rights and subject to such terms as he thinks fit, may direct that such acts by such persons or descriptions of persons and for such purposes as may be set out in the order, shall not constitute a breach of the restrictions of CA 1985, Pt XV: CA 1985, s 445(1A).

Section 445 and Pt XV in its application to orders under it, apply in relation to debentures as in relation to shares save that s 445(1A) shall not so apply: CA 1985, s 445(2).

General powers to give directions

34.46 In exercising his functions an inspector shall comply with any direction given to him by the Secretary of State under s 446A: CA 1985, s 446A(1).

The Secretary of State may give an inspector appointed under ss 431, 432(2) or 442(1) a direction:

(a) as to the subject matter of his investigation (whether by reference to a specified area of a company's operation, a specified transaction, a period of time or otherwise); or

(b) which requires the inspector to take or not to take a specified step in his investigation: CA 1985, s 446A(2).

34.47 The Secretary of State may give an inspector appointed under any provision of this Part a direction requiring him to secure that a specified report under s 437:

(a) includes the inspector's views on a specified matter;

(b) does not include any reference to a specified matter;

(c) is made in a specified form or manner; or

(d) is made by a specified date: CA 1985, s 446A(3).

34.48 A direction under s 446A:

(a) may be given on an inspector's appointment;

(b) may vary or revoke a direction previously given; and

(c) may be given at the request of an inspector: CA 1985, s 446A(4).

34.49 Under s 446A:

(a) a reference to an inspector's investigation includes any investigation he undertakes, or could undertake, under s 433(1) (power to investigate affairs of holding company or subsidiary); and

(b) 'specified' means specified in a direction under s 446A: CA 1985, s 446A(5).

Direction to terminate investigation

34.50 The Secretary of State may direct an inspector to take no further steps in his investigation: CA 1985, s 446B(1).

The Secretary of State may give a direction under s 446B to an inspector appointed under ss 432(1) or 442(3) only on the grounds that it appears to him that:

(a) matters have come to light in the course of the inspector's investigation which suggest that a criminal offence has been committed; and

(b) those matters have been referred to the appropriate prosecuting authority: CA 1985, s 446B(2).

34.51 Where the Secretary of State gives a direction under s 446, any direction already given to the inspector under s 437(1) to produce an interim report and any direction given to him under s 446A(3) in relation to such a report, shall cease to have effect: CA 1985, s 446B(3).

Where the Secretary of State gives a direction under this section, the inspector shall not make a final report to the Secretary of State unless:

(a) the direction was made on the grounds mentioned in s 446B(2) and the Secretary of State directs the inspector to make a final report to him; or

(b) the inspector was appointed under s 432(1) (appointment in pursuance of order of the court): CA 1985, s 446B(4).

An inspector shall comply with any direction given to him under s 446B: CA 1985, s 446B(5).

Under s 446B, a reference to an inspector's investigation includes any investigation he undertakes, or could undertake, under s 433(1) (power to investigate affairs of holding company or subsidiary): CA 1985, s 446B(6).

Resignation and revocation of appointment

34.52 An inspector may resign by notice in writing to the Secretary of State: CA 1985, s 446C(1).

The Secretary of State may revoke the appointment of an inspector by notice in writing to the inspector: CA 1985, s 446C(2).

Appointment of replacement inspectors

34.53 Where:

(a) an inspector resigns;

(b) an inspector's appointment is revoked; or

(c) an inspector dies,

the Secretary of State may appoint one or more competent inspectors to continue the investigation: CA 1985, s 446D(1).

34.54 An appointment under s 446D(1) shall be treated for the purposes of Pt XIV of the CA 1985 (apart from this section) as an appointment under the provision of Pt XIV of the CA 1985 under which the former inspector was appointed: CA 1985, s 446D(2).

The Secretary of State must exercise his power under s 446D(1) so as to secure that at least one inspector continues the investigation: CA 1985, s 446D(3).

Section 446D(3) does not apply if:

(a) the Secretary of State could give any replacement inspector a direction under s 446B (termination of investigation); and

(b) such a direction would (under s 446D(4)) result in a final report not being made: CA 1985, s 446D(4).

In s 446D, references to an investigation include any investigation the former inspector conducted under s 433(1) (power to investigate affairs of holding company or subsidiary): CA 1985, s 446D(5).

Obtaining information from former inspectors

34.55 Section 446E applies to a person who was appointed as an inspector:

(a) who has resigned; or

(b) whose appointment has been revoked: CA 1985, s 446E(1).

Section 446E also applies to an inspector to whom the Secretary of State has given a direction under s 446B (termination of investigation): CA 1985, s 446E(2).

34.56 The Secretary of State may direct a person to whom s 446E applies to produce documents obtained or generated by that person during the course of his investigation to:

(a) the Secretary of State; or

(b) an inspector appointed under CA 1985: CA 1985, s 446E(3).

The power under s 446E(3) to require production of a document includes the power, in the case of a document not in hard copy form, to require the production of a copy of the document:

(a) in hard copy form; or

(b) in a form from which a hard copy can be readily obtained: CA 1985, s 446E(4).

The Secretary of State may take copies of or extracts from a document produced in pursuance of s 446E: CA 1985, s 446E(5).

34.57 The Secretary of State may direct a person to whom s 446E applies to inform him of any matters that came to that person's knowledge as a result of his investigation: CA 1985, s 446E(6).

A person shall comply with any direction given to him under s 446E: CA 1985, s 446E(7).

Under s 446E:

(a) references to the investigation of a former inspector or inspector include any investigation he conducted under s 433(1) (power to investigate affairs of holding company or subsidiary); and

(b) 'document' includes information recorded in any form: CA 1985, s 446E(8).

Power to require documents and information: Informal Investigations

34.58 As formal investigations in the appointment of inspectors is rarely used in practice, the most common type of informal investigation is under s 447 and the appointment of CI investigators by the Secretary of State for BIS. The Secretary of State may act under s 447(2) and (3) in relation to a company: CA 1985, s 447(1).

The Secretary of State may give directions to the company requiring it:

(a) to produce such documents (or documents of such description) as may be specified in the directions; or

(b) to provide such information (or information of such description) as may be so specified: CA 1985, s 447(2).

34.59 The Secretary of State may authorise a person (an investigator) to require the company or any other person:

(a) to produce such documents (or documents of such description) as the investigator may specify;

(b) to provide such information (or information of such description) as the investigator may specify: CA 1985, s 447(3).

A person on whom a requirement under s 447(3) is imposed may require the investigator to produce evidence of his authority: CA 1985, s 447(4).

A requirement under s 447(2) or (3) must be complied with at such time and place as may be specified in the directions or by the investigator (as the case may be): CA 1985, s 447(5).

The production of a document in pursuance of s 447 does not affect any lien which a person has on the document: CA 1985, s 447(6).

34.60 The Secretary of State or the investigator (as the case may be) may take copies of or extracts from a document produced in pursuance of s 447.

A 'document' includes information recorded in any form: CA 1985, s 447(8).

The power under s 447 to require production of a document includes power, in the case of a document not in hard copy form, to require the production of a copy of the document:

(a) in hard copy form; or

(b) in a form from which a hard copy can be readily obtained: CA 1985, s 447(9).

There must be a genuine and bona fide decision exercised by the Secretary of State in exercising his powers to obtain certain documents as part of a company's investigation under the CA 1985

In *R v Secretary of State for Trade and Industry, ex parte Perestrello* [1981] QB 19, the court stated that the Secretary of State's powers to obtain documents must not be exercised for any ulterior motive.

See too *Attorney-General's Reference No 2 of 1998* [1999] BCC 590.

Information provided: evidence

34.61 A statement made by a person in compliance with a requirement under s 447 may be used in evidence against him: CA 1985, s 447A(1).

Subsequent use of the testimony obtained by the inspectors may be used in proceedings under s 8 of the CDDA 1986.

Evidence obtained by the Secretary of State under Pt 14 of the CA 1985 could be used against the person in subsequent disqualification proceedings under the CDDA 1986

In *R v Secretary of State for Trade and Industry ex parte McCormick* [1998] BCC 379, the applicant contended that the Secretary of State ought not to be allowed to use the evidence against him in disqualification proceedings. It was agreed that if disqualification proceedings involved a criminal charge, the Secretary of State's power to use compelled evidence ought to be exercised so as to give effect to the obligations of the UK under the Convention. That question had to be determined in accordance with national law. Although the consequences of a disqualification order were severe and had been described as penal, they did not involve a deprivation of liberty, livelihood or property. The disqualification order did not prevent the person subject to its terms from carrying on a commercial activity in his own name. Rather, its effect was to remove the privilege of doing so through the vehicle of a limited liability company. Further, the court rejected the applicant's submission that, as Art 6.1 applied to civil rights and obligations, the Secretary of State was obliged to follow the same procedure as applied in criminal proceedings. As was established by the jurisprudence of the European Court of Human Rights, the requirement of fairness did not demand the same treatment in civil proceedings as in criminal. In the former, compelled evidence in the form of discovery and interrogatories was allowed by the rules of court, but those rules were designed to produce a fair trial. Therefore, the Secretary of State was not bound to treat these proceedings as if they involved a criminal charge, and her decision to use compelled evidence did not make the proceedings unfair.

34.62 The disqualification proceedings under the CDDA 1986 are not criminal proceedings but civil in nature.

But in criminal proceedings in which the person is charged with a relevant offence:

(a) no evidence relating to the statement may be adduced by or on behalf of the prosecution; and

(b) no question relating to it may be asked by or on behalf of the prosecution,

unless evidence relating to it is adduced or a question relating to it is asked in the proceedings by or on behalf of that person: CA 1985, s 447A(2).

34.63 A relevant offence is any offence other than the following:

(a) an offence under s 451;

(b) an offence under s 5 of the Perjury Act 1911 (false statement made otherwise than on oath);

(c) an offence under s 44(2) of the Criminal Law (Consolidation) (Scotland) Act 1995 (false statement made otherwise than on oath); or

(d) an offence under Art 10 of the Perjury (Northern Ireland) Order 1979 (false statements made otherwise than on oath): CA 1985, s 447A(3).

Entry and search of premises

34.64 A justice of the peace may issue a warrant under s 448 if satisfied on information on oath given by or on behalf of the Secretary of State, or by a person appointed or authorised to exercise powers under this Part, that there are reasonable grounds for believing that there are on any premises documents whose production has been required under this CA 1985, Pt 14 and which have not been produced in compliance with the requirement: CA 1985, s 448(1).

34.65 A justice of the peace may also issue a warrant under s 448 if satisfied on information on oath given by or on behalf of the Secretary of State, or by a person appointed or authorised to exercise powers under this Part:

(a) that there are reasonable grounds for believing that an offence has been committed for which the penalty on conviction on indictment is imprisonment for a term of not less than two years and that there are, on any premises, documents relating to whether the offence has been committed,

(b) that the Secretary of State, or the person so appointed or authorised, has power to require the production of the documents under this Part, and

(c) that there are reasonable grounds for believing that if production was so required the documents would not be produced but would be removed from the premises, hidden, tampered with or destroyed: CA 1985, s 448(2).

34.66 A warrant under this s 448 shall authorise a constable, together with any other person named in it and any other constables:

(a) to enter the premises specified in the information, using such force as is reasonably necessary for the purpose;

(b) to search the premises and take possession of any documents appearing to be such documents as are mentioned in s 448(1) or (2), as the case may be, or to take, in relation to any such documents, any other steps which may appear to be necessary for preserving them or preventing interference with them;

(c) to take copies of any such documents; and

(d) to require any person named in the warrant to provide an explanation of them or to state where they may be found: CA 1985, s 448(3).

If in the case of a warrant under s 448(2) the justice of the peace is satisfied on information on oath that there are reasonable grounds for believing that there are also on the premises other documents relevant to the investigation, the warrant shall also authorise the actions mentioned in s 448(3) to be taken in relation to such documents: CA 1985, s 448(4).

34.67 A warrant under s 448 shall continue in force until the end of the period of one month beginning with the day on which it is issued: CA 1985, s 448(5).

Any documents of which possession is taken under s 448 may be retained:

(a) for a period of three months; or

(b) if within that period proceedings to which the documents are relevant are commenced against any person for any criminal offence, until the conclusion of those proceedings: CA 1985, s 448(6).

Any person who intentionally obstructs the exercise of any rights conferred by a warrant issued under this section or fails without reasonable excuse to comply with any requirement imposed in accordance with s 448(3)(d) is guilty of an offence: CA 1985, s 448(7).

34.68 A person guilty of an offence under s 448 will be liable:

(a) on conviction on indictment, to a fine;

(b) on summary conviction, to a fine not exceeding the statutory maximum: CA 1985, s 448(7A) CA 1985.

For the purposes of ss 449 and 451A (provision for security of information) documents obtained under s 448 shall be treated as if they had been obtained under the provision of this Part under which their production was or, as the case may be, could have been required: CA 1985, s 448(8).

In the application of s 448 to Scotland for the references to a justice of the peace substitute references to a justice of the peace or a sheriff, and for the references to information on oath substitute references to evidence on oath: CA 1985, s 448(9).

Under s 448, the term 'document' includes information recorded in any form: CA 1985, s 448(10).

Protection in relation to certain disclosures: information provided to Secretary of State

34.69 A person who makes a relevant disclosure is not liable by reason only of that disclosure in any proceedings relating to a breach of an obligation of confidence: CA 1985, s 448A(1).

A relevant disclosure is a disclosure which satisfies each of the following conditions:

(a) it is made to the Secretary of State otherwise than in compliance with a requirement under Pt XIV of the CA 1985;

(b) it is of a kind that the person making the disclosure could be required to make in pursuance of Pt XIV of the CA 1985;

(c) the person who makes the disclosure does so in good faith and in the reasonable belief that the disclosure is capable of assisting the Secretary of State for the purposes of the exercise of his functions under Pt XIV of the CA 1985;

(d) the information disclosed is not more than is reasonably necessary for the purpose of assisting the Secretary of State for the purposes of the exercise of those functions; and

(e) the disclosure is not one falling within s 448A(3) or (4): CA 1985, s 448A(2).

A disclosure falls within s 448A(3) if the disclosure is prohibited by virtue of any enactment whenever passed or made: CA 1985, s 448A(3).

34.70 A disclosure falls within s 448A(4) if:

(a) it is made by a person carrying on the business of banking or by a lawyer; and

(b) it involves the disclosure of information in respect of which he owes an obligation of confidence in that capacity: CA 1985, s 448A(4).

Under s 448A, the term 'enactment' has the meaning given by s 1293 of CA 2006: CA 1985, s 448A(5).

Provision for security of information obtained

34.71 Section 449 applies to information (in whatever form) obtained:

(a) in pursuance of a requirement imposed under s 447;

(b) by means of a relevant disclosure within the meaning of s 448A(2); and

(c) by an investigator in consequence of the exercise of his powers under s 453A: CA 1985, s 449(1).

34.72 Such information must not be disclosed unless the disclosure:

(a) is made to a person specified in Sch 15C; or

(b) is of a description specified in Sch 15D: CA 1985, s 449(2).

The Secretary of State may by order amend Schs 15C and 15D: CA 1985, s 449(3).

An order under s 449(3) must not amend:

(a) Sch 15C by specifying a person unless the person exercises functions of a public nature (whether or not he exercises any other function);

(b) Sch 15D by adding or modifying a description of disclosure unless the purpose for which the disclosure is permitted is likely to facilitate the exercise of a function of a public nature: CA 1985, s 449(4).

An order under s 449(3) must be made by statutory instrument subject to annulment in pursuance of a resolution of either House of Parliament: CA 1985, s 449(5).

34.73 A person who discloses any information in contravention of s 449 is guilty of an offence: CA 1985, s 449(6). A person guilty of an offence under s 449 will be liable:

(a) on conviction on indictment, to imprisonment for a term not exceeding two years or a fine (or both);

(b) on summary conviction:

  (i) in England and Wales, to imprisonment for a term not exceeding 12 months or to a fine not exceeding the statutory maximum (or both);

  (ii) in Scotland or Northern Ireland, to imprisonment for a term not exceeding six months, or to a fine not exceeding the statutory maximum (or both): CA 1985, s 449(6A).

Any information which may by virtue of s 449 be disclosed to a person specified in Sch 15C may be disclosed to any officer or employee of the person: CA 1985, s 449(8).

Section 449 does not prohibit the disclosure of information if the information is or has been available to the public from any other source: CA 1985, s 449(9).

For the purposes of s 449, information obtained by an investigator in consequence of the exercise of his powers under s 453A includes information obtained by a person accompanying the investigator in pursuance of s 449(4) in consequence of that person's accompanying the investigator: CA 1985, s 449(10).

Nothing in s 449 authorises the making of a disclosure in contravention of the Data Protection Act 1998: CA 1985, s 449(11).

Punishment for destroying, mutilating, etc company documents

34.74 An officer of a company who:

(a) destroys, mutilates or falsifies, or is privy to the destruction, mutilation or falsification of a document affecting, or relating to the company's property or affairs, or

(b) makes, or is privy to the making of, a false entry in such a document,

is guilty of an offence, unless he proves that he had no intention to conceal the state of affairs of the company or to defeat the law: CA 1985, s 450(1).

Section 450(1) applies to an officer of an authorised insurance company which is not a body corporate as it applies to an officer of a company: CA 1985, s 450(A1).

34.75 A person who, as mentioned above, fraudulently parts with, alters or makes an omission in any such document or is privy to fraudulent parting with, fraudulent altering or fraudulent making of an omission in, any such document, is guilty of an offence: CA 1985, s 450(2).

A person guilty of an offence under s 450 is liable:

(a) on conviction on indictment, to imprisonment for a term not exceeding seven years or a fine (or both);

(b) on summary conviction:

  (i) in England and Wales, to imprisonment for a term not exceeding 12 months or to a fine not exceeding the statutory maximum (or both); or

  (ii) in Scotland or Northern Ireland, to imprisonment for a term not exceeding six months, or to a fine not exceeding the statutory maximum (or both): CA 1985, s 450(3).

Under s 450, the term 'document' includes information recorded in any form: CA 1985, s 450(5).

Punishment for furnishing false information

34.76 A person commits an offence if in purported compliance with a requirement under s 447 to provide information:

(a) he provides information which he knows to be false in a material particular; or

(b) he recklessly provides information which is false in a material particular: CA 1985, s 451(1).

34.77 A person guilty of an offence under s 451 is liable:

(a) on conviction on indictment, to imprisonment for a term not exceeding two years or a fine (or both);

(b) on summary conviction:

  (i) in England and Wales, to imprisonment for a term not exceeding 12 months or to a fine not exceeding the statutory maximum (or both); or

  (ii) in Scotland or Northern Ireland, to imprisonment for a term not exceeding six months, or to a fine not exceeding the statutory maximum (or both): CA 1985, s 451(2).

Disclosure of information by Secretary of State or inspector

34.78 Section 451A applies to information obtained:

(a) under ss 434–446E;

(b) by an inspector in consequence of the exercise of his powers under s 453A: CA 1985, s 451A(1).

The Secretary of State may, if he thinks fit:

(a) disclose any information to which this section applies to any person to whom, or for any purpose for which, disclosure is permitted under s 449; or

(b) authorise or require an inspector appointed under Pt XIV of the CA 1985 to disclose such information to any such person or for any such purpose: CA 1985, s 451A(2).

34.79 Information to which s 451A applies may also be disclosed by an inspector appointed under Pt XIV of the CA 1985 to:

(a) another inspector appointed under Pt XIV of the CA 1985;

(b) a person appointed under:

  (i) s 167 of the Financial Services and Markets Act 2000 (general investigations);

  (ii) s 168 of that Act (investigations in particular cases);

  (iii) s 169(1)(b) of that Act (investigation in support of overseas regulator);

  (iv) s 284 of that Act (investigations into affairs of certain collective investment schemes); or

  (v) regulations made as a result of s 262(2)(k) of that Act (investigations into open-ended investment companies),

  to conduct an investigation; or

(c) a person authorised to exercise powers under:

  (i) s 447 of this Act; or

  (ii) s 84 of the Companies Act 1989 (exercise of powers to assist overseas regulatory authority): CA 1985, s 451A(3).

Any information which may by virtue of s 451(3) be disclosed to any person may be disclosed to any officer or servant of that person: CA 1985, s 451A(4).

34.80 The Secretary of State may, if he thinks fit, disclose any information obtained under s 444 to:

(a) the company whose ownership was the subject of the investigation;

(b) any member of the company;

(c) any person whose conduct was investigated in the course of the investigation;

(d) the auditors of the company; or

(e) any person whose financial interests appear to the Secretary of State to be affected by matters covered by the investigation: CA 1985, s 451A(5).

For the purposes of s 451A, information obtained by an inspector in consequence of the exercise of his powers under s 453A includes information obtained by a person accompanying the inspector in pursuance of s 451A(4) in consequence of that person's accompanying the inspector: CA 1985, s 451A(6).

The reference to an inspector in s 451A(2)(b) includes a reference to a person accompanying an inspector in pursuance of s 453A(4): CA 1985, s 451A(7).

Privileged information

34.81 Nothing in ss 431–446E compels the disclosure by any person to the Secretary of State or to an inspector appointed by him of information in respect of which in an action in the High Court a claim to legal professional privilege, or in an action in the Court of Session a claim to confidentiality of communications, could be maintained: CA 1985, s 452(1).

Nothing in ss 434, 443 or 446 requires a person (except as mentioned in s 452(1B) to disclose information or produce documents in respect of which he owes an obligation of confidence by virtue of carrying on the business of banking unless:

(a) the person to whom the obligation of confidence is owed is the company or other body corporate under investigation;

(b) the person to whom the obligation of confidence is owed consents to the disclosure or production; or

(c) the making of the requirement is authorised by the Secretary of State: CA 1985, s 452(1A).

Section 452(1A) does not apply where the person owing the obligation of confidence is the company or other body corporate under investigation under ss 431, 432 or 433: CA 1985, s 452(1B).

34.82 Nothing in ss 447–451:

(a) compels the production by any person of a document or the disclosure by any person of information in respect of which in an action in the High Court a claim to legal professional privilege, or in an action in the Court of Session a claim to confidentiality of communications, could be maintained;

(b) authorises the taking of possession of any such document which is in the person's possession: CA 1985, s 452(2).

34.83 The Secretary of State must not under CA 1985 s 447 require, or authorise a person to require:

(a) the production by a person carrying on the business of banking of a document relating to the affairs of a customer of his; or

(b) the disclosure by him of information relating to those affairs,

unless one of the conditions in s 452(4) is met: CA 1985, s 452(3).

The conditions are:

(a) the Secretary of State thinks it is necessary to do so for the purpose of investigating the affairs of the person carrying on the business of banking;

(b) the customer is a person on whom a requirement has been imposed under s 447; and

(c) the customer is a person on whom a requirement to produce information or documents has been imposed by an investigator appointed by the Secretary of State in pursuance of ss 171 or 173 of the Financial Services and Markets Act 2000 (powers of persons appointed under s 167 or as a result of s 168(2) to conduct an investigation): CA 1985, s 452(4).

Despite ss 452(1) and (2), a person who is a lawyer may be compelled to disclose the name and address of his client: CA 1985, s 452(5).

Investigation of overseas companies

34.84 The provisions of Pt XIV of the CA 1985 apply to bodies corporate incorporated outside the UK which are carrying on business in the UK, or have at any time carried on business there, as they apply to companies under CA 1985 but subject to the following exceptions, adaptations and modifications: CA 1985, s 453(1).

The following provisions do not apply to such bodies:

(a) s 431 (investigation on application of company or its members); and

(c) ss 442–445 (investigation of company ownership and power to obtain information as to those interested in shares): CA 1985, s 453(1A).

The other provisions of Pt XIV of the CA 1985 apply to such bodies subject to such adaptations and modifications as may be specified by regulations made by the Secretary of State: CA 1985, s 453(1B).

Regulations under s 453 are made by statutory instrument subject to annulment in pursuance of a resolution of either House of Parliament: CA 1985, s 453(2).

Power to enter and remain on premises

34.85 The policy objective for amending Pt 14 of the CA 1985 was to improve the effectiveness and efficiency of the company investigations regime. Section 453A was one of the changes designed to better equip company inspectors and investigators to uncover malpractice, by giving them the power to enter and remain on premises used for the business of the company under investigation. It also enabled some investigations to be concluded more quickly, and so free up company inspectors and investigators to move to other investigations more quickly. These benefits have contributed to engendering confidence in the UK corporate framework.

It is essential that, when this power is exercised, its use is compatible with privacy rights under Article 8 of the European Convention on Human Rights (ECHR). For that reason a number of safeguards have been provided by the new s 453B. These include the provision of a written statement of powers, rights and obligations and the drawing up of a written record following a visit to premises. Section 453B provides that the content of both this statement and the visit record be prescribed by regulations.

34.86 Previously, broad proposals for modernisation of the investigations regime were set out in a public consultation document entitled 'Company Investigations: Powers for the 21st Century' published in October 2001 and a further public consultation document 'Company investigations: Draft regulations and plans for commencement' was issued in August 2004. The results of these consultation were taken into account in the enactment of The Companies Act 1985 (Power to Enter and Remain on Premises: Procedural) Regulations 2005, SI 2005/684.

Under the CA 1985, an inspector or investigator may act under s 454(2) in relation to a company if:

(a) he is authorised to do so by the Secretary of State; and

(b) he thinks that to do so will materially assist him in the exercise of his functions under Pt XIV of the CA 1985 in relation to the company: CA 1985, s 453A(1).

34.87 An inspector or investigator may at all reasonable times:

(a) require entry to relevant premises; and

(b) remain there for such period as he thinks necessary for the purpose mentioned in s 453(1)(b): CA 1985, s 453A(2).

Relevant premises are premises which the inspector or investigator believes are used (wholly or partly) for the purposes of the company's business: CA 1985, s 453A(3).

In exercising his powers under s 453A(2), an inspector or investigator may be accompanied by such other persons as he thinks appropriate: CA 1985, s 453(4).

34.88 A person who intentionally obstructs a person lawfully acting under s 453A(2) or (4) is guilty of an offence: CA 1985, s 453A(5).

A person guilty of an offence under s 453A will be liable:

(a) on conviction on indictment, to a fine;

(b) on summary conviction, to a fine not exceeding the statutory maximum: CA 1985, s 453A(5).

An inspector is a person appointed under ss 431, 432 or 442: CA 1985, s 453A(7). An investigator is a person authorised for the purposes of s 447: CA 1985, s 453A(8).

Power to enter and remain on premises: procedural

34.89 Section 453B applies for the purposes of s 453A: CA 1985, s 453B(1).

The requirements of s 453B(3) must be complied with at the time an inspector or investigator seeks to enter relevant premises under s 453A(2)(a): CA 1985, s 453B(2).

The requirements are:

(a) the inspector or investigator must produce evidence of his identity and evidence of his appointment or authorisation (as the case may be); and

(b) any person accompanying the inspector or investigator must produce evidence of his identity: CA 1985, s 453B(3).

34.90 The inspector or investigator must, as soon as practicable after obtaining entry, give to an appropriate recipient a written statement containing such information as to:

(a) the powers of the investigator or inspector (as the case may be) under s 453A; and

(b) the rights and obligations of the company, occupier and the persons present on the premises,

as may be prescribed by regulations: CA 1985, s 453B(4).

If during the time the inspector or investigator is on the premises there is no person present who appears to him to be an appropriate recipient for the purposes of s 453B(8), the inspector or investigator must, as soon as reasonably practicable, send to the company:

(a) a notice of the fact and time that the visit took place; and

(b) the statement mentioned in s 453B(4): CA 1985, s 453B(5).

34.91 As soon as reasonably practicable after exercising his powers under s 453A(2), the inspector or investigator must prepare a written record of the visit and:

(a) if requested to do so by the company he must give it a copy of the record; or

(b) in a case where the company is not the sole occupier of the premises, if requested to do so by an occupier, he must give the occupier a copy of the record: CA 1985, s 453B(6).

The written record must contain such information as may be prescribed by regulations: CA 1985, s 453B(7).

34.92 If the inspector or investigator thinks that the company is the sole occupier of the premises, an appropriate recipient is a person who is present on the premises and who appears to the inspector or investigator to be:

(a) an officer of the company; or

(b) a person otherwise engaged in the business of the company if the inspector or investigator thinks that no officer of the company is present on the premises: CA 1985, s 453B(8).

34.93 If the inspector or investigator thinks that the company is not the occupier or sole occupier of the premises, an appropriate recipient is:

(a) a person who is an appropriate recipient for the purposes of subsection (8), and (if different)

(b) a person who is present on the premises and who appears to the inspector or investigator to be an occupier of the premises or otherwise in charge of them: CA 1985, s 453B(9).

A statutory instrument containing regulations made under s 453B is subject to annulment in pursuance of a resolution of either House of Parliament: CA 1985, s 453B(10). The Secretary of State has enacted The Companies Act 1985 (Power to Enter and Remain on Premises: Procedural) Regulations 2005, SI 2005 No 684 – see Checklist in section 34.7 of this Chapter. This statutory instrument is legally important as the regulations prescribe the content of two safeguards inserted in CA 1985 to safeguard privacy rights under Art 8 of the ECHR.

Failure to comply with certain requirements

34.94 Section 453C applies if a person fails to comply with a requirement imposed by an inspector, the Secretary of State or an investigator in pursuance of either of the following provisions:

(a) s 447; or

(b) s 453A: CA 1985, s 453C(1).

The inspector, Secretary of State or investigator (as the case may be) may certify the fact in writing to the court: CA 1985, s 453C(2).

If, after hearing:

(a) any witnesses who may be produced against or on behalf of the alleged offender; or

(b) any statement which may be offered in defence,

the court is satisfied that the offender failed without reasonable excuse to comply with the requirement, it may deal with him as if he had been guilty of contempt of the court: CA 1985, s 453C(4).

Offences by bodies corporate

34.95 Where an offence under any of ss 448, 449–451 and 453A is committed by a body corporate, every officer of the body who is in default also commits the offence. For this purpose:

(a) any person who purports to act as director, manager or secretary of the body is treated as an officer of the body; and

(b) if the body is a company, any shadow director is treated as an officer of the company: CA 1985, s 453D.

Checklist: power to enter and remain on premises

34.96 *This checklist sets out the procedural aspects governing the power of investigators and inspectors appointed by the Secretary of State for BIS to enter and remain on premises.*

Part 1 of CAICE amended (inter alia) Pt 14 of the CA 1985 and introduced (in s 453A(2)) the power for inspectors and investigators who are duly authorised by the Secretary of State to enter premises used by a company and remain there for as long as is necessary in order to exercise their statutory functions.

Sections 453B(4) and (6) of the CA 1985 (as amended) provide that (i) as soon as practicable after exercising the power to enter and remain on premises 'appropriate recipients' are to be given a statement of powers, rights and obligations ('the statement'); and (ii) as soon as reasonably practicable after the exercise of the power a written record of the visit ('the record') is to be sent to anyone entitled to request a copy who asks for it. By virtue of s 453B(4) and (7) of the CA 1985, the content of the statement and the record are to be prescribed by regulations. The statutory instrument governing the power to enter and remain on premises sets out procedural rules under para 2 dealing with the statement, and para 3 with the record.

The amendments to CA 1985 effected by CAICE come into force on 6 April 2005 including the statutory instrument.

No	Issue	Act reference
1	The provisions concerning the power of investigators and inspectors appointed by the Secretary of State for BIS to enter and remain on premises are set out in further detail by way of Statutory Instrument	The Companies Act 1985 (Power to Enter and Remain on Premises: Procedural) Regulations 2005, SI 2005 No. 684
2	**Prescribed contents of the written statement given under s 453B(4) or sent under s 453B(5) of the CA 2006** Under para 2 of the regulations, the written statement which s 453B(4) of the CA1985 requires the inspector or investigator to give to an appropriate recipient (or which s 453B(5), where it applies, requires him to send to the company) must contain the following information: (a) a statement that the inspector or investigator has been appointed or (as the case may be) authorised by the Secretary of State to carry out an investigation and a reference to the enactment under which that appointment or authorisation was made; (b) a statement that the inspector or investigator has been authorised by the Secretary of State under s 453A(1) to exercise the powers in that section;	Paragraph 2

No	Issue	Act reference
	(c) a description of the conditions which are required by s 453A(1) to be satisfied before an inspector or investigator can act under s 453A(2); (d) a description of the powers in sub-s 453A(2); (e) a statement that the inspector or investigator must, at the time he seeks to enter premises under s 453A, produce evidence of his identity and evidence of his appointment or authorisation (as the case may be); (f) a statement that any person accompanying the inspector or investigator when the inspector or investigator seeks to enter the premises must, at that time, produce evidence of his identity; (g) a statement that entry to premises under s 453A may be refused to an inspector, investigator or other person who fails to produce the evidence referred to (in the case of an inspector or investigator) in para (e) or (in the case of any other person) in para (f); (h) a statement that the company, occupier and the persons present on the premises may be required by the inspector or investigator, while he is on the premises, to comply with any powers the inspector or investigator may have by virtue of his appointment or authorisation (as the case may be) to require documents or information; (i) a statement that the inspector or investigator is not permitted to use any force in exercising his powers under s 453A and is not permitted during the course of his visit to search the premises or to seize any document or other thing on the premises; (j) a description of the effect of s 453C(2) as it relates to a requirement imposed by an inspector or investigator under s 453A; (k) a statement that it is an offence under s 453A(5) intentionally to obstruct an inspector, investigator or other person lawfully acting under s 453A; (l) a description of the inspector's or investigator's obligations under s 453B(6) and (7) to prepare a written record of the visit and to give a copy of	

No	Issue	Act reference
	the record, when requested, to the company and any other occupier of the premises; and (m) information about how any person entitled under s 453B(6) to receive a copy of that record can request it.	
3	**Prescribed contents of the written record prepared under s 453B(6) of the CA 1985** Under para 3 of the regulations, the written record which s 453B(6) of the CA 1985 requires an inspector or investigator to prepare must contain the following information: (a) the name by which the company in relation to which the powers under s 453A were exercised was registered at the time of the authorisation under s 453A(1)(a); (b) the company's registered number at that time; (c) the postal address of the premises visited; (d) the name of the inspector or investigator who visited the premises and the name of any person accompanying him; (e) the date and time when the inspector or investigator entered the premises and the duration of his visit; (f) the name (if known by the inspector or investigator) of the person to whom the inspector or investigator and any person accompanying him produced evidence of their identity under s 453B(3); (g) the name (if known by the inspector or investigator) of the person to whom the inspector or investigator produced evidence of his appointment or authorisation (as the case may be) as required by s 453B(3); (h) if the inspector or investigator does not know the name of the person to whom he produced evidence of his identity and appointment or authorisation as required by s 453B(3), an account of how he produced that evidence under that section; (i) if the inspector or investigator does not know the name of the person to whom any person accompanying the inspector or investigator	Paragraph 3

No	Issue	Act reference
	produced evidence of his identity under s 453B(3), an account of how that evidence was produced under that section; (j) the name (if known by the inspector or investigator) of the person who admitted the inspector or investigator to the premises or, if the inspector or investigator does not know that person's name, an account of how he was admitted to the premises; (k) the name (if known by the inspector or investigator) of every appropriate recipient to whom the inspector or investigator, while on the premises, gave a written statement of powers, rights and obligations as required by s 453B(4); (l) if the inspector or investigator does not know the name of a person referred to in paragraph (k), an account of how the written statement was given to that person; (m) the name (if known by the inspector or investigator) of any person physically present on the premises (to the inspector's or investigator's knowledge) at any time during the inspector's or investigator's visit (other than another inspector or investigator, a person accompanying the inspector or investigator or a person referred to in para (k)) and with whom the inspector or investigator communicated in relation to the inspector's or investigator's presence on the premises; (n) a record of any apparent failure by any person during the course of the inspector's or investigator's visit to the premises to comply with any requirement imposed by the inspector or investigator under Pt 14 of the 1985 Act; and (o) a record of any conduct by any person during the course of the inspector's or investigator's visit to the premises which the inspector or investigator believes amounted to the intentional obstruction of him, or anyone accompanying him, in the lawful exercise of the power to enter and remain on the premises under s 453A.	

Definitions

34.97

CI:	Companies Investigation (formerly CIB).
Document:	includes information recorded in any form.

35 Registrar of companies

Contents

Introduction

35.1 The Registrar of Companies occupies an important position within the regulatory structure of the company's establishment, operation and functioning process. The registrar has duties that require compliance with CA 2006 including regulations and enforcement mechanisms to ensure companies comply with the laws. Part 35 of the CA 2006 (as amended by SBEEA 2015) governs the duties and functions of the registrar. This Chapter also takes account of the Companies (Disclosure of Date of Birth Information) Regulations 2015 (SI 2015/1694).

35.2 This Chapter addresses the following issues:

- The regime under the CA 2006 in its application to registrars.
- The appointment of the company registrar.
- Functions of the registrar.
- Dealings with Companies House and the registrar.
- Proposed changes by the Government to filing requirements.

Scheme of Part 35

35.3 Section 1059A sets out the scheme for Pt 35 of the CA 2006: CA 2006, s 1059A(1).

The following provisions apply generally (to the registrar, to any functions of the registrar, or to documents delivered to or issued by the registrar under any enactment, as the case may be): CA 2006, s 1059A(2).

- ss 1060(1) and (2) and 1061–1063 (the registrar);
- ss 1068–1071 (delivery of documents to the registrar);
- ss 1072–1076 (requirements for proper delivery);
- ss 1080(1), (4) and (5) and 1092 (keeping and production of records);
- s 1083 (preservation of original documents);
- s 1084A (recording optional information on register) (as inserted by SBEEA 2015, s 95(2));
- ss 1108–1110 (language requirements: transliteration); and
- ss 1111 and 1114–1119 (supplementary provisions).

35.4 The following provisions apply in relation to companies (or for the purposes of the Companies Acts, as the case may be): CA 2006, s 1059A(3):

- s 1060(3) and (4) (references to the registrar in the Companies Acts);
- ss 1064 and 1065 (certificates of incorporation);
- s 1066 (registered numbers);
- ss 1077–1079 (public notice of receipt of certain documents);
- ss 1080(2) and (3), 1081, 1082 and 1084 (the register);
- ss 1085–1091 (inspection of the register);
- ss 1093–1098 (correction or removal of material on the register);
- s 1106 (voluntary filing of translations); and
- ss 1112 and 1113 (supplementary provisions).

35.5 The following provisions apply as indicated in the provisions concerned: CA 2006, s 1059A(4):

- s 1067 (registered numbers of UK establishments of overseas companies);
- ss 1099–1101 (the registrar's index of company names); and
- ss 1102–1105 and 1107 (language requirements: translation).

Unless the context otherwise requires, the provisions of Pt 35 apply to an overseas company as they apply to a company as defined in s 1059A(1): CA 2006, s 1059A(5).

The registrar

35.6 There is:

(a) a registrar of companies for England and Wales;

(b) a registrar of companies for Scotland; and

(c) a registrar of companies for Northern Ireland: CA 2006, s 1060(1).

The registrars must be appointed by the Secretary of State: CA 2006, s 1060(2).

In the Companies Acts, 'the registrar of companies' and 'the registrar' refer to the registrar of companies for England and Wales, Scotland or Northern Ireland, as the case may require: CA 2006, s 1060(3); and references in the Companies Acts to registration in a particular part of the UK are to registration by the registrar for that part of the UK: CA 2006, s 1060(4).

The registrar's functions

35.7 The registrar must:

(a) perform the functions conferred on the registrar by or under the Companies Acts or any other enactment; and

(b) perform such functions on behalf of the Secretary of State, in relation to the registration of companies or other matters, as the Secretary of State may from time to time direct: CA 2006, s 1061(1).

The references in CA 2006 to the functions of the registrar are to functions within s 1061(1)(a) or (b): CA 2006, s 1061(3).

The registrar's official seal

35.8 The registrar must have an official seal for the authentication of documents in connection with the performance of the registrar's functions: CA 2006, s 1062.

Fees payable to the registrar

35.9 The Secretary of State may make provision by regulations requiring the payment to the registrar of fees in respect of:

(a) the performance of any of the registrar's functions; or

(b) the provision by the registrar of services or facilities for purposes incidental to, or otherwise connected with, the performance of any of the registrar's functions: CA 2006, s 1063(1).

35.10 The matters for which fees may be charged include:

(a) the performance of a duty imposed on the registrar or the Secretary of State;

(b) the receipt of documents delivered to the registrar; and

(c) the inspection, or provision of copies, of documents kept by the registrar: CA 2006, s 1063(2).

35.11 The regulations may:

(a) provide for the amount of the fees to be fixed by or determined under the regulations;

(b) provide for different fees to be payable in respect of the same matter in different circumstances;

(c) specify the person by whom any fee payable under the regulations is to be paid;

(d) specify when and how fees are to be paid: CA 2006, s 1063(3).

In respect of the performance of functions or the provision of services or facilities:

(a) for which fees are not provided for by regulations; or

(b) in circumstances other than those for which fees are provided for by regulations,

the registrar may determine from time to time what fees (if any) are chargeable: CA 2006, s 1063(5).

Fees received by the registrar are to be paid into the Consolidated Funds: CA 2006, s 1063(6).

Public notice of issue of certificate of incorporation

35.12 The registrar must cause to be published:

(a) in the *Gazette*; or

(b) in accordance with s 1116 (alternative means of giving public notice);

notice of the issue by the registrar of any certificate of incorporation of a company: CA 2006, s 1064(1).

The notice must state the name and registered number of the company and the date of issue of the certificate: CA 2006, s 1064(2).

Section 1064 applies to a certificate of incorporation issued under:

(a) s 80 (change of name);

(b) s 88 (Welsh companies); or

(c) any provision of Pt 7 to CA 2006 (re-registration);

as well as to the certificate issued on a company's formation: CA 2006, s 1064(3).

Right to certificate of incorporation

35.13 Any person may require the registrar to provide him with a copy of any certificate of incorporation of a company, either signed by the registrar or authenticated by the registrar's seal: CA 2006, s 1065.

Company's registered numbers

35.14 The registrar must allocate to every company a number, which shall be known as the company's registered number: CA 2006, s 1066(1).

The term 'company' includes an overseas company whose particulars have been registered under s 1046, other than a company that appears to the registrar not to be required to register particulars under that section: CA 2006, s 1066(6).

Companies' registered numbers must be in such form, consisting of one or more sequences of figures or letters, as the registrar may determine: CA 2006, s 1066(2).

The registrar may, on adopting a new form of registered number, make such changes of existing registered numbers as appear necessary: CA 2006, s 1066(3).

A change of a company's registered number has effect from the date on which the company is notified by the registrar of the change: CA 2006, s 1066(4). For a period of three years beginning with that date any requirement to disclose the company's registered number imposed by regulations under s 82 or 1051 (trading disclosures) is satisfied by the use of either the old number or the new: CA 2006, s 1066(5).

Registered numbers of UK establishments of overseas companies

35.15 The registrar must allocate to every UK establishment of an overseas company whose particulars are registered under s 1046 a number, which shall be known as the UK establishment's registered number: CA 2006, s 1067(1). The term 'establishment' in relation to an overseas company means:

(a) a branch within the meaning of the Eleventh Company Law Directive (89/666/EEC); or

(b) a place of business that is not such a branch.

'UK establishment' means an establishment in the UK: CA 2006, s 1067(6).

The registered numbers of UK establishments of overseas companies must be in such form, consisting of one or more sequences of figures or letters, as the registrar may determine: CA 2006, s 1067(2).

The registrar may, on adopting a new form of registered number, make such changes of existing registered numbers as appear necessary: CA 2006, s 1067(3).

A change of the registered number of a UK establishment has effect from the date on which the company is notified by the registrar of the change: CA 2006, s 1067(4).

For a period of three years, beginning with that date, any requirement to disclose the UK establishment's registered number imposed by regulations under s 1051 (trading disclosures) is satisfied by the use of either the old number or the new: CA 2006, s 1067(5).

Registrar's requirements as to form, authentication and manner of delivery

35.16 CA 2006 requires various forms and documents to be delivered to the registrar at Companies House. In this regard, the registrar may impose requirements as to the form, authentication and manner of delivery of documents required or authorised to be delivered to the registrar under any enactment: CA 2006, s 1068(1).

Form

35.17 As regards the form of the document, the registrar may:

(a) require the contents of the document to be in a standard form; or

(b) impose requirements for the purpose of enabling the document to be scanned or copied: CA 2006, s 1068(2).

According to Companies House Guidance Booklet 'Life of a Company Part 2 – Event-driven Filings GP3' Chapter 10 sets out further details as to the form and quality of documents to be filed at Companies House.

Companies House scans the documents and paper forms that are delivered to it to produce an electronic image. It then stores the original, paper documents and uses the electronic image as the working document.

35.18 When a customer searches the company record, they see the electronic image reproduced online. Companies House specifies that the original must be legible and that it can also produce a clear copy.

When a document is submitted electronically, Companies House automatically creates an electronic image from the data provided by the customer.

Documents filed through WebFiling are formatted in accordance with specifications set out by the registrar in his rules on electronic filing as published on the Companies House website.

With regard to paper documents, generally, every paper document sent to Companies House must state the registered name and number of the company in a prominent position. There are a few exceptions to this rule, which are set out in the published registrar's rules. Paper documents should be on A4 size, plain white paper with a matt finish. The text should be black, clear, legible, and of uniform density. Letters and numbers must be clear and legible so that the Companies House can make an acceptable copy of the document. Failure to follow these guidelines is likely to result in the document being rejected. The following guidelines may assist in the preparation and filing of paper documents:

35.19 When filing in a paper form, the following instructions should be followed:

- use black ink or black type;
- use bold lettering (some elegant thin typefaces and pens give poor-quality copies);
- do not send a carbon copy;
- do not use a dot matrix printer;
- remember – photocopies can result in a grey shade that will not scan well;
- use A4 size paper with a good margin;
- supply documents in portrait format (ie with the shorter edge across the top); and
- include the company number and name.

Authentication

35.20 As regards authentication, the registrar may:

(a) require the document to be authenticated by a particular person or a person of a particular description;

(b) specify the means of authentication;

(c) require the document to contain or be accompanied by the name or registered number (or both) of the company (or other body) to which it relates: CA 2006, s 1068(3).

Manner of delivery

35.21

(a) the physical form of the document (eg hard copy or electronic form);

(b) the means to be used for delivering the document (eg by post or electronic means);

(c) the address to which the document is to be sent; and

(d) in the case of a document to be delivered by electronic means, the hardware and software to be used and any technical specifications (eg matters relating to protocol, security, anti-virus protection or encryption): CA 2006, s 1068(4).

The registrar must secure that as from 1 January 2007, all documents subject to the Directive disclosure requirements (see s 1078) may be delivered to the registrar by electronic means: CA 2006, s 1068(5).

35.22 The power conferred by s 1068 does not authorise the registrar to require documents to be delivered by electronic means (see s 1069): CA 2006, s 1068(5). Requirements imposed under this section must not be inconsistent with requirements imposed by any enactment with respect to the form, authentication or manner of delivery of the document concerned: CA 2006, s 1068(6).

But the power conferred by this section does authorise the registrar to require any document permitted or required to be delivered to the registrar under Chapter 2A of Part 8 (option to keep membership information on central register) to be delivered by electronic means: CA 2006, s 1068(6A) (as inserted by SBEEA 2015, Schedule 5, Part 2).

Power to require delivery by electronic means

35.23 The Secretary of State may make regulations requiring documents that are authorised or required to be delivered to the registrar to be delivered by electronic means: CA 2006, s 1069(1).

Any such requirement to deliver documents by electronic means is effective only if the registrar's rules have been published with respect to the detailed requirements for such delivery: CA 2006, s 1069(2).

Agreement for delivery by electronic means

35.24 The registrar may agree with a company (or other body) that documents relating to the company (or other body) that are required or authorised to be delivered to the registrar:

(a) will be delivered by electronic means, except as provided for in the agreement; and

(b) will conform to such requirements as may be specified in the agreement or specified by the registrar in accordance with the agreement: CA 2006, s 1070(1).

An agreement under s 1070 may relate to all or any description of documents to be delivered to the registrar: CA 2006, s 1070(2). Documents in relation to which an agreement is in force under this section must be delivered in accordance with the agreement: CA 2006, s 1070(3).

Document not delivered until received

35.25 A document is not delivered to the registrar until it is received by the registrar: CA 2006, s 1071(1). Provision may be made by registrar's rules as to when a document is to be regarded as received: CA 2006, s 1071(2).

Requirements for proper delivery

35.26 A document delivered to the registrar is not properly delivered unless all the following requirements are met:

(a) the requirements of the provision under which the document is to be delivered to the registrar as regards:

(i) the contents of the document; and

(ii) form, authentication and manner of delivery;

(b) any applicable requirements under:

- CA 2006, s 1068 (registrar's requirements as to form, authentication and manner of delivery);
- CA 2006, s 1069 (power to require delivery by electronic means); or
- CA 2006, s 1070 (agreement for delivery by electronic means);

(c) any requirements of Pt 35 as to the language in which the document is drawn up and delivered or as to its being accompanied on delivery by a certified translation into English;

(d) in so far as it consists of or includes names and addresses, any requirements of Pt 35 of the CA 2006 as to permitted characters, letters or symbols or as to its being accompanied on delivery by a certificate as to the transliteration of any element;

(e) any applicable requirements under s 1111 (registrar's requirements as to certification or verification);

(f) any requirement of regulations under s 1082 (use of unique identifiers); and

(g) any requirements as regards payment of a fee in respect of its receipt by the registrar: CA 2006, s 1072(1).

A document that is not properly delivered is treated for the purposes of the provision requiring or authorising it to be delivered as not having been delivered, subject to the provisions of s 1073 (power to accept documents not meeting requirements for proper delivery): CA 2006, s 1072(2).

Power to accept documents not meeting requirements for proper delivery

35.27 The registrar may accept (and register) a document that does not comply with the requirements for proper delivery: CA 2006, s 1073(1).

A document accepted by the registrar under s 1073 is treated as being received by the registrar for the purposes of s 1077 (public notice of receipt of certain documents): CA 2006, s 1073(2). No objection may be taken to the legal consequences of a document's being accepted (or registered) by the registrar under this section on the ground that the requirements for proper delivery were not met: CA 2006, s 1073(3).

The acceptance of a document by the registrar under s 1073 does not affect:

(a) the continuing obligation to comply with the requirements for proper delivery; or

(b) subject as follows, any liability for failure to comply with those requirements: CA 2006, s 1073(4).

35.28 For the purposes of:

(a) s 453 (civil penalty for failure to file accounts and reports); and

(b) any enactment imposing a daily default fine for failure to deliver the document,

the period after the document is accepted does not count as a period during which there is default in complying with the requirements for proper delivery: CA 2006, s 1073(5).

But if, subsequently:

(a) the registrar issues a notice under s 1094(4) in respect of the document (notice of administrative removal from the register); and

(b) the requirements for proper delivery are not complied with before the end of the period of 14 days after the issue of that notice,

any subsequent period of default does count for the purposes of those provisions: CA 2006, s 1073(6).

Documents containing unnecessary material

35.29 Section 1074 applies where a document delivered to the registrar contains unnecessary material: CA 2006, s 1074(1).

The term 'unnecessary material' means material that:

(a) is not necessary in order to comply with an obligation under any enactment; and

(b) is not specifically authorised to be delivered to the registrar: CA 2006, s 1074(2).

For this purpose, an obligation to deliver a document of a particular description, or conforming to certain requirements, is regarded as not extending to anything that is not needed for a document of that description or, as the case may be, conforming to those requirements: CA 2006, s 1074(3).

35.30 If the unnecessary material cannot readily be separated from the rest of the document, the document is treated as not meeting the requirements for proper delivery: CA 2006, s 1074(4).

If the unnecessary material can readily be separated from the rest of the document, the registrar may register the document either:

(a) with the omission of the unnecessary material; or

(b) as delivered: CA 2006, s 1074(5).

Informal correction of documents

35.31 A document delivered to the registrar may be corrected by the registrar if it appears to the registrar to be incomplete or internally inconsistent: CA 2006, s 1075(1). This power is exercisable only:

(a) on instructions; and

(b) if the company (or other body) to which the document relates has given (and has not withdrawn) its consent to instructions being given under s 1075: CA 2006, s 1075(2).

The following requirements must be met as regards the instructions:

(a) the instructions must be given in response to an enquiry by the registrar;

(b) the registrar must be satisfied that the person giving the instructions is authorised to do so:

  (i) by the person by whom the document was delivered; or

  (ii) by the company (or other body) to which the document relates;

(c) the instructions must meet any requirements of the registrar's rules as to:

  (i) the form and manner in which they are given; and

  (ii) authentication: CA 2006, s 1075(3).

35.32 The consent of the company (or other body) to instructions being given under s 1075 (and any withdrawal of such consent):

(a) may be in hard copy or electronic form; and

(b) must be notified to the registrar: CA 2006, s 1075(4).

Section 1075 applies in relation to documents delivered under Pt 25 (company charges) by a person other than the company (or other body) as if the references to the company (or other body) were to the company (or other body) or the person by whom the document was delivered: CA 2006, s 1075(5).

A document that is corrected under s 1075 is treated, for the purposes of any enactment relating to its delivery, as having been delivered when the correction is made: CA 2006, s 1075(6). The power conferred by this section is not exercisable if the document has been registered under s 1073 (power to accept documents not meeting requirements for proper delivery): CA 2006, s 1075(7).

Replacement of documents not meeting the requirements for proper delivery

35.33 The registrar may accept a replacement for a document previously delivered that:

(a) did not comply with the requirements for proper delivery; or

(b) contained unnecessary material (within the meaning of s 1074): CA 2006, s 1076(1).

35.34 A replacement document must not be accepted unless the registrar is satisfied that it is delivered by:

(a) the person by whom the original document was delivered; or

(b) the company (or other body) to which the original document relates,

and that it complies with the requirements for proper delivery: CA 2006, s 1076(2).

The power of the registrar to impose requirements as to the form and manner of delivery includes the power to impose requirements as to the identification of the original document and the delivery of the replacement in a form and manner enabling it to be associated with the original: CA 2006, s 1076(3).

Section 1076 does not apply where the original document was delivered under Pt 25 (company charges) (but see ss 873 and 888 (rectification of register of charges)): CA 2006, s 1076(4).

Public notice of receipt of certain documents

35.35 The registrar must cause to be published:

(a) in the *Gazette*; or

(b) in accordance with s 1116 (alternative means of giving public notice),

notice of the receipt by the registrar of any document that, on receipt, is subject to the Directive disclosure requirements (see s 1078): CA 2006, s 1077(1). This notice must state the name and registered number of the company, the description of the document and the date of receipt: CA 2006, s 1077(2).

The registrar is not required to cause notice of the receipt of a document to be published before the date of incorporation of the company to which the document relates: CA 2006, s 1077(3).

Documents subject to Directive disclosure requirements

35.36 The documents subject to the 'Directive disclosure requirements' are as follows.

The requirements referred to are those of Art 3 of the First Company Law Directive (68/151/EEC) as amended, extended and applied: CA 2006, s 1078(1).

In the case of every company:

Constitutional documents

- The company's memorandum and articles.
- Any amendment of the company's articles (including every resolution or agreement required to be embodied in or annexed to copies of the company's articles issued by the company).
- After any amendment of the company's articles, the text of the articles as amended.
- Any notice of a change of the company's name.

Directors

- The statement of proposed officers required on formation of the company.
- Notification of any change among the company's directors.
- Notification of any change in the particulars of directors required to be delivered to the registrar.
- Accounts and reports etc.
- All documents required to be delivered to the registrar under s 441 (annual accounts and reports).
- Any confirmation statement delivered by the company under s.853A.

Registered office

- Notification of any change of the company's registered office.
- Winding up.
- Copy of any winding-up order in respect of the company.
- Notice of the appointment of liquidators.
- Order for the dissolution of a company on a winding up.
- Return by a liquidator of the final meeting of a company on a winding up: CA 2006, s 1078(2).

In the case of a public company:

Share capital

- Any statement of capital and initial shareholdings.
- Any return of allotment and the statement of capital accompanying it.
- Copy of any resolution under ss 570 or 571 (disapplication of pre-emption rights).
- Copy of any report under ss 593 or 599 as to the value of a non-cash asset.
- Statement of capital accompanying notice given under s 625 (notice by company of redenomination of shares).
- Statement of capital accompanying notice given under s 627 (notice by company of reduction of capital in connection with redenomination of shares).
- Notice delivered under s 636 (notice of new name of class of shares) or s 637 (notice of variation of rights attached to shares).
- Statement of capital accompanying order delivered under s 649 (order of court confirming reduction of capital).
- Notification (under s 689) of the redemption of shares and the statement of capital accompanying it.
- Statement of capital accompanying return delivered under s 708 (notice of cancellation of shares on purchase of own shares) or s 730 (notice of cancellation of shares held as treasury shares).
- Any statement of compliance delivered under s 762 (statement that company meets conditions for issue of trading certificate).
- Any statement delivered under s. 762(1)9e) (statement of the aggregate amount paid up on shares on account of their nominal value).

Mergers and divisions

- Copy of any draft of the terms of a scheme required to be delivered to the registrar under ss 906 or 921.
- Copy of any order under ss 899 or 900 in respect of a compromise or arrangement to which Pt 27 (mergers and divisions of public companies) applies: CA 2006, s 1078(3).

In the case of a private company which applies to re-register as a public company, the statement delivered under s 94(2)(e) (statement of the aggregate amount paid up on shares on account of their nominal value): CA 2006, s 1078(3A) (as inserted by SBEEA 2015, s 98(4)(b).

Where a private company re-registers as a public company (see s 96):

(a) the last statement of capital relating to the company received by the registrar under any provision of the Companies Acts becomes subject to the Directive disclosure requirements; and

(b) s 1077 (public notice of receipt of certain documents) applies as if the statement had been received by the registrar when the re-registration takes effect: CA 2006, s 1078(4).

In the case of an overseas company, such particulars, returns and other documents required to be delivered under Pt 34 as may be specified by the Secretary of State by regulations: CA 2006, s 1078(5).

Effect of failure to give public notice

35.37 A company is not entitled to rely against other persons on the happening of any event to which s 1079 applies unless:

(a) the event has been officially notified at the material time; or

(b) the company shows that the person concerned knew of the event at the material time: CA 2006, s 1079(1).

35.38 The events are:

(a) an amendment of the company's articles;

(b) a change among the company's directors;

(c) (as regards service of any document on the company) a change of the company's registered office;

(d) the making of a winding-up order in respect of the company; or

(e) the appointment of a liquidator in a voluntary winding up of the company: CA 2006, s 1079(2).

35.39 If the material time falls:

(a) on or before the fifteenth day after the date of official notification; or

(b) where the fifteenth day was not a working day, on or before the next day that was,

the company is not entitled to rely on the happening of the event as against a person who shows that he was unavoidably prevented from knowing of the event at that time: CA 2006, s 1079(3).

35.40 The term 'official notification' means:

(a) in relation to an amendment of the company's articles, notification in accordance with s 1077 (public notice of receipt by registrar of certain documents) of the amendment and the amended text of the articles;

(b) in relation to anything else stated in a document subject to the Directive disclosure requirements, notification of that document in accordance with that section; and

(c) in relation to the appointment of a liquidator in a voluntary winding up, notification of that event in accordance with s 109 of the Insolvency Act 1986 (c 45) or art 95 of the Insolvency (Northern Ireland) Order 1989 (SI 1989 No 2405 (NI 19)): CA 2006, s 1079(4).

Notice of receipt of documents about new directors

Duty to notify directors

35.45 CA 2006, s 1079B applies whenever the registrar registers either of the following documents:

(a) the statement of proposed officers required on formation of a company, or

(b) notice under section 167 or 167D of a person having become a director of a company: CA 2006, s 1079B(1) (as inserted by SBEEA 2015, s 101(1)).

35.46 As soon as reasonably practicable after registering the document, the registrar must notify:

(a) in the case of a statement of proposed officers, the person or each person named in the statement as a director of the company, or

(b) in the case of a notice under section 167 or 167D, the person named in the document as having become a director of the company: CA 2006, s 1079B(2) (as inserted by SBEEA 2015, s 101(1)).

35.47 The notice must:

(a) state that the person is named in the document as a director of the company, and

(b) include such information relating to the office and duties of a director (or such details of where information of that sort can be found) as the Secretary of State may from time to time direct the registrar to include: CA 2006, s 1079B(3) (as inserted by SBEEA 2015, s 101(1)).

The notice may be sent in hard copy or electronic form to any address for the person that the registrar has received from either the subscribers or the company: CA 2006, s 1079B(4) (as inserted by SBEEA 2015, s 101(1))

The register

35.48 The registrar must keep records of:

(a) the information contained in documents delivered to the registrar under any enactment; and

(b) certificates issued by the registrar under any enactment: CA 2006, s 1080(1).

The records relating to companies are referred to collectively in the Companies Acts as 'the register': CA 2006, s 1080(2).

Information deriving from documents subject to the Directive disclosure requirements (see s 1078) that are delivered to the registrar on or after 1 January 2007 must be kept by the registrar in electronic form: CA 2006, s 1080(3).

35.49 Subject to that, information contained in documents delivered to the registrar may be recorded and kept in any form the registrar thinks fit, provided it is possible to inspect and produce a copy of it: CA 2006, s 1080(4).

This is sufficient compliance with any duty of the registrar to keep, file or register the document or to record the information contained in it: CA 2006, s 1080(5).

The records kept by the registrar must be such that information relating to a company or other registered body is associated with that body, in such manner as the registrar may determine, so as to enable all the information relating to the body to be retrieved: CA 2006, s 1080(6).

Annotation in the register

35.50 The registrar must place a note in the register recording:

(a) the date on which a document is delivered to the registrar;

(b) if a document is corrected under s 1075, the nature and date of the correction;

(c) if a document is replaced (whether or not material derived from it is removed), the fact that it has been replaced and the date of delivery of the replacement;

(d) if material is removed:

   (i) what was removed (giving a general description of its contents);

   (ii) under what power; and

   (iii) the date on which that was done: CA 2006, s 1081(1).

(e) If the registrar registers a document delivered by a company under section 128E that, by virtue of subsection (3)(a), (b) or (c) of that section, does not specify the relevant date, the registrar must place a note in the register recording as that date the date on which the document was registered by the registrar: CA 2006, s 1081(1A) (as inserted by SBEEA 2015, Schedule 5, Part 2).

35.51 The Secretary of State may make provision by regulations:

(a) authorising or requiring the registrar to annotate the register in such other circumstances as may be specified in the regulations; and

(b) as to the contents of any such annotation: CA 2006, s 1081(2).

No annotation is required in the case of a document that by virtue of s 1072(2) (documents not meeting requirements for proper delivery) is treated as not having been delivered: CA 2006, s 1081(3).

A note may be removed if it no longer serves any useful purpose: CA 2006, s 1081(4).

Any duty or power of the registrar with respect to annotation of the register is subject to the court's power under s 1097 (powers of court on ordering removal of material from the register) to direct:

(a) that a note be removed from the register; or

(b) that no note shall be made of the removal of material that is the subject of the court's order: CA 2006, s 1081(5).

Notes placed in the register in accordance with s 1081(1) or (1A), or in pursuance of regulations under s 1082(2), are part of the register for all purposes of the Companies Acts: CA 2006, s 1081(6) (as inserted by SBEEA 2015, Sch 5, Part 2).

Allocation of unique identifiers

35.52 The Secretary of State may make provision for the use, in connection with the register, of reference numbers ('unique identifiers') to identify each person who:

(a) is a director of a company;

(b) is secretary (or a joint secretary) of a company; or

(c) in the case of an overseas company whose particulars are registered under s 1046, holds any such position as may be specified for the purposes of s 1082 by regulations under that section: CA 2006, s 1082(1).

35.53 The regulations may:

(a) provide that a unique identifier may be in such form, consisting of one or more sequences of letters or numbers, as the registrar may from time to time determine;

(b) make provision for the allocation of unique identifiers by the registrar;

(c) require there to be included, in any specified description of documents delivered to the registrar, as well as a statement of the person's name:

  (i) a statement of the person's unique identifier; or

  (ii) a statement that the person has not been allocated a unique identifier,

(d) enable the registrar to take steps where a person appears to have more than one unique identifier to discontinue the use of all but one of them: CA 2006, s 1082(2).

The regulations may contain provision for the application of the scheme in relation to persons appointed, and documents registered, before the commencement of this Act: CA 2006, s 1082(3).

The regulations may make different provision for different descriptions of person and different descriptions of document: CA 2006, s 1082(4).

Preservation of original documents

35.54 The originals of documents delivered to the registrar in hard copy form must be kept for three years after they are received by the registrar, after which they may be destroyed provided the information contained in them has been recorded. This is subject to s 1087(3) (extent of obligation to retain material not available for public inspection): CA 2006, s 1083(1).

The registrar is under no obligation to keep the originals of documents delivered in electronic form, provided the information contained in them has been recorded: CA 2006, s 1083(2). Section 1083 applies to documents held by the registrar when the section comes into force as well as to documents subsequently received: CA 2006, s 1083(3).

Records relating to companies that have been dissolved, etc

35.55 CA 2006, s 1084 applies where:

(a) a company is dissolved. The term 'company' includes a company provisionally or completely registered under the Joint Stock Companies Act 1844 (c 110): CA 2006, s 1084(4);

(b) an overseas company ceases to have any connection with the UK by virtue of which it is required to register particulars under s 1046; or

(c) a credit or financial institution ceases to be within s 1050 (overseas institutions required to file accounts with the registrar): CA 2006, s 1084(1).

35.56 At any time after two years from the date on which it appears to the registrar that:

(a) the company has been dissolved;

(b) the overseas company has ceased to have any connection with the UK by virtue of which it is required to register particulars under s 1046; or

(c) the credit or financial institution has ceased to be within s 1050 (overseas institutions required to file accounts with the registrar),

the registrar may direct that records relating to the company or institution may be removed to the Public Record Office or, as the case may be, the Public Record Office of Northern Ireland: CA 2006, s 1084(2).

Records for which such a direction is given shall be disposed of under the enactments relating to that Office and the rules made under them: CA 2006, s 1084(3).

Section 1084 does not extend to Scotland: CA 2006, s 1084(5).

Recording of optional information on register

35.57 SBEEA 2015, Sch 5 amends the CA 2006 to give private companies the option of keeping certain information on the register kept by the registrar instead of keeping it in their own registers: SBEEA 2015, s 94.

The Secretary of State may make provision by regulations authorising a company or other body to deliver optional information of a prescribed description to the registrar: CA 2006, s 1084A(1) (as inserted by SBEEA 2015, s 95).

The term "optional information", in relation to a company or other body, means information about the company or body which, but for the regulations, the company or body would not be obliged or authorised under any enactment to deliver to the registrar: CA 2006, s 1084A(2) (as inserted by SBEEA 2015, s 95).

The regulations may, in particular, include provision:

(a) imposing requirements on a company or other body in relation to keeping any of its optional information recorded on the register up to date;

(b) about the consequences of a company or other body failing to do so: CA 2006, s 1084A(3) (as inserted by SBEEA 2015, s 95).

Inspection of the register

35.58 Any person may inspect the register: CA 2006, s 1085(1). This right of inspection extends to the originals of documents delivered to the registrar in hard copy form if, and only if, the record kept by the registrar of the contents of the document is illegible or unavailable.

The period for which such originals are to be kept is limited by s 1083(1): CA 2006, s 1085(2).

Section 1085 is subject to s 1087 (material not available for public inspection): CA 2006, s 1085(3).

Right to copy of material on the register

35.59 Any person may ask to copy any material on the register: CA 2006, s 1086(1). The fee for any such copy of material derived from a document subject to the Directive disclosure requirements (see s 1078), whether in hard copy or electronic form, must not exceed the administrative cost of providing it: CA 2006, s 1086(2).

Section 1086 is subject to s 1087 (material not available for public inspection): CA 2006, s 1086(3).

Material not available for public inspection

35.60 The following material must not be made available by the registrar for public inspection:

(a) the contents of any document sent to the registrar containing views expressed pursuant to s 56 (comments on proposal by company to use certain words or expressions in company name);

(b) protected information within s 242(1) (directors' residential addresses: restriction on disclosure by registrar) or any corresponding provision of regulations under s 1046 (overseas companies);

(ba) representations received by the registrar in response to a notice under:

- (i) s 245(2) (notice of proposal to put director's usual residential address on the public record), or
- (ii) any corresponding provision of regulations under s 1046 (overseas companies);

(bb) information to which ss 240 to 244 are applied by s 790ZF(1) (residential addresses of people with significant control over the company) or any corresponding provision of regulations under s 1046 (overseas companies);

(bc) information that, by virtue of regulations under s 790ZG or any corresponding provision of regulations under s 1046, the registrar must omit from the material on the register that is available for inspection: (as inserted by SBEEA 2015, Sch 3, Part 2);

(c) any application to the registrar under s 1024 (application for administrative restoration to the register) that has not yet been determined or was not successful;

(d) any document received by the registrar in connection with the giving or withdrawal of consent under s 1075 (informal correction of documents);

(da) information falling within s 1087A(1) (information about a person's date of birth) (as inserted by SBEEA 2015, s 96(2));

(e) any application or other document delivered to the registrar under s 1088 (application to make address unavailable for public inspection) and any address in respect of which such an application is successful;

(f) any application or other document delivered to the registrar under s 1095 (application for rectification of register);

(g) any court order under s 1096 (rectification of the register under court order) that the court has directed under s 1097 (powers of court on ordering removal of material from the register) is not to be made available for public inspection;

(ga) any application or other document delivered to the registrar under s 1097A (rectification of company registered office) other than an order or direction of the court;

(h) the contents of:

   (i) any instrument creating or evidencing a charge; or

   (ii) any certified or verified copy of an instrument creating or evidencing a charge,

   delivered to the registrar under Pt 25 (company charges) or regulations under s 1052 (overseas companies);

(i) any e-mail address, identification code or password deriving from a document delivered for the purpose of authorising or facilitating electronic filing procedures or providing information by telephone;

(j) the contents of any documents held by the registrar pending a decision of the Regulator of Community Interest Companies under:

   (i) s 36A of the Companies (Audit, Investigations and Community Enterprise) Act 2004 (eligibility for registration as community interest company);

   (ii) s 38 of that Act (eligibility for conversion to community interest company); or

   (iii) s 55 of that Act (eligibility for conversion from community interest company to charity),

   and that the registrar is not later required to record;

(k) any other material excluded from public inspection by or under any other enactment: CA 2006, s 1087(1) (as inserted by SBEEA 2015, s 99(2)).

A restriction applying by reference to material deriving from a particular description of document does not affect the availability for public inspection of the same information contained in material derived from another description of document in relation to which no such restriction applies: CA 2006, s 1087(2).

Material to which s 1087 applies need not be retained by the registrar for longer than appears to the registrar reasonably necessary for the purposes for which the material was delivered to the registrar: CA 2006, s 1087(3).

Information about a person's date of birth

35.61 CA 2006, s 1087A (as inserted by SBEEA 2015, s 96(3) is concerned with information about a person's date of birth. Information falls within CA 2006, s 1087(1) at any time ('the relevant time') if:

(a) it is DOB information;

(b) it is contained in a document delivered to the registrar that is protected at the relevant time as regards that information;

(c) the document is one in which such information is required to be stated; and

(d) if the document has more than one part, the part in which the information is contained is a part in which such information is required to be stated: CA 2006, s 1087A(1).

'DOB information' is information as to the day of the month (but not the month or year) on which a relevant person was born: CA 2006, s 1087A(2).

35.62 A 'relevant person' is an individual:

(a) who is a director of a company, or

(b) whose particulars are stated in a company's PSC register as a registrable person in relation to that company (see Part 21A): CA 2006, s 1087A(3).

A document delivered to the registrar is 'protected' at any time unless:

(a) it is an election period document;

(b) s 1087A(7) applies to it at the time; or

(c) it was registered before this section comes into force: CA 2006, s 1087A(4).

35.63 As regards DOB information about a relevant person in his or her capacity as a director of the company, each of the following is an 'election period document':

(a) a statement of the company's proposed officers delivered under s 9 in circumstances where the subscribers gave notice of election under s 167A (election to keep information on central register) in respect of the company's register of directors when the statement was delivered;

(b) a document delivered by the company under s 167D (duty to notify registrar of changes while election in force): CA 2006, s 1087A(5).

35.64 As regards DOB information about a relevant person in his or her capacity as someone whose particulars are stated in the company's PSC register, each of the following is an 'election period document':

(a) a statement of initial significant control delivered under s 9 in circumstances where the subscribers gave notice of election under s 790X in respect of the company when the statement was delivered;

(b) a document containing a statement or updated statement delivered by the company under s 790X(6)(b) or (7) (statement accompanying notice of election made after incorporation);

(c) a document delivered by the company under s 790ZA (duty to notify registrar of changes while election in force): CA 2006, s 1087A(6).

35.65 CA 2006, s 1087(7) applies to a document if:

(a) the DOB information relates to the relevant person in his or her capacity as a director of the company;

(b) an election under s 167A is or has previously been in force in respect of the company's register of directors;

(c) the document was delivered to the registrar at some point before that election took effect,

(d) the relevant person was a director of the company when that election took effect; and

(e) the document was either:

 (i) a statement of proposed officers delivered under s 9 naming the relevant person as someone who was to be a director of the company, or

 (ii) notice given under s 167 of the relevant person having become a director of the company: s 1087A(1) (CA 2006: s 1087A(7)).

Information about a person does not cease to fall within s 1087A(1) when he or she ceases to be a relevant person and, to that extent, references in this section to a relevant person include someone who used to be a relevant person: CA 2006, s 1087A(8).

Nothing in 1087A(1) obliges the registrar to check other documents or (as the case may be) other parts of the document to ensure the absence of DOB information: CA 2006 s 1087A(8).

Disclosure of DOB Information

35.66 The registrar must not disclose restricted DOB information unless:

(a) the same information about the relevant person (whether in the same or a different capacity) is made available by the registrar for public inspection as a result of being contained in another description of document in relation to which no restriction under s 1087 applies (see sub-s (2) of that section); or

(b) disclosure of the information by the registrar is permitted by sub-s (2) or another provision of this Act: CA 2006, s 1087B(1).

The registrar may disclose restricted DOB information:

(a) to a public authority specified for the purposes of this subsection by regulations made by the Secretary of State; or

(b) to a credit reference agency: CA 2006, s 1087B(2).

The Companies (Disclosure of Date of Birth Information) Regulations 2015 (SI 2015/1694), have been enacted and came into force on 10 October 2015. These Regulations specify the conditions for disclosure of date of birth information (defined as 'DOB information' in CA 2006, s 1087A to public authorities and credit reference agencies under CA 2006, s1087B.

35.67 The registrar may disclose restricted DOB information to a specified public authority where the conditions specified in SI 2015/1695, Sch 2, paras 2 and 3 are satisfied: reg 2(1).

A specified public authority shall deliver to the registrar such information or evidence as the registrar may direct for the purpose of enabling the registrar to determine in accordance with these Regulations whether to disclose restricted DOB information to a specified public authority: reg 2(2).

The registrar may require such information or evidence to be verified in such manner as the registrar may direct: reg 2(3).

The specified public authority must inform the registrar immediately of any change in respect of any statement delivered to the registrar pursuant to Sch 2 or information or evidence provided for the purpose of enabling the registrar to determine whether to disclose restricted DOB information: reg 2(4).

35.68 The public authorities specified for the purposes of s 1087B(2) are set out in Sch 1 to these Regulations: reg 2(5).

Regulation 3 provides that the registrar may disclose restricted DOB information to a credit reference agency where the conditions specified in Sch 2, paras 6–10 are satisfied: reg 3(1).

The registrar may rely on a statement delivered to the registrar by a credit reference agency under of Sch 2, para 10 as sufficient evidence of the matters stated in it: reg 3(2).

Notwithstanding paragraph (2), a credit reference agency shall deliver to the registrar such information or evidence in addition to the statement required by of Schedule 2, para 10 as the registrar may direct for the purpose of enabling the registrar to determine in accordance with these Regulations whether to disclose restricted DOB information to a credit reference agency: reg 3(3).

The registrar may require such information or evidence to be verified in such manner as the registrar may direct: reg 3(4).

35.69 The credit reference agency must inform the registrar immediately of any change in respect of any statement delivered to the registrar pursuant to Sch 2 or information or evidence provided for the purpose of enabling the registrar to determine whether to disclose restricted DOB information: reg 3(5).

CA 2006, s 243(3)–(8) (permitted use or disclosure of directors' residential addresses etc by the registrar) apply for the purposes of s 1087B(2) as for the purposes of that section (reading references there to protected information as references to restricted DOB information): CA 2006, s 1087B(3).

CA 2006, s 1087B does not apply to restricted DOB information about a relevant person in his or her capacity as someone whose particulars are stated in the company's PSC register if an application under regulations made under s 790ZG (regulations for protecting PSC particulars) has been granted with respect to that information and not been revoked: CA 2006, s 1087B(4).

'Restricted DOB information' means information falling within s 1087A(1): CA 2006, s 1087B(5).

Application to register to make address unavailable for public inspection

35.70 The Secretary of State may make provision by regulations requiring the registrar, on application, to make an address on the register unavailable for public inspection: CA 2006, s 1088(1). The regulations may make provision as to:

(a) who may make an application;

(b) the grounds on which an application may be made;

(c) the information to be included in and documents to accompany an application;

(d) the notice to be given of an application and of its outcome; and

(e) how an application is to be determined: CA 2006, s 1088(2).

Provision under s 1088(2)(e) may in particular:

(a) confer a discretion on the registrar; and

(b) provide for a question to be referred to a person other than the registrar for the purposes of determining the application: CA 2006, s 1088(3).

35.71 An application must specify the address to be removed from the register and indicate where it is on the register: CA 2006, s 1088(4).

The regulations may provide:

(a) that an address is not to be made unavailable for public inspection under s 1088 unless replaced by a service address; and

(b) that in such a case the application must specify a service address: CA 2006, s 1088(5).

Form of application for inspection or copy

35.72 The registrar may specify the form and manner in which application is to be made for:

(a) inspection under s 1085; or

(b) a copy under s 1086: CA 2006, s 1089(1).

As from 1 January 2007, applications in respect of documents subject to the Directive disclosure requirements may be submitted to the registrar in hard copy or electronic form, as the applicant chooses.

This does not affect the registrar's power under s 1089(1) above to impose requirements in respect of other matters: CA 2006, s 1089(2).

Form and manner in which copies to be provided

35.73 Copies of documents subject to the Directive disclosure requirements must be provided in hard copy or electronic form, as the applicant chooses. However, the registrar is not obliged by s 1090(2) to provide copies in electronic form of a document that was delivered to the registrar in hard copy form if:

(a) the document was delivered to the registrar on or before 31 December 1996; or

(b) the document was delivered to the registrar on or before 31 December 2006 and ten years or more have elapsed between the date of delivery and the date of receipt of the first application for a copy on or after 1 January 2007: CA 2006, s 1090(3).

Subject to this aspect, the registrar may determine the form and manner in which copies are to be provided: CA 2006, s 1090(4).

Certification of copies as accurate

35.74 Copies provided under s 1086 in hard copy form must be certified as true copies unless the applicant dispenses with such certification: CA 2006, s 1091(1). Copies provided in electronic form must not be certified as true copies unless the applicant expressly requests such certification: CA 2006, s 1091(2).

A copy provided under s 1086, certified by the registrar (whose official position it is unnecessary to prove) to be an accurate record of the contents of the original document, is in all legal proceedings admissible in evidence:

(a) as of equal validity with the original document; and

(b) as evidence (in Scotland, sufficient evidence) of any fact stated in the original document of which direct oral evidence would be admissible: CA 2006, s 1091(3).

The Secretary of State may make provision by regulations as to the manner in which such a certificate is to be provided in a case where the copy is provided in electronic form: CA 2006, s 1091(4).

Except in the case of documents that are subject to the Directive disclosure requirements (see s 1078), copies provided by the registrar may, instead of being certified in writing to be an accurate record, be sealed with the registrar's official seal: CA 2006, s 1091(5).

Issue of process for production of records kept by the registrar

35.75 No process for compelling the production of a record kept by the registrar shall issue from any court except with the permission of the court: CA 2006, s 1092(1). Any such process shall bear on it a statement that it is issued with the permission of the court: CA 2006, s 1092(2).

Registrar's notice to resolve inconsistency in the register

35.76 Where it appears to the registrar that the information contained in a document delivered to the registrar is inconsistent with other information on the register, the registrar may give notice to the company to which the document relates:

(a) stating in what respects the information contained in it appears to be inconsistent with other information on the register; and

(b) requiring the company to take steps to resolve the inconsistency: CA 2006, s 1093(1).

35.77 The notice must:

(a) state the date on which it is issued; and

(b) require the delivery to the registrar, within 14 days after that date, of such replacement or additional documents as may be required to resolve the inconsistency: CA 2006, s 1093(2).

35.78 If the necessary documents are not delivered within the period specified, an offence is committed by:

(a) the company; and

(b) every officer of the company who is in default: CA 2006, s 1093(3).

A person guilty of an offence under s 1093(3) will be liable on summary conviction to a fine not exceeding level 5 on the standard scale and, for continued contravention, a daily default fine not exceeding one-tenth of level 5 on the standard scale: CA 2006, s 1093(4).

Administrative removal of material from the register

35.79 The registrar may remove from the register anything that there was power, but no duty, to include: CA 2006, s 1094(1).

This power is exercisable, in particular, so as to remove:

(a) unnecessary material within the meaning of s 1074; and

(b) material derived from a document that has been replaced under:

- s 1076 (replacement of document not meeting requirements for proper delivery); or
- s 1093 (notice to remedy inconsistency on the register): CA 2006, s 1094(2).

35.80 Section 1094 does not authorise the removal from the register of:

(a) anything whose registration has had legal consequences in relation to the company as regards:

- its formation;
- a change of name;
- its re-registration;
- its becoming or ceasing to be a community interest company;
- a reduction of capital;
- a change of registered office;
- the registration of a charge;
- its dissolution; or
- a change in its membership particulars of which were delivered to the registrar under section 128E (duty to notify registrar of changes while election to keep information on central register is in force);

(b) an address that is a person's registered address for the purposes of s 1140 (service of documents on directors, secretaries and others): CA 2006, s 1094(3).

35.81 On or before removing any material under s 1094 (otherwise than at the request of the company), the registrar must give notice:

(a) to the person by whom the material was delivered (if the identity, and name and address of that person are known); or

(b) to the company to which the material relates (if notice cannot be given under para (a) and the identity of that company is known): CA 2006, s 1094(4).

The notice must:

(a) state what material the registrar proposes to remove, or has removed, and on what grounds; and

(b) state the date on which it is issued: CA 2006, s 1094(5).

Rectification of register on application to registrar

35.82 On application (but not if there is a valid objection to the application) the registrar must remove from the register any 'relevant material' that:

(a) derives from anything invalid or ineffective or that was done without the authority of the company or overseas company to which the material relates; or

(b) is factually inaccurate, or is derived from something that is factually inaccurate or forged: CA 2006, s 1095 and the Registrar of Companies and Applications for Striking Off Regulations 2009 (SI 2009 No 1808) regs 4 and 5.

The term 'relevant material' means material on the register that was included in, or is derived from material that was included in, a relevant company form or a relevant overseas company form delivered to the registrar by any person.

35.83 The term 'relevant company form' is:

(a) a standard form required for giving notice under s 87 (change of address of registered office), s 167 (changes relating to directors) or s 276 (changes relating to secretaries) of the Companies Act 2006; or

(b) so much of a standard form required for delivering an application under s 9 of that Act (application for registration of a company) as is required for the statement of a company's proposed officers referred to in s 9(4)(c).

35.84 A 'relevant overseas company form' is:

(a) so much of a standard form required for delivering a return under reg 4 of the Overseas Companies Regulations 2009 as is required for:

  (i) the list referred to in reg 6(1)(d) (list of directors and secretary of an overseas company);

  (ii) the names and service addresses referred to in reg 7(1)(e) (names and service addresses of persons authorised to accept service of documents on behalf of an overseas company in respect of a UK establishment); or

  (iii) the list referred to in reg 7(1)(f) (list of permanent representatives of an overseas company in respect of a UK establishment); or

(b) so much of a standard form required for delivering a return under reg 13 as is required for details of the alteration of particulars delivered under:

  (i) reg 6(1)(d) (directors and secretary);

  (ii) reg 7(1)(a) (address of UK establishment);

  (iii) reg 7(1)(e) (names and service addresses of persons authorised to accept service); or

  (iv) reg 7(1)(f) (list of permanent representatives).

An application to the registrar for the removal from the register (on the grounds in para (1)) of material that was included in a standard form required for giving notice under s 87 (change of address of registered office), or of material that is derived from material that was included in such a form, may be made by (and only by) the company to which the material relates.

35.85 An application to the registrar for the removal from the register (on the grounds in para (1)) of material that was included in, or is derived from material that was included in, so much of a standard form required for delivering a return under reg 13 of the Overseas Companies Regulations 2009 as is required for details of the alteration of particulars delivered under reg 7(1)(a) of those Regulations (address of UK establishment) may be made by (and only by) the overseas company to which the material relates.

An application to the registrar for the removal from the register on the grounds in para (1) of relevant material other than material referred to in para (5) or (6) may be made by (and only by):

(a) the person by whom the relevant company form or relevant overseas company form (as the case may be) was delivered to the registrar;

(b) the company or overseas company to which the material relates; or

(c) any other person to whom the material relates.

35.86 A 'valid objection' is:

(a) an objection made in accordance with reg 5(10) and (11) by a person to whom notice of the application was given under reg 5(2), (3), (4) or (5); or

(b) an objection made in accordance with reg 5(10) by any other person which is not an objection that the registrar is prevented from taking into account under reg 5(12).

In this regulation 'required' means required by rules made by the registrar under s 1117 of the CA 2006.

35.87 An application must:

(a) specify what is to be removed from the register and indicate where on the register it is;

(b) be accompanied by a statement that the material specified in the application complies with s 1095 and the regulations: CA 2006, s 1095(3);

(c) state the applicant's name and address;

(d) where the application concerns the address of a registered office or UK establishment, confirm that the applicant is the company or (as the case may be) the overseas company to which the relevant material which is the subject of the application relates;

(e) in any other case, state whether the applicant is:

  (i) the person delivering the form;

  (ii) the company or overseas company to which the material relates; or

  (iii) another person to whom the material relates.

35.88 The application must state whether the relevant material that is the subject of the application:

(a) is factually inaccurate or is derived from something that is factually inaccurate; or

(b) is derived from something that is forged.

The registrar must give notice of the application to:

(a) the specified person which includes the company (but only if the registrar knows the identity and name and address of that person);

(b) every person who (to the registrar's knowledge) was a director or secretary of the company at the time when the application was delivered to the registrar; and

(c) the company at the address of its registered office.

35.89 The notice by the registrar must:

(a) specify what is to be removed from the register and indicate where on the register it is;

(b) state the date on which the notice is issued;

(c) give particulars of the recipient's right to object to the application and the requirements applying to that right; and

(d) explain the effect of valid objection.

An objection to an application may be made to the registrar by any person. Such objection must be made by giving notice in writing to the registrar and the notice must state the name and address of the person making the objection and identify the application to which the objection relates before the end of the period of 28 days beginning with the date on which the registrar's notice was issued (as stated in the notice).

35.90 The registrar must not take account of an objection made by any other person after the end of the period of 28 days beginning with the date on which the notice was issued.

Where a valid objection is made to the application, the registrar must reject the application. In these circumstances, the registrar must also:

(a) send an acknowledgment of receipt to the person who made the objection;

(b) notify the applicant of the fact that an objection has been made; and

(c) notify every other person to whom the registrar gave notice (but not the person who made the objection or any other person who has made an objection).

If no valid objection is made, the registrar must notify the applicant of that fact. In these circumstances, the registrar may accept the statement as sufficient evidence that the material specified in the application should be removed from the register: CA 2006, s 1095(4).

35.91 CA 2006, 1095(4B) and (4C) apply, in place of sub-s (4), in a case where:

(a) the material specified in the application is material naming a person:

  (i) in a statement of a company's proposed officers as a person who is to be a director of the company; or

  (ii) in a notice given by a company under s 167 or 167D as a person who has become a director of the company; and

(b) the application is made by or on behalf of the person named and is accompanied by a statement that the person did not consent to act as director of the company: CA 2006, s 1095(4A) (as inserted by SBEEA 2015, s 102(1)).

If the company provides the registrar with the necessary evidence within the time required by the regulations, the registrar must not remove the material from the register: CA 2006, s 1095(4B) (as inserted by SBEEA 2015, s 102(1)).

35.92 If the company does not provide the registrar with the necessary evidence within that time:

(a) the material is conclusively presumed for the purposes of this section to be derived from something that is factually inaccurate; and

(b) the registrar must accept the applicant's statement as sufficient evidence that the material should be removed from the register: CA 2006, s 1095(4C) (as inserted by SBEEA 2015, s 102(1)).

The 'necessary evidence' is:

(a) evidence sufficient to satisfy the registrar that the person did consent to act as director of the company; plus

(b) a statement by the company that the evidence provided by it is true and is not misleading or deceptive in any material particular: CA 2006, s 1095(4D) (as inserted by SBEEA 2015, s 102(1)).

35.93 Where anything is removed from the register under s 1095 the registration of which had legal consequences as mentioned in s 1094(3), any person appearing to the court to have a sufficient interest may apply to the court for such consequential orders as appear just with respect to the legal effect (if any) to be accorded to the material by virtue of its having appeared on the register: CA 2006, s 1095(5).

In relation to the application of CA 2006, s 1095 to limited liability partnerships, see the Limited Liability Partnerships (Application of Companies Act 2006) Regulations (SI 2009/1804).

35.94 CA 2006, s 1095 applies therefore to both companies and LLPs. However, there is no similar provision applicable to limited liability partnerships established under the Limited Partnerships Act 1907 (LPA 1907). In *Bank of Beirut SAL v HRH Prince Adel El-Hashemite* [2015] EWHC 1451, two banks claimed to be victims of a fraud carried out by a person claiming to be HRH Price Adel El-Hashemite by forging documents and registering certain documents at Companies House under the LPA 1907, giving the appearance of the banks as a general partner and the Prince as a limited partner. The registrar (registrar) registered the limited partnership based on the documents received. The issue was whether the court had power to order rectification of the register and to order the registrar to delete the registration of the limited partnerships. In this regard the registrar was joined as a defendant in the action. The difficulty was that under LPA 1907, s 8C the certificate of registration issued by the registrar is 'conclusive evidence' that the limited partnership came into existence on the date of registration. Nugee J held that the establishment of fraud or forgery by themselves were not sufficient to go behind the conclusiveness of the certificate issued by the registrar. The registrar had acted in good faith in registering the limited partnership. He concluded that he had no authority under the LPA 1907 to require the Register to remove the entries relating to the limited partnerships at Companies House. Further, it was not the court's function to micromanage the process at Companies House. Moreover, the registrar had not been in breach of his public law functions in declining to remove the partnerships as if they had never existed. To do so would cause more confusion and the most appropriate course of action which the registrar had taken was to mark the register so that anyone searching was reasonably alerted to the position.

The court's control over the registrar

35.95 There have been some judicial authority for the view that even in the absence of statutory powers, the court has some control over the registrar. In *Re Calmex Limited* [1989] 1 All ER 485, the registrar had registered a winding up order which was made against Re Calmex Ltd. This order was made by mistake as it was intended to wind up an unconnected company. The court was required to consider whether it could make an order that the winding up order be removed from the register? Hoffmann J held that the court could make the order on the basis that the purpose of the register was not simply to chronicle events but to record information which might be useful to persons dealing with the company, ad that he could see no purpose in recording that the company had been the victim of mistaken identity, and that the existence of the record was a potential source of serious injustice to the company.

However, *Re Calmex* has been distinguished in other cases. In *igroup Ltd v Ocwen* [2003] EWHC 2431, the mortgage companies had delivered for registration forms containing particulars of charges to which were scheduled details of their customers' personal information. Lightman J did not make an order requiring the Registrar to remove or replace the schedules. The documents delivered to the Registrar were valid and the Registrar was under no duty to rectify them.

35.96 In *Re a Company (No 004766 of 2003)* [2004] EWHC 35, the company had delivered annual accounts for registration containing a reference to an offer under the civil procedure rules in respect of on-going litigation. The judge refused to make an order permitting the filing of revised accounts and held that the filed accounts were not a nullity and could not be said to be improperly filed.

An issue which arises is whether there can be a claim against the Registrar for negligence and breach of statutory duty where the Registrar has made an error that amounts to negligence? In *Sebry v Companies House The Registrar of Companies* [2015] EWHC 115, the claimant was a managing director in a company called "Taylor and Sons Limited" (Company). Another company was registered at Companies House under the name "Taylor and Son Limited" and a winding up order was made by the Chancery Court against this latter company but the order did not include the company number, and was received by Companies House which by error registered the order against "Taylor and Sons Limited" instead of against "Taylor and Son Limited". Communications between the Companies House and the claimant led to the ultimate removal of the winding up order against Taylor and Sons Limited, but the damage had already been inflicted by the Company's creditors and suppliers having knowledge of this order which led to the Company's administration. Edis J considered both the common law and statutory breach of duty by the Registrar.

35.97 With regard to the common law duty of care, Edis J considered that there were three approaches to the determination of existence of a duty of care at law. There were three approaches to the determination of the existence or otherwise of a duty of care at law: (a) 'incrementalism' (based on legal precedent); (b) assumption of responsibility; and (c) the 'three stage *Caparo* test'. Where the Registrar undertook to alter the status of a company on the Register which it was his duty to keep, in particular by recording a winding up order against it, he assumed a responsibility to that company (but not to anyone else) to take reasonable care to ensure that the winding up order is not registered against the wrong company. That special relationship between the Registrar and the company arose because it was foreseeable that if a company was wrongly said on the Register to be in liquidation it would suffer serious harm. The system placed a degree of trust therefore in the Registrar's staff to ensure that it did not damage companies which had no way of defending themselves against errors. When such an exercise was performed in private and behind closed doors, those doing it had truly assumed responsibility for it. *White v. Jones* [1995] 2 AC 619 made it clear that the class could be adjusted to meet considerations of practical justice and the aspect of practical justice suggested strongly that it should contain, but be limited to, the company whose record was being changed. A registrar owed a duty of care when entering a winding up order on the register to take reasonable care to ensure that the order was not registered against the wrong company. That duty was owed to any company which was not in liquidation but which was wrongly recorded on the register as having been wound up by order of the court. See too: *Hedley Byrne v Heller* [1963] 2 AC 465 and subsequently developed in *Caparo Industries v Dickman* [1990] 2 AC 605, *Murphy v Brentwood* [1991] AC 398 and *Commissioners of Customs & Excise v Barclays Bank plc* [2007] 1 AC 181.

35.98 Applying each of the three tests for the existence of a duty of care, Edis J concluded that on the facts there was a relationship between the company and Companies House, at the time when the liquidation document examiner entered the winding up order against it, which was a 'special' one. It followed that there was an assumption of responsibility and that the company was entitled to succeed on the duty issue. In the instant case, foreseeability of harm was obvious. Therefore the limbs of the 'three stage Caparo test' which were in play were proximity and whether it was fair, just and reasonable to impose a duty. Given that a duty was owed to one individual company whose identity was readily discoverable by the liquidator document examiner meant that it was fair and just to impose a duty. The class was limited and its members ascertainable at the stage when treatment was given. Further it was fair, just and reasonable to impose the duty of care. The evidence was that the company had gone into administration as a direct result of the false information published and therefore on the evidence causation had been proved.

Rectification of register under court order

35.99 The registrar must remove from the register any material:

(a) that derives from anything that the court has declared to be invalid or ineffective, or to have been done without the authority of the company; or

(b) that a court declares to be factually inaccurate, or to be derived from something that is factually inaccurate, or forged;

and that the court directs should be removed from the register: CA 2006, s 1096(1).

35.100 The court order must specify what is to be removed from the register and indicate where on the register it is: CA 2006, s 1096(2).

The court must not make an order for the removal from the register of anything the registration of which had legal consequences as mentioned in s 1094(3) unless satisfied:

(a) that the presence of the material on the register has caused, or may cause, damage to the company; and

(b) that the company's interest in removing the material outweighs any interest of other persons in the material continuing to appear on the register: CA 2006, s 1096(3).

35.101 Where in such a case the court does make an order for removal, it may make such consequential orders as appear just with respect to the legal effect (if any) to be accorded to the material by virtue of its having appeared on the register: CA 2006, s 1096(4).

A copy of the court's order must be sent to the registrar for registration: CA 2006, s 1096(5).

Section 1096 does not apply where the court has other, specific, powers to deal with the matter, for example under:

(a) the provisions of Pt 15 relating to the revision of defective accounts and reports; or

(b) ss 873 or 888 (rectification of the register of charges): CA 2006, s 1096(6).

Powers of the court on ordering removal from the register

35.102 Where the court makes an order for the removal of anything from the register under s 1096 (rectification of the register), it may give directions under s 1097: CA 2006, s 1097(1). It may direct that any note on the register that is related to the material that is the subject of the court's order shall be removed from the register: CA 2006, s 1097(2).

It may direct that its order shall not be available for public inspection as part of the register: CA 2006, s 1097(3). It may also direct:

(a) that no note shall be made on the register as a result of its order; or

(b) that any such note shall be restricted to such matters as may be specified by the court: CA 2006, s 1097(4).

35.103 The court must not give any direction under this section unless it is satisfied:

(a) that:

  (i) the presence on the register of the note or, as the case may be, of an unrestricted note; or

  (ii) the availability for public inspection of the court's order;

  may cause damage to the company; and

(b) that the company's interest in non-disclosure outweighs any interest of other persons in disclosure: CA 2006, s 1097(5).

Rectification of register relating to company registered office

35.104 The Secretary of State may make provision by regulations requiring the registrar, on application, to change the address of a company's registered office if the registrar is satisfied that the company is not authorised to use the address: CA 2006, s 1097A(1) (as inserted by SBEEA 2015, s 99(1)).

The applicant and the company must provide such information as the registrar may require for the purposes of determining such an application: CA 2006, s 1097A(2) (as inserted by SBEEA 2015, s 99(1)).

35.105 The regulations may make provision as to:

(a) who may make an application;

(b) the information to be included in and documents to accompany an application;

(c) the notice to be given of an application and of its outcome;

(d) the period in which objections to an application may be made;

(e) how an application is to be determined, including in particular the evidence, or descriptions of evidence, which the registrar may without further enquiry rely on to be satisfied that the company is authorised to use the address;

(f) the referral of the application, or any question relating to the application, by the registrar for determination by the court;

(g) the registrar requiring a company to provide an address to be the company's registered office;

(h) the nomination by the registrar of an address (a "default address") to be the company's registered office;

(i) the effect of the registration of any change: CA 2006, s 1097A(3) (as inserted by SBEEA 2015, s 99(1)).

Subject to further provision which may be made by virtue of sub-s (3)(i), the change takes effect upon it being registered by the registrar, but until the end of the period of 14 days beginning with the date on which it is registered a person may validly serve any document on the company at the address previously registered: CA 2006, s 1097A(4) (as inserted by SBEEA 2015, s 99(1)).

35.106 Provision made by virtue of sub-s (3)(i) may in particular include provision, in relation to the registration of a default address:

(a) for the suspension, for up to 28 days beginning with the date on which it is registered, of duties of the company under this Act relating to the inspection of company records or to the provision, disclosure or display of information;

(b) that the default address may not be used for the purpose of keeping the company's registers, indexes or other documents;

(c) for there to be no requirement that documents delivered to the default address for the company must be opened;

(d) for the collection of such documents by the company, or the forwarding of such documents to the company;

(e) for the circumstances in which, and the period of time after which, such documents may be destroyed;

(f) about evidence, or descriptions of evidence, that the registrar may require a company to provide if giving notice to the registrar to change the address of its registered office from a default address: CA 2006, s 1097A(5) (as inserted by SBEEA 2015, s 99(1)).

The applicant or the company may appeal the outcome of an application under this section to the court: CA 2006, s 1097A(6) (as inserted by SBEEA 2015, s 99(1)).

35.107 On an appeal, the court must direct the registrar to register such address as the registered office of the company as the court considers appropriate in all the circumstances of the case: CA 2006, s 1097A(7) (as inserted by SBEEA 2015, s 99(1)).

The regulations may make further provision about an appeal and in particular:

(a) provision about the time within which an appeal must be brought and the grounds on which an appeal may be brought,

(b) provision for the suspension, pending the outcome of an appeal, of duties of the company under this Act relating to the inspection of company records or to the provision, disclosure or display of information,

(c) further provision about directions by virtue of sub-s (7) : CA 2006, s 1097A(8) (as inserted by SBEEA 2015, s 99(1)).

The regulations may include such provision applying (including applying with modifications), amending or repealing an enactment contained in this Act as the Secretary of State considers necessary or expedient in consequence of any provision made by the regulations: CA 2006, s 1097A(9) (as inserted by SBEEA 2015, s 99(1)).

Public notice of removal of certain material from the register

35.108 The registrar must cause to be published:

(a) in the *Gazette*; or

(b) in accordance with s 1116 (alternative means of giving public notice),

notice of the removal from the register of any document subject to the Directive disclosure requirements (see s 1078) or of any material derived from such a document: CA 2006, s 1098(1). This notice must state the name and registered number of the company, the description of the document and the date of receipt: CA 2006, s 1098(2).

The registrar's index of company names

35.109 The registrar of companies must keep an index of the names of the companies and other bodies to which s 1099 applies. This is known as 'the registrar's index of company names': CA 2006, s 1099(1). It applies to:

(a) UK-registered companies;

(b) any body to which any provision of the Companies Acts applies by virtue of regulations under s 1043 (unregistered companies); and

(c) overseas companies that have registered particulars with the registrar under s 1046, other than companies that appear to the registrar not to be required to do so: CA 2006, s 1099(2).

35.110 It also applies to:

(a) limited partnerships registered in the UK;

(b) limited liability partnerships incorporated in the UK;

(c) European Economic Interest Groupings registered in the UK;

(d) open-ended investment companies authorised in the UK;

(e) societies registered under the Industrial and Provident Societies Act 1965 (c 12) or the Industrial and Provident Societies Act (Northern Ireland) 1969 (c 24 (NI)): CA 2006, s 1099(3).

35.111 The Secretary of State may by order amend s 1099(3):

(a) by the addition of any description of body; or

(b) by the deletion of any description of body: CA 2006, s 1099(4).

Right to inspect index

35.112 Any person may inspect the registrar's index of company names: CA 2006, s 1100.

Power to amend enactments relating to bodies other than companies

35.113 The Secretary of State may by regulations amend the enactments relating to any description of body for the time being within s 1099(3) (bodies other than companies whose names are to be entered in the registrar's index), so as to:

(a) require the registrar to be provided with information as to the names of bodies registered, incorporated, authorised or otherwise regulated under those enactments; and

(b) make provision in relation to such bodies corresponding to that made by:

- s 66 (company name not to be the same as another in the index); and
- ss 67 and 68 (power to direct change of company name in case of similarity to existing name): CA 2006, s 1101(1).

Application of language requirements

35.114 The provisions listed below apply to all documents required to be delivered to the registrar under any provision of:

(a) the Companies Acts; or

(b) the Insolvency Act 1986 (c 45) or the Insolvency (Northern Ireland) Order 1989 (SI 1989 No 2405 (NI 19)): CA 2006, s 1102(1).

The Secretary of State may make provision by regulations applying all or any of the listed provisions, with or without modifications, in relation to documents delivered to the registrar under any other enactment: CA 2006, s 1102(2).

35.115 The provisions are:

- s 1103 (documents to be drawn up and delivered in English);
- s 1104 (documents relating to Welsh companies);
- s 1105 (documents that may be drawn up and delivered in other languages); and
- s 1107 (certified translations): CA 2006, s 1102(3).

Documents to be drawn up and delivered in English

35.116 The general rule is that all documents required to be delivered to the registrar must be drawn up and delivered in English: CA 2006, s 1103(1). This is subject to:

- s 1104 (documents relating to Welsh companies); and
- s 1105 (documents that may be drawn up and delivered in other languages): CA 2006, s 1103(2).

Documents relating to Welsh companies

35.117 Documents relating to a Welsh company may be drawn up and delivered to the registrar in Welsh: CA 2006, s 1104(1). On delivery to the registrar any such document must be accompanied by a certified translation into English, unless it is:

(a) of a description excepted from that requirement by regulations made by the Secretary of State; or

(b) in a form prescribed in Welsh (or partly in Welsh and partly in English) by virtue of s 26 of the Welsh Language Act 1993 (c 38): CA 2006, s 1104(2).

35.118 The following documents are excepted under the Registrar of Companies and Applications for Striking Off Regulations 2009 (SI 2009 No 1803):

(a) a non-traded company's memorandum of association;

(b) a non-traded company's articles;

(c) a community interest company report prepared for a non-traded company under s 34 of the Companies (Audit, Investigations and Community Enterprise) Act 2004;

(d) a resolution or agreement which was agreed to by members of a non-traded company and to which CA 2006, Pt 3, Ch 3 applies, except for a resolution or agreement listed in para (3);

(e) annual accounts and reports of a non-traded company required to be delivered to the registrar under Pt 15 of the Companies Act 2006;

(f) a declaration referred to in regs 11(1)(b) or 12(1)(b) or (c) of the Community Interest Company Regulations 2005 which relates to a non-traded company;

(g) revised accounts and any revised report of a non-traded company, and any auditor's report on such revised accounts and reports, required to be delivered to the registrar by the Companies (Revision of Defective Accounts and Reports) Regulations 2008;

(h) a document required to be appended to the group accounts of a non-traded company by para 30(2) of Sch 6 to the Large and Medium-sized Companies and Groups (Accounts and Reports) Regulations 2008 (SI 2008 No 410) (banking groups: information as to undertaking in which shares held as a result of financial assistance operation).

35.119 The following resolutions and agreements are also excepted:

(a) a special resolution that:

- a private company should be re-registered as a public company;
- a public company should be re-registered as a private limited company;
- a private limited company should be re-registered as an unlimited company; or
- an unlimited company should be re-registered as a limited company;

(b) a special resolution agreeing to the change of a company's name;

(c) a special resolution required by s 37(6) of the Companies (Audit, Investigations and Community Enterprise) Act 2004 (requirements for an existing company to become a community interest company);

(d) a resolution or agreement as altered by an enactment other than an enactment amending the general law, required to be delivered to the registrar under s 34;

(e) a resolution or agreement as altered by an order of a court or other authority, required to be delivered to the registrar under ss 35 or 999;

(f) a special resolution under s 88(2) requiring the register to be amended so that it states that a company's registered office is to be situated in Wales;

(g) a special resolution under s 626 (reduction of capital in connection with redenomination);

(h) a special resolution under s 641(1)(a) (resolution for reducing the share capital of a private limited company supported by solvency statement);

(i) a resolution under s 664(1) that a public company should be re-registered as a private company to comply with s 662.

Where a document is properly delivered to the registrar in Welsh without a certified translation into English, the registrar must obtain such a translation if the document is to be available for public inspection.

35.120 The translation is treated as if delivered to the registrar in accordance with the same provision as the original: CA 2006, s 1104(3).

A Welsh company may deliver to the registrar a certified translation into Welsh of any document in English that relates to the company and is or has been delivered to the registrar: CA 2006, s 1104(4)

Section 1105 (which requires certified translations into English of documents delivered to the registrar in another language) does not apply to a document relating to a Welsh company that is drawn up and delivered in Welsh: CA 2006, s 1104(5).

Documents that may be drawn up and delivered in other languages

35.121 Documents may be drawn up and delivered to the registrar in a language other than English, but when delivered to the registrar they must be accompanied by a certified translation into English: CA 2006, s 1105(1).

This applies to:

(a) agreements required to be forwarded to the registrar under Ch 3 of Pt 3 (agreements affecting the company's constitution);

(b) documents required to be delivered under s 400(2)(e) or s 401(2)(f) (company included in accounts of larger group: required to deliver copy of group accounts);

(c) instruments or copy instruments required to be delivered under Pt 25 (company charges);

(d) documents of any other description specified in regulations made by the Secretary of State: CA 2006, s 1105(2). These include:

- a memorandum of association;
- a company's articles;
- a valuation report required to be delivered to the registrar under s 94(2)(d);
- any order made by a competent court in the UK or elsewhere (see the Registrar of Companies and Applications for Striking Off Regulations 2009 (SI 2009 No 1803) reg 7).
- certified copy of a debenture or other instrument creating or evidencing a charge over the property of an overseas company;
- certified copy of the company's constitution;
- copy of accounting documents; and
- copy of accounts (see the Overseas Companies (Execution of Documents and Registration of Charges) Regulations 2009 (SI 2009 No 1917), regs 8, 9,14, 15, 27, 32, 40, 45, 46 and 55).

Voluntary filing of translations

35.122 A company may deliver to the registrar one or more certified translations of any document relating to the company that is or has been delivered to the registrar: CA 2006, s 1106(1).

The Secretary of State may by regulations specify:

(a) the languages; and

(b) the descriptions of documents,

in relation to which this facility is available: Overseas Companies (Execution of Documents and Registration of Charges) Regulations 2009, s 1106(2).

35.123 The regulations must provide that it is available as from 1 January 2007:

(a) in relation to all the official languages of the European Union; and

(b) in relation to all documents subject to the Directive disclosure requirements (see s 1078): Overseas Companies (Execution of Documents and Registration of Charges) Regulations 2009, s 1106(3).

The power of the registrar to impose requirements as to the form and manner of delivery includes power to impose requirements as to the identification of the original document and the delivery of the translation in a form and manner enabling it to be associated with the original: CA 2006, s 1106(4).

Section 1106 does not apply where the original document was delivered to the registrar before this section came into force: CA 2006, s 1106(6).

Certified translations

35.124 The term 'certified translation' means a translation certified to be a correct translation: CA 2006, s 1107(1).

In the case of any discrepancy between the original language version of a document and a certified translation:

(a) the company may not rely on the translation as against a third party; but

(b) a third party may rely on the translation unless the company shows that the third party had knowledge of the original: CA 2006, s 1107(2).

A 'third party' means a person other than the company or the registrar: CA 2006, s 1107(3).

Transliteration of names and addresses: permitted characters

35.125 Names and addresses in a document delivered to the registrar must contain only letters, characters and symbols (including accents and other diacritical marks) that are permitted: CA 2006 s 1108(1).

The Secretary of State may make provision by regulations:

(a) as to the letters, characters and symbols (including accents and other diacritical marks) that are permitted; and

(b) permitting or requiring the delivery of documents in which names and addresses have not been transliterated into a permitted form: CA 2006, s 1108(2).

35.126 Under the Registrar of Companies and Applications for Striking Off Regulations 2009 (SI 2009 No 1803), the following are the permitted characters whereby all names and addresses in a document lodged with the registrar must only contain the following permitted characters and symbols (subject to the exceptions below).

The permitted characters also include:

- full stops, commas, colons, semi-colons and hyphens;
- the numerals 0, 1, 2, 3, 4, 5, 6, 7, 8 and 9.

35.127 Under reg 8 of the Registrar of Companies and Applications for Striking Off Regulations 2009 (SI 2009 No 1803), the above permitted characters and symbols do not apply to the following documents:

(a) a memorandum of association;

(b) a company's articles;

(c) an order made by a competent court in the UK or elsewhere;

(d) an agreement required to be forwarded to the registrar under CA 2006, Pt 3, Ch 3 (agreements affecting a company's constitution);

(e) a valuation report required to be delivered to the registrar under s 94(2)(d) of that Act;

(f) a document required to be delivered to the registrar under ss 400(2)(e) or 401(2)(f) of that Act (company included in accounts of larger group: required to deliver copy of group accounts);

(g) an instrument or copy instrument required to be delivered to the registrar under Pt 25 of that Act (company charges);

(h) a certified copy of the constitution of an overseas company required to be delivered to the registrar under regs 8, 14 or 15 of the Overseas Companies Regulations 2009 (SI 2009 No 1801);

(i) a copy of accounting documents of an overseas company required to be delivered to the registrar under regs 9, 32, 45 or 46 of those Regulations;

(j) a copy of the annual accounts of an overseas company, or of a credit or financial institution to which Ch 2 of Pt 6 of the Overseas Companies Regulations 2009 applies, required to be delivered to the registrar under s 441.

Transliteration of names and addresses: transliteration into roman characters

35.128 Where a name or address is or has been delivered to the registrar in a permitted form using other than roman characters, the company (or other body) to which the document relates may deliver to the registrar a transliteration into roman characters: CA 2006, s 1109(1).

The power of the registrar to impose requirements as to the form and manner of delivery includes power to impose requirements as to the identification of the original document and the delivery of the transliteration in a form and manner enabling it to be associated with the original: CA 2006, s 1109(2).

Transliteration of names and addresses: certification

35.129 The Secretary of State may make provision by regulations requiring the certification of transliterations and prescribing the form of certification: CA 2006, s 1110(1).

Different provision may be made for compulsory and voluntary transliterations: CA 2006, s 1110(2).

Registrar's requirements as to certification or verification

35.130 Where a document required or authorised to be delivered to the registrar under any enactment is required:

(a) to be certified as an accurate translation or transliteration; or

(b) to be certified as a correct copy or verified,

the registrar may impose requirements as to the person, or description of person, by whom the certificate or verification is to be given: CA 2006, s 1111(1).

The power conferred by s 1068 (registrar's requirements as to form, authentication and manner of delivery) is exercisable in relation to the certificate or verification as if it were a separate document: CA 2006, s 1111(2).

Requirements imposed under s 1111 must not be inconsistent with requirements imposed by any enactment with respect to the certification or verification of the document concerned: CA 2006, s 1111(3).

General false statement offence

35.131 It is an offence for a person knowingly or recklessly:

(a) to deliver or cause to be delivered to the registrar, for any purpose of the Companies Acts, a document; or

(b) to make to the registrar, for any such purpose, a statement,

that is misleading, false or deceptive in a material particular: CA 2006, s 1112(1).

35.132 A person guilty of an offence under , s 1112 will be liable:

(a) on conviction on indictment, to imprisonment for a term not exceeding two years or a fine (or both);

(b) on summary conviction:

  (i) in England and Wales, to imprisonment for a term not exceeding 12 months or to a fine not exceeding the statutory maximum (or both);

(ii) in Scotland or Northern Ireland, to imprisonment for a term not exceeding six months, or to a fine not exceeding the statutory maximum (or both): CA 2006, s 1112(2).

Enforcement of company's filing obligations

35.133 Section 1113 applies where a company has made default in complying with any obligation under the Companies Acts:

(a) to deliver a document to the registrar; or

(b) to give notice to the registrar of any matter: CA 2006, s 1113(1).

The registrar, or any member or creditor of the company, may give notice to the company requiring it to comply with the obligation: CA 2006, s 1113(2).

35.134 If the company fails to make good the default within 14 days after service of the notice, the registrar, or any member or creditor of the company, may apply to the court for an order directing the company and any specified officer of it, to make good the default within a specified time: CA 2006, s 1113(3).

The court's order may provide that all costs (in Scotland, expenses) of or incidental to the application are to be borne by the company or by any officers of it responsible for the default: CA 2006, s 1113(4).

Section 1113 does not affect the operation of any enactment making it an offence, or imposing a civil penalty, for the default: CA 2006, s 1113(5).

Application of provisions about documents and delivery

35.135 The following terms are defined in relation to document and delivery:

(a) 'document' means information recorded in any form; and

(b) references to delivering a document include forwarding, lodging, registering, sending, producing or submitting it or (in the case of a notice) giving it: CA 2006, s 1114(1).

Except as otherwise provided, Pt 31 applies in relation to the supply to the registrar of information otherwise than in documentary form as it applies in relation to the delivery of a document: CA 2006, s 1114(2).

Supplementary provisions relating to electronic communications

35.136 The registrar's rules may require a company (or other body) to give any necessary consents to the use of electronic means for communications by the registrar to the company (or other body) as a condition of making use of any facility to deliver material to the registrar by electronic means: CA 2006, s 1115(1).

A document that is required to be signed by the registrar or authenticated by the registrar's seal shall, if sent by electronic means, be authenticated in such manner as may be specified by the registrar's rules: CA 2006, s 1115(2).

Alternative to publication in the Gazette

35.137 Notices that would otherwise need to be published by the registrar in the *Gazette* may instead be published by such means as may from time to time be approved by the registrar in accordance with regulations made by the Secretary of State: CA 2006, s 1116(1). The Secretary of State may make provision by regulations as to what alternative means may be approved: CA 2006, s 1116(2).

The regulations may, in particular:

(a) require the use of electronic means;

(b) require the same means to be used:

  (i) for all notices or for all notices of specified descriptions; and

  (ii) whether the company (or other body) to which the notice relates is registered in England and Wales, Scotland or Northern Ireland;

(c) impose conditions as to the manner in which access to the notices is to be made available: CA 2006, s 1116(3).

Before starting to publish notices by means approved under s 1116 the registrar must publish at least one notice to that effect in the *Gazette*: CA 2006, s 1116(5).

Nothing in s 1116 prevents the registrar from giving public notice both in the *Gazette* and by means approved under this section. In that case, the requirement of public notice is met when notice is first given by either means: CA 2006, s 1116(6).

Registrar's rules

35.138 Where any provision of Pt 31 enables the registrar to make provision, or impose requirements as to any matter, the registrar may make such provision or impose such requirements by means of rules under s 1117. This is without prejudice to the making of such provision or the imposing of such requirements by other means: CA 2006, s 1117(1).

The registrar's rules:

(a) may make different provision for different cases; and

(b) may allow the registrar to disapply or modify any of the rules: CA 2006, s 1117(2).

The registrar must:

(a) publicise the rules in a manner appropriate to bring them to the notice of persons affected by them; and

(b) make copies of the rules available to the public (in hard copy or electronic form): CA 2006, s 1117(3).

Payments into the consolidated fund

35.139 Nothing in the Companies Acts or any other enactment as to the payment of receipts into the consolidated fund shall be read as affecting the operation in relation to the registrar of s 3(1) of the Government Trading Funds Act 1973 (c 63): CA 2006, s 1118.

Contracting out of the registrar's functions

35.140 Where by virtue of an order made under s 69 of the Deregulation and Contracting Out Act 1994 (c 40) a person is authorised by the registrar to accept delivery of any class of documents that are under any enactment to be delivered to the registrar, the registrar may direct that documents of that class shall be delivered to a specified address of the authorised person. Any such direction must be printed and made available to the public (with or without payment): CA 2006, s 1119(1).

A document of that class that is delivered to an address other than the specified address is treated as not having been delivered: CA 2006, s 1119(2).

The registrar's rules are not subordinate legislation for the purposes of s 71 of the Deregulation and Contracting Out Act 1994 (functions excluded from contracting out): CA 2006, s 1119(3).

Guidance booklets published by Companies House

35.141

Company aspects	
GP1	Incorporation and Names
GP2	Life of a Company – Part 1 Annual Requirements
GP3	Life of a Company – Part 2 Event Driven Filings
GP4	Strike off, Dissolution and Restoration
GP5	Late Filing Penalties
GP6	Registrar's Rules and Powers
GP7	Restricting the disclosure of your address
Limited Liability Partnerships	
GPLLP1	Limited Liability Partnership Incorporation and Names
GPLLP2	Life of a Limited Liability Partnership
GPLLP3	Limited Liability Partnership Strike off, Dissolution and Restoration
GPLLP4	Limited Liability Partnership Late Filing Penalties
GPLLP5	Limited Liability Partnerships Liquidation and Insolvency
GPLLP5s	Limited Liability Partnership Liquidation and Insolvency (Scotland)
GPLLP5n	Limited Liability Partnership Liquidation and Insolvency (Northern Ireland)

Other legislation

GPO1	Overseas Companies registered in the UK
GPO2	Limited Partnership Act
GPO3	Newspaper Libel and Registration Act
GPO4	European Economic Interest Groupings
GPO5	Conducting Business in Welsh
GPO6	The European Company: Societas Europaea (SE)
GPO7	Cross Border Mergers
GPO8	Liquidation and Insolvency
GPO8s	Liquidation and Insolvency (Scotland)
GPO8n	Liquidation and Insolvency (Northern Ireland)

Definitions

35.142

Certified translation:	a translation certified to be a correct translation.
Company:	includes an overseas company whose particulars have been registered under CA 2006 s 1046, other than a company that appears to the registrar not to be required to register particulars under that section.
Document:	information recorded in any form.
Relevant material:	material on the register that was included in, or is derived from material that was included in, a relevant company form or a relevant overseas company form delivered to the registrar by any person.
Registrar of companies and the registrar:	the registrar of companies for England and Wales, Scotland or Northern Ireland, as the case may require.

36 Offences under the Companies Acts

Contents

Introduction

36.1 Part 36 of CA 2006 addresses the offences under the Companies Acts. It comprises 13 sections.

It considers the key term 'officer in default', and identifies the situations in which individuals may be liable for a breach under the CA 2006.

The general principle adopted as to whether a company should be liable for a breach of the requirements of Companies Acts is that, where the only victims of the offence are the company or its members, the company should not be liable for the offence. On the other hand, where members or the company are potential victims, but not the only ones, then the company should be potentially liable for a breach, whether or not the offence may also harm the company or its members.

Liability of officer in default

36.2 Section 1121 of the CA 2006 sets out the liability of an 'officer in default'. It applies for the purposes of any provision of the Companies Acts to the effect that, in the event of contravention of an enactment in relation to a company, an offence is committed by every officer of the company who is in default: CA 2006, s 1121(1).

The term 'officer' includes:

(a) any director, manager or secretary; and

(b) any person who is to be treated as an officer of the company for the purposes of the provision in question: CA 2006, s 1121(2).

An officer is 'in default' for the purposes of the provision, if he authorises or permits, participates in, or fails to take all reasonable steps to prevent, the contravention: CA 2006, s 1121(3).

36.3 The term 'officer' as defined under CA 2006, s 1121(2) is not exhaustive. A person could operate as an 'officer' under another title or label other than as director, manager or secretary. An issue that arises is who can be treated as an 'officer of the company' for the purposes of CA 2006, s 1121. A chief investment officer would be caught under this provision. It would also catch sub-board managers too. The following case, to some extent, represented the approach followed under the CA 2006 in respect of corporate officers.

The rules of attribution should be applied in identifying the main decision-makers in the company

In *Meridian Global Funds Management Asia Limited v Securities Commission* [1995] 2 AC 500, the chief investment officer (CIO) of an investment management company, and its senior portfolio manager (SPM), with the company's authority but unknown to the board of directors and managing director, used funds managed by the company to acquire shares in a public company. The company thus became for a short period a substantial security holder in that public company, but the company did not give notice thereof as required by s 20(3) of the Securities Amendment Act 1988. The Securities Commission instituted proceedings in the High Court of New Zealand against the company for failing to comply with s 20. The judge made a declaration that the company was in breach of its duty to give notice under s 20(3), holding that for the purposes of s 20(4)(e) the knowledge of the CIO and SPM should be attributed to the company. The Court of Appeal of New Zealand upheld that decision on the basis that the CIO was the directing mind and will of the company and so his knowledge was attributable to the company.

The matter came up before the Privy Council. It held that a company's rights and obligations were determined by rules whereby the acts of natural persons were attributed to the company normally to be determined by reference to the primary rules of attribution generally contained in the company's constitution and implied by company law and or general rules of agency; but that, in an exceptional case, where application of those principles would defeat the intended application of a particular provision to companies, it was necessary to devise a special rule of attribution to determine whose act or knowledge or state of mind was for the purpose of that provision to be attributed to the company; that, although the description of such a person as the 'directing mind and will' of a company did not have to be apposite in every case, knowledge of an act of a company's duly authorised servant or agent, or the state of mind with which it was done, would be attributed to the company only where a true construction of the relevant substantive provision so required: see *Tesco Supermarkets Ltd v Nattrass* [1972] AC 153, HL(E) and *In Re Supply of Ready Mixed Concrete (No 2)* [1995] 1 AC 456;

Admiralty v Owners of the Steamship Divina (The Truculent) [1952] P 1, HL; *Bolton (Engineering) Co Ltd v TJ Graham & Sons Ltd* [1957] 1 QB 159, CA and [1965] P 294.

It further held that having regard to the policy of s 20 of the Act of 1988, on the true construction of s 20(4)(e), the appropriate rule of attribution to be implied was that a corporate security holder knew that it was a substantial security holder in a public company when that was known to the person who had acquired the relevant interest with the company's authority, whereupon the company was obliged to give notice under s 20(3); and that, accordingly, the CIO's knowledge of the transaction was attributable to the company irrespective of whether he could be described in a general sense as its directing mind and will, and so in failing to give notice the company had been in breach of its duty under s 20(3).

According to Lord Hoffmann, the key task was to apply the rule of attribution towards identifying the main decision maker within the company to whom liability could be attributed:

> 'Any proposition about a company necessarily involves a reference to a set of rules. A company exists because there is a rule (usually in a statute) which says that a *persona ficta* shall be deemed to exist and to have certain of the powers, rights and duties of a natural person. But there would be little sense in deeming such a *persona ficta* to exist unless there were also rules to tell one what acts were to count as acts of the company. It is therefore a necessary part of corporate personality that there should be rules by which acts are attributed to the company. These may be called "the rules of attribution".'

The company's primary rules of attribution will generally be found in its constitution, typically the articles of association, and will say things such as 'for the purpose of appointing members of the board, a majority vote of the shareholders shall be a decision of the company' or 'the decisions of the board in managing the company's business shall be the decisions of the company'. There are also primary rules of attribution which are not expressly stated in the articles but implied by company law, such as:

> '... the unanimous decision of all the shareholders in a solvent company about anything which the company under its memorandum of association has power to do shall be the decision of the company. See *Multinational Gas and Petrochemical Co v Multinational Gas and Petrochemical Services Ltd* [1983] Ch 258.)
>
> These primary rules of attribution are obviously not enough to enable a company to go out into the world and do business. Not every act on behalf of the company could be expected to be the subject of a resolution of the board or a unanimous decision of the shareholders. The company therefore builds upon the primary rules of attribution by using general rules of attribution which are equally available to natural persons, namely, the principles of agency. It will appoint servants and agents whose acts, by a combination of the general principles of agency

and the company's primary rules of attribution, count as the acts of the company. And having done so, it will also make itself subject to the general rules by which liability for the acts of others can be attributed to natural persons, such as estoppel or ostensible authority in contract and vicarious liability in tort.

It is worth pausing at this stage to make what may seem an obvious point. Any statement about what a company has or has not done, or can or cannot do, is necessarily a reference to the rules of attribution (primary and general) as they apply to that company. Judges sometimes say that a company "as such" cannot do anything; it must act by servants or agents. This may seem an unexceptionable, even banal remark. And of course the meaning is usually perfectly clear. But a reference to a company "as such" might suggest that there is something out there called the company of which one can meaningfully say that it can or cannot do something. There is in fact no such thing as the company as such, no ding an sich, only the applicable rules. To say that a company cannot do something means only that there is no one whose doing of that act would, under the applicable rules of attribution, count as an act of the company.

The company's primary rules of attribution together with the general principles of agency, vicarious liability and so forth are usually sufficient to enable one to determine its rights and obligations. In exceptional cases, however, they will not provide an answer. This will be the case when a rule of law, either expressly or by implication, excludes attribution on the basis of the general principles of agency or vicarious liability. For example, a rule may be stated in language primarily applicable to a natural person and require some act or state of mind on the part of that person "himself", as opposed to his servants or agents. This is generally true of rules of the criminal law, which ordinarily impose liability only for the *actus reus* and *mens rea* of the defendant himself. How is such a rule to be applied to a company?

One possibility is that the court may come to the conclusion that the rule was not intended to apply to companies at all; for example, a law which created an offence for which the only penalty was community service. Another possibility is that the court might interpret the law as meaning that it could apply to a company only on the basis of its primary rules of attribution, ie if the act giving rise to liability was specifically authorised by a resolution of the board or an unanimous agreement of the shareholders. But there will be many cases in which neither of these solutions is satisfactory; in which the court considers that the law was intended to apply to companies and that, although it excludes ordinary vicarious liability, insistence on the primary rules of attribution would in practice defeat that intention. In such a case, the court must fashion a special rule of attribution for the particular substantive rule. This is always a matter of interpretation: given that it was intended to apply to a company, how was it intended to apply? Whose act (or knowledge, or state of mind) was for this purpose intended to count as the act etc.

of the company? One finds the answer to this question by applying the usual canons of interpretation, taking into account the language of the rule (if it is a statute) and its content and policy.'

See too *Jetvia SA v Bilta (UK) Ltd* [2015] UKSC 23.

The term 'officer' does not include the company's auditor: *Mutual Reinsurance Co Ltd v Peat Marwick Mitchell and Co* [1997] 1 BCLC 1; and *R v Shacter* [196] 2 QB 252.

The term 'manager' is also used in the employment law context but this does not mean that every manager with such description will be an 'officer' for the purposes of liability under the CA 2006. In order to fall within the liability provisions under the CA 2006, the manager must be wholly involved in the company's management affairs as part of the company's governance structure and fully integrated within that structure which involves providing strategy and direction and aspects of decision making functions that impact the operational aspects of the corporation.

In *Gibson v Barton* (1875) LR 10 QB 329 where the court was concerned with s 26 of the Companies Act 1862 (25 & 26 Vict c 89): 'every director and manager of the company who shall knowingly and wilfully authorise or permit such default (in not forwarding an annual list of members) shall incur a like penalty'. Blackburn J said, at p 336:

> 'In what sense are the words "director" and "manager" used in that section? When the section says "director", it is plain enough a director is a director, but the words are "and manager". We have to say who is to be considered a manager. A manager would be, in ordinary talk, a person who has the management of the whole affairs of the company; not an agent who is to do a particular thing, or a servant who is to obey orders, but a person who is entrusted with power to transact the whole of the affairs of the company.'
>
> Blackburn J was referring to a person within the corporation wholly involved in its corporate governance process.

The terms 'manager' or 'officer' have a limited meaning

In *Registrar of Restrictive Trading Agreements v WH Smith & Son Ltd* [1969] 1 WLR 1460, the statutory provision there in question was s 15(3) of the Restrictive Trade Practices Act 1956:

> 'Where notice under section 14 of this Act has been given to a body corporate, an order may be made under this section for the attendance and examination of any director, manager, secretary or other officer of that body corporate; ...'

> In giving the leading judgment of the Court of Appeal, Lord Denning MR stated that the term "manager" or "officer" should not be given an extended meaning. To do so would be contrary to the spirit of the laws of England. The word "manager" referred to a person who was managing the affairs of the company as a whole. The word "officer" had a similar connotation. The only relevant "officer" here was an officer who was a "manager". In this context it meant a person who was managing in a governing role the affairs of the company itself.

36.4 Subsequent cases have, however, applied an extended definition to the term 'manager':

The term 'manager' signifies a wider meaning

In *Re A Company* [1980] Ch 138, the Court of Appeal placed an altogether wider meaning of the term 'manager' under CA 2006, s 1132:

> 'If … there is shown to be reasonable cause to believe that any person has, while an officer of a company, committed an offence in connection with the management of the company's affairs and that evidence of the commission of the offence is to be found in any books or papers of or under the control of the company, an order may be made …'

Lord Denning MR stated that the term 'officer' referred to a person in a managerial situation in regard to the company's affairs. The term should not be restricted. The general object of the Act was to enable the important officers of the state to get at the books of the company when there had been a fraud or wrongdoing. Further, whenever anyone in a superior position in a company encourages, directs or acquiesces in defrauding creditors, customers, shareholders or the like, then an offence was committed by an officer of the company in connection with the company's affairs.

> 'According to Shaw LJ, the expression "manager" should not be too narrowly construed. It should not to be equated with a managing or other director or a general manager. Any person who in the affairs of the company exercised a supervisory control which reflected the general policy of the company for the time being or which was related to the general administration of the company was in the sphere of management. He need not be a member of the board of directors. He need not be subject to specific instructions from the board. If he fulfilled a function which touched the central administration of the company, that was sufficient to constitute him an "officer" or "manager" of the company.

> ***The court will have regard to those persons in positions of real authority***
>
> In *R v Boal* [1992] QB 591, the appellant, who was employed by a company as assistant general manager of its bookshop, had responsibility for the day to day running of the shop but had been given no training in management, health and safety at work or fire precautions. On a day when he was in charge of the shop, while the general manager was away on holiday, serious breaches were found of the requirements of the fire certificate in force for the premises. The company and the appellant were charged on an indictment containing counts charging offences under s 7(4) of the Fire Precautions Act 1971 and alleging that the appellant was criminally liable as a 'manager' within s 23(1) of the Act of 1971. He was given legal advice which assumed that he was incontestably a manager within the meaning of s 23, and he pleaded guilty to some counts, was convicted on others and acquitted on one.
>
> On appeal against conviction, the Court of Appeal allowed the appeal. It held that s 23 of the Fire Precautions Act 1971 was intended to fix with criminal liability only those who were in a position of 'real authority', who had both the power and the responsibility to decide corporate policy. As the appellant could well have been regarded as responsible merely for the day to day running of the shop rather than having a governing role respecting the affairs of the company, it was likely that the defence that he was not a manager within s 23 would have prevailed if it had been advanced.

36.5 Section 1121 of the CA 2006 specifies which persons may be liable as an officer of a company for an offence committed by the company under CA 2006 or the other Companies Acts. It only applies where another provision expressly states that an offence is committed by every officer of a company who is in default.

An 'officer' of a company is defined as including a director, manager or (company) secretary, and any person who is to be treated as an officer of the company for the purposes of the provisions in question. An officer is liable for an offence when he is 'in default', meaning he authorises or permits, participates in, or fails to take all reasonable steps to prevent the offence being committed. A secretary, therefore, also now plays an important role within the company and will be treated as an 'officer' for the purposes of certain provisions of the CA 2006.

Liability of company as officer in default

36.6 Where a company is an officer of another company, it does not commit an offence as an officer in default unless one of its officers is in default: CA 2006, s 1122(1). Where any such offence is committed by a company, the officer in question also commits the offence and is liable to be proceeded against and punished accordingly: CA 2006, s 1122(2).

The terms 'officer' and 'in default' have the meanings given by s 1121: CA 2006, s 1122(3). Under this provision, where a company is an officer of another company, liability for a breach of company law can be fixed upon the company as an officer only if one of its officers is in default.

Application to bodies other than companies

36.7 Section 1121 of the CA 2006 (liability of officers in default) applies to a body other than a company as it applies to a company: CA 2006, s 1123(1).

As it applies in relation to a body corporate other than a company:

(a) the reference to a director of the company shall be read as referring:

  (i) where the body's affairs are managed by its members, to a member of the body;

  (ii) in any other case, to any corresponding officer of the body; and

(b) the reference to a manager or secretary of the company shall be read as referring to any manager, secretary or similar officer of the body: CA 2006, s 1123(2).

36.8 As it applies in relation to a partnership:

(a) the reference to a director of the company shall be read as referring to a member of the partnership; and

(b) the reference to a manager or secretary of the company shall be read as referring to any manager, secretary or similar officer of the partnership: CA 2006, s 1123(3).

36.9 As it applies in relation to an unincorporated body other than a partnership:

(a) the reference to a director of the company shall be read as referring:

  (i) where the body's affairs are managed by its members, to a member of the body;

  (ii) in any other case, to a member of the governing body; and

(b) the reference to a manager or secretary of the company shall be read as referring to any manager, secretary or similar officer of the body: CA 2006, s 1123(4).

Section 1123 of the CA 2006 provides that s 1121 applies to persons in bodies other than companies, where their role is equivalent to that of an officer of a company. It makes specific provisions for bodies corporate, partnerships and unincorporated bodies.

General provisions

Meaning of 'daily default fine'

36.10 Section 1125 of CA 2006 defines the expression 'daily default fine'. It defines what is meant in the Companies Acts where it is provided that a person guilty of an offence is liable on summary conviction to a fine not exceeding a specified amount 'and, for continued contravention, a daily default fine' not exceeding a specified amount: CA 2006, s 1125(1).

This means that the person is liable on a second or subsequent summary conviction of the offence to a fine not exceeding the latter amount for each day on which the contravention is continued (instead of being liable to a fine not exceeding the former amount): CA 2006, s 1125(2).

Consents required for certain prosecutions

36.11 Section 1126 of the CA 2006 deals with consents required for certain prosecutions. It applies to proceedings for an offence under any of the following provisions:

- s 458, 460 or 949 of CA 2006 (offences of unauthorised disclosure of information);
- s 953 of the CA of 2006 (failure to comply with rules about takeover bid documents);
- s 448, 449, 450, 451 or 453A of the CA 1985 (c 6) (offences in connection with company investigations);
- s 798 of the CA 2006 or s 455 of the CA 1985 (offence of attempting to evade restrictions on shares);
- s 1112 of this Act (general false statement offence);
- paragraph 5 or 6 of Schedule 1B to this Act (breach of certain restrictions imposed under that Schedule): CA 2006, s 1126(1) (as inserted by SBEEA 2015, Sch 3, Part 2).

36.12 No such proceedings are to be brought in England and Wales except by or with the consent of:

(a) in the case of an offence under:

  (i) CA 2006, ss 458, 460 or 949;

  (ii) CA 2006, s 953;

  (iii) CA 1985, ss 448, 449, 450, 451 or 453A; or

  (iv) CA 2006, s.1112,

  the Secretary of State or the Director of Public Prosecutions (as inserted by SBEEA 2015, Sch 3, Part 2);

(b) in the case of an offence under CA 2006, s 798 or CA 1985 s 455, the Secretary of State: CA 2006, s 1126(2).

36.13 No such proceedings are to be brought in Northern Ireland except by or with the consent of:

(a) in the case of an offence under:

  (i) CA 2006, ss 458, 460 or 949;

  (ii) CA 2006, ss 953; or

  (iii) CA 1985, ss 448, 449, 450, 451 or 453A,

  the Secretary of State or the Director of Public Prosecutions for Northern Ireland;

(b) in the case of an offence under CA 2006, s 798 or CA 1985, s 455 the Secretary of State: CA 2006, s 1126(3).

Summary proceedings: venue

36.14 Summary proceedings for any offence under the Companies Acts may be taken:

(a) against a body corporate, at any place at which the body has a place of business; and

(b) against any other person, at any place at which he is for the time being: CA 2006, s 1127(1).

This is without prejudice to any jurisdiction exercisable apart from this section: CA 2006, s 1127(2).

Summary proceedings: time limit for proceedings

36.15 Any information relating to an offence under the Companies Acts that is triable by a magistrates' court in England and Wales may be so tried if it is laid:

(a) at any time within three years after the commission of the offence; and

(b) within 12 months after the date on which evidence sufficient in the opinion of the Director of Public Prosecutions or the Secretary of State (as the case may be) to justify the proceedings comes to his knowledge: CA 2006, s 1128(1).

36.16 Summary proceedings in Scotland for an offence under the Companies Acts:

(a) must not be commenced after the expiration of three years from the commission of the offence;

(b) subject to that, may be commenced at any time:

   (i) within 12 months after the date on which evidence sufficient in the Lord Advocate's opinion to justify the proceedings came to his knowledge; or

   (ii) where such evidence was reported to him by the Secretary of State, within 12 months after the date on which it came to the knowledge of the latter: CA 2006, s 1128(2).

Section 136(3) of the Criminal Procedure (Scotland) Act 1995 (c 46) (date when proceedings deemed to be commenced) applies for the purposes of this subsection as for the purposes of that section.

36.17 A magistrates' court in Northern Ireland has jurisdiction to hear and determine a complaint charging the commission of a summary offence under the Companies Acts provided that the complaint is made:

(a) within three years from the time when the offence was committed; and

(b) within 12 months from the date on which evidence sufficient in the opinion of the Director of Public Prosecutions for Northern Ireland or the Secretary of State (as the case may be) to justify the proceedings comes to his knowledge: CA 2006, s 1128(3).

For the purposes of this section a certificate of the Director of Public Prosecutions, the Lord Advocate, the Director of Public Prosecutions for Northern Ireland or the Secretary of State (as the case may be) as to the date on which such evidence as is referred to above came to his notice is conclusive evidence: CA 2006, s 1128(4).

Legal professional privilege

36.18 In proceedings against a person for an offence under the Companies Acts, nothing in those Acts is to be taken to require any person to disclose any information that he is entitled to refuse to disclose on grounds of legal professional privilege (in Scotland, confidentiality of communications): CA 2006, s 1129.

Proceedings against unincorporated bodies

36.19 Proceedings for an offence under the Companies Acts alleged to have been committed by an unincorporated body must be brought in the name of the body (and not in that of any of its members): CA 2006, s 1130(1).

For the purposes of such proceedings:

(a) any rules of court relating to the service of documents have effect as if the body were a body corporate; and

(b) the following provisions apply as they apply in relation to a body corporate:

  (i) in England and Wales, s 33 of the Criminal Justice Act 1925 (c 86) and Sch 3 to the Magistrates' Courts Act 1980 (c 43);

  (ii) in Scotland, ss 70 and 143 of the Criminal Procedure (Scotland) Act 1995 (c 46);

  (iii) in Northern Ireland, s 18 of the Criminal Justice Act (Northern Ireland) 1945 (c 15 (NI)) and Art 166 of and Sch 4 to the Magistrates' Courts (Northern Ireland) Order 1981 (SI 1981 No 1675 (NI 26)): CA 2006, s 1130(2).

A fine imposed on an unincorporated body on its conviction of an offence under the Companies Acts must be paid out of the funds of the body: CA 2006, s 1130(3).

Imprisonment on summary conviction in England and Wales: transitory provision

36.20 Section 1131 of the CA 2006 applies to any provision of the Companies Acts that provides that a person guilty of an offence is liable on summary conviction in England and Wales to imprisonment for a term not exceeding 12 months: CA 2006, s 1131(1).

In relation to an offence committed before the commencement of s 154(1) of the Criminal Justice Act 2003 (c 44), for 'twelve months' substitute 'six months': CA 2006, s 1131(2).

Section 1131 of the CA 2006 provides for the period before the commencement of s 154(1) of the Criminal Justice Act 2003, which makes new provision about the powers of magistrates' courts in England and Wales to impose sentences of imprisonment on summary conviction. For offences committed before s 154(1) is brought into force, the maximum term of imprisonment in England and Wales for a person guilty of an offence on summary conviction under the Companies Acts is to be six months (as it is at present) instead of 13 months.

Production and inspection of documents

Production and inspection of documents where offence suspected

36.21 An application under CA 2006, s 1132 may be made:

(a) in England and Wales, to a judge of the High Court by the Director of Public Prosecutions, the Secretary of State or a chief officer of police;

(b) in Scotland, to one of the Lords Commissioners of Justiciary by the Lord Advocate;

(c) in Northern Ireland, to the High Court by the Director of Public Prosecutions for Northern Ireland, the Department of Enterprise, Trade and Investment or a chief superintendent of the Police Service of Northern Ireland: CA 2006, s 1132(1).

36.22 If on an application under this section there is shown to be reasonable cause to believe:

(a) that any person has, while an officer of a company, committed an offence in connection with the management of the company's affairs, and

(b) that evidence of the commission of the offence is to be found in any documents in the possession or control of the company,

an order under this section may be made: s 1132(2) CA 2006.

36.23 The order may:

(a) authorise any person named in it to inspect the documents in question, or any of them, for the purpose of investigating and obtaining evidence of the offence; or

(b) require the secretary of the company, or such other officer of it as may be named in the order, to produce the documents (or any of them) to a person named in the order at a place so named: CA 2006, s 1132(3).

This section applies also in relation to documents in the possession or control of a person carrying on the business of banking, so far as they relate to the company's affairs, as it applies to documents in the possession or control of the company, except that no such order as is referred to in s 1132(3)(b) may be made by virtue of this sub-s (4): CA 2006, s 1132(4).

The decision under s 1132 of a judge of the High Court, any of the Lords Commissioners of Justiciary or the High Court is not appealable: CA 2006, s 1132(5).

In this section 'document' includes information recorded in any form: CA 2006, s 1132(6).

Meaning of 'the court'

36.24 Except as otherwise provided, in the Companies Acts 'the court' means:

(a) in England and Wales, the High Court or (subject to s 1156(3)) a county court;

(b) in Scotland, the Court of Session or the sheriff court;

(c) in Northern Ireland, the High Court: CA 2006, s 1156(1).

The provisions of the Companies Acts conferring jurisdiction on 'the court' as defined above have effect subject to any enactment or rule of law relating to the allocation of jurisdiction or distribution of business between courts in any part of the UK: CA 2006, s 1156(2).

Offences under the Companies Act 1985

36.25 Section 1124 of the CA 2006 deals with amendments under the Companies Act 1985. CA 2006, Sch 3 contains amendments of the Companies Act 1985 relating to offences.

This section introduces CA 2006, Sch 4 which contains amendments to the CA relating to offences that remain in Parts 14 and 15 of the CA 1985.

Many of these amendments were necessary due to the repeal by the CA 2006 of Sch 24 to the CA 1985. Schedule 24 set out the level of punishment for offences under CA 1985. The provisions in Parts 14 and 15 have been amended so that the applicable punishments are now included alongside the description of the offence instead of in Sch 24.

36.26 Schedule 3 to the CA 2006 also makes amendments to the offences provisions remaining in Pts 14 and 15 of CA 1985 to reflect the (non-textual) changes made to the Act by the Criminal Justice Act 2003. Section 282 of the Criminal Justice Act increases from six months to 12 months, the maximum term of imprisonment to which a person is liable on summary conviction of an offence triable either way, and s 154(1) of that Act gives power to magistrates to impose a 12-month term of imprisonment. The increased penalties only apply in England and Wales; in Scotland and Northern Ireland the maximum term of imprisonment that may be imposed on summary conviction remains six months. When the Act received Royal Assent, neither s 282 nor s 154(1) of the Criminal Justice Act 2003 had come into force (which was the reason for the transitional provision in s 1131).

A number of the amendments make reference to 'the statutory maximum fine'. This was set at £5,000 at the time the Act received Royal Assent.

36.27 Schedule 3 to the CA 2006 makes only one substantive change to the offence provisions in Parts 14 and 15. This is to include a daily default fine, of one-fiftieth of the statutory maximum, for continued contravention of CA 2006, s 444(3) (failure to provide information about interests in shares).

- Level 1: £200;
- Level 2: £500;

- Level 3: £1,000;
- Level 4: £2,500;
- Level 5: £5,000.

The statutory maximum has also been set at £5,000 since the date.

36.28 The table below sets out the substantive changes made by CA 2006, Sch 3 to sections of the 1985 Act.

	1985 Act	*Subject matter*	*Change*
1	s 444(3)	Failure to give information about interests in shares etc.	Provides that the penalty for the offence on summary conviction in England and Wales is 12 months' imprisonment or the statutory maximum fine (or both), and a daily fine not exceeding one-fiftieth of the statutory maximum.
			Provides that the penalty for the offence on summary conviction in Scotland and Northern Ireland is six months' imprisonment or the statutory maximum fine (or both), and a daily fine not exceeding one-fiftieth of the statutory maximum. Provides that on conviction on indictment, a person is liable to imprisonment for a term not exceeding two or a fine (or both) years.
2	s 448(7)	Obstruction of rights conferred by a warrant or failure to comply with requirement under s 448.	A person guilty of an offence under s 448 of the CA 1985 is liable on conviction on indictment to a fine. On summary conviction to a fine not exceeding the statutory maximum.
3	s 449	Wrongful disclosure of information to which s 449 applies.	Provides that on conviction on indictment, a person is liable to imprisonment for a term not exceeding two years or a fine (or both). Provides that the penalty for the offence on summary conviction in England and Wales up to 12 months' imprisonment or the statutory maximum fine, or both. Provides that the penalty for the offence on summary conviction in Scotland and Northern Ireland is six months' imprisonment or the statutory fine, or both.

	1985 Act	*Subject matter*	*Change*
4	s 450(3)	Destruction, mutilation etc of company documents.	Provides that on conviction on indictment, a person is liable to imprisonment for a term not exceeding seven years or a fine (or both). Provides that the penalty for the offence on summary conviction in England and Wales is 12 months' imprisonment or the statutory maximum fine, or both. Provides that the penalty for the offence on summary conviction in Scotland and Northern Ireland is six months' imprisonment or the statutory maximum fine, or both.
5	s 451(2)	Provision of false information in purported compliance with s 447.	Provides that on conviction on indictment, a person is liable to imprisonment for a term not exceeding two years or a fine (or both). Provides that the penalty for the offence on summary conviction in England and Wales is 12 months' imprisonment or the statutory maximum fine, or both. Provides that the penalty for the offence on summary conviction in Scotland and Northern Ireland is six months' imprisonment or the statutory maximum fine, or both.
6	s 453A	Obstruction of inspector; etc exercising power to enter and remain on premises.	A person guilty of an offence is liable on conviction on indictment to a fine. On summary conviction to a fine not exceeding the statutory maximum.
7	s 455(1)	Attempted evasion of restrictions under Pt 15.	A person guilty of an offence is liable on conviction on indictment to a fine. On summary conviction to a fine not exceeding the statutory maximum.

Definitions

36.29

Default: where a person authorises or permits, participates in or fails to take all reasonable steps to prevent the contravention.

Officer: includes a director, manager or secretary.

37 Statutory auditors

Contents

Introduction

37.1 Part 42 of the Companies Act 2006 concerns statutory auditors.

This Chapter addresses the following aspects:

- The concept of a 'statutory auditor'.
- Who is eligible to be a statutory auditor?

- The issue of independence.
- Qualifying as a statutory auditor.
- Regulation of statutory auditors.

Main purposes of Part 42

37.2 The main purposes of Pt 42 of the CA 2006 are:

(a) to secure that only persons who are properly supervised and appropriately qualified are appointed as statutory auditors; and

(b) to secure that audits by persons so appointed are carried out properly, with integrity and with a proper degree of independence: CA 2006, s 1209.

Meaning of 'statutory auditor'

37.3 The term 'statutory auditor' is defined as:

(a) a person appointed as auditor under CA 2006, Pt 16;

(b) a person appointed as auditor under s 77 of or Sch 11 to the Building Societies Act 1986 (c 53);

(c) a person appointed as auditor of an insurer that is a friendly society under s 72 of or Sch 14 to the Friendly Societies Act 1992 (c 40);

(e) a person appointed as auditor for the purposes of reg 5 of the Insurance Accounts Directive (Lloyd's Syndicate and Aggregate Accounts) Regulations 2008 or appointed to report on the 'aggregate accounts' within the meaning of those Regulations;

(f) a person appointed as auditor of an insurance undertaking for the purposes of the Insurance Accounts Directive (Miscellaneous Insurance Undertakings) Regulations 2008;

(g) a person appointed as auditor of a bank for the purposes of the Bank Accounts Directive (Miscellaneous Banks) Regulations 2008;

(h) a person appointed as auditor of a prescribed person under a prescribed enactment authorising or requiring the appointment;

and the expressions 'statutory audit' and 'statutory audit work' are to be construed accordingly: CA 2006, s 1210(1).

37.4 The term 'audited person' means the person in respect of whom a statutory audit is conducted: CA 2006, s 1210(2).

The term 'bank' means a person who:

(a) is a credit institution within the meaning given by Art 4.1 of Directive 2006/48/EC of the European Parliament and of the Council relating to the taking up and pursuit of the business of credit institutions as last amended by Directive 2009/111/EC; and

(b) is a company or a firm as defined in Art 54 of the Treaty on the Functioning of the European Union;

The term 'friendly society' means a friendly society within the meaning of the Friendly Societies Act 1992 (c 40);

The term 'insurer' means a person who is an insurance undertaking within the meaning given by Art 2.1 of Council Directive 1991/674/EEC on the annual accounts and consolidated accounts of insurance undertakings;

The term 'prescribed' means prescribed, or of a description prescribed, by order made by the Secretary of State for the purposes of sub-s (1)(h): CA 2006, s 1210(3).

Individuals and firms: eligibility for appointment as a statutory auditor

37.5 Under CA 2006, s 1212 an individual or firm is eligible for appointment as a statutory auditor if the individual or firm:

(a) is a member of a recognised supervisory body; and

(b) is eligible for appointment under the rules of that body: CA 2006, s 1212(1).

In the cases to which s 1222 applies (individuals retaining only 1967 Act authorisation) a person's eligibility for appointment as a statutory auditor is restricted as mentioned in that section: CA 2006, s 1212(2).

Effect of ineligibility

37.6 No person may act as statutory auditor of an audited person if he is ineligible for appointment as a statutory auditor: CA 2006, s 1213(1).

If at any time during his term of office a statutory auditor becomes ineligible for appointment as a statutory auditor, he must immediately:

(a) resign his office (with immediate effect); and

(b) give notice in writing to the audited person that he has resigned by reason of his becoming ineligible for appointment: CA 2006, s 1213(2).

37.7 A person is guilty of an offence if:

(a) he acts as a statutory auditor in contravention of s 1213(1); or

(b) he fails to give the notice mentioned in para (b) of sub-s (2) in accordance with that subsection: CA 2006, s 1213(3).

37.8 A person guilty of an offence under CA 2006, s 1213(3) will be liable:

(a) on conviction on indictment, to a fine;

(b) on summary conviction, to a fine not exceeding the statutory maximum: CA 2006, s 1213(4).

37.9 A person is guilty of an offence if:

(a) he has been convicted of an offence under s 1213 (3)(a) or s 1213(5), and

(b) he continues to act as a statutory auditor in contravention of s 1213(1) CA 2006 after the conviction: CA 2006, s 1213(5).

37.10 A person is guilty of an offence if:

(a) he has been convicted of an offence under s 1213(3)(b) or s 1213(6), and

(b) he continues, after the conviction, to fail to give the notice mentioned in s 1213(2)(b): CA 2006, s 1213(6).

37.11 A person guilty of an offence under s 1213(5) or (6) will be liable:

(a) on conviction on indictment, to a fine;

(b) on summary conviction, to a fine not exceeding one-tenth of the statutory maximum for each day on which the act or the failure continues: CA 2006, s 1213(7).

In proceedings against a person for an offence under s 1213, it is a defence for him to show that he did not know and had no reason to believe that he was, or had become, ineligible for appointment as a statutory auditor: CA 2006, s 1213(8).

Independence requirement

37.12 A person may not act as statutory auditor of an audited person if one or more of CA 2006, s 1214(2), (3) and (4) apply to him: CA 2006, s 1214(1). Section 1214(2) applies if the person is:

(a) an officer or employee of the audited person; or

(b) a partner or employee of such a person, or a partnership of which such a person is a partner: CA 2006, s 1214(2).

37.13 Section 1214(3) applies if the person is:

(a) an officer or employee of an associated undertaking of the audited person; or

(b) a partner or employee of such a person, or a partnership of which such a person is a partner: CA 2006, s 1214(3).

37.14 Section 1214(4) applies if there exists, between:

(a) the person or an associate of his; and

(b) the audited person or an associated undertaking of the audited person,

a connection of any such description as may be specified by regulations made by the Secretary of State: CA 2006, s 1214(4).

37.15 An auditor of an audited person is not to be regarded as an officer or employee of the person for the purposes of s 1214(2) and (3): CA 2006, s 1214(5).

The term 'associated undertaking', in relation to an audited person, means:

(a) a parent undertaking or subsidiary undertaking of the audited person; or

(b) a subsidiary undertaking of a parent undertaking of the audited person: CA 2006, s 1214(6).

Effect of lack of independence

37.16 If at any time during his term of office a statutory auditor becomes prohibited from acting by CA 2006, s 1214(1), he must immediately:

(a) resign his office (with immediate effect); and

(b) give notice in writing to the audited person that he has resigned by reason of his lack of independence: CA 2006, s 1215(1).

37.17 A person is guilty of an offence if:

(a) he acts as a statutory auditor in contravention of CA 2006, s 1215(1); or

(b) he fails to give the notice mentioned in para (b) of sub-s (1) in accordance with s 1215: CA 2006, s 1215(2).

37.18 A person guilty of an offence under CA 2006, s 1215(2) is liable:

(a) on conviction on indictment, to a fine;

(b) on summary conviction, to a fine not exceeding the statutory maximum: CA 2006, s 1215(3).

37.19 A person is guilty of an offence if:

(a) he has been convicted of an offence under CA 2006, s 1215(2)(a) or s 1215(4); and

(b) he continues to act as a statutory auditor in contravention of CA 2006, s 1214(1) after the conviction: CA 2006, s 1215(4).

37.20 A person is guilty of an offence if:

(a) he has been convicted of an offence under CA 2006, s 1215(2)(b) or s 1215(5); and

(b) after the conviction, he continues to fail to give the notice mentioned in CA 2006, s 1215(1)(b).

37.21 A person guilty of an offence under ss 1215(4) or (5) is liable:

(a) on conviction on indictment, to a fine;

(b) on summary conviction, to a fine not exceeding one-tenth of the statutory maximum for each day on which the act or the failure continues: CA 2006, s 1215(6).

In proceedings against a person for an offence under s 1215, it is a defence for him to show that he did not know and had no reason to believe that he was, or had become, prohibited from acting as statutory auditor of the audited person by CA 2006, s 1214(1).

Effect of appointment of a partnership

37.21 Section 1216 of the CA 2006 applies where a partnership constituted under the law of:

(a) England and Wales;

(b) Northern Ireland; or

(c) any other country or territory in which a partnership is not a legal person;

is by virtue of Pt 42, Ch 2 appointed as statutory auditor of an audited person: CA 2006, s 1216(1).

37.22 Unless a contrary intention appears, the appointment is an appointment of the partnership as such and not of the partners: CA 2006, s 1216(2).

Where the partnership ceases, the appointment is to be treated as extending to:

(a) any appropriate partnership which succeeds to the practice of that partnership; or

(b) any other appropriate person who succeeds to that practice having previously carried it on in partnership: CA 2006, s 1216(3).

37.23 For the purposes of CA 2006, s 1216 (3):

(a) a partnership is to be regarded as succeeding to the practice of another partnership only if the members of the successor partnership are substantially the same as those of the former partnership; and

(b) a partnership or other person is to be regarded as succeeding to the practice of a partnership only if it or he succeeds to the whole or substantially the whole of the business of the former partnership: CA 2006, s 1216(4).

37.24 Where the partnership ceases and the appointment is not treated under s 1216(3) as extending to any partnership or other person, the appointment may with the consent of the audited person be treated as extending to an appropriate partnership, or other appropriate person, who succeeds to:

(a) the business of the former partnership; or

(b) such part of it as is agreed by the audited person is to be treated as comprising the appointment: CA 2006, s 1216(5).

37.25 For the purposes of CA 2006, s 1216, a partnership or other person is 'appropriate' if it or he:

(a) is eligible for appointment as a statutory auditor by virtue of Pt 42, Ch 2, and

(b) is not prohibited by CA 2006, s 1214(1) from acting as statutory auditor of the audited person: CA 2006, s 1216(6).

Supervisory bodies

37.26 The term 'supervisory body' means a body established in the UK (whether a body corporate or an unincorporated association) which maintains and enforces rules as to:

(a) the eligibility of persons for appointment as a statutory auditor; and

(b) the conduct of statutory audit work,

which are binding on persons seeking appointment or acting as a statutory auditor because they are members of that body: CA 2006, s 1217(1).

37.27 The rules referred to in paras 9(3)(b) (confidentiality of information) and 10C(3)(a) and (b) (bar on appointment as director or other officer) of Sch 10 must also be binding on persons who:

(a) have sought appointment or acted as a statutory auditor; and

(b) have been members of the body at any time after the commencement of this CA 2006, Pt 42: CA 2006, s 1217(1A).

The references to the members of a supervisory body are to the persons who, whether or not members of the body, are subject to its rules in seeking appointment or acting as a statutory auditor: CA 2006, s 1217(2).

37.28 The references to the rules of a supervisory body are to the rules (whether or not laid down by the body itself) which the body has power to enforce and which are relevant for the purposes of this Pt 42. This includes rules relating to the admission or expulsion of members of the body, so far as relevant for the purposes of this Part: CA 2006, s 1217(3).

Schedule 10 to the CA 2006 applies with respect to the recognition of supervisory bodies for the purposes of this Pt 42: CA 2006, s 1217(4).

Exemption from liability for damages

37.29 No person within CA 2006, s 1218(2) is to be liable in damages for anything done or omitted in the discharge or purported discharge of functions to which s 1218(1) applies: CA 2006, s 1218(1).

The persons within s 1218(2) are:

(a) any recognised supervisory body;

(b) any officer or employee of a recognised supervisory body; and

(c) any member of the governing body of a recognised supervisory body: CA 2006, s 1218(2).

37.30 Section 1218(1) of CA 2006 applies to the functions of a recognised supervisory body so far as relating to, or to matters arising out of, any of the following:

(a) rules, practices, powers and arrangements of the body to which the requirements of CA 2006, Sch 10, Pt 2 apply;

(b) the obligations with which para 20 of that Schedule requires the body to comply;

(c) any guidance issued by the body;

(d) the obligations imposed on the body by or by virtue of Pt 42: CA 2006, s 1218(3).

37.31 The reference in s 1218(3)(c) to guidance issued by a recognised supervisory body is a reference to any guidance or recommendation which is:

(a) issued or made by it to all or any class of its members or persons seeking to become members, and

(b) relevant for the purposes of Pt 42,

including any guidance or recommendation relating to the admission or expulsion of members of the body, so far as relevant for the purposes of Pt 42: CA 2006, s 1218(4).

37.32 Section 1218(1) does not apply:

(a) if the act or omission is shown to have been in bad faith; or

(b) so as to prevent an award of damages in respect of the act or omission on the ground that it was unlawful as a result of s 6(1) of the Human Rights Act 1998 (c 42) (acts of public authorities incompatible with Convention rights): CA 2006, s 1218(5).

Appropriate qualifications

37.33 A person holds an appropriate qualification if and only if:

(a) he holds a recognised professional qualification obtained in the UK;

(b) immediately before the commencement of CA 2006, Pt 42, Ch 2, he:

  (i) held an appropriate qualification for the purposes of Pt 2 of the CA 1989 (c 40) (eligibility for appointment as company auditor) by virtue of s 31(1)(a) or (c) of that Act; or

  (ii) was treated as holding an appropriate qualification for those purposes by virtue of s 31(2), (3) or (4) of that Act,

(c) immediately before the commencement of Ch 2, he:

  (i) held an appropriate qualification for the purposes of Pt III of the Companies (Northern Ireland) Order 1990 (SI 1990 No 593 (NI 5)) by virtue of Art 34(1)(a) or (c) of that Order; or

  (ii) was treated as holding an appropriate qualification for those purposes by virtue of Art 34(2), (3) or (4) of that order;

(d) he is within sub-s (2); or

...

(f) subject to any direction under CA 2006, s 1221(5), he is regarded for the purposes of Ch 2 as holding an approved third-country qualification: CA 2006, s 1219(1).

37.34 A person is within this subsection if:

(a) before 1 January 1990, he began a course of study or practical training leading to a professional qualification in accountancy offered by a body established in the UK;

(b) he obtained that qualification on or after 1 January 1990 and before 1 January 1996; and

(c) the Secretary of State approves his qualification as an appropriate qualification for the purposes of CA 2006, Pt 42, Ch 2: CA 2006, s 1219(2).

The Secretary of State may approve a qualification under CA 2006, s 1219(2)(c) only if he is satisfied that, at the time the qualification was awarded, the body concerned had adequate arrangements to ensure that the qualification was awarded only to persons educated and trained to a standard equivalent to that required, at that time, in the case of a recognised professional qualification under Pt 2 of the CA 1989 (c 40) (eligibility for appointment as company auditor): CA 2006, s 1219(3).

Qualifying bodies and recognised professional qualifications

37.35 The term 'qualifying body' means a body established in the UK (whether a body corporate or an unincorporated association) which offers a professional qualification in accountancy: CA 2006, s 1220(1).

The references to the rules of a qualifying body are to the rules (whether or not laid down by the body itself) which the body has power to enforce and which are relevant for the purposes of CA 2006, Pt 42.

37.36 This includes, so far as relevant, rules relating to:

(a) admission to or expulsion from a course of study leading to a qualification;

(b) the award or deprivation of a qualification; or

(c) the approval of a person for the purposes of giving practical training or the withdrawal of such approval: CA 2006, s 1220(2).

Schedule 11 to the CA 2006 has effect with respect to the recognition for the purposes of Pt 42 of a professional qualification offered by a qualifying body: CA 2006, s 1220(3).

Approval of third-country qualifications

37.37 The Secretary of State may declare that the following are to be regarded for the purposes of CA 2006, Pt 42, Ch 2 as holding an approved third-country qualification:

(a) persons who are qualified to audit accounts under the law of a specified third country; or

(b) persons who hold a specified professional qualification in accountancy obtained in a specified third country: CA 2006, s 1221(1).

A declaration under CA 2006, s 1221(1)(a) or (b) must be expressed to be subject to the requirement that any person to whom the declaration relates must pass an aptitude test in accordance with s 1221(7A), unless an aptitude test is not required (see CA 2006, s 1221(7B)); CA 2006, s 1221(1A).

37.38 A declaration under s 1221(1)(b) may be expressed to be subject to the satisfaction of any specified requirement or requirements: CA 2006, s 1221(2).

The Secretary of State may make a declaration under s 1221(1) only if he is satisfied that:

(a) in the case of a declaration under sub-s (1)(a), the fact that the persons in question are qualified to audit accounts under the law of the specified third country; or

(b) in the case of a declaration under sub-s (1)(b), the specified professional qualification taken with any requirement or requirements to be specified under s 1221(2),

affords an assurance of professional competence equivalent to that afforded by a recognised professional qualification: CA 2006, s 1221(3).

37.39 The Secretary of State may make a declaration under sub-s (1) only if he is satisfied that the treatment that the persons who are the subject of the declaration will receive as a result of it is comparable to the treatment which is, or is likely to be, afforded in the specified third country, or a part of it to:

(a) in the case of a declaration under CA 2006, s 1221(1)(a), some or all persons who are eligible to be appointed as a statutory auditor; and

(b) in the case of a declaration under CA 2006, s 1221(1)(b), some or all persons who hold a corresponding recognised professional qualification: CA 2006, s 1221(4).

The Secretary of State may direct that persons holding an approved third-country qualification are not to be treated as holding an appropriate qualification for the purposes of CA 2006, Pt 42, Ch 2 unless they hold such additional educational qualifications as the Secretary of State may specify for the purpose of ensuring that such persons have an adequate knowledge of the law and practice in the UK relevant to the audit of accounts: CA 2006, s 1221(5).

The Secretary of State may give different directions in relation to different approved third-country qualifications: CA 2006, s 1221(6).

37.40 The Secretary of State may, if he thinks fit, having regard to the considerations mentioned in CA 2006, s 1221(3) and (4) withdraw a declaration under s 1221(1) in relation to:

(a) persons becoming qualified to audit accounts under the law of the specified third country after such date as he may specify; or

(b) persons obtaining the specified professional qualification after such date as he may specify: CA 2006, s 1221(7).

37.41 An aptitude test required for the purposes of s 1221(1A):

(a) must test the person's knowledge of subjects:

  (i) that are covered by a recognised professional qualification;

  (ii) that are not covered by the professional qualification already held by the person; and

  (iii) the knowledge of which is essential for the pursuit of the profession of statutory auditor;

(b) may test the person's knowledge of rules of professional conduct;

(c) must not test the person's knowledge of any other matters: CA 2006,s 1221(7A).

No aptitude test is required for the purposes of s 1221(1A) if the subjects that are covered by a recognised professional qualification and the knowledge of which is essential for the pursuit of the profession of statutory auditor are covered by the professional qualification already held by the person: CA 2006, s 1221(7B).

The Secretary of State may, if he thinks fit, having regard to the considerations mentioned in CA 2006, s 1221(3) and (4) vary or revoke a requirement specified under s 1221(2) from such date as he may specify: CA 2006, s 1221(8).

Eligibility of individuals retaining only 1967 Act authorisation

37.42 A person whose only appropriate qualification is based on his retention of an authorisation originally granted by the Board of Trade or the Secretary of State under s 13(1) of the Companies Act 1967 is eligible only for appointment as auditor of an unquoted company: CA 2006, s 1222(1).

A company is 'unquoted' if, at the time of the person's appointment, neither the company, nor any parent undertaking of which it is a subsidiary undertaking, is a quoted company within the meaning of CA 2006, s 385(2): CA 2006, s 1222(2).

References to a person eligible for appointment as a statutory auditor by virtue of Pt 42 in enactments relating to eligibility for appointment as auditor of a person other than a company do not include a person to whom this section applies: CA 2006, s 1222(3).

Matters to be notified to the Secretary of State

37.43 The Secretary of State may require a recognised supervisory body or a recognised qualifying body:

(a) to notify him immediately of the occurrence of such events as he may specify in writing and to give him such information in respect of those events as is so specified;

(b) to give him, at such times or in respect of such periods as he may specify in writing, such information as is so specified: CA 2006, s 1223(1).

The notices and information required to be given must be such as the Secretary of State may reasonably require for the exercise of his functions under Pt 42: CA 2006, s 1223(2).

The Secretary of State may require information given under this section to be given in a specified form or verified in a specified manner: CA 2006, s 1223(3).

Any notice or information required to be given under s 1223 must be given in writing unless the Secretary of State specifies or approves some other manner: CA 2006, s 1223(4).

Notification of matters relevant to other EEA states

37.44 A recognised supervisory body must notify the Secretary of State of:

(a) any withdrawal of a notifiable person's eligibility for appointment as a statutory auditor; and

(b) the reasons for the withdrawal: CA 2006, s 1223A(1).

37.45 A recognised supervisory body must also notify the Secretary of State of any reasonable grounds it has for suspecting that:

(a) a person has contravened the law of the UK, or any other EEA State or part of an EEA State, implementing the Audit Directive; and

(b) the act or omission constituting that contravention took place on the territory of an EEA State other than the UK: CA 2006, s 1223A(2).

37.46 The term 'notifiable person' means a member of the recognised supervisory body in question:

(a) who is also an EEA auditor; and

(b) in respect of whom the EEA competent authority is not the recognised supervisory body itself: CA 2006, s 1223A(3).

The Secretary of State's power to call for information

37.47 The Secretary of State may by notice in writing require a person within s 1224(2) to give him such information as he may reasonably require for the exercise of his functions under Pt 42: CA 2006, s 1224(1). The persons within this subsection are:

(a) any recognised supervisory body;

(b) any recognised qualifying body; and

(c) any person eligible for appointment as a statutory auditor by virtue of CA 2006, Pt 42, Ch 2: CA 2006, s 1224(2).

The Secretary of State may require that any information which he requires under this section is to be given within such reasonable time and verified in such manner as he may specify: CA 2006, s 1224(3).

Restrictions on disclosure

37.48 CA 2006, s 1224A applies to information (in whatever form):

(a) relating to the private affairs of an individual; or

(b) relating to any particular business;

that is provided to a body to which this section applies in connection with the exercise of its functions under CA 2006, Pt 42 or ss 522–524 (notification to appropriate audit authority of resignation or removal of auditor): CA 2006, s 1224A(1).

37.49 Section 1224A applies to:

(a) a recognised supervisory body;

(b) a recognised qualifying body;

(c) a body performing functions for the purposes of arrangements within para 23(1) (independent monitoring of certain audits), para 23A(1) (independent monitoring of third-country audits) or para 24(1) (independent investigation of public interest cases) of Sch 10;

(d) the Independent Supervisor;

(e) the Secretary of State; and

(f) a body designated by the Secretary of State under CA 2006, s 1252 (delegation of the Secretary of State's functions): CA 2006, s 1224A(2).

No such information may, during the lifetime of the individual or so long as the business continues to be carried on, be disclosed without the consent of that individual or (as the case may be) the person for the time being carrying on that business: CA 2006, s 1224A(3).

37.50 Section 1224A(3) does not apply to any disclosure of information that:

(a) is made for the purpose of facilitating the carrying out by the body of any of its functions;

(b) is made to a person specified in Pt 1 of Sch 11A;

(c) is of a description specified in Pt 2 of that Sch; or

(d) is made in accordance with Pt 3 of that Schedule: CA 2006, s 1224A(4).

37.51 Section 1224A(3) does not apply to:

(a) the disclosure by an EEA competent authority of information disclosed to it by the body in reliance on s 1224A(4);

(b) the disclosure of such information by anyone who has obtained it directly or indirectly from an EEA competent authority: CA 2006, s 1224A(5).

Section 1224A does not prohibit the disclosure of information if the information is or has been available to the public from any other source: CA 2006, s 1224A(6).

Nothing in s 1224A authorises the making of a disclosure in contravention of the Data Protection Act 1998: CA 2006, s 1224A(7).

Offence of disclosure in contravention of s 1224A

37.52 A person who discloses information in contravention of CA 2006, s 1224A (restrictions on disclosure) is guilty of an offence, unless:

(a) he did not know, and had no reason to suspect, that the information had been provided as mentioned in s 1224A(1); or

(b) he took all reasonable steps and exercised all due diligence to avoid the commission of the offence: s 1224B(1).

37.53 A person guilty of an offence under this section is liable:

(a) on conviction on indictment, to imprisonment for a term not exceeding two years or a fine (or both);

(b) on summary conviction:

  (i) in Scotland, to imprisonment for a term not exceeding 12 months or to a fine not exceeding the statutory maximum, or to both;

  (ii) in England and Wales or Northern Ireland, to imprisonment for a term not exceeding three months or to a fine not exceeding the statutory maximum, or to both: CA 2006, s 1224B(2).

Enforcement: general

37.54 CA 2006, s 1225 applies if at any time it appears to the Secretary of State:

(a) in the case of a recognised supervisory body, that any requirement of CA 2006, Sch 10, Pts 2 or 3 is not satisfied;

(b) in the case of a recognised professional qualification offered by a recognised qualifying body, that any requirement of Pt 2 of Sch 11 is not satisfied; or

(c) that a recognised supervisory body or a recognised qualifying body has not complied with an obligation imposed on it by or by virtue of Pt 42 (other than an obligation to pay a financial penalty under s 1225D of the CA 2006): s 1225(1) CA 2006.

37.55 The Secretary of State may do any one or more of the following:

(a) give a direction to the body under s 1225A;

(b) make an application to the court in respect of the body under s 1225C;

(c) impose a financial penalty on the body under s 1225D: CA 2006, s 1225(2).

Section 1225A(2) is without prejudice to the powers of the Secretary of State under para 3 of Sch 10 and para 3 of Sch 11 to the CA 2006 (revocation of recognition orders): CA 2006, s 1225(3).

Directions: general

37.56 A direction under CA 2006, s 1225A is one directing a body to take such steps as the Secretary of State considers will:

(a) secure that the requirement in question is satisfied or the obligation in question is complied with; or

(b) mitigate the effect, or prevent the recurrence, of the failure to satisfy the requirement or comply with the obligation: CA 2006, s 1225A(1).

37.57 A direction under this section:

(a) may only require a body to take steps which it has power to take;

(b) may require a body to refrain from taking a particular course of action: CA 2006, s 1225A(2).

The power to give a direction under this section is subject to any provision made by or under any other enactment: CA 2006, s 1225A(3).

The Secretary of State may take such steps as the Secretary of State considers appropriate to monitor the extent to which a direction under this section is being, or has been, complied with: CA 2006, s 1225A(4).

Directions: supplementary

37.58 Before giving a direction to a body under CA 2006, s 1225A, the Secretary of State must give the body a notice (a 'notice of proposed direction') accompanied by a copy of the proposed direction: CA 2006, s 1225B(1).

A notice of proposed direction must:

(a) state that the Secretary of State proposes to give the body a direction in the form of the accompanying draft;

(b) identify the requirement or obligation in question and state why it appears to the Secretary of State that the requirement is not satisfied or the obligation has not been complied with;

(c) specify a period within which the body may make written representations with respect to the proposal: CA 2006, s 1225B(2).

37.59 The period specified under CA 2006, s 1225B(2)(c):

(a) must begin with the date on which the notice of proposed direction is given to the body; and

(b) must not be less than 14 days: CA 2006, s 1225B(3).

Written representations made by the body within the period specified under s 1225B (2)(c) must be considered by the Secretary of State: CA 2006, s 1225B(4).

After considering any such representations or, in their absence, on the expiry of the period specified under s 1225B(2)(c), the Secretary of State must decide whether to give the body the proposed direction: CA 2006, s 1225B(5).

37.60 The Secretary of State must give notice of the decision (a 'direction decision notice') to the body: CA 2006, s 1225B(6); and if the Secretary of State decides to give the proposed direction, the direction decision notice must:

(a) contain the direction;

(b) state the time at which the direction is to take effect; and

(c) specify the Secretary of State's reasons for the decision to give the direction: CA 2006, s 1225B(7).

37.61 Where the Secretary of State decides to give the proposed direction, the Secretary of State must publish the direction decision notice in such manner as the Secretary of State considers appropriate for bringing the direction to the attention of persons likely to be affected: CA 2006, s 1225B(8).

The Secretary of State may revoke a direction given to a body under s 1225A and, where doing so, must:

(a) give the body notice of the revocation; and

(b) publish the notice in the same manner as the direction decision notice was published: CA 2006, s 1225B(9).

Compliance orders

37.62 If on an application under CA 2006, s 1225C in respect of a body, the court decides that a requirement is not satisfied or an obligation has not been complied with, the court may, subject to s 1225C(2), order the body to take such steps as it considers will secure that the requirement is satisfied or the obligation is complied with: CA 2006, s 1225C(1).

Where the obligation is an obligation to comply with a direction under s 1225A, the court may not order compliance with the direction unless it also decides that:

(a) the requirement in respect of which the direction was given is not satisfied; or

(b) the obligation in respect of which the direction was given has not been complied with: CA 2006, s 1225C(2).

The term 'the court' means the High Court or, in Scotland, the Court of Session: CA 2006, s 1225C(3).

Financial penalties: general

37.63 A financial penalty imposed on a body under CA 2006, s 1225D is a financial penalty of such amount as the Secretary of State considers appropriate, subject to s 1225D(2): CA 2006, s 1225D(1).

In deciding what amount is appropriate the Secretary of State:

(a) must have regard to the nature of the requirement which is not satisfied or the obligation which has not been complied with; and

(b) must not take into account the Secretary of State's costs in discharging functions under CA 2006, Pt 42: CA 2006, s 1225D(2).

A financial penalty under this section is payable to the Secretary of State: CA 2006, s 1225D(3).

In ss 1225E–1225G, references to a penalty are to a financial penalty under this section: CA 2006, s 1225D(4).

Financial penalties: supplementary

37.64 Before imposing a penalty on a body, the Secretary of State must give the body a notice (a 'notice of proposed penalty'):

(a) stating that the Secretary of State proposes to impose a penalty and the amount of the penalty proposed;

(b) identifying the requirement or obligation in question and stating why it appears to the Secretary of State that the requirement is not satisfied or the obligation has not been complied with; and

(c) specifying a period within which the body may make written representations with respect to the proposed penalty: CA 2006, s 1225E(1).

37.65 The period specified under CA 2006, s 1225E(1)(c):

(a) must begin with the date on which the notice of proposed penalty is given to the body; and

(b) must not be less than 21 days: CA 2006, s 1225E(2).

Written representations made by the body before the end of the period specified under CA 2006, s 1225E(1)(c) must be considered by the Secretary of State: CA 2006, s 1225E(3).

37.66 After considering any such representations or, in their absence, on the expiry of the period specified under CA 2006, s 1225E(1)(c), the Secretary of State must decide:

(a) whether to impose a penalty; and

(b) where the Secretary of State decides to do so, whether to reduce the proposed amount of the penalty: CA 2006, s 1225E(4).

The Secretary of State must give notice of the decision (a 'penalty decision notice') to the body: CA 2006, s 1225E(5).

37.67 Where the Secretary of State decides to impose a penalty, the penalty decision notice must:

(a) state that the Secretary of State has imposed a penalty on the body and its amount;

(b) identify the requirement or obligation in question and state:

  (i) why it appears to the Secretary of State that the requirement is not satisfied or the obligation has not been complied with; or

  (ii) where, by that time, the requirement is satisfied or the obligation has been complied with, why it appeared to the Secretary of State when giving the notice of proposed penalty that the requirement was not satisfied or the obligation had not been complied with; and

(c) specify a time by which the penalty is required to be paid: CA 2006, s 1225E(6).

37.68 The time specified under CA 2006, s 1225E(6)(c) must be at least three months after the date on which the penalty decision notice is given to the body: CA 2006, s 1225E(7). Where the Secretary of State decides to impose a penalty, he must publish the penalty decision notice and must do so in such manner as he considers appropriate for bringing the penalty to the attention of persons likely to be affected: CA 2006, s 1225E(8).

The Secretary of State may rescind a penalty imposed on a body under CA 2006, s 1225D and, where doing so, must:

(a) give the body notice of the rescission; and

(b) publish the notice in the same manner as the penalty decision notice was published: CA 2006, s 1225E(9).

Appeals against financial penalties

37.69 A body on which a penalty is imposed may appeal to the court on one or more of the appeal grounds: CA 2006, s 1225F(1).

The appeal grounds are:

(a) that, before the giving of the notice under CA 2006, s 1225E(1), the requirement in respect of which the penalty was imposed was satisfied or the obligation in respect of which the penalty was imposed had been complied with;

(b) that, where the penalty was imposed in respect of a failure to comply with a direction under CA 2006, s 1225A, before the giving of the notice under s 1225B(6), the requirement in respect of which the direction was given was satisfied or the obligation in respect of which the direction was given had been complied with;

(c) that any of the requirements of s 1225E have not been complied with in relation to the imposition of the penalty and the interests of the body have been substantially prejudiced by the non-compliance;

(d) that the amount of the penalty is unreasonable;

(e) that it was unreasonable of the Secretary of State to require the penalty imposed to be paid by the time specified in the notice under s 1225E(5): CA 2006, s 1225F(2).

An appeal under s 1225F((1) must be made within the period of three months beginning with the day on which the notice under s 1225E(5) is given to the body in respect of the penalty: CA 2006, s 1225F(3).

37.70 On any such appeal, where the court considers it appropriate to do so in all the circumstances of the case and is satisfied of one or more of the appeal grounds, the court may:

(a) quash the penalty;

(b) substitute a penalty of such lesser amount as the court considers appropriate; or

(c) in the case of the appeal ground in s 1225F(2)(e) substitute a later time for the time specified in the notice under s 1225E(5): CA 2006, s 1225F(4).

Where the court substitutes a penalty of a lesser amount, it may require the payment of interest on the substituted penalty, accruing from the time specified in the notice under s 1225E(5) or such later time as the court considers just and equitable: CA 2006, s 1225F(5).

37.71 Where the court substitutes a later time for the time specified in the notice under s 1225E(5), it may require the payment of interest on the penalty, accruing from the substituted time or such later time as the court considers just and equitable: CA 2006, s 1225F(6).

Where the court dismisses the appeal, it may require the payment of interest on the penalty, accruing from the time specified in the notice under s 1225E(5): CA 2006, s 1225F(7).

Where the court requires the payment of interest under this section, the interest is payable at such rate as the court considers just and equitable: CA 2006, s 1225F(8).

Except as provided by this section, the validity of a penalty is not to be questioned by any legal proceedings whatever: CA 2006, s 1225F(9).

The term 'the court' means the High Court or, in Scotland, the Court of Session: CA 2006, s 1225F(10).

Recovery of financial penalties

37.72 If the whole or any part of a penalty is not paid by the time by which it is required to be paid, the unpaid balance from time to time carries interest at the rate for the time being specified in s 17 of the Judgments Act 1838 (c 110) (unless a different rate is specified by the court under CA 2006, s 1225F(8)): CA 2006, s 1225G(1).

If an appeal is made under s 1225F in relation to a penalty, the penalty is not required to be paid until the appeal has been determined or withdrawn: CA 2006, s 1225G(2).

Section 1225G(2) does not prevent the court from specifying that interest is to accrue from an earlier date under s 1225F: CA 2006, s 1225G(3).

37.73 Where a penalty, or any portion of it, has not been paid by the time when it is required to be paid and:

(a) no appeal relating to the penalty has been made under s 1225F during the period within which such an appeal can be made; or

(b) an appeal has been made under that section and has been determined or withdrawn,

the Secretary of State may recover from the body, as a debt due to the Secretary of State, any of the penalty and any interest which has not been paid: CA 2006, s 1225G(4).

Checklist: statutory auditors

37.74

No	Issue	Act reference
1	Consider whether a person falls within the definition of 'statutory auditor'.	CA 2006, s 1210
2	Ensure that eligibility for appointment as a statutory auditor is satisfied.	CA 2006, s 1212
3	Consider the effect of ineligibility for appointment as statutory auditor including duty to resign and give notice to audited person, including criminal conviction.	CA 2006, s 1213
4	Maintain duty of independence as a statutory auditor and consider effect of lack of independence.	CA 2006, ss 1214 and 1215
5	There must be a supervisory body to regulate statutory auditors.	CA 2006, s 1217
6	The Secretary of State has powers to impose sanctions on a recognised supervisory body under the enforcement provisions.	CA 2006, s 1225
7	The court has powers to impose a compliance order on a supervisory body where an obligation or requirement has not been satisfied.	CA 2006, s 1225C
8	The Secretary of State has power to impose financial penalties on a supervisory body.	CA 2006, s 1225D
9	A supervisory body has power to appeal against a financial penalty.	CA 2006, s 1225E
10	The Secretary of State may also recover financial penalty against a supervisory body as a debt due together with any interest.	CA 2006, s 1225G

Definitions

37.75

Associated undertaking: In relation to an audited person means: (a) a parent undertaking or subsidiary undertaking of an audited person; or (b) a subsidiary undertaking of a parent undertaking of the audited person.

Audited person: A person in respect of whom a statutory audited is conducted.

Court: The High Court, or in Scotland, the Court of Session.

Friendly society: A friendly society within the meaning of the Friendly Societies Act 1992.

Prescribed:	Prescribed or of a description prescribed, by order made by the Secretary of State.
Qualifying body:	A body established in the UK (whether a body corporate or an unincorporated association) which offers a professional qualification in accountancy.
Supervisory body:	A body established in the UK (whether a body corporate or an unincorporated association) which maintains and enforces rules as to the eligibility of persons for appointment as a statutory auditor; and the conduct of statutory audit work.

38 Auditors General

Contents

Introduction

38.1 Part 42, Ch 3 of the CA 2006 is concerned with the appointment and regulation of Auditors General.

This Chapter looks at the following aspects:

- How an Auditor General may be appointed.
- Control of audits.
- The role of the Independent Supervisor.
- Duties of the Auditor General.
- Reporting requirements.

Eligibility for appointment

38.2 Section 1226 of the CA 2006 concerns the eligibility of Auditors General for appointment as a statutory auditor.

The term 'Auditor General' means:

(a) the Comptroller and Auditor General;

(b) the Auditor General for Scotland;

(c) the Auditor General for Wales; or

(d) the Comptroller and Auditor General for Northern Ireland: CA 2006, s 1226(1).

Under s 1226(2) of CA 2006, an Auditor General is eligible for appointment as a statutory auditor.

This provision is subject to any suspension notice having effect under s 1234 (notices suspending eligibility for appointment as a statutory auditor): CA 2006, s 1226(3).

Conduct of audits

Individuals responsible for audit work on behalf of Auditors General

38.3 An Auditor General must secure that each individual responsible for statutory audit work on behalf of that Auditor General is eligible for appointment as a statutory auditor by virtue of Ch 2.

The Independent Supervisor

Appointment of the Independent Supervisor

38.4 The Secretary of State must appoint a body ('the Independent Supervisor') to discharge the function mentioned in s 1229(1) ('the supervision function'): CA 2006, s 1228(1).

An appointment made under s 1228 must be made by order: CA 2006, s 1228(2).

The order has the effect of making the body appointed under s 1228(1) designated under s 5 of the Freedom of Information Act 2000 (c 36) (further powers to designate public authorities): CA 2006, s 1228(3).

38.5 A body may be appointed under s 1228 only if it is a body corporate or an unincorporated association which appears to the Secretary of State:

(a) to be willing and able to discharge the supervision function; and

(b) to have arrangements in place relating to the discharge of that function which are such as to be likely to ensure that the conditions in s 1228(5) are met: CA 2006, s 1228(4).

The conditions are:

(a) that the supervision function will be exercised effectively; and

(b) where the order is to contain any requirements or other provisions specified under s 1228(6), that that function will be exercised in accordance with any such requirements or provisions: CA 2006, s 1228(5).

An order under s 1228 may contain such requirements or other provisions relating to the exercise of the supervision function by the Independent Supervisor as appear to the Secretary of State to be appropriate: CA 2006, s 1228(6).

Supervision of Auditors General

Supervision of Auditors General by the Independent Supervisor

38.6 The Independent Supervisor must supervise the performance by each Auditor General of his functions as a statutory auditor: CA 2006, s 1229(1) and must discharge that duty by:

(a) establishing supervision arrangements itself; or

(b) entering into supervision arrangements with one or more bodies: CA 2006, s 1229(2).

If the Independent Supervisor enters into supervision arrangements with one or more bodies, it must oversee the effective operation of those supervision arrangements: CA 2006, s 1229(2A).

38.7 For this purpose 'supervision arrangements' are arrangements established by the Independent Supervisor or entered into by the Independent Supervisor with a body, for the purposes of s 1229, in accordance with which the Independent Supervisor or the body does the following:

(a) determines standards relating to professional integrity and independence which must be applied by an Auditor General in statutory audit work;

(b) determines technical standards which must be applied by an Auditor General in statutory audit work and the manner in which those standards are to be applied in practice;

(c) monitors the performance of statutory audits carried out by an Auditor General;

(d) investigates any matter arising from the performance by an Auditor General of a statutory audit;

(e) holds disciplinary hearings in respect of an Auditor General which appear to be desirable following the conclusion of such investigations;

(f) decides whether (and, if so, what) disciplinary action should be taken against an Auditor General to whom such a hearing related: CA 2006, s 1229(3).

The requirements of paras 9–10A and 12–15 of Sch 10 (requirements for recognition of a supervisory body) apply in relation to supervision arrangements as they apply in relation to the rules, practices and arrangements of supervisory bodies: CA 2006, s 1229(3A).

38.8 The Independent Supervisor may enter into supervision arrangements with a body despite any relationship that may exist between the Independent Supervisor and that body: CA 2006, s 1229(4).

The Independent Supervisor must notify each Auditor General in writing of any supervision arrangements that it establishes or enters into under s 1229: CA 2006, s 1229(5) and must, at least once in every calendar year, deliver to the Secretary of State a summary of the results of any inspections conducted for the purposes of s 1229(3)(c): CA 2006, s 1229(5A).

Supervision arrangements within sub-s (3)(f) may, in particular, provide for the payment by an Auditor General of a fine to any person: CA 2006, s 1229(6).

Any fine received by the Independent Supervisor under supervision arrangements is to be paid into the Consolidated Fund: CA 2006, s 1229(7).

Duties of Auditors General in relation to supervision arrangements

38.9 Each Auditor General must:

(a) comply with any standards of the kind mentioned in s 1230(3)(a) or (b) of s 1229 determined under the supervision arrangements;

(b) take such steps as may be reasonably required of that Auditor General to enable his performance of statutory audits to be monitored by means of inspections carried out under the supervision arrangements; and

(c) comply with any decision of the kind mentioned in sub-s (3)(f) of that section made under the supervision arrangements: CA 2006, s 1230(1).

38.10 Each Auditor General must:

(a) if the Independent Supervisor has established supervision arrangements, pay to the Independent Supervisor;

(b) if the Independent Supervisor has entered into supervision arrangements with a body, pay to that body,

such proportion of the costs incurred by the Independent Supervisor or body for the purposes of the arrangements as the Independent Supervisor may notify to him in writing: CA 2006, s 1230(2).

Expenditure under s 1230(2) is, in the case of expenditure of the Comptroller and Auditor General for Northern Ireland, to be regarded as expenditure of the Northern Ireland Audit Office for the purposes of Art 6(1) of the Audit (Northern Ireland) Order 1987 (SI 1987 No 460 (NI 5)): CA 2006, s 1230(3)(b).

The term 'the supervision arrangements' means the arrangements established or entered into under s 1229: CA 2006, s 1230(4).

Reporting requirement

Reports by the Independent Supervisor

38.11 The Independent Supervisor must, at least once in each calendar year, prepare a report on the discharge of its functions (CA 2006, s 1231(1)) and must give a copy of each report prepared under s 1231(1) to the :

(1) Secretary of State;

(2) First Minister in Scotland;

(3) First Minister and the deputy First Minister in Northern Ireland;

(4) First Minister for Wales: CA 2006, s 1231(2).

The Secretary of State must lay before each House of Parliament a copy of each report received by him under s 1231(2)(a): CA 2006, s 1231(3); and the First Minister for Wales must lay before the National Assembly for Wales a copy of each report received by him under 1231(2)(d): CA 2006, s 1231(3A).

In relation to a calendar year during which an appointment of a body as the Independent Supervisor is made or revoked by an order under s 1228, s 1231applies with such modifications as may be specified in the order: CA 2006, s 1231(4).

Information

Matters to be notified to the Independent Supervisor

38.12 The Independent Supervisor may require an Auditor General:

(1) to notify the Independent Supervisor immediately of the occurrence of such events as it may specify in writing and to give it such information in respect of those events as is so specified; .

(2) to give the Independent Supervisor, at such times or in respect of such periods as it may specify in writing, such information as is so specified: CA 2006, s 1232(1).

The notices and information required to be given must be such as the Independent Supervisor may reasonably require for the exercise of the functions conferred on it by or by virtue of CA 2006, Pt 42: CA 2006, s 1232(2).

The Independent Supervisor may require information given under s 1232 to be given in a specified form or verified in a specified manner: CA 2006, s 1232(3).

Any notice or information required to be given under this section must be given in writing unless the Independent Supervisor specifies or approves some other manner: CA 2006, s 1232(4).

38.9 The Independent Supervisor's power to call for information

38.13 The Independent Supervisor may by notice in writing require an Auditor General to give it such information as it may reasonably require for the exercise of the functions conferred on it by or by virtue of CA 2006, Pt 42: CA 2006, s 1233(1).

The Independent Supervisor may require that any information which it requires under s 1233 is to be given within such reasonable time and verified in such manner as it may specify: CA 2006, s 1233(2).

Enforcement

Suspension notices

38.14 The Independent Supervisor may issue:

(1) a notice (a 'suspension notice') suspending an Auditor General's eligibility for appointment as a statutory auditor in relation to all persons, or any specified person or persons, indefinitely or until a date specified in the notice;

(2) a notice amending or revoking a suspension notice previously issued to an Auditor General: CA 2006, s 1234(1).

38.15 In determining whether it is appropriate to issue a notice under s 1234(1), the Independent Supervisor must have regard to:

(1) the Auditor General's performance of the obligations imposed on him by or by virtue of CA 2006, Pt 42; and

(2) the Auditor General's performance of his functions as a statutory auditor: CA 2006, s 1234(2).

38.16 A notice under s 1234(1) must:

(1) be in writing; and

(2) state the date on which it takes effect (which must be after the period of three months beginning with the date on which it is issued): CA 2006, s 1234(3).

Before issuing a notice under s 1234(1), the Independent Supervisor must:

(a) give written notice of its intention to do so to the Auditor General; and

(b) publish the notice mentioned in para (a) in such manner as it thinks appropriate for bringing it to the attention of any other persons who are likely to be affected: CA 2006, s 1234(4).

38.17 A notice under s 1234(4) must:

(a) state the reasons for which the Independent Supervisor proposes to act; and

(b) give particulars of the rights conferred by s 1234(6): CA 2006, s 1234(5).

A person within s 1234(7) may, within the period of three months beginning with the date of service or publication of the notice under s 1234 (4) or such longer period as the Independent Supervisor may allow, make written representations to the Independent Supervisor and, if desired, oral representations to a person appointed for that purpose by the Independent Supervisor: CA 2006, s 1234(6).

The persons within s 1234 are:

- the Auditor General; and
- any other person who appears to the Independent Supervisor to be affected: CA 2006, s 1234(7).

38.18 The Independent Supervisor must have regard to any representations made in accordance with s 1234(6) in determining:

(a) whether to issue a notice under s 1234(1); and

(b) the terms of any such notice: CA 2006, s 1234(8).

If in any case the Independent Supervisor considers it appropriate to do so in the public interest it may issue a notice under sub-s (1), without regard to the restriction in s 1234(3)(b), even if:

(a) no notice has been given or published under s 1234(4); or

(b) the period of time for making representations in pursuance of such a notice has not expired: CA 2006, s 1234(9).

On issuing a notice under s 1234(1), the Independent Supervisor must:

(a) give a copy of the notice to the Auditor General; and

(b) publish the notice in such manner as it thinks appropriate for bringing it to the attention of persons likely to be affected: CA 2006, s 1234(10).

The term 'specified' means specified in, or of a description specified in, the suspension notice in question: CA 2006, s 1234(11).

Effect of suspension notices

38.19 An Auditor General must not act as a statutory auditor at any time when a suspension notice issued to him in respect of the audited person has effect: CA 2006, s 1235(1).

If at any time during an Auditor General's term of office as a statutory auditor a suspension notice issued to him in respect of the audited person takes effect, he must immediately:

(a) resign his office (with immediate effect); and

(b) give notice in writing to the audited person that he has resigned by reason of his becoming ineligible for appointment: CA 2006, s 1235(2).

A suspension notice does not make an Auditor General ineligible for appointment as a statutory auditor for the purposes of s 1213 (effect of ineligibility: criminal offences): CA 2006, s 1235(3).

Compliance orders

38.20 If at any time it appears to the Independent Supervisor that an Auditor General has failed to comply with an obligation imposed on him by or by virtue of CA 2006, Pt 42, the Independent Supervisor may make an application to the court under s 1236: CA 2006, s 1236(1).

If on an application under this section the court decides that the Auditor General has failed to comply with the obligation in question, it may order the Auditor General to take such steps as the court directs for securing that the obligation is complied with: CA 2006, s 1236(2).

The term 'the court' means the High Court or, in Scotland, the Court of Session: CA 2006, s 1236(3).

Proceedings

Proceedings involving the Independent Supervisor

38.21 If the Independent Supervisor is an unincorporated association, any relevant proceedings may be brought by or against it in the name of any body corporate whose constitution provides for the establishment of the body: CA 2006, s 1237(1).

For this purpose 'relevant proceedings' means proceedings brought in or in connection with the exercise of any function by the body as the Independent Supervisor: CA 2006, s 1237(2).

Where an appointment under s 1228 is revoked, the revoking order may make such provision as the Secretary of State thinks fit with respect to pending proceedings: CA 2006, s 1237(3).

Checklist

38.22 *This checklist sets out an overview of the regulatory framework governing Auditors General. All references are to the CA 2006.*

No	Issue	Act reference
1	An Auditor General (as defined by CA 2006) may be eligible for appointment as a statutory auditor	CA 2006, s 1226
2	The Secretary of State must appoint an Independent Supervisor to supervise the Auditor General	CA 2006, s 1228
3	The Independent Supervisor's functions include, *inter alia*, supervising the performance by each Auditor General of his functions as a statutory auditor	CA 2006, s 1229
4	Auditor Generals have specific duties in relation to supervision arrangements	CA 2006, s 1230
5	The Independent Supervisor has a duty to prepare a report on the discharge of his functions	CA 2006, s 1231
6	Auditors General have a duty to provide certain information as required by the Independent Supervisor	CA 2006, s 1232
7	The Independent Supervisor has powers to issue suspension notices with the effect of suspending an Auditor General's eligibility for appointment as a statutory auditor	CA 2006, s 1234
8	The effect of a suspension notice is that an Auditor General cannot act as a statutory auditor and must immediately resign his office and notify the audited person to that effect	CA 2006, s 1235

No	Issue	Act reference
9	The Independent Supervisor has powers to apply to the court for a compliance order that the Auditor General has failed to comply with his obligations, and for the court to direct the Auditor General to comply with such obligations	CA 2006, s 1236
10	It is also possible to bring proceedings against the Independent Supervisor before court in connection with the exercise of its functions	CA 2006, s 1237

Definitions

38.23

Court:	High Court or, in Scotland, the Court of Session
Relevant Proceedings:	Proceedings brought in or in connection with the exercise of any function by the body as the Independent Supervisor
Suspension Notice:	A notice suspending an Auditor General's eligibility for appointment as a statutory auditor in relation to all persons, or any specified person or persons, indefinitely or until a date specified in the notice

39 Corporate manslaughter

Contents

Introduction

39.1 In English common law, the main principle concerning the criminal liability of corporations has been that those who 'controlled and managed' the affairs of the company were regarded as embodying the company itself. For a company to be convicted of manslaughter, an individual who could be identified as the embodiment of the company itself must first be shown to have been guilty of manslaughter. Only if the identified individual was found guilty could the company then be convicted. Where there was insufficient evidence to convict the individual, any prosecution of the company would generally fail.

The Corporate Manslaughter and Corporate Homicide Act 2007 ('the Act') was enacted to address the difficulties in securing corporate convictions at common law. This chapter considers the following questions:

- How does common law address the position of identifying the culpable company?
- How is liability imposed under the Act?
- When will exemptions be available?
- What factors will the jury consider in determining whether the company is culpable?
- What are the penalties once a conviction is secured for corporate manslaughter or corporate homicide?

The position before the Act

39.2 The legal position on corporate manslaughter was largely governed by common law and prosecutions under the Health and Safety at Work etc Act 1974.

Corporate responsibility and liability lies those who are he 'directing mind and will' of the corporation

At common law, the issue of identifying an individual who could be the 'directing mind and will' of the company was highlighted by Lord Reid in *Tesco Supermarkets Ltd v Nattrass* [1972] AC 153 (a case unconnected with corporate manslaughter):

> '[A corporation] must act through living persons, though not always one or the same person. Then the person who acts is not speaking or acting for the company. He is acting as the company and his mind, which directs his acts, is the mind of the company. There is no question of the company being vicariously liable ... He is an embodiment of the company. If it is a guilty mind then the guilt is the guilt of the company'. See too *R v HM Coroner for East Kent, ex parte Spooner* (1899) 88 Cr App R 10 (a company could be vicariously liable for the negligent acts or omissions of its servants or agents).'

39.3 However, in practice, one of the main difficulties has been in identifying an individual who could be the embodiment of the company and who could therefore be culpable. The problem was even more acute with larger companies which had a diffuse structure, where the responsibility for safety matters was unclear, with no one individual having overall responsibility. In these circumstances, it was almost impossible to identify specific individuals who could represent the 'directing mind and will' of the company and who also possessed the requisite *mens rea* (mental state) to be guilty of manslaughter, thereby making it difficult to attribute any criminal liability to the company: *DPP v Kent and Sussex Contractors Ltd* [1944] KB 146 (company could not be guilty of the criminal offences charged because it was not possible to impute *mens rea* to the company); *R v ICR Haulage Ltd* [1944] KB 551 (a company was not liable for the acts of its agents); *Moore v Bresler Ltd* [1944] 2 All ER 515 (the fraudulent acts of the company's officers were the acts of the company).

In some cases, liability on a corporation could be applied through attribution or agency principles but these were not determinative

Before the 2007 Act, the courts attempted to attribute liability to a corporation for corporate manslaughter through the 'identification principle' or the principle of vicarious liability: see *R v Birmingham & Gloucester Railway Co* [1842] 3 QB 223 (a company was vicariously liable for the acts of its servants); *Seaboard Offshore Ltd v Secretary of State for Transport* [1994] 1 WLR 541 (a company was held not to be vicariously liable for an offence under the Merchant Shipping Act 1988); and *R v British Steel plc* [1994] 1 WLR 1356 (vicarious liability was imposed on the company by s 31 of the Health and Safety etc Act 1974).

In the event that neither the identification nor the agency principles applied, the court could not attribute criminal liability to the corporation.

In *Meridian Global Funds Management Asia Ltd v The Securities Commission* [1995] 2 AC 500, Lord Hoffman stated that:

> 'Reference to a company "as such" might suggest that there is something out there called the company, of which one can meaningfully say that it can or cannot do something. There is in fact no such thing as the company as such ... only applicable rules. To say that a company cannot do something means only that there is no one whose doing of that act would, under the rules of attribution, count as an act of the company.'

39.4 The need for reform had been increasing for some time, due to a number of disasters where corporate culpability had been alleged. This had provoked demands for a new law on corporate manslaughter, particularly where the failure successfully to prosecute had led to a perception among the public that the law dealing with corporate manslaughter was inadequate. Some examples included: the sinking of the Herald of Free Enterprise in 1987; the King's Cross fire in 1987; the Piper Alpha oil platform disaster in 1988; the Clapham Rail crash in 1988; the sinking of the Marchioness in 1989; the Southall rail crash in 1997; Thames trains, regarding a fatal train crash at Ladbroke Grove in 1999; Transco and the fatal explosion in Larkhall in 1999; and Network Rail with a fatal derailment of a train near Hatfield.

Following a series of consultations by the previous Labour Government and by the Law Commission, the Corporate Manslaughter and Corporate Homicide Act 2007 (CMCHA 2007, 'the Act') finally received Royal Assent on 26 July 2007 and came into force on 6 April 2008 (see The Corporate Manslaughter and Corporate Homicide Act 2007 (Commencement No 1 Order) 2008 (SI 2008/401). The Act sets out the legal mechanism specifically identifying companies and other organisations who may be prosecuted, where gross negligence in the manner in which an organisation's activities were managed or organised leads to death. A wide range of organisations fall within the scope of the Act (including commercial organisations). This chapter focuses on the management systems and practices of an organisation and how it addresses its risks for the various activities it manages or organises.

The Act makes provision for a criminal offence which, in England and Wales or Northern Ireland is known as 'corporate manslaughter', and 'corporate homicide' in Scotland.

> The Act abolishes the common law offence of manslaughter by gross negligence in its application to corporations, including unincorporated associations: s 20: see *R v Bateman* (1925) 19 Cr App R 8 (gross negligence manslaughter involved a duty of care owed by the defendant to the deceased; breach of duty by the defendant; the breach caused the deceased's death and the defendant was guilty of gross negligence) and *R v Seymour* [1983] 2 AC 493 (for gross negligence manslaughter the appropriate fault term was 'recklessness') but see now *R v Adomako* [1995] 1 AC 171 (the *Bateman* test for gross negligence manslaughter was the appropriate test). However, any future prosecutions for corporate manslaughter will fall under the Act. The offence under the Act is therefore intended to complement, not replace, other forms of accountability (eg prosecutions under health and safety legislation) and is specifically linked to existing health and safety requirements.

The offence

39.5 The offence is committed where, in the particular circumstances, an organisation owes a duty to take reasonable care for a person's safety, and the way in which the activities of the organisation have been managed or organised, amounts to a gross breach of that duty and causes a person's death.

The main elements of the offence are:

- *Duty of care*

  The organisation owes a 'relevant duty of care' to the victim: CMCHA 2007, s 1(1).

- *Gross breach*

  The way in which the organisation's activities were managed or organised amounts to a gross breach of the relevant duty of care. The test is whether the conduct that constitutes the gross breach falls below what can reasonably be expected of the organisation in the circumstances: CMCHA 2007, s 1(4)(b). In practice, juries would take account of any health and safety breaches by the organisation and how serious and dangerous the failures were: CMCHA 2007, s 8.

- *Senior management*

  An organisation cannot be convicted of the offence unless a substantial element of the breach lies in the way the senior management of the organisation managed or organised its activities: CMCHA 2007, s 1(3). The term 'senior management' refers to persons who play a significant role in the making of decisions about how the whole or a substantial part of an organisation's activities are to be managed or organised; or the actual managing or organising of the whole or substantial part of those activities: CMCHA 2007, s 1(4). This definition would include top management, as well as key officers in the organisation and those in operational management roles.

- *Victim's death*

  The way in which the organisation's activities were managed or organised have caused the victim's death.

Establishing a 'relevant duty of care' by the organisation

39.6 The offence applies where the organisation owes a duty of care to its victim under the law of negligence. The statutory duties owed under health and safety legislation will not be 'relevant' duties for the offence under the Act. It will be for the judge to decide whether a duty of care was owed to the victim. The duty of care arises from specific functions or activities performed by the organisation, such as taking reasonable steps to protect a person's safety. These duties, for example, exist for the systems of work, equipment used by employees, workplace conditions, other sites occupied by an organisation and products or services supplied to customers. The term 'relevant duty of care' means any of the following duties owed by the organisation under the law of negligence:

- A duty owed to its employees or to other persons working for the organisation or performing services for it. See for example, *Wilsons & Clyde Coal Co Ltd v English* [1938] AC 57, where Lord Wright set out the general nature of an employer's obligation as 'a duty, which is personal to the employer, whether the employer be an individual, a firm or a company, and whether or not the employer takes any share in the conduct of the operations'. Accordingly, the employer's obligations comprise ensuring competent staff are appointed; the provision of adequate equipment; and the provision of a proper system and effective supervision: see too *Stafford v Antwerp Steamship Co Ltd* [1965] 2 Lloyd's Rep 104; *Hudson v Ridge Manufacturing Co Ltd* [1957] 2 QB 348; *Butter v Life Coal Co Ltd* [1912] AC 149; and *Taylor v Rover Co Ltd* [1966] 1 WLR 1491. An organisation may also owe a duty of care to those whose work it is able to control or direct, even though they are not formally employed by the organisation (eg contractors, subcontractors, secondees, or consultants).
- A duty owed as occupier of premises (but see also the duties under the Occupiers' Liability Acts 1957 and 1984 and the Defective Premises Act 1972). The term 'premises' includes land. Organisations must ensure that the buildings they occupy are in a safe condition.
- A duty owed in connection with:
  - the supply by the organisation of goods or services (whether for consideration or not). This includes a duty owed by the organisation to its customers as well as duty owed by transport suppliers to their passengers, including retailers for the safety of their products and the supply of services by the public sector such as the NHS providing medical treatment); or
  - the carrying on by the organisation of any construction or maintenance operations. This would include a duty by the organisation to ensure that adequate safety precautions are taken when repairing a road or in maintaining the roadworthiness of vehicles, as well as public utility bodies such as water authorities by, for example, ensuring that drinking water is not polluted, or the gas authorities in ensuring that there is no gas leakage; or

- the carrying on by the organisation of any other activity on a commercial basis. This ensures that any other activities not covered above are caught by virtue of their commercial activities such as mining or farming; or
- the use or keeping by the organisation of any plant, vehicle or other thing: CMCHA 2007, s 2(1).

- A duty of care also arises in respect of persons held in detention or custody. The detention can apply in the following circumstances:
  (a) being detained at a custodial institution or in a custody area at a court or police station;
  (b) being detained at a removal centre or short-term holding facility;
  (c) being transported in a vehicle, or being held in any premises in pursuance of prison escort arrangements or immigration escort arrangements;
  (d) the person is living in secure accommodation in which he has been placed; or
  (e) where the person is a detained patient. This usually arises under the Mental Health Act 1983: CMCHA 2007, s 2(2).
- The existence of a duty of care in a particular case is a matter of law for the judge to decide: CMCHA 2007, s 2(5). This reflects the legal nature of the test applied to the existence of a duty of care in the law of negligence. The judge will decide whether the circumstances of the case give rise to a duty of care and will need to make certain determinations of fact that are usually for the jury. For example, in deciding whether a corporation owes a duty of care as an employer, the judge will need to decide if the victim was an employee of the corporation. The questions of fact to be decided by the judge are likely to be uncontroversial, but will only be decided by the judge in considering issues such as duty of care. If they affect the case, this will be for the jury to decide.

Who is caught by the offence?

39.7 The offence applies to the following organisations or entities:

- Corporation – this is defined as any body corporate, whether incorporated in the UK or elsewhere. The term includes companies established under the companies legislation, but excludes sole corporations: CMCHA 2007, ss 1(2) and 25. Companies within a group structure will be treated as separate entities and are subject to the offence separately. A parent company cannot therefore be liable for the acts of its subsidiary. The offence applies to all companies and other corporate bodies operating in the UK, whether incorporated in the UK or abroad.
- Charities and voluntary organisations.
- Other public bodies such as local authorities, NHS institutions and a wide range of non-departmental public bodies.
- Organisations incorporated by Royal Charter.
- Limited liability partnerships.

- Crown Bodies – Schedule 1 to the Act specifies a list of all the Crown institutions to whom the Act applies. The offence will also apply to Crown bodies that are incorporated such as the Charity Commission, the Office of Fair Trading and the Postal Services Commission. Not many Crown institutions have separate legal personality. Where they do, it means that the application of the offence to corporations also applies to these Crown institutions. If they do not have separate legal personality, then the list in Schedule 1 sets out the institutions subject to the Act: CMCHA 2007, s 1(2).

  Section 11(1) states that an organisation that is a servant or agent of the Crown is not immune from prosecution under the Act. Therefore, the effect of ss 1 and 11 is that Crown bodies that are either bodies corporate or are listed in Schedule 1 are subject to the offence. In practice, the liability of the Crown in the law of negligence is governed by the Crown Proceedings Act 1947, which makes the Crown liable for the torts of its servants and agents. However, under the Corporate Manslaughter and Corporate Homicide Act 2007, the Crown body owes a personal duty of care to the victim. This is reinforced by the fact that Crown bodies are to be treated as owing, for the purposes of the offence, the duties of care that they would owe if they were ordinarily constituted corporate bodies: CMCHA 2007, s 11(2). The activities and functions of government departments and other Crown bodies are to be treated as those of the relevant Crown department or body: CMCHA 2007, ss 11(3) and (4). Where there are changes to the government departments, the Act provides that any prosecution will be against the body that has the responsibility for the functions connected with the death: CMCHA 2007, s 16. If the function is transferred wholly out of the public sector, then the proceedings will be against the public body which last carried out the function.

- Partnership, or a trade union or employers' association, if the organisation concerned is an employer: CMCHA 2007, s 1(2). The definition of 'partnership' extends to those covered by the Partnership Act 1890 and limited partnerships under the Limited Partnerships Act 1907, but it does not extend to limited liability partnerships under the Limited Liability Partnership Act 2000: CMCHA 2007, s 25. In law, partnerships are distinct entities from corporations and (unlike limited liability partnerships), they lack a separate legal personality for the purposes of owing a duty of care in the law of negligence. However, s 14 provides that a partnership is to be treated as owing whatever duty of care it would owe if it were a body corporate: CMCHA 2007, s 14(1). Proceedings for an offence alleged to have been committed by the partnership are to be brought in the name of the partnership, not in that of any of its members: CMCHA 2007, s 14(2). Further, a fine imposed on a partnership on conviction of an offence is to be paid out of the funds of the partnership: CMCHA 2007, s 14(3).

- The list of organisations to which the offence applies can be further extended by secondary legislation subject to an affirmative resolution procedure: CMCHA 2007, s 21.

- Police authorities, which are bodies corporate under the Police Act 1996. Although police forces are not incorporated bodies, the Act ensures that police officers are treated as the employees of the police force to impose a duty of care: CMCHA 2007, s 13(2).

- The armed forces. Section 12 defines the term 'armed forces' used in ss 4 and 6 so that it includes the Royal Navy, the army and the air force. For the purposes of s 2, a person who is a member of the armed forces is to be treated as being employed by the Ministry of Defence for the purposes of the offence: CMCHA 2007, s 12(2).

No individual liability

39.8 The offence under the Act is only concerned with corporate liability of the organisation and it does not apply to individual directors, senior managers or other individuals. Further, the Act excludes secondary liability for the offence, namely the principle under which a person may be prosecuted for an offence if they have aided, abetted, counselled or procured it. An individual cannot be guilty of aiding, abetting, counselling or procuring the commission of an offence of corporate manslaughter or corporate homicide: CMCHA 2007, s 18.

However, this does not exclude an individual's direct liability for offences such as gross negligence manslaughter, culpable homicide or health and safety offences. The Act does not change the existing law on individual liability and prosecutions against individuals will continue where there is sufficient evidence and it is in the public interest to do so.

Venue for trial

39.9 The offence will be triable only in the Crown Court in England and Wales and Northern Ireland and the High Court of Justiciary in Scotland. The trial will be by jury. An organisation that is guilty of corporate manslaughter or corporate homicide is subject to an unlimited fine: CMCHA 2007, s 1(6), but the court also has power to impose a remedial order under s 9, or a publicity order under s 10.

The exemptions – public policy decisions, exclusively public functions and statutory inspections

39.10 Section 3 of the Act excludes certain matters from the scope of the offence. These include decisions of public policy taken by public authorities, including, in particular, the allocation of public resources and strategic funding decisions, or other matters involving competing public interests: CMCHA 2007, s 3(1), but it does not exempt decisions about how resources are managed. Public authorities are defined by reference to the Human Rights Act 1998 and include public bodies such as government departments and local government bodies, as well as other bodies, some of whose functions are of a public nature. However, courts and tribunals are not covered by the new offence and are excluded.

At present, the law of negligence recognises that some decisions taken by public bodies are not justifiable (ie are not susceptible to review in the courts) as they concern decisions involving competing public priorities or other questions of public policy. This may, for example, include decisions by Primary Care Trusts about the funding of particular treatments.

39.11 There is an exemption available in respect of intrinsically public functions. In many circumstances, functions of this nature will not be covered by the categories of duty set out in s 2 of the CMCHA 2007. However, it may be possible that some functions will amount to the supply of goods or services or be performed commercially, particularly if performed by the private sector on behalf of the State. The Act ensures that an organisation will not be liable for a breach of any duty of care owed in respect of things done in the exercise of 'exclusively public functions', unless the organisation owns or is an occupier of premises: CMCHA 2007, s 3(2). This test is not confined to Crown or other public bodies, but also excludes any organisations (public or otherwise) performing that particular type of function. This does not affect questions of individual liability and prosecutions for gross negligence manslaughter and other offences will remain possible against individuals performing these functions who are themselves culpable. The management of these functions will continue to be subject to other forms of accountability such as independent investigations, public inquiries and the accountability of ministries through Parliament.

39.12 The term 'exclusively public functions' covers both functions falling within the prerogative of the Crown such as acting in a civil emergency and types of activity that, because of their nature, require a statutory or prerogative basis. They cannot be independently performed by private bodies. This looks at the nature of the activity involved. It would not cover an activity simply because it required a licence or took place on a statutory basis (eg functions relating to the custody of prisoners (the function of lawfully detaining someone requiring a statutory basis): CMCHA 2007, s 3(4). The type of activity involved must intrinsically require statutory or prerogative authority, such as licensing drugs or conducting international diplomacy. Private companies carrying out exempt functions will be in the same position as public bodies.

39.13 A commercial organisation will not be liable in respect of any duty of care owed in connection with the carrying out of statutory inspections, unless the organisation owes the duty in its capacity as an employer, or as an occupier of premises to ensure compliance with statutory standards (eg inspection activities by the health and safety enforcing authorities). It is unlikely that these bodies would owe duties of care in respect of such activities, or that these activities would be performed commercially; nor would the exercise of this function amount to a supply of services. It may be possible that the carrying out of an inspection might involve the use of equipment, so as to bring s 2(1)(c)(iv) into operation. This provision makes explicit that the performance of these functions will fall outside the scope of the offence.

The Act excludes certain activities performed by the armed forces: CMCHA 2007, s 4(1). A wide range of operational military activities will be exclusively public functions within the terms of s 3(2), which are exempt from the offence.

39.14 The offence will not apply unless the death relates to the organisation's responsibility as an employer, or to others working for the organisation. In respect of policing and law enforcement activities performed by the police and other law enforcement bodies, the Act provides a partial exemption for the police and other law enforcement bodies in respect of all categories of duty of care referred to in s 2 (ie including those duties of care owed by an organisation as an employer or occupier of premises). However, this wide exemption is available only in limited circumstances (see s 5(1) and (2).

The offence does not apply to the emergency services when responding to emergencies: CMCHA 2007, s 6(1). This does not exclude the responsibility these authorities owe to provide a safe system of work for their employees, or to secure the safety of their premises.

The offence does not apply in relation to the exercise of specific functions to protect children from harm, or in relation to the activities of probation services (or equivalent bodies in Scotland and Northern Ireland): CMCHA 2007, s 7. Local authorities and probation services will be covered by the offence by requiring them to ensure the safety of their employees or the premises they occupy.

Factors for a jury

39.15 The Act sets out the test for assessing whether the breach of duty involved a gross failure: CMCHA 2007, s 1(4)(b). The test asks whether the conduct that constitutes this failure falls far below what could reasonably have been expected. Whether this threshold has been met will be an issue for the jury to determine. The existing common law offence of gross negligence manslaughter asks whether the conduct was so negligent as to be criminal.

Section 8 applies where it is established that an organisation owed a relevant duty of care to a person, and it falls for the jury to decide whether there was a gross breach of that duty: CMCHA 2007, s 8(1). The jury is directed to consider whether the evidence shows that the organisation failed to comply with any health and safety legislation that relates to the alleged breach, and if so, how serious that failure was; and how much of a risk of death it posed: CMCHA 2007, s 8(2).

Depending upon the circumstances, the jury may take the following into account:

- the extent to which the evidence shows that there were attitudes, policies, systems or accepted practices within the organisation that were likely to have encouraged any such failure, or to have produced tolerance of it;
- any health and safety guidance that relates to the alleged breach: CMCHA 2007, s 8(3). The term 'health and safety guidance' means any code, guidance, manual or similar publication that is concerned with health and safety matters and is made or issued by an authority responsible for the enforcement of any health and safety legislation: CMCHA 2007, s 8(5). These include approved Codes of Practice. Employers are not required to follow guidance and can freely choose to implement other courses of action. However, guidance from regulatory authorities could assist the jury when considering the extent of any failures to comply with health and safety legislation and whether the organisation's conduct has fallen far below what could reasonably have been expected.

However, the jury may still have regard to any other matters they consider relevant other than those stated above: CMCHA 2007, s 8(4).

39.16 In order to provide a clearer framework for assessing an organisation's culpability, s 8 sets out a number of factors for the jury to consider. In particular, these put the management of an activity into the context of the organisation's obligations under health and safety legislation, the extent to which the organisation was in breach of these and the risk to life that is involved. Section 8 also provides for the jury to consider the wider context in which these health and safety breaches occurred, including cultural issues within the organisation such as attitudes or accepted practices that tolerated breaches. When considering breaches of health and safety, juries may also consider guidance on how those obligations should be discharged. Guidance, however, does not provide an authoritative statement of required standards. However, where breaches of relevant health and safety duties have been established, guidance may assist a jury in considering how serious this was.

Penalties

39.17 An organisation that is convicted of the offence may be subject to the following penalties:

- *Fine*

  There is no upper limit for the amount of the fine: CMCHA 2007, s 1. It will be for the criminal courts to determine the size of a fine and any sentencing guidelines (see, however, the guidelines from the Sentencing Guidelines Council below).

- *Remedial orders*

  In addition to the power under s 1 to impose an unlimited fine, s 9 gives the court the power to order an organisation convicted of an offence to take steps to remedy the management failure leading to the victim's death. This is known as a 'remedial order' which requires the organisation that is convicted of corporate manslaughter or corporate homicide to take specified steps to remedy:

  - the breach that led to the victim's death;
  - any matters that appears to the court to have resulted from the relevant breach and to have been a cause of the death; or
  - any deficiency, as regards health and safety matters, in the organisation's policies, systems or practices of which the relevant breach appears to the court to be an indication: CMCHA 2007, s 9(1).

However, a remedial order can only be made on an application by the prosecution who must specify the terms of the order. Any such order must be on terms that the court considers appropriate having regard to any representations made and any evidence adduced, in relation to that matter, by the prosecution or on behalf of the organisation: CMCHA 2007, s 9(2).

39.18 Before applying for any remedial order, the prosecution must consult such enforcement authority or authorities as it considers appropriate having regard to the nature of the relevant breach: CMCHA 2007, s 9(3). This could include the Health and Safety Executive, Office of Rail Regulation, Food Standards Agency or local authority.

The remedial order must specify a period within which the steps referred to in s 9(1) are to be taken: CMCHA 2007, s 9(3). Further, the remedial order may require the organisation to supply to an enforcement authority consulted under s 9(3) within a specified period, evidence that these steps have been taken: CMCHA 2007, s 9(4).

39.19 If an organisation fails to comply with a remedial order, it will be guilty of an offence and liable on conviction on indictment to a fine: CMCHA 2007, s 9(5). This would be the responsibility of the general prosecuting authorities, namely the Crown Prosecution Service in England and Wales, the Public Prosecution Service in Northern Ireland and the Procurator Fiscal in Scotland.

It also enables the court to order the organisation to remedy any consequence of the management failure, if it appeared to the court to have been a cause of death. For example, where the management failure related to inadequate risk assessment and monitoring procedures, the consequence of which was inadequate safety precautions resulting in death, the court would be able to order the convicted organisation to improve both its management of risk and the resulting safety precautions. Remedial orders may also require an organisation to address deficiencies in health and safety management that lie behind the relevant breach of duty. For example, if the breach is indicative of the organisation and employees generally paying little attention to health and safety management, an order could require the organisation to review and promulgate to staff its health and safety practices.

39.20 Applications for remedial orders must be made by the prosecution, having consulted the relevant health and safety regulator. The prosecution must set out the proposed terms of the order. The convicted organisation will have an opportunity to make representations to the court about the order. The order must specify how long the organisation has to comply with the required steps. This period can be extended on application. Failure to comply with a remedial order is an indictable offence for which the sanction will be an unlimited fine.

- *Publicity orders*

  A court before which an organisation is convicted of corporate manslaughter or corporate homicide may make an order, otherwise known as a 'publicity order', requiring the organisation to publicise in a specified manner the following:

  - the fact that the organisation has been convicted of the offence;
  - the specified particulars of the offence;
  - the amount of any fine imposed; and
  - the terms of any remedial order made: CMCHA 2007, s 10(1).

However, in deciding on the terms of a publicity order that it is proposing to make, the court must ascertain the views of such enforcement authority or authorities (if any) as it considers appropriate. The court must also have regard to any representations made by the prosecution or on behalf of the organisation: CMCHA 2007, s 10(2).

The publicity order must specify a period within which the requirements set out in s 10(1) are to be complied with. Further, the publicity order may require the organisation to supply to any enforcement authority whose views have been ascertained under s 10(2), evidence that those requirements have been complied with.

Section 10 was brought into force on 15 February 2010 by the Corporate Manslaughter and Corporate Homicide Act 2007 (Commencement No 2) Order 2010 (SI 2010/276).

Procedure, evidence and sentencing

39.21 In law generally, the provisions relating to criminal and court procedure and sentencing relate to the prosecution of individuals, but many of these provisions will also be applicable to corporations and similar entities. Under s 15, for the purposes of the offence of corporate manslaughter or corporate homicide all such provisions apply in the same way as they apply to corporations, to those government departments or other bodies listed in Sch 1, as well as to police forces, partnerships, trade unions, an employers' association that is not a corporation and other unincorporated associations covered by the offence: CMCHA 2007, s 15(1).

39.22 In February 2010, the Sentencing Guidelines Council issued a definitive guideline entitled *Corporate Manslaughter & Health and Safety Offences Causing Death*. Under s 172 of the Criminal Justice Act 2003, every court must have regard to the guidelines in respect of sentencing on or after 15 February 2010. The following guideline applies only to corporate manslaughter and to those health and safety offences where the offence is shown to have made a significant contribution to the cause of death. The harm involved must be very serious. The possible range of factors affecting the seriousness of the offence will be very wide. Seriousness should ordinarily be assessed first by asking the following:

(a) How foreseeable was serious injury? The more foreseeable it was, the graver the offence.

(b) How far short of the applicable standard did the defendant fall?

(c) How common is this kind of breach in this organisation? How widespread was the non-compliance? Was it isolated in extent or indicative of a systematic departure from good practice across the defendant's operations?

(d) How far up the organisation does the breach go? Usually, the higher up the responsibility for the breach, the more serious the offence: *Chargot* [2008] UKHL 73 at para 30; *Electric Gate Services Ltd* [2009] EWCA Crim 1942.

39.23 In addition, other factors are likely, if present, to aggravate the offence (the list is not exhaustive):

(a) more than one death, or very grave personal injury in addition to death;

(b) failure to heed warnings or advice, whether from officials such as the Inspectorate, or by employees (especially health and safety representatives) or other persons, or to respond appropriately to 'near misses' arising in similar circumstances;

(c) cost-cutting at the expense of safety;

(d) deliberate failure to obtain or comply with relevant licences, at least where the process of licensing involves some degree of control, assessment or observation by independent authorities with a health and safety responsibility; and

(e) injury to vulnerable persons.

In this context, vulnerable persons would include those whose personal circumstances make them susceptible to exploitation.

39.24 Conversely, the following factors, which are similarly non-exhaustive, are likely, if present, to afford mitigation:

(a) a prompt acceptance of responsibility;

(b) a high level of cooperation with the investigation, beyond that which will always be expected;

(c) genuine efforts to remedy the defect;

(d) a good health and safety record; and

(e) a responsible attitude to health and safety, such as the commissioning of expert advice or the consultation of employees or others affected by the organisation's activities.

Since corporate manslaughter requires proof of gross breach of duty and the substantial involvement of senior management, it is unlikely that the unauthorised act of an employee will significantly reduce the culpability of the defendant in that offence.

39.25 The commission of an offence may, in some cases, be solely due to the unauthorised act of an employee. In such a case, the responsibility of the organisation must be assessed (eg for inadequate supervision or training). There may be some cases where there is very little culpability within the organisation itself.

It will generally be appropriate to require the prosecution to set out in writing the facts of the case relied upon and any aggravating or mitigating features which it identifies. Further, the defence may be required to set out, in writing, any points on which it differs. If sentence is to proceed upon agreed facts, they should be set out in writing: *Friskies Petcare (UK) Ltd* [2000] EWCA Crim 95; [2000] 2 Cr App Rep (S) 401.

39.26 With respect to financial information and the size and nature of the organisation, the following guidelines apply:

(a) The law must expect the same standard of behaviour from both large and small organisations. Smallness does not by itself mitigate, and largeness does not by itself aggravate, these offences. Size may affect the approach to safety, whether because a small organisation is careless or because a large one is bureaucratic, but these considerations affect the seriousness of the offence via the assessment set out above, rather than demonstrating a direct correlation between size and culpability.

(b) A large organisation may be more at risk of committing an offence than a small one simply because it conducts very many more operations. Some large corporate groups operate as a single company whereas others are structured as separate companies for separate operations. A large organisation may be operating upon a budget as tight (or tighter) than a small one because of the demands placed upon it (eg large local authorities, hospital trusts or police forces), but so might commercial companies with a large turnover but small profit margins. However, in some instances, a large organisation may have fewer excuses for not dealing properly with matters affecting health and safety, since it has greater access to expertise, advice and training resources.

(c) Size is, however, relevant. The principal available penalty for organisations is a fine therefore a company's ability to pay must be assessed. The court should require information about the financial circumstances of the defendant. Best practice will usually be to call for financial information for a three-year period, including the year of the offence, so as to avoid any risk of atypical figures in a single year.

(d) A fixed correlation between the fine and either turnover or profit is not appropriate. The circumstances of defendant organisations and the financial consequences of the fine will vary too much; similar offences committed by companies structured in differing ways ought not to attract fines which are vastly different; a fixed correlation might provide a perverse incentive to manipulation of corporate structure.

(e) The court should, however, look carefully at turnover, profit and assets to gauge the resources of the defendant. When taking account of financial circumstances, statute (s 164(1) and (4) Criminal Justice Act 2003) allows the court either to increase or decrease the amount of a fine. It is just that a wealthy defendant should pay a larger fine than a poor one; whilst a fine is intended to inflict punishment, it should be one which the defendant is capable of paying, even if this takes a number of years.

(f) Annex A sets out the type of financial information with which, in the ordinary way, a court should expect to be provided in relation to a defendant. The primary obligation to provide it lies on the defendant. As a matter of practice, it would be helpful if the prosecution takes the preliminary step of calling upon the defendant to provide it to the court and prosecution and, if the defendant does not do so, of assembling what can be obtained from public records and furnishing that to the court. If a defendant fails to provide relevant information, the court is justified in making adverse assumptions as to its means, and may be obliged to do so.

(g) It will not ordinarily be necessary for the prosecution to embark upon analysis of the figures, as distinct from ensuring that the raw material is available to the court, and it may not in any event normally have the expertise to do so. In a few complex cases of relevant dispute the prosecution can, if genuinely necessary, undertake such analysis either in-house or by the instruction of an accountant and if it can justify the expense as part of its necessary costs those costs will ordinarily be recoverable from the defendant: Criminal Justice Act 2003, s 164(5)(b)(iii).

(h) In assessing the financial consequences of a fine, the court should consider, *inter alia*, the following factors:

- The effect on the employment of the innocent may be relevant.
- Any effect upon shareholders will, however, not normally be relevant; those who invest in and finance a company take the risk that its management will result in financial loss.
- The effect on directors will not, likewise, normally be relevant.
- Nor would it ordinarily be relevant that the prices charged by the defendant might in consequence be raised, at least unless the defendant is a monopoly supplier of public services.
- The effect upon the provision of services to the public will be relevant; although a public organisation such as a local authority, hospital trust or police force must be treated the same as a commercial company where the standards of behaviour to be expected are concerned, and must suffer a

punitive fine for breach of them, a different approach to determining the level of fine may well be justified:

> 'The Judge has to consider how any financial penalty will be paid. If a very substantial financial penalty will inhibit the proper performance by a statutory body of the public function that it has been set up to perform, that is not something to be disregarded': see *Milford Haven Port Authority* [2000] 2 Cr App R(S) 423 per Lord Bingham CJ at 433–4.

- The same considerations will be likely to apply to non-statutory bodies, or charities if they provide public services.
- The liability to pay civil compensation will ordinarily not be relevant; normally this will be provided by insurance or the resources of the defendant will be large enough to meet it from its own resources.
- The cost of meeting any remedial order will not ordinarily be relevant, except to the overall financial position of the defendant; such an order requires no more than should already have been done.
- Whether the fine will have the effect of putting the defendant out of business will be relevant: in some cases this may be an acceptable consequence.

39.27 In the case of a large organisation, the fine should be payable within 28 days. In the case of a smaller or financially stretched organisation, it is permissible to require payment to be spread over a much longer period. There is no limitation to payment within 12 months, but the first payment should be required within a short time of sentencing. An extended period for the payment of further instalments may be particularly appropriate for an organisation of limited means which has committed a serious offence and where it is undesirable that the fine should cause it to go out of business.

In some cases, it may be apparent that a broadly quantifiable saving has been made by the defendant by committing the offence. In such cases it will normally be the proper approach to ensure that the fine removes the profit and imposes an appropriate additional penalty.

39.28 In respect of the level of fines, the following guidelines apply:

- There will inevitably be a broad range of fines because of the range of seriousness involved and the differences in the circumstances of the defendants. Fines must be punitive and sufficient to have an impact on the defendant.
- Fines cannot and do not attempt to value a human life in monetary terms. Civil compensation will be payable separately. The fine is designed to punish the defendant and is therefore tailored not only to what it has done, but also to its individual circumstances.
- The offence of corporate manslaughter, because it requires gross breach at a senior level, will ordinarily involve a level of seriousness significantly greater than a health and safety offence. The appropriate fine will seldom be less than £500,000 and may be measured in millions of pounds: see *Friskies Petcare (UK) Ltd* [2000] EWCA Crim 95.

- The range of seriousness involved in health and safety offences is greater than for corporate manslaughter. However, where the offence is shown to have caused death, the appropriate fine will seldom be less than £100,000 and may be measured in hundreds of thousands of pounds or more.
- A plea of guilty should be recognised by the appropriate reduction.
- In respect of compensation the following guidelines apply:
- The assessment of compensation in cases of death will usually be complex, will involve payment of sums well beyond the powers of a criminal court, and will ordinarily be covered by insurance.
- In the vast majority of cases, the court should conclude that compensation should be dealt with in a civil court and should say that no order is made for that reason. There may be occasional cases, for example if the defendant is uninsured and payment may not otherwise be made, when consideration should be given to a compensation order in respect of bereavement and/or funeral expenses.
- On the issue of costs, the defendant ought ordinarily (subject to means) to be ordered to pay the properly incurred costs of the prosecution.

39.29 Publicity orders are available in the case of corporate manslaughter only. They may require publication in a specified manner of:

(a) the fact of conviction;

(b) specified particulars of the offence;

(c) the amount of any fine; and

(d) the terms of any remedial order.

39.30 Such an order should ordinarily be imposed in a case of corporate manslaughter. The object is deterrence and punishment.

(i) The order should specify with particularity the matters to be published in accordance with s 10(1) of CMCHA 2007. Special care should be taken with the terms of the particulars of the offence committed.

(ii) The order should normally specify the place where public announcement is to be made and consideration should be given to indicating the size of any notice or advertisement required. It should ordinarily contain a provision designed to ensure that the conviction becomes known to shareholders in the case of companies and local people in the case of public bodies. Consideration should be given to requiring a statement on the defendant's website. A newspaper announcement may be unnecessary if the proceedings are certain to receive news coverage in any event, but if an order requires publication in a newspaper it should specify the paper, the form of announcement to be made and the number of insertions required.

(iii) The prosecution should provide the court in advance of the sentencing hearing, and should serve on the defendant, a draft of the form of order suggested and the judge should personally endorse the final form of the order.

(iv) Consideration should be given to stipulating in the order that any comment placed by the defendant alongside the required announcement should be separated from it and clearly identified as such.

A publicity order is part of the penalty. Any exceptional cost of compliance should be considered in fixing the fine. It is not, however, necessary to fix the fine first and then deduct the cost of compliance.

39.31 In respect of remedial orders, the following guidelines apply.

- A remedial order is available both for corporate manslaughter and HSWA offences. A defendant ought, by the time of sentencing, to have remedied any specific failings involved in the offence and if it has not will be deprived of significant mitigation.
- However, if it has not, a remedial order should be considered if it can be made sufficiently specific to be enforceable. The prosecution is required by s 9(2) of CMCHA 2007 to give notice of the form of any such order sought, which can only be made on its application; although there is no equivalent stipulation in the HSWA it is good practice to require the same notice. The judge should personally endorse the final form of such an order.
- The cost of compliance with such an order should not ordinarily be taken into account in fixing the fine; the order requires only what should already have been done.

Annex A: Financial information expected to be provided to the court (Sentencing Guidelines Council)

39.32

(1) For companies: published audited accounts. Particular attention should be paid to (a) turnover, (b) profit before tax, (c) directors' remuneration, loan accounts and pension provision and (d) assets as disclosed by the balance sheet (note that they may be valued at cost of acquisition which may not be the same as current value). Most companies are required to lodge accounts at Companies House. Failure to produce relevant recent accounts on request may properly lead to the conclusion that the company can pay any appropriate fine.

(2) For partnerships: annual audited accounts. Particular attention should be paid to (a) turnover, (b) profit before tax, (c) partner's drawings, loan accounts and pension provision and (d) assets as above. If accounts are not produced on request, see paragraph 1.

(3) For local authorities, police and fire authorities and similar public bodies: the Annual Revenue Budget (ARB) is the equivalent of turnover and the best indication of the size of the defendant organisation (see www.local.communities.gov.uk/finance/bellwin.HTM). It is unlikely to be necessary to analyse specific expenditure or reserves unless inappropriate or grandiose expenditure is suggested. Such authorities also have attributed to them a 'Bellwin factor' which represents the level of exceptional and unforeseen expenditure that they are expected by central government to meet themselves in any one year without any claim to

recourse to central funds. But since that is arithmetically related to the ARB (currently 0.2%) it will ordinarily add little of significance beyond an indication of budgetary discipline.

(4) For health trusts: the independent regulator of NHS Foundation Trusts is Monitor. It publishes quarterly reports and annual figures for the financial strength and stability of trusts from which the annual income can be seen (see www.monitor-nhsft.gov.uk/home/our-publications). Detailed analysis of expenditure or reserves is unlikely to be called for.

Note that Monitor has significant regulatory powers including over membership of the boards of directors or governors.

(5) For 'third sector' organisations: it will be appropriate to inspect annual audited accounts. Detailed analysis of expenditure or reserves is unlikely to be called for unless there is a suggestion of unusual or unnecessary expenditure.

Relationship between the Act and health and safety legislation

39.33 A conviction for corporate manslaughter would not preclude an organisation being convicted for a health and safety offence on the same facts if this were in the interests of justice. An individual could, for example, be convicted on a secondary basis for such an offence under provisions such as s 37 of the Health and Safety at Work etc Act 1974. This does not impose any existing liabilities on individuals but ensures that existing liabilities are not reduced as an unintended consequence of the new offence.

Where in the same proceedings a charge of corporate manslaughter or corporate homicide arises out of a particular set of circumstances and a charge against the same defendant of a health and safety offence arises out of some or all of those circumstances, the jury may, if the interests of justice so require, be invited to return a verdict on each charge: CMCHA 2007, s 19(1). Further, an organisation that has been convicted of corporate manslaughter or corporate homicide arising out of a particular set of circumstances may, if the interests of justice so require, be charged with a health and safety offence arising out of some or all of those circumstances: CMCHA 2007, s 19(2). The term 'health and safety offence' means an offence under any health and safety legislation: CMCHA 2007, s 19(3).

An issue has arisen as to whether a sole director and shareholder could sue his company for injuries sustained under the health and safety rules and regulations, including the duty under s 174 of the CA 2006.

A sole director and shareholder of a company could not bring a claim for damages for breach of health and safety regulations where his breach of duty under s 174 of the CA 2006 to exercise reasonable care had prevented the company from meeting its statutory obligation

In *Brumder v Motornet Service and Repairs Limited* [2013] EWCA Civ 195, the issue for determination by the court was whether the sole director and shareholder of a company who suffered personal injuries as a result of the breach by the company of an absolute statutory obligation to maintain equipment in efficient working order, could bring a claim against the company even though he was in breach of his obligations to the company to exercise reasonable care to enable the company to fulfil that obligation?

Mr Brumder was the sole director and shareholder of Motornet Service and Repairs Ltd, a company specialising in servicing vehicles and putting them through their MOT inspections. On 8 November 2008 Mr Brumder's left ring finger was severed from his hand while he was trying to climb down to ground level from a raised hydraulic ramp in the company's workshop after the compressor in the ramp mechanism failed. An attempt to reattach the finger was unsuccessful. He appealed against the order of His Honour Judge Levey dismissing his claim for damages for the injuries sustained by him 'on account of finding that [Mr Brumder] was 100% contributorily negligent'.

> The Court of Appeal held that the sole director and shareholder could not bring a claim here as his breach of duty under s 174 of the CA 2006 to exercise reasonable care, skill and diligence had prevented the company from meeting its statutory obligation: (see *Re City Equitable Fire Insurance* [1925] Ch 407 at 427 per Romer J); and *Re D'Jan of London Ltd* [1994] 1 BCLC 561. The test under s.174 is both subjective and objective.

DPP consent for proceedings

39.34 The Director of Public Prosecution's consent is required for any proceedings for corporate manslaughter. In Scotland, the consent of the Lord Advocate will be required for all proceedings on indictment: CMCHA 2007, s 17.

Checklist

39.35 *This checklist considers the essential issues that need to be addressed by organisations and entities in ensuring full compliance with the Corporate Manslaughter and Corporate Homicide Act 2007, and matters that must be taken into account by directors, non-executive directors and key officers within the organisation in the proper discharge of their duties.*

No	Issue	Act reference
1	What are the activities of the organisation?	s 1(1)
2	Do the activities present any health and safety risks?	
3	Has a risk assessment of the organisation's activities been undertaken? If not, this should be undertaken immediately.	
4	What issues have been identified from the risk assessment that require further investigation and analysis?	

No	Issue	Act reference
5	If necessary, engage consultants and specialists to resolve the risk issues and ensure the risk assessment is ongoing, continuous and monitored by compliance officers to ensure adherence to the health and safety legislation and European directives and regulations.	
6	Set a deadline for any risks to be removed and a detailed record of the risks identified and how they were resolved.	
7	Ensure all personnel are aware of the organisation's risk-assessment policies and procedures set out in a manual, including the frequency of assessment that takes place, and the actions taken.	
8	Ensure that all proper and necessary accountability systems are in place to ensure elimination of risks.	
9	Ensure the organisation provides a safe system of work.	s 2(1)
10	Ensure the company employs competent personnel with specialist skills where the activities present a risk or are of a hazardous nature.	s 2(1)
11	Ensure the organisation provides a safe place of work and a safe means of access.	s 2(1)
12	Ensure the organisation provides and maintains adequate appliances.	s 2(1)
13	The organisation must have a proper and necessary training mechanism in place to train and update personnel.	
14	The organisation should arrange regular meetings with personnel to take into account their concerns concerning systems and work procedures.	
15	Multinational organisations should establish consistent and standard procedures for providing safe systems of work.	s 2(1)
16	The organisation's key officers including the chief operating officer (if any) must ensure that the organisation's safety policies and procedures are communicated to all staff at the workplace.	
17	Ensure that the organisation's meeting has a regular item on the agenda to address management activities with regard to the health and safety of its employees and those likely to be affected by the organisation's activities.	
18	Ensure regular health checks of key employees involved in hazardous or dangerous activities.	
19	Assess any new insurance policies to cover the types of offences contemplated by the Corporate Manslaughter and Corporate Homicide Act 2007.	

No	Issue	Act reference
20	Ensure all newly recruited key officers including non-executive directors are fully aware of the 2007 Act implications as part of their induction course, and to build in a regular programme to raise continuous awareness of the nature and scope of the offence.	
21	How are the activities managed or organised in practice?	s 1(1)
22	Who are the key people within the organisation with responsibilities for managing or organising the organisation's activities?	s 1(3)
23	Was a relevant duty of care owed to the victim?	s 2
24	Was there a gross breach of a relevant duty of care in the organisation's management and in its activities?	s 1(1)(b)
25	Did the management and organisation of the activities lead to the victim's death?	s 1(1)(a)
26	Did the relevant duty of care involve any of the following: (a) Duty to employees? (b) Duty to the occupier of the premises? (c) Duty in connection with the supply of goods or services, or any construction or maintenance operations, or carrying out other activity on a commercial basis? (d) The detention at a custodial institution or in a custody area at a court or police station? (e) Being a detained person? (f) Being detained at a removal centre or a short-term holding facility? (g) Being transported in a vehicle or being held in any premises in pursuance of prison or immigration escort agencies?	s 2(1)
27	Are there any exemptions where the duty of care will not arise? Consider: (a) public policy decisions; (b) exclusively public functions; (c) statutory inspections; (d) military activity; (e) policing and law enforcement; (f) emergencies; (g) child protection and probation functions.	ss 3–7

No	Issue	Act reference
28	Consider the factors for a jury in determining whether there was a gross management failure: (a) the test is one of reasonableness; (b) the issue is whether the conduct that constitutes management failure falls far below what could reasonably have been expected. Discretionary factors for the jury include: (a) whether there were attitudes, policies, systems or accepted practices within the organisation that were likely to have failure in management activities or organisation; (b) any health and safety guidance relating to the alleged breach; (c) any other matters considered relevant.	s 8

Guidance notes

39.36 *These guidance notes address specifically the offence of corporate manslaughter or corporate homicide based on the provisions of the Corporate Manslaughter and Corporate Homicide Act 2007. The Guidance Note is a summary form of the essential provisions of the 2007 Act.*

Note 1: Objectives

No		Tick
	The principal objectives for the offence of corporate manslaughter and corporate homicide are to:	
1.1	Ensure organisations operate high standards of systems and procedures at their workplace in full compliance with the health and safety legislation, where such hazardous or dangerous activities affect the health and safety of employees or others affected by the organisation's activities.	
1.2	Raise heightened awareness of the series of deaths and fatalities that have resulted owing to an organisation's failure in the management of its activities with unsuccessful criminal prosecutions in the past against such organisations for corporate manslaughter.	
1.3	Ensure that the present system of attributing liability by the identification principle or vicarious liability principle no longer have a place in determining corporate manslaughter, but rather to focus on the concept of 'management failure' in attributing liability to the organisation.	

No		Tick
1.4	Deter organisations and/or its officers from engaging in high-risk activities without proper safe systems and procedures at the workplace that are regularly reviewed and updated.	
1.5	Focus on those organisations that have no or inadequate systems and procedures at the workplace, and have not taken steps to minimise risk from their management activities.	

Note 2: Corporate manslaughter and corporate homicide

No		Tick
1.1	The offence of corporate manslaughter applies in England and Wales and corporate homicide in Scotland.	
1.2	The focus is on the way in which the organisation's 'activities' are managed or organised such that they cause a person's death, and amounts to a gross breach of relevant duty of care owed by the organisation to the deceased.	
1.3	The offence of corporate manslaughter or corporate homicide broadly corresponds to the individual offence of killing by gross carelessness.	
1.4	An organisation will be guilty of a criminal offence of corporate manslaughter or corporate homicide only if the way in which its activities are managed or organised by its senior management is a substantial element of the breach of relevant duty of care.	

Note 3: The existence of a 'relevant duty of care'

No		Tick
1.1	For the offence of corporate manslaughter or corporate manslaughter to apply, an organisation must owe a relevant duty of care.	
1.2	A duty of care is owed to the organisation's employees or to other persons working for the organisation or performing services for it. This would include casual workers, consultants and others hired by the organisation. A contractual relationship would be required to be demonstrated for a duty of care to be established here.	
1.3	The breach of a duty of care by the organisation must be 'gross', in that the conduct alleged to amount to a breach of that duty falls far below what can reasonably be expected of the organisation in the circumstances.	
1.4	A duty of care owed as occupier of the premises. This would extend to anyone coming on to the organisation's premises including the public.	
1.5	A duty owed by the organisation in connection with supply by the organisation of goods or services (whether for consideration or not).	

No		**Tick**
1.6	A duty owed by the organisation in the carrying on by the organisation of any construction or maintenance operations.	
1.7	The carrying on by the organisation of any other activity on a commercial basis.	
1.8	The use or keeping by the organisation of any plant, vehicle or other thing.	
1.9	A duty of care by the organisation is also owed to a person who is detained at a custodial institution or in a custody area at a court or police station; the person is detained at a removal centre or short-term holding facility; transported in a vehicle or being held in any premises, in pursuance of prison escort arrangements or immigration escort arrangements; he is living in secure accommodation in which he has been placed; or he is a detained patient.	
1.10	Certain activities or organisations will be exempt from the duty of care and these include a public authority on matters of public policy; military activities; policing and law enforcement; emergencies; child protection and probation functions.	

Note 4: Potential defendants

No		**Tick**
	Some of the potential defendants include:	
1.1	The corporation – except a corporation sole. (Note: a corporation sole is a corporation constituted in a single person in right of some office or function, which grants that person a special legal capacity to act in certain ways.) Examples of corporation soles include many Ministers of the Crown and government officers (eg the Secretary of State for Defence, a public trustee and various Anglican clergy – a bishop (but not a Roman Catholic bishop) a vicar, an archdeacon and a canon.	
1.2	Unincorporated associations, including partnerships, a trade union or employers' association, that is an employer.	
1.3	A police force.	
1.4	The Crown and various Crown bodies.	
1.5	Focus on those organisations that have no or inadequate systems and procedures at the workplace and have not taken steps to minimise risk from their management activities.	

Note 5: Factors for the jury

No	*Factors*	Tick
1.1	The jury in a case concerning corporate manslaughter or corporate homicide must have regard to certain factors only once it has been established that an organisation owed a relevant duty of care to a person, and it falls to the jury to decide whether there was a gross breach of that duty.	
1.2	The jury *must* consider whether the evidence shows that the organisation failed to comply with any health and safety legislation that relates to the alleged breach, and if so, how serious that fault was and how much of a risk of death it posed.	
1.3	The jury *may* also consider the extent to which the evidence shows that there were attitudes, policies, systems or accepted practices within the organisation that were likely to have encouraged any such failure to comply with health and safety legislation, or to have produced tolerance of it. Further, the jury may also have regard to any health and safety guidance that relates to the alleged breach.	
1.4	The jury may also have regard to any other matters they consider relevant.	

Note 6: Remedial orders and publicity orders

No	*Types of orders*	Tick
1.1	A court before which an organisation is convicted of corporate manslaughter or corporate homicide may make an order known as a 'remedial order' requiring the organisation to remedy the management failure in respect of its activities, including any matter that appears to the court to have resulted from the relevant breach or to have been a cause of the death; including any deficiency as regards health and safety matters, in the organisation's policies, systems or practices of which the relevant breach appears to the court to be an indication.	
1.2	A remedial order can only be made on the application by the prosecution specifying the terms of the proposed order.	
1.3	A remedial order must be made on such terms as the court considers appropriate having regard to any representations made, and any evidence adduced, in relation to the matter by the prosecution or on behalf of the organisation.	
1.4	A remedial order must specify the period within which the organisation is to remedy the breach and provide supporting evidence of the remedy.	
1.5	Focus on those organisations that have no or inadequate systems and procedures at the workplace and have not taken steps to minimise risk from their management activities.	

No	*Types of orders*	Tick
1.6	A court before which an organisation is convicted of corporate manslaughter or corporate homicide may make a publicity order requiring the organisation to publicise the fact that it has been convicted of an offence including the specified particulars of the offence, the amount of any fine imposed and the terms of any remedial order made.	
1.7	In deciding the terms of a publicity order, the court must ascertain the views of any such enforcement authority it considers appropriate, and have regard to the representations made by the prosecution or on behalf of the organisation.	
1.8	A publicity order must specify a period within which the imposition of the court's requirements are to be complied with, and may require the organisation to supply evidence to any enforcement authority of compliance with the publicity order.	

*Note 7: **Investigation and prosecution***

No	*The process*	Tick
1.1	Generally, the police have the task of investigating the criminal activity.	
1.2	Advice is sought from the Crown Prosecution Service.	
1.3	The Director of Public Prosecution's consent will be required for proceedings to be issued against the organisation.	
1.4	With respect to corporate manslaughter or corporate homicide, there will also be specialist enforcement authorities involved.	
1.5	The specialist authorities would include health and safety enforcement authorities and any other enforcement authorities as considered appropriate in the circumstances.	
1.6	An organisation that is guilty of corporate manslaughter or corporate homicide is liable on conviction on indictment to a fine.	

The practical application of the Corporate Manslaughter and Corporate Homicide Act 2007

39.37 Does the matter fall into a relevant category?

(1) Was the victim an employee of the organisation concerned?

(2) Were they otherwise working for the organisation or performing services for it?

(3) Was the death connected with premises occupied by the organisation?

(4) Does the death relate to:

- Goods supplied by the organisation?
- Services supplied by the organisation?

- Construction or maintenance carried out by the organisation?
- An activity pursued by the organisation commercially?
- Use or keeping by the organisation of plant, vehicles, equipment or other materials?

(5) Was the victim in the custody of the organisation?

(a) Does the matter fall into a relevant category?

(6) Was the victim an employee of the organisation concerned?

(7) Were they otherwise working for the organisation or performing services for it?

(8) Was the death connected with premises occupied by the organisation?

(9) Does the death relate to:

- Goods supplied by the organisation?
- Services supplied by the organisation?
- Construction or maintenance carried out by the organisation?
- An activity pursued by the organisation commercially?
- Use or keeping by the organisation of plant, vehicles, equipment or other materials?

(10) Was the victim in the custody of the organisation?

Significant cases under the Corporate Manslaughter and Corporate Homicide Act 2007

39.38

The first case involving corporate manslaughter under the CMCHA 2007 was *Cotswold Geotechnical Holding* which resulted in a conviction against the company following a three-week trial in 2011 at the Winchester Crown Court.

The case concerned an employee. Mr Alex Wright was 27 years old when he died on 5 September 2008. He was a geologist for Cotswold Geotechnical Holdings and was investigating soil conditions in a deep trench on a development plot in Stroud when it collapsed and killed him.

According to the Crown Prosecution Service, Mr Wright was left working alone in the 3.5 metre-deep trench to 'finish-up' when the company director left for the day. The two people who owned the development plot decided to stay at the site as they knew Mr Wright was working alone in the trench. About 15 minutes later they heard a muffled noise and then a shout for help.

While one of the plot-owners called the emergency services, the other one ran to the trench where he saw that a surge of soil had fallen in and buried Mr Wright up to his head. He climbed into the trench and removed some of the soil to enable Mr Wright to breathe. At that point, more earth fell so quickly into the pit that it covered Mr Wright completely and, despite the plot owner's best efforts, Mr Wright died of traumatic asphyxiation.

The prosecution's case was that Mr Wright was working in a dangerous trench because Cotswold Geotechnical Holdings' systems had failed to take all reasonably practicable steps to protect him from working in that way. In convicting the company, the jury found that their system of work in digging trial pits was wholly and unnecessarily dangerous. The company ignored well-recognised industry guidance that prohibited entry into excavations more than 1.2 metres deep, requiring junior employees to enter into and work in unsupported trial pits, typically from 2 to 3.5 metres deep. Mr Wright was working in just such a pit when he died.

There was no person in the dock at Winchester Crown Court during the three-week trial as it is the company, rather than an individual, which is charged with corporate manslaughter. At the trial, the director in charge did not appear owing to illness, but Mr Justice Field described the director's actions as 'extremely irresponsible and dangerous'. Justice Field stated that the company's gross breach of duty to Mr Wright was a 'grave offence'.

The case was investigated by Gloucestershire Constabulary and supported by the Health and Safety Executive.

Cotswold Geotechnical Holdings was fined and ordered to pay the fine of £385,000 with payments of £38,500 per annum over a ten-year period. In imposing the fine, Justice Field stated that this would be a deterrent for future companies to ensure they complied in all respects with health and safety at the workplace: 'It may well be that the fine in terms of its payment will put the company into liquidation. If that is the case it is unfortunate and unavoidable ... but it's a consequence of the serious breach.' This fine was less than that recommended by the Sentencing Guidelines Council of £500,000 as a starting point for such types of cases.

In *JWM Farms*, the trial proceeded at Belfast Langanside Crown Court in 2012. The case concerned Mr Robert Wilson who was an employee of JWM Farms. Mr Wilson was washing the inside of a metal bin which was on the forks of a fork lift truck. He fell on the ground with the bin falling on him resulting in his death. The company was fined £187,500 with payment over a six-month period including costs of the prosecution. The company was in a good financial position, so the appropriate fine should have been £250,000 but was reduced by 25% because the company pleaded guilty. Judge Tom Burgess stated: 'Yet again, the court is faced with an incident where common sense would have shown that a simple, reasonable and effective solution would have been available to prevent this tragedy.'

A Cheshire manufacturing firm was fined almost £480,000 for corporate manslaughter following the death of an employee. The company, *Lion Steel Equipment Ltd*, was found guilty of corporate manslaughter under the CMCHA 2007. It pleaded guilty to the offence. It was also ordered by Judge Andrew Gilbart QC to pay prosecution costs of £84,000 by Manchester Crown Court. The case concerned the death of an employee, Mr Steven Berry, who died after falling through a fragile roof panel at a site in Hyde, Cheshire in May 2008. The Crown Prosecution Service also brought individual charges of gross negligence manslaughter against the firm's three directors which were subsequently dropped in return for the company pleading guilty to corporate manslaughter.

Practical issues arising from cases under the CMCHA 2007

39.39 From the cases tried to date, it is possible to make the following observations:

- The companies were relatively small and owner-managed.
- The fines have been in the range of up to £500,000. Other penalties and sanctions under the Act have not yet been tested by the courts.
- The judge will have particular regard to the company's financial position including the number of employees, ability to pay and the impact on the company's employees in the event the company going into liquidation because of the fine (but this is not the prime concern). The fine will act as a deterrent to companies to prevent future fatalities arising.
- There appears to be an aspect of 'plea bargaining' in that if the company pleads guilty, the fine may be reduced by a certain percentage with fewer costs to pay.
- It would appear that in conjunction with corporate manslaughter charges against the company, the CPS is also pursuing charges of gross negligence manslaughter at common law against senior managers of the company. However, some cases have demonstrated that in return for a guilty plea by the company, the prosecution may agree to the removal of the risk of a personal conviction and likely prison sentence by not pursuing claims for gross negligence manslaughter against the director.
- The issue still remains in identifying the company's senior managers. The CPS is likely to put significant effort into identifying those individuals who are considered culpable and bringing individual prosecutions against them, unless plea bargaining impacts upon the decision not to prosecute the individual concerned.
- The issue remains as to the interrelationship between the CMCHA 2007 and the Health and Safety at Work etc Act 1974 and under which Act the prosecution should be brought.
- Detailed guidance will be required from higher courts (Court of Appeal and House of Lords) on the interpretation of various provisions of the CMCHA 2007. This is likely to be the case where large companies are prosecuted.
- Companies should have legal insurance in place to deal with the potential cost of any prosecution arising.
- Further regular and continuous training of senior managers is essential to raise awareness of their duties and responsibilities under the CMCHA 2007.

Definitions

39.40

Armed forces:	Any of the naval, military or air forces of the Crown raised under the law of the UK.
Construction or maintenance operations:	Operations such as construction, installation, alteration, extension, improvement, repair, maintenance, decoration cleaning, demolition, or dismantling a building or structure, or anything else that forms part of land, and any plant, vehicle or other thing.
Corporate manslaughter:	A term used to describe a criminal offence in England and Wales or Northern Ireland where the management or organisation of a particular entity or body's activities has led to a person's death.
Corporate homicide:	A term used to describe a criminal offence in Scotland where the management or organisation of a particular entity or body's activities has led to a person's death.
Corporation:	Does not include a corporation sole but includes any body corporate wherever incorporated.
Custodial institution:	A prison, a young offender institution, a secure training centre, a young offender's institution, a young offender's centre, a juvenile justice centre or a remand centre.
Detained patient:	A person detained under the Mental Health Act 1983.
Employee:	An individual who works under a contract of employment or apprenticeship (whether express or implied and, if express, whether oral or in writing).
Enforcement authority:	An authority responsible for the enforcement of any health and safety legislation.
Exclusively public function:	A function that falls within the prerogative of the Crown or is, by its nature, exercisable only with authority conferred by the exercise of that prerogative; or by or under a statutory provision.
Emergency circumstances:	Circumstances that are present or imminent and are causing or likely to cause serious harm or a worsening of such harm; or are likely to cause the death of a person.
Health and safety guidance:	Any code, guidance, manual or other similar publication that is concerned with health and safety matters and is made or issued by an authority responsible for the enforcement of any health and safety legislation.
Medical treatment:	Includes treatment or procedure of a medical or similar nature.
Partnership:	A partnership within the meaning of the Partnership Act 1890; a limited partnership registered under the Limited Partnerships Act 1907; or a firm or entity of a similar character formed under the law of a country or territory outside the UK.

Premises:	Includes land, buildings and movable structures.
Secure accommodation:	Accommodation not consisting of or forming part of a custodial institution, provided for the purpose of restricting the liberty of persons under the age of 18.
Senior management:	Persons within an organisation who play significant roles in: (a) making decisions about how the whole or a substantial part of its activities are to be managed or organised; or (b) actually managing or organising the whole or a substantial part of the activities.
Serious harm:	Serious injury to or serious illness (including mental illness) of a person; serious harm to the environment (including life and health of plants and animals); or serious harm to any building or other property.
Special forces:	Those units of the armed forces, the maintenance of whose capabilities is the responsibility of the Director of Special Forces, or which are for the time being subject to operational command of that director.
Statutory function:	A function conferred by or under a statutory provision.

40 Bribery and commercial organisations

Contents

Introduction

40.1 The Bribery Act 2010 ('the Act') received Royal Assent on 8 April 2010. The principal objective of the Act has been to reform the criminal law on bribery, with a new consolidation into a single statute of the bribery offences committed in the UK and abroad. The Act originates largely with the work of the Law Commission of England and Wales, which made significant recommendations for changes to the existing law on bribery. There are particular offences applicable to companies involved in corporate bribery.

As long ago as the declaration in the Magna Carta, bribery was considered contrary to law and considered as a moral improbity: 'We will sell to no man … either justice or right'. To this day, the concept of bribery has proved to be elusive and contentious, difficult to define and complex to apply in practice. However, despite difficulties in reaching a consensus on an appropriate definition, various initiatives have been undertaken at both national and international levels to address and tackle bribery activities.

40.2 At a national level, according to the previous Justice Secretary, the Right Honourable Jack Straw, the perception has been that:

> 'Bribery is a cancer which destroys the integrity, accountability and honesty that underpins ethical standards both in public life and in the business community. The fight against bribery is not an optional extra or a luxury to be dispensed with in testing economic times. Our current law is old, complex and fragmented … A new law will provide our investigators and prosecutors with the tools they need to deal with bribery much more effectively' (See Ministry of Justice, *Government Welcomes New Bribery Law Recommendations* 20 November 2008).

These concerns were also echoed by the Law Commission which stated that 'the damage and inefficiency caused by corruption, in either financial or social terms, should not be underestimated. The effective combating of corrupt practices requires an effective law of bribery. However, the current law is riddled with uncertainty and in need of rationalisation.' (The Law Commission, *Reforming Bribery* HC 928, 19 November 2008).

40.3 At an international level, various institutions and organisations have established rules, regulations or guidance on combating bribery practices at all levels in society.

This chapter examines the background to the law on bribery, the international initiatives to combat bribery, and analyses at a national level on the legal aspects and the practical effect, of the Act. It also considers the implications of the Act for commercial organisations either registered in the UK, or with any part of their business operating in the UK, and their potential liability including those of senior officers.

Background

40.4 The British legal system on bribery was long in need of reform – but reform of what kind? One of the principal reasons for reform has been that the system has struggled with the definition of 'bribery', with some overlapping but distinct corruption offences set out in the Public Bodies Corrupt Practices Act 1889, the Prevention of Corruption Act 1906 and the Prevention of Corruption Act 1916. These Acts were largely considered antiquated, as was some of the case law in this area. There was also pressure on the UK to update the law, particularly from the OECD and other international organisations involved in anti-corruption measures. Against this background, the law on bribery was considered fragmented and complex and in need of simplification. There was also a perceived need to codify and modernise the law.

The position at common law

40.5 At common law, bribery and attempted bribery were criminal law offences punishable by fine and/or imprisonment. There was a lack of consensus at common law as to whether bribery was regarded as a general offence, or comprised separate individual offences distinguished by the office or function involved. According to

Russell: 'Bribery is the receiving or offering [of] any undue reward by or to any person whatsoever, in a public office, in order to influence his behaviour in office, and incline him to act contrary to the known rules of honesty and integrity' *(Russell on Crime* (12th edn, 1964), p 381). A reward that is so small as not to be considered a reward at all, will not be sufficient to constitute bribery: see *Bodmin Case* (1869) 1 O'M & H 121, where Willes J stated how he had been required to swear that he would not take any gift from a man who had a plea pending, unless it was 'meat or drink, and that of small value'. See Law Commission Report, *Reforming Bribery* (Law Com No 313), 19 November 2008, p 5.

40.6 At common law, a distinction was also drawn between a bribe and a treat. In the South African case of *S v Deal Enterprises (Pty) Ltd 1978 (3) SA 302, 311*, Nicholas J stated: 'The difference between legitimate entertainment and bribery lies in the intention in which the entertainment is provided, and that is something to be inferred from all the circumstances, including the relationship between giver and recipient, their respective financial and social positions and the nature and value of the entertainment'.

The bribery offence at common law was not limited to judicial and ministerial officers, but applied also to a 'public officer', who was defined as 'an officer who discharges any duty in the discharge of which the public are interested, more clearly so if he is paid out of a fund provided by the public': See *Whitaker* [1914] 3 KB 1283 at 1296 per Lawrence J. A public officer also included a person discharging ad hoc public duties such as electors at parliamentary (*Pitt and Mead* (1762) 3 Burr 1335, 97 ER 861), or local government elections: Worrall (1890) 16 Cox CC 550. Embracery (the bribing of jurors) was also considered a common law offence.

40.7 At common law, a mental element for the bribery was also a prerequisite for the offence. The payer of the bribe must also have intended to influence the behaviour of the recipient, and incline him to act contrary to known rules of integrity and honesty. This would include the payer of the bribe acting in breach of his duties of office, but this was not always necessary. In *Gurney (1867)* 10 Cox CC 550, it was held sufficient that the defendant charged with attempting to bribe a justice of the peace, had intended to produce any effect on the justice's decision.

The legislation on corruption

40.8 The main legislative provisions dealing with corruption were the Public Bodies Corrupt Practices Act 1889; the Prevention of Corruption Act 1906; and the Prevention of Corruption Act 1916.

Section 1(1) of the Public Bodies Corrupt Practices Act 1889 made it an offence for any person alone, or in conjunction with others, corruptly to solicit or receive, for himself, or for any other person, any gift, loan, fee, reward, or advantage as an inducement to, or reward for, or otherwise on account of any member, officer or servant of a public body, doing or forbearing to do anything in respect of any matter or transaction, actual or proposed, in which the public body was concerned. Section 1(2) created a similar offence to s 1(1) in respect of anyone who gave the bribe.

40.9 Under s 1 of the Prevention of Corruption Act 1906, offences were created relating to corrupt transactions by and with agents in relation to their principal's activities. This Act also included Crown servants.

The Prevention of Corruption Act 1916 shifted the burden of proof in relation to offences under both the 1889 Act and the 1906 Act, for the defendant to show on the balance of probabilities that the money, gift or other consideration was not received corruptly: s 2.

Other specific statutory offences involving corruptions included the Honours (Prevention of Abuses) Act 1925.

Between the period 1993 and 2003 on average, 21 people were prosecuted each year under the Prevention of Corruption Acts, whereas by comparison 23,000 people were prosecuted each year for fraud between 1997 and 2001. There was, therefore, a significant difference between those prosecuted for public sector corruption and those prosecuted for private sector fraud: See Annex to the Public Administration Committee Report by Christopher Sallon WC in Propriety and Peerages, HC 153 2007-08 Annex.

Previous reform proposals

40.10 The pressure for reform of the law on bribery had emerged from various sources. In 1974, the Redcliffe-Maud Committee (appointed in 1973 by the then Prime Minister Edward Heath) reported in response to widespread disquiet about conduct in local government after several prosecutions for offences of corruption. The Committee was charged with examining local government law and practice and how it might affect the conduct of members and officers in situations involving a conflict of interest between their public functions and private interests. The Committee made several recommendations including the extension of the presumption of corruption under the Prevention of Corruption Act 1916.

40.11 As a consequence of the Poulson affair, the Salmon Committee was established in 1974. It examined the standards of conduct in central and local government in relation to the problems of conflict of interest, and the risk of corruption involving favourable treatment from a public body, and to recommend further safeguards to ensure the highest standards of probity in public life. The Commission thereafter recommended that the Prevention of Corruption Acts 1889 to 1916 insofar as they applied to the public sector, should be consolidated and amended. However, the government of the day took no further action in this regard.

40.12 A series of public corruption scandals led to the First Report of the Committee on Standards in Public Life known as the Nolan Committee (Committee on Standards in Public Life (First Report) (May 1995) Cmnd 2850), which examined concerns about standards of conduct of all holders of public office and made recommendations to ensure the highest standards of propriety in public life. The Committee considered three main areas: issues relating to Members of Parliament; ministers and civil servants; and quangos. The Committee recommended that the general principles of public life be restated namely, selflessness, integrity, objectivity, accountability, openness, honesty and leadership. In regard to the law on corruption, the Committee recommended that steps be taken to clarify the law on bribery in relation to the receipt of a bribe by an MP as recommended by the Salmon Commission together with a consolidation of the statute law on bribery (Royal Commission on Standards in Public Life (1976) Cmnd 6524, see esp para 87, which recommended the rationalisation of the statute law on bribery, see esp para 2.104).

40.13 In June 1997, the Home office published a consultation document on the prevention of corruption (The Prevention of Corruption: Consolidation and Amendment of the Prevention of Corruption Acts 1889–1916: A Government Statement (June 1997)). The government stated that there may be some justification in having a single offence of corruption, and that there was a case for extending the existing statutes to cover trustees and all situations where a person has a duty, whether express or implied, to use his impartial judgment on an issue. It also stated that it was right to consider carefully an extension to the presumption of corruption. The Home Office document also raised issues concerning the jurisdiction of the courts to deal with acts of corruption arising outside the jurisdiction, and to the issues concerning the mental element of a corruption offence.

International initiatives

OECD

40.14 There have been a number of initiatives at an international level to deal with anti-corruption issues, particularly corruption in the public sector. The Organisation for Economic Co-operation and Development (OECD), the Commonwealth Law Ministers, the G7, the United Nations, the World Trade Organisation, the International Monetary Fund, and the Organisation of American States have all been active in this area.

40.15 The OECD Ministerial Council in May 1994 adopted a recommendation on bribery in international business transactions, namely that 'Member countries take effective measures to deter, prevent and combat the bribery of foreign public officials in connection with international business transactions'. The OECD Convention on Combating Bribery of Foreign Public Officials in International Business Transactions came into force on 15 February 1999. Its purpose was to 'assure a functional equivalence among the measures taken by the Parties to sanction bribery of foreign public officials'. According to para 1 of Art 1:

> 'Each Party shall take such measures as may be necessary to establish that it is a criminal offence under its law for any person intentionally to offer, promise or give any undue pecuniary or other advantage, whether directly or through intermediaries to a foreign public official, for that official or for a third party, in order for that the official act or refrain from acting in relation to the performance of official duties, in order to obtain or retain business or other improper advantage in the conduct of international business'.

Further, under para 2 of Art 1, 'each Party shall take any measures necessary to establish that complicity in, including incitement, aiding and abetting, or authorisation of an act of bribery of a foreign public official shall be a criminal offence. Attempt and conspiracy to bribe a foreign public official shall be criminal offences to the same extent as attempt and conspiracy to bribe a public official of that Party.' The principal objective of the OECD Convention has been to target 'active' bribery in that only the payer of the bribe is caught, and not the public official in receipt of the bribe. The government complied with the Convention by its implementation into UK legislation at the time. (See Pt 12 of the Anti-Terrorism, Crime and Security Act 2001 which came into force on 14 February 2002 – ss 108–110 now repealed.)

40.16 In addition, the OECD also published a 'Recommendation of the Council for Further Combating Bribery of Foreign Public Officials in International Business Transactions' on 26 November 2009, which called on signatories to strengthen the fight against foreign bribery through awareness-raising issues in the public and private sector, for the purpose of preventing and detecting foreign bribery as well as improved cooperation between national authorities in preventing bribery. The Recommendation also sets out good practice guidance on internal controls, ethics and compliance in respect of the OECD Convention.

European Union

40.17 In June 1995, a convention was signed in the European Union requiring Member States to criminalise acts of fraud committed by their national officials where they affect the Communities' budget. The First Protocol of the Convention was adopted in September 1996. It was directed at criminalising acts of corruption involving national officials which damage or are likely to damage the Communities' financial interests. Another convention was signed in 1997 which reflected the European Union's concern to combat corruption of public officials whether or not that corruption damaged the Communities' financial interests (see The Convention on the Fight Against Corruption Involving Officials of the European Communities or Officials of Member States of the European Union).

Further in 1997, the Lima Declaration called for a concerted effort by all international organisations, national governments and others to combat corruption.

40.18 In 1999, the Group of States Against Corruption (GRECO) was established by the Council of Europe to monitor States' compliance with the organisation's anti-corruption standards through a process of mutual evaluation and peer pressure. It assists in identifying deficiencies in national anti-corruption policies, prompting the legislative, institutional and practical reforms.

40.19 There have also been a series of initiatives by the Council of Europe in addressing corruption issues (see for example, the Criminal Law Convention on Corruption, 27 January 1999; the Civil Law Convention on Corruption, 4 November 1999; Additional Protocol to the Criminal Law Convention on Corruption, 15 May 2003; Council of Europe, Committee of Ministers: Resolution (97)(24) on the Twenty Guiding Principles for the Fight Against Corruption, 6 November 1997; and Council of Europe, Committee of Ministers: Recommendation Rec (2003)4 on the Common Rules Against Corruption in the Funding of Political Parties and Electoral Campaigns, 8 April 2003).

40.20 In an effort to combat global corruption, the World Economic Forum Partnering Against Corruption Initiative (PACI) was formally launched in January 2004 by CEOs from the engineering and construction, energy and metals and mining industries. PACIs mission has been to develop multi-industry principles that would result in a competitive level playing field, based on integrity, fairness and ethical conduct. In this regard, PACI has developed 'Principles for Countering Bribery' (World Economic Forum, Partnering Against Corruption – 'Principles for Countering Bribery' (2005)). The Principles require a business enterprise to prohibit bribery in any form; and for the enterprise to commit to the continuation or implementation of an effective programme to counter bribery.

UK initiatives

Law Commission Report in 1998

40.21 In 1998, the Law Commission considered the UK's corruption laws in its report 'Legislating the Criminal Code: Corruption'. It pointed out that the law on bribery was out of date in the following main respects: first, the law was drawn from a multiplicity of sources including overlapping common law offences, and at least 11 statutes (eg, misconduct in public office: *Llewellyn-Jones* [1968] 1 QB 429; and specific bribery offences such as embracery: *Pomfriet v Brownsal* (1600) Cro Eliz 736; 78 ER 968; attempts to bribe a Privy Councillor: *Vaughan* (1769) 4 Burr 2495; 98 ER 308; attempts to bribe a police constable: *Richardson* 111 Cent Crim Ct Sess Pap 612; and the taking of a bribe by a coroner not to hold an inquest: *Harrison* (1800) 1 East PC 383). A large part of the legislation was prepared hastily in response to a contemporary problem and was neither comprehensive, nor clear and consistent. Secondly, the law depended upon a distinction between public and non-public bodies. Third, there was difficulty in ascertaining to whom the present legislation applied, such as, for example, judges, and whether they fell within the definition of an agent. The Law Commission recommended that the common law offence of bribery and the statutory offences of corruption should be replaced by a modern statute. The offences would cover corruptly conferring or offering or agreeing to confer an advantage as well as corruptly obtaining, soliciting or agreeing to obtain an advantage.

Corruption Bill 2002–2003

40.22 Following the Queen's Speech in 2002, a draft Corruption Bill was presented to Parliament. The draft Bill was criticised and rejected by the Joint Committee in 2003 particularly on the retention of the agent/principal relationship as the basis of the offence.

In December 2003, the government responded to the Joint Committee report and signalled that it did not agree with some of the views of the Joint Committee: see HL Paper 157, HC 705 2002–2003 Cm 6086. By way of a compromise, the Home Office issued a consultation paper in December 2005 setting out a new statutory agenda for bribery law: Home Office, Reform of the Prevention of Corruption Acts and SFO Powers in Cases of Bribery Against Foreign Officials, December 2005. However, in March 2007, the government announced that the outcome of the consultation process was that there was broad support for reform of the current law, but there was no consensus as to how this could be achieved.

Law Commission Consultation 2007

40.23 In November 2007, the Law Commission embarked on further consultation on the law of bribery, where it sought views on the most appropriate way forward in reforming the law on bribery, but principally favoured a modern statutory approach to bribery law: Law Commission Consultation Paper No 185. The Law Commission accepted that its earlier proposals were no longer widely acceptable in moving forward in this area. It also recommended a new offence of bribing a foreign public official.

Law Commission Report 2008

40.24 In November 2008, the Law Commission, following its consultation, prepared a report entitled *Reforming Bribery*: The Law Commission, Reforming Bribery (Law Com No 313), 19 November 2008. The report acknowledged that there was a need for reform in this area, but also recognised that there was a lack of consensus on the best approach towards reform. It recommended that the existing law, which was fragmented, should be replaced by five offences (and it recommended defences) and the extra-territorial application of the offences.

The Law Commission report highlighted some key problems with the existing law. These included fragmentation, with a lack of clarity among the different legislative and regulatory instruments; complexity and uncertainty; an imperfect distinction between public and private sector bribery; inconsistencies and uncertainties in terminology and scope; and lack of clarity as to what constituted a bribe.

Government White Paper

40.25 In March 2009, the government published a White Paper setting out a statutory agenda for reform of the bribery law: Bribery: Draft Legislation Cm 7570. This paved the way for the Bribery Act 2010. In his foreword to the White Paper, the Lord Chancellor, Jack Straw stated: 'Bribery by its very nature is insidious: if it is not kept in check it can have potentially devastating consequences.' He noted that the bribery laws were outdated and anachronistic, dating back to around the turn of the century and that the laws had never been consolidated. There were inconsistencies in language and concepts between the various provisions with some gaps in the law, with the exact scope of the common law offence being unclear, with the effect that bribery law was difficult to understand for the public and difficult to apply for the prosecutors and the courts.

The White Paper advocated a modernisation of the law to deal effectively with those who offer or accept bribes in the business or public sectors, but also to bring transparency and accountability to the UK's international business transactions. The government modelled the new legislation on the Law Commission's proposals.

Scope and extent of the Bribery Act 2010

40.26 The Act was passed by Parliament on 8 April 2010 and comprises 20 sections and two schedules. It was enacted to 'make provision about offences relating to bribery; and for connected purposes'. It sets out a new consolidated mechanism for bribery offences committed in the UK and abroad. The Act replaces the bribery offences at common law and the three Corruption Acts, namely the Public Bodies Corrupt Practices Act 1889, the Prevention of Corruption Act 1906, and the Prevention of Corruption Act 1916.

The main substantive provisions of the Act extend to England and Wales, Scotland and Northern Ireland: s 18.

Offences of bribing another person

40.27 Section 1 sets out the general offence of bribing another person. The provider of the advantage, 'P' is guilty of a criminal offence if either of the following two cases apply, namely Case 1 and Case 2:

Case 1

This applies to situations in which the advantage is intended to bring about an improper performance by another person of a 'relevant function or activity', or to reward such improper performance. Section 3 elaborates on the term 'relevant function or activity'. Section 4 elucidates on the concept of 'improper performance'.

Case 1 is applicable where P offers, promises or gives a financial or other advantage to another person: s 1(2)(a); and P intends the advantage to either:

(a) induce a person to perform improperly a relevant function or activity: s 1(2)(b)(i); or

(b) to reward a person for the improper performance of such a function or activity: s 1(2)(b)(ii).

Case 1 therefore creates a bribery offence of inducing or rewarding a person in relation to the function or activity set out in s 3 of the Act. The terms 'inducing' or 'rewarding' will be given their ordinary, natural meaning as no further guidance is provided under the Act. The wrongfulness element lies in P seeking a favour from R.

Case 2

This concerns situations where:

(a) P offers, promises or gives a financial or other advantage to another person: s 1(3)(a); and

(b) P knows or believes that the acceptance of the advantage would itself constitute the improper performance of a relevant function or activity: s 1(3)(b).

40.28 In both Cases 1 and 2, the substantive offence is that P 'offers, promises, or gives financial or other advantage'. The term 'financial or other advantage' is not defined but will be determined on the facts of the matter before the courts. The courts should apply an ordinary and natural meaning to 'financial' or 'other advantage'. The term 'financial' would relate to pecuniary or monetary aspects that are offered, promised or given to R. R need not be in actual receipt of the financial or other advantage, as P will be caught if P simply offered or promised some financial or other advantage. The term 'other advantage' would include putting R in a favourable position; benefiting R in relation to others, who would not otherwise have benefited but for the bribery. The advantage can be provided in the form of a reward for the improper conduct. It need not have been provided in advance of the improper conduct in question.

40.29 In Case 1, it does not matter whether the person to whom the advantage is offered, promised or given is the same person who is to perform, or has performed, the function or activity concerned: s 1(4). Further, in both Cases 1 and 2, it does not matter whether the advantage is offered, promised or given by P directly or through a third party: s 1(5).

Both Cases 1 and 2 are specifically concerned with the conduct of P, the payer of the bribe. P will be caught in the following situations which apply to Cases 1 and 2.

Case studies

- P provides a long-time friend from university days (who works in the same company as Y) £20,000 to give to Y, to persuade Y to send P confidential information about the company that P wants in connection with her own business.
- P tells Z who works as an employee for a rival company to supply certain information about the company that could benefit P's business significantly. In return, P says he knows the chairman of the rival company as they play golf together and will see to it that Z becomes a director within days.

Offences relating to being bribed

40.30 Section 2 sets out the offence of being bribed as it applies to a recipient or potential recipient of the bribe, who is referred to as 'R'.

R will be guilty of a criminal offence if any of the following cases apply, namely Cases, 3, 4, 5 and 6:

Case 3

This applies where R requests, agrees to receive or accepts a financial or other advantage intending that, in consequence, a relevant function or activity should be performed improperly (whether by R or another person): s 2(2).

Case 4

> This is where:
> (a) R requests, agrees to receive or accepts a financial or other advantage: s 2(3)(a); and
> (b) the request, agreement or acceptance itself constitutes the improper performance by R or a relevant function or authority: s 2(3)(b).

Case 5

> This applies where R requests, agrees to receive or accepts a financial or other advantage as a reward for the improper performance (whether by R or another person) of a relevant function or activity: s 2(4).

Case 6

> This is where, in anticipation of or in consequence of R requesting, agreeing to receive or accepting a financial or other advantage, a relevant function or activity is performed improperly by R or by another person at R's request or with R's assent or acquiescence: s 2(5). In Case 6, whether a person other than R is performing the function or activity, it also does not matter whether that person knows or believes that the performance of the function or activity is improper: s 2(8).

40.31 In Cases 3 to 6, it does not matter whether R requests, agrees to receive or accepts (or is to request, agree to receive or accept) the advantage directly or through a third party. Further, it does not matter whether the advantage is (or is to be) for the benefit of R or another person: s 2(6).

In Cases 4 to 6, it is immaterial whether R knows or believes that the performance of the function or activity is improper: s 2(7).

Under Cases 3, 4 and 5, there is a requirement that R 'requests, agrees to receive or accepts' an advantage, whether or not R actually receives it. It must then relate to the 'improper performance' of a relevant function or activity. The term 'improper performance' is set out in s 4 of the Act.

All the cases under s 2 are concerned with R's conduct, the recipient of the bribe. R will be caught under the following situations:

Case studies

> - R asks P for £15,000 if R or his colleague destroys supporting documents submitted by rival bidders for a contract P is hoping to secure with R's employer.

- R, a civil servant, asks for £4,000 for himself to process a routine application for a visa.
- R, a civil servant in the immigration department, asks P for £1,500 as a reward for having expedited P's application for a visa to come to the UK.
- R, an agent, accepts P's bid for a contract on behalf of a company because R expects P to secretly reward him personally; or R accepts an undocumented personal reward from P for accepting P's bid for the contract.
- P is well known as a provider of large 'rewards' to officials who give P's work priority. Hoping to secure some financial reward, R moves P's planning application to the top of the list for consideration. When P subsequently discovers this, P sends R a 'reward' of £2,000. Here, R and P will be caught even though there had not been any prior contact between them.
- R, a government official, has issued a visa to P. P is very grateful to have received the visa and sends R £1,500, and R banks the cheque.

Function or activity to which the bribe relates

40.32 Section 3 of the Act sets out the areas within which bribery can take place with particular reference to the function or activity that can be improperly performed for the purposes of ss 1 and 2 of the Act. The term 'relevant function or activity' is used for the purposes of the Act. Section 3 also highlights the important fact that bribery applies to both public and private functions without differentiating between the two.

The functions and activities are:

- any function of a public nature: s 3(2)(a);
- any activity connected with a business: s 3(2)(b). The term 'business' includes trade or profession: s 3(7): The term 'business' has been described as an 'etymological chameleon': *Town Investments Ltd v Department of the Environment* [1978] AC 359, p 383 per Lord Diplock. Further guidance as to the scope of the term can be obtained from s 23(2) of the Landlord and Tenant Act 1954, Pt II which states that the expression 'business' includes a trade, profession or employment, and includes any activity carried on by a body of persons, whether corporate or unincorporated. The expression would also cover NHS Hospitals: see *Hill (Patents) Ltd v University College Hospital Board of Governors* [1956] 1 QB 90;
- any activity performed in the course of a person's employment: s 3(2)(c);
- any activity performed by or on behalf of a body of persons (whether corporate or unincorporated): s 3(2)(d).

It would appear that the definition of 'function or activity' relates not only to the current activities, but also to those in the past:

Case study

- R has recently retired from his influential long service within the civil service. R is approached by P who is seeking a lucrative contract with a government department. P pays R a large sum of money to provide confidential information to P about the bidding process and criteria. Here, although R is not engaged in a profession or function, it is arguable that he would be caught under s 2 of the Act in respect of his previous activities. The transaction between R and P relates to a past conduct of a public or professional kind.

40.33 Once any of the above definitions of 'function or activity' is satisfied, the function or activity must also meet one or more of conditions A to C: s 3(1)(b). The conditions are associated with the nature of the function or activity and are based on the 'expectation' test set out in s 5.

- Condition A is that a person performing the function or activity is expected to perform it in good faith: s 3(3).
- Condition B is that the person performing the function or activity is expected to perform it impartially: s 3(4).
- Condition C is that a person performing the function or activity is in a position of trust by virtue of performing it: s 3(5).

The function or activity may be carried out either in the UK or abroad. It need not have any connection with the UK: s 3(6).

Case studies

- R is a trustee who makes grants to a company's needy former employees. R agrees to consider making grants to a needy former employee, Z, who is also a member of his own family, when Z says he has made R a beneficiary under Z's will.
- In exchange for payment, R, a security guard, agrees to allow P on the company premises at night so that P, a director of a rival company, can go through confidential papers that will assist his company's business dealings.
- R is P's former tutor, but has now retired from his university post. P was not a good student at university, but needs a glowing reference from R if she is to have any chance of securing a lucrative position. P promises R a large sum of money if R will write a reference for P. R agrees. Here, R is no longer employed by the university and has no duty to act impartially or to be in a position of trust. R will be caught, as he is in a position to act in good faith and he acted improperly in providing the misleading reference.
- The CEO of a major listed company is requested to assess the merits of taking over a smaller company. Her counterpart at the smaller company is keen that the takeover should go ahead. The latter offers the CEO of the larger

company a substantial payment if she will recommend to her shareholders that the takeover goes ahead. The CEO accepts the offer.

- An agent invites bids from contractors of behalf of the principal. The principal has told the agent that, if a large sum of money is offered 'under the table' by one of the contractors to secure the contract, it may be awarded to that contractor. The agent agrees to split the sum with the principal.
- P knows that R is likely to favour P's bid for a contract, over the bids of other competitors. P sends R £20,000 to 'make sure' that R favours P's bid even though P knows that R should evaluate the bids in good faith. R knows he is sure to accept P's bid in any event. R accepts the £20,000 without authority from his employer.
- The following would not be caught under the Bribery Act (although there may be contractual or tortious implications involved): P offers to pay R, a security guard, a higher salary, if R will leave her existing position at the end of the shift to come to work for P.

Improper performance to which the bribe relates

40.34 Section 4 defines the term 'improper performance' as performance which breaches a 'relevant expectation' as set out in condition A or B under s 3(3) and (4): s 4(1)(a) and (2)(a); or any expectation as to the manner in which, or reasons for which, a function or activity satisfying condition C under s 3(5) will be performed: s 4(2)(b). The relevant function or activity is to be treated as being performed improperly if there is a failure to perform the function or activity, and that failure is itself a breach of a relevant expectation: s 4(1)(b).

Anything that a person does (or omits to do) arising from or in connection with that person's past performance of a relevant function or activity is to be treated as being done (or omitted) by that person in the performance of that function or activity': s 4(3). This would apply to a situation where R is no longer engaged in a particular function or activity, but still carries out acts related to the previous function or activity in some form or capacity. Such acts are treated as being undertaken in the performance of the function or activity.

Expectation test

40.35 In deciding what is expected of a person performing a function or activity for the purposes of ss 3 and 4, an objective test applies, namely, what a reasonable person in the UK would expect in relation to the performance of the type of function or activity concerned: s 5(1).

In deciding what such a person would expect in relation to the performance of a function or activity, where the performance is not subject to the law of any part of the UK, any local custom or practice must not be taken into account unless it is permitted or required by the written law applicable to the country or territory concerned: s 5(2).

The term 'written law' means law contained in any written constitution, or legislation applicable to the country or territory concerned: s 5(3)(a); or any judicial decision which is applicable 'and is evidenced in published written sources': s 5(3)(b).

Bribery of foreign public officials

40.36 A separate discrete offence of bribing of foreign public officials is set out under s 6 of the Act. This aligns with the requirements of the Organisation for Economic Cooperation and Development (OECD) in its *Convention on Combating Bribery of Foreign Public Officials in International Business Transactions* (adopted 21 November 1997).

The fault element of the offence is set out in ss 6(1),(2) and (4). A person 'P' who bribes a foreign public official 'F' is guilty of an offence if P's intention is to influence F in F's capacity as a foreign public official: s 6(1). Intention is therefore a key element in this offence.

Further, P must also intend to retain a business, or an advantage in the conduct of business: s 6(2).

40.37 P bribes F if directly or through a third party, P offers, promises or gives any financial or other advantage to F, or to another person at F's request or with F's assent or acquiescence. In addition, F is neither permitted nor required by the written law applicable to F to be influenced in F's capacity as a foreign public official by the offer, promise or gift: s 6(3). This is the 'conduct' element of the offence.

The offence will also be committed if the advantage is offered to someone other than the official at the official's request, or with the officials consent or agreement.

Unlike the bribery offences of ss 1 and 2, the offence of a bribery of a foreign public official only covers the offering, promising or giving of bribes, and not the acceptance of them.

40.38 The term 'influencing' F in F's capacity as a foreign public official means influencing F in the performance of F's functions as such an official. This includes any omission to exercise those functions: s 6(4)(a); and any use of F's position as such an official, even if not within F's authority: s 6(4)(b).

'Foreign public official' is defined as an individual who holds legislative, administrative or judicial position of any kind, whether appointed or elected, of a country or territory outside the UK. In addition, the foreign public official exercises a public function for or on behalf of a country or territory outside the UK, or for any public agency or public enterprise of that country or territory, or is an official or agent of a public international organisation: s 6(5). The term 'public international organisation' is defined as an organisation whose members are any of the following:

- countries or territories;
- governments of countries or territories;
- other public international organisations;
- a mixture of any of the above: s 6(6).

Case studies

- P offers to reward a FPO if he will award P a contract, which the FPO can do in his capacity as a FPO.
- P entrusts a payment to Z, requesting that Z give it to such FPO as has the power to award the contract to P.
- P is asked by a FPO to pay T a sum of money, in exchange for the FPOs award of a contract to P.

Failure of commercial organisations to prevent bribery

40.39 Section 7 creates a strict liability offence of failing to prevent bribery which can only be committed by a relevant commercial organisation. A relevant commercial organisation 'C' will be guilty of an offence if a person 'A' associated with C, bribes another person intending to obtain or retain business for C: s 7(1)(a); or to obtain or retain an advantage in the conduct of business for C: s 7(1)(b). The main justification for the introduction of this offence is to deter commercial organisations from giving direct or indirect support to the practice or culture of bribe taking.

40.40 The term 'relevant commercial organisation' is defined as:

- a body incorporated under the law of any part of the UK and which carries on business whether there or elsewhere;
- a partnership that is formed under the law of any part of the UK and which carries on a business there or elsewhere;
- any other body corporate or partnership whether incorporated or formed which carries on business in any part of the UK: s 7(5).

'Business' is defined as including a trade or profession and includes what is done in the course of a trade or profession: s 7(5).

The term 'partnership' is defined as a partnership under the Partnership Act 1890: s 7(5)(a); or a limited partnership registered under the Limited Partnerships Act 1907: s 7(5)(b); or a firm or entity of a similar character formed under the law of a country or territory outside the UK: s 7(5).

The 'adequate procedures' defence

40.41 There is however a defence to the s 7 offence. It will be a defence for the commercial organisation to show it had adequate procedures in place to prevent persons associated with C from committing bribery offences. The existence of the defence limits the liability of commercial organisations for the s 7 offence, as the principal concern of the Act is to direct the criminal law at commercial organisations that fail to make continuing and systematic efforts to ensure that active bribery is not committed on their behalf.

The Act does not define 'adequate procedures'. However, s 9 requires the Secretary of State to publish guidance about procedures that relevant commercial organisations can put in place to prevent persons associated with them to prevent bribery taking place': s 9(1). The Secretary of State may from time to time publish revisions to guidance or a revised guidance: s 9(2). The Scottish Ministers must be consulted before publishing any guidance: s 9(3). The publication will be in such manner as the Secretary of State considers appropriate: s 9(4).

40.42 Pursuant to s 9 of the Act, the Ministry of Justice has issued guidance on bribery prevention measures which addresses the concept of 'adequate procedures' under s 9. Commercial organisations should not simply rely on this guidance, but they should also have regard to the wealth of knowledge, experience and expertise to be found outside government, by, for example, reference to the business community and non-governmental organisations, and seeking best practice examples in the particular industry in combating bribery. The guidance is designed to assist commercial organisations of all sizes and sectors understand what type of procedures they can put in place to prevent bribery from occurring within them. It is, therefore, designed to be of general application.

40.43 The guidance establishes six principles which are followed by commentary and explanation. However, the guidance is not prescriptive and it is not a 'one-size-fits-all' guidance. The issue of whether a commercial organisation had adequate procedures in place to prevent bribery in the context of a particular prosecution is a matter that can only be resolved by the courts having regard to the particular facts and circumstances of the case. The burden will be on the commercial organisation where it seeks to rely on the defence, to prove that it had adequate procedures in place to prevent bribery. Commercial organisations may be able to discharge this burden by implementing the Ministry of Justice guidance including establishing and maintaining their own policies and procedures in line with the six principles.

The six principles

40.44 The guidance is non-prescriptive. The six principles are intended to be of general application and are addressed in neutral but affirmative language. The commentary following each of the principles is expressed more broadly. Where actions or options are listed by way of examples, they are not exhaustive.

The six principles reflect UK and international good practice and they do not propose any particular procedures in themselves. They are intended to be used as a flexible guide in deciding what procedures are right for an organisation. Where the commercial organisation is small or medium sized the application of the principles is likely to suggest procedures to those that may be right for a large multinational organisation. Although the guidance sets out certain procedures, some of these may not be appropriate for the commercial organisation concerned or there may be other procedures that are appropriate for the organisation. Commercial organisations need to tailor the guidance for its policies and procedures so that they are proportionate to the nature, scale and the complexity of its activities.

Principle 1: risk assessment

40.45 This principle states that the commercial organisation regularly and comprehensively assesses the nature and extent of the risks relating to bribery to which it is exposed.

A full understanding of the bribery risks an organisation faces is the foundation of any effective efforts to prevent bribery. Although bribery risks will evolve over time, the commercial organisation's risk assessment will also therefore need to evolve over a period of time.

40.46 Accordingly, a commercial organisation must have a risk assessment procedure in place. What constitutes adequate risk assessment procedures will vary enormously depending on the size of an organisation, its activities, its customers and the markets in which it operates but organisations should consider:

- whether those undertaking the assessment are adequately skilled and equipped to do so, or whether using external professionals may be appropriate;
- How best to inform the risk assessment, for example by tapping into existing information held by the organisation, such as annual audit reports, internal investigation reports, focus groups and staff/client/customer complaints; and by analysing publicly available information on bribery issues in particular sectors or overseas markets and jurisdictions.

The factors affecting internal risk include for example deficiencies in employee knowledge of the organisation's business profile and understanding of associated bribery risks, deficiencies in employee training or skills sets, the organisation's remuneration structure or lack of clarity in the organisation's policy on gifts, entertaining and travel expenses.

40.47 External risk factors include for example:

- *Country risk* – perceived high levels of corruption as highlighted by corruption league tables published by reputable organisations, and factors such as the absence of anti-bribery legislation and implementation and a perceived lack of capacity of the government, media, local business community and civil society effectively to promote transparent procurement and investment policies;
- *Transaction risk* – transactions involving for example charitable or political contributions, licences and permits, public procurement, high value or projects with many contractors or involvement of intermediaries or agents;
- *Partnership risks* – business partners located in higher risk jurisdictions, associations with prominent public office holders, insufficient knowledge or transparency of third-party processes and controls.

Principles 2 to 6 below deal with how the risk assessment will inform the development, implementation and maintenance of effective anti-bribery policies and procedures.

Principle 2: top level commitment

40.48 The top-level management of a commercial organisation (be it a board of directors, the owners or any other equivalent body or person) are committed to preventing bribery. They establish a culture within the organisation in which bribery is never acceptable. They take steps to ensure that the organisation's policy to operate without bribery is clearly communicated to all levels of management, the workforce and any relevant external actors.

Those at the top of an organisation are in the best position to foster a culture of integrity where bribery is unacceptable within the organisation. Effective leadership in bribery prevention will take a variety of forms depending on the circumstances in which an organisation does business, but by way of example the kinds of leadership procedures that may be effective include:

- A statement of commitment to counter bribery in all parts of the organisation's operation

  Such a statement could include commitments to carry out business fairly, honestly and openly; to adopt a zero tolerance policy towards bribery and set out the consequences of breaching the provisions of the regime for employees and management or for any contractual bribery prevention provision with business partners; and to avoid doing business with others who do not commit to doing business without bribery. A top-level statement may be made public and communicated to subsidiaries and business partners.

- Reflecting commitment against bribery in the organisation's management structure

  Personal involvement of top-level managers in developing a code of conduct or ensuring anti-bribery policies are published and communicated to employees, subsidiaries and business partners helps embed an anti-bribery culture within an organisation. Maintenance of a clear top-level commitment to anti-bribery policies may be assisted by the appointment of a senior manager to oversee the development of an anti-bribery programme and to ensure its effective implementation throughout the organisation.

Principle 3: Due diligence

40.49 The commercial organisation has due diligence policies and procedures which cover all parties to a business relationship, including the organisation's supply chain, agents and intermediaries, all forms of joint venture and similar relationships and all markets in which the commercial organisation does business.

Organisations will need to know who they are doing business with if their risk assessment and mitigation are to be effective. The particular types of due diligence listed below are examples of enquiries that can help identify bribery risks associated with a particular business relationship and will enable the organisation to take appropriate preventive measures.

Location

40.50 Enquiries about the risk of bribery in a particular country in which an organisation is seeking a business relationship, the types of bribery most commonly encountered, and any information about the preventive actions which are most effective. Organisations may wish, for example, to be advised of relevant civil, administrative and criminal law and the existence of any procedures for reporting bribery to the relevant local authorities.

Business opportunity

40.51 Enquiri51es about the risks that a particular business opportunity raises (eg, establishing whether the project is to be undertaken at market prices, or has a defined legitimate objective and specification).

Business partners

40.52 Enquiries to establish whether individuals or other organisations involved in key decisions, such as intermediaries, consortium or joint venture partners, contractors or suppliers have a reputation for bribery and whether anyone associated with them is being investigated or prosecuted, or has been convicted or debarred, for bribery or related offences. Organisations may also wish to consider the risks associated with politically exposed persons where the proposed business relationship involves, or is linked to, a prominent public office holder.

Organisations may wish to ensure that enquiries are made of partners' internal anti-corruption measures.

Principle 4: clear, practical and accessible policies and procedures

40.53 The commercial organisation's policies and procedures to prevent bribery being committed on its behalf are clear, practical, accessible and enforceable. Policies and procedures take account of the roles of the whole work force from the owners or board of directors to all employees, and all people and entities over which the commercial organisation has control.

Having undertaken a risk assessment and due diligence, a commercial organisation will be in a better position to develop effective bribery prevention policies and procedures. Tapping into the expertise of its work force to develop policies can serve to secure buy-in from those who will be responsible for applying them.

Policy and procedure documentation

40.54 Organisations may wish to consider how comprehensive, clear, practical and accessible policy and procedures documentation is to all within the organisation, and to other people and entities over which it has control. Such documentation could include:

- a clear prohibition of all forms of bribery including a strategy for building this prohibition into the decision making processes of the organisation;
- guidance on making, directly or indirectly, political and charitable contributions, gifts, and appropriate levels and manner of provision of bona fide hospitality or promotional expenses to ensure that the purposes of such expenditure are ethically sound and transparent;

- advice on relevant laws and regulations;
- guidance on what action should be taken when faced with blackmail or extortion, including a clear escalation process;

The organisation's level of commitment to the Public Interest Disclosure Act 1998 (employment law protection for whistle-blowers) and an explanation of the process.

INFORMATION ON ANTI-CORRUPTION PROGRAMMES RELEVANT TO THE SECTOR.

40.55 Organisations may also wish to consider issuing a code of conduct, which sets out expected standards of behaviour and which can form part of the employment contract.

SUPPORT AND OPERATIONAL PROCEDURES

40.56 Organisations may wish to consider how existing procedures can be used for bribery prevention purposes. For example, financial and auditing controls, disciplinary procedures, performance appraisals, and selection criteria can act as an effective bribery deterrent. Other bribery prevention procedures may include modification of sales incentives to give credit for orders refused where bribery is suspected; and 'speak up' procedures to allow any employee to report allegations of bribery or breaches of corporate anti-bribery policy in a safe and confidential manner.

Managers may wish to consider the resistance to bribery of particularly vulnerable operational areas such as procurement and supply chain management mechanisms and address any issues they have identified.

MANAGEMENT OF INCIDENTS OF BRIBERY

40.57 Organisations could also consider putting in place procedures to deal with incidents of bribery, should one arise, in a prompt, consistent and appropriate manner. This could include designating a senior manager to oversee the organisation's response. The organisation will need to decide whether to refer the matter to law enforcement agencies. There may need to be oversight of the sanctions process and a communications strategy to reassure investors, employees, customers, business partners and others possibly exposed to consequences from the incident.

Principle 5: effective implementation

40.58 The commercial organisation effectively implements its anti-bribery policies and procedures and ensures they are embedded throughout the organisation. This process ensures that the development of policies and procedures reflects the practical business issues that an organisation's management and workforce face when seeking to conduct business without bribery.

Appropriate bribery prevention policies and procedures will vary enormously from organisation to organisation depending on the nature of the business, the assessment of risk and the nature of its operational and support functions. But whatever the policies they will require effective implementation if they are to be successful.

Implementation strategy

40.59 Organisations may wish to consider planning how to bring their high-level anti-bribery commitment to life. Like all corporate programmes, anti-bribery policies and procedures cannot manage the risk of bribery if left in a file on a shelf but need to be implemented through the allocation of roles and responsibilities and by setting milestones for delivery and review.

40.60 Larger organisations may wish to establish an implementation strategy that clearly sets out how policies and procedures are to be implemented across the organisation's various groups and functions, including for example:

- who will be responsible for implementation;
- how the policies and procedures will be communicated internally and externally;
- the nature of training and how it will be rolled out;
- the internal reporting of progress to top management;
- the extent to which external assurance processes will be engaged;
- the arrangements for monitoring compliance;
- the timescale of implementation;
- a clear statement of the penalties for breaches of agreed policies and procedures; and
- the date of the next review.

Internal communication

40.61 Organisations may wish to consider how best to communicate anti-bribery policies and procedures to relevant staff, and the need for bribery prevention training. If training is necessary, it could cover the bribery risks the organisation is exposed to as well as the organisation's anti-bribery policies and procedures. It can also be tailored for different functions within the organisation. Larger organisations may also wish to consider offering or even requiring the participation of business partners in anti-bribery training courses.

External communication

40.62 External communication can promote better implementation of policies and procedures as well as providing support for business partners and employees seeking to implement the organisation's policies and procedures. External communication can range from the provision of information on the organisation's website to direct face-to-face communication with key players at meetings. Messages could include an indication that employees will be subject to robust internal sanctions (in addition to any criminal justice outcome if criminal offences are committed), if they accept bribes and that corrupt vendors risk being removed from the list of approved suppliers.

Principle 6: Monitoring and review

40.63 The commercial organisation institutes monitoring and review mechanisms to ensure compliance with relevant policies and procedures and identifies any issues as they arise. The organisation implements improvements where appropriate.

Policies and procedures are likely to require monitoring and adaptation to changing circumstances or in response to any incidents involving bribery in order to remain effective. Organisations may wish to consider the following examples of monitoring and review procedures.

INTERNAL MONITORING AND REVIEW MECHANISMS

40.64 Organisations could consider what internal checks and balances are needed to monitor and review anti-bribery policies.

In smaller organisations, this might include effective financial and auditing controls that pick up potential and actual irregularities, combined perhaps with a means by which the views and comments of employees and key business partners are incorporated into the continuing improvement of anti-bribery policies.

40.65 In larger organisations, this might include financial monitoring, bribery reporting and incident management procedures. Large organisations may also wish, for example, to consider periodically reporting the result of such reviews to the Audit Committee, the Board of Directors or equivalent body. In turn, the audit committee, board or equivalent body may wish to make an independent assessment of the adequacy of anti-bribery policies and disclose their findings and recommendations for improvement in the organisation's annual report to shareholders.

40.66 Organisations could also identify appropriate ways of identifying when a review of bribery risk and the corresponding policies and procedures is necessary; for example, external trigger events like government changes, corruption convictions, or negative press reports. Where appropriate, organisations may also wish also consult the publications of relevant trade bodies or regulators that could highlight examples of good or bad practice.

40.67 Organisations may also wish to ensure that their procedures take account of external methods of issue identification and reporting as a result of the statutory requirements applying to their supporting institutions (eg money laundering regulations reporting by accountants and solicitors).

TRANSPARENCY

40.68 Transparency is an important anti-bribery tool. Secrecy within an organisation and the failure to disclose important information about specific projects can facilitate the payment, receipt and concealment of bribes. Given the challenges posed by distance and unfamiliarity with overseas customs and regulations, organisations may wish to consider how to monitor the implementation of anti-bribery procedures in overseas offices and business partners.

External verification

40.69 The senior management of higher risk and larger organisations may wish to consider whether to commission external verification or assurance of the effectiveness of anti-bribery policies, or to seek membership of one of the independently verified anti-bribery codes monitored by industrial sector associations or multilateral bodies. An independent review can be helpful in providing organisations undergoing structural change or entering new markets with an insight into the strengths and weaknesses of its anti-bribery policies and procedures and in identifying areas for improvement. It may also enhance its credibility with business partners or restore market confidence following the discovery of a bribery incident, help meet the requirements of both voluntary or industry initiatives and any future pre-qualification requirements.

40.70 However, in practice, it is expected that most companies will have written policies and procedures in place to combat bribery. Further, such policies should be communicated to employees so that they are aware of them, including communicating the policies to those associated with the commercial organisation such as subsidiaries, third parties, consultants and even in general terms and conditions of business of the commercial organisation. What is essential is that these policies are in place; they are operational; they have been communicated; and the commercial organisation has put in place steps and procedures including investigative measures to address and identify aspects of bribery, and the appropriate actions in the event of a default (including disciplinary actions). This aspect might be addressed by the risk management unit of the relevant commercial organisation, assuming this is a medium to large organisation.

40.71 It is therefore essential as a defence to the s 7 offence to show that a due diligence procedure was in place, and could be followed in respect of bribery issues. The concept of 'adequate procedures' does not mean that the commercial organisation should be saddled with disproportionate administrative burdens, and exposed to a serious form of criminal liability respecting conduct which they were helpless to prevent. A relevant commercial organisation should contribute constructively towards the reduction of bribery by the adoption of policies and procedures, and a positive attitude towards reform in their own internal systems and procedures. A commercial organisation should therefore be able to rebut the s 7 offence on the grounds that it has established an internal policy in this regard. Section 7 is aimed at commercial organisations who perpetuate the culture and practice of bribery, by operating without safeguards to promote high standards of integrity, in industries, regions or countries vulnerable to the bribery.

40.72 In establishing 'adequate procedures', the commercial organisations should be particularly wary when seeking to do business in a country that is prepared for its officials to ignore ethical standards 'if the price is right'. The procedures should forbid any facilitation payments as a matter of global policy, and that such payments are reported to senior executives and to the board. Some policies go so far as stating that if the corruption is endemic in a country's business culture, the commercial organisation may consider withdrawing or limiting its activities in that country.

40.73 In some cases, advisers are sometimes incentivised by commission payments on the successful award of sales contracts and at a percentage of the contract price.

These contracts can be of a very large monetary value and large common payments. Some advisers are tempted to obtain contracts with the aid of corrupt payments either with or without the knowledge or connivance of the company. A reputable commercial organisation should take all practical actions to prevent this happening. It should only appoint advisers where stringent control measures based upon ethical and reputational risk are followed to ensure due diligence in their selection, appointment, management and payment. Companies with multinational operations or sales should also endorse anti-corruption policies.

40.74 The adequacy of a system will depend on the size, type and resources of the company in question, location and the type of transaction involved. In a small company of fewer than five employees, it may be adequate for the director to remind employees periodically of their obligations regarding bribery.

40.75 The 'adequate procedures' defence is concerned with the courts measuring the adequacy of internal standards. Even a 'single-person' company should have adequate policies and procedures in place to address bribery issues. The procedures may not be on a par with a plc or a listed company, and internal standards and procedures will differ and vary depending upon the type, size and resources of the relevant commercial organisation including its dealing with countries where bribery is commonplace. For example, it could be argued that a 'one man' company which is extensively involved in business dealings abroad in countries where bribery is acute, will not be able to avail of the s 7 defence, if it did not have adequate procedures in place to address bribery issues even though it is a small commercial organisation in terms of size and resources, but owing to the circumstances of the business dealings, it would be failing in its duties in not establishing any anti-bribery policies and procedures. This could be compared to another 'one-man' company which hardly conducts business dealings with countries where bribery is commonplace. In these circumstances, the company may simply occasionally remind its employees that it does not tolerate bribery of any sort, or state this in the employees' contracts of employment, as well as in its terms of business with third parties. In any event, such a company will still need to demonstrate it had an 'adequate procedure' in place to address bribery issues.

40.76 There is also an obligation on the board in practice to ensure that they are proactive in meeting high standards of ethical business conduct in all the commercial organisation's activities. This should be a standard item on the agenda. There should be an explicit assessment of ethical and reputational risks in all business decisions taken by the board. Board members should themselves be exemplars of the standards and receive regular briefings on emerging issues in business ethics.

40.77 The term 'bribery' in relation to the offence under s 7 relates only to the offering, promising or giving of a bribe contrary to ss 1 and 6 and there is no corresponding offence of failure to prevent the taking of bribes. Further, the offences under ss 1 and 3 include being liable for such offences by way of aiding, abetting, counselling or procuring, in other words, secondary liability: s 7(3). There is no requirement for the prosecution to show that the person who committed the bribery offence has already been successfully prosecuted. However, the prosecution must show that the person would be guilty of the offence were that person prosecuted under the Act.

There is no requirement for A to have a close connection to the UK as set out in s 12. The courts will have jurisdiction provided C falls within the definition of 'relevant commercial organisation'.

40.78 Section 7 refers to the term 'associated person'. The definition is considered in s 8 of the Act which states that a person 'A' is associated with C for the purposes of s 7 if A performs services for, or on behalf of C: s 8(1). This ensures that s 7 relates to the actual activities being undertaken by A at the time rather than A's general position. However, the capacity in which A performs services for or on behalf of C does not matter: s 8(2). Accordingly, A may be the commercial organisation's employee, agent or subsidiary: s 8(3). Further, whether or not A is a person who performs services for or on behalf of C is to be determined by reference to all the relevant circumstances, and not merely by reference to the nature of the relationship between A and C: s 8(4). Where A is an employee of the commercial organisation, it is to be presumed unless the contrary is shown, that A is a person who performs services for or on behalf of C: s 8(5).

Case studies

- An English company, C, that has anti-bribery policies and procedures in place of which employees are periodically reminded, takes over a company (ZCo) based in a country where bribery by companies is common. Immediately following its takeover, a former employee of ZCo (now an employee of C) bribes an official to secure a contract. The employee's superior (also a former employee of ZCo) says that she was still coming to terms with C's new ways of operating, and had not fully appreciated the wholly categorical nature of the new policy. C is charged with failing to prevent bribery.
- An English company, C, wishes to do business in Redland. C employs an agent (X) living in Redland to establish business contracts on C's behalf with government officials in Redland. X bribes the officials to place contracts with C. C can show that it gave Y, their regional manager, the task of ensuring that all foreign agents complied with the company's anti-bribery policy. Y had failed in her task, as she was busy looking for a job with a rival company.

In both the above cases, the company has failed to prevent bribes from taking place and would be criminally liable under the s 7 offence. However, in both examples C will have a good defence to the charge of failing to prevent the bribery if it can show that it had adequate procedures in place designed to prevent the commission of the bribery. The individual failings of particular members of staff do not necessarily illustrate systematic failures in the way it sought to prevent the commission of bribery.

- A British company, C, with no previous experience of operating overseas, sets up a subsidiary to act on its behalf, ZCo, in a country where payment of bribes to secure contracts is commonplace. C does not have any anti-bribery policies, and does not look closely into how ZCo does its business. ZCo pays a bribe in order to secure an important contract on C's behalf. In this case, C failed to prevent bribery by someone providing services for it, who was acting on its behalf. There was no anti-bribery policy in place and hence the adequate procedure defence will not be available, and the case will be considered on the basis of failure by C to prevent bribery.

Consent to prosecution

40.79 A prosecution under the Act in England and Wales can only be brought with the consent of one of the following: the Director of Public Prosecutions; the Director of the Serious Fraud Office; or the Director of Revenue and Customs Prosecutions: s 10(1). The relevant Director must exercise the consent function personally: s 10(4). However, where the Director is unavailable (due to incapacity or because they are abroad), another person who has been designated in writing by the Director to exercise any such function may do so, but must do so personally: s 10(5) and (6). Any provisions of other legislation which would allow another person to exercise the functions of one of the Directors do not apply to the Directors' consent functions under s 10: s 10(7).

40.80 With regard to a prosecution in Northern Ireland, this can only be brought with the consent of the Director of Public Prosecutions for Northern Ireland or the Director of the Serious Fraud Office: s 10(2), (3) and (8). The Director of Public Prosecutions for Northern Ireland must exercise the consent function personally unless the consent function is exercised by the Deputy Director under s 30(4) and (7) of the Justice (Northern Ireland) Act 2002: s 10(9).

Penalties

40.81 Any offence under the Act which is committed by an individual under s 1, 2 or 6 is punishable either by a fine or imprisonment for up to ten years. It will be 12 months on summary conviction in England and Wales or six months in Northern Ireland, or both: s 11(1). An offence committed by a person other than an individual is punishable by a fine. In either case, the fine may be up to the statutory maximum (£5,000 in England and Wales and £10,000 in Scotland) if the conviction is summary, and unlimited if on indictment: s 11(2) and (3).

Although not yet in force, s 154 of the Criminal Justice Act 2003 sets the maximum sentence that can be imposed by a magistrates' court in England and Wales at 12 months. If an offence under the Bribery Act is committed before s 154 comes into force, the magistrates' court's power is limited to six months: s 11(4)(a).

Territorial application

40.82 The offences in s 1, 2 or 6 are committed in any part of the UK if any part of the conduct element takes place in that part of the UK: s 12(1). In the event all the actions concerning bribery take place abroad, they still constitute the offence if the person performing them is a British national or ordinarily resident in the UK, a body incorporated in the UK or a Scottish partnership: s 12(2), (3) and (4).

Section 12(5) of the Act states that for the purposes of the offence in s 7 (failure of commercial organisation to prevent bribery), it is immaterial where the conduct element of the offence occurs.

Where proceedings are to be taken in Scotland against a person, such proceedings may be taken in any sheriff court district in which the person is apprehended or in custody, or in such sheriff district as the Lord Advocate may determine: s 12(7), (8) and (9).

Defence for certain bribery offences

40.83 It will be a defence for a person charged with a relevant bribery offence to prove that the person's conduct was necessary for the proper exercise of any function of an intelligence service: s 13(1)(a); or the proper exercise of any function of the armed forces when engaged on active service: s 13(1)(b). It is likely that the standard of proof that the defendant would need to discharge in order to prove the defence is the balance of probabilities. 'Active service' is defined as an action or operation against the enemy which is an operation outside the British Islands for the protection of life or property; or the military occupation of a foreign country or territory: s 13(6).

40.84 The head of each intelligence service must ensure that the service has in place arrangements designed to ensure that any conduct of a member of the service which would otherwise be a relevant bribery offence is necessary for the purpose set out in s 13(1)(a). There is a similar requirement placed on the Defence Council to ensure that the armed forces have arrangements in place to ensure that the conduct of any member of the armed forces engaged on active service or a civilian subject to service discipline working in support of military personnel so engaged is necessary for a purpose set out in s 13(1)(b): s 13(3). The arrangements must be ones that the Secretary of State considers to be satisfactory: s 13(5).

40.85 Under s 13(5), a person's conduct is to be treated as necessary for the purposes of s 13(1)(a) and (b) in circumstances where the person's conduct would otherwise be an offence under s 2, and involves conduct on the part of another person which would amount to an offence under s 1 but for the defence in s 13(1). Accordingly, s 13(5) has the effect that a recipient of the bribe paid by a member of the intelligence services or armed forces is covered by the defence in any case where the person offering or paying the bribe is able to rely on the s 13 defence.

40.86 Section 13(6) provides a definition of a 'relevant bribery offence' which means an offence under ss 1 and 2 including one committed by aiding, abetting, counselling or procuring such an offence, and related inchoate offences. The term 'relevant bribery offence' does not include a s 1 offence which would also amount to an offence of bribing a foreign public official under s 6.

Offences under ss 1 and 2 by bodies corporate

40.87 Section 14 applies to individuals who consent or connive at bribery, contrary to s 1, 2 or 6, committed by a body corporate (of any kind) or Scottish partnership. It does not apply to the offence in s 7.

It must be shown that the body corporate or Scottish partnership has been guilty of an offence under s 1, 2 or 6: s 14(1). Once this is established, then a director, partner or similar senior manager of the body corporate is guilty of the same offence if he consented to or connived in the commission of the offence: s 14(2). Where a body corporate is managed by its members, the same applies to members. In respect of a Scottish partnership, the provision applies to partners: s 14(2)(a). In this respect, the body corporate or the Scottish partnership and the senior manager are both guilty of the main bribery offence. Section 14 does not create a separate offence of 'consent or connivance'. It should be noted that for a 'senior officer' or similar person to be guilty, he must have a close connection to the UK as defined in s 12(4): s 14(3). The term 'director' in relation to a body corporate whose affairs are managed by its members, means a member of the body corporate: s 14(4). A 'senior officer' in relation to a body corporate means a director, manager, secretary or other similar officer of the body corporate: s 14(4)(a); and in relation to a Scottish partnership, a partner in the partnership: s 14(4)(b). It is submitted that a company's liquidator could also be treated as a 'senior officer' and caught within s 14 of the Act, as the liquidator will effectively be managing the day-to-day corporate functions on behalf of the company.

Offences under s 7 by partnerships

40.88 Section 15 is concerned with proceedings for an offence under s 7 in relation to partnerships. These proceedings must be brought under the name of the partnership and not in the name of the partners: s 15(1). Some rules of court and statutory provisions which apply to bodies corporate are also deemed to apply to partnerships: s 15(2). Any fine imposed on the partnership on conviction must be paid out of the partnership assets: s 15(3).

Application to the Crown

40.89 The Act also applies to individuals in the public service of the Crown: s 16. These individuals will be liable to prosecution if their conduct in the discharge of their duties constitutes an offence under the Act.

Checklist

40.90 *This checklist sets out the essential aspects of the bribery offences under the Bribery Act 2010 including liability of commercial organisations for failing to prevent bribery. All references are to the Bribery Act 2010.*

No	Issue	Act reference
1	Is P offering a bribe to another person?	s 1(1)

No	Issue	Act reference
2	Is this a Case 1 offence? Is the bribe in the form of: (a) an offer; (b) a promise; (c) financial; or (d) other advantage?	s 1(2)(a)
3	Does P intend by the advantage: (a) to *induce a person* to perform improperly a relevant function or activity; or (b) to *reward* a person for the improper performance of such a function or activity?	s 1(2)(b)
4	Is this a Case 2 offence? Does P (a) offer; (b) promise; (c) give financial; or (d) other advantage to another person?	s 1(3)(a)
5	Does P know or believe that acceptance of the advantage would constitute the improper performance of a relevant function or activity?	s 1(3)(b)
6	In Case 1, It is irrelevant whether the advantage is offered, promised or given by P directly or through a third party.	s 1(4)
7	Is this a Case 3 offence? Does R (recipient) (a) request; (b) agree to receive; (c) accept a financial or other advantage? *and* Is there intention that the relevant function or activity should be performed improperly?	s 2(1) and 2(2)

No	Issue	Act reference
8	Is this a Case 4 offence? Does R: (a) request; (b) agree to receive; (c) accept a financial or other advantage? *and* Does the request, agreement or acceptance constitute the improper performance by R of a relevant function or activity?	s 2(3)
9	Is this a Case 5 offence? Does R (recipient): (a) request; (b) agree to receive; (c) accept a financial or other advantage as a reward for the improper performance of a relevant function or activity?	s 2(4)
10	Is this a Case 6 offence? Where in anticipation of or in consequence of R: (a) requesting; (b) agreeing to receive; (c) accepting a financial or other advantage; a relevant function or activity is performed improperly by (i) R; or (ii) by another person at R's request or with R's assent or acquiescence.	s 2(5)
11	In respect of Cases 3–6 it is irrelevant: (a) whether R requests, agrees to receive or accepts the advantage directly or through a third party; or (b) whether the advantage is for R's benefit or for another person.	s 2(6)
12	In Cases 4–6: It does not matter whether R knows or believes that the performance of the function or activity is improper.	s 2(7)

No	Issue	Act reference
13	In respect of Case 6: Where a person other than R is performing the function or activity, it does not matter whether that person knows or believes that the performance of the function or activity is improper.	s 2(8)
14	Is the 'function or activity': (a) of a public nature? (b) connected with a business? (c) performed in the ordinary course of a person's employment? (d) performed by or on behalf of a body or persons (whether corporate or unincorporated)?	s 3(2)
15	Does the 'function or activity' meet any of the following conditions: Condition A: the person performing the function or activity is expected to perform in good faith. Condition B: the person performing the function or activity is expected to perform it impartially. Condition C: the person performing the function or activity is in a position of trust by virtue of performing it.	s 3(3)
16	The organisation's key officers including the chief operating officer (if any) must ensure that the organisation's safety policies and procedures are communicated to all staff at the workplace.	s 7(2)
17	The function or activity will be a relevant function or activity even if it: (a) has no connection with the UK; and (b) it is performed in a country or territory outside the UK.	s 3(6)
18	Is the relevant function or activity: (a) performed improperly if performed in breach of a relevant expectation? And (b) is treated as performed improperly if there is a failure to perform the function or activity and that failure is a breach of a relevant expectation?	s 4(1)
19	'Relevant expectation' applies in relation to a function or activity which meets Conditions A, or B or C.	s 4(2)

No	Issue	Act reference
20	The 'expectation' test is a test of what a reasonable person in the UK would expect in relation to the performance of the type of function or activity concerned.	s 5(1)
21	In deciding what such a person would expect in relation to the performance of a function or activity where the performance is not subject to the law of any part of the UK, any local custom or practice is to be disregarded, unless it is permitted or required by the written law applicable to the country or territory concerned.	s 5(2)
22	Is it a bribery of a public official? A person (P) who bribes a foreign official (F) is guilty of an offence if P's intention is to influence F in F's capacity as a foreign public official. Does P also intend to obtain or retain (a) business; or (b) an advantage in the conduct of business? Does P bribe F: (a) directly or through a third party by offering, promising or giving any financial or other advantage to F or to another person at F's request or with F's assent or acquiescence; *and* (b) F is neither permitted nor required by the written law applicable to F to be influenced in F's capacity as a foreign public official by the offer, promise or gift?	s 6
23	Is a 'commercial organisation' involved? The commercial organisation will be guilty of an offence if a person (A) associated with C bribes another person intending: (a) to obtain or retain business for C; or (b) to obtain or retain an advantage in the conduct of business for C.	s 7(1)
24	Can the commercial organisation use a defence to prove it had in place 'adequate procedures' designed to prevent persons associated with C from undertaking such conduct?	s 7(2)
25	Has the organisation established and prepared a manual which also addresses practices and procedures for dealing with bribery?	s 7(2)
26	Is there induction training for staff on dealing with bribery issues?	s 2(1)
27	How often is staff training conducted on bribery issues and updates?	s 7(2)

No	Issue	Act reference
28	What internal investigative procedures exist for addressing bribery issues? Who is involved in the investigation process? How independent is the investigation?	s 7(2)
29	Is a coordinator appointed as the central person within the organisation to communicate anti-bribery policies and address such issues?	s 7(2)
30	What sanctions are in place where bribery is found to exist?	s 7(2)

Definitions

40.91

Active Service: Service in: (a) an action or operation against an enemy; or (b) an operation outside the British Islands for the protection of life or property; or (c) the military occupation of a foreign country or territory.

Armed Forces: Her Majesty's forces within the meaning of the Armed Forces Act 2006.

Business: Any trade or profession.

Devolved Legislation: An Act of the Scottish Parliament, a Measure of the National Assembly for Wales, or an Act of the Northern Ireland Assembly.

Director: In relation to a body corporate whose affairs are managed by its members means a member of the body corporate.

Enactment: Includes an Act of the Scottish Parliament and Northern Ireland legislation.

Foreign Public Official: An individual who holds a legislative, administrative or judicial position of any kind, whether appointed or elected, of a country or territory outside the UK (or any subdivision of such a country or territory); and who exercises a public function for or on behalf of a country or territory outside the UK (or any subdivision of such a country or territory); or is an official or agent of a public international organisation.

Head: In relation to the Security Service means the Director General of Security Service. In relation to the Secret Intelligence Service means the Chief of the Secret Intelligence Service. In relation to GCHQ means the Director of GCHQ.

Intelligence Service: The Security Service, the Secret Intelligence Service or GCHQ.

Partnership: A partnership under the Partnership Act 1890; or a limited partnership registered under the Limited Partnerships Act 1907; or a firm or entity of a similar character formed under the law of a country or territory outside the UK.

Public International Organisation:	An organisation whose members are any of the following: (a) countries or territories; (b) governments of countries or territories; (c) other public international organisations; (d) a mixture of any of the above.
Relevant Commercial Organisation:	It means (a) a body which is incorporated under the law of any part of the UK and which carries on a business (whether there or elsewhere); or (b) any other body corporate (whether incorporated) which carries on a business, or part of a business, in any part of the UK; or (c) a partnership which is formed under the law of any part of the UK and which carries on a business (whether there or elsewhere); or (d) any other partnership (whether formed) which carries on a business, or any part of a business, in any part of the UK. A business also includes a trade or profession.
Relevant National Authority:	In the case of a provision which would be within the legislative competence of the Scottish Parliament if it were contained in an Act of that Parliament, the Scottish Ministers; and in any other case, the Secretary of State.
Senior Officer:	In relation to a body corporate, a director, manager, secretary or other similar officer of the body corporate; and in relation to a Scottish partnership, a partner in the partnership.
Written law:	Any written constitution, or provision made by or under legislation, applicable to the country or territory concerned; or any judicial decision which is so applicable and is evidenced in published written sources.

Judicial attitudes towards bribery under the Bribery Act 2010

40.92 There have been a growing number of cases which have been the subject of prosecution under the Bribery Act 2010. Some of the cases have involved conviction of individuals while others have involved self-referrals to the court where on investigation by the companies concerned, bribery and corruption have transpired.

Munir Patel

Serious legal consequences will ensue for those convicted of bribery

This was one of the first prosecutions under the Bribery Act 2010, which concerned a magistrates' court clerk who was charged and convicted for soliciting and receiving a number of bribes including a bribe of £500 for removing a motoring offence in the official records. He was given a six-year sentence for misconduct at Southwark Crown Court, reduced on appeal to four years and three years for the bribery offence under BA 2010, s 2 running concurrently. The judge, HHJ Alistair McCreath considered Patel as the 'prime mover' in the corrupt scheme when he had been soliciting bribes for over a year and 53 instances where he had manipulated the process by removing offenders' motoring fines, penalty points and disqualifications. He stated that corrupt officials would be treated extremely harshly: 'It is important that those who are tempted to behave in this way understand that there will be serious consequences. Sentences for this sort of offence must act to deter offending of this kind.' He stated that Patel occupied an important function as a court clerk whose position 'had at its heart a duty to uphold and protect the integrity of the criminal justice process'. Further, 'the public would expect and rightly expect the courts to take strong action to protect and defend the integrity of the justice system'.

> 'A justice system in which officials are prepared to take bribes in order to allow offenders to escape the proper consequences of their offending is inherently corrupt and is one which deserves no public respect and which will attract none.'

Paul Jennings

The courts take a serious view for those convicted of corruption of public officials

Mr Paul Jennings, a former CEO of Innospec Ltd, appeared before His Honour Judge Leonard QC at Southwark Crown Court and pleaded guilty to one charge of conspiracy to corrupt Iraqi public officials and other agents of the government of Iraq. He has already admitted his part in corruption to secure supply contracts.

The charge related to allegations of conspiracy to corrupt Iraqi public officials and other agents of the government of Iraq (between 1 June 2006 and 31 May 2007) by making payments as inducements.

Other offences, already admitted to on 11 June 2012, were two charges relating to allegations of conspiracy to corrupt in that he gave or agreed to give corrupt payments to public officials and other agents of the government of Indonesia (between 14 February 2002 and 31 December 2008) and Iraq (between 1 January 2003 and 31 January 2008) as inducements to secure, or as rewards for having secured, contracts from that government for the supply of its products.

***R v Innospec* [2010] Crim LR 665**

The courts will apply appropriate penalties for those convicted of bribery and corruption

The sentencing remarks of Lord Justice Thomas called into question the authority of the Serious Fraud Office (SFO) to enter into US-style plea bargains with corporates and individuals who have committed corruption offences.

Between 2002 and 2006, Innospec Limited ('I Ltd'), a UK company and a subsidiary of US company Innospec Inc ('I Inc'), conspired with its directors and others to make corrupt payments to officials of the government of Indonesia for the supply of an anti-knock fuel additive called Tetraethyl Lead ('TEL'). I Inc paid bribes to the Iraq Ministry of Oil to sell them TEL under the UN Oil for

Food Programme. TEL has been phased out throughout most of the world due to health and environmental concerns.

In 2008, I Inc began discussions with the US Department of Justice with a view to achieving a global settlement in relation to its criminal conduct. The SFO became a party to those discussions.

In March 2010 the companies reached a plea agreement with the US and UK authorities. The settlement involved a guilty plea by I Ltd of conspiracy to corrupt and payments of $40 million in fines to the US and UK authorities. The agreed UK fine was $12.7 million, payable in part by way of civil settlement. The settlement was subject to court approval.

Thomas LJ indicated that the activities in which I Ltd had engaged were 'at the top end of serious corporate offending' and that the courts needed to impose an appropriate offence. The court considered that the fine sought from I Ltd by the SFO was only a fraction of the penalty that could be properly imposed and, under normal circumstances, would have measured 'tens of millions'.

The settlement that I Ltd had entered into with the SFO raised issues relating to the way in which a prosecutor and a court should approach sentencing in cases where an agreement had been reached between the prosecutor and offender as to penalties.

The court considered that the fine of $12.7 million was 'wholly inadequate' but still reluctantly approved it on the basis that I Ltd's management had cooperated with the SFO and had 'put that past behind them'. The judge was prepared to accept a lesser fine that would not drive I Ltd into insolvency. Thomas LJ rejected the proposition that a civil settlement would be appropriate and stated that it 'would be inconsistent with basic principles of justice for the criminality of corporations to be glossed over by a civil as opposed to a criminal sanction'.

The court was clear that the SFO did not have the authority to enter into an agreement under the laws of England and Wales as to the penalty in respect of the offence charged, and stated that the imposition of a sentence was a matter for the judiciary. This is in contrast to US law which provides a basis for a plea agreement. The court concluded that 'the Director of the SFO had no power to enter into the arrangements made and no such arrangements should be made again'.

According to Thomas LJ in: 'Those who commit such serious crimes as corruption of senior foreign government officials must not be viewed or treated in any different way to other criminals'.

Oxford Publishing Ltd

Significant fines may be imposed on organisations found guilty of bribery or corruption

The Director of the Serious Fraud Office (SFO) took action in the High Court, which has resulted in an Order that Oxford Publishing Limited (OPL) pay

£1,895,435 in recognition of sums it received which were generated through unlawful conduct related to subsidiaries incorporated in Tanzania and Kenya.

In 2011, OPL became aware of the possibility of irregular tendering practices involving its education business in East Africa. OPL acted immediately to investigate the matter, instructing independent lawyers and forensic accountants to undertake a detailed investigation.

As a result of the investigation, in November 2011 OPL voluntarily reported certain concerns in relation to contracts arising from a number of tenders which its Kenyan and Tanzanian subsidiaries, OUPEA and OUPT, entered into between the years 2007 and 2010. The SFO required OPL to follow a procedure based on the guidance contained within its published protocol document – 'The Serious Fraud Office's Approach to Dealing with Overseas Corruption'.

Because two of the tenders were funded by the World Bank, OPL also voluntarily reported on a potential breach of the World Bank's Procurement Guidelines to the World Bank.

The SFO remit was broader in its scope than the World Bank investigation in that it required investigation of all public tender contracts whether or not funded by the World Bank.

The costs of the investigation were met by OPL.

Abbot Group Limited

The court may make a recovery order for amounts received owing to bribery or corruption

This was a self-referral by Abbot Group Limited to the Scottish Crown Office and Procurator Fiscal Service. The company admitted that it had benefited from some corrupt payments made by one of its overseas subsidiaries. A civil recovery order of £5.6 million was made by entering into a civil settlement.

Mawia Mushtaq

Courts may also impose curfew on individuals sentenced for bribery

In December 2012, Mawia Mushtaq was convicted of bribery for offering a licensing officer of Oldham council bribes of £200 or £300 to achieve a 'pass certificate' on a private taxi licence test. He was sentenced to two months' imprisonment which was suspended for 12 months. He was also under a two-month curfew from 6pm to 6am.

Yang Li

Appropriate sentence may be passed on individuals found guilty of bribery

A past student at the University of Bath was convicted of bribery under s 1 of the Bribery Act 2010 by attempting to bribe his tutor with £5,000 in order to receive a pass mark for his dissertation. He was sentenced to 12 months' imprisonment and was ordered to pay £4,880 in costs.

Index

[all references are to paragraph number]